Index to Children's Poetry

SECOND SUPPLEMENT

A TITLE, SUBJECT, AUTHOR, AND FIRST LINE
INDEX TO POETRY IN COLLECTIONS
FOR CHILDREN AND YOUTH

COMPILED BY
JOHN E. AND SARA W. BREWTON

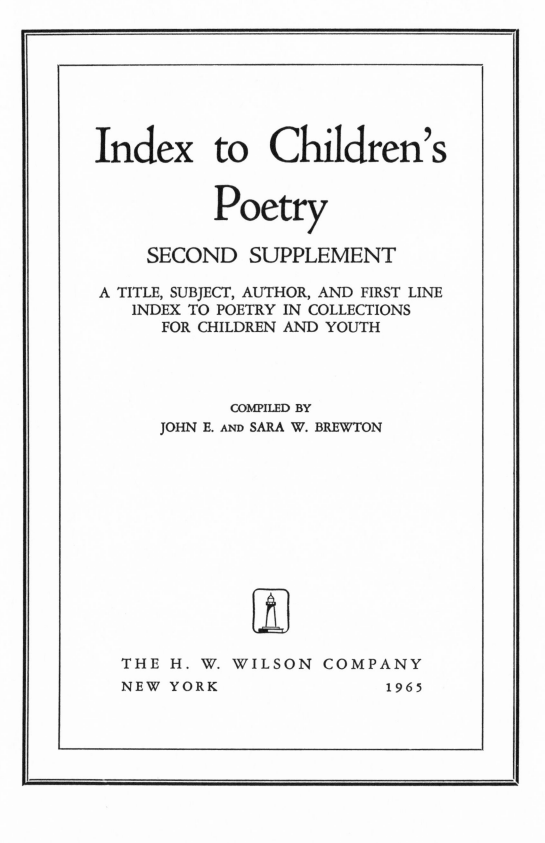

THE H. W. WILSON COMPANY
NEW YORK   1965

INDEX TO CHILDREN'S POETRY
SECOND SUPPLEMENT

Copyright 1965
By John E. Brewton and Sara W. Brewton

First Printing 1965
Second Printing 1969
Third Printing 1991

Standard Book Number 8242-0023-3
Library of Congress Catalog Card Number (42-20148)

PRINTED IN THE UNITED STATES OF AMERICA

Introduction

The INDEX TO CHILDREN'S POETRY: SECOND SUPPLEMENT is a dictionary index to 85 collections of poems for children and youth published between 1949 and 1963, with title, subject, author, and first line entries. More than 8,000 poems by approximately 1,400 authors are classified under more than 1,500 subjects. The SECOND SUPPLEMENT is an extension of the INDEX TO CHILDREN'S POETRY, published in 1942, in which more than 15,000 poems by approximately 2,500 authors are classified under more than 1,800 subjects; and of the FIRST SUPPLEMENT, published in 1954, in which more than 7,000 poems by approximately 1,300 authors are classified under more than 1,250 subjects.

Scope. The carefully selected list of books of poetry for children and youth which are indexed include collections for the very young child (e.g., books such as those classed in "Easy Books" in the *Children's Catalog*, Mother Goose, etc.); collections for the elementary school grades (e.g., the range of collections in class **821.08** in the *Children's Catalog*); and collections suitable for high-school age (e.g., such collections as those found in class **821.08** in the *Standard Catalog for High School Libraries*). In addition to anthologies or collections of poetry by more than one poet (e.g., books by John Ciardi, David McCord, etc.) are also indexed. Books partly in prose and partly in verse (e.g., *Story and Verse for Children*, Revised Edition, selected and edited by Miriam Blanton Huber) and collections of poems on one subject (e.g., *Birthday Candles Burning Bright*, compiled by Sara and John E. Brewton, and *Imagination's Other Place*, compiled by Helen Plotz) are included. The inclusion of comprehensive collections (e.g., *Favorite Poems Old and New*, compiled by Helen Ferris) gives the index a wide range.

Selection of Collections Included. Selection of the 85 collections included is based on a list of titles voted on by consulting librarians and teachers in various parts of the United States. A comprehensive list of anthologies and volumes of poetry by individual authors was sent to the selected consultants, their advice secured, and the final selection made. A list of consultants follows this Introduction.

Entries. Entries are of four types: *title, subject, author,* and *reference from first line to title.* The addition of collection symbols to title, subject and author entries makes these complete within themselves, thus obviating the necessity for cross references.

1. TITLE ENTRY. The fullest information is given in this entry. Although the symbols designating the books in which the poems are to be found are given in author and subject entries as well as in the title entries, the title entry is the only one which gives full name of author, when known, and full name of translator. References to the title entry have been made (a) from variant titles (e.g., The **three** jovial Welshmen. See "There were three jovial Welshmen"); (b) from titles of selections to the source title (e.g., The **witches'** spell. See Macbeth); and (c) from first lines (e.g., "**Spring** is the morning of the year." See The goldenrod).

The title entry includes:

(a) Title, followed by first line in parentheses when needed to distinguish between poems with the same title.

(b) Variant titles, indented under the main title. When the same poem appears in different books with different titles, one title, generally the one appearing in the most collections, has been chosen as the title entry and all variations have been indented and listed under this title.

(c) Full name of author, when known.

(d) Full name of translator.

(e) Symbols for collections in which the poem is to be found.

In order to bring together selections from a single source, selections are listed under source titles. An example follows:

> **Alice's** adventures in wonderland, sels.
> Turtle soup. *ReG*
> Beautiful soup. *DeT*

All entries subordinated under source titles are entered in their alphabetical position and referred to the source entry. Examples follow:

> **Beautiful** soup. See Alice's adventures in wonderland—Turtle soup
> **Turtle** soup. See Alice's adventures in wonderland

A group title (e.g., Limericks since Lear) under which several poems appear has been subordinated as a variant to a title under which the poem appears in another book. Otherwise it has been subordinated to its own first line. Examples follow:

> "A **silly** young fellow named Hyde." Unknown. *CoH*
> Limericks since Lear. *UnG*
> "**There** were three little birds in a wood." Unknown
> Limericks since Lear. *UnG*

2. SUBJECT ENTRY. Entries are grouped by specific subjects. For example, under **Animals** are listed the poems about animals in general, while poems about specific animals are grouped under names of animals, as **Dogs**. A single poem is often classified under a number of subject headings (e.g., The ant and the cricket, is listed under the subject headings **Ants; Fables; Crickets; Diligence;** and **Selfishness.**

Both *See* and *See also* references have been made freely to and from related subjects. These are filed at the beginning of the entries for the subject. Examples follow:

> **Agriculture.** See Farm life; Harvests and harvesting
> **Animals.** See also Aquariums; Circus; Fables; also names of classes of the animal kingdom, as Birds; also names of animals, as Elephants

In order that individual poems or selections from longer poems which have been subordinated to source titles in the title entries may be classified according to subject and may also be readily identified as to source, they have been entered under subject headings as follows:

> **Witches**
> The witches' spell. From Macbeth. W. Shakespeare. *CoPm*

iv

INTRODUCTION

Variant titles and titles of selections subordinate to source titles are treated in the same way as under the title and author entries.

The subject entry gives:

(a) Title, followed by first line in parentheses when needed to distinguish between poems with the same title.

(b) Name, including initials, of author.

(c) Symbols for collections in which the poem is to be found.

3. AUTHOR ENTRY. All titles are listed alphabetically under the name of the author. Variant titles and titles of selections subordinated under source titles are entered in their proper alphabetical place and referred to the main title or source title.

The author entry gives, under the full name of the author:

(a) Title, followed by first line in parentheses when needed to distinguish between poems with the same title.

(b) Symbols for collections in which the poem is to be found.

(c) Cross references from variant titles to main titles.

(d) Cross references from titles of selections to source titles.

4. FIRST LINE REFERENCES. The first line is always given in quotation marks, even when it is also the title. When the title differs from first line, reference is made from first line to title.

Arrangement. The arrangement is alphabetical. Articles are always retained at the beginning of title and first line, but the articles are disregarded in the alphabeting. Such entries are alphabeted by the word following the article and this word is printed in boldface (e.g., The **cat,** is filed under C). Articles in dialect have been filed under both the dialect article and under the first word after the article (e.g., Da **comica** man, is filed under C and **Da** comica man, is filed under D) except that entries which are grouped under authors and subjects are entered only under the dialect article (e.g., Da comica man, is filed only under D). Abbreviations are filed as if spelled in full (e.g., St is filed as Saint). Contractions are filed as one word (e.g., **Who'd** is filed as Whod). Hyphenated words are filed as separate words. An exception is made if the hyphen is really part of the word (e.g., **A-hunting, To-day**). To facilitate quick use the many entries beginning O and Oh have been filed together under O. Likewise, names beginning **Mac** and **Mc** have been filed together under Mac. Punctuation has been disregarded in filing.

Grades. The books have been graded and the grades are given in parentheses in the Analysis of Books Indexed and in the Key to Symbols. The grading is only approximate and is given to indicate in general the grades for which each book is suitable. A book that is comprehensive in nature and is suitable for a wide range of grades up to and beyond the twelfth grade is designated (r), reference.

Uses. The INDEX TO CHILDREN'S POETRY: SECOND SUPPLEMENT should serve as a practical reference book for all who desire to locate children's poems by subject, author, title, or first line. It should prove especially useful to librarians, teachers in elementary and secondary schools, teachers and students of children's literature, radio and television artists, parents, youth, and children. The variety of subject classifications should be particularly useful to anyone preparing programs for special occasions, to teachers planning activities around interests of children, to parents who desire to share poetry with children, and to anyone searching for poems on a given topic. The Analysis of Books Indexed, which gives in detail the contents of each book, number of poems included, number of authors represented, and number of poems in each group or classification, should prove valuable in the selection of collections for purchase or use. The comprehensiveness of the books indexed insures the usefulness of the SECOND SUPPLEMENT to those interested in poetry from the nursery through the secondary school and beyond.

Acknowledgments. The compilers thank the librarians who cooperated in answering questionnaires and in checking lists of titles to be included. Thanks are also due the publishers who generously supplied copies of their books which are included in the INDEX TO CHILDREN'S POETRY: SECOND SUPPLEMENT.

JOHN EDMUND BREWTON
SARA WESTBROOK BREWTON

Consultants

The compilers acknowledge with deep appreciation the generous assistance given by the consultants listed below.

MARJORIE E. BURNS
Supervisor, Department of
    School Libraries
Board of Education
Wilmington, Delaware

ANNIE JO CARTER
Director, Public School Libraries
Nashville, Tennessee

ADELINE CORRIGAN
Assistant to the Director
Cleveland Public Library
Cleveland, Ohio

ANNE T. EATON
New York, New York

EDITH EDMONDS
Librarian, Elementary School
Winnetka Public Schools
Winnetka, Illinois

ELVAJEAN HALL
Supervisor, Library Service
Division of Instruction
Newton Public Schools
West Newton, Massachusetts

GLADYS L. LEES
Director of School Libraries
Tacoma Public Schools
Tacoma, Washington

LUCILLE R. MENIHAN
Librarian, Baker School Library
Great Neck, New York

MILDRED R. PHIPPS
Supervisor, Work with Children
Public Library
Pasadena, California

MARIAN R. SCHROETHER
Children's Librarian
Public Library
Waukegan, Illinois

FRANCES LANDER SPAIN
Librarian, Central Florida Junior
    College
Ocala, Florida

JEAN THOMSON
Head, Branches Division
Public Library
Toronto, Ontario

MADELYN C. WANKMILLER
Head, Extension and Children's
    Department
Free Public Library
Worcester, Massachusetts

Contents

Analysis of Books of Poetry Indexed

Grades are given in parentheses at the end of each entry: (k), kindergarten or preschool grade; (1), first grade; (2), second grade, etc. Comprehensive general collections are designated (r), reference.

Aldis, Dorothy. All together; a child's treasury of verse; il. by Helen D. Jameson, Marjorie Flack, and Margaret Freeman. Putnam 1952 (1-4)
Contents: 144 poems ungrouped. Also Foreword. This book contains selections from Everything and anything; Here, there and everywhere; Hop, skip and jump; and Before things happen; as well as poems previously unpublished in book form. Indexed by first lines.

Aldis, Dorothy. Hello day; il. by Susan Elson. Putnam 1959 (1-4)
Contents: 34 poems ungrouped. Indexed by first lines and titles.

Allen, Marie Louise. Pocketful of poems; il. by Sheila Greenwald. Harper 1957 (k-3)
Contents: 22 poems ungrouped.

Anglund, Joan Walsh, comp. and il. In a pumpkin shell; a Mother Goose A B C. Harcourt 1960 (k-3)
Contents: 23 rhymes ungrouped.

Arbuthnot, May Hill, comp. Time for poetry; il. by Arthur Paul. general ed rev Scott 1961 (r)
Contents: 735 poems by 224 authors grouped as follows: Using poetry in verse choirs, 9; All sorts of people, 95; The animal fair, 125; Traveling we go, 46; Let's play, 82; How ridiculous, 87; Magic and make believe, 38; Wind and water, 55; Round the clock, 35; Round the calendar, 112; and Wisdom and beauty, 51. Also an introduction for teachers and parents on reading poetry to children and using poetry in verse choirs. Indexed by authors, first lines, and titles.

Behn, Harry. House beyond the meadow; il. by the author. Pantheon 1955 (2-4)
Contents: 7 poems ungrouped.

Behn, Harry. Windy morning; il. by the author. Harcourt 1953 (1-4)
Contents: 35 poems ungrouped.

Brewton, Sara and Brewton, John E. comps. Birthday candles burning bright; a treasury of birthday poetry; decorations by Vera Bock. Macmillan 1960 (2-8)
Contents: 206 poems by 132 authors grouped as follows: To be a birthday child, 22; Two of us, two of us, 8; When I was christened, 14; So let thy birthdays come to thee—Birthdays before seven, 39; So let thy birthdays come to thee—Seven through thirteen, 20; Cakes and candles, 14; Surprises, surprises, 11; Growing up, 32; Youth and age, 11; Birthdays through adult eyes, 15; and The birthday of the Lord, 20. Also Foreword. Indexed by authors, first lines, and titles.

Brewton, Sara and Brewton, John E. comps. Sing a song of seasons; poems about holidays, vacation days, and days to go to school; decorations by Vera Bock. Macmillan 1955 (2-8)
Contents: 224 poems by 98 authors grouped as follows: Time runs wild on the hilltops, 12; Morning is a little lass, 11; Evening is a little boy, 20; Oh! to have a birthday, 15; Fall is good, 43; Oh, the joys of winter, 52; Spring with laughter on her lips, 42; and Summer days are vacation days, 29. Also Foreword. Indexed by authors, first lines, and titles.

Brown, Helen A. and Heltman, Harry J. eds. Let's-read-together poems; an anthology of verse for choral reading in kindergarten and primary grades. Harper (Row bk) 1949 (k-3)
    Contents: 194 poems by 81 authors grouped as follows: In an introductory preface about choral reading, 13; Nursery rhymes, 27; Childhood mystery and experience, 40; Living things, 39; Nature and seasons, 43; People, 6; Religious poetry, 3; Special days, 10; Transportation, 3; and Wee folks and magic, 10. Also Something about this book; A word about choral reading; Procedures. Indexed by titles.

Brown, Helen A. and Heltman, Harry J. eds. Let's-read-together poems, 7; an anthology of verse selected and arranged for choral reading in the seventh grade. Harper (Row bk) 1950 (7)
    Contents: 48 poems by 41 authors grouped as follows: Fables, 4; Nature and seasons, 7; God's world, 7; Patriotism, 5; Special days and special people, 9; Yearnings, 4; Humorous, 8; and Sampling the ballads, 4. Also What kind of book is this? Indexed by titles.

Brown, Helen A. and Heltman, Harry J. eds. Let's-read-together poems, 8; an anthology of verse selected and arranged for choral reading in the eighth grade. Harper (Row bk) 1954 (8)
    Contents: 44 poems by 40 authors grouped as follows: Sampling the ballads, 5; Nature and seasons, 7; Inspiration, 9; Special days and special people, 6; Humorous, 6; Rules for living, 6; and Yearnings, 5. Also What kind of book is this? Indexed by titles.

Brown, Helen A. and Heltman, Harry J. eds. Read-together poems, 3; an anthology of verse for choral reading in the third grade; il. by Florence Hoopes and Mary Jo Larsen. Harper (Row bk) 1961 (3)
    Contents: 67 poems by 55 authors grouped as follows: Old rhymes, 3; Childhood mystery and experience, 21; Thoughts about things, 3; Living things, 9; Nature and seasons, 8; God's world, 4; Special days, 6; Machines and transportation, 4; and Imagination, 9. Also What kind of book is this? Indexed by titles.

Brown, Helen A. and Heltman, Harry J. eds. Read-together poems, 4; an anthology of verse for choral reading in the fourth grade; il. by Florence Hoopes and Mary Jo Larsen. Harper (Row bk) 1961 (4)
    Contents: 65 poems by 41 authors grouped as follows: Just for fun, 8; Nature and seasons, 19; Thoughts about things, 9; Living things, 8; Childhood mystery and experience, 5; God's world, 3; Special days, 4; and Imagination, 9. Also What kind of book is this? Indexed by titles.

Brown, Helen A. and Heltman, Harry J. eds. Read-together poems, 5; an anthology of verse for choral reading in the fifth grade; il. by Florence Hoopes and Mary Jo Larsen. Harper (Row bk) 1961 (5)
    Contents: 57 poems by 44 authors grouped as follows: Nature, 11; Through the senses, 9; Gaiety and fun, 14; Special days, 5; Native land, 7; Adventure, 6; and Pioneer ballads, 5. Also What kind of book is this? Indexed by titles.

Brown, Helen A. and Heltman, Harry J. eds. Read-together poems, 6; an anthology of verse for choral reading in the sixth grade; il. by Florence Hoopes and Mary Jo Larsen. Harper (Row bk) 1961 (6)
    Contents: 56 poems by 43 authors grouped as follows: Transportation, 4; Life and living, 10; Nature and seasons, 10; God's world, 5; Special days, 7; In and out of school, 5; Home, 5; and Gaiety and fun, 10. Also What kind of book is this? Indexed by titles.

Chute, Marchette. Around and about; rhymes by Marchette Chute; il. by the author. Dutton 1957 (k-3)
    Contents: 63 poems ungrouped.

Ciardi, John. I met a man; il. by Robert Osborn. Houghton 1961 (k-3)
    Contents: 33 poems ungrouped. Also Introduction.

Ciardi, John. Man who sang the sillies; il. by Edward Gorey. Lippincott 1961 (2-5)
Contents: 25 poems ungrouped.

Ciardi, John. Reason for the pelican; il. by Madeleine Gekiere. Lippincott 1959 (2-5)
Contents: 23 poems ungrouped.

Ciardi, John. You read to me, I'll read to you; il. by Edward Gorey. Lippincott 1962 (2-5)
Contents: 35 poems ungrouped.

Coatsworth, Elizabeth. Mouse chorus; il. by Genevieve Vaughan-Jackson. Pantheon 1955 (k-3)
Contents: 17 poems ungrouped.

Cole, William, ed. Humorous poetry for children; il. by Ervine Metzl. World pub 1955 (r)
Contents: 200 poems by 79 authors grouped under authors' names, which appear in alphabetical order. Also Introduction. Indexed by first lines.

Cole, William, ed. I went to the animal fair; a book of animal poems; il. by Colette Rosselli. World pub 1958 (k-3)
Contents: 35 poems by 26 authors ungrouped. Indexed by authors and titles.

Cole, William, ed. Poems for seasons and celebrations; il. by Johannes Troyer. World pub 1961 (5-12)
Contents: 141 poems by 83 authors grouped as follows: Introductory poem, 1; New Year's day, 7; Ground-hog day, 3; Lincoln's birthday, 4; Valentine's day, 8; Washington's birthday, 4; St Patrick's day, 2; Spring, 14; Easter, 4; April Fools' day, 3; Arbor day, 3; May day, 6; Mother's day, 5; Memorial day, 4; Flag day, 3; Father's day, 3; Summer, 8; The Fourth of July, 4; Labor day, 4; Autumn, 10; Columbus day, 3; Halloween, 6; Book week, 3; Veterans' day, 2; Thanksgiving, 3; Winter, 13; and Christmas, 11. Also Introduction. Indexed by authors and titles.

Cole, William, ed. Poems of magic and spells; il. by Peggy Bacon. World pub 1960 (4-12)
Contents: 90 poems by 60 authors grouped under authors' names, which appear in alphabetical order. Also Introduction. Indexed by first lines and titles.

Cole, William, ed. Story poems new and old; il. by Walter Buehr. World pub 1957 (5-12)
Contents: 92 poems by 63 authors grouped under authors' names, which appear in alphabetical order. Also Introduction. Indexed by first lines and titles.

De Angeli, Marguerite, comp. and il. Book of nursery and Mother Goose rhymes. Doubleday 1954 (k-3)
Contents: 376 rhymes ungrouped; 260 illustrations. Also Foreword. Indexed by first lines.

De La Mare, Walter, ed. Tom Tiddler's ground; a book of poetry chosen and annotated by Walter De La Mare; il. by Margery Gill. Knopf 1962 (r)
Contents: 238 poems by 92 authors ungrouped. Also Foreword by Leonard Clark; Introduction and copious notes by Walter De La Mare.

Doane, Pelagie, comp. and il. Poems of praise. Lippincott 1955 (1-5)
Contents: 117 poems by 69 authors ungrouped. Indexed by authors, first lines, and titles.

Eastwick, Ivy O. I rode the black horse far away; il. by Robert A. Jones. Abingdon 1960 (k-3)
Contents: 46 poems ungrouped.

Eaton, Anne Thaxter, comp. Welcome Christmas; a garland of poems; iL by Valenti Angelo. Viking 1955 (r)
Contents: 50 poems by 34 authors ungrouped. Also Foreword. Indexed by authors, first lines, and titles.

Farjeon, Eleanor. Children's bells; il. by Peggy Fortnum. Walck 1960 (4-8)
Contents: 240 poems grouped as follows: Introductory poem, 1; All the way to Alfriston, 6; Songs of the saints, 11; Songs of kings and heroes, 21; Martin Pippin's flower songs, 17; Young folk and old, 20; An alphabet of magic, 26; Fancies and jingles, 18; and Round the year: First quarter, 30; Second quarter, 30; Third quarter, 25; Fourth quarter, 35. Indexed by titles.

Farjeon, Eleanor. New book of days; il. by Philip Gough and M. W. Hawes. Walck 1961 (r)
Contents: 146 poems and a number of prose pieces arranged by days of the year. Also Foreword.

Ferris, Helen, ed. Favorite poems old and new; il. by Leonard Weisgard. Doubleday 1957 (r)
Contents: 726 poems by 335 authors grouped as follows: Myself and I, 35; My family and I, 47; My almanac, 58; It's fun to play, 29; Little things that creep and crawl and swim and sometimes fly, 55; Animal pets and otherwise, 42; On the way to anywhere, 34; From the good earth growing, 33; Roundabout the country, roundabout town, 42; My brother the sun, my sister the moon, the stars, and mother earth, 30; Bird-watcher, 33; People to know, friends to make, 34; Almost any time is laughing time, 66; My fancy and I, 38; Sign of my nation, great and strong, 47; From all the world to me, 55; Story time is a special time, 14; and From the family scrapbook, 34. Also Poetry at our house by Helen Ferris. Indexed by authors, first lines, and titles.

Frost, Frances Mary. Little naturalist; il. by Kurt Werth. McGraw (Whittlesey house pub) 1959 (2-5)
Contents: 23 poems ungrouped. Also Foreword by May Hill Arbuthnot.

Frost, Robert. Road not taken; an introduction to Robert Frost; a selection of Robert Frost's poems with a biographical preface and running commentary by Louis Untermeyer; il. by John O'Hara Cosgrave II. Holt 1951 (7-12)
Contents: 131 poems ungrouped. Also Robert Frost: An appreciation and a running commentary by Louis Untermeyer. Indexed by first lines and titles.

Frost, Robert. You come too; favorite poems for young readers; with wood engravings by Thomas W. Nason. Holt 1959 (5-12)
Contents: 51 poems grouped as follows: "I'm going out . . . ," 8; "The woods are lovely, dark and deep . . . ," 6; "I often see flowers . . . ," 5; "He has dust in his eyes and a fan for a wing . . . ," 11; "I was one of the children told . . . ," 5; "Men work together . . . ," 6; "We love the things we love . . . ," 5; and "I took the one less traveled by . . . ," 5. Also Foreword by Hyde Cox. Indexed by titles.

Graves, Robert. Penny fiddle; poems for children; il. by Edward Ardizzone. Doubleday 1960 (5-7)
Contents: 23 poems ungrouped.

Gregory, Horace and Zaturenska, Marya, eds. Crystal cabinet; an invitation to poetry; wood engravings by Diana Bloomfield. Holt 1962 (7-12)
Contents: 124 poems by 95 authors grouped as follows: Introductory poem, 1; Sing we for love, 18; The wind begun to rock the grass, 22; Musick, the mosaique of the air, 11; White Iope, blithe Helen, and the rest, 19; We were the heroes, 19; How many heavens, 8; I saw a peacock with a fiery tail, 11; and Eastward, into sunrise, 15. Also Foreword; Notes. Indexed by authors, first lines, and titles.

Hall, Donald, ed. Poetry sampler. Watts, F. 1962 (r)
Contents: 213 poems by 100 authors ungrouped. Also The purpose of this book. Indexed by authors and titles.

ANALYSIS OF BOOKS

Hazeltine, Alice I. and Smith, Elva S. comps. Year around; poems for children; il. by Paula Hutchison. Abingdon 1956 (3-7)
Contents: 191 poems by 117 authors grouped as follows: Introductory poem, 1; The seasons, 4; Spring, 48; Summer, 40; Autumn, 48; and Winter, 50. Indexed by authors and titles.

Hollander, John and Bloom, Harold, eds. Wind and the rain; an anthology of poems for young people. Doubleday 1961 (7-12)
Contents: 142 poems by 61 authors grouped as follows: The wind and the rain, 7; Spring, 22; Summer, 27; Fall, 35; Winter, 42; and Beyond winter, 9. Also Introduction. Indexed by authors, first lines, and titles.

Huber, Miriam Blanton, ed. Story and verse for children; il. by Lynd Ward. rev ed Macmillan 1955 (r)
Contents: Two sections of this book are devoted to poetry. The first section, Mother Goose rhymes, contains 65 rhymes; also Mother Goose rhymes: Origin and significance; Mother Goose rhymes: Suggested grades; Books of Mother Goose rhymes; and A B C books. The second section, Verse, contains 246 poems by 107 authors grouped as follows: Boys and girls, 35; Fairies and make-believe, 19; In feathers and fur and such, 43; The world and all, 53; For fun, 19; Roads to anywhere, 12; The day's work, 16; Our country, 13; Guideposts, 20; and Stories in verse, 16. Also Verse for children; References: Verse for children; Collections of verse; Books of verse. Indexed by authors and titles.

Hughes, Rosalind, comp. Let's enjoy poetry; an anthology of children's verse for kindergarten, grades 1, 2, and 3, with suggestions for teaching. Houghton 1958 (k-3)
Contents: 266 poems by 105 authors grouped as follows: Poems to teach rhythm, 32; Poems with refrain, 34; Two-part poems, 40; Line-a-child or group poems, 41; Three and more part poems, 46; and Poems for speaking in unison, 73. Also Foreword to teachers; Teaching suggestions.

Hughes, Rosalind, comp. Let's enjoy poetry; an anthology of children's verse for grades 4, 5, and 6, with suggestions for teaching. Houghton 1961 (4-6)
Contents: 201 poems by 111 authors grouped as follows: Poems to teach rhythm, 33; Poems with refrain, 31; Two-part poems, 24; Poems for sequence work, 31; Three and more part poems, 29; Poems for speaking in unison, 29; and Poems for individual work, 24. Also Foreword to teachers; Teaching suggestions.

Johnson, Edna; Sickels, Evelyn R.; and Sayers, Frances Clarke, comps. Anthology of children's literature; il. by Fritz Eichenberg. third ed Houghton 1959 (r)
Contents: Three sections of this book are devoted to poetry and a fourth section contains some poetry. The section Around the world in nursery rhymes contains 178 rhymes grouped as follows: Mother Goose nursery rhymes, 96; Mother Goose ballads, 7; John Newbery's Mother Goose, 6; Singing games, jingles, counting-out rhymes, 16; Riddles, paradoxes, tongue trippers, 18; Nursery rhymes of many lands, 28; and American chants and jingles, 7; also Introduction; Bibliography. The section Nonsense contains 44 poems by 8 authors; also Introduction; Bibliography. The section Poetry contains 208 poems by 91 authors grouped as follows: Fairies, fay, and far away, 16; Wind, woods, and weather, 64; Surge of the sea, 6; Little creatures, 26; Good day and good night, 50; Christmas, Christmas, 9; The grace of understanding, 21; and Ballads and tales, 16; also Introduction; Bibliography. The section Sacred writings and legends of the saints contains 8 songs from the Bible and 2 prayer poems. Indexed by authors, first lines, and titles.

Lines, Kathleen, comp. Lavender's blue; a book of nursery rhymes; il. by Harold Jones. Watts, F. 1954 (k-3)
Contents: 167 rhymes grouped as follows: Rock-a-bye, baby, 22; Girls and boys come out to play, 26; Old Mother Goose, 34; The lion and the unicorn, 29; A apple pie, 2; One, two, buckle my shoe, 8; Here we go round the mulberry bush, 9; The house that Jack built, 7; and If ifs and ands, 30. Also Cradle rhyme games; Nursery rhyme games. Indexed by first lines.

Livingston, Myra Cohn. I'm hiding; il. by Erik Blegvad. Harcourt 1961 (k-3)
Contents: One long poem describing favorite hiding places of children when playing this childhood game.

Livingston, Myra Cohn. Whispers and other poems; il. by Jacqueline Chwast. Harcourt 1958 (k-3)
Contents: 35 poems ungrouped.

Livingston, Myra Cohn. Wide awake and other poems; il. by Jacqueline Chwast. Harcourt 1959 (k-3)
Contents: 40 poems ungrouped.

Love, Katherine, comp. Little laughter; il. by Walter H. Lorraine. Crowell 1957 (k-4)
Contents: 77 poems by 28 authors ungrouped. Indexed by authors, first lines, and titles.

McCord, David. Far and few; rhymes of the never was and always is; il. by Henry B. Kane. Little 1952 (3-7)
Contents: 60 poems ungrouped.

McCord, David. Take sky; more rhymes of the never was and always is; il. by Henry B. Kane. Little 1962 (4-9)
Contents: 48 poems ungrouped.

McDonald, Gerald D. comp. Way of knowing; a collection of poems for boys; il. by Clare and John Ross. Crowell 1959 (7-12)
Contents: 161 poems by 116 authors grouped as follows: Come and see, 8; Stand and stare, 22; Fur, fin, and feather, 30; Live and learn, 19; Wondering, 23; Hear my tale, 13; O pioneers, 21; Rise and go, 18; and For you, 7. Also Foreword. Indexed by authors, first lines, and titles.

McEwen, Catherine Schaefer, comp. Away we go; 100 poems for the very young; il. by Barbara Cooney. Crowell 1956 (k-3)
Contents: 100 poems by 54 authors grouped as follows: Me and mine, 8; The outside world, 22; Nature and the seasons, 21; Living creatures, 12; Special days, 15; Poems for fun, 9; and Widening horizons, 13. Indexed by authors, first lines, and titles.

Manning-Sanders, Ruth, comp. Bundle of ballads; il. by William Stobbs. Lippincott 1959 (7-12)
Contents: 63 traditional ballads ungrouped. Also Introduction; Glossary. Indexed by first lines.

Milne, Alan Alexander. World of Christopher Robin; the complete When we were very young, and Now we are six; with decorations and new illustrations in full color by E. H. Shepard. Dutton 1958 (1-4)
Contents: 79 poems ungrouped. Also Just before we begin; Introduction to Now we are six.

Morrison, Lillian, comp. Yours till Niagara falls; il. by Marjorie Bauern-schmidt. Crowell 1950 (5-8)
Contents: 279 autograph rhymes grouped as follows: Roses are red, 27; What! Write in your album, 25; Look who's graduating, 16; True friends are like diamonds, 16; Listen, my friend, 28; I love you, I love you, 32; When you get married, 25; You're sitting on my head, 27; Start low, climb high, 32; Forget-me-not, 29; and Best wishes, amen, 22. Also prose autograph album entries.

Nash, Ogden, ed. Everybody ought to know; il. by Rose Shirvanian. Lippincott 1961 (r)
Contents: 136 poems by 80 authors ungrouped. Also Foreword. Indexed by authors, first lines, and titles.

ANALYSIS OF BOOKS

Nash, Ogden, ed. Moon is shining bright as day; an anthology of good-humored verse; il. by Rose Shirvanian. Lippincott 1953 (1-6)
 Contents: 180 poems by 93 authors grouped as follows: Introductory poem, 1; Has anybody seen my mouse? 64; Blum, blum, blum, 40; Over in the meadow, 30; How many miles to Babylon? 9; Four and twenty bowmen, 13; and Yonder see the morning blink, 23. Also Foreword. Indexed by authors, first lines, and titles.

Opie, Iona and Opie, Peter, comps. Oxford nursery rhyme book; with additional illustrations by Joan Hassall. Oxford 1955 (k-3)
 Contents: 800 nursery rhymes grouped as follows: Baby games and lullabies, 128; First favourites, 126; Little songs, 93; People, 95; A little learning, 88; Awakening, 76; Wonders, 59; Riddles, tricks, and trippers, 78; and Ballads and songs, 57. Also Preface; Sources of the illustrations. Indexed by first lines, refrains, and familiar titles.

Parker, Elinor, comp. 100 more story poems; il. by Peter Spier. Crowell 1960 (6-12)
 Contents: 100 poems by 67 authors grouped as follows: Just for fun, 25; Ballads old and new, 13; Battles long ago, 9; Rogues and heroes, 12; My true love hath my heart, 8; Fantasy and enchantment, 13; Birds and beasts, 11; and Christmastide, 9. Indexed by authors, first lines, and titles.

Parker, Elinor, comp. Singing and the gold; poems translated from world literature; wood engravings by Clare Leighton. Crowell 1962 (7-12)
 Contents: 205 poems by 118 authors translated from 34 languages by 107 translators grouped as follows: How sleep the brave, 8; Friendship is a sheltering tree, 9; Arise, my love, my fair one, 56; Sing a song of seasons, 46; Charm me asleep, 32; The bliss of solitude, 35; and All glorious above, 19. Also Foreword. Indexed by authors and sources, first lines, languages, titles, and translators.

Peterson, Isabel J. comp. First book of poetry; il. by Kathleen Elgin. Watts, F. 1954 (k-6)
 Contents: 81 poems by 48 authors grouped as follows: A variety of animals, 18; Interesting people, 13; Journeying far and wide, 7; The land of make-believe, 8; The world around us, 15; From season to season, 11; and Just for fun, 9. Also About poetry. Indexed by authors, first lines, and titles.

Plotz, Helen, comp. Imagination's other place; poems of science and mathematics; il. with wood engravings by Clare Leighton. Crowell 1955 (7-12)
 Contents: 124 poems by 79 authors grouped as follows: In the beginning, 38; The kingdom of number, 26; Both man and bird and beast, 38; and Watchers of the skies, 22. Also Preface and sectional introductions. Indexed by authors, first lines, and titles.

Plotz, Helen, comp. Untune the sky; poems of music and the dance; il. with wood engravings by Clare Leighton. Crowell 1957 (7-12)
 Contents: 134 poems by 105 authors grouped as follows: All instruments, 38; Singing over the earth, 21; One God is God of both, 23; Poet to dancer, 23; and Music shall untune the sky, 29. Also Preface and sectional introductions. Indexed by authors, first lines, and titles.

Read, Herbert, comp. This way, delight; a book of poetry for the young; il. by Juliet Kepes. Pantheon 1956 (5-9)
 Contents: 110 poems by 56 authors grouped as follows: Charms, 27; Songs, 43; Enchantments, 23; Escapes, 10; and Stories, 7. Also What is poetry? Indexed by authors and first lines.

Reeves, James. Blackbird in the lilac; verses for children; il. by Edward Ardizzone. Dutton 1959 (1-4)
 Contents: 53 poems grouped as follows: The blackbird in the lilac, 1; Dance and rhyme, 12; Hedge and harvest, 10; Elm trees and other people, 11; The street musician, 9; Myths and wonders, 9; and Time to go home, 1.

xvii

Reeves, James, ed. Golden land; stories, poems, songs, new and old; il. by Gillian Conway and others. Hastings house 1958 (r)
Contents: 68 poems by 24 authors ungrouped. Also Introduction and prose selections. Indexed by authors, first lines, and titles.

Reeves, James. Prefabulous animiles; il. by Edward Ardizzone. Dutton 1960 (k-4)
Contents: 13 poems ungrouped.

Reeves, James. Ragged Robin; il. by Jane Paton. Dutton 1961 (k-3)
Contents: 28 poems, 2 introductory and 1 for each of the 26 letters of the alphabet.

Reeves, James. Wandering moon; il. by Edward Ardizzone. Dutton 1960 (k-4)
Contents: 49 poems ungrouped.

Rieu, E. V. Flattered flying fish and other poems; il. by E. H. Shepard. Dutton 1962 (4-7)
Contents: 48 poems ungrouped. Also Preface.

Sandburg, Carl. Wind song; il. by William A. Smith. Harcourt 1960 (5-12)
Contents: 95 poems grouped as follows: New poems, 16; Little people, 14; Little album, 15; Corn belt, 14; Night, 12; Blossom themes, 12; and Wind, sea, and sky, 12. Also Introduction.

Smith, Janet Adam, comp. Looking glass book of verse; il. by Consuelo Joerns. Random house, distributors, 1959 (3-9)
Contents: 293 poems by 123 authors grouped as follows: Poetry, music, and dancing, 20; Night and day, seasons and weathers, 23; Beasts and birds, 34; Children, 20; Victuals and drink, 11; Some people, 6; Two countries, 18; Kings and heroes, 7; Tales, 10; Magic, 11; Fairies, nymphs, and gods, 8; Witches, charms, and spells, 14; March and battle, 10; Dirges, coronachs, and elegies, 16; Marvels and riddles, 8; Voyaging and travel, 15; The sea, 7; Love, 15; God and heaven, 21; Epigrams and reflections, 9; and History and time, 10. Also Introduction. Indexed by authors.

Smith, William Jay. Boy Blue's book of beasts; il. by Juliet Kepes. Little 1957 (k-3)
Contents: 39 poems ungrouped.

Smith, William Jay. Laughing time; il. by Juliet Kepes. Little 1955 (k-3)
Contents: 35 poems ungrouped.

Taylor, Margaret, comp. Did you feed my cow?; rhymes and games from city streets and country lanes; il. by Paul Galdone. Crowell 1956 (k-3)
Contents: 72 traditional rhymes grouped as follows: Call and response, 25; Play party, 8; Doorstep chants and rhymes, 13; Turn fast, turn slow, 12; and Street rhymes and bounce ball games, 14. Also Introduction. Indexed by first lines and titles.

Thompson, Blanche Jennings, ed. Pocketful of poems. Oxford book company 1954 (7-12)
Contents: 92 poems by 66 authors grouped as follows: I could not love thee, dear, so much, loved I not honor more, 12; Needles and pins, needles and pins, when a man marries, his trouble begins, 9; Blessed is he who has found his work; let him ask no other blessedness, 8; Nature never did betray the heart that loved her, 15; There is a destiny that makes us brothers; none goes his way alone; all that we send into the lives of others comes back into our own, 16; Character is what you are in the dark, 10; The price of wisdom is above rubies, 11; and God is our refuge and our strength; a very present help in trouble, 11. Also copious introductions and notes. Indexed by authors.

Untermeyer, Louis, ed. Golden treasury of poetry; il. by Joan Walsh Anglund. Golden press 1959 (r)
Contents: 431 poems by 178 authors grouped as follows: In the beginning, 18; Rhyme with reasons, 10; Creatures of every kind, 90; Gallery of people, 36; Unforgettable stories, 48; Laughter holding both his sides, 35; Good things in small packages, 67; Wide, wonderful world, 40; Around the year, 28; Come Christmas, 11; Sweet and low, 13; and Guiding stars, 35. Also Foreword and commentary. Indexed by authors, first lines, and titles.

ANALYSIS OF BOOKS

Untermeyer, Louis, ed.   Magic circle; stories and people in poetry; il. by Beth and Joe Krush.   Harcourt 1952   (7-12)
> *Contents*: 106 poems by 65 authors grouped as follows: Strange tales, 15; Gallant deeds, 10; Unforgettable people, 22; Our American heritage, 9; Six fables, 6; All in fun, 21; Ballads of the old days, 13; and Folk tales of our times, 10. Also Introduction and commentary. Indexed by authors and titles.

Withers, Carl and Jablow, Alta, comps.   Rainbow in the morning; il. by Abner Graboff.   Abelard-Schuman 1956   (k-3)
> *Contents*: 84 folk rhymes ungrouped.

Wood, Ray, comp.   Fun in American folk rhymes; il. by Ed Hargis.   Lippincott 1952   (k-5)
> *Contents*: 102 folk rhymes ungrouped. Also Introduction by Carl Carmer; Author's foreword. Indexed by first lines.

Worstell, Emma Vietor, comp.   Jump the rope jingles; il. by Sheila Greenwald.   Macmillan 1961   (k-3)
> *Contents*: 40 folk rhymes ungrouped. Also Foreword; Editor's note; and instructions for playing jump-rope games. Indexed by first lines.

Key to Symbols for Books Indexed

Grades are given in parentheses at the end of each entry: (k), kindergarten or preschool grade; (1), first grade; (2), second grade, etc. Comprehensive general collections are designated (r), reference.

Space is left after each symbol where the library call number may be inserted.

AlA — Aldis, D. All together. Putnam 1952 (1-4)

AlHd — Aldis, D. Hello day. Putnam 1959 (1-4)

AlP — Allen, M. L. Pocketful of poems. Harper 1957 (k-3)

AnI — Anglund, J. W. comp. and il. In a pumpkin shell. Harcourt 1960 (k-3)

ArTp — Arbuthnot, M. H. comp. Time for poetry, revised. Scott 1961 (r)

BeH — Behn, H. House beyond the meadow. Pantheon 1955 (2-4)

BeW — Behn, H. Windy morning. Harcourt 1953 (1-4)

BrBc — Brewton, S. and J. E. comps. Birthday candles burning bright. Macmillan 1960 (2-8)

BrL-k — Brown, H. A. and Heltman, H. J. eds. Let's-read-together poems. Harper (Row bk) 1949 (k-3)

BrL-7 — Brown, H. A. and Heltman, H. J. eds. Let's-read-together poems, 7. Harper (Row bk) 1950 (7)

BrL-8 — Brown, H. A. and Heltman, H. J. eds. Let's-read-together poems, 8. Harper (Row bk) 1954 (8)

BrR-3 — Brown, H. A. and Heltman, H. J. eds. Read-together poems, 3. Harper (Row bk) 1961 (3)

BrR-4 — Brown, H. A. and Heltman, H. J. eds. Read-together poems, 4. Harper (Row bk) 1961 (4)

BrR-5 — Brown, H. A. and Heltman, H. J. eds. Read-together poems, 5. Harper (Row bk) 1961 (5)

BrR-6 — Brown, H. A. and Heltman, H. J. eds. Read-together poems, 6. Harper (Row bk) 1961 (6)

BrS — Brewton, S. and J. E. comps. Sing a song of seasons. Macmillan 1955 (2-8)

ChA — Chute, M. G. Around and about. Dutton 1957 (k-3)

CiI — Ciardi, J. I met a man. Houghton 1961 (k-3)

CiM — Ciardi, J. Man who sang the sillies. Lippincott 1961 (2-5)

CiR — Ciardi, J. Reason for the pelican. Lippincott 1959 (2-5)

CiY — Ciardi, J. You read to me, I'll read to you. Lippincott 1962 (2-5)

CoH — Cole, W. ed. Humorous poetry for children. World pub 1955 (r)

CoI — Cole, W. ed. I went to the animal fair. World pub 1958 (k-3)

CoM — Coatsworth, E. Mouse chorus. Pantheon 1955 (k-3)

CoPm — Cole, W. ed. Poems of magic and spells. World pub 1960 (4-12)

CoPs — Cole, W. ed. Poems for seasons and celebrations. World pub 1961 (5-12)

CoSp — Cole, W. ed. Story poems new and old. World pub 1957 (5-12)

DeMg — De Angeli, M. comp. and il. Book of nursery and Mother Goose rhymes. Doubleday 1954 (k-3)

DeT — De La Mare, W. ed. Tom Tiddler's ground. Knopf 1962 (r)

DoP — Doane, P. comp. and il. Poems of praise. Lippincott 1955 (1-5)

EaI — Eastwick, I. O. I rode the black horse far away. Abingdon 1960 (k-3)

EaW — Eaton, A. T. comp. Welcome Christmas. Viking 1955 (r)

FaCb — Farjeon, E. Children's bells. Walck 1960 (4-8)

FaN — Farjeon, E. New book of days. Walck 1961 (r)

FeF — Ferris, H. ed. Favorite poems old and new. Doubleday 1957 (r)

FrLn — Frost, F. M. Little naturalist. McGraw (Whittlesey house pub) 1959 (2-5)

FrR — Frost, R. Road not taken. Holt 1951 (7-12)

Key to Abbreviations

at. attributed
bk book
comp. compiler, compiled
comps. compilers
ed. edition, editor
eds. editors
il. illustrated, illustrator
ils. illustrators
k kindergarten or preschool grade
pseud. pseudonym

pseuds. pseudonyms
pub publishing, publication
r reference
rev ed revised edition
sel. selection
sels. selections
tr. translator
tr. fr. translated from
trs. translators
wr. at. wrongly attributed

Directions for Use

The **title entry** is the main entry and gives the fullest information, including title (with the first line in parentheses when needed to distinguish between poems with the same title); variant titles; full name of author; translator; and symbols for collections in which the poem is to be found. **Variant titles** and titles with variant first lines are also listed in their alphabetical order, with *See* references to the main title.

> Carol ("In the bleak mid-winter") Christina
> Georgina Rossetti. *EaW*
> A Christmas carol. *BrBc* (sel.)
> A Christmas carol. See Carol ("In the bleak
> mid-winter")
> A tragic story. Adelbert von Chamisso, tr. fr.
> the German by William Makepeace Thack-
> eray. *BrL-7—CoH—DeT—FeF—NaM—*
> *UnG*

Titles of poems are grouped according to subject, in alphabetical order under a subject heading. The **subject entry** gives the title of poem; name of author with initials only; first line where needed for identification; variant titles; source title for subordinate selections; and the symbols for the collections in which the poem is to be found.

> Dogs
> Dogs ("The dogs I know") M. Chute. *ChA—*
> *HuL-1*
> Dogs ("I am his Highness' dog at Kew")
> A. Pope. *UnG*
> Elegy on the death of a mad dog. From
> The vicar of Wakefield. O. Goldsmith.
> *HaP—McW—SmLg—UnMo*
> "Every time I come to town." Unknown.
> *WoF*
> American Father Gander. *UnG*

The **author entry** gives the full name of the author; title of poem with its variants (first line in parentheses when needed for identification); and the symbols for the collections in which the poem is to be found. Included under the author entry are references from variant titles, and from titles of selections to the source title.

> Carroll, Lewis, pseud. (Charles Lutwidge Dodg-
> son)
> Alice's adventures in wonderland, sels.
> Father William. *BrBc—CoH—FeF—*
> *HuL-2—LoL—McW—UnG*
> "You are old, Father William, the
> young man said." *ArTp*
> Father William. See Alice's adventures in
> wonderland
> "You are old, Father William, the young
> man said." See Alice's adventures in
> wonderland—Father William

First lines of poems, enclosed in quotation marks, are listed in their alphabetical order with references to the title entry where all the information may be found. First lines are enclosed in quotation marks even when used as titles.

> "Away beyond the Jarboe tree." See Strange
> tree
> "On the first day of Christmas." See "The
> first day of Christmas"

When the source of a poem is more familiar than the title of the poem, or when only selections from a longer work are given, such titles are grouped under the source title. All titles subordinated to **source titles** are also entered in their alphabetical order with references to the source title.

> Alice's adventures in wonderland, sels. Lewis
> Carroll
> The lobster quadrille. *FeF—HuL-2—HuSv*
> *—NaM—PeF*
> The white rabbit's verses. *JoAc*
> The lobster quadrille. See Alice's adventures
> in wonderland
> The white rabbit's verses. See Alice's adven-
> tures in wonderland

See Key to Symbols, p. xxi

Index to Children's Poetry
Second Supplement

A., F. P. pseud. See Adams, Franklin P.
A apple pie. See "A was an apple-pie"
"A apple-pye. B bit it." See "A was an apple-pie"
The A B C bunny. Wanda Gág. *ArTp*
"A B C D." Mother Goose. *OpO*
"A, B, C, D, E, F, G." Mother Goose. *OpO*
A. E. pseud. See Russell, George William
"A for apple, big and red." See The A B C bunny
A. G. W. See W., A. G.
A is for abracadabra. Eleanor Farjeon. *FaCb*
"A is one." See Alphabet
A. W. See W., A.
"A was an apple-pie." Mother Goose. *DeMg —LiL*
  A apple pie. *JoAc*
  Apple-pye. *DeT*
  The tragical death of A, apple pie. *OpO*
"A was an archer." See "A was an archer, who shot at a frog"
"A was an archer, and shot at a frog." See "A was an archer, who shot at a frog"
"A was an archer, who shot at a frog." Mother Goose. *DeMg*
  "A was an archer." *LiL*
  Tom Thumb's picture alphabet. *OpO*
"A was once an apple-pie." Edward Lear. *ArTp*
  Nonsense alphabet. *JoAc*
Abarbanel, Clara Ruth. See Crane, Nathalia, pseud.
"The Abbé Liszt." See Liszt
Abbey, Henry
  What do we plant. *ArTp—FeF*
"The abbot of Inisfalen." William Allingham. *PaOm*
Abbots
  "The abbot of Inisfalen." W. Allingham. *PaOm*
  King John and the abbot of Canterbury. Unknown. *UnG*
Abdullah Bulbul Amir. Unknown. *CoSp*
Abe. Eleanor Farjeon. *FaCb—FaN*
"Abe he was born in the backwoods." See Abe
Abeita, Louise. See E-Yeh-Shuré
Abiding in the shadow of the Almighty. See Psalms—Psalm XCI
Abou Ben Adhem. Leigh Hunt. *BrR-6—ThP—UnG*
  Abou Ben Adhem and the angel. *FeF*
Abou Ben Adhem and the angel. See Abou Ben Adhem

"Abou Ben Adhem, may his tribe increase." See Abou Ben Adhem
About buttons. Dorothy Aldis. *BrL-k*
About candy. Dorothy Aldis. *AlA*
About Jimmy James. John Ciardi. *CiY*
"About suffering they were never wrong." See Musée des beaux arts
"About the dog days folks complain." See A dog day
"About the shark, phlegmatical one." See The Maldive shark
About the teeth of sharks. John Ciardi. *CiY*
"Above my face is a map." See Cloud-mobile
"Above the rabbit-shaken bush." See North
"Above the wary waiting world." See Christmas song
Abraham Lincoln ("Lincoln was a long man") Rosemary Carr and Stephen Vincent Benét. *ArTp—CoPs—HaY*
Abraham Lincoln ("Oh, slow to smite and swift to spare") William Cullen Bryant. *BrR-6*
Abraham Lincoln ("Remember he was poor and country-bred") Mildred Plew Meigs. *ArTp—BrR-6—PeF*
Abraham Lincoln walks at midnight. Vachel Lindsay. *BrL-8—FeF—JoAc*
Abram Brown. See "Old Abram Brown is dead and gone"
Absence. Unknown. *DeT*
A-caroling on Christmas eve. James S. Tippett. *McAw*
Accordions
  A man with a little pleated piano. W. Welles. *FeF*
Achilles
  "The horses of Achilles." E. Farjeon. *FaCb*
  "King Priam in the dark night went." E. Farjeon. *FaCb*
Achilles Deatheridge. See The Spoon River anthology
"The acorn." See Acorn cap
Acorn cap. Myra Cohn Livingston. *LiWa*
Acorns. See also Oak trees
  Acorn cap. M. C. Livingston. *LiWa*
  To an oak dropping acorns. E. Farjeon. *FaCb—FaN*
Acquainted with the night. Robert Frost *FrY—HaP*
Acquiescence Irwin Edman. *ThP*
Acrobat. See A circus garland

Acrobats
Acrobat. From A circus garland. R. Field. *HuSv*
The acrobats. D. Aldis. *AlA*
The man on the flying trapeze. Unknown. *SmLg*

The **acrobats**. Dorothy Aldis. *AlA*

"**Across** the narrow beach we flit." See The sandpiper

"**Across** the sands of Syria." See The legend of the first cam-u-el

"**Across** the seas of Wonderland to Mogadore we plodded." See Forty singing seamen

"**Across** the years he could recall." See The secret heart

Action rhyme. E. H. Adams. *HuL-1*

Actors and acting
At the theater. R. Field. *FeF*
It bids pretty fair. R. Frost. *FrR*
The make-up man. J. H. Breig. *BrR-5*

Adam and Eve
Eve. R. Hodgson. *NaE*

Adam Bell, Clym of the Clough, and William of Cloudesley. Unknown. *MaB*

Adams, E. H.
Action rhyme. *HuL-1*

Adams, Franklin P. (F. P. A., pseud.)
The rich man. *CoH*

Adams, H. M.
Johnny's farm. *HuL-1*

Adams, James Barton
The cowboy's life. at. *ArTp*

Adams, Léonie
The walk. *GrCc*

Addison, Joseph
"The spacious firmament on high." *BrL-7*

Addison, Joseph (about)
Atticus. From Epistle to Dr Arbuthnot. A. Pope. *HaP*

Addition. See Arithmetic

Address to my infant daughter. William Wordsworth. *NaE*

The **ad-dressing** of cats. T. S. Eliot. *UnG*

"**Adieu,** farewell earth's bliss." See In plague time

The **admiral's** caravan, sel. Charles Edward Carryl
The plaint of the camel. *FeF—HuSv—NaE —PeF*
The camel's complaint. *CoI—HuL-2— JoAc*
The camel's lament. *UnG*

The **admiral's** ghost. Alfred Noyes. *ArTp— CoPm—JoAc*

Adonais. Percy Bysshe Shelley. *HaP*(sel.)

Adoration of the disk. See The book of the dead

Adults
Differences. D. Aldis. *AlA*
Grown-up people. D. Aldis. *AlA*

Adventure ("It's not very far to the edge of town") Harry Behn. *ArTp*

Adventure ("The little men of meadow land") Nancy Byrd Turner. *HuSv*

Adventure and adventurers. See also Camping; Explorers and exploration; Frontier and pioneer life; Gipsies; Heroes and heroines; Hunters and hunting; Indians of America; Roads and trails; Seamen; Wayfaring life
Adventure ("It's not very far to the edge of town") H. Behn. *ArTp*
Adventure ("The little men of meadow land") N. B. Turner. *HuSv*
Adventures. A. Kramer. *BrBc*
"The bearer of evil tidings." R. Frost. *FrR*
The knight without a name. Unknown. *HoW*
Maps. D. B. Thompson. *ArTp—HuL-2*
Q is for quest. E. Farjeon. *FaCb*
Tom Twist. W. A. Butler. *CoH*
Ulysses. A. Tennyson. *HaP*

Adventures. Arthur Kramer. *BrBc*

Adventures of Isabel. Ogden Nash. *CoH— NaM*

Adversity. See Consolation; Misfortune

Advice. See also Conduct of life
Advice ("He that sweareth") H. Rhodes. *UnG*
Advice ("Question not, but live and labor") Unknown. *ThP*
Advice from an elderly mouse. E. J. Coatsworth. *CoM*
Advice to a bird, species unknown. G. S. Galbraith. *BrL-8*
Advice to a child. E. Farjeon. *FaCb*
Advice to a girl. T. Campion. *ThP*
Advice to small children. E. Anthony. *UnG*
Advice to young naturalists. L. E. Richards. *LoL*
Sage counsel. A. Quiller-Couch. *CoH— LoL*
"Three children sliding on the ice." J. Gay. *DeMg—JoAc—LiL*
Three children sliding. *OpO*
A warning. *DeT*

Advice ("He that sweareth") Hugh Rhodes. *UnG*

Advice ("Question not, but live and labor") Unknown. *ThP*

Advice from an elderly mouse. Elizabeth Jane Coatsworth. *CoM*

Advice to a bird, species unknown. Georgie Starbuck Galbraith. *BrL—8*

Advice to a child. Eleanor Farjeon. *FaCb*

Advice to a girl. Thomas Campion. *ThP*

Advice to small children. Edward Anthony. *UnG*

Advice to young naturalists. Laura E. Richards. *LoL*

Aegean sea
Santorin. J. E. Flecker. *GrCc*

Aeneas (about)
"Queen Dido is building." E. Farjeon. *FaCb*

Aeroplane. Mary McB. Green. *ArTp—PeF*

Aeroplanes. See Airplanes

Aesculapius (about)
The staff of Aesculapius. M. Moore. *PlI*

"An **airplane** has gigantic wings." See The airplane

"The **airplane** taxis down the field." See Taking off

Airplanes. See also Aviators
Aeroplane. M. M. Green. *ArTp—PeF*
The airplane. R. B. Bennett. *FeF*
At the airport. M. C. Livingston. *LiWa*
Chairoplane chant. N. B. Turner. *BrR-5*
Cockpit in the clouds. D. Dorrance. *ArTp —FeF*
Darius Green and his flying-machine. J. T. Trowbridge. *NaM*
High flight. J. G. Magee, Jr. *FeF—McW —UnMc*
Night plane. F. M. Frost. *ArTp—FeF*
Riding in an airplane. D. W. Baruch. *FeF*
"Seven sharp propeller blades." J. Ciardi. *CiR*
Silver ships. M. P. Meigs. *ArTp—BrR-5— FeF*
Taking off. M. M. Green. *ArTp—HuL-1*
    The airplane. *McAw*
To Beachey, 1912. C. Sandburg. *ArTp*
Up in the air. J. S. Tippett. *ArTp*
Wilbur Wright and Orville Wright. R. C. and S. V. Benét. *BrL-8*
The Wrights' biplane. R. Frost. *FrR*

"**Airs,** that wander and murmur round." See The siesta

Airships. See Airplanes; Aviators; Balloons

Akhmatova, Anna
The muse. *GrCc*
Upon the hard crest. *PaS*

The **Akond** of Swat. Edward Lear. *HuL-2 —LoL—UnG*

"**Ala,** mala, mink, monk." Mother Goose. *OpO*

Aladdin. James Russell Lowell. *BrR-5— CoPm—McW*

The **alarmed** skipper. James T. Fields. *UnG*

Alas, alack. Walter De La Mare. *ArTp— BrL-k—FeF—HuL-1—NaE*

"**Alas,** alas, I am so dumb." Unknown. *MoY*

"**Alas,** noble Prince Leopold, he is dead." See The death of Prince Leopold

Alaska
The cremation of Sam McGee. R. W. Service. *CoSp—UnMc*
The shooting of Dan McGrew. R. W. Service. *UnMc*

"**Albatross,** albatross, why do you fly." See The albatross and the equator

The **albatross** and the equator. E. V. Rieu. *RiF*

Albatrosses
The albatross and the equator. E. V. Rieu. *RiF*
The rime of the ancient mariner, sels. S. T. Coleridge. *HaP*(complete)—*PlU* (sel.)—*SmLg*(complete)
    The ancient mariner. *DeT*
    He prayeth best. *DoP—FeF—HuSv— ThP*
        He prayeth well. *HuL-2*
        The rime of the ancient mariner. *UnG*

The **alchemist.** A. A. Milne. *MiWc*

Aldington, Mrs Richard. See D., H., pseud.

Aldis, Dorothy (Keeley)
About buttons. *BrL-k*
About candy. *AlA*
The acrobats. *AlA*
After my bath. *AlA*
A-ha. *AlA*
All a duck needs. *AlA*
Alone. *AlA*
At night. *AlHd*
Away. *AlA*
Awful mornings. *AlA*
Bad. *AlA*
The balloon man. *AlA—ArTp*
Bare-back rider. *AlA*
Bed in winter. *AlA*
Big. *AlA*
Blum. *AlA—CoH—McAw—NaM*
Brooms. *AlA—BrR-4*
Bursting. *AlA*
Christmas dog. *AlA*
Clouds. *AlA*
The clown. *AlA*
Dangerous. *AlA*
Day-time moon. *AlA*
Differences. *AlA*
The dinner party. *AlA*
Don't tell me. *AlA*
Down on the beach. *AlA*
The dragon fly. *AlA*
A dreadful sight. *AlA*
Dresses. *AlA*
Early. *AlA*
The Easter rabbit. *AlA*
Eek eek. *AlHd*
The elephants. *AlA*
Emma's store. *AlA*
Evening walk. *AlA*
"Everybody says." *AlA—BrL-k—FeF— HuL-1*
Exactly right. *AlHd*
Feet. *AlA—BrR-4*
Fireflies. *AlHd*
First winter's day. *AlA*
Fisher man. *AlA*
Flies. *AlA*
Flower party. *AlHd*
For Christmas. *AlA—HuL-1*
For dessert. *AlHd*
Found again. *AlA*
Fourth of July night. *AlA—ArTp—BrS— McAw*
Going to sleep. *AlA*
The goldfish. *AlA—BrL-k*
Goodness me. *AlA*
The grasshoppers. *AlA—CoI—HuL-2*
Grown-up people. *AlA*
Guessing game. *AlHd*
Harebells. *AlA*
The Harpers' farm. *AlA*
Hello day. *AlHd*
Here I come. *AlA*
Hiding. *AlA—ArTp—BrL-k—FeF—JoAc*
The holiday. *AlA*
Hot weather. *AlA*
The hunter. *AlA*
I have to have it. *AlA*
I never hear. *AlA*
Ice. *ArTp—BrL-k*

The ice had all melted. *AlHd*
The ice man. *AlA—HuL-1*
If you ask me. *AlHd*
I'm a kitty. *AlHd*
I'm so big. *AlHd*
In May. *AlA—AlHd*
In spring in warm weather. *AlA—BrBc*
In the morning. *AlHd*
In the summer. *AlA—McAw*
Inch-worm. *AlHd*
Insight. *ThP*
Ironing day. *AlA*
The island. *AlA*
It was. *AlA*
Kick a little stone. *AlA*
The lazy crocuses. *AlA*
Lazy day. *AlHd*
A lazy sight. *AlA*
Like me. *AlA—McAw*
Little. *AlA—ArTp—FeF*
Little fountain. *AlA*
The little girl and the turkey. *AlA*
The little hat. *AlA*
A long time ago. *AlA*
Looking in. *AlA—HuL-1*
Looking out my window. *AlA*
A lucky thing. *AlA*
Luncheons. *AlA*
Mary Anne's luncheon. *AlA*
Mister Carrot. *AlA*
Mourning doves. *AlHd*
Mouths. *AlA*
My brother ("My brother is inside the sheet") *ArTp*
My brother ("Today I went to market with my mother") *AlHd*
My dress is pink. *AlHd*
My keys. *AlHd*
My nose. *AlA*
My pony. *AlA*
My streamer hat. *AlA*
Naughty soap song. *AlA—BrL-k*
New. *AlA*
The new house. *AlHd*
The new pet. *AlA*
Nice food. *AlA*
Night and morning. *AlA—CoPs—HaY*
No. *AlA*
No one heard him call. *AlA*
Noah's ark. *AlHd*
Not any more. *AlA*
Not that. *AlA*
The nuns. *AlA*
Oh, dear. *AlA*
On a snowy day. *AlA*
    Snow. *ArTp*
On some windy day. *AlA*
On the beach. *AlHd*
Once when I was sick. *AlA*
Our guest. *AlA*
Our little calf. *AlA*
Our little fir tree. *AlA*
Our picnic. *AlHd*
Our silly little sister. *AlA—CoH—FeF—NaE*
Our squirrel. *AlHd*
Our tame baby squirrel. *AlA*
The picnic. *AlA—ArTp—McAw*
Please. *AlA*
Polite tea party. *AlA*

Practicing. *AlA*
Proud Jane. *AlA*
Radiator lions. *AlA—JoAc*
Raining again. *AlA*
The reason. *AlA—ArTp*
A riddle: What am I. *AlA—BrL-k*
The sad monkey. *AlA*
The sad shoes. *AlA*
Saddest of all. *AlA*
The seals. *AlA—ArTp*
The secret place. *AlA*
See, I can do it. *AlA*
Setting the table. *ArTp—FeF*
Singing. *AlA*
Skipping ropes. *AlA—HuSv*
Snow. See On a snowy day
Some vegetables and flowers. *AlHd*
Somersault. *ALA*
Spring. *AlA*
The sprinkler. *AlA*
The storm. *AlA*
The story of the baby squirrel. *ArTp*
Stranger still. *AlHd*
A summer story. *AlHd*
Supper for a lion. *AlA*
Susie the milk horse. *AlA*
A tail to wag. *AlA*
Taller and older. *AlHd*
Tell me. *AlA*
That was the one. *AlA*
Then. *BrBc—HuL-1*
A thought. *AlA*
The time we like best. *AlA*
Today. *AlHd*
Train ride. *AlA*
Tree house. *AlHd*
Troubles. *BrL-k—HuSv—JoAc*
The twins. *AlA—BrBc*
Waiting. *AlA*
Watch me. *AlHd*
We know a house. *AlA*
The welcome. *AlA*
What am I. *HuSv—JoAc*
What happened. *AlA*
What I would do. *AlA*
What they are for. *AlA*
When. *AlA—BrS*
When Anabelle's it. *AlA*
When I was lost. *AlA*
When I'm invited. *AlHd*
Where is it. *AlA*
Whistle. See Whistles
Whistles. *JoAc*
    Whistle. *BrL-k*
"White flowers and white butterflies." *AlHd*
Who did it. *AlA*
Windy wash day. *AlA—ArTp—JoAc*
Winter coats. *AlA*
Winter flower store. *AlA*
Aldrich, Thomas Bailey
Marjorie's almanac. *FeF*
Memory. *ThP*
October. *UnG*
Sleepy song. *UnG*
Tiger-lilies. *UnG*
Aldridge, Richard
The pine bough. *CoPs*

Alexander, Cecil Frances
　All things beautiful. See The creation
　"All things bright and beautiful." See The creation
　The creation. *DoP—FeF*
　　All things beautiful. *BrR-3*
　　"All things bright and beautiful." *HuSv*
　　God, our maker. *DeT*
　God, our maker. See The creation
　"Once in royal David's city." *DoP*
　St Patrick's breastplate. tr. *SmLg*
Alexander, John T.
　The winning of the TV West. *McW*
"Alexander Graham Bell." See Alexander Graham Bell did not invent the telephone
Alexander Graham Bell did not invent the telephone. Robert P. Tristram Coffin. *ArTp*
Alexander the Great, King of Macedon (about)
　Alexander to his horse. E. Farjeon. *FaCb*
　Alexander's feast; or, The power of music. J. Dryden. *HoW*
　Alexandrian kings. C. P. Cavafy. *GrCc*
Alexander to his horse. Eleanor Farjeon. *FaCb*
Alexander's feast; or, The power of music. John Dryden. *HoW*
Alexander's song. See "There was a man of Thessaly"
Alexandrian kings. C. P. Cavafy, tr. by John Mavrogordato. *GrCc*
"The **Alexandrians** came in a crowd." See Alexandrian kings
Alfred, King
　Proverbs of King Alfred. *McW*
Alfred the Great, King of England
　The king's cake. E. Farjeon. *FaCb*
Algy. See "Algy met a bear"
"Algy met a bear." Unknown. *FeF*
　Algy. *NaM*
Alice. William Jay Smith. *SmL*
"Alice Corbin is gone." Carl Sandburg. *SaW*
Alice Fell. William Wordsworth. *DeT*
The **Alice** Jean. Robert Graves. *GrP*
Alice's adventures in wonderland, sels. Lewis Carroll
　Father William. *BrBc—CoH—FeF—HuL-2—LoL—McW—UnG*
　　"You are old, Father William, the young man said." *ArTp*
　"How doth the little crocodile." *ArTp—FeF—LoL—McW—NaM—SmLg*
　　The crocodile. *JoAc—UnG*
　The lobster quadrille. *FeF—HuL-2—HuSv—NaM—PeF*
　'Tis the voice of the lobster. *JoAc*
　　The voice of the lobster. *NaE*
　Turtle soup. *ReG*
　　Beautiful soup. *DeT*
　The white rabbit's verses. *JoAc*
Alighieri, Durante. See Dante
Alison Gross. Unknown. *MaB*
All a duck needs. Dorothy Aldis. *AlA*
All about boys and girls. John Ciardi. *CiY*

All about fireflies all about. David McCord. *McFf*
"All along the backwater." See The wind in the willows—Ducks' ditty
"All around the cobbler's bench." See Pop goes the weasel
All around the town, sels. Phyllis McGinley
　"B's the bus." *ArTp—FeF—LoL*
　"C is for the circus." *ArTp*
　"E is the escalator." *ArTp—LoL—McAw*
　"F is the fighting firetruck." *FeF*
　"J's the jumping jay-walker." *ArTp—FeF*
　"P's the proud policeman." *ArTp*
　"R is for the restaurant." *ArTp*
　"U is for umbrellas." *ArTp*
　"W's for windows." *ArTp*
"All but blind. " Walter De La Mare. *FeF—McW*
"All day I hear the noise of waters." See Chamber music—The noise of waters
"All day in mother's garden here." See Bedtime
All fools' day. See April fools' day
All fools' day. Unknown. *BrS*
"All happy and glad in the sunshine I stood." See Spring
"All honor to him who shall win the prize." See For those who fail
"All I do is dole out minutes." See Gallop, gallop to a rhyme
"All I need to make me happy." Unknown American Father Gander. *UnG*
"All in a glance." See N is for nixie
"All in green went my love riding." E. E. Cummings. *ReT*
"All in the April morning." See Sheep and lambs
"All in the downs the fleet was moored." See Black-eyed Susan
"All in the groves of dragon-fungus." See The chickamungus
"All in the merry month of May." See Barbara Allen
All in the morning. Unknown. *BrBc*
All in together. Unknown. *WoJ*
"All in together, girls." See All in together
"All-intellectual eye, our solar round." See To the memory of Sir Isaac Newton
"All music, sauces, feasts, delights and pleasures." See Christian ethics
"All my sheep." See Last words before winter
"All night by the rose, the rose." See The rose's scent
"All of a sudden the big nasturtiums." See The big nasturtiums
"All out of doors looked darkly in at him." See An old man's winter night
"All that I know." See My star
"All that people care about." See Picnic by the sea
All that's past. Walter De La Mare. *ReT*
"All the bells were ringing." Christina Georgina Rossetti. *ArTp*
"All the birds have come again." See Spring's arrival
"All the foul fiends and demons of the air." See Static

"**All** the little tadpoles." See Spring lullaby

"**All** the names I know from nurse." See The flowers

"**All** the others translate: the painter sketches." See The composer

All the rabbits and Robin A'Dare. **Ivy O.** Eastwick. *EaI*

"**All** the soldiers marching along." See Remembering day

"**All** the way to Alfriston." Eleanor Farjeon. *FaCb*

"**All** the world's a stage." See As you like it

All things beautiful. See The creation

"**All** things bright and beautiful." See The creation

"**All** through the garden I went and went." See The butterbean tent

All through the night. See Welsh lullaby

"**All** through the woods it's as dark as dark." See Alone

All wool. Abbie Farwell Brown. *ArTp*

"**All** work and no play makes Jack a dull boy." Mother Goose. *OpO*

"**All** ye woods, and trees, and bowers." See The god of sheep

Alle vögel sind schon da. Frances Chesterton. *PlU*

"**Alleluia.** Alleluia. Let the holy anthem rise." Unknown. *CoPs*

Allen, Marie Louise
Angleworms. *AlP*
Birthday candles. *AlP*
The circus. *AlP*
First snow. *AlP—ArTp—BrL-k*
Five years old. *AlP—BrBc—BrL-k*
Forever. *AlP*
If I were a fish. *AlP*
The lawn mower. *AlP*
Mister Hoppy-toes. *AlP*
The mitten song. *AlP—ArTp—BrL-k—HuL-1*
My zipper suit. *AlP—ArTp—BrL-k*
Rubbers and galoshes. *AlP*
Seesaw. *AlP*
Sky laundry. *AlP*
Sneezing. *AlP—BrL-k—HuL-1*
Soap bubbles. *AlP*
Stop and go. *AlP*
The telephone. *AlP*
Washing. *AlP*
What is it. *AlP*
The wind. *AlP*
Winter-wear. *AlP*

Allen, Marjorie. See Seiffert, Marjorie Allen

Allen, Sara Van Alstyne
Walk on a winter day. *HaY*

Allen, Willis Boyd
Christmastide. *DoP*

Allen-a-Dale. See Rokeby

"**Allen-a-Dale** has no fagot for burning." See Rokeby—Allen-a-Dale

Alley cat. David McCord. *McT*

Allie. Robert Graves. *FeF—GrP*

"**Allie,** call the birds in." See Allie

Alligators
"I went to the river and couldn't get across (I jumped on an alligator)." Unknown. *WoF*
The purist. O. Nash. *CoH—NaM*

Alligoshee. Mother Goose. *OpO*

Allingham, William
"The abbot of Inisfalen." *PaOm*
Amy Margaret. *BrBc*
The elf singing. *HuSv—UnG*
The fairies. *CoPm — DeT — FeF — JoAc—NaE—PaOm—PeF—ReG—SmLg*
"Up the airy mountain." *HuSv*
The fairy king. *CoPm*
"Four ducks on a pond." *HuL-2—ReT*
Homeward bound. *BrL-7*
Robin Redbreast. *NaM*
A swing song. *FeF—HuL-1—NaM—PeF*
"Up the airy mountain." See The fairies
Wishing. *FeF*

Allison, Young Ewing
Derelict. *PaOm*

Alma-Tadema, Miss Laurence (or Lawrence)
"If no one ever marries me." *BrBc—HuL-1—UnG*
Playgrounds. *McAw*
The robin. *BrL-k—HuL-1*

An **almanac.** William Sharp. *JoAc*

Almanacs
An almanac. W. Sharp. *JoAc*
The child reads an almanac. F. Jammès. *FeF*
Marjorie's almanac. T. B. Aldrich. *FeF*

"**Alone.**" Myra Cohn Livingston. *LiW*

Alone ("All through the woods it's as dark as dark") Marchette Chute. *ChA*

Alone ("From childhood's hour I have not been") Edgar Allan Poe. *HaP*

Alone ("I never had walked quite so far") Joseph Paget-Fredericks. *BrR-3—HuSv*

Alone ("I was alone the other day") Dorothy Aldis. *AlA*

Alone ("White daisies are down in the meadow") John Farrar. *HaY*

"**Alone** in the night." See Stars

"**Alone** on the lawn." See The dancing cabman

"**Along** came a new grief." See Insight

"**Along** the thousand roads of France." See The good Joan

"**Along** the valley of the Ump." See The hippocrump

Alons au bois le may cueillir. Charles d'Orleans, tr. fr. the French by William Ernest Henley. *PaS*

Alphabet
The A B C bunny. W. Gág. *ArTp*
"A B C D." Mother Goose. *OpO*
"A, B, C, D, E, F, G." Mother Goose. *OpO*
"A was an apple-pie." Mother Goose. *DeMg—LiL*
A apple pie. *JoAc*
Apple-pye. *DeT*
The tragical death of A, apple pie. *OpO* .
"A was an archer, who shot at a frog." Mother Goose. *DeMg*
"A was an archer." *LiL*
Tom Thumb's picture alphabet. *OpO*
"A was once an apple-pie." E. Lear. *ArTp*
Nonsense alphabet. *JoAc*
Alphabet. D. McCord. *McT*

"**Amy** Margaret's five years old." See Amy Margaret

Anacreon
The grasshopper. *HoW—UnG*

Anacreontics, sel. Abraham Cowley
The thirsty earth. *HoW*
    Drinking. *HaP*

Anatomy. See Body, Human; also names of parts of the body, as Hands

Ancestry. See also Heritage
The fall of J. W. Beane. O. Herford. *CoSp*
Irish. E. J. O'Brien. *BrS*
Pedigree. E. Dickinson. *UnG*
Progress. D. McCord. *PlI*
Small talk. D. Marquis. *CoSp*
Watch, America. R. Nathan. *McW*

"The **anchor** is weigh'd and the sails they are set." See Away, Rio

An **ancient** Christmas carol. Unknown. *DoP*

The **ancient** mariner. See The rime of the ancient mariner

An **ancient** prayer. Thomas Harry Basil Webb. *DoP*

"An **ancient** story I'll tell you anon." See King John and the abbot of Canterbury

"**And** a clam caught my little finger." See The little girl that lost her finger

"**And** are ye sure the news is true." See The sailor's wife

"**And** are you really come again." See Cuckoo-come-again

And back. Rodney Bennett. *HuL-1*

"**And** can the physician make sick men well." See Song

"**And** Dick said, Look what I have found." See Crescent moon

"**And** did those feet in ancient time." See Milton—Jerusalem

"**And** God stepped out on space." See The creation

"**And** Gwydion said to Math, when it was spring." See The wife of Llew

"**And** here's the happy, bounding flea." See The flea

"**And** if he's gone away, said she." See Story

"**And** in the frosty season, when the sun." See The prelude—Skating

"**And,** like a dying lady lean and pale." See The moon

"**And** mathematics, fresh as May." See Reliques

"**And** now at last I come to it: spring." See Spring, etc

"**And** now you live dispersed on ribbon roads." See The rock

"**And** once, in some swamp-forest, these." See Coal fire

"**And** Science said." See The dunce

And shall Trelawny die. Robert Stephen Hawker. *NaE*

"**And,** star and system rolling past." See In memoriam

And that's all. See "There was an old man (and he had a calf)"

"**And** then I pressed the shell." See The shell

"**And** there were in the same country shepherds." See Gospel according to Luke—Christmas eve

"**And** they had fixed the wedding day." See The thorn

"**And** what is so rare as a day in June." See The vision of Sir Launfal—A day in June

"**And** where have you been, my Mary." See The fairies of the Caldon Low

"**And** while my visitor prattled." See Translations from the Chinese — Secret thoughts

"**And** whither, black-eyed gypsies." See Followers of the sun

"**And** will King Olaf come again." Eleanor Farjeon. *FaCb*

And yet fools say. George S. Holmes. *ArTp—BrL-7*

Andersen, Hans Christian
The pearl. *PaS*

Andersen, Hans Christian (about)
Fairy gardens. E. Farjeon. *FaCb—FaN*

Anderson, Marjorie Allen
A new friend. *McAw*

Andre. Gwendolyn Brooks. *ArTp*

Andrew Jackson. Martha Keller. *UnG—UnMc*

Andrewes, Lancelot
Phillis inamorata. *GrCc*

Andriello, Amelia
Autumn eve. *BrS*

An **angel.** See "An angel came as I lay in bed"

"An **angel** came as I lay in bed." Unknown, tr. fr. the Hebrew by Rose Fyleman. *JoAc*

An **angel.** *DoP*

The **angel** in the apple tree. Winifred Welles. *HuSv*

"An **angel** living near the moon." See To Dick, on his sixth birthday

An **angel** singing. William Blake. *DoP*

"An **angel** told Mary." See A Christmas carol

Angels
Abou Ben Adhem. L. Hunt. *BrR-6—ThP—UnG*
    Abou Ben Adhem and the angel. *FeF*
"An angel came as I lay in bed." Unknown. *JoAc*
    An angel. *DoP*
The angel in the apple tree. W. Welles. *HuSv*
An angel singing. W. Blake. *DoP*
Guardian angel. E. Goudge. *DoP*
Little Breeches. J. Hay. *UnG*
Lullaby. Unknown. *DoP*

Angels in the air, sel. S. W. Partridge
Dark. *DeT*

"The **angels** to the shepherds sang." See A carol

Anger
He that is slow to anger. From Proverbs, Bible, Old Testament. *FeF*
    "He that is slow to anger is better than the mighty." *ArTp*
"Jenny was so mad." Mother Goose. *DeMg*

A poison tree. W. Blake. *CoPm*

Anger—*Continued*
"A soft answer turneth away wrath." From Proverbs, Bible, Old Testament. *ArTp*
    A merry heart. *HuSv*

The **angler's** reveille. Henry Van Dyke. *HuSv*

Angleworms. Marie Louise Allen. *AlP*

Angling. See Fishermen and fishing

Animal crackers. Christopher Morley. *ArTp—BrR-3—FeF—JoAc*

"**Animal** crackers, and cocoa to drink." See Animal crackers

Animal fair. Unknown. *CoI—NaM—UnG*

The **animal** store. Rachel Field. *ArTp—CoI—HuL-1*

Animal tracks
  The snow-bird. F. D. Sherman. *ArTp—BrS*
  Tracks. J. Farrar. *BrL-k*
  Tracks in the snow. M. Chute. *BrS—ChA*

Animals. See also Aquariums; Circus; Fables; also names of classes of the animal kingdom, as Birds; also names of animals, as Elephants
  Afreet. D. McCord. *McT*
  Allie. R. Graves. *FeF—GrP*
  The amperzand. J. Reeves. *ReP*
  Animal fair. Unknown. *CoI—NaM—UnG*
  The animals. E. Muir. *GrCc*
  Animals' houses. J. Reeves. *ReW*
  The answers. R. Clairmont. *CoH—UnG*
    When did the world begin. *McW*
  The artful ant. O. Herford. *CoH*
  At the beginning of winter. E. J. Coatsworth. *CoM*
  At the zoo ("Giraffes are tall") M. Chute. *ChA*
  At the zoo ("I've been to the zoo") M. C. Livingston. *LiW*
  Autumn. N. B. Turner. *HaY*
  Bagpipes. Mother Goose. *OpO*
  The barn. E. J. Coatsworth. *BrBc—EaW—UnG*
  The barnyard. M. Burnham. *ArTp—HuL-1*
  Bed-time story. M. Cane. *UnG*
  "Birds of a feather flock together." Mother Goose. *DeMg*
    Signs, seasons, and sense. *UnG*
  Birthday gifts. L. B. Scott and J. J. Thompson. *BrBc*
  Birthday presents. Unknown. *McAw*
  The blether. J. Reeves. *ReP*
  "Bow-wow, says the dog." Mother Goose. *AnI—DeMg—OpO*
  Brothers and sisters. E. Farjeon. *FaCb—FaN*
  "A bullfrog sat on a downy nest." Unknown. *WiRm*
  The bumblebeaver. From Mixed beasts. K. Cox. *ArTp*
  "Calico pie." E. Lear. *FeF—LoL—ReG—SmLg—UnG*
  The carnival of animals. O. Nash. *PlU* (sel.)
  Carol. D. Sayers. *EaW*
  The catipoce. J. Reeves. *ReP*
  The chickamungus. J. Reeves. *ReP—UnG*

Christ is born. J. A. Chapman. *EaW*
Christmas eve legend. F. M. Frost. *BrBc—EaW*
A Christmas folk song. L. W. Reese. *ArTp—DoP—FeF—JoAc*
Christmas in the woods. F. M. Frost. *ArTp*
Christmas song. E. E. Long. *BrS*
Coati-mundi. W. J. Smith. *SmB*
Cold-blooded creatures. E. Wylie. *PlI*
"Come hither, little puppy dog." Mother Goose. *DeMg*
The common cormorant. Unknown. *CoH—LoL—SmLg—UnG*
Conversation. A. Robinson. *BrR-3—HuL-1*
The cove. D. McCord. *McT*
Covering the subject. R. Armour. *McW*
"The cow has a cud." From Five chants. D. McCord. *McFf*
The cries of Bethlehem. E. Farjeon. *FaN*
The difference. E. Farjeon. *FaCb—FaN*
The doze. J. Reeves. *ReP—UnG*
Easter in the woods. F. M. Frost. *BrS*
"Excuse us, animals in the zoo." A. Wynne. *ArTp*
Explorers. J. Reeves. *ReBl*
The fairy swing. I. O. Eastwick. *EaI*
Familiar friends. J. S. Tippett. *BrL-k—HuL-2*
The farmyard. Unknown. *HuL-2*
A farmyard song. Mother Goose. *OpO*
Feather or fur. J. Becker. *ArTp—FeF*
The first night. L. A. Garnett. *DoP*
Fishes swim. Mother Goose. *OpO*
The four friends. A. A. Milne. *MiWc—UnG*
Four neighbors. I. O. Eastwick. *EaI*
Four things. From Proverbs, Bible, Old Testament. *FeF—UnG*
The friendly beasts. Unknown. *BrBc—BrS—CoPs—EaW—FeF*
Good morning. M. Sipe. *ArTp—BrL-k—HuL-1*
Green hill neighbors. F. M. Frost. *ArTp—FrLn*
Grim and gloomy. J. Reeves. *ReW*
The guppy. O. Nash. *JoAc*
Halloween concert. A. Fisher. *BrS*
"The hart he loves the high wood." Mother Goose. *DeMg—OpO—SmLg*
"Hey, diddle, diddle (the cat)." Mother Goose. *ArTp—BrL-k—DeMg—HuSv—JoAc—LiL—OpO*
"Higglety, pigglety, pop." S. G. Goodrich. *LoL—OpO*
The hippocrump. J. Reeves. *ReP*
"Hoddley, poddley, puddle and fogs." Mother Goose. *OpO*
"The horny-goloch is an awesome beast." Unknown. *LoL*
Hot weather. D. Aldis. *AlA*
How to tell the wild animals. C. Wells. *ArTp—CoH—FeF*
  How to know the wild animals. *UnG*
  How to tell wild animals. *UnMc*
"Hurt no living thing." C. G. Rossetti. *BrS—FeF*
I can't decide. F. M. Frost. *FrLn*

"I met a man that lived in a house." J. Ciardi. *CiI*

If they spoke. M. Van Doren. *PlI*

In come de animals. Unknown. *BrR-6*

In spring in warm weather. D. Aldis. *AlA—BrBc*

In the fashion. A. A. Milne. *MiWc*

In the stable. E. Goudge. *DoP*

The intruder. J. Reeves. *ReBl*

Johnny Crow's garden. L. L. Brooke. *ReG*

Jump or jiggle. E. Beyer. *ArTp—BrR-3—HuL-1*

Jungle night club. E. V. Rieu. *RiF*

The kangarooster. From Mixed beasts. K. Cox. *ArTp*

Laughing time. *FeF—SmL*

"Let no one suppose." J. Reeves. *ReP*

Leviathan. L. Untermeyer. *UnG*

Little things. J. Stephens. *ArTp—BrS—FeF—JoAc*

The mouse, the frog, and the little red hen. Unknown. *HuL-1*

The nimp. J. Reeves. *ReP*

Noah. Unknown. *TaD*

Noah's ark. D. Aldis. *AlHd*

Notice. D. McCord. *McFf*

The octopussycat. From Mixed beasts. K. Cox. *ArTp—FeF*

"Old Mother Shuttle." Mother Goose. *NaE*

    Mother Shuttle. *OpO*

Old Shellover. W. De La Mare. *ReG*

Open the door. M. Edey. *ArTp—BrS—HuL-1*

The osc. J. Reeves *ReP*

Others. J. Reeves. *ReW*

Our visit to the zoo. J. Pope. *HuL-2.*

"Over in the meadow." O. A. Wadsworth. *NaM*

The ox and the donkey's carol. Sister Maris Stella. *DoP*

    Ox and donkey's carol. *EaW*

Partners. J. Castiello. *McW*

Passing it along. H. F. Day. *BrR-6*

The peaceable kingdom. From Isaiah, Bible, Old Testament. *FeF*

The people. E. M. Roberts. *ArTp*

The pig's tail. N. Ault. *HuL-2*

Please, Johnny. J. Ciardi. *CiM*

"The pobble who has no toes." E. Lear. *CoH—LoL—NaM—SmLg—UnG—UnMc*

Poem for a child. J. G. E. Hopkins. *DoP*

"Pollywog on a log." Unknown. *WoF*

"The raccoon's tail has rings all round." Unknown. *WoF*

A rainy day. M. Chute. *McAw*

The reason. D. Aldis. *AlA—ArTp*

Remembering the winter. R. B. Bennett. *BrS*

A robin redbreast. From Auguries of innocence. W. Blake. *BrS*

    Things to remember. *DoP*

    Three things to remember. *FeF—NaM*

Sage counsel. A. Quiller-Couch. *CoH—LoL*

The saginsack. J. Ciardi. *CiR*

The sandhill crane. M. Austin. *ArTp—BrR-5—HuL-2*

Scat, scitten. D. McCord. *McT*

Sea song. M. Chute. *ChA*

The shape God wears. S. H. Hay. *UnG*

The silent snake. Unknown. *ArTp—FeF*

"Sing a song of sunshine." I. O. Eastwick. *BrS*

The skippery boo. E. L. Newton. *UnG*

Smoke animals. R. B. Bennett. *HuL-2*

The snitterjipe. J. Reeves. *ReP*

The snyke. J. Reeves. *ReP*

A song. Mother Goose. *OpO*

"The spangled pandemonium." P. Brown. *ArTp—LoL*

Spilt milk: Whodunit. W. J. Smith. *SmL*

Spring signs. M. C. Livingston. *LiWa*

Strange talk. L. E. Yates. *HuL-1*

A summer story. A. A. Preston. *BrR-4*

Tails ("De coon's got a long ringed bushy tail") Unknown. *CoH*

Tails ("A dog's tail") M. C. Livingston. *LiW*

Tails ("The kangaroo has a heavy tail") R. B. Bennett. *BrR-4*

There once was a puffin. F. P. Jacques. *ArTp—HuL-2*

There once was an owl. J. Ciardi. *CiR*

"Three young rats with black felt hats." Mother Goose. *DeMg—JoAc*

    Three young rats. *LoL—OpO*

Trouble at the farm. I. O. Eastwick. *HuL-1*

Under ground. J. Reeves. *ReW*

Under the ground. R. W. Bacmeister. *BrL-k—McAw*

Undersea. M. Chute. *HuL-1*

The unicorn. E. V. Rieu. *RiF*

Up the hill. W. J. Smith. *SmL*

Variation on a sentence. L. Bogan. *PlI*

"Way down yonder in the maple swamp." Unknown

    American Father Gander. *UnG*

We must be polite. C. Sandburg. *SaW*

What did you learn at the zoo. J. Ciardi. *CiY*

What they do. E. Farjeon. *FaCb—FaN*

What they like. Unknown. *HuL-1*

What you will learn about the brobinyak. J. Ciardi. *CiR—NaE*

"When a goose meets a moose." Z. Gay. *ArTp*

Who's in. E. Fleming. *BrL-k—PeF*

Wild animals. E. Fleming. *HuSv*

Wild beasts. E. Stein. *BrL-k*

Winter coats. D. Aldis. *AlA—HuL-1*

Winter in the wood. I. O. Eastwick. *HaY*

Woods' litany. E. J. Coatsworth. *EaW*

Zoo manners. E. Mathias. *HuL-1*

Animals—Care

The bells of heaven. R. Hodgson. *BrS—DeT—HaP*

The brown thrush. L. Larcom. *BrR-4—FeF*

A change of heart. V. Hobbs. *BrS*

Forbearance. R. W. Emerson. *ThP*

The frog. H. Belloc. *CoH—FeF—JoAc—LoL—NaM*

He prayeth best. From The rime of the ancient mariner. S. T. Coleridge. *DoP—FeF—HuSv—ThP*

    He prayeth well. *HuL-2*

    The rime of the ancient mariner. *UnG*

Go to the ant. From Proverbs, Bible, Old Testament. *FeF*

"Way down South where the coconuts grow." Unknown. *WiRm*

The **ant's** a centaur. See Pisan cantos

"The **ant's** a centaur in his dragon world." See Pisan cantos—The ant's a centaur

"The **ants** are walking under the ground." See The people

Any sunset. Louis Untermeyer. *UnG*

"**Anyone** lived in a pretty how town." E. E. Cummings. *HaP—NaE*

"**Anything** extra." See Our milkman

Apostrophic notes from the new-world physics. E. B. White. *PlI*

"**Apparently** the Nibelungs." See Operatic note

"An **apple** a day." Mother Goose. *DeMg*

"**Apple** blossom honey is crystal white." See Brown bear's honey song

Apple blossoms
Apple blossoms ("Apple blossoms, budding, blowing") L. Larcom. *HaY*
Apple blossoms ("Have you seen an apple orchard in the spring, in the spring") W. W. Martin. *BrR-6*
A comparison. J. Farrar. *FeF—HuL-2*
What saw I a-floating. E. Farjeon. *FaCb*

Apple blossoms ("Apple blossoms, budding, blowing") Lucy Larcom. *HaY*

Apple blossoms ("Have you seen an apple orchard in the spring, in the spring") William Wesley Martin. *BrR-6*

"**Apple** blossoms, budding, blowing." See Apple blossoms

"**Apple** blossoms look like snow." See A comparison

An **apple** gathering. Christina Georgina Rossetti. *GrCc*

"The **apple** on its bough is her desire." See Garden abstract

"**Apple-pie**, apple-pie." Mother Goose. *OpO*

Apple-pye. See "A was an apple-pie"

Apple season. Frances M. Frost. *BrS*

Apple song. Frances M. Frost. *FeF*

Apple-time. Eleanor Farjeon. *FaCb*

The **apple** tree. Beatrice Curtis Brown. *BrS*

Apple trees
The angel in the apple tree. W. Welles. *HuSv*
An apple gathering. C. G. Rossetti. *GrCc*
Apple-time. E. Farjeon. *FaCb*
The apple tree. B. C. Brown. *BrS*
Ballad of Johnny Appleseed. H. O. Oleson. *ArTp—BrS*
Garden abstract. H. Crane. *GrCc*
The hoar apple tree. E. Farjeon. *FaCb*
New Hampshire. From Landscapes. T. S. Eliot. *HaP—ReT—SmLg*
The planting of the apple tree. W. C. Bryant. *CoPs*(sel.)—*HuSv*
Twelfth night. Mother Goose. *OpO*
Up the pointed ladder. D. McCord. *McT*
"Upon Paul's steeple stands a tree." Mother Goose. *LiL—OpO*
Yer's tu thee. Unknown. *DeT*

Apples
After apple-picking. R. Frost. *FrR—FrY*
"An apple a day." Mother Goose. *DeMg*
Apple season. F. M. Frost. *BrS*
Apple song. F. M. Frost. *FeF*
Apple-time. E. Farjeon. *FaCb*
Apples. W. J. Smith. *SmL*
Apples and pears. E. L. Halsey. *HuL-1*
Apples go begging. E. Farjeon. *FaN*
August. A. C. Swinburne. *HoW*
The boys and the apple-tree. A. O'Keefe. *DeT*
The cow in apple time. R. Frost. *FrR—FrY*
Dividing. D. McCord. *McFf*
The favourite fruit. E. Farjeon. *FaCb—FaN*
"If I were an apple." Unknown. *AnI—HuL-1*
September's song. E. Farjeon. *FaCb—FaN*
Thieves in the orchard. E. Farjeon. *FaCb*
Toss me your golden ball. E. Farjeon. *FaCb*

Apples. William Jay Smith. *SmL*

Apples and pears. Eleanor L. Halsey. *HuL-1*

"The **apples** are seasoned." See Apple song

Apples go begging. Eleanor Farjeon. *FaN*

"**Apples** heavy and red." See September

Appleseed, Johnny (about). See Chapman, John

April
April ("The roofs are shining from the rain") S. Teasdale. *ArTp—CoPs—FeF—HaY—HuL-2—HuSv—JoAc*
April ("So here we are in April, in showy, blowy April") Ted Robinson. *UnG*
April ("Softly glows the sun") I. O. Eastwick. *EaI*
April ("The tulips now are pushing up") E. Tietjens. *HaY*
April and Isabella. I. O. Eastwick. *EaI*
April and May. R. W. Emerson. *JoAc*
April rain. R. Loveman. *BrR-5*
April rain song. L. Hughes. *ArTp—FeF—PeF*
April weather. M. Watts. *McAw*
The concert. P. McGinley. *HaY—ThP*
Early April. R. Frost. *HaY*
False April. E. Farjeon. *FaCb—FaN*
Lady April. R. Le Gallienne. *HaY*
Like an April day. J. S. C. Wellhaven. *PaS*
"March, blow by." E. Farjeon. *FaCb—FaN*
"Now the noisy winds are still." M. M. Dodge. *HaY*
Rain in April. E. Hammond. *BrR-3*
Rainbow in April. I. O. Eastwick. *EaI*
Song. W. Watson. *CoPs—JoAc*
April. *UnG*

April. See Song ("April, April")

April ("The roofs are shining from the rain") Sara Teasdale. *ArTp—CoPs—FeF—HaY—HuL-2—HuSv—JoAc*

April ("So here we are in April, in showy, blowy April") Ted Robinson. *UnG*

April ("Softly glows the sun") Ivy O. Eastwick. *EaI*
April ("The tulips now are pushing up") Eunice Tietjens. *HaY*
April and Isabella. Ivy O. Eastwick. *EaI*
April and May. Ralph Waldo Emerson. *JoAc*
"April, April." See Song
"April cold with dropping rain." See April and May
"An April day . . . an April day." See April weather
April fool ("I saw an elephant walking down the road") Elizabeth Jane Coatsworth. *HaY*
April fool ("Who will be an April fool") Eleanor Farjeon. *FaCb—FaN*
April fools' day
    All fools' day. Unknown. *BrS*
    April fool ("I saw an elephant walking down the road") E. J. Coatsworth. *HaY*
    April fool ("Who will be an April fool") E. Farjeon. *FaCb—FaN*
    April fools' day. M. Pomeroy. *CoPs*
    Conversation with an April fool. R. B. Bennett. *BrS*
    "Oh did you hear." S. Silverstein. *CoPs*
    The rain. Unknown. *BrR-3*
April fools' day. Marnie Pomeroy. *CoPs*
April rain. Robert Loveman. *BrR-5*
April rain song. Langston Hughes. *ArTp—FeF—PeF*
"The April rain that's pelted." See Rainy robin
April weather. Mabel Watts. *McAw*
Aquariums
    At the aquarium. M. Eastman. *FeF*
Aquarius. Eleanor Farjeon. *FaCb—FaN*
Arabian nights
    Aladdin. J. R. Lowell. *BrR-5—CoPm—McW*
    The thousand nights and one, sels. Unknown
        Haroun's favorite song. *PaS*
        Love. *PaS*
        The power of love. *PaS*
Arbor day. See also Forests and forestry; Trees; also names of trees, as Apple trees; also Chapman, John
    Arbor day ("On Arbor day") A. Wynne. *DoP*
    Arbor day ("To plant a tree. How small the twig") D. B. Thompson. *BrS—McAw*
    Planting a tree. N. B. Turner. *HaY*
    What do we plant. H. Abbey. *ArTp—FeF*
Arbor day ("On Arbor day") Annette Wynne. *DoP*
Arbor day ("To plant a tree. How small the twig") Dorothy Brown Thompson. *BrS—McAw*
The archer. C. Scollard. *FeF*
"The archer draws his bow." See Sagittarius
Archery. See also Bows and arrows; Robin Hood
    Adam Bell, Clym of the Clough, and William of Cloudesley. Unknown. *MaB*
    The archer. C. Scollard. *FeF*
    Sagittarius. E. Farjeon. *FaCb—FaN*

Archibald's example. Edwin Arlington Robinson. *GrCc*
Archie of Cawfield. Unknown. *MaB*
Archilochus
    Be still, my soul. *PaS*
Archy a low brow. Don Marquis. *CoH*
Archy confesses. Don Marquis. *NaE*
Archy, the cockroach speaks. See Certain maxims of Archy
Archy's autobiography. Don Marquis. *CoH* (sel.)
"The Arctic moon hangs overhead." See The wolf cry
Arctic regions. See also Eskimos
    The cremation of Sam McGee. R. W. Service. *CoSp—UnMc*
    A dash to the pole. W. Irwin. *CoH*
    The shooting of Dan McGrew. R. W. Service. *UnMc*
"Are all the birds imprisoned there." See Alle vögel sind schon da
"Are not two sparrows sold for a farthing." See Gospel according to Matthew— The sparrow, 2
"Are the reindeer in the rain, dear." See Conversation between Mr and Mrs Santa Claus
"Are zebras black with broad white stripes." See Zebra
"Aren't you coming out, Mary." See Mary indoors
Arethusa ("Arethusa arose") Percy Bysshe Shelley. *HoW*
Arethusa ("Arethusa the gay is departed") E. V. Rieu. *RiF*
"Arethusa arose." See Arethusa
"Arethusa the gay is departed." See Arethusa
Argumentation
    The blind men and the elephant. J. G. Saxe. *CoSp—JoAc—UnG—UnMc*
    A parable. A. C. Doyle. *BrL-7*
Argus and Ulysses. Eleanor Farjeon. *FaCb*
"Argus was a puppy." See Argus and Ulysses
Ariel's dirge. See The Tempest—"Full fathom five thy father lies"
Ariel's song. See The tempest—"Come unto these yellow sands"
Aries. Eleanor Farjeon. *FaCb—FaN*
Aristotle
    Epitaph for Chaeroneia. *PaS*
Arithmetic. See also Mathematics
    Arithmetic. C. Sandburg. *FeF* (sel.)—*McW —PlI—SaW*
    Child Margaret. C. Sandburg. *SaW*
    Counting. H. Behn. *BeW*
    Little hundred. Mother Goose. *OpO*
    A mortifying mistake. A. M. Pratt. *CoH*
    "Multiplication is vexation." Mother Goose. *DeMg*
        Signs, seasons, and sense. *UnG*
    A puzzling example. V. S. Benjamin. *BrBc*
    Roman figures. Mother Goose. *OpO*
    "There was an old man who said, Do." Unknown *FeF—PlI*
    "To think that two and two are four." A. E. Housman. *PlI*

Arithmetic. Carl Sandburg. *FeF* (sel.)—
McW—PlI—SaW
"Arithmetic is where numbers fly like
pigeons in and out of your head." See
Arithmetic
Ark of the covenant. Louise Townsend
Nicholl. *PlI*
Arlon, Laura
Slow pokes. *McAw*
Armada. See Spain—History
The Armada. Thomas Babington Macaulay.
SmLg
Armistice day. See Veterans day
Armor. See Arms and armor
Armour, Richard
Covering the subject. *McW*
Money. *McW*
Arms and armor
A fairy in armor. From The culprit fay.
J. R. Drake. *FeF*
The knight whose armour didn't squeak.
A. A. Milne. *MiWc*
Pigwiggin arms himself. From Nymphidia:
The court of fairy. M. Drayton. *NaM*
The skeleton in armor. H. W. Longfellow.
UnG—UnMc
Armstrong, Mildred Bowers. See Bowers,
Mildred
The army horse and the army jeep. John
Ciardi. *CiR*
"Army, navy (medicine)." Mother Goose.
OpO
"Army, navy (peerage)." Mother Goose.
OpO
Arnold, Matthew
Dover beach. *HaP*
The forsaken merman. *SmLg*
The last word. *HaP*
The mirror of perfection, sel.
Praise of created things. tr. *FeF*
The song of the creatures. tr. *PaS*
Praise of created things. See The mirror
of perfection
Requiescat. *HaP*
The song of the creatures. See The mirror
of perfection—Praise of created things
The song of the Muses. *HoW*
"Around, above the world of snow." See
February
"Around bend after bend." See Not of
school age
Around my room. William Jay Smith. *SmL*
"Around the rick, around the rick." Mother
Goose. *OpO*
Arran. Unknown, tr. fr. the Irish by Kuno
Meyer. *SmLg*
"Arran of the many stags." See Arran
Arrieta, Rafael Alberto
January night. *PaS*
Arrogance. See Pride and vanity
The arrogant frog and the superior bull.
Guy Wetmore Carryl. *CoSp*
The arrow and the song. Henry Wadsworth
Longfellow. *BrR-6*
"An arrow flying past." Gustavo Adolfo
Bécquer, tr. fr. the Spanish by J. M.
Cohen. *PaS*
Arrows. See Archery; Bows and arrows

Arrows of love. Chauras, tr. fr. the Sanskrit
by E. Powys Mathers. *PaS*
Art. Marchette Chute. *ChA*
Art and artists
Art. M. Chute. *ChA*
Circles. H. Behn. *LoL*
Delight in disorder. R. Herrick. *HaP*
Musée des beaux arts. W. H. Auden.
HaP
My last duchess. R. Browning. *HaP*
Ode on a Grecian urn. J. Keats. *HaP*
"Art thou gone in haste." Unknown. *ReT*
"Art thou poor, and hast thou golden slum-
bers." See Pleasant comedy of patient
Grissell—The basket-maker's song
"Art thou poor, yet hast thou golden slum-
bers." See Pleasant comedy of patient
Grissell—The basket-maker's song
The artful ant. Oliver Herford. *CoH*
Arthur, King (about)
Avalon. J. Reeves. *ReR*
Is Arthur gone to Avalon. E. Farjeon.
FaCb
The lady of Shalott. A. Tennyson. *HoW*
—UnMg
"When good King Arthur ruled this land."
Mother Goose. *DeMg—JoAc—LiL*
The bag pudding. *DeT*
King Arthur. *OpO*
Arthur. Ogden Nash. *CoH*
"Arthur O'Bower has broken his band."
Mother Goose. *OpO*
The wind. *SmLg*
"Arvin Marvin Lillisbee Fitch." John Ciardi.
CiY
"As a beauty I am not a star." See My face
"As a friend to the children, commend me
the yak." See The yak
"As a rule men are fools." Unknown. *MoY*
"As a young lobster roamed about." See
The lobster
"As beautiful Kitty one morning was trip-
ping." See Kitty of Coleraine
"As black as ink and isn't ink." Mother
Goose. *OpO*
"As gardens grow with flowers." See Eng-
lish
"As gay for you to take your father's axe."
See To a young wretch
"As he had often done before." See The inky
boys
"As he trudg'd along to school." See The
story of Johnny Head-in-air
"As I came over the humpbacked hill." See
The green fiddler
"As I came to the edge of the woods." See
Come in
"As I drive to the junction of lane and high-
way." See At Castle Boterel
"As I in hoary winter's night stood shivering
in the snow." See The burning Babe
"As I lay awake in the white moonlight."
See Sleepyhead
"As I looked out one May morning." See
The princess and the gypsies
"As I passed by a river side." See The crow
and the crane
"As I rowed out to the light-house." See
The light-house-keeper's white-mouse

"As I sat on a sunny bank." See Carol

As I walked. See "As I walked by myself"

"As I walked by myself." Mother Goose. *DeMg*
  As I walked. *DeT*
  The philosopher. *OpO*

"As I walked down the evening road." See Fox cub goes home

"As I walked out in the streets of Laredo." See The cowboy's lament

"As I walked out one evening." W. H. Auden. *HaP*

"As I walked out one morning for pleasure." See Whoopee ti yi yo, git along, little dogies

"As I walked through my garden." See Butterfly

"As I was a-hoeing, a-hoeing my lands." See The six badgers

"As I was a-walking mine alone." See Archie of Cawfield

"As I was a-walking on Westminster bridge." Mother Goose. *OpO*

"As I was a-walking one morning for pleasure." See Whoopee ti yi yo, git along, little dogies

"As I was a-walking the other day." See The shoemaker

"As I was a-walking upon a fine day." See Because I were shy

"As I was going along, long, long." Mother Goose. *DeMg—OpO*

"As I was going by candlelight." See Copper song

"As I was going by Charing cross." Mother Goose. *SmLg*
  Charles I. *OpO*
  King Charles. *DeT*

"As I was going o'er London bridge." Mother Goose. *OpO*

"As I was going o'er misty moor." See The three cats

"As I was going o'er Tipple Tine." Mother Goose. *OpO*

"As I was going to Banbury." Mother Goose. *JoAc*
  Banbury fair. *OpO*

"As I was going to Derby." Mother Goose. *DeMg—LoL*
  The Derby ram. *OpO*
  The wonderful Derby ram. *HuL-1*

"As I was going to Derby, all on a market day." See "As I was going to Derby"

"As I was going to St Ives." Mother Goose. *DeMg—HuSv—JoAc—LiL—OpO*

"As I was going to sell my eggs." Mother Goose. *DeMg—JoAc*
  Old bandy legs. *OpO*

"As I was going up Pippen hill." Mother Goose. *DeMg—OpO*

"As I was going up the hill." Mother Goose. *OpO*

"As I was going up the stair." See The little man who wasn't there

"As I was laying on the green." Unknown. *CoH*

"As I was picking a bobble-bud." John Ciardi. *CiM*

"As I was sailing down the coast." See The high Barbaree

"As I was sitting in my chair." See The perfect reactionary

"As I was standing in the street." Unknown. *CoH*

"As I was walking all alane." See The twa corbies

"As I was walking in a field of wheat." Mother Goose. *OpO*

"As I was walking mine alone." See The little wee man

"As I went by a dyer's door." See A tawnymoor

"As I went down the Portsmouth road, a careless rambling fellow." See The Portsmouth road

"As I went down to Hastings mill I lingered in my going." See Hastings mill

"As I went home on the old wood road." See Meeting

"As I went out a crow." See The last word of a bluebird

"As I went out a-walking." See The tragedy

"As I went over the water." Mother Goose. *OpO*

"As I went singing over the earth." Mary Coleridge. *PlU*

"As I went through the garden gap." Mother Goose. *DeMg*
  A cherry. *ReG*

"As I went through the North country." See York, York for my money

"As I went to Bonner." See On oath

"As I went up the apple tree." Unknown. *WiRm*

"As I went up the Brandy hill." Mother Goose. *OpO*

"As I went up the hazel-dazel." Unknown. *WoF*

"As I went walking." See Song in spring

"As I went walking down the road." Unknown. *WoF*

"As I went walking one fine Sunday." See Coati-mundi

"As it fell out on a holy-day." See John Dory

"As it fell out one May morning." See The holy well

As Joseph was awakening. See An old Christmas carol

"As Joseph was a-walking." See An old Christmas carol

"As Joseph was a-waukin'." See An old Christmas carol

"As little Jenny Wren." See Fidget

"As long as I live." See Me

"As mad sexton's bell, tolling." See Song on the water

"As many fishes as are in the sea." Unknown. *MoY*

As ocean holds the globe. Fyodor Tyutchev, tr. fr. the Russian by Babette Deutsch. *PaS*

"As ocean holds the globe in its embrace." See As ocean holds the globe

"As Pluto ruled the underworld." See Neptune

"As round as an apple." See "As round as an apple, as deep as a cup"

"**As** round as an apple, as deep as a cup." Mother Goose. *ArTp—JoAc*
"**As** round as an apple." *DeMg—OpO*
"**As** round as an apple (as deep as a pail)." Mother Goose. *OpO*
"**As** salt resolved in the ocean." Rumi, tr. fr. the Persian by A. J. Arberry. *PaS*
"**As** soft as silk." Mother Goose. *LiL—OpO*
"**As** soon as ever twilight comes." Walter De La Mare. *BrS*
"**As** soon as I'm in bed at night." See Mrs Brown
"**As** soon as the fire burns red and low." See The sleepy song
"**As** soon as they began to spark." See Fireflies
"**As** sure as comes your wedding day." Unknown. *MoY*
"**As** the cat." See Poem
"**As** the moon sinks on the mountain-edge." See Far beyond us
"**As** the racing circle closed in like a lasso." See The Painted desert—Ceremonial hunt
"**As** the years go by." Unknown *MoY*
"**As** Tommy Snooks and Bessy (or Bessie) Brooks." Mother Goose. *DeMg—JoAc—LiL*
   Tommy and Bessy. *OpO*
"**As** twilight fell." See I saw a ghost
"**As** vain to raise a voice as a sigh." See On going unnoticed
"**As** wet as a fish, as dry as a bone." See Comparisons
"**As** white as milk." Unknown
   Five very old riddles. *DeT*
"**As** William and Thomas were walking one day." See The boys and the apple-tree
"**As** years roll by." Unknown. *MoY*
"**As** you came from the holy land." See Walsinghame
As you like it, sels. William Shakespeare
   "All the world's a stage"
      From As you like it. *HaP*
      Gallery of people. *UnG*
   "Blow, blow, thou winter wind." *HoW—McW*
      Blow, blow. *DeT*
   "Under the greenwood tree." *ArTp—DeT—FeF—HoW*
      In Arden forest. *JoAc*

Asataro, Miyamori
   Lotus leaves. tr. *PaS*
Ascent to the Sierras. Robinson Jeffers. *SmLg*
"**Ashes** to ashes (dust to dust, if the Camels)." Unknown. *MoY*
"**Ashes** to ashes (dust to dust, there is no man)." Unknown. *MoY*
The **Ashtabula** disaster. Julia Moore. *NaE*
Asleep and awake. David McCord. *McFf*
"The **aspens** and the maples now." See Valentine's day
Aspinwall, Alicia
   Patrick goes to school. *BrL-k*
Aspiration. See Ambition

Asquith, Herbert
   Birthday gifts. *BrBc—BrS*
   The elephant. *ArTp*
   The hairy dog. *ArTp—BrR-4—FeF—HuSv—PeF*
   Skating. *ArTp—FeF—HuL-2—HuSv*
Asses. See Donkeys
Assyria—History
   The destruction of Sennacherib. G. G. Byron. *FeF—NaE—SmLg—UnG*
"The **Assyrian** came down like the wolf on the fold." See The destruction of Sennacherib
Astronomy. See also Moon; Planets; also names of planets, as Venus; Stars; Sun; Tides; World
   "Reason has moons, but moons not hers." R. Hodgson. *SmLg*
   "When I heard the learn'd astronomer." W. Whitman. *SmLg*
Astrophel and Stella, sel. Philip Sidney
   Leave me, O love. *HaP*
Asturias, Miguel Angel
   "The Indians come down from Mixco." *FeF*
At a concert of music. Conrad Aiken. *PlU*
At a country fair. John Holmes. *NaM*
At a solemn musick. John Milton. *PlU* (sel.)
At a window. Eleanor Farjeon. *FaCb*
"**At** an open window." See At a window
At bedtime. Myra Cohn Livingston. *LiWa*
At Belle Isle. See "At the siege of Belleisle"
"**At** Brill on the hill." Mother Goose. *OpO*
At Castle Boterel. Thomas Hardy. *HaP*
"**At** Christmas, firstling lambs are dropped." See Shepherds' carol
At daybreak. Helen Hoyt. *BrBc*
At Easter time. Laura E. Richards. *DoP*
"**At** evening when I go to bed." See Daisies
"**At** evening when the lamp is lit." See The land of story-books
At eventide. Eleanor Farjeon. *FaCb—FaN*
"**At** every proper christening." See To Patricia on her christening day
"**At** every stroke his brazen fins do take." See The whale
"**At** first he stirs uneasily in sleep." See Dog at night
"**At** first I said: I will not have, I think." See Birthday
"**At** Flores in the Azores Sir Richard Grenville lay." See The Revenge
"**At** four o'clock in the morning." See Waking time
At home. A. A. Milne. *MiWc*
At low tide. David McCord. *McFf*
"**At** low tide like this how sheer the water is." See The bight
At Matsushima. Shiki, tr. fr. the Japanese by Harold G. Henderson. *PaS*
"**At** midsummer fair on a galloping pony." See Roundabout
At Mrs Appleby's. Elizabeth Upham McWebb. *ArTp—BrS—HuSv*
At night ("I've been awake, and been awake") Marchette Chute. *ChA*

At night ("On moony nights the dogs bark shrill") Frances Cornford. *CoI*

At night ("These are the fastest shoes I know") Dorothy Aldis. *AlHd*

"At night I dreamt I was back in Ch'ang-an." See Dreaming that I went with Li and Yü to visit Yüan Chēn

"At night I reach down with my feet just to see." See Bed in winter

"At night when the cattle are sleeping." See Cowboy's meditation

"At nighttime when I go to bed." See Day song

At peace. Rumi, tr. fr. the Persian by A. J. Arberry. *PaS*

"At sunset, when the night-dews fall." See The snail

At the airport. Myra Cohn Livingston. *LiWa*

At the aquarium. Max Eastman. *FeF*

At the beginning of winter. Elizabeth Jane Coatsworth. *CoM*

"At the corner of Wood street, when daylight appears." See The reverie of poor Susan

At the dog show. Christopher Morley. *NaM*

"At the end of the street lives small Miss Wing." See Miss Wing

"At the equinox when the earth was veiled in a late rain, wreathed with wet poppies, waiting spring." See Continent's end

At the farm. John Ciardi. *CiY*

At the garden gate. David McCord. *FeF—McFf*

At the sea-side. Robert Louis Stevenson. *ArTp—FeF—JoAc*

"At the siege of Belleisle." Mother Goose. *DeMg*
  At Belle Isle. *OpO*

At the theater. Rachel Field. *FeF*

"At the top of the world, where fields of snow." See Mrs Santa Claus' Christmas present

At the zoo ("Giraffes are tall") Marchette Chute. *ChA*

At the zoo ("I've been to the zoo") Myra Cohn Livingston. *LiW*

At the zoo ("There are lions and roaring tigers, and enormous camels and things") A. A. Milne. *FeF—MiWc*

"At Viscount Nelson's lavish funeral." See 1805

At Woodward's gardens. Robert Frost. *FrR—PlI*

Atalanta
  Atalanta in Calydon, sel. A. C. Swinburne
    Chorus from Atalanta in Calydon. *HaP—NaE*

Atalanta in Calydon, sel. Algernon Charles Swinburne
  Chorus from Atalanta in Calydon. *HaP—NaE*

Athletes. See also names of sports, as Baseball
  To an athlete dying young. From A Shropshire lad. A. E. Housman. *HaP—UnMc*

Atlantic Charter, A. D. 1620-1942. See The island

Atom from atom. Ralph Waldo Emerson. *PlI*

"Atom from atom yawns as far." See Atom from atom

Atoms
  Atom from atom. R. W. Emerson. *PlI*
  Mr Attila. C. Sandburg. *PlI*

"Attend, all ye who list to hear our noble England's praise." See The Armada

Atticus. See Epistle to Dr Arbuthnot

Attila, King of the Huns
  The ride of the Huns. E. Farjeon. *FaCb*

"Attila rode with his Huns." See The ride of the Huns

Auction. John Holmes. *McW*

Auctioneer. Carl Sandburg. *SaW*

Auden, W. H.
  "As I walked out one evening." *HaP*
  Ballad. *UnMc*
  The composer. *PlU*
  Epilogue. *SmLg*
  Musée des beaux arts. *HaP*
  Night mail. *HaP*
  Numbers and faces. *PlI*(sel.)

Auguries of innocence, sels. William Blake
  SmLg (complete)
  A robin redbreast. *BrS*
    Things to remember. *DoP*
    Three things to remember. *FeF—NaM*
  "To see the world in a grain of sand." *DoP*
    Auguries of innocence. *PlI*
    To see a world. *UnG*

August
  August ("Buttercup nodded and said good-by") C. Thaxter. *FeF—HaY*
  August ("The city dwellers all complain") M. Lewis. *UnG*
  August ("There were four red apples on the bough") A. C. Swinburne. *HoW*
  August ("The yellow goldenrod is dressed") H. M. Winslow. *HaY*
  August afternoon. M. Edey. *HaY*
  August hail. J. V. Cunningham. *HaP*
  August night. E. M. Roberts. *HaY*
  August smiles. E. J. Coastworth. *BrS*
  August 28. D. McCord. *McFf*
  A dog day. R. Field. *BrS*
  The golden month. M. Doyle. *HaY*
  In August. M. Chute. *ChA—McAw*
  Mid-August. L. Driscoll. *HaY*
  The month of falling stars. E. Higginson. *HaY*

August ("Buttercup nodded and said good-by") Celia Thaxter. *FeF—HaY*

August ("The city dwellers all complain") Michael Lewis. *UnG*

August ("There were four red apples on the bough") Algernon Charles Swinburne. *HoW*

August ("The yellow goldenrod is dressed") Helen Maria Winslow. *HaY*

August afternonn. Marion Edey. *HaY*

August hail. J. V. Cunningham. *HaP*

"August is a lazy girl." See August smiles

August night. Elizabeth Madox Roberts. *HaY*

August smiles. Elizabeth Jane Coatsworth. *BrS*

August 28. David McCord. *McFf*

"Augustus was a chubby lad." See The story of Augustus who would not have any soup

Auks
The great auk's ghost. R. Hodgson. *NaM*

"The auld wife sat at her ivied door." See Ballad

Ault, Norman
The pig's tail. *HuL-2*

Aunt Eliza. See Four ruthless rhymes

Aunt Helen. T. S. Eliot. *HaP*

Aunt Maud. Unknown. *CoH—NaM*

"Auntie, will your dog bite." See Chicken in the bread tray

Aunts
Aunt Helen. T. S. Eliot. *HaP*
Aunt Maud. Unknown. *CoH—NaM*
My singing aunt. J. Reeves. *ReBl*

Auslander, Joseph
A blackbird suddenly. *ArTp*
Near dusk. *FeF*

Austin, Mary
The brown bear. *CoPs—FeF—McW*
The deer. *FeF*
A feller I know. *FeF*
"First I am frosted"
    Rhyming riddles. *ArTp*
Grizzly bear. *ArTp—FeF*
"I come more softly than a bird"
    Rhyming riddles. *ArTp*
'I have no wings, but yet I fly"
    Rhyming riddles. *ArTp*
'I never speak a word"
    Rhyming riddles. *ArTp*
"Neither spirit nor bird." tr. *PaS*
Prairie-dog town. *ArTp—FeF—HuSv*
Rathers. *FeF*
The sandhill crane. *ArTp—BrR-5—HuL-2*
A song of greatness. *ArTp—BrBc—FeF—JoAc*
Texas trains and trails. *ArTp*

Australia
Up from down under. D. McCord. *McT*
Waltzing Matilda. A. B. Paterson. *CoSp—McW*

The author. E. V. Rieu. *RiF*

Authors and authorship. See Writers and writing

Autograph album verses
"Alas, alas, I am so dumb." Unknown. *MoY*
"Ann for sale." Unknown. *MoY*
"Anna is a silver star." Unknown. *MoY*
"As many fishes as are in the sea." Unknown. *MoY*
"As sure as comes your wedding day." Unknown. *MoY*
"As the years go by." Unknown. *MoY*
"As years roll by." Unknown. *MoY*
"Ashes to ashes (dust to dust, if the Camels)." Unknown. *MoY*
"Ashes to ashes (dust to dust, there is no man)." Unknown. *MoY*
"Be good as a Christian." Unknown. *MoY*
"Best what." Unknown. *MoY*
"Beware of boys with eyes of brown." Unknown. *MoY*

"Birds on the mountain." Unknown. *MoY*
"Bless the man that takes your hand." Unknown. *MoY*
"Blue eyes, brown hair." Unknown. *MoY*
"Boys are like a box of snuff." Unknown. *MoY*
"Butter is butter." Unknown. *MoY*
"Can't think." Unknown. *MoY*
"Chicken when you're hungry." Unknown. *MoY*
"Choose not your friends." Unknown. *MoY*
"Dear Saint Anthony." Unknown. *MoY*
"Do you love me." Unknown. *CoPs*
"Don't be crooked." Unknown. *MoY*
"Don't be fretful." Unknown. *MoY*
"Don't make love at the garden gate." Unknown. *MoY*
"Don't steal this book." Unknown. *MoY*
"Dot." Unknown. *MoY*
"Down by the river (where the river flows)." Unknown. *MoY*
"East is east." Unknown. *MoY*
"Fair are the lilies." Unknown. *MoY*
"First comes love." Unknown. *MoY*
"First in your affection." Unknown. *MoY*
"First we meet." Unknown. *MoY*
"Forget me not." Unknown. *MoY*
"Forget the moon, forget the stars." Unknown. *MoY*
"Forgive me, Jane, for being bold." Unknown. *MoY*
"Four lines from a lazy poet." Unknown. *MoY*
"Frankie, Frankie, don't you blush." Unknown. *MoY*
"Friends are like melons." Unknown. *MoY*
"Friends, Romans, countrymen." Unknown. *MoY*
"Fruit is soft as soon as ripened." Unknown. *MoY*
"Ginny made some doughnuts." Unknown. *MoY*
"Girls are like a nugget of gold." Unknown. *MoY*
"Gloria is your name." Unknown. *MoY*
"Go little album, far and near." Unknown. *MoY*
"God made the men." Unknown. *MoY*
"God made the ocean." Unknown. *MoY*
"Gold is pure." Unknown. *MoY*
"Great oaks from little acorns grow." Unknown. *MoY*
"Ha, ha, ha." Unknown. *MoY*
"Henry is a proper noun." Unknown. *MoY*
"Henry was here and is now gone." Unknown. *MoY*
"I am no poet." Unknown. *MoY*
"I beg you on this page of pink." Unknown. *MoY*
"I bet my maid." Unknown. *MoY*
"I bet you I can make any fool in town." Unknown. *MoY*
"I chose blue." Unknown. *MoY*
"I climbed up the door." Unknown. *MoY*
"I like coffee, I like tea (I like you)." Unknown. *MoY*
"I love coffee, I love tea (a shoemaker's daughter)." Unknown. *MoY*

"Remember the beer." Unknown. *MoY*
"Remember the fork." Unknown. *MoY*
"Remember the fourth commandment." Unknown. *MoY*
"Remember the kid from Brooklyn." Unknown. *MoY*
"Remember the miss." Unknown. *MoY*
"Remember well and bear in mind." Unknown. *MoY*
"The rose is red." Unknown. *MoY*
"Roses are red (pickles are green)." Unknown. *MoY*
"Roses are red (they grow)." Unknown. *MoY*
"Roses are red (violets are blue, God made)." Unknown. *MoY*
"Roses are red (violets are blue, I can)." Unknown. *MoY*
"Roses are red, violets are blue (lend me)." Unknown. *MoY*
"Roses are red (violets are blue, when it)." Unknown. *MoY*
"Roses may be red." Unknown. *MoY*
"Round went the album." Unknown. *MoY*
"Sailing down the stream of life." Unknown. *MoY*
"Sitting by a stream." Unknown. *MoY*
"Sitting on a tombstone." Unknown. *MoY*
"Some blank verse from a blank mind." Unknown. *MoY*
"Some love ten." Unknown. *MoY*
"Some shoes are black." Unknown. *MoY*
"Sometimes I'm naughty." Unknown. *MoY*
"Start low." Unknown. *MoY*
"Study and work." Unknown. *MoY*
"Success and happiness run in pairs." Unknown. *MoY*
"Sugar is sweet." Unknown. *MoY*
"Sure as the grass grows round the stump." Unknown. *MoY*
"Tables are round." Unknown. *MoY*
"Take the local." Unknown. *MoY*
"Take the word pluck." Unknown. *MoY*
"Tell me quick." Unknown. *MoY*
"There are golden ships." Unknown. *MoY*
"There are seven ages of woman." Unknown. *MoY*
"There are tulips in the garden." Unknown. *MoY*
"There is a pale blue flower." Unknown. *MoY*
"There's a meter in music." Unknown. *MoY*
"Think of a fly." Unknown. *MoY*
"This book becomes a treasure rare." Unknown. *MoY*
"This is not a laundry tab." Unknown. *MoY*
"Though your tasks are many." Unknown. *MoY*
"To keep my friends." Unknown. *MoY*
"To my friend." Unknown. *MoY*
"Tom, Dick, or Harry." Unknown. *MoY*
"True friends are like diamonds." Unknown. *MoY*
"'Twas in a restaurant they first met." Unknown. *MoY*
"Twinkle, twinkle, little star (eyebrow pencil)." Unknown. *MoY*

"Two in a car." Unknown. *MoY*
"Two in a hammock." Unknown. *MoY*
"Until two nickels don't make a dime." Unknown. *MoY*
"Way back here." Unknown. *MoY*
"What is life." Unknown. *MoY*
"What, write in your album." Unknown. *MoY*
"What, write in your book." Unknown. *MoY*
"When I am dead and in my grave." Unknown. *MoY*
"When on this page." Unknown. *MoY*
"When sitting on the sofa." Unknown. *MoY*
"When the walls of earth have fallen." Unknown. *MoY*
"When times are hard." Unknown. *MoY*
"When twilight drops her curtain." Unknown. *MoY*
"When you are drinking." Unknown. *MoY*
"When you are dying." Unknown. *MoY*
"When you are hungry." Unknown. *MoY*
"When you are in the country." Unknown. *MoY*
"When you are lonely." Unknown. *MoY*
"When you are married (and have a pair)." Unknown. *MoY*
"When you are married (and have one)." Unknown. *MoY*
"When you are old (and cannot see)." Unknown. *MoY*
"When you are sick." Unknown. *MoY*
"When you are washing at a tub." Unknown. *MoY*
"When you are wealthy." Unknown. *MoY*
"When you get married (and have twenty-five)." Unknown. *MoY*
"When you get married (and live across)." Unknown. *MoY*
"When you get married (and live next door)." Unknown. *MoY*
"When you get married (and live on figs)." Unknown. *MoY*
"When you get married (and live upstairs)." Unknown. *MoY*
"When you get married (and your husband)." Unknown. *MoY*
"When you get married (don't marry a flirt)." Unknown. *MoY*
"When you get old and your dress gets purple." Unknown. *MoY*
"When you grow old." Unknown. *MoY*
"You are nice to know." Unknown. *MoY*
"You asked me to sign my autograph." Unknown. *MoY*
"You can fall from the mountains." Unknown. *MoY*
"You drink a lot of soda." Unknown. *MoY*
"You love yourself, you think you're grand." Unknown. *MoY*
"Your future lies before you." Unknown. *MoY*
"Your head is like a ball of straw." Unknown. *MoY*
"Your heart is not a plaything." Unknown. *MoY*

Automobile mechanics. Dorothy W. Baruch. *ArTp—FeF*

Automobiles. See also Taxicabs
Automobile mechanics. D. W. Baruch. *ArTp—FeF*
"Funny the way different cars start." D. W. Baruch. *BrL-k—FeF*
Motor cars. R. B. Bennett. *ArTp—FeF—JoAc*
Song for a blue roadster. R. Field. *ArTp—FeF*
Stop—go. D. W. Baruch. *ArTp—BrL-k—FeF—HuL-1*
This dim and ptolemaic man. J. P. Bishop. *PlI*
Traffic light. N. K. Duffy. *McAw*

"Automobiles." See Stop—go

Autumn. See also Seasons; September; October; November
Autumn ("Autumn's good, a cosy season") Unknown. *CoPs*
Autumn ("The leaves fall, fall as from far") R. M. Rilke. *PaS*
Autumn ("Now is the time when cheery crickets") N. B. Turner. *HaY*
Autumn ("There is wind where the rose was") W. De La Mare. *GrCc*
Autumn ("Yellow the bracken") F. Hoatson. *HuL-1*
Autumn color. T. Robinson. *HaY*
Autumn eve. A. Andriello. *BrS*
Autumn evening. J. Clare. *ReT*
Autumn fancies. Unknown. *FeF—HuSv*
Autumn fashions. E. M. Thomas. *HaY*
Autumn fires. R. L. Stevenson. *ArTp—HaY—JoAc*
Autumn season. I. O. Eastwick. *EaI*
Autumn sigheth. E. Farjeon. *FaCb—FaN*
Autumn song. E. E. Long. *BrS*
The autumn wind. Wu-ti, Emperor of Liang. *SmLg*
Autumn woods. J. S. Tippett. *ArTp—McAw*
An autumnal evening. W. Sharp. *CoPs*
Autumn's fete. A. S. McGeorge. *HaY*
Blue smoke. F. M. Frost. *BrS*
Chant for skippers. K. Gallagher. *BrS*
The cranes. Po Chü-i. *PaS*
Fall. A. Fisher. *ArTp—FeF*
Fall days. M. Conger. *BrS*
First autumn ("The crow sat black") F. M. Frost. *FrLn*
The first autumn ("Where God had walked") M. Schacht. *BrL-8*
Gathering leaves. R. Frost. *FrR—FrY*
Glimpse in autumn. J. S. Untermeyer. *JoAc*
Harvest home. A. Guiterman. *HaY*
Indian summer ("Indian summer is with us now") A. S. Draper. *HaY*
Indian summer ("These are the days when birds come back") E. Dickinson. *UnG*
An Indian summer day on the prairie. V. Lindsay. *HuSv—McW*
A leaf treader. R. Frost. *FrR*
The mist and all. D. Willson. *BrL-7—FeF—HaY—HuL-2—PeF*
"The morns are meeker than they were." E. Dickinson. *ArTp—JoAc—PeF*
Autumn. *BrR-5—FeF—HaY*

On some windy day. D. Aldis. *AlA*
Parting. Buson. *PaS*
Pirate wind. M. J. Carr. *BrS*
Robin Redbreast. W. Allingham. *NaM*
Song. R. W. Dixon. *HaY—ReT—SmLg*
Song of autumn. P. Verlaine. *PaS*
Spring and fall. G. M. Hopkins. *HaP—ReT*
To autumn ("O autumn, laden with fruit, and stained") W. Blake. *HoW*
To autumn ("Season of mists and mellow fruitfulness") J. Keats. *DeT—HaP—JoAc—UnG*
A vagabond song. B. Carman. *BrR-5—CoPs—FeF—HuL-2—JoAc—UnG*
The weather factory. N. B. Turner *BrR-4*
Autumn. See "The morns are meeker than they were"
Autumn, sel. Ann Taylor
The sound of a gun. *DeT*
Autumn ("Autumn's good, a cosy season") Unknown, tr. fr. the Irish by Frank O'Connor. *CoPs*
Autumn ("The leaves fall, fall as from far") Rainer Maria Rilke, tr. fr. the German by Jessie Lemont. *PaS*
Autumn ("Now is the time when cheery crickets") Nancy Byrd Turner. *HaY*
Autumn ("There is wind where the rose was") Walter De La Mare. *GrCc*
Autumn ("Yellow the bracken") Florence Hoatson. *HuL-1*
Autumn color. Tom Robinson. *HaY*
"Autumn comes on slippered feet." See Autumn's fete
Autumn eve. Amelia Andriello. *BrS*
Autumn evening. John Clare. *ReT*
Autumn fancies. Unknown. *FeF—HuSv*
Autumn fashions. Edith Matilda Thomas. *HaY*
Autumn fires. Robert Louis Stevenson. *ArTp—HaY—JoAc*
Autumn season. Ivy O. Eastwick. *EaI*
Autumn sigheth. Eleanor Farjeon. *FaCb—FaN*
Autumn song. Elizabeth-Ellen Long. *BrS*
The **autumn** wind. Wu-ti, Emperor of Liang, tr. fr. the Chinese by Arthur Waley. *SmLg*
"Autumn wind rises; white clouds fly." See The autumn wind
"The autumn wind's a pirate." See Pirate wind
Autumn woods. James S. Tippett. *ArTp—McAw*
An **autumnal** evening. William Sharp. *CoPs*
Autumnal spring song. Vassar Miller. *HaP*
Autumn's fete. Alice Sutton McGeorge. *HaY*
"Autumn's good, a cosy season." See Autumn
Avalon. James Reeves. *ReR*
Aviators
Darius Green and his flying-machine. J. T. Trowbridge. *NaM*
Flight. H. Vinal. *FeF—McW*
High flight. J. G. Magee, Jr. *FeF—McW—UnMc*
An Irish airman foresees his death. W. B. Yeats. *GrCc—SmLg*
Prayer for a pilot. C. Roberts. *FeF*

Awake. See The song of Solomon

"Awake, arise." See Up time

"Awake, for morning in the bowl of night." See The rubáiyát of Omar Khayyám of Naishapúr

Awake, glad heart. Henry Vaughan. *UnG*

"Awake, glad heart, get up and sing." See Awake, glad heart

"Awake, O, north wind." See The song of Solomon—Awake

Away. Dorothy Aldis. *AlA*

Away, away. See To Jane: The invitation

"Away, away, from men and towns." See To Jane: The invitation

"Away, away in the Northland." See A legend of the Northland

"Away beyond the Jarboe house." See Strange tree

"Away in a manger, no crib for a bed." See Cradle hymn

"Away in the forest, all darksome and deep." See W-o-o-o-o-o-ww

Away, Rio. Unknown. *SmLg*

Away we go. Eleanor Dennis. *McAw*

Awful mornings. Dorothy Aldis. *AlA*

"The axe has cut the forest down." See The wilderness is tamed

Ay me, alas. Thomas Weelkes. *SmLg*

"Ay me, alas, heigh ho, heigh ho." See Ay me, alas

"Ay, tear her tattered ensign down." See Old Ironsides

Aytoun, William Edmondstone
The execution of Montrose. *PaOm*

Aztecs
La noche triste. R. Frost. *FrR*

"Azzoomm, azzoomm loud and strong." See Riding in an airplane

B

B., J. P.
The cock and the sun. *BrR-3*

B is for beanseed. Eleanor Farjeon. *FaCb—HuL-1*

B. L. T., pseud. See Taylor, Bert Leston

"Baa, baa, black sheep." Mother Goose. *ArTp—BrL-k—DeMg—HuSv—JoAc—LiL—OpO*

Babcock, Donald
Program note on Sibelius. *PlU*

Babcock, Maltbie Davenport
"Be strong." *BrL-8*

Babcock, N. P.
The stranger cat. *CoH*

"The babe is cold." See Candle and star

The babes in the wood. See "My dear, do you know"

Babies. See also Childhood recollections; Children and childhood; Finger play poems; Lullabies; Mother Goose; Nursery play
Address to my infant daughter. W. Wordsworth. *NaE*

Anniversary in September. B. C. Brown. *BrBc*

At daybreak. H. Hoyt. *BrBc*

The baby. G. Macdonald. *BrBc—FeF*

"Baby and I." Mother Goose. *OpO*

Baby Kate. J. S. Newman. *CoH*

Baby-land. G. Cooper. *HuL-1*

Baby toes. C. Sandburg. *FeF*

A baby's feet. From Étude réaliste. A. C. Swinburne. *FeF*

The baby's name. T. Jenks. *BrBc*

Bartholomew. N. Gale. *BrBc*

Cradle song. A. A. Milne. *MiWc*

The crib. C. Morley. *BrBc*

February birthday. N. B. Turner. *BrBc*

"How many days has my baby to play." Mother Goose. *ArTp—OpO*

Infant joy. W. Blake. *ArTp—BrBc—BrS—FeF—ReT—UnG*

The little bird. W. De La Mare. *BrBc*

"Little Blue Shoes." K. Greenaway. *ArTp*

"Little papoose." H. Conkling. *FeF*

Naming the baby. M. Richstone. *BrBc*

Our baby. M. C. Livingston. *LiWa*

Ringely, ringely. E. L. Follen. *BrBc*

Six weeks old. C. Morley. *BrBc*

Sixteen months. C. Sandburg. *SaW*

Slippery. C. Sandburg. *ArTp—BrBc—FeF*

Strictly germ-proof. A. Guiterman. *BrL-8*

To baby. K. Greenaway. *BrL-k*

To Rose. S. Teasdale. *BrBc*

The twins. D. Aldis. *AlA—BrBc*

"What will we do with the baby-oh." Unknown. *WoF*

"Whenever a little child is born." A. C. Mason. *BrBc*

Baboons. See Monkeys

The baby. George Macdonald. *BrBc—FeF*

"Baby and I." Mother Goose. *OpO*

"Baby, baby, naughty baby." See Giant Bonaparte

Baby beds. Unknown. *HuL-1*

Baby bird. Harry Behn. *BeW*

"Baby Bobby in the tub." Unknown. *WoF*

"A baby cat is soft and sweet." See Cats

Baby chick. Aileen Fisher. *CoI*

"The Baby Christ, when He was born." See The birthday of the Lord

Baby goat. Zhenya Gay. *McAw*

The baby goes to Boston. Laura E. Richards. *ArTp—HuL-1*

Baby Kate. Joseph S. Newman. *CoH*

Baby-land. George Cooper. *HuL-1*

Baby seed song. Edith Nesbit. *FeF*

Baby seeds. Unknown. *BrR-3*

Baby song of the four winds. Carl Sandburg. *SaW*

Baby Taffy. Mother Goose. *OpO*

Baby toes. Carl Sandburg. *FeF*

A baby's feet. See Étude réaliste

"A baby's feet, like sea-shells pink." See Étude réaliste—A baby's feet

The baby's name. Tudor Jenks. *BrBc*

The Bacchae, sel. Euripides
Where shall wisdom be found, tr. fr. the Greek by Gilbert Murray. *PaS—PlU*

A bachelor of Maine. Ellen Douglas Deland. *CoH*

The **bachelor's** lament. See "When I was a little boy"

"**Back** and forth." See Horses

"**Back** and forth." Lucy Sprague Mitchell. *FeF*

"**Back** and side go bare, go bare." See Drinking song

"**Back** behind the mirror is another pussycat." See The looking-glass pussy

"**Back** in the year of 'fifty-nine." Unknown. *WoF*

Back-yard swing. Myra Cohn Livingston. *LiW*

Bacmeister, Rhoda W.
Bridges. *BrL-k—McAw*
Galoshes. *ArTp—BrL-k*
Icy. *BrL-k*
Little bug. *BrL-k*
Milk in winter. *BrL-k*
Raining. *BrL-k*
Snowstorm. *BrL-k*
Under the ground. *BrL-k—McAw*

Bacon, Josephine Dodge Daskam
Brother, lift your flag with mine. *CoPs*
The sleepy song. *HuSv*

Bacon, Leonard
Richard Tolman's universe. *PlI*

Bacon, Peggy
Hearth. *FeF*

Bad. Dorothy Aldis. *AlA*

A **bad** day by the river. E. V. Rieu. *RiF*

The **bad** kittens. Elizabeth Jane Coatsworth. *FeF*

The **bad** rider. See "I had a little pony"

Bad Sir Brian Botany. A. A. Milne. *CoH—MiWc*

The **bad-tempered** wife. Unknown. *UnMc*

Badger. John Clare. *HoW*

Badgers
Badger. J. Clare. *HoW*
The six badgers. R. Graves. *CoI—GrP—ReG*

A **bag** of chestnuts. Eleanor Farjeon. *FaCb—FaN*

A **bag** of tools. R. L. Sharpe. *ThP*

The **bag** pudding. See "When good King Arthur ruled this land"

The **bagpipe** man. Nancy Byrd Turner. *ArTp—HuL-1—HuL-2*

"The **bagpipe** man came over our hill." See The bagpipe man

Bagpipe music. Louis MacNeice. *HaP*

Bagpipers
The bagpipe man. N. B. Turner. *ArTp—HuL-1—HuL-2*
Bagpipe music. L. MacNeice. *HaP*
"A cat came fiddling out of a barn." Mother Goose. *DeMg—HuSv—JoAc*
Bagpipes. *DeT—OpO*
A cat came fiddling. *HuL-1*

Bagpipes. See "A cat came fiddling out of a barn"

Bahar
The miracle of spring. *PaS*

Bailada. Airas Nunez, tr. fr. the Portuguese by Seth G. Thornton. *PaS*

Bailey, Liberty Hyde
Farmer. *HaY*
Miracle. *HaY*

The **bailiff's** daughter of Islington. Unknown. *UnG*

The **bait.** John Donne. *GrCc*

Baker, Karle Wilson
Days. *ArTp*
Good company. *FeF*

Bakers
"Blow wind, blow, and go mill, go." Mother Goose. *ArTp—DeMg—HuSv*
"Blow, wind, blow." *HuL-1—OpO*
Charley. Mother Goose. *OpO*
Mr Cooter. E. Farjeon. *FaCb*

Balaclava, Battle of, 1854
The charge of the Light Brigade. A. Tennyson. *FeF—JoAc—UnMc*

"**Ball, ball.**" See Playing ball

Ball with Yvonne. Eleanor Farjeon. *FaCb*

Ballad ("The auld wife sat at her ivied door") Charles Stuart Calverley. *HoW*

Ballad ("O what is that sound which so thrills the ear") W. H. Auden. *UnMc*

A **ballad** for Palm Sunday. Eleanor Farjeon. *FaCb—FaN*

The **ballad** of Earl Haldan's daughter. Charles Kingsley. *HuL-2*

The **ballad** of east and west. Rudyard Kipling. *UnMc*

The **ballad** of Father Gilligan. William Butler Yeats. *McW*

A **ballad** of John Silver. John Masefield. *NaE*

Ballad of Johnny Appleseed. Helmer O. Oleson. *ArTp—BrS*

Ballad of the Epiphany. Charles Dalmon. *EaW*

Ballad of the fox. See "A fox jumped up one winter's night"

Ballad of the goodly fere. Ezra Pound. *HaP*

The **ballad** of the harp-weaver. Edna St Vincent Millay. *ArTp—CoSp—UnMc*

Ballad of the little black hound. Dora Sigerson Shorter. *CoSp*

The **ballad** of the oysterman. Oliver Wendell Holmes. *BrL-8—NaM*

Ballad of the rag-bag heart. Marjorie Allen Seiffert. *ThP*

The **ballad** of William Sycamore. Stephen Vincent Benét. *JoAc*

Ballads—American. See Cowboys—Songs; Lumbering; Mountaineer songs

Ballads—Old English and Scottish
Adam Bell, Clym of the Clough, and William of Cloudesley. Unknown. *MaB*
Alison Gross. Unknown. *MaB*
Annan water. Unknown. *MaB*
Annie of Lochroyan. Unknown. *MaB*
Archie of Cawfield. Unknown. *MaB*
The bailiff's daughter of Islington. Unknown. *UnG*
Barbara Allen. Unknown. *UnMc*
Binnorie. Unknown. *MaB*
The birth of Robin Hood. Unknown. *MaB*
The bonnie banks of Fordie. Unknown. *MaB*
The bonny earl of Murray. Unknown. *MaB*
The bonnie earl of Moray. *SmLg*

The bonny house of Airlie. Unknown. *MaB*
Brown Adam. Unknown. *MaB*
Chevy Chase. Unknown. *MaB*
Clerk Colven. Unknown. *MaB*
Clootie. Unknown. *MaB*
The crafty farmer. Unknown. *ArTp*
The crow and the crane. Unknown. *MaB*
The death of Robin Hood. Unknown. *MaB*
The demon lover. Unknown. *CoPm—MaB*
The Douglas tragedy. Unknown. *UnMc*
The duke of Gordon's daughter. Unknown. *MaB*
Earl Mar's daughter. Unknown. *MaB*
Edward, Edward. Unknown. *HaP—MaB—UnMc*
The elfin-knight. Unknown. *MaB*
Erlington. Unknown. *MaB*
The fair flower of Northumberland. Unknown. *MaB*
The falcon. Unknown. *GrCc*
The false knight upon the road. Unknown. *MaB*
The gay goshawk. Unknown. *MaB*
Get up and bar the door. Unknown. *ArTp—CoSp—JoAc—UnG—UnMc*
The gipsy laddie. Unknown. *SmLg*
Glenlogie. Unknown. *MaB*
The golden glove. Unknown. *UnMc*
The Golden Vanity. Unknown. *HoW*
The Great Silkie of Sule Skerrie. Unknown. *MaB*
Green broom. Unknown. *CoSp—ReG*
The heir of Linne. Unknown. *MaB*
How Robin Hood rescued the widow's sons. Unknown. *CoSp*
Hynd Etin. Unknown. *MaB*
Hynd Horn. Unknown. *MaB*
"I have four sisters beyond the sea." Unknown. *DeMg*
John Dory. Unknown. *MaB*
Johnie Faa. Unknown. *MaB*
Johnny Armstrong. Unknown. *UnMc*
Katherine Johnstone. Unknown. *MaB*
Kemp Oweyne. Unknown. *MaB*
King Estmere. Unknown. *MaB*
King John and the abbot of Canterbury. Unknown. *UnG*
King Orpheo. Unknown. *MaB*
Lady Elspat. Unknown. *MaB*
The little wee man. Unknown. *MaB*
The Lochmabyn harper. Unknown. *MaB*
Lord Lovel. Unknown. *CoPm—FeF*
Lord Randal. Unknown. *HuL-2*
    Lord Randall. *UnMc*
A lyke-wake dirge. Unknown. *MaB—NaE*
Maiden in the moor. Unknown. *MaB*
May Colvin. Unknown. *CoSp—MaB—UnMc*
Moy castle. Unknown. *UnG*
The old cloak. Unknown. *MaB*
Old Wichet. Unknown. *CoSp*
The outlandish knight. Unknown. *UnG*
The raggle taggle gypsies. Unknown. *ArTp—FeF—HuSv—UnG*
    The wraggle taggle gipsies. *NaE—ReT*
    The wraggle taggle gipsies, O. *HoW*

The riddling knight. Unknown. *GrCc—SmLg*
Robin Hood and Alan a Dale. Unknown. *MaB*
    Robin Hood and Allan a Dale. *UnG*
    Robin Hood and Allin a Dale. *NaM*
Robin Hood and Guy of Gisborne. Unknown. *MaB*
Robin Hood and Little John. Unknown. *HuSv—JoAc*
Robin Hood and the bishop of Hereford. Unknown. *MaB*
Robin Hood and the butcher. Unknown. *MaB*
Robin Hood and the curtal friar. Unknown. *MaB*
Robin Hood and the ranger. Unknown. *HuSv*
Robin Hood and the two priests. Unknown. *MaB*
Robin Hood rescuing the widow's three sons. Unknown. *ArTp*
    Robin Hood and the widow's sons. *UnG*
    Robin Hood and the widow's three sons. *MaB*
Sir Patrick Spens. Unknown. *HaP—JoAc—MaB—SmLg*
    Sir Patrick Spence. *ArTp*
Sweet William's ghost. Unknown. *MaB*
Tamlane. Unknown. *MaB*
True Thomas. Unknown. *CoSp—UnG—UnMc*
    Thomas the Rhymer. *MaB*
The twa corbies. Unknown. *CoSp—SmLg*
    The two corbies. *MaB*
The wife of Usher's well. Unknown. *ArTp—DeT—MaB*
Willie Mackintosh. Unknown. *MaB*
Young Bekie. Unknown. *MaB*
Young John. Unknown. *MaB*

Ballata. Unknown, tr. fr. the Italian by Dante Gabriel Rossetti. *PlU*

The **balloon** man ("The balloon man's stall") Myra Cohn Livingston. *LiW*

The **balloon** man ("He always comes on market days") Rose Fyleman. *HuL-1*

The **balloon** man ("Our balloon man has balloons") Dorothy Aldis. *AlA—ArTp*

"The **balloon** man's stall." See The balloon man

Balloon men. See Balloons

Balloons
    The balloon man ("The balloon man's stall") M. C. Livingston. *LiW*
    The balloon man ("He always comes on market days") R. Fyleman. *HuL-1*
    The balloon man ("Our balloon man has balloons") D. Aldis. *AlA—ArTp*
    "Balloons, balloons." M. C. Livingston. *LiW*
    The dirigible. R. Bergengren. *BrR-3—FeF*
    "I met a man that was all head." J. Ciardi. *CiI*
    In just spring. From Chanson innocente. E. E. Cummings. *CoH—JoAc—ReT*
        Chanson innocente. *FeF—NaM*
        "In just." *UnG*
    "Timothy Boon." I. O. Eastwick. *ArTp*

Barnum, Phineas Taylor (about)
P. T. Barnum. R. C. and S. V. Benét. *BrL-7*
The **barnyard.** Maude Burnham. *ArTp—HuL-1*
Barr, Matthias
"Moon, so round and yellow." *BrL-k*
The **barrel-organ,** sel. Alfred Noyes
Go down to Kew in lilac-time. *HuL-2*
"The **barrier** stone has rolled away." See Easter
Barrows, Marjorie
Hallowe'en song. *HuL-1*
May morning. *BrL-k*
Pine tree song. *BrR-4*
Barter. Sara Teasdale. *BrR-6—FeF—JoAc*
Barthélémon at Vauxhall. Thomas Hardy. *PlU*
Bartholomew. Norman Gale. *BrBc*
"**Bartholomew** is very sweet." See Bartholomew
Baruch, Dorothy W.
Automobile mechanics. *ArTp—FeF*
Barber's clippers. *BrR-3*
Cat. *ArTp—BrR-3*
Different bicycles. *ArTp—FeF*
"Funny the way different cars start." *BrL-k—FeF*
I would like to be—a bee. *BrBc*
Merry-go-round. *ArTp—BrL-k—HuL-1—HuSv*
On a steamer. *FeF*
Rabbits. *ArTp—BrL-k*
Riding in a motor boat. *FeF*
Riding in an airplane. *FeF*
Stop—go. *ArTp—BrL-k—FeF—HuL-1*
Bas-Quercy
Carol of the birds. *EaW*
Baseball
Casey at the bat. E. L. Thayer. *CoSp—FeF—UnMc*
Hits and runs. C. Sandburg. *SaW*
Bashō, Matsuo
On the mountain pass. *PaS*
On the road to Nara. *PaS*
Seven poems. *PaS* (sel.)
The sun path. *PaS*
Basket. Carl Sandburg. *SaW*
The **basket-maker's** song. See Pleasant comedy of patient Grissell
Basse, William
A memento for mortality. at. *SmLg*
The **bat.** Theodore Roethke. *UnG*
"**Bat,** bat, come under my hat." Mother Goose. *DeMg*
To the bat. *OpO*
Bath time. Marchette Chute. *ChA*
Bate, H. N.
The Christmas tree. tr. *EaW*
Bates, Clara Doty
Who likes the rain. *ArTp—BrR-3—HuL-1*
Bates, Katharine Lee
America the beautiful. *FeF*
Vacation. *BrR-6*
Bateson, Thomas
Sister, awake. *CoPs—GrCc*
Bathing
After a bath. A. Fisher. *McAw*
After my bath. D. Aldis. *AlA*

Anthony washes. E. V. Rieu. *RiF*
"Baby Bobby in the tub." Unknown. *WoF*
Bath time. M. Chute. *ChA*
"Connie, Connie, in the tub." Unknown. *MoY*
The footprint. J. Reeves. *ReBl*
An indignant male. A. B. Ross. *BrR-3*
"It ain't gonna rain no more." Unknown. *WoF*
"It's hard to lose a friend." Unknown. *MoY*
"Marguerite, go wash your feet." Unknown. *MoY*
Molly Grime. E. Farjeon. *FaCb—FaN*
Naughty soap song. D. Aldis. *AlA—BrL-k*
Pater's bathe. From Katawampus. E. A. Parry. *HuL-2*
Poems in praise of practically nothing. S. Hoffenstein. *NaE* (sel.)
Slippery. C. Sandburg. *ArTp—BrBc—FeF*
Soap, the oppressor. B. Johnson. *BrR-4*
Washing ("What is all this washing about") J. Drinkwater. *BrR-4—FeF—HuSv—JoAc*
Washing ("With soap and water") M. L. Allen. *AlP*
Bats
The bat. T. Roethke. *UnG*
"Bat, bat, come under my hat." Mother Goose. *DeMg*
To the bat. *OpO*
Five little bats. D. McCord. *McFf*
The witch of Willowby wood. R. B. Bennett. *CoPm*
Battle-hymn of the republic. Julia Ward Howe. *FeF—UnG*
The **battle** of Blenheim. Robert Southey. *HaP—UnG*
Battle royal. See "The lion and the unicorn"
Battles. See also Naval battles; names of battles, as Balaclava, Battle of, 1854; Warships
Fighting south of the ramparts. Unknown. *PaS*
Opportunity. E. R. Sill. *BrR-6—ThP—UnG*
Riding together. W. Morris. *McW*
Battleships. See Naval battles; Warships
Baucis and Philemon. Jonathan Swift. *CoSp*
Baudelaire, Charles
Invitation to the voyage. *PaS*
Landscape. *PaS*
Music. *PaS*
Bavarian gentians. D. H. Lawrence. *HaP—SmLg*
"The **bawl** of a steer." See The cowboy's life
"**Be** always in time." Mother Goose. *OpO*
"**Be** careful what." See Zoo manners
Be different to trees. Mary Carolyn Davies. *FeF*
"**Be** good as a Christian." Unknown. *MoY*
"**Be** kind and tender to the frog." See The frog
"**Be** kind to all dumb animals." See The cheerful cherub—Humane thought
"**Be** land ready." See Be ready
Be like the bird. Victor Hugo. *ArTp—FeF*
Wings. *JoAc*

"**Be** like the bird, who." See Be like the bird

"**Be** not afeard. The isle is full of noises."
See The tempest

Be not afraid. Robert Nathan. *BrR-5*

"**Be** not afraid because the sun goes down."
See Be not afraid

Be ready. Carl Sandburg. *SaW*

"**Be** silent, secret, and conceal." See Silentium

Be still, my soul. Archilochus, tr. fr. the
Greek by C. M. Bowra. *PaS*

"**Be** still, while the music rises about us; the
deep enchantment." See At a concert of
music

"**Be** strong." Maltbie Davenport Babcock.
BrL-8

Be thankful unto Him. See Psalms—
Psalm C

"**Be** Thou praised, my Lord, with all Thy
creatures." See The mirror of perfection—Praise of created things

"**Be** you to others kind and true." Unknown.
MoY

Beach. Myra Cohn Livingston. *LiWa*

Beach fire. Frances M. Frost. *ArTp—PeF*

Beaches. See Seashore

"A **beanseed,** a beanseed." See B is for beanseed

The **bear.** Robert Frost. *FrR*

"A **bear,** however hard he tries." See Teddy
Bear

The **bear** hunt. Margaret Widdemer. *FeF*

"The **bear** puts both arms around the tree
above her." See The bear

"A **bear** went over the mountain." Mother
Goose. *HuSv—JoAc*

Beards
"There was an old man in a tree (whose
whiskers)." E. Lear
Limericks. *JoAc*
"There was an old man named Michael
Finnegan." Unknown. *ArTp*
American Father Gander. *UnG*
"There was an old man with a beard."
E. Lear. *ArTp—CoH—WiRm*
Just as he feared. *BrR-4*
Nonsense verses. *HuSv*
Old man with a beard. *FeF*

"The **bearer** of evil tidings." Robert Frost.
FrR

Bears
"Algy met a bear." Unknown. *FeF*
Algy. *NaM*
The bear. R. Frost. *FrR*
The bear hunt. M. Widdemer. *FeF*
"A bear went over the mountain." Mother
Goose. *HuSv—JoAc*
The bears who once were giants. From
The house beyond the meadow. H.
Behn. *BeH*
"A big black bug bit a big black bear."
Unknown. *WiRm*
The brown bear. M. Austin. *CoPs—FeF*
—McW
Brown bear's honey song. K. Jackson.
McAw
"A cheerful old bear at the zoo." Unknown
Limericks since Lear. *UnG*

Furry bear. A. A. Milne. *CoI—HuSv—
MiWc—PeF*
"Fuzzy Wuzzy was a bear." Unknown.
WiRm—WoF
American Father Gander. *UnG*
Grizzly bear. M. Austin. *ArTp—FeF*
Infant innocence. A. E. Housman. *SmLg*
Last word about bears. J. Ciardi. *CiY*
Lines and squares. A. A. Milne. *MiWc*
More about bears. J. Ciardi. *CiY*
"A pleasant old bear at the zoo." Unknown. *WiRm*
Polar bear. W. J. Smith. *SmB*
The Shakespearean bear. A. Guiterman.
NaE
Still more about bears. J. Ciardi. *CiY*
Teddy Bear. A. A. Milne. *MiWc*
Teddy Bear, Teddy Bear. Unknown. *WoJ*
"Teddy Bear, Teddy Bear, turn
around." *WiRm*
"There was an old person of Ware."
E. Lear
Lear's limericks. *UnG*
Limericks. *JoAc*
Twice times. A. A. Milne. *MiWc*
Us two. A. A. Milne. *ArTp—MiWc*
Waiting. H. Behn. *ArTp—BrS—JoAc*
A warning about bears. J. Ciardi. *CiY*
"Who are you? asked the cat of the bear."
E. J. Coatsworth. *ArTp*
Winter-wear. M. L. Allen. *AlP*
W-o-o-o-o-o-ww. N. M. Hayes. *HuL-1*
The **bears** who once were giants. See The
house beyond the meadow

"The **beast** that is most fully dressed." See
Lion

Beasts. See Animals

"**Beatrice** with her freckled face." See Summer offering

"**Beau** Nash he was a gentleman." See The
Beau of Bath

The **Beau** of Bath. Eleanor Farjeon. *FaN*

Beauchamp, Kathleen. See Mansfield, Katherine, pseud.

Beaumont, Francis
Song for a dance. See Superlative dance
and song
Superlative dance and song. *PlU*
Song for a dance. *SmLg*

Beaumont, Francis and Fletcher, John
"Nose, nose, jolly red nose." *SmLg*
The river-god's song. *FeF—NaM*
Song. *ReT*
Song. See The river-god's song

"A **beautiful** place is the town of Lo-yang."
See Lo-yang

"**Beautiful** railway bridge of the silv'ry Tay."
See The Tay bridge disaster

Beautiful soup. See Alice's adventures in
wonderland—Turtle soup

"**Beautiful** soup, so rich and green." See
Alice's adventures in wonderland—
Turtle soup

"**Beautifully** Janet slept." See Janet waking

Beauty
Altar smoke. R. Grayer. *UnG*
Barter. S. Teasdale. *BrR-6—FeF—JoAc*
Beauty. E-Yeh-Shuré. *ArTp—BrR-5—FeF*
—JoAc

Behavior—*Continued*

"When Jack's a very good boy." Mother Goose. *DeMg*

"When Jacky's a good boy." *OpO*

"When Jacky's a very good boy." *NaE*

Whole duty of children. R. L. Stevenson. *NaE*

You and I. Unknown. *ThP*

"Behind him lay the gray Azores." See Columbus

Behind the gorse. Eleanor Farjeon. *FaN*

Behind the waterfall. Winifred Welles. *ArTp—CoPm—HuSv*

Behn, Harry

Adventure. *ArTp*

After rain. *BeW*

Baby bird. *BeW*

Bantam rooster. *JoAc*

The bears who once were giants. See The house beyond the meadow

Building. *BeW*

A Christmas carol. *BrBc*

Christmas morning. *BeW*

Circles. *LoL*

Counting. *BeW*

Curiosity. *BeW*

Doctor Windikin. *BeW*

The dream. *BeW*

Easter eggs. *BeW*

Enchanted summer. *BeW*

Evening. *BeW—JoAc*

The fairy and the bird. *BeW*

Far away music. *BeW*

First enchantment. See The house beyond the meadow

Flowers. *ArTp—FeF*

A friendly visit. See The house beyond the meadow

The gnome. *ArTp—BeW—FeF*

Goodbye to fairyland. See The house beyond the meadow

Grasshopper song. *BeW*

Growing up. *BrBc—BrS*

Hallowe'en. *ArTp — BrS — CoPs — FeF — HaY—HuL-2—HuSv—JoAc*

The house beyond the meadow, sels. *BeH* (complete)

The bears who once were giants

First enchantment

A friendly visit

Goodbye to fairyland

The magic map

The strangest wish

The thunder-and-lightning bug

Invitation. *FeF*

Jack Frost. *BeW*

The kite. *ArTp—BeW—FeF—JoAc*

The last leaf. *BeW*

Lesson. *BeW*

The magic map. See house beyond the meadow

Make believe. *BeW*

Mr Pyme. *ArTp—LoL*

Moon vine. *BeW*

Morning in winter. *BeW*

Morning magic. *BeW*

The mystery. *BeW*

Near and far. *BeW*

The new little boy. *BeW*

Picnic by the sea. *BeW*

Pirates. *BeW*

Pretending. *BeW—JoAc*

The sea shore. *BeW*

Shopping spree. *BeW*

Spring. *ArTp*

Spring rain. *ArTp—PeF*

The strangest wish. See The house beyond the meadow

Surprise. *BrBc*

Tea party. *BeW*

This happy day. *ArTp—HuL-1*

The thunder-and-lightning bug. See The house beyond the meadow

Trees. *ArTp—BrS—HaY—HuL-2—JoAc—PeF*

Voices. *BeW*

Waiting. *ArTp—BrS—JoAc*

Windy morning. *ArTp—BeW*

"Behold, a giant am I." See The windmill

"Behold, a new white world." See A new year

"Behold, a silly tender Babe." See New Prince, new pomp

"Behold, God is great, and we know Him not." See Job—Job, Chapter 36

"Behold her, single in the field." See The solitary reaper

"Behold the duck." See The duck

"Behold the mighty dinosaur." See The dinosaur

"Behold the supercilious nimp." See The nimp

"Behold within our Hayden planetarium." See Ode to the Hayden planetarium

Being gypsy. Barbara Young. *ArTp*

"A being stood before me in a dream." See England

Being twins. Kathryn Jackson. *BrBc*

Bel m'es quan lo vens m'alena. Arnaut Daniel, tr. fr. the Provençal by Harriet Waters Preston. *PaS*

Belief. See Faith

"Belinda lived in a little white house." See The tale of Custard the dragon

Belisarius. Henry Wadsworth Longfellow. *HoW*

Bell, Alexander Graham (about)

Alexander Graham Bell did not invent the telephone. R. P. T. Coffin. *ArTp*

Bell, Ellis, pseud. See Brontë, Emily

Bell, H. Idris

A snowy day. tr. *PaS*

Bell-horses. See "Bell horses, bell horses, what time of day"

"Bell horses, bell horses, what time of day." Mother Goose. *ArTp—OpO*

Bell-horses. *HuL-1*

What time of day. *BrS*

La **belle** dame sans merci. John Keats. *CoSp — DeT — HaP — McW — SmLg — UnG—UnMc*

Bellman, Carl Michael

Cradle song. *FeF*

Belloc, Hilaire

The big baboon. *NaM*

The dodo. *LoL*

The early morning. *McW*

The elephant. *ArTp—LoL*

The false heart. *SmLg*
The frog. *CoH—FeF—JoAc—NaM*
G. *CoH*
George who played with a dangerous toy and suffered a catastrophe of considerable dimensions. *CoH—UnG*
The hippopotamus. *CoH*
Jim. See Jim, who ran away from his nurse
Jim, who ran away from his nurse. *LoL—NaM*
 Jim. *UnMc*
The llama. *NaM—SmLg*
Matilda. *CoSp*
The microbe. *BrL-7*
The python. *NaE*
The rhinoceros. *FeF*
Sarah Byng. *GrCc*
Tarantella. *NaM—SmLg*
The vulture. *LoL*
The yak. *CoH—FeF—HuL-2—JoAc*

Bells
"As round as an apple (as deep as a pail)." Mother Goose. *OpO*
Bells ("Hard as crystal") J. Reeves. *ReG—ReW*
The bells ("Hear the sledges with the bells") E. A. Poe. *FeF* (sel.)
The bells of peace. A. Fisher. *BrS*
Canterbury bells. E. Farjeon. *FaCb*
The children's bells. E. Farjeon. *FaCb*
Christmas bells. H. W. Longfellow. *FeF—UnG*
 "I heard the bells on Christmas day." *CoPs*
Curfew must not ring tonight. R. H. Thorpe. *FeF*
Doorbells. R. Field. *ArTp—FeF—HuSv*
For whom the bell tolls. J. Donne. *ThP*
"Gay go up and gay go down." Mother Goose. *DeMg—JoAc—LiL*
 The bells of London. *NaE*
 Oranges and lemons. *OpO*
The green gnome. R. Buchanan. *CoSp*
How still the bells. E. Dickinson. *ReG*
Jingle bells. J. Pierpont. *OpO* (sel.)
"Merry are the bells, and merry would they ring." Unknown. *DeMg—DeT*
 Merry are the bells. *ArTp—LoL—NaM*
School-bell. E. Farjeon. *BrS—FeF*
Sing-song. D. McCord. *McT*
Sleigh bells at night. E. J. Coatsworth. *BrS*
Song of the engine bells. E. J. Coatsworth. *BrR-5*
Tarlingwell. J. Reeves. *ReR*
Tolling bells. Lady Kasa. *PaS*
Tom Tittlemouse. Mother Goose. *OpO*
"What are the great bells ringing." C. S. Thomas. *BrL-8*
Bells ("Hard as crystal") James Reeves. *ReG—ReW*
The **bells** ("Hear the sledges with the bells") Edgar Allan Poe. *FeF* (sel.)
"The **bells** are ringing for church this morning." See Through the window
"The **bells** are tolling." See Tolling bells
"The **bells** chime clear." See The christening

The **bells** of heaven. Ralph Hodgson. *BrS—DeT—HaP*
The **bells** of London. See "Gay go up and gay go down"
The **bells** of peace. Aileen Fisher. *BrS*
Belongings. Marchette Chute. *ChA*
"**Below** the hall." See The pine-trees in the courtyard
"**Below** the thunders of the upper deep." See The kraken
"**Ben** Battle was a soldier bold." See Faithless Nelly Gray
"**Ben** Franklin munched a loaf of bread while walking down the street." See Benjamin Franklin
Ben Franklin's head. Mark A. DeWolfe Howe. *McW*
"**Bend** low again, night of summer stars." See Summer stars
"**Beneath** the green acacia tree." See The shower
"**Beneath** the waters." See Undersea
"**Beneathe** an ancient oake one daye." See A Christmas legend
Benediktsson, Einar
 Rain. *PaS*
Benét, Rosemary Carr and Stephen Vincent
 Abraham Lincoln. *ArTp—CoPs—HaY*
 Benjamin Franklin. *ArTp—FeF*
 Captain Kidd. *HuL-2*
 Christopher Columbus. *PeF*
 Clipper ships and captains. *HuSv*
 George Washington. *FeF—UnMc*
 Nancy Hanks. *ArTp—BrR-5—BrS—FeF—HuSv—JoAc*
 Negro spirituals. *FeF*
 P. T. Barnum. *BrL-7*
 "Thomas Jefferson." *ArTp—BrL-8—FeF*
 Western wagons. *BrR-5—McW*
 Wilbur Wright and Orville Wright. *BrL-8*
Benét, Stephen Vincent
 American names. *McW—SmLg*
 The ballad of William Sycamore. *JoAc*
 Listen to the people: Independence day, 1941. *CoPs* (sel.)
 Metropolitan nightmare. *PlI*
 The mountain whippoorwill *CoSp*
 Nightmare number three. *UnMc*
Benét, William Rose
 Books et veritas. *ThP*
 Jesse James. *CoSp*
Benjamin, Virginia Sarah
 A puzzling example. *BrBc*
Benjamin Franklin. Rosemary Carr and Stephen Vincent Benét. *ArTp—FeF*
Bennett, Henry
 St Patrick was a gentleman. *BrS*
Bennett, Henry Holcomb
 The flag goes by. *ArTp—BrL-7—BrS—FeF*
Bennett, John
 The ingenious little old man. *FeF*
 The merry pieman's song. *LoL*
 The snake charmer. *BrR-3*
 A tiger's tale. *CoH*
Bennett, Mary
 The ragged girl's Sunday. *DeT*
Bennett, Peggy
 A mother is a sun. *CoPs*

"Betwixt and Between were two betwins."
    See Betwixt and Between
Bevington, Helen
    The man from Porlock. *NaE*
"Beware of boys with eyes of brown." Unknown. *MoY*
Bewick Finzer. Edwin Arlington Robinson. *GrCc*
Bewitched. Walter De La Mare. *CoPm*
Beyer, Evelyn
    Jump or jiggle. *ArTp—BrR-3—HuL-1*
    Seesaw. *BrL-k*
"Beyond the east the sunrise, beyond the west the sea." See Wander-thirst
"Beyond the great valley an odd instinctive rising." See Ascent to the Sierras
Bhartrihari
    Love in moonlight. *PaS*
    Peace. *PaS*
    Women's eyes. *PaS*
Bhasa
    The moon. *PaS*
Bialik, Chaim Nachman
    Tell him. *PaS*
Bialik, H. N.
    Bird's nest. *BrL-k*
    Blessing over food. *BrL-k—HaY*
    For Hanukkah. *ArTp*
    The grasshopper's song. *FeF—HaY*
    Rainbow. *BrR-4*
    Rocking horse. *BrL-k*
    See-saw. *BrL-k*
Bible, Old Testament
    Abiding in the shadow of the Almighty. See Psalms—Psalm XCI
    Awake. See The song of Solomon
    Be thankful unto Him. See Psalms—Psalm C
    "Bless the Lord, O my soul." See Psalms—Psalm CIII
    "But they that wait upon the Lord shall renew their strength." See Isaiah
    "Cast thy bread upon the waters." See Ecclesiastes
    "The earth abideth forever." See Ecclesiastes
    "The earth is the Lord's." See Psalms—Psalm XXIV
    "The earth is the Lord's, and the fulness thereof." See Psalms—Psalm XXIV
    "For lo, the winter is past." See The song of Solomon—The winter is past
    Four things. See Proverbs
    "Fret not thyself because of evildoers." See Psalms—Psalm XXXVII
    Genesis, Chapter 1. See Genesis
    Go to the ant. See Proverbs
    "God is our refuge and strength." See Psalms—Psalm XLVI
    The hay appeareth. See Proverbs
    He that is slow to anger. See Proverbs
    "The heavens declare the glory of God." See Psalms—Psalm XIX
    The horse. See Job
    "I will lift up mine eyes." See Psalms—Psalm CXXI
    I will sing praise. See Psalms—Psalm IX
    Job, Chapter 38. See Job
    Job, Chapter 36. See Job
    Let the nations be glad. See Psalms—Psalm LXVII

The light is sweet. See Ecclesiastes
Lo, the winter is past. See The song of Solomon—The winter is past
"The Lord is my shepherd." See Psalms—Psalm XXIII
"The Lord is my shepherd, I shall not want." See Psalms—Psalm XXIII
"Make a joyful noise unto the Lord, all ye lands." See Psalms—Psalm C
Mother of the house. See Proverbs—"Strength and honour are her clothing"
The peaceable kingdom. See Isaiah
"Praise ye the Lord (for it is)." See Psalms—Psalm CXLII
"Praise ye the Lord (praise God)." See Psalms—Psalm CL
Psalm I. See Psalms
Psalm VIII. See Psalms
Psalm IX. See Psalms
Psalm XIX. See Psalms
Psalm XXIII. See Psalms
Psalm XXIV. See Psalms
Psalm XXXVII. See Psalms
Psalm XLVI. See Psalms
Psalm LV. See Psalms
Psalm LXVII. See Psalms
Psalm LXXXIV. See Psalms
Psalm XCI. See Psalms
Psalm C. See Psalms
Psalm CIII. See Psalms
Psalm CIV. See Psalms
Psalm CVII. See Psalms
Psalm CXXI. See Psalms
Psalm CXLVII. See Psalms
Psalm CL. See Psalms
A psalm of praise. See Psalms—Psalm C
Psalm 100. See Psalms—Psalm C
Psalm one hundred fifty. See Psalms—Psalm CL
Psalm 150. See Psalms—Psalm CL
Psalm 107. See Psalms—Psalm CVII
Psalm twenty-four. See Psalms—Psalm XXIV
The rich earth. See Psalms—Psalm CIV
"A soft answer turneth away wrath." See Proverbs
The song of songs. See The song of Solomon
The sparrow, 1. See Psalms—Psalm LXXXIV
"Strength and honour are her clothing." See Proverbs
Thanksgiving. See Psalms—Psalm C
"They that go down to the sea." See Psalms—Psalm CVII
The tree and the chaff. See Psalms—Psalm I
The two paths. See Proverbs
"When I consider Thy heavens." See Psalms—Psalm VIII
Who maketh the grass to grow. See Psalms—Psalm CXLVII
Wings. See Psalms—Psalm LV
The winter is past. See The song of Solomon
A word fitly spoken. See Proverbs
Bible, New Testament
    Charity. See First epistle of Paul to the Corinthians
    Christmas eve. See Gospel according to Luke

Bible, New Testament—*Continued*
"For God hath not given us the spirit of fear." See The second epistle of Paul to Timothy
The sermon on the mount. See Gospel according to Matthew
The sparrow, 2. See Gospel according to Matthew
Tidings of great joy. See Gospel according to Luke—Christmas eve
Treasures in heaven. See Gospel according to Matthew
"Whatsoever things are true." See The epistle of Paul to the Philippians
Bible characters. See also names of Bible characters, as Adam and Eve
Bible stories. L. W. Reese. *DoP*
"Joshua fit de battle of Jericho." Unknown. *UnMc*
Noah. J. Reeves. *ReR*
"Noah an' Jonah an' Cap'n John Smith." D. Marquis. *SmLg*
Peter and John. E. Wylie. *UnMc*
Ruth. T. Hood. *GrCc*
Bible stories. Lizette Woodworth Reese. *DoP*
Bickerstaffe, Isaac
Jolly miller. See Love in a village—"There was a jolly miller"
Love in a village, sel.
"There was a jolly miller." *DeMg—UnG*
Jolly miller. *OpO*
"There was a jolly miller once." *LiL*
"There was a jolly miller." See Love in a village
"There was a jolly miller once." See Love in a village—"There was a jolly miller"
Bicycles and bicycling
Different bicycles. D. W. Baruch. *ArTp—FeF*
"Bid me to live, and I will live." See To Anthea who may command him any thing
Big. Dorothy Aldis. *AlA*
Big and little. William Jay Smith. *SmL*
"Big at both ends and small in the middle." Unknown. *WoF*
The **big** baboon. Hilaire Belloc. *NaM*
"The **big** baboon is found upon." See The big baboon
The **big** bass drum. Unknown. *HuL-1*
"A **big** black bug bit a big black bear." Unknown. *WiRm*
"Big boys do." See Big and little
Big brother. Elizabeth Madox Roberts. *FeF*
"The **big** brown hen and Mrs Duck." See A little talk
The **big** clock. Unknown. *ArTp—HuL-1*
"Big feet." See Feet
The **big** nasturtiums. Robert Beverly Hale. *CoPm*
The **big** Rock Candy mountain. Unknown. *UnMc*
"The **big** swing-tree is green again." Mary Jane Carr. *BrS*
"Big trucks for steel beams." See trucks

"Big trucks with apples." See Country trucks
Big waves and little waves. Eleanor Farjeon. *HuL-1*
"Big yellow trolley lumbers along." See There are so many ways of going places
"The bigger the box the more it holds." See Boxes and bags
The **bight.** Elizabeth Bishop. *HaP*
Bilderdijk, Willem
Prayer. *PaS*
Bill. J. L. Salzburg. *BrBc*
"Bill dug a well." See A narrative
"Bill, where does your coat belong." See If you ask me
Billy. See Four ruthless rhymes
Billy and me. Mother Goose. *OpO*
"Billy Billy Booster." Unknown. *WiRm*
Billy boy. See "Oh where have you been, Billy boy, Billy boy"
Billy-boy. Dorothy King. *HuL-1*
"Billy-boy, Billy-boy." See Billy-boy
"Billy came to see us." See Tell him to go home
"Billy, in one of his nice new sashes." See Four ruthless rhymes—Billy
Bingo has an enemy. Rose Fyleman. *BrR-5*
"Bingo is kind and friendly." See Bingo has an enemy
Binker. A. A. Milne. *MiWc*
"Binker—what I call him—is a secret of my own." See Binker
Binnorie. Unknown. *MaB*
Binns, Elsie
"Christmas is remembering." *BrBc—BrS*
"The **biplane** is the shape of human flight." See The Wrights' biplane
"The **birch** begins to crack its outer sheath." See A young birch
Birch trees
The birches ("The little birches, white and slim") W. P. Eaton. *BrL-k—HuSv*
Birches ("When I see birches bend to left and right") R. Frost. *FrR—FrY—SmLg*
Pea brush. R. Frost. *FrR—FrY*
A young birch. R. Frost. *FrY*
The **birches** ("The little birches, white and slim") Walter Prichard Eaton. *BrL-k—HuSv*
Birches ("When I see birches bend to left and right") Robert Frost. *FrR—FrY—SmLg*
Birckhead, Nancy
October. *BrL-7*
A **bird.** See "A bird came down the walk"
The **bird** ("Though the evening comes with slow steps and has signalled for all songs to cease") Rabindranath Tagore. *PaS*
Bird at dawn. Harold Monro. *UnG*
The **Bird-brain** song. John Ciardi. *CiY*
"Bird-brain took a train." See The Bird-brain song
"A **bird** came down the walk." Emily Dickinson. *ArTp*(sel.)—*BrR-3*(sel.)—*NaM*
A bird. *FeF*(sel.)—*CoI*(sel.)—*HuSv*(sel.)
"A **bird** half wakened in the lunar noon." See On a bird singing in its sleep

Bird scarer's song. Mother Goose. *OpO*

"A birdie with a yellow bill." See Time to rise

Birds. See also names of birds, as Robins

"The abbot of Inisfalen." W. Allingham. *PaOm*

"Ah poor bird." Unknown. *ReG*

Alle vögel sind schon da. F. Chesterton. *PlU*

Answer to a child's question. S. T. Coleridge. *ReT*

"As black as ink and isn't ink." Mother Goose. *OpO*

Autumn evening. J. Clare. *ReT*

Baby bird. H. Behn. *BeW*

Be like the bird. V. Hugo. *ArTp—FeF—JoAc*

The bird. R. Tagore. *PaS*

Bird at dawn. H. Monro. *UnG*

"A bird came down the walk." E. Dickinson. *ArTp*(sel.)—*BrR-3*(sel.)—*NaM*

  A bird. *FeF*(sel.)—*CoI*(sel.)—*HuSv* (sel.)

Bird scarer's song. Mother Goose. *OpO*

The birds and the telephone wires. C. P. Cranch. *BrR-5*

Birds in the forest. J. Reeves. *ReBl*

The birds' lullaby. E. P. Johnson. *HuL-2*

Birds of joy. E. Farjeon. *FaCb—FaN*

The birds on the school windowsill. E. Dainty. *HuL-1*

The bisk. J. Reeves. *ReP*

The bugle-billed bazoo. J. Ciardi. *CiR*

By Dippel woods. E. Farjeon. *FaCb*

Cape Ann. From Landscapes. T. S. Eliot. *JoAc—NaE—ReT*

Carol of the birds. Bas-Quércy. *EaW*

Cheep. E. Farjeon. *FaCb—FaN*

Children of the wind. From The people, yes. C. Sandburg. *HuSv*

The dodo. H. Belloc. *LoL*

Feather or fur. J. Becker. *ArTp—FeF*

February bird. D. Morton. *ThP*

The frog and the bird. V. Hessey. *HuL-1*

Goony bird. W. J. Smith. *SmB*

The grasshopper and the bird. J. Reeves. *ReBl*

Hark. Unknown. *DeT*

The high Barbaree. L. E. Richards. *JoAc*

Hungry morning. M. C. Livingston. *LiWa*

"I heard a bird sing." O. Herford. *ArTp—BrS—EaW—HaY—HuL-2*

"I met a man that had two birds." J. Ciardi. *CiI*

In a museum. T. Hardy. *PlU*

In Glencullen. J. M. Synge. *ReT*

"It was Saint Francis who came." A. Wynne. *DoP*

Joe. D. McCord. *ArTp—McFf*

Joy of the morning. E. Markham. *FeF*

Lady lost. J. C. Ransom. *HaP*

Little brother. A. Fisher. *BrBc—McAw*

Looking for a sunset bird in winter. R. Frost. *FrR—FrY*

Love without hope. R. Graves. *GrP*

Luncheons. D. Aldis. *AlA*

A minor bird. *FrR—FrY*

The mocking bird. I. O. Eastwick. *EaI*

Mourning doves. D. Aldis. *AlHd*

Never again would birds' song be the same. R. Frost. *FrR*

The nonny. J. Reeves. *ReP*

"Now, more near ourselves than we." E. E. Cummings. *GrCc*

On a bird singing in its sleep. R. Frost. *FrR*

"Once I saw a little bird." Mother Goose. *BrL-k—DeMg—HuSv*

  Little bird. *OpO*

Our singing strength. R. Frost. *FrR*

The pelican chorus. E. Lear. *LoL*

Praise. Mother Goose. *OpO*

Prisoned. M. C. Davies. *HuL-2*

Proud songsters. T. Hardy. *HaP*

Psalm LXXXIV. From Psalms, Bible, Old Testament

  The sparrow, 1. *FeF*

The rivals. J. Stephens. *BrR-6—FeF*

River roads. C. Sandburg. *SaW*

Rockaby, baby. W. Barnes. *DeT*

Rover and the bird. Mrs N. Crossland. *DeT*

Secrets. M. McArthur. *DeT*

The singers in a cloud. R. Torrence. *PlU*

Singing. D. Aldis. *AlA*

Song. S. T. Coleridge. *CoPs—DeT*

Spring's arrival. Unknown. *FeF*

Stupidity street. R. Hodgson. *BrS—DeT*

"There were two birds sat on a stone." Mother Goose. *DeMg*

  Two birds. *OpO*

The three singing birds. J. Reeves. *CoPm—ReBl*

Time to rise. R. L. Stevenson. *BrS—BrL-k—HuSv*

To a waterfowl. W. C. Bryant. *DeT*

"Two little dicky birds." Mother Goose. *LiL—OpO*

Warning. Mother Goose. *OpO*

"A wee bird sat upon a tree." Unknown. *JoAc*

What bird so sings. J. Lyly. *ReT*

"What does little birdie say." A. Tennyson. *BrL-k—HuL-1*

A widow bird. P. B. Shelley. *DeT—FeF*

  A song. *ReT*

Winter feast. F. M. Frost. *HaY*

Birds—Eggs and nests

Bird's nest ("Among the trees") H. N. Bialik. *BrL-k*

The bird's nest ("I know a place, in the ivy on a tree") J. Drinkwater. *HuSv—McAw—NaE*

The brown thrush. L. Larcom. *BrR-4—FeF*

"Elizabeth, Elspeth, Betsy and Bess." Mother Goose. *DeMg—JoAc—OpO*

  Elizabeth. *ReG*

The exposed nest. R. Frost. *FrY*

The green grass growing all around. Unknown. *HuL-2—NaM*

A hymn for Saturday. C. Smart. *ReG*

  A lark's nest. *SmLg*

The linnet. R. Burns. *DeT*

"A little sparrow built his nest, up in a waterspout." Unknown. *WoF*

"Look at six eggs." C. Sandburg. *FeF*

Meadow secret. F. M. Frost. *FrLn*

The birthday child. R. Fyleman. *BrBc—BrS—FeF*

Birthday garden. I. O. Eastwick. *BrBc*

Birthday gift. E. B. De Vito. *BrBc*

Birthday gifts ("Birthday, birthday; little boy has a birthday") L. B. Scott and J. J. Thompson. *BrBc*

Birthday gifts ("What will you have for your birthday") H. Asquith. *BrBc—BrS*

Birthdays. M. Chute. *BrBc—BrL-k—BrS—ChA—HuSv*

Cake. M. C. Clark. *BrBc*

A child's Christmas song. T. A. Daly. *BrBc*

Christmas birthday. G. E. Glaubitz. *BrBc—BrS*

Crab-apple. E. Talbot. *ArTp—BrBc*

Dandelions. M. Chute. *BrBc—ChA—McAw*

The end. A. A. Milne. *BrBc—BrS—MiWc*

Experience. A. Kilmer. *BrBc*

February birthday. N. B. Turner. *BrBc*

Fifth birthday gift. M. Lederer. *BrBc*

Five-in-June. L. B. Borie. *BrBc*

Five years old ("If ever there is something nice") L. B. Borie. *BrBc—BrS*

Five years old ("Please, everybody, look at me") M. L. Allen. *AlP—BrBc—BrL-k*

For a birthday. E. V. Emans. *BrBc*

For Arvia. E. A. Robinson. *BrBc*

For Maria at four. J. Becker. *BrBc*

Four. E. Gibbs. *BrBc*

Four and eight. F. Wolfe. *BrBc—BrS—HuL-1*

Gifts. H. H. Harris. *BrBc*

Growing up ("My birthday is coming tomorrow") Unknown. *BrBc—BrL-k*

Growing up ("When I was seven") H. Behn. *BrBc—BrS*

Hal's birthday. L. Larcom. *BrBc*

The hippopotamus's birthday. E. V. Rieu. *RiF*

Hurry tomorrow. I. O. Eastwick. *BrBc*

I would like to be—a bee. D. W. Baruch. *BrBc*

"I'm glad my birthday comes in May." I. O. Eastwick. *BrBc*

Little Blue Ribbons. A. Dobson. *BrBc*

Little brother's secret. K. Mansfield. *ArTp—FeF*

"Little lad, little lad, where wast thou born." Mother Goose. *DeMg*
  Little lad. *BrBc*
  "Little lad, little lad." *OpO*

Lucinda Prattle. P. Brown. *LoL*

Lucy Lavender. I. O. Eastwick. *BrBc—BrS*

Manhattan lullaby. R. Field. *BrBc*

Mary and the marigold. I. O. Eastwick. *EaI*

The miracle. E. M. Fowler. *BrBc*

"Monday's child is fair of face." Mother Goose. *BrBc—DeMg—HuSv—JoAc—LiL—SmLg*
  Birthdays. *OpO—ReG*
  Days of birth. *NaM*
  Signs, seasons, and sense. *UnG*

My birthday's in winter. Z. Gay. *BrBc*

My dress is pink. D. Aldis. *AlHd*

My sailor of seven. G. Brenan. *BrBc*

Nature at three. B. Breeser. *BrBc*

"Oh, to have a birthday." L. Lenski. *BrBc*

One, two, buckle my shoe. O. Nash. *BrBc*

Our birthday. M. Edey. *BrBc—BrS*

Our guest. D. Aldis. *AlA*

A party L. E. Richards. *BrBc—BrS*

Present. M. C. Potter. *BrBc*

A puzzling example. V. S. Benjamin. *BrBc*

Richer. A. Fisher. *BrBc*

Seven times one. J. Ingelow. *BrBc—FeF—UnG*

Seven times one are seven. R. Hillyer. *BrBc*

Seven today. I. O. Eastwick. *BrBc*

Six birthday candles shining. M. J. Carr. *BrBc*

Six in June. M. C. Davies. *BrBc*

Somebody's birthday. A. F. Brown. *BrBc*

Someone. J. Ciardi. *BrBc—CiR*

Something very elegant. A. Fisher. *BrBc*

Sons of the kings. J. Agnew. *BrBc*

Sophisticate. B. Young. *BrBc—BrS*

Telegram. W. Wise. *ArTp*

A thought. M. Chute. *ChA*

To a little sister, aged ten. A. E. Cummings. *BrBc*

To Dick, on his sixth birthday. S. Teasdale. *BrBc*

To his son, Vincent Corbet. R. Corbet. *SmLg*

Tree birthdays. M. C. Davies. *BrBc*

Un-birthday cake. A. Fisher. *BrBc*

When a fellow's four. M. J. Carr. *BrBc*

When I was six. Z. Cross. *BrBc—FeF*

"Who wants a birthday." D. McCord. *BrBc—McFf*

Written on the road. M. M. Dodge. *BrBc*

Birthdays. See "Monday's child is fair of face"

Birthdays ("We had waffles-with-syrup for breakfast") Marchette Chute. *BrBc—BrL-k—BrS—ChA—HuSv*

"Birthdays and Christmas." See A thought

The **birthplace.** Robert Frost. *FrR—FrY—SmLg*

Birthright. John Drinkwater. *GrCc*

Bishop, Elizabeth
  The bight. *HaP*
  The fish. *UnG*
  The map. *SmLg*

Bishop, John Peale
  This dim and ptolemaic man. *PlI*

Bishop, Morris
  E=MC². *PlI*
  It rolls on. *PlI*
  Ozymandias revisited. *CoH*
  Song of the pop-bottlers. *CoH—FeF*
  The tales the barbers tell. *CoH*
  We have been here before. *NaE*

Bishop Hatto. Robert Southey. *CoSp*

The **bisk.** James Reeves. *ReP*

Bison. See Buffaloes

Bithell, Jethro
  Amsterdam, sel.
    Robinson Crusoe returns to Amsterdam. tr. *FeF*

The lark's song. *HoW*
Laughing song. *ArTp — CoPs — JoAc — McW—ReT—UnG*
The little black boy. *SmLg*
The little boy found. *ArTp*
The little boy lost. *ArTp*
Little lamb. See The lamb
London. *HaP*
Love's secret. *HaP*
Milton, sel.
    Jerusalem. *NaE*
      "And did those feet in ancient time." *HaP—SmLg*
Morning. *SmLg*
Night. *DoP—FeF—HoW—ReG—UnG*
Nurse's song. *DeT—HuL-2—JoAc—ReT—UnG*
    Play time. *FeF*
The piper. See "Piping down the valleys wild"
"Piping down the valleys wild." *PlU—SmLg*
    Happy songs. *UnG*
    Introduction. *ReT*
    Introduction to Songs of innocence. *ArTp*
    The piper. *DeT*
Play time. See Nurse's song
A poison tree. *CoPm*
A robin redbreast. See Auguries of innocence
The shepherd. *ArTp—ReT—UnG*
The sick rose. *HaP*
Spring. *ArTp—FeF—HaY—JoAc—NaM—SmLg—UnG*
Spring song. *HuL-1*
Things to remember. See Auguries of innocence—A robin redbreast
Three things to remember. See Auguries of innocence—A robin redbreast
The tiger. *ArTp—DoP—FeF—HaP—UnG*
    The tyger. *McW—SmLg*
To autumn. *HoW*
"To see a world in a grain of sand." See Auguries of innocence
To spring. *HoW*
To summer. *HoW*
To the evening star. *HoW*
To winter. *HoW*
The tyger. **See The tiger**
The wild thyme. *HoW*

Blanket street. Inez Hogan. *BrBc*

Blassing, Myrtle
    Little cloud. *BrR-3*

Blenheim, Battle of, 1704
    The battle of Blenheim. R. Southey. *HaP —UnG*

"**Bless** my friends, the whole world bless." See Good night prayer

"**Bless** the four corners of this house." See House blessing

"**Bless** the Lord, O my soul." See Psalms—Psalm CIII

"**Bless** the man that takes your hand." Unknown. *MoY*

"**Bless** you, bless you, burnie-bee." Mother Goose. *JoAc—OpO*

"**Blessed** are the poor in spirit." See Gospel according to Matthew—The sermon on the mount

"**Blessed** art Thou, O God our Lord." See Blessings for Chanukah

"**Blessed** is the man that walketh not in the counsel of the ungodly." See Psalms—Psalm I

"**Blessèd** Lord, what is it to be young." David McCord. *McT*

Blessing over food. H. N. Bialik, tr. fr. the Hebrew by Jessie E. Sampter. *BrL-k—HaY*

Blessings for Chanukah. Jessie E. Sampter. *ArTp*

"**Blessings** on thee, little man." See The barefoot boy

"**Blest** be God." See Blessing over food

"**Blest** pair of sirens, pledges of heaven's joy." See At a solemn musick

The **blether**. James Reeves. *ReP*

Blicher, Steen Steensen
    The heather. *PaS*

Blind
    "All but blind." W. De La Mare. *FeF—McW*
    The blind men and the elephant. J. G. Saxe. *CoSp—JoAc—UnG—UnMc*
    The fiddler. J. Reeves. *ReBl*
    The fog. W. H. Davies. *ArTp—McW*
    Sonnet on his blindness. J. Milton. *ThP*
    Tim Turpin. T. Hood. *HoW*

"**Blind** man, blind man." See Blind man's buff

"The **blind** man lifts his violin." See The fiddler

Blind man's buff ("Blind man, blind man") Mother Goose. *OpO*

Blind man's buff ("A peacock feather") Unknown, tr. fr. the Chinese by Isaac Taylor Headland. *JoAc*

Blind-man's buff ("When silver snow decks Susan's clothes") William Blake. *HoW*

The **blind** men and the elephant. John Godfrey Saxe. *CoSp—JoAc—UnG—UnMc*

Block city. Robert Louis Stevenson. *FeF*

The **bloodhound**. Edward Anthony. *UnG*

Bloomgarden, Solomon. See Yehoash, pseud.

The **blossom**. William Blake. *ReT*

"The **blossom** that has started, Lord." See A prayer for blossoms

Blossom themes. Carl Sandburg. *SaW*

Blossoms and storm. Sadaiye, tr. fr. the Japanese by Harold G. Henderson. *PaS*

Blow, blow. See As you like it—"Blow, blow, thou winter wind"

"**Blow**, blow, thou winter wind." See As you like it

Blow, bugle, blow. See The princess—Bugle song

Blow me eyes. Wallace Irwin. *CoSp*

"**Blow** the fife and clarinet." See Jonathan Bing dances for spring

"**Blow** the fire, blacksmith." Mother Goose. *OpO*

"**Blow**, wind, blow." See "Blow wind, blow, and go mill, go"

"**Blow**, wind, blow." See Winter night

"**Blow** wind, blow, and go mill, go." Mother Goose. *ArTp—DeMg—HuSv*
    Blow, wind, blow. *HuL-1*

Blowing bubbles. See Soap bubbles
"Blows the wind to-day, and the sun and the rain are flying." See Vailima
Blue (Color)
Cheap blue. C. Sandburg. *SaW*
Blue Bell. Mother Goose. *OpO*
Blue-butterfly day. Robert Frost. *FrY*
"Blue drifted the sea; the waters of the sun." See The sea
"Blue eyes, brown hair." Unknown. *MoY*
Blue girls. John Crowe Ransom. *GrCc—HaP*
"Blue is true." Unknown
Signs, seasons, and sense. *UnG*
"Blue jay, fly to my windowsill." See Invitation
Blue jays. See Jays
Blue magic. Eleanor Farjeon. *FaCb—FaN*
A **blue** ribbon at Amesbury. Robert Frost. *FrR*
"A **blue** robe on their shoulder." See The seven fiddlers
Blue smoke. Frances M. Frost. *BrS*
"The **blue** train for the south—but the green train for us." See The green train
Blue wool monkey. Myra Cohn Livingston. *LiWa*
"The **blue** wool monkey won't sit where." See Blue wool monkey
The **bluebell**, sel. Emily Brontë
The trees are bare. *DeT*
Bluebells
Blue magic. E. Farjeon. *FaCb—FaN*
Bluebells and foxgloves. J. Reeves. *ReBl*
Bluebells and foxgloves. James Reeves. *ReBl*
"Bluebells, cockleshells, evy-ivy-o." See How many miles
"Bluebells, cockleshells, evy-ivy-over." See Dr Brown
Blueberries
Blueberries. R. Frost. *FrR—FrY* (sel.)
Blueberries. Robert Frost. *FrR—FrY* (sel.)
"A **bluebird** met a butterfly, one lovely summer day." See A summer story
"Bluebird, what do you feed on." Carl Sandburg. *SaW*
Bluebirds
"Bluebird, what do you feed on." C. Sandburg. *SaW*
The last word of a bluebird. R. Frost. *ArTp—FeF—FrY—HuSv—JoAc*
"Little horned toad." Unknown. *FeF*
"Bluff King Hal was full of beans." See Henry VIII
Blum. Dorothy Aldis. *AlA—CoH—McAw—NaM*
Blunden, Edmund
A Maltese dog. tr. *ArTp—SmLg*
Reliques. *PlI* (sel.)
Blyton, Enid
The one-legged stool. *HuL-1*
What piggy-wig found. *HuL-1*
"Bo-peep." Mother Goose. *OpO*
"Bo peeper." Mother Goose. *DeT—OpO*
"The **board** is bare." See Bread and water
Boat races. See Races and racing—Boat
The **boat** sails away. Kate Greenaway. *NaM*

"The **boat** sails away, like a bird on the wing." See The boat sails away
Boating. James Reeves. *ReBl*
Boats. Rowena Bastin Bennett. *ArTp—HuL-1*
Boats and boating. See also Canoes and canoeing; Ferries; Races and racing—Boat; Ships
The boat sails away. K. Greenaway. *NaM*
Boating. J. Reeves. *ReBl*
Boats. R. B. Bennett. *ArTp—HuL-1*
Cargoes. J. Masefield. *ArTp—FeF—HuL-2*
The crescent boat. From Peter Bell. W. Wordsworth. *ReT*
Among the stars. *UnG*
Ferry-boats. J. S. Tippett. *ArTp*
The floating old man. E. Lear. *HoW*
The flower boat. R. Frost. *FrR*
The fog horn. E. H. Newlin. *BrR-3*
Freight boats. J. S. Tippett. *FeF—HuL-2—HuSv*
Hey dorolot. Mother Goose. *OpO*
The kayak. Unknown. *FeF*
"Little Tee Wee." Mother Goose. *DeMg—OpO—WoF*
A Longford legend. Unknown. *CoSp*
Lost. C. Sandburg. *JoAc*
The moonlit stream. J. Reeves. *ReBl*
My plan. M. Chute. *BrBc—ChA—FeF*
Paddling. G. M. Higgs. *HuL-1*
Paper boats. R. Tagore. *FeF*
Riding in a motor boat. D. W. Baruch. *FeF*
Row the boat home. A. Lack. *HuL-2*
Tugs. J. S. Tippett. *FeF*
Where go the boats. R. L. Stevenson. *ArTp—BrR-3—HuL-2—SmLg*
"Boats sail on the rivers." Christina Georgina Rossetti. *ArTp—BrR-4—DoP—HuL-2—HuSv—PeF*
The bridge. *JoAc*
"Boats that carry sugar." See Freight boats
Bob Robin. Mother Goose. *OpO*
Bob White. George Cooper. *UnG*
Bobadil. James Reeves. *ReBl*
Bobbily Boo and Wollypotump. Laura E. Richards. *LoL*
"Bobbily Boo, the king so free." See Bobbily Boo and Wollypotump
Bobby Blue. John Drinkwater. *FeF*
Bobby Shafto. See "Bobby Shafto's gone to sea"
Bobby Shaftoe. See "Bobby Shafto's gone to sea"
"Bobby Shaftoe's gone to sea." See "Bobby Shafto's gone to sea"
"Bobby Shafto's gone to sea." Mother Goose. *DeMg*
Bobby Shafto. *DeT*
Bobby Shaftoe. *OpO—ReG*
"Bobby Shaftoe's gone to sea." *JoAc*
"Bobby went down to the ocean." Unknown. *WoJ*
Bobby's first poem. Norman Gale. *CoH—NaM*
Bobolinks
Robert of Lincoln. W. C. Bryant. *FeF*

Body, Human. See also names of parts of body, as Hands
The comical girl. M. Pelham. *CoH*
Doctor Emmanuel. J. Reeves. *ReW*
The girl of New York. C. Monkhouse. *CoH*
My body. W. J. Smith. *SmL*
On digital extremities. G. Burgess. *FeF*
Thanksgiving for the body. T. Traherne. *PlI*
A thought. D. Aldis. *AlA*
X-ray. L. Speyer. *PlI*
Bogan, Louise
Musician. *PlU*
Variation on a sentence. *PlI*
Boileau, Helen Houston
Home grown. *McAw*
Boilleau, Joan
I saw a ghost. *ArTp*
"The Bona Esperanza." See The frozen ships
Bonaparte, Napoleon. See Napoleon I, Emperor of France (about)
Bone, Florence
A prayer for a little home. *DoP*
Bones
Bones. W. De La Mare. *CoH*
Didn't it rain. Unknown. *TaD*
Bones. Walter De La Mare. *CoH*
"A bonnie bairn, my Patrick, the day that he was born." See Saint Patrick
The bonnie banks of Fordie. Unknown. *MaB*
The bonnie cravat. Mother Goose. *ArTp—HuL-1—OpO*
The bonnie earl of Moray. See The bonny earl of Murray
Bonny Dundee. See The doom of Devorgoil
The bonny earl of Murray. Unknown. *MaB*
The bonnie earl of Moray. *SmLg*
"The bonny heir, the well-favoured heir." See The heir of Linne
The bonny house of Airlie. Unknown. *MaB*
Boogie chant and dance. Unknown. *TaD*
A book. See "There is no frigate like a book"
A book ("A book may be a flower") Lizette Woodworth Reese. *HaY*
A book ("I'm a strange contradiction; I'm new and I'm old") Hannah More. *CoPs*
"A book may be a flower." See A book
The book of the dead, sels. Unknown, tr. fr. the Egyptian by Robert Hillyer
Adoration of the disk. *FeF*
The dead man ariseth and singeth a hymn to the sun. *PaS*
Books. See Books and reading
Books ("Books are more than words") Joseph Joel Keith. *HuSv*
Books ("What worlds of wonder are our books") Eleanor Farjeon. *HaY*
Books and reading
Adventures. A. Kramer. *BrBc*
Autumn eve. A. Andriello. *BrS*
A book ("A book may be a flower") L. W. Reese. *HaY*
A book ("I'm a strange contradiction; I'm new and I'm old") H. More. *CoPs*
Books ("Books are more than words") J. J. Keith. *HuSv*

Books ("What worlds of wonder are our books") E. Farjeon. *HaY*
Books are keys. A. E. Poulsson. *BrS*
Books et veritas. W. R. Benét. *ThP*
Decline and fall. E. V. Rieu. *RiF*
Dictionary. W. J. Smith. *SmL*
"Don't steal this book." Unknown. *MoY*
End of volume one. E. V. Rieu. *RiF*
The fairy book. A. F. Brown. *BrL-k*
Golden spurs. V. S. Miner. *BrS*
I have a book. D. McCord. *McT*
I'd leave. A. Lang. *FeF*
"If someone asks you." D. Mitchell. *CoPs*
"If this book should chance to roam." Unknown. *MoY*
"I've got a new book from my Grandfather Hyde." L. F. Jackson. *BrS—FeF*
The King of Hearts. W. J. Smith. *SmL*
The king of Spain. W. J. Smith. *SmL*
Knights and ladies. A. A. Milne. *MiWc*
The land of story-books. R. L. Stevenson. *ArTp—FeF—UnG*
"The land was white." Mother Goose. *OpO*
The library. B. A. Huff. *FeF*
"Little Bob Snooks was fond of his books." Mother Goose. *DeMg*
Magic. B. J. Thompson. *BrR-3*
Mary indoors. E. Farjeon. *ReG*
"Mary make the butter." I. O. Eastwick. *EaI*
O for a booke. Unknown. *BrS—CoPs*
On first looking into Chapman's Homer. J. Keats. *SmLg*
On opening a new book. A. B. Farwell. *HaY*
Only a book. E. Dickinson. *BrR-4*
"Our bows bended." Mother Goose. *OpO*
Picture people. M. C. Livingston. *LiW*
Sarah Byng. H. Belloc. *GrCc*
"There is no frigate like a book." E. Dickinson. *BrS—HaY*
A book. *FeF*
To Susanna, reading. E. Farjeon. *FaCb*
When mother reads aloud. Unknown. *FeF*
"Who hath a book." W. D. Nesbit. *ArTp—BrS*
"Books are bridges." See Golden spurs
Books are keys. Anne Emilie Poulsson. *BrS*
"Books are keys to wisdom's treasure." See Books are keys
"Books are more than words." See Books
Books et veritas. William Rose Benét. *ThP*
"The boomerang and kangaroo." See Up from down under
Boone, Daniel (about)
Daniel Boone. A. Guiterman. *FeF—NaM—UnMc*
Booth, Clarice Foster
Ready for winter. *McAw*
Boots. See Boots and shoes
"Boots." See Downpour
Boots and shoes. See also Shoemakers
At night. D. Aldis. *AlHd*
Black your honour's shoes. Mother Goose. *OpO*
Boots, boots, boots. L. F. Jackson. *BrL-k*

Boots and shoes—*Continued*
Choosing shoes. F. Wolfe. *ArTp—BrR-3 —HuL-1*
The cobbler. E. A. Chaffee. *ArTp*
"Cobbler, cobbler, mend my shoe." Mother Goose. *DeMg—LiL*
    Cobbler, cobbler. *OpO*
"Cock-a-doodle-doo." Mother Goose. *DeMg—HuL-1—JoAc—LiL—OpO*
Differences. D. Aldis. *AlA*
Fairy shoes. A. Wynne. *BrL-k*
Footwear. M. Justus. *HaY*
Galoshes. R. W. Bacmeister. *ArTp—BrL-k*
The giant's shoes. E. Fallis. *BrR-3*
Happiness. A. A. Milne. *ArTp—HuL-2— MiWc*
"I have lost my shoes." C. Suasnavar. *FeF*
"Little Betty Blue." Mother Goose. *DeMg —HuSv*
    Betty Blue. *OpO*
The lost shoe. W. De La Mare. *HuL-2*
Mrs Golightly. J. Reeves. *ReBl*
New. D. Aldis. *AlA*
New shoes ("I have new shoes in the fall-time") A. Wilkins. *ArTp—BrL-k*
New shoes ("When I am walking down the street") M. S. Watts. *BrR-3*
A record stride. R. Frost. *FrY*
Rubber boots. R. B. Bennett. *JoAc*
Rubbers and galoshes. M. L. Allen. *AlP*
The sad shoes. D. Aldis. *AlA*
A Scottish shoe. Mother Goose. *OpO*
Shoes. T. Robinson. *ArTp*
Shoes and stockings. A. A. Milne. *MiWc —HuL-1*
Strange footprints. V. G. Gouled. *McAw*
"There was an old woman who lived in a shoe." Mother Goose. *AnI—ArTp— DeMg—HuSv—JoAc—LiL*
    The old woman in a shoe. *OpO*
"Two brothers are we." Mother Goose. *OpO*
Velvet shoes. E. Wylie. *ArTp—BrS—FeF —HuSv—JoAc—PeF*

Boots, boots, boots. Leroy F. Jackson. *BrL-k*
Bores. Arthur Guiterman. *BrR-5*
Borie, Lysbeth Boyd
Five-in-June. *BrBc*
Five years old. *BrBc—BrS*
GraceAnAnne. *BrBc*
Just for Jesus. *DoP*
"Boss i saw a picture." See Archy a low brow
Bossidy, John Collins
Boston. *UnG*
Boston, Massachusetts
The baby goes to Boston. L. E. Richards. *ArTp—HuL-1*
Boston. J. C. Bossidy. *UnG*
Boston. John Collins Bossidy. *UnG*
"Both my little pockets jingle." See Differences
"The bottle of perfume that Willie sent." Unknown
Limericks since Lear. *UnG*

Bottles
"Around the rick, around the rick." Mother Goose. *OpO*
"He wears his hat upon his neck." Unknown. *WoF*
Song of the pop-bottlers. M. Bishop. *CoH —FeF*
Boughs are bare. Eleanor Farjeon. *FaN*
"Boughs are bare on Christmas night." See Boughs are bare
"The boughs do shake and the bells do ring." Mother Goose. *JoAc*
    Harvest. *OpO*
Bought locks. John Harington. *BrL-8*
Boumphrey, H. M.
The giraffe. *HuL-2*
Bounce ball rhymes. See Play
Bounce buckram. See "Bounce, buckram, velvet's dear"
"Bounce, buckram, velvet's dear." Mother Goose. *DeMg*
    Bounce buckram. *OpO*
Bouncing ball. Sara Ruth Watson. *BrR-3*
"The boundaries of heaven may be." See The uncharted
A boundless moment. Robert Frost. *FrR*
Bourdillon, Francis William
"The night has a thousand eyes." *ThP*
Bourinot, Arthur S.
Paul Bunyan. *FeF* (sel.)
Bourne, Vincent
The snail. *McW—UnG*
"Bow-wow, says the dog." Mother Goose. *AnI—DeMg—OpO*
"Bow, wow, wow." Mother Goose. *ArTp— DeMg—HuSv—JoAc*
Tom Tinker's dog. *OpO*
The bower of bliss. See The faerie queene
Bowers, Mildred (Mildred Bowers Armstrong)
Spring-signs. *McAw*
Bowles, Caroline Anne (Mrs Robert Southey; Caroline Southey)
Lady-bird. *HuL-2—UnG*
Bowra, C. M.
Be still, my soul. tr. *PaS*
The climb to virtue. tr. *PaS*
An eclipse. tr. *PaS*
The giraffe. tr. *FeF* (sel.)
The power of music. tr. *PlU* (sel.)
Bows and arrows
The arrow and the song. H. W. Longfellow. *BrR-6*
"I have no wings, but yet I fly." M. Austin
    Rhyming riddles. *ArTp*
"I took a bow and arrow." J. Ciardi. *CiR —NaE*
"Robin-a-Bobbin." Mother Goose. *OpO*
Boxes and bags. Carl Sandburg. *SaW*
"A boy." See In praise of Johnny Appleseed
The boy. Eleanor Farjeon. *ReG*
The boy and the wolf. Aesop, tr. fr. the Greek by Louis Untermeyer. *UnMc*
Boy Blue. See "Little Boy Blue, come blow your horn"
"A boy drove into the city, his wagon loaded down." See The little black-eyed rebel
"A boy employed to guard the sheep." See The boy and the wolf

The **boy** fishing. E. J. Scovell. *ReT*

Da **boy** from Rome. T. A. Daly. *FeF*

"**Boy** heart of Johnny Jones—aching today." See Buffalo Bill

A **boy** in church. Robert Graves. *GrP*

A **boy** of other days. See Lincoln ("There was a boy of other days")

"A **boy,** presuming on his intellect." See At Woodward's gardens

"The **boy** stood on the burning deck." See Casabianca

"The **boy** stood on the burning deck (eating peanuts)." Unknown. *WoF*
American Father Gander. *UnG*

"A **boy** that is good." See The good boy

The **boy** Washington. Dorothy Brown Thompson. *BrS*

The **boy** who laughed at Santa Claus. Ogden Nash. *CoSp—UnMc*

"A **boy** who played tunes on a comb." Unknown. *CoH*

Boyden, Polly Chase
"I stare at the cow." *CoI*
Mud. *ArTp—BrL-k*
New Mexico. *ArTp*

Boyhood. See Boys and boyhood

Boys. See Boys and boyhood

Boys and boyhood. See also Babies; Childhood recollections; Children and childhood
All about boys and girls. J. Ciardi. *CiY*
The barefoot boy. J. G. Whittier. *FeF* (sel.)
"Beware of boys with eyes of brown." Unknown. *MoY*
Big and little. W. J. Smith. *SmL*
Bill. J. L. Salzburg. *BrBc*
The boy. E. Farjeon. *ReG*
A boy in church. R. Graves. *GrP*
"Boys are like a box of snuff." Unknown. *MoY*
Boy's day. R. E. Henderson. *BrBc*
Boys' names. E. Farjeon. *ArTp—BrBc—HuL-2—JoAc*
A boy's song. J. Hogg. *DeT—FeF—HoW—McW—NaM*
A boy's summer song. P. L. Dunbar. *BrS*
Canadian boat song. Unknown. *SmLg*
The cave-boy. L. E. Richards. *FeF*
Château de Chinon. E. Farjeon. *FaCb*
Da boy from Rome. T. A. Daly. *FeF*
"Doll's boy's asleep." E. E. Cummings. *GrCc*
"Evan Kirk." J. Ciardi. *CiM*
Four. E. Gibbs. *BrBc*
The fruit plucker. S. T. Coleridge. *DeT*
In a moonlight wilderness. *SmLg*
"Grandma said such a curious thing." Unknown. *WoF*
"Jack, be nimble." Mother Goose. *AnI—ArTp—DeMg—HuSv—JoAc—LiL—OpO*
"Jenny White and Johnny Black." E. Farjeon. *FeF*
Jim Jay. W. De La Mare. *BrS—UnG*
Jittery Jim. W. J. Smith. *SmL*
Little Boy Blue. E. Field. *FeF*
The little boy found. W. Blake. *ArTp*
The little boy lost. W. Blake. *ArTp*

Little boys of Texas. R. P. T. Coffin. *McW*
Little lad. Unknown. *BrBc*
"The most of being a boy is noise." J. Ciardi. *CiM*
The new little boy. H. Behn. *BeW*
"O tan-faced prairie boy." W. Whitman. *FeF*
"Sandy Candy." Unknown. *JoAc*
Upon Pagget. R. Herrick. *SmLg*
"Wee Willie Winkie runs through the town." Mother Goose. *ArTp—DeMg—HuSv—JoAc—LiL*
"Wee Willie Winkie." *BrS*
Willie Winkie. *OpO*
"What are little boys made of, made of." Mother Goose. *DeMg—JoAc*
Natural history. *OpO*
Whistling boy. J. R. Quinn. *BrBc*

"**Boys** and girls come out to play." See "Girls and boys, come out to play"

"**Boys** and girls, we pledge allegiance." See Dianae sumus in fide

"The **boys** and girls who live in books." See Adventures

The **boys** and the apple-tree. Adelaide O'Keefe. *DeT*

"**Boys** are like a box of snuff." Unknown. *MoY*

Boy's day. Ruth Evelyn Henderson. *BrBc*

Boys' names. Eleanor Farjeon. *ArTp—BrBc—HuL-2—JoAc*

A **boy's** song. James Hogg. *DeT—FeF—HoW—McW—NaM*

A **boy's** summer song. Paul Laurence Dunbar. *BrS*

"**Bracken** on the hillside." See November

Brady's bend. Martha Keller. *CoSp*

Bragdon, Claude
"The point, the line, the surface and sphere." *PlI*

Braley, Berton
Day of rest. *ThP*
The glow within. *BrL-8*

Branch, Anna Hempstead
Her words. See Song for my mother: Her words
Mathematics or the gift of tongues. *PlI*
Song for my mother. See Song for my mother: Her words
Song for my mother: Her words. *BrS—HaY*
Her words. *FeF*
Song for my mother. *ArTp*

The **branch.** Elizabeth Madox Roberts. *JoAc*

Brand the blacksmith. James Reeves. *ReR*

"**Brand** the blacksmith with his hard hammer." See Brand the blacksmith

Brasier, Virginia
Generosity. *HuSv*
Heartbeat of democracy. *HuSv*
Wind weather. *HuSv*

"The **brass** band blares." See Circus

"**Brave** news is come to town." See Jemmy Dawson

The **brave** old duke of York. See "Oh, the grand old duke of York"

Bravery. See Courage

"The **bravest** names for fire and flames."
    See General John
Bread
    "Blow wind, blow, and go mill, go."
        Mother Goose. *ArTp—DeMg—HuSv*
    "Blow, wind, blow." *HuL-1—OpO*
    Bread. H. E. Wilkinson. *HuL-1*
    A man's bread. J. P. Peabody. *HaY*
    "This bread." E. Farjeon. *FaCb—FaN*
Bread. H. E. Wilkinson. *HuL-1*
"**Bread** and butter." Unknown
    Four questions. *WoJ*
Bread and cherries. Walter De La Mare.
    HuL-1
Bread and water. Eleanor Farjeon. *FaN*
"**Bread** is a lovely thing to eat." See Lovely
    things
"**Break,** break, break." Alfred Tennyson.
    HaP
Breakfast
    Breakfast time. J. Stephens. *BrR-3*
    The king's breakfast. A. A. Milne. *MiWc*
    Mummy slept late and daddy fixed break-
        fast. J. Ciardi. *CiY*
Breakfast time. James Stephens. *BrR-3*
"The **breaking** waves dashed high." See The
    landing of the Pilgrim Fathers
"**Breathing** something German at the end."
    See The gift to be simple
Breeser, Bettye
    Nature at three. *BrBc*
"A **breeze** discovered my open book." See
    A cloud shadow
Breig, Jean H.
    The make-up man. *BrR-5*
Breining, June
    Inexperience. *ThP*
Breitmann, Hans, pseud. See Leland, Charles
    Godfrey
Brenan, Gerald
    My sailor of seven. *BrBc*
Brentano, Clemens
    "O woodland cool." *PaS*
    Serenade. *PaS*
Breton, Nicholas
    "In the merry month of May." *HaP*
Brewer, Ebenezer Cobham
    "Little drops of water." at. *AnI—DeMg*
        Little things. *FeF—UnG*
    Little things. See "Little drops of water"
Brewster, Marietta W.
    Dandelions. *BrL-k*
Brian O'Lin. Unknown. *WoF*
"**Brian** O'Lin was an Irishman born." See
    Brian O'Lin
Brian O'Linn. Unknown. *CoH*
"**Brian** O'Linn was a gentleman born." See
    Brian O'Linn
Briar-rose. Unknown, tr. fr. the German by
    Louis Untermeyer. *HuL-2*
Brides and bridegrooms
    A lady comes to an inn. E. J. Coatsworth.
        ArTp—CoSp
    Love and a question. R. Frost. *FrR*
    The purist. O. Nash. *CoH—NaM*
    Shoes and stockings. A. A. Milne. *MiWc*
        —HuL-1
    The thorn. W. Wordsworth. *NaE*(sel.)
    A young bride. Sappho. *PaS*

The **brides'** tragedy, sel. Thomas Lovell
    Beddoes
    Song. *GrCc*
The **bridge.** See "Boats sail on the rivers"
"The **bridge** says: Come across, try me."
    See Potomac town in February
**Bridges, Madeline, pseud. (Mary Ainge de
    Vere)**
    Life's mirror. *ThP*
Bridges, Robert
    Country music. tr. *PaS*
    First spring morning. *HaY*
    A hymn of nature. *HaY*
    "I love all beauteous things." *HuL-2*
    London snow. *HaP—HoW*
    A passer-by. *HoW*
Bridges
    The Ashtabula disaster. J. Moore. *NaE*
    "Boats sail on the rivers." *ArTp—BrR-4—
        DoP—HuL-2—HuSv—PeF*
        The bridge. *JoAc*
    Bridges. R. W. Bacmeister. *BrL-k—
        McAw*
    Horatius. From Lays of ancient Rome.
        T. B. Macaulay. *SmLg*
        The fight at the bridge. *UnMc*(sel.)
    "London bridge is broken down." Mother
        Goose. *DeMg—JoAc—LiL*
        London bridge. *OpO*
    The Tay bridge disaster. W. McGonagall.
        NaE
    When a ship sails by. R. B. Bennett.
        BrR-6
Bridges. Rhoda W. Bacmeister. *BrL-k—
    McAw*
"**Bridges** are for going over water." See
    Over and under
Bridget, Saint (about)
    Saint Bridget. E. Farjeon. *FaCb*
"**Bright** is the ring of words." See Words
"**Bring** daddy home." Mother Goose. *OpO*
"**Bring** hether the pincke and purple cullam-
    bine." See The shepherd's calendar—A
    nosegay
"**Bring** me men to match my mountains."
    See The coming American
"**Bring** me now the bright flower." See
    Nightsong
"**Bring** the comb and play upon it." See
    Marching song
Brink, Carol Ryrie
    Goody O'Grumpity. *FeF*
"**Brisk** wielder of the birch and rule." See
    Snow-bound—The schoolmaster
"The **broad-backed** hippopotamus." See The
    hippopotamus
Broadcasting. Mildred D. Shacklett. *BrR-3*
"The **brobinyak** has dragon eyes." See What
    you will learn about the brobinyak
"A **broken** altar, Lord, thy servant rears."
    See The altar
"A **broken** saucer of the sea." See At low
    tide
Broken sky. Carl Sandburg. *SaW*
Bromley, Isaac H.
    The passenjare. *CoH*

Brontë, Emily (Ellis Bell, pseud.)
The bluebell, sel.
The trees are bare. *DeT*
"Fall, leaves, fall; die, flowers, away."
SmLg
The night-wind. *HaP*
That wind. *DeT*
The trees are bare. See The bluebell
"Bronwen gathered wild-flowers." See
Bronwen of the flowers
Bronwen of the flowers. Eleanor Farjeon.
FaCb
Bronwen to her magpie. Eleanor Farjeon.
FaCb
The brook. Alfred Tennyson. *DeT—FeF*
Song of the brook. *JoAc*
"The brook-edge weeds are slender grass."
See Mice under snow
A brook in the city. Robert Frost. *FrR*
"The brook wound through the woods be-
hind." See The crayfish
Brooke, L. Leslie
Johnny Crow's garden. *ReG*
Brooke, Rupert
Heaven. *McW*
The soldier. *UnMc*
Brooklyn bridge
Brooklyn bridge at dawn. R. Le Gal-
lienne. *ArTp*
Brooklyn bridge at dawn. Richard Le Gal-
lienne. *ArTp*
Brooks, Gwendolyn
Andre. *ArTp*
Cynthia in the snow. *ArTp*
Vern. *ArTp*
Brooks, Phillips
Christmas everywhere. *UnG*
"O little town of Bethlehem." *FeF—JoAc*
—ReG
Brooks, Walter R.
Ode to the pig: His tail. *LoL*
Brooks
The branch. E. M. Roberts. *JoAc*
The brook. A. Tennyson. *DeT—FeF*
Song of the brook. *JoAc*
A brook in the city. R. Frost. *FrR*
Hyla brook. R. Frost. *FrR—FrY*
The ice had all melted. D. Aldis. *AlHd*
The runaway brook. E. L. Follen. *BrL-k*
The walk. L. Adams. *GrCc*
Waters. E. H. Newlin. *BrR-4*
West-running brook. R. Frost. *FrR*
"The broom and the shovel, the poker and
tongs." See The broom, the shovel, the
poker and the tongs
The broom squire's song. Mother Goose.
OpO
The broom, the shovel, the poker and the
tongs. Edward Lear. *JoAc*
Brooms
The broom squire's song. Mother Goose.
OpO
Brooms. D. Aldis. *AlA—BrR-4*
Green broom. Unknown. *CoSp—ReG*
Brooms. Dorothy Aldis. *AlA—BrR-4*
The broomstick train. Oliver Wendell
Holmes. *CoPm(sel.)—FeF(sel.)*
"Broomsticks and witches." See Hallowe'en
Brother and sister. William Wordsworth.
DeT

Brother, lift your flag with mine. Josephine
Dodge Daskam Bacon. *CoPs*
"Brother, sing your country's anthem." See
Brother, lift your flag with mine
Brotherhood
Abou Ben Adhem. L. Hunt. *BrR-6—ThP*
—UnG
Abou Ben Adhem and the angel. *FeF*
The ballad of east and west. R. Kipling.
UnMc
Brother, lift your flag with mine. J. D. D.
Bacon. *CoPs*
Innumerable friend. M. Sarton. *McW*
Refugee in America. L. Hughes. *McW*
"Ring around the world." A. Wynne.
ArTp—HuSv—JoAc
Ring out, wild bells. From In memoriam.
A. Tennyson. *ArTp — BrL-8 — FeF —
HoW*
The sun that warms you. E. Farjeon.
FaCb—FaN
Brothers and sisters
Archie of Cawfield. Unknown. *MaB*
The bear hunt. M. Widdemer. *FeF*
Being twins. K. Jackson. *BrBc*
Betwixt and Between. H. Lofting. *BrBc*
Big brother. E. M. Roberts. *FeF*
Binnorie. Unknown. *MaB*
Brother and sister. W. Wordsworth. *DeT*
Brothers and sisters. E. Farjeon. *FaCb—
FaN*
Careless Willie. Unknown. *CoH—FeF*
Comparison. M. A. Hoberman. *BrBc*
Dick and Will. E. M. Roberts. *BrBc*
"Five little sisters walking in a row." K.
Greenaway. *NaM*
Hard lines. T. Robinson. *BrBc*
"I love you well, my little brother."
Mother Goose. *AnI*
"In go-cart so tiny." K. Greenaway. *FeF*
Little. D. Aldis. *AlA—ArTp—FeF*
Little brother. A. Fisher. *BrBc—McAw*
Little brother's secret. K. Mansfield.
ArTp—FeF
Mima. W. De La Mare. *BrBc—ReG*
"Molly, my sister, and I fell out." Mother
Goose. *DeMg*
Mumps. E. M. Roberts. *FeF—JoAc—LoL
—McAw*
My brother ("My brother is inside the
sheet") D. Aldis. *ArTp*
My brother ("Today I went to market
with my mother") D. Aldis. *AlHd*
Our silly little sister. D. Aldis. *AlA—CoH
—FeF—NaE*
Portrait. M. Chute. *ChA—McAw*
The quarrel. E. Farjeon. *FeF*
Sister Nell. Unknown. *CoH—FeF*
Sisters. E. Farjeon. *FeF*
Ten brothers. Unknown. *UnMc*
To a little sister, aged ten. A. E. Cum-
mings. *BrBc*
"Tommy was a silly boy." K. Greenaway.
ArTp
The twins ("I have two friends") K. Jack-
son. *BrBc*
The twins ("In form and feature, face and
limb") H. S. Leigh. *ArTp—BrBc—CoH
—FeF—McW—UnG—UnMc*

Brothers and sisters—*Continued*
The twins ("Likeness has made them animal and shy") K. Shapiro. *HaP*
The twins ("When one starts crying") D. Aldis. *AlA—BrBc*
Two in bed. A. B. Ross. *ArTp—FeF*
Wild grapes. R. Frost. *FrR*
Young Sammy Watkins. Unknown. *CoH*
Brothers and sisters. Eleanor Farjeon. *FaCb—FaN*
"Brow bender." Mother Goose. *DeMg*
"Brow, brow, brenty." Mother Goose. *OpO*
"Brow, brow, brinkie." Mother Goose. *DeMg*
Brown, Abbie Farwell
All wool. *ArTp*
The fairy book. *BrL-k*
The fisherman. *FeF*
On opening a new book. *HaY*
Somebody's birthday. *BrBc*
Brown, Alice
Revelation. *DoP*
Brown, Barbara and Beatrice
My kite. *BrL-k*
Brown, Beatrice Curtis
Anniversary in September. *BrBc*
The apple tree. *BrS*
Jonathan Bing. *ArTp—CoH—FeF—HuL-2 —LoL—PeF*
Jonathan Bing dances for spring. *BrS*
Jonathan Bing's tea. *McW*
Brown, Felicia Dorothea. See Hemans, Felicia Dorothea
Brown, John (about)
The portent. H. Melville. *HoW*
Brown, Kate Louise
The five-fingered maple. *HuL-1*
The little plant. *BrL-k*
Pussy willow. *BrL-k*
Brown, Margaret Wise
"Little black bug." *FeF—HuL-1*
September. *McAw*
Brown, Palmer
A dappled duck. *LoL*
Lucinda Prattle. *LoL*
"The spangled pandemonium." *ArTp— LoL*
Brown, Thomas
Doctor Fell. See "I do not like thee, Doctor Fell"
"I do not like thee, Doctor Fell." tr. *DeMg—NaM*
Doctor Fell. *OpO*
Non amo te. *PlI*
Signs, seasons, and sense. *UnG*
Non amo te. See "I do not like thee, Doctor Fell"
Brown, Thomas Edward
A garden. See My garden
I bended unto me. *CoPs*
My garden. *ThP*
A garden. *UnG*
Brown Adam. Unknown. *MaB*
"Brown and furry." See Caterpillar
The brown bear. Mary Austin. *CoPs—FeF —McW*
Brown bear's honey song. Kathryn Jackson. *McW*
"Brown bunny sits inside his burrow." See The rabbit

The brown dwarf of Rügen. John Greenleaf Whittier. *CoPm*
"Brown eyes." See Polly
Brown gold. Carl Sandburg. *SaW*
"Brown lived at such a lofty farm." See Brown's descent; or, The willy-nilly slide
Brown penny. William Butler Yeats. *GrCc —SmLg*
The brown thrush. Lucy Larcom. *BrR-4— FeF*
Browne, Patrick
The green autumn stubble. tr. *PaS*
Browne, William
Another to the same. *HoW*
Brownie. A. A. Milne. *MiWc*
Brownies. See Fairies
Browning, Elizabeth Barrett
A child's thought of God. *DoP—FeF*
The great god Pan. See A musical instrument
A musical instrument. *FeF—UnG*
The great god Pan. *HoW*
Browning, Robert
A face. *GrCc*
Home thoughts from abroad. *BrL-8—FeF —JoAc*
How the rats were destroyed. See The Pied Piper of Hamelin
How they brought the good news from Ghent to Aix. *ArTp—HuSv—UnG*
Incident of the French camp. *UnG— UnMc*
My last duchess. *HaP*
My star. *FeF—NaE*
Parting at morning. *HoW*
The Pied Piper of Hamelin. *ArTp—HuSv —JoAc—SmLg—UnG*
How the rats were destroyed. *HuL-2* (sel.)
Pippa passes, sel.
Pippa's song. *FeF*
Spring song. *UnG*
"The year's at the spring." *DoP— HaY—HuSv—ThP*
Pippa's song. See Pippa passes
Rabbi Ben Ezra. *BrBc* (sel.)
Spring song. See Pippa passes—Pippa's song
"The year's at the spring." See Pippa passes—Pippa's song
Brown's descent; or, The willy-nilly slide. Robert Frost. *CoSp—FrR—FrY—NaE*
The browny hen. Irene F. Pawsey. *HuL-1*
"A browny hen sat on her nest." See The browny hen
Bruce, Robert, King of Scotland (about)
Before Bannockburn. R. Burns. *SmLg*
Freedom. J. Barbour. *SmLg*
Brutus, Marcus Junius (about)
"This was the noblest Roman of them all." From Julius Caesar. W. Shakespeare
Gallery of people. *UnG*
A Shakespeare gallery. *UnMc*
"Bryan O'Lin had no breeches to wear." Mother Goose. *DeMg*

Bryant, William Cullen
Abraham Lincoln. *BrR-6*
The new moon. *DeT*
The planting of the apple tree. *CoPs*(sel.)
—*HuSv*
Robert of Lincoln. *FeF*
The siesta. tr. *PaS*
To a waterfowl. *DeT*
To a fringed gentian. *JoAc*

"B's the bus." See All around the town

Bubbles. Carl Sandburg. *SaW*

The **buccaneer.** Nancy Byrd Turner. *ArTp*

Buccaneers. See Pirates

Buchanan, Fannie R.
The tardy playmate. *DoP*

Buchanan, Robert
The green gnome. *CoSp*

Buckets
The old oaken bucket. S. Woodworth.
FeF (sel.)

Buckhurst, Lord. See Sackville, Thomas

Buckingham palace. A. A. Milne. *HuL-2—MiWc*

"The **buds** of April dare not yet unfold."
See Like an April day

Buff. See "I had a little dog and they called him Buff"

Buffalo Bill. See Cody, William Frederick
(about)

Buffalo Bill. Carl Sandburg. *SaW*

"**Buffalo** Bill's defunct." E. E. Cummings.
GrCc

Buffalo dusk. Carl Sandburg. *ArTp*

Buffaloes
Buffalo dusk. C. Sandburg. *ArTp*
The flower-fed buffaloes. V. Lindsay.
ArTp—FeF—HaP—JoAc—McW—ReT—SmLg
The passing of the buffalo. H. Garland.
HuSv
Water buffalo. W. J. Smith. *SmB*

"The **buffaloes** are gone." See Buffalo dusk

The **bugle-billed** bazoo. John Ciardi. *CiR*

Bugle song. See The princess

"A **bugler** named Douglas MacDougal."
See Edouard

Bugles
Bugle song. From The princess. A. Tennyson. *FeF—HuSv*
Blow, bugle, blow. *HoW—PlU*
Echo song. *DeT*
Song. *ReT*
"The splendor falls on castle walls."
ArTp
The splendour falls. *SmLg*
Edouard. O. Nash. *LoL*

Bugs. See Insects

Bugs. Will Stokes. *NaM*

Build-on rhymes
"Anna Elise, she jumped with surprise."
Mother Goose. *LoL*
"Anna Elise." *OpO*
A farmyard song. Mother Goose. *OpO*
The green grass growing all around.
Unknown. *HuL-2—NaM*
"I went downtown." Unknown. *WiRm*

"A man of words and not of deeds."
Mother Goose. *DeMg—SmLg*
A man of words. *DeT*
The man who jumped. Mother Goose.
OpO
"Obadiah." Unknown. *WoJ*
"An old woman was sweeping her house."
Unknown. *DeMg—LiL*
The old woman who bought a pig. Mother
Goose. *OpO*
"Peter Simon Suckegg." Unknown. *TaD*
Poor old lady. Unknown. *CoH—UnG*
Poor old woman. *HuL-1*
Swinging. Mother Goose. *OpO*
Tammy Tyrie. Mother Goose. *OpO*
"There was a crooked man." Mother
Goose. *BrL-k—ReG*
The crooked man. *OpO*
"There was a crooked man, and he
went a crooked mile." *DeMg—HuSv—JoAc—LiL*
"There was a man of double deed."
Mother Goose. *OpO*
"This is the house that Jack built."
Mother Goose. *DeMg—HuSv—JoAc—LiL*
The house that Jack built. *OpO*
"This is the key of the kingdom." Mother
Goose. *DeMg—OpO*
This is the key. *NaM—ReT—SmLg*
The thread was thin. Unknown. *WoJ*
Trading. Unknown. *TaD*
"Went to the river, couldn't get across."
Unknown
American Father Gander. *UnG*
"What's in there." Mother Goose. *OpO*
When I was a lad. Mother Goose. *OpO*

"Builder, in building the little house." See
The kitchen chimney

Building. Harry Behn. *BeW*

The **building** of the ship, sels. Henry Wadsworth Longfellow
Sail on, O ship of state. *FeF*
The ship of state. *BrL-7*

Buildings. Myra Cohn Livingston. *LiW*

"**Buildings** are a great suprise." See Buildings

"A **bullfrog** sat on a downy nest." Unknown.
WiRm

Bulls
The arrogant frog and the superior bull.
G. W. Carryl. *CoSp*
Hoosen Johnny. Unknown. *FeF*
Sarah Byng. H. Belloc. *GrCc*
Taurus. E. Farjeon. *FaCb—FaN*
"There was a young lady of Hull." E.
Lear
Limericks. *NaM*

The **bumblebeaver.** See Mixed beasts

"A **bumblebee** flew over the barn." See
Buzz, buzz, buzz

Bump on my knee. Myra Cohn Livingston.
LiWa

"**Bun** lies low." See The rabbit

"A **bunch** of grass, a wild rose." See That's
July

"A **bunch** of the boys were whooping it up
in the Malamute saloon." See The shooting of Dan McGrew

Bunches of grapes. Walter De La Mare. *ArTp—HuL-2—NaM*
"Bunches of grapes, says Timothy." See Bunches of grapes
"A bundle is a funny thing." See Bundles
Bundles
    Bundles. J. Farrar. *ArTp—BrL-k*
    Secrets. E. M. Fowler. *BrBc*
Bundles. John Farrar. *ArTp—BrL-k*
Bunker hill, Battle of, 1775
    Grandmother's story of Bunker hill battle. O. W. Holmes. *UnG*
    "T'other side of Duck-pond." E. Farjeon. *FaN*
Bunner, Henry Cuyler
    Grandfather Watt's private Fourth. *ArTp—CoPs—CoSp*
    One, two, three. *FeF*
Bunting, Basil
    Hymn to Venus. tr. *GrCc*
Bunyan, John
    The pilgrim. See The pilgrim's progress—Pilgrim's song
    The pilgrim's progress, sels.
        Pilgrim's song. *HoW—McW*
            The pilgrim. *ArTp—DeT—NaE*
        The shepherd boy sings in the valley of humiliation. *UnG*
    Pilgrim's song. See The pilgrim's progress
    The shepherd boy sings in the valley of humiliation. See The pilgrim's progress
    Time and eternity. *HoW*
Bunyan, Paul (about)
    How we logged Katahdin stream. D. G. Hoffman. *UnMc*
    Paul Bunyan. A. S. Bourinot. *FeF* (sel.)
    Paul's wife. R. Frost. *FrR*
The bunyip and the whistling kettle. John Manifold. *CoPm*
Burden-bearers
    Great fleas. A. De Morgan. *McW*
Burgess, Gelett
    Felicia Ropps. *ArTp—FeF*
    "I never saw a purple cow." See The purple cow
    "I wish that my room had a floor." *CoH—LoL*
        Limericks since Lear. *UnG*
    Nell the nibbler. *BrR-6*
    On digital extremities. *FeF*
    The purple cow. *ArTp—CoH—FeF*
        "I never saw a purple cow." *LoL*
    Tricky. *CoH*
Burgundian carol. Bernard De La Monnoye, tr. by Percy Dearmer. *PlU*
Burial of Sir John Moore. Charles Wolfe. *UnMc*
    The burial of Sir John Moore at Corunna, 1809. *DeT*
The burial of Sir John Moore at Corunna, 1809. See Burial of Sir John Moore
Burial of the Minnisink. Henry Wadsworth Longfellow. *GrCc*
Burials. See Funerals
"Burly dozing humble-bee." See The humble-bee
"Burn ash-wood green." Mother Goose. *DeMg*

Burnham, Maud
    The barnyard. *ArTp—HuL-1*
    The pigeons. *BrL-k*
"Burnie bee, burnie bee." Mother Goose. *DeMg*
The burning Babe. Robert Southwell. *SmLg*
Burns, Robert
    Before Bannockburn. *SmLg*
    A child's grace. *FeF—HuSv—NaM*
    "Some hae meat that canna eat." *SmLg*
    John Anderson, my jo. *HaP—HuSv—ThP*
    John Barleycorn. *SmLg*
    The linnet. *DeT*
    My heart's in the highlands. *BrR-5—FeF—McW*
    My luve's like a red, red rose. *CoPs*
        "O, my luve is like a red, red rose." *SmLg*
        A red, red rose. *HaP*
    "O, my luve is like a red, red rose." See My luve's like a red, red rose
    O, open the door to me, O. *SmLg*
    A red, red rose. See My luve's like a red, red rose
    The silver tassie. *GrCc*
    "Some hae meat that canna eat." See A child's grace
    To a mouse. *McW*
    Up in the morning early. *CoPs—DeT*
Burnshaw, Stanley
    The muse. tr. *GrCc*
Burnt Norton. T. S. Eliot. *PlU* (sel.)
Burr, Amelia Josephine
    Rain in the night. *ArTp—BrL-k*
Burro with the long ears. Unknown, tr. fr. the Navajo by Hilda Faunce Wetherill. *FeF*
Burroughs, John
    The song of the toad. *FeF*
Bursting. Dorothy Aldis. *AlA*
"Bury her deep, down deep." See Cat's funeral
A burying. Eleanor Farjeon. *FaCb*
Bus ride. See Ferry ride
Bush, Jocelyn
    The little red sled. *ArTp*
Buson
    Parting. *PaS*
Busses
    The birthday bus. M. A. Hoberman. *BrBc*
    "B's the bus." From All around the town. P. McGinley. *ArTp—FeF—LoL*
    Bus ride. From Ferry ride. S. Robinson. *FeF*
"Buster, Buster, climb the tree." Unknown. *WoJ*
"Buster's got a popper gun." See Boots, boots, boots
Busy. A. A. Milne. *MiWc*
Busy carpenters. James S. Tippett. *HuSv*
"Busy, curious, thirsty fly." See On a fly drinking from his cup
"The busy wind is out today." See My kite
"But give me holly, bold and jolly." Christina Georgina Rossetti. *ArTp*

"But hark, from the woodlands the sound of a gun." See Autumn—The sound of a gun

"But hark to the wind how it blows." T. Sturge Moore. *ArTp*

"But how many moons be in the year." See Robin Hood and the curtal friar

"But if I saw a mountain pass." See After Oliver

"But once I pass this way." See The pilgrim way

"But peaceful was the night." See On the morning of Christ's nativity

"But they that wait upon the Lord shall renew their strength." See Isaiah

Butchers
    Robin Hood and the butcher. Unknown. *MaB*

Butler, A. J.
    Plato, a musician. tr. *PlU*

Butler, George O.
    A Halloween meeting. *BrL-k*

Butler, Samuel
    The barn owl. *DeT*
    Hudibras, Canto I. *PlI* (sel.)
    Hudibras, Canto III. *PlI* (sel.)

Butler, William Allen
    Tom Twist. *CoH*

"Butter is butter." Unknown. *MoY*

The butterbean tent. Elizabeth Madox Roberts. *HuSv*

Buttercup Cow. Elizabeth Rendall. *ArTp*

"Buttercup Cow has milk for me." See Buttercup Cow

Buttercup days. A. A. Milne. *MiWc*

"Buttercup nodded and said good-by." See August

"Buttercup, the cow, had a new baby calf." See The new baby calf

Buttercups
    Buttercup days. A. A. Milne. *MiWc*
    Buttercups. W. Thorley. *FeF*
    Gold-weed. E. Farjeon. *FaCb—FaN*
    Things to remember. J. Reeves. *ReBl*

Buttercups. Wilfrid Thorley. *FeF*

"The buttercups in May." See Things to remember

Butterflies
    Blue-butterfly day. R. Frost. *FrY*
    Brother and sister. W. Wordsworth. *DeT*
    Butterfly ("As I walked through my garden") H. Conkling *ArTp*
    Butterfly ("I'm a little butterfly") Mother Goose. *OpO*
    Butterfly ("Of living creatures most I prize") W. J. Smith. *ArTp—CoI—SmB*
    The butterfly's ball. W. Roscoe. *JoAc—UnG*
    Caterpillar. C. G. Rossetti. *FeF—HuSv—JoAc—UnG*
        "Brown and furry." *BrR-4*
    The example. W. H. Davies. *DoP*
    Fairy aeroplanes. A. B. Payne. *BrL-k*
    "Fuzzy wuzzy, creepy crawly." L. S. Vanada. *ArTp—BrR-3*
    My butterfly. R. Frost. *FrR*
    Stranger still. D. Aldis. *AlHd*

To a butterfly. W. Wordsworth. *UnG*

"Was worm." M. Swenson. *UnG*

White butterflies. A. C. Swinburne. *FeF*

"White flowers and white butterflies." D. Aldis. *AlHd*

Butterfly ("As I walked through my garden") Hilda Conkling. *ArTp*

Butterfly ("I'm a little butterfly") Mother Goose. *OpO*

Butterfly ("Of living creatures most I prize") William Jay Smith. *ArTp—CoI—SmB*

The butterfly's ball. William Roscoe. *JoAc—UnG*

"A buttery, sugary, syrupy waffle." See The groaning board

"Button to chin." Mother Goose. *OpO*

Buttons
    About buttons. D. Aldis. *BrL-k*
    Buy any buttons. Mother Goose. *OpO*

"Buttons, a farthing a pair." See Buy any buttons

Butts, Mary Frances
    That's July. *HaY*
    That's June. *HaY*
    Winter night. *ArTp*

Buy any buttons. Mother Goose. *OpO*

"Buz, quoth the blue fly." See Elves' song

Buzz and hum. See Elves' song

Buzz, buzz, buzz. Unknown. *TaD*

"Buzz, quoth the blue fly." See Elves' song

"By a quiet little stream on an old mossy log." See The frog and the bird

"By day the bat is cousin to the mouse." See The bat

By Dippel woods. Eleanor Farjeon. *FaCb*

"By June our brook's run out of song and speed." See Hyla brook

"By sloth on sorrow fathered." See Lollocks

"By special lens, photo-electric cells." See A different speech

By the crib. Katharine Tynan. *EaW*

By the fire. See "Pussy sits beside the fire"

"By the little river." See The willows

"By the moon we sport and play." See Fairy song

"By the road to the contagious hospital." See Spring and all

"By the rude bridge that arched the flood." See Concord hymn

"By the sand between my toes." See Summer song

By the sea. Marchette Chute. *ChA—HuSv*

"By the sewer I lived." Unknown. *MoY*

"By the shores of Gitche Gumee." See The song of Hiawatha—Hiawatha's childhood

By way of preface. See "How pleasant to know Mr Lear"

"Bye, baby bunting." Mother Goose. *ArTp—DeMg—HuSv—JoAc—LiL—OpO—WoF*

"Bye, bye, baby bunting." Mother Goose. *OpO*

Bynner, Witter
    Looking at the moon and thinking of one far away. tr. *PaS*
    On hearing a flute at night from the wall of Shou-Hsiang. tr. *PlU*

Candles—*Continued*
"Castles and candlelight." J. Reeves. *ReR*
Green candles. H. Wolfe. *CoPm*
"Little Nancy Etticoat." Mother Goose.
  DeMg—HuSv—JoAc—LiL—OpO
    "Little Nanny Etticoat." *ArTp*
Six birthday candles shining. M. J. Carr.
  BrBc
"To make your candles last for aye."
  Mother Goose. *DeMg—DeT—OpO*
"Candles. Red tulips, sixty cents the bunch."
  See Recipe for an evening musicale

Candy
  About candy. D. Aldis. *AlA*
  "Hippety hop to the barber shop."
    Mother Goose. *ArTp*
  Pull. F. M. Frost. *BrR-6*
  Saturday morning. M. C. Livingston.
    LiWa
  The sugar man. C. D. Cole. *HuL-1*
  When candy was chocolate. W. J. Smith.
    SmL

Cane, Melville
  Bed-time story. *UnG*
  Fog, the magician. *DoP*
  Operatic note. *PlU*
  Snow toward evening. *ArTp*

Canis Major. Robert Frost. *FrR*
"A canner, exceedingly canny." Carolyn
  Wells. *FeF—WiRm*
"Canny moment, lucky fit." See The nativity
  chant

Canoes and canoeing
  The kayak. Unknown. *FeF*
  Lullaby. R. Hillyer. *FeF*
  The song my paddle sings. E. P. Johnson.
    FeF

"Canst thou love me, lady." See Love
"Can't think." Unknown. *MoY*
Canterbury bells. Eleanor Farjeon. *FaCb*
The Canterbury tales, sels. Geoffrey Chaucer
  A girlish pardoner. *HaP*
  A gluttonous rich man. *HaP*
  A greedy friar. *HaP*
  A knight. *UnG—UnMc*
    A perfect knight. *HaP*
  A miller. *UnG*
    A stout miller. *HaP*
  A parson. *HaP*
  A prioress. *UnMc*
    A polite nun. *HaP*
  A sporting monk. *HaP*
  A squire. *UnG—UnMc*
  A tasty cook. *HaP*
  The wife of Bath. *HaP*

Canton, William
  Bethlehem. *HaY*
    Carol. *EaW*
  Carol. See Bethlehem
  The crow. *UnG*

Cape Ann. See Landscapes
Cape Horn
  Cape Horn gospel (I). J. Masefield. *CoSp*
Cape Horn gospel (I). John Masefield. *CoSp*
"A capital ship for an ocean trip." See Davy
  and the goblin—A nautical ballad
Capricorn. Eleanor Farjeon. *FaCb—FaN*
"Capricorn, Capricorn." See Capricorn

Caps. See Hats
Captain Carpenter. John Crowe Ransom.
  HaP
"Captain Carpenter rose up in his prime."
  See Captain Carpenter
"Captain Fox was padding along sociably."
  See The fox and the goat
Captain Kidd ("Oh, my name was Robert
  Kidd, as I sailed, as I sailed") Un-
  known. *NaM*
Captain Kidd ("The person in the gaudy
  clothes") Rosemary Carr and Stephen
  Vincent Benét. *HuL-2*
Captain Reece. William Schwenck Gilbert.
  CoH—NaE—UnMc
"The captain stood on the carronade: First
  lieutenant, says he." See The old navy
"The captain went to sea at seventeen."
  See Clipper captain
The caravan. Madeleine Nightingale. *HuL-1*
Caravans
  The caravan. M. Nightingale. *HuL-1*
  Caravans. I. Thompson. *HuL-2*
Caravans. Irene Thompson. *HuL-2*
Cardinal birds. See Red birds
Cards (Games)
  Plain language from truthful James. B.
    Harte. *CoH*
Carducci, Giosuè
  First snowfall. *PaS*
Carefulness
  Forgotten. A. A. Milne. *MiWc*
  "Godfrey Gordon Gustavus Gore." W. B.
    Rands. *ArTp—FeF—HuL-2—PeF*
  Old cat Care. R. Hughes. *ReT*
  That'll be all right you'll find. L. De G.
    Sieveking. *CoH*
  Things that get lost. B. Johnson. *BrR-6*
Careless Willie. Unknown. *CoH—FeF*
Carelessness. See Carefulness
Carew, Thomas
  Now that the winter's gone. See The
    spring
  The spring. *GrCc—HaP—HoW*
    Now that the winter's gone. *CoPs*
Carey, Henry
  Sally in our alley. *CoPs*(sel.)
Cargoes
  Cargoes. J. Masefield. *ArTp—FeF—HuL-2*
  Country trucks. M. Shannon. *ArTp—FeF*
  Freight boats. J. S. Tippett. *FeF—HuL-2*
    —HuSv
  "I saw a ship a-sailing." Mother Goose.
    ArTp — BrR-3 — DeMg — HuSv —
    JoAc—LiL—NaM
    I saw a ship. *DeT*
    A ship a-sailing. *OpO*
  Red iron ore. Unknown. *ArTp*
Cargoes. John Masefield. *ArTp—FeF—*
  HuL-2
Carleton, Will (M.)
  The little black-eyed rebel. *FeF—UnG*
Carlin, Francis (James Francis Carlin Mac-
  Donnell)
  The Virgin's slumber song. *HaY*
Carlisle, Irene
  Cold house. *BrL-7*

Carlyle, Thomas
Today. *DoP—ThP*
Carman, Bliss
Christmas song. *CoPs*
In October. *HaY*
The joys of the road. *BrL-8*
Mr Moon. *FeF—HuL-2*
The ships of Yule. *BrBc*
A vagabond song. *BrR-5—CoPs—FeF—HuL-2—JoAc—UnG*
Where is heaven. *UnG*
Winter streams. *DeT—HaY*
Carmer, Carl
Antique shop. *FeF*
Carmichael, Alexander
Good wish. tr. *SmLg*
Carmina burana. Unknown, tr. fr. the Latin by Helen Waddell. *PaS* (sel.)
Carnations
Carnations. M. Widdemer. *ThP*

Carnations. Margaret Widdemer. *ThP*

"**Carnations** and my first love. And he was seventeen." See Carnations
Carney, Julia Fletcher
"Little drops of water." at. *AnI—DeMg*
Little things. *FeF—UnG*
Little things. See "Little drops of water"
The **carnival** of animals. Ogden Nash. *PlU* (sel.)
Carol. See "I sing of a maiden"
A **carol** ("The angels to the shepherds sang") Frederic E. Weatherly. *HaY*
Carol ("As I sat on a sunny bank") Mother Goose. *OpO*
Sunny bank; or, I saw three ships. *EaW*
Carol ("High o'er the lonely hills") Jan Struther. *EaW*
Carol ("In the bleak mid-winter") Christina Georgina Rossetti. *EaW*
A Christmas carol. *BrBc* (sel.)
My gift. *BrS* (sel.)—*FeF* (sel.)
"What can I give Him." *BrR-4* (sel.)
Carol ("Outlanders, whence come ye last") William Morris. *EaW*
Carol ("The ox said to the ass, said he, all on a Christmas night") Dorothy Sayers. *EaW*
Carol ("There was a Boy bedden in bracken") John Short. *SmLg*
Carol ("When the herds were watching") See Bethlehem
"**Carol,** brothers, carol." William Augustus Muhlenberg. *ArTp*
A **carol** for sleepy children. Sister Maris Stella. *DoP*
Carol of the birds. Bas-Quércy. *EaW*
"A **carol** round the ruddy hearth." See For Christmas day
Caroline, Caroline. James Reeves. *ReW*
"**Caroline,** Caroline sing me a song." See Caroline, Caroline
Carousal. Mother Goose. *OpO*
Carpenter. Edward Verrall Lucas. *HuSv*
Carpenters and carpentry
Busy carpenters. J. S. Tippett. *HuSv*
Carpenter. E. V. Lucas. *HuSv*
In the carpenter shop. Unknown. *UnG*

The walrus and the carpenter. From Through the looking glass. L. Carroll. *CoH — DeT — FeF — HuSv — JoAc — PeF—UnMc*
"The time has come, the walrus said." *ArTp*
Carpets and rugs
A visit from abroad. J. Stephens. *CoPm*
Carr, Mary Beale
Old Mother Ocean. *BrR-6*
Carr, Mary Jane
"The big swing-tree is green again." *BrS*
The birthday of the Lord. *BrBc*
Pirate wind. *BrS*
Six birthday candles shining. *BrBc*
When a fellow's four. *BrBc*
When a ring's around the moon. *ArTp—HuL-2*

Carriages and carts. See also Stage-coaches; Wagons
The deacon's masterpiece; or, The wonderful one-hoss shay. O. W. Holmes. *CoSp—HuSv—NaM—SmLg*
The old coach road. R. Field. *HuL-2*
Yellow wheels. J. Reeves. *ReBl*
The **carrion** crow. See "A carrion crow sat on an oak"
The **carrion** crow. See "Old Adam, the carrion crow"
"A **carrion** crow sat on an oak." Mother Goose. *DeMg—JoAc—LiL*
The carrion crow. *OpO*
The tailor and the crow. *ReG*
Carroll, Lewis, pseud. (Charles Lutwidge Dodgson)
Alice's adventures in wonderland, sels.
Father William. *BrBc—CoH—FeF—HuL-2—LoL—McW—UnG*
"You are old, Father William, the young man said." *ArTp*
"How doth the little crocodile." *ArTp—FeF—LoL—McW—NaM—SmLg*
The crocodile. *JoAc—UnG*
The lobster quadrille. *FeF—HuL-2—HuSv—NaM—PeF*
'Tis the voice of the lobster. *JoAc*
The voice of the lobster. *NaE*
Turtle soup. *ReG*
Beautiful soup. *DeT*
The white rabbit's verses. *JoAc*
Beautiful soup. See Alice's adventures in wonderland—Turtle soup
The beaver's lesson. See The hunting of the snark
The crocodile. See Alice's adventures in wonderland—"How doth the little crocodile"
Father William. See Alice's adventures in wonderland
The gardener's song. See Sylvie and Bruno
He thought he saw. See Sylvie and Bruno—The gardener's song
"How doth the little crocodile." See Alice's adventures in wonderland
Humpty Dumpty's recitation. See Through the looking glass
The hunting of the snark. *CoH* (sel.)
The beaver's lesson. *JoAc*
Jabberwocky. See Through the looking glass

Carroll, Lewis, pseud. (Charles Lutwidge Dodgson)—*Continued*
The lobster quadrille. See Alice's adventures in wonderland
The mad gardener's song. See Sylvie and Bruno—The gardener's song
The melancholy pig. See Sylvie and Bruno
A pig-tale. See Sylvie and Bruno—The melancholy pig
"Speak roughly to your little boy." *SmLg*
A strange wild song. See Sylvie and Bruno—The gardener's song
Sylvie and Bruno, sels.
    The gardener's song. *GrCc—JoAc—NaE*
    He thought he saw. *CoH—HuL-2*
    The mad gardener's song. *HoW*
    A strange wild song. *HuSv*
    The melancholy pig. *FeF*
    A pig-tale. *HoW*
"There was a young lady of station"
  Limericks since Lear. *UnG*
Through the looking glass, sels.
    Humpty Dumpty's recitation. *UnG*
    Jabberwocky. *ArTp — FeF — JoAc — UnG*
    The walrus and the carpenter. *CoH—DeT — FeF — HuSv — JoAc — PeF—UnMc*
      "The time has come, the walrus said." *ArTp*
    The white knight's song. *SmLg*
    Ways and means. *CoH*
"The time has come, the walrus said." See Through the looking glass—The walrus and the carpenter
'Tis the voice of the lobster. See Alice's adventures in wonderland
Turtle soup. See Alice's adventures in wonderland
The voice of the lobster. See Alice's adventures in wonderland—'Tis the voice of the lobster
The walrus and the carpenter. See Through the looking glass
Ways and means. See Through the looking glass—The white knight's song
The white knight's song. See Through the looking glass
The white rabbit's verses. See Alice's adventures in wonderland
"You are old, Father William, the young man said." See Alice's adventures in wonderland—Father William
Carroll, Lewis, pseud. (Charles Lutwidge Dodgson) (about)
Lewis Carroll came here to-day. E. Farjeon. *FaN*
Carrots
Mister Carrot. D. Aldis. *AlA*
"Carrots and spinach." See Nice food
"Carry me, ferryman, over the ford." See Saint Christopher
Carryl, Charles Edward
The admiral's caravan, sel.
    The plaint of the camel. *FeF—HuSv—NaE—PeF*
      The camel's complaint. *CoI—HuL-2—JoAc*
      The camel's lament. *UnG*

The camel's complaint. See The admiral's caravan—The plaint of the camel
The camel's lament. See The admiral's caravan—The plaint of the camel
Davy and the goblin, sels.
    A nautical ballad. *FeF—HuSv*
    The walloping window-blind. *CoH—LoL—NaM—UnG*
    Robinson Crusoe's story. *CoH*
The highlander's song. *CoH*
A nautical ballad. See Davy and the goblin
The plaint of the camel. See The admiral's caravan
The post captain. *CoH*
Robinson Crusoe's story. See Davy and the goblin
The walloping window-blind. See Davy and the goblin—A nautical ballad
Carryl, Guy Wetmore
The arrogant frog and the superior bull. *CoSp*
The embarrassing episode of little Miss Muffet. *CoSp—FeF*
The fearful finale of the irascible mouse. *CoH*
The gastronomic guile of Simple Simon. *UnG*
How a fisherman corked up his foe in a jar. *CoPm*
Little Red Riding Hood. *CoH*
The sycophantic fox and the gullible raven. *CoH*
Carthage, Ancient city
"Queen Dido is building." E. Farjeon. *FaCb*
Carts. See Carriages and carts
Carving
When father carves the duck. E. V. Wright. *CoH—CoPs*
Cary, Phoebe
The leak in the dike. *FeF*
A legend of the Northland. *UnG*
The naughty little robin. *BrL-k*
Casabianca ("The boy stood on the burning deck") Felicia Dorothea Hemans. *FeF—UnG*
Casabianca ("Sea, be kind to a young boy's bones") Eleanor Farjeon. *FaCb—FaN*
Casey at the bat. Ernest Lawrence Thayer. *CoSp—FeF—UnMc*
Casey Jones. T. Lawrence Seibert. *UnMc*
"Cast thy bread upon the waters." See Ecclesiastes
The castaway. William Cowper. *HaP*
Castiello, Jaime
Partners. *McW*
The castle. James Reeves. *ReW*
"A castle has." See Having
Castles
The castle. J. Reeves. *ReW*
"Castles and candlelight." J. Reeves. *ReR*
Château de Chinon. E. Farjeon. *FaCb*
Having. W. J. Smith. *SmL*
"In the sand." M. C. Livingston. *LiW*
Moy castle. Unknown. *UnG*
"Castles and candlelight." James Reeves. *ReR*
Castor oil. David McCord. *McT*

Castro, Rosalía de
"I know not what I seek eternally." *PaS*
Casual gold. Maud E. Uschold. *HaY*
"The **cat**." See A cat may look at a king
Cat ("The black cat yawns") Mary Britton Miller. *ArTp—BrR-4—HuSv—PeF*
Cat ("Cats are not at all like people") William Jay Smith. *SmB*
Cat ("I am exceedingly rich") Jan Struther. *UnG*
Cat ("My cat") Dorothy W. Baruch. *ArTp—BrR-3*
Cat ("This is a cat that sleeps at night") Sinclair Lewis. *UnG*
Cat and rat. Unknown. *TaD*
The **cat** and the fish. Thomas Gray. *HoW*
The **cat** and the moon. William Butler Yeats. *CoPm—ReT—SmLg*
A **cat** came fiddling. See "A cat came fiddling out of a barn"
"A **cat** came fiddling out of a barn." Mother Goose. *DeMg—HuSv—JoAc*
Bagpipes. *DeT—OpO*
A cat came fiddling. *HuL-1*
The **cat** heard the cat-bird. John Ciardi. *CiI*
"**Cat**, if you go outdoors you must walk in the snow." See On a night of snow
A **cat** may look at a king. Laura E. Richards. *CoI*
Cat on couch. Barbara Howes. *HaP*
"The **cat** runs races with her tail. The dog." See Signs of winter
The **cat** sat asleep. See "The cat sat asleep by the side of the fire"
"The **cat** sat asleep by the side of the fire." See "The cat sat asleep by the side of the fire"
"The **cat** sat asleep by the side of the fire." Mother Goose. *DeMg*
The cat sat asleep. *DeT*
Medley. *OpO*
"A **cat** sat quaintly by the fire." See Hearth
"The **cat** that comes to my window sill." See That cat
"The **cat** was once a weaver." See What the gray cat sings
"The **cat** went here and there." See The cat and the moon
Catalog. Rosalie Moore. *UnG*
Catbirds
The cat heard the cat-bird. J. Ciardi. *CiI*
Catch. See "Little Robin Redbreast sat upon a tree"
A catch by the hearth. Unknown. *BrL-7*
"**Catch** him, crow. Carry him, kite." Mother Goose. *OpO*
Catches
"I went up one pair of stairs." Mother Goose. *DeMg—JoAc*
The pullet. Unknown. *TaD*
Catching song. Eleanor Farjeon. *DeT—HuL-1*
Caterpillar. Christina Georgina Rossetti. *FeF—HuSv—JoAc—UnG*
"Brown and furry." *BrR-4*

Caterpillars
Caterpillar. C. G. Rossetti. *FeF—HuSv—JoAc—UnG*
"Brown and furry." *BrR-4*
Cocoon. D. McCord. *McFf*
"Fuzzy wuzzy, creepy crawly." L. S. Vanada. *ArTp—BrR-3*
Only my opinion. M. Shannon. *ArTp—FeF—HuSv*
Stranger still. D. Aldis. *AlHd*
Cathemerinon, sels. Prudentius, tr. fr. the Latin by Helen Waddell. *PaS*
"The earth is sweet with roses"
"Take him, earth, for cherishing"
Cather, Willa Sibert
Spanish Johnny. *FeF—McW*
"Catherinette." Eleanor Farjeon. *FaCb—FaN*
The catipoce. James Reeves. *ReP*
Catkin. Unknown. *BrL-k*
Cats
The ad-dressing of cats. T. S. Eliot. *UnG*
Alley cat. D. McCord. *McT*
The bad kittens. E. J. Coatsworth. *FeF*
"Barbara had a cat." Unknown. *MoY*
Cat ("The black cat yawns") M. B. Miller. *ArTp—BrR-4—HuSv—PeF*
Cat ("Cats are not at all like people") W. J. Smith. *SmB*
Cat ("I am exceedingly rich") J. Struther. *UnG*
Cat ("My cat") D. W. Baruch. *ArTp—BrR-3*
Cat ("This is a cat that sleeps at night") S. Lewis. *UnG*
The cat and the fish. T. Gray. *HoW*
The cat and the moon. W. B. Yeats. *CoPm—ReT—SmLg*
"A cat came fiddling out of a barn." Mother Goose. *DeMg—HuSv—JoAc*
Bagpipes. *DeT—OpO*
A cat came fiddling. *HuL-1*
The cat heard the cat-bird. J. Ciardi. *CiI*
A cat may look at a king. L. E. Richards. *CoI*
Cat on couch. B. Howes. *HaP*
Catalog. R. Moore. *UnG*
Cats ("A baby cat is soft and sweet") M. Chute. *ChA*
Cats ("Cats sleep") E. Farjeon. *FaCb—FaN*
Cat's funeral. E. V. Rieu. *RiF*
The cats' tea-party. F. E. Weatherly. *ArTp—CoI*
"Chang McTang McQuarter Cat." J. Ciardi. *CiY*
Choosing a kitten. Unknown. *HuSv*
Country cat. E. J. Coatsworth. *UnG*
A curse on the cat. J. Skelton. *NaE*
"Dame Trot and her cat." Mother Goose. *DeMg—HuL-1*
Dame Trot. *OpO*
Dandelion morning. F. M. Frost. *FrLn*
Diamond cut diamond E. Milne. *ArTp—SmLg*
"Diddlety, diddlety, dumpty." Mother Goose. *DeMg—LiL*
Puss up the plum tree. *OpO*
"Ding dang, bell rang." Mother Goose. *OpO*

"Who are you? asked the cat of the bear."
E. J. Coatsworth. *ArTp*
"Who's that ringing at my doorbell." Unknown. *SmLg*
Visitor. *OpO*
Who's that ringing. *HuL-1*
Witch cat. R. B. Bennett. *BrS*
Cats ("A baby cat is soft and sweet")
Marchette Chute. *ChA*
Cats ("Cats sleep") Eleanor Farjeon. *FaCb—FaN*
"Cats are not at all like people." See Cat
Cat's funeral. E. V. Rieu. *RiF*
The cats of Kilkenny. See "There once were two cats of Kilkenny"
"Cats sleep." See Cats
"Cats sleep fat and walk thin." See Catalog
The cats' tea-party. Frederic E. Weatherly. *ArTp—CoI*
Cattle. See also Bulls; Calves; Cowboys—Songs; Cows
Crossing the plains. J. Miller. *GrCc*
The herd-boy's song. Chen Shan-min. *PaS*
The ox and the ass. E. Simpson. *EaW*
The oxen. T. Hardy. *EaW—HaP*
Song. Unknown. *ReT*
"The cattle roam again across the fields." See Book of the dead—Adoration of the disk
Catullus, Gaius Valerius
Dianae sumus in fide. *GrCc*
"Cauld blaws the wind frae east to west." See Up in the morning early
The caulker. M. A. Lewis. *CoSp*
Causley, Charles
Cowboy song. *HaP*
Caution. See "Mother, may I go out to swim"
Cavafy, C. P.
Alexandrian kings. *GrCc*
Waiting for the barbarians. *GrCc*
Cavalcanti, Guido
He compares all things with his lady, and finds them wanting. *PaS*
The cave-boy. Laura E. Richards. *FeF*
Caves
The cave-boy. L. E. Richards. *FeF*
The dream. H. Behn. *BeW*
The secret cavern. M. Widdemer. *FeF*
"Caw, caw, caw." See Many crows, any owl
Cawein, Madison (Julius)
Deserted. *BrL-7*
Old Man Rain. *BrR-6—CoPs*
Cecilia, Saint (about)
Alexander's feast; or, The power of music. J. Dryden. *HoW*
A song for St Cecilia's day. J. Dryden. *PlU* (sel.)
Celanta at the well of life. George Peele. *ReT*
A voice speaks from the well. *SmLg*
A celebration of Charis, sel. Ben Jonson
"Have you seen but a bright lily grow." *SmLg*
A comparison. *DeT*
Celery. Ogden Nash. *FeF*
"Celery, raw." See Celery

The Celestial Surgeon. Robert Louis Stevenson. *UnG*
Cemeteries. See also Epitaphs; Tombs
Elegy written in a country churchyard. T. Gray. *DeT—HaP*
The heather. S. S. Blicher. *PaS*
Hide-and-seek. R. Francis. *HaP*
In a disused graveyard. R. Frost. *FrR*
Quiet fun. H. Graham. *CoH*
"The cemetery stone New England autumn." See Voices of heroes
The census-taker. Robert Frost. *FrR*
The centennial meditation of Columbia, sel. Sidney Lanier
Dear land of all my love. *HuSv*
A centipede. See "A centipede was happy quite"
The centipede ("I objurgate the centipede") Ogden Nash. *FeF*
"The centipede along the threshold crept." See The haunted house
"A centipede was happy quite." Unknown. *CoH—LoL*
A centipede. *ArTp—UnG*
The centipede. *BrR-5*
The puzzled centipede. *FeF*
Centipedes
The centipede. O. Nash. *FeF*
"A centipede was happy quite." Unknown. *CoH—LoL*
A centipede. *ArTp—UnG*
The centipede. *BrR-5*
The puzzled centipede. *FeF*
The ceremonial band. James Reeves. *ReBl*
Ceremonial hunt. See The Painted desert
Ceremonies for Christmas. Robert Herrick. *ArTp*
Certain maxims of Archy. Don Marquis. *CoH* (sel.)
Archy, the cockroach, speaks. *FeF*
Certainty. See "I never saw a moor"
Cervantes Saavedra, Miguel de (about)
Cervantes. E. C. Bentley. *NaE*
Cervantes. E. C. Bentley. *NaE*
Chaffee, Eleanor Alletta
The cobbler. *ArTp*
The difference. *BrBc*
Spring song. *BrL-7*
"Chaffinch sings at dawn." See On this day the wren and the robin stop singing
Chairoplane chant. Nancy Byrd Turner. *BrR-5*
Chairs
Nursery chairs. A. A. Milne. *MiWc*
The perfect reactionary. H. Mearns. *CoH*
The table and the chair. E. Lear. *HuSv—JoAc—UnG*
Chairs to mend. See "If I'd as much money as I could spend"
Chalmers, Patrick R.
The little young lambs. *HuL-2*
Puk-wudjies. *HuL-2*
"The tortoiseshell cat." *HuL-2*
Chamber music, sels. James Joyce
"Lean out of the window"
From Chamber music. *GrCc*
The noise of waters. *ArTp—FeF*
"All day I hear the noise of waters." *SmLg*

Chamberlayne, L. P.
The gusts of winter are gone. tr. *PaS*
Chamberlin, Enola
Home again. *McAw*
Chambers, Robert William
To nature seekers. *NaM*
The chameleon. A. P. Herbert. *CoI—FeF*
"The chameleon changes his color." See The chameleon
Chameleons. See Lizards
Chamisso, Adelbert von
A tragic story. *BrL-7—CoH—DeT—FeF—NaM—UnG*
Chan Fang-shēng
Sailing homeward. *PaS—SmLg*
Chandler, Elsie Williams
Christmas singing. *BrS*
Chang Chiu-ling
Looking at the moon and thinking of one far away. *PaS*
"Chang McTang McQuarter Cat." John Ciardi. *CiY*
Change
"If once you have slept on an island." R. Field. *HuL-2*
No single thing abides. From De rerum natura. Lucretius. *PlI*
Ozymandias. P. B. Shelley. *BrL-7—HaP—McW—SmLg—UnG*
"The world turns and the world changes." From The rock. T. S. Eliot. *ArTp*
A change of heart. Valine Hobbs. *BrS*
Change of seasons. James Steel Smith. *McAw*
"Changed is the scene: the peace." See La noche triste
Changeling. Leah Bodine Drake. *CoPm*
Changelings
Changeling. L. B. Drake. *CoPm*
The return of the fairy. H. Wolfe. *CoPm*
Chanson innocente, sels. E. E. Cummings
In just spring. *CoH—JoAc—ReT*
Chanson innocente. *FeF—NaM*
"In just." *UnG*
"Little tree"
Chanson innocente. *CoPs*
Chant for skippers. Katharine Gallagher. *BrS*
A chant out of doors. Marguerite Wilkinson. *JoAc*
Chanticleer ("High and proud on the barnyard fence") John Farrar. *ArTp—BrR-3*
Chanticleer ("Of all the birds from east to west") Katharine Tynan. *ArTp*
Chanukah
Blessings for Chanukah. J. E. Sampter. *ArTp*
Chapman, John (about)
Ballad of Johnny Appleseed. H. O. Oleson. *ArTp—BrS*
In praise of Johnny Appleseed. V. Lindsay. *HuSv*
Johnny Appleseed. *FeF* (sel.)
Chapman, John Alexander
Christ is born. *EaW*
Chapter two. Winfield Townley Scott. *GrCc*
Character. See Conduct of life
Character building. Edward Anthony. *UnG*

Charade. Mother Goose. *OpO*
The charcoal-burner. A. A. Milne. *MiWc*
"The charcoal-burner has tales to tell." See The charcoal-burner
The charge of the Light Brigade. Alfred Tennyson. *FeF—JoAc—UnMc*
Charity
Alice Fell. W. Wordsworth. *DeT*
Charity ("There is so much good in the worst of us") Unknown. *ThP*
Charity ("Though I speak with the tongues of men and of angels") From First epistle of Paul to the Corinthians, Bible, New Testament. *HuSv*
"Mrs Malone." E. Farjeon. *CoPm*
Charity ("There is so much good in the worst of us") Unknown. *ThP*
Charity ("Though I speak with the tongues of men and of angels") See First epistle of Paul to the Corinthians
Charlemagne (about)
The gay young squires. E. Farjeon. *FaCb*
Charles I, of England (about)
"As I was going by Charing cross." Mother Goose. *SmLg*
Charles I. *OpO*
King Charles. *DeT*
Charles I. See "As I was going by Charing cross"
Charles II, of England (about)
On Charles II. J. Wilmot, Earl of Rochester. *HaP—UnG*
Charles, Jack
To Chuck—concerning a rendezvous in Siam. *McW*
Charles, Robert E.
A roundabout turn. *NaM*
Charles d'Orleans (Comte d'Angoulême)
Alons au bois le may cueillir. *PaS*
The return of spring. *GrCc*
Rondeau. *PaS*
Charley. Mother Goose. *OpO*
Charley Barley. Mother Goose. *OpO*
"Charley Barley, butter and eggs." See Charley Barley
"Charley, Charley." See Charley
Charley Lee. Henry Herbert Knibbs. *McW*
"Charley over the water." Unknown. *WiRm—WoJ*
"Charley Wag, Charley Wag." Mother Goose. *JoAc*
"Charlie Wag." *OpO*
Charley Warlie. See "Charlie Warlie had a cow"
"Charlie Chaplin went to France." Unknown; wrongly attributed to Carl Withers. *NaM*
"Charlie Wag." See "Charley Wag, Charley Wag"
"Charlie Warlie had a cow." Mother Goose. *DeMg*
Charley Warlie. *OpO*
A charm for spring flowers. Rachel Field. *ArTp*
"Charm me asleep, and melt me so." See To music, to becalme his fever
A charm; or, An allay for love. Robert Herrick. *SmLg*

Charms
C is for charms. E. Farjeon. *FaCb*
A charm for spring flowers. R. Field *ArTp*
A charm; or, An allay for love. R. Herrick. *SmLg*
"Come, butter, come." Mother Goose. *DeMg* —*HuSv*
  Churning. *OpO*
"Cushy cow, bonny, let down thy milk." Mother Goose. *DeMg—HuSv—JoAc*
  Milking. *OpO*
M is for midsummer eve. E. Farjeon. *FaCb*
"One for sorrow, two for joy." Mother Goose. *OpO*
P is for philtre. E. Farjeon. *FaCb*
Rutterkin. W. Cornish. *CoPm*
A spell. J. Dryden. *HoW*
"Star-light, star-bright." Mother Goose. *ArTp—OpO*
  "Star bright, starlight." *HuSv*
T is for talisman. E. Farjeon. *FaCb*
"Thrice toss these oaken ashes in the air." T. Campion. *SmLg*
To the magpie. Mother Goose. *OpO*
The witches' charms. B. Jonson. *CoPm* (sel.)—*ReT*
  Witches' charm. *SmLg* (sel.)
The witches' spell. From Macbeth. W. Shakespeare. *CoPm*

Chase, Polly. See Boyden, Polly Chase

Chase, Victoria
The birthday cake. *BrBc*

The **chase.** Arthur Gregor. *GrCc*

Château de Chinon. Eleanor Farjeon. *FaCb*

Chatham, Earl of. See Pitt, William

"**Chatter** of birds two by two." See Prairie waters by night

Chatterton, Thomas
My love is dead. *HoW*

Chaucer, Geoffrey
The Canterbury tales, sels.
  A girlish pardoner. *HaP*
  A gluttonous rich man. *HaP*
  A greedy friar. *HaP*
  A knight. *UnG—UnMc*
    A perfect knight. *HaP*
  A miller. *UnG*
    A stout miller. *HaP*
  A parson. *HaP*
  A prioress. *UnMc*
    A polite nun. *HaP*
  A sporting monk. *HaP*
  A squire. *UnG—UnMc*
  A tasty cook. *HaP*
  The wife of Bath. *HaP*
A girlish pardoner. See The Canterbury tales
A gluttonous rich man. See The Canterbury tales
A greedy friar. See The Canterbury tales
A knight. See The Canterbury tales
A miller. See The Canterbury tales
A parson. See The Canterbury tales
A perfect knight. See The Canterbury tales —A knight
A polite nun. See The Canterbury tales— A prioress
A prioress. See The Canterbury tales
A sporting monk. See The Canterbury tales

A squire. See The Canterbury tales
A stout miller. See The Canterbury tales— A miller
A tasty cook. See The Canterbury tales
The wife of Bath. See The Canterbury tales

Chaucer, Geoffrey (about)
Sir Geoffrey Chaucer. R. Greene. *SmLg*

Chauras
Arrows of love. *PaS*
I love long black eyes. *PaS*

Cheap blue. Carl Sandburg. *SaW*

Check. James Stephens. *ArTp—BrS—PeF*
Night was creeping. *HuSv*

Cheep. Eleanor Farjeon. *FaCb—FaN*

"A **cheerful** and industrious beast." See Mixed beasts—The bumblebeaver

The **cheerful** cherub, sels. Rebecca McCann. *ThP*
  Humane thought
  Light words
  Vanity

"A **cheerful** old bear at the zoo." Unknown Limericks since Lear. *UnG*

Cheerfulness. See Happiness; Laughter; Optimism

"The **cheese-mites** asked how the cheese got there." See A parable

Chemists
The alchemist. A. A. Milne. *MiWc*

Chen Shan-min
The herd-boy's song. *PaS*
The moon in the mountains. *PaS*

Cheney, John Vance
The happiest heart. *BrL-8*

Cheney, Rowena
For color. *BrR-5*

Cherries
"As I went through the garden gap." Mother Goose. *DeMg*
  A cherry. *ReG*
Bread and cherries. W. De La Mare. *HuL-1*
Cherry stones. A. A. Milne. *MiWc*
Cherry time. S. Dayre. *BrR-3*
Eardrops. W. H. Davies. *GrCc*
Freddie and the cherry-tree. A. Hawkshawe. *HuL-1*
"Mother shake the cherry-tree." C. G. Rossetti. *ArTp*
  Let's be merry. *FeF*
Old blue saucepan. E. Farjeon. *FaN*
"Riddle me, riddle me ree." Mother Goose. *OpO*
Song for a hot day. E. J. Coatsworth. *HuSv*

"**Cherries,** ripe cherries." See Bread and cherries

A **cherry.** See "As I went through the garden gap"

"**Cherry** pie and beer." See Cherry-pie Sunday

Cherry-pie Sunday. Eleanor Farjeon. *FaN*
Cherry stones. A. A. Milne. *MiWc*
Cherry time. Sydney Dayre. *BrR-3*
Cherry tree. See "Oh, fair to see"

Cherry trees
Freddie and the cherry-tree. A. Hawkshawe. *HuL-1*
Loveliest of trees. From A Shropshire lad. A. E. Housman. *HuSv—JoAc*
"Oh, fair to see." C. G. Rossetti. *ArTp—FeF*
Cherry tree. *HaY*
"The **cherry** tree's shedding." See May morning
"A **cherry** year." Mother Goose. *OpO*
Chesterman, Hugh
Sir Nicketty Nox. *HuL-2*
Yesterday. *BrS*
Chesterton, Frances
Alle vögel sind schon da. *PlU*
Children's song of the nativity. See "How far is it to Bethlehem"
"How far is it to Bethlehem." *DoP—EaW*
Children's song of the nativity. *DeT*
Chesterton, Gilbert Keith
The Christ Child. See A Christmas carol
A Christmas carol. *ArTp—EaW*
The Christ Child. *DoP*
A dedication. *CoH*
Elegy in a country churchyard. *NaE*
The house of Christmas. *EaW*
The rolling English road. *NaE—SmLg*
"The **chestnut** man is in the street." See A bag of chestnuts
Chestnut stands. Rachel Field. *BrS*
Chestnuts
A bag of chestnuts. E. Farjeon. *FaCb—FaN*
Chestnut stands. R. Field. *BrS*
"First I am frosted." M. Austin
Rhyming riddles. *ArTp*
Chevy Chase. Unknown. *MaB*
Chewing gum. Unknown. *WoJ*
Chicago
Chicago. C. Sandburg. *SmLg*
The Windy City, sels.
Night. *SaW*
"Winds of the Windy City." *SaW*
Chicago. Carl Sandburg. *SmLg*
"**Chick**, my naggie." Mother Goose. *OpO*
Chickadee ("The chickadee in the appletree") Hilda Conkling. *ArTp*
The **chickadee** ("Piped a tiny voice hard by") Ralph Waldo Emerson. *FeF*
"The **chickadee** in the appletree." See Chickadee
Chickadees
Chickadee ("The chickadee in the appletree") H. Conkling. *ArTp*
The chickadee ("Piped a tiny voice hard by") R. W. Emerson. *FeF*
"Five little chickadees, sitting in a door." Unknown. *WoF*
I'm so big. D. Aldis. *AlHd*
The **chickamungus**. James Reeves. *ReP—UnG*
Chicken. Walter De La Mare. *ArTp*
"**Chicken** in a car." Unknown. *WiRm*
"Chicken in the car and the car won't go." *WoF*
Chicken in the bread tray. Unknown. *TaD*

"**Chicken** in the car and the car won't go." See "Chicken in a car"
"**Chicken** when you're hungry." Unknown. *MoY*
Chickens
At the farm. J. Ciardi. *CiY*
Baby chick. A. Fisher. *CoI*
Bantam rooster. H. Behn. *JoAc*
"Billy Billy Booster." Unknown. *WiRm*
A blue ribbon at Amesbury. R. Frost. *FrR*
The browny hen. I. F. Pawsey. *HuL-1*
Chanticleer ("High and proud on the barnyard fence") J. Farrar. *ArTp—BrR-3*
Chanticleer ("Of all the birds from east to west") K. Tynan. *ArTp*
Chicken. W. De La Mare. *ArTp*
Chicken in the bread tray. Unknown. *TaD*
The chickens ("Said the first little chicken") Unknown. *BrL-k—FeF—NaM*
Five little chickens. *HuL-1—UnG*
The chickens ("What a fearful battle") Unknown. *ArTp*
The clucking hen. A. Hawkshawe. *HuL-1*
Cock and hen. Mother Goose. *OpO*
The cock and the sun. J. P. B. *BrR-3*
"The cock doth crow." Mother Goose. *ArTp—DeMg—LiL—OpO*
"Cocks crow in the morn." Mother Goose. *ArTp*
Signs, seasons, and sense. *UnG*
The complete hen. E. J. Coatsworth. *UnG*
The egg. L. E. Richards. *ArTp*
Hen. W. J. Smith. *SmB*
The hen and the oriole. D. Marquis. *CoH—NaE*
The hen keeper. Mother Goose. *OpO*
The hens. E. M. Roberts. *ArTp—BrR-4—CoI—FeF—HuSv—PeF—UnG*
"Hickety, pickety, my black hen (she lays eggs for gentlemen)." Mother Goose. *AnI—DeMg—JoAc—LiL*
"Higgledy, piggledy, my black hen." *ArTp—HuSv*
My black hen. *OpO*
"Hickety-pickety, my black hen (she lays eggs for the railroad men)." Unknown. *WoF*
"I had a little hen, her name was Blue." Unknown. *WoF*
"I had a little hen, the prettiest ever seen." Mother Goose. *DeMg—JoAc—LiL*
I sometimes think. Unknown. *UnG*
To be or not to be. *CoH—NaM*
"I went to see if my old hen." Unknown. *WoF*
Janet waking. J. C. Ransom. *ReT*
The little black hen. A. A. Milne. *MiWc*
Little Blue Ben. Mother Goose. *OpO*
A little talk. Unknown. *HuL-1*
"Lock the dairy door." Mother Goose. *OpO*
Mrs Hen ("Chook, chook, chook, chook") Mother Goose. *OpO*
Mrs Hen ("Please lay me an egg, Mrs Hen") M. A. Campbell. *HuL-1*
"My mammy had a speckled hen." Unknown. *WoF*
"My Uncle Ben he has a hen." Unknown. *WiRm*
Near and far. H. Behn. *BeW*
Red rooster. H. Conkling. *JoAc*

Rise, sun. F. M. Frost. *FrLn*
"The rooster and the chicken had a fight."
Unknown. *MoY*
"See-saw, Margery Daw (the old hen flew)." Mother Goose. *DeMg—OpO*
"There was an old hen and she had a black foot." Unknown. *WoF*
To let. D. Newey-Johnson. *HuL-1*
Well, I never. Unknown. *JoAc*
The wise hen. J. Ciardi. *CiY*
The **chickens** ("Said the first little chicken") Unknown. *BrL-k—FeF—NaM*
Five little chickens. *HuL-1—UnG*
The **chickens** ("What a fearful battle") Unknown, tr. fr. the German by Rose Fyleman. *ArTp*
"The **chickens** run inside the coop." See A rainy day
"A **chieftain** to the highlands bound." See Lord Ullin's daughter
Ch'ien Wên ti, Emperor
Lo-yang. *GrCc*

Child, Lydia Maria
Thanksgiving day. *BrS—FeF—HuSv—UnG*

The **child** and the snake. Mary Lamb. *DeT*
The **child** in the train. Eleanor Farjeon. *FaCb—FaN*
"The **child** is on my shoulders." See Three spring notations on bipeds—Laughing child
Child Margaret. Carl Sandburg. *SaW*
"The **child** Margaret begins to write numbers on a Saturday morning." See Child Margaret
The **child** next door. Rose Fyleman. *FeF*
"The **child** next door has a wreath on her hat." See The child next door
The **child** reads an almanac. Francis Jammès, tr. fr. the French by Ludwig Lewisohn. *FeF*
"The **child** reads on; her basket of eggs stands by." See The child reads an almanac
"A **child** should always say what's true." See Whole duty of children
Childe Harold's pilgrimage, sel. George Gordon Byron
Roll on, thou dark blue ocean. *FeF*
Childhood. See Children and childhood
Childhood recollections
Aladdin. J. R. Lowell. *BrR-5—CoPm—McW*
Antique shop. C. Carmer. *FeF*
The barefoot boy. J. G. Whittier. *FeF* (sel.)
Brother and sister. W. Wordsworth. *DeT*
Fairy days. W. M. Thackeray. *UnG*
Fern hill. D. Thomas. *JoAc—McW—NaE—ReT—SmLg*
A girl's garden. R. Frost. *FrY*
The green door. L. B. Drake. *BrBc*
"I remember, I remember." T. Hood. *FeF—UnG*
I remember. *DeT*
The light of other days. T. Moore. *DeT*
The old familiar faces. C. Lamb. *HaP*
The old oaken bucket. S. Woodworth. *FeF* (sel.)

Sam. W. De La Mare. *ArTp—CoPm*
Sea memories. H. W. Longfellow. *FeF*
Seven times one are seven. R. Hillyer. *BrBc*
That wind. E. Brontë. *DeT*
To the dandelion. J. R. Lowell. *FeF* (sel.) *—JoAc* (sel.)
"Woodman, spare that tree." G. P. Morris. *FeF* (sel.)

Children and childhood. See also Babies; Boys and boyhood; Childhood recollections; Girls and girlhood
Ambition. A. Kilmer. *ThP*
A carol for sleepy children. Sister Maris Stella. *DoP*
"Children, when they're very sweet." J. Ciardi. *CiM*
The children's hour. H. W. Longfellow. *FeF—UnG*
A child's laughter. A. C. Swinburne. *BrBc*
A child's thought of God. E. B. Browning. *DoP—FeF*
Crayons. C. Morley. *DoP*
Differences. D. Aldis. *AlA*
The dream. Unknown. *DeT*
Experience. A. Kilmer. *BrBc*
For a child. F. S. Davis. *FeF*
Good and bad children. R. L. Stevenson. *SmLg*
The happy family. J. Ciardi. *CiM*
"Here comes a poor woman from Baby-land." Mother Goose. *DeMg*
Hiawatha's childhood. From The song of Hiawatha. H. W. Longfellow. *ArTp—FeF—HuSv—JoAc*
I'd love to be a fairy's child. R. Graves. *BrBc—FeF—HuL-2*
The ideal age for a man. M. Shannon. *BrBc*
Indian children. A. Wynne. *ArTp—HuSv—McAw*
Infant innocence. A. E. Housman. *SmLg*
Laughing child. From Three spring notations on bipeds. C. Sandburg. *SaW*
Lilliput-land. W. B. Rands. *ReG*
Little. Unknown. *HuL-1*
The man who sang the sillies. J. Ciardi. *CiM*
Middle-aged child. I. Hogan. *BrBc*
"My dear, do you know." Mother Goose. *DeMg*
The babes in the wood. *DeT*
Not of school age. R. Frost. *FrY*
Nurse's song. W. Blake. *DeT—HuL-2—JoAc—ReT—UnG*
Play time. *FeF*
Ode on intimations of immortality. W. Wordsworth. *BrBc* (sel.)
Our birth is but a sleep. *HaP* (sel.)
"Piping down the valleys wild." W. Blake. *PlU—SmLg*
Happy songs. *UnG*
Introduction. *ReT*
Introduction to Songs of innocence. *ArTp*
The piper. *DeT*
Portrait of a child settling down for an afternoon nap. C. Sandburg. *SaW*
Punkie-night. E. Farjeon. *FaCb—FaN*
"Ring around the world." A. Wynne. *ArTp—HuSv—JoAc*

Children and childhood—*Continued*

A Scottish shoe. Mother Goose. *OpO*

The stolen child. W. B. Yeats. *CoPm*

Sweeping Wendy: Study in fugue. C. Sandburg. *SaW*

Sweet story of old. J. T. Luke. *DoP*

There was a boy. From The prelude. W. Wordsworth. *SmLg*

There was a child went forth. W. Whitman. *BrBc—UnG*

"There was an old woman who lived in a shoe." Mother Goose. *AnI—ArTp—DeMg—HuSv—JoAc—LiL*

   The old woman in a shoe. *OpO*

To a child. C. Morley. *BrBc*

Treasure. E. E. Long. *BrBc*

Yankee cradle. R. P. T. Coffin. *NaE*

"**Children** born of fairy stock." See I'd love to be a fairy's child

"**Children**, if you dare to think." See Warning to children

Children of the desert. See The people, yes

Children of the wind. See The people, yes

The **children** of the wolf. Eleanor Farjeon. *FaCb*

"The **children** were shouting together." See Frolic

"**Children**, when they're very sweet." John Ciardi. *CiM*

"**Children**, you are very little." See Good and bad children

The **children's** bells. Eleanor Farjeon. *FaCb*

The **children's** hour. Henry Wadsworth Longfellow. *FeF—UnG*

The **children's** lament. E. V. Rieu. *RiF*

The **children's** song ("Land of our birth, we pledge to thee") Rudyard Kipling. *HuL-2*

The **children's** song ("The swallow has come again") Unknown, tr. fr. the Greek. *FeF*

Children's song of the nativity. See "How far is it to Bethlehem"

"**Children's** voices in the orchard." See Landscapes—New Hampshire

Child's carol. Arthur Quiller-Couch. *EaW*

A **child's** Christmas song. T. A. Daly. *BrBc*

"The **child's** cough scratches at my heart— my head." See New York, December, 1931

A **child's** day, sel. Walter De La Mare

   "Softly, drowsily." *HuL-2—JoAc*

   A child's day, Part II. *ArTp*

   A child's day begins. *HuSv*

A **child's** evening prayer. Mary Lundie Duncan. *DoP*

   The good shepherd. *HuL-1*

A **child's** grace. See "Thank you for the earth so sweet"

A **child's** grace ("Here a little child I stand") See A grace for a child

Child's grace ("I give thanks for the lovely colored year") Frances M. Frost. *BrR-6*

A **child's** grace ("Some hae meat and canna eat") Robert Burns. *FeF—HuSv—NaM*

   "Some hae meat that canna eat." *SmLg*

The **child's** hymn. Mary Howitt. *UnG*

A **child's** laughter. Algernon Charles Swinburne. *BrBc*

A **child's** prayer. John Banister Tabb. *FeF*

Child's song. See A masque

A **child's** song of Christmas. Marjorie L. C. Pickthall. *HaY*

A **child's** thought of God. Elizabeth Barrett Browning. *DoP—FeF*

A **child's** thought of harvest. Susan Coolidge. *CoPs*

A **child's** treasure. Eleanor Farjeon. *FaCb*

The **chimney** sweeper. William Blake. *DeT*

Chimney sweeps

   The chimney sweeper. W. Blake. *DeT*

Chimneys

   "Black within and red without." Mother Goose. *DeMg—JoAc—OpO*

   The kitchen chimney. R. Frost. *FrR—FrY*

China. See also Chinese

   Fighting south of the ramparts. Unknown. *PaS*

   "The king of China's daughter." E. Sitwell. *JoAc*

   Lo-yang. Emperor Ch'ien Wên-ti. *GrCc*

Chinaware. See Pottery

Chinese.

   Plain language from truthful James. B. Harte. *CoH*

A **Chinese** nursery rhyme. Unknown, tr. fr. the Chinese by Isaac Taylor Headland. *BrR-3*

The **chipmunk**. Frances M. Frost. *FrLn*

Chipmunks

   The chipmunk. F. M. Frost. *FrLn*

   Eek eek. D. Aldis. *AlHd*

   For dessert. D. Aldis. *AlHd*

   Little Charlie Chipmunk. H. C. LeCron. *ArTp—BrR-3—FeF—PeF*

Chipp, Elinor

   Wild geese. *ArTp—FeF*

Chippewa Indians. See Indians of America —Chippewa

The **chirrupy** cricket. Martha Banning Thomas. *BrR-5*

"**Chitter-chatter**." See A summer story

Chivalry. See also Knights and knighthood; Romance; also names of knights, as Arthur, King

   The glove and the lions. L. Hunt. *FeF—UnMc*

   The rhyme of the chivalrous shark. W. Irwin. *CoH*

Choice. John Farrar. *BrS*

"The **choicest** gifts at christenings." See Gifts

"**Chook**, chook, chook, chook, chook." See Mrs Hen

"**Choose** not your friends." Unknown. *MoY*

Choose something like a star. Robert Frost. *FrR*

"**Choose** the darkest part o' the grove." See A speil

Choosing

   Basket. C. Sandburg. *SaW*

   Bunches of grapes. W. De La Mare. *ArTp—HuL-2—NaM*

   Choice. J. Farrar. *BrS*

"Choose not your friends." Unknown. *MoY*

Choose something like a star. R. Frost. *FrR*

Choosing. E. Farjeon. *ArTp*

Choosing a kitten. Unknown. *HuSv*

Choosing shoes. F. Wolfe. *ArTp—BrR-3 —HuL-1*

Plain philomel. E. Farjeon. *FaCb*

The road not taken. R. Frost. *FrR—FrY —NaE—SmLg*

Vocation. R. Tagore. *FeF*

The ways. J. Oxenham. *ThP*

Choosing. Eleanor Farjeon. *ArTp*

Choosing a kitten. Unknown. *HuSv*

Choosing shoes. Ffrida Wolfe. *ArTp— BrR-3—HuL-1*

Chop-a-nose. Mother Goose. *OpO*

Chorus from Atalanta in Calydon. See Atalanta in Calydon

Chorus from Medea. See Medea

Choruses from The rock. See The rock

Christ. See Jesus Christ

The **Christ** Child. See A Christmas carol ("The Christ-Child lay on Mary's lap")

"The **Christ** Child lay in the ox's stall." See The ox and the donkey's carol

"The **Christ-Child** lay on Mary's lap." See A Christmas carol

"**Christ** hath a garden walled around." Isaac Watts. *SmLg*

Christ is born. John Alexander Chapman. *EaW*

"**Christ** keep the hollow land." See Song

The **christening** ("The bells chime clear") Walter De La Mare. *BrBc*

The **christening** ("What shall I call") A. A. Milne. *BrBc—MiWc*

Christening-day wishes for my God-child, Grace Lane Berkley II. Robert P. Tristram Coffin. *BrBc*

Christenings

The christening ("The bells chime clear") W. De La Mare. *BrBc*

The christening ("What shall I call") A. A. Milne. *BrBc—MiWc*

Christening-day wishes for my God-child, Grace Lane Berkley II. R. P. T. Coffin. *BrBc*

Gifts. H. H. Harris. *BrBc*

It really happened. E. Henley. *BrBc*

To Patricia on her christening day. E. B. Price. *BrBc*

"When I was christened." D. McCord. *BrBc*

Christian ethics. Thomas Traherne. *PlU* (sel.)

Christmas. See also Christmas trees; Santa Claus

A-caroling on Christmas eve. J. S. Tippett. *McAw*

Advice to a child. E. Farjeon. *FaCb*

After Christmas. D. McCord. *McT*

All in the morning. Unknown. *BrBc*

An ancient Christmas carol. Unknown. *DoP*

Awake, glad heart. H Vaughan. *UnG*

Ballad of the Epiphany. C. Dalmon. *EaW*

The barn. E. J. Coatsworth. *BrBc—EaW —UnG*

Before dawn. W. De La Mare. *EaW*

"Before the paling of the stars." C. G. Rossetti. *DoP—EaW—ReG*

A Christmas carol. *BrBc*

Christmas daybreak. *UnG*

Bethlehem. W. Canton. *HaY*

Carol. *EaW*

"Bethlehem-Juda, 'twas there on a morn." G. R. Woodward. *EaW*

Bethlehem of Judea. Unknown. *BrBc*

Bethlehem. *EaW*

The birthday of the Lord. M. J. Carr. *BrBc*

Birthday presents. Unknown. *McAw*

Boughs are bare. E. Farjeon. *FaN*

"Bounce, buckram, velvet's dear." Mother Goose. *DeMg*

Bounce buckram. *OpO*

Bundles. J. Farrar. *ArTp—BrL-k*

Burgundian carol. B. De La Monnoye. *PlU*

The burning Babe. R. Southwell. *SmLg*

"But give me holly, bold and jolly." C. G. Rossetti. *ArTp*

By the crib. K. Tynan. *EaW*

Candle and star. E. J. Coatsworth. *BrBc*

A carol ("The angels to the shepherds sang") F. E. Weatherly. *HaY*

Carol ("As I sat on a sunny bank") Mother Goose. *OpO*

Sunny bank; or, I saw three ships. *EaW*

Carol ("High o'er the lonely hills") J. Struther. *EaW*

Carol ("In the bleak mid-winter") C. G. Rossetti. *EaW*

A Christmas carol. *BrBc* (sel.)

My gift. *BrS* (sel.)—*FeF* (sel.)

"What can I give Him." *BrR-4* (sel.)

Carol ("Outlanders, whence come ye last") W. Morris. *EaW*

Carol ("The ox said to the ass, said he, all on a Christmas night") D. Sayers. *EaW*

Carol ("There was a Boy bedden in bracken") J. Short. *SmLg*

"Carol, brothers, carol." W. A. Muhlenberg. *ArTp*

A carol for sleepy children. Sister Maris Stella. *DoP*

Carol of the birds. Bas-Quércy. *EaW*

A catch by the hearth. Unknown. *BrL-7*

Ceremonies for Christmas. R. Herrick. *ArTp*

Child's carol. A. Quiller-Couch. *EaW*

A child's Christmas song. T. A. Daly. *BrBc*

A child's song of Christmas. M. L. C. Pickthall. *HaY*

Christ is born. J. A. Chapman. *EaW*

Christmas ("My goodness, my goodness") M. Chute. *BrS—ChA*

Christmas ("Oh, tell me, children who have seen") M. M. Dodge. *BrBc*

Christmas at Freelands. J. Stephens. *EaW*

Christmas at sea. R. L. Stevenson. *CoSp*

Christmas birthday. Grace Ellen Glaubitz. *BrBc—BrS*

"Christmas cakes." See Birthday cake

A Christmas carol. See "Before the paling of the stars"

A Christmas carol. See Carol ("In the bleak mid-winter")

Christmas carol. See "God bless the master of this house"

A Christmas carol ("An angel told Mary") Harry Behn. *BrBc*

A Christmas carol ("The Christ-Child lay on Mary's lap") Gilbert Keith Chesterton. *ArTp—EaW*
    The Christ Child. *DoP*

Christmas carol ("God bless your house this holy night") See This holy night

Christmas carol for the dog. Sister Maris Stella. *DoP*

Christmas chant. Isabel Shaw. *BrS*

"Christmas comes but once a year." Mother Goose. *DeMg—OpO*

Christmas day. Andrew Young. *EaW*

Christmas daybreak. See "Before the paling of the stars"

Christmas dog. Dorothy Aldis. *AlA*

Christmas eve ("And there were in the same country shepherds") See Gospel according to Luke

Christmas eve ("I see some waits awaiting") David McCord. *McFf*

Christmas eve ("In holly hedges starving birds") John Davidson. *EaW*

Christmas eve ("On a winter night") Marion Edey. *HaY*

Christmas eve ("On Christmas eve I turned the spit") Mother Goose. *OpO*

"Christmas eve, and twelve of the clock." See The oxen

Christmas eve in Ireland. Katharine Tynan. *EaW*

Christmas eve in the wainscoting. Elizabeth Jane Coatsworth. *CoM*

Christmas eve legend. Frances M. Frost. *BrBc—EaW*

Christmas everywhere. Phillips Brooks. *UnG*

A Christmas folk song. Lizette Woodworth Reese. *ArTp—DoP—FeF—JoAc*

Christmas greeting. See An old Christmas greeting

Christmas in the heart. Unknown. *BrS*

Christmas in the woods. Frances M. Frost. *ArTp*

"Christmas is coming." See "Christmas is coming, the geese are getting fat"

"Christmas is coming, the geese are getting fat." Mother Goose. *DeMg*
    Christmas. *ArTp*
    "Christmas is coming." *OpO*

"Christmas is remembering." Elsie Binns. *BrBc—BrS*

A Christmas legend. Oliver Herford. *CoPm*

Christmas lullaby. Ulrich Troubetzkoy. *HaY*

Christmas morning ("Christmas bells, awake and ring") Harry Behn. *BeW*

Christmas morning ("If Bethlehem were here today") Elizabeth Madox Roberts. *CoPs—DoP—HuSv—JoAc—UnG*

Christmas pageant. Margaret Fishback. *CoPs*

The Christmas pudding. Unknown. *ArTp—HuL-1*

The Christmas robin. Robert Graves. *GrCc*

Christmas singing. Elsie Williams Chandler. *BrS*

Christmas song. See Song ("Why do bells of [or for] Christmas ring")

Christmas song ("Above the wary waiting world") Bliss Carman. *CoPs*

Christmas song ("Of all the animals on earth") Elizabeth-Ellen Long. *BrS*

Christmas stocking. Eleanor Farjeon. *FaCb—FaN*

The Christmas tree. Carl August Peter Cornelius, tr. by H. N. Bate. *EaW*

Christmas trees
    The Christmas tree. C. A. P. Cornelius. *EaW*
    Christmas trees. R. Frost. *FrY*
    "Little tree." From Chanson innocente. E. E. Cummings
        Chanson innocente. *CoPs*
    The outdoor Christmas tree. A. Fisher. *BrS*
    Pine tree song. M. Barrows. *BrR-4*
    Round and round. D. B. Thompson. *BrBc—McAw*
    To a Christmas tree. F. M. Frost. *BrR-6*
    To a young wretch. R. Frost. *FrR*
    Triolet on a dark day. M. Fishback. *CoPs*

Christmas trees. Robert Frost. *FrY*

Christmastide. Willis Boyd Allen. *DoP*

"Christofero had a mind." See The great discovery

"Christofo Colombo was a hungry man." See Mysterious biography

Christopher, Saint (about)
    Saint Christopher. E. Farjeon. *FaCb*

Christopher, Robin
    One, two, three. *HuL-2*

"Christopher, Christopher, where are you going, Christopher Robin." See Journey's end

Christopher Columbus. Rosemary Carr and Stephen Vincent Benét. *PeF*

"Christopher Robin." See Sneezles

"Christopher Robin goes." See Hoppity

"Christus natus est, the cock." See Christ is born

The chronometer. A. M. Sullivan. *McW*

Chrysanthemums
    The dormouse and the doctor. A. A. Milne. *MiWc*

"Chug. Puff. Chug." See Tugs

Church-musick. George Herbert. *PlU*

Churches
    A boy in church. R. Graves. *GrP*
    Church-musick. G. Herbert. *PlU*
    "Here is the church, and here is the steeple." Mother Goose. *DeMg—OpO*
    The hippopotamus. T. S. Eliot. *HaP*
    A little girl. Mother Goose. *OpO*
    Meeting-house hill. A. Lowell. *SmLg*
    Mr Wells. E. M. Roberts. *FeF*
    Old hundred. M. Van Doren. *PlU*
    Through the window. D. McCord. *McFf*
    Tudor church music. S. T. Warner. *PlU*

Churchyards. See Cemeteries

Churning. See "Come, butter, come"

Churns and churning
"Come, butter, come." Mother Goose. *DeMg—HuSv*
    Churning. *OpO*
The fable of the magnet and the churn. From Patience. W. S. Gilbert. *FeF*

Chute, Marchette (Gaylord)
Alone. *ChA*
Ambition. *ChA*
Art. *ChA*
At night. *ChA*
At the zoo. *ChA*
Bath time. *ChA*
Belongings. *ChA*
Birthdays. *BrBc — BrL-k — BrS — ChA —HuSv*
By the sea. *ChA—HuSv*
Cats. *ChA*
Christmas. *BrS—ChA*
Cleverness. *ChA*
Cookery. *ChA*
Dandelions. *BrBc—ChA—McAw*
Dogs. *ChA—HuL-1*
Dreams. *HuL-2*
Dressing-up. *ChA*
Drinking fountain. *ChA—McAw*
Easter parade. *BrS—ChA*
Fairies. *BrL-k—ChA*
"Fourth of July." *BrS—ChA*
Going to bed. *ChA*
Hallowe'en. *ChA*
Helpfulness. *ChA*
History of New York. *ChA*
Horsemanship. *ChA*
In August. *ChA—McAw*
In winter. *ChA*
Indecision. *ChA*
"Jemima Jane." *ChA*
Magic. *ChA*
Merry-go-round. *ChA*
The mouse. *ChA*
My dog. *ArTp — BrL-k — ChA — FeF — HuL-1—McAw—PeF*
My plan. *BrBc—ChA—FeF*
My puppy. *ChA*
My ship. *ChA*
Our band. *ChA*
Our tree. *ChA*
Out walking. *ChA*
Picnics. *ChA*
Pigeons. *ChA*
The pirate cook. *BrR-6—ChA*
Playing ball. *ChA*
Playing store. *ChA*
Portrait. *ChA—McAw*
Presents. *BrS—BrR-3—ChA—NaE*
A rainy day. *McAw*
Sea song. *ChA*
Skiing. *ChA*
Sliding. *ChA—McAw*
Snowflakes. *ChA*
Speed. *ChA*
Spring. *ChA—McAw*
Spring rain. *ArTp—ChA—HuL-1—McAw*
The tea party. *ChA*
Thanksgiving. *ChA*

Thinking. *ChA*
A thought. *ChA*
Timbuctoo. *ChA*
Towns. *ChA*
Tracks in the snow. *BrS—ChA*
Undersea. *HuL-1*
Usefulness. *ChA*
Virtue. *ChA*
Weather. *ChA*

Ciardi, John
About Jimmy James. *CiY*
About the teeth of sharks. *CiY*
All about boys and girls. *CiY*
The army horse and the army jeep. *CiR*
"Arvin Marvin Lillisbee Fitch." *CiY*
"As I was picking a bobble-bud." *CiM*
At the farm. *CiY*
The Bird-brain song. *CiY*
The bugle-billed bazoo. *CiR*
The cat heard the cat-bird. *CiI*
"Chang McTang McQuarter Cat." *CiY*
"Children, when they're very sweet." *CiM*
A cool drink on a hot day. *CiY*
Dan Dunder. *CiY*
A dream about the man in the moon. *CiY*
"Evan Kirk." *CiM*
Forget. *CiI*
Guess. *CiI*
Halloween. *ArTp—CiR*
The happy family. *CiM*
Have you met this man. *CiI*
The heron. *CiR*
How much is true. *CiM*
How the frightful child grew better. *CiY*
How to tell a tiger. *CiY*
How to tell the top of a hill. *CiR*
How Woodrow got his dinner. *CiR*
I met a crow. *CiI*
I met a man down in the well. *CiI*
"I met a man I could not see." *CiI*
"I met a man right here on the pad." *CiI*
"I met a man that had two birds." *CiI*
"I met a man that lived in a house." *CiI*
"I met a man that said, Just look." *CiI*
"I met a man that showed me a trick." *CiI*
"I met a man that was all head." *CiI*
"I met a man that was coming back." *CiI*
"I met a man that was playing games." *CiI*
"I met a man that was trying to whittle." *CiI*
I met a man with three eyes. *CiI*
I sometimes think about dollar bills. *CiR*
"I took a bow and arrow." *CiR—NaE*
"I wish I could meet the man that knows." *CiI*
I wouldn't. *CiY*
It's time to get up. *CiM*
Jerry Mulligan. *CiM*
The journey. *CiY*
Last word about bears. *CiY*
The light-house-keeper's white-mouse. *CiY*
Little bits. *CiY*
Lobster music. *CiM*
"Lucifer Leverett Lightningbug." *CiR*
"The man from the woods." *CiM*
The man in the onion bed. *CiI*
A man in the woods said. *CiI*
The man that had little to say. *CiI*
The man that had no hat. *CiI*

Ciardi, John—*Continued*
The man that lived in a box. *CiI*
The man who sang the sillies. *CiM*
Margaret Nash got wet but I don't know how. *CiM*
Mind you, now. *CiY*
More about bears. *CiY*
"The most of being a boy is noise." *CiM*
Mummy slept late and daddy fixed breakfast. *CiY*
My cat, Mrs Lick-a-chin. *CiY*
My father's watch. *PlI*
My horse, Jack. *CiY*
One day. *CiY*
"The other day when I met Dick." *CiI*
The pinwheel's song. *CiR*
Please, Johnny. *CiM*
Prattle. *BrBc—CiR*
"The principal part of a python." *CiR*
Rain sizes. *CiR*
"The reason for the pelican." *CiR*
Remember. *CiI*
The river is a piece of sky. *ArTp—CiR*
A sad song. *CiY*
The saginsack. *CiR*
"Samuel Silvernose Slipperyside." *CiR*
Say yes to the music, or else. *CiM*
A sea song. *CiY*
"Seven sharp propeller blades." *CiR*
A short checklist of things to think about before being born. *CiY*
Sizes. *CiM*
The sleepy man. *CiI*
Some cook. *CiM*
Someone. *BrBc—CiR*
Someone's face. *CiM*
Sometimes I feel this way. *CiY*
Still more about bears. *CiY*
The stranger in the pumpkin. *CiM*
Summer song. *CiM*
Sylvester. *CiM*
Tell him to go home. *CiY*
Then I met another man I could not see. *CiI*
There once was an owl. *CiR*
There was a hunter from Littletown. *CiM*
There was an old man. *CiM*
"This is I at work at my desk." *CiR*
This man came from nowhere. *CiI*
This man had six eyes. *CiI*
This man lives at my house now. *CiI*
This man talked about you. *CiI*
This man went away. *CiI*
Time. *CiM*
Two lessons. *CiM*
Warning. *CiM*
A warning about bears. *CiY*
What did you learn at the zoo. *CiY*
What do you think his daddy did. *CiY*
What night would it be. *CiY*
What you will learn about the brobinyak. *CiR—NaE*
When I went to get a drink. *CiI*
Why nobody pets the lion at the zoo. *CiR*
The wise hen. *CiY*
Wouldn't you. *CiY*

Cimino, Maria
Cincirinella had a mule. tr. *FeF*

Cincirinella had a mule. Unknown, tr. fr. the Italian by Maria Cimino. *FeF*

"Cincirinella had a mule in his stall." See Cincirinella had a mule

Cinderella
After all and after all. M. C. Davies. *ArTp*
"Cinderella, dressed in red." Unknown. *WiRm*
"Cinderella, dressed in yeller." Unknown
Four questions. *WoJ*

Circles
Circles ("The things to draw with compasses") H. Behn. *LoL*
Circles ("The white man drew a small circle in the sand and told the red man") From The people, yes. C. Sandburg. *SaW*
Circles ("The things to draw with compasses") Harry Behn. *LoL*
Circles ("The white man drew a small circle in the sand and told the red man") See The people, yes

Circus. See also Animals; Clowns; also names of circus animals, as Lions
The acrobats. D. Aldis. *AlA*
Bare-back rider. D. Aldis. *AlA*
"C is for the circus." From All around the town. P. McGinley. *ArTp*
Circus ("The brass band blares") E. Farjeon. *JoAc*
The circus ("Friday came and the circus was there") E. M. Roberts. *FeF*
The circus ("When the circus starts, with the band in front") M. L. Allen. *AlP*
A circus garland, sels. R. Field
   Acrobat. *HuSv*
   The elephant. *HuSv*
   The girl on the milk-white horse. *HuSv*
   The performing seal. *HuSv*
The circus parade. O. B. Miller. *ArTp*
The clown. D. Aldis. *AlA*
The elephants. D. Aldis. *AlA*
Holding hands. L. M. Link. *ArTp—FeF—NaM*
Our circus. L. L. Randall. *ArTp*
P. T. Barnum. R. C. and S. V. Benét. *BrL-7*
The seals. D. Aldis *AlA—ArTp*
Circus ("The brass band blares") Eleanor Farjeon *JoAc*
The circus ("Friday came and the circus was there") Elizabeth Madox Roberts. *FeF*
The circus ("When the circus starts, with the band in front") Marie Louise Allen. *AlP*
A circus garland, sels. Rachel Field
   Acrobat. *HuSv*
   The elephant. *HuSv*
   The girl on the milk-white horse. *HuSv*
   The performing seal. *HuSv*
The circus parade. Olive Beaupré Miller. *ArTp*

Cities and city life. See also Streets; Towns; Village life; also names of cities, as Boston, Massachusetts
All around the town, sels. P. McGinley
  "B's the bus." *ArTp—FeF—LoL*
  "C is for the circus." *ArTp*
  "E is the escalator." *ArTp—LoL—McAw*
  "F is the fighting firetruck." *FeF*
  "J's the jumping jay-walker." *ArTp—FeF*
  "P's the proud policeman." *ArTp*
  "R is for the restaurant." *ArTp*
  "U is for umbrellas." *ArTp*
  "W's for windows." *ArTp*
America for me. H. Van Dyke. *BrR-5*
August. M. Lewis. *UnG*
A brook in the city. R. Frost. *FrR*
Bus ride. From Ferry ride. S. Robinson. *FeF*
Chestnut stands. R. Field. *BrS*
City. L. Hughes. *FeF*
City lights. R. Field. *FeF*
The city mouse and the garden mouse. C. G. Rossetti. *FeF—HuSv—UnG*
  The city mouse. *JoAc*
  "The city mouse lives in a house." *ArTp*
City rain. R. Field. *ArTp*
City streets and country roads. E. Farjeon. *ArTp—PeF*
City trees. E. St V. Millay. *FeF*
The ice-cream man. R. Field. *BrR-4—BrS—FeF*
Natura in urbe. E. B. White. *McW*
On receiving a camp catalog. M. Taylor. *BrR-6*
People. L. Lenski. *FeF*
Skyscrapers. R. Field. *BrL-k—FeF—HuSv—JoAc*
Snow in the city. R. Field. *ArTp*
Taxis. R. Field. *ArTp—FeF—HuL-2—JoAc*
Until we built a cabin. A. Fisher. *ArTp*
"Cities drowned in olden time." See Against oblivion
City. Langston Hughes. *FeF*
"City child, city child, vacation camp is calling." See On receiving a camp catalog
'City dwellers all complain." See August
"The city had withdrawn into itself." See Christmas trees
"The city has streets." See City streets and country roads
City life. See Cities and city life
City lights. Rachel Field. *FeF*
The city mouse. See The city mouse and the garden mouse
The city mouse and the garden mouse. Christina Georgina ·Rossetti. *FeF—HuSv—UnG*
  The city mouse. *JoAc*
  "The city mouse lives in a house." *ArTp*
"The city mouse lives in a house." See The city mouse and the garden mouse
The city of dreadful night. James Thomson. *HoW*
The city of falling leaves. Amy Lowell. *ArTp*

City rain. Rachel Field. *ArTp*
City streets and country roads. Eleanor Farjeon. *ArTp—PeF*
City trees. Edna St Vincent Millay. *FeF*
Civil war. See United States—History—Civil war
Clairmont, Robert
  The answers. *CoH—UnG*
    When did the world begin. *McW*
  A hero in the land of dough. *McW*
  The wheelgoround. *CoPm*
  When did the world begin. See The answers
Clams
  Have you met this man. J. Ciardi. *CiI*
  Nirvana. Unknown. *CoH*
"Clap hands, clap hands (hie, Tommy)." See Cock-a-bandy
"Clap hands, clap hands (till father)." Mother Goose. *OpO*
"Clap hands, Daddy comes." Mother Goose. *OpO*
"Clap hands, Daddy's coming." Mother Goose. *OpO*
Clapping games. See Nursery play
"Clapping her platter stood plump Bess." See Chicken
Clare, John
  Autumn evening. *ReT*
  Badger. *HoW*
  Bits of straw. *HoW*
  Clock-a-clay. *FeF—ReT*
  High summer. *GrCc*
  I am. *HaP*
  July. *UnG*
  Little Trotty Wagtail. *FeF*
  November. *UnG*
  Signs of winter. *CoPs—HoW—McW*
  Snowstorm. *HoW*
  Song's eternity. *McW—SmLg*
  Sudden shower. *CoPs*
  Summer morning. *CoPs*
  The thrush's nest. *HaP—ReT—UnG*
  Young lambs. *UnG*
Clark, Ann Nolan
  In my mother's house, sels.
    Irrigation. *HuSv*
    Mountains. *HuSv*
    "Yucca." *JoAc*
  Irrigation. See In my mother's house
  Mountains. See In my mother's house
  "Yucca." See In my mother's house
Clark, Badger
  Cottonwood leaves. *ArTp*
  The glory trail. *CoSp*
Clark, Electa
  The merry-go-round. *McAw*
Clark, Leslie Savage
  Persian proverb. *ThP*
Clark, Thomas Curtis
  The search. *DoP*
Clarke, Frances. See Sayers, Frances Clarke
The clavichord. May Sarton. *PlU*
Clean Clara. William Brighty Rands. *CoH* (sel.)
Cleanliness. See also Bathing
  Before tea. A. A. Milne. *MiWc*
  Clean Clara. W. B. Rands. *CoH*(sel.)
  Dirty Jack. Unknown. *DeT*

Cleanliness—*Continued*
  The fairies. R. Herrick. *FeF*
    Queen Mab. *ReG*
  Going too far. M. Howells. *ArTp*
  Mr Wells. E. M. Roberts. *FeF*
  Pigs. W. J. Smith. *SmB*
  Strictly germ-proof. A. Guiterman. *BrL-8*
"**Cleanly,** sir, you went to the core of the matter." See A correct compassion
Clearing at dawn. Li T'ai-po, tr. fr. the Chinese by Arthur Waley. *PaS*
Cleopatra (about)
  "Age cannot wither her, nor custom stale." From Antony and Cleopatra. W. Shakespeare
    A Shakespeare gallery. *UnMc*
Clerk Colven. Unknown. *MaB*
"**Clerk** Colven and his gay lady." See Clerk Colven
Cleveland, Elizabeth L.
  Snowflakes. *BrL-k*
Cleverness. Marchette Chute. *ChA*
"**Clickety-clack.**" See Song of the train
"**Cliffs** that rise a thousand feet." See Sailing homeward
Climb. Winifred Welles. *BrBc*
The **climb** to virtue. Simonides, tr. fr. the Greek by C. M. Bowra. *PaS*
Clipper captain. Shirley Barker. *McW*
Clipper ships and captains. Rosemary Carr and Stephen Vincent Benét. *HuSv*
Clive, Lord (about)
  Lord Clive. E. C. Bentley. *NaM*
Clock-a-clay. John Clare. *FeF—ReT*
"The **clock** in the hall." Ivy O. Eastwick. *EaI*
"**Clocks.**" See Sing-song
Clocks and watches
  The big clock. Unknown. *ArTp—HuL-1*
  "The clock in the hall." I. O. Eastwick. *EaI*
  The cuckoo-clock shop. R. Field. *HuL-2*
  The fearful finale of the irascible mouse. G. W. Carryl. *CoH*
  Four quartz crystal clocks. M. Moore. *PlI*
  "Hickory, dickory, dock (the mouse)." Mother Goose. *AnI—ArTp—BrL-k—DeMg—HuL-1—JoAc—LiL—OpO*
  I will sing you one-o. R. Frost. *FrR*
  Mr Coggs, watchmaker. E. V. Lucas. *FeF*
  My father's watch. J. Ciardi. *PlI*
  Nursery clock. M. C. Livingston. *LiWa*
  Our clock. F. Eakman. *BrS*
  The sad tale of Mr Mears. Unknown. *CoSp*
  Sing-song. D. McCord. *McT*
  Song for a little cuckoo clock. E. J. Coatsworth. *BrS*
  Time. J. Ciardi. *CiM*
  What does it matter. E. V. Rieu. *RiF*
Clootie. Unknown. *MaB*
Close shave. Mother Goose. *OpO*
"**Clothed** in yellow, red, and green." Mother Goose. *OpO*
Clothing and dress. See also names of clothing, as Boots and shoes
  About buttons. D. Aldis. *BrL-k*
  Aiken Drum. Mother Goose. *OpO—SmLg*

All wool. A. F. Brown. *ArTp*
"As soon as ever twilight comes." W. De La Mare. *BrS*
Awful mornings. D. Aldis. *AlA*
The bonnie cravat. Mother Goose. *ArTp—HuL-1—OpO*
Brian O'Lin. Unknown. *WoF*
Brian O'Linn. Unknown. *CoH*
"Bryan O'Lin had no breeches to wear." Mother Goose. *DeMg*
A dash to the pole. W. Irwin. *CoH*
Delight in disorder. R. Herrick. *HaP*
"Diddle, diddle, dumpling, my son John." Mother Goose. *HuSv—JoAc—LiL—OpO*
  Deedle, deedle, dumpling. *HuL-1*
  "Deedle, deedle, dumpling, my son John." *DeMg*
Disillusionment of ten o'clock. W. Stevens. *HaP*
Downpour. M. C. Livingston. *LiWa*
Dresses. D. Aldis. *AlA*
Dressing-up. M. Chute. *ChA*
Durenda Fair. D. McCord. *McFf*
Easter parade. M. Chute. *BrS—ChA*
"Emily, Bob, and Jane." E. Farjeon. *FaN*
Flower party. D. Aldis. *AlHd*
"The funniest sight that ever I saw." Unknown
  American Father Gander. *UnG*
Getting out of bed. E. Farjeon. *BrS*
Growing up. M. C. Livingston. *LiW*
Hair ribbons. Unknown. *BrBc—BrL-k*
Happiness. A. A. Milne. *ArTp—HuL-2—MiWc*
Having. W. J. Smith. *SmL*
"Hector Protector was dressed all in green." Mother Goose. *DeMg*
  Hector Protector. *NaM—OpO*
"Hey diddle, dinketty, poppety, pet." Mother Goose. *DeMg—OpO*
Hot weather. D. Aldis. *AlA*
The Hottentot tot. N. Levy. *HuL-2*
  Midsummer fantasy. *CoPs*
"A housewife called out with a frown." Unknown
  Limericks since Lear. *UnG*
If you ask me. D. Aldis. *AlHd*
"I'm a little Hindoo." Unknown. *CoH*
In winter. M. Chute. *ChA*
"Johnny shall have a new bonnet." Mother Goose. *DeMg—JoAc*
  Why may not I love Johnny. *OpO*
Jonathan Bing. B. C. Brown. *ArTp—CoH—FeF—HuL-2—LoL—PeF*
Kingsway. E. Farjeon. *HuL-2*
"Little Blue Apron." Unknown. *HuL-1*
Little Blue Ribbons. A. Dobson. *BrBc*
"Little boy, little boy." Unknown. *WoF*
Little boy's britches. Unknown. *TaD*
A little girl. Mother Goose. *OpO*
"Little Polly Flinders." Mother Goose. *DeMg—LiL*
  Polly Flinders. *OpO*
"Mrs Farleigh-fashion." J. Reeves. *ReW*
"The morns are meeker than they were." E. Dickinson. *ArTp—JoAc—PeF*
  Autumn. *BrR-5—FeF—HaY*
Mother. R. Fyleman. *BrL-k—BrS*
My donkey. Unknown. *ArTp—HuL-2*

"My grandmother sent me." Mother Goose. *OpO*

My zipper suit. M. L. Allen. *AlP—ArTp—BrL-k*

New clothes and old. E. Farjeon. *FaCb—FaN*

The new vestments. E. Lear. *CoH*

The old cloak. Unknown. *MaB*

"Out came the sun." E. Farjeon. *FaCb—FaN*

The perils of invisibility. W. S. Gilbert. *CoSp*

Poems in praise of practically nothing. S. Hoffenstein. *NaE* (sel.)

"Poor little fly upon the wall." Unknown. *WoF*

Pretending. M. C. Livingston. *BrBc—LiW*

"Pretty little redbird, dressed so fine." Unknown. *WiRm*

Putting on nightgown. Mother Goose. *OpO*

Ready for winter. C. F. Booth. *McAw*

Rumbo and Jumbo. Unknown. *CoH*

Sensitive Sydney. W. Irwin. *CoH*

The September gale. O. W. Holmes. *CoH* (sel.)

Silk coats. E. Farjeon. *FaN*

Silly. Mother Goose. *OpO*

"A sleeper from the Amazon." Unknown. *LoL*

Still to be neat. B. Jonson. *HaP*

"There was a young man of Bengal." Unknown
    Limericks since Lear. *UnG*

"There was an old man in a pew." E. Lear
    Limericks. *NaM*

A thought. A. A. Milne. *MiWc*

"Three little kittens." Unknown. *BrL-k—FeF—HuSv—OpO*
    The little kittens. *ArTp—HuL-1*
    "Three little kittens, they lost their mittens." *AnI—DeMg—LiL*
    "Three young rats with black felt hats." Mother Goose. *DeMg—JoAc*
    Three young rats. *LoL—OpO*

Tommy O'Linn. Mother Goose. *OpO*

Tommy Tacket. Mother Goose. *OpO*

Troubles. D. Aldis. *BrL-k—HuSv—JoAc*

The well-dressed children. R. Graves. *GrP*

"Well I never, did you ever." Unknown. *SmLg*

"What kind of pants do cowboys wear." Unknown. *WiRm*
    "What kind of pants does a cowboy wear." *WoF*

"When I was a little boy, I thought I was a bold one." Unknown. *WoF*

"When nose itches." Unknown. *WoF*

Winter-wear. M. L. Allen. *AlP*

"With flowers on my shoulders." Unknown. *WiRm*

The **cloud**. Percy Bysshe Shelley. *FeF—JoAc—PlI* (sel.)

The **cloud**-mobile. May Swenson. *UnG*

A **cloud** shadow. Robert Frost. *FrR*

Clouds. See also Weather
    "Boats sail on the rivers." C. G. Rossetti. *ArTp — BrR-4 — DoP — HuL-2 — HuSv—PeF*
    The bridge. *JoAc*

The cloud. P. B. Shelley. *FeF—JoAc—PlI* (sel.)

The cloud-mobile. M. Swenson. *UnG*

A cloud shadow. R. Frost. *FrR*

Clouds. D. Aldis. *AlA*

Job. Chapter 36. From Job, Bible, Old Testament. *PlI*

Little cloud. M. Blassing. *BrR-3*

"Low-anchored cloud." H. D. Thoreau. *PlI*

Rolling clouds. From Sky talk. C. Sandburg. *SaW*

Washday song. M. C. Livingston. *LiWa*

Watching clouds. J. Farrar. *HuSv*

"When clouds appear." Mother Goose. *OpO*
    Signs, seasons, and sense. *UnG*

"White sheep, white sheep." Unknown. *ArTp*
    Clouds. *BrL-k—HuSv*

"The **clouds**." See Washday song

Clouds. See "White sheep, white sheep"

Clouds ("If I had a spoon") Dorothy Aldis. *AlA*

"**Clouds** on the mountain." See On a mountain road

Clough, Arthur Hugh
    Columbus. *CoPs*
    Keeping on. *NaM*
    Where lies the land. *SmLg*

Clover
    Clover for breakfast. F. M. Frost. *HuSv—JoAc*
    Four-leaf clover. E. Higginson. *BrR-6—FeF*
    I found. M. C. Livingston. *LiW*

Clover for breakfast. Frances M. Frost. *HuSv—JoAc*

The **clown**. Dorothy Aldis. *AlA*

Clowns. See also Circus
    The clown. D. Aldis. *AlA*
    The king and the clown. Unknown. *UnMc*

Club fist. Unknown. *TaD*

The **clucking** hen. Anne Hawkshawe. *HuL-1*

"The **coach** is at the door at last." See Farewell to the farm

Coaches. See Carriages and carts; Stagecoaches

The **coachman**. Mother Goose. *OpO*

Coal
    "Black we are, but much admired." Mother Goose. *DeMg*
    "Black I am and much admired." *OpO*
    Coal fire. L. Untermeyer. *UnG*

Coal fire. Louis Untermeyer. *UnG*

"**Coarse**." See Archie confesses

Coates, Florence Earle
    For joy. *BrL-7*

Coati-mundi. William Jay Smith. *SmB*

Coatsworth, Elizabeth Jane
    Advice from an elderly mouse. *CoM*
    April fool. *HaY*
    At the beginning of winter. *CoM*
    August smiles. *BrS*
    The bad kittens. *FeF*
    The barn. *BrBc—EaW—UnG*
    Candle and star. *BrBc*

Coatsworth, Elizabeth Jane—*Continued*
Ceremonial hunt. See The Painted desert
Christmas eve in the wainscoting. *CoM*
"Cold winter now is in the wood." *ArTp*
The complete hen. *UnG*
Conquistador. *UnG*
Counters. *PeF*
   To think. *HuL-2*
Country cat. *UnG*
Daniel Webster's horses. *CoPm*
Easter. *HaY*
Eerily sweet. *EaW*
Epitaph. *CoM*
Ever since. *BrS*
Field mouse conference. *CoM*
Field mouse to kitchen mouse. *CoM*
Footnote to history. *BrS*
"Hard from the southeast blows the wind." *ArTp*—*HuL-2*
"He who has never known hunger." *ArTp*
"A horse would tire." *ArTp*
"How gray the rain." *ArTp*
In Walpi. See The Painted desert
The isle should have a pine tree. *BrR-4*
January. See Snow
The kangaroo. *ArTp*—*HuSv*
The lady. *UnMc*
A lady comes to an inn. *ArTp*—*CoSp*
Lullaby. *BrS*—*CoM*
March. *HaY*
"The mice of Spain." *CoM*—*LoL*
The moon will give the prize. *CoM*
The mouse. *ArTp*—*CoI*—*CoM*—*FeF*—*JoAc*—*NaM*
Mouse chorus. *CoM*
Mouse midnight. *CoM*
The Navajo. See The Painted desert
Nosegay. See "Violets, daffodils"
November. *HaY*
Oak leaves. *HuSv*
On a night of snow. *NaM*—*UnG*
The Painted desert, sels. *JoAc*
   Ceremonial hunt
   In Walpi
   The Navajo
The Pleiades. *PlI*
The rabbits' song outside the tavern. *ArTp*
The sea gull. See "The sea gull curves his wings"
"The sea gull curves his wings." *ArTp*—*PeF*
   The sea gull. *HuL-1*
Sleigh bells at night. *BrS*
Snow. *BrR-6*—*BrS*
   January. *CoPs*
Song for a hot day. *HuSv*
Song for a little cuckoo clock. *BrS*
Song for midsummer night. *HaY*
Song of the engine bells. *BrR-5*
Song of the parrot. *HuSv*
Song of the ship's cat. *BrR-4*
Song to night. *McW*
Summer rain. See "What could be lovelier than to hear"
The sun is first to rise. *HuSv*
Sunday. *McW*
"Swift things are beautiful." *ArTp*—*HuL-2*—*HuSv*
The tempest. *HuL-2*
To a guardian mouse. *CoM*

To and fro. *CoM*
To think. See Counters
"Violets, daffodils." *ArTp*
   Nosegay. *McAw*
"The warm of heart shall never lack a fire." *ArTp*
The ways of trains. *ArTp*
"What could be lovelier than to hear." *BrS*
   Summer rain. *BrR-5*
"Who are you? asked the cat of the bear." *ArTp*
Who is so pretty. *CoM*
The wilderness is tamed. *BrR-5*—*FeF*—*HuSv*
Winter. *CoM*
Winter content. *CoM*
Wise Sarah and the elf. *CoPm*
Witches' song. *CoPm*
Woods' litany. *EaW*

"Cobalt and umber and ultramarine." See The paint box
The **cobbler** ("Crooked heels") Eleanor Alletta Chaffee. *ArTp*
The **cobbler** ("Wandering up and down one day") Unknown. *HuL-2*
Cobbler, cobbler." See "Cobbler, cobbler, mend my shoe"
"Cobbler, cobbler, mend my shoe." Mother Goose. *DeMg*—*LiL*
   Cobbler, cobbler. *OpO*

Coblentz, Catherine Cate
Our history. *FeF*

Cobwebs
Of a spider. W. Thorley. *FeF*
The spider's web. C. D. Cole. *HuL-1*
Spinners in the sun. E. Farjeon. *FaCb*—*FaN*
"There was an old woman tossed up in a basket." Mother Goose. *DeMg*—*HuSv*—*JoAc*—*LiL*
   An old woman. *OpO*
   The old woman in the basket. *ReG*
   Sweeping the sky. *HuL-1*
   There was an old woman. *NaE*

Cock-a-bandy. Mother Goose. *OpO*
"Cock-a-doodle-doo." Mother Goose. *DeMg*—*HuL-1*—*JoAc*—*LiL*—*OpO*
Cock and hen. Mother Goose. *OpO*
"The cock and the hen." Unknown. *JoAc*
The **cock** and the sun. J. P. B. *BrR-3*
"Cock, cock, cock, cock." See Cock and hen
Cock-crow. See "The cock's in the wood pile a-blowing his horn"
"The cock doth crow." Mother Goose. *ArTp*—*DeMg*—*LiL*—*OpO*
"The cock had first performed and roused the dogs." See Morning overture: Chorus of dogs
"The cock is crowing." See Written in March
Cock Robin. See "Who killed Cock Robin"
Cock Robin ("Cock Robin got up early") Mother Goose. *DeT*
   Cock Robin's courtship. *OpO*
"Cock Robin got up early." See Cock Robin
Cock Robin's courtship. See Cock Robin ("Cock Robin got up early")

"A **cock** saw the sun as he climbed up the east." See The cock and the sun

"**Cockleshells.**" Ivy O. Eastwick. *EaI*

Cockpit in the clouds. Dick Dorrance. *ArTp —FeF*

Cockroaches
    Archy a low brow. D. Marquis. *CoH*
    Certain maxims of Archy. D. Marquis. *CoH* (sel.)
        Archy, the cockroach, speaks. *FeF*
    The hen and the oriole. D. Marquis. *CoH —NaE*

Cocks. See Chickens

"The **cocks** are crowing." See Eerily sweet

"**Cocks** crow." See What they do

"**Cocks** crow in the morn." Mother Goose. *ArTp*
    Signs, seasons, and sense. *UnG*

"The **cock's** in the wood pile a-blowing his horn." Mother Goose. *DeMg*
    Cock-crow. *OpO*

"The **cock's** on the wood pile." See "The cock's in the wood pile a-blowing his horn"

Cocoon. David McCord. *McFf*

The **code.** Robert Frost. *FrR—UnMc*

Cody, William Frederick (about)
    Buffalo Bill. C. Sandburg. *SaW*
    "Buffalo Bill's defunct." E. E. Cummings. *GrCc*

A **coffeepot** face. Aileen Fisher. *BrL-k*

Coffin, Robert P. Tristram
    Alexander Graham Bell did not invent the telephone. *ArTp*
    America is corn. *McW*
    America was schoolmasters. *McW*
    Christening-day wishes for my God-child, Grace Lane Berkley II. *BrBc*
    The cripple. *HuSv*
    Little boys of Texas. *McW*
    The pheasant. *ArTp*
    The secret heart. *CoPs*
    The skunk. *ArTp—FeF*
    The spider. *PlI*
    The starfish. *PlI*
    Where I took hold of life. *BrBc*
    Yankee cradle. *NaE*
    The young calves. *ArTp—HuSv*

Cohen, J. M.
    "An arrow flying past." tr. *PaS*

Cohn, Myra. See Livingston, Myra Cohn

The **coin.** Sara Teasdale. *ArTp*

"**Cold** and raw the north wind doth blow." See Winter

Cold-blooded creatures. Elinor Wylie. *PlI*

"A **cold** coming we had of it." See Journey of the Magi

Cold house. Irene Carlisle. *BrL-7*

"**Cold** reigns the summer, and grey falls the day." See Poppies

"**Cold** winter now is in the wood." Elizabeth Jane Coatsworth. *ArTp*

Cole, Charlotte Druitt
    The spider's web. *HuL-1*
    The sugar man *HuL-1*

Coleridge, Mary
    "As I went singing over the earth." *PlU*
    The deserted house. *DeT—ReT*
    I saw a stable. *EaW*
    The train. *HuL-2*

Coleridge, Samuel Taylor
    The ancient mariner. See The rime of the ancient mariner
    Answer to a child's question. *ReT*
    The desired swan-song. See Swans sing
    The devil's thoughts. at. *CoPm*
    An epigram. *UnG*
    The fruit plucker. *DeT*
        In a moonlight wilderness. *SmLg*
    He prayeth best. See The rime of the ancient mariner
    He prayeth well. See The rime of the ancient mariner—He prayeth best
    Hunting song. *ReT*
    In a moonlight wilderness. See The fruit plucker
    The knight's tomb. *SmLg*
    Kubla Khan; or, A vision in a dream. *ReT —SmLg—UnMc*
    The nightingale. *DeT*
    The raven. *HoW*
    The rime of the ancient mariner, sels. *HaP* (complete)*—PlU* (sel.)*—SmLg* (complete)
        The ancient mariner. *DeT*
        He prayeth best. *DoP—FeF—HuSv— ThP*
            He prayeth well. *HuL-2*
        The rime of the ancient mariner. *UnG*
    Song. *CoPs—DeT*
    Swan song. See Swans sing
    Swans sing. *NaE*
        The desired swan-song. *PlU*
        Swan song. *UnG*

Coleridge, Sara
    A calendar. See "January brings the snow"
    The garden year. See "January brings the snow"
    "January brings the snow." *ArTp—DeMg*
        A calendar. *UnG*
        The garden year. *DeT—HuSv*
        The months of the year. *HuL-2*
    The months of the year. See "January brings the snow"

A **college** training. Joseph C. Lincoln. *CoH*

"A **collegiate** damsel named Breeze." Unknown
    Limericks since Lear. *UnG*

The **collies.** Edward Anthony. *UnG*

Collingwood, W. G. and Stefansson, Jon
    Song to Steingerd. tr. *PaS*

Colly, my cow. Unknown. *NaE*

Colman, George
    Sir Marmaduke. *UnG*

Color. See also names of colors, as Yellow
    Autumn color. T. Robinson. *HaY*
    Black and gold. N. B. Turner. *ArTp— BrR-6—HaY—HuL-2*
    "Blue is true." Unknown
        Signs, seasons, and sense. *UnG*

Color—*Continued*
Color in the wheat. H. Garland. *JoAc*
For color. R. Cheney. *BrR-5*
Homage to the philosopher. B. Deutsch. *PlI*
Variation on a sentence. L. Bogan. *PlI*
"What is pink? a rose is pink." C. G. Rossetti. *ArTp*
  Color. *HuL-1*

Color. See "What is pink? a rose is pink"

Color in the wheat. Hamlin Garland. *JoAc*

Colum, Padraic
An old woman of the roads. *FeF—HuL-2—HuSv*
The tin-whistle player. *PlU*
Tulips. *PlI*

Columbus, Christopher (about)
Christopher Columbus. R. C. and S. V. Benét. *PeF*
Columbus ("Behind him lay the gray Azores") J. Miller. *ArTp—BrL-8—FeF—HaY—HuSv—McW*
Columbus ("Columbus sailed over the ocean blue") L. F. Jackson. *BrS*
Columbus ("How in heaven's name did Columbus get over") A. H. Clough. *CoPs*
Columbus ("An Italian boy that liked to play") A. Wynne. *ArTp*
"Columbus sailed the ocean blue." Mother Goose. *OpO*
Dark-eyed lad Columbus. N. B. Turner. *BrS*
The discovery. J. C. Squire. *CoPs—McW*
  Sonnet. *FeF*
The great discovery. E. Farjeon. *CoPs—FaCb—FaN*
Light in the darkness. A. Fisher. *HaY*
Mysterious biography. C. Sandburg. *BrS*

Columbus ("Behind him lay the gray Azores") Joaquin Miller. *ArTp—BrL-8—FeF—HaY—HuSv—McW*

Columbus ("Columbus sailed over the ocean blue") Leroy F. Jackson. *BrS*

Columbus ("How in heaven's name did Columbus get over") Arthur Hugh Clough. *CoPs*

Columbus ("An Italian boy that liked to play") Annette Wynne. *ArTp*

"Columbus sailed over the ocean blue." See Columbus

"Columbus sailed the ocean blue." Mother Goose. *OpO*

"Come all ye river-drivers, if a tale you wish to hear." See How we logged Katahdin stream

"Come all you bold sailors that follow the lakes." See Red iron ore

"Come, all you brave gallants, and listen a while." See Robin Hood and the butcher

"Come, all you rounders, if you want to hear." See Casey Jones

"Come all you young ladies and make no delay." See Sweet blooming lavender

"Come and buy." See Lemonade stand

"Come, be my valentine." See Phillis inamorata

"**Come**, bring with a noise." See Ceremonies for Christmas

"**Come**, butter, come." Mother Goose. *DeMg—HuSv*
  Churning. *OpO*

"**Come**, cried Helen, eager Helen." See Sisters

"**Come** dance a jig." Mother Goose. *OpO*

"**Come**, dear children, let us away." See The forsaken merman

"**Come** down to the water." Eleanor Farjeon. *FaCb*

"**Come** forth, O beasts. This is the day." See Brothers and sisters

"**Come**, gentlemen all, and listen a while." See Robin Hood and the bishop of Hereford

"**Come** here, my boy; hould up your head." See The Irish schoolmaster

"**Come** hither, Evan Cameron." See The execution of Montrose

"**Come** hither, little puppy dog." Mother Goose. *DeMg*

Come in. Robert Frost. *FrR—FrY*

"**Come**, let us plant the apple tree." See The planting of the apple tree

"**Come**, let us sound with melody, the praises." Thomas Campion. *PlU*

"**Come**, let's to bed." Mother Goose. *DeMg—LiL*
  Bed time. *OpO*
  To bed. *DeT*

"**Come**, let's to bed, says Sleepy-head." See "Come, let's to bed"

"**Come** listen to me, you gallants so free." See Robin Hood and Alan a Dale

Come, little leaves. George Cooper. *FeF*

"**Come**, little leaves, said the wind one day." See Come, little leaves

"**Come** live with me and be my love." See The passionate shepherd to his love

"**Come** live with mee, and bee my love." See The bait

"**Come** Mamina." See Umamina

"**Come** on, let's dance, the gay wind cried." See The dance of the leaves

"**Come** on Smarty, guess my riddle." Unknown. *WoF*

"**Come** out o' door, 'tis spring, 'tis Mäy." See Mäy

Come out with me. A. A. Milne. *MiWc*

"**Come** out with me, cried the little red sled." See The little red sled

"**Come** play with me." See To a squirrel at Kyle-na-no

"**Come**, ride with me to Toyland." Rowena Bastin Bennett. *BrS*

"**Come**, said Old Shellover." See Old Shellover

"**Come** see the two-horned jigamaree." See P. T. Barnum

"**Come** sit aneath this pinetree, whose lofty tressèd crown." See Country music

"**Come**, take up your hats, and away let us haste." See The butterfly's ball

"**Come** the little clouds out of the ice-caves." See Indian songs—Rain chant

Continent's end. Robinson Jeffers. *PlI*

Contrary Mary. See "Mary, Mary, quite contrary"

Conundrums. See Riddles

"Conveniently near to where." See The gastronomic guile of Simple Simon

Conversation
Bores. A. Guiterman. *BrR-5*
Conversation. A. Robinson. *BrR-3—HuL-1*
Conversational. Unknown. *CoH*
Little Charlie Chipmunk. H. C. LeCron. *ArTp—BrR-3—FeF—PeF*
A time to talk. R. Frost. *FrR—FrY*
The two old women of Mumbling hill. J. Reeves. *ReW*
"Whispers." M. C. Livingston. *LiW*
You'd say it was a funeral. J. Reeves. *ReW*
"You'd say it was a wedding." J. Reeves. *ReW*

Conversation ("I called to gray squirrel, Good-day, good-day") Anne Robinson. *BrR-3—HuL-1*

Conversation ("Mother, may I stay up to-night") David McCord. *McFf*

Conversation ("Mousie, mousie") Rose Fyleman. *HuL-1*

A conversation ("O dandelion, yellow as gold") See The dandelion

Conversation between Mr and Mrs Santa Claus. Rowena Bastin Bennett. *ArTp—BrS*

Conversation in the mountains. Li T'ai-po, tr. fr. the Chinese. *PaS*

Conversation with an April fool. Rowena Bastin Bennett. *BrS*

Conversational. Unknown. *CoH*

Converse, Florence
Rune of riches. *HuL-2*

Coo. See "The dove says, Coo, coo, what shall I do"

Cooke, Edmund Vance
How did you die. *ThP*
The moo-cow-moo. *NaM*

Cookery. Marchette Chute. *ChA*

Cookies. See Cakes and cookies

Cooking. Myra Cohn Livingston. *LiW*

Cooks and cooking. See also Food and eating; also names of foods, as Cakes and cookies
A bachelor of Maine. E. D. Deland. *CoH*
"Betty Botter bought some butter." Mother Goose. *JoAc—OpO*
"Betty Baker bought some butter." *WoF*
Betty Barter. *WiRm*
The Christmas pudding. Unknown. *ArTp—HuL-1*
Cookery. M. Chute. *ChA*
Cooking. M. C. Livingston. *LiW*
Goody O'Grumpity. C. R. Brink. *FeF*
His mother's cooking. L. M. Hadley. *BrR-5*
Lickety-lick. M. Justus. *McAw*
"Mary make the butter." I. O. Eastwick. *EaI*

"Mix a pancake." C. G. Rossetti. *BrL-k—HuL-1*
"O, dear, O." Unknown. *DeT*
The pirate cook. M. Chute. *BrR-6—ChA*
Some cook. J. Ciardi. *CiM*
Stirring the pudding. E. Farjeon. *FaN*
Strawberry jam. M. Justus. *FeF*
Three cooks. Mother Goose. *OpO*
The toaster. W. J. Smith. *ArTp—CoH—SmL*
What Molly Blye said. D. McCord. *McT*
"Whoo. Whoo. Who cooks for you-all." Unknown. *WoF*

A cool drink on a hot day. John Ciardi. *CiY*

"Cool waters tumble, singing as they go." See A garden

Coolidge, Dane and Mary Roberts
The war god's horse song. tr. *SmLg*

Coolidge, Mary Roberts. See Coolidge, Dane and Mary Roberts

Coolidge, Susan, pseud. (Sarah Chauncy Woolsey)
The better way. *BrR-5*
A child's thought of harvest. *CoPs*
Time to go. *DoP*

Coolness. Onitsura, tr. fr. the Japanese by Harold G. Henderson. *PaS*

Coonley, Lydia Avery. See Ward, Lydia Avery Coonley

Coons. See Raccoons

"De coon's got a long ringed bushy tail." See Tails

Cooper, Anne
The tragedy. *BrL-k*

Cooper, George
Baby-land. *HuL-1*
Bob White. *UnG*
Come, little leaves. *FeF*
Frogs at school. *CoI*
October's party. *BrS*
Only one mother. *BrS—FeF*
What robin told. *ArTp—BrL-k—BrR-3—FeF*

Cooperation. See also Brotherhood
The tuft of flowers. R. Frost. *FrR—FrY*

Coplen, Grace Wilson
Fireflies. *BrL-k*

Coppard, Alfred Edgar
Forester's song . *FeF*

Copper song. Ethel Talbot Scheffauer. *CoPm*

Coral
The coral grove. J. G. Percival. *UnG*
The coral grove. James Gates Percival. *UnG*

Corbet, Richard
The fairies' farewell. See Farewell to the fairies
Farewell to the fairies. *NaE*
The fairies' farewell. *SmLg*
To his son, Vincent Corbet. *SmLg*

Corinna. See "When to her lute Corinna sings"

Corinthians I. See First epistle of Paul to the Corinthians

Corn. Lalia Mitchell Thornton. *BrL-7*

Corn and cornfields
America is corn. R. P. T. Coffin. *McW*
Corn. L. M. Thornton. *BrL-7*
Cornhuskers. C. Sandburg. *SaW*

John Barleycorn. R. Burns. *SmLg*
Korosta katzina song. Unknown. *PaS*
The last corn shock. D. W. Dresbach. *FeF*
New corn. T'ao Ch'ien. *PaS*
A pop corn song. N. B. Turner. *BrL-k—*
FeF—HuL-1
Ripe corn. C. Sandburg. *SaW*
Cornelius, Carl August Peter
The Christmas tree. *EaW*
The **corner**. Walter De La Mare. *BrBc*
Corner-of-the-street. A. A. Milne. *MiWc*
Cornfield ridge and stream. Carl Sandburg.
SaW
Cornfields. See Corn and cornfields
Cornford, Frances
At night. *CoI*
For M.S. singing Frühlingsglaube in 1945.
PlU
For Nijinsky's tomb. *PlU*
Pre-existence. *McW*
The princess and the gypsies. *CoSp—HuL-2*
Village before sunset. *SmLg*
Cornhuskers. Carl Sandburg. *SaW*
Cornish, William
Rutterkin. *CoPm*
Cornish magic. Ann Durell. *FeF*
Coronach. See The lady of the lake
A **correct** compassion. James Kirkup. *PlI*
Cortez, Hernando (about)
La noche triste. R. Frost. *FrR*
**Cory, William (Johnson) (William John-
son-Cory)**
Heraclitus. tr. *PaS*
Cotterell, Mabel
Moon-night. tr. *PaS*
"O woodland cool." tr. *PaS*
Cotton, Charles
Evening. *HoW*
Cottonwood leaves. Badger Clark. *ArTp*
"**Could** I take me to some cavern for mine
hiding." See Hippolytus—O for the
wings of a dove
Could it have been a shadow. Monica
Shannon. *ArTp—FeF—HuSv*
"**Could** we but see men as they are." See
A window in the breast
"**Could** you tell me the way to somewhere."
See Somewhere
Counselman, Mary Elizabeth
Gift with the wrappings off. *BrL-7*
"**Count** Hubert hunted in Ardennes." See
Saint Hubert
Count that day lost. George Eliot. *ThP*
"**Count** that day lost." Unknown. *MoY*
Counters. Elizabeth Jane Coatsworth. *PeF*
To think. *HuL-2*
Counting
"Five little chickadees, sitting in a door."
Unknown. *WoF*
Ten brothers. Unknown. *UnMc*
Ten little nigger boys. Mother Goose.
OpO
Ten to one. I. O. Eastwick. *EaI*
Counting. Harry Behn. *BeW*
The **counting** man. William Vaughn Moody.
CoPm

Counting-out rhyme. Edna St Vincent
Millay. *NaE*
Counting-out rhyme for March. Frances
M. Frost. *HaY*
Counting-out rhymes
"Ah, ra, chickera." Mother Goose. *OpO*
"Ala, mala, mink, monk." Mother Goose.
OpO
Buzz, buzz, buzz. Unknown. *TaD*
"Come to dinner, little sinner." Unknown.
WiRm
The counting man. W. V. Moody. *CoPm*
Counting-out rhyme. E. St V. Millay. *NaM*
Counting-out rhyme for March. F. M.
Frost. *HaY*
"Eenie, meenie, mackeracka." Mother
Goose. *OpO*
"Eenie, meenie, minie, mo." Unknown.
WiRm
Counting-out rhymes. *FeF*
"Eenity, feenity, fickety, feg." Mother
Goose. *OpO*
"Eeny, weeny, winey, wo." Mother Goose.
OpO
"Engine, engine, number nine." Unknown.
WiRm—WoF
Engine, engine. *TaD—WoJ*
"Fireman, fireman." Unknown. *TaD*
"Fireman, fireman, number eight." *WoF*
"Hickety, pickety, i-silicity." Mother
Goose. *OpO*
"Hickety, pickety, my black hen." Mother
Goose. *AnI—DeMg—JoAc—LiL*
"Higgledy, piggledy, my black hen."
ArTp—HuSv
My black hen. *OpO*
"Hinty, minty, cuty, corn." Unknown
Counting-out rhymes. *FeF*
"Hinx, minx, the old witch winks."
Mother Goose. *DeMg*
Hinx, minx. *OpO*
Hokey pokey. Unknown. *TaD*
Ibbity, bibbity, sibbity. Unknown. *TaD*
"Ibbity-bibbity sibbity sab." Unknown.
WiRm
"Inter, mitzy, titzy, tool." Mother Goose.
OpO
"Intery, mintery, cutery, corn." Mother
Goose. *ArTp—DeMg—JoAc—OpO*
A counting-out rhyme. *DeT*
"Intry, mintry, cutry, corn." *HuSv*
"Mena, deena, deina, duss." Mother
Goose. *LiL*
"Monkey, monkey, bottle of beer." Un-
known. *WiRm—WoF*
"One potato, two potato." Unknown
Counting-out rhymes. *FeF*
"One, two, buckle my shoe." Mother
Goose. *BrL-k—DeMg—HuL-1—LiL—OpO*
"One, two." *ArTp—DeT—HuSv—
JoAc*
Signs, seasons, and sense. *UnG*
"One, two, policeman blue." Unknown,
tr. fr. the German. *JoAc*
"One, two, three, four (Mary at)."
Mother Goose. *LiL—OpO—TaD*
"One, two, three, four, five (I caught a
fish alive)." Mother Goose. *HuL-1—
LiL—OpO—WoF*

Cowboys—Songs
   Cowboy song. C. Causley. *HaP*
   The cowboy's dream. Unknown. *UnMc*
   The cowboy's lament. Unknown. *McW— UnMc*
   The cowboy's life. Unknown. *ArTp*
   Cowboy's meditation. Unknown. *BrR-5*
   Whoopee ti yi yo, git along, little dogies. Unknown. *ArTp—FeF—McW*
      Git along, little dogies. *HuSv—NaM*
      Whoopee ti yi yo. *BrR-5*
   The Zebra Dun. Unknown. *CoSp—HuSv*
The **cowboy's** dream. Unknown. *UnMc*
The **cowboy's** lament. Unknown. *McW— UnMc*
The **cowboy's** life. Unknown, attributed to James Barton Adams. *ArTp*
Cowboy's meditation. Unknown. *BrR-5*
Cowley, Abraham
   Anacreontics, sel.
      The thirsty earth. *HoW*
         Drinking. *HaP*
   Drinking. See Anacreontics—The thirsty earth
   The grasshopper. tr. *HoW—UnG*
   The thirsty earth. See Anacreontics
Cowley, Malcolm
   The long voyage. *McW*
Cowper, William
   The castaway. *HaP*
   Light shining out of darkness. *SmLg*
   The nightingale and the glowworm. *UnG*
   The poplar field. *DeT—HaP—HoW*
   The snail. tr. *McW—UnG*
   The squirrel. *UnG*
   The woodman's dog. *DeT*
Cows
   Buttercup Cow. E. Rendall. *ArTp*
   "Charlie Warlie had a cow." Mother Goose. *DeMg*
      Charley Warlie. *OpO*
   Colly, my cow. Unknown. *NaE*
   Cow ("Cows are not supposed to fly") W. J. Smith. *SmB*
   The cow ("The friendly cow all red and white") R. L. Stevenson. *ArTp—FeF— HuSv*
   The cow in apple time. R. Frost. *FrR— FrY*
   Cow time. M. Shannon. *BrS*
   Cows. J. Reeves. *CoPs—ReBl*
   "Cushy cow, bonny, let down thy milk." Mother Goose. *DeMg—HuSv—JoAc*
      Milking. *OpO*
   "Did you feed my cow." Unknown. *TaD*
   The five toes. Unknown. *JoAc*
   "Four stiff-standers." Mother Goose. *DeMg —LiL—OpO*
   Green grass and white milk. W. Welles. *ArTp*
   Hey diddle. M. C. Livingston. *LiW*
   "I had a little cow, I milked her in a gourd." Unknown. *WoF*
   "I stare at the cow." P. C. Boyden. *CoI*
   The invaders. A. A. Milne. *MiWc*
   Jonathan. Unknown. *ArTp—JoAc*
   "Milk-white moon, put the cows to sleep." C. Sandburg. *FeF—HuSv*

   Milking time. E. M. Roberts. *BrL-k—FeF*
   The moo-cow-moo. E. V. Cooke. *NaM*
   My little cow. Mother Goose. *OpO*
   The new baby calf. E. H. Newlin. *ArTp —BrL-k*
   Old cow. Unknown. *TaD*
   "Old Sam Brodie lost his cow." Unknown. *WoF*
   The old woman's three cows. Mother Goose. *OpO*
   Pretty cow. A. Taylor. *HuSv*
   The purple cow. G. Burgess. *ArTp—CoH —FeF*
      "I never saw a purple cow." *LoL*
   The robin and the cows. W. D. Howells. *UnG*
   Summer afternoon. A. A. Milne. *MiWc*
   "There was a piper had a cow." Mother Goose. *DeMg*
      The piper. *OpO*
   "There was an old man who said, How." E. Lear
      Limericks. *NaE*
      Nonsense verses. *HuSv*
Cows. James Reeves. *CoPs—ReBl*
"**Cows** are not supposed to fly." See Cow
"The **cows** low in the pasture on the hill." See The song of the robin
Cox, Kenyon
   The bumblebeaver. See Mixed beasts
   The kangarooster. See Mixed beasts
   Mixed beasts, sels.
      The bumblebeaver. *ArTp*
      The kangarooster. *ArTp*
      The octopussycat. *ArTp—FeF*
   The octopussycat. See Mixed beasts
Crab-apple. Ethel Talbot. *ArTp—BrBc*
Crab-apples
   Crabapples. C. Sandburg. *SaW*
Crabapples. Carl Sandburg. *SaW*
Crabbe, George
   The village. *HaP*
Crabs
   Cancer. E. Farjeon. *FaCb—FaN*
   Old Chang the crab. Unknown. *JoAc*
Crackers. See Cakes and cookies
Cradle hymn ("Away in a manger, no crib for a bed") Martin Luther. *ArTp— BrBc — DoP — EaW — FeF — HuL-1 —HuSv—JoAc—McAw—UnG*
Cradle hymn ("Hush, my dear, lie still and slumber") Isaac Watts. *DoP*
Cradle song ("From groves of spice") Sarojini Naidu. *FeF*
Cradle song ("Hushaba, birdie, croon, croon") Unknown. *HuL-2*
Cradle song ("Lullaby, my little one") Carl Michael Bellman. *FeF*
Cradle song ("O Timothy Tim") A. A. Milne. *MiWc*
Cradle song ("Sleep, sleep, beauty bright") William Blake. *JoAc*
A **cradle** song ("Sweet and low, sweet and low") See Sweet and low
Cradle song of the elephants. Adriano Del Valle, tr. fr. the Portuguese by Alida Malkus. *FeF*
Cradle songs. See Lullabies

The **crafty** farmer. Unknown. *ArTp*

Craigmyle, Elizabeth
Sir Olaf. tr. *CoPm*

Craik, Dinah Maria. See Mulock, Dinah Maria

Cranch, Christopher Pearse
The birds and the telephone wires. *BrR-5*

Crane, Hart
Garden abstract. *GrCc*
In shadow. *GrCc*
To Potapovitch. *PlU*

Crane, Nathalia, pseud. (Clara Ruth Abarbanel)
Destiny. *UnG*
The first story. *BrR-5*
The janitor's boy. *UnG*
Standards. *UnG*

Crane, Stephen
"I saw a man pursuing the horizon." *SmLg*
"A man said to the universe." *PlI*
"A man saw a ball of gold in the sky." *NaE*
"The wayfarer." *McW*

Cranes (Birds)
The cranes. Po Chü-i. *PaS*
The crow and the crane. Unknown. *MaB*
"My dame hath a lame tame crane." Mother Goose. *OpO*
The sandhill crane. M. Austin. *ArTp—BrR-5—HuL-2*
The cranes. Po Chü-i, tr. fr. the Chinese by Arthur Waley. *PaS*

Cranmer-byng, L. (Lancelot)
The little rain. tr. *FeF*

Crapsey, Adelaide
November night. *FeF*

The **crawdad** hole. Unknown. *TaD*

The **crayfish.** Robert Wallace. *McW*

Crayons. Christopher Morley. *DoP*

"**Created** by the poets to sing my song." See The reaper

Creation
Crayons. C. Morley. *DoP*
The creation ("All things bright and beautiful") C. F. Alexander. *DoP—FeF*
All things beautiful. *BrR-3*
"All things bright and beautiful." *HuSv*
God, our maker. *DeT*
The creation ("And God stepped out on space") J. W. Johnson. *ArTp—JoAc*
Genesis, Chapter 1. From Genesis, Bible, Old Testament. *PlI*
God's first creature was light. W. Welles. *PlI*
Job, Chapter 38. From Job, Bible, Old Testament *PlI*
Praise of created things. From The mirror of perfection. Saint Francis of Assisi. *FeF*
The song of the creatures. *PaS*
"The spacious firmament on high." J. Addison. *BrL-7*
Spell of creation. K. Raine. *McW—SmLg*
The wife of Llew. F. Ledwidge. *CoPm*

The **creation** ("All things bright and beautiful") Cecil Frances Alexander. *DoP—FeF*
All things beautiful. *BrR-3*
"All things bright and beautiful." *HuSv*
God, our maker. *DeT*
The **creation** ("And God stepped out on space") James Weldon Johnson. *ArTp—JoAc*

Creeds
A patriotic creed. E. A. Guest. *BrR-5*
School creed. Unknown. *HuL-2*

"**Creep** into thy narrow bed." See The last word

The **cremation** of Sam McGee. Robert W. Service. *CoSp—UnMc*

The **crescent** boat. See Peter Bell

Crescent moon. Elizabeth Madox Roberts. *ArTp—BrL-k—McAw*

Crew, Helen Coale
Bedtime. *BrR-3*

The **crib.** Christopher Morley. *BrBc*

Crickets
The ant and the cricket. Aesop. *DeT—UnG*
The chirrupy cricket. M. B. Thomas. *BrR-5*
Crickets ("Crickets all busy punching tickets") D. McCord. *McT*
Crickets ("What makes the crickets crick all night") H. Wing. *BrL-k*
Crickets and mice. J. J. Keith. *HuSv*
On the grasshopper and cricket. L. Hunt. *UnG*
The poetry of earth. J. Keats. *HoW*
On the grasshopper and cricket. *JoAc—UnG*
Singing. D. Aldis. *AlA*
Splinter. C. Sandburg. *ArTp—FeF*
Spring cricket. F. Rodman. *BrS—FeF*

Crickets ("Crickets all busy punching tickets") David McCord. *McT*

Crickets ("What makes the crickets crick all night") Helen Wing. *BrL-k*

"**Crickets** all busy punching tickets." See Crickets

Crickets and mice. Joseph Joel Keith. *HuSv*

"**Crickets** are making." See September is here

The **cries** of Bethlehem. Eleanor Farjeon. *FaN*

Crime and criminals
The demon of the gibbet. F. J. O'Brien. *CoPm*
The dream of Eugene Aram. T. Hood. *CoSp*
The highwayman's ghost. R. Garnett. *CoSp*
The highwaymen. J. Gay. *HoW*
Macavity: The mystery cat. T. S. Eliot. *McW*
Noonday Sun. K. and B. Jackson. *ArTp—FeF—HuL-2*
Tim Turpin. T. Hood. *HoW*

The **cripple.** Robert P. Tristram Coffin. *HuSv*

Cripple creek. Unknown. *ReG*

"**Cripple** Dick upon a stick." Mother Goose. *OpO*

Cripples
   One, two, three. H. C. Bunner. *FeF*
   The cripple. R. P. T. Coffin. *HuSv*
Crisscross. Carl Sandburg. *SaW*
Criticism. See Critics and criticism
Critics and criticism
   The owl-critic. J. T. Fields. *CoSp—NaE
   —UnG*
The crocodile. See Alice's adventures in
   wonderland—"How doth the little croc-
   odile"
The crocodile ("Crocodile once dropped a
   line") Oliver Herford. *CoH*
Crocodile ("The crocodile wept bitter tears")
   William Jay Smith. *SmB*
"Crocodile once dropped a line." See The
   crocodile
"The crocodile wept bitter tears." See Croc-
   odile
Crocodiles
   The crocodile ("Crocodile once dropped a
   line") O. Herford. *CoH*
   Crocodile ("The crocodile wept bitter
   tears") W. J. Smith. *SmB*
   "How doth the little crocodile." From
   Alice's adventures in wonderland. L.
   Carroll. *ArTp—FeF—LoL—McW—NaM
   —SmLg*
      The crocodile. *JoAc—UnG*
   The monkeys and the crocodile. L. E.
   Richards. *ArTp—BrR-4—FeF—HuL-1—
   JoAc—PeF*
   The purist. O. Nash. *CoH—NaM*
"Crocus for Saint Valentine." See Fair maid
   of February
"The crocus, while the days are dark." See
   The year
Crocuses
   Crocuses. Jōsa. *ArTp*
   The lazy crocuses. D. Aldis. *AlA*
   Saffron Walden. E. Farjeon. *FaN*
Crocuses. Jōsa. *ArTp*
The croodin doo. Mother Goose. *OpO*
"Crooked as a rainbow." Unknown. *WiRm*
"Crooked heels." See The cobbler
The crooked man. See "There was a
   crooked man"
"A crop of suns has sprung up overnight."
   See Dandelion morning
Croquet
   The time we like best. D. Aldis. *AlA*
Cross, Marian Evans Lewes. See Eliot,
   George, pseud.
Cross, Zora
   When I was six. *BrBc—FeF*
"Cross-patch." Mother Goose. *DeMg—JoAc
   —LiL—NaE—OpO*
Crossing the bar. Alfred Tennyson. *BrL-8
   —ThP*
Crossing the plains. Joaquin Miller. *GrCc*
Crossing the river. Unknown, tr. fr. the
   Chinese by Arthur Waley. *PaS*
"Crossing the river I pluck hibiscus-flowers."
   See Crossing the river
Crossland, Mrs Newton
   Rover and the bird. *DeT*
Crotchet castle, sel. Thomas Love Peacock
   The priest and the mulberry tree. *CoSp—
   DeT*

Crouch, Pearl Riggs
   A story in the snow. *ArTp—BrR-3*
The crow. William Canton. *UnG*
The crow and the crane. Unknown. *MaB*
The crow and the fox. Jean De La Fon-
   taine, tr. fr. the French by Edward
   Marsh. *BrL-7—UnMc*
"The crow sat black." See First autumn
"A crow sat perched upon an oak." See The
   crow and the fox
Crowell, Grace Noll
   "The day will bring some lovely thing."
   ArTp
Crows
   Bores. A. Guiterman. *BrR-5*
   "A carrion crow sat on an oak." Mother
   Goose. *DeMg—JoAc—LiL*
      The carrion crow. *OpO*
      The tailor and the crow. *ReG*
   The crow. W. Canton. *UnG*
   The crow and the crane. Unknown. *MaB*
   The crow and the fox. J. De La Fontaine.
   BrL-7—UnMc
   Crows. D. McCord. *ArTp—McFf*
   Dust of snow. R. Frost. *ArTp—FrR—FrY
   —NaM—ThP*
   First autumn. F. M. Frost. *FrLn*
   Fox and crow. W. J. Smith. *SmB*
   The frog and the crow. Unknown. *ReG*
   I met a crow. J. Ciardi. *CiI*
   I sometimes think. Unknown. *UnG*
      To be or not to be. *CoH—NaM*
   Johnny Crow's garden. L. L. Brooke. *ReG*
   Many crows, any owl. D. McCord. *McT*
   North. F. M. Frost. *FrLn*
   "Old Adam, the carrion crow." T. L.
   Beddoes. *CoPm*
      The carrion crow. *HoW*
   "On the first of March." Mother Goose.
   OpO
   Short song. Mother Goose. *OpO*
Crows. David McCord. *ArTp—McFf*
Crucifixion. See Easter; Jesus Christ
"The crumbs from our breakfast let's scatter
   abroad." See Rover and the bird
Crusades
   Choruses from The rock. T. S. Eliot.
   GrCc
"Cry, baby, cry (put your)." Mother Goose.
   DeMg
"Cry-baby, cry (wipe your)." Unknown
   American Father Gander. *UnG*
Crying
   Crocodile. W. J. Smith. *SmB*
   "Cry, baby, cry (put your)." Mother
   Goose. *DeMg*
   "Cry-baby, cry (wipe your)." Unknown
   American Father Gander. *UnG*
   The jokesmith's vacation. D. Marquis.
   CoH
   The man in the onion bed. J. Ciardi. *CiI*
The crystal cabinet. William Blake. *GrCc—
   SmLg*
The cuckoo. See "The cuckoo is a merry
   bird"
"Cuckoo, cherry tree." Mother Goose.
   DeMg—OpO
The cuckoo-clock shop. Rachel Field. *HuL-2*

Cuckoo-come-again. Eleanor Farjeon. *FaCb*

The cuckoo comes. Eleanor Farjeon. *FaCb—FaN*

"The cuckoo comes in April." Mother Goose. *OpO*

"Cuck-oo, cuck-oo." Unknown
Three cuckoo rhymes. *DeT*

"Cuckoo, cuckoo, what do you do." Mother Goose. *LiL*
To the cuckoo. *OpO*

"The cuckoo he's a fine bird." See "The cuckoo is a merry bird"

"The cuckoo is a merry bird." Mother Goose. *DeMg*
The cuckoo. *OpO*
Three cuckoo rhymes. *DeT*

Cuckoo-shoes. Eleanor Farjeon. *FaCb*

"Cuckoo-shoes aren't cuckoos' shoes." See Cuckoo-shoes

Cuckoos
Cuckoo-come-again. E. Farjeon. *FaCb*
The cuckoo comes. E. Farjeon. *FaCb—FaN*
"The cuckoo comes in April." Mother Goose. *OpO*
"Cuck-oo, cuck-oo." Unknown
Three cuckoo rhymes. *DeT*
"Cuckoo, cuckoo, what do you do." Mother Goose. *LiL*
To the cuckoo. *OpO*
"The cuckoo is a merry bird." Mother Goose. *DeMg*
The cuckoo. *OpO*
Three cuckoo rhymes. *DeT*
Cuckoo-shoes. E. Farjeon. *FaCb*
"Far in dark woods away." Unknown
Three cuckoo rhymes. *DeT*
The missing cuckoo. E. V. Rieu. *RiF*
To the cuckoo. W. Wordsworth. *UnG*

Culbertson, Anne V.
He understood. *BrL-8*

Cullen, Countee
Incident. *JoAc*
The unknown color. *FeF*
The wakeupworld. *JoAc*

The culprit fay, sels. Joseph Rodman Drake
Elfin song. *CoPm*
A fairy in armor. *FeF*

Cummings, Alison Elizabeth
To a little sister, aged ten. *BrBc*

Cummings, E. (Edward) E. (Erstlin)
"All in green went my love riding." *ReT*
"Anyone lived in a pretty how town." *HaP—NaE*
"Buffalo Bill's defunct." *GrCc*
"The Cambridge ladies who live in furnished souls." *HaP*
Chanson innocente, sels.
In just spring. *CoH—JoAc*
Chanson innocente. *FeF—NaM*
"In just." *UnG*
"Little tree"
Chanson innocente. *CoPs*
"Doll's boy's asleep." *GrCc*
"In just." See Chanson innocente—In just spring
In just spring. See Chanson innocente
"Lady will you come with me into." *ReT*
"Little tree." See Chanson innocente

"Now, more near ourselves than we." *GrCc*
Poem. *CoPs*
"Who knows if the moon's." *CoPm*

Cunningham, Allan
Hame, hame, hame. *DeT*
A sea song. See "A wet sheet and a flowing sea"
"A wet sheet and a flowing sea." *ArTp—BrL-8—McW*
A sea song. *JoAc*

Cunningham, J. V.
August hail. *HaP*
For my contemporaries. *HaP*

"Cup of warm milk, Baby Jesus." See Birthday presents

"Cup, what's up." See Food and drink

The cupboard. Walter De La Mare. *ArTp—BrL-k—FeF—HuL-1*

Cupboards
The cupboard. W. De La Mare. *ArTp—BrL-k—FeF—HuL-1*
"Old Mother Hubbard." Mother Goose. *AnI—DeMg—HuSv—JoAc—LiL—UnG*
Old Mother Hubbard and her dog. *OpO*
"What's in the cupboard." Mother Goose. *JoAc—OpO*

Cupid
The vow to Cupid. Unknown. *PaS*

"Curbstones are to balance on." See What they are for

Curfew. See Bells

Curfew. Henry Wadsworth Longfellow. *McW* (sel.)

Curfew must not ring tonight. Rosa Hartwick Thorpe. *FeF*

"The curfew tolls the knell of parting day." See Elegy written in a country churchyard

Curiosity. Harry Behn. *BeW*

"Curious, curious Tiggady Rue." See Tiggady Rue

Curious something. Winifred Welles. *ArTp*

"Curly Locks, Curly Locks." Mother Goose. *DeMg—JoAc—OpO*
"Curly Locks, Curly Locks, wilt thou be mine." *LiL*

A curse on the cat. John Skelton. *NaE*

Curtis, Natalie
Korosta katzina song. tr. *PaS*

"Curves of sand." See The sea shore

Cushing, Frank
The locust. tr. *FeF*

"Cushy cow, bonny, let down thy milk." Mother Goose. *DeMg—HuSv—JoAc*
Milking. *OpO*

"Cut them on Monday, you cut them for health." See Finger nails

"Cut thistles in May." Mother Goose. *OpO*

Cutler, Charlotte Yoder
Hallowe'en scare. *McAw*

The cutty wren. Unknown. *HoW*

Cycle. Langston Hughes. *FeF*

Cymbeline, sels. William Shakespeare
Fear no more. *DeT—HaP*
Fidele's dirge. *SmLg*
Hark, hark the lark. *FeF*
"Hark, hark, the lark at heaven's gate sings." *SmLg*
A morning song. *JoAc*

Cynthia in the snow. Gwendolyn Brooks. *ArTp*
Cynthia's revels, sel. Ben Jonson
    Hymn to Diana. *HoW*

D

D. D. W. See W., D. D.
D. F. See F., D.
D., H., pseud. (Hilda Doolittle; Mrs Richard Aldington)
    A song from Cyprus. *GrCc*
    Stars wheel in purple. *GrCc*
    Storm. *ArTp*
D is for dragon. Eleanor Farjeon. *FaCb*
Da boy from Rome. T. A. Daly. *FeF*
Dabbling in the dew. Unknown. *HuL-2*
The dachshund. Edward Anthony. *UnG*
Daddy. Rose Fyleman. *BrS*
"Daddy bought a rat trap." Unknown. *WiRm*
Daddy fell into the pond. Alfred Noyes. *CoH—FeF*
"Daddy fixed the breakfast." See Mummy slept late and daddy fixed breakfast
"Daffadowndilly." Mother Goose. *ArTp*
    "Daffy-down-dilly has come up to town." *DeMg*
    "Daffy-down-dilly is new come to town." *OpO*
Daffodils
    "Daffadowndilly." Mother Goose. *ArTp*
    "Daffy-down-dilly has come up to town." *DeMg*
    "Daffy-down-dilly is new come to town." *OpO*
    "Daffodils." From The winter's tale. W. Shakespeare. *ArTp*
    Daffodils ("I wandered lonely as a cloud") W. Wordsworth. *BrL-8—FeF—HaP—HuSv—JoAc—UnG*
        "I wandered lonely as a cloud." *ReT*
    Daffodils ("In spite of cold and chills") Kikuriō. *ArTp*
    Daffodowndilly. A. A. Milne. *MiWc*
    "Growing in the vale." C. G. Rossetti. *ArTp*
    Hello. L. A. Garnett. *BrS*
    "I saw green banks of daffodil." E. W. Tennant. *ArTp*
    The Lent lily. From A Shropshire lad. A. E. Housman. *CoPs*
    To daffodils. R. Herrick. *JoAc—NaE*
"Daffodils." See The winter's tale
Daffodils ("I wandered lonely as a cloud") William Wordsworth. *BrL-8 — FeF — HaP—HuSv—JoAc—UnG*
    "I wandered lonely as a cloud." *ReT*
Daffodils ("In spite of cold and chills") Kikuriō. *ArTp*
Daffodowndilly. A. A. Milne. *MiWc*
"Daffy-down-dilly has come up to town." See "Daffadowndilly"
"Daffy-down-dilly is new come to town." See "Daffadowndilly"
Dafydd Ap Gwilym
    A snowy day. *PaS*

Dahlias
    "A maiden caught stealing a dahlia." Unknown. *CoH*
Dainty, Evelyn
    The birds on the school windowsill. *HuL-1*
Dainty little maiden. Alfred Tennyson. *HuL-2*
"Dainty little maiden, whither would you wander." See Dainty little maiden
The dairymaid and her milk-pot. Jean De La Fontaine, tr. fr. the French by Marianne Moore. *JoAc*
Daisies
    Daisies. F. D. Sherman. *BrR-3—HuL-1*
    The stars, the dark, and the daisies. I. O. Eastwick. *EaI*
    With a daisy. E. Dickinson. *PlI*
Daisies. Frank Dempster Sherman. *BrR-3—HuL-1*
Dalmon, Charles
    Ballad of the Epiphany. *EaW*
Daly, June
    The wildebeest. *FeF*
Daly, T. (Thomas) A. (Augustine)
    A child's Christmas song. *BrBc*
    Da boy from Rome. *FeF*
    Leetla Giorgio Washeenton. *CoPs—FeF*
    Mia Carlotta. *BrL-7*
"Dame, dame, the watch is set." See The witches' charms
Dame get up. See "Dame, get up and bake your pies"
"Dame, get up and bake your pies." Mother Goose. *DeMg—JoAc*
    Dame get up. *HuL-1*
    On Christmas day. *OpO*
The dame of Dundee. Mother Goose. *OpO*
Dame Trot. See "Dame Trot and her cat"
"Dame Trot and her cat." Mother Goose. *DeMg—HuL-1*
    Dame Trot. *OpO*
Dan Dunder. John Ciardi. *CiY*
"Dan Dunder is a blunder." See Dan Dunder
Dana, Katherine Floyd. See Wadsworth, Olive A., pseud.
Dance. See "Dance, Thumbkin, dance"
The dance ("In Breughel's great picture, The Kermess") William Carlos Williams. *SmLg*
The dance ("Robin is a lovely lad") Thomas Campion. *SmLg*
"Dance a baby diddy." Mother Goose. *OpO*
"Dance, little baby, dance up high." Mother Goose. *DeMg—OpO*
The dance of the leaves. Isla Paschal Richardson. *BrR-3*
Dance song. Unknown, tr. fr. the Chinese by Arthur Waley. *SmLg*
"Dance, Thumbkin, dance." Mother Goose. *DeMg—LiL—OpO*
    Dance. *DeT*
"Dance to the beat of the rain, little fern." See Fern song
"Dance to your daddie." See "Dance to your daddy"

"Dance to your daddy." Mother Goose. *DeMg—JoAc—LiL—OpO*
"Dance to your daddie." *ArTp*

The dancer at Cruachan and Cro-Patrick. William Butler Yeats. *PlU*

Dancers. See Dances and dancing

Dances and dancing. See also names of dancers, as Pavlova, Anna
African dance. L. Hughes. *FeF*
Bailada. A. Nunez. *PaS*
Ballroom dancing class. P. McGinley. *NaM*
Boogie chant and dance. Unknown. *TaD*
The butterfly's ball. W. Roscoe. *JoAc—UnG*
"Cock-a-doodle-doo." Mother Goose. *DeMg—HuL-1—JoAc—LiL—OpO*
"Come unto these yellow sands." From The tempest. W. Shakespeare. *DeT*
Ariel's song. *ReT—SmLg*
The dance ("In Breughel's great picture, The Kermess") W. C. Williams. *SmLg*
The dance ("Robin is a lovely lad") T. Campion. *SmLg*
Dance song. Unknown. *SmLg*
The dancer at Cruachan and Cro-Patrick. W. B. Yeats. *PlU*
Dancing ("A hop, a skip, and off you go") E. Farjeon. *HuSv*
Dancing ("Wide sleeves sway") Yang Kuei-Fei. *FeF*
The dancing cabman. J. B. Morton. *NaM*
The dancing seal. W. W. Gibson. *CoPm*
The Dick Johnson reel. J. Falstaff. *NaE*
The elves' dance. T. Ravencroft. *DeT—FeF—JoAc*
The fairy ball. R. Fyleman. *HuL-1*
Fairy song. J. Lyly. *DeT*
For Nijinsky's tomb. F. Cornford. *PlU*
Four for Sir John Davies. T. Roethke. *PlU* (sel.)
A frolic. P. L. Dunbar. *BrR-5*
Furry-dance. E. Farjeon. *FaCb—FaN*
Harp music. R. Humphries. *PlU*
"He met old Dame Trot with a basket of eggs." Mother Goose. *DeMg*
Homage to Vaslav Nijinsky J. Kirkup. *PlU*
"I cannot dance upon my toes." E. Dickinson. *PlU*
The Irish dancer. Unknown. *SmLg*
Jessica dances. E. Farjeon. *FaCb*
Jim Crow. Mother Goose. *OpO*
Jonathan Bing dances for spring. B. C. Brown. *BrS*
Lines written for Gene Kelly to dance to. C. Sandburg. *SaW*
The lobster quadrille. From Alice's adventures in wonderland. L. Carroll. *FeF—HuL-2—HuSv—NaM—PeF*
The looking-glass. R. Kipling. *GrCc—NaE*
Love restored. B. Jonson. *PlU* (sel.)
Marco Polo. Unknown. *WoJ*
Merrily danced the Quaker's wife. Mother Goose. *OpO*
Miss Petal. J. Reeves. *ReW*
"My Cousin German came from France." Unknown. *SmLg*

My papa's waltz. T. Roethke. *HaP*
Off the ground. W. De La Mare. *CoSp—HuL-2*
Orchestra. J. Davies. *PlU* (sel.)
A pavane for the nursery. W. J. Smith. *CoPs*
Pediment: Ballet. L. T. Nicholl. *PlU*
A piper. S. O'Sullivan. *ArTp—FeF—HuL-2—NaM*
Poet to dancer. B. Kavinoky. *PlU*
The potatoes' dance. V. Lindsay. *FeF*
Say there, fellow. Unknown. *TaD*
Shadow dance. I. O. Eastwick. *ArTp—HuL-2*
A song of dagger-dancing. Tu Fu. *PlU* (sel.)
Sonnets to Orpheus. R. M. Rilke. *PlU* (sel.)
Spanish dancer. Unknown. *WoJ*
"Stocking and shirt." J. Reeves. *ReW*
Superlative dance and song. F. Beaumont. *PlU*
Song for a dance. *SmLg*
The swan. S. Spender. *PlU*
Tarantella. H. Belloc. *NaM—SmLg*
To Potapovitch. H. Crane. *PlU*
The two mice. J. Reeves. *ReBl*
Vaudeville dancer. J. H. Wheelock. *PlU*
Waltzing it. W. T. Moncrieff. *PlU*
"When you sing." From The winter's tale. W. Shakespeare
The winter's tale. *PlU*
When young Melissa sweeps. N. B. Turner. *FeF*
Where shall we dance. G. Mistral. *PaS*
Where shall wisdom be found. From The Bacchae. Euripides. *PlU*
The witch's ballad. W. B. Scott. *NaE*

Dancing. See Dances and dancing

Dancing ("A hop, a skip, and off you go") Eleanor Farjeon. *HuSv*

Dancing ("Wide sleeves sway") Yang Kuei-Fei, tr. fr. the Chinese by Florence Ayscough and Amy Lowell. *FeF*

The dancing cabman. J. B. Morton. *NaM*

"Dancing dancing down the street." See Rain

"Dancing, prancing." See Signs of Christmas

The dancing seal. Wilfrid Wilson Gibson. *CoPm*

The dandelion ("O dandelion, yellow as gold") Unknown. *BrL-k*
A conversation. *HuL-1*

Dandelion ("O little soldier with the golden helmet") Hilda Conkling. *ArTp—FeF—JoAc*

The dandelion ("There was a pretty dandelion") E. J. H. Goodfellow. *BrL-k*

Dandelion morning. Frances M. Frost. *FrLn*

Dandelions
Casual gold. M. E. Uschold. *HaY*
The dandelion ("O dandelion, yellow as gold") Unknown. *BrL-k*
A conversation. *HuL-1*
Dandelion ("O little soldier with the golden helmet") H. Conkling. *ArTp—FeF—JoAc*

Dandelions—*Continued*
The dandelion ("There was a pretty dandelion") E. J. H. Goodfellow. *BrL-k*
Dandelion morning. F. M. Frost. *FrLn*
Dandelions ("I'm picking my mother a present") M. Chute. *BrBc—ChA—McAw*
Dandelions ("Over the climbing meadow") F. M. Frost. *ArTp*
Dandelions ("When I went out to play today") M. W. Brewster. *BrL-k*
A lucky thing. D. Aldis. *AlA*
To the dandelion. J. R. Lowell. *FeF* (sel.) —*JoAc* (sel.)
The tragedy. A. Cooper. *BrL-k*
Who did it. D. Aldis. *AlA*
The young dandelion. D. M. Mulock. *UnG*
Dandelions ("I'm picking my mother a present") Marchette Chute. *BrBc—ChA —McAw*
Dandelions ("Over the climbing meadows") Frances M. Frost. *ArTp*
Dandelions ("When I went out to play today") Marietta W. Brewster. *BrL-k*
Dangerous. Dorothy Aldis. *AlA*
Daniel, Arnaut
Bel m'es quan lo vens m'alena. *PaS*
Daniel Boone. Arthur Guiterman. *FeF— NaM—UnMc*
"Daniel Boone at twenty-one." See Daniel Boone
Daniel Webster's horses. Elizabeth Jane Coatsworth. *CoPm*
Danny Deever. Rudyard Kipling. *UnMc*
"Danny was a rascal." See The buccaneer
Dante (Durante Alighieri)
Within her eyes. *PaS*
Danyel, John
"Can doleful notes to mesur'd accents set." *PlU*
Daphne
Daphne. M. Zaturenska. *GrCc*
Daphne. Marya Zaturenska. *GrCc*
Daphnis to Ganymede. Richard Barnfield. *ReT*
A dappled duck. Palmer Brown. *LoL*
"A dappled duck with silver feet." See A dappled duck
Dappled Grey. Mother Goose. *OpO*
"A dappled horse stood at the edge of the meadow." See The grey horse
"Darby and Joan, to Dunmow go." See Flitch of bacon
"Darby and Joan were dressed in black." See Alligoshee
Darcy, Louise
Lincoln learning. *BrR-5*
"Dare to be true." George Herbert. *UnG*
"Dare we despair? Through all the nights and days." See He leads us still
"A daring young lady of Guam." Unknown Limericks since Lear. *UnG*
Darius Green and his flying-machine. John Townsend Trowbridge. *NaM*
Dark. See Angels in the air
"The dark blue wind." See Sleep impression
"Dark brown is the river." See Where go the boats

"The dark danced over the daisies." See The stars, the dark, and the daisies
Dark Danny. Ivy O. Eastwick. *ArTp—FeF —HuL-2*
"Dark Danny has eyes." See Dark Danny
"Dark, darker grew the leaden sky." See Angels in the air—Dark
Dark-eyed lad Columbus. Nancy Byrd Turner. *BrS*
The dark hills. Edwin Arlington Robinson. *HaP*
"Dark hills at evening in the west." See The dark hills
"Dark house, by which once more I stand." See In memoriam
"Dark house, dark lonely grave." See The grave
"The dark is kind and cozy." See God's dark
"Dark red roses in a honeyed wind swinging." See June
The darkling thrush. Thomas Hardy. *HaP— NaE*
Darley, George
Nepenthe, sel.
The phoenix. *GrCc—HoW*
"O blest unfabled incense tree." *SmLg*
"O blest unfabled incense tree." See Nepenthe—The phoenix
The phoenix. See Nepenthe
The sea-ritual. *HoW*
"Darling of gods and men, beneath the gliding stars." See Hymn to Venus
Darwin, Erasmus
The whale. *UnG*
"Darwin and Mendel laid on man the chains." See Progress
A dash to the pole. Wallace Irwin. *CoH*
"Dashing out." See Ocean call
Dates (Fruit)
Dates. Unknown. *FeF*
Dates. Unknown, tr. fr. the Arabian by E. Powys Mathers. *FeF*
"The daughter of the farrier." Unknown Limericks since Lear. *UnG*
Davenant, Sir William
"Wake all the dead, what ho, what ho." *SmLg*
David, King of Israel (about)
"King David and King Solomon." Unknown
Rhymed chuckles. *UnG*
A song to David. C. Smart. *PlU* (sel.)
Davidson, John
Christmas eve. *EaW*
A runnable stag. *HoW—NaE*
Davies, Sir John
Homely meats. *SmLg*
Orchestra. *PlU* (sel.)
Davies, Mary Carolyn
After all and after all. *ArTp*
Be different to trees. *FeF*
"The day before April." *ArTp—DoP—FeF*
The fishing pole. *FeF*
I'll wear a shamrock. *ArTp—BrS—HaY*
June. *BrC*
A new year. *HaY*
Prisoned. *HuL-2*
Six in June. *BrBc*
Tree birthdays. *BrBc*

Davies, William Henry
Eardrops. *GrCc*
The elements. *McW*
The example. *DoP*
The fog. *ArTp—McW*
Leisure. *ArTp—FeF—HuL-2—McW—NaM*
The rain. *ArTp—DeT*
Sheep. *CoSp*
A thought. *NaM*
Davis, Dorothy Marie
Debtor. *BrL-8*
Davis, Fannie Stearns (Fanny Stearns Gifford)
For a child. *FeF*
Davis, Florence Boyce
This and that. *FeF*
Davis, Helen Bayley
Jack Frost. *BrR-4*
Davis, Thomas Osborne
My land. *BrR-5*
Davy, Sir Humphry (about)
"Sir Humphry Davy." E. C. Bentley. *PlI*
Davy and the goblin, sels. Charles Edward Carryl
A nautical ballad. *FeF—HuSv*
The walloping window-blind. *CoH—LoL—NaM—UnG*
Robinson Crusoe's story. *CoH*
"Davy Davy Dumpling." See Davy Dumpling
Davy Dumpling. Mother Goose. *OpO*
Dawn came running. Ivy O. Eastwick. *EaI*
Dawn song—St Patrick's day. Violet Alleyn Storey. *HaY*
"Dawn turned on her purple pillow." See A December day
Day, Clarence
"Man is but a castaway." *PlI*
Day, Holman F.
Passing it along. *BrR-6*
Day. See also Bed-time; Evening; Morning; Night
Confusion. M. C. Livingston. *LiW*
Day and night. A. Lindsay. *HuL-2*
The day is dancing. R. B. Bennett. *BrR-6*
Day song. E. Hammond. *McAw*
"The day will bring some lovely thing." G. N. Crowell. *ArTp*
Hello day. D. Aldis. *AlHd*
Round the clock. D. A. Lord. *DoP*
Sometimes. R. Fyleman. *BrS*
Today. T. Carlyle. *DoP—ThP*
The two spirits. P. B. Shelley. *HoW*
"Will there really be a morning." E. Dickinson. *BrS*
Morning. *FeF—PeF*
Yesterday. H. Chesterman. *BrS*
A **day.** See "I'll tell you how the sun rose"
Day and night. Anne Lindsay. *HuL-2*
"The day before April." Mary Carolyn Davies. *ArTp—DoP—FeF*
"Day by day I float my paper boats one by one down the running stream." See Paper boats
Day-dreamer. Unknown, tr. fr. the German by Louis Untermeyer. *ArTp*
A **day** in June. See The vision of Sir Launfal
The day is dancing. Rowena Bastin Bennett. *BrR-6*

"The **day** is dancing with the wind." See The day is dancing
"The **day** is done." See Evening hymn
Day-Lewis, Cecil
One and one. *PlU*
"Day of glory. Welcome day." See The fourth of July
Day of rest. Berton Braley. *ThP*
Day song. Eleanor Hammond. *McAw*
Day-time moon. Dorothy Aldis. *AlA*
"The day will bring some lovely thing." Grace Noll Crowell. *ArTp*
"A day with sky so wide." See The motion of the earth
Daybreak ("Daybreak comes first") Carl Sandburg. *SaW*
Daybreak ("A wind came up out of the sea") Henry Wadsworth Longfellow. *DeT—McW*
"Daybreak comes first." See Daybreak
Dayre, Sydney
Cherry time. *BrR-3*
Days. See Days of the week
Days. Karle Wilson Baker. *ArTp*
"The days are clear." Christina Georgina Rossetti. *ArTp*
Stay, June, stay. *HaY*
"The days are gone." See Older grown
"The day's grown old, the fainting sun." See Evening
Days in the month. See "Thirty days hath September"
Days of birth. See "Monday's child is fair of face"
Days of the week
Days. K. W. Baker. *ArTp*
December. A. Fisher. *BrS*
Every week song. M. C. Livingston. *LiWa*
Finger nails. Mother Goose. *OpO*
"How many days has my baby to play." Mother Goose. *ArTp—OpO*
"Monday's child is fair of face." Mother Goose. *BrBc—DeMg—HuSv—JoAc—LiL—SmLg*
Birthdays. *OpO—ReG*
Days of birth. *NaM*
Signs, seasons, and sense. *UnG*
Open the door. M. Edey. *ArTp—BrS—HuL-1*
Page ix. G. Stein. *McW*
Sally Lun Lundy. D. McCord. *McT*
"Sneeze on Monday, sneeze for danger." Mother Goose. *LiL*
"If you sneeze on Monday, you sneeze for danger." *DeMg*
"Sneeze on a Monday, you sneeze for danger." *NaE*
Sneezing. *ReG*
"Solomon Grundy." Mother Goose. *DeMg—HuL-1—JoAc—LiL—OpO*
Birthday rhyme. *BrBc*
"They that wash on Monday." Mother Goose. *DeMg—LiL*
Days of the week—Monday
Plow-Monday. E. Farjeon. *FaCb—FaN*
Days of the week—Tuesday
Pancake Tuesday. E. Farjeon. *FaCb*
"Run to church with a frying pan." *FaN*

Janet waking. J. C. Ransom. *ReT*
Journal. E. St V. Millay. *PlI* (sel.)
Kind valentine. D. Schubert. *GrCc*
The king and the clown. Unknown. *UnMc*
The knight's leap. C. Kingsley. *CoSp*
Let be at last. E. Dowson. *HaP*
Little Boy Blue. E. Field. *FeF*
The little peach. E. Field. *CoH*
Little Willie. Unknown. *NaM*
  Rhymed chuckles. *UnG*
A lyke-wake dirge. Unknown. *MaB*
The mill. E. A. Robinson. *HaP*
"My dear, do you know." Mother Goose. *DeMg*
  The babes in the wood. *DeT*
No single thing abides. From De rerum natura. Lucretius. *PlI*
No swan so fine. M. Moore. *GrCc*
Of an ancient spaniel in her fifteenth year. C. Morley. *McW*
"Old Abram Brown is dead and gone." Mother Goose. *DeMg*
  Abram Brown. *OpO*
  Old Abram Brown. *DeT*
Old men. O. Nash. *NaE*
Old Roger. Unknown. *HuL-2*
"On nights like this all cities are alike." R. M. Rilke. *GrCc*
On the death of Ianthe. W. S. Landor. *GrCc*
On the death of Mr Purcell. J. Dryden. *PlU*
On the university carrier. J. Milton. *SmLg*
Pet Marjorie. E. Farjeon. *FaN*
The phantom-wooer. T. L. Beddoes. *HoW*
Pirate passes. E. V. Rieu. *RiF*
"Proud Maisie is in the wood." From The heart of Midlothian. W. Scott. *SmLg*
The raven. Nicharchus. *PlU*
The reaper. R. Duncan. *GrCc*
Remembrance. V. Zhukovsky. *PaS*
Requiem. R. L. Stevenson. *HaP—McW—ThP—UnG*
Requiescat. M. Arnold. *HaP*
Richard Cory. E. A. Robinson. *CoSp—SmLg—ThP*
A round. Unknown. *SmLg*
Seven poems. M. Bashō. *PaS* (sel.)
Shameful death. W. Morris. *UnG—UnMc*
The silver swan. Unknown. *SmLg*
"A slumber did my spirit seal." W. Wordsworth. *SmLg*
The snows of yester-year. F. Villon. *HoW*
The soldier. R. Brooke. *UnMc*
Soldier, rest. From The lady of the lake. W. Scott. *McW—NaM*
  "Soldier, rest, thy warfare o'er." *DeT*
The son. R. Torrence. *McW*
Song ("The glories of our blood and state") From Contention of Ajax and Ulysses. J. Shirley. *GrCc*
Song ("I had a dove and the sweet dove died") J. Keats. *FeF—ReT*
  I had a dove. *CoI—DeT*
Springfield mountain. Unknown. *WoF*
Tears, idle tears. From The princess. A. Tennyson. *HaP*
They are not long. E. Dowson. *HaP*
Things. A. Kilmer. *ThP*

"This troubled world is sighing now." Unknown
  Rhymed chuckles. *UnG*
Time to go. S. Coolidge. *DoP*
To an athlete dying young. From A Shropshire lad. A. E. Housman. *HaP—UnMc*
To sleep. J. Kochanowski. *PaS*
To the fringed gentians. W. C. Bryant. *JoAc*
Tom Bowling. C. Dibdin. *DeT*
The twa corbies. Unknown. *CoSp—SmLg*
  The two corbies. *MaB*
Tywater. R. Wilbur. *HaP*
Upon a maid. R. Herrick. *SmLg*
Vailima. R. L. Stevenson. *DeT*
The valiant. From Julius Caesar. W. Shakespeare. *ThP*
"Wake all the dead, what ho, what ho." W. Davenant. *SmLg*
"When I am dead, my dearest." C. G. Rossetti. *HaP*
"When I have fears that I may cease to be." J. Keats. *HaP—UnG*
"When thou must home to shades of underground." T. Campion. *GrCc*
  When thou must home. *HaP*
"Who killed Cock Robin." Mother Goose. *DeMg—DeT—JoAc*
  Cock Robin. *UnG*
  Death and burial of Cock Robin. *OpO*
The wife of Usher's well. Unknown. *ArTp—DeT—MaB*
The witch. R. Southey. *HoW*
With wavering feet I walked. V. Solovyov. *PaS*
The wreck of the Hesperus. H. W. Longfellow. *FeF*

Death and burial of Cock Robin. See "Who killed Cock Robin"

Death and General Putnam. Arthur Guiterman. *CoPm*

Death and immortality. See also Immortality
After sunset. G. H. Conkling. *ThP*
The conclusion. W. Raleigh. *NaE*
Death be not proud. J. Donne. *HaP*
Epilogue. H. Melville. *PlI*
Homage to the philosopher. B. Deutsch. *PlI*

In memoriam, sels. A. Tennyson
  "And, star and system rolling past" In memoriam. *PlI*
  "Dark house, by which once more I stand" From In memoriam. *HaP*
  "I trust I have not wasted breath" In memoriam. *PlI*
  Ring out, wild bells. *ArTp—BrL-8—FeF—HoW*

Man's mortality. Unknown. *SmLg*
Not to die. Simonides. *PaS*
The onset. R. Frost. *FrR*
"Remember, though the telescope extend." G. Dillon. *PlI*
Virtue. G. Herbert. *HaP*

Death be not proud. John Donne. *HaP*

"Death, be not proud, though some have called thee." See Death be not proud

Death from cancer. Robert Lowell *HaP*

The **death** of Prince Leopold. William Mc-Gonagall. *NaE*

The **death** of Robin Hood ("Give me my bow, said Robin Hood") Eugene Field. *CoSp*

The **death** of Robin Hood ("When Robin Hood and Little John") Unknown. *MaB*

"**Death** of Sir Nihil, book the nth." See Tywater

The **death** of the hired man. Robert Frost. *FrR—FrY—UnMc*

The **death** of the old year. Alfred Tennyson. *CoPs* (sel.)

Death's jest book, sel. Thomas Lovell Beddoes
   Sea song. *UnG*

De Ayala, Ramon Perez
   "She was a pretty little girl." *FeF*

"**Deborah** danced, when she was two." See Experience

"The **debt** is paid." See The past

Debtor. Dorothy Marie Davis. *BrL-8*

Deceit
   Atticus. From Epistle to Dr Arbuthnot. A. Pope. *HaP*
   The boy and the wolf. Aesop. *UnMc*
   Deceiver. Mother Goose. *OpO*
   The fair flower of Northumberland. Unknown. *MaB*
   The fox and the goat. J. De La Fontaine. *JoAc*
   The frog and the crow. Unknown. *ReG*
   Johnny Armstrong. Unknown. *UnMc*
   The outlandish knight. Unknown. *UnG*
   The spider and the fly. M. Howitt. *DeT—FeF—PeF*

Deceiver. Mother Goose. *OpO*

December
   December ("Dimmest and brightest month am I") C. G. Rossetti. *HaY*
   December ("Down swept the chill wind from the mountain peak") From The vision of Sir Launfal. J. R. Lowell. *UnG*
   December ("I like days") A. Fisher. *BrS*
   A December day. S. Teasdale. *HaY*
   "I heard a bird sing." O. Herford. *ArTp—BrS—EaW—HaY—HuL-2*
   The long night moon: December. F. M. Frost. *HaY*

December ("Dimmest and brightest month am I") Christina Georgina Rossetti. *HaY*

December ("Down swept the chill wind from the mountain peak") See The vision of Sir Launfal

December ("I like days") Aileen Fisher. *BrS*

A **December** day. Sara Teasdale. *HaY*

Decline and fall. E. V. Rieu. *RiF*

"The **decline** and fall of the empire of Rome." See Decline and fall

Decoration day. See Memorial day

Decoration day. Henry Wadsworth Longfellow. *CoPs*

"A **decrepit** old gasman, named Peter." Unknown. *CoH*

A **dedication.** Gilbert Keith Chesterton. *CoH*

Deedle, deedle, dumpling. See "Diddle, diddle, dumpling, my son John"

"**Deedle,** deedle, dumpling, my son John." See "Diddle, diddle, dumpling, my son John"

"**Deep** black against the dying glow." See An autumnal evening

"**Deep** in the jungles of Jam-kaïk." See The snyke

"**Deep** in the shadowy cellar where." See Storm cellar

"**Deep** in the wave is a coral grove." See The coral grove

Deer
   Child's song. From A masque. T. Moore. *GrCc*
   The cripple. R. P. T. Coffin. *HuSv*
   The deer. M. Austin. *FeF*
   Earthy anecdote. W. Stevens. *ReT*
   The faun. E. Pound. *SmLg*
   Green afternoon. F. M Frost. *ArTp—FrLn*
   Meeting. R. Field. *HuL-2*
   Mrs Caribou. W. J. Smith. *CoPm—SmL*
   The nymph and her fawn. A. Marvell. *SmLg*
   A runnable stag. J. Davidson. *HoW—NaE*
   Two look at two. R. Frost. *FrR*

The **deer.** Mary Austin. *FeF*

Deirdre. James Stephens. *GrCc*

Dekker, Thomas
   The basket-maker's song. See Pleasant comedy of patient Grissell
   O sweet content. See Pleasant comedy of patient Grissell—The basket-maker's song
   Pleasant comedy of patient Grissell, sel.
      The basket-maker's song. *ReT*
      O sweet content. *DeT*

De La Mare, Walter (Walter Ramal; Walter Rand, pseuds.)
   Alas, alack. *ArTp—BrL-k—FeF—HuL-1—NaE*
   "All but blind." *FeF—McW*
   All that's past. *ReT*
   "As soon as ever twilight comes." *BrS*
   Autumn. *GrCc*
   The bandog. *ArTp—NaE*
   The barber's. *BrR-3—JoAc*
   The bee's song. *LoL*
   Before dawn. *EaW*
   Berries. *ArTp*
   Bewitched. *CoPm*
   Bones. *CoH*
   Bread and cherries. *HuL-1*
   Bunches of grapes. *ArTp—HuL-2—NaM*
   Chicken. *ArTp*
   A child's day, sel.
      "Softly, drowsily." *HuL-2—JoAc*
      A child's day, Part II. *ArTp*
      A child's day begins. *HuSv*
   A child's day begins. See A child's day—"Softly, drowsily"
   The christening. *BrBc*
   The corner. *BrBc*
   The cupboard. *ArTp—BrL-k—FeF—HuL-1*
   The dunce. *PlI*
   Eeka, neeka. *McW*
   Faint music. *SmLg*

"**Dickery,** dickery, dare." Mother Goose. *DeMg*
  The flying pig. *OpO*
Dickey Diller and his wife. Unknown. *GrCc*
Dickinson, Emily
  The Amherst train. See "I like to see it lap the miles"
  Autumn. See "The morns are meeker than they were"
  A bird. See "A bird came down the walk"
  "A bird came down the walk." *ArTp*(sel.) —*BrR-3*(sel.)—*NaM*
    A bird. *FeF*(sel.)—*CoI*(sel.)—*HuSv* (sel.)
  A book. See "There is no frigate like a book"
  Certainty. See "I never saw a moor"
  A day. See "I'll tell you how the sun rose"
  "Farther in summer than the birds." *HaP*
  The grass. *FeF*
  "The heart asks pleasure first." *HaP*
  "Hope is the thing with feathers." *ArTp*— *NaM*
  How still the bells. *ReG*
  The hummingbird. *UnG*
  "I cannot dance upon my toes." *PlU*
  I know some lonely houses. *CoPm*—*McW*
  "I like to see it lap the miles." *NaM*
    The Amherst train. *SmLg*
    The locomotive. *FeF*
  "I never saw a moor." *ArTp*—*DoP*—*FeF*— *HuL-2*—*JoAc*—*NaE*
    Certainty. *UnG*
  "I started early, took my dog." *ReT*
  "If I can stop one heart from breaking." *BrR-4*
  "I'll tell you how the sun rose." *BrS*— *NaM*
    A day. *UnG*
    Poem. *ReT*
    The sun. *HuSv*
    Sunrise and sunset. *BrR-6*
  "I'm nobody. Who are you." *ArTp*—*UnG*
    A nobody. *UnMc*
  Indian summer. *UnG*
  "Lightly stepped a yellow star." *NaM*
  The little tippler. *NaE*
  The locomotive. See "I like to see it lap the miles"
  March. *HaY*
  Morning. See "Will there really be a morning"
  "The morns are meeker than they were." *ArTp*—*JoAc*—*PeF*
    Autumn. *BrR-5*—*FeF*—*HaY*
  "Musicians wrestle everywhere." *PlU*
  A nobody. See "I'm nobody. Who are you"
  Once a child. *PlI*
  Only a book. *BrR-4*
  Our little kinsmen. *FeF*—*PlI*
  Pedigree. *UnG*
  "A secret told." *ThP*
  The snake. *UnG*
  The snow. *UnG*
  The sun. See "I'll tell you how the sun rose"
  Sunrise and sunset. See "I'll tell you how the sun rose"

"Surgeons must be very careful." *PlI*
"There is no frigate like a book." *BrS*— *HaY*
  A book. *FeF*
"There's a certain slant of light." *HaP*— *SmLg*
"To hear an oriole sing." *PlU*
We never know how high. *McW*
"Will there really be a morning." *BrS*
  Morning. *FeF*—*PeF*
"The wind begun to rock the grass." *GrCc*
With a daisy. *PlI*
  A word. *ArTp*
Dickinson, G. Lowes
  No joy without love. tr. *PaS*
Dicky. Robert Graves. *GrP*
Dicky Dilver. Mother Goose. *OpO*
"**Dicky** set out for Wisdom hall." See Gallop away
Dictionary. William Jay Smith. *SmL*
"A **dictionary's** where you can look things up." See Dictionary
"**Did** a blowing cherry blossom drift in." See At daybreak
Did you ever. Unknown. *WoJ*
"**Did** you ever attempt to shampoo." See Advice to young naturalists
"**Did** you ever ever ever." Unknown. *WiRm*
"**Did** you ever go a-fishing on a sunny day." See Did you ever
"**Did** you ever hear of the curate who mounted his mare." See Crotchet castle —The priest and the mulberry tree
"**Did** you ever (iver, over)." Unknown. *TaD*
"**Did** you ever pat a baby goat." See Baby goat
"**Did** you ever think how queer." See A birthday
"**Did** you feed my cow." Unknown. *TaD*
Did you see my wife. Mother Goose. *OpO*
"**Did** you see my wife, did you see, did you see." See Did you see my wife
"**Did** you tackle that trouble that came your way." See How did you die
"**Diddle,** diddle, dumpling, my son John." Mother Goose. *HuSv*—*JoAc*—*LiL*—*OpO*
  Deedle, deedle, dumpling. *HuL-1*
"**Deedle,** deedle, dumpling, my son John." *DeMg*
"**Diddlety,** diddlety, dumpty." Mother Goose. *DeMg*—*LiL*
  Puss up the plum tree. *OpO*
Diddling. James Reeves. *ReBl*
Didn't it rain. Unknown. *TaD*
"**Didn't** it rain, rain, rain, rain, rain, rain." See Didn't it rain
"**Die,** pussy, die." See Stopping the swing
The **difference.** ("I know that he is ten years old") Eleanor Alletta Chaffee. *BrBc*
The **difference** ("Outside") Myra Cohn Livingston. *LiW*
The **difference** (" 'Twixt optimist and pessimist") Unknown. *UnG*
The **difference** ("Your eye may see") Eleanor Farjeon. *FaCb*—*FaN*
Differences. Dorothy Aldis. *AlA*

"**Do** you love me." Unknown. *CoPs*

"**Do** you remember." See To James

"**Do** you remember an inn, Miranda." See Tarantella

"**Do** you remember, when you were first a child." See Message from home

"**Do** you want apples." See Apples go begging

Dob and Mob. See "There was a man and his name was Dob"

Dobell, Sydney
Keith of Ravelston. *DeT*

Dobson, (Henry) Austin
Little Blue Ribbons. *BrBc*
Song of the sea wind. *HuL-2*

Dock, William
The naked world. tr. *PlI*
The wheel. tr. *PlI*

Docks. Carl Sandburg. *SaW*

Dr Brown. Unknown. *WoJ*

Doctor Emmanuel. James Reeves. *ReW*

"**Doctor** Emmanuel Harrison-Hyde" See Doctor Emmanuel

"**Doctor** Faustus was a good man." Mother Goose. *DeMg—LiL*
Doctor Foster. *OpO*

Doctor Fell. See "I do not like thee, Doctor Fell"

"**A doctor** fell in a deep well." Unknown
Rhymed chuckles. *UnG*

Doctor Foster. See "Doctor Faustus was a good man"

Doctor Foster. See "Doctor Foster went to Gloucester"

Doctor Foster ("Old Doctor Foster") Mother Goose. *OpO*

"**Doctor** Foster is a good man." See "Doctor Faustus was a good man"

"**Doctor** Foster went to Glo'ster." See "Doctor Foster went to Gloucester"

"**Doctor** Foster went to Gloucester." Mother Goose. *DeMg—JoAc*
Doctor Foster. *OpO*
"Doctor Foster went to Glo'ster." *LiL*

"**Dr** John Hearty." James Reeves. *ReW*

Dr Klimwell's fall. David McCord. *McT*

Doctor Windikin. Harry Behn. *BeW*

Doctors
A correct compassion. J. Kirkup. *PlI*
Doctor Emmanuel. J. Reeves. *ReW*
"A doctor fell in a deep well." Unknown
Rhymed chuckles. *UnG*
"Dr John Hearty." J. Reeves. *ReW*
Doctor Windikin. H. Behn. *BeW*
The dormouse and the doctor. A. A. Milne. *MiWc*
Heart specialist. E. Lieberman. *PlI*
"I do not like thee, Doctor Fell." Martial. *DeMg—NaM*
Doctor Fell. *OpO*
Signs, seasons, and sense. *UnG*
On a doctor named Isaac Letsome. Unknown. *UnG*
Sneezles. A. A. Milne. *MiWc*
Song. Unknown. *ReT*
The staff of Aesculapius. M. Moore. *PlI*
"Surgeons must be very careful." E. Dickinson. *PlI*

Dodge, Mary Mapes
Christmas. *BrBc*
In trust. *BrS*
Melons. *ArTp*
"Now the noisy winds are still." *HaY*
Snowflakes. *BrL-k—HuL-1*
The sweet, red rose. *BrBc*
"When I am big, I mean to buy." *BrBc*
Written on the road. *BrBc*

Dodgson, Charles Lutwidge. See Carroll, Lewis, pseud.

The dodo. Hilaire Belloc. *LoL*

"**The dodo** used to walk around." See The dodo

"**Does** the road wind up-hill all the way." See Up-hill

Dog. William Jay Smith. *SmB*

"**A dog** and a cat went out together." Mother Goose. *DeMg*

Dog at night. Louis Untermeyer. *UnG*

A dog day. Rachel Field. *BrS*

"**The dog** fox rolls on his lolling tongue." See The hunt

"**The dog** is man's best friend." See An introduction to dogs

"**Dog** means dog." See Blum

"**The doggies** went to the mill." Mother Goose. *OpO*

Dogs
The animal store. R. Field. *ArTp—CoI—HuL-1*
Argus and Ulysses. E. Farjeon. *FaCb*
At night. F. Cornford. *CoI*
At the dog show. C. Morley. *NaM*
Ballad of the little black hound. D. S. Shorter. *CoSp*
The bandog. W. De La Mare. *ArTp—NaE*
Beth Gêlert. W. R. Spencer. *UnG*
Bingo has an enemy. R. Fyleman. *BrR-5*
Birthday gift. E. B. De Vito. *BrBc*
The bloodhound. E. Anthony. *UnG*
Blue Bell. Mother Goose. *OpO*
"Bow, wow, wow." Mother Goose. *ArTp—DeMg—HuSv—JoAc*
Tom Tinker's dog. *OpO*
The buccaneer. N. B. Turner. *ArTp*
Certain maxims of Archy. D. Marquis. *CoH* (sel.)
Archy, the cockroach, speaks. *FeF*
Christmas carol for the dog. Sister Maris Stella. *DoP*
Christmas dog. D. Aldis. *AlA*
The collies. E. Anthony. *UnG*
The dachshund. E. Anthony. *UnG*
Dog. W. J. Smith. *SmB*
"A dog and a cat went out together." Mother Goose. *DeMg*
Dog at night. L. Untermeyer. *UnG*
A dog day. R. Field. *BrS*
Dogs ("The dogs I know") M. Chute. *ChA—HuL-1*
Dogs ("I am his Highness' dog at Kew") A. Pope. *UnG*
Dogs ("O little friend, your nose is ready; you sniff") H. Monro. *UnG*
Dogs and weather. W. Welles. *ArTp—FeF—HuL-2—HuSv*

The lost doll. From The water babies. C. Kingsley. *FeF—NaM*

A mortifying mistake. A. M. Pratt. *CoH*

Polite tea party. D. Aldis. *AlA*

"She was a pretty little girl." R. P. De Ayala. *FeF*

"Doll's boy's asleep." E. E. Cummings. *GrCc*

Dolor. Theodore Roethke. *HaP*

Dolphins
Arethusa. E. V. Rieu. *RiF*

Donegal, Ireland
Springtime in Donegal. M. R. Stevenson. *HuSv*

"The **dong** with a luminous nose." Edward Lear. *CoPm—HoW*

Donian, Mitchell
"If someone asks you." *CoPs*

The **donkey.** Unknown. *BrBc*

"**Donkey,** donkey, do not bray." Mother Goose. *OpO*

Donkeys
Burro with the long ears. Unknown. *FeF*
The donkey. Unknown. *BrBc*
The fable of the old man, the boy, and the donkey. I. Serraillier. *ReG*
Francis Jammès: A prayer to go to Paradise with the donkeys. R. Wilbur. *ArTp*
"If I had a donkey that wouldn't go." Mother Goose. *DeMg—JoAc*
Kindness. *OpO*
My donkey. Unknown. *ArTp—HuL-2*
Nicholas Nye. W. De La Mare. *ReG*
The ox and the ass. E. Simpson. *EaW*
"Tom saw a cross fellow was beating an ass." Mother Goose. *DeMg*

Donne, John
The bait. *GrCc*
Death be not proud. *HaP*
For whom the bell tolls. *ThP*
Hymne to God my God, in my sicknesse. *PlU* (sel.)
Song. *HaP*
The whale. *HaP*

"**Don't** be crooked." Unknown. *MoY*

"**Don't** be fretful." Unknown. *MoY*

Don't-Care. Unknown. *DeT*

"**Don't-Care,** he didn't care." See Don't-Care

"**Don't** make love at the garden gate." Unknown. *MoY*

"**Don't** shirk." See Good advice

"**Don't** steal this book." Unknown. *MoY*

Don't tell me. Dorothy Aldis. *AlA*

"**Don't** tell your friends about your indigestion." See Of tact

"**Don't** you think it's probable." See Little talk

"**Doodledy,** doodledy, doodledy, dan." Mother Goose. *OpO*

Doolittle, Esther Hull
Secret. *HaY*

Doolittle, Hilda. See D., H., pseud.

The **doom** of Devorgoil, sel. Walter Scott
Bonny Dundee. *SmLg*

The **door.** David McCord. *McFf*

"The **door** is shut fast." See Who's in

Doorbells. See Bells

Doorbells. Rachel Field. *ArTp—FeF—HuSv*

Doors
The door. D. McCord. *McFf*
Doorbells. R. Field. *ArTp—FeF—HuSv*
Doors. C. Sandburg. *SaW*
"Godfrey Gordon Gustavus Gore." W. B. Rands. *ArTp—FeF—HuL-2—PeF*
Joan's door. E. Farjeon. *BrBc*
The man who hid his own front door. E. MacKinstry. *ArTp—FeF*
The revolving door. N. Levy. *CoH*
Some one. W. De La Mare. *ArTp—BrL-k —HuL-2—HuSv—JoAc—NaM*
Someone. *FeF*

Doors. Carl Sandburg. *SaW*

The **Dorchester** giant. Oliver Wendell Holmes. *FeF*

D'Orleans, Charles. See Charles d'Orleans

Dormice
The christening. A. A. Milne. *BrBc— MiWc*
The dormouse and the doctor. A. A. Milne. *MiWc*
The elf and the dormouse. O. Herford. *ArTp—FeF—HuL-1—PeF—UnG*

The **dormouse** and the doctor. A. A. Milne. *MiWc*

Dorothea, Saint (about)
For a picture of St Dorothea. G. M. Hopkins. *GrCc*
Saint Dorothea. E. Farjeon. *FaCb*

"**Dorothea** to Theophilus: I send." See Saint Dorothea

Dorrance, Dick
Cockpit in the clouds. *ArTp—FeF*

Dorset, Earl of (Lord Buckhurst). See Sackville, Thomas, Earl of Dorset (Lord Buckhurst)

"**Dot.**" Unknown. *MoY*

"**Dot** is five and Jack is ten." See A puzzling example

"**Double** bubble gum bubbles double." Unknown. *WiRm*

"The **double** moon." See River moons

Double-u. See "Heigh ho, my heart is low"

The **Douglas** tragedy. Unknown. *UnMc*

The **dove** and the ant. Jean De La Fontaine, tr. fr. the French by Marianne Moore. *JoAc*

"**Dove-colored,** the shadows melt and mingle." See Twilight

The **dove** says. See "The dove says, Coo, coo, what shall I do"

"The **dove** says, Coo, coo, what shall I do." Mother Goose. *DeMg*
Coo. *DeT*
The dove says. *OpO*

Dover, England
Dover beach. M. Arnold. *HaP*

Dover beach. Matthew Arnold. *HaP*

Doves. See Pigeons

"The **dove's** a bore, exclaimed the crow." See Bores

Dowd, Emma C.
Fun in a garret. *ArTp—BrR-3*

"**Down.**" See The grasshopper

"**Down** a sunny Easter meadow." Nancy Byrd Turner. *BrS*

"Down by the corner of the street." See Corner-of-the-street

Down by the pond. A. A. Milne. *MiWc*

"Down by the river (where the green grass grows)." Mother Goose. *OpO*

"Down by the river (where the river flows)." Unknown. *MoY*

Down by the sea. David McCord. *McT*

"Down cellar, said the cricket." See The potatoes' dance

"Down, down." Eleanor Farjeon. *ArTp*

"Down in our cellar on a Monday and a Tuesday." See Old Ellen Sullivan

"Down in the meadow, spread with dew." See Revelation

Down in the valley. Unknown. *TaD—WoJ*

"Down in the valley where the green grass grows." See Down in the valley

Down on my tummy. Myra Cohn Livingston. *LiWa*

Down on the beach. Dorothy Aldis. *AlA*

"Down on the beach where it's shining and wet." See Down on the beach

"Down swept the chill wind from the mountain peak." See The vision of Sir Launfal—December

"Down the slide." See Sliding

"Down the star-stairs fell." See Dr Klimwell's fall

"Down the street, down the street, flying down the street." See Jonathan Bing's tea

"Down the street the old man came." See Kingcups in town

"Down with the lambs." Mother Goose. *OpO*

"Downhill I came, hungry, and yet not starved." See The owl

Downpour. Myra Cohn Livingston. *LiWa*

Dowson, Ernest
  Let be at last. *HaP*
  "The sky is up above the roof." tr. *FeF*
  They are not long. *HaP*

Doyle, Sir Arthur Conan
  A parable. *BrL-7*

Doyle, Marion
  The golden month. *HaY*
  The month of the Thunder Moon. *HaY*
  The wind. *BrR-3*

The doze. James Reeves. *ReP—UnG*

"A dozen machines." See A time for building

Dragon. William Jay Smith. *SmB*

Dragon flies
  The dragon fly ("A dragon fly upon my knee") D. Aldis. *AlA*
  A dragon-fly ("When the heat of the summer") E. Farjeon. *FeF*

The dragon fly ("A dragon fly upon my knee") Dorothy Aldis. *AlA*

A dragon-fly (When the heat of the summer") Eleanor Farjeon. *FeF*

"A dragon fly upon my knee." See The dragon fly

"A dragon named Ernest Belflour." See Dragon

Dragonflies. See Dragon flies

Dragons
  D is for dragon. E. Farjeon. *FaCb*
  Dragon. W. J. Smith. *SmB*
  A dream of governors. L. Simpson. *HaP*
  "A knight and a lady." Mother Goose. *HuL-1*
  Knight-in-armour. A. A. Milne. *MiWc*
  A modern dragon. R. B. Bennett. *ArTp*
  The Princess Priscilla. E. V. Rieu. *RiF*
  Sir Eglamour. S. Rowlands. *McW—SmLg*
  The tale of Custard the dragon. O. Nash. *FeF—UnG*
  The toaster. W. J. Smith. *ArTp—CoH—SmL*
  Us two. A. A. Milne. *ArTp—MiWc*

Drake, Sir Francis (about)
  The admiral's ghost. A. Noyes. *ArTp—CoPm—JoAc*
  Drake's drum. H. Newbolt. *DeT*

Drake, Joseph Rodman
  The culprit fay, sels.
    Elfin song. *CoPm*
    A fairy in armor. *FeF*
  Elfin song. See The culprit fay
  A fairy in armor. See The culprit fay

Drake, Leah Bodine
  Changeling. *CoPm*
  The green door. *BrBc*

"Drake he's in his hammock an' a thousand mile away." See Drake's drum

Drake's drum. Henry Newbolt. *DeT*

"Drank lonesome water." See Lonesome water

Draper, A. S.
  Indian summer. *HaY*

"Draw a pail of water." Mother Goose. *DeMg—LiL—NaM—OpO*

Drawing
  Circles. H. Behn. *LoL*
  Mr Blob. E. V. Rieu. *RiF*

Drayton, Michael
  Agincourt. *SmLg*
  Calm. *DeT*
  Nymphidia: The court of fairy, sel.
    Pigwiggin arms himself. *NaM*
  Pigwiggin arms himself. See Nymphidia: The court of fairy
  The poet's paradise. *HoW*
  Since there's no help. *HaP*

A dreadful sight. Dorothy Aldis. *AlA*

The dream ("One night I dreamed") Harry Behn. *BeW*

Dream ("The sandman put it in his sack") Myra Cohn Livingston. *LiWa*

The dream ("There was a lady fair and gay") Unknown. *DeT*

A dream about the man in the moon. John Ciardi. *CiY*

The dream of Eugene Aram. Thomas Hood. *CoSp*

A dream of governors. Louis Simpson. *HaP*

Dream-pedlary. Thomas Lovell Beddoes. *HoW*

Dreams to sell. *HuL-2*

"Dreaming of a prince." See After all and after all

"Dreaming of honeycombs to share." See Waiting

Dreaming that I went with Li and Yü to visit Yüan Chēn. Po Chü-i, tr. fr. the Chinese by Arthur Waley. *PaS*

"Dreaming when dawn's left hand was in the sky." See The rubáiyát of Omar Khayyám of Naishapúr

Dreams. See also Visions
  After all and after all. M. C. Davies. *ArTp*
  Andre. G. Brooks. *ArTp*
  The army horse and the army jeep. J. Ciardi. *CiR*
  "Arvin Marvin Lillisbee Fitch." J. Ciardi. *CiY*
  The cave-boy. L. E. Richards. *FeF*
  The concert. J. S. Newman. *CoH*
  The cowboy's dream. Unknown. *UnMc*
  Crab-apple. E. Talbot. *ArTp—BrBc*
  Cradle song. S. Naidu. *FeF*
  Disillusionment of ten o'clock. W. Stevens. *HaP*
  The dream ("One night I dreamed") H. Behn. *BeW*
  Dream ("The sandman put it in his sack") M. C. Livingston. *LiWa*
  The dream ("There was a lady fair and gay") Unknown. *DeT*
  A dream about the man in the moon. J. Ciardi. *CiY*
  The dream of Eugene Aram. T. Hood. *CoSp*
  Dream-pedlary. T. L. Beddoes. *HoW*
    Dreams to sell. *HuL-2*
  Dreaming that I went with Li and Yü to visit Yüan Chēn. Po Chü-i. *PaS*
  Dreams. M. Chute. *HuL-2*
  "Friday night's dream." Mother Goose. *DeMg—WiRm*
  "Hold fast your dreams." L. Driscoll. *ArTp—BrBc—FeF*
  "Little cat." L. E. Richards. *HuL-1*
  The little dreamer. Unknown. *BrL-k*
  Mary and her kitten. E. Farjeon. *DeT*
  The moonlit stream. J. Reeves. *ReBl*
  Paradise. C. G. Rossetti. *DoP*
  Poem. H. von Hofmannsthal. *PaS*
  Tomorrow. R. B. Bennett. *HuL-2*
  What did I dream. R. Graves. *GrP*
  Where dreams are made. B. Johnson. *BrR-4*

Dreams. Marchette Chute. *HuL-2*

"Dreams are made in the moon, my dear." See Where dreams are made

"Dreams, graves, pools, growing." See So to speak

Dreams to sell. See Dream-pedlary

Dreidel song. Efraim Rosenzweig. *ArTp*

Dresbach, Glenn Ward
  The last corn shock. *FeF*

Dress. See Clothing and dress

The **dress** of spring. May Justus. *HaY*

Dresses. Dorothy Aldis. *AlA*

Dressing-up. Marchette Chute. *ChA*

"Drink to me only with thine eyes." See Song, to Celia

Drinking. See Drinks and drinking

Drinking. See Anacreontics—The thirsty earth

Drinking fountain. Marchette Chute. *ChA—McAw*

Drinking song. John Still. *HoW*

Drinking vessels. Laura E. Richards. *LoL*

Drinks and drinking
  Billy and me. Mother Goose. *OpO*
  Bobbily Boo and Wollypotump. L. E. Richards. *LoL*
  Cherry-pie Sunday. E. Farjeon. *FaN*
  A cool drink on a hot day. J. Ciardi. *CiY*
  Drinking fountain. M. Chute. *ChA—McAw*
  Drinking song. J. Still. *HoW*
  Drinking vessels. L. E. Richards. *LoL*
  Food and drink. D. McCord. *McT*
  Hunger and thirst. B. Young. *McAw*
  John Barleycorn. R. Burns. *SmLg*
  King's-cup. E. Farjeon. *FaCb*
  Lemonade stand. D. B. Thompson. *BrS*
  "Little Kathleen took a drink." Unknown. *MoY*
  Lord Alcohol. T. L. Beddoes. *HoW*
  "The man in the moon drinks claret." Mother Goose. *OpO*
  Margie. Unknown. *WoJ*
  Mr Flood's party. E. A. Robinson. *HaP—NaE*
  "Molly, my sister, and I fell out." Mother Goose. *DeMg*
  "Roses are blue." Unknown. *MoY*
  "Round about, round about (maggotty pie)." Mother Goose. *OpO*
  "Said the monkey to the owl." Unknown. *WoF*
  Seamen three. From Nightmare abbey. T. L. Peacock. *HoW*
  The thirsty earth. From Anacreontics. A. Cowley. *HoW*
    Drinking. *HaP*
  When I went to get a drink. J. Ciardi. *CiI*

Drinkwater, John
  The bird's nest. *HuSv—McAw—NaE*
  Birthright. *GrCc*
  Bobby Blue. *FeF*
  I want to know. *FeF*
  Old woman in May. *HuL-2*
  Puzzles. *McW*
  The sun. *ArTp—FeF—PeF*
  Tiptoe Night. *BrS*
  Twos. *JoAc*
  The wagon in the barn. *BrR-4—PeF*
  Washing. *BrR-4—FeF—HuSv—JoAc*

Driscoll, Louise
  "Hold fast your dreams." *ArTp—BrBc—FeF*
  July meadow. *HaY*
  Mid-August. *HaY*
  November garden. *HaY*
  Thanksgiving. *HaY*

"Droning a drowsy syncopated tune." See The weary blues

A **drop** of dew. Andrew Marvell. *DeT*

Droste-Hülshoff, Annette von
  The pond. *PaS*

Drowning
  Annan water. Unknown. *MaB*
  Binnorie. Unknown. *MaB*
  The bunyip and the whistling kettle. J. Manifold. *CoPm*
  Lord Ullin's daughter. T. Campbell. *FeF*

Drowning—*Continued*
The outlandish knight. Unknown. *UnG*
The sands of Dee. From Alton Locke.
C. Kingsley. *CoPm—DeT—JoAc*
The tide. H. W. Longfellow. *HoW*
"The tide rises, the tide falls." *DeT*

"Drowsily come the sheep." See Slumber song

Drowsy. Carl Sandburg. *SaW*

The **drum** ("The drum's a very quiet fellow")
John Farrar. *BrR-3*

The **drum** ("I'm a beautiful red, red drum")
Eugene Field. *BrR-6*

A **drumlin** woodchuck. Robert Frost. *FrR—
FrY—McW*

The **drummer-boy** and the shepherdess. William Brighty Rands. *NaM*

"Drummer-boy, drummer-boy, where is your drum." See The drummer-boy and the shepherdess

Drummers and drums
The drum ("The drum's a very quiet fellow") J. Farrar. *BrR-3*
The drum ("I'm a beautiful red, red drum") E. Field. *BrR-6*
The drummer-boy and the shepherdess. W. B. Rands. *NaM*

Drummond, William Henry
The wreck of the Julie Plante. *FeF*

Drummond, William, of Hawthornden
To his lute. *PlU*

Drums. See Drummers and drums

"The drum's a very quiet fellow." See The drum

The **dry** salvages, sel. T. S. Eliot
"I do not know much about gods; but I think that the river." *ArTp*

Dryads. See Fairies

Dryden, John
Alexander's feast; or, The power of music. *HoW*
George Villiers, Duke of Buckingham. *HaP*
Ode to Maecenas. tr. *PaS* (sel.)
Today and tomorrow. *UnG* (sel.)
On the death of Mr Purcell. *PlU*
A song for St Cecilia's day, 1687. *PlU* (sel.)
A spell. *HoW*
Today and tomorrow. See Ode to Maecenas

The **duck** ("Behold the duck") Ogden Nash. *NaM*

The **duck** ("If I were in a fairy tale") Edith King. *BrL-k—HuSv*

"A duck and a drake." Mother Goose. *DeMg*
Ducks and drakes. *OpO*

The **duck** and the kangaroo. Edward Lear. *HuL-2—JoAc*

"The duck is whiter than whey is." See Quack

Ducks
All a duck needs. D. Aldis. *AlA*
At the farm. J. Ciardi. *CiY*
Charley Barley. Mother Goose. *OpO*
A dappled duck. P. Brown. *LoL*
The duck ("Behold the duck") O. Nash. *NaM*

The duck ("If I were in a fairy tale") E. King. *BrL-k—HuSv*
"A duck and a drake." Mother Goose. *DeMg*
Ducks and drakes. *OpO*
The duck and the kangaroo. E. Lear. *HuL-2—JoAc*
The ducks. A. Wilkins. *ArTp*
Ducks at dawn. J. S. Tippett. *ArTp—BrS*
Ducks' ditty. From The wind in the willows. K. Grahame. *ArTp—BrR-3—FeF—JoAc—McW—NaM—PeF*
"Four ducks on a pond." W. Allingham. *HuL-2—ReT*
The hunter. O. Nash. *NaE*
"I saw a ship a-sailing." Mother Goose. *ArTp — BrR-3 — DeMg — HuSv — JoAc—LiL—NaM*
I saw a ship. *DeT*
A ship a-sailing. *OpO*
"Jemima Jane." M. Chute. *ChA*
A little talk. Unknown. *HuL-1*
Natura in urbe. E. B. White. *McW*
The new duckling. A. Noyes. *FeF*
"Oh, what have you got for dinner, Mrs Bond." Mother Goose. *DeMg*
Dilly dilly. *OpO*
Old Ducky Quackerel. L. E. Richards. *BrR-5*
Quack. W. De La Mare. *ArTp—CoI*
Railroad ducks. F. M. Frost. *FrLn*
Regent's park. R. Fyleman. *BrR-4*
In the park. *HuSv*
Sing-song rhyme. Unknown. *BrS—HuL-1*
Swimming. C. Scollard. *FeF*
That duck. B. MacI. *McAw*
Who likes the rain. C. D. Bates. *ArTp—BrR-3—HuL-1*

The **ducks.** Alice Wilkins. *ArTp*

Ducks and drakes. See "A duck and a drake"

Ducks at dawn. James S. Tippett. *ArTp—BrS*

Ducks' ditty. See The wind in the willows

The **duel.** Eugene Field. *ArTp—FeF—HuSv—NaM*

Duels
The duel. E. Field. *ArTp—FeF—HuSv—NaM*

Duffy, Nona Keen
Our milkman. *McAw*
Spring is in the making. *HaY*
Traffic light. *McAw*

Duggan, Eileen
Juniper. *DoP*

The **duke.** Unknown. *DeT*

Duke o' York. See "Oh, the grand old duke of York"

"The duke of Cum-ber-land." See The duke

"The duke of Gordon had three daughters." See The duke of Gordon's daughter

The **duke** of Gordon's daughter. Unknown. *MaB*

The **duke** of Plaza-Toro. See The gondoliers

Dum and Dee. See "Tweedledum and Tweedledee"

The **dumb** soldier. Robert Louis Stevenson. *UnG*

The **dumb** wife cured. Unknown. *UnMc*

E

Dunbar, Paul Laurence
  A boy's summer song. *BrS*
  An easy-goin' fellow. *BrR-6*
  A frolic. *BrR-5*
  Philosophy. *BrL-8*
  Song of summer. *BrL-8*

Duncan, Mary Lundie
  A child's evening prayer. *DoP*
    The good shepherd. *HuL-1*
  The good shepherd. See A child's evening prayer

Duncan, Robert
  The reaper. *GrCc*

The **dunce** ("And Science said") Walter De La Mare. *PlI*

The **dunce** ("Ring the bells, ring") Mother Goose. *OpO*

Dunkirk, Battle of, 1940
  Dunkirk. R. Nathan. *UnMc*

Dunkirk. Robert Nathan. *UnMc*

Dunstan, Saint (about)
  The devil. Mother Goose. *OpO*

Durell, Ann
  Cornish magic. *FeF*

Durenda Fair. David McCord. *McFf*

Durfey, Thomas
  "I'll sail upon the dog-star." *SmLg*

"**During** the strike, the ponies were brought up." See The ponies

During wind and rain. Thomas Hardy. *HaP*

Durston, Georgia Roberts
  The hippopotamus. *ArTp*
  The wolf. *ArTp*

"The **dusky** night rides down the sky." See A-hunting we will go

Dust
  A peck of gold. R. Frost. *FrY*

"**Dust** always blowing about the town." See A peck of gold

Dust of snow. Robert Frost. *ArTp—FrR—FrY—NaM—ThP*

Dust to dust. Thomas Hood. *UnG*

The **dustman.** Clive Sansom. *HuL-1*

A **Dutch** picture. Henry Wadsworth Longfellow. *NaM*

Duty. See also Conduct of life
  Casabianca. D. F. Hemans. *FeF—UnG*
  Duty of the student. E. Anthony. *UnG*
  Jim Bludso of the Prairie Belle. J. Hay. *BrL-8—UnMc*
  The leak in the dike. P. Cary. *FeF*
  Ode to duty. E. V. Rieu. *RiF*
  Whole duty of children. R. L. Stevenson. *NaE*

Duty of the student. Edward Anthony. *UnG*

Dwarfs
  The brown dwarf of Rügen. J. G. Whittier. *CoPm*

Dyer, Edward
  "My mind to me a kingdom is." *HaP*

"**Dying** leaf and dead leaf." See Myfanwy among the leaves

The **dying** swan. Alfred Tennyson. *HoW*

The **dynasts,** sel. Thomas Hardy
  We be the king's men. *HuL-2*
  Men who march away. *DeT*

$E = MC^2$. Morris Bishop. *PlI*

E is for elf. Eleanor Farjeon. *FaCb*

"**E** is the escalator." See All around the town

E-Yeh-Shuré (Louise Abeita)
  Beauty. *ArTp—BrR-5—FeF—JoAc*

"**Each** morning when the dawn returns." See The firetender

The **eagle.** Alfred Tennyson. *ArTp—FeF—HoW—ReT—SmLg—ThP—UnG*

"An **eagle** flew from north to south." Unknown. *MoY*

Eagle on the mountain crest. Hilda Conkling. *DoP*

"**Eagle,** why soarest thou above that tomb." See Plato's tomb

Eagles
  The eagle. A. Tennyson. *ArTp—FeF—HoW—ReT—SmLg—ThP—UnG*
  Eagle on the mountain crest. H. Conkling. *DoP*

Eakman, Florence
  Our clock. *BrS*

Eardrops. William Henry Davies. *GrCc*

Earl Mar's daughter. Unknown. *MaB*

"**Earlier,** earlier." See Change of seasons

Early. Dorothy Aldis. *AlA*

Early April. Robert Frost. *HaY*

The **early** bird. Jessamine Sykes Reilly. *BrR-4*

"An **early** dew woos the half-opened flowers." See The thousand nights and one—Haroun's favorite song

"**Early,** early, comes the dark." See Witches' song

Early, early Easter day. Aileen Fisher. *BrS—McAw*

"**Early** in the morning." Louis Simpson. *HaP*

"**Early** in the morning, before the day began." See The angel in the apple tree

"**Early** in the morning, let's go to the country." Unknown. *WiRm*

The **early** morning. Hilaire Belloc. *McW*

"**Early** the next morning, I woke up hearing a sound." See The house beyond the meadow—The strangest wish

"**Early** this morning when earth was empty." See Egg to eat

"**Early** to bed and early to rise." See "Early to bed, early to rise"

"**Early** to bed, early to rise." Mother Goose. *AnI*

"**Early** to bed and early to rise." *LiL*

Ears
  Eardrops. W. H. Davies. *GrCc*

Earth. See World

"The **earth** abideth forever." See Ecclesiastes

Earth and sea. Alexander Sergeyevich Pushkin, tr. fr. the Russian by Cecil Kisch. *PaS*

Earth and sky. Eleanor Farjeon. *CoPs—EaW—HuL-2*

A rainbow piece. *EaI*
A rainy piece. *EaI*
The robber. *BrS*
Sea-shell. *EaI*
Seven today. *BrBc*
Shadow dance. *ArTp—HuL-2*
"Sing a song of moonlight." *BrS*
"Sing a song of sunshine." *BrS*
Snow everywhere. *EaI*
Snow in spring. *EaI*
Snow picture. *EaI*
Snowflake world. *EaI*
The stars, the dark, and the daisies. *EaI*
"Stay, Christmas." *BrS*
The sunlight ran on little feet. *EaI*
Ten to one. *EaI*
The three horses. *EaI*
"Timothy Boon." *ArTp*
Trouble at the farm. *HuL-1*
Under the moon. *EaI*
Waking time. *ArTp—BrS*
"Where are you going." *EaI*
Where's Mary. *ArTp*
"The wind came running." *EaI*
The window box. *EaI*
Winter in the wood. *HaY*
Yellow balloon. *EaI*

An **easy-goin'** feller. Paul Laurence Dunbar. *BrR-6*

"**Eat** no green apples or you'll droop." See Advice to small children

Eating. See Food and eating

Eaton, Arthur Wentworth Hamilton
The phantom light of the Baie des Chaleurs. *CoPm*

Eaton, Burnham
Late winter on our beach. *McAw*

Eaton, Walter Prichard
The birches. *BrL-k—HuSv*
The willows. *FeF*

Eberhart, Richard
"Go to the shine that's on a tree." *PlU*
The groundhog. *HaP*

Ecclesiastes, sels. Bible, Old Testament
"Cast thy bread upon the waters." *ArTp*
"The earth abideth forever." *FeF*
The light is sweet. *FeF*

Echo. Unknown. *BrL-k*

Echo song. See The princess—Bugle song

Echoes
Bugle song. From The princess. A. Tennyson. *FeF—HuSv*
Blow, bugle, blow. *HoW—PlU*
Echo song. *DeT*
Song. *ReT*
"The splendor falls on castle walls." *ArTp*
The splendour falls. *SmLg*
Echo. Unknown. *BrL-k .*
Heaven. G. Herbert. *GrCc*
I met a man down in the well. J. Ciardi. *CiI*
"I met a man I could not see." J. Ciardi. *CiI*

The **echoing** (ecchoing) green. William Blake. *CoPs—HoW—JoAc*

An **eclipse.** Pindar, tr. fr. the Greek by C. M. Bowra. *PaS*

"**Eddington's** universe goes phut." See Richard Tolman's universe

The **Eddystone** light. Unknown. *CoSp*

Edelman, Katherine
Irish grandmother. *BrS*
Night train. *BrR-6*

Eden, Helen Parry
Four-paws. *DeT*

Edey, Marion
The ant village. *ArTp—FeF*
August afternoon. *HaY*
Christmas eve. *HaY*
The jolly woodchuck. *ArTp—CoI—FeF—HuL-1*
The little fox. *ArTp*
Midsummer night. *HaY*
Open the door. *ArTp—BrS—HuL-1*
Our birthday. *BrBc—BrS*
So many monkeys. *ArTp*
"Trot along, pony." *ArTp*

Edison, Thomas (about)
And yet fools say. G. S. Holmes. *ArTp—BrL-7*

Edman, Irwin
Acquiescence. *ThP*

Edmonds, J. M.
Night. tr. *PaS*

Edouard. Ogden Nash. *LoL*

Edward, Lord Herbert of Cherbury
Melander supposed to love Susan, but did love Ann. *GrCc*

Edward, Edward. Unknown. *HaP—MaB—UnMc*

Edward Lear went away to-day. Eleanor Farjeon. *FaN*

Edwards, E. D.
The herd-boy's song. tr. *PaS*
The moon in the mountains. tr. *PaS*
On a mountain road. tr. *PaS*
Pear-trees by the fence. tr. *PaS*
The white egret. tr. *PaS*

Eek eek. Dorothy Aldis. *AlHd*

Eeka, neeka. Walter De La Mare. *McW*

"**Eeka,** neeka, leeka, lee." See Eeka, neeka

The **eel.** Ogden Nash. *FeF—JoAc*

Eels
The eel. O. Nash. *FeF—JoAc*
A sad song. J. Ciardi. *CiY*

"**Eency** weency spider climbed the water spout." Unknown. *DeMg*

"**Eenie,** meenie, mackeracka." Mother Goose. *OpO*

"**Eenie,** meenie, minie, mo." Unknown. *WiRm*
Counting-out rhymes. *FeF*

"**Eenity,** feenity, fickety, feg." Mother Goose. *OpO*

"**Eeny,** meeny, miney, mo." See The counting man

"**Eeny,** weeny, winey, wo." Mother Goose. *OpO .*

Ee-oh. See "A fox jumped up one winter's night"

Eerily sweet. Elizabeth Jane Coatsworth. *EaW*

"**Eftsoons** they heard a most melodious sound." See The faerie queene—The bower of bliss

The **egg.** Laura E. Richards. *ArTp*

"An **egg** of humble sphere." See The prodigal egg

Egg to eat. James Reeves. *ReR*

Eggs. See also Birds—Eggs and nests
"As I was walking in a field of wheat." Mother Goose. *OpO*
Easter eggs. H. Behn. *BeW*
The egg. L. E. Richards. *ArTp*
Egg to eat. J. Reeves. *ReR*
"Humpty Dumpty sat on a wall." Mother Goose. *DeMg—HuSv—JoAc—LiL—OpO*
Humpty Dumpty. *BrL-k*
The importance of eggs. D. McCord. *McT*
"In marble halls as white as milk." Mother Goose. *DeMg—JoAc—OpO*
"In marble walls as white as milk." *HuSv*
The little black hen. A. A. Milne. *MiWc*
Mrs Hen. M. A. Campbell. *HuL-1*
The prodigal egg. Unknown. *CoH*
"There was an old man of Thermopylae." E. Lear
Limericks. *NaE*

"**Eggs,** butter, bread." Mother Goose. *DeMg*

Egrets. See Herons

Egypt
Ozymandias. P. B. Shelley. *BrL-7—HaP—McW—SmLg—UnG*
"The **Egyptians** say, The sun has twice." See Hudibras, Canto III

Eichendorff, Joseph von
Moon-night. *PaS*
Nocturne. *PaS*

"**Eight** o'clock." Christina Georgina Rossetti. *ArTp*

1805. Robert Graves. *NaE—SmLg*

Eighth street west. Rachel Field. *BrS*

Einstein, Albert (about)
Einstein, 1929. A. MacLeish. *PlI*
The gift to be simple. H. Moss. *PlI*

Einstein, 1929. Archibald MacLeish. *PlI*

Elaine. Edna St Vincent Millay. *ThP*

Elderton, William
York, York for my money. *ReG*

Eldorado. Edgar Allan Poe. *HoW—McW—SmLg*

"**Elected** silence, sing to me." See The habit of perfection

Electricity
And yet fools say. G. S. Holmes. *ArTp—BrL-7*

Elegies. See Laments

Elegy. Chidiock Tichborne. *HaP*
The spring is past. *DeT* (sel.)

Elegy for Lucy Lloyd. Llewelyn Goch, tr. fr. the Welsh by Ernest Rhys. *PaS*

Elegy in a country churchyard. Gilbert Keith Chesterton. *NaE*

Elegy on the death of a mad dog. See The vicar of Wakefield

Elegy on the death of Mme Anna Pavlova. E. H. W. Meyerstein. *PlU* (sel.)

Elegy written in a country churchyard. Thomas Gray. *DeT—HaP*

The **elements.** William Henry Davies. *McW*

The **elephant** ("Here comes the elephant") Herbert Asquith. *ArTp*

The **elephant** ("When people call this beast to mind") Hilaire Belloc. *ArTp—LoL*

Elephant ("When you put me up on the elephant's back") William Jay Smith. *SmB*

The **elephant** ("With wrinkled hide and great frayed ears") See A circus garland

*The **elephant** always carries his trunk." See The elephant's trunk

"The **elephant** has a great big trunk." Unknown. *WiRm*

"The **elephant** he started in and made tremendous fuss." See Passing it along

Elephants
The blind men and the elephant. J. G. Saxe. *CoSp—JoAc—UnG—UnMc*
The circus. M. L. Allen. *AlP*
Cradle song of the elephants. A. Del Valle. *FeF*
The elephant ("Here comes the elephant") H. Asquith. *ArTp*
The elephant ("When people call this beast to mind") H. Belloc. *ArTp—LoL*
Elephant ("When you put me up on the elephant's back") W. J. Smith. *SmB*
The elephant ("With wrinkled hide and great frayed ears") From A circus garland. R. Field. *HuSv*
"The elephant has a great big trunk." Unknown. *WiRm*
The elephants. D. Aldis. *AlA*
The elephant's trunk. A. Wilkins. *ArTp*
Eletelephony. L. E. Richards. *ArTp—CoI—FeF—JoAc—LoL—PeF*
Holding hands. L. M. Link. *ArTp—FeF—NaM*
"I asked my mother for fifteen cents." Unknown. *ArTp*
American Father Gander. *UnG*
I asked my mother. *NaM*
"I asked my mother for fifty cents." *JoAc*
In the middle. D. McCord. *McFf*
Let's pretend. J. S. Tippett. *McAw*
Some questions to be asked of a rajah, perhaps by the Associated Press. P. Newman. *CoH*
Way down South. Unknown. *NaE*
"Way down South where the coconuts grow." Unknown. *WiRm*

The **elephants.** Dorothy Aldis. *AlA*

The **elephant's** trunk. Alice Wilkins. *ArTp*

"**Elephants** walking." See Holding hands

Eletelephony. Laura E. Richards. *ArTp—CoI—FeF—JoAc—LoL—PeF*

Elevator. Unknown. *WoJ*

Elevators
Elevator. Unknown. *WoJ*
Lift-boy. R. Graves. *GrP*
Song: Lift-boy. *GrCc*

The **elf** and the dormouse. Oliver Herford. *ArTp—FeF—HuL-1—PeF—UnG*

"**Elf.** Elf. Elf." See E is for elf

"An **elf** sat on a twig." See The elf singing

The **elf** singing. William Allingham. *HuSv—UnG*

The **elfin-knight.** Unknown. *MaB*

Elfin song. See The culprit fay

Eliot, George, pseud. (Marian [or Mary
    Ann] Evans Lewes Cross)
  Count that day lost. *ThP*
Eliot, T. (Thomas) S. (Stearns)
  The ad-dressing of cats. *UnG*
  "And now you live dispersed on ribbon
    roads." See The rock
  Aunt Helen. *HaP*
  Burnt Norton. *PlU* (sel.)
  Cape Ann. See Landscapes
  Choruses from The rock. See The rock
  Cousin Nancy. *HaP*
  The dry salvages, sel.
    "I do not know much about gods; but
      I think that the river." *ArTp*
  Four quartets. *PlI* (sel.)
  Growltiger's last stand. *SmLg*
  The hippopotamus. *HaP*
  "I do not know much about gods; but I
    think that the river." See The dry
    salvages
  "If humility and purity be not in the
    heart." See The rock
  Journey of the Magi. *HaP—SmLg*
  Landscapes, sels.
    Cape Ann. *JoAc—NaE—ReT—SmLg*
    New Hampshire. *HaP—ReT—SmLg*
    Rannoch, by Glencoe. *SmLg*
    Usk. *SmLg*
    Virginia. *HaP—SmLg*
  Macavity: The mystery cat. *ArTp—McW*
  The naming of cats. *CoH*
  New Hampshire. See Landscapes
  The old Gumbie cat. *UnG*
  Prelude I. *ArTp*
    Prelude. *NaM*
  Rannoch, by Glencoe. See Landscapes
  The rock, sels.
    "And now you live dispersed on
      ribbon roads." *ArTp*
    Choruses from The rock. *GrCc*
    "If humility and purity be not in the
      heart." *ArTp*
    "The world turns and the world
      changes." *ArTp*
  The Rum Tum Tugger. *ArTp—FeF—NaE*
  Skimbleshanks: The railway cat. *SmLg*
  The song of the Jellicles. *LoL—SmLg*
  Usk. See Landscapes
  Virginia. See Landscapes
  "The world turns and the world changes."
    See The rock
The elixir. George Herbert. *SmLg*
"Eliza Ottley, seventy-five." See The true
    tale of Eliza Ottley
Elizabeth. See "Elizabeth, Elspeth, Betsy
    and Bess"
"Elizabeth Ann." See Explained
Elizabeth at the piano. Horace Gregory.
    PlU
"Elizabeth cried." Eleanor Farjeon. *McAw*
"Elizabeth, Elspeth, Betsy and Bess."
    Mother Goose. *DeMg—JoAc—OpO*
  Elizabeth. *ReG*
"Elizabeth, Elspeth, Betty and Bess." See
    "Elizabeth, Elspeth, Betsy and Bess"
"Elizabeth of Hungary." See The princesses'
    carol

Elliott, F. Ann
  Pictures. *HuL-2*
Elsie Marley. See "Elsie Marley is grown
    so fine"
"Elsie Marley is grown so fine." Mother
    Goose. *DeMg*
  Elsie Marley. *OpO*
Elves. See Fairies
The elves' dance. Thomas Ravenscroft. *DeT*
    —FeF—JoAc
Elves' song. Ben Jonson. *DeT*
  Buzz and hum. *OpO*
Emans, Elaine V.
  Birthday. *BrBc*
  For a birthday. *BrBc*
The embarrassing episode of little Miss
    Muffet. Guy Wetmore Carryl. *CoSp—
    FeF*
"Emerald April, September's gold." See
    Song of the seasons
"An emerald is as green as grass." Christina
    Georgina Rossetti. *ArTp*
  Precious stones. *DeT—UnG*
"The emeralds are singing on the grasses."
    See How many heavens
Emerson, Ralph Waldo
  "Announced by all the trumpets of the
    sky." *ArTp*
    The snow storm. *HoW*
  April and May. *JoAc*
  Atom from atom. *PlI*
  The chickadee. *FeF*
  Concord hymn. *FeF—HuSv*
  Fable. See The mountain and the squirrel
  Flower chorus. *HuL-2*
  Forbearance. *ThP*
  "Give all to love." *McW* (sel.)
  The humble-bee. *FeF* (sel.)
  "The mountain and the squirrel." *FeF—
    UnG*
    Fable. *BrR-4*
  Music. *UnG*
  A nation's strength. *FeF*
  The past. *SmLg*
  The rhodora. *UnG*
  The snow storm. See "Announced by all
    the trumpets of the sky"
  Spring prayer. *HuL-2*
  Two rivers. *GrCc*
  Wealth. *PlI*
"Emily, Bob, and Jane." Eleanor Farjeon.
    FaN
Emily Jane. Laura E. Richards. *HuL-1*
Emma's store. Dorothy Aldis. *AlA*
"Emmeline." See Before tea
Emmett, Dan D.
  Dixie. *FeF* (sel.)
The emperor of ice-cream. Wallace Stevens.
    HaP
The emperors of Rome. Eleanor Farjeon.
    FaCb
The emperor's rhyme. A. A. Milne. *MiWc*
The enchanted shirt. John Hay. *HuL-2—
    UnG—UnMc*
Enchanted summer. Harry Behn. *BeW*
Enchantment
  Alison Gross. Unknown. *MaB*
  Bewitched. W. De La Mare. *CoPm*

Entropy. Theodore Spencer. *PlI*

"Envied by us all." See Maple leaves

Envoy. See "Matthew, Mark, Luke, and John"

Envy. See Jealousy

"An epicure, dining at Crewe." Unknown. *CoH—LoL*

Limericks. *BrL-7*

Limericks since Lear. *UnG*

An epigram. Samuel Taylor Coleridge. *UnG*

Epigram on Handel and Bononcini. John Byrom. *PlU*

Epilogue ("If Luther's day expand to Darwin's year") Herman Melville. *PlI*

Epilogue ("O where are you going, said reader to rider") W. H. Auden. *SmLg*

The epistle of Paul to the Philippians, sel. Bible, New Testament

"Whatsoever things are true." *ArTp*

Epistle to be left in the earth. Archibald MacLeish. *PlI*

Epistle to Dr Arbuthnot, sel. Alexander Pope
Atticus. *HaP*

Epitaph ("Here lies a mouse of gentle ways") Elizabeth Jane Coatsworth. *CoM*

An epitaph ("Under this sod and beneath these trees") Unknown. *NaM*

Epitaph for a Concord boy. Stanley Young. *McW*

Epitaph for Chaeroneia. Aristotle, tr. fr. the Greek by C. R. Kennedy. *PaS*

Epitaph intended for Sir Isaac Newton. Alexander Pope. *PlI*

Epitaph on a Jacobite. Thomas Babington Macaulay. *DeT*

An epitaph on Salathiel Pavy. Ben Jonson. *HaP*

An epitaph upon the celebrated Claudy Philips, musician, who died very poor. Samuel Johnson. *PlU*

Epitaphs
A dead liar speaks. M. Lewis. *UnG*
Epitaph ("Here lies a mouse of gentle ways") E. J. Coatsworth. *CoM*
An epitaph ("Under this sod and beneath these trees") Unknown. *NaM*
Epitaph for a Concord boy. S. Young. *McW*
Epitaph for Chaeroneia. Aristotle. *PaS*
Epitaph intended for Sir Isaac Newton. A. Pope. *PlI*
Epitaph on a Jacobite. T. B. Macaulay. *DeT*
An epitaph on Salathiel Pavy. B. Jonson. *HaP*
An epitaph upon the celebrated Claudy Philips, musician, who died very poor. S. Johnson. *PlU*
"Here I lie at the chancel door." Unknown
Four country epitaphs. *UnG*
Here lies. Unknown. *UnG*
"Here lies father, mother, sister, and I." Unknown
Four country epitaphs. *UnG*
"Here lies me and my three daughters." Unknown
Four country epitaphs. *UnG*

"Here lies the body of Jonathan Pound." Unknown
Four country epitaphs. *UnG*
An old man's epitaph. E. Farjeon. *FaCb— FaN*
On a dentist. Unknown. *UnG*
On a doctor named Isaac Letsome. Unknown. *UnG*
On a man named Merideth. Unknown. *UnG*
On a thieving locksmith. Unknown. *UnG*
On a tired housewife. Unknown. *NaE*
On Charles II. J. Wilmot, Earl of Rochester. *HaP—UnG*
On John Bun. Unknown. *UnG*
On Leslie Moore. Unknown. *UnG*
On Martha Snell. Unknown. *UnG*
On Prince Frederick. Unknown. *UnG*
On Richard Dent, landlord. Unknown. *UnG*
On Skugg. B. Franklin. *UnG*
On stubborn Michael Shay. Unknown. *UnG*
On the university carrier. J. Milton. *SmLg*
The Spoon River anthology, sels. E. L. Masters
Achilles Deatheridge. *UnMc*
Anne Rutledge. *CoPs—HaP*
Fiddler Jones. *PlU—SmLg*
Petit, the poet. *HaP—SmLg*
William Jones. *PlI*

The equinox. Henry Wadsworth Longfellow. *DeT*

"Ere the moon begins to rise." See Sleepy song

"Ere yet the sun is high." See The iris

The erl-king. Johann Wolfgang von Goethe, tr. fr. the German by Walter Scott. *UnMc*

Erlington. Unknown. *MaB*

"Erlington had a fair daughter." See Erlington

"Ernest was an elephant, a great big fellow." See The four friends

Escalators
"E is the escalator." From All around the town. P. McGinley. *ArTp—McAw*

Escape. Elinor Wylie, *JoAc—ReT*

Escape at bedtime. Robert Louis Stevenson. *ArTp—BrR-5—PeF—UnG*

Escapes
Charley Lee. H. H. Knibbs. *McW*
Escape. E. Wylie *JoAc—ReT*
Escape at bedtime. R. L. Stevenson. *ArTp —BrR-5—PeF—UnG*

Eskimos
The kayak. Unknown. *FeF*
Novel experience. C. Wells. *BrR-3*

An essay on man. Alexander Pope. *HaP* (sel.)—*PlI* (sel.)
Vice. *ThP* (sel.)

The eternal. Esaias Tegnér, tr. fr. the Swedish by Charles Wharton Stork. *PaS*

Eternity. See Time

"Eternity is like unto a ring." See Time and eternity

Etiquette
Etiquette. W. S. Gilbert. *CoH—UnMc*
"Excuse us, animals in the zoo." A. Wynne. *ArTp*
"Hearts, like doors, will ope with ease." Mother Goose. *OpO*
"Hold up your head." Mother Goose. *OpO*
"I eat my peas with honey." Unknown. *NaE*
Peas. *CoH—FeF*
"Joe, Joe, strong and able." Unknown. *WoF*
Manners. M. G. Van Rensselaer. *FeF*
"Manners in the dining room." Mother Goose. *OpO*
"Of a little take a little." Mother Goose. *OpO*
Of courtesy. A. Guiterman. *ArTp*
Proverbs. *ThP*
Please. D. Aldis. *AlA*
Politeness. A. A. Milne. *MiWc*
"There was an old man from Antigua." Unknown. *CoH*
Tony the turtle. E. V. Rieu. *HuL-2—RiF*
We must be polite. C. Sandburg. *SaW*
When I'm invited. D. Aldis. *AlHd*
Whole duty of children. R. L. Stevenson. *NaE*
"Wilful waste brings woeful want." Mother Goose. *OpO*
Zoo manners. E. Mathias. *HuL-1*
Etiquette. William Schwenck Gilbert. *CoH—UnMc*
Étude réaliste, sel. Algernon Charles Swinburne
A baby's feet. *FeF*
Euclid of Alexandria (about)
Euclid. V. Lindsay. *PlI*
"Euclid alone has looked on beauty bare." E. St V. Millay. *PlI*
Euclid. Vachel Lindsay. *PlI*
"Euclid alone has looked on beauty bare." Edna St Vincent Millay. *PlI*
Eulalie. Edgar Allan Poe. *NaE*
Euripides
The Bacchae, sel.
Where shall wisdom be found. *PaS—PlI*
The beginning of day. *PaS*
Chorus from Medea. See Medea
Hippolytus, sel.
O for the wings of a dove. *PaS*
Medea, sel.
Chorus from Medea. *PaS*
O for the wings of a dove. See Hippolytus
Where shall wisdom be found. See The Bacchae
Europe. See also names of European countries, as France
America for me. H. Van Dyke. *BrR-5*
The king rides forth. E. Farjeon. *FaCb—FaN*
European war, 1914-1918. See also Veterans day
Everyone sang. S. Sassoon. *CoPs—McW*
In Flanders fields. J. McCrae. *BrS*
The spires of Oxford. W. M. Letts. *BrL-7*
These fought. E. Pound. *HaP*

Euterpe (about)
New chitons for old gods. D. McCord. *PlU* (sel.)
"Euterpe, you must think us common queer." See New chitons for old gods
Eutychides. Lucilius, tr. by Edwin Arlington Robinson. *PlU*
"Eutychides, who wrote the songs." See Eutychides
Euwer, Anthony
My face. *CoH*
Limericks since Lear. *UnG*
"Evan Kirk." John Ciardi. *CiM*
Evans, Sebastian
The seven fiddlers. *CoPm*
Eve, Beatrice
The shower. *DeT*
Eve. See Adam and Eve
Eve. Ralph Hodgson. *NaE*
"Eve, with her basket, was." See Eve
"Even my tombstone gives the truth away." See A dead liar speaks
"Even now." See I love long black eyes
"Even such is time, that takes in trust." See The conclusion
"Even though." See Scat, scitten
Evening. See also Night
"As soon as ever twilight comes." W. De La Mare. *BrS*
At eventide. E. Farjeon. *FaCb—FaN*
"Beauty is most at twilight's close." P. Lagerkvist. *PaS*
The dark hills. E. A. Robinson. *HaP*
Evening ("The day's grown old, the fainting sun") C. Cotton. *HoW*
Evening ("Now the drowsy sun shine") H. Behn. *BeW—JoAc*
Evening at the farm. J. Trowbridge. *FeF*
Evening on the farm. *NaM*
Evening hymn ("The day is done") E. M. Roberts. *ArTp*
Evening hymn ("I hear no voice, I feel no touch") Unknown. *BrL-k—DoP*
Evening hymn for a little family. A. and J. Taylor. *DoP*
Evening in a sugar orchard. R. Frost. *FrR*
Evening landscape. P. de Mont. *PaS*
Evening prayer. H. Hagedorn. *DoP*
Evening song. From The faithful shepherdess. J. Fletcher. *DeT*
Evening waterfall. C. Sandburg. *GrCc*
"Hard from the southeast blows the wind." E. J. Coatsworth. *ArTp—HuL-2*
"I'll tell you how the sun rose." E. Dickinson. *BrS—NaM*
A day. *UnG*
Poem. *ReT*
The sun. *HuSv*
Sunrise and sunset. *BrR-6*
"Now the day is over." S. Baring-Gould. *DeT*
Prelude I. T. S. Eliot. *ArTp*
Prelude. *NaM*
The sun is first to rise. E. J. Coatsworth. *HuSv*
"This is my rock." D. McCord. *BrS—FeF—HuSv—McFf*
Twilight. F. Tyutchev. *PaS*
Village before sunset. F. Cornford. *SmLg*

Evening ("The day's grown old, the fainting sun") Charles Cotton. *HoW*

Evening ("Now the drowsy sun shine") Harry Behn. *BeW—JoAc*

Evening at the farm. John Townsend Trowbridge. *FeF*

Evening on the farm. *NaM*

Evening hymn ("The day is done") Elizabeth Madox Roberts. *ArTp*

Evening hymn ("I hear no voice, I feel no touch") Unknown. *BrL-k—DoP*

An evening hymn for a little family. Ann and Jane Taylor. *DoP*

Evening in a sugar orchard. Robert Frost. *FrR*

Evening landscape. Pol de Mont, tr. fr. the Flemish by Jethro Bithell. *PaS*

Evening on the farm. See Evening at the farm

Evening prayer. Hermann Hagedorn. *DoP*

"Evening red and morning grey." Mother Goose. *OpO*

Signs, seasons, and sense. *UnG*

Evening song. See The faithful shepherdess

Evening walk. Dorothy Aldis. *AlA*

Evening waterfall. Carl Sandburg. *GrCc*

"Evenings." See Setting the table

"Ever, ever, not ever so terrible." See Castor oil

Ever since. Elizabeth Jane Coatsworth. *BrS*

"Every branch big with it." See Snow in the suburbs

"Every button has a door." See About buttons

"Every lady in this land." Mother Goose. *DeMg—OpO*

"Every morning." See Park play

"Every morning when the sun." See This happy day

"Every night as I go to bed." See Waltzing mice

"Every rose on the little tree." See The little rose tree

"Every Thursday morning." See The dustman

"Every time I climb a tree." See Five chants

"Every time I come to town." Unknown. *WoF*

American Father Gander. *UnG*

"Every time the bucks went clattering." See Earthy anecdote

"Every valley drinks." See Winter rain

Every week song. Myra Cohn Livingston. *LiWa*

"Every where." See Snowy morning

"Everybody says." Dorothy Aldis. *AlA—BrL-k—FeF—HuL-1*

Everybody stared. Ivy O. Eastwick. *EaI*

"Everybody's in the ocean." See Down by the sea

"Everyone grumbled. The sky was grey." See Daddy fell into the pond

"Everyone is tight asleep." See Morning

Everyone sang. Siegfried Sassoon. *CoPs—McW*

"Everyone suddenly burst out singing." See Everyone sang

"Everyone's bursting outdoors, outdoors." See Spring

"Everything is black and gold." See Black and gold

"Everything's been different." See The birthday child

"Everywhere, everywhere, Christmas tonight." See Christmas everywhere

"Everywhere the wind blows." See Springsigns

Ewing, Juliana Horatia

For good luck. *FeF*

A friend in the garden. *BrR-3—FeF—HuSv*

Gifts. *ThP*

Ex ore infantium. Francis Thompson. *DoP*

Exactly right. Dorothy Aldis. *AlHd*

The example. William Henry Davies. *DoP*

Excelsior. Henry Wadsworth Longfellow. *FeF*

"Excuse us, animals in the zoo." Annette Wynne. *ArTp*

The execution of Montrose. William Edmondstone Aytoun. *PaOm*

Expectans expectavi. Charles Hamilton Sorley. *SmLg*

Experience. Aline Kilmer. *BrBc*

Explained. A. A. Milne. *MiWc*

An explanation of the grasshopper. Vachel Lindsay. *FeF—HuSv*

Explanation, on coming home late. Richard Hughes. *ReT*

Exploration. See Explorers and exploration

Explorers. James Reeves. *ReBl*

Explorers and exploration. See also names of explorers, as Columbus, Christopher

A dash to the pole. W. Irwin. *CoH*

Four quartets. T. S. Eliot. *PlI* (sel.)

The unexplorer. E. St V. Millay. *NaM*

The exposed nest. Robert Frost. *FrY*

The extraordinary dog. Nancy Byrd Turner. *ArTp*

Extremes. James Whitcomb Riley. *BrL-k—FeF*

"Eye winker." Mother Goose. *DeMg--OpO*

Eyes

Five eyes. W. De La Mare. *CoI*

A pair of sea-green eyes. H. MacDiarmid. *GrCc*

The powerful eyes o' Jeremy Tait. I. Irwin. *CoSp*

Sweeping Wendy: Study in fugue. C. Sandburg. *SaW*

"There was a man in our town." Mother Goose. *DeMg*

"There was a man of Thessaly." Mother Goose. *LiL*

Alexander's song. *JoAc*

Man of Thessaly. *OpO*

"There was a young lady whose eyes." E. Lear. *CoH*

Women's eyes. Bhartrihari. *PaS*

The eyes of God. Gabriel Setoun. *DoP*

F

F., D.

The sower. tr. *FeF*

F. P. A., pseud. See Adams, Franklin P.

F is for fairy queen. Eleanor Farjeon. *FaCb*

"F is the fighting firetruck." See All around the town

"Fa, fe, fi, fo, fum." See "Fe, fi, fo, fum"

Fable. See "The mountain and the squirrel"

The fable of the magnet and the churn. See Patience

The fable of the old man, the boy, and the donkey. Ian Serraillier. *ReG*

Fables

The ant and the cricket. Aesop. *DeT—UnG*

At Woodward's garden. R. Frost. *FrR—Pll*

The blind men and the elephant. J. G. Saxe. *CoSp—JoAc—UnG—UnMc*

The boy and the wolf. Aesop. *UnMc*

The camel and the flotsam. J. De La Fontaine. *JoAc*

The crow and the fox. J. De La Fontaine. *BrL-7—UnMc*

The dairymaid and her milk-pot. J. De La Fontaine. *JoAc*

The dove and the ant. J. De La Fontaine. *JoAc*

The enchanted shirt. J. Hay. *HuL-2—UnG—UnMc*

The fable of the magnet and the churn. From Patience. W. S. Gilbert. *FeF*

The fable of the old man, the boy, and the donkey. I. Serraillier. *ReG*

The fearful finale of the irascible mouse. G. W. Carryl. *CoH*

Fox and crow. W. J. Smith. *SmB*

The fox and the goat. J. De La Fontaine. *JoAc*

The frog who wanted a king. Aesop. *UnG*
  The frogs who wanted a king. *UnMc*

The greedy fox and the elusive grapes. Aesop. *UnMc*
  The fox and the grapes. *UnG*

How a fisherman corked up his foe in a jar. G. W. Carryl. *CoPm*

Little Red Riding Hood. G. W. Carryl. *CoH*

"The mountain and the squirrel." R. W. Emerson. *FeF—UnG*
  Fable. *BrR-4*

"The mouse that gnawed the oak tree down." V. Lindsay. *BrL-7*

The mouse, the frog, and the little red hen. Unknown. *HuL-1*

The new duckling. A. Noyes. *FeF*

The swan and goose. Aesop. *PlU*
  The swan and the goose. *FeF*

The sycophantic fox and the gullible raven. G. W. Carryl. *CoH*

A face. Robert Browning. *GrCc*

Faces

A coffeepot face. A. Fisher. *BrL-k*

Curious something. W. Welles. *ArTp*

A face. R. Browning. *GrCc*

My face. A. Euwer. *CoH*
  Limericks since Lear. *UnG*

Numbers and faces. W. H. Auden. *Pll* (sel.)

The old familiar faces. C. Lamb. *HaP*

Phizzog. C. Sandburg. *ArTp*

"Roses are red (pickles are green)." Unknown. *MoY*

"Roses are red (they grow)." Unknown. *MoY*

Someone's face. J. Ciardi. *CiM*

Under a hat rim. C. Sandburg. *SaW*

Factories

A lone striker. R. Frost. *FrR*

The faerie queene, sels. Edmund Spenser
  The bower of bliss. *PlU*
  Old January. *HaY*

"The faery beam upon you." See Gipsy song

Failure. See also Misfortune
  For those who fail. J. Miller. *BrL-8*
  How did you die. E. V. Cooke. *ThP*
  The star-splitter. R. Frost. *FrR—PlI*

"Fain would I live in safest freedom." August Graf von Platen, tr. fr. the German by Edwin Morgan. *PaS*

Faint music. Walter De La Mare. *SmLg*

"Faintly at first, and low." See Symphony: First movement

"Fair are the lilies." Unknown. *MoY*

"Fair daffodils, we weep to see." See To daffodils

The fair flower of Northumberland. Unknown. *MaB*

Fair maid of February. Eleanor Farjeon. *FaCb—FaN*

"A fair maid sat in her bower-door." See Young John

"The fair maid who, the first of May." Mother Goose. *DeMg*

"Fair maiden, white and red." See Celanta at the well of life

"Fair now is the springtide, now earth lies beholding." See The message of the March wind

"Fair stood the wind for France." See Agincourt

Fairies

Adventure. N. B. Turner. *HuSv*

Arethusa. P. B. Shelley. *HoW*

The bee's song. W. De La Mare. *LoL*

La belle dame sans merci. J. Keats. *CoSp — DeT — HaP — McW — SmLg — UnG—UnMc*

Berries. W. De La Mare. *ArTp*

"The best game the fairies play." R. Fyleman. *ArTp*

The brown dwarf of Rügen. J. G. Whittier. *CoPm*

Brownie. A. A. Milne. *MiWc*

Bugle song. From The princess. A. Tennyson. *FeF—HuSv*
  Blow, bugle, blow. *HoW—PlU*
  Echo song. *DeT*
  Song. *ReT*
  "The splendor falls on castle walls." *ArTp*
  The splendour falls. *SmLg*

Buttercups. W. Thorley. *FeF*

The canary. R. Fyleman. *HuL-1*

The child next door. R. Fyleman. *FeF*

"Come unto these yellow sands." From The tempest. W. Shakespeare. *DeT*
  Ariel's song. *ReT—SmLg*

Conversation with an April fool. R. B. Bennett. *BrS*

Cornish magic. A. Durell. *FeF*

Could it have been a shadow. M. Shannon. *ArTp—FeF—HuSv*

Crab-apple. E. Talbot. *ArTp—BrBc*

The culprit fay, sels. J. R. Drake
  Elfin song. *CoPm*
  A fairy in armor. *FeF*
E is for elf. E. Farjeon. *FaCb*
The elf and the dormouse. O. Herford.
  ArTp—FeF—HuL-1—PeF—UnG
The elf singing. W. Allingham. *HuSv—UnG*
The elfin-knight. Unknown. *MaB*
The elves' dance. T. Ravenscroft. *DeT—FeF—JoAc*
Elves' song. B. Jonson. *DeT*
The erl-king. J. W. von Goethe. *UnMc*
An explanation of the grasshopper. V. Lindsay. *FeF—HuSv*
F is for fairy queen. E. Farjeon. *FaCb*
Fairies ("I cannot see fairies") H. Conkling. *ArTp—BrL-k*
The fairies ("If ye will with Mab find grace") R. Herrick. *FeF*
  Queen Mab. *ReG*
Fairies ("There are fairies at the bottom of our garden") R. Fyleman. *HuL-1—HuSv—JoAc—PeF*
The fairies ("Up the airy mountain") W. Allingham. *CoPm—DeT—FeF—JoAc—NaE—PaOm—PeF—ReG—SmLg*
  "Up the airy mountain." *HuSv*
Fairies ("You can't see fairies unless you're good") M. Chute. *BrL-k—ChA*
"The fairies have never a penny to spend." R. Fyleman. *FeF*
The fairies of the Caldon Low. M. Howitt. *ReG*
Fairies' song. L. Hunt. *CoPm*
Fairy aeroplanes. A. B. Payne. *BrL-k*
The fairy and the bird. H. Behn. *BeW*
The fairy ball. R. Fyleman. *HuL-1*
The fairy book. A. F. Brown. *BrL-k*
Fairy days. W. M. Thackeray. *UnG*
Fairy gardens. E. Farjeon. *FaCb—FaN*
The fairy king. W. Allingham. *CoPm*
Fairy lullaby. From A midsummer-night's dream. W. Shakespeare. *FeF—UnG*
  You spotted snakes. *JoAc*
Fairy music. F. Ledwidge. *HaY*
Fairy shoes. A. Wynne. *BrL-k*
Fairy song ("By the moon we sport and play") J. Lyly. *DeT*
Fairy song ("Shed no tear. O, shed no tear") J. Keats. *FeF*
The fairy thorn. S. Ferguson. *DeT*
"A fairy went a-marketing." R. Fyleman. *HuL-1—JoAc*
"Faith, I wish I were a leprechaun." M. Ritter. *ArTp—FeF—HuL-2*
Fantasy. R. M. Skidmore. *CoPm*
Farewell to fairies. R. Corbet. *NaE—NaM*
  The fairies' farewell. *SmLg*
For a mocking voice. E. Farjeon. *ArTp—CoPm*
For good luck. J. H. Ewing. *FeF*
Frost fairies. C. Kuck. *BrR-3*
The gnome. H. Behn. *ArTp—BeW—FeF*
The goblin. Unknown. *ArTp—JoAc*
Goblin feet. J. R. R. Tolkien. *CoPm—FeF*
A goblinade. F. P. Jacques. *ArTp—HuL-1*
Green candles. H. Wolfe. *CoPm*
The green fiddler. R. Field. *CoSp*
The green gnome. R. Buchanan. *CoSp*

Have you watched the fairies. R. Fyleman. *ArTp—HuL-1—PeF*
The house beyond the meadow, sels. H. Behn. *BeH* (complete)
  The bears who once were giants
  First enchantment
  A friendly visit
  Goodbye to fairyland
  The magic map
  The strangest wish
  The thunder-and-lightning bug
How to tell goblins from elves. M. Shannon. *ArTp—FeF*
"I keep three wishes ready." A. Wynne. *ArTp—PeF*
I'd love to be a fairy's child. R. Graves. *BrBc—FeF—HuL-2*
"If you never talked with fairies." E. M. Fowler. *BrBc*
"If you see a fairy ring." Unknown. *HuL-1*
In the hours of darkness. J. Flexner. *FeF*
K is for kobold. E. Farjeon. *FaCb*
King Orpheo. Unknown. *MaB*
The leprahaun. R. D. Joyce. *CoPm*
The light-hearted fairy. Mother Goose. *BrR-4—FeF—HuL-2*
The lion of winter. From A midsummer-night's dream. W. Shakespeare. *HoW*
  Puck speaks. *ReT*
  Puck's song. *NaM*
The little elf. J. K. Bangs. *BrBc—BrL-k—HuL-1—JoAc—McW—PeF—UnG*
  The little elfman. *ArTp*
The little land. R. L. Stevenson. *HuSv—JoAc*
Little Orphant Annie. J. W. Riley. *FeF—HuSv—NaM*
The little wee man. Unknown. *MaB*
Lollocks. R. Graves. *NaE*
The Lorelei. H. Heine. *CoPm*
  The Loreley. *UnG*
Mab. From The satyr. B. Jonson. *HoW*
The man who hid his own front door. E. MacKinstry. *ArTp—FeF*
Midsummer magic. I. O. Eastwick. *ArTp*
Midsummer night. M. Edey. *HaY*
Mr Moon. B. Carman. *FeF—HuL-2*
The mocking fairy. W. De La Mare. *NaM*
Morning magic. H. Behn. *BeW*
N is for nixie. E. Farjeon. *FaCb*
Of a spider. W. Thorley. *FeF*
The one-legged stool. E. Blyton. *HuL-1*
Our guest. D. Aldis. *AlA*
"Over hill, over dale." From A midsummer-night's dream. W. Shakespeare. *DeT—JoAc—ReT*
  Fairy's wander-song. *FeF*
Overheard on a saltmarsh. H. Monro. *ArTp — CoPm — FeF — HuL-2 — JoAc —NaM—ReT*
The perils of invisibility. W. S. Gilbert. *CoSp*
Pigwiggin arms himself. From Nymphidia: The court of fairy. M. Drayton. *NaM*
Please. R. Fyleman. *BrL-k*
The plumpuppets. C. Morley. *ArTp—FeF*
The pointed people. R. Field. *FeF*
Puk-wudjies. P. R. Chalmers. *HuL-2*
Queen Mab ("A little fairy comes at night") T. Hood. *HuSv*

Fairies—*Continued*

Queen Mab ("Oh, then, I see Queen Mab hath been with you") From Romeo and Juliet. W. Shakespeare. *FeF—JoAc*
  Gallery of people. *UnG*
  A Shakespeare gallery. *UnMc*
R is for Robin Goodfellow. E. Farjeon. *FaCb*
The rainbow fairies. L. M. Hadley. *BrL-k*
The return of the fairy. H. Wolfe. *CoPm*
Rilloby-rill. H. Newbolt. *HuL-2—ReG*
Robin Goodfellow. B. Jonson. *ReG*
The seven ages of elf-hood. R. Field. *BrBc*
Sir Olaf. J. G. von Herder. *CoPm*
Sleepyhead. W. De La Mare. *ArTp*
Some one. W. De La Mare. *ArTp—BrL-k —HuL-2—HuSv—JoAc—NaM*
  Someone. *FeF*
Sometimes. R. Fyleman. *BrS*
Song for a midsummer night. E. J. Coatsworth. *HaY*
The spider's web. C. D. Cole. *HuL-1*
Stocking fairy. W. Welles. *ArTp—FeF— HuL-2*
The stolen child. W. B. Yeats. *CoPm*
Tamlane. Unknown. *MaB*
Teddy's wonderings. J. K. Bangs. *BrBc*
To a little sister, aged ten. A. E. Cummings. *BrBc*
"Troll sat alone on his seat of stone." From The hobbit. J. R. R. Tolkien. *LoL*
True Thomas. Unknown. *CoSp—UnG— UnMc*
  Tom the Rhymer. *MaB*
Twinkletoes. A. A. Milne. *MiWc*
Very nearly. Q. Scott-Hopper. *FeF*
When a ring's around the moon. M. J. Carr. *ArTp—HuL-2*
When I was six. Z. Cross. *BrBc—FeF*
Where dreams are made. B. Johnson. *BrR-4*
"Where the bee sucks, there suck I." From The tempest. W. Shakespeare. *ArTp*
  Where the bee sucks. *JoAc—ReT*
Wise Sarah and the elf. E. J. Coatsworth. *CoPm*
Yesterday in Oxford street. R. Fyleman. *ArTp—PeF*

Fairies ("I cannot see fairies") Hilda Conkling. *ArTp—BrL-k*

The fairies ("If ye will with Mab find grace") Robert Herrick. *FeF*
  Queen Mab. *ReG*

Fairies ("There are fairies at the bottom of our garden") Rose Fyleman. *HuL-1— HuSv—JoAc—PeF*

The fairies ("Up the airy mountain") William Allingham. *CoPm—DeF—FeF— JoAc—NaE—PaOm—PeF—ReG—SmLg*
  "Up the airy mountain." *HuSv*

Fairies ("You can't see fairies unless you're good") Marchette Chute. *BrL-k—ChA*

"The fairies have never a penny to spend." Rose Fyleman. *FeF*

The fairies of the Caldon Low. Mary Howitt. *ReG*

Fairies' song. Leigh Hunt. *CoPm*

"The fairies, too, have aeroplanes." See Fairy aeroplanes

Fairlop Friday. Eleanor Farjeon. *FaN*

Fairs
Animal fair. Unknown. *CoI—NaM—UnG*
"As I was going to Banbury." Mother Goose. *JoAc*
  Banbury fair. *OpO*
At a country fair. J. Holmes. *NaM*
Banbury fair. E. G. Millard. *HuL-1*
Billy-boy. D. King. *HuL-1*
A blue ribbon at Amesbury. R. Frost. *FrR*
Caravans. I. Thompson. *HuL-2*
"Come up, my horse, to Budleigh fair." Mother Goose. *OpO*
"Gee up, Neddy, to the fair." Mother Goose. *OpO*
"Jill came from the fair." E. Farjeon. *ArTp*
Mother Niddity Nod. Mother Goose. *OpO*
"Oh dear, what can the matter be." Mother Goose. *DeMg*
  What can the matter be. *OpO*
Roundabout. J. Reeves. *ReW*
"Simple Simon met a pieman." Mother Goose. *DeMg—HuSv—JoAc—LiL*
  Simple Simon. *ReG—UnG*
  Simple Simon and the pieman. *OpO*
Widdecombe fair. Unknown. *CoPm*
  Widdicombe fair. *NaM*

Fairy aeroplanes. Anne Blackwell Payne. *BrL-k*

The fairy and the bird. Harry Behn. *BeW*

The fairy ball. Rose Fyleman. *HuL-1*

The fairy book. Abbie Farwell Brown. *BrL-k*

Fairy days. William Makepeace Thackeray. *UnG*

Fairy gardens. Eleanor Farjeon. *FaCb— FaN*

A fairy in armor. See The culprit fay

The fairy king. William Allingham. *CoPm*

"The fairy king was old." See The fairy king

Fairy lullaby. See A midsummer-night's dream

Fairy music. Francis Ledwidge. *HaY*

Fairy shoes. Annette Wynne. *BrL-k*

Fairy song ("By the moon we sport and play") John Lyly. *DeT*

Fairy song ("Shed no tear. O, shed no tear") John Keats. *FeF*

The fairy swing. Ivy O. Eastwick. *EaI*

The fairy thorn. Samuel Ferguson. *DeT*

"A fairy went a-marketing." Rose Fyleman. *HuL-1—JoAc*

Fairy's wander-song. See A midsummer-night's dream—"Over hill, over dale"

Faith
The country faith. N. Gale. *DoP—HuL-2*
Fidele's dirge. From Cymbeline. W. Shakespeare. *SmLg*
Geneviève. E. Farjeon. *FaCb*
"I never saw a moor." E. Dickinson. *ArTp—DoP—FeF—HuL-2—JoAc—NaE*
  Certainty. *UnG*
Innate helium. R. Frost. *PlI*
Into my own. R. Frost. *FrR*

Light in the darkness. A. Fisher. *HaY*

Little Breeches. J. Hay. *UnG*

The sacred order. M. Sarton. *PlI*

St Patrick's breastplate. Unknown. *SmLg*

Sitting by a bush in broad daylight. R. Frost. *FrR*

The waterfall. H. Vaughan. *HoW*

"Faith, I wish I were a leprechaun." Margaret Ritter. *ArTp—FeF—HuL-2*

The faithful shepherdess, sel. John Fletcher

Evening song. *DeT*

Faithless Nelly Gray. Thomas Hood. *CoH*

The falcon. Unknown. *GrCc*

Falconry. See Falcons and falconry

Falcons and falconry

The falcon. Unknown. *GrCc*

Fall. See Autumn

Fall. Aileen Fisher. *ArTp—FeF*

Fall days. Marion Conger. *BrS*

"Fall, leaves, fall; die, flowers, away." Emily Brontë. *SmLg*

The fall of J. W. Beane. Oliver Herford. *CoSp*

The fall of the plum blossoms. Rankō. *ArTp*

Falling snow. Unknown. *ArTp—PeF*

The falling star. Sara Teasdale. *ArTp—HuL-1—HuSv—NaM—PeF*

Fallis, Edwina

The giant's shoes. *BrR-3*

September. *ArTp—BrR-4—HaY—HuL-2*

Wise Johnny. *ArTp—BrL-k—BrS*

False April. Eleanor Farjeon. *FaCb—FaN*

"False April, drest in green." See False April

The false heart. Hilaire Belloc. *SmLg*

The false knight upon the road. Unknown. *MaB*

"False Sir John a-wooing came." See May Colvin

Falsehood. See Truthfulness and falsehood

Falstaff, Jake

The Dick Johnson reel. *NaE*

Fame

Elegy written in a country churchyard. T. Gray. *DeT—HaP*

I think continually of those. S. Spender. *HaP*

"I'm nobody. Who are you." E. Dickinson. *ArTp—UnG*

A nobody. *UnMc*

A memento for mortality. Attributed to W. Basse. *SmLg*

The triumph. E. Farjeon. *FaN*

X-roads. J. Reeves. *ReR*

Familiar friends. James S. Tippett. *BrL-k—HuL-2*

Family. See also Children and childhood; Fathers and fatherhood; Home and family life; Married life; Mothers and motherhood; Relatives; also names of relatives, as Uncles

About Jimmy James. J. Ciardi. *CiY*

Andre. G. Brooks. *ArTp*

Mummy slept late and daddy fixed breakfast. J. Ciardi. *CiY*

Our baby. M. C. Livingston. *LiWa*

A short checklist of things to think about before being born. J. Ciardi. *CiY*

The son. R. Torrence. *McW*

Family life. See Home and family life

Fancy. See The merchant of Venice

Fanshawe, Catherine Maria

Enigma on the letter h. *UnG*

Fantasy. Ruth Mather Skidmore. *CoPm*

"Far as creation's ample range extends." See An essay on man

Far away. David McCord. *McFf*

"Far-away is very far." See Away

Far away music. Harry Behn. *BeW*

"Far away music is never so far." See Far away music

Far beyond us. Unknown, tr. fr. the Japanese by Ishii and Obata. *PaS*

"Far from far." See Bobadil

"Far in dark woods away." Unknown

Three cuckoo rhymes. *DeT*

"Far off, far off." See Song of the parrot

"Fare you well." See Farewell to summer

"Farewell and adieu to you, fair Spanish ladies." See Spanish ladies

"Farewell, I'm fading, cried." See Indispensability

"Farewell rewards and fairies." See Farewell to the fairies

A farewell to Agassiz. Oliver Wendell Holmes. *PlI*

Farewell to summer. Eleanor Farjeon. *FaCb—FaN*

Farewell to the fairies. Richard Corbet. *NaE—NaM*

The fairies' farewell. *SmLg*

Farewell to the farm. Robert Louis Stevenson. *ArTp—FeF*

Farewell to the old year. Eleanor Farjeon. *BrS*

Farewells

Away, Rio. Unknown. *SmLg*

Farewell to summer. E. Farjeon. *FaCb—FaN*

Farewell to the fairies. R. Corbet. *NaE—NaM*

The fairies' farewell. *SmLg*

Farewell to the farm. R. L. Stevenson. *ArTp—FeF*

Farewell to the old year. E. Farjeon. *BrS*

Good-by and keep cold. R. Frost. *FrR—FrY—UnG*

Goodbye to fairyland. From The house beyond the meadow. H. Behn. *BeH*

Last song. J. Guthrie. *ArTp—HuL-1*

Parting. Buson. *PaS*

Parting at morning. R. Browning. *HoW*

The silver tassie. R. Burns. *GrCc*

Since there's no help. M. Drayton. *HaP*

"Summer sunshine." M. A. Lathbury. *HaY*

To Chuck—concerning a rendezvous in Siam. J. Charles. *McW*

Farjeon, Eleanor

A is for abracadabra. *FaCb*

Abe. *FaCb—FaN*

Advice to a child. *FaCb*

After harvest. *FaCb—FaN*

Alexander to his horse. *FaCb*

Jessica dances. *FaCb*
"Jill came from the fair." *ArTp*
Joan's corner. *FaCb*
Joan's door. *BrBc*
John of the fountain. *FaN*
July's song. *FaCb—FaN*
June's song. *FaCb—FaN*
K is for kobold. *FaCb*
The keys of heaven. *FaCb*
The kindness. *FaCb—FaN*
King Olaf's gold. *FaCb*
"King Priam in the dark night went."
  FaCb
The king rides forth. *FaCb—FaN*
King Xerxes and the sea. *FaCb*
Kingcups in town. *FaCb—FaN*
The king's cake. *FaCb*
King's-cup. *FaCb*
Kingsway. *HuL-2*
A kitten. *ArTp—HuL-2—ReG*
L is for Lorelei. *FaCb*
Lady day. *FaCb—FaN*
Lady-slippers. *FaCb*
Lady's bedstraw. *FaCb*
Leo. *FaCb—FaN*
Lewis Carroll came here to-day. *FaN*
Libra. *FaCb—FaN*
"Light the lamps up, lamplighter." *BrS—
  HuL-2*
Loganberry spooks. *FaCb—FaN*
The London owl. *FaCb*
London sparrow. *ReG*
Low and high. *FaCb—FaN*
M is for midsummer eve. *FaCb*
"March, blow by." *FaCb—FaN*
March speaks. *FaCb—FaN*
"March, you old blusterer." *FaCb—FaN*
Mary and her kitten. *DeT*
Mary indoors. *ReG*
May-day in June. *FaCb—FaN*
May's song. *FaCb—FaN*
Meeting Mary. *BrBc*
Memorial garden (Canterbury). *FaCb—
  FaN*
A memory. *FaCb—FaN*
Milkmaids. *FaCb*
Minnie. *UnG*
Mr Cooter. *FaCb*
"Mrs Malone." *CoPm*
"Mrs Peck-Pigeon." *ArTp—BrL-k—HuSv
  —JoAc*
Molly Grime. *FaCb—FaN*
"Moon-come-out." *ArTp—McAw*
"The moon upon her watch-tower." *FaCb*
A morning song. *FaCb—FaN*
The Mother's song. *DoP*
The mother's tale. *BrBc—DoP*
Myfanwy among the leaves. *FaCb*
N is for nixie. *FaCb*
Narcissus fields. *FaCb—FaN*
Neptune. *FaCb—FaN*
New clothes and old. *FaCb—FaN*
News, news. *BrS*
The next holiday. *FaCb*
Night-piece. *FaCb*
"The night will never stay." *BrR-6—BrS—
  FeF—HuL-2—HuSv—JoAc—PeF*
Norman William. *FaCb*
November's song. *FaCb—FaN*
Now every child. *BrBc*

"Now, says Time." *FaCb—FaN*
A nursery song for Shepherdswell in Kent.
  FaN
O is for once upon a time. *FaCb*
Oak apple day. *FaCb—FaN*
October's song. *CoPs—FaCb—FaN*
Old blue saucepan. *FaN*
"The old man sweeps the leaves." *FaCb*
An old man's epitaph. *FaCb—FaN*
"Oliver Goldsmith." *FaCb—FaN*
On Queen Anne. *FaN*
On the staircase. *BrS*
On this day the wren and the robin stop
  singing. *FaN*
One lime. *DeT—FaCb*
Open eye, pimpernel. *FaCb—FaN*
The other child. *FaCb*
"Out came the sun." *FaCb—FaN*
"Over the garden wall." *BrR-4—HuSv*
P is for philtre. *FaCb*
Pancake Tuesday. *FaCb*
  "Run to church with a frying pan."
    FaN
Peep-primrose. *FaCb—FaN*
Pegasus. *FaCb—FaN*
Pet Marjorie. *FaN*
Piecrust. *FaCb—FaN*
Pisces. *FaCb—FaN*
Plain philomel. *FaCb—FaN*
Plow-Monday. *FaCb—FaN*
A pointless tale. *FaCb—FaN*
Poppies. *FaCb—FaN*
A prayer for blossoms. *FaCb*
A prayer for little things. *JoAc*
Presents from heaven. *FaCb—FaN*
The princesses' carol. *FaCb—FaN*
Punkie-night. *FaCb—FaN*
Q is for quest. *FaCb*
The quarrel. *FeF*
"Queen Dido is building." *FaCb*
Queen's lace. *FaCb*
The quest. *FaCb*
A quill for John Stow. *FaN*
R is for Robin Goodfellow. *FaCb*
"Ragged Robin." *FaN*
Randolph Caldecott. *FaN*
Remember the grotto. *FaCb—FaN*
Remembrance. *FaCb*
The ride of the Huns. *FaCb*
The riding of the kings. *DoP—HaY*
Robin-run-by-the-wall. *FaCb*
A round for the new year. *FaCb*
"Run to church with a frying pan." See
  Pancake Tuesday
The running. *FaCb*
S is for sandman. *FaCb*
Saffron Walden. *FaN*
Sagittarius. *FaCb—FaN*
Said Hengist to Horsa. *FaCb*
Sailor. *PeF*
Saint Bridget. *FaCb*
Saint Christopher. *FaCb*
Saint Dorothea. *FaCb*
Saint Francis. *FaCb*
Saint Giles. *FaCb*
Saint Hubert. *FaCb*
Saint Joseph. *FaCb*
Saint Martin. *FaCb*
Saint Nicholas. *FaCb*
Saint Patrick. *FaCb*

Farjeon, Eleanor—*Continued*
Saint Simeon Stylites. *FaCb*
Saint Swithin's wish. *FaCb—FaN*
The sands. *FaCb*
School-bell. *BrS—FeF*
Scorpio. *FaCb—FaN*
Scotland's Mary. *FaN*
September's song. *FaCb—FaN*
Seventh son. See "Seventh son of seventh son"
"Seventh son of seventh son." *FaCb*
    Seventh son. *FaN*
Shadows. *DeT*
The sheepfold. *FaCb*
The shell. *FaCb*
"The shepherd and the king." *ArTp*
Shepherds. *FaCb*
Shepherd's purse. *FaCb*
Silk coats. *FaN*
Sisters. *FeF*
Six green singers. *EaW*
Skate and sled. *FaCb—FaN*
Somebody and naebody. *FaN*
A song for September. *FaCb*
Song of the very poor. tr. *FaCb—FaN*
"The sounds in the morning." *JoAc*
The spendthrift. *FaCb—FaN*
Spinners in the sun. *FaCb—FaN*
Spring night in a village. *FaCb*
Stirring the pudding. *FaN*
Summer offering. *FaCb*
The sun that warms you. *FaCb—FaN*
Sweet Robin Herrick. *FaCb—FaN*
T is for talisman. *FaCb*
Taurus. *FaCb—FaN*
There isn't time. *FeF—HuL-2*
Thieves in the orchard. *FaCb*
"This bread." *FaCb—FaN*
This holy night. *DoP*
    Christmas carol. *HuL-2*
"Three little puffins." *ArTp—LoL*
Three miles to Penn. *FaCb*
"The tide in the river." *ArTp*
To an oak dropping acorns. *FaCb—FaN*
To Susanna, reading. *FaCb*
Toad-flax. *FaCb*
A toast for Doctor Sam. *FaN*
Toss me your golden ball. *FaCb*
"T'other side of Duck-pond." *FaN*
Traveller's joy. *FaCb*
The trees and the wind. *FaCb*
The triumph. *FaN*
The true tale of Eliza Ottley. *FaCb*
"Two young lambs." *FaCb—FaN*
U is for unicorn. *FaCb*
Under my lean-to. *FaCb—FaN*
Up the hill, down the hill. *CoPs—FaCb—FaN*
"Upon an Easter morning." *CoPs—FaCb—FaN*
V is for Valhalla. *FaCb*
Vegetables. *FeF*
Virgo. *FaCb—FaN*
W is for witch. *FaCb*
Welcome to the new year. *HaY*
"What is poetry? Who knows." *HaY*
"What is time." *FaCb—FaN*
What saw I a-floating. *FaCb*
What they do. *FaCb—FaN*

When Hannibal crossed the Alps. *FaCb—HuL-2*
The white blackbirds. *FaCb*
"Who's that bleating." *FaCb—FaN*
Wild thyme. *BrS*
Wildflowers. *DoP*
Window boxes. *FeF*
X is for xoanon. *FaCb*
Y is for Yggdrasil. *FaCb*
The yew-tree. *FaCb*
Z is for Zoroaster. *FaCb*

Farjeon, Eleanor and Herbert
Henry VIII. *CoSp*

Farjeon, Herbert. See Farjeon, Eleanor and Herbert

Farm animals. See Animals; also names of farm animals, as Cows

Farm boy after summer. Robert Francis. *HaP*

Farm life. See also Country life; Fields; Harvests and harvesting; Plows and plowing; also names of farm products, as Wheat
At the farm. J. Ciardi. *CiY*
The barnyard. M. Burnham. *ArTp—HuL-1*
Behind the gorse. E. Farjeon. *FaN*
Brown's descent; or, The willy-nilly slide. R. Frost. *CoSp—FrR—FrY—NaE*
Cleverness. M. Chute. *ChA*
"The cock's in the wood pile a-blowing his horn." Mother Goose. *DeMg*
    Cock-crow. *OpO*
The code. R. Frost. *FrR—UnMc*
Corn. L. M. Thornton. *BrL-7*
The crafty farmer. Unknown. *ArTp*
Evening at the farm. J. Trowbridge. *FeF*
    Evening on the farm. *NaM*
Farewell to the farm. R. L. Stevenson. *ArTp—FeF*
Farm boy after summer. R. Francis. *HaP*
Farmer. L. H. Bailey. *HaY*
"A farmer went trotting upon his gray mare." Mother Goose. *ArTp—DeMg—JoAc*
    "A farmer went riding." *BrL-k—HuSv*
    "A farmer went trotting." *HuL-1—LiL—NaE*
    The mischievous raven. *OpO*
The farmyard. Unknown. *HuL-2*
A farmyard song. Mother Goose. *OpO*
Father. F. M. Frost. *ArTp—BrS—FeF—HuSv*
Fern hill. D. Thomas. *JoAc—McW—NaE—ReT—SmLg*
"Fodder in the barn loft." Unknown. *WoF*
The grindstone. R. Frost. *FrR*
The happy farmer. Unknown. *UnG*
The Harpers' farm. D. Aldis. *AlA*
Harvest. M. M. Hutchinson. *HuL-2*
"Hay is for horses." Mother Goose. *OpO*
"Here's a health to the barley mow." Mother Goose. *DeMg*
High summer. J. Clare. *GrCc*
The housekeeper. R. Frost. *FrR*
"I will go with my father a-ploughing." J. Campbell. *ArTp—BrS—FeF*
"If I was a farmer, I'd have an easy time." Unknown. *WoF*

Improved farm land. C. Sandburg. *SaW*

In spring in warm weather. D. Aldis. *AlA—BrBc*

Irrigation. From In my mother's house. A. N. Clark. *HuSv*

John. D. McCord. *McFf*

Johnny's farm. H. M. Adams. *HuL-1*

Korosta katzina song. Unknown. *PaS*

The last corn shock. G. W. Dresbach. *FeF*

The legends of evil. R. Kipling. *NaM*

Mending wall. R. Frost. *FrR—FrY—HaP*

Mowing. R. Frost. *FrR*

"My father left me three acres of land." Mother Goose. *DeMg*
    Mad farmer's song. *HuL-2*
    Three acres of land. *OpO*

"My land is fair for any eyes to see." J. Stuart. *ArTp—FeF*

"My maid Mary." Mother Goose. *DeMg—OpO*

New farm tractor. C. Sandburg. *FeF*

Off the ground. W. De La Mare. *CoSp—HuL-2*

Old farmer Buck. Unknown. *CoH*

"Once there lived a little man." Unknown. *HuL-1*

"One for the cut worm." Unknown. *WoF*

The pasture. R. Frost. *ArTp—BrR-4—FeF—FrR — FrY — HuL-2 — HuSv — JoAc—NaM—PeF*

The ploughboy in luck. Mother Goose. *OpO*
    The silly. *DeT*

Ploughing on Sunday. W. Stevens. *FeF—ReT*

Putting in the seed. R. Frost. *FrR*

She opens the barn door every morning. C. Sandburg. *SaW*

The six badgers. R. Graves. *CoI—GrP—ReG*

The sower. R. O. Figueroa. *FeF*

Springfield mountain. Unknown. *WoF*

Summer morning. From Prairie. C. Sandburg. *SaW*

A time to talk. R. Frost. *FrR—FrY*

To call our own. J. Stuart. *ThP*

Trouble at the farm. I. O. Eastwick. *HuL-1*

Un. J. Reeves. *ReR*

When. D. Aldis. *AlA—BrS*

Where I took hold of life. R. P. T. Coffin. *BrBc*

"Whistle and hoe." Unknown. *WoF*

A witch. W. Barnes. *CoPm*
    A country witch. *UnG*

Yellow wheels. J. Reeves. *ReBl*

Farmer. Liberty Hyde Bailey. *HaY*

"Farmer, is the harvest ready." See Bread

"A farmer was plowing. his field one day." See The bad-tempered wife

"A farmer went riding." See "A farmer went trotting upon his gray mare"

"A farmer went trotting." See "A farmer went trotting upon his gray mare"

"A farmer went trotting upon his gray mare." Mother Goose. *ArTp—DeMg—JoAc*

"A farmer went riding." *BrL-k—HuSv*

"A farmer went trotting." *HuL-1—LiL—NaE*

The mischievous raven. *OpO*

Farmers. See Farm life

Farms and farming. See Farm life

"The farmhouse lingers, though averse to square." See A brook in the city

Th farmyard. Unknown. *HuL-2*

A farmyard song. Mother Goose. *OpO*

Farrar, Canon
"I am only one." *ThP*

Farrar, John (Chipman)
Alone. *HaY*

Bundles. *ArTp—BrL-k*

Chanticleer. *ArTp—BrR-3*

Choice. *BrS*

A comparison. *FeF—HuL-2*

The drum. *BrR-3*

Moral song. *BrL-k—HuL-1*

Morning at the beach. *HuL-1*

Prayer. *DoP*

Roller skates. *FeF*

Song for a camper. *HaY*

Tracks. *BrL-k*

Watching clouds. *HuSv*

"Farther in summer than the birds." Emily Dickinson. *HaP*

A farthing. Mother Goose. *OpO*

A farthing and a penny. James Reeves. *ReW*

Fashions. See Clothing and dress

"Faster than fairies, faster than witches." See From a railway carriage

The fastidious serpent. Henry Johnstone. *CoH—LoL*

"Fat father robin." David McCord. *McFf*

"Fat green frog sits by the pond." See Grandfather frog

"Fat torpedoes in bursting jackets." See Fourth of July

Fate
Destiny. N. Crane. *UnG*

Fate is unfair. D. Marquis. *NaE*

Invictus. W. E. Henley. *UnG*

Song. From Contention of Ajax and Ulysses. J. Shirley. *GrCc*

"When in disgrace with fortune and men's eyes." From Sonnets. W. Shakespeare. *HaP*

The winds of fate. E. W. Wilcox. *BrL-8*

Fate is unfair. Don Marquis. *NaE*

The fate of the Cabbage Rose. Wallace Irwin. *CoH*

Father ("His eyes can be quite old and stern") Mildred Weston. *CoPs*

Father ("My father's face is brown with sun") Frances Frost. *ArTp—BrS—FeF—HuSv*

Father and I in the woods. David McCord. *McFf*

"Father and I went down to camp." See "Yankee Doodle went to town"

"Father calls me William, sister calls me Will." See Jest 'fore Christmas

"Father, father, where are you going." See The little boy lost

Father Greybeard. Mother Goose. *OpO*

Father Grumble. Unknown. *BrR-5*

"**Father** lighted candles for me." See For Hanukkah

"**Father** said, Call him Anthony." See Naming the baby

Father Short. Mother Goose. *OpO*

"**Father** Short came down the lane." See Father Short

"**Father**, we thank Thee for the night." See A prayer

Father William. See Alice's adventures in wonderland

Fathers and fatherhood
Address to my infant daughter. W. Wordsworth. *NaE*
"As I went up the Brandy hill." Mother Goose. *OpO*
Automobile mechanics. D. W. Baruch. *ArTp—FeF*
Birthday gift. E. B. De Vito. *BrBc*
A college training. J. C. Lincoln. *CoH*
Daddy. R. Fyleman. *BrS*
Daddy fell into the pond. A. Noyes. *CoH —FeF*
Dear old dad. L. P. *BrR-6*
"Do not go gentle into that good night." D. Thomas. *HaP*
Epitaph for a Concord boy. S. Young. *McW*
Father ("His eyes can be quite old and stern") M. Weston. *CoPs*
Father ("My father's face is brown with sun") F. M. Frost. *ArTp—BrS—FeF— HuSv*
Father and I in the woods. D. McCord. *McFf*
Father's story. E. M. Roberts. *CoPs— FeF*
The hero. L. F. Jackson. *BrS*
"I will go with my father a-ploughing." J. Campbell. *ArTp—BrS—FeF*
"I wish I could meet the man that knows." J. Ciardi. *CiI*
Irish. E. J. O'Brien. *BrS*
It was. D. Aldis. *AlA*
Lord Ullin's daughter. T. Campbell. *FeF*
My papa's waltz. T. Roethke. *HaP*
The old man and Jim. J. W. Riley. *CoSp*
Request number. G. N. Sprod. *CoH*
The secret heart. R. P. T. Coffin. *CoPs*
Six and thirty. D. E. Stevenson. *BrBc*
To my son, aged three years and five months. T. Hood. *FeF*
A parental ode to my son, aged three years and five months. *CoH* (sel.)
Walking. G. E. Glaubitz. *McAw*
What happened. D. Aldis. *AlA*
When father carves the duck. E. V. Wright. *CoH—CoPs*
A wonderful man. A. Fisher. *BrS*

"**Father's** gone a-flailing." Mother Goose. *OpO*

Father's story. Elizabeth Madox Roberts. *CoPs—FeF*

The **faun**. Ezra Pound. *SmLg*

The **favourite** fruit. Eleanor Farjeon. *FaCb —FaN*

Fawcett, Edgar
"January is here." *HaY*
Oriole. *UnG*

"**Fe**, fi, fo, fum." Mother Goose. *NaE*
"Fa, fe, fi, fo, fum." *DeMg*
The giant. *OpO*

Fear
Advice from an elderly mouse. E. J. Coatsworth. *CoM*
Alone. M. Chute. *ChA*
Be not afraid. R. Nathan. *BrR-5*
The camel and the flotsam. J. De La Fontaine. *JoAc*
The city of dreadful night. J. Thomson. *HoW*
Dicky. R. Graves. *GrP*
Do you fear the wind. H. Garland. *ArTp —JoAc*
The duke of Plaza-Toro. From The gondoliers. W. S. Gilbert. *CoH—FeF*
The fear. R. Frost. *FrR*
Fear no more. From Cymbeline. W. Shakespeare. *DeT—HaP*
Fidele's dirge. *SmLg*
"For God hath not given us the spirit of fear." From The second epistle of Paul to Timothy, Bible, New Testament. *ArTp*
A hundred collars. R. Frost. *FrR*
A little maid. Mother Goose. *OpO*
Looking out my window. D. Aldis. *AlA*
Passing it along. H. F. Day. *BrR-6*
The river-god's song. F. Beaumont and J. Fletcher. *FeF—NaM*
Song. *ReT*
The scaredy. Mother Goose. *OpO*
The sick child. R. L. Stevenson. *CoPs— DeT*
Snake. D. H. Lawrence. *ArTp—HaP*
Storm fear. R. Frost. *FrR*
The valiant. From Julius Caesar. W. Shakespeare. *ThP*
When I was lost. D. Aldis. *AlA*

The **fear**. Robert Frost. *FrR*

Fear no more. See Cymbeline

"**Fear** no more the heat o' the sun." See Cymbeline—Fear no more

The **fearful** finale of the irascible mouse. Guy Wetmore Carryl. *CoH*

Fearing, Kenneth
Dirge. *HaP*

"**Feather** on feather." See Snow in spring

Feather or fur. John Becker. *ArTp—FeF*

Feathers. Mother Goose. *OpO*

"The **feathers** of the willow." See Song

February
February ("Around, above the world of snow") J. B. Bensel. *UnG*
February ("February,—fortnights two") F. D. Sherman. *HaY*
February ("Will winter never be over") A. D. T. Whitney. *HaY*
February birthday. N. B. Turner. *BrBc*
"February, tall and trim." A. N. Gilmore. *HaY*
February twilight. S. Teasdale. *BrR-4— FeF—HaY—HuL-1—PeF*
In February. J. A. Symonds. *HaY*
Potomac town in February. C. Sandburg. *McW—NaE*
When. D. Aldis. *AlA—BrS*

February ("Around, above the world of snow") James Berry Bensel. *UnG*

February ("February,—fortnights two") Frank Dempster Sherman. *HaY*

February ("Will winter never be over") Adeline D. T. Whitney. *HaY*

February bird. David Morton. *ThP*

February birthday. Nancy Byrd Turner. *BrBc*

"February-fill-the-dyke." Ivy O. Eastwick. *EaI*

"February,—fortnights two." See February

"February, tall and trim." Anna Neil Gilmore. *HaY*

February twilight. Sara Teasdale. *BrR-4—FeF—HaY—HuL-1—PeF*

Feeney, Leonard
Wind. *UnG*

Feet
A baby's feet. From Étude réaliste. A. C. Swinburne. *FeF*
The barefoot boy. J. G. Whittier. *FeF* (sel.)
Barefoot days. R. Field. *FeF—HaY—HuL-2*
Corner-of-the-street. A. A. Milne. *MiWc*
"Every lady in this land." Mother Goose. *DeMg—OpO*
Fate is unfair. D. Marquis. *NaE*
Feet ("Big feet") I. Thompson. *HuL-1*
Feet ("Feet are very special things") M. C. Livingston. *LiW*
Feet ("There are things") D. Aldis. *AlA—BrR-4*
Mrs Button. J. Reeves. *ReBl*

Feet ("Big feet") Irene Thompson. *HuL-1*

Feet ("Feet are very special things") Myra Cohn Livingston. *LiW*

Feet ("There are things") Dorothy Aldis. *AlA—BrR-4*

"Feet are very special things." See Feet

Felicia Ropps. Gelett Burgess. *ArTp—FeF*

"Felicity in the air." See Memory of flowers

A feller I know. Mary Austin. *FeF*

Fellowship. See Friendship

"Fence posts wear marshmallow hats." See On a snowy day

Fences
Mending wall. R. Frost. *FrR—FrY—HaP*
"The pickety fence." From Five chants. D. McCord. *McFf*

"Ferdinand De Soto lies." See The distant runners

Ferguson, Sir Samuel
Dear dark head. tr. *PaS*
The fairy thorn. *DeT*

Fern hill. Dylan Thomas. *JoAc—McW—NaE—ReT—SmLg*

Fern song. John Banister Tabb. *DoP*

Ferns
Fern song. J. B. Tabb. *DoP*

Ferries
"Back and forth." L. S. Mitchell. *FeF*
Ferry-boats. J. S. Tippett. *ArTp*
The ferryman. C. G. Rossetti. *HuL-1*
Recuerdo. E. St V. Millay. *NaE*
The seven fiddlers. S. Evans. *CoPm*

Ferry boats. See Ferries

Ferry-boats. James S. Tippett. *ArTp*

"Ferry me across the water." See The ferryman

Ferry ride, sel. Selma Robinson
Bus ride. *FeF*

The ferryman. Christina Georgina Rossetti. *HuL-1*

Festivals. See Fairs

Fet, Afanasy
"A magic landscape." *PaS*
"A few leaves stay for awhile on the trees." See The last leaf

"Fiddle de dee, fiddle de dee." Mother Goose. *DeMg*
The fly and the bumble-bee. *HuL-1*
Song. *WiRm*

"Fiddle dee dee, fiddle dee dee." See "Fiddle de dee, fiddle de dee"

The fiddler ("The blind man lifts his violin") James Reeves. *ReBl*

A fiddler ("Once was a fiddler. Play could he") Walter De La Mare. *PlU*

"The fiddler and his wife." Mother Goose. *OpO*

Fiddler Jones. See The Spoon River anthology

The fiddler of Dooney. William Butler Yeats. *ArTp—PlU—SmLg*

Fidele's dirge. See Cymbeline—Fear no more

Fidget. Mother Goose. *OpO*

Field, Eugene
Christmas song. See Song
The death of Robin Hood. *CoSp*
The drum. *BrR-6*
The duel. *ArTp—FeF—HuSv—NaM*
The fly-away horse. *UnG*
Jest 'fore Christmas. *FeF*
The limitations of youth. *BrR-6*
Little Boy Blue. *FeF*
The little peach. *CoH*
A new year idyl. *CoPs* (sel.)
The night wind. *BrR-4—FeF*
Orkney lullaby. *UnG*
The Rock-a-by Lady. *ArTp*
Song. *ArTp—DoP—HuL-1*
Christmas song. *HaY*
"Why do the bells of Christmas ring." *BrL-k*
Song of the all-wool shirt. *CoSp*
"Why do the bells of Christmas ring." See Song
Wynken, Blynken, and Nod. *FeF—HuL-1—HuSv—JoAc—UnG*

Field, Rachel (Lyman)
Acrobat. See A circus garland
The animal store. *ArTp—CoI—HuL-1*
At the theater. *FeF*
Barefoot days. *FeF—HaY—HuL-2*
A birthday. *BrBc—BrS*
A charm for spring flowers. *ArTp*
Chestnut stands. *BrS*
A circus garland, sels.
Acrobat. *HuSv*
The elephant. *HuSv*
The girl on the milk-white horse. *HuSv*
The performing seal. *HuSv*
City lights. *FeF*

"Toe Tipe." Mother Goose. *OpO*
"Tom Thumbkin." Mother Goose. *OpO*
"Tommy Tibule." Mother Goose. *OpO*

Fingers. See also Finger-play poems
"Every lady in this land." Mother Goose. *DeMg—OpO*
Finger nails. Mother Goose. *OpO*
The little girl that lost a finger. G. Mistral. *FeF*
The story of little Suck-a-thumb. H. Hoffmann. *NaE*

Finis. Henry Newbolt. *ArTp*

Fink, William W.
Larrie O'Dee. *BrL-8*

Finnigan to Flannigan. Strickland W. Gillilan. *CoSp*

Fir trees
Our little fir tree. D. Aldis. *AlA*

Fire. See Also Firemen; Fireplaces
Autumn fires. R. L. Stevenson. *ArTp—HaY—JoAc*
Beach fire. F. M. Frost. *ArTp—PeF*
"Burn ash-wood green." Mother Goose. *DeMg*
Coal fire. L. Untermeyer. *UnG*
Earthy anecdote. W. Stevens. *ReT*
Fire. J. Reeves. *ReW*
Fire and ice. R. Frost. *FrR—FrY*
"Fire, fire (cried Mrs McGuire)." Unknown. *WoF*
"Fire, fire (false alarm)." Unknown. *MoY*
Fire, fire ("Fire, fire, said the town crier") Mother Goose. *OpO*
Hearth song. R. U. Johnson. *HaY*
"Jeremiah, blow the fire." Mother Goose. *OpO*
Jim Bludso. J. Hay. *BrL-8—UnMc*
Matilda. H. Belloc. *CoSp—SmLg*
Movies in the fire. M. D. Shacklett. *BrR-4*

Fire. James Reeves. *ReW*
Fire and ice. Robert Frost. *FrR—FrY*
"Fire, fire (cried Mrs McGuire)." Unknown. *WoF*
"Fire, fire (false alarm)." Unknown. *MoY*
Fire, fire ("Fire, fire, said the town crier") Mother Goose. *OpO*
"Fire, fire, said the town crier." See Fire, fire

Fire-flies. See Fireflies

Fireflies
All about fireflies all about. D. McCord. *McFf*
Fireflies ("As soon as they began to spark") D. Aldis. *AlHd*
Fireflies ("I like to chase the fireflies") G. W. Coplen. *BrL-k*
Fireflies ("Little lamps of the dusk") C. Hall. *FeF*
Fireflies ("Oh, who is lost tonight") W. Welles. *JoAc*
Fireflies in the garden. R. Frost. *FrR—FrY*
Firefly. E. M. Roberts. *ArTp—HuL-1—JoAc*
Glowworm. D. McCord. *McT*

"Lucifer Leverett Lightningbug." J. Ciardi. *CiR*
Fireflies ("As soon as they began to spark") Dorothy Aldis. *AlHd*
Fireflies ("I like to chase the fireflies") Grace Wilson Coplen. *BrL-k*
Fireflies ("Little lamps of the dusk") Carolyn Hall. *FeF*
Fireflies ("Oh, who is lost tonight") Winifred Welles. *JoAc*
Fireflies in the garden. Robert Frost. *FrR—FrY*
Firefly. Elizabeth Madox Roberts. *ArTp—HuL-1—JoAc*
"Fireman, fireman." Unknown. *TaD*
"Fireman, fireman, number eight." *WoF*
"Fireman, fireman, number eight." See "Fireman, fireman"

Firemen
"F is the fighting firetruck." From All around the town. P. McGinley. *FeF*
"Fire, fire (cried Mrs McGuire)." Unknown. *WoF*
"Fire, fire (false alarm)." Unknown. *MoY*
"Fireman, fireman." Unknown. *TaD*
"Fireman, fireman, number eight." *WoF*

Fireplaces
Hearth. P. Bacon. *FeF*

The firetender. David McCord. *McFf*

Fireworks
Choice. J. Farrar. *BrS*
Fireworks. J. Reeves. *CoPs—ReBl*
"Fourth of July." M. Chute. *BrS—ChA*
Fourth of July. R. Field. *BrS*
Fourth of July night ("The little boat at anchor") C. Sandburg. *SaW*
Fourth of July night ("Pin wheels whirling round") D. Aldis. *AlA—ArTp—BrS—McAw*
Fourth of July song. L. Lenski. *BrS*
"If I had a firecracker." S. Silverstein. *CoPs*
"I've got a rocket." Unknown. *BrS—JoAc*
The pinwheel's song. J. Ciardi. *CiR*

Fireworks. James Reeves. *CoPs—ReBl*
"Firm in the good brown earth." See Planting a tree
"First, April, she with mellow showers." See The succession of the four sweet months
First autumn ("The crow sat black") Frances M. Frost. *FrLn*
The first autumn ("Where God had walked") Marshall Schacht. *BrL-8*
The first bee. See The snowdrop
"First came the Indians." See History of New York
First catch your hare. Eleanor Farjeon. *FaCb—FaN*
First Christmas night of all. Nancy Byrd Turner. *BrBc*
"First comes love." Unknown. *MoY*
"The first day of Christmas." Mother Goose. *DeMg*
"On the first day of Christmas." *LiL*
The twelve days of Christmas. *JoAc—OpO*
First departure. Frances M. Frost. *BrS*

November. *BrS*
Otherwise. *HuL-1*
The outdoor Christmas tree. *BrS*
The picnic box. *McAw*
Richer. *BrBc*
The snowman's resolution. *PeF*
Something very elegant. *BrBc*
Un-birthday cake. *BrBc*
Until we built a cabin. *ArTp*
Valentine's day. *HaY*
Wearing of the green. *HaY*
Winter circus. *HaY*
A wonderful man. *BrS*
"Fisher, in your bright bark rowing." See The fisherman
Fisher man. Dorothy Aldis. *AlA*
The fisherman ("Fisher, in your bright bark rowing") Unknown, tr. fr. the Portuguese by Anne Higginson Spicer. *FeF*
The fisherman ("The fisherman goes out at dawn") Abbie Farwell Brown. *FeF*
The fisherman ("The little boy is fishing") David McCord. *McFf*
"The fisherman goes out at dawn." See The fisherman
"A fisherman lived on the shore." See How a fisherman corked up his foe in a jar
"The fisherman's swapping a yarn for a yarn." See The flower boat
Fishermen and fishing
The angler's reveille. H. Van Dyke. *HuSv*
A bad day by the river. E. V. Rieu. *RiF*
The ballad of the oysterman. O. W. Holmes. *BrL-8—NaM*
Blackfriars. E. Farjeon. *HuL-1*
The boy fishing. E. J. Scovell. *ReT*
The crawdad hole. Unknown. *TaD*
The crayfish. R. Wallace. *McW*
Did you ever. Unknown. *WoJ*
Down by the pond. A. A. Milne. *MiWc*
Fisher man. D. Aldis. *AlA*
The fisherman ("Fisher, in your bright bark rowing") Unknown. *FeF*
The fisherman ("The fisherman goes out at dawn") A. F. Brown. *FeF*
The fisherman ("The little boy is fishing") D. McCord. *McFf*
Fishing. Unknown. *JoAc*
The fishing pole. M. C. Davies. *FeF*
Fishing Simon. Unknown. *TaD*
The flower boat. R. Frost. *FrR*
Fun with fishing. E. Tietjens. *FeF*
How a fisherman corked up his foe in a jar. G. W. Carryl. *CoPm*
"If I ever marry." Unknown. *WoF*
A man in the woods said. J. Ciardi. *CiI*
"Noah an' Jonah an' Cap'n John Smith." D. Marquis. *SmLg*
Old Ducky Quackerel. L. E. Richards. *BrR-5*
Salutation. E. Pound. *SmLg*
The sea wolf. V. McDougal. *FeF*
Some fishy nonsense. L. E. Richards. *ArTp*
Trebizond, Jonah, and the minnows. H. Wolfe. *HuL-2*
"Two boys went fishing one bright summer day." Unknown. *WiRm*

"When the wind is in the east." Mother Goose. *DeMg—LiL—OpO*
Signs, seasons, and sense. *UnG*
Where. D. McCord. *McT*
Wynken, Blynken, and Nod. E. Field. *FeF—HuL-1—HuSv—JoAc—UnG*
Yonder. J. Reeves. *ReR*
"The fishermen say, when your catch is done." See The sea wolf
Fishes swim. Mother Goose. *OpO*
"Fishes swim in water clear." See Fishes swim
Fishing. See Fishermen and fishing
Fishing. Unknown, tr. fr. the Danish by Rose Fyleman. *JoAc*
The fishing pole. Mary Carolyn Davies. *FeF*
"A fishing pole's a curious thing." See The fishing pole
Fishing Simon. Unknown. *TaD*
"Fishy, fish in the brook." Unknown. *WiRm*
American Father Gander. *UnG*
Fitts, Dudley
Ya se van los pastores. *GrCc*
Fitzgerald, Edward
The rubáiyát of Omar Khayyám of Naishapúr. tr. *HaP* (sel.)—*PaS* (sel.)
Wake. *FeF* (sel.)
Wake. See The rubáiyát of Omar Khayyám of Naishapúr
Fitzgerald, Margaret M.
The golden mean. tr. *PaS*
Fitzgerald, Robert
Memory of flowers. *GrCc*
Music. tr. *PaS*
Five chants. David McCord. *McFf*
I. "Every time I climb a tree." *ArTp—UnG*
II. "Monday morning back to school"
III. "The pickety fence"
IV. "The cow has a cud"
V. "Thin ice"
"Five ducks in the pond." See Railroad ducks
Five eyes. Walter De La Mare. *CoI*
The five-fingered maple. Kate Louise Brown. *HuL-1*
Five-in-June. Lysbeth Boyd Borie. *BrBc*
Five little bats. David McCord. *McFf*
"Five little bats flew out of the attic." See Five little bats
"Five little chickadees, sitting in a door." Unknown. *WoF*
Five little chickens. See The chickens ("Said the first little chicken")
"Five little monkeys." See The monkeys and the crocodile
"Five little pussy-cats, invited out to tea." See The cats' tea-party
"Five little sisters walking in a row." Kate Greenaway. *NaM*
"Five little squirrels." Unknown. *HuL-1 WiRm*
"Five little squirrels sat up in a tree." *JoAc*
"Five little squirrels sat up in a tree." See "Five little squirrels"
"Five minutes, five minutes more, please." See Bedtime

"Five-ten-twenty. Loud and clear." See When Anabelle's it

The five toes. Unknown, tr. fr. the Chinese by Isaac Taylor Headland. *JoAc*

Five trees. Eleanor Farjeon. *FaCb—FaN*

Five years old ("If ever there is something nice") Lysbeth Boyd Borie. *BrBc—BrS*

Five years old ("Please, everybody, look at me") Marie Louise Allen. *AlP—BrBc—BrL-k*

Flaccus, Quintus Horatius. See Horace

The flag. Shelley Silverstein. *CoPs*

The flag goes by. Henry Holcomb Bennett. *ArTp—BrL-7—BrS—FeF*

Flag song. Lydia Avery Coonley Ward. *HaY*

The flag we fly. Aileen Fisher. *HaY*

Flags
Brother, lift your flag with mine. J. D. D. Bacon. *CoPs*

Flags—United States
The flag. S. Silverstein. *CoPs*
The flag goes by. H. H. Bennett. *ArTp—BrL-7—BrS—FeF*
Flag song. L. A. C. Ward. *HaY*
The flag we fly. A. Fisher. *HaY*
Hang out the flags. J. S. Tippett. *BrS*
Quilt. J. Updike. *McW*
The star-spangled banner. F. S. Key. *FeF*

Flannan isle. Wilfrid Wilson Gibson. *CoSp*

The flattered flying fish. E. V. Rieu. *RiF*

The flattered lightning bug. Don Marquis. *CoSp*

The flea. Roland Young. *McW*

"A flea and a fly got caught in a flue." See "A flea and a fly in a flue"

"A flea and a fly in a flue." Unknown. *CoH—LoL—WiRm*
The flea and the fly. *FeF*
Limericks since Lear. *UnG*

The flea and the fly. See "A flea and a fly in a flue"

Fleas
Certain maxims of Archy. D. Marquis. *CoH* (sel.)
Archy, the cockroach, speaks. *FeF*
The flea. R. Young. *McW*
"A flea and a fly in a flue." Unknown. *CoH—LoL—WiRm*
The flea and the fly. *FeF*
Limericks since Lear. *UnG*
Great fleas. A. De Morgan. *McW*
In the middle. D. McCord. *McFf*
Small talk. D. Marquis. *CoSp*

Flecker, James Elroy
Lord Arnaldos. *CoSp*
Mignon. See Wilhelm Meister
The old ships. *DeT—NaE*
Santorin. *GrCc*
Wilhelm Meister, sel.
Mignon. tr. *PaS*

"Fled are those times, when, in harmonious strains." See The village

Fleming, Elizabeth
The hurdy-gurdy. *HuL-2*
The patchwork quilt. *HuL-2*
The steeple. *HuL-2*
Who's in. *BrL-k—PeF*
Wild animals. *HuSv*

Fleming, Marjorie
A melancholy lay. See Three turkeys
Three turkeys. *ReT*
A melancholy lay. *SmLg*
To a monkey. *UnG*

Fletcher, John
Evening song. See The faithful shepherdess
The faithful shepherdess, sel.
Evening song. *DeT*
The god of sheep. *SmLg*
Song in the wood. *ReT*

Fletcher, John Gould
Lincoln. *JoAc*

Flexner, James
In the hours of darkness. *FeF*

Flies
"Fiddle de dee, fiddle de dee." Mother Goose. *DeMg*
The fly and the bumble-bee. *HuL-1*
Song. *WiRm*
"A flea and a fly in a flue." Unknown. *CoH—LoL—WiRm*
The flea and the fly. *FeF*
Limericks since Lear. *UnG*
Flies. D. Aldis. *AlA*
The fly ("How large unto the tiny fly") W. De La Mare. *HuL-2—ReG*
The fly ("Little fly") W. Blake. *HaP—UnG*
The fly ("The Lord in His wisdom made the fly") O. Nash. *FeF*
"The fly made a visit to the grocery store." Unknown. *WoF*
"I wish I could meet the man that knows." J. Ciardi. *CiI*
On a fly drinking from his cup. W. Oldys. *UnG*
"Poor little fly upon the wall." Unknown. *WoF*
The spider and the fly. M. Howitt. *DeT—FeF—PeF*
A trapped fly. R. Herrick. *HoW*
"Will you walk into my parlor." Unknown. *WiRm*

Flies. Dorothy Aldis. *AlA*

"Flies walk on ceilings." See Flies

Flight. Harold Vinal. *FeF*

Flint, Annie Johnson
God's promises. *BrR-6—ThP*

Flitch of bacon. Eleanor Farjeon. *FaN*

The floating old man. Edward Lear. *HoW*

"A flock of swallows have gone flying south." See August 28

"A flock of white sheep." Unknown
Five very old riddles. *DeT*

The floor and the ceiling. William Jay Smith. *CoH*

Flores, Kate
Love song. tr. *PaS*
"Lovely as a flower." tr. *PaS*
"The moldering hulk." tr. *PaS*
"The white moon." tr. *PaS*

Florists
The flower-cart man. R. Field. *BrS*
"A maiden caught stealing a dahlia." Unknown. *CoH*

"Flour of England, fruit of Spain." Mother Goose. *DeMg—OpO*

Flower, Robin
Pangur Bán. tr. *PaS—SmLg*
The **flower** boat. Robert Frost. *FrR*
The **flower**-cart man. Rachel Field. *BrS*
Flower chorus. Ralph Waldo Emerson. *HuL-2*
The **flower**-fed buffaloes. Vachel Lindsay. *ArTp — FeF — HaP — JoAc — McW — ReT—SmLg*
"The **flower**-fed buffaloes of the spring." See The flower-fed buffaloes
"**Flower** in the crannied wall." Alfred Tennyson. *DoP—FeF—ThP*
Flower party. Dorothy Aldis. *AlHd*
The **flowering** hills. Eleanor Farjeon. *FaCb —FaN*
Flowers. See also Gardens and gardening; Plants; Trees; also names of flowers, as Roses
At Easter time. L. E. Richards. *DoP*
Blossom themes. C. Sandburg. *SaW*
Blossoms and storm. Sadaiye. *PaS*
Bronwen of the flowers. E. Farjeon. *FaCb*
Cathemerinon, sels. Prudentius. *PaS*
  "The earth is sweet with roses"
  "Take him, earth, for cherishing"
A charm for spring flowers. R. Field. *ArTp*
Cuckoo-shoes. E. Farjeon. *FaCb*
Cycle. L. Hughes. *FeF*
Dainty little maiden. A. Tennyson. *HuL-2*
The dormouse and the doctor. A. A. Milne. *MiWc*
Early. D. Aldis. *AlA*
First thought. M. C. Livingston. *LiWa*
The flower boat. R. Frost. *FrR*
The flower-cart man. R. Field. *BrS*
Flower chorus. R. W. Emerson. *HuL-2*
The flower-fed buffaloes. V. Lindsay. *ArTp — FeF — HaP — JoAc — McW —ReT—SmLg*
"Flower in the crannied wall." A. Tennyson. *DoP—FeF—ThP*
Flower party. D. Aldis. *AlHd*
The flowering hills. E. Farjeon. *FaCb—FaN*
The flowers ("All the names I know from nurse") R. L. Stevenson. *FeF*
Flowers ("We planted a garden") H. Behn. *ArTp—FeF*
Flowers and frost. J. Reeves. *ReR*
Flowers of middle summer. From The winter's tale. W. Shakespeare. *HaY*
Flowers tell months. C. Sandburg. *SaW*
"I looked before me and behind." E. Farjeon. *FaCb*
I'd leave. A. Lang. *FeF*
If I should ever by chance. E. Thomas. *NaM—SmLg*
I'll twine white violets. Meleager. *PaS*
In desert places. Sister Mary Madeleva. *UnG*
In my garden. Unknown. *HuL-1*
Jack-hide-in-the-hedge. E. Farjeon. *FaCb*
The keys of heaven. E. Farjeon. *FaCb*
Kingcups in town. E. Farjeon. *FaCb—FaN*
King's-cup. E. Farjeon. *FaCb*
Lady's bedstraw. E. Farjeon. *FaCb*
The last flower. J. T. Moore. *CoPs*

The last mowing. R. Frost. *FrY*
Late October. S. Teasdale. *BrL-7—CoPs —HaY*
A lucky thing. D. Aldis. *AlA*
"Mary, Mary, quite contrary." Mother Goose. *ArTp—HuL-1—JoAc—LiL*
  Contrary Mary. *OpO*
  "Mistress Mary." *BrL-k*
  "Mistress Mary, quite contrary." *DeMg—HuSv*
Memory of flowers. R. Fitzgerald. *GrCc*
Milkmaids. E. Farjeon. *FaCb*
More than flowers we have brought. N. B. Turner. *BrS*
My delight. Unknown. *ReG*
A nosegay. From The shepherd's calendar. E. Spenser. *DeT*
A passing glimpse. R. Frost. *FrR—FrY*
Planting flowers on the eastern embankment. Po Chü-i. *PaS*
A prayer for blossoms. E. Farjeon. *FaCb*
The procession. M. Widdemer. *HaY*
The question. P. B. Shelley. *DeT*
"Ragged Robin." E. Farjeon. *FaN*
Revelation. A. Brown. *DoP*
Robin-run-by-the-wall. E. Farjeon. *FaCb*
Solomon and the bees. J. G. Saxe. *UnG*
Some vegetables and flowers. D. Aldis. *AlHd*
Song in spring. L. Ginsberg. *HaY*
The sprinkler. D. Aldis. *AlA*
Summer offering. E. Farjeon. *FaCb*
"Through storm and wind." Mother Goose. *OpO*
Time to go. S. Coolidge. *DoP*
To the sun from a flower. G. Gezelle. *FeF*
  To the sun. *PaS*
Traveller's joy. E. Farjeon. *FaCb*
The tuft of flowers. R. Frost. *FrR—FrY*
A violet bank. From A midsummer-night's dream. W. Shakespeare. *FeF*
"Violets, daffodils." E. J. Coatsworth. *ArTp*
  Nosegay. *McAw*
"White flowers and white butterflies." D. Aldis. *AlHd*
The wild thyme. W. Blake. *HoW*
Wildflowers. E. Farjeon. *DoP*
Wind and window flower. R. Frost. *FrR*
The window box. I. O. Eastwick. *EaI*
Window boxes. E. Farjeon. *FeF*
Winter flower store. D. Aldis. *AlA*
The **flowers** ("All the names I know from nurse") Robert Louis Stevenson. *FeF*
Flowers ("We planted a garden") Harry Behn. *ArTp—FeF*
"The **flowers** all are sleeping." See Little sandman's song
Flowers and frost. James Reeves. *ReR*
"**Flowers** are yellow." See Flowers and frost
"**Flowers** every night." See At peace
Flowers of middle summer. See The winter's tale
Flowers tell months. Carl Sandburg. *SaW*
The **flute-players.** Jean-Joseph Rabéarivelo, tr. fr. the French by Dorothy Blair. *PaS*
Flute-priest song for rain. Amy Lowell. *PlU* (sel.)

Flute song. Unknown, tr. fr. the Greek by T. F. Higham. *PaS*

Flutes
  The flute-players. Jean-Joseph Rabéari-velo. *PaS*
  Flute-priest song for rain. A. Lowell. *PlU* (sel.)
  Flute song. Unknown. *PaS*
  A musical instrument. E. B. Browning. *FeF—UnG*
    The great god Pan. *HoW*
  On hearing a flute at night from the wall of Shou-Hsiang. Li Yi. *PlU*

"A fluttering swarm." See Blossoms and storm

Flux. Carl Sandburg. *SaW*

The **fly** ("How large unto the tiny **fly**") Walter De La Mare. *HuL-2—ReG*

The **fly** ("Little **fly**") William Blake. *HaP—UnG*

The **fly** ("The Lord in His wisdom made the fly") Ogden Nash. *FeF*

The **fly** and the bumble-bee. See "Fiddle de dee, fiddle de dee"

"Fly away, fly away, over the sea." See The swallow

The **fly-away** horse. Eugene Field. *UnG*

"Fly away Peter." Mother Goose. *LiL*

"The fly made a visit to the grocery store." Unknown. *WoF*

"Fly, roadster, fly." See Song for a blue roadster

"Fly, white butterflies, out to sea." See White butterflies

The **Flying** Dutchman. Charles Godfrey Leland. *CoPm*

"Flying high on silver bars." See The acrobats

Flying kite. Frank Dempster Sherman. *BrR-4*
  A kite. *ArTp* (sel.)

The **flying** pig. See "Dickery, dickery, dare"

Flying saucers
  Go fly a saucer. D. McCord. *FeF* (sel.)—*PlI*

The **flying** squirrel. Rowena Bastin Bennett. *BrR-4*

"A flying squirrel is the strangest thing." See The flying squirrel

Foal. Mary Britton Miller. *ArTp—CoI*

"Fodder in the barn loft." Unknown. *WoF*

Fog
  Fog ("The fog comes") C. Sandburg. *ArTp—FeF—HuSv—JoAc—PeF—UnG*
  The fog ("I saw the fog grow thick") W. H. Davies. *ArTp—McW*
  The fog horn. E. H. Newlin. *BrR-3*
  Fog, the magician. M. Cane. *DoP*
  River fog. Fukayabu Kiyowara. *FeF*

Fog ("The fog comes") Carl Sandburg. *ArTp—FeF—HuSv—JoAc—PeF—UnG*

The **fog** ("I saw the fog grow thick") William Henry Davies. *ArTp—McW*

"The fog comes." See Fog

The **fog** horn. Edith H. Newlin. *BrR-3*

Fog, the magician. Melville Cane. *DoP*

"Foggy, foggy, over the water." See The fog horn

Folklore. See Ballads—Old English and Scottish; Cowboys—Songs; Legends; Mountaineer songs; Mythology—Greek and Roman

"The folks at my house half the time are thinkin' about dirt." See Soap, the oppressor

Follen, Eliza Lee (Cabot)
  The little kittens. See "Three little kittens"
  The moon. *BrL-k*
  Ringely, ringely. *BrBc*
  The runaway brook. *BrL-k*
  "Three little kittens." at. *BrL-k—FeF—HuSv—OpO*
    The little kittens. *ArTp—HuL-1*
    "Three little kittens, they lost their mittens." *AnI—DeMg—LiL*
  "Three little kittens, they lost their mittens." See "Three little kittens"

"Follow my Bangalorey man." Mother Goose. *HuL-1—ReG*
  My Bangalorey man. *OpO*

Followers of the sun. Eleanor Farjeon. *FaCb—FaN*

Fontaine, Jean De La. See La Fontaine, Jean De

Fontainebleau. Sara Teasdale. *GrCc*

Food and eating. See also Cooks and cooking; also names of foods, as Cakes and cookies
  After the party. W. Wise. *FeF*
  The ant and the cricket. Unknown. *DeT*
  Baby Kate. J. S. Newman. *CoH*
  "Bananas and cream." D. McCord. *McT*
  Blessing over food. H. N. Bialik. *BrL-k—HaY*
  "Bluebird, what do you feed on." C. Sandburg. *SaW*
  Bobbily Boo and Wollypotump. L. E. Richards. *LoL*
  "The boy stood on the burning deck (eating peanuts)." Unknown. *WoF*
    American Father Gander. *UnG*
  Bread and water. E. Farjeon. *FaN*
  Celery. O. Nash. *FeF*
  "Charley Wag, Charley Wag." Mother Goose. *JoAc*
    "Charlie Wag." *OpO*
  A child's grace. R. Burns. *FeF—HuSv—NaE*
    "Some hae meat that canna eat." *SmLg*
  The Christmas pudding. Unknown. *ArTp—HuL-1*
  Country trucks. M. Shannon. *ArTp—FeF*
  The cupboard. W. De La Mare. *ArTp—BrL-k—FeF—HuL-1*
  Davy Dumpling. Mother Goose. *OpO*
  The dessert. M. Lamb. *DeT*
  The eel. O. Nash. *FeF—JoAc*
  Egg to eat. J. Reeves. *ReR*
  The embarrassing episode of little Miss Muffet. G. W. Carryl. *CoSp—FeF*
  "An epicure, dining at Crewe." Unknown. *CoH—LoL*
    Limericks. *BrL-7*
    Limericks since Lear. *UnG*

Fairlop Friday. E. Farjeon. *FaN*

Field mouse to kitchen mouse. E. J. Coatsworth. *CoM*

"Fodder in the barn loft." Unknown. *WoF*

Food and drink. D. McCord. *McT*

For dessert. D. Aldis. *AlHd*

The gastronomic guile of Simple Simon. G. W. Carryl. *UnG*

Giraffe. W. J. Smith. *SmB*

The giraffe and the woman. L. E. Richards. *CoI*

The golden palace. Unknown. *GrCc*

Goody O'Grumpity. C. R. Brink. *FeF*

The grandiloquent goat. C. Wells. *LoL—NaM*

Greedy Tom. Mother Goose. *OpO*

Griselda. E. Farjeon. *UnG*

The groaning board. Unknown. *CoH*

"Handy spandy, Jack-a-Dandy." Mother Goose. *DeMg*

"Hannah Bantry, in the pantry." Mother Goose. *DeMg*
    "Hannah Bantry." *OpO*

The hasty pudding. J. Barlow. *SmLg*

"He who has never known hunger." E. J. Coatsworth. *ArTp*

"Hey ding a ding." Mother Goose. *OpO*

"Hokey, pokey, whisky, thum." Mother Goose. *OpO*

Homely meats. J. Davies. *SmLg*

"Hot cross buns." Mother Goose. *DeMg—JoAc—OpO*

Hunger and thirst. B. Young. *McAw*

"I eat my peas with honey." Unknown. *NaE*
    Peas. *CoH—FeF*

"I had a little pup, his name was Spot." Unknown. *WoF*

"I must remember." S. Silverstein. *CoPs*

The ice-cream man. R. Field. *BrR-4—BrS—FeF*

"If all the world were apple pie." Mother Goose. *AnI—DeMg*
    "If all the world was apple pie." *JoAc—LoL*

"If I were an apple." Unknown. *AnI—HuL-1*

"I'm going to Lady Washington's." Unknown. *JoAc*

In honor of Taffy Topaz. C. Morley. *ArTp*

"Isabel Jones & Curabel Lee." D. McCord. *McFf—UnG*

"Jack Sprat could eat no fat." Mother Goose. *DeMg—JoAc—LiL*
    Jack Sprat. *OpO*

James and the shoulder of mutton. A. O'Keefe. *DeT*

Jerry Mulligan. J. Ciardi. *CiM*

The king's breakfast. A. A. Milne. *MiWc*

Little bits. J. Ciardi. *CiY*

"Little fishes in a brook." Mother Goose. *OpO*

The little girl and the turkey. D. Aldis. *AlA*

"Little Jack Horner." Mother Goose. *BrL-k—DeMg—HuSv—JoAc—LiL*
    Jack Horner. *OpO*

"Little King Boggen, he built a fine hall." Mother Goose. *HuSv*

"Little King Pippen he built a fine hall." Mother Goose. *DeMg*
    King Pippin. *LoL—OpO*

"Little Miss Muffet." Mother Goose. *ArTp — BrL-k — DeMg — HuSv — JoAc—LiL*
    Miss Muffet. *OpO*

Lobster music. J. Ciardi. *CiM*

"A long time ago." T'ao Ch'ien. *SmLg*

"Mama, mama, look at little Sam." Unknown. *WiRm*

The man in the onion bed. J. Ciardi. *CiI*

Maple feast. F. M. Frost. *BrS*

Mary Anne's luncheon. D. Aldis. *AlA*

Millions of strawberries. G. Taggard. *ArTp—FeF—NaM—UnG*

Minnie. E. Farjeon. *UnG*

Miss T. W. De La Mare. *ArTp—BrR-4—JoAc—NaM*

"Mr East gave a feast." Mother Goose. *JoAc*
    Mr East's feast. *OpO*

Mr Finney's turnip. Unknown. *CoH—LoL*

"Mrs Peck-Pigeon." E. Farjeon. *ArTp—BrL-k—HuSv—JoAc*

"Mix a pancake." C. G. Rossetti. *BrL-k—HuL-1*

Mouse. H. Conkling. *ArTp—BrL-k—HuSv*

Mumfludgeons. E. V. Rieu. *RiF*

Mummy slept late and daddy fixed breakfast. J. Ciardi. *CiY*

Neighborly. V. A. Storey. *ArTp—HuL-1*

Nell the nibbler. G. Burgess. *BrR-6*

Nice food. D. Aldis. *AlA*

"O, dear, O." Unknown. *DeT*

"Oh, what have you got for dinner, Mrs Bond." Mother Goose. *DeMg*
    Dilly dilly. *OpO*

"Old Mother Hubbard." Mother Goose. *AnI—DeMg—HuSv—JoAc—LiL—UnG*
    Old Mother Hubbard and her dog. *OpO*

"The other day when I met Dick." J. Ciardi. *CiI*

Our joyful feast. G. Wither. *BrS*

Out walking. M. Chute. *ChA*

"Over the water and over the lea." Mother Goose. *DeMg*
    Over the water to Charley. *DeT*
    Over the water to Charlie. *OpO*

A parable. A. C. Doyle. *BrL-7*

A party. L. E. Richards. *BrBc—BrS*

"Pease porridge hot." Mother Goose. *ArTp—BrL-k—DeMg—JoAc—LiL—OpO*
    "Pease pudding hot." *HuL-1*

The picnic. D. Aldis. *AlA—ArTp—McAw*

Picnic day. R. Field. *ArTp—BrS*

Picnics. M. Chute. *ChA*

The pigs. J. Taylor. *DeT*

"The Queen of Hearts." Mother Goose. *AnI—DeMg—JoAc—LiL—OpO*

"R is for the restaurant." From All around the town. P. McGinley. *ArTp*

Rice pudding. A. A. Milne. *MiWc*

"Robin the Bobbin, the big-bellied Ben." Mother Goose. *DeMg*
    Robin the Bobbin. *OpO*

"Rumpty-iddity, row, row, row." Mother Goose. *OpO*

For Anna. Myra Cohn Livingston. *LiWa*

For Anne Gregory. William Butler Yeats. *GrCc—HaP*

For Arvia. Edwin Arlington Robinson. *BrBc*

For Christmas ("I want a puppy dog") Dorothy Aldis. *AlA—HuL-1*

For Christmas ("Now not a window small or big") Rachel Field. *BrR-6*

For Christmas day. Eleanor Farjeon. *ArTp —DoP—HuL-2*

For dessert. Dorothy Aldis. *AlHd*

"For each and every joyful thing." See For joy

"For echo is the soul of the voice exerting itself in hollow places." See The instruments

For every evil. See "For every evil under the sun"

"For every evil under the sun." William Hazlitt. *DeMg—LiL—OpO*
   For every evil. *NaE—ThP—UnG*

For February twelfth. Muriel M. Gessner. *HaY*

"For flowers that bloom about our feet." See Spring prayer

"For forty years, for forty-one." See This dim and ptolemaic man

"For God hath not given us the spirit of fear." See The second epistle of Paul to Timothy

For good luck. Juliana Horatia Ewing. *FeF*

For Hanukkah. H. N. Bialik. *ArTp*

"For I will consider my cat Jeoffry." See My cat Jeoffry

For joy. Florence Earle Coates. *BrL-7*

"For life and health and strength." See God's gift

"For, lo, the winter is past." See The song of Solomon—The winter is past

For M. S. singing Frühlingsglaube in 1945. Frances Cornford. *PlU*

"For many, many days together." See Riding together

For Maria at four. John Becker. *BrBc*

"For me who go." See Parting

"For mother-love and father-care." See We thank Thee

For my contemporaries. J. V. Cunningham. *HaP*

For Nijinsky's tomb. Frances Cornford. *PlU*

For once, then, something. Robert Frost. *FrR*

"For sixty years the pine lumber barn." See The people, yes—Prairie barn

For snow. Eleanor Farjeon. *JoAc*

For the conjunction of two planets. Adrienne Cecile Rich. *PlI*

For the eightieth birthday of a great singer. Edward Shanks. *PlU*

"For the feast of trumpets should be kept up." See Jubilate agno

For those who fail. Joaquin Miller. *BrL-8*

For Vicki at seven. Sydney King Russell. *BrBc*

"For want of a nail." See "For want of a nail, the shoe was lost"

"For want of a nail, the shoe was lost." Mother Goose. *DeMg—LiL*
   "For want of a nail." *OpO*
   The horseshoe nail. *ThP*
   Tremendous trifles. *UnG*

"For when it dawn'd—they dropped their arms." See The rime of the ancient mariner

For whom the bell tolls. John Donne. *ThP*

For you. Carl Sandburg. *McW*

Forbearance. Ralph Waldo Emerson. *ThP*

Forbes, Ella C.
   Glad earth. *HaY*

The forbidden play. Robert Graves. *GrP*

"The force that through the green fuse drives the flower." Dylan Thomas. *PlI*

Foreign lands. Robert Louis Stevenson. *HuL-1*

Foresters. See Forests and forestry

Forester's song. Alfred Edgar Coppard. *FeF*

"The forest's afire." See October's song

Forests and forestry. See also Lumbering; Trees
   Alons au bois le may cueillir. Charles d'Orleans. *PaS*
   Autumn woods. J. S. Tippett. *ArTp— McAw*
   By Dippel woods. E. Farjeon. *FaCb*
   The charcoal-burner. A. A. Milne. *MiWc*
   Christmas in the woods. F. M. Frost. *ArTp*
   "Cold winter now is in the wood." E. J. Coatsworth. *ArTp*
   Come in. R. Frost. *FrR—FrY*
   Dirge in woods. G. Meredith. *HoW*
   Forester's song. A. E. Coppard. *FeF*
   Green rain. M. Webb. *FeF*
   "Hie away, hie away." From Waverley. W. Scott. *ArTp*
    Hie away. *NaM*
   In hardwood groves. R. Frost. *FrR*
   In the woods alone. Unknown. *PaS*
   The intruder. J. Reeves. *ReBl*
   Kilcash. F. O'Connor. *ReT*
   Laughing song. W. Blake. *ArTp—CoPs— JoAc—McW—ReT—UnG*
   October's song. E. Farjeon. *CoPs—FaCb —FaN*
   Peace. Bhartrihari. *PaS*
   "The plants stand silent round me." J. Jorgensen. *PaS*
   The poplar field. W. Cowper. *DeT—HaP —HoW*
   Song. J. Milton. *ReT*
   Song in the wood. J. Fletcher. *ReT*
   A song of Sherwood. A. Noyes. *ArTp— FeF—JoAc*
   Stopping by woods on a snowy evening. R. Frost. *ArTp—BrL-8—BrS—CoPs— FeF — FrR — FrY — HaP — HuL-2 — HuSv — JoAc — McW — NaM — PeF —ReT—SmLg*
   'Tis merry in greenwood. From Harold the Dauntless. W. Scott. *FeF*
   To a young wretch. R. Frost. *FrR*
   To Jane: The invitation. P. B. Shelley. *ReT*
    Away, away. *UnG*

"Four things a man must learn to do." See Four things

Four things to do. See Four things ("There be four things which are little upon the earth")

Four wrens. Mother Goose. *OpO*

"Four years old when the blackberries come." See Hal's birthday

"Fourteen angels round my bed." See Lullaby

Fourth of July
  American hill. F. M. Frost. *BrR-6*
  Choice. J. Farrar. *BrS*
  "Fourth of July." M. Chute. *BrS—ChA*
  The fourth of July ("Day of glory. Welcome day") J. Pierpont. *HaY*
  Fourth of July ("Fat torpedoes in bursting jackets") R. Field. *BrS*
  Fourth of July night ("The little boat at anchor") C. Sandburg. *SaW*
  Fourth of July night ("Pin wheels whirling round") D. Aldis. *AlA—ArTp—BrS—McAw*
  Fourth of July song. L. Lenski. *BrS*
  Grandfather Watts's private Fourth. H. C. Bunner. *ArTp—CoPs—CoSp*
  "If I had a firecracker." S. Silverstein. *CoPs*
  "I've got a rocket." Unknown. *BrS—JoAc*
  Listen to the people: Independence day, 1941. S. V. Benét. *CoPs* (sel.)
  Prayer on fourth of July. N. B. Turner. *HaY*

"Fourth of July." Marchette Chute. *BrS—ChA*

The fourth of July ("Day of glory. Welcome day") John Pierpont. *HaY*

Fourth of July ("Fat torpedoes in bursting jackets") Rachel Field. *BrS*

Fourth of July night ("The little boat at anchor") Carl Sandburg. *SaW*

Fourth of July night ("Pin wheels whirling round") Dorothy Aldis. *AlA—ArTp—BrS—McAw*

Fourth of July song. Lois Lenski. *BrS*

Fowler, E. Kathryn. See Fowler, Elsie Melchert

Fowler, Elsie Melchert
  "If you never talked with fairies." *BrBc*
  If you've never. *BrR-4—HuL-1*
  The miracle. *BrBc*
  Secrets. *BrBc*

The fox. See "A fox jumped up one winter's night"

"A fox and a hen went out one day." See The wise hen

Fox and crow. William Jay Smith. *SmB*

"The fox and his wife they had a great strife." See "A fox jumped up one winter's night"

The fox and the goat. Jean De La Fontaine, tr. fr. the French by Marianne Moore. *JoAc*

The fox and the grapes. See The greedy fox and the elusive grapes

Fox cub goes home. Frances M. Frost. *FrLn*

Fox hunting. See Hunters and hunting

"A fox jumped up one winter's night." Mother Goose. *DeMg*
  Ballad of the fox. *UnG*
  Ee-oh. *DeT*
  The fox. *CoSp*
  The fox's foray. *OpO*
  A visit from Mr Fox. *HuSv*

"The fox set out in hungry plight." See "A fox jumped up one winter's night"

Fox-Smith, Cicely
  Hastings mill. *McW*
  The Portsmouth road. *HuL-2*

"The fox went out on a chilly night." See "A fox jumped up one winter's night"

"A fox went out one chilly night." See "A fox jumped up one winter's night"

Foxes
  The crow and the fox. J. De La Fontaine. *BrL-7—UnMc*
  Four little foxes. L. Sarett. *ArTp—CoPs—FeF—HaY—McW—UnG*
  Fox and crow. W. J. Smith. *SmB*
  The fox and the goat. J. De La Fontaine. *JoAc*
  Fox cub goes home. F. M. Frost. *FrLn*
  "A fox jumped up one winter's night." Mother Goose. *DeMg*
    Ballad of the fox. *UnG*
    Ee-oh. *DeT*
    The fox. *CoSp*
    The fox's foray. *OpO*
    A visit from Mr Fox. *HuSv*
  The foxes. F. M. Frost. *FrLn*
  The greedy fox and the elusive grapes. Aesop. *UnMc*
    The fox and the grapes. *UnG*
  The hunt. L. Kent. *McW*
  The little fox. M. Edey. *ArTp*
  Night of wind. F. M. Frost. *ArTp—FeF*
  "Put your finger in foxy's hole." Mother Goose. *LiL—OpO*
  The sychophantic fox and the gullible raven. G. W. Carryl. *CoH*
  The three foxes. A. A. Milne. *HuSv—MiWc—NaM*
  The wise hen. J. Ciardi. *CiY*

The foxes. Frances M. Frost. *FrLn*

"The foxglove by the cottage door." See Four and eight

Foxgloves (Flower)
  Bluebells and foxgloves. J. Reeves. *ReBl*
  Four and eight. F. Wolfe. *BrBc—BrS—HuL-1*

The fox's foray. See "A fox jumped up one winter's night"

France
  The good Joan. L. W. Reese. *ArTp—FeF—NaM*

France—History. See also European war, 1914-1918; Naval battles; Warships; World war, 1939-1945; also names of battles, as Waterloo, Battle of, 1815
  Casabianca. E. Farjeon. *FaCb—FaN*
  Incident of the French camp. R. Browning. *UnG—UnMc*
  "The king of France went up the hill." Mother Goose. *DeMg*
    The king of France. *OpO*
  "A maiden's wondrous fame, I sing." Unknown, tr. fr. the French. *JoAc*

Frontier and pioneer life—*Continued*

The flower-fed buffaloes. V. Lindsay. *ArTp — FeF — HaP — JoAc — McW —ReT—SmLg*

In praise of Johnny Appleseed. V. Lindsay. *HuSv*
  Johnny Appleseed. *FeF* (sel.)

John Day, frontiersman. Y. Winters. *HaP*

John Sutter. Y. Winters. *HaP*

The Oregon trail. A. Guiterman. *FeF*

The Oregon trail: 1851. J. Marshall. *HuSv*

The pioneer ("He could not breathe in a crowded place") W. B. Ruggles. *BrR-5*

The pioneer ("Long years ago I blazed a trail") A. Guiterman. *ArTp*

The society upon the Stanislow. B. Harte. *UnMc*

Song of the settlers. J. West. *FeF*

The wilderness is tamed. E. J. Coatsworth. *BrR-5—FeF—HuSv*

Frost, Frances M.

American hill. *BrR-6*

Apple season. *BrS*

Apple song. *FeF*

Beach fire. *ArTp—PeF*

Blue smoke. *BrS*

Child's grace. *BrR-6*

The chipmunk. *FrLn*

Christmas eve legend. *BrBc—EaW*

Christmas in the woods. *ArTp*

Clover for breakfast. *HuSv—JoAc*

Counting-out rhyme for March. *HaY*

Cover. *BrL-k*

Dandelion morning. *FrLn*

Dandelions. *ArTp*

Easter in the woods. *BrS*

Father. *ArTp—BrS—FeF—HuSv*

First autumn. *FrLn*

First departure. *BrS*

Fox cub goes home. *FrLn*

The foxes. *FrLn*

Green afternoon. *ArTp—FrLn*

Green hill neighbors. *ArTp—FrLn*

Growing. *BrBc*

The hummingbird. *FrLn*

I can't decide. *FrLn*

Kentucky birthday: February 12, 1815. *BrS—HaY*

The little whistler. *ArTp—HuSv—JoAc—PeF*

The long night moon: December. *HaY*

Mailbox wren. *FrLn*

Maple feast. *BrS*

Meadow secret. *FrLn*

Mice under snow. *FrLn*

Night heron. *FrLn*

Night of wind. *ArTp—FeF*

Night plane. *ArTp—FeF*

North. *FrLn*

Otter creek. *FrLn*

The porcupine. *FrLn*

Pull. *BrR-6*

The rabbits. *FrLn*

Railroad ducks. *FrLn*

Rainy robin. *FrLn*

Rise, sun. *FrLn*

School is out. *BrS*

The snail. *FrLn*

Sniff. *BrS*

The snowman. *BrL-k*

Song for December thirty-first. *HaY*

Spring in hiding. *HaY*

Spring lullaby. *FrLn*

To a Christmas tree. *BrR-6*

Trains at night. *ArTp*

Valentine for earth. *ArTp—FrLn*

Weather vanes. *BrS*

White season. *ArTp—FeF*

Winter feast. *HaY*

Frost, Robert

Acquainted with the night. *FrY—HaP*

After apple-picking. *FrR—FrY*

At Woodward's gardens. *FrR—PlI*

The bear. *FrR*

"The bearer of evil tidings." *FrR*

Bereft. *FrR*

Birches. *FrR—FrY—SmLg*

The birthplace. *FrR—FrY—SmLg*

Blue-butterfly day. *FrY*

A blue ribbon at Amesbury. *FrR*

Blueberries. *FrR—FrY* (sel.)

A boundless moment. *FrR*

A brook in the city. *FrR*

Brown's descent; or, The willy-nilly slide. *CoSp—FrR—FrY—NaE*

Canis Major. *FrR*

The census-taker. *FrR*

Choose something like a star. *FrR*

Christmas trees. *FrY*

A cloud shadow. *FrR*

The code. *FrR—UnMc*

Come in. *FrR—FrY*

A considerable speck. *FrR*

The cow in apple time. *FrR—FrY*

The death of the hired man. *FrR—FrY—UnMc*

Departmental. *FrR—FrY*

Design. *FrR*

A drumlin woodchuck. *FrR—FrY—McW*

Dust of snow. *ArTp—FrR—FrY—NaM—ThP*

Early April. *HaY*

Evening in a sugar orchard. *FrR*

The exposed nest. *FrY*

The fear. *FrR*

The figure in the doorway. *FrR*

Fire and ice. *FrR—FrY*

Fireflies in the garden. *FrR—FrY*

The flower boat. *FrR*

For once, then, something. *FrR*

The freedom of the moon. *FrY*

Gathering leaves. *FrR—FrY*

Ghost house. *FrR*

The gift outright. *FrR—McW—SmLg*

A girl's garden. *FrY*

Going for water. *FrR—FrY*

Good-by and keep cold. *FrR—FrY—UnG*

Good hours. *FrR—FrY*

The grindstone. *FrR*

The gum-gatherer. *FrR*

Happiness makes up in height for what it lacks in length. *FrR*

The hardship of accounting. *FrR—SmLg*

The hill wife. *FrR*

A hillside thaw. *FrR—FrY*

Home burial. *FrR*

The housekeeper. *FrR*

A hundred collars. *FrR*

Hyla brook. *FrR—FrY*

"The **frugal** snail, with forecast of repose." See The snail

Fruit. See also Orchards; also names of fruits, as Apples
Counters. E. J. Coatsworth. *PeF*
    To think. *HuL*
The favourite fruit. E. Farjeon. *FaCb—* *—FaN*
The pawpaw patch. Unknown. *TaD*
Pomona. W. Morris. *HoW*
"**Fruit** is soft as soon as ripened." Unknown. *MoY*
The **fruit** plucker. Samuel Taylor Coleridge. *DeT*
    In a moonlight wilderness. *SmLg*
"**Fudge**, fudge, call the judge." See Elevator

Fukayabu Kiyowara
River-fog. *FeF*
"**Full** fathom five thy father lies." See The tempest
"**Full** knee-deep lies the winter snow." See The death of the old year
"**Full** many a magic island lies within the seas of coral." See Pirates on Funafuti
Full moon. See "Girls and boys, come out to play"
Full moon ("One night as Dick lay fast asleep") Walter De La Mare. *ArTp—* *JoAc*
Full moon ("She was wearing the coral taffeta trousers") V. Sackville-West. *NaM*
Fun in a garret. Emma C. Dowd. *ArTp* *—BrR-3*
Fun with fishing. Eunice Tietjens. *FeF*
Funebrial reflections. Ogden Nash. *PlI*
Funeral hymn. Unknown, tr. fr. the Sanskrit by Arthur A. Macdonell. *PaS*
The **funeral** rites of the rose. Robert Herrick. *HaP*

Funerals. See also Death; Grief; Laments
Burial of Sir John Moore. C. Wolfe. *UnMc*
    The burial of Sir John Moore at Corunna, 1809. *DeT*
Burial of the Minnisink. H. W. Longfellow. *GrCc*
Cat's funeral. E. V. Rieu. *RiF*
1805. R. Graves. *NaE—SmLg*
Funeral hymn. Unknown. *PaS*
The funeral rites of the rose. R. Herrick. *HaP*
Home burial. R. Frost. *FrR*
Robin Hood's funeral. A. Munday. *HoW*
    Song. *ReT*
The sea-ritual. G. Darley. *HoW*
"A silly young fellow named Hyde." Unknown. *CoH*
    Limericks since Lear. *UnG*
"Who killed Cock Robin." Mother Goose. *DeMg—DeT—JoAc*
    Cock Robin. *UnG*
Death and burial of Cock Robin. *OpO*
"The **funniest** sight I've ever seen." Unknown. *WoF*
"The **funniest** sight that ever I saw." Unknown
    American Father Gander. *UnG*
"**Funny**, how Felicia Ropps." See Felicia Ropps

"**Funny** Mister Hoppy-toes." See Mister Hoppy-toes
The **funny** old man and his wife. D'A. W. Thompson. *BrR-4*
"**Funny** the way different cars start." Dorothy W. Baruch. *BrL-k—FeF*
Furniture. See names of furniture, as Beds
"**Furrow** by furrow, the brown earth lies." See Corn
Furry bear. A. A. Milne. *CoI—HuSv—* *MiWc—PeF*
"A **furry** coat has the bear to wear." See The pig's tail
Furry-dance. Eleanor Farjeon. *FaCb—FaN*
"The **furry**-men in Helston." See Furry-dance
"The **furry** moth explores the night." See The explorers
"**Fuzzy** wuzzy, creepy crawly." Lillian Schulz Vanada. *ArTp—BrR-3*
"**Fuzzy** Wuzzy was a bear." Unknown. *WiRm—WoF*
    American Father Gander. *UnG*

Fyleman, Rose
An angel. See "An angel came as I lay in bed"
"An angel came as I lay in bed." tr. *JoAc*
    An angel. *DoP*
The balloon man. *HuL-1*
"The best game the fairies play." *ArTp*
Bingo has an enemy. *BrR-5*
The birthday child. *BrBc—BrS—FeF*
The canary. *HuL-1*
The chickens. tr. *ArTp*
The child next door. *FeF*
Conversation. *HuL-1*
Daddy. *BrS*
The dentist. *ArTp*
Fairies. *HuL-1—HuSv—JoAc—PeF*
"The fairies have never a penny to spend." *FeF*
The fairy ball. *HuL-1*
"A fairy went a-marketing." *HuL-1—JoAc*
Fishing. tr. *JoAc*
The frog. *HuL-1*
The goblin. tr. *ArTp—JoAc*
Have you watched the fairies. *ArTp—* *HuL-1—PeF*
Husky hi. tr. *ArTp—JoAc*
If only. *HuSv*
In the park. See Regent's park
Jonathan. tr. *ArTp—JoAc*
Little girl. tr. *JoAc*
Mary Middling. *BrL-k—HuL-1*
"Me, ray, doh." tr. *JoAc*
Mice. *ArTp — BrL-k — FeF — HuL-1* *—HuSv — NaE — PeF*
Mrs Brown. *ArTp—BrL-k—HuL-1*
Momotara. tr. *ArTp—HuL-2*
Mother. *BrL-k—BrS*
Mushrooms. tr. *JoAc*
My donkey. tr. *ArTp—HuL-2*
My policeman. *ArTp—BrL-k*
The new neighbor. *ArTp*
New year's day. tr. *JoAc*
October. *BrS*
Please. *BrL-k*
Regent's park. *BrR-4*
    In the park. *HuSv*
Shop windows. *ArTp*

Singing-time.   *ArTp—BrS—DoP—McAw*
Sometimes. *BrS*
The spring. *FeF*
To the shop. tr. *JoAc*
Twelfth night. tr. *JoAc*
Very lovely. *ArTp*
Well, I never. tr. *JoAc*
Witch, witch. *HuL-1*
Yesterday in Oxford street.   *ArTp—PeF*

G

G. Hilaire Belloc. *CoH*
G is for giant. Eleanor Farjeon. *FaCb*
"G stands for gnu, whose weapons of defence." See G
"Gabble-gabble, brethren, gabble-gabble."
    See A boy in church
Gág, Wanda
    The A B C bunny. *ArTp*
Gahan, Edward F.
    Immense hour. tr. *PaS*
"Gaily bedight." See Eldorado
Galbraith, Georgie Starbuck
    Advice to a bird, species unknown. *BrL-8*
Gale, Mrs Henry Gordon
    The icicle. *BrL-k*
Gale, Norman
    Bartholomew. *BrBc*
    Bobby's first poem. *CoH—NaM*
    The country faith. *DoP—HuL-2*
    Thanks. *GoP—UnG*
Gallagher, Dorothy Hamilton
    Morning. *BrS*
Gallagher, Katharine
    Chant for skippers. *BrS*
    Poison ivy. *BrS*
Gallop away. Unknown. *HuL-1*
Gallop, gallop to a rhyme. Monica Shannon.
    BrS
Galoshes. Rhoda W. Bacmeister. *ArTp—
    BrL-k*
Games. See also Finger-play poems; Nursery play; Sportsmanship; also names
    of games, as Baseball
Alligoshee. Mother Goose. *OpO*
American jump. Unknown. *OpO*
"The best game the fairies play." R. Fyleman. *ArTp*
Blind man's buff ("Blind man, blind man")
    Mother Goose. *OpO*
Blind man's buff ("A peacock feather")
    Unknown. *JoAc*
Blind-man's buff ("When silver snow decks
    Susan's clothes") W. Blake. *HoW*
"Bo-peep." Mother Goose. *OpO*
The bonnie cravat. Mother Goose. *ArTp—
    HuL-1—OpO*
Cat and rat. Unknown. *TaD*
Charade. Mother Goose. *OpO*
"Charlie Chaplin went to France." Unknown. *NaM*
Chicken in the bread tray. Unknown. *TaD*
Club fist. Unknown. *TaD*
Cock-a-bandy. Mother Goose. *OpO*

The crawdad hole. Unknown. *TaD*
"Did you feed my cow." Unknown. *TaD*
Didn't it rain. Unknown. *TaD*
"Draw a pail of water." Mother Goose.
    DeMg—LiL—NaM—OpO
"A duck and a drake." Mother Goose. *DeMg*
    Ducks and drakes. *OpO*
"East side, West side, all around the town."
    From The sidewalks of New York. C. V.
    Lawlor and J. W. Blake. *WoF*
"Eggs, butter, bread." Mother Goose. *DeMg*
Fishing Simon. Unknown. *TaD*
Forget. J. Ciardi. *CiI*
"Go tell Aunt Rhodie." Unknown. *TaD*
    "Go tell Aunt Rhoda." *WoF*
Green grass. Mother Goose. *OpO*
Guess. J. Ciardi. *CiI*
Guessing game. D. Aldis. *AlHd*
Ha ha thisaway. Unknown. *TaD*
Hambone. Unknown. *TaD*
"Handy dandy." Mother Goose. *OpO*
"Handy dandy, riddledy ro." Mother Goose.
    DeMg
Head and shoulders, Baby. Unknown. *TaD*
"Henry was a worthy king." Unknown.
    NaM
Here comes a wooer. Mother Goose. *OpO*
"Here we come gathering nuts in May."
    Mother Goose. *LiL*
    Nuts an' may. *NaE*
"Here we go dancing jingo-ring." Mother
    Goose. *OpO*
"Here we go round ring by ring." Mother
    Goose. *OpO*
"Here we go round the mulberry bush."
    Mother Goose. *DeMg—LiL*
Here's a poor widow. Mother Goose. *OpO*
"Hickory, dickory, sacara down." Mother
    Goose. *DeMg*
"How many miles to Babylon." Mother
    Goose. *DeMg — HuL-1 — JoAc — LiL
    — NaM — OpO — SmLg — WiRm*
"I am a gold lock." Mother Goose. *JoAc*
"I am a pretty little Dutch girl." Unknown.
    TaD
"I met a man that had two birds." J.
    Ciardi. *CiI*
"I met a man that said, Just look." J.
    Ciardi. *CiI*
"I met a man that was playing games."
    J. Ciardi. *CiI*
"I sent a letter to my love." Mother
    Goose. *LiL*
"I went up one pair of stairs." Mother
    Goose. *DeMg—JoAc*
In my lady's garden. Unknown. *TaD*
The jingo-ring. Unknown. *HuL-1*
King of the castle. Mother Goose. *OpO*
"Lady Queen Anne she sits in the sun."
    Mother Goose. *JoAc*
Li'l Liza Jane. Unknown. *TaD*
The little boy and the old man. Unknown.
    TaD
Little boy's britches. Unknown. *TaD*
"London bridge is broken down." Mother
    Goose. *DeMg—JoAc—LiL*
    London bridge. *OpO*
"Margery Mutton-pie and Johnny Bo-
    peep." Mother Goose. *DeMg—OpO*
Ma's gonna buy me. Unknown. *TaD*

Games—*Continued*
"The miller he grinds his corn, his corn."
    Mother Goose. *DeMg*
        A hop, skip, and a jump. *HuL-1*
Miss Jennie Jones. Unknown. *TaD*
Miss Mary Mac. Unknown. *TaD*
Mister Rabbit. Unknown. *TaD*
Motions. Unknown. *TaD*
My horse. Unknown. *TaD*
"Nievie nievie nick nack." Mother Goose.
    OpO
"Not last night, but the night before."
    Unknown. *WiRm*
Old cow. Unknown. *TaD*
The old grey goose. Unknown. *ReG*
    The gray goose. *TaD*
"Old Molly Hare." Unknown. *TaD*
Old Ponto. Unknown. *TaD*
Old Rattler. Unknown. *TaD*
One, two, three. H. C. Bunner. *FeF*
The pawpaw patch. Unknown. *TaD*
"Peep, squirrel, peep." Unknown. *TaD*
"Peter Rabbit—ha, ha." Unknown. *TaD*
Pick-a-back. Mother Goose. *OpO*
The pony. Unknown. *TaD*
Pop goes the weasel. Unknown. *HuL-1—
    JoAc—OpO—TaD*
        "Up and down the city road." *NaE*
Pullman porter. Unknown. *TaD*
"Red stockings, blue stockings." Mother
    Goose. *OpO*
Remember. J. Ciardi. *CiI*
Ring-a-ring. K. Greenaway. *BrL-k—FeF
    —NaM*
"Ring-a-ring o' roses." Mother Goose.
    DeMg—LiL—OpO
"A ring, a ring o' roses." Mother Goose.
    OpO
"Round about the rosebush." Mother
    Goose. *OpO*
Run, squirrel, run. Unknown. *TaD*
"Sally go round the sun." Mother Goose.
    OpO
Sally Waters. Mother Goose. *OpO*
Scottish castle. Mother Goose. *OpO*
"Sissy in the barn." Unknown. *TaD*
"Strut, Miss Susie." Unknown. *TaD*
There was an old dog. Unknown. *DeT*
"Tit, tat, toe." Mother Goose. *OpO*
"Titty cum tawtay." Mother Goose. *OpO*
Trading. Unknown. *TaD*
When Anabelle's it. D. Aldis. *AlA*
"Who did." Unknown. *TaD*
Woodchopper's song. Unknown. *TaD*
"A **garbage** man is a garbage man." See
    Like me
A **garden** ("Cool waters tumble, singing as
    they go") Sappho, tr. fr. the Greek by
    T. F. Higham. *PaS*
A **garden** ("A garden is a lovesome thing,
    God wot") See My garden
The **garden** ("How vainly men themselves
    amaze") Andrew Marvell. *HaP*
Garden abstract. Hart Crane. *GrCc*
A **garden** at night. James Reeves. *ReBl*
"A **garden** is a lovesome thing, God wot."
    See My garden
The **garden** seat. Thomas Hardy. *GrCc*

The **garden** year. See "January brings the
    snow"
Gardner, Isabella
    The masked shrew. *PlI*
Gardeners. See also Gardens and gardening
    The gardener's song. From Sylvie and
        Bruno. L. Carroll. *GrCc—JoAc—NaE*
            He thought he saw. *CoH—HuL-2*
    The mad gardener's song. *HoW*
        A strange wild song. *HuSv*
    "Jonathan Jo." A. A. Milne. *MiWc*
    Nature's hired man. J. K. Bangs. *BrR-6*
    "Old Quin Queeribus." N. B. Turner.
        ArTp—BrR-4—CoH—HuL-1—NaE
    Poor Rumble. J. Reeves. *ReBl*
The **gardener's** song. See Sylvie and Bruno
Gardens and gardening. See also Gardeners
    At the garden gate. D. McCord. *FeF—
        McFf*
    At Woodward's gardens. R. Frost. *FrR—
        PlI*
    Birthday garden. I. O. Eastwick. *BrBc*
    The butterbean tent. E. M. Roberts. *HuSv*
    Child's song. From A masque. T. Moore.
        GrCc
    A farthing. Mother Goose. *OpO*
    A friend in the garden. J. H. Ewing.
        BrR-3—FeF—HuSv
    A garden ("Cool waters tumble, singing
        as they go") Sappho. *PaS*
    The garden ("How vainly men themselves
        amaze") A. Marvell. *HaP*
    Garden abstract. H. Crane. *GrCc*
    A garden at night. J. Reeves. *ReBl*
    The garden seat. T. Hardy. *GrCc*
    A girl's garden. R. Frost. *FrY*
    Go down to Kew in lilac time. From The
        barrel-organ. A. Noyes. *HuL-2*
    Home grown. H. H. Boileau. *McAw*
    In my garden. Unknown. *HuL-1*
    In my lady's garden. Unknown. *TaD*
    In the garden. I. Orleans. *HuL-1*
    Johnny Crow's garden. L. L. Brooke.
        ReG
    "Mary, Mary, quite contrary." Mother
        Goose. *ArTp—HuL-1—JoAc—LiL*
            Contrary Mary. *OpO*
            "Mistress Mary." *BrL-k*
            "Mistress Mary, quite contrary."
                DeMg—HuSv
    Maytime magic. M. Watts. *McAw*
    Memorial garden (Canterbury). E. Far-
        jeon. *FaCb—FaN*
    My garden. T. E. Brown. *ThP*
        A garden. *UnG*
    November garden. L. Driscoll. *HaY*
    "Old Quin Queeribus." N. B. Turner.
        ArTp—BrR-4—CoH—HuL-1—NaE
    Old Shellover. W. De La Mare. *ReG*
    Thy garden. Mu'tamid, King of Seville.
        PaS
    Vegetables. E. Farjeon. *FeF*
    Window boxes. E. Farjeon. *FeF*
Garland, Hamlin
    Color in the wheat. *JoAc*
    Do you fear the wind. *ArTp—JoAc*
    Horses chawin' hay. *HuSv*
    My prairies. *FeF*

The passing of the buffalo. *HuSv*
Plowing: A memory. *HuSv*
The plowman of today. *HuSv*
A **garland** for Agatha Blyth. Eleanor Farjeon. *FaCb—FaN*
Garnett, Louise Ayres
The first night. *DoP*
Hello. *BrS*
The moon. *BrS*
Garnett, Richard
The highwayman's ghost. *CoSp*
Who was it. tr. *PaS*
Garrison, Theodosia (Pickering)
Memorial day. *CoPs*
The poplars. *HuSv*
Shade. *BrL-7*
Garstin, Crosbie
The figure-head. *CoSp*
Gasetsu
The iris. *ArTp*
The **gastronomic** guile of Simple Simon. Guy Wetmore Carryl. *UnG*
Gates and doors. Joyce Kilmer. *EaW*
"**Gather** up the ribbons, give the 'orn a toot." See The phantom mail coach
Gather ye rosebuds. Robert Herrick. *HaP—ReG*
"**Gather** ye rosebuds while ye may." See Gather ye rosebuds
Gathering leaves. Robert Frost. *FrR—FrY*
Gay, John
Black-eyed Susan. *DeT*
The highwaymen. *HoW*
Three children sliding. See "Three children sliding on the ice"
"Three children sliding on the ice." *DeMg—JoAc—LiL*
   Three children sliding. *OpO*
   A warning. *DeT*
A warning. See "Three children sliding on the ice"
Youth's the season. *HoW*
Gay, Zhenya
Baby goat. *McAw*
My birthday's in winter. *BrBc*
"When a goose meets a moose." *ArTp*
"The world is full of wonderful smells." *ArTp*
"**Gay** go up and gay do down." Mother Goose. *DeMg—JoAc—LiL*
The bells of London. *NaE*
Oranges and lemons. *OpO*
The **gay** goshawk. Unknown. *MaB*
The **gay** young squires. Eleanor Farjeon. *FaCb*
"**Gee** up, Neddy, to the fair." Mother Goose. *OpO*
Geese
Feathers. Mother Goose. *OpO*
"A fox jumped up one winter's night." Mother Goose. *DeMg*
   Ballad of the fox. *UnG*
   Ee-oh. *DeT*
   The fox. *CoSp*
   The fox's foray. *OpO*
   A visit from Mr Fox. *HuSv*
"Go tell Aunt Rhodie." Unknown. *TaD*
"Go tell Aunt Rhoda." *WoF*

"Goodness. Gracious. Have you heard the news." Unknown. *WoF*
"Goosey, goosey, gander." *DeMg—JoAc—LiL*
   Goosey gander. *OpO*
   Goosie gander. *BrL-k*
"Gray goose and gander." Mother Goose. *JoAc—LiL—OpO*
The grey goose. Unknown. *McW*
Harbingers. E. Tatum. *BrR-6*
The new and the old. Shiki. *PaS*
The old grey goose. Unknown. *ReG*
   The gray goose. *TaD*
Something better. D. McCord. *McFf*
"Something told the wild geese." R. Field. *ArTp — BrS — CoPs — HaY — HuL-2 —HuSv—JoAc—McW*
The swan and goose. Aesop. *PlU*
   The swan and the goose. *FeF*
"Three grey geese in a green field grazing." Mother Goose. *OpO*
"V." D. McCord. *McFf*
Why does it snow. L. E. Richards. *BrS*
Wild geese ("I have heard the curlew crying") K. Tynan. *UnG*
Wild geese ("I heard the wild geese flying") E. Chipp. *ArTp—FeF*
Wild geese ("Where bright waters flood the spring shore") Shēn Yo. *PaS*
Gemini. Eleanor Farjeon. *FaCb—FaN*
"**Gemini-Jiminy,** heavenly twins." See Gemini
Gems. See Precious stones
The **General** Elliott. Robert Graves. *GrP*
General John. William Schwenck Gilbert. *CoH—UnG*
General store. Rachel Field. *HuSv—JoAc*
Generosity. Virginia Brasier. *HuSv*
Genesis, sel. Bible, Old Testament
Genesis, Chapter 1. *PlI*
Genesis, Chapter 1. See Genesis
Geneviève. Eleanor Farjeon. *FaCb*
Gentians
Bavarian gentians. D. H. Lawrence. *HaP—SmLg*
Fringed gentians. A. Lowell. *FeF*
To the fringed gentian. W. C. Bryant. *JoAc*
Gentle name. Selma Robinson. *BrBc—NaM*
"**Gently** dip, but not too deep." See Celanta at the well of life
"**Gently** the river bore us." See Boating
"**Gently** we're gliding over the stream." See Row the boat home
Geography
Counters. E. J. Coatsworth. *PeF*
   To think. *HuL-2*
Geography. E. Farjeon. *BrR-6—FeF*
"Geography, geography is such a pleasant study." Unknown. *WoF*
Lines written for Gene Kelly to dance to. C. Sandburg. *SaW*
Physical geography. L. T. Nicholl. *PlI*
The snuff-boxes. Unknown. *CoSp*
Geography. Eleanor Farjeon. *BrR-6—FeF*
"**Geography,** geography is such a pleasant study." Unknown. *WoF*
Geometry. See Mathematics

"George and Martha Washington." See Picture people

"George lives in an apartment and." See Radiator lions

George Villiers, Duke of Buckingham. John Dryden. *HaP*

George Washington ("George Washington is tops with me") Shelley Silverstein. *CoPs*

George Washington ("George Washington, the farmer") James S. Tippett. *HaY*

George Washington ("Sing hey, for bold George Washington") Rosemary Carr and Stephen Vincent Benét. *FeF—UnMc*

"George Washington is tops with me." See George Washington

"George Washington, the farmer." See George Washington

George who played with a dangerous toy and suffered a catastrophe of considerable dimensions. Hilaire Belloc. *CoH—UnG*

Georgie Porgie. See "Georgie Porgie, pudding and pie"

"Georgie Porgie, pudding and pie." Mother Goose. *DeMg—JoAc—LiL*
  Georgie Porgie. *OpO*

The germ. Ogden Nash. *NaM*

German slumber song. Karl Simrock, tr. fr. the German by Louis Untermeyer. *UnG*

"The Germans live in Germany." See Home

Germs
  The germ. O. Nash. *NaM*
  Strictly germ-proof. A. Guiterman. *BrL-8*

Gessner, Muriel M.
  For February twelfth. *HaY*

"Get ready your money and come to me." See "Young lambs to sell. Young lambs to sell"

Get up and bar the door. Unknown. *ArTp—CoSp—JoAc—UnG—UnMc*

Get up, get up. Unknown. *CoH*

"Get up, get up, you lazy-head." See Get up, get up

"Get up, our Anna dear, from the weary spinning wheel." See The fairy thorn

Getting back. Dorothy Brown Thompson. *BrS*

Getting out of bed. Eleanor Farjeon. *BrS*

Gezelle, Guido
  To the sun. See To the sun from a flower
  To the sun from a flower. *FeF*
    To the sun. *PaS*

Ghost house. Robert Frost. *FrR*

The ghost that Jim saw. Bret Harte. *CoPm*

"A ghost, that loved a lady fair." See The phantom-wooer

Ghosts
  The admiral's ghost. A. Noyes. *ArTp—CoPm—JoAc*
  Cape Horn gospel (I). J. Masefield. *CoSp*
  Dicky. R. Graves. *GrP*
  The fall of J. W. Beane. O. Herford. *CoSp*
  The garden seat. T. Hardy. *GrCc*
  Ghost house. R. Frost. *FrR*
  The ghost that Jim saw. B. Harte. *CoPm*

The ghost's lament. Unknown. *MaB*
    The ghost song. *SmLg*
  Hallowe'en. E. Farjeon. *FaCb—FaN*
  The haunted house. T. Hood. *HoW*
  The haunted palace. E. A. Poe. *HoW*
  The highwayman's ghost. R. Garnett. *CoSp*
  I saw a ghost. J. Boilleau. *ArTp*
  Keith of Ravelston. S. Dobell. *DeT*
  Loganberry spooks. E. Farjeon. *FaCb—FaN*
  Meet-on-the-road. Unknown. *CoPm*
  Molly Malone. Unknown. *UnMc*
  Molly Means. M. Walker. *CoSp*
  Old Christmas. R. Helton. *CoPm—UnMc*
  The old ghost. T. L. Beddoes. *HoW*
  The old wife and the ghost. J. Reeves. *CoPm—ReBl*
  Pat's fiddle. J. Reeves. *ReBl*
  The phantom light of the Baie des Chaleurs. A. W. H. Eaton. *CoPm*
  The phantom mail coach. L. O. Welcome. *CoPm*
  The phantom-wooer. T. L. Beddoes. *HoW*
  Sir Roderic's song. W. S. Gilbert. *CoPm*
  "Sitting on a tombstone." Unknown. *MoY*
  Sweet William's ghost. Unknown. *MaB*
  "Three little ghostesses." Mother Goose. *WiRm*
    Three ghostesses. *OpO*
  Trees in the moonlight. J. Reeves. *ReBl*
  The two old women of Mumbling hill. J. Reeves. *ReW*
  The two spirits. P. B. Shelley. *HoW*
  Waltzing Matilda. A. B. Paterson. *McW*
  Widdecombe fair. Unknown. *CoPm*
    Widdicombe fair. *NaM*
  The wife of Usher's well. Unknown. *ArTp—DeT—MaB*
  The witch of Coös. R. Frost. *FrR*

The ghost's lament. Unknown. *MaB*
  The ghost's song. *SmLg*

The ghost's song. See The ghost's lament

Ghoulies and ghosties. See Litany for Halloween

The giant. See "Fe, fi, fo, fum"

The giant ("There came a giant to my door") Charles Mackay. *BrR-6*

Giant Bonaparte. Mother Goose. *OpO*

Giant Thunder. James Reeves. *ReBl*

"Giant Thunder, striding home." See Giant Thunder

Giants
  The bears who once were giants. From The house beyond the meadow. H. Behn. *BeH*
  The Dorchester giant. O. W. Holmes. *FeF*
  "Fe, fi, fo, fum." Mother Goose. *NaE*
    "Fa, fe, fi, fo, fum." *DeMg*
      The giant. *OpO*
  G is for giant. E. Farjeon. *FaCb*
  The giant. C. Mackay. *BrR-6*
  Giant Bonaparte. Mother Goose. *OpO*
  The giant's shoes. E. Fallis. *BrR-3*
  Magic. M. Chute. *ChA*
  Momotara. Unknown. *ArTp—HuL-2*
  Song. D. McCord. *McFf*

The giant's shoes. Edwina Fallis. *BrR-3*

Gibbs, Elise
Four. *BrBc*

Gibbs. Muriel Rukeyser. *PlI* (sel.)

Gibson, Wilfrid Wilson
The dancing seal. *CoPm*
Flannan isle. *CoSp*
Luck. *NaM*
The ponies. *McW*

Gifford, Fannie Stearns. See Davis, Fannie Stearns

Gift for the queen. Mother Goose. *OpO*

The **gift** outright. Robert Frost. *FrR—McW—SmLg*

The **gift** to be simple. Howard Moss. *PlI*

Gift with the wrappings off. Mary Elizabeth Counselman. *BrL-7*

Gifts ("The choicest gifts at christenings") Hazel Harper Harris. *BrBc*

Gifts ("Give a man a horse he can ride") James Thomson. *ThP*

Gifts ("You ask me what—since we must part") Juliana Horatia Ewing. *ThP*

Gifts and giving. See also Charity; Thankfulness
Anniversary in September. B. C. Brown. *BrBc*
Betsy Jane's sixth birthday. A. Noyes. *BrBc—BrS*
Birthday gift. E. B. De Vito. *BrBc*
Birthday gifts ("Birthday, birthday; little boy has a birthday") L. B. Scott and J. J. Thompson. *BrBc*
Birthday gifts ("What will you have for your birthday") H. Asquith. *BrBc—BrS*
Birthday presents. Unknown. *McAw*
Carol. C. G. Rossetti. *EaW*
A Christmas carol. *BrBc* (sel.)
My gift. *BrS* (sel.)—*FeF* (sel.)
"What can I give Him." *BrR-4* (sel.)
Daphnis to Ganymede. R. Barnfield. *ReT*
Emily Jane. L. E. Richards. *HuL-1*
Fifth birthday gift. M. Lederer. *BrBc*
"The first day of Christmas." Mother Goose. *DeMg*
"On the first day of Christmas." *LiL*
The twelve days of Christmas. *JoAc—OpO*
For a birthday. E. V. Emans. *BrBc*
For Christmas. D. Aldis. *AlA—HuL-1*
Generosity V. Brasier. *HuSv*
Gift for the queen. Mother Goose. *OpO*
The gift outright. R. Frost. *FrR—McW—SmLg*
Gift with the wrappings off. M. E. Counselman. *BrL-7*
Gifts ("The choicest gifts at christenings") H. H. Harris. *BrBc*
Gifts ("Give a man a horse he can ride") J. Thomson. *ThP*
Gifts ("You ask me what—since we must part") J. H. Ewing. *ThP*
God giveth all things. Unknown. *DoP*
God's providence. N. B. Turner. *DoP*
A hinted wish. Martial. *BrL-8*
The hippopotamus's birthday. E. V. Rieu. *RiF*

I could give all to time. R. Frost. *FrR*

"I have four sisters beyond the sea." Unknown. *DeMg*
"Little girl, little girl, where have you been." Mother Goose. *DeMg*
Little girl. *HuL-1—OpO*
The lover's gifts. Mother Goose. *OpO*
Night song at Amalfi. S. Teasdale. *ThP*
Of giving. A. Guiterman. *ArTp*
Proverbs. *ThP*
Present. M. C. Potter. *BrBc*
Presents. M. Chute. *BrR-3—BrS—ChA—HuSv—NaE*
Presents from heaven. E. Farjeon. *FaCb—FaN*
Sailor. E. Farjeon. *PeF*
Secrets. E. M. Fowler. *BrBc*
Short sermon. Unknown. *ArTp*
Summer offering. E. Farjeon. *FaCb*
Surprise. H. Behn. *BrBc*
Surprises. J. C. Soule. *BrBc*
A ternarie of littles, upon a pipkin of jelly sent to a lady. R. Herrick. *SmLg*
To Patricia on her christening day. E. B. Price. *BrBc*
Waltzing mice. D. McCord. *McFf*
What shall I give. E. Thomas. *SmLg*
X is for xoanon. E. Farjeon. *FaCb*

Gilbert, Ann Taylor. See Taylor, Ann

Gilbert, Sir William Schwenck
Captain Reece. *CoH—NaE—UnMc*
The duke of Plaza-Toro. See The gondoliers
Etiquette. *CoH—UnMc*
The fable of the magnet and the churn. See Patience
General John. *CoH—UnG*
The gondoliers, sel.
The duke of Plaza-Toro. *CoH—FeF*
There lived a king. *CoSp*
Iolanthe, sel.
The Lord Chancellor's song. *CoH*
The Lord Chancellor's song. See Iolanthe
My name is John Wellington Wells. See The sorcerer
Patience, sel.
The fable of the magnet and the churn. *FeF*
The perils of invisibility. *CoSp*
The pirates of Penzance, sel.
The policeman's lot. *CoH*
The policeman's lot. See The pirates of Penzance
Ruddigore, sel.
Sir Roderic's song. *CoPm*
Sir Roderic's song. See Ruddigore
The sorcerer, sel.
My name is John Wellington Wells. *CoPm*
There lived a king. See The gondoliers
"There was a young man of St Bees." *CoH*
The yarn of the Nancy Bell. *CoH—HuSv—NaE—NaM—SmLg—UnG*

Giles, Saint (about)
Saint Giles. E. Farjeon. *FaCb*

Gillilan, Strickland W.
Finnigin to Flannigan. *CoSp*

"Gilly Silly Jarter." See Silly

Pretty Maid Marion. I. O. Eastwick. *HuL-1*
Ruth. T. Hood. *GrCc*
"There is a garden in her face." T. Campion. *ReT*
To Mistress Margaret Hussey. J. Skelton. *HaP—ReT*
  "Merry Margaret." *UnG*
  Mistress Margaret Hussey. *SmLg*
Tradja of Norway.⁻ Unknown. *JoAc*
"What are little boys made of, made of." Mother Goose. *DeMg—JoAc*
  Natural history. *OpO*
"Girls and boys, come out to play." Mother Goose. *ArTp—DeMg—HuSv—LiL—NaM*
"Boys and girls come out to play." *JoAc—OpO*
  Full moon. *DeT*
  Girls and boys. *HuL-1*
"Girls are like a nugget of gold." Unknown. *MoY*
A girl's garden. Robert Frost. *FrY*
Girls' names. Eleanor Farjeon. *ArTp—BrBc—HuL-2—JoAc*
Git along, little dogies. See Whoopee ti yi yo, git along, little dogies
"Giuseppe, da barber, ees greata for mash." See Mia Carlotta
"Give a man a horse he can ride." See Gifts
"Give all to love." Ralph Waldo Emerson. *McW* (sel.)
"Give me a good digestion, Lord, and also something to digest." See An ancient prayer
"Give me a philtre, a philtre." See P is for philtre
"Give me my bow, said Robin Hood." See The death of Robin Hood
"Give me that man, that dares bestride." See His cavalier
"Give me the dance of your boughs, O trees." See Song to a tree
Give me the splendid silent sun. Walt Whitman. *FeF—JoAc*
"Give me the splendid silent sun with all its beams full-dazzling." See Give me the splendid silent sun
"Give me your tired, your poor." See The new colossus
"Give to me the life I love." See The vagabond
Giving. See Gifts and giving
Glad earth. Ella C. Forbes. *HaY*
"Glad that I live am I." See A little song of life
Gladde things. Unknown. *ArTp*
The gladness of the May. William Wordsworth. *HaY*
Glaubitz, Grace Ellen
  Christmas birthday. *BrBc—BrS*
  Walking. *McAw*
The gleaners. Eleanor Farjeon. *FaCb—FaN*
Glenlogie. Unknown. *MaB*
Glimpse in autumn. Jean Starr Untermeyer. *JoAc*
"Glinting on the roadway." See The magical picture
"The gloom of death is on the raven's wing." See The raven

"Gloria is your name." Unknown. *MoY*
"The glories of our blood and state." See Contention of Ajax and Ulysses—Song
"Glorious the sun in mid-career." Christopher Smart. *SmLg*
"The glory and the ardour of the stage." See Elegy on the death of Mme Anna Pavlova
"Glory be to God for dappled things." See Pied beauty
The glory trail. Badger Clark. *CoSp*
The glove and the lions. Leigh Hunt. *FeF—UnMc*
Gloves. See also Mittens
  The glove and the lions. L. Hunt. *FeF—UnMc*
  The golden glove. Unknown. *UnMc*
The glow within. Berton Braley. *BrL-8*
Glow-worms. See Fireflies
Glowworm. David McCord. *McT*
A gluttonous rich man. See The Canterbury tales
Gnat. Rosalie Moore. *UnG*
Gnats
  Gnat. R. Moore. *UnG*
The gnome. Harry Behn. *ArTp—BeW—FeF*
Gnomes. See Fairies
The gnu. Samuel Hoffenstein. *CoH*
"The gnu is a remarka-bul." See The gnu
Gnus. See Antelopes
"Go and catch a falling star." See Song
"Go and tell Aunt Nancy." See The old grey goose
"Go call old Rattler." See Old Rattler
"Go down to Kew in lilac-time, in lilac-time, in lilac-time." See The barrel-organ—Go down to Kew in lilac-time
"Go, fetch to me a pint o' wine." See The silver tassie
Go fly a saucer. David McCord. *FeF* (sel.) *—PlI*
"Go little album, far and near." Unknown. *MoY*
"Go, lovely rose." Edmund Waller. *HaP*
"Go roll a prairie up like cloth." See The merry miner
"Go tell Aunt Nancy." See The old grey goose
"Go tell Aunt Rhoda." See "Go tell Aunt Rhodie"
"Go tell Aunt Rhodie." Unknown. *TaD*
  "Go tell Aunt Rhoda." *WoF*
"Go to bed first." Mother Goose. *OpO*
"Go to bed late." Mother Goose. *OpO*
"Go to bed, Tom." Mother Goose. *OpO*
"Go to sleep and good night." See German slumber song
Go to the ant. See Proverbs, Bible, Old Testament
"Go to the ant, thou sluggard." See Proverbs, Bible, Old Testament—Go to the ant
"Go to the shine that's on a tree." Richard Eberhart. *PlU*

The **goatherd**. Grace Hazard Conkling. *ArTp*

Goats
Baby goat. Zhenya Gay. *McAw*
The fox and the goat. J. De La Fontaine. *JoAc*
The goatherd. G. H. Conkling. *ArTp*
The grandiloquent goat. C. Wells. *LoL—NaM*
Old Hogan's goat. Unknown. *CoI—TaD*
The sad goat. Unknown. *McW*

The **goblin**. Unknown, tr. fr. the French by Rose Fyleman. *ArTp—JoAc*

Goblin feet. J. R. R. Tolkien. *CoPm—FeF*

"The **goblin** has a wider mouth." See How to tell goblins from elves

"A **goblin** lives in our house, in our house, in our house." See The goblin

A **goblinade**. Florence Page Jaques. *ArTp—HuL-1*

Goblins. See Fairies

"**Goblins** on the doorstep." See This is Halloween

Goch, Llewelyn
Elegy for Lucy Lloyd. *PaS*

God. See also Faith; Hymns; Jesus Christ; Psalms
The altar. G. Herbert. *HaP*
"As salt resolved in the ocean." Rumi. *PaS*
The ballad of Father Gilligan. W. B. Yeats. *McW*
Bermudas. A. Marvell. *SmLg*
Blessings for Chanukah. J. E. Sampter. *ArTp*
The Celestial Surgeon. R. L. Stevenson. *UnG*
A child's thought of God. E. B. Browning. *DoP—FeF*
"Come, let us sound with melody, the praises." T. Campion. *PlU*
Crayons. C. Morley. *DoP*
The creation ("All things bright and beautiful") C. F. Alexander. *DoP—FeF*
    All things beautiful. *BrR-3*
    "All things bright and beautiful." *HuSv*
    God, our Maker. *DeT*
The creation ("And God stepped out on space") J. W. Johnson. *ArTp—JoAc*
"The day before April." M. C. Davies. *ArTp—DoP—FeF*
"Do you know how many stars." Unknown. *DoP*
Eagle on the mountain crest. H. Conkling. *DoP*
An eclipse. Pindar. *PaS*
The elixir. G. Herbert. *SmLg*
Evening hymn. Unknown. *BrL-k—DoP*
Expectans expectavi. C. H. Sorley. *SmLg*
Explained. A. A. Milne. *MiWc*
The eyes of God. G. Setoun. *DoP*
The first autumn. M. Schacht. *BrL-8*
"Flower in the crannied wall." A. Tennyson. *DoP—FeF—ThP*
The fly. O. Nash. *FeF*
For a child. F. S. Davis. *FeF*
For joy. F. E. Coates. *BrL-7*
Geneviève. E. Farjeon. *FaCb*
"Glorious the sun in mid-career." C. Smart. *SmLg*

God careth. Unknown. *DoP*
God giveth all things. Unknown. *DoP*
God is everywhere. Unknown. *DoP*
God is like this. R. B. Bennett. *BrR-4*
God is so good. J. Taylor. *DoP*
The god of galaxies. M. Van Doren. *PlI*
God's dark. J. Martin. *BrR-3—DoP*
God's gift. Unknown. *DoP*
God's house. A. Wynne. *DoP*
God's promises. A. J. Flint. *BrR-6—ThP*
God's providence. N. B. Turner. *DoP*
God's world. From Renascence. E. St V. Millay. *CoPs—JoAc—UnG*
Good night ("Good night. Good night") V. Hugo. *ArTp—BrS—DoP—FeF*
Good night ("On tip-toe comes the gentle dark") D. M. Pierce. *ArTp—BrS*
The grasshopper's song. H. N. Bialik. *FeF—HaY*
How many heavens. E. Sitwell. *GrCc*
How nice. M. D. Thayer. *DoP*
I have sought Thee daily. S. Ibn-Gabirol. *PaS*
"I only know a glowing warmth." O. B. Miller. *DoP*
In desert places. Sister Mary Madeleva. *UnG*
In the morning. C. Loftus. *DoP*
Invocation. Unknown. *PaS*
Job, Chapter 36. From Job, Bible, Old Testament. *PlI*
The lamb. W. Blake. *DoP—FeF—JoAc—McW—SmLg—UnG*
    Little lamb. *HuSv*
"Let us with a gladsome mind." J. Milton. *DeT*
    Praise the Lord. *SmLg*
Light shining out of darkness. W. Cowper. *SmLg*
The little boy found. W. Blake. *ArTp*
The little boy lost. W. Blake. *ArTp*
Mathematics or the gift of tongues. A. H. Branch. *PlI*
My garden. T. E. Brown. *ThP*
    A garden. *UnG*
Not all there. R. Frost. *FrR*
Out in the fields with God. Unknown. *DoP—UnG*
Peace. H. Vaughan. *GrCc—SmLg*
The pelican. P. De Thaun, tr. by R. Wilbur. *McW*
Pied beauty. G. M. Hopkins. *McW—ReT—UnG*
Pippa's song. From Pippa passes. R. Browning. *FeF*
    Spring song. *UnG*
    "The year's at the spring." *DoP—HaY—HuSv—ThP*
Poem for a child. J. G. E. Hopkins. *DoP*
The pulley. G. Herbert. *HaP*
Puzzles. J. Drinkwater. *McW*
Rain. E. Benediktsson. *PaS*
The rainbow. D. McCord. *FeF—McFf*
Reality. A. De Vere. *DoP*
The rebellious vine. H. Monro. *McW*
Revelation. A. Brown. *DoP*
St Teresa's book-mark. Saint Teresa of Avila. *PaS*
The sandpiper. C. Thaxter. *FeF—JoAc*
Science in God. R. Herrick. *PlI*

The search. T. C. Clark. *DoP*
The shape God wears. S. H. Hay. *UnG*
The silence of God. O. Sitwell. *McW*
"Sing a song of joy." T. Campion. *PlU*
Sitting by a bush in broad sunlight. R. Frost. *FrR*
A song in praise of the Lord. Unknown. *DoP*
Spring. D. A. Lord. *DoP*
Thanksgivings for the beauty of His providence. T. Traherne. *SmLg*
The tiger. W. Blake. *ArTp—DoP—FeF—HaP—UnG*
    The tyger. *McW—SmLg*
To a waterfowl. W. C. Bryant. *DeT*
"To music bent, is my retired mind." T. Campion. *PlU*
To the Supreme Being. Michelangelo Buonarroti. *PaS*
The unseen power. Rumi. *PaS*
Variation on a Polish folk song. M. Zaturenska. *GrCc*
The voice of God. J. Stephens. *DoP*
Welsh lullaby. Unknown. *UnG*
The whisperer. J. Stephens. *DoP*
"Who is that a-walking in the corn." F. Johnson. *GrCc*
Who taught them. Unknown. *DoP*
Wildflowers. E. Farjeon. *DoP*
Wind in the pine. L. Sarett. *BrL-7*
The young mystic. L. Untermeyer. *BrR-5*
"God be here, God be there." See New year
"God be merciful unto us, and bless us." See Psalms—Psalm LXVII
"God bless the corners of this house." See A house blessing
"God bless the field and bless the furrow." See The robin's song
"God bless the master of this house." Mother Goose. *DeMg—HuSv—OpO*
Christmas carol. *ArTp—BrS*
A grace. *NaM*
"God bless this house from thatch to floor." Mother Goose. *OpO*
"God bless your house this holy night." See This holy night
God careth. Unknown. *DoP*
God, give us men. Josiah Gilbert Holland. *ThP*
"God, give us men. A time like this demands." See God, give us men
"God gives so many lovely things." See God's providence
God giveth all things. Unknown. *DoP*
"God has a way of making flowers grow." See In desert places
"God hath not promised." See God's promises
God is everywhere. Unknown. *DoP*
God is like this. Rowena Bastin Bennett. *BrR-4*
"God is our refuge and strength." See Psalms—Psalm XLVI
God is so good. Jane Taylor. *DoP*
"God is so good that He will hear." See God is so good

"God made the bees (and the bees make)." Unknown
Signs, seasons, and sense. *UnG*
"God made the bees (the bees made)." Unknown. *MoY*
"God made the men." Unknown. *MoY*
"God made the ocean." Unknown. *MoY*
"God moves in a mysterious way." See Light shining out of darkness
The god of galaxies. Mark Van Doren. *PlI*
"The god of galaxies has more to govern." See The god of galaxies
"God of grave nights." See A chant out of doors
"God of our fathers, known of old." See Recessional
The god of sheep. John Fletcher. *SmLg*
God, our maker. See The creation
God rest ye merry, gentlemen. Dinah Maria Mulock. *JoAc*
"God rest ye merry, gentlemen; let nothing you dismay." See God rest ye merry, gentlemen
"God send us a little home." See A prayer for a little home
"God, though this life is but a wraith." See Prayer
"God watches o'er us all the day." See The eyes of God
"Godfrey Gordon Gustavus Gore." William Brighty Rands. *ArTp—FeF—HuL-2—PeF*
Godiva, Lady (about)
Leofric and Godiva. W. S. Landor. *GrCc*
Gods and goddesses. See also Mythology—Greek and Roman; also names of gods and goddesses, as Neptune; Diana
Country gods. Comêtas. *SmLg*
The river-god's song. F. Beaumont and J. Fletcher. *FeF—NaM*
Song. *ReT*
God's dark. John Martin. *BrR-3—DoP*
"God's deathless plaything rolls an eye." See Leviathan
God's first creature was light. Winifred Welles. *PlI*
God's gift. Unknown. *DoP*
God's house. Annette Wynne. *DoP*
"God's house is wide and very tall." See God's house
God's promises. Annie Johnson Flint. *BrR-6—ThP*
God's providence. Nancy Byrd Turner. *DoP*
God's world. See Renascence
"Goes through the mud." Mother Goose. *OpO*
Goethals, George Washington (about)
Goethals, the prophet engineer. P. Mackaye. *HuSv*
Goethals, the prophet engineer. Percy Mackaye. *HuSv*
Goethe, Johann Wolfgang von
The erl-king. *UnMc*
Mignon. See Wilhelm Meister
Wilhelm Meister, sel.
Mignon. *PaS*
Gogarty, Oliver St John
Verse. *SmLg*

Going back again. Robert Lytton. *NaE*

Going for water. Robert Frost. *FrR—FrY*

"Going, the wild things of our land." See The passing of the buffalo

"Going through the hop-fields." See A nursery song for Shepherdswell in Kent

Going to bed. Marchette Chute. *ChA*

Going to sleep. Dorothy Aldis. *AlA*

Going too far. Mildred Howells. *ArTp*

Gold (Color)
  The golden month. M. Doyle. *HaY*
  Haze gold. C. Sandburg. *SaW*
  King Olaf's gold. E. Farjeon. *FaCb*
  Nothing gold can stay. R. Frost. *FrR*
  Winter gold. C. Sandburg. *SaW*

Gold (Metal). See also Money
  The alchemist. A. A. Milne. *MiWc*
  The golden touch. E. Farjeon. *FaCb—FaN*
  King Olaf's gold. E. Farjeon. *FaCb*
  A peck of gold. R. Frost. *FrY*

"Gold as morning, still as sheaves." See Enchanted summer

"Gold buttons in the garden today." See Flowers tell months

"Gold fell the autumn leaf." See The hoar apple tree

Gold-fish. See Goldfish

"Gold is pure." Unknown. *MoY*

"Gold locks, and black locks." See The barber's

"Gold, red and green flies." See Near dusk

"The gold scales of heaven." See Libra

Gold-weed. Eleanor Farjeon. *FaCb—FaN*

"The golden days are over." See End of volume one

The golden glove. Unknown. *UnMc*

"The golden hair that Gulla wears." See Bought locks

The golden mean. Horace, tr. fr. the Latin by Margaret M. Fitzgerald. *PaS*

The golden month. Marion Doyle. *HaY*

The golden palace. Unknown, tr. fr. the Chinese by Arthur Waley. *GrCc*

The golden rule. Annette Wynne. *DoP*

"The golden rule is the rule of three." See The golden rule

Golden spurs. Virginia Scott Miner. *BrS*

The golden touch. Eleanor Farjeon. *FaCb—FaN*

"The golden tree." See Autumn season

The Golden Vanity. Unknown. *HoW*

Goldenrod
  The goldenrod. F. D. Sherman. *FeF*

The goldenrod. Frank Dempster Sherman. *FeF*

"The goldenrod is yellow." See September

Goldfish
  The goldfish. D. Aldis. *AlA—BrL-k*

The goldfish. Dorothy Aldis. *AlA—BrL-k*

Goldsmith, Oliver
  The deserted village, sel.
    The village schoolmaster. *HaP*
  Elegy on the death of a mad dog. See The vicar of Wakefield

The vicar of Wakefield, sel.
  Elegy on the death of a mad dog. *HaP* —*McW—SmLg—UnMc*

The village schoolmaster. See The deserted village

Goldsmith, Oliver (about)
  "Oliver Goldsmith." E. Farjeon. *FaCb—FaN*

Goldwing moth. Carl Sandburg. *SaW*

"A goldwing moth is between the scissors." See Goldwing moth

The gondoliers, sel. William Schwenck Gilbert
  The duke of Plaza-Toro. *CoH—FeF*
  There lived a king. *CoSp*

Gone. Walter De La Mare. *GrCc*

"Gone is the city, gone the day." See The right kind of people

"Gone were but the winter." See Spring quiet

Good advice. Unknown, tr. fr. the German by Louis Untermeyer. *ArTp*

"Good afternoon, Sir Smasham Uppe." See Sir Smasham Uppe

Good and bad children. Robert Louis Stevenson. *SmLg*

"Good, better, best." Mother Goose. *MoY—OpO*

"Good Bishop Valentine." Eleanor Farjeon. *CoPs—FaCb—FaN*

The good boy. Mother Goose. *OpO*

Good-by and keep cold. Robert Frost. *FrR—FrY—UnG*

"Good-bye, good-bye to summer." See Robin Redbreast

Good company. Karle Wilson Baker. *FeF*

"The good dame looked from her cottage." See The leak in the dike

Good Friday. Mother Goose. *OpO*

"Good fortune, and good fortune." See The blackbird in the lilac

Good hours. Robert Frost. *FrR—FrY*

The good humor man. Phyllis McGinley. *NaM*

The good Joan. Lizette Woodworth Reese. *ArTp—FeF—NaM*

The good little girl. A. A. Milne. *MiWc*

"Good manners may in seven words be found." See Of courtesy

"Good master and mistress." Unknown. *NaE*

Good morning. Muriel Sipe. *ArTp—BrL-k —HuL-1*

Good morning, America, sel. Carl Sandburg
  Sky prayers. *SaW*

"Good morning, cat." Myra Cohn Livingston. *LiWa*

"Good morning, Father Francis." Mother Goose. *OpO*

"Good morning, Life—and all." See A greeting

"Good-morning, merry sunshine." See Merry sunshine

"Good morning, mistress and master." See May day

Good-morning poems. See Wake-up poems

"Good morning, sky." See The tardy playmate

"Good morrow, good morrow, dear Herb-man Robert." See Herb-Robert

"Good morrow, little rose-bush." See The sweet, red rose

"Good morrow, 'tis St Valentine's day." See Hamlet—Song

"Good morrow to the day so fair." See The mad maid's song

"Good morrow to you, Valentine." Mother Goose. *OpO*

Good name. See Othello

"Good name in man and woman, dear my lord." See Othello—Good name

"Good news to tell." See The corner

Good night ("Good night. Good night") Victor Hugo. *ArTp—BrS—DoP—FeF*

Good night ("Here's a body—there's a bed") Thomas Hood. *BrS—JoAc*

Good night ("On tip-toe comes the gentle dark") Dorothy Mason Pierce. *ArTp—BrS*

"Good night, God bless you." Mother Goose. *OpO*

"Good night. Good night." See Good night

Good-night poems. See also Bed-time
  Good night ("Good night. Good night") V. Hugo. *ArTp—BrS—DoP—FeF*
  Good night ("Here's a body—there's a bed") T. Hood. *BrS—JoAc*
  Good night ("On tip-toe comes the gentle dark") D. M. Pierce. *ArTp—BrS*
  "Good night, God bless you." Mother Goose. *OpO*
  Good night prayer. H. Johnstone. *DoP*
  "Good night, sweet repose." Mother Goose. *OpO*
  Last song. J. Guthrie. *ArTp—HuL-1*
  "Now say good night." D. McCord. *McT*

Good night prayer. Henry Johnstone. *DoP*

"Good night, sweet repose." Mother Goose. *OpO*

"Good people all, of every sort." See The vicar of Wakefield—Elegy on the death of a mad dog

A good play. Robert Louis Stevenson. *ArTp—FeF—NaM*

"The good rain knows when to fall." See The rain at night

The good shepherd. See A child's evening prayer

"A good sword and a trusty hand." See And shall Trelawny die

"A good time is coming, I wish it were here." See When Santa Claus comes

Good wish. Unknown, tr. fr. the Gaelic by Alexander Carmichael. *SmLg*

Goodbye to fairyland. See The house beyond the meadow

Goodfellow, Mrs E. J. H.
  The dandelion. *BrL-k*

Goodness. See Conduct of life

"Goodness. Gracious. Have you heard the news." Unknown. *WoF*

Goodness me. Dorothy Aldis. *AlA*

Goodrich, Samuel Griswold (Peter Parley, pseud.)
  "Higglety, pigglety, pop." *LoL—OpO*

"Goody goody Gout." Unknown. *TaD*

Goody O'Grumpity. Carol Ryrie Brink. *FeF*

Goony bird. William Jay Smith. *SmB*

Goose, moose and spruce. David McCord. *McT*

Goosey gander. See "Goosey, goosey, gander (whither)"

"Goosey, goosey, gander (whither)." Mother Goose. *DeMg—JoAc—LiL*
  Goosey gander. *OpO*
  Goosie gander. *BrL-k*

"Goosey, goosey gander (who stands yonder)." See Betsy Baker

Goosie gander. See "Goosey, goosey, gander (whither)"

Goring, J. H.
  Home. *NaM*

Gorter, Herman
  The sea. *PaS*

Gospel according to Luke, sel. Bible, New Testament
  Christmas eve. *BrBc—BrS*
    Tidings of great joy. *FeF*

Gospel according to Matthew, sels. Bible, New Testament
  The sermon on the mount. *UnG*
  The sparrow, 2. *FeF*
  Treasures in heaven. *UnG*

Gossip
  Fortunes in tea-cups. E. Farjeon. *FaCb—FaN*
  The gossips. Mother Goose. *OpO*
  "It cost little Gossip her income for shoes." Mother Goose. *DeMg*
  "My Lady Wind, my Lady Wind." Mother Goose. *DeMg*

The gossips. Mother Goose. *OpO*

"Gossips sitting at their brew." See Fortunes in tea-cups

Goudge, Elizabeth
  Guardian angel. *DoP*
  In the stable. *DoP*
  Thanksgiving for the earth. *DoP—HaY*

Gould, Benjamin Apthorp (about)
  A welcome to Benjamin Apthorp Gould. O. W. Holmes. *PlI*

Gould, Elizabeth
  My new rabbit. *HuL-1*

Gould, Gerald
  Wander-thirst. *ArTp—BrL-7—HuL-2*

Gouled, Vivian G.
  Strange footprints. *McAw*

Government
  The building of the ship, sels. H. W. Longfellow
    Sail on, O ship of state. *FeF*
    The ship of state. *BrL-7*
  "What constitutes a state." W. Jones. *BrL-7*

Grace—At meals
  Blessing over food. H. N. Bialik. *BrL-k—HaY*
  A child's grace. R. Burns. *FeF—HuSv—NaE*
    "Some hae meat that canna eat." *SmLg*

Grace. Unknown. *OpO*

Grace—At meals—*Continued*
  A grace for a child. R. Herrick. *FeF—NaM—ReT*
    A child's grace. *SmLg*
    A grace. *DeT*
  "Hurly, hurly, roon the table." Unknown. *SmLg*
  "Thank you for the earth so sweet." Unknown. *AnI*
    A child's grace. *BrL-k—HuL-1*
A grace. See "God bless the master of this house"
A grace ("Here a little child I stand") See A grace for a child
Grace ("God bless our meat") Unknown. *OpO*
"Grace and beauty has the maid." See Song
A grace for a child. Robert Herrick. *FeF—NaM—ReT*
    A child's grace. *SmLg*
    A grace. *DeT*
"Grace, Grace, dressed in lace." Unknown. *WoJ*
GraceAnAnne. Lysbeth Boyd Borie. *BrBc*
"The grade surmounted, we were riding high." See The figure in the doorway
Graduation. See School
Graham, Harry
  Aunt Eliza. See Four ruthless rhymes
  Billy. See Four ruthless rhymes
  Common sense. See Four ruthless rhymes—Mr Jones
  Four ruthless rhymes. *UnMc*
    Aunt Eliza
    Billy
    Mr Jones
      Common sense. *CoH*
    Nurse
      Tragedy. *CoH*
  Mr Jones. See Four ruthless rhymes
  Nurse. See Four ruthless rhymes
  Patience. *CoH—NaM*
  Presence of mind. *CoH*
  Quiet fun. *CoH*
  Tragedy. See Four ruthless rhymes—Nurse
Grahame, Kenneth
  Christmas carol. See The wind in the willows
  Ducks' ditty. See The wind in the willows
  The song of Mr Toad. See The wind in the willows
  The wind in the willows, sels.
    Christmas carol. *FeF*
    Carol. *EaW*
    Ducks' ditty. *ArTp—BrR-3—FeF—JoAc—McW—NaM—PeF*
    The song of Mr Toad. *CoH—FeF*
    "The world has held great heroes." *LoL*
  "The world has held great heroes." See The wind in the willows—The song of Mr Toad
Grain. See names of grain, as Wheat
Grammar
  The purist. O. Nash. *CoH—NaM*
  Two lessons. J. Ciardi. *CiM*

"The grand old duke of York." See "Oh, the grand old duke of York"
"Grandfa' Grig." See Grig's pig
Grandfather frog. Louise Seaman Bechtel. *ArTp*
"Grandfather Grasshopper." Myra Cohn Livingston. *LiWa*
Grandfather Watts's private Fourth. Henry Cuyler Bunner. *ArTp—CoPs—CoSp*
"Grandfather Watts used to tell us boys." See Grandfather Watts's private Fourth
Grandfathers
  Grandfather frog. L. S. Bechtel. *ArTp*
  "Grandfather Grasshopper." M. C. Livingston. *LiWa*
  Grandfather Watts's private Fourth. H. C. Bunner. *ArTp—CoPs—CoSp*
  "I've got a new book from my Grandfather Hyde." L. F. Jackson. *BrS—FeF*
  Thanksgiving day. L. M. Child. *BrS—FeF—HuSv—UnG*
"Grandfather's grandfather folded his letter." See The mail goes through
The grandiloquent goat. Carolyn Wells. *LoL—NaM*
"Grandma has a habit." Unknown. *MoY*
"Grandma said such a curious thing." Unknown. *WoF*
Grandmother ostrich. William Jay Smith. *SmL*
"Grandmother ostrich goes to bed." See Grandmother ostrich
Grandmothers
  Afternoon with grandmother. B. A. Huff. *FeF*
  "Amy Elizabeth Ermyntrude Annie." Q. Scott-Hopper. *ArTp—HuL-1*
  The cupboard. W. De La Mare. *ArTp—BrL-k—FeF—HuL-1*
  "Grandma has a habit." Unknown. *MoY*
  "Grandma said such a curious thing." Unknown. *WoF*
  Grandmother ostrich. W. J. Smith. *SmL*
  Grandmother's story of Bunker hill battle. O. W. Holmes. *UnG*
  Growing old. R. Henderson. *BrBc*
  Halloween. M. Lawson. *ArTp—BrS*
  Irish grandmother. K. Edelman. *BrS*
  Mr Tom Narrow. J. Reeves. *ReW*
  Old log house. J. S. Tippett. *FeF*
  The sampler. N. B. Turner. *BrBc*
  Thanksgiving day. L. M. Child. *BrS—FeF—HuSv—UnG*
Grandmother's story of Bunker hill battle. Oliver Wendell Holmes. *UnG*
"Granny, I saw a witch go by." See Halloween
Grant, Ulysses Simpson (about)
  Achilles Deatheridge. From The Spoon River anthology. E. L. Masters. *UnMc*
  The aged stranger. B. Harte. *UnMc*
Grapes
  Grapes. A. S. Pushkin. *PaS*
  The greedy fox and the elusive grapes. Aesop. *UnMc*
    The fox and the grapes. *UnG*
  Wild grapes. R. Frost. *FrR*

Grapes. Alexander Sergeyevich Pushkin, tr. fr. the Russian by Avrahm Yarmolinsky. *PaS*

Grass
The grass. E. Dickinson. *FeF*
The grass on the mountain. Unknown. *FeF*
The grasses. J. Reeves. *ReW*
Grassroots. C. Sandburg. *SaW*
Green grass. J. Reeves. *ReR*
The lawn mower. M. L. Allen. *AlP*
Lawn song. M. C. Livingston. *LiWa*
Spring grass. C. Sandburg. *FeF*
Summer grass. C. Sandburg. *SaW*
The **grass.** Emily Dickinson. *FeF*
"**Grass** clutches at the dark dirt with finger holds." See Grassroots
"The **grass** grows long in the meadow." See July meadow
The **grass** on the mountain. Unknown, tr. fr. the Paiute by Mary Austin. *FeF*
"The **grass** so little has to do." See The grass
"The **grass** still is pale, and spring is yet only a wind stirring." See Only the wind says spring
The **grasses.** James Reeves. *ReW*
"The **grasses** nod together." See The grasses
The **grasshopper** ("Down") David McCord. *LoL—McFf*
The **grasshopper** ("Happy insect, what can be") Anacreon, tr. fr. the Greek by Abraham Cowley. *HoW—UnG*
The **grasshopper** and the bird. James Reeves. *ReBl*
Grasshopper Green. Unknown. *BrR-4—FeF —HuL-1*
"**Grasshopper** Green is a comical chap." See Grasshopper Green
"The **grasshopper** said." See The grasshopper and the bird
"**Grasshopper** settin' on a sweet potato vine." Unknown. *WoF*
Grasshopper song. Harry Behn. *BeW*
"The **grasshopper,** the grasshopper." See An explanation of the grasshopper
Grasshoppers
An explanation of the grasshopper. V. Lindsay. *FeF—HuSv*
"Grandfather Grasshopper." M. C. Livingston. *LiWa*
The grasshopper ("Down") D. McCord. *LoL—McFf*
The grasshopper ("Happy insect, what can be") Anacreon. *HoW—UnG*
The grasshopper and the bird. J. Reeves. *ReBl*
Grasshopper Green. Unknown. *BrR-4—FeF —HuL-1*
"Grasshopper settin' on a sweet potato vine." Unknown. *WoF*
Grasshopper song. H. Behn. *BeW*
The grasshoppers. D. Aldis. *AlA—CoI— HuL-2*
The grasshopper's song. H. N. Bialik. *FeF —HaY*
My grasshopper. M. C. Livingston. *LiWa*
On the grasshopper and cricket. L. Hunt. *UnG*

The poetry of earth. J. Keats. *HoW*
On the grasshopper and cricket. *JoAc —UnG*
Rilloby-rill. H. Newbolt. *HuL-2—ReG*
"The voice that beautifies the land." Unknown. *PaS*
Way down South. Unknown. *NaE*
The **grasshoppers.** Dorothy Aldis. *AlA— CoI—HuL-2*
"**Grasshoppers** dancing." See Grasshopper song
"**Grasshoppers** four a-fiddling went." See Rilloby-rill
The **grasshopper's** song. H. N. Bialik, tr. fr. the Hebrew by Jessie Sampter. *FeF —HaY*
Grassroots. Carl Sandburg. *SaW*
Gratitude. See Thankfulness
The **grave.** T. Gwynn Jones, tr. fr. the Welsh by Ernest Rhys. *PaS*
Graves, Robert
The Alice Jean. *GrP*
Allie. *FeF—GrP*
The bedpost. *GrP*
A boy in church. *GrP*
The Christmas robin. *GrCc*
Dicky. *GrP*
1805. *NaE—SmLg*
The forbidden play. *GrP*
The General Elliott. *GrP*
Henry and Mary. *GrP*
The hills of May. *GrP*
"How and why." *GrP*
I'd love to be a fairy's child. *BrBc—FeF— HuL-2*
In the wilderness. *GrP*
Jock o' Binnorie. *GrP*
King Stephen. *McW*
The legs. *HaP*
Lift-boy. *GrP*
　Song: Lift-boy. *GrCc*
Lollocks. *NaE*
Lost love. *SmLg*
Love without hope. *GrP*
The magical picture. *GrP*
One hard look. *GrP*
The penny fiddle. *GrP*
The pumpkin. *CoPm—ReG*
Robinson Crusoe. *GrP*
The six badgers. *CoI—GrP—ReG*
Song: Lift-boy. See Lift-boy
To Juan at the winter solstice. *HaP*
Vain and careless. *GrP*
Warning to children. *GrP—SmLg*
The well-dressed children. *GrP*
What did I dream. *GrP*
Wild strawberries. *SmLg*
Graves. See Tombs
Graveyards. See Cemeteries
Gray, Thomas
The cat and the fish. *HoW*
Elegy written in a country churchyard. *DeT —HaP*
Gray (Color)
Grey. J. Reeves. *ReW*
"A **gray** cat, very wilful, took a notion once to wander." See The resolute cat
The **gray** goose. Unknown. *TaD*

"Gray goose and gander." Mother Goose. *JoAc—LiL—OpO*

Grayer, Rosalie
Altar smoke. *UnG*

"Great A, little a (bouncing B)." Mother Goose. *DeMg—JoAc—LiL—OpO*

"Great A, little a (this is pancake day)." Mother Goose. *DeMg*

"Great A was alarmed at B's bad behavior." Mother Goose. *OpO*

"Great are the fallen of Thermopylae." See The Greek dead at Thermopylae

The **great** auk's ghost. Ralph Hodgson. *NaM*

"The **great** auk's ghost rose on one leg." See The great auk's ghost

Great Britain. See England

The great discovery. Eleanor Farjeon. *CoPs —FaCb—FaN*

Great fleas. Augustus De Morgan. *McW*

"**Great** fleas have little fleas upon their backs to bite 'em." See Great fleas

The **great** god Pan. See A musical instrument

"**Great-grandmother** talks by the hour to me." See Irish grandmother

"**Great** oaks from little acorns grow." Unknown. *MoY*

"The **great** Overdog." See Canis Major

"The **great** Pacific railway." See The railroad cars are coming

The **great** panjandrum. See The great panjandrum himself

The great panjandrum himself. Samuel Foote. *JoAc—LoL—NaM*
The great panjandrum. *CoH—SmLg*

The **Great** Silkie of Sule Skerrie. Unknown. *MaB*

"**Great,** wide, beautiful, wonderful world." See The wonderful world

"The **greatest** poem ever known." See To a child

Greece
The Greek dead at Thermopylae. Simonides. *PaS*
Ode on a Grecian urn. J. Keats. *HaP*

Greed. See Selfishness

Greed. Mother Goose. *OpO*

The **greedy** fox and the elusive grapes. Aesop, tr. fr. the Greek by Louis Untermeyer. *UnMc*
The fox and the grapes, tr. fr. the Greek by Joseph Lauren. *UnG*

A **greedy** friar. See The Canterbury tales

Greedy Tom. Mother Goose. *OpO*

The **Greek** dead at Thermopylae. Simonides, tr. fr. the Greek by T. F. Higham. *PaS*

Greek mythology. See Mythology—Greek and Roman

Green, Mary McB.
Aeroplane. *ArTp—PeF*
Taking off. *ArTp—HuL-1*
The airplane. *McAw*

Green (Color)
A pair of sea-green eyes. G. MacDiarmid. *GrCc*

Green afternoon. Frances M. Frost. *ArTp —FrLn*

The **green** autumn stubble. Unknown, tr. fr. the Irish by Patrick Browne. *PaS*

Green broom. Unknown. *CoSp—ReG*

Green candles. Humbert Wolfe. *CoPm*

"**Green** cheese, yellow laces." See Twirling

The **green** door. Leah Bodine Drake. *BrBc*

"A **green** eye—and a red—in the dark." See The train

"**Green-eyed** Care." See Old cat Care

The **green** fiddler. Rachel Field. *CoSp*

The **green** gnome. Robert Buchanan. *CoSp*

Green grass ("A dis, a dis, a green grass") Mother Goose. *OpO*

Green grass ("Green grass is all I hear") James Reeves. *ReR*

Green grass and white milk. Winifred Welles. *ArTp*

The **green** grass growing all around. Unknown. *HuL-2—NaM*

"**Green grass** is all I hear." See Green grass

"**Green** grow'th the holly." Unknown. *EaW*

Green hill neighbors. Frances M. Frost. *ArTp—FrLn*

"A **green** hobgoblin." See A goblinade

"The **green** leaf dances now." Eleanor Farjeon. *FaCb*

"**Green** leaves, what are you doing." See The five-fingered maple

The **green** linnet. William Wordsworth. *DeT*

"**Green** little vaulter in the sunny grass." See On the grasshopper and cricket

"**Green** mistletoe." See Winter

Green moth. Winifred Welles. *ArTp—FeF —HuSv*

Green rain. Mary Webb. *FeF*

"**Green** rushes with red shoots." See Plucking the rushes

The **green** silk bug. Aileen Fisher. *McAw*

The **green** train. E. V. Rieu. *RiF*

Greenaway, Kate
The boat sails away. *NaM*
"Five little sisters walking in a row." *NaM*
"Higgledy, piggledy, see how they run." *ArTp*
"In go-cart so tiny." *FeF*
"In the pleasant green garden." *ArTp*
"Jump—jump—jump." *ArTp*
The little jumping girls. *FeF*
"Little Blue Shoes." *ArTp*
The little jumping girls. See "Jump—jump —jump"
Little Phillis. *BrBc*
Little wind. See "Little wind, blow on the hill-top"
"Little wind, blow on the hill-top." *ArTp*
Little wind. *JoAc*
"Oh, Susan Blue." *ArTp*
Susan Blue. *HuL-1*
Older grown. *BrBc*
Ring-a-ring. *BrL-k—FeF—NaM*
"School is over." *ArTp—HuL-1*
Susan Blue. See "Oh, Susan Blue"
To baby. *BrL-k*
"Tommy was a silly boy." *ArTp*

Will you. See "Will you be my little wife"
"Will you be my little wife." *NaM*
    Will you. *BrS*
Greene, Robert
    Sir Geoffrey Chaucer. *SmLg*
Greenfield, Marjorie H.
    Things I like. *HuL-1*
"**Greensleeves** was all my joy." See A new
    courtly sonnet of the Lady Greensleeves
Greenwell, Dora
    If ye would hear. *EaW*
A **greeting**. Charles Kingsley. *McW*
Greetings. See also Wake-up poems
    "As I was going up Pippen hill." Mother
    Goose. *DeMg—OpO*
    Good morning. M. Sipe. *ArTp—BrL-k—*
    HuL-1
    A greeting. C. Kingsley. *McW*
    An old Christmas greeting. Unknown. *ArTp*
    —FeF—HuL-1
    "One misty, moisty morning." Mother Goose.
    ArTp—DeMg—HuSv—JoAc—LiL—OpO
    Politeness. A. A. Milne. *MiWc*
    The tardy playmate. F. R. Buchanan. *DoP*
Gregor, Arthur
    The chase. *GrCc*
Gregory, Horace
    Dianae sumus in fide. tr. *GrCc*
    Elizabeth at the piano. *PlU*
    Voices of heroes. *GrCc*
Gregory Griggs. See "Gregory Griggs,
    Gregory Griggs"
"**Gregory Griggs**, Gregory Griggs." Mother
    Goose. *DeMg*
    Gregory Griggs. *OpO*
A **grenadier**. Mother Goose. *OpO*
"**Grendel** came to Heorot." See Beowulf
    the Goth
Grenville, Sir Richard (about)
    The Revenge. A. Tennyson. *UnMc*
Gretchen. Unknown, tr. fr. the Dutch. *JoAc*
Grey. James Reeves. *ReW*
"The **grey** cathedral towers." See Memorial
    garden (Canterbury)
The **grey** goose. Unknown. *McW*
"**Grey** goose and gander." See "Gray goose
    and gander"
The **grey** horse. James Reeves. *ReW*
"**Grey** is the sky, and grey the woodman's
    cot." See Grey
Grief. See also Consolation; Laments
    Bereft. R. Frost. *FrR*
    Birds of joy. E. Farjeon. *FaCb—FaN*
    Dolor. T. Roethke. *HaP*
    "The earth late choked with showers." T.
    Lodge. *HaP*
    Herb-Robert. E. Farjeon. *FaCb*
    Home burial. R. Frost. *FrR*
    Insight. D. Aldis. *ThP*
    The melancholy pig. From Sylvie and
    Bruno. L. Carroll. *FeF*
      A pig tale. *HoW*
    "My grief on the sea." Unknown. *PaS*
    My November guest. R. Frost. *FrR*
    Proverbs of King Alfred. King Alfred.
    McW
    Song. From The brides' tragedy. T. L.
    Beddoes. *GrCc*

Sorrow. A. De Vere. *HoW*
Spring and fall. G. M. Hopkins. *HaP—*
    ReT
"Tears flow in my heart." P. Verlaine. *PaS*
Griffins
    Yet gentle will the griffin be. V. Lindsay.
    HuSv
Grig's pig. Mother Goose. *OpO*
Grim and gloomy. James Reeves. *ReW*
Grinding. Mother Goose. *OpO*
The **grindstone**. Robert Frost. *FrR*
Griselda. Eleanor Farjeon. *UnG*
"**Griselda** is greedy, I'm sorry to say." See
    Griselda
Grist mills. See Mills
Griswold, Mariana. See Van Rensselaer,
    Mariana Griswold
Grizzly bear. Mary Austin. *ArTp—FeF*
"The **grizzly** bear is huge and wild." See
    Infant innocence
The **groaning** board. Unknown. *CoH*
Ground hog day. See Candelmas day
Ground hog day. Marnie Pomeroy. *CoPs*
Ground hogs. See Woodchucks
"The **ground** is hard, and o'er the fallows
    now." See High summer
The **groundhog**. Richard Eberhart. *HaP*
"**Grow** old along with me." See Rabbi Ben
    Ezra
Growing. Frances M. Frost. *BrBc*
"**Growing** in the vale." Christina Georgina
    Rossetti. *ArTp*
Growing old. Rose Henderson. *BrBc*
Growing up
    Adventures. A. Kramer. *BrBc*
    "As the years go by." Unknown. *MoY*
    Big. D. Aldis. *AlA*
    Comparison. M. A. Hoberman. *BrBc*
    The difference. E. Farjeon. *FaCb—FaN*
    The end. A. A. Milne. *BrBc—BrS—MiWc*
    Growing. F. M. Frost. *BrBc*
    Growing up ("I'm growing very big and
    tall") E. K. Wallace. *BrBc*
    Growing up ("I've got shoes with grown
    up laces") A. A. Milne. *BrBc—MiWc*
    Growing up ("My birthday is coming to-
    morrow") Unknown. *BrBc—BrL-k*
    Growing up ("Now I am six and going on
    seven") A. Guiterman. *BrBc*
    Growing up ("When I am old and grow
    a bit") M. C. Livingston. *LiW*
    Growing up ("When I was seven") H.
    Behn. *BrBc—BrS*
    How tall. D. McCord. *McT*
    "I used to think." I. O. Eastwick. *EaI*
    An impetuous resolve. J. W. Riley. *BrBc*
    Joan's door. E. Farjeon. *BrBc*
    Lesson. H. Behn. *BeW*
    Mary and the marigold. I. O. Eastwick. *EaI*
    My plan. M. Chute. *BrBc—ChA—FeF*
    Not that. D. Aldis. *AlA*
    Older grown. K. Greenaway. *BrBc*
    Plans. D. B. Thompson. *BrBc—HuL-1*
    Prattle. J. Ciardi. *BrBc—CiR*
    Sophisticate. B. Young. *BrBc—BrS*
    The sweet, red rose. M. M. Dodge. *BrBc*

H

H. D., pseud. See D., H., pseud.

H., H., pseud. See Jackson, Helen Hunt

H is for happily ever after. Eleanor Farjeon. *FaCb*

"Ha, ha, ha." Unknown. *MoY*

Ha ha thisaway. Unknown. *TaD*

"Ha, sir, I have seen you sniffing and snoozling." See The faun

Habit
 Meditatio. E. Pound. *SmLg*

The habit of perfection. Gerard Manley Hopkins. *PlU* (sel.)

Habits of the hippopotamus. Arthur Guiterman. *ArTp—CoH*

"Had I been Norman William." See Norman William

"Had we but world enough, and time." See To his coy mistress

Hadley, Lizzie M.
 His mother's cooking. *BrR-5*
 The rainbow fairies. *BrL-k*

The hag. Robert Herrick. *CoPs—HoW—SmLg—UnG*

"The hag is astride." See The hag

Hagedorn, Hermann
 Evening prayer. *DoP*

Hail
 August hail. J. V. Cunningham. *HaP*
 Indispensability. A. Guiterman. *McW*
 The whirl-blast. W. Wordsworth. *DeT*

"Hail to thee, blithe spirit." See To a skylark

"Haily Paily." Unknown. *JoAc*

Hair
 The barber's. W. De La Mare. *BrR-3—JoAc*
 Bought locks. J. Harington. *BrL-8*
 "Curly Locks, Curly Locks." Mother Goose. *DeMg—JoAc—OpO*
  "Curly Locks, Curly Locks, wilt thou be mine." *LiL*
 "Gregory Griggs, Gregory Griggs." Mother Goose. *DeMg*
  Gregory Griggs. *OpO*
 "Johnny has a nickel." Unknown. *WiRm*
 "There was a little girl, and she had a little curl." Mother Goose. *AnI—DeMg*
  Jemima. *SmLg—UnG*
  The little girl. *OpO*
  There was a little girl. *NaE*
 A tragic story. A. von Chamisso. *BrL-7—CoH—DeT—FeF—NaM—UnG*

Hair ribbons. Unknown. *BrBc—BrL-k*

The hairy dog. Herbert Asquith. *ArTp—BrR-4—FeF—HuSv—PeF*

Hale, Robert Beverly
 The big nasturtiums. *CoPm*

Hale, Sarah Josepha (Buell)
 "Mary had a little lamb." See Mary's lamb
 Mary's lamb. *FeF—JoAc—OpO—UnG*
  "Mary had a little lamb." *BrL-k—DeMg—LiL*

"Half a league, half a league." See The charge of the Light Brigade

"Half a pound o' tuppenny rice." See Pop goes the weasel

"Half a pound of blackberries." Eleanor Farjeon. *FaCb*

"Half the time they munched the grass, and all the time they lay." See Cows

Halfway down. A. A. Milne. *FeF—MiWc*

"Halfway down the stairs." See Halfway down

"Halfway up a certain tree." See The secret place

Hall, Carolyn
 Fireflies. *FeF*

Hall and Knight; or, $z+b+x=y+b+z$. E. V. Rieu. *CoH—RiF*

Hallam, Arthur Henry (about)
 In memoriam, sels. A. Tennyson
  "And, star and system rolling past"
   In memoriam. *PlU*
  "Dark house, by which once more I stand"
   From In memoriam. *HaP*
  "I trust I have not wasted breath"
   In memoriam. *PlU*
  Ring out, wild bells. *ArTp—BrL-8—FeF—HoW*

Hallowe'en
 Black and gold. N. B. Turner. *ArTp—BrR-6—HaY—HuL-2*
 The goblin. Unknown. *ArTp—JoAc*
 The hag. R. Herrick. *CoPs—HoW—SmLg—UnG*
 Hallowe'en ("Broomsticks and witches") M. Chute. *ChA*
 Halloween ("Granny, I saw a witch go by") M. A. Lawson. *ArTp—BrS*
 Hallowe'en ("On Hallowe'en the old ghosts come") E. Farjeon. *FaCb—FaN*
 Halloween ("Ruth says apples have learned to bob") J. Ciardi. *ArTp—CiR*
 Halloween ("The sky was yellow") I. O. Eastwick. *EaI*
 Hallowe'en ("Tonight is the night") H. Behn. *ArTp—BrS—CoPs—FeF—HaY—HuL-2—HuSv—JoAc*
 Halloween ("Who raps at my window") M. Pomeroy. *CoPs*
 Halloween concert. A. Fisher. *BrS*
 Hallowe'en indignation meeting. M. Fishback. *CoPs*
 A Halloween meeting. G. O. Butler. *BrL-k*
 Hallowe'en scare. C. Y. Cutler. *McAw*
 Hallowe'en song. M. Barrows. *HuL-1*
 "Hey-how for Hallowe'en." Unknown. *SmLg*
 If you've never. E. M. Fowler. *BrR-4—HuL-1*
 Litany for Halloween. Unknown. *BrS*
  Ghoulies and ghosties. *CoPs*
 Mr Halloween. D. McCord. *McT*
 Mr Macklin's jack o'lantern. D. McCord. *FeF—McFf*
 October. N. Birckhead. *BrL-7*
 October magic. M. C. Livingston. *LiW*
 On Halloween. S. Silverstein. *CoPs*
 A riddle: What am I. D. Aldis. *AlA—BrL-k*
 The ride-by-nights. W. De La Mare. *ArTp—BrS—FeF—HuL-2*

Gladde things. Unknown. *ArTp*

The gladness of the May. W. Wordsworth. *HaY*

The grasshopper. Anacreon. *HoW—UnG*

The happiest heart. J. V. Cheney. *BrL-8*

Happiness. A. A. Milne. *ArTp—HuL-2— MiWc*

Happiness makes up in height for what it lacks in length. R. Frost. *FrR*

The happy farmer. Unknown. *UnG*

The happy hedgehog. E. V. Rieu. *RiF*

Happy thought. R. L. Stevenson. *ArTp*

The happy townland. W. B. Yeats. *ReT*

Heaven. L. Hughes. *ArTp*

How happy the soldier. Unknown. *SmLg*

"I know not what I seek eternally." R. de Castro. *PaS*

If all the skies. H. Van Dyke. *DoP*

"I'm glad the sky is painted blue." Unknown. *LoL*

I've learned to sing. G. D. Johnson. *BrL-8*

"Jog on, jog on, the foot-path way." From The winter's tale. W. Shakespeare. *ArTp —SmLg*

Joy. H. Conkling. *DoP*

Laughing song. W. Blake. *ArTp—CoPs— JoAc—McW—ReT—UnG*

The light-hearted fairy. Mother Goose. *BrR-4—FeF—HuL-2*

A little song of life. L. W. Reese. *BrR-6 —DoP—FeF—HuL-2*

"Merry are the bells, and merry would they ring." Unknown. *DeMg—DeT*

Merry are the bells. *ArTp—LoL—NaM*

The merry man of Paris. Unknown. *BrR-4*

O happy. Unknown. *DeT*

Ode to Maecenas. Horace. *PaS* (sel.)

Today and tomorrow. *UnG* (sel.)

"Peace and joy." S. Silverstein. *CoPs*

A piper. S. O'Sullivan. *ArTp—FeF—HuL-2 —NaM*

"Piping down the valleys wild." W. Blake. *PlU—SmLg*

Happy songs. *UnG*

Introduction. *ReT*

Introduction to Songs of innocence. *ArTp*

The piper. *DeT*

Recuerdo. E. St V. Millay. *NaE*

Salutation. E. Pound. *SmLg*

Spring. W. Blake. *ArTp—FeF—HaY— JoAc—NaM—SmLg—UnG*

The sun. J. Drinkwater. *ArTp—FeF—PeF*

"There was a jolly miller." From Love in a village. I. Bickerstaffe. *DeMg—UnG*

Jolly Miller. *OpO*

"There was a jolly miller once." *LiL*

This happy day. H. Behn. *ArTp—HuL-1*

"Where are you going." I. O. Eastwick. *EaI*

The world's music. G. Setoun. *DoP*

Happiness. A. A. Milne. *ArTp—HuL-2— MiWc*

Happiness makes up in height for what it lacks in length. Robert Frost. *FrR*

"The happiness of hedgehogs." See The happy hedgehog

The happy family. John Ciardi. *CiM*

The happy farmer. Unknown. *UnG*

The happy hedgehog. E. V. Rieu. *RiF*

"Happy insect, what can be." See The grasshopper

Happy new year. Mildred Evans Roberts. *McAw*

"Happy new year. Happy new year." Unknown. *CoPs*

"Happy somebody." See Somebody and naebody

Happy songs. See "Piping down the valleys wild"

The happy thank-you day. Unknown. *BrR-3*

"The happy thank-you day has come." See The happy thank-you day

"Happy the man, and happy he alone." See Ode to Maecenas

Happy thought. Robert Louis Stevenson. *ArTp*

The happy townland. William Butler Yeats. *ReT*

Harbingers. Edith Tatum. *BrR-6*

Harbors

Docks. C. Sandburg. *SaW*

"Hard and black is my home." See Fire

"Hard as crystal." See Bells

"Hard by the Wildbrooks I met Mary." See Meeting Mary

"Hard from the southeast blows the wind." Elizabeth Jane Coatsworth. *ArTp— HuL-2*

Hard lines. Tom Robinson. *BrBc*

The hardship of accounting. Robert Frost. *FrR—SmLg*

Hardy, Thomas

At Castle Boterel. *HaP*

Barthélémon at Vauxhall. *PlU*

The darkling thrush. *HaP—NaE*

During wind and rain. *HaP*

The dynasts, sel.

We be the king's men. *HuL-2*

Men who march away. *DeT*

The field of Waterloo. *SmLg*

The garden seat. *GrCc*

Heredity. *PlI*

In a museum. *PlU*

In the evening. *PlI*

In time of the breaking of nations. *HaP*

Men who march away. See The dynasts— We be the king's men

"O I won't lead a homely life." *PlU*

The oxen. *EaW—HaP*

Proud songsters. *HaP*

The Roman road. *GrCc*

The self-unseeing. *GrCc*

Snow in the suburbs. *ReT*

Waiting both. *McW*

We be the king's men. See The dynasts

Weathers. *DeT—HuL-2—NaE—SmLg*

A woman driving. *GrCc*

The hare. Walter De La Mare. *ArTp*

Harebells

Harebells. D. Aldis. *AlA*

Harebells. Dorothy Aldis. *AlA*

"The harebells shaking out their blue." See Harebells

Harington, Sir John

Bought locks. *BrL-8*

Hark. Unknown. *DeT*

"Hark, hark." See "Hark, hark, the dogs do bark"

"Hark, hark, the dogs do bark." Mother Goose. *AnI—ArTp—LiL*
"Hark, hark." *DeMg—JoAc—OpO*

Hark, hark the lark. See Cymbeline

"Hark, hark, the lark at heaven's gate sings." See Cymbeline—Hark, hark the lark

"Hark to a perfectly pointless tale." See A pointless tale

"Harken how the flute complains." See Serenade

Harold the Dauntless, sel. Walter Scott
'Tis merry in greenwood. *FeF*

Haroun's favorite song. See The thousand nights and one

Harp music. Rolfe Humphries. *PlU*

The harper of Chao. Po Chü-i, tr. fr. the Chinese by Arthur Waley. *PlU*

The Harpers' farm. Dorothy Aldis. *AlA*

Harps
Harp music. R. Humphries. *PlU*
The Lochmabyn harper. Unknown. *MaB*
My dog Tray. *UnG*
The Irish harper. *DeT*
"There was a young lady whose chin." E. Lear. *ArTp*

Harrington, Sarah Jane S.
Lullaby. *BrL-k—HuL-1*

Harris, Hazel Harper
Gifts. *BrBc*

Harry Parry. Mother Goose. *OpO*

"The hart he loves the high wood." Mother Goose. *DeMg—OpO—SmLg*

Harte, (Francis) Bret
The aged stranger. *UnMc*
The ghost that Jim saw. *CoPm*
Plain language from truthful James. *CoH*
The society upon the Stanislow. *UnMc*
The spelling bee at Angels. *CoSp*

Harvest. See "The boughs do shake and the bells do ring"

Harvest ("I saw the farmer plough the field") M. M. Hutchinson. *HuL-2*

Harvest home. Arthur Guiterman. *HaY*

Harvest sunset. Carl Sandburg. *SaW*

Harvests and harvesting
After apple-picking. R. Frost. *FrR—FrY*
After harvest. E. Farjeon. *FaCb—FaN*
"The boughs do shake and the bells do ring." Mother Goose. *JoAc*
Harvest. *OpO*
Brown gold. C. Sandburg. *SaW*
A child's thought of harvest. S. Coolidge. *CoPs*
Cornhuskers. C. Sandburg. *SaW*
The gleaners. E. Farjeon. *FaCb—FaN*
Harvest. M. M. Hutchinson. *HuL-2*
Harvest home. A. Guiterman. *HaY*
Harvest sunset. C. Sandburg. *SaW*
Haystacks. C. Sandburg. *SaW*
Haytime. I. F. Pawsey. *HuL-1*
Hunger-harvest. E. Farjeon. *FaCb—FaN*
The last corn shock. G. W. Dresbach. *FeF*
The last mowing. R. Frost. *FrY*

The mowers. M. B. Benton. *HaY*
Mowing. R. Frost. *FrR*
The sheaves. E. A. Robinson. *HaP*
The solitary reaper. W. Wordsworth. *HaP—PlU—ReT*
The tuft of flowers. R. Frost. *FrR—FrY*
"Willy boy, Willy boy, where are you going." Mother Goose. *DeMg—HuSv*
Willie boy, Willie boy. *HuL-1*

"Has anybody seen my Mopser." See The bandog

"Has anybody seen my mouse." See Missing

"Has anyone a shoe box." See If I had a cardboard box

Hashin
Loneliness. *PaS*

"Hast thou given the horse strength." See Job—The horse

"Hast thou named all the birds without a gun." See Forbearance

"Hast thou then survived." See Address to my infant daughter

"Haste." See Poor Richard's wisdom

Hastings mill. Cicely Fox-Smith. *McW*

The hasty pudding. Joel Barlow. *SmLg*

Hate
The vindictives. R. Frost. *FrR*

Hats
Hats ("Hats, where do you belong") C. Sandburg. *SaW*
Hats ("Round or square") W. J. Smith. *SmL*
The little hat. D. Aldis. *AlA*
The man that had no hat. J. Ciardi. *CiI*
My streamer hat. D. Aldis. *AlA*
The Quangle Wangle's hat. E. Lear. *JoAc*
Under a hat rim. C. Sandburg. *SaW*
What's the difference. O. F. Pearre. *BrL-8*

Hats ("Hats, where do you belong") Carl Sandburg. *SaW*

Hats ("Round or square") William Jay Smith. *SmL*

"Hats off." See The flag goes by

"Hats, where do you belong." See Hats

The haunted house. Thomas Hood. *HoW*

The haunted palace. Edgar Allan Poe. *HoW*

"Have fair fallen, O fair, fair have fallen, so dear." See Henry Purcell

"Have you been at sea on a windy day." See A windy day

"Have you ever heard the wind go Yooooo." See The night wind

"Have you ever in your life seen a possum play possum." See Opossum

"Have you had your tonsils out." See The new neighbor

"Have you heard of the dreadful fate." See The Ashtabula disaster

"Have you heard of the wonderful one-hoss shay." See The deacon's masterpiece; or, The wonderful one-hoss shay

"Have you heard the blinking toad." See The song of the toad

Have you met this man. John Ciardi. *CiI*

"Have you met this man? He has no head." See Have you met this man

"**Have** you seen a little dog anywhere about." See My dog

"**Have** you seen an apple orchard in the spring, in the spring." See Apple blossoms

"**Have** you seen but a bright lily grow." See A celebration of Charis

"**Have** you seen Yggdrasil, the Sacred Tree." See Y is for Yggdrasil

Have you watched the fairies. Rose Fyleman. *ArTp—HuL-1—PeF*

"**Have** you watched the fairies when the rain is done." See Have you watched the fairies

Having. William Jay Smith. *SmL*

"**Having** a wheel and four legs of its own." See The grindstone

"**Having** been tenant long to a rich Lord." See Redemption

Hawker, Robert Stephen
And shall Trelawny die. *NaE*

Hawks
The gay goshawk. Unknown. *MaB*

Hawkshawe, Anne (or Hawkshaw, Ann) (Aunt Effie, pseud.)
The clucking hen. *HuL-1*
Freddie and the cherry-tree. *HuL-1*

Hay, John
The enchanted shirt. *HuL-2—UnG—UnMc*
Jim Bludso. *BrL-8—UnMc*
Little Breeches. *UnG*

Hay, Sara Henderson
The shape God wears. *UnG*

Hay
The code. R. Frost. *FrR—UnMc*
The hay appeareth. From Proverbs, Bible, Old Testament. *FeF*
Haystacks. C. Sandburg. *SaW*
Haytime. I. F. Pawsey. *HuL-1*
Horses chawin' hay. H. Garland. *HuSv*
A lazy sight. D. Aldis. *AlA*
The mowers. M. B. Benton. *HaY*
Mowing. R. Frost. *FrR*
Willy boy. Mother Goose. *OpO*

The **hay** appeareth. See Proverbs, Bible, Old Testament

"The **hay** appeareth, and the tender grass sheweth itself." See Proverbs, Bible, Old Testament—The hay appeareth

"**Hay** is for horses." Mother Goose. *OpO*

Hayes, Nancy M.
The shiny little house. *HuL-1*
W-o-o-o-o-o-ww. *HuL-1*

"The **hay's** long cut." See Hunger-harvest

Haystacks. Carl Sandburg. *SaW*

Haytime. Irene F. Pawsey. *HuL-1*

Haze gold. Carl Sandburg. *SaW*

Hazlitt, William
For every evil. See "For every evil under the sun"
"For every evil under the sun." *DeMg—LiL—OpO*
For every evil. *NaE—ThP—UnG*

"**He** always comes on market days." See The balloon man

"**He** ate and drank the precious words." See Only a book

"**He** burst from bed." See Boy's day

"**He** came." See Paul Bunyan

"**He** came all so still." See An ancient Christmas carol

"**He** came and took me by the hand." See The mystery

"**He** came from Malta; and Eumêlus says." See A Maltese dog

"**He** captured light and caged it in a glass." See And yet fools say

"**He** clasps the crag with crooked hands." See The eagle

He comforts himself. See Translations from the Chinese

He compares all things with his lady, and finds them wanting. Guido Cavalcanti, tr. fr. the Italian by Dante Gabriel Rossetti. *PaS*

"**He** could not breathe in a crowded place." See The pioneer

"**He** did not want to do it." See No

"**He** does not hear the struck string." See Music God

"**He** entered the shop." See Birthday gift

"**He** fell in victory's fierce pursuit." See The General Elliott

"**He** halted in the wind, and—what was that." See A boundless moment

"**He** has come, he is here." See The return

"**He** has dust in his eyes and a fan for a wing." See One guess

"**He** has no broomstick, but you dare not say." See Mr Halloween

"**He** has opened all his parcels but the largest and the last." See The hippopotamus's birthday

"**He** has outsoared the shadow of our night." See Adonais

He, haw, hum. See "John Cook he had a little gray mare"

"**He** huffs from the north." See March wind

"**He** is a fool who thinks by force or skill." Unknown. *MoY*

"**He** is always standing there." See My policeman

"**He** is gone on the mountain." See The lady of the lake—Coronach

"**He** is not John the gardener." See A friend in the garden

"**He** is said to have been the last Red man." See The vanishing Red

"**He** is so small, he does not know." See Six weeks old

"**He** is white as Helvellyn when winter is well in." See The white rabbit

"**He** isn't all Indian." See Our hired man

"**He** killed the noble Mudjokivis." See The modern Hiawatha

"**He** killed the noble Mudjokovis." See The modern Hiawatha

He leads us still. Arthur Guiterman. *BrL-7*

"**He** lies upon his bed." See Einstein, 1929

"**He** loves me." Mother Goose. *OpO*

"**He** met old Dame Trot with a basket of eggs." Mother Goose. *DeMg*

"**He** must not laugh at his own wheeze." See The humorist

"He never used to notice me." See The policeman

"He, of his gentleness." See In the wilderness

"He played by the river when he was young." See Washington

He prayeth best. See The rime of the ancient mariner

"He prayeth best, who loveth well." See The rime of the ancient mariner—He prayeth best

He prayeth well. See The rime of the ancient mariner—He prayeth best

"He put away his tiny pipe." See Spring cricket

"He put his acorn helmet on." See The culprit fay—A fairy in armor

"He quickly arms him for the field." See Nymphidia: The court of fairy—Pigwiggin arms himself

"He ran right out of the woods to me." See The story of the baby squirrel

"He ran up the candlestick." See A Chinese nursery rhyme

"He rises and begins to round." See The lark ascending

"He said: Awake my soul, and with the sun." See Barthélémon at Vauxhall

"He sat at the dinner table there." See His mother's cooking

"He saw her from the bottom of the stairs." See Home burial

"He sits upon the music box." See The sad monkey

"He snipped away, his scissors bright." See Oh, dear

"He stood alone within the spacious square." See The city of dreadful night

"He stood on his head by the wild seashore." See His mother-in-law

"He struggled to kiss her. She struggled the same." See Old-fashioned love

"He that dwelleth in the secret place of the Most High." See Psalms—Psalm XCI

"He that goes a-borrowing." See Poor Richard's wisdom

"He that is down needs fear no fall." See The pilgrim's progress—The shepherd boy sings in the valley of humiliation

He that is slow to anger. See Proverbs, Bible, Old Testament

"He that is slow to anger is better than the mighty." See Proverbs, Bible, Old Testament—He that is slow to anger

"He that lies at the stock." See Three a-bed

"He that sweareth." See Advice

"He that would thrive." Mother Goose. DeMg—OpO

"He thought he kept the universe alone." See The most of it

He thought he saw. See Sylvie and Bruno—The gardener's song

"He thought he saw an elephant." See Sylvie and Bruno—The gardener's song

He understood. Anne V. Culbertson. BrL-8

"He used to be a fairy once." See The canary

"He walked three miles to school each day." See Dear old dad

"He was a man as hot as whiskey." See Andrew Jackson

"He was a rat, and she was a rat." See The two rats

"He was a stickler about paying debts." See Debtor

"He was a wizard's son." See A love story

"He was, through boyhood's storm and shower." See A dedication

"He wears a big hat, big spurs, and all that." See The cowboy

"He wears his hat upon his neck." Unknown. WoF

"He went down to the woodshed." See No one heard him call

"He went to the wood and caught it." Mother Goose. OpO

"He who has never known hunger." Elizabeth Jane Coatsworth. ArTp

He who knows. Unknown. ThP—UnG
   "He who knows and knows that he knows." MoY

"He who knows and knows that he knows." See He who knows

"He who knows not, and knows not that he knows not." See He who knows

He will praise his lady. Guido Guinicelli, tr. fr. the Italian by Dante Gabriel Rossetti. PaS

"He woke me with his tiny trill." See Bantam rooster

"He would declare and could himself believe." See Never again would birds' song be the same

Head and shoulders, Baby. Unknown. TaD

"Head and shoulders, Baby—one, two, three." See Head and shoulders, Baby

"Head bumper." Mother Goose. OpO

"Head the ship for England." See Homeward bound

Headlam, Walter
   In the spring. tr. PaS
   A window in the breast. tr. PaS

Headland, Isaac Taylor
   Blind man's buff. tr. JoAc
   A Chinese nursery rhyme. tr. BrR-3
   The five toes. tr. JoAc
   Lady bug. tr. JoAc
   Old Chang the crab. tr. JoAc
   Thistle-seed. tr. JoAc

"A headlight searches a snowstorm." See Prairie—Limited crossing Wisconsin

"Heap on more wood—the wind is chill." See Marmion—Old Christmastide

"Hear, O my son, and receive my sayings." See Proverbs, Bible, Old Testament—The two paths

"Hear the carols." See Know it is Christmas

"Hear the sledges with the bells." See The bells

Hearing the early oriole. Po Chü-i, tr. fr. the Chinese by Arthur Waley. PlU

"Hearken to me, gentlemen." See King Estmere

The heart. Unknown, tr. fr. the French by Louis Untermeyer. UnMc

"The heart asks pleasure first." Emily Dickinson. HaP

"**Heart,** my heart, with griefs confounded whence you no deliv'rance find." See Be still, my soul

The **heart** of Midlothian, sel. Walter Scott "Proud Maisie is in the wood." *SmLg*

Heart specialist. Elias Lieberman. *PlI*

Heartbeat of democracy. Virginia Brasier. *HuSv*

Hearth. Peggy Bacon. *FeF*

Hearth song. Robert Underwood Johnson. *HaY*

"The **hearthfire** cast a flickering light." See Lincoln learning

Hearts
The false heart. H. Belloc. *SmLg*
The heart. Unknown. *UnMc*
Heart specialist. E. Lieberman. *PlI*
"Hearts were made to give away." A. Wynne. *ArTp*
The shape of the heart. L. T. Nicholl. *PlI*

"**Hearts,** like doors, will ope with ease." Mother Goose. *OpO*

"**Hearts** were made to give away." Annette Wynne. *ArTp*

The **heather.** Steen Steensen Blicher, tr. fr. the Danish by Charles Wharton Stork. *PaS*

Heaven
The bells of heaven. R. Hodgson. *BrS— DeT—HaP*
A blackbird suddenly. J. Auslander. *ArTp*
The child reads an almanac. F. Jammès. *FeF*
"Christ hath a garden walled around." I. Watts. *SmLg*
Conversation in the mountains. Li T'ai-po. *PaS*
The cowboy's dream. Unknown. *UnMc*
The happy townland. W. B. Yeats. *ReT*
Heaven ("Fish—fly-replete, in depth of June") R. Brooke. *McW*
Heaven ("Heaven is") L. Hughes. *ArTp*
Heaven ("O who will show me those delights on high") G. Herbert. *GrCc*
Heaven-haven. G. M. Hopkins. *HaP— McW*
How many heavens. E. Sitwell. *GrCc*
"I never saw a moor." E. Dickinson. *ArTp — DoP — FeF — HuL-2 — JoAc —NaE*
Certainty. *UnG*
I will give you. W. Blake. *DoP*
Jerusalem. Unknown. *SmLg*
Paradise C. G. Rossetti. *DoP*
Peace. H. Vaughan. *GrCc—SmLg*
The poet's paradise. M. Drayton. *HoW*
"The sky is up above the roof." P. Verlaine. *FeF*
Skylark and nightingale. C. G. Rossetti. *HuL-2*
Heaven is heaven. *HaY*
Swing low, sweet chariot. Unknown. *FeF —SmLg*
"To see the world in a grain of sand." From Auguries of innocence. W. Blake. *DoP*
Auguries of innocence. *PlI*
The uncharted. R. Field. *BrR-6*
Where is heaven. B. Carman. *UnG*

Heaven ("Fish—fly-replete, in depth of June") Rupert Brooke. *McW*

Heaven ("Heaven is") Langston Hughes. *ArTp*

Heaven ("O who will show me those delights on high") George Herbert. *GrCc*

Heaven-haven. Gerard Manley Hopkins. *HaP—McW*

"**Heaven** is." See Heaven

Heaven is heaven. See Skylark and nightingale

"**Heaven** is in my hand, and I." See A blackbird suddenly

"The **heavens** declare the glory of God." See Psalms—Psalm XIX

"The **heavens** first in tune I'll set." See Microcosmus

"The **heavens** themselves, the planets and this center." See Troilus and Cressida

Hector Protector. See "Hector Protector was dressed all in green"

"**Hector** Protector was dressed all in green." Mother Goose. *DeMg*
Hector Protector. *NaM—OpO*

Hedgehogs
The happy hedgehog. E. V. Rieu. *RiF*

Hee, haw, hum. See "John Cook he had a little gray mare"

"**He-hi,** gimme a piece of pie." Unknown *WoF*

"**Heigh** ho, my heart is low." Mother Goose. *OpO*
Double-u. *DeT*

The **height** of the ridiculous. Oliver Wendell Holmes. *BrL-8—CoH—HuSv—NaM*

Heine, Heinrich
The Lorelei. *CoPm*
The Loreley. *UnG*
The Loreley. See The Lorelei
"Lovely as a flower." *PaS*
A meeting. *CoPm*
"The sea hath its pearls." *PaS*
Who was it. *PaS*

The **heir** of Linne. Unknown. *MaB*

Heirs
The heir of Linne. Unknown. *MaB*

Helburn, Theresa
Mother. *FeF*

Hello. Louise Ayres Garnett. *BrS*

"**Hello** chickadee-dee-dee." See I'm so big

Hello day. Dorothy Aldis. *AlHd*

"**Hello** windy, springtime day." See Hello day

"**Help,** help." See Trouble at the farm

"**Help.** Murder. Police." Unknown. *WoF*

Helpfulness. See Service

Helpfulness. Marchette Chute. *ChA*

Heltery-skeltery. Eleanor Farjeon. *FaCb— FaN*

Helton, Roy
Lonesome water. *CoPm—McW*
Old Christmas. *CoPm—UnMc*

Hemans, Felicia Dorothea (Felicia Dorothea Brown)
Casabianca. *FeF—UnG*
The landing of the Pilgrim Fathers. *ArTp —BrR-5—FeF—UnG*

"Here comes a poor woman from Baby-land." Mother Goose. *DeMg*

Here comes a wooer. Mother Goose. *OpO*

"Here comes Mary Anne." See Mary Anne's luncheon

"Here comes my lady with her little baby." Mother Goose. *OpO*

"Here comes the elephant." See The elephant

Here comes the teacher. Unknown. *WoJ*

"Here comes the teacher with the big fat stick." See Here comes the teacher

"Here further up the mountain slope." See The birthplace

"Here hangs a garland." See A garland for Agatha Blyth

"Here I am, here I come." See Here I come

"Here I am with my rabbits." See The rabbit man

Here I come. Dorothy Aldis. *AlA*

"Here I go up in my swing." See Swing song

"Here I lie at the chancel door." Unknown Four country epitaphs. *UnG*

"Here in a quiet and dusty room they lay." See The seed shop

"Here in the country's heart." See The country faith

"Here in the German." See Disenchanted

"Here in the minster tower." See Tudor church music

"Here in the mountains the moon I love." See The moon in the mountains

"Here is a thing my heart wishes." See Poems done on a late night car—Home

"Here is an apple, ripe and red." See Dividing

"Here is the ancient floor." See The self-unseeing

"Here is the church, and here is the steeple." Mother Goose. *DeMg—OpO*

"Here lie I, Martin Eldinbrodde." See Here lies

Here lies. Unknown. *UnG*

"Here lies a great and mighty king." See On Charles II

Here lies a lady. John Crowe Ransom. *NaE*

"Here lies a lady of beauty and high degree." See Here lies a lady

"Here lies a mouse of gentle ways." See Epitaph

"Here lies a poor woman who was always tired." See On a tired housewife

"Here lies father, mother, sister, and I." Unknown Four country epitaphs. *UnG*

"Here lies Fred." See On Prince Frederick

"Here lies John Bun." See On John Bun

"Here lies me and my three daughters." Unknown Four country epitaphs. *UnG*

"Here lies old Hobson, death hath broke his girt." See On the university carrier

"Here lies one blown out of breath." See On a man named Merideth

"Here lies our Sovereign Lord and King." See On Charles II

"Here lies Richard Dent." See On Richard Dent, landlord

"Here lies the body of Jonathan Pound." Unknown Four country epitaphs. *UnG*

"Here lies the body of Michael Shay." See On stubborn Michael Shay

"Here lies what's left." See On Leslie Moore

"Here on the mountain pass." See On the mountain pass

Here she is. Mary Britton Miller. *ArTp*

"Here she lies, in bed of spice." See Upon a maid

Here sits. See "Here sits the Lord Mayor"

"Here sits the Lord Mayor." Mother Goose. *DeMg—LiL—OpO*

Here sits. *DeT*

"Here Skugg lies snug." See On Skugg

"Here the crow starves, here the patient stag." See Landscapes—Rannoch, by Glencoe

"Here we bring new water." See A new year carol

"Here we come a-caroling." Unknown. *ArTp—FeF*

"Here we come a-piping." Unknown. *BrS—JoAc*

"Here we come a-wassailing." See The wassail song

"Here we come gathering nuts an' may." See "Here we come gathering nuts in May"

"Here we come gathering nuts in May." Mother Goose. *LiL*

Nuts an' may. *NaE*

"Here we go dancing jingo-ring." Mother Goose. *OpO*

"Here we go round ring by ring." Mother Goose. *OpO*

"Here we go round the jingo-ring." See The jingo-ring

"Here we go round the mulberry bush." Mother Goose. *DeMg—LiL*

"Here where the dead lie hidden." See Hide-and-seek

Heredity. Thomas Hardy. *PlI*

"Here's A, B, and C." See A learned song

"Here's a ball for baby." Mother Goose. *LiL*

"Here's a body—there's a bed." See Good night

"Here's a clean year." See A new year

"Here's a health to the barley mow." Mother Goose. *DeMg*

"Here's a large one for the lady." See The broom squire's song

Here's a poor widow. Mother Goose. *OpO*

"Here's a poor widow from Babylon." See Here's a poor widow

"Here's a summer, heavy and hard." See Elegy for Lucy Lloyd

"Here's an adventure. What awaits." See On opening a new book

"Here's an example from." See The example

"Here's Finiky Hawkes." See Black your honour's boots
"Here's flowery taffeta for Mary's new gown." See The well-dressed children
"Here's Lady day." See Lady day
"Here's November." See Enter November
"Here's spring." Eleanor Farjeon. *FaCb*
"Here's Sulky Sue." Mother Goose. *DeMg*
    Sulky Sue. *OpO*
"Here's the mail, sort it quick." See A sure sign
"Here's the mould of a musical bird long passed from light." See In a museum
"Here's to good old Boston." See Boston
"Here's to the man who invented stairs." See Stairs
"Here's to thee, old apple tree." See Twelfth night
"Here's to you as good as you are." See You and I
"Here's two or three jolly boys." See Eastertide

Herford, Oliver
    The artful ant. *CoH*
    A Christmas legend. *CoPm*
    The crocodile. *CoH*
    The elf and the dormouse. *ArTp—FeF—HuL-1—PeF—UnG*
    The fall of J. W. Beane. *CoSp*
    "I heard a bird sing." *ArTp—BrS—EaW—HaY—HuL-2*
    Japanesque. *CoH*
    Kitten's night thoughts. *BrL-k*
    A love story. *CoPm*
    "My sense of sight is very keen" After Oliver. *CoH*
    Stairs. *CoH*
    The unfortunate giraffe. *CoH*

Heritage
    Birthright. J. Drinkwater. *GrCc*
    Heredity. T. Hardy. *Pll*
    The legacy. Mother Goose. *OpO*
    The ploughboy in luck. Mother Goose. *OpO*
        The silly. *DeT*
    To his son, Vincent Corbet. R. Corbet. *SmLg*

Hermits
    The hermit's song. Unknown. *PaS*
    The hermit's song. Unknown, tr. fr. the Irish by Frank O'Connor. *PaS*

The **hero.** Leroy F. Jackson. *BrS*
A **hero** in the land of dough. Robert Clairmont. *McW*
Hero of Astley's. Eleanor Farjeon. *FaN*
Heroes and heroines. See also Explorers and exploration; Mythology—Greek and Roman; Romance; also names of heroes and heroines, as Nelson, Horatio; Joan of Arc
    Barbara Frietchie. J. G. Whittier. *CoPs—FeF—JoAc—UnG—UnMc*
    Beowulf the Goth. E. Farjeon. *FaCb*
    Casabianca ("The boy stood on the burning deck") F. D. Hemans. *FeF—UnG*
    Casabianca ("Sea, be kind to a young boy's bones") E. Farjeon. *FaCb—FaN*
    The charge of the Light Brigade. A. Tennyson. *FeF—JoAc—UnMc*

    The Golden Vanity. Unknown. *HoW*
    The hero. L. F. Jackson. *BrS*
    A hero in the land of dough. R. Clairmont. *McW*
    Hero of Astley's. E. Farjeon. *FaN*
    "Heroes on horseback." J. Reeves. *ReR*
    Horatius. From Lays of ancient Rome. T. B. Macaulay. *SmLg*
        The fight at the bridge. *UnMc* (sel.)
    I think continually of those. S. Spender. *HaP*
    Incident of the French camp. R. Browning. *UnG—UnMc*
    Johnny Armstrong. Unknown. *UnMc*
    The leak in the dike. P. Cary. *FeF*
    Little Giffen. F. O. Ticknor. *UnMc*
    The minstrel-boy. T. Moore. *UnG*
    A nation's strength. R. W. Emerson. *FeF*
    Not to die. Simonides. *PaS*
    The prisoner of Chillon. G. G. Byron. *UnMc*
    A song of greatness. M. Austin. *ArTp—BrBc—FeF—JoAc*
    The triumph. E. Farjeon. *FaN*
    Voices of heroes. H. Gregory. *GrCc*
    We never know how high. E. Dickinson. *McW*

"**Heroes** on horseback." James Reeves. *ReR*
Heroism. See Heroes and heroines
The **heron.** John Ciardi. *CiR*
"The **heron** has two wooden legs." See The heron

Herons
    The heron. J. Ciardi. *CiR*
    Night heron. F. M. Frost. *FrLn*
    The white egret. Li T'ai-po. *PaS*

Herrick, Robert
    Ceremonies for Christmas. *ArTp*
    A charm; or, An allay for love. *SmLg*
    A child's grace. See A grace for a child
    Delight in disorder. *HaP*
    The fairies. *FeF*
        Queen Mab. *ReG*
    The four sweet months. See The succession of the four sweet months
    The funeral rites of the rose. *HaP*
    Gather ye rosebuds. *HaP—ReG*
    A grace. See A grace for a child
    A grace for a child. *FeF—NaM—ReT*
        A child's grace. *SmLg*
        A grace. *DeT*
    The hag. *CoPs—HoW—SmLg—UnG*
    His cavalier. *GrCc*
    His prayer to Ben Jonson. *HaP*
    Humility. *UnG*
    July: The succession of the four sweet months. See The succession of the four sweet months
    The mad maid's song. *HoW*
    An ode for Ben Jonson. *HaP*
    Queen Mab. See The fairies
    Science in God. *Pll*
    The succession of the four sweet months. *HaY*
        The four sweet months. *HoW*
        July: The succession of the four sweet months. *FeF*
    A ternarie of littles, upon a pipkin of jelly sent to a lady. *SmLg*

A thanksgiving to God for his house. *DeT*
To Anthea who may command him any thing. *GrCc*
To daffodils. *JoAc—NaE*
To music, to becalme his fever. *PlU* (sel.)
To musick. *PlU*
A trapped fly. *HoW*
Upon a maid. *SmLg*
Upon Pagget. *SmLg*
"What God gives, and what we take." *JoAc*
The white island. *HoW*
Herrick, Robert (about)
Sweet Robin Herrick. E. Farjeon. *FaCb —FaN*
"The **herring** loves the merry moonlight." Walter Scott. *SmLg*
Hers. Eleanor Farjeon. *FaCb*
"**He's** made of wool and cannot run." See Christmas dog
"**He's** nothing much but fur." See A kitten
Hessey, Vera
The frog and the bird. *HuL-1*
Hey diddle. Myra Cohn Livingston. *LiW*
"**Hey** diddle diddle (and hey)." Mother Goose. *OpO*
"**Hey**, diddle, diddle (the cat)." Mother Goose. *ArTp — BrL-k — DeMg — HuSv—JoAc—LiL—OpO*
"**Hey** diddle, dinketty, poppety, pet." Mother Goose. *DeMg—OpO*
"**Hey** diddle dout." See My little maid
"**Hey** ding a ding." Mother Goose. *OpO*
Hey dorolot. Mother Goose. *OpO*
"**Hey**, dorolot, dorolot." See Hey dorolot
"**Hey-how** for Hallowe'en." Unknown. *SmLg*
"**Hey**, my kitten, my kitten." Mother Goose. *DeMg—OpO*
"**Hey**, my lad, ho, my lad." See Welcome to the new year
Hey, my pony. Eleanor Farjeon. *FeF*
"**Hey** nonny no." See A round
"**Hey**, the little postman." See The postman
Heywood, Thomas
Pack, clouds, away. See The rape of Lucrece
The rape of Lucrece, sel.
Pack, clouds, away. *ReT*
"**Hezekiah** Bettle was a bachelor of Maine." See A bachelor of Maine
Hiawatha's childhood. See The song of Hiawatha
"**Hick-a-more**, hack-a-more." Mother Goose. *ArTp—JoAc—OpO*
"**Hickamore-hackamore**." Unknown. *WoF*
"**Hickety**, pickety, i-silicity." Mother Goose. *OpO*
"**Hickety**, pickety, my black hen (she lays eggs for gentlemen)." Mother Goose. *AnI—DeMg—JoAc—LiL*
"Higgledy, piggledy, my black hen." *ArTp —HuSv*
My black hen. *OpO*
"**Hickety-pickety**, my black hen (she lays eggs for the railroad men)." Unknown. *WoF*

"**Hickory**, dickory, dock (the mouse)." Mother Goose. *AnI—ArTp—BrL-k— DeMg—HuL-1—JoAc—LiL—OpO*
"**Hickory**, dickory, sacara down." Mother Goose. *DeMg*
Hicky, Daniel Whitehead
Wisdom. *BrBc*
Hide-and-seek. Robert Francis. *HaP*
"**Hide** in the hedge, Jack." See Jack-hide-in-the-hedge
"**Hide** not your talents; they for use were made." See Poor Richard's wisdom
Hiding
A-ha. D. Aldis. *AlA*
Hide-and-seek. R. Francis. *HaP*
Hiding. D. Aldis. *AlA—ArTp—BrL-k— FeF—JoAc*
Jack-hide-in-the-hedge. E. Farjeon. *FaCb*
The rabbit. E. M. Roberts. *ArTp—PeF— UnG*
When Anabelle's it. D. Aldis. *AlA*
Hiding. Dorothy Aldis. *AlA—ArTp—BrL-k —FeF—JoAc*
"**A hiding** tuft, a green-barked yew-tree." See The hermit's song
Hie away. See Waverley—"Hie away, hie away"
"**Hie** away, hie away." See Waverley
"**Hie**, hie, says Anthony." See Puss in the pantry
"**Hie** to the market, Jenny come trot." Mother Goose. *OpO*
Hiems. See Love's labor's lost—"When icicles hang by the wall"
Higginson, Anne
The fisherman. tr. *FeF*
Higginson, Ella
Four-leaf clover. *BrR-6—FeF*
The month of falling stars. *HaY*
"**Higgledy-piggledy** here we lie." See Charade
"**Higgledy**, piggledy, my black hen." See "Hickety, pickety, my black hen"
"**Higgledy**, piggledy, see how they run." Kate Greenaway. *ArTp*
"**Higglety**, pigglety, pop." Samuel Griswold Goodrich. *LoL—OpO*
Higgs, Gertrude Monro
Paddling. *HuL-1*
"**High**." See The grasshoppers
"**High** adventure." See Maps
"**High** and proud on the barnyard fence." See Chanticleer
The **high** Barbaree. Laura E. Richards. *JoAc*
"**High** diddle ding, did you hear the bells ring." See Parliament soldiers
"**High** diddle doubt, my candle's out." Mother Goose. *DeMg*
High flight. John Gillespie Magee, Jr. *FeF —McW—UnMc*
"**High** in the flowering catalpa trees." See Fox and crow
"**High** o'er the lonely hills." See Carol
"**High** on a banyan tree in a row." See Monkey
"The **high** skip." Mother Goose. *LiL*
High summer. John Clare. *GrCo*

A **high** tide on the coast of Lincolnshire. Jean Ingelow. *DeT*

"**High** up, high." See Back-yard swing

"**High** up on the lonely mountains." See A night with a wolf

"**High** upon the lonely down." See The sheepfold

Higham, T. F.
Country gods. tr. *SmLg*
Flute song. tr. *PaS*
A garden. tr. *PaS*
The Greek dead at Thermopylae. tr. *PaS*
How can man die better. tr. *PaS*

"**Higher**." See At the airport

"**Higher** than a house." Mother Goose. *ArTp—OpO*
"**Higher** than a house, higher than a tree." *DeMg*

"**Higher** than a house, higher than a tree." See "Higher than a house"

The **highlander's** song. Charles Edward Carryl. *CoH*

"**Highly** beloved and intimate was he." See The Canterbury tales—A greedy friar

"**Highty**, tighty, paradighty." Mother Goose. *OpO*

The **highwayman**. Alfred Noyes. *BrL-8* (sel.)—*FeF—UnG—UnMc*

The **highwayman's** ghost. Richard Garnett. *CoSp*

Highwaymen. See Crime and criminals

The **highwaymen**. John Gay. *HoW*

Hill, Mildred J.
"When you send a valentine." *BrR-3—McAw*

"**Hill** blue among the leaves in summer." See Cheap blue

"A **hill** full, a hole full." Mother Goose. *ArTp—DeMg*

The **hill** wife. Robert Frost. *FrR*

Hills. See also Mountains
After sunset. G. H. Conkling. *ThP*
Afternoon on a hill. E. St V. Millay. *ArTp—FeF—HuSv—PeF*
The dark hills E. A. Robinson. *HaP*
The flowering hills. E. Farjeon. *FaCb—FaN*
Hills. H. Conkling. *HuSv*
The hills of May. R. Graves. *GrP*
A hillside thaw. R. Frost. *FrR—FrY*
How to tell the top of a hill. J. Ciardi. *CiR*
Journey's end. A. A. Milne. *MiWc*
Lonesome water. R. Helton. *CoPm—McW*
Up the hill. W. J. Smith. *SmL*

Hills. Hilda Conkling. *HuSv*

"The **hills** are going somewhere." See Hills

"The **hills** are high." See In the country

The **hills** of May. Robert Graves. *GrP*

A **hillside** thaw. Robert Frost. *FrR—FrY*

Hillyer, Robert (Silliman)
Adoration of the disk. See The book of the dead

The book of the dead, sels.
Adoration of the disk. tr. *FeF*
The dead man ariseth and singeth a hymn to the sun. tr. *PaS*

The dead man ariseth and singeth a hymn to the sun. See The book of the dead

Lullaby. *FeF*

"The **plants** stand silent round me." tr. *PaS*

The relic. *PlU*

Seven times one are seven. *BrBc*

"So ghostly then the girl came in." *GrCc*

"There is a charming land." tr. *FeF*

Hilsabeck, Emily M.
A hurry-up word. *McAw*
Quiet please. *McAw*

Hinkson, Katharine Tynan. See Tynan, Katharine

A **hinted** wish. Martial, tr. fr. the Latin by Samuel Johnson. *BrL-8*

"**Hinty**, minty, cuty, corn." Unknown
Counting-out rhymes. *FeF*

Hinx, minx. See "Hinx, minx, the old witch winks"

"**Hinx**, minx, the old witch winks." Mother Goose. *DeMg*
Hinx, minx. *OpO*

"**Hippety-hop**, goes the kangaroo." See Up the hill

"**Hippety** hop to the barber shop." Mother Goose. *ArTp*

A **hippity**, hippity hop. Unknown. *HuL-1*

"A **hippity**, hippity, hippity hop, heigho." See A hippity, hippity hop

"**Hippity-hop**." See Away we go

Hippity hop to bed. Leroy F. Jackson. *ArTp—BrL-k*

The **hippocrump**. James Reeves. *ReP*

Hippolytus, sel. Euripides
O for the wings of a dove, tr. fr. the Greek by Gilbert Murray. *PaS*

Hippopotami
Habits of the hippopotamus. A. Guiterman. *ArTp—CoH*
The hippopotamus ("The broad-backed hippopotamus") T. S. Eliot. *HaP*
Hippopotamus ("The hippopotamus—hippo for short") W. J. Smith. *SmB*
The hippopotamus ("I shoot the hippopotamus") H. Belloc. *CoH*
The hippopotamus ("In the squdgy river") G. R. Durston. *ArTp*
The hippopotamus's birthday. E. V. Rieu. *RiF*

The **hippopotamus** ("The broad-backed hippopotamus") T. S. Eliot. *HaP*

Hippopotamus ("The hippopotamus—hippo for short") William Jay Smith. *SmB*

The **hippopotamus** ("I shoot the hippopotamus") Hilaire Belloc. *CoH*

The **hippopotamus** ("In the squdgy river") Georgia Roberts Durston. *ArTp*

"The **hippopotamus**—hippo for short." See Hippopotamus

"The **hippopotamus** is strong." See Habits of the hippopotamus

The **hippopotamus's** birthday. E. V. Rieu. *RiF*

"His bronze shone like a haze." See Eagle on the mountain crest

His cavalier. Robert Herrick. *GrCc*

"His eyes are quickened so with grief." See Lost love

"His eyes can be quite old and stern." See Father

"His face was the oddest that ever was seen." See The strange man

"His golden locks time hath to silver turned." See Polyhymnia

"His house is a haven where fingers dare." See Heart specialist

"His house was never short of bake-meat pies." See The Canterbury tales—A gluttonous rich man

"His iron arm had spent its force." See Death and General Putnam

His mother-in-law. Walter Parke. *CoH*

His mother's cooking. Lizzie M. Hadley. *BrR-5*

"His name it is Pedro-Pablo-Ignacio-Juan." See A feller I know

"His nightly song will scarce be missed." See Alley cat

"His nose is short and scrubby." See My dog

His prayer to Ben Jonson. Robert Herrick. *HaP*

"His stature was not very tall." See Sir Geoffrey Chaucer

"His tail is remarkably long." See Mixed beasts—The kangarooster

History. See also subdivision History under names of countries, as France—History
Our history. C. C. Coblentz. *FeF*
Verse. O. St J. Gogarty. *SmLg*

History of New York. Marchette Chute *ChA*

Hits and runs. Carl Sandburg. *SaW*

"Hitty Pitty within the wall." Mother Goose. *OpO*

Ho Chih-yuan
Ninth moon. tr. *PaS*

"Ho, for taxis green or blue." See Taxis

"Ho, for the Pirate Don Durk of Dowdee." See The Pirate Don Durk of Dowdee

"Ho, laughs the winter." See March

"Ho-ah, ho." See March speaks

The hoar apple tree. Eleanor Farjeon. *FaCb*

Hoatson, Florence
Autumn. *HuL-1*

"Hob, shoe, hob; hob, shoe, hob." Mother Goose. *OpO*

The hobbit, sels. J. R. R. Tolkien
"Roads go ever on and on." *FeF*
"Roads go ever ever on." *ArTp—BrR-5*
"There is an inn, a merry old inn." *LoL*
"Troll sat alone on his seat of stone." *LoL*

"Hobbled to market an old man and his boy." See The fable of the old man, the boy, and the donkey

Hobbs, Valine
A change of heart. *BrS*

Hobby-horses
The huntsmen. W. De La Mare. *ArTp—BrS—HuL-1—HuSv*

"I had a little hobby horse." Mother Goose. *DeMg*
My hobby horse. *OpO*

Hoberman, Mary Ann
The birthday bus. *BrBc*
Comparison. *BrBc*

"Hoddley, poddley, puddle and fogs." Mother Goose. *OpO*

"Hoddy doddy." Mother Goose. *OpO*

Hodgson, Ralph
The bells of heaven. *BrS—DeT—HaP*
Eve. *NaE*
The great auk's ghost. *NaM*
The mystery. *DoP*
"Reason has moons, but moons not hers." *SmLg*
Stupidity street. *BrS—DeT*
"Time, you old gipsy man." *BrS—FeF—McW—NaM—ReT*

Hoffenstein, Samuel
The gnu. *CoH*
Poems in praise of practically nothing. *NaE* (sel.)

Hoffman, Daniel G.
How we logged Katahdin stream. *UnMc*

Hoffmann, (August) Heinrich
The inky boys. *DeT*
The story of Augustus. See The story of Augustus who would not have any soup
The story of Augustus who would not have any soup. *DeT—NaM*
The story of Augustus. *ArTp*
The story of Johnny Head-in-air. *ArTp*
The story of little Suck-a-thumb. *NaE*

Hofmannstal, Hugo von
Poem. *PaS*

"Hog butcher for the world." See Chicago

Hogan, Inez
Blanket street. *BrBc*
Middle-aged child. *BrBc*

Hogg, James
A boy's song. *DeT—FeF—HoW—McW—NaM*

Hogs. See Pigs

Hokey pokey. Unknown. *TaD*

"Hokey pokey, hanky panky." See Hokey pokey

"Hokey, pokey, whisky, thum." Mother Goose. *OpO*

"Hold fast your dreams." Louise Driscoll. *ArTp—BrBc—FeF*

"Hold up your head." Mother Goose. *OpO*

Holding hands. Lenore M. Link. *ArTp—FeF—NaM*

Holiday ("Where are you going") Ella Young. *ArTp—HuL-2*

The holiday ("Yesterday our postman stuck") Dorothy Aldis. *AlA*

Holidays. See also names of holidays, as Christmas; Fourth of July
Holiday ("Where are you going") E. Young. *ArTp—HuL-2*
The holiday ("Yesterday our postman stuck") D. Aldis. *AlA*
"I must remember." S. Silverstein. *CoPs*
The next holiday. E. Farjeon. *FaCb*

Holland, Josiah Gilbert
God, give us men. *ThP*

Holland, Rupert Sargent
When I grow up. *BrBc—BrR-5*
Holland
A Dutch picture. H. W. Longfellow.
NaM
The leak in the dike. P. Cary. *FeF*
"The hollow winds begin to blow." See
Signs of rain
Holly. See Holly trees
"The holly and the ivy." Unknown. *DeT*
"Holly dark: pale mistletoe." See Nowel
Holly trees
"But give me holly, bold and jolly." C. G.
Rossetti. *ArTp*
"Green grow'th the holly." Unknown.
EaW
"Highty, tighty, paradighty." Mother
Goose. *OpO*
"The holly and the ivy." Unknown. *DeT*
"The holly's up, the house is all bright." See
The Christmas tree
Holm, Saxe, pseud. See Jackson, Helen
Hunt
Holmes, George S.
And yet fools say. *ArTp—BrL-7*
Holmes, John
At a country fair. *NaM*
Auction. *McW*
Old men and young men. *McW*
Rhyme of rain. *McW*
Holmes, Oliver Wendell
The ballad of the oysterman. *BrL-8—NaM*
The broomstick train. *CoPm* (sel.)—*FeF*
(sel.)
The deacon's masterpiece; or, The won-
derful one-hoss shay. *CoSp—HuSv—*
NaM—SmLg
The Dorchester giant. *FeF*
A farewell to Agassiz. *PlI*
Grandmother's story of Bunker hill battle.
UnG
The height of the ridiculous. *BrL-8—CoH*
—HuSv—NaM
The last leaf. *FeF—McW*
Old Ironsides. *FeF—UnMc*
"Said a great Congregational preacher."
UnG
The September gale. *CoH* (sel.)
A welcome to Dr Benjamin Apthorp
Gould. *PlI*
Holy lullaby. See "Sleep, baby, sleep (thy
father guards)"
The holy well. Unknown. *SmLg*
Homage to Diana. Walter Raleigh. *HoW*
Homage to the philosopher. Babette
Deutsch. *PlI*
"Homage to thee, O Ra, at thy tremendous
rising." See The book of the dead—The
dead man ariseth and singeth a hymn to
the sun
Homage to Vaslav Nijinsky. James Kirkup.
PlU
Home. See Home and family life
Home ("The Germans live in Germany")
J. H. Goring. *NaM*
Home ("Here is a thing my heart wishes")
See Poems done on a late night car
Home again. Enola Chamberlin. *McAw*

Home and family life. See also Family;
Home-sickness; Housekeepers and house-
keeping
"Bessy Bell and Mary Gray." Mother
Goose. *DeMg*
Bessy and Mary. *OpO*
The birthplace. R. Frost. *FrR—FrY—*
SmLg
Blueberries. R. Frost. *FrR—FrY* (sel.)
"The cat sat asleep by the side of the fire."
Mother Goose. *DeMg*
The cat sat asleep. *DeT*
Medley. *OpO*
A catch by the hearth. Unknown. *BrL-7*
The children's hour. H. W. Longfellow.
FeF—UnG
Christmas singing. E. W. Chandler. *BrS*
"Cross-patch." Mother Goose. *DeMg—*
JoAc—LiL—NaE—OpO
The death of the hired man. R. Frost.
FrR—FrY—UnMc
"God bless the master of this house."
Mother Goose. *DeMg—HuSv—OpO*
Christmas carol. *ArTp—BrS*
A grace. *NaM*
Grey. J. Reeves. *ReW*
Hame, hame, hame. A. Cunningham. *DeT*
The happy family. J. Ciardi. *CiM*
Hers. E. Farjeon. *FaCb*
Hiding. D. Aldis. *AlA—ArTp—BrL-k—*
FeF—JoAc
Home ("The Germans live in Germany")
J. H. Goring. *NaM*
Home ("Here is a thing my heart wishes")
From Poems done on a late night car.
C. Sandburg. *SaW*
Home again. Enola Chamberlin. *McAw*
Jest 'fore Christmas. E. Field. *FeF*
The lake isle of Innisfree. W. B. Yeats.
FeF—JoAc
The little bird. W. De La Mare. *BrBc*
Mr Nobody. Unknown. *BrR-4—CoPm—*
FeF—HuL-1—HuSv
Mrs Brown. R. Fyleman. *ArTp—BrL-k—*
HuL-1
No one heard him call. D. Aldis. *AlA*
An old woman of the roads. P. Colum.
FeF—HuL-2—HuSv
A prayer for a little home. F. Bone. *DoP*
Reading the book of hills and seas. T'ao
Ch'ien. *PaS*
"Remember the fourth commandment."
Unknown. *MoY*
Roofs J. Kilmer. *BrL-8*
Sailing homeward. Chan Fang-shēng.
PaS—SmLg
A serious step lightly taken. R. Frost.
FrR
Snow-bound, sels. J. G. Whittier
The schoolmaster. *UnG*
The snow. *HuSv*
Snow-bound. *HoW*
The uncle. *UnG*
"Unwarmed by any sunset light"
Lines from Snow-bound. *JoAc*
Song. H. W. Longfellow. *DeT*
"There was a man and his name was
Dob." Mother Goose. *DeMg*
Dob and Mob. *OpO*
"Time to go home." J. Reeves. *ReBl*

Vacation time. R. B. Bennett. *BrS*
"The warm of heart shall never lack a fire."
   E. J. Coatsworth. *ArTp*
"What does the bee do." C. G. Rossetti.
   ArTp—HuL-1
      What do they do. *FeF*
Wild thyme. E. Farjeon. *BrS*
Wilful homing. R. Frost. *FrR*
Home burial. Robert Frost. *FrR*
"Home from college came the stripling, calm
   and cool and debonair." See A college
   training
Home grown. Helen Houston Boileau.
   McAw

Home-sickness
The blackbird in the lilac. J. Reeves. *ReBl*
The fields of Ballyclare. D. A. McCarthy.
   BrL-7
Home-sickness. J. Kerner. *PaS*
Home thoughts from abroad. R. Brown-
   ing. *BrL-8—FeF—JoAc*
Homesick blues. L. Hughes. *McW*
The oak and the ash. Unknown. *SmLg*
On hearing a flute at night from the wall
   of Shou-Hsiang. Li Yi. *PlU*

Home-sickness. Justinus Kerner, tr. fr. the
   German by James Clarence Mangan.
   PaS
"Home they brought her sailor son." See
   The recognition
Home thoughts from abroad. Robert
   Browning. *BrL-8—FeF—JoAc*
Homely meats. John Davies. *SmLg*
Homer (about)
   On first looking into Chapman's Homer.
   J. Keats. *SmLg*
Homesick blues. Langston Hughes. *McW*
Homeward bound. William Allingham.
   BrL-7
Honesty. See Truthfulness and falsehood
Honey. See also Bees
   Brown bear's honey song. K. Jackson.
   McAw
The honey bee. Don Marquis. *CoH*
"The honey bee is sad and cross." See The
   honey bee
"The hoo-hah and the rinky-dink." See A
   cool drink on a hot day
Hood, Thomas
   The dream of Eugene Aram. *CoSp*
   Dust to dust. *UnG*
   Faithless Nelly Gray. *CoH*
   Good night. *BrS—JoAc*
   The haunted house. *HoW*
   I remember. See "I remember, I re-
      member"
   "I remember, I remember." *FeF—UnG*
      I remember. *DeT*
   Little piggy. *HuL-1*
   No. *CoH—UnG*
   A parental ode to my son, aged three
      years and five months. See To my son,
      aged three years and five months
   Precocious piggy. *BrL-k*
   Queen Mab. *HuSv*
   Ruth. *GrCc*
   She is far from the land. *HoW*
   The song of the shirt. *UnMc*

Tim Turpin. *HoW*
To my son, aged three years and five
   months. *FeF*
      A parental ode to my son, aged three
      years and five months. *CoH* (sel.)
Hooft, Pieter Corneliszoon
   Thus spoke my love. *PaS*
Hoosen Johnny. Unknown. *FeF*
"A hop, a skip, and off you go." See Danc-
   ing
"Hop and skip." See Robin
A hop, skip, and a jump. See "The miller he
   grinds his corn, his corn"
Hope
   The darkling thrush. T. Hardy. *HaP—
      NaE*
   Fairy song. J. Keats. *FeF*
   Hope. G. Herbert. *GrCc*
   "Hope is the thing with feathers." E.
      Dickinson. *ArTp—NaM*
   Keeping on. A. H. Clough. *NaM*
Hope. George Herbert. *GrCc*
"Hope is the thing with feathers." Emily
   Dickinson. *ArTp—NaM*
Hopi Indians. See Indians of America—
   Hopi
Hopkins, Gerard Manley
   For a picture of St Dorothea. *GrCc*
   The habit of perfection. *PlU* (sel.)
   Heaven-haven. *HaP—McW*
   Henry Purcell. *PlU*
   On a piece of music. *PlU*
   Pied beauty. *McW—ReT—UnG*
   Spring and fall. *HaP—ReT*
   The starlight night. *ReT*
Hopkins, J. G. E.
   Poems for a child. *DoP*
Hopper, Nora
   June. *HaY*
Hopping frog. Christina Georgina Rossetti.
   ReG
"Hopping frog, hop here and be seen." See
   Hopping frog
Hoppity. A. A. Milne. *ArTp—MiWc*
Horace (Quintus Horatius Flaccus)
   Call to youth. *PaS*
   The golden mean. *PaS*
   Ode to Maecenas. *PaS* (sel.)
      Today and tomorrow. *UnG* (sel.)
   To a girl. *HoW*
   Today and tomorrow. See Ode to
      Maecenas
Horatius. See Lays of ancient Rome
The horn. James Reeves. *ReBl*
Horne, Frank
   To James. *BrBc*
Hornets
   The white-tailed hornet. R. Frost. *FrR*
"The horny-goloch is an awesome beast."
   Unknown. *LoL*
The horse ("Hast thou given the horse
   strength") See Job
The horse ("I will not change my horse with
   any that treads") See King Henry V
Horse racing. See Rides and riding—Horse
"A horse would tire." Elizabeth Jane Coats-
   worth. *ArTp*

The **horseman**. Walter De La Mare. *ArTp*
　—*HuL-1*

Horsemanship. Marchette Chute. *ChA*

Horses. See also Rides and riding—Horse

Alexander to his horse. E. Farjeon. *FaCb*

The army horse and the army jeep. J.
　Ciardi. *CiR*

"As I was standing in the street." Un-
　known. *CoH*

Bare-back rider. D. Aldis. *AlA*

Charley Lee. H. H. Knibbs. *McW*

Daniel Webster's horses. E. J. Coatsworth.
　CoPm

Dappled Grey. Mother Goose. *OpO*

The distant runners. M. Van Doren.
　SmLg

"A farmer went trotting upon his gray
　mare." Mother Goose. *ArTp—DeMg—
　JoAc*
　　"A farmer went riding." *BrL-k—HuSv*
　　"A farmer went trotting." *HuL-1—
　　LiL—NaE*
　　The mischievous raven. *OpO*

The fly-away horse. E. Field. *UnG*

Foal. M. B. Miller. *ArTp—CoI*

The four horses. J. Reeves. *ReW*

The grey horse. J. Reeves. *ReW*

Hey, my pony. E. Farjeon. *FeF*

The horse ("Hast thou given the horse
　strength") From Job, Bible, Old Testa-
　ment. *FeF—UnG*

The horse ("I will not change my horse
　with any that treads") From King
　Henry V. W. Shakespeare. *UnG*

The horseman. W. De La Mare. *ArTp—
　HuL-1*

Horsemanship. M. Chute. *ChA*

Horses ("Back and forth") A. Fisher.
　McAw

The horses ("Barely a twelvemonth
　after") E. Muir. *HaP*

Horses ("Those lumbering horses in the
　steady plough") E. Muir. *SmLg*

Horses chawin' hay. H. Garland. *HuSv*

"The horses of Achilles." E. Farjeon.
　FaCb

"The horses of the sea." C. G. Rossetti.
　FeF

"Heroes on horseback." J. Reeves. *ReR*

Husky hi. Unknown. *ArTp—JoAc*

"I had a little horse (his name was
　Dapple-gray)." Unknown. *WoF*

"I had a little pony." Mother Goose.
　*BrL-k — DeMg — DeT — HuL-1 —
　HuSv—JoAc—LiL*
　　The bad rider. *OpO*

"I went to the river and couldn't get
　across (I paid five dollars)." Unknown.
　WoF

In Lincoln lane. Mother Goose. *OpO*

"John Cook he had a little gray mare."
　Mother Goose. *DeMg*
　　He, haw, hum. *HuL-1*
　　Hee haw, hum. *DeT*
　　John Cook's mare. *ReG*
　　The last will and testament of the
　　grey mare. *OpO*

Kentucky Belle. C. F. Woolson. *CoSp—
　UnG—UnMc*

The leap of Roushan Beg. H. W. Long-
　fellow. *HuSv*

Little nag. Mother Goose. *OpO*

"A little old man came riding by." Un-
　known
　　American Father Gander. *UnG*

"Little pony, little pony." Unknown.
　JoAc

The milkman's horse. Unknown. *BrL-k—
　CoI—HuL-1*

Money works wonders. Mother Goose.
　OpO

My horse. Unknown. *TaD*

My horse, Jack. J. Ciardi. *CiY*

My pony. D. Aldis. *AlA*

Noonday Sun. K. and B. Jackson. *ArTp—
　FeF—HuL-2*

Old Ponto. Unknown. *TaD*

On a clergyman's horse. Unknown. *UnG*

"One white foot, buy him." Unknown.
　WoF

The ponies. W. W. Gibson. *McW*

The pony. Unknown. *TaD*

Poor old horse. Unknown. *ReG*

The priest and the mulberry tree. From
　Crotchet castle. T. L. Peacock. *CoSp—
　DeT*

The runaway. R. Frost. *ArTp—FeF—FrR
　—FrY—HuL-2—HuSv—SmLg—UnG*

"See, see, what shall I see." Mother
　Goose. *OpO*

"Shoe a little horse." Mother Goose.
　DeMg—LiL—OpO

Sing-song. D. McCord. *McT*

Susie the milk horse. D. Aldis. *AlA*

The three horses. I. O. Eastwick. *EaI*

To the shop. Unknown. *JoAc*

"Trot along, pony." M. Edey. *ArTp*

The war god's horse song. Unknown.
　SmLg

Widdecombe fair. Unknown. *CoPm*
　　Widdicombe fair. *NaM*

The Zebra Dun. Unknown. *CoSp—HuSv*

Horses ("Back and forth") Aileen Fisher.
　McAw

The **horses** ("Barely a twelvemonth after")
　Edwin Muir. *HaP*

Horses ("Those lumbering horses in the
　steady plough") Edwin Muir. *SmLg*

Horses chawin' hay. Hamlin Garland. *HuSv*

"The **horses** of Achilles." Eleanor Farjeon.
　FaCb

"The **horses** of the sea." Christina Georgina
　Rossetti. *FeF*

"The **horses**, the pigs, and the chickens."
　See Familiar friends

The **horseshoe**. See From a very little
　sphinx—"Wonder where this horseshoe
　went"

The **horseshoe** nail. See "For want of a nail,
　the shoe was lost"

Horseshoes. See also Blacksmiths and blacksmithing
"For want of a nail, the shoe was lost." Mother Goose. *DeMg—LiL*
  "For want of a nail." *OpO*
  The horseshoe nail. *ThP*
  Tremendous trifles. *UnG*
"Wonder where this horseshoe went." From From a very little sphinx. E. St V. Millay. *ArTp*
  The horseshoe. *HuSv*
  Wonder where. *PeF*

Hospitality
Baucis and Philemon. J. Swift. *CoSp*
"Hot boiled beans and very good butter." Mother Goose. *DeMg*
"Hot cross buns." Mother Goose. *DeMg—JoAc—OpO*
"Hot cross buns, hot cross buns (one a penny)." See Good Friday
"The hot May night is like July." See Spring night in a village
The hot pease man. Mother Goose. *OpO*
Hot weather. Dorothy Aldis. *AlA*
A hot-weather song. Don Marquis. *HuSv*
The Hottentot tot. Newman Levy. *HuL-2*
  Midsummer fantasy. *CoPs*

Houghton, George Washington Wright
The March winds. *HaY*

Houghton, Lord. See Milne, Richard Monckton

The hound. Sidney Lanier. *CoPm*
"The hound was cuffed, the hound was kicked." See The hound
"Hour after hour." See People
Hours of idleness. George Gordon Byron. *NaE*
Hours of sleep. Unknown. *UnG*
The house and the road. Josephine Preston Peabody. *BrR-5*
"The house at the corner." Myra Cohn Livingston. *LiWa*
The house beyond the meadow, sels. Harry Behn. *BeH* (complete)
  The bears who once were giants
  First enchantment
  A friendly visit
  Goodbye to fairyland
  The magic map
  The strangest wish
  The thunder-and-lightning bug
House blessing ("Bless the four corners of this house") Arthur Guiterman. *ArTp*
A house blessing ("God bless the corners of this house") Unknown. *ThP*
The house cat. Annette Wynne. *BrL-k—HuSv*
"The house cat sits." See The house cat
"A house full, a hole full." See "A house full, a yard full"
"A house full, a yard full." Mother Goose. *LiL*
  "A house full, a hole full." *OpO*
"The house had gone to bring again." See The need of being versed in country things

"The house is made of gopher wood." Unknown. *WiRm*
The house of Christmas. Gilbert Keith Chesterton. *EaW*
"The house of the mouse." Lucy Sprague Mitchell. *ArTp—CoI*
The house on the hill. Edwin Arlington Robinson. *FeF—HaP*
The house that Jack built. See "This is the house that Jack built"
"The house that we live in was built in a place." See Portrait of a house
The house with nobody in it. Joyce Kilmer. *HuSv*
The housekeeper. Robert Frost. *FrR*
Housekeepers and housekeeping. See also Servants
The fairies. R. Herrick. *FeF*
  Queen Mab. *ReG*
Helpfulness. M. Chute. *ChA*
"High diddle doubt, my candle's out." Mother Goose. *DeMg*
The housekeeper. R. Frost. *FrR*
I like housecleaning. D. B. Thompson. *FeF*
"I married my wife by the light of the moon." Mother Goose. *DeMg*
Mrs Button. J. Reeves. *ReBl*
Mrs Gilfillan. J. Reeves. *ReBl*
On a tired housewife. Unknown. *NaE*
"One, two, three, four (mama scrubbed)." Unknown. *WoF*
Wash the dishes. Mother Goose. *OpO*
Washing up. Mother Goose. *OpO*
When young Melissa sweeps. N. B. Turner. *FeF*

Housekeeping. See Housekeepers and housekeeping

Houses
Animals' houses. J. Reeves. *ReW*
Bobadil. J. Reeves. *ReBl*
Buildings. M. C. Livingston. *LiW*
The census-taker. R. Frost. *FrR*
Cold house. I. Carlisle. *BrL-7*
Conversation. R. Fyleman. *HuL-1*
Deserted. M. Cawein. *BrL-7*
The deserted house. M. Coleridge. *DeT—ReT*
The difference. M. C. Livingston. *LiW*
Doorbells. R. Field. *ArTp—FeF—HuSv*
The floor and the ceiling. W. J. Smith. *CoH*
Fun in a garret. E. C. Dowd. *ArTp—BrR-3*
Ghost house. R. Frost. *FrR*
The goblin. Unknown. *ArTp—JoAc*
The haunted house. T. Hood. *HoW*
The haunted palace. E. A. Poe. *HoW*
The house and the road. J. P. Peabody. *BrR-5*
"The house at the corner." M. C. Livingston. *LiWa*
House blessing ("Bless the four corners of this house") A. Guiterman. *ArTp*
A house blessing ("God bless the corners of this house") Unknown. *ThP*
"The house of the mouse." L. S. Mitchell. *ArTp—CoI*

Houses—*Continued*
    The house on the hill. E. A. Robinson.
        FeF—HaP
    The house with nobody in it. J. Kilmer.
        HuSv
    I built my hut. T'ao Ch'ien. *PaS*
    I know some lonely houses. E. Dickinson.
        CoPm—McW
    "I wish that my room had a floor." G.
        Burgess. *CoH—LoL*
        Limericks since Lear. *UnG*
    If I had a cardboard box. A. Fisher.
        McAw
    Johnny Fife and Johnny's wife. M. P.
        Meigs. *ArTp—BrL-7—HuL-1*
    The kitchen chimney. R. Frost. *FrR—FrY*
    "Lady will you come with me into." E. E.
        Cummings. *ReT*
    Little girl. Unknown. *JoAc*
    May is building her house. R. Le Gal-
        lienne. *HaY*
    Mr Bellairs. J. Reeves. *ReBl*
    The need of being versed in country
        things. R. Frost. *FrR—HaP*
    The new house. D. Aldis. *AlHd*
    Old log house. J. S. Tippett. *FeF*
    The playhouse key. R. Field. *FeF*
    Portrait of a house. E. V. Rieu. *RiF*
    Prairie-dog town. M. Austin. *ArTp—FeF*
        —HuSv
    Prayer for this house. L. Untermeyer.
        BrR-6—FeF—HuL-2
    Saddest of all. D. Aldis. *AlA*
    The shepherd's hut. A. Young. *ReT*
    The shiny little house. N. M. Hayes.
        HuL-1
    Solitude. A. A. Milne. *MiWc*
    Song for a little house. C. Morley. *BrR-6*
        —FeF—HuSv—JoAc
    Stairs. O. Herford. *CoH*
    A thanksgiving to God for his house.
        R. Herrick. *DeT*
    This holy night. E. Farjeon. *DoP*
        Christmas carol. *HuL-2*
    "This is the house that Jack built." Mother
        Goose. *DeMg—HuSv—JoAc—LiL*
        The house that Jack built. *OpO*
    To a guardian mouse. E. J. Coatsworth.
        CoM
    Tree house. D. Aldis. *AlHd*
    Two houses. E. Thomas. *SmLg*
    Vicary square. J. Reeves. *ReW*
    We know a house. D. Aldis. *AlA*
    Who's in. E. Fleming. *BrL-k—PeF*
    The wrong house. A. A. Milne. *MiWc*
"**The houses** are haunted." See Disillusion-
    ment of ten o'clock
"**A housewife** called out with a frown." Un-
    known
    Limericks since Lear. *UnG*
Housman, Alfred Edward
    Infant innocence. *SmLg*
    Inhuman Henry; or, Cruelty to fabulous
        animals. *CoH*
    "Into my heart an air that kills." See A
        Shropshire lad
    "Is my team ploughing." See A Shrop-
        shire lad
    The Lent lily. See A Shropshire lad

Loveliest of trees. See A Shropshire lad
    March. *SmLg*
    Old age. tr. *PaS*
    Revolution. *PlI*
    The shades of night. *CoH*
    A Shropshire lad, sels.
        "Into my heart an air that kills"
            A Shropshire lad. *NaE*
        "Is my team ploughing." *HaP*
        The Lent lily. *CoPs*
        Loveliest of trees. *HuSv—JoAc*
        To an athlete dying young. *HaP—*
            UnMc
        "When I was one-and-twenty." *BrBc*
    To an athlete dying young. See A Shrop-
        shire lad
    "To think that two and two are four." *PlI*
    "When I was one-and-twenty." See A
        Shropshire lad
    "Yonder see the morning blink." *NaM*
Hovey, Richard
    The sea gypsy. *BrL-7—FeF—UnG*
How a fisherman corked up his foe in a jar.
    Guy Wetmore Carryl. *CoPm*
"**How** all's to one thing wrought." See On a
    piece of music
"**How** am I to withhold my soul." See Love
    song
"**How** and why." Robert Graves. *GrP*
"**How** bright on the blue." See The kite
"**How** can a man's life keep its course." See
    The way of life
How can man die better. Tyrtaeus, tr. fr. the
    Greek by T. F. Higham. *PaS*
"**How** cool the breeze." See Coolness
"**How** dear to this heart are the scenes of my
    childhood." See The old oaken bucket
"**How** did that duck." See That duck
How did you die. Edmund Vance Cooke.
    ThP
"**How** do robins build their nests." See
    What robin told
"**How** do you like to go up in a swing." See
    The swing
"**How** doth the little busy bee." Isaac Watts.
    FeF
    The bee. *UnG*
    Little busy bee. *HuSv*
"**How** doth the little crocodile." See Alice's
    adventures in wonderland
"**How** falls it, oriole, thou hast come to fly."
    See Oriole
"**How** far is it to Bethlehem." Frances
    Chesterton. *DoP—EaW*
    Children's song of the nativity. *DeT*
"**How** far, today." See Far away
"**How** gray the rain." Elizabeth Jane Coats-
    worth. *ArTp*
How happy the soldier. Unknown. *SmLg*
"**How** happy the soldier who lives on his
    pay." See How happy the soldier
"**How** in heaven's name did Columbus get
    over." See Columbus
"**How** it sings, sings, sings." See Song of the
    sea wind
"**How** large unto the tiny fly." See The fly
"**How** lost is the little fox at the borders of
    night." See Night of wind

"How loudly and how surely the musician plays." See The musician

"How lovely in the English wood." See Five trees

"How many candles shall we light." See Birthday candles

How many carriages. Unknown. *WoJ*

"How many days has my baby to play." Mother Goose. *ArTp—OpO*

"How many dear companions who enlivened for us." See Remembrance

"How many fairy gardens, Hans." See Fairy gardens

How many heavens. Edith Sitwell. *GrCc*

How many miles. Unknown. *WoJ*

"How many miles to Babylon." Mother Goose. *DeMg — HuL-1 — JoAc — LiL —NaM—OpO—SmLg—WiRm*

"How many nights, oh, how many nights." See New year's day

"How many seconds in a minute." Christina Georgina Rossetti. *BrS*

"How many silk coats is to-day." See Silk coats

"How mighty a wizard." See Z is for Zoroaster

"How much do you love me." Unknown. *WoF*

How much is true. John Ciardi. *CiM*

"How much wood would a wood-chuck chuck." Mother Goose. *ArTp—HuSv—JoAc—WiRm*

If a woodchuck would chuck. *FeF*

How nice. Mary Dixon Thayer. *DoP*

"How nice it is, dear God, to know." See How nice

"How odd it would be if ever a tapir." See Tapir

"How old is thirty-six, about." See Prattle

"How pleasant to know Mr Lear." Edward Lear. *CoH—UnG*

By way of preface. *HaP*

How Robin Hood rescued the widow's sons. See Robin Hood rescuing the widow's three sons

"How she held up the horses' heads." See A woman driving

"How should I your true love know." See Hamlet—Ophelia's song

"How should I your true love know." See An old song ended

"How silent comes the water round that bend." See "I stood tiptoe upon a little hill"—Minnows

"How smooth's your brow, my lady Elspat." See Lady Elspat

How still the bells. Emily Dickinson. *ReG*

"How still the bells in steeples stand." See How still the bells

"How sweet is the shepherd's sweet lot." See The shepherd

How tall. David McCord. *McT*

"How tall, they say." See How tall

How the frightful child grew better. John Ciardi. *CiY*

"How the mountains talked together." See A farewell to Agassiz

How the rats were destroyed. See The Pied Piper of Hamelin

How they brought the good news from Ghent to Aix. Robert Browning. *ArTp —HuSv—UnG*

"How time reverses." See For my contemporaries

How to ask and have. Samuel Lover. *BrR-6*

How to know the wild animals. See How to tell the wild animals

How to tell a tiger. John Ciardi. *CiY*

How to tell goblins from elves. Monica Shannon. *ArTp—FeF*

How to tell the top of a hill. John Ciardi. *CiR*

How to tell the wild animals. Carolyn Wells. *ArTp—CoH—FeF*

How to know the wild animals. *UnG*

How to tell wild animals. *UnMc*

How to tell wild animals. See How to tell the wild animals

How to write a letter. Elizabeth Turner. *NaM*

"How vainly men themselves amaze." See The garden

How we logged Katahdin stream. Daniel G. Hoffman. *UnMc*

How Woodrow got his dinner. John Ciardi. *CiR*

Howard, Winifred
A windy day. *FeF*

Howe, Julia Ward
Battle-hymn of the republic. *FeF—UnG*

Howe, Mark A. De Wolfe
Ben Franklin's head. *McW*

Howells, Mildred
Going too far. *ArTp*

Howells, William Dean
The robin and the cows. *UnG*

Howes, Barbara
Cat on couch. *HaP*

"However they talk, whatever they say." See Motto

Howitt, Mary
The child's hymn. *UnG*
The fairies of the Caldon Low. *ReG*
The lion. *FeF*
September. *HuL-2*
The spider and the fly. *DeT—FeF—PeF*
The true story of the web-spinner. *DeT*

Howitt, William
The wind in a frolic. *NaM—ReG*

"How's your father, came the whisper." See Conversational

"Hoyda, hoyda, jolly rutterkin." See Rutterkin

Hoyt, Helen
At daybreak. *BrBc*

Hubert, Saint (about)
Saint Hubert. E. Farjeon. *FaCb*

Hucksters. See Peddlers and venders

Hudibras, Canto I. Samuel Butler. *PlI* (sel.)

Hudibras, Canto III. Samuel Butler. *PlI* (sel.)

Huff, Barbara A.
Afternoon with grandmother. *FeF*
The library. *FeF*

Hughes, Asa
First snowfall. tr. *PaS*
Hughes, Langston
African dance. *FeF*
April rain song. *ArTp—FeF—PeF*
City. *FeF*
Cycle. *FeF*
Heaven. *ArTp*
Homesick blues. *McW*
"In time of silver rain." *ArTp*
Life is fine. *McW*
Mother to son. *BrBc—HuSv—PeF*
Proposition. tr. *FeF*
Refugee in America. *McW*
Snail. *ArTp*
The weary blues. *PlU*
Wisdom. *ArTp*
Youth. *BrBc*
Hughes, Richard
Explanation, on coming home late. *ReT*
Old cat Care. *ReT*
Winter. *ReT*
Hughes, William R.
The wind's song. tr. *PaS*
Hugo, Victor (Marie, Vicomte)
Be like the bird. *ArTp—FeF*
Wings. *JoAc*
Good night. *ArTp—BrS—DoP—FeF*
Wings. See Be like the bird
Human body. See Body, Human
Human race. See Man
A human instinct. See Translations from the Chinese
The **human** seasons. John Keats. *HoW*
Humane thought. See The cheerful cherub
The **humble-bee.** Ralph Waldo Emerson. *FeF* (sel.)
Humble pomp. See New Prince, new pomp
"**Humble** we must be, if to heaven we go." See Humility
Hume, Tobias
Soldier's song. *HoW*
Humility
Ben Franklin's head. M. A. De Wolfe Howe. *McW*
Humility. R. Herrick. *UnG*
"If humility and purity be not in the heart." From The rock. T. S. Eliot. *ArTp*
Low and high. E. Farjeon. *FaCb—FaN*
Recessional. R. Kipling. *BrL-7*
The shepherd boy sings in the valley of humiliation. From The pilgrim's progress. J. Bunyan. *UnG*
Humility. Robert Herrick. *UnG*
The **humming** bird. Harry Kemp. *FeF*
Humming birds
The humming bird. H. Kemp. *FeF*
The hummingbird ("A route of evanescence") E. Dickinson. *UnG*
The hummingbird ("The smallest bird in the wide world") F. M. Frost. *FrLn*
The **hummingbird** ("A route of evanescence") Emily Dickinson. *UnG*
The **hummingbird** ("The smallest bird in the wide world") Frances M. Frost. *FrLn*
The **humorist.** Keith Preston. *NaE*

Humorists
The height of the ridiculous. O. W. Holmes. *BrL-8—CoH—HuSv—NaM*
The humorist. K. Preston. *NaE*
Humphries, Rolfe
Harp music. *PlU*
Static. *PlU*
Variation on a theme by Francis Kilvert. *PlU*
Humpty Dumpty. See "Humpty Dumpty sat on a wall"
"**Humpty** Dumpty sat on a wall." Mother Goose. *DeMg—HuSv—JoAc—LiL—OpO*
Humpty Dumpty. *BrL-k*
Humpty Dumpty's recitation. See Through the looking glass
A **hundred** collars. Robert Frost. *FrR*
"**Hundreds** of stars in the pretty sky." See Only one mother
Hunger and thirst. Barbara Young. *McAw*
Hunger-harvest. Eleanor Farjeon. *FaCb—FaN*
Hungry morning. Myra Cohn Livingston. *LiWa*
Hunt, Helen. See Jackson, Helen Hunt
Hunt, (James Henry) Leigh
Abou Ben Adhem. *BrR-6—ThP—UnG*
Abou Ben Adhem and the angel. *FeF*
Abou Ben Adhem and the angel. See Abou Ben Adhem
Fairies' song. *CoPm*
Fish to man. *NaM*
The glove and the lions. *FeF—UnMc*
Jenny kissed me. *BrBc*
On the grasshopper and cricket. *UnG*
The story of Rimini. *NaE* (sel.)
The **hunt.** Louis Kent. *McW*
The **hunt** is up. Unknown. *DeT*
"The **hunt** is up, the hunt is up." See The hunt is up
The **hunter** ("Bang bang, he is a hunter") Dorothy Aldis. *AlA*
The **hunter** ("The hunter crouches in his blind") Ogden Nash. *NaE*
The **hunter** ("The tiny young hunter arose with the morn") David McCord. *McFf*
"A **hunter** cried out when he spotted a tiger." See Tiger
"The **hunter** crouches in his blind." See The hunter
Hunters and hunting. See also Falcons and falconry
A-hunting we will go. *DeT*
"All in green went my love riding." E. E. Cummings. *ReT*
All the rabbits and Robin A'Dare. I. O. Eastwick. *EaI*
The chase. A. Gregor. *GrCc*
Chevy-Chase. Unknown. *MaB*
The cutty wren. Unknown. *HoW*
Dangerous. D. Aldis. *AlA*
Friar's hunting song. T. L. Peacock. *UnG*
The old friar remembers. *DeT*
The grey goose. Unknown. *McW*
The hunt. L. Kent. *McW*
The hunt is up. Unknown. *DeT*
The hunter ("Bang bang, he is a hunter") D. Aldis. *AlA*
The hunter ("The hunter crouches in his blind") O. Nash. *NaE*

The hunter ("The tiny young hunter arose with the morn") D. McCord. *McFf*

The hunting of the snark. L. Carroll. *CoH* (sel.)
> The beaver's lesson. *JoAc*

Hunting song ("Up, up, ye dames, and lasses gay") S. T. Coleridge. *ReT*

Hunting song ("Waken, lords and ladies gay") W. Scott. *HoW—NaE*

The intruder. J. Reeves. *ReBl*

Like as a huntsman. E. Spenser. *HaP*

Lord Arnaldos. J. E. Flecker. *CoSp*

"A man went a-hunting at Reigate." Mother Goose. *DeMg*

One-eyed gunner. Mother Goose. *OpO*

"Possum up a gum tree." Unknown. *WiRm*

A runnable stag. J. Davidson. *HoW—NaE*

There was a hunter from Littletown. J. Ciardi. *CiM*

"There was a little man, and he had a little gun." Mother Goose. *DeMg—JoAc*
> Sam, the sportsman. *OpO*
> "There was a little man." *HuL-1—LiL*

"There were three jovial Welshmen." Mother Goose. *DeMg—JoAc*
> "There were three jovial huntsmen." *HuSv*
> The three huntsmen. *PaOm*
> "Three jolly huntsmen." *UnG*
> The three jovial Welshmen. *OpO*
> The three Welshmen. *NaM*

The three jolly hunters. J. W. Riley. *McW*

The wren hunt. Mother Goose. *OpO*

Hunting. See Hunters and hunting

"Hunting my cat along the evening brook." See Night heron

The hunting of the snark. Lewis Carroll. *CoH* (sel.)
> The beaver's lesson. *JoAc*

Hunting song ("Up, up, ye dames, and lasses gay") Samuel Taylor Coleridge. *ReT*

Hunting song ("Waken, lords and ladies gay") Walter Scott. *HoW—NaE*

The huntsmen. Walter De La Mare. *ArTp—BrS—HuL-1—HuSv*

The hurdy-gurdy. Elizabeth Fleming. *HuL-2*

"Hurly, hurly, roon the table." Unknown. *SmLg*

Hurnard, James
Winter. *CoPs*

The hurricane. Pales Matos, tr. fr. the Spanish by Alida Malkus. *FeF*

"Hurry to bless the hands that play." See The players ask for a blessing on the psalteries and on themselves

Hurry tomorrow. Ivy O. Eastwick. *BrBc*

A hurry-up word. Emily M. Hilsabeck. *McAw*

"Hurt no living thing." Christina Georgina Rossetti. *BrS—FeF*

Husbands. See Married life

"Hush-a-ba birdie, croon, croon." Mother Goose. *OpO*

"Hush-a-baa, baby." Mother Goose. *OpO*

"Hush-a-by, baby." See Italian lullaby

"Hush-a-bye a baa lamb." Mother Goose. *OpO*

"Hush-a-bye, baby (daddy is near)." Mother Goose. *DeMg*

"Hush-a-bye, baby, on the tree top." Mother Goose. *DeMg—HuSv—JoAc—LiL—OpO*

"Hush-a-bye, baby (the beggar)." Mother Goose. *OpO*

"Hush-a-bye, baby, they're gone to milk." Mother Goose. *OpO*

"Hush, baby, my doll, I pray you don't cry." Mother Goose. *DeMg*

"A hush had fallen on the birds." See The young calves

"Hush, little baby, don't say a word." Mother Goose. *OpO*

"Hush, my baby, do not cry." Mother Goose. *OpO*

"Hush, my dear, lie still and slumber." See Cradle hymn

"Hush now, my little one, and sleep." See Christmas lullaby

"Hush thee, my babby." Mother Goose. *DeMg—OpO*

"Hushaba, birdie, croon, croon." See Cradle song

"Hushaby, don't you cry." Unknown. *WoF*

"Hushie ba, burdie beeton." Mother Goose. *OpO*

Husky hi. Unknown, tr. fr. the Norwegian by Rose Fyleman. *ArTp—JoAc*

"Husky hi, husky hi." See Husky hi

Hussey, N. E.
Toad the tailor. *HuL-1*

Hutchinson, M. M.
Harvest. *HuL-2*
My new umbrella. *HuL-1*
Ten little Indian boys. *HuL-1*

Hutchison, Collister
Winter night. *ArTp*

Hyde, Douglas
"My grief on the sea." tr. *PaS*

Hyder iddle. Mother Goose. *OpO*

"Hyder iddle diddle dell." See Hyder iddle

Hyla brook. Robert Frost. *FrR—FrY*

A hymn for Saturday. Christopher Smart. *ReG*
> A lark's nest. *SmLg*

A hymn of nature. Robert Bridges. *HaY*

Hymn of Pan. Percy Bysshe Shelley. *SmLg*

Hymn to Diana. See Cynthia's revels

Hymn to the sun. Michael Roberts. *SmLg*

Hymn to Venus. Lucretius, tr. fr. the Latin by Basil Bunting. *GrCc*

Hymne to God my God, in my sicknesse. John Donne. *PlU* (sel.)

Hymns
"Alleluia. Alleluia. Let the holy anthem rise." Unknown. *CoPs*
Battle-hymn of the republic. J. W. Howe. *FeF—UnG*
The child's hymn. M. Howitt. *UnG*

Hymns—*Continued*

Cradle hymn ("Away in a manger, no crib for a bed") M. Luther. *ArTp—BrBc—DoP — EaW — FeF — HuL-1 — HuSv —JoAc—McAw—UnG*

Cradle hymn ("Hush, my dear, lie still and slumber") I. Watts. *DoP*

The dead man ariseth and singeth a hymn to the sun. From The book of the dead. Unknown. *PaS*

Evening hymn ("The day is done") E. M. Roberts. *ArTp*

Evening hymn ("I hear no voice, I feel no touch") Unknown. *BrL-k—DoP*

An evening hymn for a little family. A. and J. Taylor. *DoP*

Funeral hymn. Unknown. *PaS*

Hymn of Pan. P. B. Shelley. *SmLg*

Hymn to Diana. From Cynthia's revels. B. Jonson *HoW*

Hymn to the sun. M. Roberts. *SmLg*

Hymn to Venus. Lucretius. *GrCc*

Hymne to God my God, in my sicknesse. J. Donne. *PlU* (sel.)

Lead Kindly Light. J. H. Newman. *BrL-7*

"Let us with a gladsome mind." J. Milton. *DeT*

    Praise the Lord. *SmLg*

Light shining out of darkness. W. Cowper. *SmLg*

"Now the day is over." S. Baring-Gould. *DeT*

"O little town of Bethlehem." P. Brooks. *FeF—JoAc—ReG*

Old hundredth. T. Ken. *PlU*

Recessional. R. Kipling. *BrL-7*

"The spacious firmament on high." J. Addison. *BrL-7*

"There were three little birds in a wood." Unknown

    Limericks since Lear. *UnG*

Hynd Etin. Unknown. *MaB*

Hynd Horn. Unknown. *MaB*

"**Hynd** Horn's bound, love, and Hynd Horn's free." See Hynd Horn

I

"I act monkey motions." See Motions

"I always shout when grandma comes." See Afternoon with grandmother

"I always thought, old witch." See A Halloween meeting

"I am." See Nirvana

I am ("I am willowy boughs") Hilda Conkling. *ArTp—FeF*

I am ("I am: yet what I am none cares or knows") John Clare. *HaP*

"I am a bold fellow." See The young dandelion

"I am a gentleman in a dustcoat trying." See Piazza piece

"I am a gold lock." Mother Goose. *JoAc*

"I am a little Dutch girl." See Little Dutch girl

"I am a pretty little Dutch girl." Unknown. *TaD*

"I am a pretty wench." See Plaint

"I am a very little girl." See Little Phillis

"I am an American." Elias Lieberman. *FeF*

"I am asked to the ball to-night, to-night." See The fairy ball

"I am cold and alone." See The boy fishing

"I am exceedingly rich." See Cat

"I am fevered with the sunset." See The sea gypsy

"I am his Highness' dog at Kew." See Dogs

"I am no poet." Unknown. *MoY*

"I am of Ireland." See The Irish dancer

"I am off down the road." See Goblin feet

"I am only one." Canon Farrar. *ThP*

"I am out on the wind." See Changeling

"I am poor and old and blind." See Belisarius

"I am riding on a limited express, one of the crack trains of the nation." See Limited

"I am the ancient apple-queen." See Pomona

"I am the cat of cats. I am." See Kitty: What she thinks of herself

"I am the dog world's best detective." See The bloodhound

"I am the family face." See Heredity

"I am the rooftree and the keel." See Tapestry trees

"I am the sister of him." See Little

"I am the turquoise woman's son." See The war god's horse song

"I am tired of this barn, said the colt." See The barn

"I am willowy boughs." See I am

"I am: yet what I am none cares or knows." See I am

"I am Pangur Bán, my cat." See Pangur Bán

I asked my mother. See "I asked my mother for fifteen cents"

"I asked my mother for fifteen cents." Unknown. *ArTp*

    American Father Gander. *UnG*

    I asked my mother. *NaM*

    "I asked my mother for fifty cents." *JoAc*

"I asked my mother for fifty cents." See "I asked my mother for fifteen cents"

"I asked the heaven of stars." See Night song at Amalfi

"I ate my egg. I ate my toast." See Goodness me

"I bear a basket lined with grass." See For a picture of St Dorothea

"I been t'inkin' 'bout de preachah; whut he said de othah night." See Philosophy

"I beg you on this page of pink." Unknown. *MoY*

"I believe a leaf of grass is no less than the journey-work of the stars." See Song of myself

I bended unto me. Thomas Edward Brown. *CoPs*

"I bended unto me a bough of may." See I bended unto me

"I bent unto the ground." See The voice of God

"I bet my maid." Unknown. *MoY*

"I bet you I can make any fool in town." Unknown. *MoY*

"I bind unto myself today." See St Patrick's breastplate

"I boiled hot water in an urn." Unknown, after Nicarchus. *JoAc*

"I bought me a parrot in Trinidad." See Parrot

"I bring fresh showers for the thirsting flowers." See The cloud

"I bring you my rose." See June's song

I built my hut. T'ao Ch'ien, tr. fr. the Chinese by Arthur Waley. *PaS*

"I built my hut in a zone of human habitation." See I built my hut

"I called to gray squirrel, Good-day, good-day." See Conversation

"I came an errand one cloud-blowing evening." See The census-taker

"I came on them yesterday—merely by chance." See Pussy willows

"I came to look, and lo." See The fall of the plum blossoms

"I can bridle a horse." See Cleverness

"I can get through a doorway without any key." See The wind

"I can play." See Lamplighter barn

"I can run faster than you." See Watch me

"I can see a picture." See Pictures

"I cannot dance upon my toes." Emily Dickinson. *PlU*

"I cannot see fairies." See Fairies

"I cannot see the wind at all." See God is like this

"I cannot sleep or take the air." See A snowy day

"I cannot tell why this imagined." See The Lorelei

I can't decide. Frances M. Frost. *FrLn*

"I can't decide which I like best." See I can't decide

"I can't remember where I'd been." See The green door

"I carefully spade up the ground." See Home grown

"I carry bits of bread along." See Out walking

"I caught a fish and I." See What happened

"I caught a tremendous fish." See The fish

"I certainly have been a help." See Helpfulness

"I chose blue." Unknown. *MoY*

"I climbed up on the merry-go-round." See Merry-go-round

"I climbed up the door." Unknown. *MoY*

"I come from haunts of coot and hern." See The brook

"I come from Salem county." See Cowboy song

"I come more softly than a bird." Mary Austin
Rhyming riddles. *ArTp*

"I come to see Miss Jennie Jones." See Miss Jennie Jones

I could give all to time. Robert Frost. *FrR*

"I could not keep love down." See The thousand nights and one—The power of love

"I creep across enchanted land." See Indecision

"I dance and dance without any feet." See Spells

"I do not know much about gods; but I think that the river." See The dry salvages

"I do not like thee, Doctor Fell." Martial, tr. fr. the Latin by Thomas Brown. *DeMg—NaM*
Doctor Fell. *OpO*
Non amo te. *PlI*
Signs, seasons, and sense. *UnG*

"I do not love thee, Doctor Fell." See "I do not like thee, Doctor Fell"

"I don't go much on religion." See Little Breeches

"I don't know who they are." See The pointed people

"I don't know why." Myra Cohn Livingston. *LiW*

"I don't like the look of little Fan, mother." See Little Fan

"I don't mind eels." See The eel

"I dote the baple buds are swellig." See Kerchoo

"I dream'd that I walk'd in Italy." See Going back again

"I dreamed a dream next Tuesday night." Unknown
Rhymed chuckles. *UnG*

"I dreamed I was a cave-boy." See The cave-boy

"I dreamed that, as I wandered by the way." See The question

"I dreamed the fairies wanted me." See Crab-apple

"I drive boys out." See January's song

"I dwell in a lonely house I know." See Ghost house

"I dwelt alone." See Eulalie

"I eat my peas with honey." Unknown. *NaE*
Peas. *CoH—FeF*

"I fasted for some forty days on bread and buttermilk." See The pilgrim

"I feel so exceedingly lazy." See A hot-weather song

"I feel very sorry for." See Not any more

"I flew my kite." See Kite

I found. Myra Cohn Livingston. *LiW*

"I found a dimpled spider, fat and white." See Design

"I found a four-leaf clover." See I found

"I found a little beetle, so that Beetle was his name." See Forgiven

"I found ten kinds of wild flowers growing." See Late October

"I gather thyme upon the sunny hills." See Immalee

"I gave to hope a watch of mine; but he." See Hope

"I give thanks for the lovely colored year." See Child's grace

"I give you now Professor Twist." See The purist

"I got a valentine from Timmy." See Valentine

"I got me flowers to straw Thy way." See Easter

"I guess today." See John plans

"I had a cat and the cat pleased me." See A farmyard song

"I had a dog." See "I had a little dog and they called him Buff"

"I had a dog, his name was Rover." Unknown. *WiRm*

I had a dove. See Song ("I had a dove and the sweet dove died")

"I had a dove and the sweet dove died." See Song

"I had a dream last night. I dreamed." See Andre

"I had a feeling in my neck." See Mumps

"I had a little cow." See My little cow

"I had a little cow, I milked her in a gourd." Unknown. *WoF*

"I had a little dog and his name was Blue Bell." See Blue Bell

"I had a little dog and they called him Buff." Mother Goose. *DeMg*
Buff. *OpO*

"I had a little dog, his name was Tim." Unknown. *WoF*

"I had a little hen, her name was Blue." Unknown. *WoF*

"I had a little hen, the prettiest ever seen." Mother Goose. *DeMg—JoAc—LiL*

"I had a little hobby horse." Mother Goose. *DeMg*
My hobby horse. *OpO*

"I had a little horse (his name was Dapplegray)." Unknown. *WoF*

"I had a little horse (his name was Dappled Grey)." See Dappled Grey

"I had a little husband." Mother Goose. *DeMg—JoAc—NaE*
Little husband. *OpO*

"I had a little monkey." See "I had a little monkey, I sent him to the country"

"I had a little monkey, I sent him to the country." Unknown. *WoF*
"I had a little monkey." *WiRm*

"I had a little moppet." Mother Goose. *DeMg*
Little moppet. *OpO*

"I had a little mule, her name was Jenny." Unknown. *WoF*

"I had a little nag." See Little nag

"I had a little nut tree." Mother Goose. *DeMg—DeT—HuL-1—JoAc—OpO—ReG*
"I had a little nut tree; nothing would it bear." *AnI—ArTp—HuSv—LiL*
The nut tree. *NaM*

"I had a little nut tree; nothing would it bear." See "I had a little nut tree"

"I had a little pig, his name was Ben." Unknown. *WoF*

"I had a little pig, I fed him in a trough." Unknown. *WoF*

"I had a little pony." Mother Goose. *BrL-k — DeMg — DeT — HuL-1 — HuSv — JoAc—LiL*
The bad rider. *OpO*

"I had a little pup, his name was Spot." Unknown. *WoF*

"I had a little sweetheart no bigger than my thumb." Unknown. *WoF*

"I had a little wife." See My little wife

"I had a new tea set." See The tea party

"I had a penny." See Market square

"I had for my winter evening walk." See Good hours

"I had two eels once that I taught." See A sad song

"I had two pigeons bright and gay." Mother Goose. *OpO*

"I had written to Aunt Maud." See Aunt Maud

"I hailed the bus and I went for a ride." See Ferry ride—Bus ride

I have a book. David McCord. *McT*

"I have a book that has no cover." See I have a book

"I have a dog." See Notice

"I have a funny Airedale dog." See My Airedale dog

"I have a fur cap." See Ready for winter

"I have a garden of my own." See A masque—Child's song

"I have a golden ball." See Rune of riches

"I have a Gumbie cat in mind, her name is Jennyanydots." See The old Gumbie cat

"I have a house where I go." See Solitude

"I have a little doll so small." See Exactly right

"I have a little pony." See My pony

"I have a little pony." See To the shop

"I have a little pussy." See Catkin

"I have a little shadow that goes in and out with me." See My shadow

"I have a little sister." See "I have a little sister, they call her Peep-peep"

"I have a little sister, they call her Peep-peep." Mother Goose. *ArTp—DeMg—HuSv—JoAc—OpO*
Five very old riddles. *DeT*
"I have a little sister." *LiL*

"I have a little teddy bear." See My teddy bear

"I have a little turtle." See Lost

"I have a little valentine." See My valentine

"I have a little window box." See The window box

"I have a new umbrella." See My new umbrella

"I have a set of little keys." See My keys

"I have a white cat whose name is Moon." See Moon

"I have a white dog." See My dog, Spot

"I have an uncle I don't like." See Manners

"I have an understanding with the hills." See After sunset

"I have been in the woods alone." See In the woods alone

"I have been one acquainted with the night." See Acquainted with the night

"I have been treading on leaves all day until I am autumn-tired." See A leaf treader

"I have closed my books and hidden my slate." See Vacation

"I have desired to go." See Heaven-haven

"I have fallen in love with American names." See American names

"I have four sisters beyond the sea." Unknown. *DcMg*

"I have had playmates, I have had companions." See The old familiar faces

"I have heard a lady this night." See Bewitched

"I have heard talk of the bold Robin Hood." See Robin Hood and the two priests

"I have heard the curlew crying." See Wild geese

"I have known the inexorable sadness of pencils." See Dolor

"I have lost my shoes." Constantino Suasnavar, tr. by M. L. *FeF*

"I have new shoes in the fall-time." See New shoes

"I have no dog, but it must be." See My dog

"I have no name." See Infant joy

"I have no wings, but yet I fly." Mary Austin
Rhyming riddles. *ArTp*

"I have one head that wants to be good." See Sometimes I feel this way

"I have praised many loved ones in my song." See Mother

"I have seen old ships sail like swans asleep." See The old ships

I have sought Thee daily. Solomon Ibn-Gabirol, tr. fr. the Hebrew by Israel Zangwill. *PaS*

"I have sought Thee daily at dawn and twilight." See I have sought Thee daily

I have to have it. Dorothy Aldis. *AlA*

"I have to jump up." See Wide awake

"I have to live with myself, and so." See Myself

"I have to think." See At bedtime

"I have two friends." See The twins

"I have wished a bird would fly away." See A minor bird

"I hear a sudden cry of pain." See The snare

I hear America singing. Walt Whitman. *ArTp — BrL-7 — BrR-5 — CoPs — FeF —HuSv—JoAc—SmLg—UnG*

"I hear America singing, the varied carols I hear." See I hear America singing

"I hear leaves drinking rain." See The rain

"I hear no voice, I feel no touch." See Evening hymn

"I hear the engine pounding." See The ways of trains

"I hear you, little bird." See Joy of the morning

"I heard a." See Certain maxims of Archy

"I heard a bird at dawn." See The rivals

"I heard a bird sing." Oliver Herford. *ArTp —BrS—EaW—HaY—HuL-2*

"I heard a cry in the night." See Message

"I heard a horseman." See The horseman

"I heard a mouse." See The mouse

"I heard a red-winged black-bird singing." See A June day

"I heard a voice that cried, Make way for those who died." See The march

"I heard an angel singing." See An angel singing

"I heard an old farm wife." See The son

"I heard the bells on Christmas day." See Christmas bells

"I heard the old, old men say." See The old men admiring themselves in the water

"I heard the wild geese flying." See Wild geese

"I hid my heart." See The robber

"I hoe and I plow." See Farmer

"I hope you got." See Remember

"I hunted for boards for a tree house." See Tree house

"I imagine him still with heavy brow." See Beethoven's death mask

I is for invisibility. E. Farjeon. *FaCb*

"I keep three wishes ready." Annette Wynne. *ArTp—PeF*

"I kissed my darling at the zoo." See The prodigy

"I knew a most superior camper." See The bunyip and the whistling kettle

"I knew an old lady." See Antique shop

"I knew no woman, child, or man." See By Dippel woods

"I knew that you were coming, June, I knew that you were coming." See June

"I know." See October magic

"I know a bank whereon the wild thyme blows." See A midsummer-night's dream—A violet bank

"I know a boy who went to meet the morning." See Morning

"I know a funny little man." See Mr Nobody

"I know a grove." See The nightingale

"I know a little cupboard." See The cupboard

"I know a place." Myra Cohn Livingston. *LiW*

"I know a place, in the ivy on a tree." See The bird's nest

"I know a place where the sun is like gold." See Four-leaf clover

"I know all about boys, I do." See All about boys and girls

"I know four winds with names like some strange tune." See Weather words

"I know, I know, I know it." See Spring song

"I know it's pretty. What of that." See My streamer hat

"I know not what I seek eternally." Rosalía de Castro, tr. fr. the Spanish by Muriel Kittel. *PaS*

I know some lonely houses. Emily Dickinson. *CoPm—McW*

"I know some lonely houses off the road." See I know some lonely houses

"I know something I won't tell." Unknown. *WiRm*

"I love you, I like you." See Love

"I love you, I love you (I do)." Unknown. *MoY*

"I love you, I love you (I love you so well)." Unknown. *MoY*

"I love you, I love you (with my heart)." Unknown. *MoY*

"I love you once." Unknown. *MoY*

"I love you well, my little brother." Mother Goose. *AnI*

I. M. Margaritae sorori. William Ernest Henley. *HaP*

"I made a swing." See The fairy swing

"I made believe fly." See Make believe

"I married my wife by the light of the moon." Mother Goose. *DeMg*

"I meant to do my work to-day." Richard Le Gallienne. *ArTp—BrR-5—HuL-2—JoAc—UnG*

"I meet few bears and few meet me." See Last word about bears

I met a crow. John Ciardi. *CiI*

"I met a little elf-man, once." See The little elf

"I met a man as I went walking." See Puppy and I

"I met a man at one o'clock who said, Hello, at two." See The man that had little to say

I met a man down in the well. John Ciardi. *CiI*

"I met a man I could not see." John Ciardi. *CiI*

"I met a man in an onion bed." See The man in the onion bed

"I met a man on my way to town." See This man lives at my house now

"I met a man right here on the pad." John Ciardi. *CiI*

"I met a man that had no hat." See The man that had no hat

"I met a man that had six eyes." See This man had six eyes

"I met a man that had two birds." John Ciardi. *CiI*

"I met a man that lived in a box." See The man that lived in a box

"I met a man that lived in a house." John Ciardi. *CiI*

"I met a man that looked about." See The sleepy man

"I met a man that said he knew." See This man talked about you

"I met a man that said, Just look." John Ciardi. *CiI*

"I met a man that showed me a trick." John Ciardi. *CiI*

"I met a man that was all head." John Ciardi. *CiI*

"I met a man that was all mine." See This man went away

"I met a man that was coming back." John Ciardi. *CiI*

"I met a man that was playing games." John Ciardi. *CiI*

"I met a man that was trying to whittle." John Ciardi. *CiI*

"I met a man that was very wise." See I met a man with three eyes

"I met a man with a triple-chin." See The man who sang the sillies

I met a man with three eyes. John Ciardi. *CiI*

"I met a strange woman." See C is for charms

"I met a traveller from an antique land." See Ozymandias

"I met a traveller from an antique land." See Ozymandias revisited

"I met a wizened woman." See W is for witch

"I met Louisa in the shade." See Louisa

"I met Mr Catfish going up stream." Unknown. *WiRm*

"I met you as a stranger." Unknown. *MoY*

"I moved them up close to my bed last night." See The lazy crocuses

"I mun be married a Sunday." Nicholas Udall. *GrCc*

"I must be mad, or very tired." See Meeting-house hill

"I must go down to the seas again, to the lonely sea and the sky." See Sea-fever

"I must go walk the wood so wild." See The wood so wild

"I must laugh and dance and sing." See Youth

"I must not think of thee; and, tired yet strong." See Renouncement

"I must remember." Shelley Silverstein. *CoPs*

"I need a little stick when I." See I have to have it

"I need not your needles." Mother Goose. *OpO*

"I never dared be radical when young." See Precaution

"I never did, I never did, I never did like." See Independence

"I never even hear." See Whistles

"I never got a telegram before." See Telegram

"I never had walked quite so far." See Alone

"I never have seen the snow so white." See Christmas birthday

I never hear. Dorothy Aldis. *AlA*

"I never hear my mother come." See I never hear

"I never quite saw fairyfolk." See Very nearly

"I never saw a moor." Emily Dickinson. *ArTp—DoP—FeF—HuL-2—JoAc—NaE* Certainty. *UnG*

"I never saw a puppy that." See Hot weather

"I never saw a purple cow." See The purple cow

"I never speak a word." Mary Austin Rhyming riddles. *ArTp*

"I objurgate the centipede." See The centipede

"I often see flowers from a passing car." See A passing glimpse

"I often sit and wish that I." See Flying kite

"I often wish I were a king." See If I were king

"I once had a sweet little doll, dears." See The water babies—The lost doll

"I once thought that snowflakes were feathers." See Snowflakes

"I only know a glowing warmth." Olive Beaupré Miller. *DoP*

"I peeled bits of straw and I got switches too." See Bits of straw

"I peeped through the window." Mother Goose. *OpO*

"I played I was two polar bears." See The bear hunt

"I plucked pink blossoms from mine appletree." See An apple gathering

"I, proclaiming that there is." See The dancer at Cruachan and Cro-Patrick

"I put on a pair of overshoes." See Around my room

"I quarreled with my brother." See The quarrel

"I rather like new clothes." See New clothes and old

"I read with varying degrees." See Journal

"I recognized him by his skips and hops." See Pan and the cherries

"I recollect a nurse call'd Ann." See The terrible infant

"I regret that before people can be reformed they have to be sinners." See Piano tuner, untune me that tune

I remember. See "I remember, I remember"

"I remember, as if it were yesterday." See One and one

"I remember black winter waters." See New Hampshire again

"I remember how I once heard." See Harbingers

"I remember how we stood." See The last corn shock

"I remember, I remember." Thomas Hood. *FeF—UnG*

I remember. *DeT*

"I remember the Chillicothe ball players." See Hits and runs

"I reside at Table mountain, and my name is Truthful James." See The society upon the Stanislow

"I restore the primal line." See November's song

"I rolled the dough out very thin." See Cookery

"I run from California." See Pullman porter

"I, said the duck, I call it fun." See Who likes the rain

"I said, This horse, sir, will you shoe." See Rhyme for a simpleton

"I said to a bug in the sink." See When I went to get a drink

"I said to heart, How goes it? Heart replied." See The false heart

"I sat by the sea." Ivy O. Eastwick. *EaI*

"I saw a donkey." See The donkey

"I saw a fishpond all on fire." Mother Goose. *JoAc—OpO*

"I saw a fly within a bead." See A trapped fly

I saw a ghost. Joan Boilleau. *ArTp*

"I saw a gnome." See The gnome

"I saw a light, Columbus said." See Light in the darkness

"I saw a little snail." See Little snail

"I saw a little squirrel." See A little squirrel

"I saw a man down in the well." See I met a man down in the well

"I saw a man pursuing the horizon." Stephen Crane. *SmLg*

I saw a peacock. See "I saw a peacock with a fiery tail"

"I saw a peacock with a fiery tail." Mother Goose. *DeMg—LoL—SmLg*

I saw a peacock. *GrCc—PlI*

Not so impossible. *UnG*

The wonder of wonders. *OpO*

"I saw a proud, mysterious cat." See The mysterious cat

I saw a ship. See "I saw a ship a-sailing"

"I saw a ship a-sailing." Mother Goose. *ArTp — BrR-3 — DeMg — HuSv — JoAc—LiL—NaM*

I saw a ship. *DeT*

A ship a-sailing. *OpO*

"I saw a ship a-sailing, a-sailing, a-sailing." See An old song re-sung

"I saw a snail." See Little snail

I saw a stable. Mary Coleridge. *EaW*

"I saw a stable, low and very bare." See I saw a stable

"I saw a star slide down the sky." See The falling star

"I saw a thing, and stopped to wonder." See The pine bough

"I saw an elephant walking down the road." See April fool

"I saw an old man by the wayside." See Traveller's joy

"I saw dawn creep across the sky." See A summer morning

"I saw eternity the other night." See A vision

"I saw green banks of daffodil." E. Wyndham Tennant. *ArTp*

"I saw her plucking cowslips." See The witch

"I saw him once before." See The last leaf

"I saw my face in the coffeepot." See A coffeepot face

"I saw the devil's darning needle." See Devil's darning needle

"I saw the ewes lying." See Lambs

"I saw the farmer plough the field." See Harvest

"I saw the fog grow thick." See The fog

"I saw the lovely arch." See The rainbow

"I saw the spires of Oxford." See The spire of Oxford

I saw three ships. See "I saw three ships come sailing by"

"I saw three ships come sailing by." Mother Goose. *DeMg—JoAc—LiL*

I saw three ships. *HuL-1—UnG*

Three ships. *OpO*

"I saw with open eyes." See Stupidity street

"I saw you toss the kites on high." See The wind

"I say to lick a candy stick." See About candy

"I scarcely think." See The zoo

"I see a lot of cowboys." See Squaw talk

"I see some waits awaiting." See Christmas eve

"I see the moon." Mother Goose. *ArTp—DeMg—OpO*
  The moon. *DoP*
  Signs, seasons, and sense. *UnG*
  Sun and moon. *HuL-1*

"I see the twelve fair months go by." See A burying

"I see two fish swim in the sky." See Pisces

"I seem to see." See Queer

"I seen a dunce of a poet once, a-writin' a little book." See Tricky

"I sent a letter to my love." Mother Goose. *LiL*

"I set a jumpy mouse trap." See A change of heart

"I shall not miss the roses, fading." See Grapes

"I shape the vessel of my life." See Misdirection

"I shoot the hippopotamus." See The hippopotamus

"I shot an arrow into the air." See The arrow and the song

"I should like to buy you a birthday present, said Billy to Betsy Jane." See Betsy Jane's sixth birthday

"I should like to rise and go." See Travel

"I sing of a maiden." Unknown. *DeT—MaB—SmLg—UnG*
  Carol. *ReT*

"I sing the praise of honored wars." See Soldier's song

"I slip and I slide." See Icy

"I somersault just like a clown." See Somersault

I sometimes think. Unknown. *UnG*
  To be or not to be. *CoH—NaM*

I sometimes think about dollar bills. John Ciardi. *CiR*

"I sometimes think I'd rather crow." See I sometimes think

"I sometimes think when I'm alone." See I sometimes think about dollar bills

"I sometimes wonder where he lives." See Echo

"I sought his love in sun and stars." See The search

"I sought immortality." See The crib

"I sowed the seeds of love." See The seeds of love

"I spot the hills." See Theme in yellow

"I sprang to the stirrup, and Joris, and he." See How they brought the good news from Ghent to Aix

"I stand most humbly." See Wisdom

"I stare at the cow." Polly Chase Boyden. *CoI*

"I started early, took my dog." Emily Dickinson. *ReT*

"I stayed the night for shelter at a farm." See The witch of Coös

"I stood beside a hill." See February twilight

"I stood on a corner chewing gum." See Chewing gum

"I stood one day by the breezy bay." See A nautical extravaganza

"I stood tiptoe upon a little hill," sels. John Keats
  Minnows. *FeF—JoAc—UnG*
  Sweet peas. *JoAc*

I strove with none. Walter Savage Landor. *HaP*

"I strove with none, for none was worth my strife." See I strove with none

"I studied my tables over and over, and backward and forward, too." See A mortifying mistake

"I taste a liquor never brewed." See The little tippler

"I tell yeh whut. The chankin'." See Horses chawin' hay

"I tell you a tale tonight." See The admiral's ghost

"I thank Thee, God, for color." See For color

"I thank you, God." See Thanksgiving

"I thank you, God." Ilo Orleans. *DoP—HuL-1*

"I think about the elephant and flea." See In the middle

I think continually of those. Stephen Spender. *HaP*

"I think continually of those who were truly great." See I think continually of those

"I think flowers can see." See Thoughts of a little girl

"I think I am a muffin man. I haven't got a bell." See Busy

"I think I remember this moorland." See We have been here before

"I think if I should wait some night in an enchanted forest." See Fantasy

"I think it must be very nice." See Penguin

"I think mice." See Mice

"I think that I shall never see." See Song of the open road

"I think that I shall never see." See Trees

"I think that many owls say Who-o." See Owls talking

"I think when I read that sweet story of old." See Sweet story of old

"I thought I could saw, and I thought I could plane." See Carpenter

"I thought I heard the old man say." See Leave her, Johnny, leave her

"I thought I saw white clouds, but no." See Lilies

"I thought, I thought, I thought in vain." Unknown. *MoY*

"I told the sun that I was glad." See The sun

"I, too, dislike it: there are things that are important beyond all this fiddle." See Poetry

"I took a bow and arrow." John Ciardi. *CiR—NaE*

"I took a lump of clay in my hand." See This man came from nowhere

"I took away the ocean once." See The shell

"I took money and bought flowering trees." See Planting flowers on the eastern embankment

"I took the pail for water when the sun was high." See The star in the pail

"I trust I have not wasted breath." See In memoriam

"I turned to speak to God." See Not all there

"I use my feet a lot for walking." See Usefulness

"I used to think." Ivy O. Eastwick. *EaI*

"I wake in the morning early." See Singingtime

"I walked down alone Sunday after church." See Pea brush

"I wander thro' each charter'd street." See London

"I wander through the silent night." See Nocturne

"I wandered by the brook-side." See Song

"I wandered lonely as a cloud." See Daffodils

"I want a little witch cat." See Witch cat

"I want a puppy dog." See For Christmas

"I want a soldier." See At home

"I want to be new, said the duckling." See The new duckling

I want to know. John Drinkwater. *FeF*

"I want to know why when I'm late." See I want to know

"I want to learn to whistle." See Whistles

"I want to write a book of chaste and simple verse." See Landscape

"I want to write something original." Unknown. *MoY*

I want you to meet. David McCord. *McT*

"I wanted a rifle for Christmas." See Presents

"I wanted to have a cowboy suit." See Dressing-up

"I was alone the other day." See Alone

"I was angry with my friend." See The poison tree

"I was born in Illinois." See My fathers came from Kentucky

"I was in a hooker once, said Karlssen." See Cape Horn gospel (I)

"I was standing on the corner." Unknown. *TaD*

"I was the one they chose: See, he's the." See A riddle: What am I

"I was the patriarch of the shining land." See John Sutter

"I was the third man running in a race." See The service

"I was up so tiptoe early." See Early

"I was with Grant, the stranger said." See The aged stranger

"I watched a little snowflake." See Snow fairies

"I watched the dear little blossoms." See Cherry time

"I went down to the river." See Life is fine

"I went down to the shouting sea." See Sand-between-the-toes

"I went down town an' met Miss Brown." See The thread was thin

"I went downtown." Unknown. *WiRm*

"I went into a house, and it wasn't a house." See The wrong house

"I went into a sort of house." See The wheelgoround

"I went into my grandmother's garden." See A farthing

"I went into my grandmother's garden." See Swinging

"I went into my stable, to see what I might see." See Old Wichet

"I went into the flea circus." See Small talk

"I went out to the hazel wood." See The song of wandering Aengus

"I went out to the woods to-day." See Paradox

"I went through a forest without a tree." See The journey

"I went to bring." See The skippery boo

"I went to Noke." Mother Goose. *OpO*

"I went to see if my old hen." Unknown. *WoF*

"I went to the animal fair." See Animal fair

"I went to the river." See Trading

"I went to the river and couldn't get across (I jumped on an alligator)." Unknown. *WoF*

"I went to the river and couldn't get across (I paid five dollars)." Unknown. *WoF*

"I went to the toad that lies under the wall." Mother Goose. *OpO*

"I went to the woods and got it." Unknown. *WoF*

"I went to turn the grass once after one." See The tuft of flowers

"I went up one pair of stairs." Mother Goose. *DeMg—JoAc*

"I went visiting Miss Melinda." See Strawberry jam

"I whispered, I am too young." See Brown penny

I will arise and go now. Ogden Nash. *McW*

"I will arise and go now, and go to Innisfree." See The lake isle of Innisfree

"I will be a lion." See Wild beasts

"I will be the gladdest thing." See Afternoon on a hill

"I will build you a house." See Little girl

"I will gallop along with a stick for a horse." See A stick for a horse

"I will gather the sunshine in my hands." See Down on my tummy

"I will give you." See Presents from heaven

I will give you. William Blake. *DoP*

"I will give you the end of a golden string." See I will give you

"I will go walking on Eighth street." See Eighth street west

"I will go with my father a-ploughing." Joseph Campbell. *ArTp—BrS—FeF*

"I will lift up mine eyes." See Psalms—Psalm CXXXI

"I will make you brooches and toys for your delight." See My valentine

"I will not change my horse with any that treads." See King Henry V—The horse

"I will not say, Forget-me-not." Unknown. *MoY*

"I will praise Thee, O Lord, with my whole heart." See Psalms—Psalm IX

I will sing praise. See Psalms—Psalm IX

I will sing you one-o. Robert Frost. *FrR*

"I, Willie Wastle." See Scottish castle

I wish. Nancy Byrd Turner. *BrS*

"I wish, how I wish, that I had a little house." See The shiny little house

"I wish I could meet the man that knows." John Ciardi. *CiI*

"I wish I had a great big ball." See Bouncing ball

"I wish I had been His apprentice." See In the carpenter shop

"I wish I had two little mouths." See Mouths

"I wish I loved the human race." See The wishes of an elderly man

"I wish I was in de land ob cotton." See Dixie

"I wish I were a bunny." Unknown. *MoY*

"I wish I were an elephant." Unknown. *MoY*

"I wish my heart." See Ballad of the ragbag heart

"I wish she'd give away my plate." See What I would do

"I wish that my room had a floor." Gelett Burgess. *CoH—LoL*

Limericks since Lear. *UnG*

"I wish they would hurry up their trip to Mars." See A projection

"I wish, when summer's drawing near about the end of May." See I wish

"I wish you all that pen and ink." See Thanksgiving wishes

"I wish you health." Unknown. *MoY*

"I wish you luck." Unknown. *MoY*

"I, with my mind's eye, see." See Islands

I woke up. Unknown. *WoJ*

"I woke up Monday morning." See I woke up

I wonder. Mariana Griswold Van Rensselaer. *BrL-k*

"I wonder about the trees." See The sound of the trees

I wonder as I wander. Unknown. *JoAc*

"I wonder as I wander out under the sky." See I wonder as I wander

"I wonder if the engine." See Engine

"I wonder if the sap is stirring yet." See The first spring day

"I wonder if the stars are fire." See I wonder

"I wonder if there's anywhere." See Teddy's wonderings

"I wonder what spendthrift chose to spill." See March

"I wonder where the rabbits go." See Tracks

"I won't be my father's Jack." Mother Goose. *DeMg —OpO—PlU*

"I would I were beneath a tree." See The three woulds

"I would, if I could." Mother Goose. *DeMg —OpO*

I would like to be—a bee. Dorothy W. Baruch. *BrBc*

I wouldn't. John Ciardi. *CiY*

"I write on white." Unknown. *MoY*

"I write upon this page of blue." Unknown. *MoY*

"I write what I know on one side of the paper." See Paper II

"I wrote some lines once on a time." See The height of the ridiculous

Ibbity, bibbity, sibbity. Unknown. *TaD*

"Ibbity, bibbity, sibbity, sa." See Ibbity, bibbity, sibbity

"Ibbity-bibbity sibbity sab." Unknown. *WiRm*

Iberia. Leo Kirschenbaum. *PlU*

Ibn-Gabriol, Solomon
  I have sought Thee daily. *PaS*

Ibycus
  In the spring. *PaS*

Ice
  "As I was going o'er London bridge." Mother Goose. *OpO*
  Fire and ice. R. Frost. *FrR—FrY*
  Ice. D. Aldis. *ArTp—BrL-k*
  The ice man. D. Aldis. *AlA—HuL-1*
  The icicle. H. G. Gale. *BrL-k*
  Icy. R. W. Bacmeister. *BrL-k*
  "Lives in winter." Mother Goose. *ArTp*

Ice. Dorothy Aldis. *ArTp—BrL-k*

"Ice cream city." Unknown. *MoY*

The ice-cream man. Rachel Field. *BrR-4— BrS—FeF*

"Ice cream, soda, ginger ale, pop." Unknown. *TaD—WoJ*

The ice had all melted. Dorothy Aldis. *AlHd*

"The ice had all melted and I went to look." See The ice had all melted

The ice man. Dorothy Aldis. *AlA—HuL-1*

Ichihara, Prince
  Solitary pine. *PaS*

The icicle. Mrs Henry Gordon Gale. *BrL-k*

"An icicle hung on a red brick wall." See The icicle

"Ickle ockle, blue bockle." Mother Goose. *OpO*

Icky bicky. Unknown. *WoJ*

The icosasphere. Marianne Moore. *PlI*

Icy. Rhoda W. Bacmeister. *BrL-k*

"I'd forgotten her eyes were so blue." See Found again

I'd leave. Andrew Lang. *FeF*

"I'd leave all the hurry." See I'd leave

"I'd like a different dog." See Dogs and weather

"I'd like to be a cowboy an' ride a fiery hoss." See The limitations of youth

"I'd like to be a dentist with a plate upon the door." See The dentist

"I'd like to be a lighthouse." Rachel Field *HuL-1*

"I'd like to be a make-up man." See The make-up man
"I'd like to run like a rabbit in hops." See Rabbit
"I'd like to slide my sled to bed." See Wishful
I'd love to be a fairy's child. Robert Graves. *BrBc—FeF—HuL-2*
"I'd rather have fingers than toes." See On digital extremities
The ideal age for a man. Monica Shannon. *BrBc*
Ideals. See also Ambition; Conduct of life; Dreams
Choose something like a star. R. Frost. *FrR*
Excelsior. H. W. Longfellow. *FeF*
Idleness. See also Leisure
The camel's hump. From Just-so stories. R. Kipling. *NaE*
"Elsie Marley is grown so fine." Mother Goose. *DeMg*
Elsie Marley. *OpO*
A hot-weather song. D. Marquis. *HuSv*
Lazy day. D. Aldis. *AlHd*
The mouse, the frog, and the little red hen. Unknown. *HuL-1*
The sluggard. I. Watts. *NaM*
Sunning. J. S. Tippett. *ArTp—BrR-4—BrS—HuL-2*
Tired Tim. W. De La Mare. *ArTp—FeF—HuL-2—JoAc—NaE—PeF*
Where's Mary. I. O. Eastwick. *ArTp*
If. Rudyard Kipling. *UnG*
"If a knife falls, a gentleman calls." See Company
"If a man who turnips cries." Samuel Johnson. *DeMg*
The turnip seller. *NaE*
The turnip vendor. *OpO*
"If a pig wore a wig." Christina Georgina Rossetti. *JoAc*
"If a task is once begun." See Always finish
If a woodchuck would chuck. See "How much wood would a wood-chuck chuck"
If all the seas. See "If all the seas were one sea"
"If all the seas were one sea." Mother Goose. *DeMg—HuSv—JoAc—LoL—OpO*
If all the seas. *ReG*
If all the skies. Henry Van Dyke. *DoP*
"If all the skies were sunshine." See If all the skies
"If all the trees were one tree." Unknown. *WiRm*
"If all the verse what i have wrote." See Archy's autobiography
"If all the world and love were young." See The nymph's reply to the shepherd
"If all the world was apple pie." See "If all the world were apple pie"
"If all the world was paper." Mother Goose. *OpO*
"If all the world were apple pie." Mother Goose. *AnI—DeMg*
"If all the world was apple pie." *JoAc—LoL*
If all were rain. Christina Georgina Rossetti. *BrR-3*

"If all were rain and never sun." See If all were rain
"If bees stay at home." Mother Goose. *OpO*
Signs, seasons, and sense. *UnG*
"If Bethlehem were here today." See Christmas morning
"If bluebells could be rung." See Bluebells and foxgloves
"If buttercups buzz'd after the bee." Unknown. *SmLg*
"If Candlemas day be dry and fair." Unknown. *CoPs*
"If Candlemas day be fair and bright." Unknown. *CoPs—DeMg*
"If ever a husband you shall see." Unknown. *MoY*
"If ever in a foreign land." See J is for jinn
"If ever there is something nice." See Five years old
"If ever there lived a Yankee lad." See Darius Green and his flying-machine
"If ever you should go by chance." See How to tell the wild animals
"If everyone had a flying machine." See Chairoplane chant
"If flowers ever gave a party." See Flower party
"If history is hard, don't sit and croak." See Reflection
"If humility and purity be not in the heart." See The rock
"If I." See I would like to be—a bee
"If I." See Wouldn't you
"If I can stop one heart from breaking." Emily Dickinson. *BrR-4*
"If I could be a gypsy boy." See The caravan
"If I could be where I wish to be." See Spring song
"If I could climb the garden wall." See There
"If I could smell smells with my ears." See Curious something
"If I ever marry." Unknown. *WoF*
If I had a cardboard box. Aileen Fisher. *McAw*
"If I had a darter." Unknown. *WiRm*
"If I had a donkey that wouldn't go." Mother Goose. *DeMg—JoAc*
Kindness. *OpO*
"If I had a firecracker." Shelley Silverstein. *CoPs*
"If I had a hundred dollars to spend." See The animal store
"If I had a ship." See The island
"If I had a spoon." See Clouds
"If I had just one penny." See Choice
"If I have faltered more or less." See The Celestial Surgeon
"If I should be so lucky." See Shepherd's purse
"If I should die, think only this of me." See The soldier
"If I should die tonight." Ben King. *CoH*
If I should ever by chance. Edward Thomas. *NaM—SmLg*
"If I should ever by chance grow rich." See If I should ever by chance

"If I started out to go." See Towns

"If I was a farmer, I'd have an easy time." Unknown. *WoF*

"If I were a bear." See Furry bear

If I were a fish. Marie Louise Allen. *AlP*

"If I were a giant." See G is for giant

"If I were a head of lettuce." Unknown. *MoY*

"If I were a pilgrim child." Rowena Bastin Bennett. *HaY*

"If I were a queen." Christina Georgina Rossetti. *BrS*

"If I were an apple." Unknown. *AnI—HuL-1*

"If I were in a fairy tale." See The duck

"If I were John and John were me." See A thought

If I were king. A. A. Milne. *MiWc*

"If I were Lord of Tartary." See Tartary

"If I were the wind." See Yellow balloon

If I'd as much money. See "If I'd as much money as I could spend"

"If I'd as much money as I could spend." Mother Goose. *JoAc—LiL*
Chairs to mend. *OpO*
If I'd as much money. *HuL-1*
Old clothes, any old clo', clo'. *OpO*

"If I'd as much money as I could tell." See "If I'd as much money as I could spend"

"If ifs and ands." Mother Goose. *DeMg—LiL*

"If in heaven." Unknown. *MoY*

"If in some green-shaded woodland bed." See I is for invisibility

"If it were not for the voice." See Shui Shū —Nakatsukasa

"If life were a thing that money could buy." Unknown. *MoY*

"If little mice have birthdays." See Birthday cake

"If Luther's day expand to Darwin's year." See Epilogue

"If Mary goes far out to sea." See Stately verse

"If Mother Nature patches." See Sewing

"If music and sweet poetry agree." See To his friend Master R. L., in praise of music and poetry

"If music be the food of love, play on." See Twelfth night

"If Nancy Hanks." See Nancy Hanks

"If no one ever marries me." Laurence Alma-Tadema. *BrBc—HuL-1—UnG*

"If once you have slept on an island." Rachel Field. *HuL-2*

"If one could have that little head of hers." See A face

If only. Rose Fyleman. *HuSv*

"If only I'd some money." See If only

"If people ask me." See Politeness

If pigs could fly. James Reeves. *ReBl*

"If pigs could fly, I'd fly a pig." See If pigs could fly

"If quarrel you must, good men of Bere." See Behind the gorse

"If so be a toad be laid." See A charm; or, An allay for love

"If someone asks you." Donian Mitchell. *CoPs*

"If someone, something, somehow, as man dreams." See A musical critic anticipates eternity

"If the butterfly courted the bee." See Topsyturvey-world

"If the golden-crested wren." See A child's laughter

"If the oak is out before the ash." Mother Goose. *OpO*

"If the moon shines." See What night would it be

"If there were a boys' camp." Unknown *MoY*

"If there were dreams to sell." See Dreampedlary

"If there were, oh, an Hellespont of cream." See Homely meats

If they spoke. Mark Van Doren. *PlI*

"If this book should chance to roam." Unknown. *MoY*

"If thou art sleeping, maiden." See Song

"If thou wilt come and dwell with me at home." See Daphnis to Ganymede

"If we meet a gorilla." See We must be polite

"If when the wind blows." See Daniel Webster's horses

"If wisdom's ways you wisely seek." Unknown. *MoY*

"If wishes were horses." Mother Goose. *DeMg—LiL—OpO*

"If writing in albums." Unknown. *MoY*

"If ye will with Mab find grace." See The fairies

If ye would hear. Dora Greenwell. *EaW*

"If ye would hear the angels sing." See If ye would hear

"If you are a gentleman." Mother Goose. *OpO*

"If you are low with humbleness." See Low and high

If you ask me. Dorothy Aldis. *AlHd*

"If you can keep your head when all about you." See If

If you ever. Unknown. *CoI*

"If you ever ever ever ever ever." See If you ever

"If you ever, ever, ever meet a grizzly bear." See Grizzly bear

"If you feel for it pressing back the glossy leaves." See Orange trees by night

"If you get to heaven." Unknown. *MoY*

"If you happen to meet." See Advice from an elderly mouse

"If you have a notion." Unknown. *MoY*

"If you haven't got a pony." See Horsemanship

"If you love me as I love you." Unknown. *DeMg—MoY*

"If you never talked with fairies." Elsie Melchert Fowler. *BrBc*

"If you of all the fruits that be." See The favourite fruit

"If you see a fairy ring." Unknown. *HuL-1*

"If you see a monkey in a tree." Unknown. *MoY*

"If you see a package." See Secrets

"If you should bid me make a choice." See The windmill

"If you sit down at set of sun." See Count that day lost

"If you sneeze on Monday, you sneeze for danger." See "Sneeze on Monday, sneeze for danger"

"If you want a taste." Unknown. *MoY*

"If you were a fish." Unknown. *MoY*

"If you were as big as a giant flea." See Sizes

"If you were to ask me why I dwell among green mountains." See Conversation in the mountains

"If you would reap praise, sow the seeds." See Poor Richard's wisdom

"If your husband is thirsty." Unknown. *MoY*

If you've never. Elsie Melchert Fowler. *BrR-4—HuL-1*

"If you've never seen an old witch." See If you've never

"Ignore dull days; forget the showers." See Lesson from a sun-dial

"I'll be right there, says the little man. Please note." See What am I up to

"I'll buy you a tartan bonnet." Mother Goose *OpO*

"I'll eat when I'm hungry." Unknown American Father Gander. *UnG*

"I'll lie, said Swithin." See Saint Swithin's wish

"I'll need—for April's thirty days." See April and Isabella

"I'll sail upon the dog-star." Thomas Durfey. *SmLg*

"I'll sing you a song—nine verses long." See A song

"I'll sing you a song—the days are long." See A song

"I'll sing you a song (though not very long)." Mother Goose. *DeMg*

I'll tell. Mother Goose. *OpO*

"I'll tell my own daddy." See I'll tell

"I'll tell thee everything I can." See Through the looking glass—The white knight's song

"I'll tell you a lie, and it's almost true." See How much is true

"I'll tell you a story." Mother Goose. *DeMg —JoAc—LiL*
Jack a nory. *OpO*

"I'll tell you how the sun rose." Emily Dickinson. *BrS—NaM*
A day. *UnG*
Poem. *ReT*
The sun. *HuSv*
Sunrise and sunset. *BrR-6*

"I'll tell you of a sailor now, a tale that can't be beat." See The story of Samuel Jackson

"I'll tell you the truth, father, though your heart bleed." See The forbidden play

I'll twine white violets. Meleager, tr. fr. the **Greek by Goldwin Smith.** *PaS*

"I'll twine white violets and the myrtle green." See I'll twine white violets

I'll wear a shamrock. Mary Carolyn Davies. *ArTp—BrS—HaY*

Illness. See Sickness

Ilott, **Percy H.**
The witch. *HuL-1*

"I'm a beautiful red, red drum." See The drum

I'm a kitty. Dorothy Aldis. *AlHd*

"I'm a kitty sounding pretty." See I'm a kitty

"I'm a lean dog, a keen dog, a wild dog, and lone." See Lone dog

"I'm a little butterfly." See Butterfly

"I'm a little Hindoo." Unknown. *CoH*

"I'm a little teapot, short and stout." Unknown. *WoF*

"I'm a sailor all dressed in blue." Unknown. *TaD*

"I'm a strange contradiction, I'm new and I'm old." See A book

"I'm always told to hurry up." See Going to bed

"I'm called by the name of a man." Mother Goose. *OpO*

"I'm fishing." See Down by the pond

"I'm glad my birthday comes in May." Ivy O. Eastwick. *BrBc*

"I'm glad our house is a little house." See Song for a little house

"I'm glad that I." See The park

"I'm glad that I was good today." See Thanksgiving

"I'm glad the sky is painted blue." Unknown. *LoL*

"I'm glad the stars are over me." See Stars

"I'm going out to clean the pasture spring." See The pasture

"I'm going to Lady Washington's." Unknown. *JoAc*

"I'm going to school tomorrow, just." See Patrick goes to school

"I'm growing very big and tall." See Growing up

"I'm hiding, I'm hiding." See Hiding

"I'm hungry, oh so hungry." See The birds on the school windowsill

"I'm in a 10 der mood today." See O i c

"I'm king of the hill." See King of the hill

"I'm nobody. Who are you." Emily Dickinson. *ArTp—UnG*
A nobody. *UnMc*

"I'm not a Northern beauty." Unknown. *MoY*

"I'm painting a picture." See Art

"I'm picking my mother a present." See Dandelions

"I'm pretty old." See Five-in-June

"I'm seven years old." See Middle-aged child

I'm so big. Dorothy Aldis. *AlHd*

"I'm something I have never been." See Something very elegant

"I'm sure that no one ever knows." See Underneath the clothes

"I'm the cat." See Cat and rat

"I'm the king of the castle." See King of the castle

"I'm the toughest boy in the city." Unknown. *MoY*

"I'm three years old and like to wear." See Hair ribbons

"I'm very good at skiing." See Skiing

"I'm wild and woolly and full of fleas." Unknown. *WoF*

Immalee. Christina Georgina Rossetti. *ReT*

Immense hour. Juan Ramón Jiménez, tr. fr. the Spanish by Edward F. Gahan. *PaS*

An immorality. Ezra Pound. *GrCc—HaP*

Immortality. See also Death and immortality
  The crib. C. Morley. *BrBc*
  Ode on intimations of immortality. W. Wordsworth. *BrBc* (sel.)
    Our birth is but a sleep. *HaP* (sel.)
  A song of always. E. Rosenzweig. *ArTp*
  Words. R. L. Stevenson. *UnG*

Impatience. See Patience

An impetuous resolve. James Whitcomb Riley. *BrBc*

The importance of eggs. David McCord. *McT*

Improved farm land. Carl Sandburg. *SaW*

"In a blue, blue bonnet." See The summer party

"In a corner of the bedroom is a great big curtain." See Brownie

"In a cottage in Fife." Mother Goose. *DeMg —LoL*
  Two comical folk. *OpO*

In a desert town. Lionel Stevenson. *HuSv*

In a disused graveyard. Robert Frost. *FrR*

"In a far land upon a day." See The riding of the kings

"In a hole of the heel of an old brown stocking." See Stocking fairy

"In a huge hoary mansion." See Mr Bellairs

"In a little white house." See The return of the fairy

"In a milkweed cradle." See Baby seeds

In a moonlight wilderness. See The fruit plucker

In a museum. Thomas Hardy. *PlU*

In a poem. Robert Frost. *FrR*

"In a shady nook one moonlit night." See The leprahaun

"In a Vermont bedroom closet." See A record stride

"In after years when this you see." Unknown. *MoY*

"In all his glory, Solomon." See A lily of the field

"In all the Eastern hemisphere." See The fall of J. W. Beane

"In all the good Greek of Plato." See Survey of literature

"In all the oldest legends, one day under the spell." See The house beyond the meadow—Goodbye to fairyland

"In all the parish not a dame dared stir." See The Canterbury tales—The wife of Bath

"In ancient times, as story tells." See Baucis and Philemon

In Arden forest. See As you like it—"Under the greenwood tree"

In August. Marchette Chute. *ChA—McAw*

"In autumn down the beechwood path." See Beech leaves

"In autumn every maple tree." See On some windy day

"In Avalon lies Arthur yonder." See Avalon

"In Baltimore there lived a boy." See The boy who laughed at Santa Claus

"In Breughel's great picture, The Kermess." See The dance

"In Brittany there lived a lad." See The heart

"In Buckinghamshire hedgerows." See The icosasphere

"In burnished armor." See Starling

"In came the moon and covered me with wonder." See A thrush in the moonlight

"In careless patches through the wood." See The invaders

"In Central park." Unknown. *MoY*

In come de animals. Unknown. *BrR-6*

"In come de animals two by two." See In come de animals

"In days of old." Unknown. *MoY*

"In days of old, when Englishmen were—men." See Italian opera

"In December I remember." See Hungry morning

In desert places. Sister Mary Madeleva. *UnG*

"In Dublin's fair city where the girls are so pretty." See Molly Malone

"In enterprise of martial kind." See The gondoliers—The duke of Plaza-Toro

"In every hour, in every mood." See Leofric and Godiva

"In far Tibet." See I will arise and go now

In February. John Addington Symonds. *HaY*

"In February there are days." See When

"In February when few gusty flakes." See Ground hog day

"In fiction tales we keep performing." See The collies

"In fir tar is." Mother Goose. *DeMg—OpO*

In Flanders fields. John McCrae. *BrS*

"In Flanders fields the poppies blow." See In Flanders fields

In foreign parts. Laura E. Richards. *CoH— LoL*

"In form and feature, face and limb." See The twins

"In French there is a little word." Unknown. *MoY*

"In fury and terror." See The tempest

In Glencullen. John M. Synge. *ReT*

"In go-cart so tiny." Kate Greenaway. *FeF*

In grato jubilo. David McCord. *PlU*

"In Hans' old mill his three black cats." See Five eyes

In Hardin county, 1809. Lulu E. Thompson. *CoPs—CoSp*

In hardwood groves. Robert Frost. *FrR*

"In his grandmother's garden was a cake with seven candles." See Seven times one are seven

"In holly hedges starving birds." See Christmas eve

In honor of Taffy Topaz. Christopher Morley. *ArTp*

"In jail they give you coffee." Unknown. *MoY*

"In January the spirit dreams." See An almanac

In June. Nora Perry. *HaY*

"In June, amid the golden fields." See The groundhog

"In just." See Chanson innocente—In just spring

In just spring. See Chanson innocente

"In late summer the wild geese." See August hail

In Lincoln lane. Mother Goose. *OpO*

"In many places here and." See Fate is unfair

"In marble halls as white as milk." Mother Goose. *DeMg—JoAc—OpO*

"In marble walls as white as milk." *HuSv*

"In marble walls as white as milk." See "In marble halls as white as milk"

In March. See Written in March

"In March come the March winds." See The March winds

"In mathematicks he was greater." See Hudibras, Canto I

"In May." Ivy O. Eastwick. *EaI*

In May. Dorothy Aldis. *AlA—AlHd*

"In May, when sea-winds pierced our solitudes." See The rhodora

In memoriam, sels. Alfred Tennyson
 "And, star and system rolling past" In memoriam. *PlI*
 "Dark house, by which once more I stand" From In memoriam. *HaP*
 "I trust I have not wasted breath" In memoriam. *PlI*
 Ring out, wild bells. *ArTp—BrL-8—FeF—HoW*

"In men whom men condemn as ill." See Byron

"In Mildenhall is a hurdy-gurdy." See The hurdy-gurdy

"In moving-slow he has no peer." See The sloth

"In my craft or sullen art." Dylan Thomas. *HaP*

In my garden. Unknown. *HuL-1*

In my lady's garden. Unknown. *TaD*

"In my little garden." See In my garden

In my mother's house, sels. Ann Nolan Clark
 Irrigation. *HuSv*
 Mountains. *HuSv*
 "Yucca." *JoAc*

In neglect. Robert Frost. *FrR*

"In Nottingham there lives a tanner." See Robin Hood and the tanner

In October. Bliss Carman. *HaY*

"In October, when they know." See Winter coats

"In olden days to knit and sew." Unknown. *MoY*

"In orchard set yer ladders." See September's song

In plague time. Thomas Nashe. *SmLg*
 "Adieu, farewell earth's bliss." *HaP*

In praise of Johnny Appleseed. Vachel Lindsay. *HuSv*
 Johnny Appleseed. *FeF* (sel.)

In praise of llamas. Arthur Guiterman. *CoH*

In praise of Neptune. Thomas Campion. *HoW*

In praise of water. Nancy Byrd Turner. *HuL-2*

"In Saturday market, there's eggs a-plenty." See Saturday market

In school-days. John Greenleaf Whittier. *FeF* (sel.)

"In search through gardens, woods." See The chase

In shadow. Hart Crane. *GrCc*

"In sixteen hundred and sixty-six." Mother Goose. *OpO*

"In spite of cold and chills." See Daffodils

In spring. Eduard Mörike, tr. fr. the German by Vernon Watkins. *PaS*

"In spring I look gay." Mother Goose. *OpO*

In spring in warm weather. Dorothy Aldis. *AlA—BrBc*

"In springtime when the leaves are young." See Seasons

"In summer I am very glad." See Playgrounds

"In summer when the woods be bright." See Robin Hood and Guy of Gisborne

"In summer's mellow midnight." See The night-wind

In the bazaars of Hyderabad. Sarojini Naidu. *FeF*

"In the beginning God created the heaven and the earth." See Genesis—Genesis, Chapter 1

"In the big-flaked sugar-snow." See Maple feast

"In the black furrow of a field." See The hare

"In the bleak mid-winter." See Carol

"In the blossom-land Japan." See An old song

In the carpenter shop. Unknown. *UnG*

"In the city of Rome." See Candlemas day

In the clear cold. Sergey Yesenin, tr. fr. the Russian by Babette Deutsch. *PaS*

"In the clear cold the dales grow blue and tremble." See In the clear cold

In the country. Ivy O. Eastwick. *EaI*

"In the courtyard grows a rare tree." See A rare tree

"In the cowslip pips I lie." See Clock-a-clay

In the dark. A. A. Milne. *MiWc*

"In the days that are long gone." See X is for xoanon

"In the deep kingdom under ground." See Under ground

"In the drinking well." See Four ruthless rhymes—Aunt Eliza

In the dumps. See "We are all in the dumps"

"In the early, shivery dark." See Milk in winter

In the evening. Thomas Hardy. *PlI*

"In the evening, when the world knew he was dead." See In the evening

"In the family drinking well." See Sister Nell

"In the far corner." See The blackbird

In the fashion. A. A. Milne. *MiWc*

"In the fold." See The little young lambs

In the garden. Ilo Orleans. *HuL-1*

"In the gray dawning across the white lake." See Wild March

"In the greenest of our valleys." See The haunted palace

"In the greenhouse lives a wren." See Little friend

"In the harbor, in the island, in the Spanish seas." See Trade winds

"In the heart of a seed." See The little plant

In the hours of darkness. James Flexner. *FeF*

"In the jolly, jolly spring." See What the toys are thinking

"In the long flat panhandle of Texas." See The people, yes—Night too has numbers

"In the long lake's mirror." See From the mailboat passing by

"In the maple-sugar bush." See March

"In the mellowy orchards, rich and ripe." See The snitterjipe

"In the merry month of May." Nicholas Breton. *HaP*

In the middle. David McCord. *McFf*

"In the middle of the sea." See Ambition

"In the mirror." See Reflection

"In the month of June the grass grows high." See Reading the book of hills and seas

In the morning ("In the morning every day") Dorothy Aldis. *AlHd*

In the morning ("When, in the morning, fresh from sleep") Cecilia Loftus. *DoP*

"In the morning every day." See In the morning

"In the morning her dress is of palest green." See Tree gowns

"In the morning the city." See City

"In the morning, very early." See Barefoot days

"In the morning when the sun." See Daytime moon

"In the motionless haze of interior heat." See Recital

"In the old deep sing-song of the sea." See Old deep sing-song

"In the other gardens." See Autumn fires

"In the pale sunshine, with frail wings unfurled." See The snowdrop—The first bee

In the park. See Regent's park

"In the pleasant green garden." Kate Greenaway. *ArTp*

"In the sand." Myra Cohn Livingston. *LiW*

"In the season of spring is the season of growing." See In the spring

In the spring ("In the season of spring is the season of growing") Ibycus, tr. fr. the Greek by Walter Headlam. *PaS*

In the spring ("Now the bright crocus flames, and now") Meleager, tr. fr. the Greek by Andrew Lang. *PaS*

"In the squdgy river." See The hippopotamus

In the stable. Elizabeth Goudge. *DoP*

"In the storms of life." Unknown. *MoY*

"In the stronghold of his will fighting his last battle still." See Pirate passes

In the summer. Dorothy Aldis. *AlA—McAw*

"In the summer, in the evenings." See In the summer

"In the summer palace the fireflies have lost their way. The sky is like water." See Ninth moon

"In the time of violets." See Over, under, over

"In the very early morning." See The rabbits

In the week when Christmas comes. Eleanor Farjeon. *ArTp—BrL-7—BrS—HuL-2*

In the wilderness. Robert Graves. *GrP*

"In the winter the rabbits match their pelts to the earth." See White season

"In the winter time we go." See White fields

In the woods alone. Unknown, tr. fr. the Latin by Helen Waddell. *PaS*

"In the woods the bluebells seem." See Blue magic

"In this book I'll gladly sign." Unknown. *MoY*

"In this world, the Isle of Dreams." See The white island

"In Timbuctoo." See Timbuctoo

"In time of silver rain." Langston Hughes. *ArTp*

In time of the breaking of nations. Thomas Hardy. *HaP*

In trust. Mary Mapes Dodge. *BrS*

"In Vicary square at Tithe-on-Trent." See Vicary square

"In Waikee-waik." See The bisk

In Walpi. See The Painted desert

In winter. Marchette Chute. *ChA*

"In winter I get up at night." See Bed in summer

"In winter time our flower store." See Winter flower store

"In winter, when it's cold and snows." See Winter-wear

"In winter, when the fields are white." See Through the looking glass—Humpty Dumpty's recitation

"In woods are words." See Words

"In Xanadu did Kubla Khan." See Kubla Khan; or, A vision in a dream

"In years to come." Unknown. *MoY*

Inch-worm. Dorothy Aldis. *AlHd*

The Inchcape rock. Robert Southey. *UnG*

Incident. Countee Cullen. *JoAc*

Incident of the French camp. Robert Browning. *UnG—UnMc*

Inns and taverns

The General Elliott. R. Graves. *GrP*

A lady comes to an inn. E. J. Coatsworth. *ArTp—CoSp*

The rabbits' song outside the tavern. E. J. Coatsworth. *ArTp*

Tarantella. H. Belloc. *NaM—SmLg*

"There is an inn, a merry old inn." From The hobbit. J. R. R. Tolkien. *LoL*

Innumerable friend. May Sarton. *McW*

Insanity

The dancing seal. W. W. Gibson. *CoPm*

Tom o' Bedlam's song. Unknown. *HaP—NaE*

Roaring mad Tom. *HoW*

Tom o' Bedlam. *McW—SmLg*

Inscription for an old bed. William Morris. *HoW*

Inscription on the Statue of Liberty. See The new colossus

Inscriptions. See Epitaphs

Insects. See also names of insects, as Ants

"A big black bug bit a big black bear." Unknown. *WiRm*

Bugs. W. Stokes. *NaM*

A considerable speck. R. Frost. *FrR*

Devil's darning needle. C. L. McCoy. *BrR-3*

End-of-summer poem. R. B. Bennett. *BrS—FeF*

The flattered lightning bug. D. Marquis. *CoSp*

The green silk bug. A. Fisher. *McAw*

I want you to meet. D. McCord. *McT*

Lady bug. Unknown. *JoAc*

"Little black bug." M. W. Brown. *FeF—HuL-1*

Little bug. R. W. Bacmeister. *BrL-k*

Little talk. A. Fisher. *FeF*

Near dusk. J. Auslander. *FeF*

The spit-bug. W. H. Matchett. *McW*

Tea party. H. Behn. *BeW*

"There was a young man of St Bees." W. S. Gilbert. *CoH*

The thunder-and-lightning bug. From The house beyond the meadow. H. Behn. *BeH*

When I went to get a drink. J. Ciardi. *CiI*

"The **inside** of a whirlpool." See Warning

Insight. Dorothy Aldis. *ThP*

The **instruments.** Christopher Smart. *HoW*

"**Inter,** mitzy, titzy, tool." Mother Goose. *OpO*

"**Interminable** palaces front on the green parterres." See Fontainebleau

"**Intery,** mintery, cutery, corn." Mother Goose. *ArTp—DeMg—JoAc—OpO*

A counting-out rhyme. *DeT*

"Intry, mintry, cutry, corn." *HuSv*

"**Into** any little room." See Sleep song

"**Into** my head." See A dream about the man in the moon

"**Into** my heart an air that kills." See A Shropshire lad

"**Into** my heart's treasury." See The coin

Into my own. Robert Frost. *FrR*

"**Into** the basin put the plums." See The Christmas pudding

"**Into** the endless dark." See City lights

"**Into** the fountain." See The fountain

"**Into** the scented woods we'll go." See Green rain

Introduction. See "Piping down the valleys wild"

An **introduction** to dogs. Ogden Nash. *NaM—UnG*

Introduction to Songs of innocence. See "Piping down the valleys wild"

The **intruder.** James Reeves. *ReBl*

"**Intry,** mintry, cutry, corn." See "Intery, mintery, cutery, corn"

The **invaders.** A. A. Milne. *MiWc*

Inventions. See Inventors and inventions

Inventors and inventions. See also names of inventions, as Telephones; also names of inventors, as Bell, Alexander Graham

Alexander Graham Bell did not invent the telephone. R. P. T. Coffin. *ArTp*

And yet fools say. G. S. Holmes. *ArTp—BrL-7*

Darius Green and his flying-machine. J. T. Trowbridge. *NaM*

Stairs. O. Herford. *CoH*

The **investment.** Robert Frost. *FrR*

Invictus. William Ernest Henley. *UnG*

"The **invisible** atoms of the air." See Rima

The **invisible** playmate. Margaret Widdemer. *FeF*

Invitation. Harry Behn. *FeF*

Invitation to Bess. Eleanor Farjeon. *FaCb—FaN*

Invitation to the voyage. Charles Baudelaire, tr. fr. the French by Richard Wilbur. *PaS*

Invocation. Unknown, tr. fr. the Sotho (African) by G. H. Franz. *PaS*

"**Io.** Paean. Io, sing." See The triumph of the whale

Iolanthe, sel. William Schwenck Gilbert

The Lord Chancellor's song. *CoH*

Ipsey wipsey. Mother Goose. *OpO*

"**Ipsey** wipsey spider." See Ipsey wipsey

Ireland

"The abbot of Inisfalen." W. Allingham. *PaOm*

Christmas eve in Ireland. K. Tynan. *EaW*

I'll wear a shamrock. M. C. Davies. *ArTp—BrS—HaY*

Irish. E. J. O'Brien. *BrS*

Irish grandmother. K. Edelman. *BrS*

Kitty of Coleraine. Unknown. *CoSp*

A Longford legend. Unknown. *CoSp*

Red Hanrahan's song about Ireland. W. B. Yeats. *SmLg*

St Patrick was a gentleman. H. Bennett. *BrS*

The wearin' of the green. Unknown. *CoPs*

Ireland—History

Bronwen to her magpie. E. Farjeon. *FaCb*

The **iris.** Gasetsu. *ArTp*

Irises

The iris. Gasetsu. *ArTp*

Irish
  Brian O'Lin. Unknown. *WoF*
  An Irish airman foresees his death. W. B.
    Yeats. *GrCc—SmLg*
  The Irish dancer. Unknown. *SmLg*
  The Irish schoolmaster. J. A. Sidney. *CoH*
  My dog Tray. T. Campbell. *UnG*
    The Irish harper. *DeT*
Irish. Edward J. O'Brien. *BrS*
An **Irish** airman foresees his death. William
    Butler Yeats. *GrCc—SmLg*
The **Irish** dancer. Unknown. *SmLg*
Irish grandmother. Katherine Edelman.
    BrS
The **Irish** harper. See My dog Tray
The **Irish** schoolmaster. James A. Sidney.
    CoH
Iron (Metal)
  Red iron ore. Unknown. *ArTp*
Ironing day. Dorothy Aldis. *AlA*
Irwin, Wallace (Hashimura Togo, pseud.)
  Blow me eyes. *CoSp*
  A dash to the pole. *CoH*
  The fate of the Cabbage Rose. *CoH*
  A nautical extravagance. See A nautical
    extravaganza
  A nautical extravaganza. *CoSp*
    A nautical extravagance. *HuSv*
  The powerful eyes o' Jeremy Tait. *CoSp*
  The rhyme of the chivalrous shark. *CoH*
  Sensitive Sydney. *CoH*
"**Is** a caterpillar ticklish." See Only my
    opinion
"**Is** Arthur gone." See Is Arthur gone to
    Avalon
Is Arthur gone to Avalon. Eleanor Far-
    jeon. *FaCb*
"**Is** it, I wonder, a rum thing." See The boy
"**Is** it not so, brother." See The sun that
    warms you
"**Is** John Smith within." Mother Goose.
    DeMg—OpO
"**Is** Mary in the dairy." See Where's Mary
"**Is** my team ploughing." See A Shropshire
    lad
"**Is** some such word." See Propriety
"**Is** that dance slowing in the mind of man."
    See Four for Sir John Davies
Is the moon tired. Christina Georgina Ros-
    setti. *HuSv*
"**Is** the moon tired? She looks so pale."
    See Is the moon tired
"**Is** there anybody there? said the traveler."
    See The listeners
"**Is** there anything." See Wise Sarah and
    the elf
"**Isabel** Jones & Curabel Lee." David Mc-
    Cord. *McFf—UnG*
"**Isabel** met an enormous bear." See Ad-
    ventures of Isabel
Isaiah, sels. Bible, Old Testament
  "But they that wait upon the Lord shall
    renew their strength." *ArTp*
  The peaceable kingdom. *FeF*
Ise, Lady
  "The rains of spring" *ArTp*

Ishii and Obata
  Far beyond us. tr. *PaS*
  Once only. tr. *PaS*
  Solitary pine. tr. *PaS*
  Tolling bells. tr. *PaS*
The island, sel. Francis Brett Young
  Atlantic Charter, A. D. 1620-1942. *ArTp—
    JoAc*
The island ("If I had a ship") A. A. Milne.
    MiWc
The island ("They mowed the meadow
    down below") Dorothy Aldis. *AlA*
Islands. See also names of islands, as Ber-
    muda
  Ambition. M. Chute. *ChA*
  Arran. Unknown. *SmLg*
  At Matsushima. Shiki. *PaS*
  Flannan isle. W. W. Gibson. *CoSp*
  "If once you have slept on an island." R.
    Field. *HuL-2*
  The island ("If I had a ship") A. A. Milne.
    MiWc
  The island ("They mowed the meadow
    down below") D. Aldis. *AlA*
  Islands. J. Reeves. *ReR*
  The isle should have a pine tree. E. J.
    Coatsworth. *BrR-4*
  The lake isle of Innisfree. W. B. Yeats.
    FeF—JoAc
  Pirates on Funafuti. E. V. Rieu. *RiF*
  The story of Samuel Jackson. C. G. Le-
    land. *CoSp*
Islands. James Reeves. *ReR*
"**Islands** all around." See At Matsushima
"**Islands** and peninsulas, continents and
    capes." See Geography
The isle should have a pine tree. Elizabeth
    Jane Coatsworth. *BrR-4*
"**Isn't** it strange." See A bag of tools
"**Isn't** it strange some people make." See
    Some people
"**It** ain't gonna rain no more." Unknown.
    WoF
It bids pretty fair. Robert Frost. *FrR*
"**It** came upon the midnight clear." Ed-
    mund Hamilton Sears. *FeF*
"**It** chanced to be our washing day." See
    The September gale
"**It** costs little Gossip her income for shoes."
    Mother Goose. *DeMg*
It couldn't be done. Edgar A. Guest. *BrL-8*
"**It** doesn't breathe." See My nose
"**It** fell about the Martinmas time." See
    Get up and bar the door
"**It** fell on a day, and a bonny summer day."
    See The bonny house of Airlie
"**It** hasn't a scratch, it hasn't a spot." See
    New
"**It** is a curious thing that you." See The
    kangaroo
"**It** is a windy day." See Weather
"**It** is blue-butterfly day here in spring."
    See Blue-butterfly day
"**It** is Christmas in the mansion." See
    Christmas in the heart
"**It** is colder now." See Epistle to be left
    in the earth
"**It** is getting dark and time he drew to a
    house." See Willful homing

It is July. Susan Hartley Swett. *HaY*

"It is memory speaking, preternaturally clear." See Elizabeth at the piano

It is not far. See Night ("Stars over snow")

"It is not growing like a tree." See A Pindaric ode: To the immortal memory and friendship of that noble pair, Sir Lucius Cary and Sir Henry Morrison —The noble nature

"It is portentous, and a thing of state." See Abraham Lincoln walks at midnight

"It is queer to think that many people." See The man with the rake

"It is raining." Lucy Sprague Mitchell. *ArTp* —*HuL-2*

"It is so smooth." See Sea-shell

"It is the day of all the year." See Mothering Sunday

"It is the duty of the student." See Duty of the student

"It is the month of falling stars." See The month of falling stars

"It is very nice to know." See A thought

"It isn't just on Mother's day." See Mother's day

"It isn't raining rain to me." See April rain

"It little profits that an idle king." See Ulysses

"It looks like any building." See The library

"It matters not how piteously you plead." See Acquiescence

"It ought to come in April." See Wearing of the green

"It rained on Anne." See No drip of rain

"It rained quite a lot, that spring. You woke in the morning." See Metropolitan nightmare

It really happened. Elizabeth Henley. *BrBc*

It rolls on. Morris Bishop. *PlI*

"It seemed that a giant." See Strange footprints

"It seems a shame." See The last flower

"It sifts from leaden sieves." See The snow

"It snowed in spring on earth so dry and warm." See Our singing strength

"It sushes." See Cynthia in the snow

"It takes a good speller." See Spelling bee

"It takes a little island." See The isle should have a pine tree

"It tickles." Myra Cohn Livingston. *LiWa*

"It tickles me." Unknown. *MoY*

"It troubled me as once I was." See Once a child

It was. Dorothy Aldis. *AlA*

"It was a jolly bed in sooth." See Us idle wenches

"It was a knight in Scótland born." See The fair flower of Northumberland

"It was a summer evening." See The battle of Blenheim

"It was a tall young oysterman lived by the riverside." See The ballad of the oysterman

"It was amusing on that antique grass." See Recorders in Italy

"It was an old, old, old, old lady." See One, two, three

"It was Earl Haldan's daughter." See The ballad of Earl Haldan's daughter

"It was fifty years ago." See The fiftieth birthday of Agassiz

"It was in a pleasant time." See Earl Mar's daughter

"It was late in the night when the squire came home." See The gipsy laddie

"It was laughing time, and the tall giraffe." See Laughing time

"It was long I lay." See I will sing you one-o

"It was many and many a year ago." See Annabel Lee

"It was midnight on the back porch." Unknown. *MoY*

"It was much later in life he rose." See Gibbs

"It was my thirtieth year to heaven." See October

"It was on a merry time." Mother Goose. *DeMg*

"It was on a Sunday morning." See The gray goose

"It was on a Wednesday night, the moon was shining bright." See Jesse James

"It was on Christmas day." See All in the morning

"It was Saint Francis who came." Annette Wynne. *DoP*

"It was six men of Indostan." See The blind men and the elephant

"It was the schooner Hesperus." See The wreck of the Hesperus

"It was the time when lilies blow." See Lady Clare

"It were as if the heavens." See Moon-night

"An Italian boy that liked to play." See Columbus

Italian lullaby. Unknown, tr. fr. the Italian. *FeF*

Italian opera. James Miller. *PlU* (sel.)

Italians
  Da boy from Rome. T. A. Daly. *FeF*
  Mia Carlotta. T. A. Daly *BrL-7*

Italy
  A bag of chestnuts. E. Farjeon. *FaCb*— *FaN*

"It's a dark and dreary season." See Triolet on a dark day

"It's a very odd thing." See Miss T

"It's cold, said the cricket." See Halloween concert

"It's coming, boys." See In trust

"It's former green is blue and thin." See The garden seat

"It's fun to .clean house." See I like housecleaning

"It's funny how often they say to me, Jane." See The good little girl

"It's good to be back." See In the garden

"It's hard to lose a friend." Unknown. *MoY*

"It's midsummer day." See Haytime

"It's nice to be hungry." See Hunger and thirst

"It's no go the merrygoround, it's no go the rickshaw." See Bagpipe music

"It's not very far to the edge of town." See Adventure

"It's once I courted as pretty a lass." Mother Goose. *OpO*

"It's raining, it's pouring." Mother Goose. *OpO*

"It's raining, it's raining." Mother Goose. *OpO*

"It's raining, raining, raining." See Raining

"It's springtime in Donegal." See Springtime in Donegal

It's time to get up. John Ciardi. *CiM*

"It's very cold." See Field mouse conference

"Itt rely is ridikkelus." See Bobby's first poem

"I've asked Professor Swigly Brown." See Write me a verse

"I've been awake, and been awake." See At night

"I've been bad and I'm in bed." See Bad

"I've been to the zoo." See At the zoo

"I've broken lots of eggs, I guess." See The importance of eggs

"I've brushed my hair, and made myself." See Virtue

"I've got a box." See Belongings

"I've got a new book from my Grandfather Hyde." Leroy F. Jackson. *BrS—FeF*

"I've got a rocket." Unknown. *BrS—JoAc*

"I've got shoes with grown up laces." See Growing up

"I've had my supper." See In the dark

"I've known the spring in England." See The fields of Ballyclare

I've learned to sing. Georgia Douglas Johnson. *BrL-8*

"I've learned to sing a song of hope." See I've learned to sing

"I've noticed how the woolly lamb." See All wool

"I've often heard my mother say." See The unknown color

"I've said goodbye to the three black kittens." See First departure

"I've seen caravans." See Caravans

"I've seen one flying saucer. Only when." See Go fly a saucer

"I've seen you where you never were." Mother Goose. *DeMg*
Five very old riddles. *DeT*

"I've tried the new moon tilted in the air." See The freedom of the moon

"I've watched the clouds by day and night." See Watching clouds

"I've watched you now a full half-hour." See To a butterfly

Ives. Muriel Rukeyser. *PlU* (sel.)

Ivy
"Hitty Pitty within the wall." Mother Goose. *OpO*
"The holly and the ivy." Unknown. *DeT*
Poison ivy. K. Gallagher. *BrS*

Izembō
A shower. *ArTp*

J

J. P. B. See B., J. P.

J is for jinn. Eleanor Farjeon. *FaCb*

"Ja-Nez—burro with the long ears." See Burro with the long ears

Jabberwocky. See Through the looking glass

Jack a nory. See "I'll tell you a story"

"Jack and Gye." Mother Goose. *OpO*

Jack and Jill. See "Jack and Jill went up the hill"

Jack and Jill and old Dame Dob. See "Jack and Jill went up the hill"

"Jack and Jill went up the hill." Mother Goose. *ArTp—DeMg—HuSv—JoAc—LiL*
Jack and Jill. *BrL-k*
Jack and Jill and old Dame Dob. *OpO*

"Jack, be nimble." Mother Goose. *AnI—ArTp—DeMg—HuSv—JoAc—LiL—OpO*

Jack Frost ("Look out, look out") Cicely E. Pike. *HuL-1*

Jack Frost ("Someone painted pictures on my") Helen Bayley Davis. *BrR-4*

Jack Frost ("Swift and busy, brash and bold") Harry Behn. *BeW*

Jack Frost ("When Jack Frost comes—oh, the fun") Unknown. *BrL-k*

Jack-hide-in-the-hedge. Eleanor Farjeon. *FaCb*

Jack Horner. See "Little Jack Horner"

"Jack Horner was a pretty lad." See Little Jack Horner

"A Jack-in-the-box." See Jack-in-the-box

Jack-in-the-box. William Jay Smith. *SmL*

"Jack-in-the-pulpit." Ivy O. Eastwick. *HaY*

Jack in the pulpit. Mother Goose. *OpO*

"Jack in the pulpit, out and in." See Jack in the pulpit

Jack-in-the-pulpits
"Jack-in-the-pulpit." I. O. Eastwick. *HaY*
Jack in the pulpit. Mother Goose. *OpO*

"Jack, Jack, pump the water." Unknown. *TaD*

Jack-o'-lanterns. See Hallowe'en

Jack Sprat. See "Jack Sprat could eat no fat"

"Jack Sprat could eat no fat." Mother Goose. *DeMg—JoAc—LiL*
Jack Sprat. *OpO*

"Jack Sprat (had a cat)." See Jack Sprat's cat

Jack Sprat's cat. Mother Goose. *OpO*

Jack Sprat's pig. Mother Goose. *OpO*

Jack Tar. Émile Jacot. *HuL-1*

"Jack Tar, sailor man." See Jack Tar

Jackson, Andrew (about)
Andrew Jackson. M. Keller. *UnG—UnMc*

Jackson, Helen Hunt (H. H., pseud.; Helen Hunt; Saxe Holme, pseud.)
October's bright blue weather. *CoPs*
September. *FeF—UnG*
September days are here. *HaY*
September days are here. See September

Jackson, Kathryn
  Being twins. *BrBc*
  Brown bear's honey song. *McAw*
  Things of summer. *McAw*
  The twins. *BrBc*

Jackson, Kathryn and Byron
  Noonday Sun. *ArTp—FeF—HuL-2*
  Open range. *ArTp—FeF*

Jackson, Leroy F.
  Boots, boots, boots. *BrL-k*
  Columbus. *BrS*
  The hero. *BrS*
  Hippity hop to bed. *ArTp—BrL-k*
  "I've got a new book from my Grandfather Hyde." *BrS—FeF*
  Old Father Annum. *BrS*
  Simple Sam. *CoPs*

"**Jacky**, come give me thy fiddle." Mother Goose. *OpO—PlU*

Jacky Jingle. Mother Goose. *OpO*

Jacob, Ruth Apprich
  Waiting. *BrBc*

Jacobson, Ethel
  A jolly noise. *McAw*
  Words from the bottom of a well. *ThP*

Jacot, Émile
  Jack Tar. *HuL-1*

James II, King of England (about)
  Epitaph on a Jacobite. T. B. Macaulay. *DeT*

James, Jesse (about)
  Jesse James ("It was on a Wednesday night, the moon was shining bright") Unknown. *HoW*
  Jesse James ("Jesse James was a lad who killed many a man") Unknown. *UnMc*
  Jesse James ("Jesse James was a two-gun man") W. R. Benét. *CoSp*

James and the shoulder of mutton. Adelaide O'Keefe. *DeT*

"**James** has hated motorists ever since the day." See That'll be all right you'll find

"**James James.**" See Disobedience

Jammès, Francis
  Amsterdam, sel.
    Robinson Crusoe returns to Amsterdam. *FeF*
  A child reads an almanac. *FeF*
  Robinson Crusoe returns to Amsterdam. See Amsterdam

Jammès, Francis (about)
  Francis Jammès: A prayer to go to Paradise with the donkeys. R. Wilbur. *ArTp*

"**Jan., Jan.**, is a jeweler-man." See January snow

"**Jane's** too old." See Proud Jane

Janet waking. John Crowe Ransom. *ReT*

"**Janie** now, Janie ever." Unknown. *MoY*

The **janitor's** boy. Nathalia Crane. *UnG*

January
  January ("January, bleak and drear") F. D. Sherman. *HaY*
  January ("January sparkles") S. S. Lambdin. *HaY*
  January ("A silver sky is faintly etched") M. Lewis. *UnG*

"**January** is here." E. Fawcett. *HaY*
January snow. A. Fisher. *HaY*
January's song. E. Farjeon. *FaCb—FaN*
Old January. From The faerie queene. E. Spenser. *HaY*
Snow. E. J. Coatsworth. *BrR-6—BrS*
  January. *CoPs*
The wind of January. C. G. Rossetti. *HaY*
January. See Snow ("A snow can come as quietly")
January ("January, bleak and drear") Frank Dempster Sherman. *HaY*
January ("January sparkles") Sylvia S. Lambdin. *HaY*
January ("A silver sky is faintly etched") Michael Lewis. *UnG*
"**January**, bleak and drear." See January
"**January** brings the snow." Sara Coleridge. *ArTp—DeMg*
  A calendar. *UnG*
  The garden year. *DeT—HuSv*
  The months of the year. *HuL-2*
"**January** cold and desolate." See The months
"**January** is here." Edgar Fawcett. *HaY*
January night. Rafael Alberto Arrieta, tr. fr. the Spanish by Muna Lee de Muñoz Marin. *PaS*
"**January** night, quiet and luminous." See January night
January 1. Marnie Pomeroy. *CoPs*
"**January** shivers." See Calendar
January snow. Aileen Fisher. *HaY*
"**January** sparkles." See January
January's song. Eleanor Farjeon. *FaCb—FaN*
Japan
  Japanesque. O. Herford. *CoH*
  Momotara. Unknown. *ArTp—HuL-2*
  An old song. Hehoash. *PaS*
Japanesque. Oliver Herford. *CoH*
Jaques, Florence Page
  A goblinade. *ArTp—HuL-1*
  There once was a puffin. *ArTp—HuL-2*
Jargon. James Reeves. *ReR*
"**Jay-bird**, jay-bird, settin' on a rail." Unknown
  American Father Gander. *UnG*
Jaybird. Unknown. *CoH*
"**Jaybird** a-sitting on a hickory limb." See Jaybird
"**Jaybird** pulls the turnin' plow." Unknown. *WoF*
"**Jaybird** settin' on a barbed-wire fence." Unknown. *WoF*
Jays
  August 28. D. McCord. *McFf*
  Invitation. H. Behn. *FeF*
  Jaybird. Unknown. *CoH*
  "Jaybird pulls the turnin' plow." Unknown. *WoF*
  "Jaybird settin' on a barbed-wire fence." Unknown. *WoF*
Jealousy
  Advice to a girl. T. Campion. *ThP*
  Binnorie. Unknown. *MaB*
  Richard Cory. E. A. Robinson. *CoSp—SmLg—ThP*

Jeffers, Robinson
Ascent to the Sierras. *SmLg*
Continent's end. *PlI*
Jefferson, Thomas (about)
"Thomas Jefferson." R. C. and S. V. Benét. *ArTp—BrL-8—FeF*
"Jellicle cats come out to-night." See The song of the Jellicles
The jellyfish. Ogden Nash. *FeF*
Jemima. See "There was a little girl, and she had a little curl"
"Jemima is my name." See Mima
"Jemima Jane." Marchette Chute. *ChA*
Jemmy Dawson. Mother Goose. *OpO*
Jenks, Tudor
The baby's name. *BrBc*
Jenner, Edward
Signs of rain. *DeT*
"Jennifer's my other name." See My other name
Jennings, Elizabeth
Music and words. *PlU*
"Jenny, come tie my." See The bonnie cravat
Jenny kissed me. Leigh Hunt. *BrBc*
"Jenny kissed me when we met." See Jenny kissed me
"Jenny was so mad." Mother Goose. *DeMg*
"Jenny White and Johnny Black." Eleanor Farjeon. *FeF*
Jenny Wren. See "Jenny Wren fell sick"
"Jenny Wren fell sick." Mother Goose. *JoAc*
Jenny Wren. *NaE*
Little Jenny Wren. *HuL-1*
Ungrateful Jenny. *OpO*
"Jeremiah, blow the fire." Mother Goose. *OpO*
Jeremy's secrets. Barbara E. Todd. *BrBc*
"Jeremy's six, so his sisters say." See Jeremy's secrets
"Jerry Hall." Mother Goose. *DeMg—OpO*
Jerry Mulligan. John Ciardi. *CiM*
"Jerry Mulligan came to see me." See Jerry Mulligan
"Jersey girls are pretty." Unknown. *MoY*
Jerusalem
Jerusalem ("And did those feet in ancient time") From Milton. W. Blake. *NaE*
"And did those feet in ancient time." *HaP—SmLg*
Jerusalem ("Jerusalem, my happy home") Unknown. *SmLg*
Jerusalem ("And did those feet in ancient time") See Milton
Jerusalem ("Jerusalem, my happy home") Unknown. *SmLg*
"Jerusalem, Joppa, Jericho." See Jargon
"Jerusalem, my happy home." See Jerusalem
Jesse James ("It was on a Wednesday night, the moon was shining bright") Unknown. *HoW*
Jesse James ("Jesse James was a lad who killed many a man") Unknown. *UnMc*
Jesse James ("Jesse James was a two-gun man") William Rose Benét. *CoSp*

"Jesse James was a lad who killed many a man." See Jesse James
"Jesse James was a two-gun man." See Jesse James
Jessica dances. Eleanor Farjeon. *FaCb*
Jest 'fore Christmas. Eugene Field. *FeF*
"Jesu." See A page's road song
Jesus Christ. See also Christmas; Easter; God
All in the morning. Unknown. *BrBc*
Ballad of the goodly fere. E. Pound. *HaP*
The child's hymn. M. Howitt. *UnG*
The ending of the year. E. Farjeon. *EaW*
Ex ore infantium. F. Thompson. *DoP*
Guests. Unknown. *NaE*
The holy well. Unknown. *SmLg*
In the carpenter shop. Unknown. *UnG*
Lambs. K. Tynan. *DeT*
Loving Jesus. C. Wesley. *DoP*
Mother and Child. I. O. Eastwick. *BrS*
The Mother's song. E. Farjeon. *DoP*
My example. C. Wesley. *DoP*
The mystery. R. Hodgson. *DoP*
"Once in royal David's city." C. F. Alexander. *DoP*
Redemption. G. Herbert. *HaP*
Saint Joseph. E. Farjeon. *FaCb*
Sheep and lambs. K. Tynan. *DoP*
Spanish lullaby. Unknown. *DoP*
Sweet story of old. J. T. Luke. *DoP*
"Jesus, I kneel down to say." See Just for Jesus
"Jesus our brother, strong and good." See The friendly beasts
"Jesus, tender Shepherd, hear me." See A child's evening prayer
"Jill came from the fair." Eleanor Farjeon. *ArTp*
Jim. See Jim, who ran away from his nurse
Jim Bludso. John Hay. *BrL-8—UnMc*
Jim Crow. Mother Goose. *OpO*
Jim Jay. Walter De La Mare. *BrS—UnG*
"Jim says a sailor man." See When we are men
Jim, who ran away from his nurse. Hilaire Belloc. *LoL—NaM*
Jim. *UnMc*
Jiménez, Juan Ramón
Immense hour. *PaS*
Nightfall. *PaS*
"Jiminy jiminy jukebox. Wheatcakes. Crumbs." See Mole
"Jimmy James when he was three." See About Jimmy James
"Jimmy the Mowdy." See Greedy Tom
Jingle bells. James Pierpont. *OpO* (sel.)
"Jingle bells, jingle bells." See Jingle bells
The jingo-ring. Unknown. *HuL-1*
Jippy and Jimmy. Laura E. Richards. *ArTp—BrR-4—HuL-1*
"Jippy and Jimmy were two little dogs." See Jippy and Jimmy
Jittery Jim. William Jay Smith. *SmL*
"Joan has a corner in a garden." See Joan's corner
Joan of Arc (about)
The good Joan. L. W. Reese. *ArTp—FeF—NaM*
The maid. T. G. Roberts. *NaM*

Joan's corner. Eleanor Farjeon. *FaCb*

Joan's door. Eleanor Farjeon. *BrBc*

Job, sels. Bible, Old Testament
The horse. *FeF—UnG*
Job, Chapter 36. *PlI*
Job, Chapter 38. *PlI*

Job, Chapter 36. See Job

Job, Chapter 38. See Job

Jock o' Binnorie. Robert Graves. *GrP*

Jock o' Hazeldean. See Guy Mannering

Joe. David McCord. *ArTp—McFf*

"Joe, Joe, broke his toe." Unknown. *WoF*

"Joe, Joe, hurt his toe." Unknown. *WiRm*

"Joe, Joe, strong and able." Unknown. *WoF*

"Jog on, jog on, the foot-path way." See The winter's tale

John. David McCord. *McFf*

John Anderson, my jo. Robert Burns. *HaP —HuSv—ThP*

"John Anderson, my jo, John." See John Anderson, my jo

John Barleycorn. Robert Burns. *SmLg*

"John comes in with a basket." See John

"John Cook had a little grey mare." See "John Cook he had a little gray mare"

"John Cook he had a little gray mare." Mother Goose. *DeMg*
He, haw, hum. *HuL-1*
Hee, haw, hum. *DeT*
John Cook's mare. *ReG*
The last will and testament of the grey mare. *OpO*

John Cook's mare. See "John Cook he had a little gray mare"

John Day, frontiersman. Yvor Winters. *HaP*

John Dory. Unknown. *MaB*

"John had." See Happiness

John Henry. Unknown. *UnMc*

"John Henry was a little baby." See John Henry

"John is the tallest—he's ever so high." See Comparison

John Jiggy Jag. See "Little John Jiggy Jag"

"John Littlehouse the redhead was a large ruddy man." See The blacksmith's serenade

John of the fountain. Eleanor Farjeon. *FaN*

"John of the fountain was born in July." See John of the fountain

John plans. Dorothy Mason Pierce. *BrBc*

"John says to John." Unknown. *WiRm*

"John Smith, fellow fine." Mother Goose. *OpO*

"John Smith's a very guid man." Unknown. *JoAc*

John Sutter. Yvor Winters. *HaP*

John Watts. Mother Goose. *OpO*

Johnie Faa. Unknown. *MaB*

"Johnnie Crack and Flossie Snail." See Under milk wood

"Johnnie Norrie." Mother Goose. *OpO*

Johnny. Emma Rounds. *CoH*

Johnny Appleseed. See In praise of Johnny Appleseed

"Johnny Appleseed, Johnny Appleseed." See In praise of Johnny Appleseed

Johnny Armstrong. See "Johnny Armstrong killed a calf"

Johnny Armstrong ("There was a man in Westmoreland") Unknown. *UnMc*

"Johnny Armstrong killed a calf." Mother Goose. *DeMg*

Johnny Armstrong. *OpO*

"Johnny Crow." See Johnny Crow's garden

Johnny Crow's garden. L. Leslie Brooke. *ReG*

Johnny Fife and Johnny's wife. Mildred Plew Meigs. *ArTp—BrL-7—HuL-1*

"Johnny had a little dove." See Johnny's farm

"Johnny has a nickel." Unknown. *WiRm*

"Johnny is a buttercup." Unknown. *MoY*

"Johnny made a custard." See Some cook

Johnny Morgan. See "Little Johnny Morgan"

"Johnny on the ocean." Unknown. *TaD*

"Johnny shall have a new bonnet." Mother Goose. *DeMg—JoAc*
Why may not I love Johnny. *OpO*

"Johnny used to find content." See Johnny

Johnny's farm. H. M. Adams. *HuL-1*

Johnson, Burges
The service. *BrL-8*
Soap, the oppressor. *BrR-4*
Things that get lost. *BrR-6*
Where dreams are made. *BrR-4*

Johnson, E. Pauline
The birds' lullaby. *HuL-2*
The song my paddle sings. *FeF*

Johnson, Fenton
"Who is that a-walking in the corn." *GrCc*

Johnson, Georgia Douglas
I've learned to sing. *BrL-8*

Johnson, James Weldon
The creation. *ArTp—JoAc*
O black and unknown bards. *PlU*

Johnson, Lionel
To Morfydd. *ReT*

Johnson, Robert Underwood
Hearth song. *HaY*

Johnson, Samuel
An epitaph upon the celebrated Claudy Philips, musician, who died very poor. *PlU*
A hinted wish. tr. *BrL-8*
"If a man who turnips cries." *DeMg*
The turnip seller. *NaE*
The turnip vendor. *OpO*
The turnip seller. See "If a man who turnips cries"
The turnip vendor. See "If a man who turnips cries"

Johnson, Samuel (about)
A toast for Doctor Sam. E. Farjeon. *FaN*

Johnstone, Henry (Lord Johnstone)
The fastidious serpent. *CoH—LoL*
Good night prayer. *DoP*

Johnstone, Lord. See Johnstone, Henry

The jokesmith's vacation. Don Marquis. *CoH*

"A jolly fat frog did in the river swim, O."
See The frog and the crow

"A jolly little pig once lived in a sty." See
The three little pigs

Jolly miller. See Love in a village—"There
was a jolly miller"

A jolly noise. Ethel Jacobson. *McAw*

The jolly tester. See "I love sixpence, jolly
little sixpence"

Jolly Wat. Unknown. *MaB*

The jolly woodchuck. Marion Edey. *ArTp*
—*CoI*—*FeF*—*HuL-1*

Jonathan. Unknown, tr. fr. the Dutch by
Rose Fyleman. *ArTp*—*JoAc*

Jonathan Bing. Beatrice Curtis Brown.
ArTp—*CoH*—*FeF*—*HuL-2*—*LoL*—*PeF*

Jonathan Bing dances for spring. Beatrice
Curtis Brown. *BrS*

Jonathan Bing's tea. Beatrice Curtis Brown.
McW

"Jonathan Blake." See After the party

"Jonathan Gee." See Jonathan

"Jonathan Jo." A. A. Milne. *MiWc*

Jones, John Luther (about)
    Casey Jones. T. L. Seibert. *UnMc*

Jones, T. Gwynn
    The grave. *PaS*

Jones, Sir William
    "What constitutes a state." *BrL-7*

Jonson, Ben
    Another birthday. *HoW*
    Buzz and hum. See Elves' song
    A celebration of Charis, sel.
        "Have you seen but a bright lily
            grow." *SmLg*
            A comparison. *DeT*
    A comparison. See A celebration of Charis
        —"Have you seen but a bright lily
        grow"
    Cynthia's revels, sel.
        Hymn to Diana. *HoW*
    Elves' song. *DeT*
        Buzz and hum. *OpO*
    An epitaph on Salathiel Pavy. *HaP*
    Gipsy song. *SmLg*
    "Have you seen but a bright lily grow."
        See A celebration of Charis
    Hymn to Diana. See Cynthia's revels
    Love restored. *PlU* (sel.)
    Mab. See The satyr
    The noble nature. See A Pindaric ode: To
        the immortal memory and friendship of
        that noble pair, Sir Lucius Cary and Sir
        Henry Morrison
    A Pindaric ode: To the immortal memory
        and friendship of that noble pair, Sir
        Lucius Cary and Sir Henry Morrison,
        sel.
        The noble nature. *BrR-6*
    Robin Goodfellow. *ReG*
    The satyr, sel.
        Mab. *HoW*
    Song, to Celia. *HaP*
    Still to be neat. *HaP*
    Witches' charm. See The witches' charms
    The witches' charms. *CoPm* (sel.)—*ReT*
        Witches' charm. *SmLg* (sel.)

Jonson, Ben (about)
    His prayer to Ben Jonson. R. Herrick. *HaP*
    An ode for Ben Jonson. R. Herrick. *HaP*

Jorgensen, Johannes
    "The plants stand silent round me." *PaS*

Jōsa
    Crocuses. *ArTp*

Joseph, Saint (about)
    Saint Joseph. E. Farjeon. *FaCb*

Jōsō
    Winter. *PaS*

Josh's song. Myra Cohn Livingston. *LiWa*

"Joshua fit de battle of Jericho." Unknown.
    UnMc

Journal. Edna St Vincent Millay. *PlI* (sel.)

The journey. John Ciardi. *CiY*

Journey of the Magi. T. S. Eliot. *HaP*—
    SmLg

Journey's end. A. A. Milne. *MiWc*

Joy. See Happiness

Joy. Hilda Conkling. *DoP*

"Joy is not a thing you can see." See Joy

"Joy, joy, joy, that on my quiet day." See
    Variation on a Polish folk song

Joy of the morning. Edwin Markham. *FeF*

Joyce, James
    "All day I hear the noise of waters." See
        Chamber music—The noise of waters
    Chamber music, sels.
        "Lean out of the window"
            From Chamber music. *GrCc*
        The noise of waters. *ArTp*—*FeF*
            "All day I hear the noise of waters."
            SmLg
    "Lean out of the window." See Chamber
        music
    The noise of waters. See Chamber music

Joyce, Robert Dwyer
    The leprahaun. *CoPm*

Joys. James Russell Lowell. *HuL-2*

The joys of the road. Bliss Carman. *BrL-8*

"J's the jumping jay-walker." See All
    around the town

Jubilate agno. Christopher Smart. *PlU*
    (sel.)

Julius Caesar, sels. William Shakespeare
    "This was the noblest Roman of them all"
        Gallery of people. *UnG*
        A Shakespeare gallery. *UnMc*
    The valiant. *ThP*
    "Why man, he doth bestride the narrow
        world"
        A Shakespeare gallery. *UnMc*

July
    It is July. S. H. Swett. *HaY*
    July ("Loud is the summer's busy song")
        J. Clare. *UnG*
    July ("Now ripened berries fill") L.
        Tatyanicheva. *PaS*
    July meadow. L. Driscoll. *HaY*
    July's song. E. Farjeon. *FaCb*—*FaN*
    The month of the Thunder Moon. M. Doyle.
        HaY
    The mowers. M. B. Benton. *HaY*
    That's July. M. F. Butts. *HaY*

July ("Loud is the summer's busy song")
    J. Clare. *UnG*

July ("Now ripened berries fill") Lyudmila Tatyanicheva, tr. fr. the Russian by Babette Deutsch. *PaS*

"July is just in the nick of time." See The mowers

July meadow. Louise Driscoll. *HaY*

July: The succession of the four sweet months. See The succession of the four sweet months

July's song. Eleanor Farjeon. *FaCb—FaN*

The Jumblies. Edward Lear. *ArTp—CoH —HoW—JoAc—LoL—NaE—ReG*

"Jump—jump—jump." Kate Greenaway. *ArTp*
    The little jumping girls. *FeF*

Jump or jiggle. Evelyn Beyer. *ArTp—BrR —HuL-1*

Jump-rope rhymes. See Play

Jumping Joan. See "Here am I, little jumping Joan"

June
    A day in June. From The vision of Sir Launfal. J. R. Lowell. *FeF—HuSv*
    June. *UnG*
    "The days are clear." C. G. Rossetti. *ArTp*
    Stay, June, stay. *HaY*
    In June. N. Perry. *HaY*
    June ("Dark red roses in a honeyed wind swinging") N. Hopper. *HaY*
    June ("I knew that you were coming, June, I knew that you were coming") D. Malloch. *HaY*
    June ("The merry-go-round") M. C. Davies. *BrS*
    A June day. S. Teasdale. *HaY*
    June's song. E. Farjeon. *FaCb—FaN*
    May-day in June. E. Farjeon. *FaCb—FaN*
    "The sun has long been set." W. Wordsworth. *HaY*
    That's June. M. F. Butts. *HaY*

June ("And what is so rare as a day in June") See The vision of Sir Launfal— A day in June

June ("Dark red roses in a honeyed wind swinging") Nora Hopper. *HaY*

June ("I knew that you were coming, June, I knew that you were coming") Douglas Malloch. *HaY*

June ("The merry-go-round") Mary Carolyn Davies. *BrS*

A June day. Sara Teasdale. *HaY*

June's song. Eleanor Farjeon. *FaCb—FaN*

Jungle life
    Jungle night club. E. V. Rieu. *RiF*

"Jungle necklaces are hung." See Here she is

Jungle night club. E. V. Rieu. *RiF*

Juniper. Eileen Duggan. *DoP*

Juniper trees
    Juniper. E. Duggan. *DoP*

Just as he feared. See "There was an old man with a beard"

"Just as my fingers on these keys." See Peter Quince at the clavier

"Just as soon as summer's done." See The weather factory

"Just as the light is fading." See The time we like best

Just because. David McCord. *McT*

"Just before bed." See The mother's tale

Just for Jesus. Lysbeth Boyd Borie. *DoP*

"Just once, in far off Labrador." See Novel experience

"Just see those pin wheels whirling round." See Fourth of July night

Just-so stories, sels. Rudyard Kipling
    The camel's hump. *NaE*
    The sing-song of old man kangaroo. *FeF*

"Just the place for a snark, the Bellman cried." See The hunting of the snark

"Just the way that people do." See Some vegetables and flowers

Just watch. Myra Cohn Livingston. *LiW*

"Just when I'm ready to." See Naughty soap song

Justus, May
    The dress of spring. *HaY*
    Footwear. *HaY*
    Lickety-lick. *McAw*
    "Remember September." *BrS—HaY*
    Signs of Christmas. *McAw*
    Spring song. *McAw*
    Strawberry jam. *FeF*
    Winds a-blowing. *BrR-5*
    Witchwood. *BrS*

K

K is for kobold. Eleanor Farjeon. *FaCb*

Kalamazoo, Michigan
    Kalamazoo. V. Lindsay. *GrCc*

Kalamazoo. Vachel Lindsay. *GrCc*

The kangaroo ("It is a curious thing that you") Elizabeth Jane Coatsworth. *ArTp —HuSv*

Kangaroo ("A tough kangaroo named Hopalong Brown") William Jay Smith. *SmB*

"The kangaroo has a heavy tail." See Tails

Kangaroos
    The duck and the kangaroo. E. Lear. *HuL-2 —JoAc*
    The kangaroo ("It is a curious thing that you") E. J. Coatsworth. *ArTp—HuSv*
    Kangaroo ("A tough kangaroo named Hopalong Brown") W. J. Smith. *SmB*
    The sing-song of old man kangaroo. From Just-so stories. R. Kipling. *FeF*
    Sylvester. J. Ciardi. *CiM*
    Up from down under. D. McCord. *McT*

The kangarooster. See Mixed beasts

Kasa, Lady
    Tolling bells. *PaS*

Katawampus, sel. E. A. Parry
    Pater's bathe. *HuL-2*

Katherine Johnstone. Unknown. *MaB*

"Kate's eyes were sea-green. She was one of the last." See A pair of sea-green eyes

Kavinoky, Bernice
    Poet to dancer. *PlU*

Kay. James Reeves. *ReR*

"Kay, Kay." See Kay

The kayak. Unknown. *FeF*

Keats, John
La belle dame sans merci. *CoSp—DeT—HaP—McW—SmLg—UnG—UnMc*
Endymion, sel.
    A thing of beauty. *HuSv*
Fairy song. *FeF*
The human seasons. *HoW*
I had a dove. See Song
"I stood tiptoe upon a little hill," sels.
    Minnows. *FeF—JoAc—UnG*
    Sweet peas. *JoAc*
Meg Merrilies. *ArTp—FeF—HuL-2—HuSv—SmLg*
    Old Meg. *ReT*
Minnows. See "I stood tiptoe upon a little hill"
The naughty boy. See "There was a naughty boy"
Ode on a Grecian urn. *HaP*
Old Meg. See Meg Merrilies
On first looking into Chapman's Homer. *SmLg*
On the grasshopper and cricket. See The poetry of earth
The poetry of earth. *HoW*
    On the grasshopper and cricket. *JoAc—UnG*
Robin Hood. *GrCc*
Song. *FeF—ReT*
    I had a dove. *CoI—DeT*
Sweet peas. See "I stood tiptoe upon a little hill"
"There was a naughty boy." *CoH—DeMg—NaM—SmLg*
    The naughty boy. *HuL-2—ReG*
A thing of beauty. See Endymion
To autumn. *DeT—HaP—JoAc—UnG*
"When I have fears that I may cease to be." *HaP—UnG*

Keats, John (about)
Adonais. P. B. Shelley. *HaP* (sel.)
"The keen stars were twinkling." See To Jane

"Keep conscience clear." See Poor Richard's wisdom

Keep the pot a-boilin'. Unknown. *WoJ*

"Keep the pot a-boilin' just for Marie." See Keep the pot a-boilin'

Keeping on. Arthur Hugh Clough. *NaM*

Keith, A. Berriedale
The moon. tr. *PaS*

Keith, Joseph Joel
Books. *HuSv*
Crickets and mice. *HuSv*

Keith of Ravelston. Sydney Dobell. *DeT*

Keller, Martha
Andrew Jackson. *UnG—UnMc*
Brady's bend. *CoSp*

Kemp, Harry (Hibbard)
The humming bird. *FeF*

Kemp Oweyne. Unknown. *MaB*

Ken, Thomas
Old hundredth. *PlU*

Kennedy, C. R.
Epitaph for Chaeroneia. tr. *PaS*

Kennedy, Marian
Sleepy song. *McAw*
Snowflakes. *McAw*

Kent, Louis
The hunt. *McW*
The toad. *McW*

"Kenton and Deborah, Michael and Rose." See Ambition

Kentucky
My fathers came from Kentucky. V. Lindsay. *GrCc*
Kentucky Belle. Constance Fenimore Woolson. *CoSp—UnG—UnMc*
Kentucky birthday: February 12, 1815. Frances M. Frost. *BrS—HaY*

Keppel, Caroline
Robin Adair. *DeT*

Keppel, David
Trouble. *ThP*

Kerchoo. Margaret Fishback. *CoPs*

Kerner, Justinus
Home-sickness. *PaS*

Kettles. See Pots and pans

Key, Francis Scott
The star-spangled banner. *FeF*

Keys. See Locks and keys

The keys of Canterbury. Unknown. *JoAc*

The keys of heaven. Eleanor Farjeon. *FaCb*

Khayyám, Omar. See Omar Khayyám

Kick a little stone. Dorothy Aldis. *AlA*

Kidd, Captain (about)
Captain Kidd ("Oh, my name was Robert Kidd, as I sailed, as I sailed") Unknown. *NaM*
Captain Kidd ("The person in the gaudy clothes") R. C. and S. V. Benét. *HuL-2*

Kikuriō
Daffodils. *ArTp*

Kilcash. Frank O'Connor. *ReT*

The Kilkenny cats. See "There once were two cats of Kilkenny"

Kilmer, Aline
Ambition. *ThP*
Experience. *BrBc*
Things. *ThP*

Kilmer, Joyce
Easter. *ArTp*
Gates and doors. *EaW*
The house with nobody in it. *HuSv*
Roofs. *BrL-8*
Trees. *FeF*

Kilvert, Francis (about)
Variation on a theme by Francis Kilvert. R. Humphries. *PlU*

"The kind of grass that a spit-bug chooses." See The spit-bug

Kind valentine. David Schubert. *GrCc*

"The kindliest thing God ever made." See Shade

Kindness. See also Animals—Care; Service; Sympathy
Count that day lost. G. Eliot. *ThP*
The kindness. E. Farjeon. *FaCb—FaN*
"The warm of heart shall never lack a fire." E. J. Coatsworth. *ArTp*

Kindness. See "I love little pussy"

Kindness. See "If I had a donkey that wouldn't go"

The kindness ("The kindness done")
Eleanor Farjeon. *FaCb—FaN*
"The kindness done." See The kindness
Kindness to animals. See Animals—Care
Kindness to animals ("Little children,
never give") Unknown. *UnG*
Do as you'd be done by. *DeT*
Kindness to animals ("Riddle cum diddle
cum dido") Laura E. Richards. *ArTp*
—*HuL-1*
King, Ben
The cow slips away. *CoH*
"If I should die tonight." *CoH*
The pessimist. *CoH—McW*
That cat. *CoH*
King, Dorothy
Billy-boy. *HuL-1*
Gipsy man. *HuL-1*
King, E. L. M.
Robin's song. *ArTp*
King, Edith
The duck. *BrL-k—HuSv*
The rabbit. *BrL-k—HuSv*
King, Stoddard
Matters of taste. *ThP*
"King Alfred he could sing a song." See
The king's cake
"King and queen of the pelicans we." See
The pelican chorus
The king and the clown. Unknown, tr. fr.
the Persian by Michael Lewis. *UnMc*
King Arthur. See Arthur, King (about)
King Arthur. See "When good King Arthur
ruled this land"
"The king asked." See The king's break-
fast
King Charles. See "As I was going by
Charing cross"
"King Charles the First walked and talked."
Mother Goose. *OpO*
"King David and King Solomon." Unknown
Rhymed chuckles. *UnG*
"King Duncan had a fool called Leery." See
Jock o' Binnorie
King Estmere. Unknown. *MaB*
"King Francis was a hearty king, and loved
a royal sport." See The glove and the
lions
"King Frost rides forth in Europe." See
The king rides forth
"The king had taken captive in some war
a band." See The house beyond the
meadow—The bears who once were
giants
King Henry VIII, sel. William Shakespeare
or John Fletcher
Orpheus. *PlU*
Music. *SmLg*
King Henry V, sels. William Shakespeare
The horse. *UnG*
"Once more unto the breach, dear friends,
once more"
From King Henry the Fifth. *HaP*
King Hilary and the beggarman. A. A.
Milne. *MiWc*
King John and the abbot of Canterbury.
Unknown. *UnG*
"King John was not a good man." See King
John's Christmas

King John's Christmas. A. A. Milne. *MiWc*
King Lear, sel. William Shakespeare
"With hey, ho, the wind and the rain."
ArTp
"King Midas had the golden touch." See
The golden touch
"The king of China's daughter." Edith Sit-
well. *JoAc*
The king of France. See "The king of
France went up the hill"
"The king of France went up the hill."
Mother Goose. *DeMg*
The king of France. *OpO*
The King of Hearts. William Jay Smith.
SmL
"The king of Peru." See The emperor's
rhyme
The king of Spain. William Jay Smith. *SmL*
King of the castle. Mother Goose. *OpO*
King of the hill. Unknown. *TaD*
King Olaf's gold. Eleanor Farjeon. *FaCb*
"A king once lived, a thousand years ago."
See Château de Chinon
King Orpheo. Unknown. *MaB*
King Pippin. See "Little King Pippin he
built a fine hall"
"King Priam in the dark night went."
Eleanor Farjeon. *FaCb*
The king rides forth. Eleanor Farjeon. *FaCb*
—*FaN*
"The king sent for his wise men all." See W
"King Siegfried sat in his lofty hall." See
The three songs
"The king sits in Dumferling town." See
Sir Patrick Spens
"The king sits in Dunfermline town." See
Sir Patrick Spens
King Stephen. Robert Graves. *McW*
"King Stephen had a story teller and gave
him princely pay." See King Stephen
"The king walked in his garden green."
See The three singing birds
"The king was sick. His cheek was red."
See The enchanted shirt
King Xerxes and the sea. Eleanor Farjeon.
FaCb
"King Xerxes saw the sea." See King
Xerxes and the sea
Kingcups in town. Eleanor Farjeon. *FaCb*
—*FaN*
Kingdom cove. James Reeves. *ReBl*
"The Kingdom of Number is all bound-
aries." See Numbers and faces
Kings. See Kings and rulers
Kings and rulers. See also Princes and
princesses; also names of kings and
rulers, as David, King of Israel
The Akond of Swat. E. Lear. *HuL-2—
LoL—UnG*
Alexandrian kings. C. P. Cavafy. *GrCc*
Bronwen to her magpie. E. Farjeon. *FaCb*
Buckingham palace. A. A. Milne. *HuL-2
—MiWc*
A cat may look at a king. L. E. Richards.
CoI
The ceremonial band. J. Reeves. *ReBl*
A dream of governors. L. Simpson. *HaP*

Jenny kissed me. L. Hunt. *BrBc*

"A kiss is a germ." Unknown. *MoY*

"Old woman, old woman, shall we go a-shearing." Mother Goose. *ArTp—DeMg—OpO*

The prodigy. A. P. Herbert. *NaE*

She called him Mr. Unknown. *FeF*

Limericks since Lear. *UnG*

"There are tulips in the garden." Unknown. *MoY*

"There was a little boy and a little girl." Mother Goose. *DeMg—OpO*

"Trip upon trenchers, and dance upon dishes." Mother Goose. *DeMg*

A melancholy song. *OpO*

"Two in a hammock." Unknown. *MoY*

"When sitting on the sofa." Unknown. *MoY*

"Willy, Willy Wilkin." Mother Goose. *OpO*

The kitchen chimney. Robert Frost. *FrR—FrY*

The kite ("How bright on the blue") Harry Behn. *ArTp—BeW—FeF—JoAc*

Kite ("I flew my kite") David McCord. *McT*

A kite ("I often sit and wish that I") See Flying kite

The kite ("My kite is three feet broad, and six feet long") Adelaide O'Keefe. *DeT*

"A kite, a sky, and a good firm breeze." See Kite days

Kite days. Mark Sawyer. *BrS—McAw*

"Kite on the end of the twine." See Three signs of spring

Kites

Flying kite. F. D. Sherman. *BrR-4*

A kite. *ArTp* (sel.)

The kite ("How bright on the blue") H. Behn. *ArTp—BeW—FeF—JoAc*

Kite ("I flew my kite") D. McCord. *McT*

A kite ("I often sit and wish that I") Unknown. *ArTp*

The kite ("My kite is three feet broad, and six feet long") A. O'Keefe. *DeT*

Kite days. M. Sawyer. *BrS—McAw*

My kite. B. and B. Brown. *BrL-k*

Three signs of spring. D. McCord. *McT*

Wind on the hill. A. A. Milne. *MiWc*

Kittel, Muriel

"I know not what I seek eternally." tr. *PaS*

"Tears flow in my heart." tr. *PaS*

A kitten ("He's nothing much but fur") Eleanor Farjeon. *ArTp—HuL-2—ReG*

The kitten ("The trouble with a kitten is") Ogden Nash. *FeF—NaM*

The kitten at play. William Wordsworth. *FeF*

The kitten playing with the falling leaves. *UnG*

The kitten playing with the falling leaves. See The kitten at play

Kittens. See Cats

"Kittens have paws they don't have pawses." See Just because

"The kitten's in the dairy." See Mary and her kitten

Kitten's night thoughts. Oliver Herford. *BrL-k*

The kitty. Elizabeth Prentiss. *BrL-k—NaM*

Kitty of Coleraine. Unknown. *CoSp*

Kitty: What she thinks of herself. William Brighty Rands. *NaM*

Knibbs, Henry Herbert

Charley Lee. *McW*

"Knife and a fork." Unknown. *WiRm*

"Knife and a fork and a bottle and a cork." *WoF*

"Knife and a fork and a bottle and a cork." See "Knife and a fork"

A knight. See The Canterbury tales

"A knight and a lady." Mother Goose. *HuL-1*

"The knight from the world's end." See A dream of governors

Knight-in-armour. A. A. Milne. *MiWc*

"A knight there was, and that a worthy man." See The Canterbury tales—A knight

The knight whose armour didn't squeak. A. A. Milne. *MiWc*

The knight without a name. Unknown. *HoW*

Knighthood. See Knights and knighthood

Knights and knighthood. See also Arthur, King; Chivalry; Romance

Bad Sir Brian Botany. A. A. Milne. *CoH—MiWc*

Clootie. Unknown. *MaB*

Eldorado. E. A. Poe. *HoW—McW—SmLg*

The false knight upon the road. Unknown. *MaB*

Kay. J. Reeves. *ReR*

"A knight and a lady." Mother Goose. *HuL-1*

Knight-in-armour. A. A. Milne. *MiWc*

The knight whose armour didn't squeak. A. A. Milne. *MiWc*

The knight without a name. Unknown. *HoW*

Knights and ladies. A. A. Milne. *MiWc*

The knight's leap. C. Kingsley. *CoSp*

The knight's tomb. S. T. Coleridge. *SmLg*

Lochinvar. From Marmion. W. Scott. *BrL-7 — CoSp — FeF — HuSv — JoAc — NaE — UnG — UnMc*

The outlandish knight. Unknown. *UnG*

The riddling knight. Unknown. *GrCc—SmLg*

Sir Eglamour. S. Rowlands. *McW—SmLg*

Sir Marmaduke. G. Colman. *UnG*

Sir Nicketty Nox. H. Chesterman. *HuL-2*

Sir Olaf. J. G. von Herder. *CoPm*

Knights and ladies. See Knights and knighthood

Knights and ladies. A. A. Milne. *MiWc*

The knight's leap. Charles Kingsley. *CoSp*

Knights of the Round Table. See Arthur, King; Knights and knighthood

The knight's tomb. Samuel Taylor Coleridge. *SmLg*

"Knock at the doorie." Mother Goose. *OpO*

"Knock on the door." Unknown. *WoF*

Know it is Christmas. Lois Snelling. *BrBc*

"Know then thyself, presume not God to scan." See An essay on man

"Knowest thou the land where bloom the lemon trees." See Wilhelm Meister—Mignon

Knowledge
At Woodward's garden. R. Frost. *FrR—PlI*
Circles. From The people, yes. C. Sandburg. *SaW*
Curiosity. H. Behn. *BeW*
He who knows. Unknown. *ThP—UnG*
"He who knows and knows that he knows." *MoY*
I want to know. J. Drinkwater. *FeF*
Inexperience. J. Breining. *ThP*
"Men say they know many things." H. D. Thoreau. *PlI*
To and fro. E. J. Coatsworth. *CoM*
"When land is gone and money spent." Mother Goose. *OpO*
Why. W. J. Smith. *SmL*
Wild grapes. R. Frost. *FrR*
"The kobold's a miner." See K is for kobold
Kochanowski, Jan
To sleep. *PaS*
Kochin Shū, sel. Unknown, tr. fr. the Chinese by Arthur Waley
Ono no yoshiki. *PaS*
"kool uoy nehW." See Mirror
Korosta katzina song. Unknown, tr. fr. the Hopi by Natalie Curtis. *PaS*
The **kraken.** Alfred Tennyson. *HoW*
Krakens
The kraken. A. Tennyson. *HoW*
Kramer, Arthur
Adventures. *BrBc*
Kubla Khan; or, A vision in a dream. Samuel Talyor Coleridge. *ReT—SmLg—UnMc*
Kuck, Clara
Frost fairies. *BrR-3*

L

L., C. G.
The master. *PlI*
L., M.
"I have lost my shoes." tr. *FeF*
The little girl that lost a finger. tr. *FeF*
L. P. See P., L.
L is for Lorelei. Eleanor Farjeon. *FaCb*
"**La-la-llamas** rate as mammals." See In praise of llamas
Labor. See Work
Labor day. See Work
Labor day. Marnie Pomeroy. *CoPs*
The **laboratory** midnight. Revel Denney. *PlI*
Laborers. See Work
Lack, Agnes
Row the boat home. *HuL-2*
Lack wit. Mother Goose. *OpO*
"A **lad** once walked in Warwick woods." See F is for fairy queen
"**Ladies** and gentlemen and children, too." See Boogie chant and dance
"**Ladies** and gentlemen, I'll tell you a fact." Unknown. *WoF*
"**Ladies** at a ball." See Glimpse in autumn

"**Lads** and lasses, up and out." See The next holiday
The **lady.** Elizabeth Jane Coatsworth. *UnMc*
"**Lady.**" Mother Goose. *OpO*
Lady April. Richard Le Gallienne. *HaY*
Lady-bird. Caroline Anne Bowles; also attributed to Charlotte T. Smith. *HuL-2—UnG*
"**Lady-bird,** lady-bird, fly away home." See Lady-bird
Lady-birds. See Beetles
Lady bug. Unknown, tr. fr. the Chinese by Isaac Taylor Headland. *JoAc*
"**Lady-bug,** lady-bug, fly away, do." See Lady bug
Lady bugs. See Beetles
Lady Clare. Alfred Tennyson. *CoSp—FeF—HuSv—UnG*
A **lady** comes to an inn. Elizabeth Jane Coatsworth. *ArTp—CoSp*
Lady day. Eleanor Farjeon. *FaCb—FaN*
Lady Elspat. Unknown. *MaB*
The **lady** in love. See "There was a lady loved a swine"
"**Lady, Lady Landers.**" Unknown. *JoAc*
Lady lost. John Crowe Ransom. *HaP*
"**Lady,** lovely lady." See Vain and careless
Lady Moon. Richard Monckton Milnes, Lord Houghton. *BrR-3—HuL-2—NaM*
"**Lady Moon,** Lady Moon, where are you roving." See Lady Moon
The **lady** of Leigh. E. V. Rieu. *RiF*
The **lady** of Shalott. Alfred Tennyson. *HoW—UnMc*
The **lady** of the lake, sels. Walter Scott
Coronach. *HoW*
Soldier, rest. *McW—NaM*
"Soldier, rest, thy warfare o'er." *DeT*
"**Lady** Queen Anne she sits in the sun." Mother Goose. *JoAc*
Queen Anne. *OpO*
"The **lady** sat in a flood of tears." See Lady-slippers
Lady-slippers. Eleanor Farjeon. *FaCb*
"**Lady,** the shepherds are all gone." See Ya se van los pastores
"A **lady** who lived in Uganda." See The panda
"**Lady** will you come with me into." E. E. Cummings. *ReT*
"**Ladybird,** ladybird (fly away home)." Mother Goose. *DeMg—LiL*
To the ladybird. *FeF—OpO*
"**Ladybird,** ladybird (where)." Ivy O. Eastwick. *EaI*
Ladybirds. See Beetles
Lady's bedstraw. Eleanor Farjeon. *FaCb*
Lady's slippers (Flower)
Lady-slippers. E. Farjeon. *FaCb*
La Fontaine, Jean de
The camel and the flotsam. *JoAc*
The crow and the fox. *BrL-7—UnMc*
The dairymaid and her milk-pot. *JoAc*
The dove and the ant. *JoAc*
The fox and the goat. *JoAc*
La Fontaine, Jean de (about)
John of the fountain. E. Farjeon. *FaN*

Lagerkvist, Pär
"Beauty is most at twilight's close." *PaS*
"A laird, a lord." Mother Goose. *OpO*
The **lake** isle of Innisfree. William Butler
Yeats. *FeF—JoAc*

Lakes
Daddy fell into the pond. A. Noyes. *CoH
—FeF*
Down by the pond. A. A. Milne. *MiWc*
From the mailboat passing by. D. McCord.
McFf
The pond. A. von Droste-Hülshoff. *PaS*
Something better. D. McCord. *McFf*
The **lama**. Ogden Nash. *CoH—FeF—LoL*
"The one-l lama." *SmLg*

Lamb, Charles
The old familiar faces. *HaP*
The snail. *NaM—UnG*
The triumph of the whale. *PlI* (sel.)

Lamb, Mary
The child and the snake. *DeT*
The dessert. *DeT*
The **lamb**. William Blake. *DoP—FeF—
JoAc—McW—SmLg—UnG*
Little lamb. *HuSv*

"Lamb of God, I look to Thee." See My
example

Lambdin, Sylvia S.
January. *HaY*

Lambert, James H., Jr
The tale of a dog. *CoI*

Lambs. See also Sheep
The first lamb. E. Farjeon. *FaCb—FaN*
The lamb. W. Blake. *DoP—FeF—JoAc—
McW—SmLg—UnG*
Little lamb. *HuSv*
Lambs. K. Tynan. *DeT*
The little young lambs. P. R. Chalmers.
HuL-2
"Mary had a little lamb (her father)." Un-
known. *MoY*
Mary's lamb. S. J. Hale. *FeF—JoAc—
OpO—UnG*
"Mary had a little lamb." *BrL-k—
DeMg—LiL*
The pet lamb. W. Wordsworth. *DeT* (sel.)
Sheep and lambs. K. Tynan. *DoP*
"Two young lambs." E. Farjeon. *FaCb—
FaN*
Woolly lambkins. C. G. Rossetti. *HuSv*
Young lambs. J. Clare. *UnG*
"Young lambs to sell. Young lambs to
sell." Mother Goose. *DeMg*
The toy lamb seller. *OpO*

Lambs. Katharine Tynan. *DeT*

The **lament** of the white mouse. E. V. Rieu.
RiF

Laments. See also Death
Adonais. P. B. Shelley. *HaP* (sel.)
"Call for the robin-redbreast and the wren."
From The white devil. J. Webster. *SmLg*
A dirge. *ReT*
Coronach. From The lady of the lake. W.
Scott. *HoW*
The cowboy's lament. Unknown. *McW—
UnMc*
Dirge ("1-2-3 was the number he played
but today the number came 3-2-1") K.
Fearing. *HaP*

A dirge ("Rough wind, that moanest loud")
P. B. Shelley. *HoW*
Dirge ("We do lie beneath the grass")
T. L. Beddoes. *HoW*
Dirge in woods. G. Meredith. *HoW*
Elegy. C. Tichborne. *HaP*
The spring is past. *DeT* (sel.)
Elegy for Lucy Lloyd. L. Goch. *PaS*
Elegy on the death of a mad dog. From
The vicar of Wakefield. O. Goldsmith.
HaP—McW—SmLg—UnMc
Elegy written in a country churchyard. T.
Gray. *DeT—HaP*
"Full fathom five thy father lies." From
The tempest. W. Shakespeare. *SmLg*
Ariel's dirge. *NaE—ReT*
The ghost's lament. Unknown. *MaB*
The ghost's song. *SmLg*
The lament of the white mouse. E. V. Rieu.
RiF
A lyke-wake dirge. Unknown. *MaB—NaE*
Requiem. R. L. Stevenson. *HaP—McW—
ThP—UnG*
The sea-ritual. G. Darley. *HoW*
Song on the water. T. L. Beddoes. *SmLg*
The sparrow's dirge. J. Skelton. *SmLg*
"Wake all the dead, what ho, what ho."
W. Davenant. *SmLg*

Lamplighter barn. Myra Cohn Livingston.
LiWa

Lamplighters
"Light the lamps up, lamplighter." E.
Farjeon. *BrS—HuL-2*

Lampson, Frederick Locker. See Locker-
Lampson, Frederick

"Lancaster bore him—such a little town."
See A hundred collars

Lancelot, Sir (Lancelot du Lac) (about)
The lady of Shalott. A. Tennyson. *HoW—
UnMg*

"Land lies in water, it is shadowed green."
See The map
The **land** of counterpane. Robert Louis
Stevenson. *FeF—HuSv—JoAc—NaE*
The **land** of Ho-Ho-Hum. William Jay
Smith. *SmL*
The **land** of Nod. Robert Louis Stevenson.
UnG
"Land of our birth, we pledge to thee." See
The children's song
The **land** of story-books. Robert Louis
Stevenson. *ArTp—FeF—UnG*
"The land was ours before we were the
land's." See The gift outright
"The land was white." Mother Goose. *OpO*
The **land** where hate should die. Denis A.
McCarthy. *BrL-8*
The **landing** of the Pilgrim Fathers. Felicia
Dorothea Hemans. *ArTp—BrR-5—FeF
—UnG*

Landor, Walter Savage
I strove with none. *HaP*
Leofric and Godiva. *GrCc*
On music. *GrCc*
On the death of Ianthe. *GrCc*
Past ruined Ilion. *HaP*

Landscape ("I want to write a book of
chaste and simple verse") Charles
Baudelaire, tr. fr. the French by George
Dillon. *PaS*

Landscape ("See the trees lean to the wind's way of learning") Carl Sandburg. *SaW*

Landscapes, sels. T. S. Eliot
Cape Ann. *JoAc—NaE—ReT—SmLg*
New Hampshire. *HaP—ReT—SmLg*
Rannoch, by Glencoe. *SmLg*
Usk. *SmLg*
Virginia. *HaP—SmLg*

The landsman. Moschus, tr. fr. the Greek by Percy Bysshe Shelley. *PaS*

Lang, Andrew
I'd leave. *FeF*
In the spring. tr. *PaS*
Love in May. tr. *PaS*

Language. See also Words
"As I was laying on the green." Unknown. *CoH*
Ball with Yvonne. E. Farjeon. *FaCb*
A different speech. L. T. Nicholl. *PlI*
English. E. Farjeon. *HuL-2*
Goose, moose and spruce. D. McCord. *McT*
Just because. D. McCord. *McT*
"Latin is a dead language." Unknown. *MoY*

Lanier, Sidney
The centennial meditation of Columbia, sel.
Dear land of all my love. *HuSv*
Dear land of all my love. See The centennial meditation of Columbia
The hound. *CoPm*

"Lantern light." Ivy O. Eastwick. *EaI*

"A lantern light from deeper in the barn." See The fear

Lanterns
Brown's descent; or, The willy-nilly slide. R. Frost. *CoSp—FrR—FrY—NaE*
"Lantern light." I. O. Eastwick. *EaI*

Lao-tzu
The way of life. *McW*

Lape, Fred
Midsummer pause. *CoPs*

Larcom, Lucy
Apple blossoms. *HaY*
The brown thrush. *BrR-4—FeF*
Hal's birthday. *BrBc*

The lark ascending. George Meredith. *HoW*

Larks
Hark, hark the lark. From Cymbeline. W. Shakespeare. *FeF*
"Hark, hark, the lark at heaven's gate sings." *SmLg*
A morning song. *JoAc*
A hymn for Saturday. C. Smart. *ReG*
A lark's nest. *SmLg*
The lark ascending. G. Meredith. *HoW*
The lark's song. W. Blake. *HoW*
Meadow secret. F. M. Frost. *FrLm*
Rabbit and lark. J. Reeves. *ReW*
The skylark. C. G. Rossetti. *UnG*
Skylark and nightingale. C. G. Rossetti. *HuL-2*
Heaven is heaven. *HaY*
To a skylark. P. B. Shelley. *FeF*

A lark's nest. See A hymn for Saturday
The lark's song. William Blake. *HoW*

Larrie O'Dee. William W. Fink. *BrL-8*

"Lars Porsena of Clusium." See Lays of Ancient Rome—Horatius

The last buccaneer. See The old buccaneer

The last chantey. Rudyard Kipling. *SmLg*

The last corn shock. Glenn Ward Dresbach. *FeF*

"Last evening when I went to bed." See Our birthday

The last flower. John Travers Moore. *CoPs*

"Last in your book, but first in your heart." Unknown. *MoY*

The last leaf ("A few leaves stay for a while on the trees") Harry Behn. *BeW*

The last leaf ("I saw him once before") Oliver Wendell Holmes. *FeF—McW*

The last mowing. Robert Frost. *FrY*

"Last night as I lay on the prairie." See The cowboy's dream

"Last night I crept across the snow." See Prayer

"Last night I heard a rat-tat-too." See Rain riders

"Last night I saw you in the sky." See Starfish

"Last night in the open shippen." See Christmas day

"Last night, the rain was busy." See Sky laundry

"Last night the thunder began to roll." See Broadcasting

"Last night, while we were fast asleep." See New year's day

"The last of October." See Fall

"The last snow is going." See Spring

Last song. James Guthrie. *ArTp—HuL-1*

"Last week I played." See Surprise

The last will and testament of the grey mare. See "John Cook he had a little gray mare"

The last word. Matthew Arnold. *HaP*

Last word about bears. John Ciardi. *CiY*

The last word of a bluebird. Robert Frost. *ArTp—FeF—FrY—HuSv—JoAc*

Last words before winter. Louis Untermeyer. *UnG*

"Late in March in the high-wind sky." See Late winter on our beach

"Late in the winter came one day." See Blossom themes

"A late lark twitters from the quiet skies." See I. M. Margaritae sorori

"Late lies the wintry sun a-bed." See Wintertime

Late October. Sara Teasdale. *BrL-7—CoPs—HaY*

Late winter on our beach. Burnham Eaton. *McAw*

Lathbury, Mary A. (Artemisia)
"Summer sunshine." *HaY*

"Latin is a dead language." Unknown. *MoY*

Laughing child. See Three spring notations on bipeds

Laughing song. William Blake. *ArTp—CoPs—JoAc—McW—ReT—UnG*

Laughing time. William Jay Smith. *FeF—SmL*

Laughter
Bursting. D. Aldis. *AlA*
A child's laughter. A. C. Swinburne. *BrBc*
Crocodile. W. J. Smith. *SmB*
The funny old man and his wife. D'A. W. Thompson. *BrR-4*

The height of the ridiculous. O. W. Holmes. *BrL-8—CoH—HuSv—NaM*

Laughing child. From Three spring notations on bipeds. C. Sandburg. *SaW*

Laughing song. W. Blake. *ArTp—CoPs—JoAc—McW—ReT—UnG*

Laughing time. W. J. Smith. *FeF—SmL*

The merry man of Paris. Unknown. *BrR-4*

"The laughter of the lesser lynx." See The lesser lynx

Lauk a mercy. See "There was an old woman, as I've heard tell"

Laundresses and laundrymen. See Laundry

Laundry

Ironing day. D. Aldis. *AlA*

Old Ellen Sullivan. W. Welles. *FeF*

Sky laundry. M. L. Allen. *AlP*

"Stocking and shirt." J. Reeves. *ReW*

"They that wash on Monday." Mother Goose. *DeMg—LiL*

Wash-day ("This is the way we wash our clothes") L. McCrea. *HuL-1*

Washday ("Mrs Ocean takes in washing") E. F. Upson. *BrR-3*

Washing day ("The old woman must stand") Mother Goose. *OpO*

Washing day ("Water and soap") L. F. Taylor. *HuL-1*

Windy wash day. D. Aldis. *AlA—ArTp—JoAc*

Laundrymen. See Laundry

Laura. Thomas Campion. *PlU*

Lauren, Joseph

The fox and the grapes. tr. *UnG*

The frog who wanted a king. tr. *UnG*

The frogs who wanted a king. *UnMc*

The frogs who wanted a king. See The frog who wanted a king

Lavender (Flower)

Sweet blooming lavender. Mother Goose. *OpO*

"Lavender's blue, diddle, diddle." Mother Goose. *DeMg—JoAc*

"Lavender's blue, dilly, dilly." *LiL*

Love song. *OpO*

"Lavender's blue, dilly, dilly." See "Lavender's blue, diddle, diddle"

Lawlor, Charles V. and Blake, J. W.

"East side, West side, all around the town." See The sidewalks of New York

The sidewalks of New York, sel.

"East side, West side, all around the town." *WoF*

"Lawn as white as driven snow." See The winter's tale—The pedlar

The lawn mower. Marie Louise Allen. *AlP*

"The lawn mower is cutting and cutting the grass." See The lawn mower

Lawn song. Myra Cohn Livingston. *LiWa*

Lawrence, D. H.

Bavarian gentians. *HaP—SmLg*

Snake. *ArTp—HaP*

Lawson, Marie A.

Halloween. *ArTp—BrS*

"Lay me on an anvil, O God." See Prayers of steel

"Lay not up for yourselves treasures upon earth." See Gospel according to Matthew—Treasures in heaven

Laycock, G. Kenneth

"Beauty is most at twilight's close." tr. *PaS*

Lays of ancient Rome, sel. Thomas Babington Macaulay

Horatius. *SmLg*

The fight at the bridge. *UnMc* (sel.)

Lazarus, Emma

Inscription on the Statue of Liberty. See The new colossus

The new colossus. *FeF*

Inscription on the Statue of Liberty. *BrL-8* (sel.)

Laziness. See Idleness

The lazy crocuses. Dorothy Aldis. *AlA*

Lazy day. Dorothy Aldis. *AlHd*

"Lazy deuks that sit i' the coal-neuks." Mother Goose. *OpO*

A lazy sight. Dorothy Aldis. *AlA*

Lead Kindly Light. John Henry Newman. *BrL-7*

"Lead, Kindly Light, amid the encircling gloom." See Lead Kindly Light

A leaf treader. Robert Frost. *FrR*

The leak in the dike. Phoebe Cary. *FeF*

Leamy, Edmund

The ticket agent. *HuSv*

"Lean and tall and stringy are the Navajo." See The Painted desert—The Navajo

"The lean coyote, prowler of the night." See Sunrise

"Lean out of the window." See Chamber music

"Lean out the window: down the street." See A man with a little pleated piano

"Leaning his chin in his small hard hands." See Kentucky birthday: February 12, 1815

The leap of Roushan Beg. Henry Wadsworth Longfellow. *HuSv*

Lear, Edward

"A was once an apple-pie." *ArTp*

Nonsense alphabet. *JoAc*

The Akond of Swat. *HuL-2—LoL—UnG*

The broom, the shovel, the poker and the tongs. *JoAc*

By way of preface. See "How pleasant to know Mr Lear"

"Calico pie." *FeF—LoL—ReG—SmLg—UnG*

The courtship of the Yonghy-Bonghy-Bo. *HoW—JoAc—NaE—UnG*

The dong with a luminous nose. *CoPm—HoW*

The duck and the kangaroo. *HuL-2—JoAc*

The floating old man. *HoW*

"How pleasant to know Mr Lear." *CoH—UnG*

By way of preface. *HaP*

Incidents in the life of my Uncle Arly. *CoH—NaM*

The Jumblies. *ArTp—CoH—HoW—JoAc—LoL—NaE—ReG*

Just as he feared. See "There was an old man with a beard"

"Mr and Mrs Discobbolos." *JoAc*

The new vestments. *CoH*

Nonsense alphabet. See "A was once an apple-pie"

Old man with a beard. See "There was an old man with a beard"

"**Leaves** make a slow." See Spring rain

"The **leaves** said, It's spring." See What the leaves said

"The **leaves**, the little birds, and I." See The little shepherd's song

LeCron, Helen Cowles
Little Charlie Chipmunk. *ArTp—BrR-3—FeF—PeF*
The secret. *BrL-k*

Lederer, Marjorie
Fifth birthday gift. *BrBc*

Ledoux, Louis V.
Slumber song. *FeF*

Ledwidge, Francis
Fairy music. *HaY*
The wife of Llew. *CoPm*

Leetla Giorgio Washeenton. T. A. Daly. *CoPs—FeF*

Leezie Lindsay. Unknown. *SmLg*

Left out. A. G. W. *BrR-3*

"**Leg** over leg." Mother Goose. *DeMg—LiL—OpO*

The **legacy**. Mother Goose. *OpO*

Le Gallienne, Richard
Brooklyn bridge at dawn. *ArTp*
"I meant to do my work to-day." *ArTp—BrR-5—HuL-2—JoAc—UnG*
Lady April. *HaY*
May is building her house. *HaY*

A **legend** of Okeefinokee. Laura E. Richards. *CoSp*

The **legend** of the first cam-u-el. Arthur Guiterman. *CoH*

A **legend** of the Northland. Phoebe Cary. *UnG*

Legends. See also Mythology
Brady's bend. M. Keller. *CoSp*
A Christmas legend. O. Herford. *CoPm*
The fairies of the Caldon low. M. Howitt. *ReG*
The knight's leap. C. Kingsley. *CoSp*
A legend of Okeefinokee. L. E. Richards. *CoSp*
The legend of the first cam-u-el. A. Guiterman. *CoH*
The Lorelei. H. Heine. *CoPm*
The Loreley. *UnG*
Paul's wife. R. Frost. *FrR*
The pelican. P. De Thaun, tr. by R. Wilbur. *McW*
The Pied Piper of Hamelin. R. Browning. *ArTp—HuSv—JoAc—SmLg—UnG*
How the rats were destroyed. *HuL-2* (sel.)
Santorin. J. E. Flecker. *GrCc*
The woman's tongue tree. A. Guiterman. *CoPm*

The **legends** of evil. Rudyard Kipling. *NaM*

Legge, J. G.
Rondeau. tr. *PaS*

"**Legree's** big house was white and green." See Simon Legree—A Negro sermon

Legs
The legs. R. Graves. *HaP*
The legs. Robert Graves. *HaP*

Leigh, Henry Sambrooke
The twins. *ArTp—BrBc—CoH—FeF—McW—UnG—UnMc*

Leishman, J. B.
Sonnets to Orpheus. tr. *PlU* (sel.)

Leisure. See also Idleness
Leisure. W. H. Davies. *ArTp—FeF—HuL-2—McW—NaM*
Leisure. William Henry Davies. *ArTp—FeF—HuL-2—McW—NaM*

"The **Leith** police dismisseth us." Mother Goose. *OpO*

Leland, Charles Godfrey (Hans Breitmann, pseud.)
The Flying Dutchman. *CoPm*
The story of Samuel Jackson. *CoSp*

Lemonade stand. Dorothy Brown Thompson. *BrS*

Lemont, Jessie
Autumn. tr. *PaS*

Lenski, Lois
Fourth of July song. *BrS*
"Oh, to have a birthday." *BrBc*
People. *FeF*

Lent
The Lent lily. From A Shropshire lad. A. E. Housman. *CoPs*

The **Lent** lily. See A Shropshire lad

Leo. Eleanor Farjeon. *FaCb—FaN*

Leofric and Godiva. Walter Savage Landor. *GrCc*

Leonard, William Ellery
The Lorelei. tr. *CoPm*
The swan and goose. tr. *PlU*
The swan and the goose. *FeF*

Leontius
Plato, a musician. *PlU*

Leopardi, Giacomo
The infinite. *PaS*

The **leprahaun**. Robert Dwyer Joyce. *CoPm*

Lermontov, Mikhail Yuryevich
Composed while under arrest. *PaS*
The **lesser** lynx. E. V. Rieu. *RiF*

Lesson. Harry Behn. *BeW*

Lesson from a sun-dial. Unknown, tr. fr. the German by Louis Untermeyer. *ArTp*

Let be at last. Ernest Dowson. *HaP*

"**Let** be at last; give over words and sighing." See Let be at last

"**Let** every Roman boy be taught to know." See Call to youth

"**Let** it be understood that I am Don Juan Gomez." See Conquistador

"**Let** it rain." See The engineer

"**Let** me be your baby, south wind." See Baby song of the four winds

"**Let** me but do my work from day to day." See Work

"**Let** me go where'er I will." See Music

"**Let** me not to the marriage of true minds." See Sonnets

"**Let** me sit here by this adobe wall." See Summer comes

"**Let** me tell you the story of how I began." See Lift-boy

"**Let** no one suppose." James Reeves. *ReP*

"**Let** nothing disturb thee." See St Theresa's book-mark

Let others share. Edward Anthony. *UnG*

"**Let** others share your toys, my son." See Let others share

"Let the crows go by hawking their caw and caw." See River roads

"Let the green succotash with thee contend." See The hasty pudding

"Let the mighty and great." See The happy farmer

Let the nations be glad. See Psalms—Psalm LXVII

"Let the rain kiss you." See April rain song

"Let us forget these principalities." See Innumerable friend

"Let us take the road." See The highwaymen

"Let us walk in the white snow." See Velvet shoes

"Let us with a gladsome mind." John Milton. *DeT*
 Praise the Lord. *SmLg*

Let's be merry. See "Mother shake the cherry-tree"

Let's carol. Rowena Bastin Bennett. *BrR-6*

"Let's carol in the city streets." See Let's carol

"Let's dance now, all of us, all of us, oh my maidens." See Bailada

"Let's go to the wood, says this pig." Mother Goose. *OpO*

Let's pretend. James S. Tippett. *McAw*

"Let's pretend we're elephants." See Let's pretend

"A letter is a gypsy elf." Annette Wynne. *BrR-5*

Letters and letter writing
 Aunt Maud. Unknown. *CoH—NaM*
 How to write a letter. E. Turner. *NaM*
 "I sent a letter to my love." Mother Goose. *LiL*
 Jack-hide-in-the-hedge. E. Farjeon. *FaCb*
 "A letter is a gypsy elf." A. Wynne. *BrR-5*
 Mr Ibister. Mother Goose. *OpO*
 Night mail. W. H. Auden. *HaP*
 O i c. Unknown. *CoH*
 A thought. M. Chute. *ChA*
 "When times are hard." Unknown. *MoY*

Letters of the alphabet. See Alphabet

Letts, Winifred M.
 The spires of Oxford. *BrL-7*

Lettuce
 Soliloquy of a tortoise on revisiting the lettuce beds after an interval of one hour while supposed to be sleeping in a clump of blue hollyhocks. E. V. Rieu. *RiF*

Leviathan. Louis Untermeyer. *UnG*

Levy, Newman
 The Hottentot tot. *HuL-2*
  Midsummer fantasy. *CoPs*
 Midsummer fantasy. See The Hottentot tot
 The revolving door. *CoH*

Lewis, Eiluned
 Dew on the grass, sel.
  "We who were born." *BrBc—FeF*
 "We who were born." See Dew on the grass

Lewis, Emily
 My dog. *HuL-1*

Lewis, M. A.
 The caulker. *CoSp*

Lewis, Michael
 August. *UnG*
 A dead liar speaks. *UnG*
 January. *UnG*
 The king and the clown. tr. *UnMc*

Lewis, Sinclair
 Cat. *UnG*

Lewis Carroll came here to-day. Eleanor Farjeon. *FaN*

Lewisohn, Ludwig
 The child reads an almanac. tr. *FeF*
 The youth dreams. tr. *PaS*

Li Ho
 Ninth moon. *PaS*

Li Po. See Li T'ai-po

Li T'ai-po (Li Po or Rihaku)
 Clearing at dawn. *PaS*
 Conversation in the mountains. *PaS*
 The river-merchant's wife: A letter. *GrCc—HaP*
 The white egret. *PaS*

Li Yi
 On hearing a flute at night from the wall of Shou-Hsiang. *PlU*

Liberty
 Battle-hymn of the republic. J. W. Howe. *FeF—UnG*
 "Fain would I live in safest freedom." A. G. von Platen. *PaS*
 Freedom. J. Barbour. *SmLg*
 Heartbeat of democracy. V. Brasier. *HuSv*
 The new colossus. E. Lazarus. *FeF*
  Inscription on the Statue of Liberty. *BrL-8* (sel.)
 Peter and Percival; or, The penguin's revolt. E. V. Rieu. *RiF*
 Refugee in America. L. Hughes. *McW*
 Song of the settlers. J. West. *FeF*
 A stanza on freedom. J. R. Lowell. *McW—ThP*
 To Althea from prison. R. Lovelace. *HaP*
 "When a man hath no freedom to fight for at home." G. G. Byron. *HaP*

Libra. Eleanor Farjeon. *FaCb—FaN*

Libraries. See Books and reading

The library. Barbara A. Huff. *FeF*

Lickety-lick. May Justus. *McAw*

"Lickety, lickety, lickety-lick." See Lickety-lick

"Lie on this green and close your eyes." See Village sounds

Lieberman, Elias
 Heart specialist. *PlU*
 "I am an American." *FeF*

Life
 "All the world's a stage." From As you like it. W. Shakespeare
  From As you like it. *HaP*
  Gallery of people. *UnG*
 "An arrow flying past." G. A. Bécquer. *PaS*
 "As I walked out one evening." W. H. Auden. *HaP*
 Auction. J. Holmes. *McW*
 Barter. S. Teasdale. *BrR-6—FeF—JoAc*
 Celanta at the well of life. G. Peele. *ReT*
  A voice speaks from the well. *SmLg*
 The census-taker. R. Frost. *FrR*
 Climb. W. Welles. *BrBc*

Like as a huntsman. Edmund Spenser. *HaP*

"Like as a huntsman after weary chase." See Like as a huntsman

"Like as the damask rose you see." See Man's mortality

Like me. Dorothy Aldis. *AlA—McAw*

"Like small curled feathers, white and soft." See While shepherds watched

"Like the sweet apple which reddens upon the topmost bough." See A young bride

"Likeness has made them animal and shy." See The twins

Likes and dislikes
All about boys and girls. J. Ciardi. *CiY*
Animal crackers. C. Morley. *ArTp—BrR-3 —FeF—JoAc*
Bunches of grapes. W. De La Mare. *ArTp —HuL-2—NaM*
Dr Klimwell's fall. D. McCord. *McT*
The favourite fruit. E. Farjeon. *FaCb— FaN*
Give me the splendid silent sun. W. Whitman. *FeF—JoAc*
"The hart he loves the high road." Mother Goose. *DeMg—OpO—SmLg*
I can't decide. F. M. Frost. *FrLn*
"I do not like thee, Doctor Fell." Martial. *DeMg—NaM*
    Doctor Fell. *OpO*
    Non amo te. *PlI*
    Signs, seasons, and sense. *UnG*
I like housecleaning. D. B. Thompson. *FeF*
Independence. A. A. Milne. *MiWc*
"Jenny White and Johnny Black." E. Farjeon. *FeF*
Joan's corner. E. Farjeon. *FaCb*
Matters of taste. S. King. *ThP*
"Me like ice cream." Unknown. *WiRm*
Mice. R. Fyleman. *ArTp—BrL-k—FeF— HuL-1—HuSv—NaE—PeF*
My prairies. H. Garland. *FeF*
Noise. J. Pope. *HuL-2*
Page ix. G. Stein. *McW*
Rathers. M. Austin. *FeF*
The Rum Tum Tugger. T. S. Eliot. *ArTp —FeF—NaE*
Things I like. M. H. Greenfield. *HuL-1*
Tiger-lilies. *UnG*
What kind of music. J. Reeves. *ReW*
What they like. Unknown. *HuL-1*
The zoo. H. Wolfe. *CoH—McW—NaM*

"Li'l boy." See Little boy's britches

"Li'l girl, li'l girl." See The pony

Li'l Liza Jane. Unknown. *TaD*

The **lilac.** Humbert Wolfe. *FeF*

Lilacs
The barrel-organ, sel. A. Noyes
    Go down to Kew in lilac time. *HuL-2*
The lilac. H. Wolfe. *FeF*
May day. M. C. Livingston. *LiWa*

Lilies. See also Water-lilies
"Have you seen but a bright lily grow." From A celebration of Charis. B. Jonson. *SmLg*
    A comparison. *DeT*
The Lent lily. From A Shropshire lad. A. E. Housman. *CoPs*

Lilies. Shikō. *ArTp*
A lily of the field. J. B. Tabb. *DoP*
On Easter day. C. Thaxter. *FeF—HaY*
Tiger-lilies. T. B. Aldrich. *UnG*
Tiger lily. D. McCord. *McFf*

Lilies. Shikō, tr. fr. the Japanese by Olive Beaupré Miller. *ArTp*

"Lilies are white." Mother Goose. *LiL*
You shall be queen. *OpO*

Lilliput-land. William Brighty Rands. *ReG*

A **lily** of the field. John Banister Tabb. *DoP*

Limericks. See also entries under Lear, Edward, beginning There was
Arthur. O. Nash. *CoH*
The barber of Kew. C. Monkhouse. *CoH*
"The bottle of perfume that Willie sent." Unknown
    Limericks since Lear. *UnG*
"A boy who played tunes on a comb." Unknown. *CoH*
"A canner, exceedingly canny." C. Wells. *FeF—WiRm*
"A cheerful old bear at the zoo." Unknown
    Limericks since Lear. *UnG*
"A collegiate damsel named Breeze." Unknown
    Limericks since Lear. *UnG*
"A daring young lady of Guam." Unknown
    Limericks since Lear. *UnG*
"The daughter of the farrier." Unknown
    Limericks since Lear. *UnG*
"A decrepit old gasman, named Peter." Unknown. *CoH*
Edouard. O. Nash. *LoL*
Edward Lear went away to-day. E. Farjeon. *FaN*
"An epicure, dining at Crewe." Unknown. *CoH—LoL*
    Limericks. *BrL-7*
    Limericks since Lear. *UnG*
"A flea and a fly in a flue." Unknown. *CoH —LoL—WiRm*
    The flea and the fly. *FeF*
    Limericks since Lear. *UnG*
The girl of New York. C. Monkhouse. *CoH*
"A girl who weighed many an oz." Unknown
    Limericks since Lear. *UnG*
The grandiloquent goat. C. Wells. *LoL— NaM*
"A handsome young noble of Spain." Unknown
    Limericks since Lear. *UnG*
"A housewife called out with a frown." Unknown
    Limericks since Lear. *UnG*
I met a crow. J. Ciardi. *CiI*
"A maiden caught stealing a dahlia." Unknown. *CoH*
My face. A. Euwer. *CoH*
    Limericks since Lear. *UnG*
On digital extremities. G. Burgess. *FeF*
"An opera star named Maria." Unknown
    Limericks since Lear. *UnG*
The panda. W. J. Smith. *SmL*
"A pleasant old bear at the zoo." Unknown. *WiRm*
Relativity. Unknown. *ArTp—PlI*
    Limericks. *BrL-7*
    A young lady named Bright. *FeF*

"Said a great Congregational preacher."
O. W. Holmes. *UnG*
She called him Mr. Unknown. *FeF*
    Limericks since Lear. *UnG*
"A silly young fellow named Hyde." Unknown. *CoH*
    Limericks since Lear. *UnG*
"A sleeper from the Amazon." Unknown. *LoL*
The snake charmer. J. Bennett. *BrR-3*
Stein song. Unknown. *ThP*
"There once was a man of Calcutta." Unknown. *LoL*
"There was a faith-healer of Deal." Unknown
    Limericks since Lear. *UnG*
"There was a girl from Havana." Unknown. *MoY*
"There was a thick-headed marine." Unknown
    Limericks since Lear. *UnG*
"There was a young girl of Asturias." Unknown
    Limericks since Lear. *UnG*
"There was a young lady from Woosester."
Unknown
    Limericks since Lear. *UnG*
"There was a young lady of Niger." C.
Monkhouse. *LoL*
    The young lady of Niger. *FeF*
"There was a young lady of station." L.
Carroll
    Limericks since Lear. *UnG*
"There was a young man from Trinity."
Unknown. *PlI*
"There was a young man of Bengal." Unknown
    Limericks since Lear. *UnG*
"There was a young man of Herne bay."
Unknown. *CoH*
"There was a young man of St Bees." W.
S. Gilbert. *CoH*
"There was a young man so benighted."
Unknown. *CoH*
"There was a young person named Tate."
C. Wells
    Limericks since Lear. *UnG*
"There was a young prince in Bombay."
W. Parke. *CoH*
"There was an old lady of Steen." Unknown
    Limericks. *BrL-7*
"There was an old man from Antigua."
Unknown. *CoH*
"There was an old man from the Rhine."
Unknown
    Limericks since Lear. *UnG*
"There was an old man named Michael
Finnegan." Unknown. *ArTp*
    American Father Gander. *UnG*
"There was an old man of Blackheath."
Unknown. *CoH—LoL*
"There was an old man of Peru." Unknown. *WiRm*
"There was an old man of Tarentum." Unknown. *CoH—LoL*
"There was an old man of Tobago." Mother
Goose. *DeMg*
"There was an old man who said, Do."
Unknown. *FeF—PlI*

"There was an old man with a beard."
Unknown. *WiRm*
"There was an old person of Tring." Unknown. *CoH*
"There was an old stupid who wrote." W.
Parke. *CoH*
"There was once a young lady of Ryde."
Unknown
    Limericks. *NaE*
"There were three little birds in a wood."
Unknown
    Limericks since Lear. *UnG*
"There's a girl out in Ann Arbor, Mich."
Unknown
    Limericks since Lear. *UnG*
"A tutor who tooted a (or the) flute." C.
Wells. *CoH—LoL*
    Limericks since Lear. *UnG*
    The tutor. *NaM*
The unfortunate giraffe. O. Herford. *CoH*
When I went to get a drink. J. Ciardi. *CiI*
Limes
One lime. E. Farjeon. *DeT—FaCb*
The **limitations** of youth. Eugene Field.
BrR-6
Limited. Carl Sandburg. *SmLg*
Limited crossing Wisconsin. See Prairie
Lincoln, Abraham (about)
Abe. E. Farjeon. *FaCb—FaN*
Abraham Lincoln ("Lincoln was a long
man") R. C. and S. V. Benét. *ArTp—CoPs—HaY*
Abraham Lincoln ("Oh, slow to smite and
swift to spare") W. C. Bryant. *BrR-6*
Abraham Lincoln ("Remember he was poor
and country-bred") M. P. Meigs. *ArTp—BrR-6—PeF*
Abraham Lincoln walks at midnight. V.
Lindsay. *BrL-8—FeF—JoAc*
Anne Rutledge. From The Spoon River
anthology. E. L. Masters. *CoPs—HaP*
For February twelfth. M. M. Gessner. *HaY*
He leads us still. A. Guiterman. *BrL-7*
In Hardin county, 1809. L. E. Thompson.
CoPs—CoSp
Kentucky birthday: February 12, 1815.
Frances M. Frost. *BrS—HaY*
Lincoln ("Like a gaunt, scraggly pine")
J. G. Fletcher. *JoAc*
Lincoln ("There was a boy of other days")
N. B. Turner. *ArTp—FeF*
    A boy of other days. *BrR-5*
Lincoln learning. L. Darcy. *BrR-5*
Nancy Hanks. R. C. and S. V. Benét. *ArTp—BrR-5—BrS—FeF—HuSv—JoAc*
O captain, my captain. W. Whitman. *FeF—HuSv—SmLg*
Prairie. K. N. Llewellyn. *HaY*
A reply to Nancy Hanks. J. Silberger. *ArTp*
"Would I might rouse the Lincoln in you
all." V. Lindsay. *CoPs*
Lincoln, Joseph C.
A college training. *CoH*
Lincoln ("Like a gaunt, scraggly pine")
John Gould Fletcher. *JoAc*
Lincoln ("There was a boy of other days")
Nancy Byrd Turner. *ArTp—FeF*
A boy of other days. *BrR-5*
Lincoln learning. Louise Darcy. *BrR-5*

"Lincoln was a long man." See Abraham Lincoln
The Lincolnshire poacher. Unknown. *DeT*
The poacher. *HoW*
Lindsay, Lady Anne (Lady Anne Barnard)
Day and night. *HuL-2*
Lindsay, Vachel (Nicholas)
Abraham Lincoln walks at midnight. *BrL-8—FeF—JoAc*
The blacksmith's serenade. *CoSp*
Euclid. *PlI*
An explanation of the grasshopper. *FeF—HuSv*
The flower-fed buffaloes. *ArTp—FeF—HaP—JoAc—McW—ReT—SmLg*
In praise of Johnny Appleseed. *HuSv*
Johnny Appleseed. *FeF* (sel.)
An Indian summer day on the prairie. *HuSv—McW*
Johnny Appleseed. See In praise of Johnny Appleseed
Kalamazoo. *GrCc*
The little turtle. *ArTp—BrL-k—FeF—HuL-1—HuSv—JoAc*
"The moon's the north wind's cooky." *FeF—HuSv—JoAc—NaE—UnG*
"The mouse that gnawed the oak tree down." *BrL-7*
My fathers came from Kentucky. *GrCc*
The mysterious cat. *ArTp—CoI—FeF—HuSv—JoAc—PeF*
The potatoes' dance. *FeF*
Simon Legree—A Negro sermon. *SmLg*
What the rattlesnake said. *JoAc*
"Would I might rouse the Lincoln in you all." *CoPs*
Yet gentle will the griffin be. *HuSv*
Lindsay, Vachel (Nicholas) (about)
My fathers came from Kentucky. V. Lindsay. *GrCc*
The line-gang. Robert Frost. *FrR*
"The line-storm clouds fly tattered and swift." See A line-storm song
A line-storm song. Robert Frost. *FrR—GrCc*
Lines and squares. A. A. Milne. *MiWc*
Lines to Dr Ditmars. Kenneth Allan Robinson. *PlI*
Lines written after the discovery by the author of the germ of yellow fever. Ronald Ross. *PlI*
Lines written for Gene Kelly to dance to. Carl Sandburg. *SaW*
Link, Lenore M.
Holding hands. *ArTp—FeF—NaM*
Link rhymes. See Build-on rhymes
The linnet. Robert Burns. *DeT*
Linnets
The green linnet. W. Wordsworth. *DeT*
The lilac. H. Wolfe. *FeF*
The linnet. R. Burns. *DeT*
Lion ("The beast that is most fully dressed") William Jay Smith. *SmB*
The lion ("When lion sends his roaring forth") Mary Howitt. *FeF*
"The lion and the unicorn." Mother Goose. *AnI—DeMg—JoAc—LiL—NaE*
Battle royal. *OpO*

"The lion finds it difficult to get a game of cards." See The revoke
"A lion has a tail and a very fine tail." See In the fashion
"The lion is the beast to fight." See Sage counsel
"The lion jumped over the desert." See A sad case of misapplied concentration
The lion of winter. See A midsummer-night's dream
"The lion with his flaming mane." See Leo
Lions
Advice from an elderly mouse. E. J. Coatsworth. *CoM*
The glory trail. B. Clark. *CoSp*
The glove and the lions. L. Hunt. *FeF—UnMc*
"A handsome young noble of Spain." Unknown
Limericks since Lear. *UnG*
Leo. E. Farjeon. *FaCb—FaN*
The lesser lynx. E. V. Rieu. *RiF*
Lion ("The beast that is most fully dressed") W. J. Smith. *SmB*
The lion ("When lion sends his roaring forth") M. Howitt. *FeF*
"The lion and the unicorn." Mother Goose. *AnI—DeMg—JoAc—LiL—NaE*
Battle royal. *OpO*
Radiator lions. D. Aldis. *AlA—JoAc*
The revoke. E. V. Rieu. *RiF*
A sad case of misapplied concentration. L. De G. Sieveking. *CoH*
Supper for a lion. D. Aldis. *AlA*
Why nobody pets the lion at the zoo. J. Ciardi. *CiR*
"Lipstick and rouge." Unknown. *MoY*
"Listen." See The giraffe
"Listen." See November night
"Listen, children, listen, won't you come into the night." See Who calls
"Listen—I'll say you a." See Chapter two
"Listen. It is the summer's self that ambles." See The good humor man
"Listen, my children, and you shall hear." See Tales of a wayside inn—Paul Revere's ride
"Listen my children and you shall hear (of the midnight ride of Sally dear)." Unknown. *MoY*
"Listen my friend before we part." Unknown. *MoY*
"Listen to me, as when ye heard our father." See Canadian boat song
"Listen to me, you silly bird." See Advice to a bird, species unknown
Listen to the people: Independence day, 1941. Stephen Vincent Benét. *CoPs* (sel.)
The listeners. Walter De La Mare. *FeF—ReT—UnMc*
Lister, R. P.
The musician. *PlI*
Liszt, Abbé (about)
Liszt. E. C. Bentley. *PlI*
Liszt. E. C. Bentley. *PlI*
Litany for Halloween. Unknown. *BrS*
Ghoulies and ghosties. *CoPs*
Little ("I am the sister of him") Dorothy Aldis. *AlA—ArTp—FeF*

Little ("When God makes a lovely thing") Unknown. *HuL-1*

"**Little** Ann and her mother were walking one day." See A true story

"**Little** Betty Blue." Mother Goose. *DeMg—HuSv*

Betty Blue. *OpO*

"**Little** Betty Pringle she had a pig." Mother Goose. *DeMg*

Betty Pringle's pig. *OpO*

Little Billee. William Makepeace Thackeray. *DeT—SmLg*

"**Little** Billy Breek." Mother Goose. *OpO*

"The **little** birches, white and slim." See The birches

Little bird. See "Once I saw a little bird"

The **little** bird ("My dear Daddie bought a mansion") Walter De La Mare. *BrBc*

"**Little** bird of paradise." Mother Goose. *OpO*

"**Little** birds sing with their beaks." See Singing

"A **little** bit of blowing." See Thoughts for a cold day

Little bits. John Ciardi. *CiY*

The **little** black boy. William Blake. *SmLg*

"**Little** black bug." Margaret Wise Brown. *FeF—HuL-1*

"De **little** black bull kem down de medder." See Hoosen Johnny

"The **little** black dog ran round the house." Mother Goose. *OpO*

The **little** black-eyed rebel. Will Carleton. *FeF—UnG*

The **little** black hen. A. A. Milne. *MiWc*

"**Little** Blue Apron." Unknown. *HuL-1*

Little Blue Ben. Mother Goose. *OpO*

"**Little** Blue Ben, who lives in the glen." See Little Blue Ben

Little Blue Betty. Mother Goose. *OpO*

"**Little** Blue Betty lived in a den." See Little Blue Betty

Little Blue Ribbons. Austin Dobson. *BrBc*

"**Little** Blue Ribbons. We call her that." See Little Blue Ribbons

"**Little** Blue Shoes." Kate Greenaway. *ArTp*

Little Bo-peep. See "Little Bo-peep has lost her sheep"

Little Bo-peep and Little Boy Blue. A. A. Milne. *MiWc*

"**Little** Bo-peep has lost her sheep." Mother Goose. *ArTp—DeMg—HuSv—JoAc—LiL*

Little Bo-peep. *BrL-k—OpO*

"The **little** boat at anchor." See Fourth of July night

"**Little** Bob Robin." See Bob Robin

"**Little** Bob Snooks was fond of his books." Mother Goose. *DeMg*

"**Little** boots and big boots." See Rubber boots

The **little** boy and the old man. Unknown. *TaD*

"**Little** Boy Blue." See "Little Boy Blue, come blow your horn"

Little Boy Blue. Eugene Field. *FeF*

"**Little** Boy Blue, come blow your horn." Mother Goose. *ArTp—HuSv—LiL*

Boy Blue. *OpO*

"**Little** Boy Blue." *BrL-k—DeMg—JoAc*

The **little** boy found. William Blake. *ArTp*

"The **little** boy is fishing." See The fisherman

"**Little** boy kneels at the foot of the bed." See Vespers

"**Little** boy, little boy." Unknown. *WoF*

The **little** boy lost. William Blake. *ArTp*

"The **little** boy lost in the lonely fen." See The little boy found

"A **little** boy once played so loud." See Extremes

"The **little** boy stopped in the middle of the hayfield." See Railroad reverie

"A **little** boy was dreaming." See The little dreamer

Little boy's britches. Unknown. *TaD*

Little boys of Texas. Robert P. Tristram Coffin. *McW*

"The **little** boys of Texas prance." See Little boys of Texas

Little Breeches. John Hay. *UnG*

Little brother. Aileen Fisher. *BrBc—McAw*

Little brother's secret. Katherine Mansfield. *ArTp—FeF*

"**Little** brown brother, oh, little brown brother." See Baby seed song

Little bug. Rhoda W. Bacmeister. *BrL-k*

Little busy bee. See "How doth the little busy bee"

"The **little** cares that fretted me." See Out in the fields with God

"**Little** cat." Laura E. Richards. *HuL-1*

"The **little** caterpillar creeps." See Cocoon

Little Charlie Chipmunk. Helen Cowles LeCron. *ArTp—BrR-3—FeF—PeF*

"**Little** Charlie Chipmunk was a talker. Mercy me." See Little Charlie Chipmunk

"A **little** Child." See Bethlehem of Judea

"**Little** children, never give." See Kindness to animals

Little cloud. Myrtle Blassing. *BrR-3*

"**Little** cloud, little cloud, as you float in the sky." See Little cloud

"A **little** cock sparrow sat on a green tree." Mother Goose. *DeMg—LiL—OpO*

"**Little** colts caper and kick up their heels." See In spring in warm weather

The **little** creature. Walter De La Mare. *NaE*

"**Little** Dickey Diller." See Dickey Diller and his wife

"**Little** Dicky Dilver." See Dicky Dilver

"**Little** Dove." See Mary's lullaby

The **little** dreamer. Unknown. *BrL-k*

"**Little** drop of dew." See A dewdrop

"**Little** drops of dew." Unknown. *MoY*

"**Little** drops of water." Ebenezer Cobham Brewer; also attributed to Julia Fletcher Carney. *AnI—DeMg*

Little things. *FeF—UnG*

Little Dutch girl. Unknown. *WoJ*

"**Little** Dutch Gretchen sat in the kitchen." See Gretchen

"The **little** elephant was crying." See Cradle song of the elephants

The **little** elf. John Kendrick Bangs. *BrBc* — *BrL-k* — *HuL-1* — *JoAc* — *McW* — *PeF* — *UnG*

The little elfman. *ArTp*

The **little** elfman. See The little elf

"A **little** fairy comes at night." See Queen Mab

Little Fan. James Reeves. *CoPm—ReW*

"**Little** fishes in a brook." Mother Goose. *OpO*

"The **little** flowers came through the ground." See At Easter time

"**Little** fly." See The fly

"**Little** folks, little folks." Unknown. *AnI*

Little fountain. Dorothy Aldis. *AlA*

The **little** fox. Marion Edey. *ArTp*

Little friend. Mother Goose. *OpO*

Little Garaine. Gilbert Parker. *FeF*

"**Little** General Monk." Mother Goose. *OpO*

Little Giffen. Francis Orray Ticknor. *UnMc*

Little girl. See "Little girl, little girl, where have you been"

The **little** girl. See "There was a little girl, and she had a little curl"

Little girl ("I will build you a house") Unknown, tr. fr. the Arabian by Rose Fyleman. *JoAc*

A **little** girl ("When I was a little girl") Mother Goose. *OpO*

The **little** girl and the turkey. Dorothy Aldis. *AlA*

"**Little** girl, be careful what you say." Carl Sandburg. *SaW*

"**Little** girl, little girl, where have you been." Mother Goose. *DeMg*
Little girl. *HuL-1—OpO*

"The **little** girl said." See The little girl and the turkey

The **little** girl that lost a finger. Gabriela Mistral, tr. fr. the Spanish by M. L. *FeF*

"A **little** girl went for a walk." See A summer walk

"A **little** girl with golden hair." See The stranger cat

"The **little** girl's frocks are frilly." See Ballroom dancing class

"The **little** girls that live next door." See GraceAnAnne

"A **little** green frog lived under a log." See Strange talk

"A **little** green frog once lived in a pool." See The frog

"**Little** green inch-worm." See Inch-worm

The **little** green orchard. Walter De La Mare. *ArTp—NaE*

Little Gustava. Celia Thaxter. *FeF*

"**Little** Gustava sits in the sun." See Little Gustava

The **little** hat. Dorothy Aldis. *AlA*

"The **little** hedgerow birds." See An old man

"**Little** Hermogenes is so small." Lucilius. *JoAc*

"**Little** horned toad." Unknown, tr. fr. the Navajo by Hilda Faunce Wetherill. *FeF*

Little hundred. Mother Goose. *OpO*

Little husband. See "I had a little husband"

"**Little** Jack Dandy-prat." Mother Goose. *OpO*

"**Little** Jack Horner." See Teasing

"**Little** Jack Horner." Mother Goose. *BrL-k* —*DeMg—HuSv—JoAc—LiL*
Jack Horner. *OpO*

Little Jack Horner ("Jack Horner was a pretty lad") Unknown. *DeT*

"**Little** Jack Jingle." Mother Goose. *DeMg*

"**Little** Jack Sprat." See Jack Sprat's pig

"**Little** Jenny Wren." See "Jenny Wren fell sick"

"The **little** Jesus came to town." See A Christmas folk song

"**Little** Jesus, wast Thou shy." See Ex ore infantium

"**Little** Jimmy Jimsonweed." Unknown. *WoF*

Little John Bottlejohn. Laura E. Richards. *CoPm—HuL-1—LoL*

"**Little** John Bottlejohn lived on the hill." See Little John Bottlejohn

"**Little** John Jiggy Jag." Mother Goose. *DeMg*
John Jiggy Jag. *OpO*

"**Little** Johnny-jump-up said." See Wise Johnny

"**Little** Johnny Morgan." Mother Goose. *DeMg*
Johnny Morgan. *OpO*

The **little** jumping girls. See "Jump—jump —jump"

Little jumping Joan. See "Here am I, little jumping Joan"

"**Little** Kathleen took a drink." Unknown. *MoY*

"**Little** King Boggen, he built a fine hall." Mother Goose. *HuSv*

"**Little** King Pippin he built a fine hall." Mother Goose. *DeMg*
King Pippin. *LoL—OpO*

"**Little** kings and queens of May." See For good luck

The **little** kittens. See "Three little kittens"

Little lad. See "Little lad, little lad, where wast thou born"

"**Little** lad, little lad." See "Little lad, little lad, where wast thou born"

"**Little** lad, little lad, where wast thou born." Mother Goose. *DeMg*
Little lad. *BrBc*
"Little lad, little lad." *OpO*

"The **little** lady lairdie." Mother Goose. *OpO*

"**Little** Lady Wren." Tom Robinson. *ArTp* —*FeF*

Little lamb. See The lamb

"**Little** lamb, who made thee." See The lamb

"**Little** lambs, little lambs." See Baby beds

"**Little** lamps of the dusk." See Fireflies

The **little** land. Robert Louis Stevenson. *HuSv—JoAc*

"A **little** light is going by." See Firefly

"Little Lucy Lavender." See Lucy Lavender

A little maid. Mother Goose. *OpO*

"Little maid, pretty maid." Mother Goose. *OpO*

The little man and the little maid. Mother Goose. *OpO*

"Little man in coal pit." See Putting on nightgown

The little man who wasn't there. Hughes Mearns. *CoH—FeF*

"The little men of meadow land." See Adventure

Little Minnie Mystery. James Reeves. *ReBl*

"Little Minnie Mystery has packets and parcels." See Little Minnie Mystery

"Little Miss Muffet." Mother Goose. *ArTp—BrL-k—DeMg—HuSv—JoAc—LiL*
  Miss Muffet. *OpO*

"Little Miss Muffet discovered a tuffet." See The embarrassing episode of little Miss Muffet

"Little miss, pretty miss." Mother Goose. *DeMg—OpO*

"Little Mister Polliwog." See Ways of traveling

Little moppet. See "I had a little moppet"

"A little mountain spring I found." See The spring

"Little mouse in gray velvet." See Mouse

Little nag. Mother Goose. *OpO*

"Little Nancy Etticoat." Mother Goose. *DeMg—HuSv—JoAc—LiL—OpO*
  "Little Nanny Etticoat." *ArTp*

"Little Nanny Etticoat." See "Little Nancy Etticoat"

"The little newt." See The newt

"A little old man came riding by." Unknown
  American Father Gander. *UnG*

"A little old man of Derby." See Man of Derby

"A little old man of the sea." See The ingenious little old man

"A little old woman." See Behind the waterfall

Little Orphant Annie. James Whitcomb Riley. *FeF—HuSv—NaM*

"Little Orphant Annie's come to our house to stay." See Little Orphant Annie

"Little papoose." Hilda Conkling. *FeF*

"A little party in the house." See A musical at home

The little peach. Eugene Field. *CoH*

"A little peach in the orchard grew." See The little peach

Little Phillis. Kate Greenaway. *BrBc*

"A little piece of earth to call our own." See To call our own

"Little pig." Mother Goose. *OpO*

Little piggy. Thomas Hood. *HuL-1*

"Little pines upon the hill." See Pine tree song

The little plant. Kate Louise Brown. *BrL-k*

"Little Poll Parrot." See Poll Parrot

"Little Polly Flinders." Mother Goose. *DeMg—LiL*
  Polly Flinders. *OpO*

"Little pony, little pony." Unknown, tr. fr. the Mexican. *JoAc*

"Little pretty Nancy girl." Mother Goose. *OpO*

"The little priest of Felton." See The priest of Felton

"A little prince of long ago." See Sons of the kings

Little puppy. Unknown, tr. fr. the Navajo by Hilda Faunce Wetherill. *FeF*

"Little puppy with the black spots." See Little puppy

Little pussy. See "I love little pussy"

The little rain ("Oh, she is good, the little rain, and well she knows our need") Tu Fu, tr. fr. the Chinese by L. Cranmer-Byng. *FeF*

Little rain ("When I was making myself a game") Elizabeth Madox Roberts. *ArTp—BrR-4*

"The little red hen does not write with a pen." See Hen

Little Red Riding Hood. Guy Wetmore Carryl. *CoH*

The little red sled. Jocelyn Bush. *ArTp*

"The little road says go." See The house and the road

"Little Robin Redbreast." See "Little Robin Redbreast sat upon a tree"

"Little Robin Redbreast." See Visitor

"Little Robin Redbreast (sat upon a hill)." Mother Goose. *DeMg*

"Little Robin Redbreast (sat upon a rail)." Mother Goose. *DeMg—HuSv*
  Niddle noddle. *OpO*

"Little Robin Redbreast sat upon a tree." Mother Goose. *DeMg—LiL*
  Catch. *OpO*

"Little Robin Redbreast." *HuL-1*

The little rose tree. Rachel Field. *ArTp—BrL-k—FeF*

"A little saint best fits a little shrine." See A ternarie of littles, upon a pipkin of jelly sent to a lady

Little sandman's song. Unknown, tr. fr. the German by Louis Untermeyer. *HuL-2*

"A little seed." See Maytime magic

The little shepherd's song. William Alexander Percy. *HaY*

"Little ships must keep the shore." Unknown. *DeMg*

"The little shoes that fairies wear." See Fairy shoes

Little sketch. Carl Sandburg. *SaW*

"Little snail." See Snail

Little snail. Hilda Conkling. *ArTp—FeF—JoAc*

A little song of life. Lizette Woodworth Reese. *BrR-6—DoP—FeF—HuL-2*

"The little songs of summer are all gone today." See End-of-summer poem

"A little sparrow built his nest, up in a waterspout." Unknown. *WoF*

A little squirrel. Unknown. *ArTp*

"Little squirrel in the park." See Don't tell me

Little star. See The star

"Little striped chipmunk, there you sit." See Eek eek

"Little strokes." See Poor Richard's wisdom

A little talk ("The big brown hen and Mrs Duck") Unknown. *HuL-1*

Little talk ("Don't you think it's probable") Aileen Fisher. *FeF*

"Little Tee Wee." Mother Goose. *DeMg—OpO—WoF*

Little things, Importance of
"For want of a nail, the shoe was lost." Mother Goose. *DeMg—LiL*
    "For want of a nail." *OpO*
    The horseshoe nail. *ThP*
    Tremendous trifles. *UnG*
"Little drops of water." E. C. Brewer; also attributed to J. F. Carney. *AnI—DeMg*
    Little things. *FeF—UnG*
The little things. Unknown. *ThP*
One hard look. R. Graves. *GrP*

Little things. See "Little drops of water"

Little things ("Little things, that run, and quail") James Stephens. *ArTp—BrS—FeF—JoAc*

The little things. ("Oh, it's just the little homely things") Unknown. *ThP*

"Little things, that run, and quail." See Little things

The little tippler. Emily Dickinson. *NaE*

"Little Tom Dogget." See Colly, my cow

"Little Tom Tittlemouse." See Tom Tittlemouse

"Little Tommy Tacket." See Tommy Tacket

"Little Tommy Tittlemouse." Mother Goose. *AnI—DeMg*
    Tommy Tittlemouse. *OpO*

"Little Tommy Tucker." Mother Goose. *DeMg—JoAc—LiL*
    Tommy Tucker. *OpO*

"The little toy dog is covered with dust." See Little Boy Blue

"Little Tradja of Norway." See Tradja of Norway

"Little tree." See Chanson innocente

Little Trotty Wagtail. John Clare. *FeF*

"Little Trotty Wagtail, he went in the rain." See Little Trotty Wagtail

The little turtle. Vachel Lindsay. *ArTp—BrL-k—FeF—HuL-1—HuSv—JoAc*

The little valley in spring. Onitsura, tr. fr. the Japanese by Harold G. Henderson. *PaS*

The little wee man. Unknown. *MaB*

The little whistler. Frances M. Frost. *ArTp—HuSv—JoAc—PeF*

"Little white feathers." See Snowflakes

"The little white mermaidens live in the sea." See The mermaidens

"A little wild bird sometimes at my ear." See Ballata

Little Willie ("Little Willie from his mirror") Unknown. *NaM*
    Rhymed chuckles. *UnG*

Little Willie ("Willie saw some dynamite") Unknown. *FeF*

"Little Willie from his mirror." See Little Willie

Little wind. See "Little wind, blow on the hill-top"

"Little wind, blow on the hill-top." Kate Greenaway. *ArTp*
    Little wind. *JoAc*

"Little winter cottontails." See The outdoor Christmas tree

The little woman and the pedlar. See "There was an old woman, as I've heard tell"

The little young lambs. Patrick R. Chalmers. *HuL-2*

"Live so that you tempt not the sea relentless." See The golden mean

"Live thy life." See The oak

"Lives in winter." Mother Goose. *ArTp*

"The living come with grassy tread." See In a disused graveyard

Livingston, Myra Cohn
Acorn cap. *LiWa*
"Alone." *LiW*
At bedtime. *LiWa*
At the airport. *LiWa*
At the zoo. *LiW*
Back-yard swing. *LiW*
The balloon man. *LiW*
"Balloons, balloons." *LiW*
Beach. *LiWa*
Blue wool monkey. *LiWa*
Buildings. *LiW*
Bump on my knee. *LiWa*
Calendar. *LiWa*
Confusion. *LiW*
Cooking. *LiW*
The difference. *LiW*
Discovery. *LiW*
Down on my tummy. *LiWa*
Downpour. *LiWa*
Dream. *LiWa*
Every week song. *LiWa*
Feet. *LiW*
First thought. *LiWa*
For Anna. *LiWa*
"Good morning, cat." *LiWa*
"Grandfather Grasshopper." *LiWa*
Growing up. *LiW*
Hey diddle. *LiW*
"The house at the corner." *LiWa*
Hungry morning. *LiWa*
"I don't know why." *LiW*
I found. *LiW*
"I know a place." *LiW*
"In the sand." *LiW*
"It tickles." *LiWa*
Josh's song. *LiWa*
Just watch. *LiW*
Lamplighter barn. *LiWa*
Lawn song. *LiWa*
May day. *LiWa*
"The merry-go-round." *LiW*
"Mrs Spider." *LiWa*
Moon. *LiWa*
Morning. *LiW*

The mourning dove. *LiW*
My grasshopper. *LiWa*
My name. *LiWa*
My other name. *LiW*
"The night." *LiW*
Night song. *LiW*
Nursery clock. *LiWa*
Ocean call. *LiWa*
October at five. *LiWa*
October magic. *LiW*
Our baby. *LiWa*
Picture people. *LiW*
Pincushion cactus. *LiW*
The plumber man. *LiWa*
Pretending. *BrBc—LiW*
Pussy willow. *LiWa*
Rain. *LiW*
Reflection. *LiWa*
"A rock." *LiWa*
Saturday morning. *LiWa*
Seaweed. *LiWa*
Sliding. *BrS—LiW*
Spring signs. *LiWa*
Tails. *LiW*
Thought on a star. *LiW*
A time for building. *LiWa*
Train windows. *LiW*
Washday song. *LiWa*
"Whispers." *LiW*
Wide awake. *LiWa*
Winter and summer. *LiW*
Lizards
  The chameleon. A. P. Herbert. *CoI—FeF*
  Sally and Manda. A. B. Campbell. *CoI*
The llama. Hilaire Belloc. *NaM—SmLg*
"The llama is a woolly sort of fleecy hairy
  goat." See The llama
Llamas
  In praise of llamas. A. Guiterman. *CoH*
  The lama. O. Nash. *CoH—FeF—LoL*
    "The one-l lama." *SmLg*
  The llama. H. Belloc. *NaM—SmLg*
Llewellyn, K. N.
  Prairie. *HaY*
"Lo, Mary, look what's here." See Saint
  Joseph
Lo, the winter is past. See The song of
  Solomon—The winter is past
Lo-yang. Emperor Ch'ien Wēn-ti, tr. fr.
  the Chinese by Arthur Waley. *GrCc*
The lobster. Unknown. *UnG*
Lobster music. John Ciardi. *CiM*
The lobster quadrille. See Alice's adventures
  in wonderland
Lobsters
  The lobster. Unknown. *UnG*
  Lobster music. J. Ciardi. *CiM*
  There was a hunter from Littletown. J.
    Ciardi. *CiM*
  'Tis the voice of the lobster. From Alice's
    adventures in wonderland. L. Carroll.
    JoAc
    The voice of the lobster. *NaE*
"The Loch Achray was a clipper tall." See
  The yarn of the Loch Achray
Lochinvar. See Marmion
The Lochmabyn harper. Unknown. *MaB*
"Lock the dairy door." Mother Goose. *OpO*

Locker-Lampson, Frederick
  A terrible infant. *CoH*
Locks and keys
  "I am a gold lock." Mother Goose. *JoAc*
  "Lock the dairy door." Mother Goose. *OpO*
  My keys. D. Aldis. *AlHd*
  The playhouse key. R. Field. *FeF*
  "This is the key of the kingdom." Mother
    Goose. *DeMg—OpO*
    This is the key. *NaM—ReT—SmLg*
The locomotive. See "I like to see it lap
  the miles"
Locomotives. See Railroads
The locust. Unknown, tr. fr. the Zuni by
  Frank Cushing. *FeF*
"Locust, locust, playing a flute." See The
  locust
Locusts (Insect)
  The locust. Unknown. *FeF*
Lodge, Thomas
  "The earth late choked with showers." *HaP*
Lofting, Hugh
  Betwixt and Between. *BrBc*
  Mister Beers. *FeF*
Lofton, Blanche De Good
  Song of the seasons. *HaY*
Loftus, Cecilia
  In the morning. *DoP*
Loganberries
  Loganberry spooks. E. Farjeon. *FaCb—
    FaN*
Loganberry spooks. Eleanor Farjeon. *FaCb
  —FaN*
Logging. See Lumbering
Logic
  The deacon's masterpiece; or, The wonder-
    ful one-hoss shay. O. W. Holmes. *CoSp
    —HuSv—NaM—SmLg*
Lollocks. Robert Graves. *NaE*
London, England
  The children's bells. E. Farjeon. *FaCb*
  Composed upon Westminster bridge. W.
    Wordsworth. *ArTp—SmLg*
    Upon Westminster bridge. *HaP*
  "Gay go up and gay go down." Mother
    Goose. *DeMg—JoAc—LiL*
    The bells of London. *NaE*
    Oranges and lemons. *OpO*
  "In sixteen hundred and sixty-six." Mother
    Goose. *OpO*
  London. W. Blake. *HaP*
  "London bridge is broken down." Mother
    Goose. *DeMg—JoAc—LiL*
    London bridge. *OpO*
  The London owl. E. Farjeon. *FaCb*
  London snow. R. Bridges. *HaP—HoW*
  The oak and the ash. Unknown. *SmLg*
  A quill for John Stow. E. Farjeon. *FaN*
  Regent's park. R. Fyleman. *BrR-4*
    In the park. *HuSv*
  "Which is the way to London town." Un-
    known. *HuL-1*
  Yesterday in Oxford street. R. Fyleman.
    ArTp—PeF
  York, York for my money. W. Elderton.
    ReG
London. William Blake. *HaP*
London bridge. See "London bridge is
  broken down"

"Look, can you cook." See What Molly Blye said

"Look, everyone, look." See Easter joy

"Look, I see a buffalo." See Noah's ark

"Look, I'm a lawn mower, mowing the grass." See Lawn song

"Look. Look at me." See Tree birthdays

"Look, look, the spring is come." See First spring morning

"Look not for beauty." Unknown. *MoY*

"Look out how you use proud words." See Primer lesson

"Look out, look out." See Jack Frost

"Look out. Look out, boys. Clear the track." See The broomstick train

"Look out. Look out. You've spilt the ink." See April fools' day

"Look round: You see a little supper room." See De cœnatione micæ

"Look, there's a robin." See Little brother

Looking at the moon and thinking of one far away. Chang Chiu-ling, tr. fr. the Chinese by Witter Bynner. *PaS*

"Looking back over the years." See A fool and his money

Looking for a sunset bird in winter. Robert Frost. *FrR—FrY*

The looking-glass. Rudyard Kipling. *GrCc —NaE*

The looking-glass pussy. Margaret Widdemer. *BrR-3*

Looking in. Dorothy Aldis. *AlA—HuL-1*

Looking out my window. Dorothy Aldis. *AlA*

"Loping along on the day's patrol." See The sheepherder

Lord, Daniel A.
  Rain. *DoP*
  Round the clock. *DoP*
  Spring. *DoP*

Lord Alcohol. Thomas Lovell Beddoes. *HoW*

Lord Arnaldos. James Elroy Flecker. *CoSp*

The Lord Chancellor's song. See Iolanthe

Lord Clive. E. C. Bentley. *NaM*

"Lord, I'm just a little boy." See A child's Christmas song

"The Lord in His wisdom made the fly." See The fly

"The Lord is my shepherd." See Psalms— Psalm XXIII

"The Lord is my shepherd, I shall not want." See Psalms—Psalm XXIII

Lord Lovel. Unknown. *CoPm—FeF*

"Lord Lovel he stood at his castle-gate." See Lord Lovel

"Lord, make me a channel of Thy peace." See A prayer

"Lord of sea and earth and air." See Prayer for a pilot

"Lord of the mountain." See Navaho prayer

"Lord, purge our eyes to see." Christina Georgina Rossetti. *JoAc*

"Lord Rameses of Egypt sighed." See Birthright

Lord Randal. Unknown. *HuL-2*
  Lord Randall. *UnMc*

"Lord Rumbo was immensely rich." See Rumbo and Jumbo

"Lord, Thou hast given me a cell." See A thanksgiving to God for his house

Lord Ullin's daughter. Thomas Campbell. *FeF*

"Lord, who createdst man in wealth and store." See Easter-wings

"Lords of the nursery." See Forgotten

The Lorelei. Heinrich Heine, tr. fr. the German by William Ellery Leonard. *CoPm*

The Loreley, tr. fr. the German by Louis Untermeyer. *UnG*

The Loreley. See The Lorelei

Lost ("Desolate and lone") Carl Sandburg. *JoAc*

Lost ("I have a little turtle") David McCord. *McFf*

The lost cat. E. V. Rieu. *RiF*

The lost doll. See The water babies

Lost love. Robert Graves. *SmLg*

The lost shoe. Walter De La Mare. *HuL-2*

Lost time. Ffrida Wolfe. *HuL-2*

Lotus
  Lotus leaves. Mitsukuni. *PaS*

Lotus leaves. Mitsukuni, tr. fr. the Japanese by Miyamori Asataro. *PaS*

"Loud is the summer's busy song." See July

Louisa. William Wordsworth. *GrCc*

Love. See also Romance
  Absence. Unknown. *DeT*
  Advice to a girl. T. Campion. *ThP*
  "All in green went my love riding." E. E. Cummings. *ReT*
  Another to the same. W. Browne. *HoW*
  Answer to a child's question. S. T. Coleridge. *ReT*
  An apple gathering. C. G. Rossetti. *GrCc*
  Arrows of love. Chauras. *PaS*
  "Art thou gone in haste." Unknown. *ReT*
  "As I walked out one evening." W. H. Auden. *HaP*
  At a concert of music. C. Aiken. *PlU*
  At Castle Boterel. T. Hardy. *HaP*
  The bait. J. Donne. *GrCc*
  Ballad. W. H. Auden. *UnMc*
  Ballad of the rag-bag heart. M. A. Seiffert. *ThP*
  Bel m'es quan lo vens m'alena. A. Daniel. *PaS*
  La belle dame sans merci. J. Keats. *CoSp— DeT—HaP—McW—SmLg—UnG—UnMc*
  A birthday. C. G. Rossetti. *HoW—ReT*
  Bits of straw. J. Clare. *HoW*
  Black-eyed Susan. J. Gay. *DeT*
  Black diamond. N. Gumilyov. *PaS*
  "Bobby Shafto's gone to sea." Mother Goose. *DeMg*
    Bobby Shafto. *DeT*
    Bobby Shaftoe. *OpO—ReG*
    "Bobby Shaftoe's gone to sea." *JoAc*
  Brown penny. W. B. Yeats. *GrCc—SmLg*
  "Can you make a cambric shirt." Mother Goose. *JoAc*
    "Can you make me a cambric shirt." *DeMg*
    The lover's tasks. *OpO*

"My grief on the sea." Unknown. *PaS*

My heart's is in the highlands. R. Burns. *BrR-5—FeF—McW*

My horse, Jack. J. Ciardi. *CiY*

My luve's like a red, red rose. R. Burns. *CoPs*

"O, my luve is like a red, red rose." *SmLg*

A red, red rose. *HaP*

My valentine. R. L. Stevenson. *BrS—FeF*

I will make you brooches. *HuL-2*

Romance. *CoPs*

"Neither spirit nor bird." Unknown. *PaS*

"The night has a thousand eyes." F. W. Bourdillon. *ThP*

Night song at Amalfi. S. Teasdale. *ThP*

No joy without love. Mimnermus. *PaS*

"Not marble, nor the gilded monuments." From Sonnets. W. Shakespeare. *HaP*

"Oh dear, what can the matter be." Mother Goose. *DeMg*

O, open the door to me, O. R. Burns. *SmLg*

Old-fashioned love. Unknown. *UnMc*

An old song ended. D. G. Rossetti. *GrCc*

Once only. Ato Tobira. *PaS*

"One day while I was walking." Unknown. *TaD*

"One I love, two I love." Mother Goose. *DeMg—LiL—OpO*

Ono no yoshiki. From Kokin Shū. Unknown. *PaS*

"Over the water and over the lea." Mother Goose. *DeMg*

Over the water to Charley. *DeT*

Over the water to Charlie. *OpO*

Paradox. J. B. Rittenhouse. *ThP*

The passionate shepherd to his love. C. Marlowe. *HaP—ReT*

Past ruined Ilion. W. S. Landor. *HaP*

A pavane for the nursery. W. J. Smith. *CoPs*

The pearl. H. C. Andersen. *PaS*

People hide their love. Wu-ti, Emperor of Liang. *PaS*

Perfect love. Sana'i. *PaS*

The phantom-wooer. T. L. Beddoes. *HoW*

Piazza piece. J. C. Ransom. *HaP*

Plucking the rushes. Unknown. *PaS*

The power of love. From The thousand nights and one. Unknown. *PaS*

Queen's lace. E. Farjeon. *FaCb*

The question. P. B. Shelley. *DeT*

A rare tree. Unknown. *PaS*

Renouncement. A. Meynell. *ThP*

The return. S. Teasdale. *ThP*

Revelation. R. Frost. *FrR*

Rima. G. A. Bécquer. *PaS*

The river-god's song. F. Beaumont and J. Fletcher. *FeF—NaM*

The robber. I. O. Eastwick. *BrS*

Robin Adair. C. Keppel. *DeT*

"The rose is red, the rose is white." Mother Goose. *OpO*

"The rose is red, the violet's blue." Mother Goose. *DeMg—HuSv—OpO*

"Roses are red (violets are blue, sugar is)." Mother Goose. *MoY—OpO*

"Roses may be red." Unknown. *MoY*

Ruth. T. Hood. *GrCc*

"Sabrina fair." From Comus. J. Milton. *SmLg*

Sailor and tailor. Unknown. *DeT*

Sally in our alley. H. Carey. *CoPs* (sel.)

"The sea hath its pearls." H. Heine. *PaS*

The seeds of love. Unknown. *HoW—SmLg*

Seeds. *DeT*

"Shall I compare thee to a summer's day." From Sonnets. W. Shakespeare. *HaP*

The siesta. Unknown. *PaS*

The silver tassie. R. Burns. *GrCc*

The simple ploughboy. Unknown. *SmLg*

Since there's no help. M. Drayton. *HaP*

A skater's valentine. A. Guiterman. *BrS*

"So, we'll go no more a-roving." G. G. Byron. *HaP*

So late into the night. *HoW*

We'll go no more a-roving. *GrCc*

Song ("Go and catch a falling star") J. Donne. *HaP*

Song ("Grace and beauty has the maid") G. Vicente. *PaS*

Song ("I wandered by the brook-side") R. M. Milnes, Lord Houghton. *DeT*

Song ("O mistress mine, where are you roaming") W. Shakespeare. *GrCc*

A song from Cyprus. H. D. *GrCc*

A song-offering. R. Tagore. *PaS*

Song, to Celia. B. Jonson. *HaP*

Song to Steingerd. C. Ogmundarson. *PaS*

The spinning wheel. J. F. Waller. *CoSp*

Story. D. Parker. *UnMc*

The story of Rimini. L. Hunt. *NaE* (sel.)

A subaltern's love-song. J. Betjeman. *NaE*

The telephone. R. Frost. *FrR—FrY*

"That time of year thou mayst in me behold." From Sonnets. W. Shakespeare. *HaP*

"Thrice toss these oaken ashes in the air." T. Campion. *SmLg*

Thus spoke my love. P. C. Hooft. *PaS*

Thy garden. Mu'tamid, King of Seville. *PaS*

To a girl ("What slender youth bedewed with liquid odours") Horace. *HoW*

To a girl ("Why came I so untimely forth") E. Waller. *HoW*

To Althea from prison. R. Lovelace. *HaP*

To Anthea who may command him any thing. R. Herrick. *GrCc*

To earthward. R. Frost. *FrR*

To his coy mistress. A. Marvell. *HaP*

Tolling bells. Lady Kasa. *PaS*

Two look at two. R. Frost. *FrR*

Umamina. B. W. Vilikazi. *PaS*

"Up street and down street." Mother Goose. *OpO*

Upon the hard crest. A. Akhmatova. *PaS*

Valentine promise. Unknown. *CoPs*

The vow to Cupid. Unknown. *PaS*

Walsinghame. W. Raleigh. *SmLg*

"As you came from the holy land." *HaP*

"Western wind, when will thou blow." Unknown. *SmLg*

"When I was one-and-twenty." From A Shropshire lad. A. E. Housman. *BrBc*

"When in disgrace with fortune and men's eyes." From Sonnets. W. Shakespeare. *HaP*

Love—*Continued*
"When in the chronicle of wasted time."
    From Sonnets. W. Shakespeare. *SmLg*
    Sonnet CVI. *GrCc*
"When to her lute Corinna sings." T.
    Campion. *GrCc*
    Corinna. *PlU*
"The white moon." P. Verlaine. *PaS*
Who was it. H. Heine. *PaS*
"Who'll that be." K. Patchen. *McW*
Why so pale and wan. J. Suckling. *NaE*
Wind and window flower. R. Frost. *FrR*
The wind's song. E. Mörike. *PaS*
With thee conversing. J. Milton. *HoW*
Within her eyes. Dante. *PaS*
Women's eyes. Bhartrihari. *PaS*
The wood so wild. Unknown. *HoW*
Young John. Unknown. *MaB*

Love—**Courtship.** See Courtship

Love—**Humor**
The ballad of the oysterman. O. W. Holmes.
    BrL-8—*NaM*
Because I were shy. Unknown. *CoSp*
Blow me eyes. W. Irwin. *CoSp*
The courtship of Billy Grimes. Unknown.
    BrL-7
"Don't make love at the garden gate." Un-
    known. *MoY*
The fable of the magnet and the churn.
    From Patience. W. S. Gilbert. *FeF*
Faithless Nelly Gray. T. Hood. *CoH*
"I love you, I love you (I do)." Unknown.
    MoY
"I love you, I love you (I love you so
    well)." Unknown. *MoY*
"I love you, I love you (with my heart)."
    Unknown. *MoY*
The maid of Timbuctoo. L. E. Richards.
    HuL-2
Mia Carlotta. T. A. Daly. *BrL-7*
"My love for you." Unknown. *MoY*
"Pigs love pumpkins." Unknown. *MoY*
Save the tiger. A. P. Herbert. *CoH*
A seaside romance. D. Marquis. *CoH*
The shades of night. A. E. Housman. *CoH*
"You can fall from the mountains." Un-
    known. *MoY*

Love—**Love and death**
Annabel Lee. E. A. Poe. *CoSp*—*DeT*—
    FeF—*HuSv*—*JoAc*—*SmLg*—*UnG*—*UnMc*
Ballad of the little black hound. D. S.
    Shorter. *CoSp*
Barbara Allen. Unknown. *UnMc*
A high tide on the coast of Lincolnshire.
    J. Ingelow. *DeT*
The lady of Shalott. A. Tennyson. *HoW*
    —*UnMc*
Lord Lovel. Unknown. *CoPm*—*FeF*
Lord Randal. Unknown. *HuL-2*
    Lord Randall. *UnMc*
Lord Ullin's daughter. T. Campbell. *FeF*
Lucy. W. Wordsworth. *UnMc*
"Lydia is gone this many a year." L. W.
    Reese. *GrCc*
The mad maid's song. R. Herrick. *HoW*
Morning star. Plato. *PaS*
Music I heard. From Discordants. C. Aiken.
    ThP
My love is dead. T. Chatterton. *HoW*

Ophelia's song. From Hamlet. W. Shake-
    speare. *DeT*
The raven. E. A. Poe. *SmLg*
"So ghostly then the girl came in." R.
    Hillyer. *GrCc*
Song on the water. T. L. Beddoes. *SmLg*
Tim Turpin. T. Hood. *HoW*
Us idle wenches. Unknown. *GrCc*
Vittoria Colonna. H. W. Longfellow. *GrCc*

Love—**Maternal.** See Mothers and mother-
    hood

Love—**Plaints and protests**
The figure-head. C. Garstin. *CoSp*
The green autumn stubble. Unknown. *PaS*
A lover's lament. Unknown. *PaS*
The man on the flying trapeze. Unknown.
    SmLg
Mariana. A. Tennyson. *HoW*
A new courtly sonnet of the Lady Green-
    sleeves. Unknown. *SmLg*
The nymph's reply to the shepherd. W.
    Raleigh. *HaP*
"O woodland cool." C. Brentano. *PaS*
Song. E. Sitwell. *GrCc*
Tell him. C. N. Bialik. *PaS*

Love—**Wedded love.** See Married life

Love ("Canst thou love me, lady") Charles
    Stuart Calverley. *CoH*
Love ("I love you, I like you") William
    Jay Smith. *SmL*
Love ("Love must think in music sweetly")
    Ludwig Tieck, tr. fr. the German by
    Herman Salinger. *PaS*
Love ("Love was before the light began")
    See The thousand nights and one
Love and a question. Robert Frost. *FrR*
"**Love** and forgetting might have carried
    them." See Two look at two
"**Love** at the lips was touch." See To earth-
    ward
Love in a village, sel. Isaac Bickerstaffe
    "There was a jolly miller." *DeMg*—*UnG*
    Jolly miller. *OpO*
    "There was a jolly miller once." *LiL*
Love in May. Jean Passerat, tr. fr. the
    French by Andrew Lang. *PaS*
Love in moonlight. Bhartrihari, tr. fr. the
    Sanskrit by Paul Elmer More. *PaS*
"**Love** many." Unknown. *MoY*
"**Love** must think in music sweetly." See
    Love
Love restored. Ben Jonson. *PlU* (sel.)
The **love-sick** frog. See "A frog he would
    a-wooing go"
Love song. See "Lavender's blue, diddle,
    diddle"
Love song ("How am I to withhold my
    soul") Rainer Maria Rilke, tr. fr. the
    German by Kate Flores. *PaS*
A **love** story. Oliver Herford. *CoPm*
"**Love** thy God and love Him only." See
    Reality
"**Love** was before the light began." See
    The thousand nights and one—Love
Love will find out the way. Unknown.
    HoW—*SmLg*
Love without hope. Robert Graves. *GrP*
"**Love** without hope, as when the young
    bird-catcher." See Love without hope

Lucy Lavender. Ivy O. Eastwick. *BrBc—
BrS*
Lucy Locket. See "Lucy Locket lost her
pocket"
"Lucy Locket lost her pocket." Mother
Goose. *DeMg—JoAc—LiL*
Lucy and Kitty. *OpO*
Lucy Locket. *BrL-k*
Lucy McLockett. Phyllis McGinley. *BrBc*
(sel.)
Luke, Jemima Thompson
Sweet story of old. *DoP*
Lullabies
The birds' lullaby. E. P. Johnson. *HuL-2*
"Bye, baby bunting." Mother Goose. *ArTp—
DeMg—HuSv—JoAc—LiL—OpO—WoF*
"Bye, bye, baby bunting." Mother Goose.
OpO
Can ye sew cushions. Unknown. *SmLg*
Christmas lullaby. U. Troubetzkoy. *HaY*
Cradle hymn. I. Watts. *DoP*
Cradle song ("From groves of spice") S.
Naidu. *FeF*
Cradle song ("Hushaba, birdie, croon,
croon") Unknown. *HuL-2*
Cradle song ("Lullaby, my little one")
C. M. Bellman. *FeF*
Cradle song ("O Timothy Tim") A. A.
Milne. *MiWc*
Cradle song ("Sleep, sleep, beauty bright")
W. Blake. *JoAc*
Cradle song of the elephants. A. Del Valle.
FeF
Fairy lullaby. From A midsummer-night's
dream. W. Shakespeare. *FeF—UnG*
You spotted snakes. *JoAc*
"Father's gone a-flailing." Mother Goose.
OpO
The fly-away horse. E. Field. *UnG*
German slumber song. K. Simrock. *UnG*
Giant Bonaparte. Mother Goose. *OpO*
"Hush-a-ba birdie, croon, croon." Mother
Goose. *OpO*
"Hush-a-baa, baby." Mother Goose. *OpO*
"Hush-a-bye a baa lamb." Mother Goose.
OpO
"Hush-a-bye, baby (daddy is near)." Mother
Goose. *DeMg*
"Hush-a-bye, baby, on the tree top." Mother
Goose. *DeMg—HuSv—JoAc—LiL—OpO*
"Hush-a-bye, baby (the beggar)." Mother
Goose. *OpO*
"Hush-a-bye, baby, they're gone to milk."
Mother Goose. *OpO*
"Hush, baby, my doll, I pray you don't
cry." Mother Goose. *DeMg*
"Hush, little baby, don't say a word."
Mother Goose. *OpO*
"Hush thee, my babby." Mother Goose.
DeMg—OpO
"Hushaby, don't you cry." Unknown. *WoF*
"Hushie ba, burdie beeton." Mother Goose.
OpO
"I'll buy you a tartan bonnet." Mother
Goose. *OpO*
An Indian lullaby. Unknown. *JoAc*
Italian lullaby. Unknown. *FeF*
"The little lady lairdie." Mother Goose.
OpO
Little sandman's song. Unknown. *HuL-2*

Lullaby ("Fourteen angels round my
bed") Unknown. *DoP*
Lullaby ("The long canoe") R. Hillyer.
FeF
Lullaby ("Lullaby, oh, lullaby") C. G. Ros-
setti. *HuL-1*
Lullaby ("Sleep, mouseling, sleep") E. J.
Coatsworth. *BrS—CoM*
Lullaby ("Sleep, my little one, sleep")
S. J. S. Harrington. *BrL-k—HuL-1*
Lullaby for a naughty girl. E. V. Rieu. *RiF*
Lullaby of an infant chief. W. Scott. *FeF
—JoAc—UnG*
Manhattan lullaby. R. Field. *BrBc*
Mary's lullaby. I. O. Eastwick. *McAw*
Nurse's song. Unknown. *ReT*
Orkney lullaby. E. Field. *UnG*
Presents from heaven. E. Farjeon. *FaCb—
FaN*
The Rock-a-by Lady. E. Field. *ArTp*
"Rock-a-bye, baby (thy cradle is green)."
Mother Goose. *DeMg—JoAc—LiL—OpO*
Rockaby, baby ("The rook's nest do rock
on the tree-top") W. Barnes. *DeT*
Seal lullaby. R. Kipling. *ArTp—BrR-5—
FeF—JoAc*
The shell. E. Farjeon. *FaCb*
Sleep, baby boy. Unknown. *FeF*
"Sleep, baby, sleep (thy father guards)."
Mother Goose. *LiL*
Holy lullaby. *UnG*
"Sleep, baby, sleep (thy father watches the
sheep)." Unknown. *BrL-k—BrR-3—FeF
—JoAc*
The sleepy song ("As soon as the fire
burns red and low") J. D. D. Bacon. *HuSv*
Sleepy song ("Ere the moon begins to rise")
T. B. Aldrich. *UnG*
Sleepy song ("Mother sings a sleepy-song")
M. Kennedy. *McAw*
Slumber song. L. V. Ledoux. *FeF*
Spanish lullaby. Unknown. *DoP*
Spring lullaby. F. M. Frost. *FrLn*
Sweet and low. A. Tennyson. *FeF—HuL-2
—HuSv—JoAc—UnG*
A cradle song. *DeT*
Song. *ReT*
The Virgin's slumber song. F. Carlin. *HaY*
Welsh lullaby. Unknown. *UnG*
All through the night. *FeF*
"What does little birdie say." A. Tenny-
son. *BrL-k—HuL-1*
Wynken, Blynken, and Nod. E. Field. *FeF
—HuL-1—HuSv—JoAc—UnG*
The yew-tree. E. Farjeon. *FaCb*
Lullaby ("Fourteen angels round my bed")
Unknown, tr. fr. the Flemish. *DoP*
Lullaby ("The long canoe") Robert Hillyer.
FeF
Lullaby ("Lullaby, oh, lullaby") Christina
Georgina Rossetti. *HuL-1*
Lullaby ("Sleep, mouseling, sleep") Eliza-
beth Jane Coatsworth. *BrS—CoM*
Lullaby ("Sleep, my little one, sleep")
Sarah Jane S. Harrington. *BrL-k—
HuL-1*
Lullaby for a naughty girl. E. V. Rieu. *RiF*
"Lullaby, my little one." See Cradle song
Lullaby of an infant chief. Walter Scott.
FeF—JoAc—UnG

"**Lullaby,** oh, lullaby." See Lullaby
"**Lully,** lulley, lully, lulley." See The falcon
Lumbering. See also Forests and forestry
How we logged Katahdin stream. D. G. Hoffman. *UnMc*
When the drive goes down. D. Malloch. *HuSv*
Woodchopper's song. Unknown. *TaD*
Lumberjacks. See Lumbering
Luncheon
Luncheons. D. Aldis. *AlA*
Mary Anne's luncheon. D. Aldis. *AlA*
Nice food. D. Aldis. *AlA*
Luncheons. Dorothy Aldis. *AlA*
Lutes
The harper of Chao. Po Chü-i. *PlU*
Orpheus. From King Henry VIII. W. Shakespeare or J. Fletcher. *PlU*
Music. *SmLg*
To his lute. W. Drummond, of Hawthornden. *PlU*
"When to her lute Corinna sings." T. Campion. *GrCc*
Corinna. *PlU*
"Why, then thou canst not break her to the lute." From The taming of the shrew. W. Shakespeare
The taming of the shrew. *PlU*
Luther, Martin
Cradle hymn. *ArTp—BrBc—DoP—EaW—FeF—HuL-1—HuSv—JoAc—McAw—UnG*
"**Lydia** is gone this many a year." Lizette Woodworth Reese. *GrCc*
Lying awake. Barbara Young. *McAw*
A **lyke-wake** dirge. Unknown. *MaB—NaE*
Lyly, John
Fairy song. *DeT*
What bird so sings. *ReT*
Lynxes
The lesser lynx. E. V. Rieu. *RiF*
Lytton, Robert
Going back again. *NaE*

M

M. L. See L., M.
"**M** I crooked letter, crooked letter I." Unknown. *WiRm*
M is for midsummer eve. Eleanor Farjeon. *FaCb*
Mab. See The satyr
Mabel. Unknown. *WoJ*
"**Mabel,** Mabel." See Mabel
"**Mabel,** Mabel, set the table." Unknown. *WoF*
McArthur, Molly
Secrets. *DeT*
Macaulay, Lord. See Macaulay, Thomas Babington, Lord
Macaulay, Thomas Babington, Lord
The Armada. *SmLg*
Epitaph on a Jacobite. *DeT*
The fight at the bridge. See Lays of ancient Rome—Horatius

Horatius. See Lays of ancient Rome
Lays of ancient Rome, sel.
Horatius. *SmLg*
The fight at the bridge. *UnMc*
Macavity: The mystery cat. T. S. Eliot. *ArTp—McW*
"**Macavity's** a mystery cat: he's called the Hidden Paw." See Macavity: The mystery cat
Macbeth, sel. William Shakespeare
The witches' spell. *CoPm*
McCann, Rebecca
The cheerful cherub, sels. *ThP*
Humane thought
Light words
Vanity
Humane thought. See The cheerful cherub
Light words. See The cheerful cherub
Vanity. See The cheerful cherub
McCarthy, Denis A. (Aloysius)
The fields of Ballyclare. *BrL-7*
The land where hate should die. *BrL-8*
MacCathmhaoil, Seosamh, pseud. See Campbell, Joseph
McCord, David
Afreet. *McT*
After Christmas. *McT*
All about fireflies all about. *McFf*
Alley cat. *McT*
Alphabet. *McT*
Asleep and awake. *McFf*
At low tide. *McFf*
At the garden gate. *FeF—McFf*
August 28. *McFf*
"Bananas and cream." *McT*
"Blessèd Lord, what is it to be young." *McT*
Castor oil. *McT*
Christmas eve. *McFf*
Cocoon. *McFf*
Compass song. *McFf*
Conversation. *McFf*
The cove. *McT*
"The cow has a cud." See Five chants
Crickets. *McT*
Crows. *ArTp—McFf*
Dividing. *McFf*
Dr Klimwell's fall. *McT*
The door. *McFf*
Down by the sea. *McT*
Durenda Fair. *McFf*
"Every time I climb a tree." See Five chants
Far away. *McFf*
"Fat father robin." *McFf*
Father and I in the woods. *McFf*
The firetender. *McFf*
The fisherman. *McFf*
Five chants. *McFf*
    I. "Every time I climb a tree." *ArTp —UnG*
    II. "Monday morning back to school"
    III. "The pickety fence"
    IV. "The cow has a cud"
    V. "Thin ice"
Five little bats. *McFf*
Food and drink. *McT*
A fool and his money. *McT*
Fred. *ArTp—McFf*
From the mailboat passing by. *McFf*

"W's for windows." See All around the town

McGonagall, William
The death of prince Leopold. *NaE*
The Tay bridge disaster. *NaE*

Machado, Antonio
"The moldering hulk." *PaS*

Machinery. See also names of machines, as Steam shovels
John Henry. Unknown. *UnMc*
Near and far. H. Behn. *BeW*
Nightmare number three. S. V. Benét. *UnMc*
The secret of the machines. R. Kipling. *HuSv*
A time for building. M. C. Livingston. *LiWa*

McHugh, Vincent
Ode in a night of overhanging weather. *McW*

MacI., Brittan
That duck. *McAw*

MacIntyre, C. F.
"On nights like this all cities are alike." tr. *GrCc*

Mackay, Charles
The giant. *BrR-6*
No enemies. *UnG*

McKay, Lois Weakley
Night. *BrS*

Mackaye, Percy
Goethals, the prophet engineer. *HuSv*

"Mackerel sky." Mother Goose. *OpO*

MacKinstry, Elizabeth
The man who hid his own front door. *ArTp—FeF*

MacLeish, Archibald
Einstein, 1929. *Pll*
The end of the world. *HaP*
Epistle to be left in the earth. *Pll*
Reply to Mr Wordsworth. *Pll* (sel.)
The silent slain. *GrCc*

Macleod, Fiona, pseud. See Sharp, William

McLeod, Irene Rutherford
Lone dog. *ArTp—DeT—FeF*

MacNaghten, Hugh Vibart
Call to youth. tr. *PaS*

MacNeice, Louis
Bagpipe music. *HaP*

McVan, Alice Jane
Song. tr. *PaS*

McWebb, Elizabeth Upham
At Mrs Appleby's. *ArTp—BrS—HuSv*

Macy, Arthur
The peppery man. *FeF*

Mad farmer's song. See "My father left me three acres of land"

The **mad** gardener's song. See Sylvie and Bruno—The gardener's song

The **mad** maid's song. Robert Herrick. *HoW*

Madeleva, Sister Mary
In desert places. *UnG*

Magee, John Gillespie, Jr
High flight. *FeF—McW—UnMc*

"**Maggie** and Milly and Molly and May." See Poem

Magic. See also Enchantment
A is for abracadabra. E. Farjeon. *FaCb*

Aladdin. J. R. Lowell. *BrR-5—CoPm—McW*
Blue magic. E. Farjeon. *FaCb—FaN*
The conjuror. E. V. Lucas. *BrBc*
Crab-apple. E. Talbot. *ArTp—BrBc*
The fairy king. W. Allingham. *CoPm*
I is for invisibility. E. Farjeon. *FaCb*
J is for jinn. E. Farjeon. *FaCb*
A love story. O. Herford. *CoPm*
Magic ("Magic is what") M. Chute. *ChA*
Magic ("Oh, a bottle of ink, a bottle of ink") B. J. Thompson. *BrR-3*
The magic seeds. J. Reeves. *ReBl*
Midsummer magic. I. O. Eastwick. *ArTp*
My name is John Wellington Wells. From The sorcerer. W. S. Gilbert. *CoPm*
Otherwise. A. Fisher. *HuL-1*
P is for philtre. E. Farjeon. *FaCb*
Prologue for a magician. A. Guiterman. *CoPm*
The pumpkin. R. Graves. *CoPm—ReG*
Queer things. J. Reeves. *CoPm—ReW*
Thanksgiving magic. R. B. Bennett. *ArTp—BrS*
A visit from abroad. J. Stephens. *CoPm*
Who goes with Fergus. W. B. Yeats. *SmLg*
Magic ("Magic is what") Marchette Chute. *ChA*
Magic ("Oh, a bottle of ink, a bottle of ink") Blanche Jennings Thompson. *BrR-3*

"Magic is what." See Magic

"A magic landscape." Afanasy Fet, tr. fr. the Russian by Babette Deutsch. *PaS*

The magic map. See The house beyond the meadow

The magic piper. E. L. Marsh. *BrS—HuL-2*

The magic seeds. James Reeves. *ReBl*

The magical picture. Robert Graves. *GrP*

Magicians
The conjuror. E. V. Lucas. *BrBc—CoPm*
Prologue for a magician. A. Guiterman. *CoPm*

"A magnet hung in a hardware shop." See Patience—The fable of the magnet and the churn

Magnets
The fable of the magnet and the churn. From Patience. W. S. Gilbert. *FeF*

"Magpie, magpie, flutter and flee." See To the magpie

Magpies
Bronwen to her magpie. E. Farjeon. *FaCb*
To the magpie. Mother Goose. *OpO*
"Two magpies sat on a garden rail." D'A. W. Thompson. *NaM*

The **maid.** Theodore Goodridge Roberts. *NaM*

The **maid** of Timbuctoo. Laura E. Richards. *HuL-2*

"The **maiden** caught me in the wild." See The crystal cabinet

"A **maiden** caught stealing a dahlia." Unknown. *CoH*

Maiden in the moor. Unknown. *MaB*

"**Maiden** in the moor lay." See Maiden in the moor

"The **maidens** came." See Song

"A maiden's wondrous fame, I sing." Unknown, tr. fr. the French. *JoAc*

The mail goes through. Nancy Byrd Turner. *BrR-6*

Mail service. See also Letters and letter writing; Mailmen

From the mailboat passing by. D. McCord. *McFf*

The mail goes through. N. B. Turner. *BrR-6*

Night mail. W. H. Auden. *HaP*

The phantom mail coach. L. O. Welcome. *CoPm*

Stamp battalion. E. V. Lucas. *HuSv*

A sure sign. N. B. Turner. *ArTp—BrR-4*

Mailbox wren. Frances M. Frost. *FrLn*

Mailmen

"Eight o'clock." C. G. Rossetti. *ArTp*

The holiday. D. Aldis. *AlA*

My valentine. I. O. Eastwick. *EaI*

On their appointed rounds. Unknown. *FeF*

The postman ("Hey, the little postman") L. E. Richards. *ArTp*

The postman ("Rat-a-tat-tat, rat-a-tat-tat") C. Sansom. *HuL-1*

The postman ("The whistling postman swings along") Unknown. *FeF*

Mair, Charles

Winter. *CoPs* (sel.)

"Make a joyful noise unto the Lord, all ye lands." See Psalms—Psalm C

Make believe. Harry Behn. *BeW*

"Make me, dear Lord, polite and kind." See A child's prayer

"Make three-fourths of a cross." Mother Goose. *OpO*

The make-up man. Jean H. Breig. *BrR-5*

"Making toast at the fireside." See Four ruthless rhymes—Nurse

"Making toast by the fireside." See Four ruthless rhymes—Nurse

The Maldive shark. Herman Melville. *SmLg*

Malkus, Alida

Cradle song of the elephants. tr. *FeF*

The hurricane. tr. *FeF*

"She was a pretty little girl." tr. *FeF*

Malloch, Douglas

June. *HaY*

Three words. *ThP*

When the drive goes down. *HuSv*

Mallock, W. H.

De rerum natura, sel.

No single thing abides. tr. *PlI*

No single thing abides. See De rerum natura

A Maltese dog. Tymnès, tr. fr. the Greek by Edmund Blunden. *ArTp—SmLg*

"Mama, mama, look at little Sam." Unknown. *WiRm*

Man. See also Woman

"All the world's a stage." From As you like it. W. Shakespeare

From As you like it. *HaP*

Gallery of people. *UnG*

The bear. R. Frost. *FrR*

Cold-blooded creatures. E. Wylie. *PlI*

Covering the subject. R. Armour. *McW*

The difference. E. Farjeon. *FaCb—FaN*

An essay on man. A. Pope. *HaP* (sel.)— *PlI* (sel.)

Vice. *ThP*

Fish to man. L. Hunt. *NaM*

"Flower in the crannied wall." A. Tennyson. *DoP—FeF—ThP*

"God made the men." Unknown. *MoY*

Journal. E. St V. Millay. *PlI* (sel.)

"Man is but a castaway." C. Day. *PlI*

"A man said to the universe." S. Crane. *PlI*

Meditatio. E. Pound. *SmLg*

Poem. H. von Hofmannsthal. *PaS*

Progress. D. McCord. *PlI*

Psalm VIII. From Psalms, Bible, Old Testament. *PlI*

Psalm eight. *PaS*

"When I consider thy heavens." *FeF*

The pulley. G. Herbert. *HaP*

Sand dunes. R. Frost. *FrR*

Smoke stack. A. M. Sullivan. *McW*

The term. W. C. Williams. *ReT*

This dim and ptolemaic man. J. P. Bishop. *PlI*

What a piece of work is a man. Sophocles. *PaS*

What am I, Life. J. Masefield. *PlI*

"When that I was and a little tiny boy." From Twelfth night. W. Shakespeare. *McW*

The wind and the rain. *HoW*

The wishes of an elderly man. W. Raleigh. *CoH—SmLg*

"The man bent over his guitar." See The man with the blue guitar

"Man, born to toil, in his labour rejoiceth." See A hymn of nature

"A man, encountering a camel." See The camel and the flotsam

Man for Mars. David McCord. *McT*

The man from Porlock. Helen Bevington. *NaE*

"The man from the woods." John Ciardi. *CiM*

The man in the moon ("The man in the moon as he sails the sky") Unknown. *BrR-5*

The man in the moon ("Said the Raggedy Man on a hot afternoon") James Whitcomb Riley. *CoH*

"The man in the moon as he sails the sky." See The man in the moon

"The man in the moon (came tumbling down)." Mother Goose. *DeMg—LiL*

The man in the moon. *OpO*

"The man in the moon drinks claret." Mother Goose. *OpO*

"The man in the moon was caught in a trap." Mother Goose. *OpO*

"The man in the mune." Mother Goose. *OpO*

The man in the onion bed. John Ciardi. *CiI*

A man in the wilderness. See "A man in the wilderness asked me"

"A man in the wilderness asked me." Mother Goose. *DeMg—JoAc—LiL*

A man in the wilderness. *OpO*

"The man in the wilderness said to me." *SmLg*

"The man in the wilderness said to me."
See "A man in the wilderness asked me"

A man in the woods said. John Ciardi. *CiI*

"Man is but a castaway." Clarence Day.
PlI

"The man knocked strongly at the door."
See The man from Porlock

A man must live. Charlotte Perkins Stetson.
ThP

"A man must live. We justify." See A
man must live

Man of Derby. Mother Goose. *OpO*

"The man of life upright." Thomas
Campion. *HaP*

Man of Thessaly. See "There was a man
of Thessaly"

A man of words. See "A man of words
and not of deeds"

"A man of words and not of deeds." Mother
Goose. *DeMg—SmLg*

A man of words. *DeT*

The man on the flying trapeze. Unknown.
SmLg

"A man said to the universe." Stephen
Crane. *PlI*

"A man saw a ball of gold in the sky."
Stephen Crane. *NaE*

"A man so various, that he seemed to be."
See George Villiers, Duke of Buckingham

The man that had little to say. John Ciardi.
CiI

The man that had no hat. John Ciardi. *CiI*

The man that lived in a box. John Ciardi.
CiI

"Man, the egregious egoist." See Cold-
blooded creatures

"A man was sitting underneath a tree." See
Seumas Beg

"A man went a-hunting at Reigate." Mother
Goose. *DeMg*

"A man went down to Panama." See
Goethals, the prophet engineer

The man who hid his own front door.
Elizabeth MacKinstry. *ArTp—FeF*

The man who jumped. Mother Goose. *OpO*

The man who sang the sillies. John Ciardi.
CiM

A man with a little pleated piano. Winifred
Welles. *FeF*

The man with nought. See "There was a
man and he had nought"

The man with the blue guitar. Wallace
Stevens. *PlU* (sel.)

The man with the rake. See Translations
from the Chinese

Mangan, James Clarence
Home-sickness. tr. *PaS*

Manhattan lullaby. Rachel Field. *BrBc*

Manifold, John
The bunyip and the whistling kettle. *CoPm*
Fife tune. *SmLg*

Manners. See Etiquette

Manners. Mariana Griswold Van Rensselaer.
FeF

"Manners in the dining-room." Mother
Goose. *OpO*

A man's bread. Josephine Preston Peabody.
HaY

Man's mortality. Unknown. *SmLg*

Mansfield, Katherine, pseud. (Kathleen
Beauchamp)
Little brother's secret. *ArTp—FeF*

Manual system. Carl Sandburg. *ArTp*

"Many a long, long year ago." See The
alarmed skipper

"Many a ship is lost at sea." Unknown. *MoY*

"Many a tree is found in the wood." See
A salute to trees

"Many birds and the beating of wings."
See Margaret

Many crows, any owl. David McCord. *McT*

"Many have written before me." Unknown.
MoY

"Many love music but for music's sake."
See On music

The map. Elizabeth Bishop. *SmLg*

Maple feast. Frances M. Frost. *BrS*

"The maple is a dainty maid." See Autumn
fancies

Maple leaves. Shikō, tr. fr. the Japanese
by Harold G. Henderson. *PaS*

"The maple owned that she was tired." See
Autumn fashions

Maple trees
The five-fingered maple. K. L. Brown.
HuL-1
Maple feast. F. M. Frost. *BrS*
Maple leaves. Shikō. *PaS*
October. T. B. Aldrich. *UnG*
On some windy day. D. Aldis. *AlA*
"The maples flare among the spruces." See
Harvest home

Maps
The cloud-mobile. M. Swenson. *UnG*
The magic map. From The house beyond
the meadow. H. Behn. *BeH*
The map. E. Bishop. *SmLg*
Maps. D. B. Thompson. *ArTp—HuL-2*

Maps. Dorothy Brown Thompson. *ArTp—
HuL-2*

March
Counting-out rhyme for March. F. M.
Frost. *HaY*
March ("Dear March, come in") E.
Dickinson. *HaY*
March ("Ho, laughs the winter") A.
Guiterman. *HaY*
March ("I wonder what spendthrift chose
to spill") C. Thaxter. *UnG*
March ("In the maple-sugar bush") E. J.
Coatsworth. *HaY*
March ("March is a worker, busy and
merry") E. Hammond. *BrR-4*
March ("The sun at noon to higher air")
A. E. Housman. *SmLg*
"March, blow by." E. Farjeon. *FaCb—
FaN*
March speaks. E. Farjeon. *FaCb—FaN*
March wind. M. E. Uschold. *HaY*
The March winds. G. W. W. Houghton.
HaY
"March, you old blusterer." E. Farjeon.
FaCb—FaN
Wild March. C. F. Woolson. *HaY*

March—*Continued*
Written in March. W. Wordsworth. *ArTp*
— *BrR-6* — *FeF* — *HaY* — *HuL-2* —
McW — *ReG* — *ReT* — *UnG*
In March. *DeT*
March. *JoAc*
The merry month of March. *NaE*—
NaM
March ("The cock is crowing") See Written
in March
March ("Dear March, come in") Emily
Dickinson. *HaY*
March ("Ho, laughs the winter") Arthur
Guiterman. *HaY*
The **march** ("I heard a voice that cried,
Make way for those who died") J. C.
Squire. *CoPs*
March ("I wonder what spendthrift chose
to spill") Celia Thaxter. *UnG*
March ("In the maple-sugar bush") Eliza-
beth Jane Coatsworth. *HaY*
March ("March is a worker, busy and
merry") Eleanor Hammond. *BrR-4*
March ("The sun at noon to higher air")
Alfred Edward Housman. *SmLg*
"**March**, blow by." Eleanor Farjeon. *FaCb*
—*FaN*
"**March** is a worker, busy and merry." See
March
"**March**, march, head erect." See Marching
March speaks. Eleanor Farjeon. *FaCb*—
FaN
March wind. Maud E. Uschold. *HaY*
The **March** winds. George Washington
Wright Houghton. *HaY*
"**March** winds and April showers." Mother
Goose. *DeMg*—*LiL*—*OpO*
Signs, seasons, and sense. *UnG*
"**March**, you old blusterer." Eleanor
Farjeon. *FaCb*—*FaN*
Marching. See also Parades
Fife tune. J. Manifold. *SmLg*
The march. J. C. Squire. *CoPs*
Marching. Mother Goose. *OpO*
Marching song. R. L. Stevenson. *ArTp*—
FeF
"Oh, the grand old duke of York." Mother
Goose. *DeMg*—*LiL*
The brave old duke of York. *OpO*
Duke o' York. *HuL-1*
"The grand old duke of York." *ArTp*
"Oh, the brave old duke of York." *JoAc*
Marching. Mother Goose. *OpO*
Marching song. Robert Louis Stevenson.
ArTp—*FeF*
"**Marcia** and I went over the curve." See
Millions of strawberries
Marco Polo. Unknown. *WoJ*
"**Marco** Polo went to France." See Marco
Polo
Margaret. Carl Sandburg. *SaW*
"**Margaret**, are you grieving." See Spring
and fall
"**Margaret** Nash." See Margaret Nash got
wet but I don't know how
Margaret Nash got wet but I don't know
how. John Ciardi. *CiM*
"**Margery** Mutton-pie and Johnny Bo-peep."
Mother Goose. *DeMg*—*OpO*

Margie. Unknown. *WoJ*
"**Margie** drank some marmalade." See
Margie
"**Marguerite**, go wash your feet." Unknown.
MoY
"**Maria** intended a letter to write." See How
to write a letter
"**Maria**, when you were only one." See For
Maria at four
Mariana. Alfred Tennyson. *HoW*
Marigolds
"Five little sisters walking in a row." K.
Greenaway. *NaM*
Mary and the marigold. I. O. Eastwick. *EaI*
Marin, Muna Lee de Muñoz
January night. tr. *PaS*
Maris, Sister Stella
A carol for sleepy children. *DoP*
Christmas carol for the dog. *DoP*
Ox and donkey's carol. See The ox and
the donkey's carol
The ox and the donkey's carol. *DoP*
Ox and donkey's carol. *EaW*
Marjorie's almanac. Thomas Bailey Aldrich.
FeF
"**Mark** how the lark and linnet sing." See
On the death of Mr Purcell
Market square. A. A. Milne. *JoAc*—*MiWc*
Markets and marketing. See also Shops and
shopkeepers
"As I was going to Banbury." Mother
Goose. *JoAc*
Banbury fair. *OpO*
The child reads an almanac. F. Jammès.
FeF
"A fairy went a-marketing." R. Fyleman.
HuL-1—*JoAc*
"Hie to the market, Jenny come trot."
Mother Goose. *OpO*
"I had a little dog and they called him
Buff." Mother Goose. *DeMg*
Buff. *OpO*
In the bazaars of Hyderabad. S. Naidu. *FeF*
Market square. A. A. Milne. *JoAc*—*MiWc*
Mrs Golightly. J. Reeves. *ReBl*
My brother. D. Aldis. *AlHd*
Saturday market. C. Mew. *FeF* (sel.)
"There was an old woman, as I've heard
tell." Mother Goose. *ArTp*—*JoAc*—*LiL*
Lauk a mercy. *DeT*
The little woman and the pedlar. *OpO*
The old woman. *UnG*
"There was a little woman." *DeMg*
There was an old woman. *BrR-3*—*CoPs*
—*CoSp*—*NaM*
"To market, to market, to buy a fat pig."
Mother Goose. *ArTp*—*DeMg*—*HuSv*—
JoAc—*LiL*
To market. *HuL-1*
"To market, to market." *OpO*
"To market, to market, to buy a plum bun."
Mother Goose. *DeMg*
"To market, to market." *OpO*
"Trit trot to market to buy a penny doll."
Mother Goose. *OpO*
"Upon a cock-horse to market I'll trot."
Mother Goose. *OpO*

Markham, Edwin
Joy of the morning. *FeF*
A prayer. *DoP—HuSv*
The right kind of people. *BrL-8*
Song to a tree. *FeF*

Marlowe, Christopher
The passionate shepherd to his love. *HaP*
—ReT

Marmion, sels. Walter Scott
Lochinvar. *BrL-7—CoSp—FeF—HuSv—*
JoAc—NaE—UnG—UnMc
Old Christmastide. *BrS*
"Heap on more wood—the wind is
chill." *ArTp*

Marquis, Don (Donald Robert Perry Marquis)
Archy a low brow. *CoH*
Archy confesses. *NaE*
Archy, the cockroach, speaks. See Certain
maxims of Archy
Archy's autobiography. *CoH* (sel.)
Certain maxims of Archy. *CoH* (sel.)
Archy, the cockroach, speaks. *FeF*
Fate is unfair. *NaE*
The flattered lightning bug. *CoSp*
The hen and the oriole. *CoH—NaE*
The honey bee. *CoH*
A hot-weather song. *HuSv*
The jokesmith's vacation. *CoH*
"Noah an' Jonah an' Cap'n John Smith."
SmLg
A seaside romance. *CoH*
Small talk. *CoSp*

"Marquita had blossom fists." See Portrait
of a child settling down for an afternoon nap

Marriage. See also Brides and bridegrooms;
Courtship; Married life
"Bless the man that takes your hand." Un-
known. *MoY*
"Bless you, bless you, burnie-bee." Mother
Goose. *JoAc—OpO*
"A cat came fiddling out of a barn." Mother
Goose. *DeMg—HuSv—JoAc*
Bagpipes. *DeT—OpO*
A cat came fiddling. *HuL-1*
The comedy of Billy and Betty. Mother
Goose. *OpO*
"The daughter of the farrier." Unknown
Limericks since Lear. *UnG*
"Fiddle de dee, fiddle de dee." Mother
Goose. *DeMg*
The fly and the bumble-bee. *HuL-1*
Song. *WiRm*
"First comes love." Unknown. *MoY*
Gather ye rosebuds. R. Herrick. *HaP—ReG*
"Gloria is your name." Unknown. *MoY*
Harry Parry. Mother Goose. *OpO*
"I know where I'm going." Unknown. *GrCc*
—NaM
"I mun be married a Sunday." N. Udall.
GrCc
"I saw three ships come sailing by." Mother
Goose. *DeMg—JoAc—LiL*
I saw three ships. *HuL-1—UnG*
Three ships. *OpO*
"Ice cream, soda, ginger ale, pop." Unknown.
TaD—WoJ
"If I ever marry." Unknown. *WoF*

"If no one ever marries me." L. Alma-
Tadema. *BrBc—HuL-1—UnG*
"Janie now, Janie ever." Unknown. *MoY*
Jemmy Dawson. Mother Goose. *OpO*
"Mirror, mirror, tell me." Unknown
Signs, seasons, and sense. *UnG*
Mr Punchinello. Unknown. *DeT—JoAc*
The monkey's wedding. Unknown. *WoF*
The mouse who lived on a hill. Unknown.
TaD
"Needles and pins (triplets)." Unknown.
MoY
"On Saturday night shall be my care."
Mother Goose. *OpO*
Sailor. E. Farjeon. *PeF*
"Scissors and string, scissors and string."
Mother Goose. *OpO*
Song. Unknown. *ReT*
To Mr Punchinello. Mother Goose. *OpO*
"Tom, Dick, or Harry." Unknown. *MoY*
"Two in a car." Unknown. *MoY*
Wedding ("Pussicat, wussicat, with a white
foot") Mother Goose. *OpO*
The wedding ("This year") Mother Goose.
OpO
What care I. Mother Goose. *OpO*
"What is life." Unknown. *MoY*
Words from the bottom of a well. E.
Jacobson. *ThP*

Married life
Acquiescence. I. Edman. *ThP*
"As sure as comes your wedding day." Un-
known. *MoY*
The bad-tempered wife. Unknown. *UnMc*
Dickey Diller and his wife. Unknown. *GrCc*
Dicky Dilver. Mother Goose. *OpO*
Did you see my wife. Mother Goose. *OpO*
The dumb wife cured. Unknown. *UnMg*
Dust to dust. T. Hood. *UnG*
Father Grumble. Unknown. *BrR-5*
Flitch of bacon. E. Farjeon. *FaN*
The funny old man and his wife. D'A. W.
Thompson. *BrR-4*
Get up and bar the door. Unknown. *ArTp*
—CoSp—JoAc—UnG—UnMc
"Help. Murder. Police." Unknown. *WoF*
The hill wife. R. Frost. *FrR*
Home burial. R. Frost. *FrR*
"I had a little husband." Mother Goose.
DeMg—JoAc—NaE
Little husband. *OpO*
"I love sixpence, jolly little sixpence."
Mother Goose. *DeMg—JoAc*
"I love sixpence, pretty little sixpence."
LiL
The jolly tester. *OpO*
"I married my wife by the light of the
moon." Mother Goose. *DeMg*
"If your husband is thirsty." Unknown.
MoY
Jack in the pulpit. Mother Goose. *OpO*
"Jack Sprat could eat no fat." Mother
Goose. *DeMg—LiL*
Jack Sprat. *OpO*
Jacky Jingle. Mother Goose. *OpO*
John Anderson, my jo. R. Burns. *HaP—*
HuSv—ThP
Johnny Fife and Johnny's wife. M. P.
Meigs. *ArTp—BrL-7—HuL-1*
"Little Jack Jingle." Mother Goose. *DeMg*

Married life—*Continued*
  Mr Kartoffel. J. Reeves. *ReW*
  "My little wife." Mother Goose. *OpO*
  "Needles and pins, needles and pins." Mother Goose. *DeMg*
      Signs, seasons, and sense. *UnG*
  "Now you're married you must obey." Unknown
      Signs, seasons, and sense. *UnG*
  "O I won't lead a homely life." T. Hardy. *PlU*
  The old cloak. Unknown. *MaB*
  Old Wichet. Unknown. *CoSp*
  Paul's wife. R. Frost. *FrR*
  "Peter, Peter, pumpkin eater." Mother Goose. *AnI—DeMg—JoAc—LiL*
      Peter. *OpO*
  "Riddledy Bob and Jimson Weed." Unknown *WoF*
  The river-merchant's wife: A letter. Li T'ai-po. *GrCc—HaP*
  The sailor's wife. W. J. Mickle. *DeT*
  "There was an old bachelor who lived all alone." Unknown. *WoF*
  "There was an old man who lived in a wood." Mother Goose. *DeMg—HuSv*
      The old man who lived in a wood. *NaM*
  "There was an old woman in Surrey." Mother Goose. *DeMg*
  "Tommy Trot, a man of law." Mother Goose. *DeMg*
      Tommy Trot. *OpO*
  The usual way. F. E. Weatherly. *BrL-7*
  We have been together. E. Byron. *ThP*
  "When I was a bachelor, I lived by myself." Mother Goose. *LiL*
  "When I was a little boy." Mother Goose. *BrL-k*
      The bachelor's lament. *OpO*
      "When I was a little boy I lived by myself." *DeMg*
  "When you are married (and have a pair)." Unknown. *MoY*
  "When you are married (and have one)." Unknown. *MoY*
  "When you are married (and have twenty-five)." Unknown. *MoY*
  "When you get married (and live across)." Unknown. *MoY*
  "When you get married (and live next door)." Unknown. *MoY*
  "When you get married (and live on figs)." Unknown. *MoY*
  "When you get married (and live upstairs)." Unknown. *MoY*
  "When you get married (and your husband)." Unknown. *MoY*
  "When you get married (don't marry a flirt)." Unknown. *MoY*
  The wife of Llew. F. Ledwidge. *CoPm*
Marryat, Frederick
  The old navy. *CoSp—DeT*
"Marry him for love, my dear." See Words from the bottom of a well
Marsh, E. L.
  The magic piper. *BrS—HuL-2*
Marsh, Edward
  The crow and the fox. tr. *BrL-7—UnMc*
Marshall, James
  The Oregon trail: 1851. *HuSv*

Martial (Marcus Valerius Martialis)
  De cœnatione micæ. *SmLg*
  Doctor Fell. See "I do not like thee, Doctor Fell"
  A hinted wish. *BrL-8*
  "I do not like thee, Doctor Fell." *DeMg—NaM*
      Doctor Fell. *OpO*
      Non amo te. *PlI*
      Signs, seasons, and sense. *UnG*
  Non amo te. See "I do not like thee, Doctor Fell"
Martialis, Marcus Valerius. See Martial
Martin, Saint (about)
  Saint Martin. E. Farjeon. *FaCb*
Martin, Billie Eckert
  Surprise. *McAw*
Martin, John
  God's dark. *BrR-3—DoP*
Martin, Sarah Catherine
  "Old Mother Hubbard." at. *AnI—DeMg—HuSv—JoAc—LiL—UnG*
      Old Mother Hubbard and her dog. *OpO*
  Old Mother Hubbard and her dog. See "Old Mother Hubbard"
Martin, William Wesley
  Apple blossoms. *BrR-6*
Marvell, Andrew
  Bermudas. *SmLg*
  A drop of dew. *DeT*
  The garden. *HaP*
  Musicks empire. *GrCc*
  The nymph and her fawn. *SmLg*
  To his coy mistress. *HaP*
Mary, Queen of Scots (about)
  Scotland's Mary. E. Farjeon. *FaN*
Mary, Virgin (about)
  "I sing of a maiden." Unknown. *DeT—MaB—SmLg—UnG*
      Carol. *ReT*
  Lady day. E. Farjeon. *FaCb—FaN*
  A lily of the field. J. B. Tabb. *DoP*
  Mary's lullaby. I. O. Eastwick. *McAw*
  Mother and Child. I. O. Eastwick. *BrS*
  The Mother's song. E. Farjeon. *DoP*
  Virgo. E. Farjeon. *FaCb—FaN*
Mary and her kitten. Eleanor Farjeon. *DeT*
Mary and the marigold. Ivy O. Eastwick. *EaI*
"Mary Ann." See Present
Mary Anne's luncheon. Dorothy Aldis. *AlA*
"Mary had a little car." Unknown. *MoY*
"Mary had a little lamb." See Mary's lamb
"Mary had a little lamb (her father)." Unknown. *MoY*
"Mary had a parrot." Unknown. *MoY*
"Mary had a pretty bird." Mother Goose. *DeMg*
      The pretty bird. *DeT*
"Mary has a thingamajig clamped on her ears." See Manual system
Mary indoors. Eleanor Farjeon. *ReG*
"Mary is a gentle name." See Gentle name
"Mary McGuire's our cook, you know." See This and that
"Mary make the butter." Ivy O. Eastwick. *EaI*

"Mary, Mary come and listen a minute." See
  The musical box
"Mary, Mary, is a star." Unknown. *WiRm*
"Mary, Mary, quite contrary." Mother
  Goose. *ArTp—HuL-1—JoAc—LiL*
  Contrary Mary. *OpO*
  "Mistress Mary." *BrL-k*
  "Mistress Mary, quite contrary." *DeMg—
    HuSv*
Mary Middling. Rose Fyleman. *BrL-k—
  HuL-1*
"**Mary** Middling had a pig." See Mary Mid-
  dling
"**Mary** sat musing on the lamp-flame at the
  table." See The death of the hired man
Mary's lamb. Sarah Josepha Hale. *FeF—
  JoAc—OpO—UnG*
  "Mary had a little lamb." *BrL-k—DeMg
    —LiL*
Mary's lullaby. Ivy O. Eastwick. *McAw*
Ma's gonna buy me. Unknown. *TaD*
Masefield, John
  A ballad of John Silver. *NaE*
  Cape Horn gospel (I). *CoSp*
  Cargoes. *ArTp—FeF—HuL-2*
  An old song re-sung. *NaE*
  Roadways. *BrR-5*
  Sea-fever. *ArTp — BrL-8 — FeF—HuL-2 —
    HuSv—JoAc—PeF*
  Spanish waters. *FeF—McW*
  Trade winds. *HuL-2*
  A wanderer's song. *JoAc*
  What am I, Life. *PlI*
  The yarn of the Loch Achray. *CoSp*
The **masked** shrew. Isabella Gardner. *PlI*
Mason, Agnes Carter
  "Whenever a little child is born." *BrBc*
Mason, W. L.
  My Airedale dog. *PeF*
A **masque**, sel. Thomas Moore
  Child's song. *GrCc*
The **master**. C. G. L. *PlI*
Master and man. See "Master I have, and
  I am his man"
"**Master** I have, and I am his man." Mother
  Goose. *ArTp*
  Master and man. *OpO*
The **master** speed. Robert Frost. *FrR*
"**Master**, whose fire kindled our glad sur-
  prise." See The master
Masters, Edgar Lee
  Achilles Deatheridge. See The Spoon
    River anthology
  Anne Rutledge. See The Spoon River
    anthology
  Fiddler Jones. See The Spoon River an-
    thology
  Petit, the poet. See The Spoon River an-
    thology
  The Spoon River anthology, sels.
    Achilles Deatheridge. *UnMc*
    Anne Rutledge. *CoPs—HaP*
    Fiddler Jones. *PlU—SmLg*
    Petit, the poet. *HaP—SmLg*
    William Jones. *PlI*
  William Jones. See The Spoon River an-
    thology
"**Masters** in this hall." William Morris. *EaW*

Matchett, William H.
  The spit-bug. *McW*
Mathematics. See also Arithmetic
  E = MC². M. Bishop. *PlI*
  Euclid. V. Lindsay. *PlI*
  Gibbs. M. Rukeyser. *PlI* (sel.)
  Hall and Knight; or, z+b+x=y+b+z.
    E. V. Rieu. *CoH—RiF*
  Hudibras, Canto I. S. Butler. *PlI* (sel.)
  The icosasphere M. Moore. *PlI*
  Mathematics or the gift of tongues. A. H.
    Branch. *PlI*
  Numbers and faces. W. H. Auden. *PlI*
    (sel.)
  Plane geometry. E. Rounds. *PlI*
  "The point, the line, the surface and
    sphere." C. Bragdon. *PlI*
  Reliques. E. Blunden. *PlI* (sel.)
  "There was a young man from Trinity."
    Unknown. *PlI*
  Tulips. P. Colum. *PlI*
Mathematics or the gift of tongues. Anna
  Hempstead Branch. *PlI*
Mather, Cotton (about)
  Ben Franklin's head. M. A. De Wolfe
    Howe. *McW*
Mathers, E. Powys
  Arrows of love. tr. *PaS*
  Dates. tr. *FeF*
  Haroun's favorite song. See The thousand
    nights and one
  I love long black eyes. tr. *PaS*
  Love. See The thousand nights and one
  The power of love. See The thousand
    nights and one
  The thousand nights and one, sels.
    Haroun's favorite song. tr. *PaS*
    Love. tr. *PaS*
    The power of love. tr. *PaS*
Mathias, Eileen
  Zoo manners. *HuL-1*
Matilda. Hilaire Belloc. *CoSp—SmLg*
"**Matilda** told such dreadful lies." See
  Matilda
Matos, Pales
  The hurricane. *FeF*
"**Matter** is indestructible." See Smoke stack
"**Matter** whose movement moves us all."
  See Entropy
Matters of taste. Stoddard King. *ThP*
"**Matthew**, Mark, Luke, and John." Mother
  Goose. *DeMg—HuL-1—OpO—SmLg*
  Envoy. *DeT*
  Signs, seasons, and sense. *UnG*
"**Matthew**, Mark, Luke, and John (hold my
  horse)." See Pick-a-back
Matthews, Washington
  "The voice that beautifies the land." tr.
    PaS
Mavrogordato, John
  Alexandrian kings. tr. *GrCc*
  Waiting for the barbarians. tr. *GrCc*
May
  April and May. R. W. Emerson. *JoAc*
  "The fair maid who, the first of May."
    Mother Goose. *DeMg*
  Fairy music. F. Ledwidge. *HaY*
  The gladness of the May. W. Words-
    worth. *HaY*

May—*Continued*
"In May." I. O. Eastwick. *EaI*
In May. D. Aldis. *AlA—AlHd*
Invitation to Bess. E. Farjeon. *FaCb—FaN*
Love in May. J. Passerat. *PaS*
Maÿ. W. Barnes. *CoPs*
May day ("A delicate fabric of bird song") S. Teasdale. *CoPs*
May day ("Good morning, mistress and master") Mother Goose. *OpO*
May day ("So soft came the breath") M. C. Livingston. *LiWa*
A May day carol. Unknown. *CoPs*
May-day song. *UnG*
May-day in June. E. Farjeon. *FaCb—FaN*
May is building her house. R. Le Gallienne. *HaY*
May morning ("The cherry tree's shedding") M. Barrows. *BrL-k*
May morning ("Now the bright morning star, day's harbinger") J. Milton. *HaY*
May mornings. I. O. Eastwick. *BrS—EaI*
May's song. E. Farjeon. *FaCb—FaN*
Maytime magic M. Watts. *McAw*
The next holiday. E. Farjeon. *FaCb*
Sister, awake. Unknown. *CoPs*
Song. S. T. Coleridge. *CoPs—DeT*
"There is but one May in the year." C. G. Rossetti. *ArTp—HuL-2*
'Tis merry in greenwood. From Harold the Dauntless. W. Scott. *FeF*
Maÿ. William Barnes. *CoPs*
May Colvin. Unknown. *CoSp—MaB—UnMc*
May day. See May
May day ("A delicate fabric of bird song") Sara Teasdale. *CoPs*
May day ("Good morning, mistress and master") Mother Goose. *OpO*
May day ("So soft came the breath") Myra Cohn Livingston. *LiWa*
A **May** day carol. Unknown. *CoPs*
May-day song. *UnG*
May-day in June. Eleanor Farjeon. *FaCb—FaN*
May-day song. See A May day carol
"**May** God above send down a dove." Unknown. *MoY*
May is building her house. Richard Le Gallienne. *HaY*
"**May** is building her house. With apple blooms." See May is building her house
"**May** Margaret sits in her bower door." See Hynd Etin
May morning ("The cherry tree's shedding") Marjorie Barrows. *BrL-k*
May morning ("Now the bright morning star, day's harbinger") John Milton. *HaY*
May mornings. Ivy O. Eastwick. *BrS—EaI*
"**May** mornings are merry." See May mornings
"**May** nothing evil cross this door." See Prayer for this house
May thirtieth. Unknown. *CoPs*
"**May** you always be happy." Unknown. *MoY*
"**May** you always be the same." Unknown. *MoY*

"**May** you always meet Dame Fortune." Unknown. *MoY*
"**May** you gently float." Unknown. *MoY*
"**May** your cheeks retain their dimples." Unknown. *MoY*
"**May** your future be as bright." Unknown. *MoY*
"**May** your joys be as deep as the ocean." Unknown. *MoY*
"**May** your life be like arithmetic." Unknown. *MoY*
"**May** your life be long and sunny." Unknown. *MoY*
"**May** your life be strewn with roses." Unknown. *MoY*
"**May** your luck ever spread." Unknown. *MoY*
"**May** your record be as clean." Unknown. *MoY*
Mayo, E. L.
The mole. *McW*
May's song. Eleanor Farjeon. *FaCb—FaN*
Maytime magic. Mabel Watts. *McAw*
Me. Walter De La Mare. *BrBc—FeF*
"**Me** and my puppy." See My puppy
"**Me** and my wife and a bob-tail dog." Unknown. *WoF*
"**Me** father was the keeper of the Eddystone light." See The Eddystone light
"**Me** like ice cream." Unknown. *WiRm*
"**Me**, ray, doh." Unknown, tr. fr. the German by Rose Fyleman. *JoAc*
Mead, Stella
When we are men. *HuL-1*
"**The meadow** and I have a secret." See Meadow secret
Meadow larks. See Larks
Meadow secret. Frances M. Frost. *FrLn*
Meadows. See Fields
Meals. See Breakfast; Dinner; Luncheon; Supper
"**Meanwhile** the Tuscan army." See Lays of ancient Rome—Horatius—The fight at the bridge
Mearns, Hughes
The little man who wasn't there. *CoH—FeF*
The perfect reactionary. *CoH*
Measles
The old sow took the measles. Unknown. *WoF*
"**Measure** me, sky." Leonora Speyer. *BrBc—FeF—JoAc*
Measurement. A. M. Sullivan. *McW*
Meat. See Food and eating
Medea, sel. Euripides
Chorus from Medea, tr. fr. the Greek by Frederic Prokosch. *PaS*
Medicine
Bump on my knee. M. C. Livingston. *LiWa*
Castor oil. D. McCord. *McT*
Meditatio. Ezra Pound. *SmLg*
Meditations of a tortoise dozing under a rosetree near a beehive at noon while a dog scampers about and a cuckoo calls from a distant wood. E. V. Rieu. *RiF*

Medley. See "The cat sat asleep by the side of the fire"

"Meet Ladybug." See I want you to meet

"Meet me in Usk." See Rendez-vous with a beetle

Meet-on-the-road. Unknown. *CoPm*

Meeting ("As I went home on the old wood road") Rachel Field. *HuL-2*

A meeting ("Under the linden the music is gay") Heinrich Heine, tr. fr. the German by Louis Untermeyer. *CoPm*

Meeeting-house hill. Amy Lowell. *SmLg*

Meeting Mary. Eleanor Farjeon. *BrBc*

Meeting the Easter bunny. Rowena Bastin Bennett. *ArTp—BrS—BrL-k*

Meg Merrilies. John Keats. *ArTp—FeF—HuL-2—HuSv—SmLg*
Old Meg. *ReT*

Meigs, Mildred Plew (Mildred Plew Merryman)
Abraham Lincoln. *ArTp—BrR-6—PeF*
Johnny Fife and Johnny's wife. *ArTp—BrL-7—HuL-1*
The Pirate Don Durk of Dowdee. *ArTp—HuL-2—PeF*
Silver ships. *ArTp—BrR-5—FeF*

A melancholy lay. See Three turkeys

The melancholy pig. See Sylvie and Bruno

A melancholy song. See "Trip upon trenchers, and dance upon dishes"

Melander supposed to love Susan, but did love Ann. Edward, Lord Herbert of Cherbury. *GrCc*

Meleager
The gusts of winter are gone. *PaS*
I'll twine white violets. *PaS*
In the spring. *PaS*

"Mellow the moonlight to shine is beginning." See The spinning wheel

Melons
Melons. M. M. Dodge. *ArTp*

Melons. Mary Mapes Dodge. *ArTp*

"Melons, melons." See Melons

Melville, Herman
Epilogue. *PlI*
The Maldive shark. *SmLg*
The portent. *HoW*
The returned volunteer to his rifle. *GrCc*
Shiloh. *HoW*
We fish. *UnG*

A memento for mortality. Attributed to William Basse. *SmLg*

Memorial day
Decoration day. H. W. Longfellow. *CoPs*
The march. J. C. Squire. *CoPs*
May thirtieth. Unknown. *CoPs*
Memorial day. T. Garrison. *CoPs*
More than flowers we have brought. N. B. Turner. *BrS*
Remembering day. M. W. Saunders. *HaY*

Memorial day. Theodosia Garrison. *CoPs*

Memorial garden (Canterbury). Eleanor Farjeon. *FaCb—FaN*

Memories. See also Childhood recollections
Against oblivion. H. Newbolt. *DeT*
At Castle Boterel. T. Hardy. *HaP*
"Four ducks on a pond." W. Allingham. *HuL-2—ReT*

Incident. C. Cullen. *JoAc*
Memory. T. B. **Aldrich.** **ThP**
Memory of flowers. R. Fitzgerald. *GrCc*
Mingram Mo. D. McCord. *McT*
"Music, when soft voices die." P. B. Shelley. *HaP*
Night. H. de Regnier. *PaS*
Recorders in Italy. A. C. Rich. *PlU*
Remembrance V. Zhukovsky. *PaS*
The self-unseeing. T. Hardy. *GrCc*
Tears, idle tears. From The princess. A. Tennyson. *HaP*
"When to the sessions of sweet silent thought." From Sonnets. W. Shakespeare. *JoAc*

Memories of childhood. See Childhood recollections

Memory ("My mind lets go a thousand things") Thomas Bailey Aldrich. *ThP*

A memory ("That October morning") Eleanor Farjeon. *FaCb—FaN*

Memory of flowers. Robert Fitzgerald. *GrCc*

Men—Portraits. See People—Portraits—Men

"Men have heard the bison bellow on the transatlantic plains." See The giraffe

"Men say they know many things." Henry David Thoreau. *PlI*

"The men that worked for England." See Elegy in a country churchyard

Men who march away. See The dynasts—We be the King's men

"Mena, deena deina, duss." Mother Goose *LiL*

Mending wall. Robert Frost. *FrR—FrY—HaP*

The merchant of Venice, sels. William Shakespeare
Fancy. *FeF*
The quality of mercy. *BrL-8—ThP*

Merchants. See Shops and Shopkeepers

"Merciful God, who readst my inmost mind." See Prayer

Mercy. See Sympathy

Meredith, George
Dirge in woods. *HoW*
The lark ascending. *HoW*
Lucifer in starlight. *HaP*
The woods of Westermain. *McW* (sel.)

Merivale, John Hermann
Not to die. tr. *PaS*

The mermaid. Alfred Tennyson. *CoPm—FeF—UnG*

A mermaid song. James Reeves. *ReW*

The mermaidens. Laura E. Richards. *HuSv*

Mermaids and mermen
Cape Horn gospel (I). J. Masefield. *CoSp*
Clerk Colven. Unknown. *MaB*
The Eddystone light. Unknown. *CoSp*
The figure-head. C. Garstin. *CoSp*
The forsaken merman. M. Arnold. *SmLg*
Little John Bottlejohn. L. E. Richards. *CoPm—HuL-1—LoL*
A meeting. H. Heine. *CoPm*
The mermaid. A. Tennyson. *CoPm—FeF—UnG*
A mermaid song. J. Reeves. *ReW*
The mermaidens. L. E. Richards. *HuSv*
The merman. A. Tennyson. *CoPm—FeF—UnG*

Mermaids and mermen—*Continued*
 Sam. W. De La Mare. *ArTp—CoPm*
 Very nearly. Q. Scott-Hopper. *FeF*
The merman. Alfred Tennyson. *CoPm—FeF*
 —UnG
Mermen. See Mermaids and mermen
Merrill, Herbert
 Storm cellar. *BrR-5*
 Windy weather. *BrL-8*
 Winter night. *BrL-7*
Merrily danced the Quaker's wife. Mother
 Goose. *OpO*
"Merrily swinging on brier and weed." See
 Robert of Lincoln
Merry are the bells. See "Merry are the
 bells, and merry would they ring"
"Merry are the bells, and merry would they
 ring." Unknown. *DeMg—DeT*
 Merry are the bells. *ArTp—LoL—NaM*
"The merry-go-round." See June
"The merry-go-round." Myra Cohn Liv-
 ingston. *LiW*
Merry-go-round ("I climbed up on the
 merry-go-round") Dorothy W. Baruch.
 ArTp—BrL-k—HuL-1—HuSv
The merry-go-round ("Oh, the merry-go-
 round") Electa Clark. *McAw*
Merry-go-round ("Oh, the merry-go-round
 goes round and round") Marchette
 Chute. *ChA*
Merry-go-rounds
 At a country fair. J. Holmes. *NaM*
 June. M. C. Davies. *BrS*
 "The merry-go-round." M. C. Livingston.
 LiW
 Merry-go-round ("I climbed up on the
 merry-go-round") D. W. Baruch. *ArTp*
 BrL-k—HuL-1—HuSv
 The merry-go-round ("Oh, the merry-go-
 round") E. Clark. *McAw*
 Merry-go-round ("Oh, the merry-go-
 round goes round and round") M.
 Chute. *ChA*
 Roundabout. J. Reeves. *ReW*
 A roundabout turn. R. E. Charles. *NaM*
A merry heart. See Proverbs—"A soft
 answer turneth away wrath"
"Merry it was in the green forest." See
 Adam Bell, Clym of the Clough, and
 William of Cloudesley
The merry man of Paris. Unknown. *BrR-4*
"Merry Margaret." See To Mistress Mar-
 garet Hussey
"Merry Margaret, as midsummer flower."
 See To Mistress Margaret Hussey
"Merry, merry sparrow." See The blossom
The merry miner. Unknown. *HuSv*
The merry month of March. See Written in
 March
A merry note. See Love's labor's lost—
 "When icicles hang by the wall"
The merry pieman's song. John Bennett.
 LoL
Merry sunshine. Unknown. *BrL-k*
Merryman, Mildred Plew. See Meigs,
 Mildred Plew

Mertins, Louis
 Indian songs, sels. *HuSv*
  Prayer to the sun god
  Rain chant
 Prayer to the sun god. See Indian songs
 Rain chant. See Indian songs
Message. Sara Teasdale. *ThP*
Message from home. Kathleen Raine. *PlI*
The message of the March wind. William
 Morris. *HoW*
"The meteor's arc of quiet; a voiceless rain."
 See Faint music
Metropolitan nightmare. Stephen Vincent
 Benét. *PlI*
Mew, Charlotte
 Saturday market. *FeF* (sel.)
"Mexican Jo and Mexican Jane." See Rak-
 ing walnuts in the rain
Mexicans
 Ambition. E. Agnew. *ArTp*
 A feller I know. M. Austin. *FeF*
 The goatherd G. H. Conkling. *ArTp*
 Raking walnuts in the rain. M. Shannon.
 BrS
Mexico
 "The Indians come down from Mixco."
 M. A. Asturias. *FeF*
 La noche triste. R. Frost. *FrR*
Meyer, Kuno
 Arran. tr. *SmLg*
 The fort of Rathangan. tr. *SmLg*
 Summer is gone. tr. *SmLg*
Meyerstein, E. H. W.
 Elegy on the death of Mme Anne Pavlova.
 PlI (sel.)
 England. *DeT*
Meynell, Alice
 Renouncement. *ThP*
Mfeka, R. M.
 Umamina. tr. *PaS*
Mia Carlotta. T. A. Daly. *BrL-7*
Mice
 Advice from an elderly mouse. E. J.
 Coatsworth. *CoM*
 Birthday cake. A. Fisher. *BrBc*
 "A cat came fiddling out of a barn."
 Mother Goose. *DeMg—HuSv—JoAc*
  Bagpipes. *DeT*
  A cat came fiddling. *HuL-1*
 A change of heart. V. Hobbs. *BrS*
 A Chinese nursery rhyme. Unknown.
 BrR-3
 Christmas eve in the wainscoting. E. J.
 Coatsworth. *CoM*
 The city mouse and the garden mouse.
 C. G. Rossetti. *FeF—HuSv—UnG*
  The city mouse. *JoAc*
  "The city mouse lives in a house."
  ArTp
 Conversation. R. Fyleman. *HuL-1*
 Crickets and mice. J. J. Keith. *HuSv*
 Epitaph. E. J. Coatsworth. *CoM*
 The fearful finale of the irascible mouse.
 G. W. Carryl. *CoH*
 The field mouse. W. Sharp. *FeF—NaM*
 Field mouse conference. E. J. Coatsworth.
 CoM
 Field mouse to kitchen mouse. E. J.
 Coatsworth. *CoM*

The frog and the mouse. Unknown. *HoW*
"Good master and mistress." Unknown. *NaE*
"Good morning, cat." M. C. Livingston. *LiWa*
"Hickory, dickory, dock (the mouse)." Mother Goose. *AnI — ArTp — BrL-k — DeMg—HuL-1—JoAc—LiL—OpO*
"The house of the mouse." L. S. Mitchell. *ArTp—CoI*
I wouldn't. J. Ciardi. *CiY*
John Watts. Mother Goose. *OpO*
The lament of the white mouse. E. V. Rieu. *RiF*
The light-house-keeper's white-mouse. J. Ciardi. *CiY*
"Little black bug." M. W. Brown. *FeF—HuL-1*
Lullaby. E. J. Coatsworth. *BrS—CoM*
Mice. R. Fyleman. *ArTp—BrL-k—FeF—HuL-1—HuSv—NaE—PeF*
"The mice of Spain." E. J. Coatsworth. *CoM—LoL*
Mice under snow. F. M. Frost. *FrLn*
Missing. A. A. Milne. *CoI—MiWc—NaM—PeF*
The moon will give the prize. E. J. Coatsworth. *CoM*
The mouse ("I heard a mouse") E. J. Coatsworth. *ArTp — CoI — CoM — FeF—JoAc—NaM*
Mouse ("Little mouse in gray velvet") H. Conkling. *ArTp—BrL-k—HuSv*
The mouse ("A mouse lives in our kitchen") M. Chute. *ChA*
Mouse and mouser. Mother Goose. *OpO*
Mouse chorus. E. J. Coatsworth. *CoM*
Mouse midnight. E. J. Coatsworth. *CoM*
"The mouse that gnawed the oak tree down." V. Lindsay. *BrL-7*
The mouse who lived on a hill. Unknown. *TaD*
The old wife and the ghost. J. Reeves. *CoPm—ReBl*
The prince. W. De La Mare. *LoL*
Pussy and the mice. Mother Goose. *NaM*
    Three little mice. *HuL-1*
"Six little mice sat down to spin." Mother Goose. *JoAc*
    Six little mice. *OpO*
"Some little mice sat in a barn to spin." Mother Goose. *DeMg*
    Some little mice. *BrL-k*
"There was a wee bit mousikie." Unknown. *NaM*
"There was an old woman (lived under a hill, she put a mouse)." Mother Goose. *DeMg*
    An old woman. *OpO*
"Three blind mice, see how they run." Mother Goose. *AnI—DeMg*
    "Three blind mice." *LiL—OpO*
To a guardian mouse. E. J. Coatsworth. *CoM*
To a mouse. R. Burns. *McW*
To and fro. E. J. Coatsworth. *CoM*
Tom Tittlemouse. Mother Goose. *OpO*
The two mice. J. Reeves. *ReBl*
Waltzing mice. D. McCord. *McFf*
Well, I never. Unknown. *JoAc*

Who is so pretty. E. J. Coatsworth. *CoM*
Winter. E. J. Coatsworth. *CoM*
Winter content. E. J. Coatsworth. *CoM*
The witch of Willowby wood. R. B. Bennett. *CoPm*
Mice. Rose Fyleman. *ArTp—BrL-k—FeF—HuL-1—HuSv—NaE—PeF*
"The mice of Spain." Elizabeth Jane Coatsworth. *CoM—LoL*
Mice under snow. Frances M. Frost. *FrLn*
Michelangelo Buonarroti
    To the Supreme Being. *PaS*
Mick. James Reeves. *ReBl*
"Mick my mongrel-o." See Mick
Mickle, William Julius
    The sailor's wife. *DeT*
The microbe. Hilaire Belloc. *BrL-7*
"The microbe is so very small." See The microbe
Microbes
    The microbe. H. Belloc. *BrL-7*
    The microbes. Unknown. *CoH*
    Strictly germ-proof. A. Guiterman. *BrL-8*
The microbes. Unknown. *CoH*
Microcosmus. Thomas Nabbes. *PlU* (sel.)
Mid-August. Louise Driscoll. *HaY*
"Mid seaweed on a sultry strand, ten thousand years ago." See The first story
"'Mid the mountains Euganean." See The rooks
Midas
    The golden touch. E. Farjeon. *FaCb—FaN*
Middle-aged child. Inez Hogan. *BrBc*
Middle ages. See Arthur, King; Crusades; Knights and knighthood; Minstrels and troubadours
Midnight. Thomas Sackville. *DeT*
"Midnight, December thirty-first." See Song for December thirty-first
"The midnight plane with its riding lights." See Night plane
"Midnight was come, and every vital thing." See Midnight
"Midsummer eve, a year ago, my mother she commanded." See Midsummer magic
Midsummer fantasy. See The Hottentot tot
Midsummer magic. Ivy O. Eastwick. *ArTp*
Midsummer night. Marion Edey. *HaY*
A midsummer-night's dream, sels. William Shakespeare
    Fairy lullaby. *FeF—UnG*
        You spotted snakes. *JoAc*
    The lion of winter. *HoW*
    Puck speaks. *ReT*
    Puck's song. *NaM*
    "Over hill, over dale." *DeT—JoAc—ReT*
        Fairy's wander-song. *FeF*
    A violet bank. *FeF*
Midsummer pause. Fred Lape. *CoPs*
"A mighty creature is the germ." See The germ
Mignon. See Wilhelm Meister
Migration—Birds. See Birds—Migration

Milk
Frozen milk bottles. O. B. Miller. *BrL-k*
Green grass and white milk. W. Welles. *ArTp*
"I had a little cow, I milked her in a gourd." Unknown. *WoF*
Milk for the cat. H. Monro. *JoAc—ReT—UnG*
Milk in winter. R. W. Bacmeister. *BrL-k*
Milking time. E. M. Roberts. *BrL-k—FeF*
Spilt milk: Whodunit. W. J. Smith. *SmL*
Milk for the cat. Harold Monro. *JoAc—ReT—UnG*
Milk in winter. Rhoda W. Bacmeister. *BrL-k*
"**Milk-white** moon, put the cows to sleep." Carl Sandburg. *FeF—HuSv*
Milking. See "Cushy cow, bonny, let down thy milk"
Milking time. Elizabeth Madox Roberts. *BrL-k—FeF*
The **milkmaid.** See "Where are you going to, my pretty maid"
Milkmaids
Dabbling in the dew. Unknown. *HuL-2*
The dairymaid and her milk-pot. J. de La Fontaine. *JoAc*
"Where are you going to, my pretty maid." Mother Goose. *DeMg—LiL*
The milkmaid. *OpO*
"Where are you going, my pretty maid." *HuL-1—JoAc*
Milkmaids. Eleanor Farjeon. *FaCb*
The **milkman's** horse. Unknown. *BrL-k—CoI—HuL-1*
Milkmen
The milkman's horse. Unknown. *BrL-k—CoI—HuL-1*
Our milkman. N. K. Duffy. *McAw*
Psalm of those who go forth before daylight. C. Sandburg. *NaM*
Those who go forth before daylight. *HuSv*
Susie the milk horse. D. Aldis. *AlA*
The **mill.** Edwin Arlington Robinson. *HaP*
Millard, Edith G.
Banbury fair. *HuL-1*
Millay, Edna St Vincent
Afternoon on a hill. *ArTp—FeF—HuSv—PeF*
The ballad of the harp-weaver. *ArTp—CoSp—UnMc*
City trees. *FeF*
Counting-out rhyme. *NaM*
Elaine. *ThP*
"Euclid alone has looked on beauty bare." *PlI*
From a very little sphinx, sel.
"Wonder where this horseshoe went." *ArTp*
The horseshoe. *HuSv*
Wonder where. *PeF*
God's world. See Renascence
The horseshoe. See From a very little sphinx—"Wonder where this horseshoe went"
Journal. *PlI* (sel.)
On hearing a symphony of Beethoven. *PlI*

Portrait by a neighbor. *ArTp—FeF—HuL-2—NaM—PeF*
Recuerdo. *NaE*
Renascence, sel.
God's world. *CoPs—JoAc—UnG*
Travel. *ArTp—FeF—HuL-2—HuSv—NaM*
The unexplorer. *NaM*
Vacation song. *HaY*
Wonder where. See From a very little sphinx—"Wonder where this horseshoe went"
"Wonder where this horseshoe went." See From a very little sphinx
Miller, Cincinnatus Heine (or Hiner). See Miller, Joaquin
Miller, Helen Janet
Only the wind says spring. *UnG*
Miller, James
Italian opera. *PlU* (sel.)
Miller, Joaquin, pseud. (Cincinnatus Heine [or Hiner] Miller)
Byron. *ThP*
Columbus. *ArTp — BrL-8 — FeF — HaY — HuSv—McW*
Crossing the plains. *GrCc*
For those who fail. *BrL-8*
Miller, Mary Britton
Cat. *ArTp—BrR-4—HuSv—PeF*
Foal. *ArTp—CoI*
Here she is. *ArTp*
Shore. *ArTp—McAw*
"A son just born." *ArTp*
Miller, Olive Beaupré
The circus parade. *ArTp*
Frozen milk bottles. *BrL-k*
"I only know a glowing warmth." *DoP*
Lilies. tr. *ArTp*
"The rains of spring." tr. *ArTp*
A shower. tr. *ArTp*
When blue sky smiles. *BrL-k*
Miller, Thomas
The spring walk. *DeT*
Miller, Vassar
Autumnal spring song. *HaP*
Miller, William
Spring. *CoPs* (sel.)
A **miller.** See The Canterbury tales
"The **miller** he grinds his corn, his corn." Mother Goose. *DeMg*
A hop, skip, and a jump. *HuL-1*
"The **miller,** stout and sturdy as the stones." See The Canterbury tales—A miller
"The **miller** was a chap of sixteen stone." See The Canterbury tales—A miller
Millers
"Blow wind, blow, and go mill, go." Mother Goose. *ArTp—DeMg—HuSv*
"Blow, wind, blow." *HuL-1—OpO*
Five eyes. W. De La Mare. *CoI*
"God made the bees." Unknown
Signs, seasons, and sense. *UnG*
The mill. E. A. Robinson. *HaP*
"The miller he grinds his corn, his corn." Mother Goose. *DeMg*
A hop, skip, and a jump. *HuL-1*
"O the little rusty dusty miller." Mother Goose. *OpO*

"There was a jolly miller." From Love in a village. I. Bickerstaffe. *DeMg—UnG*

Jolly miller. *OpO*
"There was a jolly miller once." *LiL*
"There was an old woman (lived under a hill, she put a mouse)." Mother Goose. *DeMg*

An old woman. *OpO*
The vanishing Red. R. Frost. *FrR*
The windmill ("Behold, a giant am I") H. W. Longfellow. *NaM*
The windmill ("If you should bid me make a choice") E. V. Lucas. *DeT—HuL-2*

"The miller's wife had waited long." See The mill

"Millery, millery, dustipole." See To the puss moth

Millions of strawberries. Genevieve Taggard. *ArTp—FeF—NaM—UnG*

Mills
Five eyes. W. De La Mare. *CoI*
Grinding. Mother Goose. *OpO*
Sandy. Mother Goose. *OpO*
The vanishing Red. R. Frost. *FrR*
"When the wind blows." Mother Goose. *OpO*
The windmill ("Behold, a giant am I") H. W. Longfellow. *NaM*
The windmill ("If you should bid me make a choice") E. V. Lucas. *DeT—HuL-2*

Milne, A. (Alan) A. (Alexander)
The alchemist. *MiWc*
At home. *MiWc*
At the zoo. *FeF—MiWc*
Bad Sir Brian Botany. *CoH—MiWc*
Before tea. *MiWc*
Binker. *MiWc*
Brownie. *MiWc*
Buckingham palace. *HuL-2—MiWc*
Busy. *MiWc*
Buttercup days. *MiWc*
The charcoal-burner. *MiWc*
Cherry stones. *MiWc*
The christening. *BrBc—MiWc*
Come out with me. *MiWc*
Corner-of-the-street. *MiWc*
Cradle song. *MiWc*
Daffodowndilly. *MiWc*
"Diana Fitzpatrick Mauleverer James." See Miss James
Disobedience. *MiWc*
The dormouse and the doctor. *MiWc*
Down by the pond. *MiWc*
The emperor's rhyme *MiWc*
The end. *BrBc—BrS—MiWc*
The engineer. *MiWc*
Explained. *MiWc*
Forgiven. *MiWc—PeF*
Forgotten. *MiWc*
The four friends. *MiWc—UnG*
The friend. *MiWc*
Furry bear. *CoI—HuSv—MiWc—PeF*
The good little girl. *MiWc*
Growing up. *BrBc—MiWc*
Halfway down. *FeF—MiWc*
Happiness. *ArTp—HuL-2—MiWc*
Hoppity. *ArTp—MiWc*
If I were king. *MiWc*

In the dark. *MiWc*
In the fashion. *MiWc*
Independence. *MiWc*
The invaders. *MiWc*
The island. *MiWc*
"Jonathan Jo." *MiWc*
Journey's end. *MiWc*
King Hilary and the beggarman. *MiWc*
King John's Christmas. *MiWc*
The king's breakfast. *MiWc*
Knight-in-armour. *MiWc*
The knight whose armour didn't squeak. *MiWc*
Knights and ladies. *MiWc*
Lines and squares. *MiWc*
The little black hen. *MiWc*
Little Bo-peep and Little Boy Blue. *MiWc*
Market square. *JoAc—MiWc*
The mirror. *MiWc*
Miss James. *NaM*
"Diana Fitzpatrick Mauleverer James." *ArTp*
Missing. *CoI—MiWc—NaM—PeF*
The morning walk. *MiWc*
Nursery chairs. *MiWc*
The old sailor. *MiWc*
Pinkle Purr. *MiWc*
Politeness. *MiWc*
Puppy and I. *ArTp—FeF—HuL-1—MiWc—PeF*
Rice pudding. *MiWc*
Sand-between-the-toes. *MiWc*
Shoes and stockings. *MiWc—HuL-1*
Sneezles. *MiWc*
Solitude. *MiWc*
Spring morning. *MiWc*
Summer afternoon. *MiWc*
Swing song. *MiWc*
Teddy Bear. *MiWc*
A thought. *MiWc*
The three foxes. *HuSv—MiWc—NaM*
Twice times. *MiWc*
Twinkletoes. *MiWc*
Us two. *ArTp—MiWc*
Vespers. *MiWc*
Waiting at the window. *MiWc*
Water-lilies. *MiWc*
Wind on the hill. *MiWc*
The wrong house. *MiWc*

Milne, Ewart
Diamond cut diamond. *ArTp—SmLg*

Milnes, Richard Monckton, Lord Houghton
Lady Moon. *BrR-3—HuL-2—NaM*
Song. *DeT*

Milton, John
At a solemn musick. *PlU* (sel.)
Comus, sels.
"Sabrina fair." *SmLg*
"The star that bids the shepherd fold." *SmLg*
"Let us with a gladsome mind." *DeT*
Praise the Lord. *SmLg*
May morning. *HaY*
On the morning of Christ's nativity. *SmLg*
On the university carrier. *SmLg*
Praise the Lord. See "Let us with a gladsome mind"
"Sabrina fair." See Comus
Song. *ReT*

Milton, John—*Continued*
Sonnet on his blindness. *ThP*
"The star that bids the shepherd fold."
See Comus
A table richly spread. *SmLg*
To a girl. tr. *HoW*
With thee conversing. *HoW*
Milton, sel. William Blake
Jerusalem. *NaE*
"And did those feet in ancient time."
HaP—SmLg
Mima. Walter De La Mare. *BrBc—ReG*
Mimnermus
No joy without love. *PaS*
Mind. See also Wisdom
A considerable speck. R. Frost. *FrR*
Mind. R. Wilbur. *HaP*
Minnie. E. Farjeon. *UnG*
"My mind to me a kingdom is." E. Dyer.
HaP
Mind. Richard Wilbur. *HaP*
"Mind in its purest play is like some bat."
See Mind
Mind you, now. John Ciardi. *CiY*
"Mine eyes have seen the glory of the coming
of the Lord." See Battle-hymn of the re-
public
Miner, Virginia Scott
Golden spurs. *BrS*
Miners. See Mines and mining
Mines and mining
Buttercups. W. Thorley. *FeF*
K is for kobold. E. Farjeon. *FaCb*
The merry miner. Unknown. *HuSv*
The ponies. W. W. Gibson. *McW*
Mingram Mo. David McCord. *McT*
Ministers of the gospel
Bishop Hatto. R. Southey. *CoSp*
Doctor Foster. Mother Goose. *OpO*
On a clergyman's horse. Unknown. *UnG*
Praying and preaching. Unknown. *UnG*
Robin Hood and the bishop of Hereford. Un-
known. *MaB*
Snow. R. Frost. *FrR*
Miniver Cheevy. Edwin Arlington Robinson.
HaP—SmLg—UnMc
"Miniver Cheevy, child of scorn." See Mini-
ver Cheevy
Minnie. Eleanor Farjeon. *UnG*
"Minnie and Mattie." Christina Georgina
Rossetti. *ArTp*
"Minnie can't make her mind up." See
Minnie
Minnows. See "I stood tiptoe upon a little
hill"
A minor bird. Robert Frost. *FrR—FrY*
The minstrel-boy. Thomas Moore. *UnG*
"The minstrel-boy to the war is gone." See
The minstrel-boy
Minstrels and troubadours
The minstrel-boy. T. Moore. *UnG*
My dog Tray. T. Campbell. *UnG*
The Irish harper. *DeT*
The miracle ("Mother took") Elsie Mel-
chert Fowler. *BrBc*
Miracle ("Yesterday the twig was brown
and bare") Liberty Hyde Bailey. *HaY*

The **miracle** of spring. Bahar, tr. fr. the
Persian by A. J. Arberry. *PaS*
Miracles
The ballad of Father Gilligan. W. B.
Yeats. *McW*
Little Breeches. J. Hay. *UnG*
The miracle ("Mother took") E. M.
Fowler. *BrBc*
Miracle ("Yesterday the twig was brown
and bare") L. H. Bailey. *HaY*
Miracles. From Song of myself. W. Whit-
man. *HuSv—JoAc—McW—UnG*
Miracles. See Song of myself
The **mirror** ("Between the woods the after-
noon") A. A. Milne. *MiWc*
The **mirror** ("I look in the mirror, and what
do I see") William Jay Smith. *SmL*
Mirror ("kool uoy nehW") John Updike.
McW
The **mirror** of perfection, sel. Saint Francis
of Assisi
Praise of created things, tr. fr. the Italian
by Matthew Arnold. *FeF*
The song of the creatures. *PaS*
"Mirror, mirror, tell me." Unknown
Signs, seasons, and sense. *UnG*
Mirrors. See also Reflections (Mirrored)
The looking-glass. R. Kipling. *GrCc—NaE*
The mirror ("I look in the mirror, and
what do I see") W. J. Smith. *SmL*
Mirror ("kool uoy nehW") J. Updike. *McW*
"Mirror, mirror, tell me." Unknown
Signs, seasons, and sense. *UnG*
Reflection. M. C. Livingston. *LiWa*
A thought. W. H. Davies. *NaM*
The **mischievous** raven. See "A farmer went
trotting upon his gray mare"
Misdirection. Eleanor Slater. *ThP*
"Misery me." See The lady of Leigh
Misfortune
The three unlucky men. J. Reeves. *ReBl*
"When in disgrace with fortune and men's
eyes." From Sonnets. W. Shakespeare.
HaP
The **misfortunes** of Elphin, sel. Thomas
Love Peacock
The war-song of Dinas Vawr. *CoSp—HoW
—NaE*
"Miss Helen Slingsby was my maiden aunt."
See Aunt Helen
"Miss J. Hunter Dunn, Miss J. Hunter
Dunn." See A subaltern's love-song
Miss James. A. A. Milne. *NaM*
"Diana Fitzpatrick Mauleverer James."
ArTp
Miss Jennie Jones. Unknown. *TaD*
Miss Mary Mac. Unknown. *TaD*
"Miss Mary Mac, Mac, Mac." See Miss
Mary Mac
"Miss, Miss, little Miss, miss." See Misses
Miss Muffet. See "Little Miss Muffet"
"Miss Nancy Ellicott." See Cousin Nancy
"Miss One, Two, and Three." See The
gossips
Miss Petal. James Reeves. *ReW*
Miss T. Walter De La Mare. *ArTp—BrR-4
JoAc—NaM*

Miss Wing. James Reeves. *ReBl*

Misses. Unknown. *WoJ*

Missing. A. A. Milne. *CoI—MiWc—NaM—PeF*

The missing cuckoo. E. V. Rieu. *RiF*

Mist. See also Fog
"A hill full, a hole full." Mother Goose. *ArTp—DeMg*
The mist and all. D. Willson. *BrL-7—FeF—HaY—HuL-2—PeF*
The mist and all. Dixie Willson. *BrL-7—FeF—HaY—HuL-2—PeF*

"Mr and Mrs Discobbolos." Edward Lear. *JoAc*

Mr Attila. Carl Sandburg. *PlI*

"Mr Baker, Mr Baker, the good old shoe-maker." Unknown. *WoF*

"Mister Beedle Baddlebug." See Tea party

Mister Beers. Hugh Lofting. *FeF*

Mr Bellairs. James Reeves. *ReBl*

Mr Blob. E. V. Rieu. *RiF*

Mister Carrot. Dorothy Aldis. *AlA*

Mr Coggs, watchmaker. Edward Verrall Lucas. *FeF*

Mr Cooter. Eleanor Farjeon. *FaCb*

"Mr Cooter who kneads and bakes." See Mr Cooter

"Mr East gave a feast." Mother Goose. *JoAc*
Mr East's feast. *OpO*

Mr East's feast. See "Mr East gave a feast"

"Mr Finney had a turnip." See Mr Finney's turnip

Mr Finney's turnip. Unknown. *CoH—LoL*

Mr Flood's party. Edwin Arlington Robinson. *HaP—NaE*

"Mr Froggie went a-courtin' an' he did ride." See Frog went a-courtin'

Mr Halloween. David McCord. *McT*

Mister Hoppy-toes. Marie Louise Allen. *AlP*

Mr Ibister. Mother Goose. *OpO*

"Mr Ibister, and Betsy his sister." See Mr Ibister

Mr Jones. See Four ruthless rhymes

Mr Kartoffel. James Reeves. *ReW*

"Mr Kartoffel's a whimsical man." See Mr Kartoffel

"Mr Macklin takes his knife." See Mr Macklin's jack o'lantern

Mr Macklin's jack o'lantern. David McCord. *FeF—McFf*

Mr Moon. Bliss Carman. *FeF—HuL-2*

Mr Nobody. Unknown. *BrR-4—CoPm—FeF—HuL-1—HuSv*

Mr Punchinello. Unknown. *DeT—JoAc*

Mr Pyme. Harry Behn. *ArTp—LoL*

Mister Rabbit. Unknown. *TaD*

"Mister Rabbit, Mister Rabbit." See Mister Rabbit

Mr Tom Narrow. James Reeves. *ReW*

Mr Wells. Elizabeth Madox Roberts. *FeF*

Mistletoe
A Christmas legend. O. Herford. *CoPm*

Mistral, Gabriela
The little girl that lost a finger. *FeF*
Where shall we dance. *PaS*

Mrs Brown. Rose Fyleman. *ArTp—BrL-k—HuL-1*

Mrs Button. James Reeves. *ReBl*

Mrs Caribou. William Jay Smith. *CoPm—SmL*

"Mrs Farleigh-fashion." James Reeves. *ReW*

Mrs Gilfillan. James Reeves. *ReBl*

Mrs Golightly. James Reeves. *ReBl*

"Mrs Golightly's goloshes." See Mrs Golightly

Mrs Hen ("Chook, chook, chook, chook, chook") Mother Goose. *OpO*

Mrs Hen ("Please lay me an egg, Mrs Hen") M. A. Campbell. *HuL-1*

Mrs MacQueen. Walter De La Mare. *HuL-2*

"Mrs Malone." Eleanor Farjeon. *CoPm*

Mistress Margaret Hussey. See To Mistress Margaret Hussey

"Mistress Mary." See "Mary, Mary, quite contrary." Mother Goose

Mistress Mary ("Mistress Mary, quite contrary") William Jay Smith. *SmL*

"Mistress Mary, quite contrary." See Mary, Mary, quite contrary." Mother Goose

"Mistress Mary, quite contrary." See Mistress Mary. William Jay Smith

"Mrs Mason bought a basin." See Mrs Mason's basin

Mrs Mason's basin. Mother Goose. *OpO*

"Mrs Ocean takes in washing." See Washday

"Mrs Peck-Pigeon." Eleanor Farjeon. *ArTp—BrL-k—HuSv—JoAc*

Mrs Santa Claus' Christmas present. Alice S. Morris. *CoPs*

Mrs Snipkin and Mrs Wobblechin. Laura E. Richards. *ArTp—CoH—HuL-1—HuSv—JoAc*

"Mrs Spider." Myra Cohn Livingston. *LiWa*

Mrs Utter. James Reeves. *ReW*

Mitchell, Lucy Sprague
"Back and forth." *FeF*
"The house of the mouse." *ArTp—CoI*
"It is raining." *ArTp—HuL-2*

Mitsukuni
Lotus leaves. *PaS*

The mitten song. Marie Louise Allen. *AlP—ArTp—BrL-k—HuL-1*

Mittens. See also Gloves
The mitten song. M. L. Allen. *AlP—ArTp—BrL-k—HuL-1*
"Three little kittens." Unknown. *BrL-k—FeF—HuSv—OpO*
The little kittens. *ArTp—HuL-1*
"Three little kittens, they lost their mittens." *AnI—DeMg—LiL*

"Mix a pancake." Christina Georgina Rossetti. *BrL-k—HuL-1*

Mixed beasts, sels. Kenyon Cox
The bumblebeaver. *ArTp*
The kangarooster. *ArTp*
The octopussycat. *ArTp—FeF*

Mockery. Katherine Dixon Riggs. *BrR-4—PeF*

The **mocking** bird. Ivy O. Eastwick. *EaI*

"The **mocking** bird sat mocking." See The mocking bird

Mocking birds
A legend of Okeefinokee. L. E. Richards. *CoSp*
"Look at six eggs." C. Sandburg. *FeF*
The mocking bird. I. O. Eastwick. *EaI*

The **mocking** fairy. Walter De La Mare. *NaM*

A **modern** dragon. Rowena Bastin Bennett. *ArTp*

The **modern** Hiawatha. George A. Strong. *CoH—FeF—NaM*

"The **moldering** hulk." Antonio Machado, tr. fr. the Spanish by Kate Flores. *PaS*

Mole ("Jiminy jiminy jukebox. Wheatcakes. Crumbs") William Jay Smith. *SmB*

The **mole** ("When the mole goes digging") E. L. Mayo. *McW*

Moles (Animals)
"All but blind." W. De La Mare. *FeF—McW*
Mole ("Jiminy jiminy jukebox. Wheatcakes. Crumbs") W. J. Smith. *SmB*
The mole ("When the mole goes digging") E. L. Mayo. *McW*

"**Moll-in-the-wad** and I fell out." Mother Goose. *OpO*

Molly Grime. Eleanor Farjeon. *FaCb—FaN*

Molly Malone. Unknown. *UnMc*

Molly Means. Margaret Walker. *CoSp*

Molly Mock-Turtle. William Jay Smith. *SmL*

"**Molly** Mock-Turtle of Ocean View." See Molly Mock-Turtle

"**Molly**, my sister, and I fell out." Mother Goose. *DeMg*

Molly Pitcher. Kate Brownlee Sherwood. *UnG*

Momotara. Unknown, tr. fr. the Japanese by Rose Fyleman. *ArTp—HuL-2*

Moncrieff, William Thomas
Waltzing it. *PlU*

"**Monday** morning back to school." See Five chants

"**Monday's** child is fair of face." Mother Goose. *BrBc—DeMg—HuSv—JoAc—LiL —SmLg*
Birthdays. *OpO—ReG*
Days of birth. *NaM*
Signs, seasons, and sense. *UnG*

Money. See also Wealth
A farthing and a penny. J. Reeves. *ReW*
A fool and his money. D. McCord. *McT*
The hardship of accounting. R. Frost. *FrR —SmLg*
A hero in the land of dough. R. Clairmont. *McW*
"I love sixpence, jolly little sixpence." Mother Goose. *DeMg—JoAc*
"I love sixpence, pretty little sixpence." *LiL*
The jolly tester. *OpO*
I sometimes think about dollar bills. J. Ciardi. *CiR*
"If I should die tonight." B. King. *CoH*
Money. R. Armour. *McW*

Proposition. N. Guillén. *FeF*
Shepherd's purse. E. Farjeon. *FaCb*
This man went away. J. Ciardi. *CiI*

Money. Richard Armour. *McW*

Money works wonders. Mother Goose. *OpO*

Monkey. William Jay Smith. *SmB*

"The **monkey** married the baboon's sister." See The monkey's wedding

"**Monkey,** monkey, bottle of beer." Unknown *WiRm—WoF*

"**Monkey** monkey moo." See So many monkeys

"**Monkey** was a-settin' on a railroad track." Unknown
American Father Gander. *UnG*

Monkeys
At Woodward's gardens. R. Frost. *FrR— PlI*
Ay me, alas. T. Weelkes. *SmLg*
The big baboon. H. Belloc. *NaM*
Blue wool monkey. M. C. Livingston. *LiWa*
"I had a little monkey, I sent him to the country." Unknown. *WoF*
"I had a little monkey." *WiRm*
"I know something I won't tell." Unknown. *WiRm*
"If you see a monkey in a tree." Unknown. *MoY*
The legends of evil. R. Kipling. *NaM*
"Little General Monk." Mother Goose. *OpO*
Monkey. W. J. Smith. *SmB*
"Monkey was a-settin' on a railroad track." Unknown
American Father Gander. *UnG*
The monkeys. E. O. Thompson. *ArTp*
The monkeys and the crocodile. L. E. Richards. *ArTp — BrR-4 — FeF—HuL-1— JoAc—PeF*
The monkey's wedding. Unknown. *WoF*
The sad monkey. D. Aldis. *AlA*
"Said the monkey to the owl." Unknown. *WoF*
The ship of Rio. W. De La Mare. *ArTp— LoL*
So many monkeys. M. Edey. *ArTp*
To a monkey. M. Fleming. *UnG*
"Well I never, did you ever." Unknown. *SmLg*
"When you talk to a monkey." R. B. Bennett. *BrR-3*

The **monkeys.** Edith Osborne Thompson. *ArTp*

The **monkeys** and the crocodile. Laura E. Richards. *ArTp—BrR-4—FeF—HuL-1— JoAc—PeF*

The **monkey's** wedding. Unknown. *WoF*

Monkhouse, Cosmo
The barber of Kew. *CoH*
The girl of New York. *CoH*
"There was a young lady of Niger." *LoL*
The young lady of Niger. *FeF*
The young lady of Niger. See "There was a young lady of Niger"

Monks. See Friars

Monmouth, Battle of, 1778
Molly Pitcher. K. B. Sherwood. *UnG*

Monro (or Munro), Harold
Bird at dawn. *UnG*
Dogs. *UnG*
Milk for the cat. *JoAc—ReT—UnG*
Overheard on a saltmarsh. *ArTp—CoPm—FeF—HuL-2—JoAc—NaM—ReT*
The rebellious vine. *McW*

Mont, Pol de
Evening landscape. *PaS*

The **month** of falling stars. Ella Higginson. *HaY*

"A **month** of gold: gold flowers, gold sun."
See The golden month

The **month** of the Thunder Moon. Marion Doyle. *HaY*

Months. See also names of months, as January
An almanac. W. Sharp. *JoAc*
A burying. E. Farjeon. *FaCb*
Calendar. M. C. Livingston. *LiWa*
Flowers tell months. C. Sandburg. *SaW*
"January brings the snow." S. Coleridge. *ArTp—DeMg*
A calendar. *UnG*
The garden year. *DeT—HuSv*
The months of the year. *HuL-2*
The months. C. G. Rossetti. *FeF*
The succession of the four sweet months. R. Herrick. *HaY*
The four sweet months. *HoW*
July: The succession of the four sweet months. *FeF*
"Thirty days hath September." Mother Goose. *DeMg—HuSv—JoAc—LiL*
Days in the month. *OpO*
Signs, seasons, and sense. *UnG*

The **months.** Christina Georgina Rossetti. *FeF*

The **months** of the year. See "January brings the snow"

Montrose, James Graham (about)
The execution of Montrose. W. E. Aytoun. *PaOm*

Monuments. See Tombs

The **moo-cow-moo.** Edmund Vance Cooke. *NaM*

"**Moo,** says Mrs Cow." See What they like

Moody, William Vaughn
The counting man. *CoPm*

Moon
At night. F. Cornford. *CoI*
Auctioneer. C. Sandburg. *SaW*
The cat and the moon. W. B. Yeats. *CoPm—ReT—SmLg*
Crescent moon. E. M. Roberts. *ArTp—BrL-k—McAw*
Day-time moon. D. Aldis. *AlA*
A different speech. L. T. Nicholl. *PlI*
A dream about the man in the moon. J. Ciardi. *CiY*
The early morning. H. Belloc. *McW*
Euclid. V. Lindsay. *PlI*
The freedom of the moon. R. Frost. *FrY*
Full moon ("One night as Dick lay fast asleep") W. De La Mare. *ArTp—JoAc*
Full moon ("She was wearing the coral taffeta trousers") V. Sackville-West. *NaM*

"I see the moon." Mother Goose. *ArTp—DeMg—OpO*
The moon. *DoP*
Signs, seasons, and sense. *UnG*
Sun and moon. *HuL-1*
Is the moon tired. C. G. Rossetti. *HuSv*
Lady Moon. R. M. Milnes, Lord Houghton. *BrR-3—HuL-2—NaM*
Looking at the moon and thinking of one far away. Chang Chiu-ling. *PaS*
The man in the moon ("The man in the moon as he sails the sky") Unknown. *BrR-5*
The man in the moon ("Said the Raggedy Man on a hot afternoon") J. W. Riley. *CoH*
"The man in the moon (came tumbling down)." Mother Goose. *DeMg—LiL*
The man in the moon. *OpO*
"The man in the moon drinks claret." Mother Goose. *OpO*
"The man in the moon was caught in a trap." Mother Goose. *OpO*
"The man in the mune." Mother Goose. *OpO*
"Milk-white moon, put the cows to sleep." C. Sandburg. *FeF—HuSv*
Mr Moon. B. Carman. *FeF—HuL-2*
Mockery. K. D. Riggs. *BrR-4—PeF*
The moon ("And, like a dying lady lean and pale") P. B. Shelley. *SmLg*
The moon ("I like to sit on our doorsill") M. Morgan. *BrL-k*
The moon ("The moon came up") I. O. Eastwick. *EaI*
Moon ("The moon is sharp with her pointed ends") M. C. Livingston. *LiWa*
The moon ("O look at the moon") E. L. Follen. *BrL-k*
The moon ("See how the sky") L. A. Garnett. *BrS*
The moon ("When its rays fall on its cheeks the cat licks them, thinking them milk") Bhasa. *PaS*
"Moon-come-out." E. Farjeon. *ArTp—McAw*
The moon in the mountains. Chen Shan-Min. *PaS*
"Moon, moon." Mother Goose. *OpO*
"The moon shines bright." Mother Goose. *OpO*
Nanny. *DeT*
"Moon, so round and yellow." M. Barr. *BrL-k*
"The moon upon her watch-tower." E. Farjeon. *FaCb*
Moon vine. H. Behn. *BeW*
The moon will give the prize. E. J. Coatsworth. *CoM*
Moonlight. M. E. Uschold. *HuSv*
"The moon's the north wind's cooky." V. Lindsay. *FeF—HuSv—JoAc—NaE—UnG*
Moths and moonshine. J. Reeves. *ReR*
The new moon. W. C. Bryant. *DeT*
Night song. M. C. Livingston. *LiW*
Ninth moon. Li Ho. *PaS*
O Lady Moon. C. G. Rossetti. *DeT*
"Oh, moon, little moon." Unknown. *JoAc*
The old coon-dog dreams. K. Porter. *UnG*

The fox and the goat. tr. *JoAc*
The icosasphere. *PlI*
No swan so fine. *GrCc*
Poetry. *HaP*
Propriety. *PlU*
Silence. *HaP*
The staff of Aesculapius. *PlI*
Moore, Ora Clayton
The playing leaves. *BrL-k*
Moore, Rosalie
Catalog. *UnG*
Gnat. *UnG*
Moore, T. (Thomas) Sturge
"But hark to the wind how it blows."
ArTp
Moore, Thomas
Child's song. See A masque
The light of other days. *DeT*
A masque, sel.
      Child's song. *GrCc*
The minstrel-boy. *UnG*
Moral song. John Farrar. *BrL-k—HuL-1*
More, Hannah
A book. *CoPs*
More, Paul Elmer
Love in moonlight. tr. *PaS*
Peace. tr. *PaS*
More about bears. John Ciardi. *CiY*
"More precious than Aladdin's jewels." See
Treasure
More than flowers we have brought. Nancy
Byrd Turner. *BrS*
Morgan, Edwin
"Fain would I live in safest freedom." tr.
PaS
Morgan, May
The moon. *BrL-k*
Mörike, Eduard
In spring. *PaS*
The wind's song. *PaS*
Morland, Harold
Rima. tr. *PaS*
Morley, Christopher
Animal crackers. *ArTp—BrR-3—FeF—JoAc*
At the dog show. *NaM*
Crayons. *DoP*
The crib. *BrBc*
He comforts himself. See Translations from
the Chinese
A human instinct. See Translations from
the Chinese
In honor of Taffy Topaz. *ArTp*
The man with the rake. See Translations
from the Chinese
Of an ancient spaniel in her fifteenth year.
McW
The plumpuppets. *ArTp—FeF*
Secret thoughts. See Translations from the
Chinese
Six weeks old. *BrBc*
Smells. *BrR-5*
Smells, Junior. *ArTp—BrL-k*
Song for a little house. *BrR-6—FeF—HuSv*
—*JoAc*
To a child. *BrBc*
Translations from the Chinese, sels. *NaE*
      He comforts himself
      A human instinct
      The man with the rake
      Secret thoughts

Morning. See also Wake-up poems
Awful mornings. D. Aldis. *AlA*
The beginning of day. Euripides. *PaS*
City. L. Hughes. *FeF*
Dawn came running. I. O. Eastwick. *EaI*
Daybreak ("Daybreak comes first") C. Sandburg. *SaW*
Daybreak ("A wind came up out of the
sea") H. W. Longfellow. *DeT—McW*
Ducks at dawn. J. S. Tippett. *ArTp—BrS*
Early. D. Aldis. *AlA*
The early morning. H. Belloc. *McW*
Hark, hark the lark. From Cymbeline. W.
Shakespeare. *FeF*
      "Hark, hark, the lark at heaven's gate
      sings." *SmLg*
A morning song. *JoAc*
"I'll tell you how the sun rose." E. Dickinson. *BrS—NaM*
      A day. *UnG*
      Poem. *ReT*
      The sun. *HuSv*
      Sunrise and sunset. *BrR-6*
Joy of the morning. E. Markham. *FeF*
May morning. J. Milton. *HaY*
May mornings. I. O. Eastwick. *BrS—EaI*
Morning ("Everyone is tight asleep") M. C.
Livingston. *LiW*
Morning ("I know a boy who went to meet
the morning") D. H. Gallagher. *BrS*
Morning ("To find the western path") W.
Blake. *SmLg*
Morning ("When the ploughman, as he
goes") C. S. Calverley. *CoH* (sel.)
Morning in winter. H. Behn. *BeW*
Morning magic. H. Behn. *BeW*
A morning song· E. Farjeon. *FaCb—FaN*
Night and morning. D. Aldis. *AlA—CoPs—
HaY*
November morning. E. Stein. *HaY*
Pack, clouds, away. From The rape of
Lucrece. T. Heywood. *ReT*
Reveille. M. O'Connor. *BrR-6*
"Sing a song of sunshine." I. O. Eastwick.
BrS
Singing-time. R. Fyleman. *ArTp—BrS—DoP
—McAw*
Sister, awake. T. Bateson. *CoPs—GrCc*
"Softly, drowsily." From A child's day. W.
De La Mare. *HuL-2—JoAc*
      A child's day, Part II. *ArTp*
      A child's day begins. *HuSv*
"The sounds in the morning." E. Farjeon.
JoAc
Spring morning. A. A. Milne. *MiWc*
"Summer morning." B. Young. *McAw*
Summer morning ("I love to peep out on a
summer's morn") J. Clare. *CoPs*
A summer morning ("I saw dawn creep
across the sky") R. Field. *ArTp—BrR-4—
HuSv—PeF*
The sun is first to rise. E. J. Coatsworth.
HuSv
Up in the morning early. R. Burns. *CoPs—
DeT*
The valley's singing day. R. Frost. *PlU*
"Will there really be a morning." E. Dickinson. *BrS*
      Morning. *FeF—PeF*

Morning—*Continued*

Windy morning. H. Behn. *ArTp—BeW*

Waking time. I. O. Eastwick. *ArTp—BrS*

"Yonder see the morning blink." A. E. Housman. *NaM*

Morning. See "Will there really be a morning"

Morning ("Everyone is tight asleep") Myra Cohn Livingston. *LiW*

Morning ("I know a boy who went to meet the morning") Dorothy Hamilton Gallagher. *BrS*

Morning ("To find the western path") William Blake. *SmLg*

Morning ("When the ploughman, as he goes") Charles Stuart Calverley. *CoH* (sel.)

Morning at the beach. John Farrar. *HuL-1*

The morning glory. Confucius, tr. fr. the Chinese by Helen Waddell. *PaS*

"The morning glory climbs above my head." See The morning glory

"Morning has broken." See A morning song

Morning in winter. Harry Behn. *BeW*

"The morning is cheery, my boys, arouse." See Reveille

Morning magic. Harry Behn. *BeW*

Morning overture: Chorus of dogs. Pearl Strachan. *UnG*

"The morning sits outside afraid." See Night and morning

A morning song ("Hark, hark, the lark at heaven's gate sings") See Cymbeline—Hark, hark the lark

A morning song ("Morning has broken") Eleanor Farjeon. *FaCb—FaN*

Morning star. Plato, tr. fr. the Greek by Percy Bysshe Shelley. *PaS*

"The morning that the world began." See Why nobody pets the lion at the zoo

The morning walk. A. A. Milne. *MiWc*

"The morns are meeker than they were." Emily Dickinson. *ArTp—JoAc—PeF*

Autumn. *BrR-5—FeF—HaY*

Morris, Alice S.

Mrs Santa Claus' Christmas present. *CoPs*

Morris, George Perkins (or Pope)

"Woodman, spare that tree." *FeF* (sel.)

Morris, Hilda

"November wears a Paisley shawl." *HaY*

Morris, William

Carol. *EaW*

Inscription for an old bed. *HoW*

"Masters in this hall." *EaW*

The message of the March wind. *HoW*

Pomona. *HoW*

Riding together. *McW*

Shameful death. *UnG—UnMc*

Song. *ReT*

Tapestry trees. *FeF*

"Mortality, behold and fear." See A memento for mortality

A mortifying mistake. Anna M. Pratt. *CoH*

Morton, David

February bird. *ThP*

Old ships. *HuSv*

Morton, J. B.

The dancing cabman. *NaM*

Moschus

The landsman. *PaS*

"Moses supposes his toeses are roses." Mother Goose. *OpO*

Moss, Howard

The gift to be simple. *PlI*

"Most chivalrous fish of the ocean." See The rhyme of the chivalrous shark

"The most of being a boy is noise." John Ciardi. *CiM*

The most of it. Robert Frost. *HaP*

"Most worthy of praise were the virtuous ways." See Little Red Riding Hood

Mother ("I have praised many loved ones in my song") Theresa Helburn. *FeF*

Mother ("When mother comes each morning") Rose Fyleman. *BrL-k—BrS*

Mother and child ("I love you") See The people, yes

Mother and Child ("When Jesus was a little Child") Ivy O. Eastwick. *BrS*

"The mother cow looked up and great surprise." See Green afternoon

Mother Goose

A apple pie. See "A was an apple-pie"

"A B C D." *OpO*

"A, B, C, D, E, F, G." *OpO*

"A was an apple-pie." *DeMg—LiL*

A apple pie. *JoAc*

Apple-pye. *DeT*

The tragical death of A, apple pie. *OpO*

"A was an archer, who shot at a frog." *DeMg*

"A was an archer." *LiL*

Tom Thumb's picture alphabet. *OpO*

Abram Brown. See "Old Abram Brown is dead and gone"

"Ah, ra, chickera." *OpO*

Aiken Drum. *OpO*

"Ala, mala, mink, monk." *OpO*

Alexander's song. See "There was a man of Thessaly"

"All work and no play makes Jack a dull boy." *OpO*

Alligoshee. *OpO*

And that's all. See "There was an old man (and he had a calf)"

"Anna Elise." See "Anna Elise, she jumped with surprise"

"Anna Elise, she jumped with surprise." *LoL*

"Anna Elise." *OpO*

"An apple a day." *DeMg*

"Apple-pie, apple-pie." *OpO*

Apple-pye. See "A was an apple-pie"

"Army, navy (medicine)." *OpO*

"Army, navy (peerage)." *OpO*

"Around the rick, around the rick." *OpO*

"Arthur O'Bower has broken his band." *OpO*

The wind. *SmLg*

"As black as ink and isn't ink." *OpO*

As I walked. See "As I walked by myself"

"As I walked by myself." *DeMg*

As I walked. *DeT*

The philosopher. *OpO*

"As I was a-walking on Westminster bridge." *OpO*

"As I was going along, long, long." *DeMg—OpO*

"As I was going by Charing cross." *SmLg*
   Charles I. *OpO*
   King Charles. *DeT*
"As I was going o'er London bridge. *OpO*
"As I was going o'er Tipple Tine." *OpO*
"As I was going to Banbury." *JoAc*
   Banbury fair. *OpO*
"As I was going to Derby." *DeMg—LoL*
   The Derby ram. *OpO*
   The wonderful Derby ram. *HuL-1*
"As I was going to St Ives." *DeMg—HuSv—
   JoAc—LiL—OpO*
"As I was going to sell my eggs." *DeMg—
   JoAc*
   Old bandy legs. *OpO*
"As I was going up Pippen hill." *DeMg—
   OpO*
"As I was going up the hill." *OpO*
"As I was walking in a field of wheat." *OpO*
"As I went over the water." *OpO*
"As I went through the garden gap." *DeMg*
   A cherry. *ReG*
"As I went up the Brandy hill." *OpO*
"As round as an apple." See "As round as an
   apple, as deep as a cup"
"As round as an apple, as deep as a cup."
   ArTp—JoAc
   "As round as an apple." *DeMg—OpO*
"As round as an apple (as deep as a pail)."
   OpO
"As soft as silk." *LiL—OpO*
"As Tommy Snooks and Bessy (or Bessie)
   Brooks." *DeMg—JoAc—LiL*
   Tommy and Bessy. *OpO*
At Belle Isle. See "At the siege of Belleisle"
"At Brill on the hill." *OpO*
"At the siege of Belleisle." *DeMg*
   At Belle Isle. *OpO*
"Baa, baa, black sheep." *ArTp—BrL-k—
   DeMg—HuSv—JoAc—LiL—OpO*
The babes in the wood. See "My dear, do
   you know"
"Baby and I." *OpO*
Baby Taffy. *OpO*
The bachelor's lament. See "When I was a
   little boy"
The bad rider. See "I had a little pony"
The bag pudding. See "When good King
   Arthur ruled this land"
Bagpipes. See "A cat came fiddling out of a
   barn"
Ballad of the fox. See "A fox jumped up one
   winter's night"
Banbury fair. See "As I was going to Ban-
   bury"
Barber, barber. See "Barber, barber, shave
   a pig"
"Barber, barber, shave a pig." *DeMg—JoAc
   —LiL*
   Barber, barber. *NaE*
   Pig shaving. *OpO*
Barney Bodkin. *OpO*
"Bat, bat, come under my hat." *DeMg*
   To the bat. *OpO*
Battle royal. See "The lion and the unicorn"
"Be always in time." *OpO*
"A bear went over the mountain." *HuSv—
   JoAc*
Bed time. See "Come, let's to bed"

Bell-horses. See "Bell horses, bell horses,
   what time of day"
"Bell-horses, bell horses, what time of day."
   ArTp—OpO
   Bell-horses. *HuL-1*
   What time of day. *BrS*
The bells of London. See "Gay go up and
   gay go down"
Bessy and Mary. See "Bessy Bell and Mary
   Gray"
"Bessy Bell and Mary Gray." *DeMg*
   Bessy and Mary. *OpO*
Betsy Baker. *OpO*
"Betty Baker bought some butter." See
   "Betty Botter bought some butter"
Betty Barter. See "Betty Botter bought
   some butter"
Betty Blue. See "Little Betty Blue"
"Betty Botter bought some butter." *JoAc—
   OpO*
   "Betty Baker bought some butter." *WoF*
   Betty Barter. *WiRm*
Betty Pringle's pig. See "Little Betty Pringle
   she had a pig"
Billy and me. *OpO*
Billy boy. See "Oh where have you been,
   Billy boy, Billy boy"
Bird scarer's song. *OpO*
"Birds of a feather flock together." *DeMg*
   Signs, seasons, and sense. *UnG*
Birthday rhyme. See "Solomon Grundy"
Birthdays. See "Monday's child is fair of
   face"
"Black I am and much admired." See
   "Black we are, but much admired"
"Black we are, but much admired." *DeMg*
   "Black I am and much admired." *OpO*
"Black within and red without." *DeMg—
   JoAc—OpO*
Black your honour's shoes. *OpO*
"Bless you, bless you, burnie-bee." *JoAc—
   OpO*
Blind man's buff. *OpO*
"Blow the fire, blacksmith." *OpO*
"Blow, wind, blow." See "Blow wind, blow,
   and go mill, go"
"Blow wind, blow, and go mill, go." *ArTp—
   DeMg—HuSv*
   "Blow, wind, blow." *HuL-1—OpO*
Blue Bell. *OpO*
"Bo-peep." *OpO*
"Bo-peeper." *DeT—OpO*
Bob Robin. *OpO*
Bobby Shaftoe. See "Bobby Shafto's gone
   to sea"
"Bobby Shaftoe's gone to sea." See Bobby
   Shafto's gone to sea"
"Bobby Shafto's gone to sea." *DeMg*
   Bobby Shafto. *DeT*
   Bobby Shaftoe. *OpO—ReG*
   "Bobby Shaftoe's gone to sea." *JoAc*
The bonnie cravat. *OpO*
"The boughs do shake and the bells do ring."
   JoAc
   Harvest. *OpO*
Bounce buckram. See "Bounce, buckram, vel-
   vet's dear"
"Bounce, buckram, velvet's dear." *DeMg*
   Bounce buckram. *OpO*

Mother Goose—*Continued*
"Bow-wow, says the dog." *AnI—DeMg—OpO*
"Bow, wow, wow." *ArTp—DeMg—HuSv—JoAc*
    Tom Tinker's dog. *OpO*
Boy Blue. See "Little Boy Blue, come blow your horn"
"Boys and girls come out to play." See "Girls and boys, come out to play"
The brave old duke of York. See "Oh, the grand old duke of York"
"Bring daddy home." *OpO*
The broom squire's song. *OpO*
"Brow bender." *DeMg*
"Brow, brow, brenty." *OpO*
"Brow, brow, brinkie." *DeMg*
"Bryan O'Lin had no breeches to wear." *DeMg*
Buff. See "I had a little dog and they called him Buff"
"Burn ash-wood green." *DeMg*
"Burnie bee, burnie bee." *DeMg*
Butterfly. *OpO*
"Button to chin." *OpO*
Buy any buttons. *OpO*
By the fire. See "Pussy sits beside the fire"
"Bye, baby bunting." *ArTp—DeMg—HuSv—JoAc—LiL—OpO—WoF*
"Bye, bye, baby bunting." *OpO*
"Can you keep a secret." *LiL*
"Can you make a cambric shirt." *JoAc*
    "Can you make me a cambric shirt." *DeMg*
    The lover's tasks. *OpO*
"Can you make me a cambric shirt." See "Can you make a cambric shirt"
Carol. *OpO*
    Sunny bank; or, I saw three ships. *EaW*
Carousal. *OpO*
The carrion crow. See "A carrion crow sat on an oak"
"A carrion crow sat on an oak." *DeMg—JoAc—LiL*
    The carrion crow. *OpO*
    The tailor and the crow. *ReG*
A cat came fiddling. See "A cat came fiddling out of a barn"
"A cat came fiddling out of a barn." *DeMg—HuSv—JoAc*
    Bagpipes. *DeT—OpO*
    A cat came fiddling. *HuL-1*
The cat sat asleep. See "The cat sat asleep by the side of the fire"
"The cat sat asleep by the side of the fire." *DeMg*
    The cat sat asleep. *DeT*
    Medley. *OpO*
Catch. See "Little Robin Redbreast sat upon a tree"
"Catch him, crow. Carry him, kite." *OpO*
The cats of Kilkenny. See "There once were two cats of Kilkenny"
Caution. See "Mother, may I go out to swim"
Chairs to mend. See "If I'd as much money as I could spend"
Charade. *OpO*

Charles I. See "As I was going by Charing cross"
Charley. *OpO*
Charley Barley. *OpO*
"Charley Wag, Charley Wag." *JoAc*
    "Charlie Wag." *OpO*
Charley Warlie. See "Charlie Warlie had a cow"
"Charlie Wag." See "Charley Wag, Charley Wag"
"Charlie Warlie had a cow." *DeMg*
    Charley Warlie. *OpO*
A cherry. See "As I went through the garden gap"
"A cherry year." *OpO*
"Chick, my naggie." *OpO*
Chop-a-nose. *OpO*
Christmas. See "Christmas is coming, the geese are getting fat"
Christmas carol. See "God bless the master of this house"
"Christmas comes but once a year." *DeMg—OpO*
Christmas eve. *OpO*
"Christmas is coming." See "Christmas is coming, the geese are getting fat"
"Christmas is coming, the geese are getting fat." *DeMg*
    Christmas. *ArTp*
    "Christmas is coming." *OpO*
Churning. See "Come, butter, come"
"Clap hands, clap hands (till father)." *OpO*
"Clap hands, Daddy comes." *OpO*
"Clap hands, Daddy's coming." *OpO*
Close shave. *OpO*
"Clothed in yellow, red, and green." *OpO*
The coachman. *OpO*
Cobbler, cobbler. See "Cobbler, cobbler, mend my shoe"
"Cobbler, cobbler, mend my shoe." *DeMg—LiL*
    Cobbler, cobbler. *OpO*
Cock-a-bandy. *OpO*
"Cock-a-doodle-doo." *DeMg—HuL-1—JoAc—LiL—OpO*
Cock and hen. *OpO*
Cock-crow. See "The cock's in the wood pile a-blowing his horn"
"Cocks crow in the morn." *ArTp*
    Signs, seasons, and sense. *UnG*
"The cock doth crow." *ArTp—DeMg—LiL—OpO*
Cock Robin. See "Who killed Cock Robin"
Cock Robin ("Cock Robin got up early") *DeT*
    Cock Robin's courtship. *OpO*
Cock Robin's courtship. See Cock Robin
"The cock's in the wood pile a-blowing his horn." *DeMg*
    Cock-crow. *OpO*
"Columbus sailed the ocean blue." *OpO*
"Come, butter, come." *DeMg—HuSv*
    Churning. *OpO*
"Come dance a jig." *OpO*
"Come hither, little puppy dog." *DeMg*
"Come, let's to bed." *DeMg—LiL*
    Bed time. *OpO*
    To bed. *DeT*
"Come up, my horse, to Budleigh fair." *OpO*

"Come when you're called." *DeMg—OpO*
The comedy of Billy and Betty. *OpO*
Contrary Mary. See "Mary, Mary, quite contrary"
Coo. See "The dove says, Coo, coo, what shall I do"
Courtship. *OpO*
"A cow and a calf." *OpO*
"Cripple Dick upon a stick." *OpO*
The croodin doo. *OpO*
The crooked man. See "There was a crooked man"
"Cross-patch." *DeMg—JoAc—LiL—NaE—OpO*
"Cry, baby, cry (put your)." *DeMg*
The cuckoo. See "The cuckoo is a merry bird"
"Cuckoo, cherry tree." *DeMg—OpO*
"The cuckoo comes in April." *OpO*
"Cuckoo, cuckoo, what do you do." *LiL*
　To the cuckoo. *OpO*
"The cuckoo is a merry bird." *DeMg*
　The cuckoo. *OpO*
　Three cuckoo rhymes. *DeT*
"Curly Locks, Curly Locks." *DeMg—JoAc—OpO*
　"Curly Locks, Curly Locks, wilt thou be mine." *LiL*
"Cushy cow, bonny, let down thy milk." *DeMg—HuSv—JoAc*
　Milking. *OpO*
"Cut thistles in May." *OpO*
"Daffadowndilly." *ArTp*
　"Daffy-down-dilly has come up to town." *DeMg*
　"Daffy-down-dilly is new come to town." *OpO*
"Daffy-down-dilly has come up to town." See "Daffadowndilly"
"Daffy-down-dilly is new come to town." See "Daffadowndilly"
Dame get up. See "Dame, get up and bake your pies"
"Dame, get up and bake your pies." *DeMg—JoAc*
　Dame get up. *HuL-1*
　On Christmas day. *OpO*
The dame of Dundee. *OpO*
Dame Trot. See "Dame Trot and her cat"
"Dame Trot and her cat." *DeMg—HuL-1*
　Dame Trot. *OpO*
Dance. See "Dance, Thumbkin, dance"
"Dance a baby diddy." *OpO*
"Dance, little baby, dance up high." *DeMg—OpO*
"Dance, Thumbkin, dance." *DeMg—LiL—OpO*
　Dance. *DeT*
"Dance to your daddie." See "Dance to your daddy"
"Dance to your daddy." *DeMg—JoAc—LiL—OpO*
　"Dance to your daddie." *ArTp*
Dappled Grey. *OpO*
Davy Dumpling. *OpO*
Days in the month. See "Thirty days hath September"
Days of birth. See "Monday's child is fair of face"

Death and burial of Cock Robin. See "Who killed Cock Robin"
Deceiver. *OpO*
Deedle, deedle, dumpling. See "Diddle, diddle, dumpling, my son John"
"Deedle, deedle, dumpling, my son John." See "Diddle, diddle, dumpling, my son John"
The Derby ram. See "As I was going to Derby"
The devil. *OpO*
"Dickery, dickery, dare." *DeMg*
　The flying pig. *OpO*
Dicky Dilver. *OpO*
Did you see my wife. *OpO*
"Diddle, diddle, dumpling, my son John." *HuSv—JoAc—LiL—OpO*
　Deedle, deedle, dumpling. *HuL-1*
　"Deedle, deedle, dumpling, my son John." *DeMg*
"Diddlety, diddlety, dumpty." *DeMg—LiL*
　Puss up the plum tree. *OpO*
"A diller, a dollar." See "A diller, a dollar, a ten o'clock scholar"
"A diller, a dollar, a ten o'clock scholar." *ArTp*
　"A diller, a dollar." *DeMg—JoAc—LiL*
　Ten o'clock scholar. *OpO*
Dilly dilly. See "Oh, what have you got for dinner, Mrs Bond"
"Ding dang, bell rang." *OpO*
"Ding, dong, bell." *ArTp—BrL-k—DeMg—HuL-1—JoAc—LiL—OpO*
"Dingle dingle doosey." *OpO*
Dob and Mob. See "There was a man and his name was Dob"
"Doctor Faustus was a good man." *DeMg—LiL*
　Doctor Foster. *OpO*
Doctor Foster. See "Doctor Faustus was a good man"
Doctor Foster. See "Doctor Foster went to Gloucester"
Doctor Foster ("Old Doctor Foster") *OpO*
"Doctor Foster went to Glo'ster." See "Doctor Foster went to Gloucester"
"Doctor Foster went to Gloucester." *DeMg—JoAc*
　Doctor Foster. *OpO*
　"Doctor Foster went to Glo'ster." *LiL*
"A dog and a cat went out together." *DeMg*
"The doggies went to the mill." *OpO*
"Donkey, donkey, do not bray." *OpO*
"Doodledy, doodledy, doodledy, dan." *OpO*
Double-u. See "Heigh ho, my heart is low"
The dove says. See "The dove says, Coo, coo, what shall I do"
"The dove says, Coo, coo, what shall I do." *DeMg*
　Coo. *DeT*
　The dove says. *OpO*
"Down by the river (where the green grass grows)." *OpO*
"Down with the lambs." *OpO*
"Draw a pail of water." *DeMg—LiL—NaM—OpO*
"A duck and a drake." *DeMg*
　Ducks and drakes. *OpO*

"Girls and boys, come out to play." *ArTp* —*DeMg—HuSv—LiL—NaM*
    "Boys and girls come out to play." *JoAc—OpO*
    Full moon. *DeT*
    Girls and boys. *HuL-1*
"Go to bed first." *OpO*
"Go to bed late." *OpO*
"Go to bed, Tom." *OpO*
"God bless the master of this house." *DeMg—HuSv—OpO*
    Christmas carol. *ArTp—BrS*
    A grace. *NaM*
"God bless this house from thatch to floor." *OpO*
"Goes through the mud." *OpO*
"Good, better, best." *MoY—OpO*
The good boy. *OpO*
Good Friday. *OpO*
"Good morning, Father Francis." *OpO*
"Good morrow to you, Valentine." *OpO*
"Good night, God bless you." *OpO*
"Good night, sweet repose." *OpO*
Goosey gander. See "Goosey, goosey, gander (whither)"
"Goosey, goosey, gander (whither)." *DeMg —JoAc—LiL*
    Goosey gander. *OpO*
    Goosie gander. *BrL-k*
Goosie gander. See "Goosey, goosey, gander (whither)"
The gossips. *OpO*
A grace. See "God bless the master of this house"
"The grand old duke of York." See "Oh, the grand old duke of York"
"Gray goose and gander." *JoAc—LiL— OpO*
"Great A, little a (bouncing B)." *DeMg— JoAc—LiL—OpO*
"Great A, little a (this is pancake day)." *DeMg*
"Great A was alarmed at B's bad behavior." *OpO*
Greed. *OpO*
Greedy Tom. *OpO*
Green grass. *OpO*
Gregory Griggs. See "Gregory Griggs, Gregory Griggs"
"Gregory Griggs, Gregory Griggs." *DeMg*
    Gregory Griggs. *OpO*
A grenadier. *OpO*
Grig's pig. *OpO*
Grinding. *OpO*
The guinea-pig. See "There was a little guinea-pig"
Gunpowder plot day. See "Please to remember"
"Handy dandy." *OpO*
"Handy dandy, riddledy ro." *DeMg*
"Handy spandy, Jack-a-Dandy." *DeMg*
"Hannah Bantry." See "Hannah Bantry, in the pantry"
"Hannah Bantry, in the pantry." *DeMg*
    "Hannah Bantry." *OpO*
"Hark, hark." See "Hark, hark, the dogs do bark"
"Hark, hark, the dogs do bark." *AnI— ArTp—LiL*
    "Hark, hark." *DeMg—JoAc—OpO*

Harry Parry. *OpO*
"The hart he loves the high wood." *DeMg —OpO—SmLg*
Harvest. See "The boughs do shake and the bells do ring"
"Hay is for horses." *OpO*
He, haw, hum. See "John Cook he had a little gray mare"
"He loves me." *OpO*
"He met old Dame Trot with a basket of eggs." *DeMg*
"He that would thrive." *DeMg—OpO*
"He went to the wood and caught it." *OpO*
"Head bumper." *OpO*
"Hearts, like doors, will ope with ease." *OpO*
Hector Protector. See "Hector Protector was dressed all in green"
"Hector Protector was dressed all in green." *DeMg*
    Hector Protector. *NaM—OpO*
Hee, haw, hum. See "John Cook he had a little gray mare"
"Heigh ho, my heart is low." *OpO*
    Double-u. *DeT*
The hen keeper. *OpO*
"Here am I." See "Here am I, little jumping Joan"
"Here am I, little jumping Joan." *LiL*
    "Here am I." *DeMg*
    Jumping Joan. *OpO*
    Little jumping Joan. *ArTp*
"Here are my (or the) lady's knives and forks." *LiL—OpO*
"Here comes a poor woman from Babyland." *DeMg*
Here comes a wooer. *OpO*
"Here comes my lady with her little baby." *OpO*
"Here is the church, and here is the steeple." *DeMg—OpO*
Here sits. See "Here sits the Lord Mayor"
"Here sits the Lord Mayor." *DeMg—LiL —OpO*
    Here sits. *DeT*
"Here we come gathering nuts in May." *LiL*
    Nuts an' may. *NaE*
"Here we go dancing jingo-ring." *OpO*
"Here we go round ring by ring." *OpO*
"Here we go round the mulberry bush." *DeMg—LiL*
"Here's a ball for baby." *LiL*
"Here's a health to the barley mow." *DeMg*
Here's a poor widow. *OpO*
"Here's Sulky Sue." *DeMg*
    Sulky Sue. *OpO*
"Hey diddle diddle (and hey)." *OpO*
"Hey, diddle, diddle (the cat)." *ArTp— BrL-k—DeMg—HuSv—JoAc—LiL—OpO*
"Hey diddle, dinketty, poppety, pet." *DeMg —OpO*
"Hey ding a ding." *OpO*
Hey dorolot. *OpO*
"Hey, my kitten, my kitten." *DeMg—OpO*
"Hick-a-more, hack-a-more." *ArTp—JoAc —OpO*

"I saw three ships come sailing by." *DeMg*
  —*JoAc*—*LiL*
    I saw three ships. *HuL-1*—*UnG*
    Three ships. *OpO*
"I see the moon." *ArTp*—*DeMg*—*OpO*
    The moon. *DoP*
    Signs, seasons, and sense. *UnG*
    Sun and moon. *HuL-1*
"I sent a letter to my love." *LiL*
"I went to Noke." *OpO*
"I went to the toad that lies under the wall." Mother Goose. *OpO*
"I went up one pair of stairs." *DeMg*—*JoAc*
"I won't be my father's Jack." *DeMg*—*OpO*—*PlU*
"I would, if I could." *DeMg*—*OpO*
"Ickle ockle, blue bockle." *OpO*
If a woodchuck would chuck. See "How much wood would a wood-chuck chuck"
If all the seas. See "If all the seas were one sea"
"If all the seas were one sea." *DeMg*—*HuSv*—*JoAc*—*LoL*—*OpO*
    If all the seas. *ReG*
"If all the world was apple pie." See "If all the world were apple pie"
"If all the world was paper." *OpO*
"If all the world were apple pie." *AnI*—*DeMg*
    "If all the world was apple pie." *JoAc*—*LoL*
"If bees stay at home." *OpO*
    Signs, seasons, and sense. *UnG*
"If I had a donkey that wouldn't go." *DeMg*—*JoAc*
    Kindness. *OpO*
If I'd as much money. See "If I'd as much money as I could spend"
"If I'd as much money as I could spend." *JoAc*—*LiL*
    Chairs to mend. *OpO*
    If I'd as much money. *HuL-1*
    Old clothes, any old clo', clo'. *OpO*
"If ifs and ands." *DeMg*—*LiL*
"If the oak is out before the ash." *OpO*
"If wishes were horses." *DeMg*—*LiL*—*OpO*
"If you are a gentleman." *OpO*
"If you sneeze on Monday, you sneeze for danger." See "Sneeze on Monday, sneeze for danger"
"I'll buy you a tartan bonnet." *OpO*
"I'll sing you a song (though not very long)." *DeMg*
I'll tell. *OpO*
"I'll tell you a story." *DeMg*—*JoAc*—*LiL*
    Jack a nory. *OpO*
"I'm called by the name of a man." *OpO*
"In a cottage in Fife." *DeMg*—*LoL*
    Two comical folk. *OpO*
"In fir tar is." *DeMg*—*OpO*
In Lincoln lane. *OpO*
"In marble halls as white as milk." *DeMg*—*JoAc*—*OpO*
    "In marble walls as white as milk." *HuSv*
"In marble walls as white as milk." See "In marble halls as white as milk"
"In sixteen hundred and sixty-six." *OpO*

"In spring I look gay." *OpO*
In the dumps. See "We are all in the dumps"
Inducements. See "Whistle, daughter, whistle"
"Inter, mitzy, titzy, tool." *OpO*
"Intery, mintery, cutery, corn." *ArTp*—*DeMg*—*JoAc*—*OpO*
    A counting-out rhyme. *DeT*
    "Intry, mintry, cutry, corn." *HuSv*
"Intry, mintry, cutry, corn." See "Intery, mintery, cutery, corn"
Ipsey wipsey. *OpO*
"Is John Smith within." *DeMg*—*OpO*
"It cost little Gossip her income for shoes." *DeMg*
"It was on a merry time." *DeMg*
"It's once I courted as pretty a lass." *OpO*
"It's raining, it's pouring." *OpO*
"It's raining, it's raining." *OpO*
"I've seen you where you never were." *DeMg*
    Five very old riddles. *DeT*
Jack a nory. See "I'll tell you a story"
"Jack and Gye." *OpO*
Jack and Jill. See "Jack and Jill went up the hill"
Jack and Jill and old Dame Dob. See "Jack and Jill went up the hill"
"Jack and Jill went up the hill." *ArTp*—*DeMg*—*HuSv*—*JoAc*—*LiL*
    Jack and Jill. *BrL-k*
    Jack and Jill and old Dame Dob. *OpO*
"Jack, be nimble." *AnI*—*ArTp*—*DeMg*—*HuSv*—*JoAc*—*LiL*—*OpO*
Jack Horner. See "Little Jack Horner"
Jack in the pulpit. *OpO*
Jack Sprat. See "Jack Sprat could eat no fat"
"Jack Sprat could eat no fat." *DeMg*—*JoAc*—*LiL*
    Jack Sprat. *OpO*
Jack Sprat's cat. *OpO*
Jack Sprat's pig. *OpO*
"Jacky, come give me thy fiddle." *OpO*—*PlU*
Jacky Jingle. *OpO*
Jemima. See "There was a little girl, and she had a little curl"
Jemmy Dawson. *OpO*
"Jenny was so mad." *DeMg*
Jenny Wren. See "Jenny Wren fell sick"
"Jenny Wren fell sick." *JoAc*
    Jenny Wren. *NaE*
    Little Jenny Wren. *HuL-1*
    Ungrateful Jenny. *OpO*
"Jeremiah, blow the fire." *OpO*
"Jerry Hall." *DeMg*—*OpO*
Jim Crow. *OpO*
"John Cook he had a little gray mare." *DeMg*
    He, haw, hum. *HuL-1*
    Hee, haw, hum. *DeT*
    John Cook's mare. *ReG*
    The last will and testament of the grey mare. *OpO*
John Cook's mare. See "John Cook he had a little gray mare"

"Little lad, little lad." See "Little lad, little lad, where wast thou born"
"Little lad, little lad, where wast thou born." *DeMg*
  Little lad. *BrBc*
  "Little lad, little lad." *OpO*
"The little lady lairdie." *OpO*
A little maid. *OpO*
"Little maid, pretty maid." *OpO*
The little man and the little maid. *OpO*
"Little Miss Muffet." *ArTp—BrL-k—DeMg—HuSv—JoAc—LiL*
  Miss Muffet. *OpO*
"Little miss, pretty miss." *DeMg—OpO*
Little moppet. See "I had a little moppet"
Little nag. *OpO*
"Little Nancy Etticoat." *DeMg—HuSv—JoAc—LiL—OpO*
  "Little Nanny Etticoat." *ArTp*
"Little Nanny Etticoat." See "Little Nancy Etticoat"
"Little pig." *OpO*
"Little Polly Flinders." *DeMg—LiL*
  Polly Flinders. *OpO*
"Little pretty Nancy girl." *OpO*
"Little Robin Redbreast (sat upon a hill)." *DeMg*
"Little Robin Redbreast (sat upon a rail)." *DeMg—HuSv*
  Niddle noddle. *OpO*
"Little Robin Redbreast sat upon a tree." *DeMg—LiL*
  Catch. *OpO*
  "Little Robin Redbreast." *HuL-1*
"Little Tee Wee." *DeMg—OpO—WoF*
"Little Tommy Tittlemouse." *AnI—DeMg*
  Tommy Tittlemouse. *OpO*
"Little Tommy Tucker." *DeMg—JoAc—LiL*
  Tommy Tucker. *OpO*
The little woman and the pedlar. See "There was an old woman, as I've heard tell"
"Lives in winter." *ArTp*
"Lock the dairy door." *OpO*
London bridge. See "London bridge is broken down"
"London bridge is broken down." *DeMg—JoAc—LiL*
  London bridge. *OpO*
"Long legs, crooked thighs." *DeMg—JoAc—LiL—OpO*
"A long-tailed pig, or a short-tailed pig." *DeMg*
The love-sick frog. See "A frog he would a-wooing go"
Love song. See "Lavender's blue, diddle, diddle"
The lover's gifts. *OpO*
The lover's tasks. See "Can you make a cambric shirt"
Lucy and Kitty. See "Lucy Locket lost her pocket"
Lucy Locket. See "Lucy Locket lost her pocket"
"Lucy Locket lost her pocket." *DeMg—JoAc—LiL*
  Lucy and Kitty. *OpO*
  Lucy Locket. *BrL-k*
"Mackerel sky." *OpO*

Mad farmer's song. See "My father left me three acres of land"
"Make three-fourths of a cross." *OpO*
"The man in the moon (came down too soon)." See "The man in the moon (came tumbling down)"
"The man in the moon (came tumbling down)." *DeMg—LiL*
  The man in the moon. *OpO*
"The man in the moon drinks claret." *OpO*
"The man in the moon was caught in a trap." *OpO*
"The man in the mune." *OpO*
A man in the wilderness. See "A man in the wilderness asked me"
"A man in the wilderness asked me." *DeMg—JoAc—LiL*
  A man in the wilderness. *OpO*
  "The man in the wilderness said to me." *SmLg*
"The man in the wilderness said to me." See "A man in the wilderness asked me"
Man of Derby. *OpO*
Man of Thessaly. See "There was a man of Thessaly"
A man of words. See "A man of words and not of deeds"
"A man of words and not of deeds." *DeMg—SmLg*
  A man of words. *DeT*
"A man went a-hunting at Reigate." *DeMg*
The man who jumped. *OpO*
The man with nought. See "There was a man and he had nought"
"Manners in the dining-room." *OpO*
"March winds and April showers." *DeMg—LiL—OpO*
  Signs, seasons, and sense. *UnG*
Marching. *OpO*
"Margery Mutton-pie and Johnny Bo-peep." *DeMg—OpO*
"Mary had a pretty bird." *DeMg*
  The pretty bird. *DeT*
"Mary, Mary, quite contrary." *ArTp—HuL-1—JoAc—LiL*
  Contrary Mary. *OpO*
  "Mistress Mary." *BrL-k*
  "Mistress Mary, quite contrary." *DeMg—HuSv*
Master and man. See "Master I have, and I am his man"
"Master I have, and I am his man." *ArTp*
  Master and man. *OpO*
"Matthew, Mark, Luke, and John." *DeMg—HuL-1—OpO—SmLg*
  Envoy. *DeT*
  Signs, seasons, and sense. *UnG*
May day. *OpO*
Medley. See "The cat sat asleep by the side of the fire"
A melancholy song. See "Trip upon trenchers, and dance upon dishes"
"Mena, deena, deina, duss." *LiL*
Merrily danced the Quaker's wife. *OpO*
Milking. See "Cushy cow, bonny, let down thy milk"
The milkmaid. See "Where are you going to, my pretty maid"

Mother Goose—*Continued*
"The miller he grinds his corn, his corn."
    DeMg
        A hop, skip, and a jump. *HuL-1*
The mischievous raven. See "A farmer
    went trotting upon his gray mare"
Miss Muffet. See "Little Miss Muffet"
"Mr East gave a feast." *JoAc*
    Mr East's feast. *OpO*
Mr East's feast. See "Mr East gave a
    feast"
Mr Ibister. *OpO*
Mrs Hen. *OpO*
"Mistress Mary." See "Mary, Mary, quite
    contrary"
"Mistress Mary, quite contrary." See "Mary,
    Mary, quite contrary"
Mrs Mason's basin. *OpO*
"Moll-in-the-wad and I fell out." *OpO*
"Molly, my sister, and I fell out." *DeMg*
"Monday's child is fair of face." *BrBc—*
    DeMg—HuSv—JoAc—LiL—SmLg
        Birthdays. *OpO—ReG*
        Days of birth. *NaM*
        Signs, seasons, and sense. *UnG*
Money works wonders. *OpO*
The moon. See "I see the moon"
"Moon, moon." *OpO*
"The moon shines bright." *OpO*
    Nanny. *DeT*
"Moses supposes his toeses are roses." *OpO*
"Mother, may I go out to swim." *FeF*
    Caution. *OpO*
Mother Niddity Nod. *OpO*
Mother Shuttle. See "Old Mother Shuttle"
Mothering Sunday. *OpO*
Mouse and mouser. *OpO*
"Multiplication is vexation." *DeMg*
    Signs, seasons, and sense. *UnG*
My Bangalorey man. See "Follow my
    Bangalorey man"
My black hen. See "Hickety, pickety, my
    black hen"
"My dame hath a lame tame crane." *OpO*
"My dear, do you know." *DeMg*
    The babes in the wood. *DeT*
"My father left me three acres of land."
    DeMg
        Mad farmer's song. *HuL-2*
        Three acres of land. *OpO*
"My father was a Frenchman." *OpO*
"My grandmother sent me." *OpO*
My hobby horse. See "I had a little hobby
    horse"
"My Lady Wind, my Lady Wind." *DeMg*
My little cow. *OpO*
My little maid. *OpO*
"My little old man and I fell out." *DeMg*
    —JoAc—OpO
My little wife. *OpO*
"My maid Mary." *DeMg—OpO*
My mammy's maid. *OpO*
"My mother said." *OpO*
    "My mother said that I never should."
        SmLg
"My mother said that I never should." See
    "My mother said"
Nancy Cock. *OpO*

Nanny. See "The moon shines bright"

Natural history. See "What are little boys
    made of, made of"
"Nauty Pauty Jack-a-Dandy." *OpO*
A needle and thread. See "Old Mother
    Twitchett had (or has) but one eye"
"Needles and pins, needles and pins." *DeMg*
    Signs, seasons, and sense. *UnG*
New year. *OpO*
Niddle noddle. See "Little Robin Red-
    breast (sat upon a rail)"
"Nievie nievie nick nack." *OpO*
The north wind. See "The north wind doth
    blow"
"The north wind doth blow." *DeMg—HuL-1
    —HuSv—JoAc—LiL*
    The north wind. *OpO*
Not so impossible. See "I saw a peacock
    with a fiery tail"
Nothing-at-all. See "There was an old
    woman called Nothing-at-all"
Now I lay me. See "Now I lay me down
    to sleep (I pray)"
"Now I lay me down to sleep (I pray)."
    OpO
    Now I lay me. *HuL-1*
The nut tree. See "I had a little nut tree"
Nuts an' may. See "Here we come gather-
    ing nuts in May"
"Oh dear, what can the matter be." *DeMg*
    What can the matter be. *OpO*
"Oh, do you know the muffin-man." *DeMg*
"Oh that I were." *OpO*
"Oh, the brave old duke of York." See
    "Oh, the grand old duke of York"
"Oh, the grand old duke of York." *DeMg
    —LiL*
    The brave old duke of York. *OpO*
    Duke o' York. *HuL-1*
    "The grand old duke of York." *ArTp*
    "Oh, the brave old duke of York."
        JoAc
"O the little rusty dusty miller." *OpO*
"Oh, what have you got for dinner, Mrs
    Bond." *DeMg*
    Dilly dilly. *OpO*
"Oh where have you been, Billy boy, Billy
    boy." *DeMg*
    Billy boy. *OpO*
    The young thing. *HuL-2*
"Of a little take a little." *OpO*
"Of all the gay birds that e'er I did see."
    DeMg
"Of all the sayings in this world." *OpO*
Old Abram Brown. See "Old Abram
    Brown is dead and gone"
"Old Abram Brown is dead and gone."
    DeMg
    Abram Brown. *OpO*
    Old Abram Brown. *DeT*
Old bandy legs. See "As I was going to
    sell my eggs"
Old Boniface. *OpO*
"Old Boniface he loved good cheer." See
    Old Boniface
"Old chairs to mend. Old chairs to mend."
    DeMg
Old clothes, any old clo', clo'. See "If
    I'd as much money as I could spend"
"Old farmer Giles." *OpO*

"Old King Cole." *BrL-k—DeMg—JoAc—LiL—OpO*

"An old maid, an old maid." *OpO*

The old man who lived in a wood. See "There was an old man who lived in a wood"

Old Mother Goose and the golden egg. See "Old Mother Goose (when she)"

"Old Mother Goose (when she)." *DeMg—JoAc—LiL*

   Old Mother Goose and the golden egg. *OpO*

"Old Mother Hubbard." *AnI—DeMg—HuSv—JoAc—LiL—UnG*

   Old Mother Hubbard and her dog. *OpO*

Old Mother Hubbard and her dog. See "Old Mother Hubbard"

"Old Mother Shuttle." *NaE*

   Mother Shuttle. *OpO*

"Old Mother Twitchett had (or has) but one eye." *ArTp—DeMg—LiL—OpO*

   A needle and thread. *ReG*

Old pudding-pie woman. See "There was an old woman (sold puddings and pies)"

The old woman in a shoe. See "There was an old woman who lived in a shoe"

The old woman in the basket. See "There was an old woman tossed up in a basket"

"Old woman, old woman, shall we go a-shearing." *ArTp—DeMg—OpO*

The old woman who bought a pig. *OpO*

The old woman's three cows. *OpO*

On Christmas day. See "Dame, get up and bake your pies"

On oath. *OpO*

"On Saturday night shall be my care." *OpO*

"On the first day of Christmas." See "The first day of Christmas"

"On the first of March." *OpO*

"Once I saw a little bird." *BrL-k—DeMg—HuSv*

   Little bird. *OpO*

"One-erum, two-erum." *OpO*

"One-ery, two-ery, ickery, Ann." *OpO*

   Counting-out rhymes. *FeF*

"One-ery, two-ery, tickery, seven." *OpO*

One-eyed gunner. *OpO*

"One for money." See "One for the money"

"One for sorrow, two for joy." *OpO*

"One for the money." *HuSv*

   "One for money." *OpO*

"One I love, two I love." *DeMg—LiL—OpO*

"One misty, moisty morning." *ArTp—DeMg—HuSv—JoAc—LiL—OpO*

"One thing at a time." *OpO*

"One to make ready." *DeMg—LiL—OpO*

"One, two." See "One, two, buckle my shoe"

"One, two, buckle my shoe." *BrL-k—DeMg—HuL-1—LiL—OpO*

   "One, two." *ArTp—DeT—HuSv—JoAc*

   Signs, seasons, and sense. *UnG*

One-two-three. See "One, two, three, four, five (I caught a hare alive)"

"One, two, three, four, five (I caught a fish alive)." *HuL-1—LiL—OpO—WoF*

"One, two, three, four, five (I caught a hare alive)." *ArTp—DeMg*

   One-two-three. *DeT*

"One, two, three, four, five, six, seven (all good children)." *DeMg*

"One, two, three, four (Mary at)." *LiL—OpO—TaD*

"One, two, whatever you do." *OpO*

Oranges and lemons. See "Gay go up and gay go down"

"Our bow's bended." *OpO*

Over the hills and far away. *HuL-1*

"Over the water and over the lea." *DeMg*

   Over the water to Charley. *DeT*

   Over the water to Charlie. *OpO*

Over the water to Charley. See "Over the water and over the lea"

Over the water to Charlie. See "Over the water and over the lea"

An owl in an oak. See "There was an owl lived in an oak"

Parliament soldiers. *OpO*

Pat-a-cake. See "Pat-a-cake, pat-a-cake baker's man"

"Pat-a-cake, pat-a-cake, baker's man." *DeMg—HuSv—JoAc—LiL—OpO*

   Pat-a-cake. *BrL-k*

"Patience is a virtue." *OpO*

"Pease porridge hot." *ArTp—BrL-k—DeMg—JoAc—LiL—OpO*

   "Pease pudding hot." *HuL-1*

"Pease pudding hot." See "Pease porridge hot"

Peg. See "There was an old woman, her name it was Peg"

"Penny and penny." *OpO*

Peter. See "Peter, Peter, pumpkin eater"

"Peter, Peter, pumpkin eater." *AnI—DeMg—JoAc—LiL*

   Peter. *OpO*

"Peter Piper pick'd a peck of pepper." See "Peter Piper picked a peck of pickled pepper"

"Peter Piper picked a peck of pickled pepper." *DeMg—HuSv—LiL—OpO*

   Peter Piper. *FeF*

   "Peter Piper pick'd a peck of pepper." *JoAc*

Peter White. See "Peter White will ne'er go right"

"Peter White will ne'er go right." *DeMg*

   Peter White. *OpO*

"The pettitoes are little feet." *OpO*

The philosopher. See "As I walked by myself"

Pick-a-back. *OpO*

Pig shaving. See "Barber, barber, shave a pig"

The piper. See "There was a piper had a cow"

Pit, pat. See "Pit, pat, well-a day"

"Pit, pat, well-a day." *DeMg*

   Pit, pat. *OpO*

Plaint. *OpO*

"Please to remember." *DeMg*

   Gunpowder plot day. *OpO*

   "Please to remember the fifth of November." *LiL*

"Please to remember the fifth of November." See "Please to remember"

The ploughboy in luck. *OpO*

   The silly. *DeT*

Mother Goose—*Continued*

Poll Parrot. *OpO*

Polly Flinders. See "Little Polly Flinders"

"Polly put the kettle on." *DeMg—LiL*
  Tea-time. *OpO*

"Poor old Robinson Crusoe." *DeMg*
  Robinson Crusoe. *OpO*

Poringer. See "What is the rhyme for poringer"

Praise. *OpO*

The pretty bird. See "Mary had a pretty bird"

Prevarication. *OpO*

The priest of Felton. *OpO*

"Punch and Judy." *DeMg—OpO*

"Purple, yellow, red and green." *DeMg—OpO*

Puss in the pantry. *OpO*

Puss up the plum tree. See "Diddlety, diddlety, dumpty"

Pussy and the mice. *NaM*
  Three little mice. *HuL-1*

Pussy cat. *OpO*

Pussy cat Mole. See "Pussy cat Mole jumped over a coal"

"Pussy cat Mole jumped over a coal." *DeMg*
  Pussy cat Mole. *OpO*

"Pussy-cat, pussy-cat." See "Pussy cat, pussy cat, where have you been"

"Pussy cat, pussy cat, where have you been." *DeMg—HuSv—LiL*
  "Pussy-cat, pussy-cat." *ArTp—HuL-1 —JoAc*
  A traveller. *OpO*

"Pussy sits beside the fire." *DeMg*
  By the fire. *OpO*

"Put your finger in foxy's hole." *LiL—OpO*

Putting on nightgown. *OpO*

Queen Anne. See "Lady Queen Anne she sits in the sun"

"The Queen of Hearts." *AnI—DeMg—JoAc —LiL—OpO*

The rabbit man. *OpO*

The rain. See "Rain on the green grass"

"Rain before seven." *OpO*
  Signs, seasons, and sense. *UnG*

"Rain on the green grass." *OpO*
  The rain. *ArTp*

"Rain, rain, go away." *AnI—ArTp—DeMg —JoAc—OpO*

"Rain, rain, go to Spain." *LiL—OpO*

A rat. See "There was a rat, for want of stairs"

"A red sky at night." *LiL—OpO*

"Red stockings, blue stockings." *OpO*

"Rich man." *DeMg*
  Rich man, poor man. *WoJ*

Rich man, poor man. See "Rich man"

"Rich man, poor man, beggarman, thief." See "Rich man"

"Richard Dick upon a stick." *OpO*

"A riddle, a riddle." See "A riddle, a riddle, as I suppose"

"A riddle, a riddle, as I suppose." *ArTp— DeMg*
  "A riddle, a riddle." *OpO*

"Riddle me, riddle me ree." *OpO*

"Ride a cock horse." See "Ride a cock-horse to Banbury cross (to see a)"

"Ride a cock-horse to Banbury cross (to see a)." *DeMg—HuSv—JoAc—LiL—OpO*

"Ride a cock horse." *ArTp—BrL-k— HuL-1—OpO*

"Ride a cock-horse (to Banbury cross to see what)." *OpO*

"Ride away, ride away." *ArTp—OpO*

"Rigadoon, rigadoon, now let him fly." *OpO*

"A ring, a ring o' roses." *OpO*

"Ring-a-ring o' roses." *DeMg—LiL—OpO*

"Ring the bell." *DeMg—OpO*

Robert Barnes. See "Robert Barnes, fellow fine"

"Robert Barnes, fellow fine." *DeMg—OpO*
  Robert Barnes. *HuL-1*

"Robert Rowley rolled a round roll 'round." *HuSv—OpO*

"Robin-a-Bobbin." *OpO*

"A robin and a robin's son." *OpO*

"Robin and Richard." See "Robin and Richard were two pretty men"

"Robin and Richard were two pretty men." *DeMg*
  "Robin and Richard." *OpO*

"Robin Hood." *OpO*

"Robin Hood, Robin Hood." *DeMg—OpO*

"Robin the Bobbin." See "Robin the Bobbin, the big-bellied Ben"

"Robin the Bobbin, the big-bellied Ben." *DeMg*
  "Robin the Bobbin." *OpO*

Robinson Crusoe. See "Poor old Robinson Crusoe"

"Rock-a-bye, baby (thy cradle is green)." *DeMg—JoAc—LiL—OpO*

Roger and Dolly. *OpO*

Roman figures. *OpO*

"The rose is red, the grass is green." *OpO*

"The rose is red, the rose is white." *OpO*

"The rose is red, the violet's blue." *DeMg —HuSv—OpO*

"Rosemary green, and lavender blue." *DeMg*

"Roses are red (violets are blue, sugar is)." *MoY—OpO*

"Round about, round about (catch a wee mouse)." *OpO*

"Round about, round about, here sits the hare." *OpO*

"Round about, round about (maggotty pie)." *OpO*

"Round about the rosebush." *OpO*

"Round about there." *OpO*

"Round and round the cornfield." *LiL*

"Round and round the garden." *OpO*

"Round and round the rugged rock." *OpO —WiRm*

"Rub-a-dub-dub." *DeMg—JoAc—LiL—OpO*

"Rumpty-iddity, row, row, row." *OpO*

"Runs all day and never walks." *ArTp*

"St Swithin's day, if thou dost rain." *DeMg —LiL*
  Signs, seasons, and sense. *UnG*

"St Thomas's day is past and gone." *OpO*

"Sally go round the sun." *OpO*

Sally Waters. *OpO*

Sam, the sportsman. See "There was a little man, and he had a little gun"

Sandy. *OpO*

"Sandy Kildandy." *OpO*

"Say well and do well." *OpO*

The scaredy. *OpO*

"Scissors and string, scissors and string." *OpO*

Scottish castle. *OpO*

A Scottish cat. *OpO*

A Scottish shoe. *OpO*

"See a pin and pick it up." *DeMg—JoAc—LiL*
Signs, seasons, and sense. *UnG*

"See-saw, down in my lap." *OpO*

"See-saw, Margery Daw (Jacky shall have a new master)." *DeMg—JoAc—LiL—OpO*

"See-saw, Margery Daw (sold her bed)." *OpO*

"See-saw, Margery Daw (the old hen flew)." *DeMg—OpO*

"See-saw, sacradown." *DeMg—JoAc—OpO*

"See, see, what shall I see." Mother Goose. *OpO*

A ship a-sailing. See "I saw a ship a-sailing"

"Shoe a little horse." *DeMg—LiL—OpO*

"Shoe the colt, shoe the colt." *OpO*

"A shoemaker makes shoes without leather." *OpO*

Short song. *OpO*

Shrovetide. *OpO*

Silly ("Gilly Silly Jarter") *OpO*

The silly ("My daddy is dead, and I can't tell you how") See The ploughboy in luck

Simple Simon. See "Simple Simon met a pieman"

Simple Simon and the pieman. See "Simple Simon met a pieman"

"Simple Simon met a pieman." *DeMg—HuSv—JoAc—LiL*
Simple Simon. *ReG—UnG*
Simple Simon and the pieman. *OpO*

"Sing a song of sixpence." *ArTp—BrL-k—DeMg—HuSv—JoAc—LiL—OpO*

Sing jigmijole. *OpO*

"Sing, sing." See "Sing, sing, what shall I sing"

"Sing, sing, what shall I sing." *DeMg—LiL*
"Sing, sing." *OpO*

Six little mice. See "Six little mice sat down to spin"

"Six little mice sat down to spin." *JoAc*
Six little mice. *OpO*

"Sleep, baby, sleep (thy father guards)." *LiL*
Holy lullaby. *UnG*

"Smiling girls, rosy boys." *DeMg*
The gingerbread man. *OpO*

Snail hunters. See "Four and twenty tailors"

"Snail, snail." *DeMg—JoAc*
To the snail. *OpO*

"Sneeze on a Monday, you sneeze for danger." See "Sneeze on Monday, sneeze for danger"

"Sneeze on Monday, sneeze for danger." *LiL*
"If you sneeze on Monday, you sneeze for danger." *DeMg*
"Sneeze on a Monday, you sneeze for danger." *NaE*
Sneezing. *ReG*

Sneezing. See "Sneeze on Monday, sneeze for danger"

Snow and sun. See "White bird featherless"

"Soldier brave, sailor true." *OpO*

"Solomon Grundy." *DeMg—HuL-1—JoAc—LiL—OpO*
Birthday rhyme. *BrBc*

Some little mice. See "Some little mice sat in a barn to spin"

"Some little mice sat in a barn to spin." *DeMg*
Some little mice. *BrL-k*

A song ("I'll sing you a song—nine verses long") *OpO*

A song ("I'll sing you a song—the days are long") *OpO*

"The sow came in with the saddle." *OpO*

"The Spanish Armada met its fate." *OpO*

Spin dame. *OpO*

"Spring is showery, flowery, bowery." *ArTp*

The squirrel. See "The winds they did blow"

"Star bright, starlight." See Star-light, star-bright"

"Star-light, star-bright." *ArTp—OpO*
"Star bright, starlight." *HuSv*

Stopping the swing. *OpO*

"Sukey, you shall be my wife." *OpO*

Sulky Sue. See "Here's Sulky Sue"

Sun and moon. See "I see the moon"

Sunny bank; or, I saw three ships. See Carol ("As I sat on a sunny bank")

"A sunshiny shower." *DeMg—LiL—OpO*
Signs, seasons, and sense. *UnG*

The swan. See "Swan swam over the sea"

"Swan swam over the sea." *DeMg—OpO*
The swan. *FeF*

"Swan, swim over the sea." *WiRm*

"Swan, swim over the sea." See "Swan swam over the sea"

"A swarm of bees in May." *DeMg—LiL—OpO*

Sweeping the sky. See "There was an old woman tossed up in a basket"

Sweet blooming lavender. *OpO*

Swinging. *OpO*

"Tae titly." *OpO*

"Taffy was a Welshman." *DeMg—OpO*

The tailor and the crow. See "A carrion crow sat on an oak"

"The tailor of Bicester." *OpO*

A tale. *OpO*

Tammy Tyrie. *OpO*

A tawnymoor. *OpO*

Tea-time. See "Polly put the kettle on"

Teasing. *OpO*

"Tell-tale-tit." *DeMg*

Ten little nigger boys. *OpO*

Ten o'clock scholar. See "A diller, a dollar, a ten o'clock scholar"

"Terence McDiddler." *OpO*

"A thatcher of Thatchwood went to Thatchet a-thatching." *DeMg—OpO*

"Theophilus Thistle, the successful thistle sifter." *DeMg*
Theophilus Thistledown. *LoL*
"Theophilus Thistledown, the successful thistle sifter." *OpO*

Theophilus Thistledown. See "Theophilus Thistle, the successful thistle sifter"

Mother Goose—*Continued*

"Theophilus Thistledown, the successful thistle sifter." See "Theophilus Thistle, the successful thistle sifter"

"There once were two cats of Kilkenny." *DeMg*
  The cats of Kilkenny. *UnG*
  The Kilkenny cats. *CoH—LoL*

"There was a bee." *DeMg*

"There was a crooked man." *BrL-k—ReG*
  The crooked man. *OpO*
  "There was a crooked man, and he went a crooked mile." *DeMg—HuSv—JoAc—LiL*

"There was a crooked man, and he went a crooked mile." See "There was a crooked man"

"There was a fat man of Bombay." *DeMg*

"There was a girl in our town." *DeMg—OpO*

"There was a king, and he had three daughters." *OpO*

"There was a king met a king." *OpO*

There was a lady. See "There was a lady loved a swine"

"There was a lady loved a swine." *DeMg*
  The lady in love. *OpO*
  There was a lady. *DeT*

"There was a little boy and a little girl." *DeMg—OpO*

There was a little girl. See "There was a little girl, and she had a little curl"

"There was a little girl, and she had a little curl." *AnI—DeMg*
  Jemima. *SmLg—UnG*
  The little girl. *OpO*
  There was a little girl. *NaE*

"There was a little guinea-pig." *DeMg*
  The guinea-pig. *LoL—OpO—UnG*

"There was a little man." See "There was a little man, and he had a little gun"

"There was a little man, and he had a little gun." *DeMg—JoAc*
  Sam, the sportsman. *OpO*
  "There was a little man." *HuL-1—LiL*

"There was a little woman." See "There was an old woman, as I've heard tell"

"There was a man and he had nought." *DeMg*
  The man with nought. *OpO*
  There was a man. *DeT*

"There was a man and his name was Dob." *DeMg*
  Dob and Mob. *OpO*

"There was a man in our town." *DeMg*

"There was a man of double deed." *OpO*

"There was a man of Thessaly." *LiL*
  Alexander's song. *JoAc*
  Man of Thessaly. *OpO*

"There was a man rode through our town." *OpO*

"There was a man who had no eyes." *OpO*

There was a monkey. See "There was a monkey climbed up a tree"

"There was a monkey climbed up a tree." *DeMg*
  There was a monkey. *DeT—OpO*

"There was a piper had a cow." *DeMg*
  The piper. *OpO*

"There was a rat, for want of stairs." *DeMg*
  A rat. *OpO*

"There was a thing a full month old." *OpO*

"There was an old man (and he had a calf)." *DeMg—JoAc*
  And that's all. *DeT—OpO*

"There was an old man of Tobago." *DeMg*

"There was an old man who lived in a wood." *DeMg—HuSv*
  The old man who lived in a wood. *NaM*

"There was an old woman (and nothing she had)." *OpO*

"There was an old woman, and what do you think." *DeMg—LiL—SmLg*
  An old woman. *OpO*
  "There was an old woman." *JoAc*

"There was an old woman, as I've heard tell." *ArTp—JoAc—LiL*
  Lauk a mercy. *DeT*
  The little woman and the pedlar. *OpO*
  The old woman. *UnG*
  "There was a little woman." *DeMg*
  There was an old woman. *BrR-3—CoPs—CoSp—NaM*

"There was an old woman called Nothing-at-all." *DeMg*
  Nothing-at-all. *OpO*

"There was an old woman had three sons." *JoAc*

"There was an old woman, her name it was Peg." *DeMg*
  Peg. *OpO*

"There was an old woman in Surrey." *DeMg*

"There was an old woman (lived under a hill, she put a mouse)." *DeMg*
  An old woman. *OpO*

"There was an old woman (lived under the hill and if she's not gone)." *DeMg—JoAc—LiL*
  Under a hill. *OpO*

"There was an old woman (sold puddings and pies)." *DeMg*
  Old pudding-pie woman. *OpO*

"There was an old woman tossed up in a basket." *DeMg—HuSv—JoAc—LiL*
  An old woman. *OpO*
  The old woman in the basket. *ReG*
  Sweeping the sky. *HuL-1*
  There was an old woman. *NaE*

"There was an old woman who lived in a shoe." *AnI—ArTp—DeMg—HuSv—JoAc—LiL*
  The old woman in a shoe. *OpO*

"There was an old woman who rode on a broom." *DeMg*

There was an owl. See "There was an owl lived in an oak"

"There was an owl lived in an oak." *DeMg*
  An owl in an oak. *OpO*
  Signs, seasons, and sense. *UnG*
  There was an owl. *HuL-1*

"There were three jovial huntsmen." See "There were three jovial Welshmen"

"There were three jovial Welshmen." *DeMg—JoAc*

"There were three jovial huntsmen." *HuSv*

The three huntsmen. *PaOm*

"Three jolly huntsmen." *UnG*

The three jovial Welshmen. *OpO*

The three Welshmen. *NaM*

"There were three sisters in a hall." *OpO*

"There were two birds sat on a stone." *DeMg*

Two birds. *OpO*

"There were two blackbirds." *DeMg*

"They that wash on Monday." *DeMg—LiL*

"Thirty days hath September." *DeMg—HuSv—JoAc—LiL*

Days in the month. *OpO*

Signs, seasons, and sense. *UnG*

"Thirty white horses." See "Thirty white horses upon a red hill"

"Thirty white horses upon a red hill." *ArTp—DeMg*

"Thirty white horses." *JoAc—OpO*

"Twenty white horses." *HuSv*

"This is the house that Jack built." *DeMg—HuSv—JoAc—LiL*

The house that Jack built. *OpO*

This is the key. See "This is the key of the kingdom"

"This is the key of the kingdom." *DeMg—OpO*

This is the key. *NaM—ReT—SmLg*

"This is the way the ladies ride." *ArTp—DeMg—LiL—OpO*

"This is Willy Walker, and that's Tam Sim." *OpO*

"This little pig had a rub-a-dub." *OpO*

"This little pig went to market." *DeMg—HuSv—JoAc—LiL—OpO*

"Thomas a Tattamus took two tees." *DeMg*

Three a-bed. *DeT—OpO*

Three acres of land. See "My father left me three acres of land"

Three against one. *OpO*

"Three blind mice." See "Three blind mice, see how they run"

"Three blind mice, see how they run." *AnI—DeMg*

"Three blind mice." *LiL—OpO*

Three brethren from Spain. *OpO*

We are three lords. *HuL-1*

Three cooks. *OpO*

"Three crooked cripples went through Cripplegate." Mother Goose. *OpO*

Three ghostesses. See "Three little ghostesses"

"Three grey geese in a green field grazing." *OpO*

The three huntsmen. See "There were three jovial Welshmen"

"Three jolly huntsmen." See "There were three jovial Welshmen"

The three jovial Welshmen. See "There were three jovial Welshmen"

"Three little ghostesses." *WiRm*

Three ghostesses. *OpO*

Three little mice. See Pussy and the mice

"Three little princes." *FaN*

Three ships. See "I saw three ships come sailing by"

The three Welshmen. See "There were three jovial Welshmen"

"Three wise men of Gotham." *DeMg—JoAc—LiL*

The wise men of Gotham. *OpO*

Three young rats. See "Three young rats with black felt hats"

"Three young rats with black felt hats." *DeMg—JoAc*

Three young rats. *LoL—OpO*

"Through storm and wind." *OpO*

"Thumb bold." *OpO*

"Thumb he." *OpO*

"Thumbikin, Thumbikin, broke the barn." Mother Goose. *OpO*

"Tickly, tickly, on your knee." *OpO*

Tiddle liddle. *OpO*

"Timothy Titus took two ties." *OpO*

"Tinker, tailor." *OpO*

"Tit, tat, toe." *OpO*

"Titty cum tawtay." *OpO*

To bed. See "Come, let's to bed"

"To make your candles last for aye." *DeMg—DeT—OpO*

To market. See "To market, to market, to buy a fat pig"

"To market, to market, to buy a fat pig." *ArTp—DeMg—HuSv—JoAc—LiL*

To market. *HuL-1*

"To market, to market." *OpO*

"To market, to market, to buy a plum bun." *DeMg*

"To market, to market." *OpO*

To Mr Punchinello. *OpO*

"To sleep easy all night." *OpO*

To the bat. See "Bat, bat, come under my hat"

To the cuckoo. See "Cuckoo, cuckoo, what do you do"

To the ladybird. See "Ladybird, ladybird (fly away home)"

To the magpie. *OpO*

To the puss moth. *OpO*

To the snail. See "Snail, snail"

To the snow. *OpO*

"Toe Tipe." *OpO*

"Toe, trip and go." *OpO*

Tom Brown's Indians. *OpO*

"Tom, he was a piper's son." *ArTp—DeMg*

Tom, the piper's son. *OpO*

"Tom saw a cross fellow was beating an ass." *DeMg*

Tom, the piper's son. See "Tom, he was a piper's son"

Tom, the piper's son. See "Tom, Tom, the piper's son (stole a pig)"

"Tom Thumbkin." *OpO*

Tom Thumb's picture alphabet. See "A was an archer, who shot at a frog"

Tom Tinker's dog. See "Bow, wow, wow"

Tom Tittlemouse. *OpO*

"Tom, Tom, the piper's son (he learnt to play)." See Over the hills and far away

"Tom, Tom, the piper's son (stole a pig)." *BrL-k—DeMg—JoAc—LiL*

Tom, the piper's son. *OpO*

Mother Goose—*Continued*

Tommy and Bessy. See "As Tommy Snooks and Bessy (or Bessie) Brooks"

Tommy O'Linn. *OpO*

Tommy Tacket. *OpO*

"Tommy Tibule." *OpO*

Tommy Tittlemouse. See "Little Tommy Tittlemouse"

Tommy Trot. See "Tommy Trot, a man of law"

"Tommy Trot, a man of law." *DeMg*
   Tommy Trot. *OpO*

Tommy Tucker. See "Little Tommy Tucker"

Tommy's shop. *OpO*

The toy lamb seller. See "Young lambs to sell. Young lambs to sell"

The tragical death of A, apple pie. See "A was an apple-pie"

A traveller. See "Pussy cat, pussy cat, where have you been"

Tremendous trifles. See "For want of a nail, the shoe was lost"

"Trip upon trenchers, and dance upon dishes." *DeMg*
   A melancholy song. *OpO*

"Trit trot to market to buy a penny doll." *OpO*

"A trot, and a canter, a gallop, and over." *OpO*

"Tweedledum and Tweedledee." *DeMg—LiL*
   Dum and Dee. *OpO*

Twelfth night. *OpO*

The twelve days of Christmas. See "The first day of Christmas"

"Twelve pears hanging high." *DeMg—OpO*

"Twenty white horses." See "Thirty white horses upon a red hill"

Twirling. *OpO*

Two birds. See "There were two birds sat on a stone"

"Two bodies have I." *OpO*

"Two brothers are we." *OpO*

Two comical folk. See "In a cottage in Fife"

"Two legs sat on three legs." See "Two legs sat upon three legs"

"Two legs sat upon three legs." *DeMg—LiL—OpO*
   "Two legs sat on three legs." *JoAc*

"Two little dicky birds." *LiL—OpO*

"Two little dogs." *OpO*

Under a hill. See "There was an old woman (lived under the hill and if she's not gone)"

Ungrateful Jenny. See "Jenny Wren fell sick"

"Up street and down street." *OpO*

"Up the wooden hill." *OpO*

Up time. *OpO*

"Upon a cock-horse to market I'll trot." *OpO*

"Upon my word and honour." *DeMg*

"Upon Paul's steeple stands a tree." *LiL—OpO*

A visit from Mr Fox. See "A fox jumped up one winter's night"

Visitor. See "Who's that ringing at my doorbell"

"Walk down the path." *LiL*

Warm hands. See "Warm hands, warm"

"Warm hands, warm." *LiL*
   Warm hands. *OpO*

Warning. *OpO*

Wash the dishes. *OpO*

Washing day. *OpO*

Washing up. *OpO*

"We are all in the dumps." *DeMg*
   In the dumps. *OpO*

We are three lords. See Three brethren from Spain

Wedding ("Pussicat, wussicat, with a white foot") *OpO*

The wedding ("This year") *OpO*

"Wee Willie Winkie." See "Wee Willie Winkie runs through the town"

"Wee Willie Winkie runs through the town." *ArTp—DeMg—HuSv—JoAc—LiL*
   "Wee Willie Winkie." *BrS*
   Willie Winkie. *OpO*

"What are little boys made of, made of." *DeMg—JoAc*
   Natural history. *OpO*

What can the matter be. See "Oh dear, what can the matter be"

What care I. *OpO*

"What do they call you." *DeMg*

"What God never sees." *OpO*

"What is the rhyme for porringer." *OpO*
   Poringer. *ReG*

What time of day. See "Bell horses, bell horses, what time of day"

"What's in the cupboard." *JoAc—OpO*

"What's in there." *OpO*

What's the news. See "What's the news of the day"

"What's the news of the day." *DeMg*
   What's the news. *OpO*

"When a twister a-twisting, will twist him a twist." *DeMg—OpO*

"When clouds appear." *OpO*
   Signs, seasons, and sense. *UnG*

"When good King Arthur ruled this land." *DeMg—JoAc—LiL*
   The bag pudding. *DeT*
   King Arthur. *OpO*

"When I was a bachelor, I lived by myself." *LiL*

When I was a lad. *OpO*

"When I was a little boy." *BrL-k*
   The bachelor's lament. *OpO*
   "When I was a little boy I lived by myself." *DeMg*

"When I was a little boy I lived by myself." See "When I was a little boy"

"When I was a little boy (my mammy kept)." *OpO*

"When Jack's a very good boy." *DeMg*
   "When Jacky's a good boy." *OpO*
   "When Jacky's a very good boy." *NaE*

"When Jacky's a good boy." See "When Jack's a very good boy"

"When Jacky's a very good boy." See "When Jack's a very good boy"

"When land is gone and money spent." *OpO*

"When the clouds are upon the hills." *OpO*

"When the dew is on the grass." *OpO*

"When the wind blows." *OpO*

"When the wind is in the east." *DeMg—LiL—OpO*
Signs, seasons, and sense. *UnG*
"Where are you going, my pretty maid."
See "Where are you going to, my pretty maid"
"Where are you going to, my pretty maid." *DeMg—LiL*
The milkmaid. *OpO*
"Where are you going, my pretty maid." *HuL-1—JoAc*
Where is he. See "Where, oh, where has my little dog gone"
"Where, oh, where has my little dog gone." *WoF*
Where is he. *OpO*
"Whistle, daughter, whistle." *DeMg*
Inducements. *OpO*
"White bird featherless." *OpO*
Snow and sun. *ReG*
"Who killed Cock Robin." *DeMg—DeT—JoAc*
Cock Robin. *UnG*
Death and burial of Cock Robin. *OpO*
Who's that ringing. See "Who's that ringing at my doorbell"
"Who's that ringing at my doorbell." *SmLg*
Visitor. *OpO*
Who's that ringing. *HuL-1*
Whose little pigs. *OpO*
Why may not I love Johnny. See "Johnny shall have a new bonnet"
"Wilful waste brings woeful want." *OpO*
"William McTrimbletoe." *OpO*
"William the Conqueror, ten sixty-six." *OpO*
Willie boy, Willie boy. See "Willy boy, Willy boy, where are you going"
Willie Winkie. See "Wee Willie Winkie runs through the town"
Willy boy. *OpO*
"Willy boy, Willy boy, where are you going." *DeMg—HuSv*
Willie boy, Willie boy. *HuL-1*
"Willy, Willy Wilkin." *OpO*
Willy Wood. *OpO*
The wind. See "Arthur O'Bower has broken his band"
"The winds they did blow." *DeT*
The squirrel. *OpO*
"Wine and cakes for gentlemen." *OpO*
"Winter's thunder." *LiL*
Signs, seasons, and sense. *UnG*
The wise men of Gotham. See "Three wise men of Gotham"
"A wise old owl lived in an oak." *DeMg—LiL—OpO*
"A woman, a spaniel, and walnut tree." *DeMg*
The wonder of wonders. See "I saw a peacock with a fiery tail"
The wonderful Derby ram. See "As I was going to Derby"
The wren hunt. *OpO*
Yankee Doodle. See "Yankee Doodle went to town"
"Yankee Doodle came to town." See "Yankee Doodle went to town"

"Yankee Doodle went to town." *HuSv—JoAc*
Yankee Doodle. *FeF—OpO*
"Yankee Doodle came to town." *DeMg*
You shall be queen. See "Lilies are white"
"Young lambs to sell. Young lambs to sell." *DeMg*
The toy lamb seller. *OpO*
The young thing. See "Oh where have you been, Billy boy, Billy boy"
"Z, Y, X, and W, V." *OpO*
Mother Goose (about)
"Old Mother Goose (when she)." Mother Goose. *DeMg—JoAc—LiL*
Old Mother Goose and the golden egg. *OpO*
Mother Goose characters (about)
The embarrassing episode of little Miss Muffet. G. W. Carryl. *CoSp—FeF*
The gastronomic guile of Simple Simon. G. W. Carryl. *UnG*
Little Bo-peep and Little Boy Blue. A. A. Milne. *MiWc*
Little Jack Horner. Unknown. *DeT*
"Mother, I want to be married." See Mr Punchinello
A mother is a sun. Peggy Bennett. *CoPs*
"A mother is a sun. A gentle fire." See A mother is a sun
"Mother likes the frocks and hats." See Shop windows
"Mother, may I go out to swim." Mother Goose. *FeF*
Caution. *OpO*
"Mother, may I stay up tonight." See Conversation
"Mother, mother, I am ill." Unknown. *TaD*
"Mother, mother, I feel sick." See How many carriages
Mother Niddity Nod. Mother Goose. *OpO*
Mother of the house. See Proverbs—"Strength and honour are her clothing"
"Mother, oh mother, where shall we hide us." See Others
"Mother says I'm six." See Hard lines
"Mother shake the cherry-tree." Christina Georgina Rossetti. *ArTp*
Let's be merry. *FeF*
"Mother sings a sleepy-song." See Sleepy song
Mother to son. Langston Hughes. *BrBc—HuSv—PeF*
"Mother took." See The miracle
Motherhood. See Mothers and motherhood
Mothering Sunday. Mother Goose. *OpO*
Mothers and motherhood. See also Home and family life
The ballad of the harp-weaver. E. St V. Millay. *ArTp—CoSp—UnMc*
Dandelions. M. Chute. *BrBc—ChA—McAw*
The dinner party. D. Aldis. *AlA*
Disobedience. A. A. Milne. *MiWc*
Dresses. D. Aldis. *AlA*
First thought. M. C. Livingston. *LiWa*
His mother-in-law. W. Parke. *CoH*
His mother's cooking. L. M. Hadley. *BrR-5*

"Mousie, mousie." See Conversation

Mouths. Dorothy Aldis. *AlA*

Movies in the fire. Mildred D. Shacklett. *BrR-4*

Moving
Moving. E. Tietjens. *ArTp—HuL-2*
The new house. D. Aldis. *AlHd*

Moving. Eunice Tietjens. *ArTp—HuL-2*

"The moving moon went up the sky." See The rime of the ancient mariner—The ancient mariner

"Moving with you." See Poet to dancer

The mowers. Myron B. Benton. *HaY*

Mowing. See Farm life; Harvests and harvesting

Mowing. Robert Frost. *FrR*

Moy castle. Unknown. *UnG*

Mozart, Wolfgang Amadeus (about)
Mozart, 1935. W. Stevens. *PlU*

Mozart, 1935. Wallace Stevens. *PlU*

Mozart perhaps. John Hall Wheelock. *PlU*

"Much have I travell'd in the realms of gold." See On first looking into Chapman's Homer

Mud
Cooking. M. C. Livingston. *LiW*
"I know a place." M. C. Livingston. *LiW*
Mud. P. C. Boyden. *ArTp—BrL-k*

Mud. Polly Chase Boyden. *ArTp—BrL-k*

"Mud is very nice to feel." See Mud

Muhlenberg, William Augustus
"Carol, brothers, carol." *ArTp*

Muir, Edwin
The animals. *GrCc*
The horses ("Barely a twelvemonth after") *HaP*
Horses ("Those lumbering horses in the steady plough") *SmLg*

"The mulberry is a double tree." See Banjo boomer

Mulberry trees
Banjo boomer. W. Stevens. *McW*
The priest and the mulberry tree. From Crotchet castle. T. L. Peacock. *CoSp—DeT*

Mules
Cincirinella had a mule. Unknown. *FeF*
Ever since. E. J. Coatsworth. *BrS*
"I had a little mule, her name was Jenny." Unknown. *WoF*
"There was a man of our town." Unknown. *TaD*

Mulock, Dinah Maria (Dinah Maria Craik)
The blackbird. *UnG*
Friendship. *ThP*
God rest ye merry, gentlemen. *JoAc*
The new year. *HaY*
The young dandelion. *UnG*

"Multiplication is vexation." Mother Goose. *DeMg*

Signs, seasons, and sense. *UnG*

Mumfludgeons. E. V. Rieu. *RiF*

Mummy slept late and daddy fixed breakfast. John Ciardi. *CiY*

Mumps
Mumps. E. M. Roberts. *FeF—JoAc—LoL—McAw*

Mumps. Elizabeth Madox Roberts. *FeF—JoAc—LoL—McAw*

Munday, Anthony
Robin Hood's funeral. *HoW*
Song. *ReT*
Song. See Robin Hood's funeral

Munro, Harold. See Monro, Harold

"The murmur of the mourning ghost." See Keith of Ravelston

"A murmuring in empty shells." See The relic

Murray, Sir Gilbert
The Bacchae, sel.
Where shall wisdom be found. tr. *PaS—PlU*
Hippolytus, sel.
O for the wings of a dove. tr. *PaS*
O for the wings of a dove. See Hippolytus
Where shall wisdom be found. See The Bacchae

The muse. Anna Akhmatova, tr. fr. the Russian by Stanley Burnshaw. *GrCc*

Musée des beaux arts. W. H. Auden. *HaP*

"Musetta of the mountains." James Reeves. *ReW*

Museums
In a museum. T. Hardy. *PlU*

Mushrooms
Mushrooms. Unknown. *JoAc*
The one-legged stool. E. Blyton. *HuL-1*
The toadstool wood. J. Reeves. *ReBl*

Mushrooms. Unknown, tr. fr. the Russian by Rose Fyleman. *JoAc*

Music and musicians. See also Bands (Music); Minstrels and troubadours; Singing; also names of musical instruments, as Pianos; also names of types of musicians, as Pipers; also names of musicians, as Beethoven, Ludwig van
Alexander's feast; or, The power of music. J. Dryden. *HoW*
Alle vögel sind schon da. F. Chesterton. *PlU*
At a concert of music. C. Aiken. *PlU*
At a solemn musick. J. Milton. *PlU* (sel.)
The bagpipe man. N. B. Turner. *ArTp—HuL-1—HuL-2*
Bagpipe music. L. MacNeice. *HaP*
The big bass drum. Unknown. *HuL-1*
The bower of bliss. From The faerie queene. E. Spenser. *PlU*
Burnt Norton. T. S. Eliot. *PlU* (sel.)
"Can doleful notes to mesur'd accents set." J. Danyel. *PlU*
The carnival of animals. O. Nash. *PlU* (sel.)
The ceremonial band. J. Reeves. *ReBl*
Church-musick. G. Herbert. *PlU*
Come ye sons of art. H. Purcell. *PlU* (sel.)
The composer. W. H. Auden. *PlU*
The concert ("I left my chambers to attend") J. S. Newman. *CoH*
The concert ("When leaves of April glisten") P. McGinley. *HaY—ThP*
Country music. Plato. *PaS*
The desert music. W. C. Williams. *PlU* (sel.)

Music ("On music drawn away, a seaborne mariner") Charles Baudelaire, tr. fr. the French by Robert Fitzgerald. *PaS*

Music ("Orpheus with his lute made trees") See King Henry VIII—Orpheus

Music and words. Elizabeth Jennings. *PlU*

"Music can not stay." See Pediment: Ballet

Music God. Mark Van Doren. *PlU*

Music I heard. See Discordants

"Music I heard with you was more than music." See Discordants—Music I heard

"The music, the." See The desert music

"Music, when soft voices die." Percy Bysshe Shelley. *HaP*

A musical at home. E. V. Rieu. *RiF*

The musical box. James Reeves. *ReW*

A musical critic anticipates eternity. Siegfried Sassoon. *PlU*

A musical instrument. Elizabeth Barrett Browning. *FeF—UnG*

The great god Pan. *HoW*

Musical instruments. See also names of musical instruments, as Pianos
The clavichord. M. Sarton. *PlU*
The hurdy-gurdy. E. Fleming. *HuL-2*
The instruments. C. Smart. *HoW*
The orchestra. N. B. Turner. *BrR-5*

The musician ("How loudly and how surely the musician plays") R. P. Lister. *PlU*

Musician ("Where have these hands been") Louise Bogan. *PlU*

Musicians. See Music and musicians

"Musicians wrestle everywhere." Emily Dickinson. *PlU*

"Musick, thou Queen of Heaven, carecharming-spel." See To musick

Musicks empire. Andrew Marvell. *GrCc*

Mu'tamid, King of Seville
Thy garden. *PaS*

Muth, Eleanor
Night enchantment. *BrS*

My Airedale dog. W. L. Mason. *PeF*

My Bangalorey man. See "Follow my Bangalorey man"

My bed is a boat. Robert Louis Stevenson. *HuSv*

"My bed is like a little boat." See My bed is a boat

"My birthday is coming and I will be six." See The birthday bus

"My birthday is coming tomorrow." See Growing up

My birthday's in winter. Zhenya Gay. *BrBc*

"My birthday's in winter when it's snowy and cold." See My birthday's in winter

"My bishop's eyes I've never seen." See Praying and preaching

My black hen. See "Hickety, pickety, my black hen"

My body. William Jay Smith. *SmL*

My brother ("My brother is inside the sheet") Dorothy Aldis. *ArTp*

My brother ("Today I went to market with my mother") Dorothy Aldis. *AlHd*

"My brother is inside the sheet." See My brother

My butterfly. Robert Frost. *FrR*

"My button gloves are very white." See Easter parade

"My cat." See Cat

My cat Jeoffry. Christopher Smart. *HaP—HoW—UnG*

My cat, Mrs Lick-a-chin. John Ciardi. *CiY*

"My cat, washing her tail's tip, is a whorl." See Cat on couch

"My child, my sister, dream." See Invitation to the voyage

"My clothing was once of the linsey woolsey fine." See Poor old horse

"My counterpane is soft as silk." See A child's song of Christmas

"My country, 'tis of thee." See America

"My Cousin German came from France." Unknown. *SmLg*

"My dad was a soldier and fought in the wars." See The hero

"My daddy is dead, and I can't tell you how." See The ploughboy in luck

"My daddy smells like tobacco and books." See Smells, Junior

"My daddy went a-huntin'." See The grey goose

"My dame hath a lame tame crane." Mother Goose. *OpO*

"My darling little goldfish." See The goldfish

"My dear Daddie bought a mansion." See The little bird

"My dear, do you know." Mother Goose. *DeMg*
The babes in the wood. *DeT*

"My dear, when you." See For Vicki at seven

My delight. Unknown. *ReG*

"My delight's in pansies-o." See My delight

My dog ("Have you seen a little dog anywhere about") Emily Lewis. *HuL-1*

My dog ("His nose is short and scrubby") Marchette Chute. *ArTp—BrL-k—ChA—FeF—HuL-1—McAw—PeF*

My dog ("I have no dog, but it must be") John Kendrick Bangs. *HuSv*

My dog, Spot. Rodney Bennett. *HuL-1*

My dog Tray. Thomas Campbell. *UnG*
The Irish harper. *DeT*

"My dog's so furry I've not seen." See The hairy dog

My donkey. Unknown, tr. fr. the French by Rose Fyleman. *ArTp—HuL-2*

"My donkey, my dear." See My donkey

My dress is pink. Dorothy Aldis. *AlHd*

"My dress is pink. My shoes are white." See My dress is pink

My example. Charles Wesley. *DoP*

My face. Anthony Euwer. *CoH*
Limericks since Lear. *UnG*

"My father and mother were Irish." See Irish

"My father bought an undershirt." See Song of the all-wool shirt

"My father carries a pearl-handled knife." See A wonderful man

"**My** father died a month ago." **See The** legacy

"**My** father has a pair of shoes." **See Shoes**

"**My** father he died, but I can't tell you how." See The ploughboy in luck

"**My** father he left me three acres of land." See "My father left me three acres of land"

"**My** father, he was a mountaineer." See The ballad of William Sycamore

"**My** father left me three acres of land." Mother Goose. *DeMg*

Mad farmer's song. *HuL-2*

Three acres of land. *OpO*

"**My** father used to say." See Silence

"**My** father was a Frenchman." Mother Goose. *OpO*

My fathers came from Kentucky. Vachel Lindsay. *GrCc*

"**My** father's face is brown with sun." See Father

My father's watch. John Ciardi. *PlI*

My funny umbrella. Alice Wilkins. *BrL-k*

My garden. Thomas Edward Brown. *ThP*

A garden. *UnG*

My gift. See Carol ("In the bleak midwinter")

"**My** goodness, my goodness." See Christmas

"**My** grandmother sent me." Mother Goose. *OpO*

My grasshopper. Myra Cohn Livingston. *LiWa*

"**My** grasshopper died." See My grasshopper

"**My** grief on the sea." Unknown, tr. fr. the Irish by Douglas Hyde. *PaS*

"**My** hair is gray, but not with years." See The prisoner of Chillon

"**My** heart is like a singing bird." See A birthday

My heart leaps up. William Wordsworth. *BrBc—HaP—JoAc*

"**My** heart leaps up when I behold." *ArTp*

"**My** heart leaps up when I behold." See My heart leaps up

"**My** heart went out to Mr Blob the moment that we met." See Mr Blob

My heart's in the highlands. Robert Burns. *BrR-5—FeF—McW*

"**My** heart's in the highlands, my heart is not here." See My heart's in the highlands

My hobby horse. See "I had a little hobby horse"

"**My** home is a house." See The country child

My horse. Unknown. *TaD*

My horse, Jack. John Ciardi. *CiY*

"**My** horse, Jack, ran off to sea." See My horse, Jack

"**My** house has crickets." See Crickets and mice

My inside-self. Rachel Field. *FeF*

"**My** inside-self and my outside-self." See My inside-self

My keys. Dorothy Aldis. *AlHd*

My kite. Barbara and Beatrice Brown. *BrL-k*

"**My** kite is three feet broad, and six feet long." See The kite

"**My** kitten walks on velvet feet." See Night

"**My** lady carries love within her eyes." See Within her eyes

"**My** lady shan't lie between linen." See Lady's bedstraw

"**My** Lady Wind, my Lady Wind." Mother Goose. *DeMg*

My land. Thomas Osborne Davis. *BrR-5*

"**My** land is fair for any eyes to see." Jesse Stuart. *ArTp—FeF*

My last duchess. Robert Browning. *HaP*

My little birds. Unknown, tr. by Henrietta Siksek-Su'ad. *FeF*

"**My** little breath, under the willows by the water-side we used to sit." See A lover's lament

My little cow. Mother Goose. *OpO*

My little maid. Mother Goose. *OpO*

"**My** little old man and I fell out." Mother Goose. *DeMg—JoAc—OpO*

"**My** little snowman has a mouth." See Snowman

My little wife. Mother Goose. *OpO*

"**My** long two-pointed ladder's sticking through a tree." See After apple-picking

"**My** love." See Kokin Shū—Ono no yoshiki

"**My** love for you." Unknown. *MoY*

My love is dead. Thomas Chatterton. *HoW*

"**My** love, my love, thus spoke **my love to** me." See Thus spoke my love

"**My** love sent me a chicken without e'er a bone." See The lover's gifts

"**My** love within a forest walked alone." See Love in moonlight

"**My** lute, be as thou wast when thou didst grow." See To his lute

My luve's like a red, red rose. Robert Burns. *CoPs*

"O, my luve is like a red, red rose." *SmLg*

A red, red rose. *HaP*

"**My** maid Mary." Mother Goose. *DeMg—OpO*

"**My** mammy had a speckled hen." Unknown. *WoF*

My mammy's maid. Mother Goose. *OpO*

"**My** mill grinds pepper and spice." See Grinding

"**My** mind lets go a thousand things." See Memory

"**My** mind to me a kingdom is." Edward Dyer. *HaP*

"**My** mother and your mother." See Chop-a-nose

"**My** mother and your mother." See Icky bicky

"**My** mother bore me in the southern wild." See The little black boy

"**My** mother has the prettiest tricks." See Song for my mother: Her words

"**My** mother said." Mother Goose. *OpO*

"My mother said that I never should." *SmLg*

"**My** mother said that I never should." **See** "My mother said"

"My mother says I'm growing up." See Not that

"My mother sends our neighbors things." See Neighborly

"My mother whistled softly." See The little whistler

"My music-loving self this afternoon." See Sheldonian soliloquy

My name. Myra Cohn Livingston. *LiWa*

"My name, I said, is Peleg Doddleding." See A seaside romance

"My name is Alice, and my husband's name is Allen." See Alphabet routine

"My name is Bill." See Bill

My name is John Wellington Wells. See The sorcerer

"My name is most especially." See My name

"My name is Yon Yonson." See Endless story

My new rabbit. Elizabeth Gould. *HuL-1*

My new umbrella. M. M. Hutchinson. *HuL-1*

My nose. Dorothy Aldis. *AlA*

My November guest. Robert Frost. *FrR*

My old man. Unknown. *TaD*

"My old man number one." See My old man

My other name. Myra Cohn Livingston. *LiW*

"My pa held me up to the moo-cow-moo." See The moo-cow-moo

My papa's waltz. Theodore Roethke. *HaP*

My people. Carl Sandburg. *SaW*

"My people are gray." See My people

"My piggy bank broke, and now it's spent." See Shopping spree

"My plaid away, my plaid away." See The elfin-knight

My plan. Marchette Chute. *BrBc—ChA—FeF*

My playmate. John Greenleaf Whittier. *DeT*

"My plot of earth as yet is bare." See Peep-primrose

My policeman. Rose Fyleman. *ArTp—BrL-k*

My pony. Dorothy Aldis. *AlA*

"My poor old shoes are on the floor." See The sad shoes

"My pop keeps a lollipop shop." Unknown. *WiRm*

"My poplars are like ladies trim." See The poplars

My prairies. Hamlin Garland. *FeF*

"My pretty bird with plumage black." See Bronwen to her magpie

"My prime of youth is but a frost of cares." See Elegy

My puppy. Marchette Chute. *ChA*

"My robe is noiseless while I tread the earth." See The swan

"My rocking horse rocks and rocks." See Rocking horse

My sailor of seven. Gerald Brenan. *BrBc*

"My sailor of seven, your ship be a clipper." See My sailor of seven

"My saucer had a spoon and cup." See A long time ago

My secret. John Banister Tabb. *McW*

"My sense of sight is very keen." Oliver Herford
After Oliver. *CoH*

My shadow. Robert Louis Stevenson. *ArTp — BrL-k — FeF — HuL-1 — HuSv — JoAc—PeF*

My ship. Marchette Chute. *ChA*

"My ship has been a buccaneer." See My ship

"My shoes fall on the house-top that is so far beneath me." See Climb

My singing aunt. James Reeves. *ReBl*

"My son Augustus, in the street, one day." See Quiet fun

"My Sorrow, when she's here with me." See My November guest

"My soul, there is a country." See Peace

My star. Robert Browning. *FeF—NaE*

My streamer hat. Dorothy Aldis. *AlA*

"My sweetheart's a sailor." See Sailor

"My tail is not impressive." See Ode to the pig: His tail

My task. Robert Louis Stevenson. *ThP*

My teddy bear. Bette Olgin. *McAw*

"My thoughts are as a garden-plot, that knows." See Thy garden

"My tidings for you: the stag bells." See Summer is gone

My true love. Ivy O. Eastwick. *BrS*

"My two white rabbits." See Rabbits

"My typewriter, I gather from her lettered row on top." See Qwerty-ù-i-op

"My Uncle Ben he has a hen." Unknown. *WiRm*

"My Uncle Ben, who's been." See Kiph

"My Uncle James has sailed as far." See Uncle James

My valentine ("I have a little valentine") Mary Catherine Parsons. *ArTp—BrL-k—HuL-1*

My valentine ("I will make you brooches and toys for your delight") Robert Louis Stevenson. *BrS—FeF*
I will make you brooches. *HuL-2*
Romance. *CoPs*

My valentine ("Oh, who will be my valentine") Ivy O. Eastwick. *EaI*

My zipper suit. Marie Louise Allen. *AlP—ArTp—BrL-k*

"My zipper suit is bunny brown." See My zipper suit

Myfanwy among the leaves. Eleanor Farjeon. *FaCb*

Myself. Unknown. *ThP*

Mysterious biography. Carl Sandburg. *BrS*

The mysterious cat. Vachel Lindsay. *ArTp—CoI—FeF—HuSv—JoAc—PeF*

The mystery ("He came and took me by the hand") Ralph Hodgson. *DoP*

The mystery ("Next year I will go to school") Harry Behn. *BeW*

Nanny. See "The moon shines bright"

Napoleon. Walter De La Mare. *SmLg*

Napoleon Bonaparte I, Emperor of France (about)
Incident of the French camp. R. Browning. *UnG—UnMc*
Napoleon. W. De La Mare. *SmLg*

Narcissus fields. Eleanor Farjeon. *FaCb—FaN*

Narcissuses. See also Daffodils
Narcissus fields. E. Farjeon. *FaCb—FaN*

A narrative. Theodore Spencer. *McW*

"A narrow fellow in the grass." See The snake

Nash, Beau (about)
The Beau of Bath. E. Farjeon. *FaN*

Nash, Ogden
Adventures of Isabel. *CoH—NaM*
Arthur. *CoH*
The boy who laughed at Santa Claus. *CoSp—UnMc*
The camel. *LoL*
The carnival of animals. *PlU* (sel.)
Celery. *FeF*
The centipede. *FeF*
The duck. *NaM*
Edouard. *LoL*
The eel. *FeF—JoAc*
The fly. *FeF*
Funebrial reflections. *PlI*
The germ. *NaM*
The guppy. *JoAc*
The hunter. *NaE*
I will arise and go now. *McW*
An introduction to dogs. *NaM—UnG*
The jellyfish. *FeF*
The kitten. *FeF—NaM*
The lama. *CoH—FeF—LoL*
    "The one-l lama." *SmLg*
The octopus. *ArTp—CoH*
Old men. *NaE*
"The one-l lama." See The lama
One, two, buckle my shoe. *BrBc*
The panther. *FeF—LoL—NaM*
Piano tuner, untune me that tune. *PlU*
The purist. *CoH—NaM*
The rhinoceros. *CoH—UnG*
Song of the open road. *ThP*
The tale of Custard the dragon. *FeF—UnG*
The Wapiti. *NaM*

Nashe (or Nash), Thomas
"Adieu, farewell earth's bliss." See In plague time
In plague time. *SmLg*
    "Adieu, farewell earth's bliss." *HaP*
Spring. *DeT—HoW*

Nasturtiums
The big nasturtiums. R. B. Hale. *CoPm*

Nathan, Robert
Be not afraid. *BrR-5*
Dunkirk. *UnMc*
Watch, America. *McW*

A nation's strength. Ralph Waldo Emerson. *FeF*

The nativity chant. Walter Scott. *SmLg*

Natura in urbe. E. B. White. *McW*

Natural history. See "What are little boys made of, made of"

Nature. See also Country life; Wayfaring life
Altar smoke. R. Grayer. *UnG*
The birds and the telephone wires. C. P. Cranch. *BrR-5*
Bits of straw. J. Clare. *HoW*
A boy's song. J. Hogg. *DeT—FeF—HoW—McW—NaM*
A chant out of doors. M. Wilkinson. *JoAc*
Composed while under arrest. M. Y. Lermontov. *PaS*
Dark Danny. I. O. Eastwick. *ArTp—FeF—HuL-2*
Epitaph intended for Sir Isaac Newton. A. Pope. *PlI*
"Fain would I live in safest freedom." A. G. von Platen. *PaS*
"Farther in summer than the birds." E. Dickinson. *HaP*
Flower chorus. R. W. Emerson. *HuL-2*
"Go to the shine that's on a tree." R. Eberhart. *PlU*
"Hie away, hie away." From Waverley. W. Scott. *ArTp*
    Hie away. *NaM*
"I don't know why." M. C. Livingston. *LiW*
"I meant to do my work to-day." R. Le Gallienne. *ArTp—BrR-5—HuL-2—JoAc—UnG*
Immalee. C. G. Rossetti. *ReT*
The little tippler. E. Dickinson. *NaE*
Message from home. K. Raine. *PlI*
Natura in urbe. E. B. White. *McW*
Nature at three. B. Breeser. *BrBc*
A nature note. R. Frost. *FrY*
Nothing gold can stay. R. Frost. *FrR*
One, two, three. R. Christopher. *HuL-2*
Puzzles. J. Drinkwater. *McW*
The question in the cobweb. A. Reid. *McW*
Sewing. Unknown. *BrR-4*
The sweetness of nature. Unknown. *GrCc*
There was a boy. From The prelude. W. Wordsworth. *SmLg*
Thoughts of a little girl. M. Enriqueta. *FeF*
To Jane: The invitation. P. B. Shelley. *ReT*
    Away, away. *UnG*
To nature seekers. R. W. Chambers. *NaM*
Vacation. K. L. Bates. *BrR-6*
The voice of God. J. Stephens. *DoP*
William Jones. From The Spoon River anthology. E. L. Masters. *PlI*
The world is too much with us. W. Wordsworth. *ThP*

"Nature and nature's laws lay hid in night." See Epitaph intended for Sir Isaac Newton

Nature at three. Bettye Breeser. *BrBc*

A nature lesson. Carolyn Wells. *BrR-3*

"Nature needs five." See Hours of sleep

A nature note. Robert Frost. *FrY*

"Nature's first green is gold." See Nothing gold can stay

Nature's hired man. John Kendrick Bangs. *BrR-6*

The naughty boy. See "There was a naughty boy"

The naughty little robin. Phoebe Cary. *BrL-k*

Naughty soap song. Dorothy Aldis. *AlA— BrL-k*

A nautical ballad. See Davy and the goblin

A nautical extravagance. See A nautical extravaganza

A nautical extravaganza. Wallace Irwin. *CoSp*

A nautical extravaganza. *HuSv*

"Nauty Pauty Jack-a-Dandy." Mother Goose. *OpO*

Navaho prayer. Edward S. Yeomans. *HuSv*

The Navajo. See The Painted desert

Navajo Indians. See Indians of America— Navajo

Naval battles. See also Warships
The Armada. T. B. Macaulay. *SmLg*
Casabianca ("The boy stood on the burning deck") F. D. Hemans. *FeF—UnG*
Casabianca ("Sea, be kind to a young boy's bones") E. Farjeon. *FaCb—FaN*
The old navy. F. Marryat. *CoSp—DeT*
An old-time sea-fight. From Song of myself. W. Whitman. *UnMc*
The Revenge. A. Tennyson. *UnMc*
The Shannon and the Chesapeake. Unknown. *DeT*
"Some years of late, in eighty-eight." Unknown. *SmLg*

Neale, John Mason
"O'er the hill and o'er the vale." *EaW*

"Near a pure rivulet a dove came down and drank." See The dove and the ant

Near and far. Harry Behn. *BeW*

Near dusk. Joseph Auslander. *FeF*

"Near where I live there is a lake." See Fringed gentians

"Near Wookey hole in days gone by." See The three unlucky men

"Nearly any child will share." See Generosity

The need of being versed in country things. Robert Frost. *FrR—HaP*

A needle and thread. See "Old Mother Twitchett had (or has) but one eye"

Needles
"I need not your needles." Mother Goose. *OpO*
"Old Mother Twitchett had (or has) but one eye." Mother Goose. *ArTp—DeMg— LiL—OpO*
A needle and thread. *ReG*
"Needles and pins, needles and pins." Mother Goose. *DeMg*
Signs, seasons, and sense. *UnG*
"Needles and pins (triplets)." Unknown. *MoY*

Negro spirituals
"Joshua fit de battle of Jericho." Unknown. *UnMc*
Swing low, sweet chariot. Unknown. *FeF —SmLg*

Negro spirituals (about)
Negro spirituals. R. C. and S. V. Benét. *FeF*
O black and unknown bards. J. W. Johnson. *PlU*

Negro spirituals. Rosemary Carr and Stephen Vincent Benét. *FeF*

Negroes. See also Dialect—American— Negro; Negro spirituals; Slavery
Incident. C. Cullen. *JoAc*
The little black boy. W. Blake. *SmLg*
Mother to son. L. Hughes. *BrBc—HuSv —PeF*
Negro spirituals. R. C. and S. V. Benét. *FeF*
O black and unknown bards. J. W. Johnson. *PlU*

"A neighbor of mine in the village." See A girl's garden

Neighborly. Violet Alleyn Storey. *ArTp— HuL-1*

Neighbors
The child next door. R. Fyleman. *FeF*
Four neighbors. I. O. Eastwick. *EaI*
Mending wall. R. Frost. *FrR—FrY—HaP*
Neighborly. V. A. Storey. *ArTp—HuL-1*
A new friend. M. A. Anderson. *McAw*
The new little boy. H. Behn. *BeW*
The new neighbor. R. Fyleman. *ArTp*
Portrait by a neighbor. E. St V. Millay. *ArTp—FeF—HuL-2—NaM—PeF*

"Neither in halls, nor yet in bowers." See Song

"Neither snow, nor rain." See On their appointed rounds

"Neither spirit nor bird." Unknown, tr. fr. the Shoshone by Mary Austin. *PaS*

Nell the nibbler. Gelett Burgess. *BrR-6*

Nelson, Horatio (about)
The admiral's ghost. A. Noyes. *ArTp— CoPm—JoAc*
1805. R. Graves. *NaE—SmLg*

Nepenthe, sel. George Darley
The phoenix. *GrCc—HoW*
"O blest unfabled incense tree." *SmLg*

Neptune
In praise of Neptune. T. Campion. *HoW*
Neptune. E. Farjeon. *FaCb—FaN*

Neptune. Eleanor Farjeon. *FaCb—FaN*

Nesbit, Edith (Edith Nesbit Bland)
Baby seed song. *FeF*
Summer song. *CoPs*

Nesbit, Wilbur D.
"Who hath a book." *ArTp—BrS*

"Never a thrill—a greater thrill." See Night train

Never again would birds' song be the same. Robert Frost. *FrR*

"Never ask of money spent." See The hardship of accounting

"Never burn witchwood, my old granny said." See Witchwood

"Never forget this when the talk is clever." See The sacred order

"Never love unless you can." See Advice to a girl

"Never seek to tell thy love." See Love's secret

"Never shall a young man." See For Anne Gregory

"Never stroll away from camp." See Mind
you, now
"Never talk down to a glowworm." See
Glowworm
"Never talk to me of waltzing it." See
Waltzing it
Never two songs the same. Carl Sandburg.
SaW
New. Dorothy Aldis. AlA
The new and the old. Shiki, tr. fr. the
Japanese by Harold G. Henderson. PaS
The new baby calf. Edith H. Newlin. ArTp
—BrL-k
New chitons for old gods. David McCord.
PlU (sel.)
New clothes and old. Eleanor Farjeon.
FaCb—FaN
The new colossus. Emma Lazarus. FeF
Inscription on the Statue of Liberty.
BrL-8 (sel.)
New corn. T'ao Ch'ien, tr. fr. the Chinese
by Arthur Waley. PaS
A new courtly sonnet of the Lady Green-
sleeves. Unknown. SmLg
The new duckling. Alfred Noyes. FeF
New farm tractor. Carl Sandburg. FeF
A new friend. Marjorie Allen Anderson.
McAw
New Hampshire
New Hampshire. From Landscapes. T. S.
Eliot. HaP—ReT—SmLg
New Hampshire again. C. Sandburg.
SaW
New Hampshire. See Landscapes
New Hampshire again. Carl Sandburg.
SaW
The new house. Dorothy Aldis. AlHd
"The new house was empty. No curtains at
all." See The new house
The new little boy. Harry Behn. BeW
"A new little boy moved in next door." See
The new little boy
New Mexico
New Mexico. P. C. Boyden. ArTp
New Mexico. Polly Chase Boyden. ArTp
The new moon. William Cullen Bryant.
DeT
The new neighbor. Rose Fyleman. ArTp
The new pet. Dorothy Aldis. AlA
New Prince, new pomp. Robert Southwell.
ReT
Humble pomp. UnG
New shoes ("I have new shoes in the fall-
time") Alice Wilkins. ArTp—BrL-k
New shoes ("When I am walking down the
street") Marjorie Seymour Watts.
BrR-3
"New shoes, new shoes." See Choosing
shoes
New snow. Catharine Bryant Rowles. HaY
The new vestments. Edward Lear. CoH
New year
A burying. E. Farjeon. FaCb
The death of the old year. A. Tennyson.
CoPs (sel.)
Farewell to the old year. E. Farjeon. BrS
Happy new year ("Hang the new calen-
dar") M. E. Roberts. McAw

"Happy new year. Happy new year."
Unknown. CoPs
"Here we come a-caroling." Unknown.
ArTp—FeF
In trust. M. M. Dodge. BrS
January 1. M. Pomeroy. CoPs
"The moon upon her watch-tower." E.
Farjeon. FaCb
A new year ("Behold, a new white
world") D. S. Shorter. HaY
New year ("God be here, God be there")
Mother Goose. OpO
A new year ("Here's a clean year") M. C.
Davies. HaY
The new year ("Who comes dancing over
the snow") D. M. Mulock. HaY
A new year carol. Unknown. CoPs—DeT
—ReT
A new year idyl. E. Field. CoPs (sel.)
New year's day ("How many nights, oh,
how many nights") Unknown. JoAc
New year's day ("Last night, while we
were fast asleep") R. Field. ArTp
News, news. E. Farjeon. BrS
Old Father Annum. L. F. Jackson. BrS
Older grown. K. Greenaway. BrBc
Ring out, wild bells. From In memoriam.
A. Tennyson. ArTp—BrL-8—FeF—HoW
A round for the new year. E. Farjeon.
FaCb
The snowman's resolution. A. Fisher.
PeF
Song for December thirty-first. F. M.
Frost. HaY
Song of the very poor. Unknown. FaCb—
FaN
Up the hill, down the hill. E. Farjeon.
CoPs—FaCb—FaN
The wassail song. Unknown. CoPs—DeT
Welcome to the new year. E. Farjeon.
HaY
A new year ("Behold, a new white world")
Dora Sigerson Shorter. HaY
New year ("God be here, God be there")
Mother Goose. OpO
A new year ("Here's a clean year") Mary
Carolyn Davies. HaY
The new year ("Who comes dancing over
the snow") Dinah Maria Mulock. HaY
A new year carol. Unknown. CoPs—DeT—
ReT
A new year idyl. Eugene Field. CoPs (sel.)
New year's day ("How many nights, oh,
how many nights") Unknown, tr. fr. the
Japanese by Rose Fyleman. JoAc
New year's day ("Last night, while we were
fast asleep") Rachel Field. ArTp
New York (City)
"East side, West side, all around the
town." From The sidewalks of New
York. C. V. Lawlor and J. W. Blake.
WoF
History of New York. M. Chute. ChA
Manhattan lullaby. R. Field. BrBc
Metropolitan nightmare. S. V. Benét. PlI
Rhyme of rain. J. Holmes. McW
School days in New Amsterdam. A.
Guiterman. FeF
New York, December, 1931. Babette
Deutsch. PlI

Nocturne in a deserted brickyard. C. Sandburg. *SaW*

Questions at night. L. Untermeyer. *FeF—UnG*

Rain in the night. A. J. Burr. *ArTp—BrL-k*

Silver. W. De La Mare. *ArTp—BrS—CoPm — FeF — HuL-2 — HuSv — JoAc—McW—UnG*

Sometimes. R. Fyleman. *BrS*

Song for midsummer night. E. J. Coatsworth. *HaY*

Song to night. E. J. Coatsworth. *McW*

Spring night in a village. E. Farjeon. *FaCb*

"The star that bids the shepherd fold." From Comus. J. Milton. *SmLg*

The starlight night. G. M. Hopkins. *ReT*

Summer night. Shiki. *PaS*

Tiptoe Night. J. Drinkwater. *BrS*

To night. P. B. Shelley. *HoW*

The two spirits. P. B. Shelley. *HoW*

"Watchman, what of the night." A. C. Swinburne. *HoW*

Window. C. Sandburg. *SaW*

Windy nights. R. L. Stevenson. *ArTp—BrR-4—BrS—DeT—GrCc—HuL-1*

Winter night. M. F. Butts. *ArTp*

"The night." Myra Cohn Livingston. *LiW*

Night ("The moon is gone") Sappho, tr. fr. the Greek by J. M. Edmonds. *PaS*

Night ("My kitten walks on velvet feet") Lois Weakley McKay. *BrS*

Night ("Night gathers itself into a ball of dark yarn") See The Windy City

Night ("An odorous shade lingers the fair day's ghost") Henri de Regnier, tr. fr. the French by Seumas O'Sullivan. *PaS*

Night ("Stars over snow") Sara Teasdale. *ArTp—DoP—FeF—JoAc—PeF—ThP*
It is not far. *HuSv*

Night ("The sun descending in the west") William Blake. *DoP—FeF—HoW—ReG—UnG*

Night and morning. Dorothy Aldis. *AlA—CoPs—HaY*

Night enchantment. Eleanor Muth. *BrS*

"Night from a railroad car window." See Window

"Night gathers itself into a ball of dark yarn." See The Windy City—Night

"The night has a thousand eyes." Francis William Bourdillon. *ThP*

Night heron. Frances M. Frost. *FrLn*

"Night is come." See Finis

"Night is something watching." See Song to night

Night mail. W. H. Auden. *HaP*

Night of wind. Frances M. Frost. *ArTp—FeF*

Night-piece. Eleanor Farjeon. *FaCb*

Night plane. Frances M. Frost. *ArTp—FeF*

Night song. Myra Cohn Livingston. *LiW*

Night song at Amalfi. Sara Teasdale. *ThP*

"The night the green moth came for me." See Green moth

Night thought. E. V. Rieu. *RiF*

Night thought of a tortoise suffering from insomnia on a lawn. E. V. Rieu. *RiF*

Night too has numbers. See The people, yes

Night train. Katherine Edelman. *BrR-6*

"The night was coming very fast." See The hens

Night was creeping. See Check

"The night was creeping on the ground." See Check

"The night was thick and hazy." See Davy and the goblin—Robinson Crusoe's story

"The night will never stay." Eleanor Farjeon. *BrR-6—BrS—FeF—HuL-2—HuSv—JoAc—PeF*

The night wind ("Have you ever heard the wind go Yooooo") Eugene Field. *BrR-4—FeF*

The night-wind ("In summer's mellow midnight") Emily Brontë. *HaP*

A night with a wolf. Bayard Taylor. *UnG*

Nightfall. Juan Ramón Jiménez, tr. fr. the Spanish by Eloise Roach. *PaS*

"Nightfall. The coolness of my watered garden." See Nightfall

Nightingale, Madeleine
  The caravan. *HuL-1*
  The scissor-man. *ArTp*
  Underneath the clothes. *HuL-1*

The nightingale. Samuel Taylor Coleridge. *DeT*

The nightingale and the glowworm. William Cowper. *UnG*

"A nightingale that all day long." See The nightingale and the glowworm

Nightingales
  Nakatsukasa. From Shui Shū. Unknown. *PaS*
  The nightingale. S. T. Coleridge. *DeT*
  The nightingale and the glowworm. W. Cowper. *UnG*
  Plain philomel. E. Farjeon. *FaCb—FaN*
  The quest. E. Farjeon. *FaCb*
  Skylark and nightingale. C. G. Rossetti. *HuL-2*
    Heaven is heaven. *HaY*
  A song from Cyprus. H. D. *GrCc*

Nightmare abbey, sel. Thomas Love Peacock
  Seamen three. *HoW*

Nightmare number three. Stephen Vincent Benét. *UnMc*

Nightsong. Carl Sandburg. *SaW*

Nijinsky, Vaslav (about)
  For Nijinsky's tomb. F. Cornford. *PlU*
  Homage to Vaslav Nijinsky. J. Kirkup. *PlU*

"Nijinsky's ashes here in peace repose." See For Nijinsky's tomb

The nimp. James Reeves. *ReP*

"Nine-o'clock bell." See School-bell

Ninth moon. Li Ho, tr. fr. the Chinese by Ho Chih-yuan. *PaS*

Nirvana. Unknown. *CoH*

No ("He did not want to do it") Dorothy Aldis. *AlA*

No ("No sun—no moon") Thomas Hood. *CoH—UnG*

"No Chuck, you were wrong." See To Chuck—concerning a rendezvous in Siam

No drip of rain. Ivy O. Eastwick. *McAw*

"No early buds of laughing spring." See Valentine

No enemies. Charles Mackay. *UnG*

"No house of stone." See The elements

"No human singing can." See Music and words

No joy without love. Mimnermus, tr. fr. the Greek by G. Lowes Dickinson. *PaS*

"No, little brown bird, go away." See Prisoned

"No man is an island entire of itself." See For whom the bell tolls

"No man is born into the world whose work." See Work

"No matter what we are and who." See Routine

"No one can tell me." See Wind on the hill

No one heard him call. Dorothy Aldis. *AlA*

"No quarrel ever stirred." See Of quarrels

No second Troy. William Butler Yeats. *HaP*

No single thing abides. See De rerum natura

"No single thing abides; but all things flow." See De rerum natura—No single thing abides

"No sky at all." See Loneliness

"No speed of wind or water rushing by." See The master speed

"No stir in the air, no stir in the sea." See The Inchcape rock

"No sun—no moon." See No

No swan so fine. Marianne Moore. *GrCc*

"No, those days are gone away." See Robin Hood

"No, 'twasn't here dat tree firs' grew." See The woman's tongue tree

"No water so still as the." See No swan so fine

Noah
    The dog's cold nose. A. Guiterman. *BrL-7—CoSp*
    The legends of evil. R. Kipling. *NaM*
    Noah ("Noah was an admiral") J. Reeves. *ReR*
    Noah ("Well, old man Noah built the ark") Unknown. *TaD*
    "Noah an' Jonah an' Cap'n John Smith." D. Marquis. *SmLg*
    Noah's ark. D. Aldis. *AlHd*

Noah ("Noah was an admiral") James Reeves. *ReR*

Noah ("Well, old man Noah built the ark") Unknown. *TaD*

"Noah an' Jonah an' Cap'n John Smith." Don Marquis. *SmLg*

"Noah was an admiral." See Noah

Noah's ark. Dorothy Aldis. *AlHd*

"Noble is he who falls in front of battle." See How can man die better

The noble nature. See A Pindaric ode: To the immortal memory and friendship of that noble pair, Sir Lucius Cary and Sir Henry Morrison

A nobody. See "I'm nobody. Who are you"

"Nobody knows." Ivy O. Eastwick. *EaI*

La noche triste. Robert Frost. *FrR*

Nocturne. Joseph von Eichendorff, tr. fr. the German by Herman Salinger. *PaS*

Nocturne in a deserted brickyard. Carl Sandburg. *SaW*

Nod. Walter De La Mare. *JoAc—ReT—UnG*

Noël, Thomas
    Old winter. *CoPs*

Noise. See Sounds

Noise. Jessie Pope. *HuL-2*

The noise of waters. See Chamber music

"A noiseless patient spider." Walt Whitman. *HaP—NaE*
    The spider. *HoW*

"The noisiest bird that ever grew." See The bugle-billed bazoo

Non amo te. See "I do not like thee, Doctor Fell"

The nonny. James Reeves. *ReP*

"The nonny-bird I love particularly." See The nonny

Nonsense. See also Limericks; Mother Goose; also entries under Carroll, Lewis; Lear, Edward; Richards, Laura E.
    Adventures of Isabel. O. Nash. *CoH—NaM*
    Alas, alack. W. De La Mare. *ArTp—BrL-k—FeF—HuL-1—NaE*
    "Algy met a bear." Unknown. *FeF*
        Algy. *NaM*
    The amperzand. J. Reeves. *ReP*
    "Anyone lived in a pretty how town." E. E. Cummings. *HaP—NaE*
    "As I was picking a bobble-bud." J. Ciardi. *CiM*
    "Back in the year of 'fifty-nine." Unknown. *WoF*
    Ballad. C. S. Calverley. *HoW*
    The bisk. J. Reeves. *ReP*
    The blether. J. Reeves. *ReP*
    "A bullfrog sat on a downy nest." Unknown. *WiRm*
    The bumblebeaver. From Mixed beasts. K. Cox. *ArTp*
    "By the sewer I lived." Unknown. *MoY*
    The catipoce. J. Reeves. *ReP*
    The chickamungus. J. Reeves. *ReP—UnG*
    The concert. J. S. Newman. *CoH*
    A cool drink on a hot day. J. Ciardi. *CiY*
    The cow slips away. B. King. *CoH*
    The doze. J. Reeves. *ReP—UnG*
    Eeka, neeka. W. De La Mare. *McW*
    The emperor's rhyme. A. A. Milne. *MiWc*
    The floor and the ceiling. W. J. Smith. *CoH*
    The giraffe. H. M. Boumphrey. *HuL-2*
    "Grandma has a habit." Unknown. *MoY*
    The great panjandrum himself. S. Foote. *JoAc—LoL—NaM*
        The great panjandrum. *CoH—SmLg*

The grey goose. Unknown. *McW*

The highlander's song. C. E. Carryl. *CoH*

The hippocrump. J. Reeves. *ReP*

The Hottentot tot. N. Levy. *HuL-2*
  Midsummer fantasy. *CoPs*

How Woodrow got his dinner. J. Ciardi. *CiR*

"I asked my mother for fifteen cents." Unknown. *ArTp*
  American Father Gander. *UnG*
  I asked my mother. *NaM*
  "I asked my mother for fifty cents." *JoAc*

"I boiled hot water in an urn." Unknown, after Nicarchus. *JoAc*

"I dreamed a dream next Tuesday night." Unknown
  Rhymed chuckles. *UnG*

"I know something I won't tell." Unknown. *WiRm*

"I met a man that lived in a house." J. Ciardi. *CiI*

"I took a bow and arrow." J. Ciardi. *CiR* —*NaE*

I will arise and go now. O. Nash. *McW*

"I wish that my room had a floor." G. Burgess. *CoH—LoL*
  Limericks since Lear. *UnG*

"Ice cream city." Unknown. *MoY*

"If a pig wore a wig." C. G. Rossetti. *JoAc*

The ingenious little old man. J. Bennett. *FeF*

Japanesque. O. Herford. *CoH*

The jellyfish. O. Nash. *FeF*

Jerry Mulligan. J. Ciardi. *CiM*

"Joe, Joe, broke his toe." Unknown. *WoF*

"Johnnie Crack and Flossie Snail." From Under milk wood. D. Thomas. *FeF*
  From Under milk wood. *CoH*

Jonathan. Unknown. *ArTp—JoAc*

Jonathan Bing. B. C. Brown. *ArTp—CoH* —*FeF—HuL-2—LoL—PeF*

Jonathan Bing's tea. B. C. Brown. *McW*

The journey. J. Ciardi. *CiY*

The kangarooster. From Mixed beasts. K. Cox. *ArTp*

The land of Ho-Ho-Hum. W. J. Smith. *SmL*

Little Billee. W. M. Thackeray. *DeT— SmLg*

"Little Hermogenes is so small." Lucilius. *JoAc*

The little man who wasn't there. H. Mearns. *CoH—FeF*

"Look at Marcus and take warning." Lucilius. *JoAc*

The man that had little to say. J. Ciardi. *CiI*

The man who sang the sillies. J. Ciardi. *CiM*

Margaret Nash got wet but I don't know how. J. Ciardi. *CiM*

Mister Beers. H. Lofting. *FeF*

Mr Kartoffel. J. Reeves. *ReW*

Mr Punchinello. Unknown. *DeT—JoAc*

Mr Tom Narrow. J. Reeves. *ReW*

Mrs Caribou. W. J. Smith. *CoPm—SmL*

Mistress Mary. W. J. Smith. *SmL*

The modern Hiawatha. G. A. Strong. *CoH—FeF—NaM*

Molly Mock-Turtle. W. J. Smith. *SmL*

A nature lesson. C. Wells. *BrR-3*

A nautical ballad. From Davy and the goblin. C. E. Carryl. *FeF—HuSv*
  The walloping window-blind. *CoH— LoL—NaM—UnG*

The nimp. J. Reeves. *ReP*

The nonny. J. Reeves. *ReP*

"Now I lay me down to sleep (with a)." Unknown. *MoY*

"Oh, I've paddled on the ocean." Unknown. *MoY*

The octopussycat. From Mixed beasts. K. Cox. *ArTp—FeF*

One bright morning. Unknown. *NaE*

The osc. J. Reeves. *ReP*

"The ostrich is a silly bird." M. E. W. Freeman. *ArTp — CoH — FeF — LoL — McW*

Over and under. W. J. Smith. *SmL*

"An owl and an eel and a frying pan." Unknown. *WiRm*

The panther. O. Nash. *FeF—LoL—NaM*

"A peanut sat on a railroad track." Unknown. *MoY*

Pick me up. W. J. Smith. *SmL*

The pig's tail. N. Ault. *HuL-2*

The pilgrim. W. B. Yeats. *HaP*

The post captain. C. E. Carryl. *CoH*

The purple cow. G. Burgess. *ArTp—CoH* —*FeF*
  "I never saw a purple cow." *LoL*

Rhyme. D. McCord. *McFf*

Rhyme for a simpleton. Unknown. *CoH*

"Roses are red (violets are blue, I can)." Unknown. *MoY*

"Roses are red (violets are blue, so's your)." Unknown. *MoY*

The saginsack. J. Ciardi. *CiR*

"Said a chamber-maid to a sleeping guest." Unknown. *MoY*

Say yes to the music, or else. J. Ciardi. *CiM*

A sea song. J. Ciardi. *CiY*

The snitterjipe. J. Reeves. *ReP*

The snyke. J. Reeves. *ReP*

The song of the dumb waiter. J. Reeves. *ReW*

Stein song. Unknown. *ThP*

The strange man. Unknown. *FeF*

Sylvester. J. Ciardi. *CiM*

The tale of Custard the dragon. O. Nash. *FeF—UnG*

Tea party. H. Behn. *BeW*

That'll be all right you'll find. L. De G. Sieveking. *CoH*

"There is an inn, a merry old inn." From The hobbit. J. R. R. Tolkien. *LoL*

There was a hunter from Littletown. J. Ciardi. *CiM*

"There was an old woman sat spinning." Unknown
  American Father Gander. *UnG*

The three jolly hunters. J. W. Riley. *McW*

Tom Twist. W. A. Butler. *CoH*

Topsyturvey-world. W. B. Rands. *ReG*

Nonsense—*Continued*
  A tragic story. A. von Chamisso. *BrL-7—CoH—DeT—FeF—NaM—UnG*
  "Two little boys late one night." Unknown. *MoY*
  Uriconium. J. Reeves. *ReBl*
  The Wapiti. O. Nash. *NaM*
  What you will learn about the brobinyak. J. Ciardi. *CiR—NaE*
  When candy was chocolate. W. J. Smith. *SmL*
  "Yesterday upon the stair." Unknown. *WiRm*
  Young Sammy Watkins. Unknown. *CoH*
  Zachary Zed. J. Reeves. *ReR*
Nonsense alphabet. See "A was once an apple-pie"
Noonday Sun. Kathryn and Byron Jackson. *ArTp—FeF—HuL-2*
Norman William. Eleanor Farjeon. *FaCb*
Norsemen
  The skeleton in armor. H. W. Longfellow. *UnG—UnMc*
North, Christopher (about)
  To Christopher North. A. Tennyson. *NaE*
North. Frances M. Frost. *FrLn*
"A north-country maid up to London had stray'd." See The oak and the ash
"North, south, east, and west." See Compass song
The north wind. See "The north wind doth blow"
"The north wind doth blow." Mother Goose. *DeMg — HuL-1 — HuSv — JoAc—LiL*
  The north wind. *OpO*
"The north wind is a beggar." See Winds a-blowing
"North winds send hail, south winds bring rain." See The winds
Norway. See also Norsemen
  Tradja of Norway. Unknown. *JoAc*
"Nose, nose (jolly red nose)." See Prevarication
"Nose, nose, jolly red nose." Francis Beaumont and John Fletcher. *SmLg*
Nosegay. See "Violets, daffodils"
A nosegay ("Bring hether the pincke and purple cullambine") See The shepherd's calendar
Noses
  The dog's cold nose. A. Guiterman. *BrL-7—CoSp*
  The dong with a luminous nose. E. Lear. *CoPm—HoW*
  My nose. D. Aldis. *AlA*
  "Nose, nose, jolly red nose." F. Beaumont and J. Fletcher. *SmLg*
  "Peter White will ne'er go right." Mother Goose. *DeMg*
    Peter White. *OpO*
  Prevarication. Mother Goose. *OpO*
  "There is a young lady, whose nose." E. Lear
    Limericks. *JoAc*
  "There was a young lady whose nose." E. Lear. *FeF*
    Limericks. *JoAc*

"There was an old man on whose nose." E. Lear
    Limericks. *JoAc*
"Not a cabin in the glen shuts its door tonight." See Christmas eve in Ireland
"Not a drum was heard, not a funeral note." See Burial of Sir John Moore
Not all there. Robert Frost. *FrR*
Not any more. Dorothy Aldis. *AlA*
"Not born to the forest are we." See Twelfth night—Song of the camels
"Not every man has gentians in his house." See Bavarian gentians
"Not gold, but only man can make." See A nation's strength
"Not in all of time, I think." See What do you think his daddy did
"Not last night, but the night before." Unknown. *WiRm*
"Not like the brazen giant of Greek fame." See The new colossus
"Not like the rose shall our friendship wither." Unknown. *MoY*
"Not marble, nor the gilded monuments." See Sonnets
Not of school age. Robert Frost. *FrY*
Not so impossible. See "I saw a peacock with a fiery tail"
Not that. Dorothy Aldis. *AlA*
"Not that the pines were darker there." See The long voyage
"Not the bells of churches, housed in their towers." See Song of the engine bells
Not to die. Simonides, tr. fr. the Greek by John Hermann Merivale. *PaS*
"Not what you get, but what you give." See Of giving
Nothing-at-all. See "There was an old woman called Nothing-at-all"
Nothing gold can stay. Robert Frost. *FrR*
"Nothing in the sky is high." See Asleep and awake
"Nothing is real. The world has lost its edges." See Scarcely spring
"Nothing to do but work." See The pessimist
Notice. David McCord. *McFf*
"Nought have I to bring." See November
Novel experience. Carolyn Wells. *BrR-3*
November
  Enter November. E. Farjeon. *FaCb—FaN*
  Hearth song. R. U. Johnson. *HaY*
  My November guest. R. Frost. *FrR*
  No. T. Hood. *CoH—UnG*
  November ("Bracken on the hillside") A. Fisher. *BrS*
  November ("Nought have I to bring") C. G. Rossetti. *HaY*
  November ("November comes") E. J. Coatsworth. *HaY*
  November ("The shepherds almost wonder where they dwell") J. Clare. *UnG*
  November garden. L. Driscoll. *HaY*
  November morning. E. Stein. *HaY*
  November night. A. Crapsey. *FeF*
  November rain. M. E. Uschold. *HaY*

"November wears a Paisley shawl." H. Morris. *HaY*

November's song. E. Farjeon. *FaCb—FaN*

Things to remember. J. Reeves. *ReBl*

Weather vanes. F. M. Frost. *BrS*

November ("Bracken on the hillside") Aileen Fisher. *BrS*

November ("Nought have I to bring") Christina Georgina Rossetti. *HaY*

November ("November comes") Elizabeth Jane Coatsworth. *HaY*

November ("The shepherds almost wonder where they dwell") John Clare. *UnG*

"November comes." See November

November garden. Louise Driscoll. *HaY*

November morning. Evaleen Stein. *HaY*

November night. Adelaide Crapsey. *FeF*

November rain. Maud E. Uschold. *HaY*

"November should be cold and grey." See Weather vanes

"November wears a Paisley shawl." Hilda Morris. *HaY*

November's song. Eleanor Farjeon. *FaCb —FaN*

"Now and again I like to see." See The complete hen

"Now as I was young and easy under the apple boughs." See Fern hill

"Now birds that sleep in brittle trees." See Woods' litany

"Now chant birds in every bush." See Hark

"Now come the rosy dogwoods." See In October

"Now condescend, Almighty King." See An evening hymn for a little family

"Now every breath of air." See The trees and the wind

Now every child. Eleanor Farjeon. *BrBc*

"Now every child that dwells on earth." See Now every child

"Now everything is ready, child, and ready I'm for you." See Song before supper

"Now fades the last long streak of snow." See Spring

"Now I am six and going on seven." See Growing up

"Now I can catch and throw a ball." See Big

"Now I go down here and bring up a moon." See Auctioneer

Now I lay me. See "Now I lay me down to sleep (I pray)"

"Now I lay me down to sleep (I pray)." Mother Goose. *OpO*

Now I lay me. *HuL-1*

"Now I lay me down to sleep (with a)." Unknown. *MoY*

"Now independent, beautiful, and proud." See Night-piece

"Now is come midsummer night." See Song for midsummer night

"Now is the time when cheery crickets." See Autumn

"Now jump from *forget*, and where should you land." See Forget

"Now lighted windows climb the dark." See Manhattan lullaby

"Now, more near ourselves than we." E. E. Cummings. *GrCc*

"Now not a window small or big." See For Christmas

"Now on the Arun mists rise up like sleep." See A song for September

"Now, pray, where are you going, child? said Meet-on-the-Road." See Meet-on-the-Road

"Now ripened berries fill." See July

"Now say good night." David McCord. *McT*

"Now, says Time." Eleanor Farjeon. *FaCb —FaN*

"Now so high." See The swing

"Now that the hearth is crowned with smiling fire." See Another birthday

Now that the winter's gone. See The spring ("Now that the winter's gone, the earth hath lost")

"Now that the winter's gone, the earth hath lost." See The spring

"Now the bright crocus flames, and now." See In the spring

"Now the bright morning star, day's harbinger." See May morning

"Now the day is over." Sabine Baring-Gould. *DeT*

"Now the drowsy sun shine." See Evening

"Now the hungry lion roars." See A midsummer-night's dream—The lion of winter

"Now the joys of the road are chiefly these." See The joys of the road

"Now the last apple." See After harvest

"Now the little rivers go." See Winter streams

"Now the noisy winds are still." Mary Mapes Dodge. *HaY*

"Now the small birds come to feast." See Winter feast

"Now the sweet-voiced nightingale." See The beginning of day

"Now the widow McGee, and Larrie O'Dee." See Larrie O'Dee

"Now the wild bees that hive in the rocks." See The brown bear

"Now there is none of the living who can remember." See Epitaph for a Concord boy

"Now think of words. Take sky." See Take sky

"Now time throws off his cloak again." See The return of spring

"Now touch the air softly." See A pavane for the nursery

"Now what do you think." See Jacky Jingle

"Now what shall I send to the earth to-day." See Sunbeams

"Now when I could not find the road." See The shepherd's hut

"Now you get a line and I'll get a pole, Honey." See The crawdad hole

"Now you're married you must obey." Unknown

Signs, seasons, and sense. *UnG*

Nowel. Walter De La Mare. *EaW*

"Now's the time for mirth and play." See A hymn for Saturday

Noyes, Alfred
The admiral's ghost. *ArTp—CoPm—JoAc*
The barrel-organ, sel.
    Go down to Kew in lilac time. *HuL-2*
Betsy Jane's sixth birthday. *BrBc—BrS*
Daddy fell into the pond. *CoH—FeF*
Forty singing seamen. *CoSp*
Go down to Kew in lilac time. See The barrel-organ
The highwayman. *BrL-8* (sel.)*—FeF—UnG —UnMc*
The new duckling. *FeF*
A song of Sherwood. *ArTp—FeF—JoAc*
Song of the wooden-legged fiddler. *HuL-2*
Numbers and faces. W. H. Auden. *PlI* (sel.)

Nunez, Airas
Bailada. *PaS*

Nuns
The nuns. D. Aldis. *AlA*
The nuns. Dorothy Aldis. *AlA*

Nurse. See Four ruthless rhymes

Nursery chairs. A. A. Milne. *MiWc*

Nursery clock. Myra Cohn Livingston. *LiWa*

Nursery play
"Apple-pie, apple-pie." Mother Goose. *OpO*
"Bo peeper." Mother Goose. *DeT—OpO*
"Bring daddy home." Mother Goose. *OpO*
"Brow bender." Mother Goose. *DeMg*
"Brow, brow, brenty." Mother Goose. *OpO*
"Brow, brow, brinkie." Mother Goose. *DeMg*
"Can you keep a secret." Mother Goose. *LiL*
"Catch him, crow. Carry him, kite." Mother Goose. *OpO*
"Chick, my naggie." Mother Goose. *OpO*
Chop-a-nose. Mother Goose. *OpO*
"Clap hands, clap hands (till father)." Mother Goose. *OpO*
"Clap hands, Daddy comes." Mother Goose. *OpO*
"Clap hands, Daddy's coming." Mother Goose. *OpO*
"Come dance a jig." Mother Goose. *OpO*
"Come up, my horse, to Budleigh fair." Mother Goose. *OpO*
"Cripple Dick upon a stick." Mother Goose. *OpO*
"Cuckoo, cherry tree." Mother Goose. *DeMg—OpO*
"Dance a baby diddy." Mother Goose. *OpO*
"Dance, little baby, dance up high." Mother Goose. *DeMg—OpO*
"Dance to your daddy." Mother Goose. *DeMg—JoAc—LiL—OpO*
    "Dance to your daddie." *ArTp*
"Deedle, deedle, dumpling, my son John." Mother Goose. *DeMg*
    Deedle, deedle, dumpling. *HuL-1*
"The doggies went to the mill." Mother Goose. *OpO*
"Donkey, donkey, do not bray." Mother Goose. *OpO*
"Eye winker." Mother Goose. *DeMg—OpO*

"A farmer went trotting upon his gray mare." Mother Goose. *ArTp—DeMg— JoAc*
"A farmer went riding." *BrL-k—HuSv*
"A farmer went trotting." *HuL-1—LiL —NaE*
    The mischievous raven. *OpO*
Father Greybeard. Mother Goose. *OpO*
The five toes. Unknown. *JoAc*
"Fly away Peter." Mother Goose. *LiL*
"Follow my Bangalorey man." Mother Goose. *HuL-1—ReG*
    My Bangalorey man. *OpO*
Foot play. Mother Goose. *OpO*
"From here to there." Mother Goose. *OpO*
"From Wibbleton to Wobbleton is fifteen miles." Mother Goose. *OpO*
"Gee up, Neddy, to the fair." Mother Goose. *OpO*
"Good morning, Father Francis." Mother Goose. *OpO*
"Great A, little a (bouncing B)." Mother Goose. *DeMg—JoAc—LiL—OpO*
"Great A, little a (this is pancake day)." Mother Goose. *DeMg*
"Head bumper." Mother Goose. *OpO*
"Here comes my lady with her little baby." Mother Goose. *OpO*
"Here sits the Lord Mayor." Mother Goose. *DeMg—LiL—OpO*
    Here sits. *DeT*
"Here's a ball for baby." Mother Goose. *LiL*
"Hey diddle diddle (and hey)." Mother Goose. *OpO*
"Hey, my kitten, my kitten." Mother Goose. *DeMg—OpO*
"Hie to the market, Jenny come trot." Mother Goose. *OpO*
A hippity, hippity hop. Unknown. *HuL-1*
"Hob, shoe, hob; hob, shoe, hob." Mother Goose. *OpO*
"How many days has my baby to play." Mother Goose. *ArTp—OpO*
"Hush, my baby, do not cry." Mother Goose. *OpO*
"If you are a gentleman." Mother Goose. *OpO*
"Is John Smith within." Mother Goose. *DeMg—OpO*
"John Smith, fellow fine." Mother Goose. *OpO*
"Knock at the doorie." Mother Goose. *OpO*
"Knock on the door." Unknown. *WoF*
"Leg over leg." Mother Goose. *DeMg— LiL—OpO*
"The man in the mune." Mother Goose. *OpO*
"Master I have, and I am his man." Mother Goose. *ArTp*
    Master and man. *OpO*
"My father was a Frenchman." Mother Goose. *OpO*
"Old farmer Giles." Mother Goose. *OpO*
"An old maid, an old maid." Mother Goose. *OpO*

"Pat-a-cake, pat-a-cake, baker's man." Mother Goose. *DeMg—HuSv—JoAc—LiL—OpO*
  Pat-a-cake. *BrL-k*
A pavane for the nursery. W. J. Smith. *CoPs*
"Pease porridge hot." Mother Goose. *ArTp—BrL-k—DeMg—JoAc—LiL—OpO*
  "Pease pudding hot." *HuL-1*
"Richard Dick upon a stick." Mother Goose. *OpO*
"Ride a cock-horse to Banbury cross (to see a)." Mother Goose. *DeMg—HuSv—JoAc—LiL—OpO*
  "Ride a cock horse." *ArTp—BrL-k—HuL-1—OpO*
"Ride a cock-horse (to Banbury cross to see what)." Mother Goose. *OpO*
"Ride away, ride away." Mother Goose. *ArTp—OpO*
"Rigadoon, rigadoon, now let him fly." Mother Goose. *OpO*
"Ring the bell." Mother Goose. *DeMg—OpO*
"Robert Barnes, fellow fine." Mother Goose. *DeMg—OpO*
  Robert Barnes. *HuL-1*
"A robin and a robin's son." Mother Goose. *OpO*
"Round about, round about (catch a wee mouse)." Mother Goose. *OpO*
"Round about, round about, here sits the hare." Mother Goose. *OpO*
"Round about there." Mother Goose. *OpO*
"Round and round the cornfield." Mother Goose. *LiL*
"Round and round the garden." Mother Goose. *OpO*
"See-saw, down in my lap." Mother Goose. *OpO*
"Shoe a little horse." Mother Goose. *DeMg—LiL—OpO*
"Shoe the colt, shoe the colt." Mother Goose. *OpO*
"Tae tidy." Mother Goose. *OpO*
"This is the way the ladies ride." Mother Goose. *ArTp—DeMg—LiL—OpO*
"This is Willy Walker, and that's Tam Sim." Mother Goose. *OpO*
"Tickly, tickly, on your knee." Mother Goose. *OpO*
"To market, to market, to buy a fat pig." Mother Goose. *ArTp—DeMg—HuSv—JoAc—LiL*
  To market. *HuL-1*
  "To market, to market." *OpO*
"To market, to market, to buy a plum bun." Mother Goose. *DeMg*
  "To market, to market." *OpO*
"Toe, trip and go." Mother Goose. *OpO*
"Trit trot to market to buy a penny doll." Mother Goose. *OpO*
"A trot, and a canter, a gallop, and over." Mother Goose. *OpO*
"Two little dicky birds." Mother Goose. *LiL—OpO*
"Upon a cock-horse to market I'll trot." Mother Goose. *OpO*
"Walk down the path." Mother Goose. *LiL*

"Warm hands, warm." Mother Goose. *LiL*
  Warm hands. *OpO*
"Who's that ringing at my doorbell." Unknown. *SmLg*
  Who's that ringing. *HuL-1*
Nursery rhymes. See Mother Goose
A nursery song for Shepherdswell in Kent. Eleanor Farjeon. *FaN*
Nurses and nursing
  Forgiven. A. A. Milne. *MiWc—PeF*
  Nurse. From Four ruthless rhymes. H. Graham. *UnMc*
    Tragedy. *CoH*
  Nurse's song. W. Blake. *DeT—HuL-2—JoAc—ReT—UnG*
    Play time. *FeF*
  The terrible infant. F. Locker-Lampson. *CoH*
Nurse's song ("Sleep, baby, sleep") Unknown, tr. fr. the German. *ReT*
Nurse's song ("When the voices of children are heard on the green") William Blake. *DeT—HuL-2—JoAc—ReT—UnG*
  Play time. *FeF*
Nursing. See Nurses and nursing
The nut tree. See "I had a little nut tree"
Nutmeg trees
  "The king of China's daughter." E. Sitwell. *JoAc*
Nuts. Unknown. *DeT*
Nuts an' may. See "Here we come gathering nuts in May"
Nuts and nutting. See also names of nuts, as Walnuts
  "Here we come gathering nuts in May." Mother Goose. *LiL*
    Nuts an' may. *NaE*
  Nuts. Unknown. *DeT*
The **nymph** and her fawn. Andrew Marvell. *SmLg*
"**Nymph**, nymph, what are your beads." See Overheard on a saltmarsh
Nymphidia: The court of fairy, sel. Michael Drayton
  Pigwiggin arms himself. *NaM*
Nymphs. See Fairies
The **nymph's** reply to the shepherd. Walter Raleigh. *HaP*

O

"**Oh.**" See All the rabbits and Robin A'Dare
"**Oh,** a bottle of ink, a bottle of ink." See Magic
"**Oh,** a wonderful horse is the fly-away horse." See The fly-away horse
"**O** Alison Gross that lives in yon tower." See Alison Gross
"**O** all you little blackey tops." See Bird scarer's song
"**Oh,** Aunt Jenny." Unknown. *WiRm*
"**O** autumn, laden with fruit, and stained." See To autumn

"O Lady Moon, your horns point to the east." See O Lady Moon

"O little friend, your nose is ready; you sniff." See Dogs

"Oh, little loveliest lady mine." See A valentine

"O little soldier with the golden helmet." See Dandelion

"O little town of Bethlehem." Phillips Brooks. *FeF—JoAc—ReG*

"Oh, long long." See The grass on the mountain

"O look at the moon." See The moon

"O Lord." See Thanksgiving for the body

"O Lord our Lord." See Psalms—Psalm VIII

"O lovely O most charming pug." See To a monkey

"O lyre of gold, Apollo's." See The power of music

"O madam, I will give to you." See The keys of Canterbury

"Oh, Mary, come and call the cattle home." See Alton Locke—The sands of Dee

"Oh, Mrs Cottontail." Unknown. *WiRm*

"O mistress mine, where are you roaming." See Twelfth night—Song

"Oh, moon, little moon." Unknown, tr. fr. the Mexican. *JoAc*

"O moon, Mr Moon." See Mr Moon

"O most high, almighty, good Lord God." See The mirror of perfection—Praise of created things

"Oh, mother, I shall be married to Mr Punchinello." See To Mr Punchinello

"O mother, lay your hand on my brow." See The sick child

"O mouse." See To a guardian mouse

"O my agèd Uncle Arly." See Incidents in the life of my Uncle Arly

"O, my luve is like a red, red rose." See My luve's like a red, red rose

"O my luve's like a red, red rose." See My luve's like a red, red rose

"Oh, my name is John Wellington Wells." See The sorcerer—My name is John Wellington Wells

"Oh, my name was Robert Kidd, as I sailed, as I sailed." See Captain Kidd

O nay. James Reeves. *ReR*

"O nay. O nay. O nay." See O nay

"Oh, ninna and anninia." See Sleep, baby boy

"Oh, now that it's vacation time." See Vacation time

"Oh, once there was a pirate bold." See The pirate cook

"O, open the door, some pity to show." See O, open the door to me, O

O, open the door to me, O. Robert Burns. *SmLg*

"O Paddy dear, and did ye hear the news that's goin' round." See The wearin' of the green

"Oh peace, my Penelope: slaps are the fate." See Lullaby for a naughty girl

"Oh, pleasant, pleasant were the days." See Brother and sister

"O quick quick quick, quick hear the song-sparrow." See Landscapes—Cape Ann

"Oh, rare Harry Parry." See Harry Parry

"O rose, thou art sick." See The sick rose

"Oh, St Patrick was a gentleman." See St Patrick was a gentleman

"O say, can you see, by the dawn's early light." See The star-spangled banner

"Oh send to me an apple that hasn't any kernel." Unknown, tr. fr. the Welsh by Gwyn Williams. *SmLg*

"O shadow." See Shadow dance

"Oh, she is good, the little rain, and well she knows our need." See The little rain

"O sing unto my roundelay." See My love is dead

"Oh sky, you look so drear." See Earth and sky

"Oh, slow to smite and swift to spare." See Abraham Lincoln

"Oh, so cool." See Moral song

"O solitary pine, how many." See Solitary pine

"Oh, somebody come." See In my lady's garden

"Oh, Spanish composers may seem quite castizo." See Iberia

"O spring the long-desired." See Carmina burana

"O star, the fairest one in sight." See Choose something like a star

"Oh, stormy stormy world." See Happiness makes up in height for what it lacks in length

"Oh, such a commotion under the ground." See Flower chorus

"O sun and skies and clouds of June." See October's bright blue weather

"O sun, when I stand in my green leaves." See To the sun from a flower

"Oh, Susan Blue." Kate Greenaway. *ArTp* Susan Blue. *HuL-1*

O sweet content. See Pleasant comedy of patient Grissell—The basket-maker's song

"O tan-faced prairie-boy." Walt Whitman. *FeF*

"Oh, tell me, children who have seen." See Christmas

"Oh that I had wings like a dove." See Psalms—Psalm LV

"Oh that I were." Mother Goose. *OpO*

"Oh, that last day in Lucknow fort." See The relief of Lucknow

"Oh, the brave old duke of York." See "Oh, the grand old duke of York"

"Oh, the comfort—the inexpressible comfort of feeling safe with a person." See Friendship

"Oh the falling snow." See For snow

Oh, the funniest thing. Unknown. *NaE*

"Oh, the funniest thing I've ever seen." See Oh, the funniest thing

"Oh, the gen'ral raised the devil with the kernel, so 'tis said." See Bugs

"Oh, the girl that I loved she was handsome." See The man on the flying trapeze

"Oh, the grand old duke of York." Mother Goose. *DeMg—LiL*
The brave old duke of York. *OpO*
Duke o' York. *HuL-1*
"The grand old duke of York." *ArTp*
"Oh, the brave old duke of York." *JoAc*

"O the little rusty dusty miller." Mother Goose. *OpO*

"Oh, the merry-go-round." See The merry-go-round

"Oh, the merry-go-round goes round and round." See Merry-go-round

"O the ploughboy was a-ploughing." See The simple ploughboy

"O the raggedy man. He works fer pa." See The raggedy man

"Oh, the slopes all seemed to run." See The running

"Oh, the swift plunge into the cool, green dark." See Swimmers

"Oh, then, I see Queen Mab hath been with you." See Romeo and Juliet—Queen Mab

"Oh, there once was a puffin." See There once was a puffin

"O there were three jolly hunters." See The three jolly hunters

"Oh, these spring days." See On the road to Nara

"O thou, that sit'st upon a throne." See A song to David

"O thou, who passest through our valleys in." See To summer

"O thou, who plumed with strong desire." See The two spirits

"O thou with dewy locks, who lookest down." See To spring

"O Timothy Tim." See Cradle song

"Oh, 'tis of a bold major a tale I'll relate." See A Longford legend

"Oh, 'tis time I should talk to your mother." See How to ask and have

"Oh, to be in England." See Home thoughts from abroad

"Oh, to have a birthday." Lois Lenski. *BrBc*

"O, to have a little house." See An old woman of the roads

"Oh, we can play on the big bass drum." See The big bass drum

"O well is me, my gay goshawk." See The gay goshawk

"Oh, what a heavy sigh." See Dicky

"O, what a noble mind is here o'erthrown." See Hamlet

"O what can ail thee, knight-at-arms." See La belle dame sans merci

"Oh, what can you do with a Christmas pup." See Gift with the wrappings off

"Oh, what fun." See Twenty-one

"Oh, what have you got for dinner, Mrs Bond." Mother Goose. *DeMg*
Dilly dilly. *OpO*

"O what is that sound which so thrills the ear." See Ballad

"Oh, what shall my blue eyes go to see." See To baby

"Oh, what's the good of staying up and yawning." See Night thought

"Oh, when to the heart of man." Robert Frost. *ThP*

"O where are you going." See The false knight upon the road

"O where are you going, said reader to rider." See Epilogue

"Oh, where are you going, says Milder to Malder." See The cutty wren

"Oh, where are you going to, my pretty little dear." See Dabbling in the dew

"Oh where have you been, Billy boy, Billy boy." Mother Goose. *DeMg*
Billy boy. *OpO*
The young thing. *HuL-2*

"O where have you been, Lord Randal, my son." See Lord Randal

"Oh, where have you been, my long, long love." See The demon lover

"O where have you been, my long-lost love." See The demon lover

"Oh where, oh where has my little dog gone." See "Where, oh, where has my little dog gone"

"Oh, where the white quince blossom swings." See Japanesque

"Oh, who can sleep." See Night enchantment

"Oh, who is lost tonight." See Fireflies

"Oh, who is so merry, so merry, heigh ho." See The light-hearted fairy

"Oh, who will be my valentine." See My valentine

"O who will shoe my bonny foot." See Annie of Lochroyan

"O who will show me those delights on high." See Heaven

"O who would wish the wind to blow." See Brown Adam

"O wild west wind, thou breath of autumn's being." See Ode to the west wind

"O Willie's large of limb and bone." See The birth of Robin Hood

"O wind, why do you never rest." Christina Georgina Rossetti. *ArTp*

"O winter, bar thine adamantine doors." See To winter

"O woodland cool." Clemens Brentano, tr. fr. the German by Mabel Cotterell. *PaS*

"O world, I cannot hold thee close enough." See Renascence—God's world

"Oh would you know why Henry sleeps." See Inhuman Henry; or, Cruelty to fabulous animals

"Oh, you gotta get a glory." See The glow within

"O, young Lochinvar is come out of the west." See Marmion—Lochinvar

The oak. Alfred Tennyson. *FeF*

The oak and the ash. Unknown. *SmLg*

Oak apple day. Eleanor Farjeon. *FaCb—FaN*

Oak leaves. Elizabeth Jane Coatsworth. *HuSv*

Oak trees
"The mouse that gnawed the oak tree down." V. Lindsay. *BrL-7*
The oak. A. Tennyson. *FeF*
Oak apple day. E. Farjeon. *FaCb—FaN*
Oak leaves. E. J. Coatsworth. *HuSv*
The raven. S. T. Coleridge. *HoW*
To an oak dropping acorns. E. Farjeon. *FaCb—FaN*

"Obadiah." Unknown. *WoJ*

Obata. See Ishii and Obata

Obedience. See also Behavior
"Come when you're called." Mother Goose. *DeMg—OpO*
Disobedience. A. A. Milne. *MiWc*
The grasshoppers. D. Aldis. *AlA—CoI—HuL-2*
Jim, who ran away from his nurse. H. Belloc. *LoL—NaM*
   Jim. *UnMc*
King Hilary and the beggarman. A. A. Milne. *MiWc*
The naughty little robin. P. Cary. *BrL-k*
W-o-o-o-o-o-ww. N. M. Hayes. *HuL-1*

O'Brien, Edward J.
Irish. *BrS*

O'Brien, Fitz-James
The demon of the gibbet. *CoPm*

"Obscurest night involved the sky." See The castaway

Occupations. See also names of occupations, as Carpenters and carpentry
Cherry stones. A. A. Milne. *MiWc*
An impetuous resolve. J. W. Riley. *BrBc*
John plans. D. M. Pierce. *BrBc*
Psalm of those who go forth before daylight. C. Sandburg. *NaM*
   Those who go forth before daylight. *HuSv*
"Rub-a-dub-dub." Mother Goose. *DeMg—JoAc—LiL—OpO*
Vocation. R. Tagore. *FeF*
"When I grow up." W. Wise. *BrBc*
When we are men. S. Mead. *HuL-1*

Ocean
"Break, break, break." A. Tennyson. *HaP*
By the sea. M. Chute. *ChA—HuSv*
Christmas at sea. R. L. Stevenson. *CoSp*
The coral grove. J. G. Percival. *UnG*
Down by the sea. D. McCord. *McT*
Earth and sea. A. S. Pushkin. *PaS*
The Eddystone light. Unknown. *CoSp*
Grim and gloomy. J. Reeves. *ReW*
"I sat by the sea." I. O. Eastwick. *EaI*
"I started early, took my dog." E. Dickinson. *ReT*
King Xerxes and the sea. E. Farjeon. *FaCb*
The last chantey. R. Kipling. *SmLg*
The little girl that lost a finger. G. Mistral. *FeF*
"The moldering hulk." A. Machado. *PaS*
Ocean call. M. C. Livingston. *LiWa*
Old deep sing-song. C. Sandburg. *SaW*
Old Mother Ocean. M. B. Carr. *BrR-6*
Roll on, thou dark blue ocean. From Childe Harold's pilgrimage. G. G. Byron. *FeF*
Sam. W. De La Mare. *ArTp—CoPm*
Sand-between-the-toes. A. A. Milne. *MiWc*

The sands of Dee. From Alton Locke. C. Kingsley. *CoPm—DeT—JoAc*
The sea ("Blue drifted the sea; the waters of the sun") H. Gorter. *PaS*
The sea ("The sea is a hungry dog") J. Reeves. *ReW*
Sea memories. H. W. Longfellow. *FeF*
The sea-ritual. G. Darley. *HoW*
Sea shell. A. Lowell. *FeF—HuL-2—HuSv*
Sea song ("Once a little doodle bug") M. Chute. *ChA*
A sea song ("There was a man out your way") J. Ciardi. *CiY*
Sea song ("To sea, to sea, the calm is o'er") From Death's jest book. T. L. Beddoes. *UnG*
Sea wisdom. C. Sandburg. *SaW*
Seaweed. M. C. Livingston. *LiWa*
The secret of the sea. H. W. Longfellow. *UnG*
Song of the sea wind. A. Dobson. *HuL-2*
Song of the wave. R. Frost. *FrR*
"Three wise men of Gotham." Mother Goose. *DeMg—JoAc—LiL*
   The wise man of Gotham. *OpO*
The tide. H. W. Longfellow. *HoW*
   "The tide rises, the tide falls." *DeT*
Undersea. M. Chute. *HuL-1*
The uses of ocean. O. Seaman. *CoH*
A wanderer's song. J. Masefield. *JoAc*
Washday. E. F. Upson. *BrR-3*
Waters. E. H. Newlin. *BrR-4*

Ocean call. Myra Cohn Livingston. *LiWa*

O'Connor, Frank
Autumn. tr. *CoPs*
The blackbird by Belfast lough. tr. *PaS*
The hermit's song. tr. *PaS*
Kilcash. *ReT*
The sweetness of nature. tr. *GrCc*

O'Connor, Michael
Reveille. *BrR-6*

October
Fall. A. Fisher. *ArTp—FeF*
In October. B. Carman. *HaY*
Late October. S. Teasdale. *BrL-7—CoPs—HaY*
A memory. E. Farjeon. *FaCb—FaN*
October ("O hushed October morning mild") R. Frost. *FrR—GrCc*
October ("October turned my maple's leaves to gold") T. B. Aldrich. *UnG*
October ("A springful of larks in a rolling") D. Thomas. *HaY*
   Poem in October. *GrCc*
October ("The summer is over") R. Fyleman. *BrS*
October ("When October horns are blowing") N. Birckhead. *BrL-7*
October magic. M. C. Livingston. *LiW*
October morning. J. J. Piatt. *HaY*
October night. A. L. Dean. *HaY*
October winds. V. D. Randall. *HaY*
October's bright blue weather. H. H. Jackson. *CoPs*
October's party. G. Cooper. *BrS*
October's song. E. Farjeon. *CoPs—FaCb—FaN*

October ("O hushed October morning mild") Robert Frost. *FrR—GrCc*

October ("October turned my maple's leaves to gold") Thomas Bailey Aldrich. *UnG*

October ("A springful of larks in a rolling") Dylan Thomas. *HaY*
Poem in October. *GrCc*

October ("The summer is over") Rose Fyleman. *BrS*

October ("When October horns are blowing") Nancy Birckhead. *BrL-7*

October at five. Myra Cohn Livingston. *LiWa*

"October gave a party." See October's party

October magic. Myra Cohn Livingston. *LiW*

October morning. John James Piatt. *HaY*

"October morning. How the sun." See October morning

October night. Agnes Louise Dean. *HaY*

"October turned my maple's leaves to gold." See October

October winds. Virginia D. Randall. *HaY*

"October winds are new and clean." See October winds

October's bright blue weather. Helen Hunt Jackson. *CoPs*

October's party. George Cooper. *BrS*

October's song. Eleanor Farjeon. *CoPs—FaCb—FaN*

The octopus. Ogden Nash. *ArTp—CoH*

Octopuses
The octopus. O. Nash. *ArTp—CoH*

The octopussycat. See Mixed beasts

An ode for Ben Jonson. Robert Herrick. *HaP*

Ode in a night of overhanging weather. Vincent McHugh. *McW*

Ode on a Grecian urn. John Keats. *HaP*

Ode on intimations of immortality. William Wordsworth. *BrBc* (sel.)
Our birth is but a sleep. *HaP* (sel.)

Ode to duty. E. V. Rieu. *RiF*

Ode to Maecenas. Horace, tr. fr. the Latin by John Dryden. *PaS* (sel.)
Today and tomorrow. *UnG* (sel.)

Ode to the Hayden planetarium. Arthur Guiterman. *PlI*

Ode to the pig: His tail. Walter R. Brooks. *LoL*

Ode to the west wind. Percy Bysshe Shelley. *HaP*

"An odorous shade lingers the fair day's ghost." See Night

Odors
"The bottle of perfume that Willie sent." Unknown
Limericks since Lear. *UnG*
Mr Wells. E. M. Roberts. *FeF*
One lime. E. Farjeon. *DeT—FaCb*
The rose's scent. Unknown. *HoW*
Smells. C. Morley. *BrR-5*
Smells, Junior. C. Morley. *ArTp—BrL-k*
Sniff. F. M. Frost. *ArTp—BrS*
"The world is full of wonderful smells." Z. Gay. *ArTp*

Odysseus. See Ulysses

Oehlenschlager, Adam
"There is a charming land." *FeF*

"O'er the hill and o'er the vale." John Mason Neale. *EaW*

"O'er the smooth enamel'd green." See Song

"Of a little take a little." Mother Goose *OpO*

Of a spider. Wilfrid Thorley. *FeF*

"Of all creatures." See Quiet

"Of all the animals on earth." See Christmas song

"Of all the birds from east to west." See Chanticleer

"Of all the gay birds that e'er I did see." Mother Goose. *DeMg*

"Of all the girls that are so smart." See Sally in our alley

"Of all the knights in Appledore." See The knight whose armour didn't squeak

"Of all the rides since the birth of time." See Skipper Ireson's ride

"Of all the sayings in this world." Mother Goose. *OpO*

"Of all the ships upon the blue." See Captain Reece

Of an ancient spaniel in her fifteenth year. Christopher Morley. *McW*

"Of animals' houses." See Animals' houses

"Of course I'm me but after that." See Pretending

Of courtesy. Arthur Guiterman. *ArTp*
Proverbs. *ThP*

"Of Edenhall, the youthful lord." See The luck of Edenhall

Of giving. Arthur Guiterman. *ArTp*
Proverbs. *ThP*

"Of gladde things there be four, ay four." See Gladde things

"Of Hilary the great and good." See King Hilary and the beggarman

"Of living creatures most I prize." See Butterfly

"Of Neptune's empire let us sing." See In praise of Neptune

Of quarrels. Arthur Guiterman. *ArTp*
Proverbs. *ThP*

Of tact. Arthur Guiterman. *NaM*

"Of white and tawny, black as ink." See Variation on a sentence

Off the ground. Walter De La Mare. *CoSp—HuL-2*

"Off with sleep, love, up from bed." See Love in May

"Oft I had heard of Lucy Gray." See Lucy Gray; or, Solitude

"Oft in the stilly night." See The light of other days

"Often and often my mother says." See For dessert

"Often I think of the beautiful town." See Sea memories

Ogmundarson, Cormac
Song to Steingerd. *PaS*

O'Keefe (or O'Keeffe), Adelaide
The boys and the apple-tree. *DeT*
James and the shoulder of mutton. *DeT*
The kite. *DeT*
Tom at dinner. *DeT*

Olaf, King of Norway (about)
"And will King Olaf come again." E. Farjeon. *FaCb*
King Olaf's gold. E. Farjeon. *FaCb*
Old Abram Brown. See "Old Abram Brown is dead and gone"
"Old Abram Brown is dead and gone." Mother Goose. *DeMg*
Abram Brown. *OpO*
Old Abram Brown. *DeT*
"Old Adam, the carrion crow." Thomas Lovell Beddoes. *CoPm*
The carrion crow. *HoW*
Old age. See also Birthdays; Childhood recollections; Youth and age
All that's past. W. De La Mare. *ReT*
At a country fair. J. Holmes. *NaM*
The last leaf. O. W. Holmes. *FeF—McW*
Old age. Sophocles. *PaS*
An old man. W. Wordsworth. *SmLg*
An old man's epitaph. E. Farjeon. *FaCb —FaN*
An old man's winter night. R. Frost. *FrR*
Old men. O. Nash. *NaE*
The old men admiring themselves in the water. W. B. Yeats. *SmLg*
Poor old horse. Unknown. *ReG*
Rabbi Ben Ezra. R. Browning. *BrBc* (sel.)
The relic. R. Hillyer. *PlU*
Sir Nicketty Nox. H. Chesterman. *HuL-2*
Solitary pine. Prince Ichihara. *PaS*
When you are old. W. B. Yeats. *HaP*
Old age. Sophocles, tr. fr. the Greek by Alfred Edward Housman. *PaS*
"Old Archibald, in his eternal chair." See Archibald's example
Old bandy legs. See "As I was going to sell my eggs"
"Old battle field, fresh with spring flowers again." See Seven poems
Old blue saucepan. Eleanor Farjeon. *FaN*
Old Boniface. Mother Goose. *OpO*
"Old Boniface he loved good cheer." See Old Boniface
"The old brown thorn-trees break in two high over Cummen strand." See Red Hanrahan's song about Ireland
The **old** buccaneer. Charles Kingsley. *NaE —NaM*
The last buccaneer. *UnG*
Old cat Care. Richard Hughes. *ReT*
"Old chairs to mend. Old chairs to mend." Mother Goose. *DeMg*
Old Chang the crab. Unknown, tr. fr. the Chinese by Isaac Taylor Headland. *JoAc*
Old Christmas. Roy Helton. *CoPm—UnMc*
An **old** Christmas carol. Unknown. *DoP*
As Joseph was awakening. *DeT*
"As Joseph was a-walking." *HuSv*
An **old** Christmas greeting. Unknown. *ArTp—FeF—HuL-1*
Christmas greeting. *BrS*
Old Christmastide. See Marmion
The **old** cloak. Unknown. *MaB*
Old clothes, any old clo', clo'. See "If I'd as much money as I could spend"

The **old** coach road. Rachel Field. *HuL-2*
The **old** coon-dog dreams. Kenneth Porter. *UnG*
Old cow. Unknown. *TaD*
"Old cow, old cow." See Old cow
Old Dan'l. L. A. G. Strong. *CoPs*
Old deep sing-song. Carl Sandburg. *SaW*
"Old Dick Johnson, gentleman, adventurer." See The Dick Johnson reel
"Old Doctor Foster." See Doctor Foster
"Old Doctor Windikin." See Doctor Windikin
"Old dog lay in the summer sun." See Sunning
Old Ducky Quackerel. Laura E. Richards. *BrR-5*
"Old Ducky Quackerel went to catch some mackerel." See Old Ducky Quackerel
"Old Eben Flood, climbing alone one night." See Mr Flood's party
Old Ellen Sullivan. Winifred Welles. *FeF*
"Old Euclid drew a circle." See Euclid
The **old** familiar faces. Charles Lamb. *HaP*
Old farmer Buck. Unknown. *CoH*
"Old farmer Buck, he bought him a duck." See Old farmer Buck
"Old farmer Giles." Mother Goose. *OpO*
Old-fashioned love. Unknown. *UnMg*
Old Father Annum. Leroy F. Jackson. *BrS*
"Old Father Annum on New year's day." See Old Father Annum
"Old Father Greybeard." See Father Greybeard
The **old** friar remembers. See Friar's hunting song
The **old** ghost. Thomas Lovell Beddoes. *HoW*
The **old** grey goose. Unknown. *ReG*
The **old** Gumbie cat. T. S. Eliot. *UnG*
Old Hogan's goat. Unknown. *CoI—TaD*
"Old Hogan's goat was feeling fine." See Old Hogan's goat
"The old house leans upon a tree." See Deserted
Old hundred. Mark Van Doren. *PlU*
Old hundredth. Thomas Ken. *PlU*
Old Ironsides. See Warships
Old Ironsides. Oliver Wendell Holmes. *FeF—UnMc*
Old January. See The faerie queene
"Old Joe Brown, he had a wife." Unknown American Father Gander. *UnG*
"Old King Cole." Mother Goose. *BrL-k— DeMg—JoAc—LiL—OpO*
"The old king of Dorchester." See The ceremonial band
"Old lions." See Ode in a night of overhanging weather
Old log house. James S. Tippett. *FeF*
"An old maid, an old maid." Mother Goose. *OpO*
An **old** man. William Wordsworth. *SmLg*
The **old** man and Jim. James Whitcomb Riley. *CoSp*

An old woman. See "There was an old woman, and what do you think"

The old woman. See "There was an old woman, as I've heard tell"

The old woman and the pig. Unknown. *TaD*

"Old woman by the hedgerow." See Old woman in May

The old woman in a shoe. See "There was an old woman who lived in a shoe"

Old woman in May. John Drinkwater. *HuL-2*

The old woman in the basket. See "There was an old woman tossed up in a basket"

"The old woman must stand." See Washing day

An old woman of the roads. Padraic Colum. *FeF—HuL-2—HuSv*

"Old woman, old woman, shall we go a-shearing." Mother Goose. *ArTp—DeMg—OpO*

"An old woman was sweeping her house." Unknown. *DeMg—LiL*

"An old woman went to market and bought a pig." See The old woman who bought a pig

The old woman who bought a pig. Mother Goose. *OpO*

The old woman's three cows. Mother Goose. *OpO*

"Old year is out." See Song of the very poor

Older grown. Kate Greenaway. *BrBc*

"The older the tree." Unknown. *MoY*

Oldys, William
 On a fly drinking from his cup. *UnG*

O'Leary. Unknown. *WoJ*

Oleson, Helmer O.
 Ballad of Johnny Appleseed. *ArTp—BrS*

Olgin, Bette
 My teddy bear. *McAw*

"Oliver Goldsmith." Eleanor Farjeon. *FaCb—FaN*

Omar Khayyám
 The rubáiyát of Omar Khayyám of Naishapúr. *HaP* (sel.)—*PaS* (sel.)
  Wake. *FeF* (sel.)
 Wake. See The rubáiyát of Omar Khayyám of Naishapúr

Omnibuses. See Busses

On a bird singing in its sleep. Robert Frost. *FrR*

On a clergyman's horse. Unknown. *UnG*

"On a cold dark night when the wind is high." See Pull

On a dentist. Unknown. *UnG*

On a doctor named Isaac Letsome. Unknown. *UnG*

On a fly drinking from his cup. William Oldys. *UnG*

On a Friday morn. Unknown. *DeT*

"On a Friday morn, as we set sail." See On a Friday morn

"On a hill there blooms a palm." See Tell him

"On a little green knoll." See Old log house

On a man named Merideth. Unknown. *UnG*

On a mountain road. Wu Ch'ing-jen, tr. fr. the Chinese by E. D. Edwards. *PaS*

On a night of snow. Elizabeth Jane Coatsworth. *NaM—UnG*

On a piece of music. Gerard Manley Hopkins. *PlU*

On a railroad right of way. Carl Sandburg *SaW*

On a snowy day. Dorothy Aldis. *AlA*
Snow. *ArTp*

"On a starr'd night Prince Lucifer uprose." See Lucifer in starlight

On a steamer. Dorothy W. Baruch. *FeF*

"On a stone chair in the market-place." See The statue

On a thieving locksmith. Unknown. *UnG*

On a tired housewife. Unknown. *NaE*

On a tree fallen across the road. Robert Frost. *FrR*

"On a white field." See The sower

"On a winter night." See Christmas eve

"On Arbor day." See Arbor day

"On board the Shannon frigate." See The Shannon and the Chesapeake

"On certain days my mother says." See A tail to wag

"On Charles II. John Wilmot, Earl of Rochester. *HaP—UnG*

On Christmas day. See "Dame, get up and bake your pies"

"On Christmas eve." See A-caroling on Christmas eve

"On Christmas eve I turned the spit." See Christmas eve

On Christmas morn. See Words from an old Spanish carol

On digital extremities. Gelett Burgess. *FeF*

On Easter days. Celia Thaxter. *FeF—HaY*

"On Easter morn." See Easter. Elizabeth Jane Coatsworth

"On Easter morn." See Easter. Hilda Conkling

"On Easter morn at early dawn." See Meeting the Easter bunny

"On either side the river lie." See The lady of Shalott

On first hearing Beethoven. George Barker. *PlU*

On first looking into Chapman's Homer. John Keats. *SmLg*

"On glossy wires artistically bent." See Waspish

On going unnoticed. Robert Frost. *FrR*

On Halloween. Shelley Silverstein. *CoPs*

"On Halloween I'll go to town." See On Halloween

"On Hallowe'en my friends and I." See Hallowe'en scare

"On Hallowe'en the old ghosts come." See Hallowe'en

On hearing a flute at night from the wall of Shou-Hsiang. Li Yi, tr. by Witter Bynner. *PlU*

On hearing a symphony of Beethoven. Edna St Vincent Millay. *PlU*

On John Bun. Unknown. *UnG*

On Leslie Moore. Unknown. *UnG*

"On March the eight, as sure as fate." See Hero of Astley's

On Martha Snell. Unknown. *UnG*

"On Monday, Monday." See My true love

"On moony nights the dogs bark shrill." See At night

On music. Walter Savage Landor. *GrCc*

"On music drawn away, a sea-borne mariner." See Music

"On nights like this all cities are alike." Rainer Maria Rilke, tr. fr. the German by C. F. MacIntyre. *GrCc*

"On oak apple day in Wishford." See Oak apple day

On oath. Mother Goose. *OpO*

On opening a new book. Abbie Farwell Brown. *HaY*

"On powdery wings the white moths pass." See A garden at night

On Prince Frederick. Unknown. *UnG*

On Queen Anne. Eleanor Farjeon. *FaN*

On receiving a camp catalog. Millicent Taylor. *BrR-6*

On Richard Dent, landlord. Unknown. *UnG*

"On Saturday night shall be my care." Mother Goose. *OpO*

"On Shillingstone green." See May-day in June

On Skugg. Benjamin Franklin. *UnG*

"On some awful mornings." See Awful mornings

On some windy day. Dorothy Aldis. *AlA*

"On Springfield mow-wow-wowntain." See Springfield mountain

"On stormy days." See Brooms

On stubborn Michael Shay. Unknown. *UnG*

"On summer mornings when it's hot." See The milkman's horse

"On Sunday morning, then he comes." See Mr Wells

"On Sunday mornings the fisher man." See Fisher man

"On sunny slope and beechen swell." See Burial of the Minnisink

On the beach. Dorothy Aldis. *AlHd*

"On the coast of Coromandel." See The courtship of Yonghy-Bonghy-Bo

On the death of Ianthe. Walter Savage Landor. *GrCc*

On the death of Mr Purcell. John Dryden. *PlU*

"On the Eastern way at the city of Lo-yang." See Song

"On the eighth of March it was, some people say." See The birth of Saint Patrick

"On the fifth day of April." See A quill for John Stow

"On the first day of Christmas." See "The first day of Christmas"

"On the first of March." Mother Goose. *OpO*

"On the Fourth of July, we always go." See American hill

On the frozen lake. See The prelude—Skating

On the grasshopper and cricket ("Green little vaulter in the sunny grass") Leigh Hunt. *UnG*

On the grasshopper and cricket ("The poetry of earth is never dead") See The poetry of earth

"On the grassy banks." See Woolly lambkins

"On the green banks of Shannon when Sheelah was nigh." See My dog Tray

"On the island of Skip-scoop-anellie." See Skip-scoop-anellie

"On the lips of the child Janet float changing dreams." See Sixteen months

On the morning of Christ's nativity. John Milton. *SmLg*

On the mountain pass. Matsuo Bashō, tr. fr. the Japanese by Harold G. Henderson. *PaS*

On the road to Nara. Matsuo Bashō, tr. fr. the Japanese by Harold G. Henderson. *PaS*

"On the shores of Lake Michigan." See The people, yes—Children of the wind

On the staircase. Eleanor Farjeon. *BrS*

"On the top of the crumpetty tree." See The Quangle Wangle's hat

On the university carrier. John Milton. *SmLg*

"On the wall." See October at five

"On the wall beside the kitchen door." See Growing

"On the wind of January." See The wind of January

On their appointed rounds. Unknown. *FeF*

On this day the wren and the robin stop singing. Eleanor Farjeon *FaN*

"On this leaf." Unknown. *MoY*

"On this page." Unknown. *MoY*

"On this page of beautiful pink." Unknown. *MoY*

"On tilted toes he tries to reach." See Nature at three

"On tip-toe comes the gentle dark." See Good night

"On wan dark night on Lac St Pierre." See The wreck of the Julie Plante

"On Willy's birthday, as you see." See A party

"On yonder hill there stands a creature." See The one answer

"Once." See On a steamer

"Once a big molicepan." Unknown. *FeF*

"Once a boy espied a rose." See Briar-rose

Once a child. Emily Dickinson. *PlI*

"Once a jolly swagman camped by a billabong." See Waltzing Matilda

"Once a little doodle bug." See Sea song

"Once a mouse, a frog, and a little red hen." See The mouse, the frog, and the little red hen

"Once a raveled baby bird." See Baby bird

"Once I had a green door." See Joan's door

"**Once** I had a striped cat." Unknown. *WiRm*

"**Once** I saw a little bird." Mother Goose. *BrL-k—DeMg—HuSv*
Little bird. *OpO*

"**Once** I saw a little boat, and a pretty, pretty boat." See A song for Hal

"**Once** I was a monarch's daughter." Unknown. *DeT*

"**Once** I was a pirate." See Dreams

"**Once** in a dream I saw the flowers." See Paradise

"**Once** in a while a curious weed unknown to me." See The Spoon River anthology —William Jones

"**Once** in royal David's city." Cecil Frances Alexander. *DoP*

"**Once**, in the city of Kalamazoo." See Kalamazoo

"**Once** more, once more, Inarimé." See Vittoria Colonna

"**Once** more Orion and the sister Seven." See A welcome to Dr Benjamin Apthorp Gould

"**Once** more unto the breach, dear friends, once more." See King Henry V

"**Once** my heart was a summer rose." See Song

"**Once** on a time an artful ant." See The artful ant

"**Once**, on a time and in a place." See The arrogant frog and the superior bull

"**Once** on a time—'twas long ago." See The youth and the northwind

Once only. Ato Tobira, tr. fr. the Japanese by Ishii and Obata. *PaS*

"**Once**—only once." See Once only

"**Once** riding in old Baltimore." See Incident

"**Once** Steeple Bumpstead had a steeple." See The steeple

"**Once** there lived a little man." Unknown. *HuL-1*

"**Once** there was a little girl." See That was the one

"**Once** there was a little kitty." See The kitty

"**Once** there was a spaniel." See Bed-time story

"**Once** there was a robin." See The naughty little robin

"**Once** there was an elephant." See Eletelephony

"**Once**, twice, thrice." See Shrovetide

"**Once** upon a midnight dreary, while I pondered, weak and weary." See The raven

"**Once** upon a time." See Mr Pyme

"**Once** upon a time." See O is for once upon a time

"**Once** upon a time, in a wee little house." See The funny old man and his wife

"**Once** upon a time there were three little foxes." See The three foxes

"**Once** was a fiddler. Play could he." See A fiddler

Once when I was sick. Dorothy Aldis. *AlA*

"**Once** when the snow of the year was beginning to fall." See The runaway

One and one. Cecil Day-Lewis. *PlU*

The **one** answer. Unknown. *UnG*

One bright morning. Unknown. *NaE*

"**One** bright morning in the middle of the night." See One bright morning

"**One** cannot have enough." See Soliloquy of a tortoise on revisiting the lettuce beds after an interval of one hour while supposed to be sleeping in a clump of blue hollyhocks

One day. John Ciardi. *CiY*

"**One** day, a fine day, a high-flying-sky day." See The cat heard the cat-bird

"**One** day as I was riding by." See My horse

"**One** day I built a castle in the sand." See The castle

"**One** day I saw a downy duck." See Good morning

"**One** day it rained so hard the grass became so green." See The house beyond the meadow—The magic map

"**One** day little Tom in his clean pin-afore." See Tom at dinner

"**One** day, mamma said: Conrad dear." See The story of little Suck-a-thumb

"**One** day, Saint Nicholas made a complaint." See Left out

"**One** day, the vine." See The rebellious vine

"**One** day there reached me from the street." See The goatherd

"**One** day while I was walking." Unknown. *TaD*

"**One-erum**, two-erum." Mother Goose. *OpO*

"**One-ery**, two-ery, ickery, Ann." Mother Goose. *OpO*
Counting-out rhymes. *FeF*

"**One-ery**, two-ery, tickery, seven." Mother Goose. *OpO*

One-eyed gunner. Mother Goose. *OpO*

"**One** for anger." Unknown. *DeMg*

"**One** for money." See "One for the **money**"

"**One** for sorrow, two for joy." Mother Goose. *OpO*

"**One** for the cut worm." Unknown. *WoF*

"**One** for the money." Mother Goose. *HuSv*
"One for money." *OpO*

One guess. Robert Frost. *FrY*

One hard look. Robert Graves. *GrP*

"**One** I love, two I love." Mother Goose. *DeMg—LiL—OpO*

"**One** is a creeper and sleepy in his shell." See Guess

"The **one-1** lama." See The lama

The **one-legged** stool. Enid Blyton. *HuL-1*

One lime. Eleanor Farjeon. *DeT—FaCb*

"**One** lime in Alfriston made sweet." See One lime

"**One** little Indian boy making a canoe." See Ten little Indian boys

"**One** misty, moisty morning." Mother Goose. *ArTp—DeMg—HuSv—JoAc—LiL —OpO*

"**One** moonlight night a ship drove in." See The Alice Jean

"One morning in spring." See Fife tune

"One morning, one morning, one morning in May." See The rebel soldier

"One morning our dear little fir tree was bored." See Our little fir tree

"One night as Dick lay fast asleep." See Full moon

"One night came on a hurricane." See The sailor's consolation

"One night I dreamed." See The dream

"One night I dreamed I was locked in my father's watch." See My father's watch

"One night I heard my old dog bark." Unknown. *WoF*

"One night upon the southern sea." See The silence of God

"One night when I was sick I lay." See Once when I was sick

"One of my wishes is that those dark trees." See Into my own

"One of the chairs is South America." See Nursery chairs

"One old Oxford ox opening oysters." Unknown. *DeMg*

"One ought not to have to care." See The hill wife

"One potato, two potato." Unknown Counting-out rhymes. *FeF*

"One road leads to London, one road leads to Wales." See Roadways

"One ship drives east and another drives west." See The winds of fate

"One star is Minnesota." See The flag

"One summer night a little raccoon." See Raccoon

"One summer's day a fox was passing through." See The greedy fox and the elusive grapes

"One summer's day in the month of May." See The big Rock Candy mountain

"One thing at a time." Mother Goose. *OpO*

"One thing has a shelving bank." See A drumlin woodchuck

"One to make ready." Mother Goose. *DeMg —LiL—OpO*

"One, two." See "One, two, buckle my shoe"

"One, two, buckle my shoe." Mother Goose. *BrL-k—DeMg—HuL-1—LiL—OpO*
"One, two." *ArTp—DeT—HuSv—JoAc*
Signs, seasons, and sense. *UnG*
One, two, buckle my shoe. Ogden Nash. *BrBc*

"One, two, policeman blue." Unknown, tr. fr. the German. *JoAc*

One-two-three. See "One, two, three, four, five (I caught a hare alive)"

"One, two, three." See Sing-song rhyme

"One, two, three (I love coffee)." See Billy and me

"One, two, three ("It was an old, old, old, old lady") Henry Cuyler Bunner. *FeF*

One, two, three ("Out of the earth come good things") Robin Christopher. *HuL-2*

"One, two, three, four, five (I caught a fish alive)." Mother Goose. *HuL-1—LiL— OpO—WoF*

"One, two, three, four, five (I caught a hare alive)." Mother Goose. *ArTp—DeMg*
One-two-three. *DeT*

"One, two, three, four, five, six, seven (all good children)." Mother Goose. *DeMg*

"One, two, three, four (mama scrubbed)." Unknown. *WoF*

"One, two, three, four (Mary at)." Mother Goose. *LiL—OpO—TaD*

"One, two, three O'Leary." See O'Leary

"One, two, three, to the wood goes she." Unknown, tr. fr. the French. *JoAc*

"1-2-3 was the number he played but today the number came 3-2-1." See Dirge

"One, two, whatever you do." Mother Goose. *OpO*

"One white foot, buy him." Unknown. *WoF*

"One winter night." See Moon vine

"Onery, twoery." Unknown. *DeMg*

"One's none." See Little hundred

"Onezall, twozall, zitterzall, zee." Unknown. *WoF*

Onions
The man in the onion bed. J. Ciardi. *CiI*

Onitsura
Coolness. *PaS*
The little valley in spring. *PaS*

"Only a bell, a bird, the stillness break." See Immense hour

Only a book. Emily Dickinson. *BrR-4*

"Only a man harrowing clods." See In time of the breaking of nations

Only my opinion. Monica Shannon. *ArTp— FeF—HuSv*

Only one mother. George Cooper. *BrS— FeF*

"The only real airship." See The dirigible

"Only the clock." See Mouse midnight

Only the wind says spring. Helen Janet Miller. *UnG*

Ono no yoshiki. See Kokin Shū

The onset. Robert Frost. *FrR*

"An open door says, Come in." See Doors

Open eye, pimpernel. Eleanor Farjeon. *FaCb—FaN*

"Open eye, pimpernel, chin-in-the-dust." See Open eye, pimpernel

"An open foe may prove a curse." See Poor Richard's wisdom

Open range. Kathryn and Byron Jackson. *ArTp—FeF*

An open secret. Unknown. *BrR-4*

"Open the barn door, farm woman." See She opens the barn door every morning

Open the door. Marion Edey. *ArTp—BrS— HuL-1*

"Open the door and who'll come in." See Open the door

"Open the gate." Unknown. *MoY*

"Opens like a barn door." Unknown. *WiRm*

"An opera star named Maria." Unknown Limericks since Lear. *UnG*

Operatic note. Melville Cane. *PlU*

Ophelia's song. See Hamlet

Opossum. William Jay Smith. *SmB—UnG*

Opossums
Opossum. W. J. Smith. *SmB—UnG*
"Possum up a gum tree." Unknown. *WiRm*
Shoot that possum down. Unknown. *TaD*

Opportunity. See also Success
Opportunity. E. R. Sill. *BrR-6—ThP—UnG*

Opportunity. Edward Rowland Sill. *BrR-6—ThP—UnG*

Optimism. See also Happiness; Laughter; Success
April rain. R. Loveman. *BrR-5*
The difference. Unknown. *UnG*
Keeping on. A. H. Clough. *NaM*
The optimist. Unknown. *UnG*
Pippa's song. From Pippa passes. R. Browning. *FeF*
    Spring song. *UnG*
    "The year's at the spring." *DoP—HaY—HuSv—ThP*

The **optimist**. Unknown. *UnG*

"The **optimist** fell ten stories." See The optimist

"**Or** from what spring doth your opinion rise." See Orchestra

Orange tree by night. Sacheverell Sitwell. *GrCc*

Orange trees
Orange tree by night. S. Sitwell. *GrCc*

Oranges
Oranges. Unknown. *DeT*
"What is pink? a rose is pink." C. G. Rossetti. *ArTp*
    Color. *HuL-1*

Oranges. Unknown. *DeT*

Oranges and lemons. See "Gay go up and gay go down"

Orchards
Evening in a sugar orchard. R. Frost. *FrR*
Good-by and keep cold. R. Frost. *FrR—FrY—UnG*
The little green orchard. W. De La Mare. *ArTp—NaE*

Orchestra ("Or from what spring doth your opinion rise") John Davies. *PlU* (sel.)

The **orchestra** ("The violin's a lady, at her window clear she sings") Nancy Byrd Turner. *BrR-5*

Orderliness
Caesar's good order. E. Farjeon. *FaCb*
Delight in disorder. R. Herrick. *HaP*
Microcosmus. T. Nabbes. *PlU* (sel.)

The **ordinary** dog. Nancy Byrd Turner. *ArTp*

Oregon trail
The Oregon trail: 1851. J. Marshall. *HuSv*
The Oregon trail: 1843. A. Guiterman. *FeF*

The **Oregon** trail: 1851. James Marshall. *HuSv*

The **Oregon** trail: 1843. Arthur Guiterman. *FeF*

Organ grinders
Go down to Kew in lilac-time. From The barrel-organ. A. Noyes. *HuL-2*
The sad monkey. D. Aldis. *AlA*
The shower. B. Eve. *DeT*

Oriole. Edgar Fawcett. *UnG*

Orioles
Hearing the early oriole. Po Chü-i. *PlU*
The hen and the oriole. D. Marquis. *CoH—NaE*

Oriole. E. Fawcett. *UnG*
"To hear an oriole sing." E. Dickinson. *PlU*

Orkney lullaby. Eugene Field. *UnG*

Orleans, Charles d' (Comte d'Angoulême). See Charles d'Orleans

Orleans, Ilo
The frog on the log. *McAw*
"I thank You, God." *DoP—HuL-1*
In the garden. *HuL-1*
"Upon the beach." *ArTp*

Orphans
Alice Fell. W. Wordsworth. *DeT*
Little Orphant Annie. J. W. Riley. *FeF—HuSv—NaM*

Orpheus
Orpheus. From King Henry VIII. W. Shakespeare or J. Fletcher. *PlU*
    Music. *SmLg*
Sonnets to Orpheus. R. M. Rilke. *PlU* (sel.)

Orpheus. See King Henry VIII

"**Orpheus** with his lute made trees." See King Henry VIII—Orpheus

Osborn, Mary I.
The swing. *HuL-1*

The **osc**. James Reeves. *ReP*

"The **ostrich** is a silly bird." Mary E. Wilkins Freeman. *ArTp—CoH—FeF—LoL—McW*

Ostriches
Grandmother ostrich. W. J. Smith. *SmL*
"The ostrich is a silly bird." M. E. W. Freeman. *ArTp — CoH — FeF — LoL—McW*

O'Sullivan, Seumas, pseud. (James Starkey)
Night. tr. *PaS*
A piper. *ArTp—FeF—HuL-2—NaM*

Othello, sel. William Shakespeare
Good name. *ThP*

The **other** child. Eleanor Farjeon. *FaCb*

"The **other** day when I met Dick." John Ciardi. *CiI*

"**Other** people whistle." See Where is it

Others. James Reeves. *ReW*

"**Others** taunt me with having knelt at well-curbs." See For once, then, something

Otherwise. Aileen Fisher. *HuL-1*

Otter creek. Frances M. Frost. *FrLn*

Otterburne, Battle of, 1388
Chevy Chase. Unknown. *MaB*

Otters
Otter creek. F. M. Frost. *FrLn*

"**Ouphe** and goblin, imp and sprite." See The culprit fay—Elfin song

Our baby. Myra Cohn Livingston. *LiWa*

"**Our** baby came home." See Our baby

"**Our** balloon man has balloons." See The balloon man

Our band. Marchette Chute. *ChA*

"**Our** barn roof has three lovely holes." See Three lovely holes

Our birth is but a sleep. See Ode on intimations of immortality

"**Our** birth is but a sleeping and a forgetting." See Ode on intimations of immortality

Our birthday. Marion Edey. *BrBc—BrS*

"Our bow's bended." Mother Goose. *OpO*

"Our brother Clarence goes to school." See Big brother

"Our brother says that Will was born." See Dick and Will

Our circus. Laura Lee Randall. *ArTp*

"Our city's sons and daughters." See School days in New Amsterdam

Our clock. Florence Eakman. *BrS*

"Our clock is a little house on the wall." See Our clock

"Our eyes have met." Unknown. *MoY*

"Our fountain." See Little fountain

Our guest. Dorothy Aldis. *AlA*

Our hired man. Monica Shannon. *FeF*

Our history. Catherine Cate Coblentz. *FeF*

"Our history sings of centuries." See Our history

Our hold on the planet. Robert Frost. *FrR*

Our joyful feast. George Wither. *BrS*

Our little calf. Dorothy Aldis. *AlA*

"Our little calf is woollier." See Our little calf

Our little fir tree. Dorothy Aldis. *AlA*

Our little kinsmen. Emily Dickinson. *FeF—PlI*

"Our little kinsmen after rain." See Our little kinsmen

Our milkman. Nona Keen Duffy. *McAw*

"Our Mr Toad." David McCord. *ArTp—JoAc—McFf*

Our picnic. Dorothy Aldis. *AlHd*

Our silly little sister. Dorothy Aldis. *AlA—CoH—FeF—NaE*

Our singing strength. Robert Frost. *FrR*

Our squirrel. Dorothy Aldis. *AlHd*

Our tame baby squirrel. Dorothy Aldis. *AlA*

Our tree. Marchette Chute. *ChA*

"Our twelve months go round and round." See January 1

"Our uncle called us on the phone." See Surprise

"Our uncle, innocent of books." See Snowbound—The uncle

Our visit to the zoo. Jessie Pope. *HuL-2*

"Out came the sun." Eleanor Farjeon. *FaCb—FaN*

"Out from the beach the ships I see." See The white ships

"Out goes the rat." Unknown
Counting-out rhymes. *FeF*

"Out in the fields which were green last May." See A child's thought of harvest

Out in the fields with God. Unknown. *DoP—UnG*

"Out in the late amber afternoon." See In shadow

"Out in the sunshine fair and free." See Written on the road

"Out of his cottage to the sun." See Old Dan'l

"Out of me unworthy and unknown." See The Spoon River anthology—Anne Rutledge

"Out of my window." See For Anna

"Out of the bosom of the air." See Snowflakes

"Out of the cleansing night of stars and tides." See Brooklyn bridge at dawn

"Out of the earth come good things." See One, two, three

"Out of the factory chimney, tall." See Smoke animals

"Out of the focal and foremost fire." See Little Giffen

"Out of the mud two strangers came." See Two tramps in mud time

"Out of the night that covers me." See Invictus

"Out of the North the wild news came." See The revolutionary rising

"Out of the window." See Night song

"Out of your treasury, dear year." See The spendthrift

"Out on the breeze." See Flag song

"Out they came from Liberty, out across the plains." See The Oregon trail: 1851

"Out upon it, I have loved." See The constant lover

Out walking. Marchette Chute. *ChA*

"Out walking in the frozen swamp one gray day." See The wood-pile

"Out West is windy." See New Mexico

The outdoor Christmas tree. Aileen Fisher. *BrS*

Outdoor life. See Adventure and adventurers; Camping; Country life; Gipsies; Nature; Roads and trails; Wayfaring life; also names of outdoor sports, as Hunters and hunting

"Outlanders, whence come ye last." See Carol

The outlandish knight. Unknown. *UnG*

"An outlandish knight came out of the North." See The outlandish knight

Outlaws. See Crime and criminals

"The outlook wasn't brilliant for the Mudville nine that day." See Casey at the bat

"Outside." See The difference

The oven bird. Robert Frost. *FrR—FrY—PlU*

Over and under. William Jay Smith. *SmL*

"Over back where they speak of life as staying." See The investment

"Over hill, over dale." See A midsummer-night's dream

"Over in the corner there's a person standing." See Guardian angel

"Over in the meadow." Olive A. Wadsworth. *NaM*

"Over the beaches of the sky." See Cancer

"Over the briny wave I go." See The kayak

"Over the climbing meadow." See Dandelions

"Over the garden wall." Eleanor Farjeon. *BrR-4—HuSv*

"Over the hill the farm boy goes." See Evening at the farm

Over the hills and far away. Mother Goose. *HuL-1*

"**Over** the hilltop." See Virgo

"**Over** the lotus leaves." See Lotus leaves

"**Over** the mountains." See Love will find out the way

"**Over** the mountains." See Trains

"**Over** the river." See Ferry-boats

"**Over** the river and through the wood." See Thanksgiving day

"**Over** the water an old ghost strode." See The old ghost

"**Over** the water and over the lea." Mother Goose. *DeMg*

  Over the water to Charley. *DeT*

  Over the water to Charlie. *OpO*

Over the water to Charley. See "Over the water and over the lea"

Over the water to Charlie. See "Over the water and over the lea"

"**Over** this hearth—my father's seat." See The returned volunteer to his rifle

Over, under, over. Ivy O. Eastwick. *EaI*

"**Overhead** at sunset all heard the choir." See The singers in a cloud

Overheard on a saltmarsh. Harold Monro. *ArTp — CoPm — FeF — HuL-2 — JoAc—NaM—ReT*

"The **overlord** of roaches." See A bad day by the river

Owen, Wilfred

  Anthem for doomed youth. *NaE*

The **owl** ("Downhill I came, hungry, and yet not starved") Edward Thomas. *HaP*

The **owl** ("The owl that lives in the old oak tree") William Jay Smith. *CoI—SmL*

The **owl** ("When cats run home and light is come") Alfred Tennyson. *NaM—SmLg—UnG*

  Song: The owl. *FeF—ReT*

  The white owl. *DeT*

"An **owl** and an eel and a frying pan." Unknown. *WiRm*

"The **owl** and the eel and the warming-pan." Laura E. Richards. *JoAc—NaE*

The **owl** and the pussycat. Edward Lear. *ArTp — CoI — FeF — HaP — HuL-1 — HuSv — JoAc — NaM — PeF — ReG —SmLg—UnG*

"The **owl** and the pussycat went to sea." See The owl and the pussycat

The **owl-critic**. James T. Fields. *CoSp—NaE—UnG*

"The **owl** is abroad, the bat and the toad." See The witches' charms

"The **owl** that lives in the old oak tree." See The owl

Owls

  The barn owl. S. Butler. *DeT*

  The frog on the log. I. Orleans. *McAw*

  The little fox. M. Edey. *ArTp*

  The London owl. E. Farjeon. *FaCb*

  Many crows, any owl. D. McCord. *McT*

  "Of all the gay birds that e'er I did see." Mother Goose. *DeMg*

  "Once I was a monarch's daughter." Unknown. *DeT*

  The owl ("Downhill I came, hungry, and yet not starved") E. Thomas. *HaP*

  The owl ("The owl that lives in the old oak tree") W. J. Smith. *CoI—SmL*

The owl ("When cats run home and light is come") A. Tennyson. *NaM—SmLg—UnG*

  Song: The owl. *FeF—ReT*

  The white owl. *DeT*

The owl and the pussycat. E. Lear. *ArTp — CoI — FeF — HaP — HuL-1 — HuSv — JoAc — NaM — PeF — ReG — SmLg —UnG*

The owl-critic. J. T. Fields. *CoSp—NaE —UnG*

Owls talking. D. McCord. *McFf*

"Said the monkey to the owl." Unknown. *WoF*

The scaredy. Mother Goose. *OpO*

"There was an old man of Dumbree." E. Lear

  Lear's limericks. *UnG*

"There was an owl lived in an oak." Mother Goose. *DeMg*

  An owl in an oak. *OpO*

  Signs, seasons, and sense. *UnG*

  There was an owl. *HuL-1*

"When icicles hang by the wall." From Love's labor's lost. W. Shakespeare. *CoPs—FeF—HaP—JoAc*

  Hiems. *SmLg*

  A merry note. *HoW*

  Winter. *McW*

The white owl. F. J. Patmore. *CoPm*

"A wise old owl lived in an oak." Mother Goose. *DeMg—LiL—OpO*

Owls talking. David McCord. *McFf*

Ox and donkey's carol. See The ox and the donkey's carol

The **ox** and the ass. Edith Simpson. *EaW*

The **ox** and the donkey's carol. Sister Maris Stella. *DoP*

  Ox and donkey's carol. *EaW*

"The **ox** said to the ass, said he, all on a Christmas night." See Carol

Oxen. See Cattle

The **oxen**. Thomas Hardy. *EaW—HaP*

Oxenham, John

  The ways. *ThP*

Oxford, England

  The spires of Oxford. W. M. Letts. *BrL-7*

Oysters

  The ballad of the oysterman. O. W. Holmes. *BrL-8—NaM*

  How much is true. J. Ciardi. *CiM*

  "Seven sharp propeller blades." J. Ciardi. *CiR*

Ozymandias. Percy Bysshe Shelley. *BrL-7 —HaP—McW—SmLg—UnG*

Ozymandias revisited. Morris Bishop. *CoH*

P

P., L.

  Dear old dad. *BrR-6*

P is for philtre. Eleanor Farjeon. *FaCb*

P. T. Barnum. Rosemary Carr and Stephen Vincent Benét. *BrL-7*

"**P U** umpkin." Unknown. *WiRm*

Pack, clouds, away. See The rape of Lucrece

"Pack, clouds, away, and welcome day." See The rape of Lucrece—Pack, clouds, away

Paddling. Gertrude Monro Higgs. *HuL-1*

"Paddy, in want of a dinner one day." See Paddy O'Rafther

Paddy O'Rafther. Samuel Lover. *CoSp*

Page, Curtis Hidden
Seven poems. tr. *PaS* (sel.)

Page ix. Gertrude Stein. *McW*

A page's road song. William Alexander Percy. *HaY*

Paget-Fredericks, Joseph
Alone. *BrR-3—HuSv*

"Pagget, a school-boy, got a sword, and then." See Upon Pagget

Pain
"There was a faith-healer of Deal." Unknown
Limericks since Lear. *UnG*

The paint box. E. V. Rieu. *RiF*

Painted desert
The Painted desert, sels. E. J. Coatsworth. *JoAc*
Ceremonial hunt
In Walpi
The Navajo
The Painted desert, sels. Elizabeth Jane Coatsworth. *JoAc*
Ceremonial hunt
In Walpi
The Navajo

"The Painted Lady butterfly." See Stranger still

Paintings and pictures
Art. M. Chute. *ChA*
The dance. W. C. Williams. *SmLg*
A Dutch picture. H. W. Longfellow. *NaM*
A face. R. Browning. *GrCc*
For a picture of St Dorothea. G. M. Hopkins. *GrCc*
"I met a man right here on the pad." J. Ciardi. *CiI*
Mr Blob. E. V. Rieu. *RiF*
The paint box. E. V. Rieu. *RiF*
Picture people ("George and Martha Washington") R. B. Bennett. *HaY*
Picture people ("I like to peek") M. C. Livingston. *LiW*
Pictures. F. A. Elliott. *HuL-2*

A pair of sea-green eyes. Hugh MacDiarmid. *GrCc*

Paiute Indians. See Indians of America—Paiute

Palm Sunday
A ballad for Palm Sunday. E. Farjeon. *FaCb—FaN*

Palmer, T. H.
Try, try again. *FeF*

Pan
Ballad of the Epiphany. C. Dalmon. *EaW*
The god of sheep. J. Fletcher. *SmLg*
Hymn of Pan. P. B. Shelley. *SmLg*
A musical instrument. E. B. Browning. *FeF—UnG*
The great god Pan. *HoW*
Pan and the cherries. P. Fort. *CoPm*

Pan and the cherries. Paul Fort, tr. fr. the French by Jethro Bithell. *CoPm*

Panama canal
Goethals, the prophet engineer. P. Mackaye. *HuSv*

Pancake Tuesday. Eleanor Farjeon. *FaCb*
"Run to church with a frying pan." *FaN*

The panchatantra, sel. Unknown
True friendship, tr. fr. the Sanskrit by Arthur W. Ryder. *PaS*

The panda. William Jay Smith. *SmL*

Pandas
The panda. W. J. Smith. *SmL*

Pangur Bán. Unknown, tr. fr. the Gaelic by Robin Flower. *PaS—SmLg*

Pansies
Wise Johnny. E. Fallis. *ArTp—BrL-k—BrS*

The panther. Ogden Nash. *FeF—LoL—NaM*

"The panther is like a leopard." See The panther

Panthers
The panther. O. Nash. *FeF—LoL—NaM*

Paper
Paper. J. Reeves. *ReR*
Paper I. C. Sandburg. *SaW*
Paper II. C. Sandburg. *SaW*

Paper. James Reeves. *ReR*

Paper boats. Rabindranath Tagore. *FeF*

"Paper is two kinds, to write on, to wrap with." See Paper I

"Paper makes a picture-book." See Paper

Paper I. Carl Sandburg. *SaW*

Paper II. Carl Sandburg. *SaW*

A parable. Arthur Conan Doyle. *BrL-7*

Parades
The circus parade. O. B. Miller. *ArTp*
The flag goes by. H. H. Bennett. *ArTp—BrL-7—BrS—FeF*

Paradise. See Heaven

Paradise. Christina Georgina Rossetti. *DoP*

"A paradise on earth is found." See The poet's paradise

Paradox. Jessie B. Rittenhouse. *ThP*

A parental ode to my son, aged three years and five months. See To my son, aged three years and five months

Parents and parenthood. See Family; Fathers and fatherhood; Home and family life; Mothers and motherhood

The park. James S. Tippett. *ArTp—BrL-k—HuL-1*

Park play. James S. Tippett. *McAw*

Parke, Walter
His mother-in-law. *CoH*
"There was a young prince in Bombay." *CoH*
"There was an old stupid who wrote." *CoH*

Parker, Dorothy
Story. *UnMc*

Parker, Sir (Horatio) Gilbert
Little Garaine. *FeF*

Parks
Fairy gardens. E. Farjeon. *FaCb—FaN*
The park. J. S. Tippett. *ArTp—BrL-k—HuL-1*

Park play. J. S. Tippett. *McAw*
Regent's park. R. Fyleman. *BrR-4*
In the park. *HuSv*
Parley, Peter, pseud. See Goodrich, Samuel Griswold
Parliament soldiers. Mother Goose. *OpO*
Parodies
"The boy stood on the burning deck (eating peanuts)." Unknown. *WoF*
American Father Gander. *UnG*
Father William. From Alice's adventures in wonderland. L. Carroll. *BrBc—CoH—FeF—HuL-2—LoL—McW—UnG*
"You are old, Father William, the young man said." *ArTp*
"How doth the little crocodile." From Alice's adventures in wonderland. L. Carroll. *ArTp—FeF—LoL—McW—NaM—SmLg*
The crocodile. *JoAc—UnG*
Lewis Carroll came here to-day. E. Farjeon. *FaN*
The modern Hiawatha. G. A. Strong. *CoH—FeF—NaM*
Ozymandias revisited. M. Bishop. *CoH*
The shades of night. A. E. Housman. *CoH*
"Will you walk into my parlor." Unknown. *WiRm*
Parrot ("I bought me a parrot in Trinidad") William Jay Smith. *SmB*
Parrot ("A parrot I bought in Zambezi") William Jay Smith. *SmB*
"A **parrot** I bought in Zambezi." See Parrot
Parrots
"Clothed in yellow, red, and green." Mother Goose. *OpO*
"Mary had a parrot." Unknown. *MoY*
Parrot ("I bought me a parrot in Trinidad") W. J. Smith. *SmB*
Parrot ("A parrot I bought in Zambezi") W. J. Smith. *SmB*
Poll Parrot. Mother Goose. *OpO*
Song of the parrot. E. J. Coatsworth. *HuSv*
Parry, (Judge) E. A.
Katawampus, sel.
Pater's bathe. *HuL-2*
Pater's bathe. See Katawampus
A **parson.** See The Canterbury tales
Parsons, Mary Catherine
My valentine. *ArTp—BrL-k—HuL-1*
Parties
After the party. W. Wise. *FeF*
The artful ant. O. Herford. *CoH*
Betty at the party. Unknown. *BrBc—HuL-1*
Carousal. Mother Goose. *OpO*
The dinner party. D. Aldis. *AlA*
Flower party. D. Aldis. *AlHd*
A frolic. P. L. Dunbar. *BrR-5*
I would like to be—a bee. D. W. Baruch. *BrBc*
Mother's party. A. Fisher. *BrBc*
My dress is pink. D. Aldis. *AlHd*
October's party. G. Cooper. *BrS*
A party. L. E. Richards. *BrBc—BrS*
The revoke. E. V. Rieu. *RiF*
The summer party. J. Reeves. *ReW*

"There was a young man so benighted." Unknown. *CoH*
Waiting. J. Reeves. *ReW*
Parting. See Farewells
Parting. Buson, tr. fr. the Japanese by Harold G. Henderson. *PaS*
Parting at morning. Robert Browning. *HoW*
Partners. Jaime Castiello. *McW*
Partridge, S. W.
Angels in the air, sel.
Dark. *DeT*
Dark. See Angels in the air
"**Partridge** berry, bittersweet." See Counting-out rhyme for March
Partridges and quails
Bob White. G. Cooper. *UnG*
A party. Laura E. Richards. *BrBc—BrS*
"**Pass** one window, ty-de-o." Unknown. *WoF*
The **passenjare.** Isaac H. Bromley. *CoH*
A **passer-by.** Robert Bridges. *HoW*
Passerat, Jean
Love in May. *PaS*
A **passing** glimpse. Robert Frost. *FrR—FrY*
Passing it along. Holman F. Day. *BrR-6*
The **passing** of the buffalo. Hamlin Garland. *HuSv*
The **passionate** shepherd to his love. Christopher Marlowe. *HaP—ReT*
Past. See Time—Past
The **past.** Ralph Waldo Emerson. *SmLg*
"The **past** is a dream." Unknown. *MoY*
Past ruined Ilion. Walter Savage Landor. *HaP*
"**Past** ruined Ilion Helen lives." See Past ruined Ilion
The **pasture.** Robert Frost. *ArTp—BrR-4—FeF—FrR—FrY—HuL-2—HuSv—JoAc—NaM—PeF*
Pat-a-cake. See "Pat-a-cake, pat-a-cake, baker's man"
"**Pat-a-cake,** pat-a-cake, baker's man." Mother Goose. *DeMg—HuSv—JoAc—LiL—OpO*
Pat-a-cake. *BrL-k*
"**Pat** Flyn had sixty-seven hats." See What's the difference
A **patch** of old snow. Robert Frost. *FrR—FrY*
Patchen, Kenneth
"Who'll that be." *McW*
The **patchwork** quilt. Elizabeth Fleming. *HuL-2*
Pater's bathe. See Katawampus
Paterson, Andrew Barton
Waltzing Matilda. *CoSp—McW*
Patience. See also Perseverance
James and the shoulder of mutton. A. O'Keefe. *DeT*
"A noiseless patient spider." W. Whitman. *HaP—NaE*
The spider. *HoW*
Patience. H. Graham. *CoH—NaM*
"**Patience** is a virtue." Mother Goose. *OpO*
Tom at dinner. A. O'Keefe. *DeT*

Peas
  The hot pease man. Mother Goose. *OpO*
  Pea brush. R. Frost. *FrR—FrY*

Peas. See "I eat my peas with honey"

"Pease porridge hot." Mother Goose. *ArTp*
  —BrL-k—DeMg—JoAc—LiL—OpO
  "Pease pudding hot." *HuL-1*

"Pease pudding hot." See "Pease porridge hot"

"Peck." See Baby chick

A **peck** of gold. Robert Frost. *FrY*

"Peckerwood pecking on the old church steeple." Unknown. *WoF*

Peddlers and venders
  Apples and pears. E. L. Halsey. *HuL-1*
  A bag of chestnuts. E. Farjeon. *FaCb—FaN*
  The balloon man ("The balloon man's stall") M. C. Livingston. *LiW*
  The balloon man ("He always comes on market days") R. Fyleman. *HuL-1*
  The balloon man ("Our balloon man has balloons") D. Aldis. *AlA—ArTp*
  The blackbird in the lilac. J. Reeves. *ReBl*
  Bread and cherries. W. De La Mare. *HuL-1*
  The broom squire's song. Mother Goose. *OpO*
  Buy any buttons. Mother Goose. *OpO*
  Chestnut stands. R. Field. *BrS*
  The flower-cart man. R. Field. *BrS*
  Good Friday. Mother Goose. *OpO*
  The good humor man. P. McGinley. *NaM*
  Green broom. Unknown. *CoPs—ReG*
  "Half a pound of blackberries." E. Farjeon. *FaCb*
  Herb-Robert. E. Farjeon. *FaCb*
  "Hot cross buns." Mother Goose. *DeMg —JoAc—OpO*
  The hot pease man. Mother Goose. *OpO*
  The ice-cream man. R. Field. *BrR-4—BrS —FeF*
  The ice man. D. Aldis. *AlA—HuL-1*
  "If a man who turnips cries." S. Johnson. *DeMg*
    The turnip seller. *NaE*
    The turnip vendor. *OpO*
  "If I'd as much money as I could spend." Mother Goose. *JoAc—LiL*
    Chairs to mend. *OpO*
    If I'd as much money. *HuL-1*
    Old clothes, any old clo', clo'. *OpO*
  Lemonade stand. D. B. Thompson. *BrS*
  "Little Johnny Morgan." Mother Goose. *DeMg*
    Johnny Morgan. *OpO*
  Melons. M. M. Dodge. *ArTp*
  The merry pieman's song. J. Bennett. *LoL*
  Mr Tom Narrow. J. Reeves. *ReW*
  Molly Malone. Unknown. *UnMc*
  "Oh, do you know the muffin-man." Mother Goose. *DeMg*
  "Old chairs to mend. Old chairs to mend." Mother Goose. *DeMg*
  Old woman in May. J. Drinkwater. *HuL-2*
  A pedlar ("Fine knacks for ladies, cheap, choice, brave, and new") Unknown. *HoW*

The pedlar ("Lawn as white as driven snow") From The winter's tale. **W.** Shakespeare. *HoW*
The rabbit man. Mother Goose. *OpO*
"Smiling girls, rosy boys." Mother Goose. *DeMg*
  The gingerbread man. *OpO*
Sweet blooming lavender. Mother Goose. *OpO*
"There was an old woman (sold puddings and pies)." Mother Goose. *DeMg*
  Old pudding-pie woman. *OpO*
"Young lambs to sell. Young lambs to sell." Mother Goose. *DeMg*
  The toy lamb seller. *OpO*

Pedigree. Emily Dickinson. *UnG*

"The pedigree of honey." See Pedigree

Pedigrees. See Ancestry

Pediment: Ballet. Louise Townsend Nicholl. *PlU*

A **pedlar** ("Fine knacks for ladies, cheap, choice, brave, and new") Unknown. *HoW*

The **pedlar** ("Lawn as white as driven snow") See The winter's tale

Pedlars. See Peddlers and venders

Peele, George
  Celanta at the well of life. *ReT*
    A voice speaks from the well. *SmLg*
  "His golden locks time hath to silver turned." See Polyhymnia
  Polyhymnia, sel.
    "His golden locks time hath to silver turned." *HaP*
  A voice speaks from the well. See Celanta at the well of life
  "When as the rye reach to the chin." *SmLg*

Peep-primrose. Eleanor Farjeon. *FaCb—FaN*

"Peep, squirrel, peep." Unknown. *TaD*

Peg. See "There was an old woman, her name it was Peg"

Pegasus
  Pegasus. E. Farjeon. *FaCb—FaN*

Pegasus. Eleanor Farjeon. *FaCb—FaN*

Pelham, M.
  The comical girl. *CoH*

The **pelican.** Philippe De Thaun, tr. by Richard Wilbur. *McW*

The **pelican** chorus. Edward Lear. *LoL*

Pelicans
  The pelican. P. De Thaun. *McW*
  The pelican chorus. E. Lear. *LoL*
  "The reason for the pelican." J. Ciardi. *CiR*

"Pellicanus is the word." See The pelican

Penguin. William Jay Smith. *SmB*

Penguins
  Penguin. W. J. Smith. *SmB*
  Peter and Percival; or, The penguins' revolt. E. V. Rieu. *RiF*

"Penny and penny." Mother Goose. *OpO*

The **penny** fiddle. Robert Graves. *GrP*

"A penny is heavier than the shrew." See The masked shrew

"A **penny**, kind lady." See Remember the grotto
People
Cat. W. J. Smith. *SmB*
Dog. W. J. Smith. *SmB*
My people. C. Sandburg. *SaW*
The people ("The ants are walking under the ground") E. M. Roberts. *ArTp*
People ("Hour after hour") W. J. Smith. *SmL*
People ("Tall people, short people") L. Lenski. *FeF*
Picture people. M. C. Livingston. *LiW*
The right kind of people. E. Markham. *BrL-8*
Some people. R. Field. *FeF*
Then as now. W. De La Mare. *McW*
People—Portraits. See also Boys and boyhood; Girls and girlhood
The Canterbury tales, sels. G. Chaucer
A girlish pardoner. *HaP*
A gluttonous rich man. *HaP*
A greedy friar. *HaP*
A knight. *UnG—UnMc*
A perfect knight. *HaP*
A miller. *UnG*
A stout miller. *HaP*
A parson. *HaP*
A prioress. *UnMc*
A polite nun. *HaP*
A sporting monk. *HaP*
A squire. *UnG—UnMc*
A tasty cook. *HaP*
The wife of Bath. *HaP*
People—Portraits—Men
Archibald's example. E. A. Robinson. *GrCc*
Bewick Finzer. E. A. Robinson. *GrCc*
The figure in the doorway. R. Frost. *FrR*
Hemmed-in males. W. C. Williams. *HaP*
A hundred collars. R. Frost. *FrR*
The last leaf. O. W. Holmes. *FeF—McW*
Lighthearted William. W. C. Williams. *HaP*
Miniver Cheevy. E. A. Robinson. *HaP—SmLg—UnMc*
Mr Bellairs. J. Reeves. *ReBl*
Mr Pyme. H. Behn. *ArTp—LoL*
Old Dan'l. L. A. G. Strong. *CoPs*
Richard Cory. E. A. Robinson. *CoSp—SmLg—ThP*
The village blacksmith. H. W. Longfellow. *FeF—HuSv—UnG*
People—Portraits—Women
At a window. E. Farjeon. *FaCb*
Aunt Helen. T. S. Eliot. *HaP*
Cousin Nancy. T. S. Eliot. *HaP*
Deirdre. J. Stephens. *GrCc*
Garden abstract. H. Crane. *GrCc*
Here lies a lady. J. C. Ransom. *NaE*
In shadow. H. Crane. *GrCc*
Mrs MacQueen. W. De La Mare. *HuL-2*
My last duchess. R. Browning. *HaP*
Portrait by a neighbor. E. St V. Millay. *ArTp—FeF—HuL-2—NaM—PeF*
The silken tent. R. Frost. *FrR*
Tiggady Rue. D. McCord. *McFf*
To a fair lady, playing with a snake. E. Waller. *GrCc*
A woman driving. T. Hardy. *GrCc*

People—Size
"The daughter of the farrier." Unknown
Limericks since Lear. *UnG*
"A girl who weighed many an oz." Unknown
Limericks since Lear. *UnG*
How tall. D. McCord. *McT*
"I had a little sweetheart no bigger than my thumb." Unknown. *WoF*
"Jerry Hall." Mother Goose. *DeMg—OpO*
Little. D. Aldis. *AlA—ArTp—FeF*
The little elf. J. K. Bangs. *BrBc—BrL-k—HuL-1—JoAc—McW—PeF—UnG*
The little elfman. *ArTp*
"Little Hermogenes is so small." Lucilius. *JoAc*
Mrs Snipkin and Mrs Wobblechin. L. E. Richards. *ArTp—CoH—HuL-1—HuSv—JoAc*
"Old Joe Brown, he had a wife." Unknown
American Father Gander. *UnG*
Sizes. J. Ciardi. *CiM*
Teddy Bear. A. A. Milne. *MiWc*
"There was an old man, who when little." E. Lear
Lear's limericks. *UnG*
Limericks. *JoAc*
The **people** ("The ants are walking under the ground") Elizabeth Madox Roberts. *ArTp*
People ("Hour after hour") William Jay Smith. *SmL*
People ("Tall people, short people") Lois Lenski. *FeF*
"**People** expect old men to die." See Old men
People hide their love. Wu-ti, Emperor of Liang, tr. fr. the Chinese by Arthur Waley. *PaS*
"The **people** of Diddling." See Diddling
"The **people** of Spain think Cervantes." See Cervantes
"**People** simper and drawl." See Gnat
"**People** who know tigers." See How to tell a tiger
"The **people** who live across the way." Unknown. *WoF*
The **people**, yes, sels. Carl Sandburg
American yarns. *HuSv*
Yarns. *UnG*
Children of the desert. *SaW*
Children of the wind. *HuSv*
Circles. *SaW*
Mother and child. *SaW*
Niagara. *SaW*
Night too has numbers. *SaW*
Prairie barn. *SaW*
Proverbs. *SaW*
The **peppery** man. Arthur Macy. *FeF*
"The **peppery** man was cross and thin." See The peppery man
"**Perched** on the public wires the careless birds." See The birds and the telephone wires
Percival, James Gates
The coral grove. *UnG*

Percy, William Alexander
The little shepherd's song. *HaY*
A page's road song. *HaY*
"The **Percy** out of Northumberland." See
Chevy Chase
A **perfect** knight. See The Canterbury tales
—A knight
Perfect love. Sana'i, tr. fr. the Persian by
A. J. Arberry. *PaS*
The **perfect** reactionary. Hughes Mearns.
CoH
"**Perfection** ever rising to perfection." See
Invocation
The **performing** seal. See A circus garland
The **perils** of invisibility. William Schwenck
Gilbert. *CoSp*

Permanence
Smoke stack. A. M. Sullivan. *McW*
Song's eternity. J. Clare. *McW—SmLg*
"Violets, daffodils." E. J. Coatsworth.
ArTp

"**Perrette's** milk-pot fitted her head-mat just
right." See The dairymaid and her
milk-pot

Perry, Nora
The coming of the spring. *HaY*
In June. *HaY*

Perseverance
Columbus. J. Miller. *ArTp—BrL-8—FeF
—HaY—HuSv—McW*
Eldorado. E. A. Poe. *HoW—McW—
SmLg*
Keeping on. A. H. Clough. *NaM*
Mother to son. L. Hughes. *BrBc—HuSv
—PeF*
"The mouse that gnawed the oak tree
down." V. Lindsay. *BrL-7*
On a tree fallen across the road. R.
Frost. *FrR*
Try, try again. T. H. Palmer. *FeF*

Persia
Alexander's feast; or, The power of music.
J. Dryden. *HoW*
The rubáiyát of Omar Khayyám of Nai-
shapúr. O. Khayyám. *HaP* (sel.)—
PaS (sel.)
Wake. *FeF* (sel.)

Persian proverb. Leslie Savage Clark.
ThP

"The **person** in the gaudy clothes." See
Captain Kidd

Pessimism. See also Failure; Optimism
The difference. Unknown. *UnG*
The pessimist. B. King. *CoH—McW*

The **pessimist.** Ben King. *CoH—McW*

The **pet** lamb. William Wordsworth. *DeT*
(sel.)

Pet Marjorie. Eleanor Farjeon. *FaN*

"**Pet** Marjorie, wee croodlin dove." See
Pet Marjorie

Peter. See "Peter, Peter, pumpkin eater"

Peter and John. Elinor Wylie. *UnMc*

"**Peter** and Percival lived in a place." See
Peter and Percival; or, The penguins'
revolt

Peter and Percival; or, The penguins' revolt.
E. V. Rieu. *RiF*

Peter Bell, sel. William Wordsworth
The crescent boat. *ReT*
Among the stars. *UnG*
"**Peter,** Peter, pumpkin eater." Mother
Goose. *AnI—DeMg—JoAc—LiL*
Peter. *OpO*
Peter Piper. See "Peter Piper picked a peck
of pickled pepper"
"**Peter** Piper pick'd a peck of pepper." See
"Peter Piper picked a peck of pickled
pepper"
"**Peter** Piper picked a peck of pickled
pepper." Mother Goose. *DeMg—HuSv
—LiL—OpO*
Peter Piper. *FeF*
"Peter Piper pick'd a peck of pepper."
JoAc
Peter Quince at the clavier. Wallace
Stevens. *GrCc*
"**Peter** Rabbit—ha, ha." Unknown. *TaD*
"**Peter** Simon Suckegg." Unknown. *TaD*
Peter White. See "Peter White will ne'er
go right"
"**Peter** White will ne'er go right." Mother
Goose. *DeMg*
Peter White. *OpO*

Petit, the poet. See The Spoon River anthology

Pets. See also names of animals, as Dogs
The goldfish. D. Aldis. *AlA—BrL-k*
"Jemima Jane." M. Chute. *ChA*
Lost. D. McCord. *McFf*
Mary's lamb. S. J. Hale. *FeF—JoAc—
OpO—UnG*
"Mary had a little lamb." *BrL-k—
DeMg—LiL*
My new rabbit. E. Gould. *HuL-1*
The new pet. D. Aldis. *AlA*
The pet lamb. W. Wordsworth. *DeT*
(sel.)
Pets. Unknown. *WiRm*
The python. H. Belloc. *NaE*
Radiator lions. D. Aldis. *AlA—JoAc*
The tale of Custard the dragon. O. Nash.
FeF—UnG
The yak. H. Belloc. *CoH—FeF—HuL-2—
JoAc*

Pets. Unknown. *WiRm*

"The **pettitoes** are little feet." Mother
Goose. *OpO*

The **phantom** light of the Baie des Chaleurs.
Arthur Wentworth Hamilton Eaton.
CoPm

The **phantom** mail coach. L. O. Welcome.
CoPm

The **phantom**-wooer. Thomas Lovell Beddoes. *HoW*

Phantoms. See Ghosts

The **pheasant** ("A pheasant cock sprang into
view") Robert P. Tristram Coffin. *ArTp*

The **pheasant** ("See, from the brake the
whirring pheasant springs") Alexander
Pope. *UnG*

"A **pheasant** cock sprang into view." See
The pheasant

Pheasants
The pheasant ("A pheasant cock sprang
into view") R. P. T. Coffin. *ArTp*

Pheasants—*Continued*
The pheasant ("See, from the brake the whirring pheasant springs") A. Pope. *UnG*

Philippians. See The epistle of Paul to the Philippians

"Philips, whose touch harmonious could remove." See An epitaph upon the celebrated Claudy Philips, musician, who died very poor

Phillis inamorata. Lancelot Andrewes. *GrCc*

The philosopher. See "As I walked by myself"

Philosophy. Paul Laurence Dunbar. *BrL-8*

Phizzog. Carl Sandburg. *ArTp*

"Phoebe's getting old they say." See Anniversary in September

Phoenix
The phoenix. From Nepenthe. G. Darley. *GrCc—HoW*
"O blest unfabled incense tree." *SmLg*

The phoenix. See Nepenthe

Physical geography. Louise Townsend Nicholl. *PlI*

The piano. James Reeves. *ReBl*

Piano tuner, untune me that tune. Ogden Nash. *PlU*

Pianos
Elizabeth at the piano. H. Gregory. *PlU*
The piano. J. Reeves. *ReBl*
Practicing. D. Aldis. *AlA*

Piatt, John James
October morning. *HaY*

Piatt, Sara M. B.
Self-comforted. *DeT*

Piazza piece. John Crowe Ransom. *HaP*

Pick-a-back. Mother Goose. *OpO*

Pick me up. William Jay Smith. *SmL*

"Pick me up with a pile of blocks." See Pick me up

"The pickety fence." See Five chants

Pickthall, Marjorie L. C.
A child's song of Christmas. *HaY*

The picnic. Dorothy Aldis. *AlA—ArTp—McAw*

The picnic box. Aileen Fisher. *McAw*

Picnic by the sea. Harry Behn. *BeW*

Picnic day. Rachel Field. *ArTp—BrS*

Picnics
Beach fire. F. M. Frost. *ArTp—PeF*
Growing up. H. Behn. *BrBc—BrS*
"I met a man that showed me a trick." J. Ciardi. *CiI*
Our picnic. D. Aldis. *AlHd*
The picnic. D. Aldis. *AlA—ArTp—McAw*
The picnic box. A. Fisher. *McAw*
Picnic by the sea. H. Behn. *BeW*
Picnic day. R. Field. *ArTp—BrS*
Picnics. M. Chute. *ChA*
A rainy piece. I. O. Eastwick. *EaI*

Picnics. Marchette Chute. *ChA*

Picture people ("George and Martha Washington") Rowena Bastin Bennett. *HaY*

Picture people ("I like to peek") Myra Cohn Livingston. *LiW*

Pictures. See Paintings and pictures

Pictures. F. Ann Elliott. *HuL-2*

Piecrust. Eleanor Farjeon. *FaCb—FaN*

Pied beauty. Gerard Manley Hopkins. *McW—ReT—UnG*

The Pied Piper of Hamelin. Robert Browning. *ArTp—HuSv—JoAc—SmLg—UnG*
How the rats were destroyed. *HuL-2* (sel.)

Pierce, Dorothy Mason
Good night. *ArTp—BrS*
John plans. *BrBc*
Sprinkling. *ArTp—BrL-k*

Pierpont, James
Jingle bells. *OpO* (sel.)

Pierpont, John
The fourth of July. *HaY*

Pies
"A was an apple-pie." Mother Goose. *DeMg—LiL*
A apple pie. *JoAc*
Apple-pye. *DeT*
The tragical death of A, apple pie. *OpO*
"Calico pie." E. Lear. *FeF—LoL—ReG—SmLg—UnG*
Cherry-pie Sunday. E. Farjeon. *FaN*
The fastidious serpent. H. Johnstone. *CoH—LoL*
"He-hi, gimme a piece of pie." Unknown. *WoF*
Little bits. J. Ciardi. *CiY*
"The Queen of Hearts." Mother Goose. *AnI—DeMg—JoAc—LiL—OpO*
"Simple Simon met a pieman." Mother Goose. *DeMg—HuSv—JoAc—LiL*
Simple Simon. *ReG—UnG*
Simple Simon and the pieman. *OpO*
The tale of a tart. F. E. Weatherly. *HuL-1*
"There was an old woman (sold puddings and pies)." Mother Goose. *DeMg*
Old pudding-pie woman. *OpO*

Pig. William Jay Smith. *SmB*

Pig shaving. See "Barber, barber, shave a pig"

A pig tale ("Poor Jane Higgins") James Reeves. *ReBl*

A pig-tale ("There was a pig that sat alone") See Sylvie and Bruno—The melancholy pig

Pigeons
Bores. A. Guiterman. *BrR-5*
The dove and the ant. J. De La Fontaine. *JoAc*
"The dove says, Coo, coo, what shall I do." Mother Goose. *DeMg*
Coo. *DeT*
The dove says. *OpO*
"I had two pigeons bright and gay." Mother Goose. *OpO*
"Mrs Peck-Pigeon." E. Farjeon. *ArTp—BrL-k—HuSv—JoAc*
The mourning dove. M. C. Livingston. *LiW*
Mourning doves. D. Aldis. *AlHd*
Pigeons ("Pigeons do") M. Chute. *ChA*
The pigeons ("Ten snowy white pigeons are standing in line") M. Burnham. *BrL-k*

Psalm LV. From Psalms, Bible, Old Testament
  Wings. *FeF*
Song. J. Keats. *FeF—ReT*
  I had a dove. *CoI—DeT*

Pigeons ("Pigeons do") Marchette Chute. *ChA*

The **pigeons** ("Ten snowy white pigeons are standing in line") Maud Burnham. *BrL-k*

"Pigeons do." See Pigeons

"Piggy-wig found he had four little feet." See What piggy-wig found

Pigs
  Alice. W. J. Smith. *SmL*
  "Barber, barber, shave a pig." Mother Goose. *DeMg—JoAc—LiL*
    Barber, barber. *NaE*
    Pig shaving. *OpO*
  "Dickery, dickery, dare." Mother Goose. *DeMg*
    The flying pig. *OpO*
  Grig's pig. Mother Goose. *OpO*
  "I had a little pig, his name was Ben." Unknown. *WoF*
  "I had a little pig, I fed him in a trough." Unknown. *WoF*
  "If a pig wore a wig." C. G. Rossetti. *JoAc*
  If pigs could fly. J. Reeves. *ReBl*
  Jack Sprat's pig. Mother Goose. *OpO*
  "Let's go to the wood, says this pig." Mother Goose. *OpO*
  "Little Betty Pringle she had a pig." Mother Goose. *DeMg*
    Betty Pringle's pig. *OpO*
  Little piggy. T. Hood. *HuL-1*
  "A long-tailed pig, or a short-tailed pig." Mother Goose. *DeMg*
  Mary Middling. R. Fyleman. *BrL-k—HuL-1*
  The melancholy pig. From Sylvie and Bruno. L. Carroll. *FeF*
    A pig-tale. *HoW*
  Ode to the pig: His tail. W. R. Brooks. *LoL*
  The old sow took the measles. Unknown. *WoF*
  The old woman and the pig. Unknown. *TaD*
  The old woman who bought a pig. Mother Goose. *OpO*
  On oath. Mother Goose. *OpO*
  A pig tale. J. Reeves. *ReBl*
  The pigs ("Do look at those pigs as they lie in the straw") J. Taylor. *DeT*
  Pigs ("Pigs are always awfully dirty") W. J. Smith. *SmB*
  The pig's tail. N. Ault. *HuL-2*
  Precocious piggy. T. Hood. *BrL-k*
  "Sheep and shoat were walking through the pasture." Unknown. *WiRm*
  "There was a lady loved a swine." Mother Goose. *DeMg*
    The lady in love. *OpO*
    There was a lady. *DeT*
  "This little pig had a rub-a-dub." Mother Goose. *OpO*
  "This little pig says, I'm goin' to steal some corn." Unknown. *WoF*

"This little pig went to market." Mother Goose. *DeMg—HuSv—JoAc—LiL—OpO*
The three little pigs. A. Scott-Gatty. *HuL-1*
The unknown color. C. Cullen. *FeF*
"Upon my word and honour." Mother Goose. *DeMg*
What piggy-wig found. E. Blyton. *HuL-1*
"What shall we do for bacon now." Unknown. *WoF*
Whose little pigs. Mother Goose. *OpO*
The **pigs.** Jane Taylor. *DeT*
"Pigs are always awfully dirty." See Pigs
"Pigs love pumpkins." Unknown. *MoY*
The **pig's** tail. Norman Ault. *HuL-2*
Pigwiggin arms himself. See Nymphidia: The court of fairy

Pike, Cicely E.
  Jack Frost. *HuL-1*
The **pilgrim** ("I fasted for some forty days on bread and buttermilk") William Butler Yeats. *HaP*
The **pilgrim** ("Who could true valour see") See The pilgrim's progress—Pilgrim's song

Pilgrim Fathers. See also Thanksgiving day; United States—History—Colonial period
  "If I were a pilgrim child." R. B. Bennett. *HaY*
  The landing of the Pilgrim Fathers. F. D. Hemans. *ArTp—BrR-5—FeF—UnG*
  The pilgrims came. A. Wynne. *McAw*
The **pilgrim** way. Unknown. *ThP*
The **pilgrims** came. Annette Wynne. *McAw*
"The pilgrims came across the sea." See The pilgrims came
The **pilgrim's** progress, sels. John Bunyan
  Pilgrim's song. *HoW—McW*
    The pilgrim. *ArTp—DeT—NaE*
  The shepherd boy sings in the valley of humiliation. *UnG*
Pilgrim's song. See The pilgrim's progress

Pilots and piloting. See Aviators

A **pin** has a head. Christina Georgina Rossetti. *BrR-4*
"A pin has a head, but has no hair." See A pin has a head
"Pin wheels whirling round." See Fourth of July night

Pincushion cactus. Myra Cohn Livingston. *LiW*

Pindar
  An eclipse. *PaS*
  The power of music. *PlU* (sel.)

A **Pindaric** ode: To the immortal memory and friendship of that noble pair, Sir Lucius Cary and Sir Henry Morrison, sel. Ben Jonson
  The noble nature. *BrR-6*

Pine trees
  The isle should have a pine tree. E. J. Coatsworth. *BrR-4*
  The pine bough. R. Aldridge. *CoPs*
  Pine tree song. M. Barrows. *BrR-4*
  The pine-trees in the courtyard. Po Chü-i. *PaS*
  Solitary pine. Prince Ichihara. *PaS*

The **pine** bough. Richard Aldridge. *CoPs*

Pine tree song. Marjorie Barrows. *BrR-4*

The **pine-trees** in the courtyard. Po Chü-i, tr. fr. the Chinese by Arthur Waley. *PaS*

"The **pines** are white-powdered." See New snow

"The **pines** were dark on Ramoth hill." See My playmate

Pinkle Purr. A. A. Milne. *MiWc*

Pins
"See a pin and pick it up." Mother Goose. *DeMg—JoAc—LiL*
   Signs, seasons, and sense. *UnG*
A song. Mother Goose. *OpO*
"Tim, Tim, sat on a pin." Unknown. *WoJ*

The **pinwheel's** song. John Ciardi. *CiR*

The **pioneer** ("He could not breathe in a crowded place") William B. Ruggles. *BrR-5*

The **pioneer** ("Long years ago I blazed a trail") Arthur Guiterman. *ArTp*

Pioneer life. See Frontier and pioneer life

"**Piped** a tiny voice hard by." See The chickadee

The **piper.** See "Piping down the valleys wild"

The **piper.** See "There was a piper had a cow"

A **piper** ("A piper in the streets today") Seumas O'Sullivan. *ArTp—FeF—HuL-2 —NaM*

"A **piper** in the streets today." See A piper

Pipers
"As I was going up the hill." Mother Goose. *OpO*
The bagpipe man. N. B. Turner. *ArTp— HuL-1—HuL-2*
"Doodledy, doodledy, doodledy, dan." Mother Goose. *OpO*
"He met old Dame Trot with a basket of eggs." Mother Goose. *DeMg*
"Here we come a-piping." Unknown. *BrS—JoAc*
The magic piper. E. L. Marsh. *BrS— HuL-2*
Over the hills and far away. Mother Goose. *HuL-1*
The Pied Piper of Hamelin. R. Browning. *ArTp—HuSv—JoAc—SmLg—UnG*
   How the rats were destroyed. *HuL-2* (sel.)
A piper. S. O'Sullivan. *ArTp—FeF— HuL-2—NaM*
"Piping down the valleys wild." W. Blake. *PlU—SmLg*
   Happy songs. *UnG*
   Introduction. *ReT*
   Introduction to Songs of innocence. *ArTp*
   The piper. *DeT*
"There was a piper had a cow." Mother Goose. *DeMg*
   The piper. *OpO*
"Tom, he was a piper's son." *ArTp— DeMg*
   Tom, the piper's son. *OpO*
"Tom saw a cross fellow was beating an ass." Mother Goose. *DeMg*

"**Piping** down the valleys wild." William Blake. *PlU—SmLg*
   Happy songs. *UnG*
   Introduction. *ReT*
   Introduction to Songs of innocence. *ArTp*
   The piper. *DeT*

"**Piping** hot, smoking hot." See The hot pease man

Pippa passes, sel. Robert Browning
   Pippa's song. *FeF*
      Spring song. *UnG*
      "The year's at the spring." *DoP— HaY—HuSv—ThP*

Pippa's song. See Pippa passes

The **pirate** cook. Marchette Chute. *BrR-6— ChA*

The **Pirate** Don Durk of Dowdee. Mildred Plew Meigs. *ArTp—HuL-2—PeF*

Pirate passes. E. V. Rieu. *RiF*

Pirate story. Robert Louis Stevenson. *ArTp—FeF—JoAc—UnG*

Pirate wind. Mary Jane Carr. *BrS*

Pirates. See also names of pirates, as Kidd, Captain
A ballad of John Silver. J. Masefield. *NaE*
Captain Kidd ("Oh, my name was Robert Kidd, as I sailed, as I sailed") Unknown. *NaM*
Captain Kidd ("The person in the gaudy clothes") R. C. and S. V. Benét. *HuL-2*
Derelict. Y. E. Allison. *PaOm*
A Dutch picture. H. W. Longfellow. *NaM*
John Dory. Unknown. *MaB*
The old buccaneer. C. Kingsley. *NaE— NaM*
   The last buccaneer. *UnG*
The phantom light of the Baie des Chaleurs. A. W. H. Eaton. *CoPm*
The pirate cook. M. Chute. *BrR-6—ChA*
The Pirate Don Durk of Dowdee. M. P. Meigs. *ArTp—HuL-2—PeF*
Pirate passes. E. V. Rieu. *RiF*
Pirate story. R. L. Stevenson. *ArTp— FeF—JoAc—UnG*
Pirates. H. Behn. *BeW*
Pirates on Funafuti. E. V. Rieu. *RiF*
Spanish waters. J. Masefield. *FeF—McW*
The tale of Custard the dragon. O. Nash. *FeF—UnG*

Pirates. Harry Behn. *BeW*

The **pirates** of Penzance, sel. William Schwenck Gilbert
   The policeman's lot. *CoH*

Pirates on Funafuti. E. V. Rieu. *RiF*

Pisan cantos, sel. Ezra Pound
   The ant's a centaur. *HaP*

Pisces. Eleanor Farjeon. *FaCb—FaN*

Pit, pat. See "Pit, pat, well-a day"

"**Pit,** pat, well-a day." Mother Goose. *DeMg*
   Pit, pat. *OpO*

Pitcher, Molly (about)
   Molly Pitcher. K. B. Sherwood. *UnG*

Pitt, William, Earl of Chatham
   The sailor's consolation. at. *CoH—DeT— HuSv*

Pitter, Ruth
The viper. *GrCc*
"Pitter patter, falls the rain." See The umbrella brigade
"Pity poor Rumble: he is growing wheezy." See Poor Rumble
"Pixies, slipping, dipping, stealing." See Cornish magic
Plain language from truthful James. Bret Harte *CoH*
Plain philomel. Eleanor Farjeon. *FaCb—FaN*
The plain was grassy, wild and bare." See The dying swan
Plains. See Prairies
Plaint. Mother Goose. *OpO*
The plaint of the camel. See The admiral's caravan
Plane geometry. Emma Rounds. *PlI*
Planets. See also Moon; Stars; World
For the conjunction of two planets. A. C. Rich. *PlI*
Our hold on the planet. R. Frost. *FrR*
Valentine for earth. F. M. Frost. *ArTp—FrLn*
Plans. Dorothy Brown Thompson. *BrBc—HuL-1*
Planting a tree. Nancy Byrd Turner. *HaY*
Planting flowers on the eastern embankment. Po Chü-i, tr. fr. the Chinese by Arthur Waley. *PaS*
The planting of the apple tree. William Cullen Bryant. *CoPs* (sel.)*—HuSv*
Plants. See also names of plants, as Dandelions
The little plant. K. L. Brown. *BrL-k*
"The plants stand silent round me." Johannes Jorgensen, tr. fr. the Danish by Robert Hillyer. *PaS*

Platen, August Graf von
"Fain would I live in safest freedom." *PaS*

Plato
Country music. *PaS*
Morning star. *PaS*

Plato (about)
Plato, a musician. Leontius. *PlU*
Plato's tomb. Unknown. *SmLg*

Plato, a musician. Leontius, tr. by A. J. Butler. *PlU*

Plato's tomb. Unknown, tr. fr. the Greek by Percy Bysshe Shelley. *SmLg*

Play. See also Counting-out rhymes; Finger-play poems; Games; Nursery play; Playmates
A-ha. D. Aldis. *AlA*
All a duck needs. D. Aldis. *AlA*
All in together. Unknown. *WoJ*
"All work and no play makes Jack a dull boy." Mother Goose. *OpO*
Allie. R. Graves. *FeF—GrP*
Alone. D. Aldis. *AlA*
Alphabet routine. Unknown. *WoJ*
"Amos and Andy." Unknown. *TaD*
The archer. C. Scollard. *FeF*
At the sea-side. R. L. Stevenson. *ArTp—FeF—JoAc*
August afternoon. M. Edey. *HaY*
Away we go. E. Dennis. *McAw*

Ball with Yvonne. E. Farjeon. *FaCb*
Banana split. Unknown. *TaD*
Bath time. M. Chute. *ChA*
The bear hunt. M. Widdemer. *FeF*
"The best game the fairies play." R. Fyleman. *ArTp*
Blanket street. I. Hogan. *BrBc*
Block city. R. L. Stevenson. *FeF*
"Bobby went down to the ocean." Unknown. *WoJ*
Bobby's first poem. N. Gale. *CoH—NaM*
Bouncing ball. S. R. Watson. *BrR-3*
A boy's song. J. Hogg. *DeT—FeF—HoW—McW—NaM*
"Bread and butter." Unknown
Four questions. *WoJ*
Building. H. Behn. *BeW*
Bump on my knee. M. C. Livingston. *LiWa*
"Buster, Buster, climb the tree." Unknown. *WoJ*
Busy. A. A. Milne. *MiWc*
The castle. J. Reeves. *ReW*
Catching song. E. Farjeon. *DeT—HuL-1*
Chairoplane chant. N. B. Turner. *BrR-5*
Chant for skippers. K. Gallagher. *BrS*
"Charley over the water." Unknown. *WiRm—WoJ*
Chewing gum. Unknown. *WoJ*
"Cinderella, dressed in red." Unknown. *WiRm*
"Cinderella, dressed in yeller." Unknown
Four questions. *WoJ*
Come, little leaves. G. Cooper. *FeF*
Come out with me. A. A. Milne. *MiWc*
Dangerous. D. Aldis. *AlA*
Did you ever. Unknown. *WoJ*
"Dingle dingle doosey." Mother Goose. *OpO*
Discovery. M. C. Livingston. *LiW*
Dr Brown. Unknown. *WoJ*
Down in the valley. Unknown. *TaD—WoJ*
Down on the beach. D. Aldis. *AlA*
The drum. E. Field. *BrR-6*
The echoing (ecchoing) green. W. Blake. *CoPs—HoW—JoAc*
Elevator. Unknown. *WoJ*
"Elizabeth cried." E. Farjeon. *McAw*
"Engine, engine, number nine." Unknown. *WiRm—WoF*
Engine, engine. *TaD—WoJ*
The engineer. A. A. Milne. *MiWc*
"Every time I climb a tree." From Five chants. D. McCord. *ArTp—McFf—UnG*
Extremes. J. W. Riley. *BrL-k—FeF*
Far away. D. McCord. *McFf*
For Anna. M. C. Livingston. *LiWa*
Foreign lands. R. L. Stevenson. *HuL-1*
Forgotten. A. A. Milne. *MiWc*
Frolic. G. W. Russell. *FeF*
Fun in a garret. E. C. Dowd. *ArTp—BrR-3*
The girl with the ball. E. Farjeon. *FaCb*
"Girls and boys, come out to play." Mother Goose. *ArTp—DeMg—HuSv—LiL—NaM*
"Boys and girls come out to play." *JoAc—OpO*
Full moon. *DeT*
Girls and boys. *HuL-1*

Play—*Continued*

A good play. R. L. Stevenson. *ArTp—FeF—NaM*
"Grace, Grace, dressed in lace." Unknown. *WoJ*
Green grass. J. Reeves. *ReR*
"Gypsy, gypsy, lived in a tent." Unknown. *WiRm*
Halfway down. A. A. Milne. *FeF—MiWc*
Henry and Mary. R. Graves. *GrP*
"Here am I, little jumping Joan." Mother Goose. *LiL*
 "Here am I." *DeMg*
 Jumping Joan. *OpO*
 Little jumping Joan. *ArTp*
Here comes the teacher. Unknown. *WoJ*
Hers. E. Farjeon. *FaCb*
Hide-and-seek. R. Francis. *HaP*
Hiding. D. Aldis. *AlA—ArTp—BrL-k—FeF—JoAc*
"Higgledy, piggledy, see how they run." K. Greenaway. *ArTp*
"The high skip." Mother Goose. *LiL*
Hoppity. A. A. Milne. *ArTp—MiWc*
Horsemanship. M. Chute. *ArTp—MiWc*
How many carriages. Unknown. *WoJ*
How many miles. Unknown. *WoJ*
The hunter. D. Aldis. *AlA*
Husky hi. Unknown. *ArTp—JoAc*
I have to have it. D. Aldis. *AlA*
"I know a place." M. C. Livingston. *LiW*
I like housecleaning. D. B. Thompson. *FeF*
I love coffee. Unknown. *TaD*
 I like coffee, I like tea. *WoJ*
"I met a man that was coming back." J. Ciardi. *CiI*
"I was standing on the corner." Unknown. *TaD*
I woke up. Unknown. *WoJ*
"Ice cream, soda, ginger ale, pop." Unknown. *TaD—WoJ*
"Ickle ockle, blue bockle." Mother Goose. *OpO*
Icky bicky. Unknown. *WoJ*
Icy. R. W. Bacmeister. *BrL-k*
If I had a cardboard box. A. Fisher. *McAw*
If I were a fish. M. L. Allen. *AlP*
"I'm a sailor all dressed in blue." Unknown. *TaD*
In just spring. From Chanson innocente. E. E. Cummings. *CoH—JoAc—ReT*
 Chanson innocente. *FeF—NaM*
 "In just." *UnG*
Indecision. M. Chute. *ChA*
The island. D. Aldis. *AlA*
"Jack be nimble." Mother Goose. *AnI—ArTp—DeMg—HuSv—JoAc—LiL—OpO*
"Jack, Jack, pump the water." Unknown. *TaD*
Joan's corner. E. Farjeon. *FaCb*
"Johnny on the ocean." Unknown. *TaD*
"Jump—jump—jump." K. Greenaway. *ArTp*
 The little jumping girls. *FeF*
Just watch. M. C. Livingston. *LiW*
Keep the pot a-boilin'. Unknown. *WoJ*
Kick a little stone. D. Aldis. *AlA*
King of the hill. Unknown. *TaD*
The kitten at play. W. Wordsworth. *FeF*
 The kitten playing with the falling leaves. *UnG*

Knight-in-armour. A. A. Milne. *MiWc*
Lamplighter barn. M. C. Livingston. *LiWa*
The land of counterpane. R. L. Stevenson. *FeF—HuSv—JoAc—NaE*
The land of story-books. R. L. Stevenson. *ArTp—FeF—UnG*
Lawn song. M. C. Livingston. *LiWa*
"Lazy deuks that sit i' the coal-neuks." Mother Goose. *OpO*
Let's pretend. J. S. Tippett. *McAw*
Like me. D. Aldis. *AlA—McAw*
Lines and squares. A. A. Milne. *MiWc*
Little Dutch girl. Unknown. *WoJ*
The little land. R. L. Stevenson. *HuSv—JoAc*
The lost doll. From The water babies. C. Kingsley. *FeF—NaM*
Mabel. Unknown. *WoJ*
"Mabel, Mabel, set the table." Unknown. *WoF*
Make believe. H. Behn. *BeW*
Man for Mars. D. McCord. *McT*
Marching song. R. L. Stevenson. *ArTp—FeF*
Marco Polo. Unknown. *WoJ*
Margie. Unknown. *WoJ*
Misses. Unknown. *WoJ*
Mister Hoppy-toes. M. L. Allen. *AlP*
Mrs Brown. R. Fyleman. *ArTp—BrL-k—HuL-1*
"Mother, mother, I am ill." Unknown. *TaD*
My old man. Unknown. *TaD*
My other name. M. C. Livingston. *LiW*
My ship. M. Chute. *ChA*
Nursery chairs. A. A. Milne. *MiWc*
Nurse's song. W. Blake. *DeT—HuL-2—JoAc—ReT—UnG*
 Play time. *FeF*
"Obadiah." Unknown. *WoJ*
"Old man Daisy." Unknown. *WoJ*
O'Leary. Unknown. *WoJ*
One, two, three. H. C. Bunner. *FeF*
"Over the garden wall." E. Farjeon. *BrR-4—HuSv*
Paper boats. R. Tagore. *FeF*
Park play. J. S. Tippett. *McAw*
Pick me up. W. J. Smith. *SmL*
Pirate story. R. L. Stevenson. *ArTp—FeF—JoAc—UnG*
Pirates. H. Behn. *BeW*
Playgrounds. L. Alma-Tadema. *McAw*
The playhouse key. R. Field. *FeF*
Playing ball. M. Chute. *ChA*
Playing store. M. Chute. *ChA*
Poem. E. E. Cummings. *CoPs*
Postman, postman. Unknown. *TaD*
Pretending. H. Behn. *BeW—JoAc*
"Rich man." Mother Goose. *DeMg*
 Rich man, poor man. *WoJ*
Rocking horse. H. N. Bialik. *BrL-k*
"Rooms for rent." Unknown. *WoJ*
Run a little. J. Reeves. *ReBl*
Sailor John. D. McCord. *McT*
"Sally Rand." Unknown. *WoJ*
"Salt, pepper, sugar, cider." Unknown. *WiRm*
"School is over." K. Greenaway. *ArTp—HuL-1*
The secret cavern. M. Widdemer. *FeF*
See-saw. H. N. Bialik. *BrL-k*

"See-saw, Margery Daw (Jacky shall have a new master)." Mother Goose. *DeMg—JoAc—LiL—OpO*

"See-saw, Margery Daw (sold her bed)." Mother Goose. *OpO*

"See-saw, sacradown." Mother Goose. *DeMg—OpO*

Seesaw ("Seesaw; up and down") M. L. Allen. *AlP*

Seesaw ("Up and down") E. Beyer. *BrL-k*

The ships of Yule. B. Carman. *BrBc*

Shoot that possum down. Unknown. *TaD*

Shore. M. B. Miller. *ArTp—McAw*

Skipping along alone. W. Welles. *ArTp—HuL-2*

Skipping ropes. D. Aldis. *AlA—HuSv*

Sliding ("Down the slide") M. Chute. *ChA—McAw*

Sliding ("We can slide") M. C. Livingston. *BrS—LiW*

So run along and play. D. McCord. *McT*

Soap bubbles. Unknown. *BrL-k*

Somersault. D. Aldis. *AlA*

Spanish dancer. Unknown. *WoJ*

Spinning top. F. D. Sherman. *BrL-k*

Spring. D. Aldis. *AlA*

Squaw talk. D. McCord. *McT*

A stick for a horse. S. Fountain. *HuL-1*

"Sugar and cream." Unknown
  Four questions. *WoJ*

A tail to wag. D. Aldis. *AlA*

Teddy Bear, Teddy Bear. Unknown. *WoJ*
  "Teddy Bear, Teddy Bear, turn around." *WiRm*

That was the one. D. Aldis. *AlA*

There once was a puffin. F. P. Jaques. *ArTp—HuL-2*

This man came from nowhere. J. Ciardi. *CiI*

Thoughts of a little girl. M. Enriqueta. *FeF*

The thread was thin. Unknown. *WoJ*

"Three children sliding on the ice." J. Gay. *DeMg—JoAc—LiL*
  Three children sliding. *OpO*
  A warning. *DeT*

"Tillie the toiler sat on a boiler." Unknown. *WoJ*

"Tim, Tim, sat on a pin." Unknown. *WoJ*

The time we like best. D. Aldis. *AlA*

Tom Twist. W. A. Butler. *CoH*

"Tommy was a silly boy." K. Greenaway. *ArTp*

Toss me your golden ball. E. Farjeon. *FaCb*

Tree house. D. Aldis. *AlHd*

Twirling. Mother Goose. *OpO*

Underneath the clothes. M. Nightingale. *HuL-1*

"Upon the beach." I. Orleans. *ArTp*

Us two. A. A. Milne. *ArTp—MiWc*

The wagon in the barn. J. Drinkwater. *BrR-4—PeF*

Watch me. D. Aldis. *AlHd*

We know a house. D. Aldis. *AlA*

What they are for. D. Aldis. *AlA*

What to do. W. Wise. *ArTp*

"Where are you going." I. O. Eastwick. *EaI*

Wild beasts. E. Stein. *BrL-k*

"Play on the seashore." See Shore

"The play seems out for an almost infinite run." See It bids pretty fair

Play time. See Nurse's song

The players ask for a blessing on the psalteries and on themselves. William Butler Yeats. *PlU*

Playgrounds. Laurence Alma-Tadema. *McAw*

The playhouse key. Rachel Field. *FeF*

Playing ball. Marchette Chute. *ChA*

The playing leaves. Ora Clayton Moore. *BrL-k*

Playing store. Marchette Chute. *ChA*

Playmates
  Binker. A. A. Milne. *MiWc*
  Buttercup days. A. A. Milne. *MiWc*
  The invisible playmate. M. Widdemer. *FeF*
  My playmate. J. G. Whittier. *DeT*
  The other child. E. Farjeon. *FaCb*
  The tardy playmate. F. R. Buchanan. *DoP*
  Us two. A. A. Milne. *ArTp—MiWc*

Pleasant comedy of patient Grissell, sel. Thomas Dekker.
  The basket-maker's song. *ReT*
  O sweet content. *DeT*

"The pleasant isle of Rügen looks the Baltic water o'er." See The brown dwarf of Rügen

"A pleasant old bear at the zoo." Unknown. *WiRm*

Please ("Please be careful where you tread") Rose Fyleman. *BrL-k*

Please ("Please is a wonderful word. When I say it") Dorothy Aldis. *AlA*

"Please be careful where you tread." See Please

"Please, everybody, look at me." See Five years old

"Please God, take care of little things." See A prayer for little things

"Please is a wonderful word. When I say it." See Please

Please, Johnny. John Ciardi. *CiM*

"Please lay me an egg, Mrs Hen." See Mrs Hen

"Please let's stop." See Saturday morning

"Please to remember." Mother Goose. *DeMg*
  Gunpowder plot day. *OpO*
  "Please to remember the fifth of November." *LiL*

"Please to remember the fifth of November." See "Please to remember"

The **Pleiades.** Elizabeth Jane Coatsworth. *PlI*

The **ploughboy** in luck. Mother Goose. *OpO*
  The silly. *DeT*

Ploughing on Sunday. Wallace Stevens. *FeF—ReT*

Ploughs. See Plows and plowing

The **plover.** Unknown, tr. fr. the Swahili by Alice Werner. *PaS*

"Plover, my lover, how lightly you hover." See The plover

Plovers
  The plover. Unknown. *PaS*

Plow-Monday. Eleanor Farjeon. *FaCb—FaN*

The poet's paradise. M. Drayton. *HoW*
Prose and poesy: A rural misadventure. T. R. Ybarra. *CoH*
Ragged Robin. J. Reeves. *ReR*
A reply. M. Prior. *UnG*
Song's eternity. J. Clare. *McW—SmLg*
Take sky. D. McCord. *McT*
"There is no frigate like a book." E. Dickinson. *BrS—HaY*
    A book. *FeF*
"There was an old stupid who wrote." W. Parke. *CoH*
Thirteen ways of looking at a blackbird. W. Stevens. *HaP*
"This is I at work at my desk." J. Ciardi. *CiR*
To a child. C. Morley. *BrBc*
To Christopher North. A. Tennyson. *NaE*
To his friend Master R. L., in praise of music and poetry. R. Barnfield. *PlU*
To the thawing wind. R. Frost. *FrR*
Trees. J. Kilmer. *FeF*
Tricky. G. Burgess. *CoH*
Verse. O. St J. Gogarty. *SmLg*
W. J. Reeves. *ReBl—ReG*
"What is poetry? Who knows." E. Farjeon. *HaY*
Wild strawberries. R. Graves. *SmLg*
Write me a verse. D. McCord. *McT*

The poet's paradise. Michael Drayton. *HoW*
"The point, the line, the surface and sphere." Claude Bragdon. *PlU*
"The pointed houses lean so you would swear." See Amsterdam — Robinson Crusoe returns to Amsterdam
The pointed people. Rachel Field. *FeF*
A pointless tale. Eleanor Farjeon. *FaCb—FaN*

Poison ivy. Katharine Gallagher. *BrS*
A poison tree. William Blake. *CoPm*

Polar bear. William Jay Smith. *SmB*
"The polar bear never makes his bed." See Polar bear

Police
Action rhyme. E. H. Adams. *HuL-1*
Bobby Blue. J. Drinkwater. *FeF*
Copper song. E. T. Scheffauer. *CoPm*
"The Leith police dismisseth us." Mother Goose. *OpO*
My policeman. R. Fyleman. *ArTp—BrL-k*
"Once a big molicepan." Unknown. *FeF*
The policeman. M. S. Watts. *ArTp*
"Policeman, policeman (do your duty)." Unknown. *MoY*
"Policeman, policeman, don't catch me." Unknown. *WiRm*
The policeman's lot. W. S. Gilbert. *CoH*
"P's the proud policeman." From All around the town. P. McGinley. *ArTp*
Psalm of those who go forth before daylight. C. Sandburg. *NaM*
    Those who go forth before daylight. *HuSv*
The policeman. Marjorie Seymour Watts. *ArTp*
"The policeman buys shoes slow and careful." See Psalm of those who go forth before daylight

"Policeman, policeman (do your duty)." Unknown. *MoY*
"Policeman, policeman, don't catch me." Unknown. *WiRm*
"The policeman walks with heavy tread." See Action rhyme
The policeman's lot. See The pirates of Penzance
A polite nun. See The Canterbury tales—A prioress
Polite tea party. Dorothy Aldis. *AlA*
Politeness. See Etiquette
Politeness. A. A. Milne. *MiWc*
Poll Parrot. Mother Goose. *OpO*
Polly. William Brighty Rands. *UnG*
Polly Flinders. See "Little Polly Flinders"
"Polly put the kettle on." Mother Goose. *DeMg—LiL*
    Tea-time. *OpO*
"Pollywog on a log." Unknown. *WoF*
Polyhymnia, sel. George Peele
    "His golden locks time hath to silver turned." *HaP*
Pomeroy, Marnie
    April fools' day. *CoPs*
    Ground hog day. *CoPs*
    Halloween. *CoPs*
    January 1. *CoPs*
    Labor day. *CoPs*
Pomona. William Morris. *HoW*
The pond. Annette von Droste-Hülshoff, tr. fr. the German by Herman Salinger. *PaS*
Ponds. See Lakes
Ponies. See Horses
The ponies. Wilfrid Wilson Gibson. *McW*
The pony. Unknown. *TaD*
Poor. See also Beggars; Charity
    Bagpipe music. L. MacNeice. *HaP*
    The ballad of the harp-weaver. E. St V. Millay. *ArTp—CoSp—UnMc*
    Bishop Hatto. R. Southey. *CoSp*
    "If life were a thing that money could buy." Unknown. *MoY*
    The investment. R. Frost. *FrR*
    Mrs Utter. J. Reeves. *ReW*
    The song of the shirt. T. Hood. *UnMc*
    Song of the very poor. Unknown. *FaCb—FaN*
    "There's snow on the fields." C. G. Rossetti. *DeT*
    A true story. A. Taylor. *DeT*
"Poor Crusoe saw with fear-struck eyes." See The footprint
"Poor Jane Higgins." See A pig tale
"Poor little fly upon the wall." Unknown. *WoF*
"Poor little Ida." Unknown. *MoY*
"Poor little Lucy." See The lost shoe
"Poor Martha Snell, she's gone away." See On Martha Snell
"Poor Mrs Utter." See Mrs Utter
Poor old horse. Unknown. *ReG*
"Poor old Jonathan Bing." See Jonathan Bing

Poor old lady. Unknown. *CoH—UnG*
Poor old woman. *HuL-1*
"**Poor** old lady, she swallowed a fly." See Poor old lady
"**Poor** old Robinson Crusoe." Mother Goose. *DeMg*
Robinson Crusoe. *OpO*
Poor old woman. See Poor old lady
Poor Richard's wisdom. Benjamin Franklin. *UnG*
Poor Rumble. James Reeves. *ReBl*
"The **poor** Son of Mary." See Spanish lullaby
"**Poor** tired Tim. It's sad for him." See Tired Tim
"**Pop** bottles pop-bottles." See Song of the pop-bottlers
A **pop** corn song. Nancy Byrd Turner. *BrL-k—FeF—HuL-1*
Pop goes the weasel. Unknown. *HuL-1—JoAc—OpO—TaD*
"Up and down the city road." *NaE*
Popcorn. See Corn and cornfields
Pope, Alexander
Atticus. See Epistle to Dr Arbuthnot
Dogs. *UnG*
Epistle to Dr Arbuthnot, sel.
Atticus. *HaP*
Epitaph intended for Sir Isaac Newton. *PlI*
An essay on man. *HaP* (sel.)—*PlI* (sel.)
Vice. *ThP*
The pheasant. *UnG*
Vice. See An essay on man
Pope, Jessie
Noise. *HuL-2*
Our visit to the zoo. *HuL-2*
The **poplar** field. William Cowper. *DeT—HaP—HoW*
Poplar trees
The poplar field. W. Cowper. *DeT—HaP—HoW*
The poplars. T. Garrison. *HuSv*
The **poplars**. Theodosia Garrison. *HuSv*
"The **poplars** are felled; farewell to the shade." See The poplar field
Popocatepetl
A bachelor of Maine. E. D. Deland. *CoH*
Poppies
In Flanders fields. J. McCrae. *BrS*
Poppies. E. Farjeon. *FaCb—FaN*
Poppies. Eleanor Farjeon. *FaCb—FaN*
The **porcupine**. Frances M. Frost. *FrLn*
Porcupines
"Little Billy Breek." Mother Goose. *OpO*
The porcupine. F. M. Frost. *FrLn*
Poringer. See "What is the rhyme for porringer"
Porpoises. See Dolphins
The **portent**. Herman Melville. *HoW*
Porter, Kenneth
The old coon-dog dreams. *UnG*
Portrait ("Always in a hurry") Marchette Chute. *ChA—McAw*
Portrait by a neighbor. Edna St Vincent Millay. *ArTp—FeF—HuL-2—NaM—PeF*

Portrait of a child settling down for an afternoon nap. Carl Sandburg. *SaW*
Portrait of a house. E. V. Rieu. *RiF*
The **Portsmouth** road. Cicely Fox-Smith. *HuL-2*
Possessions. See Wealth
"**Possum** on the 'simmon." See Shoot that possum down
"**Possum** up a gum tree." Unknown. *WiRm*
"The **post-boy** drove with fierce career." See Alice Fell
The **post** captain. Charles Edward Carryl. *CoH*
Postal service. See Mail service
The **postman** ("Hey, the little postman") Laura E. Richards. *ArTp*
The **postman** ("Rat-a-tat-tat, rat-a-tat-tat") Clive Sansom. *HuL-1*
The **postman** ("The whistling postman swings along") Unknown. *FeF*
Postman, postman. Unknown. *TaD*
"**Postman**, postman, do your duty." See Postman, postman
Postmen. See Mailmen
Potatoes
The potatoes' dance. V. Lindsay. *FeF*
This man had six eyes. J. Ciardi. *CiI*
The **potatoes'** dance. Vachel Lindsay. *FeF*
Potomac town in February. Carl Sandburg. *McW—NaE*
Pots and pans
"Hoddy doddy." Mother Goose. *OpO*
"If ifs and ands." Mother Goose. *DeMg—LiL*
"I'm a little teapot, short and stout." Unknown. *WoF*
Mrs Mason's basin. Mother Goose. *OpO*
Old blue saucepan. E. Farjeon. *FaN*
"Polly put the kettle on." Mother Goose. *DeMg—LiL*
Tea-time. *OpO*
Potter, Miriam Clark
Cake. *BrBc*
Present. *BrBc*
Pottery
Bible stories. L. W. Reese. *DoP*
Drinking vessels. L. E. Richards. *LoL*
Kitty of Coleraine. Unknown. *CoSp*
Ode on a Grecian urn. J. Keats. *HaP*
Poulsson, Anne Emilie
Books are keys. *BrS*
Sunbeams. *BrR-3*
Poultry. See names of kinds of poultry, as Chickens
Pound, Ezra
The ant's a centaur. See Pisan cantos
Ballad of the goodly fere. *HaP*
The faun. *SmLg*
The gypsy. *ReT*
An immorality. *GrCc—HaP*
Meditatio. *SmLg*
Pisan cantos, sel.
The ant's a centaur. *HaP*
The river-merchant's wife: A letter, tr. *GrCc—HaP*
Salutation. *SmLg*
These fought. *HaP*

"Poussie, poussie, baudrons." See A Scottish cat

Poverty. See Poor

The power of love. See The thousand nights and one

The power of music. Pindar, tr. fr. the Greek by H. T. Wade-Gery and C. M. Bowra. *PlU* (sel.)

"Power of raven be thine." See Good wish

The powerful eyes o' Jeremy Tait. Wallace Irwin. *CoSp*

Practicing. Dorothy Aldis. *AlA*

Prairie, sels. Carl Sandburg
Limited crossing Wisconsin. *SaW*
Songs. *SaW*
Summer morning. *SaW*

Prairie ("When that Abe Lincoln was a boy") K. N. Llewellyn. *HaY*

Prairie barn. See The people, yes

Prairie-dog town. Mary Austin. *ArTp—FeF —HuSv*

Prairie-dogs
Prairie-dog town. M. Austin. *ArTp—FeF —HuSv*

"Prairie goes to the mountain." See Open range

Prairie waters by night. Carl Sandburg. *SaW*

Prairies
Crossing the plains. J. Miller. *GrCc*
An Indian summer day on the prairie. V. Lindsay. *HuSv—McW*
My prairies. H. Garland. *FeF*
Open range. K. and B. Jackson. *ArTp— FeF*
Prairie, sels. C. Sandburg
Limited crossing Wisconsin. *SaW*
Songs. *SaW*
Summer morning. *SaW*
Prairie ("When that Abe Lincoln was a boy") K. N. Llewellyn. *HaY*
Prairie barn. From The people, yes. C. Sandburg. *SaW*
Prairie-dog town. M. Austin. *ArTp—FeF —HuSv*
Prairie waters by night. C. Sandburg. *SaW*

Praise. Mother Goose. *OpO*

"Praise God from whom all blessings flow." See Old hundredth

Praise of created things. See The mirror of perfection

Praise the Lord. See "Let us with a gladsome mind"

"Praise ye the Lord (for it is)." See Psalms —Psalm CXLVII

"Praise ye the Lord (praise God)." See Psalms—Psalm CL

"Praised be Diana's fair and harmless light." See Homage to Diana

"Praised be our Lord for our brother the sun." See Thanksgiving for the earth

Pratt, Anna M. (Maria)
A mortifying mistake. *CoH*
The turkey's opinion. *BrR-4*

Prattle. John Ciardi. *BrBc—CiR*

Pray, Frances
Compensation. *BrR-5*

A prayer ("Father, we thank Thee for the night") Unknown. *BrR-3*

Prayer ("God, though this life is but a wraith") Louis Untermeyer. *UnG*

Prayer ("Last night I crept across the snow") John Farrar. *DoP*

A prayer ("Lord, make me a channel of Thy peace") Saint Francis of Assisi. *BrL-7*

Prayer ("Merciful God, who readst my inmost mind") Willem Bilderdijk, tr. fr. the Dutch by A. J. Barnouw. *PaS*

A prayer ("Teach me, Father, how to go") Edwin Markham. *DoP—HuSv*

Prayer ("Whatever comes my way today") Unknown. *ThP*

Prayer for a child. William Hawley Smith. *DoP*

A prayer for a little home. Florence Bone. *DoP*

Prayer for a pilot. Cecil Roberts. *FeF*

A prayer for blossoms. Eleanor Farjeon. *FaCb*

A prayer for little things. Eleanor Farjeon. *JoAc*

Prayer for miracle. Anna Wickham. *UnG*

Prayer for this house. Louis Untermeyer. *BrR-6—FeF—HuL-2*

A prayer in spring. Robert Frost. *FrR—HaY*

The prayer of Cyrus Brown. Sam Walter Foss. *CoH*

Prayer on fourth of July. Nancy Byrd Turner. *HaY*

Prayer to the sun god. See Indian songs

"Prayer unsaid, and mass unsung." See The sea-ritual

Prayers. See also Grace—At meals; Hymns
An ancient prayer. T. H. B. Webb. *DoP*
At eventide. E. Farjeon. *FaCb—FaN*
Blessing over food. H. N. Bialik. *BrL-k— HaY*
The Celestial Surgeon. R. L. Stevenson. *UnG*
A chant out of doors. M. Wilkinson. *JoAc*
A child's evening prayer. M. L. Duncan. *DoP*
The good shepherd. *HuL-1*
Child's grace. F. M. Frost. *BrR-6*
A child's prayer. J. B. Tabb. *FeF*
An evening hymn for a little family. A. and J. Taylor. *DoP*
Evening prayer. H. Hagedorn. *DoP*
Ex ore infantium. F. Thompson. *DoP*
For color. R. Cheney. *BrR-5*
Francis Jammès: A prayer to go to Paradise with the donkeys. R. Wilbur. *ArTp*
"God bless this house from thatch to floor." Mother Goose. *OpO*
God is so good. J. Taylor. *DoP*
Good night prayer. H. Johnstone. *DoP*
He prayeth best. From The rime of the ancient mariner. S. T. Coleridge. *DoP— FeF—HuSv—ThP*
He prayeth well. *HuL-2*
The rime of the ancient mariner. *UnG*
House blessing ("Bless the four corners of this house") A. Guiterman. *ArTp*

Pretending ("When I put on my mother's clothes") Myra Cohn Livingston. *BrBc —LiW*

The **pretty** bird. See "Mary had a pretty bird"

Pretty cow. Ann Taylor. *HuSv*

"**Pretty** John Watts." See John Watts

"**Pretty** little redbird, dressed so fine." Unknown. *WiRm*

Pretty Maid Marion. Ivy O. Eastwick. *HuL-1*

"**Pretty** Maid Marion, where have you been." See Pretty Maid Marion

"**Pretty** maid, pretty maid." See Gift for the queen

Prevarication. Mother Goose. *OpO*

"**Priam** is the king of ashes." See Troy

Price, Edith Ballinger
To Patricia on her christening day. *BrBc*

Pride and vanity. See also Conceit
The ant's a centaur. From Pisan cantos. E. Pound. *HaP*
The arrogant frog and the superior bull. G. W. Carryl. *CoSp*
Conquistador. E. J. Coatsworth. *UnG*
The crow and the fox. J. De La Fontaine. *BrL-7—UnMc*
A dappled duck. P. Brown. *LoL*
The destruction of Sennacherib. G. G. Byron. *FeF—NaE—SmLg—UnG*
Easter parade. M. Chute. *BrS—ChA*
"Elsie Marley is grown so fine." Mother Goose. *DeMg*
The fall of J. W. Beane. O. Herford. *CoSp*
The flattered flying fish. E. V. Rieu. *RiF*
The flattered lightning bug. D. Marquis. *CoSp*
Fox and crow. W. J. Smith. *SmB*
The glory trail. B. Clark. *CoSp*
The glove and the lions. L. Hunt. *FeF— UnMc*
The lobster. Unknown. *UnG*
"Lucifer Leverett Lightningbug." J. Ciardi. *CiR*
The new duckling. A. Noyes. *FeF*
No second Troy. W. B. Yeats. *HaP*
The old cloak. Unknown. *MaB*
Ozymandias. P. B. Shelley. *BrL-7—HaP —McW—SmLg—UnG*
Primer lesson. C. Sandburg. *FeF—HuSv —NaM*
Proud Jane. D. Aldis. *AlA*
Recessional. R. Kipling. *BrL-7*
"Samuel Silvernose Slipperyside." J. Ciardi. *CiR*
Song. From Contention of Ajax and Ulysses. J. Shirley. *GrCc*
The spider and the fly. M. Howitt. *DeT —FeF—PeF*
Teddy Bear. A. A. Milne. *MiWc*
"The tortoiseshell cat." P. R. Chalmers. *HuL-2*
Vain. J. Reeves. *ReR*
Vain and careless. R. Graves. *GrP*
Vanity. From The cheerful cherub. R. McCann. *ThP*

The wind and the moon. G. Macdonald. *NaM—UnG*
X-roads. J. Reeves. *ReR*

Prideaux, Tom
Skip-scoop-anellie. *CoH*

The **priest** of Felton. Mother Goose. *OpO*

Priests
The ballad of Father Gilligan. W. B. Yeats. *McW*
The lama. O. Nash. *CoH—FeF—LoL*
"The one-l lama." *SmLg*
The priest and the mulberry tree. From Crotchet castle. T. L. Peacock. *CoSp— DeT*
The priest of Felton. Mother Goose. *OpO*
Robin Hood and the two priests. Unknown. *MaB*

Primer lesson. Carl Sandburg. *FeF—HuSv —NaM*

Primroses
Peep-primrose. E. Farjeon. *FaCb—FaN*

The **prince.** Walter De La Mare. *LoL*

Princes and princesses
After all and after all. M. C. Davies. *ArTp*
The princess and the gypsies. F. Cornford. *CoSp—HuL-2*
The Princess Priscilla. E. V. Rieu. *RiF*
The princesses' carol. E. Farjeon. *FaCb— FaN*
The song of the mad prince. W. De La Mare. *GrCc—SmLg*
Sons of the kings. J. Agnew. *BrBc*
Vain. J. Reeves. *ReR*

The **princess,** sels. Alfred Tennyson
Bugle song. *FeF—HuSv*
Blow, bugle, blow. *HoW—PlU*
Echo song. *DeT*
Song. *ReT*
"The splendor falls on castle walls." *ArTp*
The spendour falls. *SmLg*
Tears, idle tears. *HaP*
"This world was once a fluid haze of light" The princess. *PlI*

The **princess** and the gypsies. Frances Cornford. *CoSp—HuL-2*

The **Princess** Priscilla. E. V. Rieu. *RiF*

Princesses. See Princes and princesses

The **princesses'** carol. Eleanor Farjeon. *FaCb—FaN*

"The **principal** part of a python." John Ciardi. *CiR*

Prior, Matthew
A reply. *UnG*

A **prioress.** See The Canterbury tales

Prisoned. Mary Carolyn Davies. *HuL-2*

The **prisoner** of Chillon. George Gordon Byron. *UnMc*

Prisoners. See Prisons and prisoners

Prisons and prisoners
"In jail they give you coffee." Unknown. *MoY*
The prisoner of Chillon. G. G. Byron. *UnMc*
To Althea from prison. R. Lovelace. *HaP*

The **procession.** Margaret Widdemer. *HaY*

The **prodigal** egg. Unknown. *CoH*

The **prodigy.** A. P. Herbert. *NaE*

Professions. See names of professions, as Doctors

Program note on Sibelius. Donald Babcock. *PlU*

Progress. David McCord. *PlU*

A **projection.** Reed Whittemore. *McW*

Prokosch, Frederic
　Chorus from Medea. See Medea
Medea, sel.
　　Chorus from Medea. tr. *PaS*

Prologue for a magician. Arthur Guiterman. *CoPm*

Prologue to The family of man, sel. Carl Sandburg
　Names. *SaW*

Prometheus unbound. Percy Bysshe Shelley. *PlI* (sel.)

Promises
　Piecrust. E. Farjeon. *FaCb—FaN*

"The **proper** way for a man to pray." See The prayer of Cyrus Brown

Proposition. Nicolás Guillén, tr. fr. the Spanish by Langston Hughes. *FeF*

Propriety. Marianne Moore. *PlU*

Prose and poesy: A rural misadventure. Thomas R. Ybarra. *CoH*

Proserpine
　Pluto and Proserpine. J. Reeves. *ReBl*

Proud Jane. Dorothy Aldis. *AlA*

"**Proud** Maisie is in the wood." See The heart of Midlothian

"**Proud** peacock glitters in the sun." See Plain philomel

Proud songsters. Thomas Hardy. *HaP*

Proverbs. See also Superstitions
　"An apple a day." Mother Goose. *DeMg*
　"Birds of a feather flock together." Mother Goose. *DeMg*
　　Signs, seasons, and sense. *UnG*
　"Burn ash-wood green." Mother Goose. *DeMg*
　"Button to chin." Mother Goose. *OpO*
　"Cast thy bread upon the waters." From Ecclesiastes, Bible, Old Testament. *ArTp*
　Day-dreamer. Unknown. *ArTp*
　"Early to bed, early to rise." Mother Goose. *AnI*
　　"Early to bed and early to rise." *LiL*
　Four things. From Proverbs, Bible, Old Testament. *FeF—UnG*
　"Go to bed late." Mother Goose. *OpO*
　Go to the ant. From Proverbs, Bible, Old Testament. *FeF*
　Good advice. Unknown. *ArTp*
　"Good, better, best." Mother Goose. *MoY —OpO*
　The hay appeareth. From Proverbs, Bible, Old Testament. *FeF*
　He that is slow to anger. From Proverbs, Bible, Old Testament. *FeF*
　　"He that is slow to anger is better than the mighty." *ArTp*
　"He that would thrive." Mother Goose. *DeMg—OpO*

He who knows. Unknown. *ThP—UnG*
　"He who knows and knows that he knows." *MoY*

"If ifs and ands." Mother Goose. *DeMg— LiL*

"If wishes were horses." Mother Goose. *DeMg—LiL—OpO*

Lesson from a sun-dial. Unknown. *ArTp*

"Little ships must keep the shore." Unknown. *DeMg*

Motto. Unknown. *ArTp*

"Of all the sayings in this world." Mother Goose. *OpO*

Of courtesy. A. Guiterman. *ArTp*
　Proverbs. *ThP*

Of giving. A. Guiterman. *ArTp*
　Proverbs. *ThP*

Of quarrels. A. Guiterman. *ArTp*
　Proverbs. *ThP*

Of tact. A. Guiterman. *NaM*

"One thing at a time." Mother Goose. *OpO*

"One, two, whatever you do." Mother Goose. *OpO*

"Patience is a virtue." Mother Goose. *OpO*

"Penny and penny." Mother Goose. *OpO*

Persian proverb. L. S. Clark. *ThP*

Poor Richard's wisdom. B. Franklin. *UnG*

Proverbs. From The people, yes. C. Sandburg. *SaW*

Proverbs of King Alfred. King Alfred. *McW*

"Say well and do well." Mother Goose. *OpO*

Short sermon. Unknown. *ArTp*

"Small skill is gained by those who cling to ease." Unknown
　Signs, seasons, and sense. *UnG*

"A soft answer turneth away wrath." From Proverbs, Bible, Old Testament. *ArTp*
　A merry heart. *HuSv*

"A swarm of bees in May." Mother Goose. *DeMg—LiL—OpO*

"To sleep easy all night." Mother Goose. *OpO*

"True success is that which makes." A. Guiterman
　Proverbs. *ThP*

"Wilful waste brings woeful want." Mother Goose. *OpO*

"Winning, never boast; and, losing." A. Guiterman
　Proverbs. *ThP*

"A woman, a spaniel, and walnut tree." Mother Goose. *DeMg*

A word fitly spoken. From Proverbs, Bible, Old Testament. *FeF*

Proverbs. See The people, yes

Proverbs, sels. Bible, Old Testament
　Four things. *FeF—UnG*
　Go to the ant. *FeF*
　The hay appeareth. *FeF*
　He that is slow to anger. *FeF*
　　"He that is slow to anger is better than the mighty." *ArTp*
　"A soft answer turneth away wrath." *ArTp*
　　A merry heart. *HuSv*

Q

Q is for quest. Eleanor Farjeon. *FaCb*

Quack. Walter De La Mare. *ArTp—CoI*

"Quack. Quack." See Ducks at dawn

Quails. See Partridges and quails

"The Quaker's wife got up to bake." See Merrily danced the Quaker's wife

The quality of mercy. See The merchant of Venice

"The quality of mercy is not strained." See The merchant of Venice—The quality of mercy

The Quangle Wangle's hat. Edward Lear. *JoAc*

The quarrel. Eleanor Farjeon. *FeF*

Quarrels and quarreling. See also Fights
  Behind the gorse. E. Farjeon. *FaN*
  Mrs Snipkin and Mrs Wobblechin. L. E. Richards. *ArTp—CoH—HuL-1—HuSv—JoAc*
  "Moll-in-the-wad and I fell out." Mother Goose. *OpO*
  "My little old man and I fell out." Mother Goose. *DeMg—JoAc—OpO*
  Of quarrels. A. Guiterman. *ArTp*
  Proverbs. *ThP*
  The quarrel. E. Farjeon. *FeF*
  The quarrelsome kittens. Unknown. *BrL-k—HuL-1*
  "Tweedledum and Tweedledee." Mother Goose. *DeMg—LiL*
    Dum and Dee. *OpO*
"Quarrels never could last long." See Poor Richard's wisdom

The quarrelsome kittens. Unknown. *BrL-k—HuL-1*

"Queen and huntress, chaste and fair." See Cynthia's revels—Hymn to Diana

Queen Anne. See "Lady Queen Anne she sits in the sun"

"Queen Anne is—Pho." See On Queen Anne

"Queen Anne, Queen Anne, has washed her lace." See Queen Anne's lace

Queen Anne's lace
  Queen Anne's lace. M. L. Newton. *BrR-4—FeF—NaM*
  Queen's lace. E. Farjeon. *FaCb*
  Queen Anne's lace. Mary Leslie Newton. *BrR-4—FeF—NaM*

"Queen Bess was Harry's daughter. Stand forward partners all." See The looking-glass

"Queen Dido is building." Eleanor Farjeon. *FaCb*

Queen Mab ("If ye will with Mab find grace") See The fairies

Queen Mab ("A little fairy comes at night") Thomas Hood. *HuSv*

Queen Mab ("Oh, then, I see Queen Mab hath been with you") See Romeo and Juliet

"The queen netted lace." See Queen's lace

"The Queen of Hearts." Mother Goose. *AnI—DeMg—JoAc—LiL—OpO*

The queen of the Nile. William Jay Smith. *SmL*

Queens. See Kings and rulers

Queen's lace. Eleanor Farjeon. *FaCb*

Queer. David McCord. *McT*

Queer things. James Reeves. *CoPm—ReW*

The quest. Eleanor Farjeon. *FaCb*

The question. Percy Bysshe Shelley. *DeT*

The question in the cobweb. Alastair Reid. *McW*

"Question not, but live and labor." See Advice

Questions at night. Louis Untermeyer. *FeF—UnG*

Quiet. James Reeves. *ReR*

Quiet fun. Harry Graham. *CoH*

"Quiet, my horse, be quiet." See Alexander to his horse

Quiet please. Emily M. Hilsabeck. *McAw*

A quill for John Stow. Eleanor Farjeon. *FaN*

Quiller-Couch, Sir Arthur
  Child's carol. *EaW*
  Sage counsel. *CoH—LoL*

Quilt. John Updike. *McW*

"The quilt that covers all of us, to date." See Quilt

Quilts
  The patchwork quilt. E. Fleming. *HuL-2*
  Quilt. J. Updike. *McW*

Quinn, John Robert
  Whistling boy. *BrBc*

"Quinquireme of Nineveh from distant Ophir." See Cargoes

"Quite unexpectedly as Vasserot." See The end of the world

Qwerty-ú-i-op. Arthur Guiterman. *CoH*

R

R is for Robin Goodfellow. Eleanor Farjeon. *FaCb*

"R is for the restaurant." See All around the town

Rabbi Ben Ezra. Robert Browning. *BrBc* (sel.)

The rabbit ("Brown bunny sits inside his burrow") Edith King. *BrL-k—HuSv*

The rabbit ("Bun lies low") Ivy O. Eastwick. *EaI*

Rabbit ("I'd like to run like a rabbit in hops") Tom Robinson. *FeF*

The rabbit ("When they said the time to hide was mine") Elizabeth Madox Roberts. *ArTp—PeF—UnG*

Rabbit and lark. James Reeves. *ReW*

A rabbit as king of the ghosts. Wallace Stevens. *ReT*

"The rabbit came bounding." See Poem for a child

The rabbit man. Mother Goose. *OpO*

Rabbits
  The A B C bunny. W. Gág. *ArTp*
  Adventure. N. B. Turner. *HuSv*

The child in the train. E. Farjeon. *FaCb*
—*FaN*
"Early in the morning, let's go to the country." Unknown. *WiRm*
Engine. J. S. Tippett. *BrL-k*
"Engine, engine, number nine." Unknown. *WiRm—WoF*
    Engine, engine. *TaD—WoJ*
The engineer. A. A. Milne. *MiWc*
Finnigin to Flannigan. S. W. Gillilan. *CoSp*
From a railway carriage. R. L. Stevenson. *ArTp—FeF—HuL-2—PeF—ReG*
The ghost that Jim saw. B. Harte. *CoPm*
The green train. E. V. Rieu. *RiF*
Homesick blues. L. Hughes. *McW*
"I like to see it lap the miles." E. Dickinson. *NaM*
    The Amherst train. *SmLg*
    The locomotive. *FeF*
John Henry. Unknown. *UnMc*
Limited. C. Sandburg. *SmLg*
Limited crossing Wisconsin. From Prairie. C. Sandburg. *SaW*
A modern dragon. R. B. Bennett. *ArTp*
"Monkey was a-settin' on a railroad track." Unknown
    American Father Gander. *UnG*
The new and the old. Shiki. *PaS*
Night mail. W. H. Auden. *HaP*
Night train. K. Edelman. *BrR-6*
Old Hogan's goat. Unknown. *CoI—TaD*
On a railroad right of way. C. Sandburg. *SaW*
"Pass one window, ty-de-o." Unknown. *WoF*
The passenjare. I. H. Bromley. *CoH*
"A peanut sat on a railroad track." Unknown. *MoY*
Pod. C. Sandburg. *SaW*
Pullman porter. Unknown. *TaD*
The railroad cars are coming. Unknown. *FeF*
Railroad ducks. F. M. Frost. *FrLn*
Railroad reverie. E. R. Young. *BrR-6*
Rhyme of the rail. J. G. Saxe. *NaM*
The sad goat. Unknown. *McW*
Skimbleshanks: The railway cat. T. S. Eliot. *SmLg*
Song of the engine bells. E. J. Coatsworth. *BrR-5*
Song of the train. D. McCord. *FeF—JoAc—McFf*
The Tay bridge disaster. W. McGonagall. *NaE*
Texas trains and trails. M. Austin. *ArTp*
The ticket agent. E. Leamy. *HuSv*
The train. M. Coleridge. *HuL-2*
Train ride. D. Aldis. *AlA*
Train windows. M. C. Livingston. *LiW*
Trains. J. S. Tippett. *ArTp—BrR-3—FeF—HuL-1*
Trains at night. F. M. Frost. *ArTp*
Travel. E. St V. Millay. *ArTp—FeF—HuL-2—HuSv—NaM*
The ways of trains. E. J. Coatsworth. *ArTp*
Window. C. Sandburg. *SaW*
Railways. See Railroads

Rain
After rain. H. Behn. *BeW*
April and Isabella. I. O. Eastwick. *EaI*
April rain. R. Loveman. *BrR-5*
April rain song. L. Hughes. *ArTp—FeF—PeF*
Children of the desert. From The people, yes. C. Sandburg. *SaW*
City rain. R. Field. *ArTp*
Didn't it rain. Unknown. *TaD*
"Doctor Foster went to Gloucester." Mother Goose. *DeMg—JoAc*
    Doctor Foster. *OpO*
    "Doctor Foster went to Glo'ster." *LiL*
Downpour. M. C. Livingston. *LiWa*
During wind and rain. T. Hardy. *HaP*
"Emily, Bob, and Jane." E. Farjeon. *FaN*
"Evening red and morning grey." Mother Goose. *OpO*
    Signs, seasons, and sense. *UnG*
"February-fill-the-dyke." I. O. Eastwick. *EaI*
Fern song. J. B. Tabb. *DoP*
Flute-priest song for rain. A. Lowell. *PlU* (sel.)
Footwear. M. Justus. *HaY*
"How gray the rain." E. J. Coatsworth. *ArTp*
"If bees stay at home." Mother Goose. *OpO*
    Signs, seasons, and sense. *UnG*
"In time of silver rain." L. Hughes. *ArTp*
"It ain't gonna rain no more." Unknown. *WoF*
"It is raining." L. S. Mitchell. *ArTp—HuL-2*
"It's raining, it's pouring." Mother Goose. *OpO*
"It's raining, it's raining." Mother Goose. *OpO*
"Jemima Jane." M. Chute. *ChA*
Korosta katzina song. Unknown. *PaS*
The little rain ("Oh, she is good, the little rain, and well she knows our need") Tu Fu. *FeF*
Little rain ("When I was making myself a game") E. M. Roberts. *ArTp—BrR-4*
My funny umbrella. A. Wilkins. *BrL-k*
No drip of rain. I. O. Eastwick. *McAw*
November rain. M. E. Uschold. *HaY*
Old Man Rain. M. Cawein. *BrR-6—CoPs*
One day. J. Ciardi. *CiY*
Rain ("Dancing dancing down the street") E. Young. *ArTp*
The rain ("I hear leaves drinking rain") W. H. Davies. *ArTp—DeT*
Rain ("I like to look out of my window and see") H. Wing. *BrL-k*
Rain ("Rain and rain is all I see") J. Reeves. *ReR*
The rain ("The rain came down in torrents") Unknown. *BrR-3*
Rain ("The rain is raining all around") R. L. Stevenson. *ArTp—BrL-k—HuSv—JoAc*
The rain ("The rain, they say, is a mousegray horse") R. B. Bennett. *JoAc*

The **rainbow** ("The rainbow arches in the sky") David McCord. *FeF—McFf*

Rainbow ("The shower has stopped") H. N. Bialik, tr. fr. the Hebrew by Jessie Sampter. *BrR-4*

"The **rainbow** arches in the sky." See The rainbow

"**Rainbow** at night." Unknown. *WiRm*

Signs, seasons, and sense. *UnG*

The **rainbow** fairies. Lizzie M. Hadley. *BrL-k*

Rainbow in April. Ivy O. Eastwick. *EaI*

"**Rainbow** in the morning." Unknown. *WiRm*

A **rainbow** piece. Ivy O. Eastwick. *EaI*

Rainbows

"Boats sail on the rivers." C. G. Rossetti. *ArTp—BrR-4—DoP—HuL-2—HuSv—PeF*

The bridge. *JoAc*

Bubbles. C. Sandburg. *SaW*

If all were rain. C. G. Rossetti. *BrR-3*

My heart leaps up. W. Wordsworth. *BrBc—HaP—JoAc*

"My heart leaps up when I behold." *ArTp*

"Purple, yellow, red, and green." Mother Goose. *DeMg—OpO*

The rainbow ("I saw the lovely arch") W. De La Mare. *ArTp*

The rainbow ("The rainbow arches in the sky") D. McCord. *FeF—McFf*

Rainbow ("The shower has stopped") H. N. Bialik. *BrR-4*

"Rainbow at night." Unknown. *WiRm*

Signs, seasons, and sense. *UnG*

The rainbow fairies. L. M. Hadley. *BrL-k*

Rainbow in April. I. O. Eastwick. *EaI*

"Rainbow in the morning." Unknown. *WiRm*

A rainbow piece. I. O. Eastwick. *EaI*

Skipping ropes. D. Aldis. *AlA—HuSv*

Raindrops. Isla Paschal Richardson. *BrL-k*

Raine, Kathleen

Message from home. *PlI*

Rock. *PlI* (sel.)

Shells. *PlI*

Spell of creation. *McW—SmLg*

Water. *PlI* (sel.)

Raining. Rhoda W. Bacmeister. *BrL-k*

Raining again. Dorothy Aldis. *AlA*

"**Raining** again. And raining again." See Raining again

"**Raining**, raining." See Rain in the night

"The **rains** of spring." Lady Ise, tr. fr. the Japanese by Olive Beaupré Miller. *ArTp*

A **rainy** day. Marchette Chute. *McAw*

Rainy day song. Violet Alleyn Storey. *HaY*

A **rainy** piece. Ivy O. Eastwick. *EaI*

Rainy robin. Frances M. Frost. *FrLn*

Raking walnuts in the rain. Monica Shannon. *BrS*

Raleigh, Sir Walter (1861-1922)

The wishes of an elderly man. *CoH—SmLg*

Raleigh, Sir Walter (1552-1618)

"As you came from the holy land." See Walsinghame

The conclusion. *NaE*

Homage to Diana. *HoW*

The nymph's reply to the shepherd. *HaP*

Walsinghame. *SmLg*

"As you came from the holy land." *HaP*

Ramal, Walter, pseud. See De La Mare, Walter

"**Rampant ram.**" See Aries

Rand, Walter, pseud. See De La Mare, Walter

Randall, Laura Lee

Our circus. *ArTp*

Randall, Virginia D.

October winds. *HaY*

Randolph Caldecott. Eleanor Farjeon. *FaN*

Rands, William Brighty

Clean Clara. *CoH* (sel.)

The drummer-boy and the shepherdess. *NaM*

Gipsy Jane. *FeF—PeF*

Gypsy Jane. *ArTp—HuL-2*

"Godfrey Gordon Gustavus Gore." *ArTp—FeF—HuL-2—PeF*

Gypsy Jane. See Gipsy Jane

Kitty: What she thinks of herself. *NaM*

Lilliput-land. *ReG*

Polly. *UnG*

Topsyturvey-world. *ReG*

The wonderful world. *ArTp*

Rankō (or Reinkō)

The fall of the plum blossoms. *ArTp*

Plum trees. *FeF*

Rannoch, by Glencoe. See Landscapes

Ransom, John Crowe

Blue girls. *GrCc—HaP*

Captain Carpenter. *HaP*

Here lies a lady. *NaE*

Janet waking. *ReT*

Lady lost. *HaP*

Piazza piece. *HaP*

Survey of literature. *SmLg*

The **rape** of Lucrece, sel. Thomas Heywood

Pack, clouds, away. *ReT*

A **rare** tree. Unknown, tr. fr. the Chinese. *PaS*

A **rat.** See "There was a rat, for want of stairs"

"**Rat-a-tat-tat,** rat-a-tat-tat." See The postman

Rathers. Mary Austin. *FeF*

Rats

Bishop Hatto. R. Southey. *CoSp*

Five eyes. W. De La Mare. *CoI*

The Pied Piper of Hamelin. R. Browning. *ArTp—HuSv—JoAc—SmLg—UnG*

How the rats were destroyed. *HuL-2* (sel.)

"There was a rat, for want of stairs." Mother Goose. *DeMg*

A rat. *OpO*

The two rats. Unknown. *HuL-1*

"**Rats** are a great deal bigger." See Mouse chorus

The **raven** ("The gloom of death is on the raven's wing") Nicharchus, tr. by Edwin Arlington Robinson. *PlU*

Flowers and frost. *ReR*
The footprint. *ReBl*
The four horses. *ReW*
The four letters. *ReBl*
A garden at night. *ReBl*
Giant Thunder. *ReBl*
The grasses. *ReW*
The grasshopper and the bird. *ReBl*
Green grass. *ReR*
Grey. *ReW*
The grey horse. *ReW*
Grim and gloomy. *ReW*
"Heroes on horseback." *ReR*
The hippocrump. *ReP*
The horn. *ReBl*
If pigs could fly. *ReBl*
The intruder. *ReBl*
Islands. *ReR*
Jargon. *ReR*
Kay. *ReR*
Kingdom cove. *ReBl*
"Let no one suppose." *ReP*
Little Fan. *CoPm—ReW*
Little Minnie Mystery. *ReBl*
Long. *ReR*
The magic seeds. *ReBl*
A mermaid song. *ReW*
Mick. *ReBl*
Miss Petal. *ReW*
Miss Wing. *ReBl*
Mr Bellairs. *ReBl*
Mr Kartoffel. *ReW*
Mr Tom Narrow. *ReW*
Mrs Button. *ReBl*
"Mrs Farleigh-fashion." *ReW*
Mrs Gilfillan. *ReBl*
Mrs Golightly. *ReBl*
Mrs Utter. *ReW*
The moonlit stream. *ReBl*
Moths and moonshine. *ReR*
"Musetta of the mountains." *ReW*
The musical box. *ReW*
My singing aunt. *ReBl*
The nimp. *ReP*
Noah. *ReR*
The nonny. *ReP*
O nay. *ReR*
Old Moll. *ReW*
The old wife and the ghost. *CoPm—ReBl*
The osc. *ReP*
Others. *ReW*
Paper. *ReR*
Pat's fiddle. *ReBl*
The piano. *ReBl*
A pig tale. *ReBl*
Pluto and Proserpine. *ReBl*
Poor Rumble. *ReBl*
Queer things. *CoPm—ReW*
Quiet. *ReR*
Rabbit and lark. *ReW*
Ragged Robin. *ReR*
Rain. *ReR*
Roundabout. *ReW*
Rum lane. *ReBl*
Run a little. *ReBl*
The sea. *ReW*
Seeds. *ReBl*
Shiny. *ReW*
Sky, sea, shore. *ReR*
Slowly. *ReW*
The snail. *ReW*

The snitterjipe. *ReP*
Snow palace. *ReW*
The snyke. *ReP*
The song of D. *ReR*
The song of the dumb waiter. *ReW*
Spells. *CoPm—ReG—ReW*
The statue. *ReBl—ReG*
"Stocking and shirt." *ReW*
Stones by the sea. *ReW*
The street musician. *ReBl*
The summer party. *ReW*
Tarlingwell. *ReR*
Things to remember. *ReBl*
The three singing birds. *CoPm—ReBl*
The three unlucky men. *ReBl*
"Time to go home." *ReBl*
The toadstool wood. *ReBl*
Tree gowns. *ReW*
Trees in the moonlight. *ReBl*
Troy. *ReBl*
Twenty-six letters. *ReR*
The two mice. *ReBl*
The two old women of Mumbling hill. *ReW*
Under ground. *ReW*
Un. *ReR*
Uriconium. *ReBl*
Vain. *ReR*
Vicary square. *ReW*
Village sounds. *ReW*
W. *ReBl—ReG*
Waiting. *ReW*
The wandering moon. *ReW*
What kind of music. *ReW*
The wind. *ReW*
Words. *ReR*
X-roads. *ReR*
Yellow wheels. *ReBl*
Yonder. *ReR*
You'd say it was a funeral. *ReW*
"You'd say it was a wedding." *ReW*
Zachary Zed. *ReR*

Reflection ("If history is hard, don't sit and croak") Unknown. *ThP*

Reflection ("In the mirror") Myra Cohn Livingston. *LiWa*

Reflections (Mirrored)
A coffeepot face. A. Fisher. *BrL-k*
"I've seen you where you never were." Mother Goose. *DeMg*
  Five very old riddles. *DeT*
The looking-glass pussy. M. Widdemer. *BrR-3*
The magical picture. R. Graves. *GrP*
The mirror ("Between the woods the afternoon") A. A. Milne. *MiWc*
Mirror ("kool uoy nehW") J. Updike. *McW*
Reflection. M. C. Livingston. *LiWa*
A thought. W. H. Davies. *NaM*

Refugee in America. Langston Hughes. *McW*

Regent's park. Rose Fyleman. *BrR-4*
In the park. *HuSv*

Regnier, Henri de
Night. *PaS*

Reid, Alastair
The question in the cobweb. *McW*
A spell for sleeping. *ReG*

Reilly, Jessamine Sykes
   The early bird. *BrR-4*
Reindeer. See Deer
Relatives. See also names of relatives, as
      Uncles
   A catch by the hearth. Unknown. *BrL-7*
   "Everybody says." D. Aldis. *AlA—BrL-k
      —FeF—HuL-1*
   The hero. L. F. Jackson. *BrS*
   Manners. M. G. Van Rensselaer. *FeF*
   Smells, Junior. C. Morley. *ArTp—BrL-k*
   Willie the poisoner. Unknown. *CoH*
Relativity. Unknown. *ArTp—PlU*
   Limericks. *BrL-7*
   A young lady named Bright. *FeF*
The **relic.** Robert Hillyer. *PlU*
The **relief** of Lucknow. Robert Traill Spence
      Lowell. *CoSp*
"Religious faith is a most filling vapor." See
      Innate helium
Reliques. Edmund Blunden. *PlI* (sel.)
Remember. John Ciardi. *CiI*
"Remember A." Unknown. *MoY*
"Remember Grant." Unknown. *MoY*
"Remember he was poor and country-bred."
      See Abraham Lincoln
"Remember me at the river." Unknown.
      MoY
"Remember me in all your wishes." Un-
      known. *MoY*
"Remember me is all I ask." Unknown.
      MoY
"Remember me (when this you see)." Un-
      known. *MoY*
"Remember September." May Justus. *BrS
      —HaY*
"Remember the beer." Unknown. *MoY*
"Remember the fork." Unknown. *MoY*
"Remember the fourth commandment." Un-
      known. *MoY*
Remember the grotto. Eleanor Farjeon.
      FaCb—FaN
"Remember the kid from Brooklyn." Un-
      known. *MoY*
"Remember the miss." Unknown. *MoY*
"Remember, though the telescope extend."
      George Dillon. *PlI*
"Remember well and bear in mind." Un-
      known. *MoY*
Remembrance
   "As years roll by." Unknown. *MoY*
   "Dot." Unknown. *MoY*
   "Forget me not." Unknown. *MoY*
   "Forget the moon, forget the stars." Un-
      known. *MoY*
   "I will not say, Forget-me-not." Un-
      known. *MoY*
   "If writing in albums." Unknown. *MoY*
   "If you have a notion." Unknown. *MoY*
   "In Central park." Unknown. *MoY*
   "In French there is a little word." Un-
      known. *MoY*
   "On this leaf." Unknown. *MoY*
   "Remember Grant." Unknown. *MoY*
   "Remember me at the river." Unknown.
      MoY
   "Remember me in all your wishes." Un-
      known. *MoY*

"Remember me is all I ask." Unknown.
      MoY
"Remember me (when this you see)."
      Unknown. *MoY*
"Remember the kid from Brooklyn." Un-
      known. *MoY*
"Remember the miss." Unknown. *MoY*
Remembrance ("How many dear com-
      panions who enlivened for us") V.
      Zhukovsky. *PaS*
Remembrance ("I know the beech has got
      its red") E. Farjeon. *FaCb*
"There is a pale blue flower." Unknown.
      MoY
"Think of a fly." Unknown. *MoY*
"When I am dead and in my grave." Un-
      known. *MoY*
"When on this page." Unknown. *MoY*
"When you are drinking." Unknown. *MoY*
"When you are dying." Unknown. *MoY*
"When you are in the country." Unknown.
      MoY
"When you are old (and cannot see)."
      Unknown. *MoY*
"When you are washing at a tub." Un-
      known. *MoY*
"When you are wealthy." Unknown. *MoY*
"When you get old and your dress gets
      purple." Unknown. *MoY*
"When you grow old." Unknown. *MoY*
Remembering day. Mary Wight Saunders.
      HaY
Remembering the winter. Rowena Bastin
      Bennett. *BrS*
"Remembering the winter, the squirrel goes
      nutting." See Remembering the winter
Remembrance ("How many dear companions
      who enlivened for us") Vasily Zhukov-
      sky, tr. fr. the Russian by Babette
      Deutsch. *PaS*
Remembrance ("I know the beech has got
      its red") Eleanor Farjeon. *FaCb*
Renascence, sel. Edna St Vincent Millay
   God's world. *CoPs—JoAc—UnG*
Rendall, Elizabeth
   Buttercup Cow. *ArTp*
Rendez-vous with a beetle. E. V. Rieu. *RiF*
Renouncement. Alice Meynell. *ThP*
Repentance
   Paddy O'Rafther. S. Lover. *CoSp*
A **reply.** Matthew Prior. *UnG*
Reply to Mr Wordsworth. Archibald Mac-
      Leish. *PlI* (sel.)
A **reply** to Nancy Hanks. Julius Silberger.
      ArTp
Reptiles. See Crocodiles; Lizards; Snakes
Request number. G. N. Sprod. *CoH*
Requiem. Robert Louis Stevenson. *HaP—
      McW—ThP—UnG*
Requiems. See Laments
Requiescat. Matthew Arnold. *HaP*
The **resolute** cat. Nancy Byrd Turner.
      HuL-1
Retribution. See also Punishment
   Bad Sir Brian Botany. A. A. Milne. *CoH
      —MiWc*
   Barbara Allen. Unknown. *UnMc*
   Bishop Hatto. R. Southey. *CoSp*

The demon lover. Unknown. *CoPm—MaB*
The destruction of Sennacherib. G. G. Byron. *FeF—NaE—SmLg—UnG*
The Inchcape rock. R. Southey. *UnG*
May Colvin. Unknown. *CoSp—MaB—UnMc*
The Pied Piper of Hamelin. R. Browning. *ArTp—HuSv—JoAc—SmLg—UnG*
How the rats were destroyed. *HuL-2* (sel.)
The story of Augustus who would not have any soup. H. Hoffmann. *DeT—NaM*
The story of Augustus. *ArTp*
The vindictives. R. Frost. *FrR*
The **return.** Sara Teasdale. *ThP*
The **return** of spring. Charles d'Orleans, tr. by Henry Wadsworth Longfellow. *GrCc*
The **return** of the fairy. Humbert Wolfe. *CoPm*
The **returned** volunteer to his rifle. Herman Melville. *GrCc*
Reveille. Michael O'Connor. *BrR-6*
Revelation ("Down in the meadow, spread with dew") Alice Brown. *DoP*
Revelation ("We make ourselves a place apart") Robert Frost. *FrR*
Revenge
The hound. S. Lanier. *CoPm*
Old Christmas. R. Helton. *CoPm—UnMc*
The raven. S. T. Coleridge. *HoW*
Shameful death. W. Morris. *UnG—UnMc*
The three songs. B. Taylor. *CoSp*
Vengence on cats. J. Skelton. *HaP*
The **Revenge.** Alfred Tennyson. *UnMc*
Revere, Paul (about)
Paul Revere's ride. From Tales of a wayside inn. H. W. Longfellow. *ArTp—BrL-7 — CoSp — FeF — HuSv — JoAc —SmLg—UnG*
The **reverie** of poor Susan. William Wordsworth. *DeT—HoW*
The **revoke.** E. V. Rieu. *RiF*
Revolution. Alfred Edward Housman. *PlI*
The **revolutionary** rising. Thomas Buchanan Read. *BrL-8*
The **revolving** door. Newman Levy. *CoH*
Rexroth, Kenneth
The infinite. tr. *PaS*
Rhine river
L is for Lorelei. E. Farjeon. *FaCb*
The Lorelei. H. Heine. *CoPm*
The Loreley. *UnG*
"The **rhino** is a homely beast." See The rhinoceros
The **rhinoceros** ("The rhino is a homely beast") Ogden Nash. *CoH—UnG*
The **rhinoceros** ("Rhinoceros, your hide looks all undone") Hilaire Belloc. *FeF*
Rhinoceros ("You may hang your hat on the nose of the rhino") William Jay Smith. *SmB*
"**Rhinoceros,** your hide looks all undone." See The rhinoceros
Rhinoceroses
The rhinoceros ("The rhino is a homely beast") O. Nash. *CoH—UnG*
The rhinoceros ("Rhinoceros, your hide looks all undone") H. Belloc. *FeF*

Rhinoceros ("You may hang your hat on the nose of the rhino") W. J. Smith. *SmB*
Rhodes, Hugh
Advice. *UnG*
The **rhodora.** Ralph Waldo Emerson. *UnG*
Rhodoras
The rhodora. R. W. Emerson. *UnG*
Rhyme. David McCord. *McFf*
Rhyme for a simpleton. Unknown. *CoH*
Rhyme of rain. John Holmes. *McW*
The **rhyme** of the chivalrous shark. Wallace Irwin. *CoH*
Rhyme of the rail. John Godfrey Saxe. *NaM*
Rhys, Ernest
Elegy for Lucy Lloyd. tr. *PaS*
The grave. tr. *PaS*
Rice pudding. A. A. Milne. *MiWc*
Rich, Adrienne Cecile
For the conjunction of two planets. *PlI*
Recorders in Italy. *PlU*
The **rich** earth. See Psalms—Psalm CIV
The **rich** man. Franklin P. Adams. *CoH*
"**Rich** man." Mother Goose. *DeMg*
Rich man, poor man. *WoJ*
"A **rich** man bought a swan and goose." See The swan and goose
"The **rich** man has his motorcar." See The rich man
Rich man, poor man. See "Rich man"
Richard Cory. Edwin Arlington Robinson. *CoSp—SmLg—ThP*
"**Richard** Dick upon a stick." Mother Goose. *OpO*
"**Richard** has been sent to bed." See Dirge for a bad boy
Richard Tolman's universe. Leonard Bacon. *PlI*
Richards, Laura E. (Elizabeth)
Advice to young naturalists. *LoL*
Antonio. *ArTp—CoH—NaM—PeF*
At Easter time. *DoP*
The baby goes to Boston. *ArTp—HuL-1*
Bobbily Boo and Wollypotump. *LoL*
A cat may look at a king. *CoI*
The cave-boy. *FeF*
Drinking vessels. *LoL*
The egg. *ArTp*
Eletelephony. *ArTp — CoI — FeF — JoAc —LoL—PeF*
Emily Jane. *HuL-1*
The giraffe and the woman. *CoI*
The high Barbaree. *JoAc*
In foreign parts. *CoH—LoL*
Jippy and Jimmy. *ArTp—BrR-4—HuL-1*
Kindness to animals. *ArTp—HuL-1*
A legend of Okeefinokee. *CoSp*
"Little cat." *HuL-1*
Little John Bottlejohn. *CoPm—HuL-1—LoL*
The maid of Timbuctoo. *HuL-2*
The mermaidens. *HuSv*
Mrs Snipkin and Mrs Wobblechin. *ArTp —CoH—HuL-1—HuSv—JoAc*
The monkeys and the crocodile. *ArTp— BrR-4—FeF—HuL-1—JoAc—PeF*
Old Ducky Quackerel. *BrR-5*

Richards, Laura E. (Elizabeth)—*Continued*
"The owl and the eel and the warming-pan." *JoAc—NaE*
A party. *BrBc—BrS*
The postman. *ArTp*
The shark. *CoH*
Some fishy nonsense. *ArTp*
A song for Hal. *HuL-2*
Talents differ. *ArTp—HuL-1*
The umbrella brigade. *ArTp—HuL-2—JoAc*
A valentine. *BrR-5—HaY*
Was she a witch. *BrL-k*
Why does it snow. *BrS*

Richardson, Isla Paschal
The dance of the leaves. *BrR-3*
Raindrops. *BrL-k*
Snow fairies. *BrL-k*

Richer. Aileen Fisher. *BrBc*

Riches. See Wealth

Richstone, May
Naming the baby. *BrBc*

"A **riddle**, a riddle." See "A riddle, a riddle, as I suppose"

"A **riddle**, a riddle." Unknown. *WiRm*

"A **riddle**, a riddle, as I suppose." Mother Goose. *ArTp—DeMg*
"A riddle, a riddle." *OpO*

"**Riddle** cum diddle cum dido." See Kindness to animals

"**Riddle** me, riddle me ree." Mother Goose. *OpO*

A **riddle**: What am I. Dorothy Aldis. *AlA —BrL-k*

"**Riddledy** Bob and Jimson Weed." Unknown. *WoF*

Riddles
"Around the rick, around the rick." Mother Goose. *OpO*
"Arthur O'Bower has broken his band." Mother Goose. *OpO*
The wind. *SmLg*
"As black as ink and isn't ink." Mother Goose. *OpO*
"As I was a-walking on Westminster bridge." Mother Goose. *OpO*
"As I was going o'er London bridge." Mother Goose. *OpO*
"As I was going o'er Tipple Tine." Mother Goose. *OpO*
"As I was going to St Ives." Mother Goose. *DeMg—HuSv—JoAc—LiL—OpO*
"As I was walking in a field of wheat." Mother Goose. *OpO*
"As I went through the garden gap." Mother Goose. *DeMg*
A cherry. *ReG*
"As I went up the hazel-dazel." Unknown. *WoF*
"As round as an apple, as deep as a cup." Mother Goose. *ArTp—JoAc*
"As round as an apple." *DeMg—OpO*
"As round as an apple (as deep as a pail)." Mother Goose. *OpO*
"As soft as silk." Mother Goose. *LiL—OpO*
"As white as milk." Unknown
Five very old riddles. *DeT*
"Big at both ends and small in the middle." Unknown. *WoF*

"Black we are, but much admired." Mother Goose. *DeMg*
"Black I am and much admired." *OpO*
"Black within and red without." Mother Goose. *DeMg—JoAc—OpO*
A book. H. More. *CoPs*
"Clothed in yellow, red, and green." Mother Goose. *OpO*
"Come on Smarty, guess my riddle." Unknown. *WoF*
"Crooked as a rainbow." Unknown. *WiRm*
"Elizabeth, Elspeth, Betsy and Bess." Mother Goose. *DeMg—JoAc—OpO*
Elizabeth. *ReG*
Enigma on the letter h. C. M. Fanshawe. *UnG*
"The fiddler and his wife." Mother Goose. *OpO*
"First I am frosted." M. Austin
Rhyming riddles. *ArTp*
"A flock of white sheep." Unknown
Five very old riddles. *DeT*
"Flour of England, fruit of Spain." Mother Goose. *DeMg—OpO*
"Formed long ago, yet made today." Mother Goose. *OpO*
"Four stiff-standers." Mother Goose. *DeMg—LiL—OpO*
"Goes through the mud." Mother Goose. *OpO*
Have you met this man. J. Ciardi. *CiI*
"He wears his hat upon his neck." Unknown. *WoF*
"He went to the wood and caught it." Mother Goose. *OpO*
"Hick-a-more, hack-a-more." Mother Goose. *ArTp—JoAc—OpO*
"Hickamore-hackamore." Unknown. *WoF*
"Higher than a house." Mother Goose. *ArTp—OpO*
"Higher than a house, higher than a tree." *DeMg*
"Highty, tighty, paradighty." Mother Goose. *OpO*
"A hill full, a hole full." Mother Goose. *ArTp—DeMg*
"Hitty Pitty within the wall." Mother Goose. *OpO*
"Hoddy doddy." Mother Goose. *OpO*
"A house full, a yard full." Mother Goose. *LiL*
"A house full, a hole full." *OpO*
"I come more softly than a bird." M. Austin
Rhyming riddles. *ArTp*
"I have a little sister, they call her Peep-peep." Mother Goose. *ArTp—DeMg—HuSv—JoAc—OpO*
Five very old riddles. *DeT*
"I have a little sister." *LiL*
"I have four sisters beyond the sea." Unknown. *DeMg*
"I have no wings, but yet I fly." M. Austin
Rhyming riddles. *ArTp*
"I met a man I could not see." J. Ciardi. *CiI*
"I met a man that showed me a trick." J. Ciardi. *CiI*

"I met a man that was all head." J. Ciardi. *CiI*

I met a man with three eyes. J. Ciardi. *CiI*

"I never speak a word." M. Austin Rhyming riddles. *ArTp*

"I went to the woods and got it." Unknown. *WoF*

"I'm called by the name of a man." Mother Goose. *OpO*

"In fir tar is." Mother Goose. *DeMg—OpO*

"In marble halls as white as milk." Mother Goose. *DeMg—JoAc—OpO*
"In marble walls as white as milk." *HuSv*

"In spring I look gay." Mother Goose. *OpO*

"I've seen you where you never were." Mother Goose. *DeMg*
Five very old riddles. *DeT*

"The land was white." Mother Goose. *OpO*

"Little Billy Breek." Mother Goose. *OpO*

"Little bird of paradise." Mother Goose. *OpO*

"Little Nancy Etticoat." Mother Goose. *DeMg—HuSv—JoAc—LiL—OpO*
"Little Nanny Etticoat." *ArTp*

"Lives in winter." Mother Goose. *ArTp*

"Long legs, crooked thighs." Mother Goose. *DeMg—JoAc—LiL—OpO*

"A man in the wilderness asked me." Mother Goose. *DeMg—JoAc—LiL*
A man in the wilderness. *OpO*
"The man in the wilderness said to me." *SmLg*

"Oh send to me an apple that hasn't any kernel." Unknown. *SmLg*

"Old Mother Twitchett had (or has) but one eye." Mother Goose. *ArTp—DeMg—LiL—OpO*
A needle and thread. *ReG*

One guess. R. Frost. *FrY*

"Opens like a barn door." Unknown. *WiRm*

"Purple, yellow, red and green." Mother Goose. *DeMg—OpO*

"A riddle, a riddle." Unknown. *WiRm*

"A riddle, a riddle, as I suppose." Mother Goose. *ArTp—DeMg*
"A riddle, a riddle." *OpO*

"Riddle me, riddle me ree." Mother Goose. *OpO*

A riddle: What am I. D. Aldis. *AlA—BrL-k*

The riddling knight. Unknown. *GrCc—SmLg*

"Round and round the rugged rock." Mother Goose. *OpO—WiRm*

"Runs all day and never walks." Mother Goose. *ArTp*

"A shoemaker makes shoes without leather." Mother Goose. *OpO*

"Something lives on yonder hill." Unknown. *WiRm*

"A son just born." M. B. Miller. *ArTp*

Spells. J. Reeves. *CoPm—ReG—ReW*

Then I met another man I could not see. J. Ciardi. *CiI*

"There was a girl in our town." Mother Goose. *DeMg—OpO*

"There was a king met a king." Mother Goose. *OpO*

"There was a little green house." Unknown
Five very old riddles. *DeT*

"There was a man rode through our town." Mother Goose. *OpO*

"There was a man who had no eyes." Mother Goose. *OpO*

"There was a thing a full month old." Mother Goose. *OpO*

"There were three sisters in a hall." Mother Goose. *OpO*

"Thirty white horses upon a red hill." Mother Goose. *ArTp—DeMg*
"Thirty white horses." *JoAc—OpO*
"Twenty white horses." *HuSv*

This man had six eyes. J. Ciardi. *CiI*

This man lives at my house now. J. Ciardi. *CiI*

This man went away. J. Ciardi. *CiI*

"Thomas a Tattamus took two tees." Mother Goose. *DeMg*

"Timothy Titus took two ties." Mother Goose. *OpO*

To be answered in our next issue. Unknown. *McW*

"Twelve pears hanging high." Mother Goose. *DeMg—OpO*

"Two bodies have I." Mother Goose. *OpO*

"Two brothers are we." Mother Goose. *OpO*

"Two legs sat upon three legs." Mother Goose. *DeMg—LiL—OpO*
"Two legs sat on three legs." *JoAc*

The vowels. J. Swift. *DeT*

What am I. D. Aldis. *HuSv—JoAc*

"What God never sees." Mother Goose. *OpO*

"White bird featherless." Mother Goose. *OpO*
Snow and sun. *ReG*

The riddling knight. Unknown. *GrCc—SmLg*

"Ride a cock horse." See "Ride a cock-horse to Banbury cross (to see a)"

"Ride a cock-horse to Banbury cross (to see a)." Mother Goose. *DeMg—HuSv—JoAc—LiL—OpO*
"Ride a cock horse." *ArTp—BrL-k—HuL-1—OpO*

"Ride a cock-horse (to Banbury cross to see what)." Mother Goose. *OpO*

"Ride away, ride away." Mother Goose. *ArTp—OpO*

The ride-by-nights. Walter De La Mare. *ArTp—BrS—FeF—HuL-2*

The ride of the Huns. Eleanor Farjeon. *FaCb*

Riders. Robert Frost. *FrR*

Rides and riding
Baby toes. C. Sandburg. *FeF*
Bus ride. From Ferry ride. S. Robinson. *FeF*
Different bicycles. D. Baruch. *ArTp—FeF*
Hey, my pony. E. Farjeon. *FeF*
"Listen my children and you shall hear (of the midnight ride of Sally dear)." Unknown. *MoY*

The ancient mariner. *DeT*
He prayeth best. *DoP—FeF—HuSv—ThP*
  He prayeth well. *HuL-2*
  The rime of the ancient mariner. *UnG*
Ring-a-ring. Kate Greenaway. *BrL-k—FeF
  —NaM*
"Ring-a-ring o' roses." Mother Goose. *DeMg
  —LiL—OpO*
"A ring, a ring o' roses." Mother Goose.
  OpO
"Ring-a-ring of little boys." See Ring-a-ring
"Ring around the world." Annette Wynne.
  ArTp—HuSv—JoAc
Ring out, wild bells. See In memoriam
"Ring out, wild bells, to the wild sky." See
  In memoriam—Ring out, wild bells
"Ring, sing, ring, sing, pleasant Sabbath
  bells." See The green gnome
"Ring the bell." Mother Goose. *DeMg—
  OpO*
"Ring the bells, ring." See The dunce
"Ring—ting, I wish I were a primrose." See
  Wishing
Ringely, ringely. Eliza Lee Follen. *BrBc*
"Ringely, ringely, dah-re-roon." See Ringely,
  ringely
Ripe corn. Carl Sandburg. *SaW*
Rise, sun. Frances M. Frost. *FrLn*
"Rise up, rise up, Lord Douglas, she says."
  See The Douglas tragedy
Rittenhouse, Jessie B.
  Paradox. *ThP*
Ritter, Margaret
  "Faith, I wish I were a leprechaun." *ArTp
  —FeF—HuL-2*
The **rivals.** James Stephens. *BrR-6—FeF*
River-fog. Fukayabu Kiyowara, tr. fr. the
  Japanese by Arthur Waley. *FeF*
The **river-god's** song. Francis Beaumont and
  John Fletcher. *FeF—NaM*
  Song. *ReT*
The **river** is a piece of sky. John Ciardi.
  ArTp—CiR
The **river-merchant's** wife: A letter. Li T'ai-
  po, tr. fr. the Chinese by Ezra Pound.
  GrCc—HaP
River moons. Carl Sandburg. *SaW*
River roads. Carl Sandburg. *SaW*
Rivers. See also names of rivers, as Rio
  Grande river
  "Crooked as a rainbow." Unknown. *WiRm*
  Explanation, on coming home late. R.
  Hughes. *ReT*
  "I do not know much about gods; but I
  think that the river." From The dry
  salvages. T. S. Eliot. *ArTp*
  "I went to the river and couldn't get across
  (I paid five dollars)." Unknown. *WoF*
  "Me and my wife and a bob-tail dog."
  Unknown. *WoF*
  Otter creek. F. M. Frost. *FrLn*
  River-fog. Fukayabu Kiyowara. *FeF*
  The river-god's song. F. Beaumont and
  J. Fletcher. *FeF—NaM*
    Song. *ReT*
  The river is a piece of sky. J. Ciardi. *ArTp
  —CiR*
  River moons. C. Sandburg. *SaW*

River roads. C. Sandburg. *SaW*
  "Runs all day and never walks." Mother
  Goose. *ArTp*
  "The tide in the river." E. Farjeon. *ArTp*
  Two rivers ("Says Tweed to Till") Un-
  known. *MaB*
  Two rivers ("Thy summer voice, Mus-
  ketaquit") R. W. Emerson. *GrCc*
  Waters. E. H. Newlin. *BrR-4*
  Where go the boats. R. L. Stevenson.
  ArTp—BrR-3—HuL-2—SmLg
  Winter streams. B. Carman. *DeT—HaY*
Roach, Eloise
  Nightfall. tr. *PaS*
"The **road** is wide and the stars are out and
  the breath of night is sweet." See Roofs
"A **road** like brown ribbon." See September
"A **road** might lead to anywhere." See
  Roads
The **road** not taken. Robert Frost. *FrR—
  FrY—NaE—SmLg*
The **road** to town. H. M. Sarson. *HuL-1*
"The **road** to town goes up and down."
  See The road to town
Roads. Rachel Field. *BrR-6—FeF—HuL-2
  —HuSv—McW—PeF*

Roads and trails. See also Streets; Way-
  faring life
  "Afoot and light-hearted, I take to the
  open road." From Song of the open
  road. W. Whitman. *ArTp*
  City streets and country roads. E. Farjeon.
  ArTp—PeF
  The house and the road. J. P. Peabody.
  BrR-5
  The joys of the road. B. Carman. *BrL-8*
  The legs. R. Graves. *HaP*
  The old coach road. R. Field. *HuL-2*
  On a mountain road. Wu Ch'ing-jen. *PaS*
  On a tree fallen across the road. R. Frost.
  FrR
  Oregon trail: 1851. J. Marshall. *HuSv*
  The Oregon trail: 1843. A. Guiterman.
  FeF
  The pioneer. A. Guiterman. *ArTp*
  The Portsmouth road. C. Fox-Smith.
  HuL-2
  River roads. C. Sandburg. *SaW*
  The road not taken. R. Frost. *FrR—FrY
  —NaE—SmLg*
  The road to town. H. M. Sarson. *HuL-1*
  Roads. R. Field. *BrR-6—FeF—HuL-2—
  HuSv—McW—PeF*
  "Roads go ever on and on." From The
  hobbit. J. R. R. Tolkien. *FeF*
    "Roads go ever ever on." *ArTp—
    BrR-5*
  Roadways. J. Masefield. *BrR-5*
  The rolling English road. G. K. Chesterton.
  NaE—SmLg
  The Roman road. T. Hardy. *GrCc*
  Silver ships. M. P. Meigs. *ArTp—BrR-5
  —FeF*
  Song of the open road. O. Nash. *ThP*
  Texas trains and trails. M. Austin. *ArTp*
  A time for building. M. C. Livingston.
  LiWa
  Wander-thirst. G. Gould. *ArTp—BrL-7—
  HuL-2*
  The way through the woods. R. Kipling.
  FeF—HaP—ReT—SmLg

"Roads go ever ever on." See The hobbit—
"Roads go ever on and on"
"Roads go ever on and on." See The hobbit
Roadways. John Masefield. *BrR-5*
Roaring mad Tom. See Tom o' Bedlam's song
"Roaring wind, soaring wind." See The wind's song
The robber. Ivy O. Eastwick. *BrS*
Robert Barnes. See "Robert Barnes, fellow fine"
"Robert Barnes, fellow fine." Mother Goose. *DeMg—OpO*
Robert Barnes. *HuL-1*
Robert of Lincoln. William Cullen Bryant. *FeF*
"Robert Rowley rolled a round roll 'round." Mother Goose. *HuSv—OpO*
Roberts, Cecil
Prayer for a pilot. *FeF*
Roberts, Elizabeth Madox
August night. *HaY*
Big brother. *FeF*
The branch. *JoAc*
The butterbean tent. *HuSv*
Christmas morning. *CoPs—DoP—HuSv—JoAc—UnG*
The circus. *FeF*
Crescent moon. *ArTp—BrL-k—McAw*
Dick and Will. *BrBc*
Evening hymn. *ArTp*
Father's story. *CoPs—FeF*
Firefly. *ArTp—HuL-1—JoAc*
The hens. *ArTp—BrR-4—CoI—FeF—HuSv—PeF—UnG*
Little rain. *ArTp—BrR-4*
Milking time. *BrL-k—FeF*
Mr Wells. *FeF*
Mumps. *FeF—JoAc—LoL—McAw*
The people. *ArTp*
The rabbit. *ArTp—PeF—UnG*
Strange tree. *FeF*
The twins. *ArTp—BrBc—McAw*
Water noises. *BrR-4—McAw*
The woodpecker. *ArTp—BrL-k—FeF—HuSv*
Roberts, Michael
Hymn to the sun. *SmLg*
St Gervais. *SmLg*
Roberts, Mildred Evans
Happy New year. *McAw*
Roberts, Theodore Goodridge
The maid. *NaM*
Robin ("Hop and skip") Tom Robinson. *BrL-k*
Robin ("Robin sang sweetly") Unknown. *HuL-2*
The robin ("When father takes his spade to dig") Laurence Alma-Tadema. *BrL-k—HuL-1*
"Robin-a-Bobbin." Mother Goose. *OpO*
Robin Adair. Caroline Keppel. *DeT*
"A robin and a robin's son." Mother Goose. *OpO*
"Robin and Richard." See "Robin and Richard were two pretty men"
"Robin and Richard were two pretty men." Mother Goose. *DeMg*
"Robin and Richard." *OpO*

The robin and the cows. William Dean Howells. *UnG*
"The robin and the redbreast." See Warning
"The robin and the wren." See Greed
"A robin back from the sunny south." See The early bird
Robin Goodfellow. Ben Jonson. *ReG*
"Robin Goodfellow, come home." See R is for Robin Goodfellow
Robin Hood
The birth of Robin Hood. Unknown. *MaB*
The death of Robin Hood ("Give me my bow, said Robin Hood") E. Field. *CoSp*
The death of Robin Hood ("When Robin Hood and Little John") Unknown. *MaB*
"Robin Hood." Mother Goose. *OpO*
Robin Hood. J. Keats. *GrCc*
Robin Hood and Alan a Dale. Unknown. *MaB*
Robin Hood and Allan a Dale. *UnG*
Robin Hood and Allin a Dale. *NaM*
Robin Hood and Guy of Gisborne. Unknown *MaB*
Robin Hood and Little John. Unknown. *HuSv—JoAc*
Robin Hood and the bishop of Hereford. Unknown. *MaB*
Robin Hood and the butcher. Unknown. *MaB*
Robin Hood and the curtal friar. Unknown. *MaB*
Robin Hood and the ranger. Unknown. *HuSv*
Robin Hood and the tanner. Unknown. *UnMc*
Robin Hood and the two priests. Unknown. *MaB*
Robin Hood rescuing the widow's three sons. Unknown. *ArTp*
How Robin Hood rescued the widow's sons. *CoSp*
Robin Hood and the widow's sons. *UnG*
Robin Hood and the widow's three sons. *MaB*
"Robin Hood, Robin Hood." Mother Goose. *DeMg—OpO*
Robin Hood's funeral. A. Munday. *HoW*
Song. *ReT*
A song of Sherwood. A. Noyes. *ArTp—FeF—JoAc*
"Robin Hood." Mother Goose. *OpO*
Robin Hood. John Keats. *GrCc*
Robin Hood and Alan a Dale. Unknown. *MaB*
Robin Hood and Allan a Dale. *UnG*
Robin Hood and Allin a Dale. *NaM*
Robin Hood and Allan a Dale. See Robin Hood and Alan a Dale
Robin Hood and Allin a Dale. See Robin Hood and Alan a Dale
Robin Hood and Guy of Gisborne. Unknown. *MaB*
Robin Hood and Little John. Unknown. *HuSv—JoAc*
Robin Hood and the bishop of Hereford. Unknown. *MaB*
Robin Hood and the butcher. Unknown. *MaB*

Robin Hood and the curtal friar. Unknown. *MaB*

Robin Hood and the ranger. Unknown. *HuSv*

Robin Hood and the tanner. Unknown. *UnMc*

Robin Hood and the two priests. Unknown. *MaB*

Robin Hood and the widow's sons. See Robin Hood rescuing the widow's three sons

Robin Hood and the widow's three sons. See Robin Hood rescuing the widow's three sons

Robin Hood rescuing the widow's three sons. Unknown. *ArTp*
  How Robin Hood rescued the widow's sons. *CoSp*
  Robin Hood and the widow's sons. *UnG*
  Robin Hood and the widow's three sons. *MaB*

"Robin Hood, Robin Hood." Mother Goose. *DeMg—OpO*

Robin Hood's funeral. Anthony Munday. *HoW*
  Song. *ReT*

"Robin is a lovely lad." See The dance

"The robin of the red breast." Unknown. *CoPm*
  Bad luck. *DeT*

"Robin rashly kissed my hand." See He understood

Robin Redbreast ("Good-bye, good-bye to summer") William Allingham. *NaM*

A robin redbreast ("A robin redbreast in a cage") See Auguries of innocence

"A robin redbreast in a cage." See Auguries of innocence—A robin redbreast

Robin-run-by-the-wall. Eleanor Farjeon. *FaCb*

"Robin sang sweetly." See Robin

"The robin sings in the elm." See The robin and the cows

"Robin the Bobbin." See "Robin the Bobbin, the big-bellied Ben"

"Robin the Bobbin, the big-bellied Ben." Mother Goose. *DeMg*
  "Robin the Bobbin." *OpO*

"Robin was a king of men." See Ragged Robin

"Robinets and Jenny Wrens." See Praise

Robins
  Betsy Robin. W. J. Smith. *SmL*
  The blossom. W. Blake. *ReT*
  Bob Robin. Mother Goose. *OpO*
  The Christmas robin. R. Graves. *GrCc*
  Cock Robin. Mother Goose. *DeT*
    Cock Robin's courtship. *OpO*
  The early bird. J. S. Reilly. *BrR-4*
  "Fat father robin." D. McCord. *McFf*
  Greed. Mother Goose. *OpO*
  "It was on a merry time." Mother Goose. *DeMg*
  "Jenny Wren fell sick." Mother Goose. *JoAc*
    Jenny Wren. *NaE*
    Little Jenny Wren. *HuL-1*
    Ungrateful Jenny. *OpO*
  "Little Robin Redbreast (sat upon a hill)." Mother Goose. *DeMg*

"Little Robin Redbreast (sat upon a rail)." Mother Goose. *DeMg—HuSv*
  Niddle noddle. *OpO*

"Little Robin Redbreast sat upon a tree." Mother Goose. *DeMg—LiL*
  "Little Robin Redbreast." *HuL-1*

"My dear, do you know." Mother Goose. *DeMg*
  The babes in the wood. *DeT*

The naughty little robin. P. Cary. *BrL-k*

"The north wind doth blow." Mother Goose. *DeMg—HuL-1—HuSv—JoAc—LiL*
  The north wind. *OpO*

On this day the wren and the robin stop singing. E. Farjeon. *FaN*

"Pit, pat, well-a day." Mother Goose. *DeMg*
  Pit, pat. *OpO*

Ragged Robin. J. Reeves. *ReR*

Rainy robin. F. M. Frost. *FrLn*

Robin ("Hop and skip") T. Robinson. *BrL-k*

Robin ("Robin sang sweetly") Unknown. *HuL-2*

The robin ("When father takes his spade to dig") L. Alma-Tadema. *BrL-k—HuL-1*

The robin and the cows. W. D. Howells. *UnG*

"The robin of the red breast." Unknown. *CoPm*
  Bad luck. *DeT*

Robin Redbreast. W. Allingham. *NaM*

The robin's song ("God bless the field and bless the furrow") C. L. Fraser. *NaM*

Robin's song ("Robin's song is crystal clear") E. L. M. King. *ArTp*

The secret. Unknown. *ArTp—BrL-k—HuL-1*

The song of the robin. B. Bergquist. *BrL-k*

Talents differ. L. E. Richards. *ArTp—HuL-1*

Visitor. Mother Goose. *OpO*

What robin told. G. Cooper. *ArTp—BrL-k—BrR-3—FeF*

"Who killed Cock Robin." Mother Goose. *DeMg—DeT—JoAc*
  Cock Robin. *UnG*
  Death and burial of Cock Robin. *OpO*

"Wrens and robins in the hedge." C. G. Rossetti. *ArTp*

"Robins in the treetop." See Marjorie's almanac

The robin's song ("God bless the field and bless the furrow") C. Lovat Fraser. *NaM*

Robin's song ("Robin's song is crystal clear") E. L. M. King. *ArTp*

"Robin's song is crystal clear." See Robin's song

Robinson, Anne
  Conversation. *BrR-3—HuL-1*

Robinson, Edwin Arlington
  Archibald's example. *GrCc*
  Bewick Finzer. *GrCc*
  The dark hills. *HaP*
  Eutychides. tr. *PlU*
  For Arvia. *BrBc*
  The house on the hill. *FeF—HaP*
  The mill. *HaP*
  Miniver Cheevy. *HaP—SmLg—UnMc*

Jock o' Hazeldean. From Guy Mannering. W. Scott. *DeT*
Keith of Ravelston. S. Dobell. *DeT*
Kubla Khan; or, A vision in a dream. S. T. Coleridge. *ReT—SmLg—UnMc*
Lady Clare. A. Tennyson. *CoSp—FeF—HuSv—UnG*
Lochinvar. From Marmion. W. Scott. *BrL-7 — CoSp — FeF — HuSv — JoAc — NaE — UnG — UnMc*
Old Christmas. R. Helton. *CoPm—UnMc*
The phantom light of the Baie des Chaleurs. A. W. H. Eaton. *CoPm*
Romance. W. J. Turner. *BrBc—CoPm—ReT*
The singing leaves. J. R. Lowell. *HuSv*
Sir Olaf. J. G. Von Herder. *CoPm*
The spinning wheel. J. F. Waller. *CoSp*
The three singing birds. J. Reeves. *CoPm—ReBl*
The Turkish lady. Unknown. *UnMc*
Romance. Walter J. Turner. *BrBc—CoPm—ReT*
Rome
The Roman road. T. Hardy. *GrCc*
Rome—History
The children of the wolf. E. Farjeon. *FaCb*
The emperors of Rome. E. Farjeon. *FaCb*
Horatius. From Lays of ancient Rome. T. B. Macaulay. *SmLg*
    The fight at the bridge. *UnMc* (sel.)
Waiting for the barbarians. C. P. Cavafy. *GrCc*
When Hannibal crossed the Alps. E. Farjeon. *FaCb—HuL-2*
Romeo and Juliet, sels. William Shakespeare
Queen Mab. *FeF—JoAc*
    Gallery of people. *UnG*
    A Shakespeare gallery. *UnMc*
"Soft, what light through yonder window breaks"
    A Shakespeare gallery. *UnMc*
Rondeau. Charles d'Orleans, tr. fr. the French by J. G. Legge. *PaS*
Roofs. Joyce Kilmer. *BrL-8*
"The **roofs** are shining from the rain." See April
Rooks
The rooks. P. B. Shelley. *DeT*
The **rooks.** Percy Bysshe Shelley. *DeT*
"The **rook's** nest do rock on the tree-top." See Rockaby, baby
"The **room** was low and small and kind." See Bible stories
"**Rooms** for rent." Unknown. *WoJ*
"The **rooster** and the chicken had a fight." Unknown. *MoY*
"The **rooster** with the scarlet comb." See Rise, sun
"**Roots** spring from my feet, Apollo, like a tree." See Daphne
Roscoe, William
The butterfly's ball. *JoAc—UnG*
"**Rose-cheeked** Laura, come." See Laura
The **rose** family. Robert Frost. *FrY*
"The **rose** is a rose." See The rose family
"The **rose** is red." Unknown. *MoY*

"The **rose** is red, the grass is green." Mother Goose. *OpO*
"The **rose** is red, the rose is white." Mother Goose. *OpO*
"The **rose** is red, the violet's blue." Mother Goose. *DeMg—HuSv—OpO*
"The **rose** was sick and smiling died." See The funeral rites of the rose
"**Rose,** when I remember you." See To Rose
"**Rosemary** green, and lavender blue." Mother Goose. *DeMg*
Rosenzweig, Efraim
Dreidel song. *ArTp*
A song of always. *ArTp*
Roses
Briar-rose. Unknown. *HuL-2*
Durenda Fair. D. McCord. *McFf*
The funeral rites of the rose. R. Herrick. *HaP*
"Go, lovely rose." E. Waller. *HaP*
June's song. E. Farjeon. *FaCb—FaN*
The little rose tree. R. Field. *ArTp—BrL-k—FeF*
The mystery. R. Hodgson. *DoP*
The rose family. R. Frost. *FrY*
The rose's scent. Unknown. *HoW*
The sick rose. W. Blake. *HaP*
The sweet, red rose. M. M. Dodge. *BrBc*
"**Roses** are blue." Unknown. *MoY*
"**Roses** are red (pickles are green)." Unknown. *MoY*
"**Roses** are red (they grow)." Unknown. *MoY*
"**Roses** are red (violets are blue, God made)." Unknown. *MoY*
"**Roses** are red (violets are blue, I can)." Unknown. *MoY*
"**Roses** are red, violets are blue (lend me)." Unknown. *MoY*
"**Roses** are red (violets are blue, so's your)." Unknown. *MoY*
"**Roses** are red (violets are blue, sugar is)." Mother Goose. *MoY—OpO*
"**Roses** are red (violets are blue, when it)." Unknown. *MoY*
"**Roses** may be red." Unknown. *MoY*
"**Roses** red and jonquils gold." See One, two, buckle my shoe
The **rose's** scent. Unknown. *HoW*
Ross, Abram Bunn
An indignant male. *BrR-3*
Two in bed. *ArTp—FeF*
Ross, Sir Ronald
Lines written after the discovery by the author of the germ of yellow fever. *PlI*
Rossetti, Christina Georgina
"All the bells were ringing." *ArTp*
An apple gathering. *GrCc*
"Before the paling of the stars." *DoP—EaW—ReG*
    A Christmas carol. *BrBc*
    Christmas daybreak. *UnG*
A birthday. *HoW—ReT*
"Boats sail on the rivers." *ArTp—BrR-4—DoP—HuL-2—HuSv—PeF*
    The bridge. *JoAc*
The bridge. See "Boats sail on the rivers"
"Brown and furry." See Caterpillar

Rounds, Emma
Johnny. *CoH*
Plane geometry. *PlI*
Rounds
"Ah poor bird." Unknown. *ReG*
"Row, row, row your boat." Unknown. *ReG*
"Turn again Whittington." Unknown. *ReG*
"A route of evanescence." See The hummingbird
Routine. Arthur Guiterman. *CoH*
Rover and the bird. Mrs Newton Crossland. *DeT*
"A row of pearls." See Seeds
"Row, row, row your boat." Unknown. *ReG*
Row the boat home. Agnes Lack. *HuL-2*
"Row to the fishing-ground, row away." See Fishing
Rowlands, Samuel
Sir Eglamour. *McW—SmLg*
Rowles, Catharine Bryant
New snow. *HaY*
"Rub-a-dub-dub." Mother Goose. *DeMg——JoAc—LiL—OpO*
The **rubáiyát** of Omar Khayyám of Naishapúr. Omar Khayyám, tr. fr. the Persian by Edward Fitzgerald. *HaP* (sel.)—*PaS* (sel.)
Wake. *FeF* (sel.)
Rubber boots. Rowena Bastin Bennett. *JoAc*
Rubbers and galoshes. Marie Louise Allen. *AlP*
"Rubbers are for rainy days." See Rubbers and galoshes
Ruddigore, sel. William Schwenck Gilbert
Sir Roderic's song. *CoPm*
Ruggles, William B.
The pioneer. *BrR-5*
Rugs. See Carpets and rugs
Rukeyser, Muriel
Gibbs. *PlI* (sel.)
Ives. *PlU* (sel.)
Rulers. See Kings and rulers
Rum lane. James Reeves. *ReBl*
The **Rum** Tum Tugger. T. S. Eliot. *ArTp—FeF—NaE*
"The Rum Tum Tugger is a curious cat." See The Rum Tum Tugger
"Rumble, rumble, rumble, goes the gloomy L." See Roller skates
Rumbo and Jumbo. Unknown. *CoH*
Rumi
"As salt resolved in the ocean." *PaS*
At peace. *PaS*
The unseen power. *PaS*
"A rumpled sheet." See The term
"Rumpty-iddity, row, row, row." Mother Goose. *OpO*
Run a little. James Reeves. *ReBl*
"Run a little this way." See Run a little
"Run by the wall, robin." See Robin-run-by-the-wall
"Run, rabbit, run." See Heltery-skeltery
Run, squirrel, run. Unknown. *TaD*
"Run to church with a frying-pan." See Pancake Tuesday

The **runaway.** Robert Frost. *ArTp—FeF—FrR—FrY—HuL-2—HuSv—SmLg—UnG*
The **runaway** brook. Eliza Lee Follen. *BrL-k*
Rune of riches. Florence Converse. *HuL-2*
A **runnable** stag. John Davidson. *HoW—NaE*
Runners and running. See Races and racing—Foot
The **running.** Eleanor Farjeon. *FaCb*
"Runs all day and never walks." Mother Goose. *ArTp*
Russell, George William (A. E., pseud.)
Frolic. *FeF*
Russell, Sydney King
For Vicki at seven. *BrBc*
Russia
Abdullah Bulbul Amir. Unknown. *CoSp*
Ruth. Thomas Hood. *GrCc*
"Ruth and Johnnie." Unknown. *ThP*
"Ruth says apples have learned to bob." See Halloween
Rutledge, Anne (about)
Anne Rutledge. From The Spoon River anthology. E. L. Masters. *CoPs—HaP*
Rutterkin. William Cornish. *CoPm*
"Rutterkin is come unto our town." See Rutterkin
Ryder, Arthur W.
The panchatantra, sel.
True friendship. tr. *PaS*
True friendship. See The panchatantra
Women's eyes. tr. *PaS*

S

S is for sandman. Eleanor Farjeon. *FaCb*
Sabin, Edwin L.
Easter. *CoPs*
"Sabrina fair." See Comus
Sackville, Thomas, Earl of Dorset (Lord Buckhurst)
Midnight. *DeT*
Sackville-West, V.
Full moon. *NaM*
The **sacred** order. May Sarton. *PlI*
A **sad** case of misapplied concentration. L. De Giberne Sieveking. *CoH*
The **sad** goat. Unknown. *McW*
The **sad** monkey. Dorothy Aldis. *AlA*
The **sad** shoes. Dorothy Aldis. *AlA*
A **sad** song. John Ciardi. *CiY*
The **sad** tale of Mr Mears. Unknown. *CoSp*
Sadaiye
Blossoms and storm. *PaS*
Saddest of all. Dorothy Aldis. *AlA*
"The **safest** feeling." See Going to sleep
Safety
"J's the jumping jay-walker." From All around the town. P. McGinley. *ArTp—FeF*
Stop and go. M. L. Allen. *AlP*
"Stop, look, and listen." Unknown. *HuL-1*
A warning. J. Gay. *DeT*
Saffron Walden. Eleanor Farjeon. *FaN*

Sage counsel. Arthur Quiller-Couch. *CoH—LoL*

The **saginsack.** John Ciardi. *CiR*

"The **saginsack** has radio horns." See The saginsack

Sagittarius. Eleanor Farjeon. *FaCb—FaN*

"**Said** a chamber-maid to a sleeping guest." Unknown. *MoY*

"**Said** a crow in the top of a tree." See I met a crow

"**Said** a great Congregational preacher." Oliver Wendell Holmes. *UnG*

"**Said** Day to Night." See Day and night

"**Said** grandpa to Tommy White." See A nature lesson

Said Hengist to Horsa. Eleanor Farjeon. *FaCb*

"**Said** Hengist to Horsa, I see a white coast." See Said Hengist to Horsa

"**Said** Mr Smith, I really cannot." See Bones

"**Said** old Father Tiber, a-wandering by." See The children of the wolf

"**Said** Orville Wright to Wilbur Wright." See Wilbur Wright and Orville Wright

"**Said** Pluto the king." See Pluto and Proserpine

"**Said** Simple Sam: Does Christmas come." See Simple Sam

"**Said** the duck to the kangaroo." See The duck and the kangaroo

"**Said** the first little chicken." See The chickens

"**Said** the monkey to the owl." Unknown. *WoF*

"**Said** the queen of the Nile." See The queen of the Nile

"**Said** the Raggedy Man on a hot afternoon." See The man in the moon

"**Said** the shark to the flying fish over the phone." See The flattered flying fish

"**Said** the table to the chair." See The table and the chair

"**Said** the wind to the moon, I will blow you out." See The wind and the moon

Sail on, O ship of state. See The building of the ship

"**Sail** on. Sail on. O ship of state." See The building of the ship—Sail on, O ship of state

Sailing. See also Boats and boating; Ships
Gone. W. De La Mare. *GrCc*
Sailing homeward. C. Fang-Shēng. *PaS—SmLg*
"A wet sheet and a flowing sea." A. Cunningham. *ArTp—BrL-8—McW*
A sea song. *JoAc*

"**Sailing** down the stream of life." Unknown. *MoY*

Sailing homeward. Chan Fang-Shēng, tr. fr. the Chinese by Arthur Waley. *PaS—SmLg*

Sailor. Eleanor Farjeon. *PeF*

Sailor and tailor. Unknown. *DeT*

Sailor John. David McCord. *McT*

"A **sailor** lad and a tailor lad." See Sailor and tailor

"A **sailor** went to sea." Unknown. *WiRm*

Sailors. See Seamen

The **sailor's** consolation. Attributed to Charles Dibdin; also attributed to William Pitt. *CoH—DeT—HuSv*

The **sailor's** wife. William Julius Mickle. *DeT*

Saint Bridget. Eleanor Farjeon. *FaCb*

"**Saint** Bridget she was beautiful." See Saint Bridget

Saint Cecelia's day
A song for St Cecelia's day, 1687. J. Dryden. *PlU* (sel.)

Saint Christopher. Eleanor Farjeon. *FaCb*

Saint Dorothea. Eleanor Farjeon. *FaCb*

"**St** Dunstan, as the story goes." See The devil

Saint Francis. Eleanor Farjeon. *FaCb*

St Gervais. Michael Roberts. *SmLg*

Saint Giles. Eleanor Farjeon. *FaCb*

Saint Hubert. Eleanor Farjeon. *FaCb*

Saint James' day
Remember the grotto. E. Farjeon. *FaCb—FaN*

Saint Joseph. Eleanor Farjeon. *FaCb*

Saint Martin. Eleanor Farjeon. *FaCb*

Saint Nicholas. See Santa Claus

Saint Nicholas. Eleanor Farjeon. *FaCb*

Saint Patrick. Eleanor Farjeon. *FaCb*

St Patrick was a gentleman. Henry Bennett. *BrS*

St Patrick's breastplate. Unknown, tr. fr. the Irish by Cecil Frances Alexander. *SmLg*

Saint Patrick's day. See Patrick, Saint

"**St** Patrick's day is with us." See I'll wear a shamrock

"**St** Patrick's day it is—it is." See Dawn song—St Patrick's day

Saint Simeon Stylites. Eleanor Farjeon. *FaCb*

St Swithin's day. See Swithin, Saint

"**St** Swithin's day, if thou dost rain." Mother Goose. *DeMg—LiL*
Signs, seasons, and sense. *UnG*

Saint Swithin's wish. Eleanor Farjeon. *FaCb—FaN*

St Teresa's book-mark. Saint Teresa of Avila, tr. fr. the Spanish by Henry Wadsworth Longfellow. *PaS*

"**St** Thomas's day is past and gone." Mother Goose. *OpO*

Saint Valentine's day
"Good Bishop Valentine." E. Farjeon. *CoPs—FaCb—FaN*
"Good morrow to you, Valentine." Mother Goose. *OpO*
"Hearts were made to give away." A. Wynne. *ArTp*
My valentine ("I have a little valentine") M. C. Parsons. *ArTp—BrL-k—HuL-1*
My valentine ("I will make you brooches and toys for your delight") R. L. Stevenson. *BrS—FeF*
I will make you brooches. *HuL-2*
Romance. *CoPs*
My valentine ("Oh, who will be my valentine") I. O. Eastwick. *EaI*
Phillis inamorata. L. Andrewes. *GrCc*

The robber. I. O. Eastwick. *BrS*
"The rose is red, the violet's blue." Mother Goose. *DeMg—HuSv—OpO*
A skater's valentine. A. Guiterman. *BrS*
Song. From Hamlet. W. Shakespeare. *BrS—FeF*
A sure sign. N. B. Turner. *ArTp—BrR-4*
A valentine ("Frost flowers on the window glass") E. Hammond. *ArTp—HaY*
Valentine ("I got a valentine from Timmy") S. Silverstein. *CoPs*
Valentine ("No early buds of laughing spring") C. W. T. *HaY*
A valentine ("Oh, little loveliest lady mine") L. E. Richards. *BrR-5—HaY*
Valentine promise. Unknown. *CoPs*
Valentine's day. A. Fisher. *HaY*
"When you send a valentine." M. J. Hill. *BrR-3—McAw*
Saints. See names of saints, as Francis, of Assisi, Saint
Salamanders
Down by the pond. A. A. Milne. *MiWc*
The newt. D. McCord. *ArTp—McFf*
Sally and Manda. A. B. Campbell. *CoI*
Sandman. See also Lullabies; Sleep
Little sandman's song. Unknown. *HuL-2*
S is for sandman. E. Farjeon. *FaCb*
Salinger, Herman
Love. tr. *PaS*
Nocturne. tr. *PaS*
The pond. tr. *PaS*
Serenade. tr. *PaS*
Sally and Manda. Alice B. Campbell. *CoI*
"**Sally** and Manda are two little lizards." See Sally and Manda
"**Sally** go round the sun." Mother Goose. *OpO*
Sally in our alley. Henry Carey. *CoPs* (sel.)
Sally Lun Lundy. David McCord. *McT*
"**Sally** Rand." Unknown. *WoJ*
"**Sally,** Sally Waters." See Sally Waters
Sally Waters. Mother Goose. *OpO*
"The **saloon** is gone up the creek." See Hemmed-in males
"**Salt,** pepper, sugar, cider." Unknown. *WiRm*
Salutation. Ezra Pound. *SmLg*
A **salute** to trees. Henry Van Dyke. *HuSv*
Salzburg, J. L.
Bill. *BrBc*
Sam. Walter De La Mare. *ArTp—CoPm*
Sam, the sportsman. See "There was a little man, and he had a little gun"
"The **same** gold of summer was on the winter hills." See Winter gold
"The **same** leaves over and over again." See In hardwood groves
The **sampler** ("A strange, strange thing it is to know") Rachel Field. *BrBc*
The **sampler** ("When great-grandmother was ten years old") Nancy Byrd Turner. *BrBc*
Sampter, Jessie E.
Bird's nest. tr. *BrL-k*
Blessing over food. tr. *BrL-k—HaY*
Blessings for Chanukah. *ArTp*
The grasshopper's song. tr. *FeF—HaY*

Rainbow. tr. *BrR-4*
Rocking horse. tr. *BrL-k*
See-saw. tr. *BrL-k*
Samuel, Maurice
Tell him. tr. *PaS*
"**Samuel** Silvernose Slipperyside." John Ciardi. *CiR*
Sana'i
Perfect love. *PaS*
"The **sand** below the border-mountain lies like snow." See On hearing a flute at night from the wall of Shou-Hsiang
Sand-between-the-toes. A. A. Milne. *MiWc*
Sand dunes. Robert Frost. *FrR*
"**Sand** of the sea runs red." See Flux
Sandburg, Carl
"Alice Corbin is gone." *SaW*
American yarns. See The people, yes
Arithmetic. *FeF* (sel.)—*McW—PlI—SaW*
Auctioneer. *SaW*
Baby song of the four winds. *SaW*
Baby toes. *FeF*
Basket. *SaW*
Be ready. *SaW*
Bee song. *SaW*
"Between two hills." *SaW*
Blossom themes. *SaW*
"Bluebird, what do you feed on." *SaW*
Boxes and bags. *SaW*
Broken sky. *SaW*
Brown gold. *SaW*
Bubbles. *SaW*
Buffalo Bill. *SaW*
Buffalo dusk. *ArTp*
Cheap blue. *SaW*
Chicago. *SmLg*
Child Margaret. *SaW*
Children of the desert. See The people, yes
Children of the wind. See The people, yes
Circles. See The people, yes
Cornfield ridge and stream. *SaW*
Cornhuskers. *SaW*
Crabapples. *SaW*
Crisscross. *SaW*
Daybreak. *SaW*
Docks. *SaW*
Doors. *SaW*
Drowsy. *SaW*
Evening waterfall. *GrCc*
Flowers tell months. *SaW*
Flux. *SaW*
Fog. *ArTp—HuSv—JoAc—PeF—UnG*
For you. *McW*
Fourth of July night. *SaW*
Frog songs. *SaW*
From the shore. *SaW*
Goldwing moth. *SaW*
Good morning, America, sel.
Sky prayers. *SaW*
Grassroots. *SaW*
Harvest sunset. *SaW*
Hats. *SaW*
Haystacks. *SaW*
Haze gold. *SaW*
Hits and runs. *SaW*
Home. See Poems done on a late night car
Improved farm land. *SaW*
Landscape. *SaW*

Conversation between Mr and Mrs Santa Claus. R. B. Bennett. *ArTp—BrS*
Left out. A. G. W. *BrR-3*
Mrs Santa Claus' Christmas present. A. S. Morris. *CoPs*
Saint Nicholas. E. Farjeon. *FaCb*
A visit from St Nicholas. C. C. Moore. *ArTp—BrS—FeF—HuSv—JoAc—UnG*
When Santa Claus comes. Unknown. *BrL-k*

Santa Fe, New Mexico
Santa Fe sketch. C. Sandburg. *SaW*
Santa Fe sketch. Carl Sandburg. *SaW*

Santorin. James Elroy Flecker. *GrCc*

Sappho
A garden. *PaS*
Night. *PaS*
A young bride. *PaS*

Sarah Byng. Hilaire Belloc. *GrCc*

Sarett, Lew
Four little foxes. *ArTp—CoPs—FeF—HaY —McW—UnG*
The sheepherder. *FeF*
Wind in the pine. *BrL-7*
The wolf cry. *FeF*

Sargent, William D.
Wind-wolves. *ArTp*

Sarson, H. M.
Lovely things. *HuL-2*
The road to town. *HuL-1*

Sarton, May
The clavichord. *PlU*
Innumerable friend. *McW*
The sacred order. *PlI*

Sassafras
Witchwood. M. Justus. *BrS*

Sassoon, Siegfried
Everyone sang. *CoPs—McW*
A musical critic anticipates eternity. *PlU*
Sheldonian soliloquy. *PlU*

Saturday. See Days of the week—Saturday

Saunders, Mary Wight
Remembering day. *HaY*

Saturday market. Charlotte Mew. *FeF* (sel.)

Saturday morning. Myra Cohn Livingston. *LiWa*

The satyr, sel. Ben Jonson
Mab. *HoW*

"Savage lion in the zoo." See Supper for a lion

Save the tiger. A. P. Herbert. *CoH*

"Saw, saw." See Twelfth night

Sawyer, Frederick William
The recognition. *BrR-6*

Sawyer, Mark
Kite days. *BrS—McAw*

Sawyer, Ruth
On Christmas morn. See Words from an old Spanish carol
Words from an old Spanish carol. tr. *EaW*
On Christmas morn. *FeF*

Saxe, John Godfrey
The blind men and the elephant. *CoSp— JoAc—UnG—UnMc*
Rhyme of the rail. *NaM*
Solomon and the bees. *UnG*
The youth and the northwind. *CoSp*

"Say in one breath." Unknown. *DeMg*

"Say not the struggle nought availeth." See Keeping on

Say there, fellow. Unknown. *TaD*

"Say there, fellow, you can't talk." See Say there, fellow

"Say well and do well." Mother Goose. *OpO*

Say yes to the music, or else. John Ciardi. *CiM*

Sayers, Dorothy
Carol. *EaW*

Sayers, Frances Clarke
Who calls. *BrL-7—BrS*

"Says Tweed to Till." See Two rivers

"A scandalous man." See Mr Tom Narrow

Scandinavia. See Denmark; Norway; Norsemen

Scarcely spring. Louis Untermeyer. *UnG*

The scaredy. Mother Goose. *OpO*

Scat, scitten. David McCord. *McT*

Schacht, Marshall
The first autumn. *BrL-8*

Scheffauer, Ethel Talbot
Copper song. *CoPm*

Schlichter, Norman C.
A sledding song. *FeF*

School. See also Teachers and teaching
Big brother. E. M. Roberts. *FeF*
"Birds on the mountain." Unknown. *MoY*
Christmas pageant. M. Fishback. *CoPs*
"A collegiate damsel named Breeze." Unknown
Limericks since Lear. *UnG*
"The cow has a cud." From Five chants. D. McCord. *McFf*
Dear old dad. L. P. *BrR-6*
"A diller, a dollar, a ten o'clock scholar." Mother Goose. *ArTp*
"A diller, a dollar." *DeMg—JoAc—LiL*
Ten o'clock scholar. *OpO*
Duty of the student. E. Anthony. *UnG*
"An eagle flew from north to south." Unknown. *MoY*
First departure. F. M. Frost. *BrS*
"First we meet." Unknown. *MoY*
"Friends, Romans, countrymen." Unknown. *MoY*
Frogs at school. G. Cooper. *CoI*
Getting back. D. B. Thompson. *BrS*
"God made the bees." Unknown. *MoY*
I wish. N. B. Turner. *BrS*
"In days of old." Unknown. *MoY*
In school-days. J. G. Whittier. *FeF* (sel.)
In winter. M. Chute. *ChA*
"Latin is a dead language." Unknown. *MoY*
"Learn when young and not when old." Unknown. *MoY*
The lonely street. W. C. Williams. *GrCc*
Lost time. F. Wolfe. *HuL-2*
Mary's lamb. S. J. Hale. *FeF—JoAc— OpO—UnG*
"Mary had a little lamb." *BrL-k— DeMg—LiL*
May mornings. I. O. Eastwick. *BrS—EaI*
"Monday morning back to school." From Five chants. D. McCord. *McFf*
A mortifying mistake. A. M. Pratt. *CoH*
The mystery. H. Behn. *BeW*
Not of school age. R. Frost. *FrY*

Rokeby, sel.
    Allen-a-dale. *CoSp*
Soldier, rest. See The lady of the lake
"Soldier, rest, thy warfare o'er." See The lady of the lake—Soldier, rest
'Tis merry in greenwood. See Harold the Dauntless
Waverley, sel.
    "Hie away, hie away." *ArTp*
    Hie away. *NaM*
Scott, William Bell
    The witch's ballad. *NaE*
Scott, Winfield Townley
    Chapter two. *GrCc*
Scott-Hopper, Queenie
    "Amy Elizabeth Ermyntrude Annie." *ArTp* —*HuL-1*
    Very nearly. *FeF*
Scottish castle. Mother Goose. *OpO*
A Scottish cat. Mother Goose. *OpO*
A Scottish shoe. Mother Goose. *OpO*
Scovell, E. J.
    The boy fishing. *ReT*
"A scraping sound: The grasshopper." See The grasshopper's song
The scribe. Walter De La Mare. *SmLg*
Sculptors. See Sculpture and sculpturing
Sculpture and sculpturing. See also Statues
    Ozymandias. P. B. Shelley. *BrL-7*—*HaP*— *McW*—*SmLg*—*UnG*
Sea. See Ocean
The sea ("Blue drifted the sea; the waters of the sun") Herman Gorter, tr. fr. the Flemish by A. J. Barnouw. *PaS*
The sea ("The sea is a hungry dog") James Reeves. *RcW*
"Sea, be kind to a young boy's bones." See Casabianca
Sea-fever. John Masefield. *ArTp*—*BrL-8*— —*FeF*—*HuL-2*—*HuSv*—*JoAc*—*PeF*
The sea gull. See "The sea gull curves his wings"
"The sea gull curves his wings." Elizabeth Jane Coatsworth. *ArTp*—*PeF*
    The sea gull. *HuL-1*
Sea gulls. See Gulls
The sea gypsy. Richard Hovey. *BrL-7*— *FeF*—*UnG*
"The sea hath its pearls." Heinrich Heine, tr. fr. the German by Henry Wadsworth Longfellow. *PaS*
"The sea is a hungry dog." See The sea
"The sea is calm tonight." See Dover beach
Sea life. See Ocean; Seamen
"The sea lions flap." See The seals
Sea memories. Henry Wadsworth Longfellow. *FeF*
The sea-ritual. George Darley. *HoW*
Sea-shell ("It is so smooth") Ivy O. Eastwick. *EaI*
Sea shell ("Sea shell, sea shell") Amy Lowell. *FeF*—*HuL-2*—*HuSv*
"Sea shell, sea shell." See Sea shell
Sea shells. See Shells
The sea shore. Harry Behn. *BeW*

A sea song. See "A wet sheet and a flowing sea"
Sea song ("Once a little doodle bug") Marchette Chute. *ChA*
A sea song ("There was a man out your way") John Ciardi. *CiY*
Sea song ("To sea, to sea, the calm is o'er") See Death's jest book
"Sea sunsets, give us keepsakes." See Good morning, America—Sky prayers
"The sea was always the sea." See Sea wisdom
"Sea waves are green and wet." See Sand dunes
Sea wisdom. Carl Sandburg. *SaW*
The sea wolf. Violet McDougal. *FeF*
Seafaring life. See Ocean; Seamen
Seal. William Jay Smith. *SmB*—*UnG*
Seal lullaby. Rudyard Kipling. *ArTp*— *BrR-5*—*FeF*—*JoAc*
Seals (Animals)
    The dancing seal. W. W. Gibson. *CoPm*
    The Great Silkie of Sule Skerrie. Unknown. *MaB*
    The performing seal. From A circus garland. R. Field. *HuSv*
    "Samuel Silvernose Slipperyside." J. Ciardi. *CiR*
    Seal. W. J. Smith. *SmB*—*UnG*
    Seal lullaby. R. Kipling. *ArTp*—*BrR-5*— *FeF*—*JoAc*
    The seals. D. Aldis. *AlA*—*ArTp*
The seals. Dorothy Aldis. *AlA*—*ArTp*
"The seals all flap." See The seals
Seaman, Owen
    The uses of ocean. *CoH*
Seamen. See also Naval battles; Ocean; Ships
    The alarmed skipper. J. T. Fields. *UnG*
    Away, Rio. Unknown. *SmLg*
    Black-eyed Susan. J. Gay. *DeT*
    Cape Horn gospel (I). J. Masefield. *CoSp*
    Captain Reece. W. S. Gilbert. *CoH*—*NaE* —*UnMc*
    Christmas at sea. R. L. Stevenson. *CoSp*
    Clipper captain. S. Barker. *McW*
    Clipper ships and captains. R. C. and S. V. Benét. *HuSv*
    A dash to the pole. W. Irwin. *CoH*
    The fate of the Cabbage Rose. W. Irwin. *CoH*
    Forty singing seamen. A. Noyes. *CoSp*
    The frozen ships. E. Farjeon. *FaN*
    Hasting's mill. C. F. Smith. *McW*
    Homeward bound. W. Allingham. *BrL-7*
    Jack Tar. E. Jacot. *HuL-1*
    The last chantey. R. Kipling. *SmLg*
    Leave her, Johnny, leave her. Unknown. *HuL-2*
    Little Billee. W. M. Thackeray. *DeT*
    Lord Arnaldos. J. E. Flecker. *CoSp*
    Luck. W. W. Gibson. *NaM*
    A nautical ballad. From Davy and the goblin. C. E. Carryl. *FeF*—*HuSv*
        The walloping window-blind. *CoH*— *LoL*—*NaM*—*UnG*
    A nautical extravaganza. W. Irwin. *CoSp*
        A nautical extravagance. *HuSv*

Seamen—*Continued*
The old sailor. A. A. Milne. *MiWc*
On a Friday morn. Unknown. *DeT*
The post captain. C. E. Carryl. *CoH*
The powerful eyes o' Jeremy Tait. W. Irwin. *CoSp*
Psalm CVII. From Psalms, Bible, Old Testament
    Psalm 107. *McW*
    "They that go down to the sea." *FeF*
The recognition. F. W. Sawyer. *BrR-6*
The rime of the ancient mariner, sels. S. T. Coleridge. *HaP* (complete)—*PlU* (sel.)—*SmLg* (complete)
    The ancient mariner. *DeT*
    He prayeth best. *DoP—FeF—HuSv—ThP*
    He prayeth well. *HuL-2*
    The rime of the ancient mariner. *UnG*
Roadways. J. Masefield. *BrR-5*
Sailor. E. Farjeon. *PeF*
Sailor and tailor. Unknown. *DeT*
Sailor John. D. McCord. *McT*
"A sailor went to sea." Unknown. *WiRm*
The sailor's consolation. Attributed to C. Dibdin; also attributed to W. Pitt. *CoH—DeT—HuSv*
The sailor's wife. W. J. Mickle. *DeT*
Sea-fever. J. Masefield. *ArTp—BrL-8—FeF—HuL-2—HuSv—JoAc—PeF*
The sea gypsy. R. Hovey. *BrL-7—FeF—UnG*
Sea song. From Death's jest book. T. L. Beddoes. *UnG*
Seamen three. From Nightmare abbey. T. L. Peacock. *HoW*
Sensitive Sydney. W. Irwin. *CoH*
Seumas Beg. J. Stephens. *FeF—NaE*
Sheep. W. H. Davies. *CoSp*
Song of the wooden-legged fiddler. A. Noyes. *HuL-2*
Spanish ladies. Unknown. *SmLg*
The story of Samuel Jackson. C. G. Leland. *CoSp*
Tom Bowling. C. Dibdin. *DeT*
A wanderer's song. J. Masefield. *JoAc*
"A wet sheet and a flowing sea." A. Cunningham. *ArTp—BrL-8—McW*
    A sea song. *JoAc*
A windy day. W. Howard. *FeF*
The yarn of the Loch Achray. J. Masefield. *CoSp*
The yarn of the Nancy Bell. W. S. Gilbert. *CoH—HuSv—NaE—NaM—SmLg—UnG*

Seamen three. See Nightmare abbey
"**Seamen** three. What men ye be." See Nightmare abbey—Seamen three
The **search**. Thomas Curtis Clark. *DoP*
Sears, Edmund Hamilton
"It came upon the midnight clear." *FeF*

Seashore. See also Ocean
At low tide. D. McCord. *McFf*
At the sea-side. R. L. Stevenson. *ArTp—FeF—JoAc*
Beach. M. C. Livingston. *LiWa*
Beach fire. F. M. Frost. *ArTp—PeF*
The bight. E. Bishop. *HaP*
The black pebble. J. Reeves. *ReBl*
By the sea. M. Chute. *ChA—HuSv*
Down by the sea. D. McCord. *McT*

Down on my tummy. M. C. Livingston. *LiWa*
Down on the beach. D. Aldis. *AlA*
Flux. C. Sandburg. *SaW*
From the shore. C. Sandburg. *SaW*
The girl with the ball. E. Farjeon. *FaCb*
"I sat by the sea." I. O. Eastwick. *EaI*
"In the sand." M. C. Livingston. *LiW*
Kingdom cove. J. Reeves. *ReBl*
Late winter on our beach. B. Eaton. *McAw*
"Little Blue Apron." Unknown. *HuL-1*
Morning at the beach. J. Farrar. *HuL-1*
My horse, Jack. J. Ciardi. *CiY*
On the beach. D. Aldis. *AlHd*
Picnic by the sea. H. Behn. *BeW*
Poem. E. E. Cummings. *CoPs*
Sand-between-the-toes. A. A. Milne. *MiWc*
Sand dunes. R. Frost. *FrR*
The sea shore. H. Behn. *BeW*
Seaweed. M. C. Livingston. *LiWa*
Shore. M. B. Miller. *ArTp—McAw*
Skipping along alone. W. Welles. *ArTp—HuL-2*
Sky, sea, shore. J. Reeves. *ReR*
Stones by the sea. J. Reeves. *ReW*
Summer song. J. Ciardi. *CiM*
Trebetherick. J. Betjeman. *NaE*
"Upon the beach." I. Orleans. *ArTp*

Seaside. See Seashore
A **seaside** romance. Don Marquis. *CoH*
"**Season** of mists and mellow fruitfulness." See To autumn
Seasons. See also Autumn; Spring; Summer; Winter; also names of months, as January
Apple season. F. M. Frost. *BrS*
At Mrs Appleby's. E. U. McWebb. *ArTp—BrS—HuSv*
Autumn fires. R. L. Stevenson. *ArTp—HaY—JoAc*
Autumnal spring song. V. Miller. *HaP*
A boundless moment. R. Frost. *FrR*
The brown bear. M. Austin. *CoPs—FeF—McW*
Change of seasons. J. S. Smith. *McAw*
The children's song. Unknown. *FeF*
Come, little leaves. G. Cooper. *FeF*
Compass song. D. McCord. *McFf*
Cornfield ridge and stream. C. Sandburg. *SaW*
Derelict. Y. E. Allison. *PaOm*
The fairy and the bird. H. Behn. *BeW*
"Fall, leaves, fall; die, flowers, away." E. Brontë. *SmLg*
February bird. D. Morton. *ThP*
Footwear. M. Justus. *HaY*
Four seasons. R. B. Bennett. *BrS*
The frost pane. D. McCord. *HuSv—JoAc—McFf*
The goldenrod. F. D. Sherman. *FeF*
Hello day. D. Aldis. *AlHd*
The human seasons. J. Keats. *HoW*
"January brings the snow." S. Coleridge. *ArTp—DeMg*
    A calendar. *UnG*
    The garden year. *DeT—HuSv*
    The months of the year. *HuL-2*
Landscape. C. Baudelaire. *PaS*
The leaves. D. McCord. *McT*
March. A. Guiterman. *HaY*

Marjorie's almanac. T. B. Aldrich. *FeF*
Never two songs the same. C. Sandburg. *SaW*
New corn. T'ao Ch'ien. *PaS*
Ninth moon. Li Ho. *PaS*
O dear me. W. De La Mare. *ArTp*
Ode to the west wind. P. B. Shelley. *HaP*
Our tree. M. Chute. *ChA*
The oven bird. R. Frost. *FrY—FrR—PlU*
The poetry of earth. J. Keats. *HoW*
    On the grasshopper and cricket. *JoAc —UnG*
The procession. M. Widdemer. *HaY*
Rain. M. C. Livingston. *LiW*
Remembrance. E. Farjeon. *FaCb*
Robin. Unknown. *HuL-2*
Seasons. C. G. Rossetti. *HaY*
"Something told the wild geese." R. Field. *ArTp — BrS — CoPs — HaY — HuL-2 — HuSv — JoAc — McW*
Song. W. Morris. *ReT*
The song of the four winds. T. L. Peacock. *HoW*
Song of the seasons. B. De Good Lofton. *HaY*
"Spring is showery, flowery, bowery." Mother Goose. *ArTp*
The succession of the four sweet months. R. Herrick. *HaY*
    The four sweet months. *HoW*
    July: The succession of the four sweet months. *FeF*
Summer comes. E. Agnew. *BrS*
"Summer sunshine." M. A. Lathbury. *HaY*
Thoughts for a cold day. Unknown. *HuL-1*
Today. D. Aldis. *AlHd*
What the leaves said. Unknown. *HuL-1*
When. D. Aldis. *AlA—BrS*
"When as the rye reach to the chin." G. Peele. *SmLg*
"When the days begin to lengthen." Mother Goose
    Signs, seasons, and sense. *UnG*
Winter night. C. Hutchison. *ArTp*
The year. C. Patmore. *ReT*
    The year's round. *DeT*

Seasons. Christina Georgina Rossetti. *HaY*
"A seated statue of himself he seems." See Farm boy after summer
Seaweed. Myra Cohn Livingston. *LiWa*
"Seaweed from high tide." See Seaweed
The second epistle of Paul to Timothy, sel. Bible, New Testament
    "For God hath not given us the spirit of fear." *ArTp*
Secret ("I know why lilies ring their bells") Esther Hull Doolittle. *HaY*
The secret ("We have a secret, just we three") Unknown. *ArTp—BrL-k—HuL-1*
The secret ("Where did they come from, said Peter to Jane") Helen Cowles LeCron. *BrL-k*
The secret cavern. Margaret Widdemer. *FeF*
The secret heart. Robert P. Tristram Coffin. *CoPs*
The secret of the machines. Rudyard Kipling. *HuSv*

The secret of the sea. Henry Wadsworth Longfellow. *UnG*
The secret place. Dorothy Aldis. *AlA*
The secret sits. Robert Frost. *FrR*
Secret thoughts. See Translations from the Chinese
"A secret told." Emily Dickinson. *ThP*
Secrets
    "Can you keep a secret." Mother Goose. *LiL*
    Jeremy's secrets. B. E. Todd. *BrBc*
    Little brother's secret. K. Mansfield. *ArTp —FeF*
    Meadow secret. F. M. Frost. *FrLn*
    My secret. J. B. Tabb. *McW*
    An open secret. Unknown. *BrR-4*
    Robin-run-by-the-wall. E. Farjeon. *FaCb*
    Secret ("I know why lilies ring their bells") E. H. Doolittle. *HaY*
    The secret ("We have a secret, just we three") Unknown. *ArTp—BrL-k—HuL-1*
    The secret ("Where did they come from, said Peter to Jane") H. C. LeCron. *BrL-k*
    The secret cavern. M. Widdemer. *FeF*
    The secret place. D. Aldis. *AlA*
    The secret sits. R. Frost. *FrR*
    "A secret told." E. Dickinson. *ThP*
    Secrets ("Birds sang at twilight") M. McArthur. *DeT*
    Secrets ("If you see a package") E. M. Fowler. *BrBc*
Secrets ("Birds sang at twilight") Molly McArthur. *DeT*
Secrets ("If you see a package") Elsie Melchert Fowler. *BrBc*
"See a pin and pick it up." Mother Goose. *DeMg—JoAc—LiL*
    Signs, seasons, and sense. *UnG*
"See, from the brake the whirring pheasant springs." See The pheasant
"See how he dives." See Seal
"See how the orient dew." See A drop of dew
"See how the sky." See The moon
See, I can do it. Dorothy Aldis. *AlA*
"See, I can do it all myself." See See, I can do it
"See, I have picked you a flower, mother." See First thought
"See on the lawn how they're getting their luncheon." See Luncheons
See-saw. H. N. Bialik, tr. fr. the Hebrew by Jessie Sampter. *BrL-k*
"See-saw, down in my lap." Mother Goose. *OpO*
"See-saw, Margery Daw (Jacky shall have a new master)." Mother Goose. *DeMg— JoAc—LiL—OpO*
"See-saw, Margery Daw (sold her bed)." Mother Goose. *OpO*
"See-saw, Margery Daw (the old hen flew)." Mother Goose. *DeMg—OpO*
"See-saw, sacradown." Mother Goose. *DeMg —JoAc—OpO*
"See-saw, see-saw." See See-saw
"See, see, what shall I see." Mother Goose. *OpO*

"See the kitten on the wall." See The kitten at play

"See the pretty snowflakes." See Falling snow

"See the trees lean to the wind's way of learning." See Landscape

"See you the ferny ride that steals." See Puck's song

The seed shop. Muriel Stuart. *UnG*

Seeds
B is for beanseed. E. Farjeon. *FaCb—HuL-1*
Baby seed song. E. Nesbit. *FeF*
Baby seeds. Unknown. *BrR-3*
Lesson. H. Behn. *BeW*
The little plant. K. L. Brown. *BrL-k*
The magic seeds. J. Reeves. *ReBl*
Maytime magic. M. Watts. *McAw*
Moon vine. H. Behn. *BeW*
"One for the cut worm." Unknown. *WoF*
Putting in the seed. R. Frost. *FrR*
The seed shop. M. Stuart. *UnG*
Seeds ("A row of pearls") J. Reeves. *ReBl*
Seeds ("The seeds I sowed") W. De La Mare. *ArTp—HuSv*
Tillie. W. De La Mare. *ArTp—CoPm—HuL-2*

Seeds ("I sowed the seeds of love") See The seeds of love

Seeds ("A row of pearls") James Reeves. *ReBl*

Seeds ("The seeds I sowed") Walter De La Mare. *ArTp—HuSv*

"The seeds I sowed." See Seeds

The seeds of love. Unknown. *HoW—SmLg*
Seeds. *DeT*

"Seemingly more." See Whistling boy

Seesaw ("Seesaw; up and down") Marie Louise Allen. *AlP*

Seesaw ("Up and down") Evelyn Beyer. *BrL-k*

"Seesaw; up and down." See Seesaw

Seibert, T. Lawrence
Casey Jones. *UnMc*

Seiffert, Marjorie Allen (Marjorie Allen)
Ballad of the rag-bag heart. *ThP*

Self
"As I walked by myself." Mother Goose. *DeMg*
As I walked. *DeT*
The philosopher. *OpO*
"Everybody says." D. Aldis. *AlA—BrL-k—FeF—HuL-1*
I am ("I am willowy boughs") H. Conkling. *ArTp—FeF*
I am ("I am: yet what I am none cares or knows") J. Clare. *HaP*
Me. W. De La Mare. *BrBc—FeF*
My inside-self. R. Field. *FeF*
Myself. Unknown. *ThP*

Self-comforted. Sara M. B. Piatt. *DeT*

The self-unseeing. Thomas Hardy. *GrCc*

Selfishness
The ant and the cricket. Aesop. *DeT—UnG*
Greed. Mother Goose. *OpO*
The greedy fox and the elusive grapes. Aesop. *UnMc*
The fox and the grapes. *UnG*

Greedy Tom. Mother Goose. *OpO*
Griselda. E. Farjeon. *UnG*
A legend of the Northland. P. Cary. *UnG*
Let others share. E. Anthony. *UnG*
The pigs. J. Taylor. *DeT*
The vindictives. R. Frost. *FrR*

Sennacherib
The destruction of Sennacherib. G. G. Byron. *FeF—NaE—SmLg—UnG*

Senses. See also names of senses, as Sight
After Oliver ("But if I saw a mountain pass") Unknown. *CoH*
After Oliver ("Why, Ollie, that you failed in this") Unknown. *CoH*
"My sense of sight is very keen." O. Herford
After Oliver. *CoH*
Queer. D. McCord. *McT*
Things of summer. K. Jackson. *McAw*

Sensitive Sydney. Wallace Irwin. *CoH*

"The sentencing goes blithely on its way." See In a poem

September
"Remember September." M. Justus. *BrS—HaY*
September ("Apples heavy and red") M. W. Brown. *McAw*
September ("The goldenrod is yellow") H. H. Jackson. *FeF—UnG*
September days are here. *HaY*
September ("A road like brown ribbon") E. Fallis. *ArTp—BrR-4—HaY—HuL-2*
September ("There are twelve months throughout the year") M. Howitt. *HuL-2*
September is here. E. B. Reed. *HaY*
September's song. E. Farjeon. *FaCb—FaN*
A song for September. E. Farjeon. *FaCb*
Watching the moon. D. McCord. *HaY—McFf*

September ("Apples heavy and red") Margaret Wise Brown. *McAw*

September ("The goldenrod is yellow") Helen Hunt Jackson. *FeF—UnG*
September days are here. *HaY*

September ("A road like brown ribbon") Edwina Fallis. *ArTp—BrR-4—HaY—HuL-2*

September ("There are twelve months throughout the year") Mary Howitt. *HuL-2*

September days are here. See September ("The goldenrod is yellow")

"September evenings such as these." See Watching the moon

The September gale. Oliver Wendell Holmes. *CoH* (sel.)

September is here. Edward Bliss Reed. *HaY*

September's song. Eleanor Farjeon. *FaCb—FaN*

Serenade. Clemens Brentano, tr. fr. the German by Herman Salinger. *PaS*

"Serene the silver fishes glide." See At the aquarium

A serious step lightly taken. Robert Frost. *FrR*

The sermon on the mount. See Gospel according to Matthew

Slumber song. L. V. Ledoux. *FeF*
"Who's that bleating." E. Farjeon. *FaCb—FaN*
Sheep ("Thousands of sheep, soft-footed, black-nosed sheep") Carl Sandburg. *SaW*
Sheep ("When I was once in Baltimore") William Henry Davies. *CoSp*
Sheep and lambs. Katharine Tynan. *DoP*
"Sheep and shoat were walking through the pasture." Unknown. *WiRm*
The sheepfold. Eleanor Farjeon. *FaCb*
The sheepherder. Lew Sarett. *FeF*
"The sheets were frozen hard, and they cut the naked hand." See Christmas at sea
Sheldonian soliloquy. Siegfried Sassoon. *PlU*
The shell ("Am I thy ocean, pretty babe") Eleanor Farjeon. *FaCb*
The shell ("And then I pressed the shell") James Stephens. *NaM*
The shell ("I took away the ocean once") David McCord. *JoAc—McFf*

Shelley, Percy Bysshe
Adonais. *HaP* (sel.)
Arethusa. *HoW*
Away, away. See To Jane: The invitation
The cloud. *FeF—JoAc—PlI* (sel.)
A dirge. *HoW*
Hymn of Pan. *SmLg*
The landsman. tr. *PaS*
The moon. *SmLg*
Morning star. tr. *PaS*
"Music, when soft voices die." *HaP*
Ode to the west wind. *HaP*
Ozymandias. *BrL-7—HaP—McW—SmLg—UnG*
Plato's tomb. tr. *SmLg*
Prometheus unbound. *PlI* (sel.)
The question. *DeT*
The rooks. *DeT*
To a skylark. *FeF*
To Jane. *ReT*
To Jane: The invitation. *ReT*
    Away, away. *UnG*
To night. *HoW*
The two spirits. *HoW*
A widow bird. *DeT—FeF*
    A song. *ReT*

Shellfish. See names of shellfish, as Lobsters
Shells
"Cockleshells." I. O. Eastwick. *EaI*
Footnote to history. E. J. Coatsworth. *BrS*
Sea-shell ("It is so smooth") I. O. Eastwick. *EaI*
Sea shell ("Sea shell, sea shell") A. Lowell. *FeF—HuL-2—HuSv*
The shell ("Am I thy ocean, pretty babe") E. Farjeon. *FaCb*
The shell ("And then I pressed the shell") J. Stephens. *NaM*
The shell ("I took away the ocean once") D. McCord. *JoAc—McFf*
Shells. K. Raine. *PlI*

Shells. Kathleen Raine. *PlI*
Shēn Yo
Wild geese. *PaS*

The **shepherd.** William Blake. *ArTp—ReT—UnG*
"The **shepherd** and the king." Eleanor Farjeon. *ArTp*
The **shepherd** boy sings in the valley of humiliation. See The pilgrim's progress
"**Shepherd,** good shepherd, the wind's blowing cold." See The first lamb
Shepherdesses. See Shepherds and shepherdesses
Shepherds. Eleanor Farjeon. *FaCb*
"**Shepherds** all, and maidens fair." See The faithful shepherdess—Evening song
"The **shepherds** almost wonder where they dwell." See November
Shepherds and shepherdesses
Christmas eve. From Gospel according to Luke, Bible, New Testament. *BrBc—BrS*
    Tidings of great joy. *FeF*
The drummer-boy and the shepherdess. W. B. Rands. *NaM*
Evening song. From The faithful shepherdess. J. Fletcher. *DeT*
The first lamb. E. Farjeon. *FaCb—FaN*
Little Bo-peep and Little Boy Blue. A. A. Milne. *MiWc*
"Little Bo-peep has lost her sheep." Mother Goose. *ArTp—DeMg—HuSv—JoAc—LiL*
    Little Bo-peep. *BrL-k—OpO*
"Little Boy Blue, come blow your horn." Mother Goose. *ArTp—HuSv—LiL*
    Boy Blue. *OpO*
"Little Boy Blue." *BrL-k—DeMg—JoAc*
The little shepherd's song. W. A. Percy. *HaY*
The little young lambs. P. R. Chalmers. *HuL-2*
Nod. W. De La Mare. *JoAc—ReT—UnG*
A nursery song for Shepherdswell in Kent. E. Farjeon. *FaN*
The nymph's reply to the shepherd. W. Raleigh. *HaP*
The passionate shepherd to his love. C. Marlowe. *HaP—ReT*
Psalm XXIII. From Psalms, Bible, Old Testament
    "The Lord is my shepherd." *FeF—HuSv—JoAc*
    "The Lord is my shepherd, I shall not want." *ArTp*
"A red sky at night." Mother Goose. *LiL—OpO*
The sheepfold. E. Farjeon. *FaCb*
The sheepherder. L. Sarett. *FeF*
The shepherd. W. Blake. *ArTp—ReT—UnG*
Shepherds. E. Farjeon. *FaCb*
Shepherds' carol. M. Stanley-Wrench. *EaW*
The shepherd's hut. A. Young. *ReT*
"Shepherds, in the field abiding." G. R. Woodward. *EaW*
The shepherd's tale. E. Simpson. *EaW*
While shepherds watched. M. Deland. *DoP*
    While shepherds watched their flocks by night. *EaW*
Ya se van los pastores. D. Fitts. *GrCc*
The **shepherd's** calendar, sel. Edmund Spenser
A nosegay. *DeT*
Shepherds' carol. Margaret Stanley-Wrench. *EaW*
The **shepherd's** hut. Andrew Young. *ReT*

"Shepherds, in the field abiding." George Ratcliffe Woodward. *EaW*

Shepherd's purse. Eleanor Farjeon. *FaCb*

The shepherd's tale. Edith Simpson. *EaW*

Sherman, Frank Dempster
Daisies. *BrR-3—HuL-1*
A dewdrop. *BrL-k*
February. *HaY*
Flying kite. *BrR-4*
A kite. *ArTp* (sel.)
The goldenrod. *FeF*
January. *HaY*
A kite. See Flying kite
The snow-bird. *ArTp—BrS*
Spinning top. *BrL-k*
Vacation song. *BrR-6*
Wizard frost. *HaY—JoAc*

Sherwood, Kate Brownlee
Molly Pitcher. *UnG*

"Sherwood in the twilight, is Robin Hood awake." See A song of Sherwood

"She's funny, she's funny." See Un-birthday cake

Shiki
At Matsushima. *PaS*
The new and the old. *PaS*
Summer night. *PaS*

Shikō
Lilies. *ArTp*
Maple leaves. *PaS*

Shiloh. Herman Melville. *HoW*

"Shine on me, oh, you gold, gold sun." See Vacation song

Shiny. James Reeves. *ReW*

"Shiny are the chestnut leaves." See Shiny

The shiny little house. Nancy M. Hayes. *HuL-1*

The ship. J. C. Squire. *DeT*

A ship a-sailing. See "I saw a ship a-sailing"

The ship of Rio. Walter De La Mare. *ArTp—LoL*

The ship of state. See Sail on, O ship of state

Ships. See also Boats and boating; Ocean; Seamen; Shipwrecks; Warships
Cargoes. J. Masefield. *ArTp—FeF—HuL-2*
Clipper ships and captains. R. C. and S. V. Benét. *HuSv*
Derelict. Y. E. Allison. *PaOm*
Docks. C. Sandburg. *SaW*
Far beyond us. Unknown. *PaS*
The figure-head. C. Garstin. *CoSp*
The flying Dutchman. C. G. Leland. *CoPm*
The frozen ships. E. Farjeon. *FaN*
The Golden Vanity. Unknown. *HoW*
A good play. R. L. Stevenson. *ArTp—FeF—NaM*
"A horse would tire." E. J. Coatsworth. *ArTp*
"I met a man that was trying to whittle." J. Ciardi. *CiI*
"I saw a ship a-sailing." Mother Goose. *ArTp — BrR-3 — DeMg — HuSv — JoAc—LiL—NaM*
  I saw a ship. *DeT*
  A ship a-sailing. *OpO*

"I saw three ships come sailing by." Mother Goose. *DeMg—JoAc—LiL*
  1 saw three ships. *HuL-1—UnG*
  Three ships. *OpO*
"Little ships must keep the shore." Unknown. *DeMg*
"The moldering hulk." A. Machado. *PaS*
My ship. M. Chute. *ChA*
The old ships ("I have seen old ships sail like swans asleep") J. E. Flecker. *DeT—NaE*
Old ships ("There is a memory stays upon old ships") D. Morton. *HuSv*
On a steamer. D. W. Baruch. *FeF*
A passer-by. R. Bridges *HoW*
Red iron ore. Unknown. *ArTp*
She is far from the land. T. Hood. *HoW*
The ship. J. C. Squire. *DeT*
The ship of Rio. W. De La Mare. *ArTp—LoL*
The ships of Yule. B. Carman. *BrBc*
Song of the ship's cat. E. J. Coatsworth. *BrR-4*
When a ship sails by. R. B. Bennett. *BrR-6*
Where lies the land. A. H. Clough. *SmLg*
Whistles. R. Field. *ArTp—HuSv*
The white ships. D. McCord. *McFf*
"The wind has such a rainy sound." C. G. Rossetti. *ArTp—HuL-2*

The ships of Yule. Bliss Carman. *BrBc*

Shipwrecks
The Alice Jean. R. Graves. *GrP*
The caulker. M. A. Lewis *CoSp*
Etiquette. W. S. Gilbert. *CoH—UnMc*
The fate of the Cabbage Rose. W. Irwin. *CoH*
The Flying Dutchman. C. G. Leland. *CoPm*
The Inchcape rock. R. Southey. *UnG*
An old song re-sung. J. Masefield. *NaE*
On a Friday morn. Unknown. *DeT*
The phantom light of the Baie des Chaleurs. A. W. H. Eaton. *CoPm*
The silence of God. O. Sitwell. *McW*
Sir Patrick Spens. Unknown. *HaP—JoAc—MaB—SmLg*
  Sir Patrick Spence. *ArTp*
Skipper Ireson's ride. J. G. Whittier. *CoSp*
The story of Samuel Jackson. C. G. Leland. *CoSp*
The wreck of the Hesperus. H. W. Longfellow. *FeF*
The wreck of the Julie Plante. W. H. Drummond. *FeF*
The yarn of the Loch Achray. J. Masefield. *CoSp*
The yarn of the Nancy Bell. W. S. Gilbert. *CoH—HuSv—NaE—NaM—SmLg—UnG*

Shirley, James
Contention of Ajax and Ulysses, sel.
  Song. *GrCc*
Song. See Contention of Ajax and Ulysses

Shirts
The enchanted shirt. J. Hay. *HuL-2—UnG—UnMc*
Song of the all-wool shirt. E. Field. *CoSp*
The song of the shirt. T. Hood. *UnMc*
"Stocking and shirt." J. Reeves. *ReW*

"Shoe a little horse." Mother Goose. *DeMg—LiL—OpO*

"**Shoe** the colt, shoe the colt." Mother Goose. *OpO*

The **shoemaker**. Unknown. *FeF*

"A **shoemaker** makes shoes without leather." Mother Goose. *OpO*

Shoemakers. See also Boots and shoes
The cobbler ("Crooked heels") E. A. Chaffee. *ArTp*
The cobbler ("Wandering up and down one day") Unknown. *HuL-2*
"Cobbler, cobbler, mend my shoe." Mother Goose. *DeMg—LiL*
Cobbler, cobbler. *OpO*
"Faith, I wish I were a leprechaun." M. Ritter. *ArTp—FeF—HuL-2*
"Goodness. Gracious. Have you heard the news." Unknown. *WoF*
The leprahaun. R. D. Joyce. *CoPm*
"Mr Baker, Mr Baker, the good old shoemaker." Unknown. *WoF*
The shoemaker. Unknown. *FeF*

Shoes. See Boots and shoes

Shoes. Tom Robinson. *ArTp*

Shoes and stockings. A. A. Milne. *MiWc—HuL-1*

"**Shoon-a-shoon.**" See The Virgin's slumber song

Shoot that possum down. Unknown. *TaD*

The **shooting** of Dan McGrew. Robert W. Service. *UnMc*

Shop windows. Rose Fyleman. *ArTp*

Shopkeepers. See Shops and shopkeepers

Shopping. See Markets and marketing; Peddlers and venders; Shops and shopkeepers

Shopping spree. Harry Behn. *BeW*

Shops and shopkeepers. See also names of shops and shopkeepers, as Barbers and barbershops
The animal store. R. Field. *ArTp—CoI—HuL-1*
The cobbler. E. A. Chaffee. *ArTp*
Counters. E. J. Coatsworth. *PeF*
To think. *HuL-2*
The cuckoo-clock shop. R. Field. *HuL-2*
Eighth street west. R. Field. *BrS*
Emma's store. D. Aldis. *AlA*
A farthing and a penny. J. Reeves. *ReW*
Felicia Ropps. G. Burgess. *ArTp—FeF*
"The fly made a visit to the grocery store." Unknown. *WoF*
Fun in a garret. E. C. Dowd. *ArTp—BrR-3*
General store. R. Field. *HuSv—JoAc*
"Handy spandy, Jack-a-Dandy." Mother Goose. *DeMg*
"Hey diddle, dinketty, poppety, pet." Mother Goose. *DeMg—OpO*
"John says to John." Unknown. *WiRm*
Miss Wing. J. Reeves. *ReBl*
Mr Coggs, watchmaker. E. V. Lucas. *FeF*
Mr Cooter. E. Farjeon. *FaCb*
"My pop keeps a lollipop shop." Unknown. *WiRm*
Playing store. M. Chute. *ChA*
The seed shop. M. Stuart. *UnG*
Shop windows. R. Fyleman. *ArTp*
Shopping spree. H. Behn. *BeW*
Stupidity street. R. Hodgson. *BrS—DeT*

Sunday. E. J. Coatsworth. *McW*
To the shop. Unknown. *JoAc*
Tommy's shop. Mother Goose. *OpO*
Winter flower store. D. Aldis. *AlA*

Shore. See Seashore

Shore. Mary Britton Miller. *ArTp—McAw*

Short, John
Carol. *SmLg*

Shorter, Dora Sigerson (Dora Sigerson)
Ballad of the little black hound. *CoSp*
A new year. *HaY*

A **short** checklist of things to think about before being born. John Ciardi. *CiY*

Short sermon. Unknown, tr. fr. the German by Louis Untermeyer. *ArTp*

Short-song. Mother Goose. *OpO*

"A **short** word and a short word is long." See Long

Shoshone Indians. See Indians of America—Shoshone

The **shower** ("Between the green acacia tree") Beatrice Eve. *DeT*

A **shower** ("Shower came") Izembō, tr. fr. the Japanese by Olive Beaupré Miller. *ArTp*

"**Shower** came." See A shower

"The **shower** has stopped." See Rainbow

"The **shreek** is a shiverous beast." See Please, Johnny

Shrews
The masked shrew. I. Gardner. *PlI*

"The **shrilling** locust slowly sheathes." See The beetle

A **Shropshire** lad, sels. Alfred Edward Housman
"Into my heart an air that kills"
A Shropshire lad. *NaE*
"Is my team ploughing." *HaP*
The Lent lily. *CoPs*
Loveliest of trees. *HuSv—JoAc*
To an athlete dying young. *HaP—UnMc*
"When I was one-and-twenty." *BrBc*

Shrovetide. Mother Goose. *OpO*

Shūi Shū, sel. Unknown, tr. fr. the Japanese by Arthur Waley
Nakatsukasa. *PaS*

The **sick** child. Robert Louis Stevenson. *CoPs—DeT*

The **sick** rose. William Blake. *HaP*

Sickness. See also names of diseases, as Mumps
Advice to small children. E. Anthony. *UnG*
Blanket street. I. Hogan. *BrBc*
The dormouse and the doctor. A. A. Milne. *MiWc*
Hymne to God my God, in my sicknesse. J. Donne. *PlU* (sel.)
In plague time. T. Nashe. *SmLg*
"Adieu, farewell earth's bliss." *HaP*
"Jenny Wren fell sick." Mother Goose. *JoAc*
Jenny Wren. *NaE*
Little Jenny Wren. *HuL-1*
Ungrateful Jenny. *OpO*
The land of counterpane. R. L. Stevenson. *FeF—HuSv—JoAc—NaE*
Lines written after the discovery by the author of the germ of yellow fever. R. Ross. *PlI*

"If I had a firecracker." *CoPs*

"Oh did you hear." *CoPs*

On Halloween. *CoPs*

"Peace and joy." *CoPs*

"There you sit." *CoPs*

Valentine. *CoPs*

"Simeon lived." See Saint Simeon Stylites

"Simon Danz has come home again." See A Dutch picture

Simon Legree—A Negro sermon. Vachel Lindsay. *SmLg*

"Simon took his hook and pole." See Fishing Simon

"Simon Zelotes speaketh it somewhile after the Crucifixion." See Ballad of the goodly fere

Simonides

The climb to virtue. *PaS*

The Greek dead at Thermopylae. *PaS*

Not to die. *PaS*

"Simple her way of smiling was and coy." See The Canterbury tales—A prioress

The simple ploughboy. Unknown. *SmLg*

Simple Sam. Leroy F. Jackson. *CoPs*

Simple Simon. See "Simple Simon met a pieman"

Simple Simon and the pieman. See "Simple Simon met a pieman"

"Simple Simon met a pieman." Mother Goose. *DeMg—HuSv—JoAc—LiL*

Simple Simon. *ReG—UnG*

Simple Simon and the pieman. *OpO*

Simpson, Edith

The ox and the ass. *EaW*

The shepherd's tale. *EaW*

Simpson, Louis

A dream of governors. *HaP*

"Early in the morning." *HaP*

Simrock, Karl

German slumber song. *UnG*

Sin

"For every evil under the sun." W. Hazlitt. *DeMg—LiL—OpO*

Vice. From An essay on man. A. Pope. *ThP*

"Since Helen's beauty set great wars apace." See Scotland's Mary

"Since I am comming to that Holy roome." See Hymne to God my God, in my sicknesse

"Since rain is good for crops in May." See Rain

Since there's no help. Michael Drayton. *HaP*

"Since there's no help, come let us kiss and part." See Since there's no help

Sincerity. See Conduct of life

"Sing a song of joy." Thomas Campion. *PlU*

"Sing a song of laughter." See The giraffe and the woman

"Sing a song of monkeys." See The monkeys

"Sing a song of moonlight." Ivy O. Eastwick. *BrS*

"Sing a song of picnics." See Picnic day

"Sing a song of pop corn." See A pop corn song

"Sing a song of rockets." See Fourth of July song

"Sing a song of scissor-men." See The scissor-man

"Sing a song of sixpence." Mother Goose. *ArTp — BrL-k — DeMg — HuSv — JoAc — LiL — OpO*

"Sing a song of sunshine." Ivy O. Eastwick. *BrS*

"Sing a song of winter." See A sledding song

"Sing hey, for bold George Washington." See George Washington

"Sing hey. Sing hey." See An old Christmas greeting

Sing jigmijole. Mother Goose. *OpO*

"Sing jigmijole, the pudding bowl." See Sing jigmijole

"Sing me to sleep." See The snake and the snake-charmer

"Sing, sing." See "Sing, sing, what shall I sing"

"Sing, sing, what shall I sing." Mother Goose. *DeMg—LiL*

"Sing, sing." *OpO*

Sing-song. David McCord. *McT*

The sing-song of old man kangaroo. See Just-so stories

Sing-song rhyme. Unknown. *BrS—HuL-1*

"Sing to us, cedars; the twilight is creeping." See The birds' lullaby

"Sing we all merrily." See A catch by the hearth

"Sing we for love and idleness." See An immorality

"The singers have hushed their notes of clear song." See The harper of Chao

The singers in a cloud. Ridgely Torrence. *PlU*

Singing

"As I was going along, long, long." Mother Goose. *DeMg—OpO*

"As I went singing over the earth." M. Coleridge. *PlU*

Ballata. Unknown. *PlU*

Bee song. C. Sandburg. *SaW*

Birds in the forest. J. Reeves. *ReBl*

The blackbird. H. Wolfe. *ArTp—FeF—HuSv—JoAc*

Caroline, Caroline. J. Reeves. *ReW*

Come in. R. Frost. *FrR—FrY*

"The day before April." M. C. Davies. *ArTp—DoP—FeF*

The elf singing. W. Allingham. *HuSv—UnG*

Everyone sang. S. Sassoon. *CoPs—McW*

For M. S. singing Frühlingsglaube in 1945. F. Cornford. *PlU*

For the eightieth birthday of a great singer. E. Shanks. *PlU*

I hear America singing. W. Whitman. *ArTp — BrL-7 — BrR-5 — CoPs — FeF — HuSv — JoAc — SmLg — UnG*

"I heard a bird sing." O. Herford. *ArTp—BrS—EaW—HaY—HuL-2*

"I'll sing you a song (though not very long)." Mother Goose. *DeMg*

Joy of the morning. E. Markham. *FeF*

The lark's song. W. Blake. *HoW*

Laura. T. Campion. *PlU*

Six in June. Mary Carolyn Davies. *BrBc*
Six little mice. See "Six little mice sat down to spin"
"Six little mice sat down to spin." Mother Goose. *JoAc*
  Six little mice. *OpO*
"Six long slim slick sycamore saplings." Unknown. *WiRm*
"The six month child." See Slippery
Six o'clock bells. Unknown. *ReG*
"Six o'clock bells ringing." See Six o'clock bells
Six weeks old. Christopher Morley. *BrBc*
Sixteen months. Carl Sandburg. *SaW*
Size. See also People—Size
  Gnat. R. Moore. *UnG*
  Measurement. A. M. Sullivan. *McW*
  A ternarie of littles, upon a pipkin of jelly sent to a lady. R. Herrick. *SmLg*
  Way down South. Unknown. *NaE*
Sizes. John Ciardi. *CiM*
Skate and sled. Eleanor Farjeon. *FaCb—FaN*
A skater's valentine. Arthur Guiterman. *BrS*
Skating
  Roller skates. J. Farrar. *FeF*
  Skate and sled. E. Farjeon. *FaCb—FaN*
  A skater's valentine. A. Guiterman. *BrS*
  Skating ("And in the frosty season, when the sun") From The prelude. W. Wordsworth. *UnG*
    On the frozen lake. *SmLg*
  Skating ("When I try to skate") H. Asquith. *ArTp—FeF—HuL-2—HuSv*
  Wings and wheels. N. B. Turner. *ArTp—HuSv*
Skating ("And in the frosty season, when the sun") See The prelude
Skating ("When I try to skate") Herbert Asquith. *ArTp—FeF—HuL-2—HuSv*
"Skedaddle." See A hurry-up word
The skeleton in armor. Henry Wadsworth Longfellow. *UnG—UnMc*
Skeletons
  The skeleton in armor. H. W. Longfellow. *UnG—UnMc*
Skelton, John
  A curse on the cat. *NaE*
  "Merry Margaret." See To Mistress Margaret Hussey
  Mistress Margaret Hussey. See To Mistress Margaret Hussey
  The sparrow's dirge. *SmLg*
  To Mistress Margaret Hussey. *HaP—ReT*
    "Merry Margaret." *UnG*
    Mistress Margaret Hussey. *SmLg*
  Vengence on cats. *HaP*
Skidmore, Ruth Mather
  Fantasy. *CoPm*
Skiing
  January. M. Lewis. *UnG*
  Patience. H. Graham. *CoH—NaM*
  Skiing. M. Chute. *ChA*
Skiing. Marchette Chute. *ChA*
Skimbleshanks: The railway cat. T. S. Eliot. *SmLg*
"Skimming lightly, wheeling still." See Shiloh

"Skinny Mrs Snipkin." See Mrs Snipkin and Mrs Wobblechin
Skip-scoop-anellie. Tom Prideaux. *CoH*
Skipper Ireson's ride. John Greenleaf Whittier. *CoSp*
The skippery boo. Earl L. Newton. *UnG*
Skipping along alone. Winifred Welles. *ArTp—HuL-2*
Skipping ropes. Dorothy Aldis. *AlA—HuSv*
"Skitter, skatter." See Who is so pretty
The skunk. Robert P. Tristram Coffin. *ArTp—FeF*
Skunks
  The skunk. R. P. T. Coffin. *ArTp—FeF*
Sky
  Broken sky. C. Sandburg. *SaW*
  Compensation. F. Pray. *BrR-5*
  Coolness. Onitsura. *PaS*
  Earth and sky. E. Farjeon. *CoPs—EaW—HuL-2*
  "Mackerel sky." Mother Goose. *OpO*
  "A red sky at night." Mother Goose. *LiL—OpO*
  The river is a piece of sky. J. Ciardi. *ArTp—CiR*
  Sky laundry. M. L. Allen. *AlP*
  Sky prayers. From Good morning, America. C. Sandburg. *SaW*
  Sky, sea, shore. J. Reeves. *ReR*
  "The sky is up above the roof." Paul Verlaine, tr. fr. the French by Ernest Dowson. *FeF*
Sky-larks. See Larks
Sky laundry. Marie Louise Allen. *AlP*
"The sky of gray is eaten in six places." See Broken sky
Sky prayers. See Good morning, America
Sky, sea, shore. James Reeves. *ReR*
"Sky so bright." See A song in praise of the Lord
Sky talk, sel. Carl Sandburg
  Rolling clouds. *SaW*
"The sky was yellow." See Halloween
The skylark. Christina Georgina Rossetti. *UnG*
Skylark and nightingale. Christina Georgina Rossetti. *HuL-2*
  Heaven is heaven. *HaY*
Skylarks. See Larks
Skyscrapers
  Prayers of steel. C. Sandburg. *FeF*
  Skyscrapers. R. Field. *BrL-k—FeF—HuSv—JoAc*
Skyscrapers. Rachel Field. *BrL-k—FeF—HuSv—JoAc*
Slater, Eleanor
  Misdirection. *ThP*
Slavery
  Simon Legree—A Negro sermon. V. Lindsay. *SmLg*
  A stanza on freedom. J. R. Lowell. *McW—ThP*
A sledding song. Norman C. Schlichter. *FeF*
Sleds and sleighs
  Jingle bells. J. Pierpont. *OpO* (sel.)
  The little red sled. E. Farjeon. *FaCb—FaN*

Sleds and sleighs—*Continued*
Skate and sled. E. Farjeon. *FaCb—FaN*
A sledding song. N. C. Schlichter. *FeF*
Sleigh bells at night. E. J. Coatsworth. *BrS*
Sleep. See also Bed-time; Dreams; Lullabies; Sandman
Asleep and awake. D. McCord. *McFf*
Baby beds. Unknown. *HuL-1*
"Doll's boy's asleep." E. E. Cummings. *GrCc*
Drowsy. C. Sandburg. *SaW*
Going to sleep. D. Aldis. *AlA*
Hours of sleep. Unknown. *UnG*
"If once you have slept on an island." R. Field. *HuL-2*
The land of Nod. R. L. Stevenson. *UnG*
The Lord Chancellor's song. From Iolanthe. W. S. Gilbert. *CoH*
Midnight. T. Sackville. *DeT*
Natura in urbe. E. B. White. *McW*
Night enchantment. E. Muth. *BrS*
Nod. W. De La Mare. *JoAc—ReT—UnG*
S is for sandman E. Farjeon. *FaCb*
Sheep. C. Sandburg. *SaW*
The siesta. Unknown. *PaS*
Sleep impression. C. Sandburg. *SaW*
Sleep song. C. Sandburg. *SaW*
The sleepy man. J. Ciardi. *CiI*
Sleepyhead. W. De La Mare. *ArTp*
A spell for sleeping. A. Reid. *ReG*
Things. W. J. Smith. *SmL*
To sleep. J. Kochanowski. *PaS*
"To sleep easy all night." Mother Goose. *OpO*
Voices. H. Behn. *BeW*
What I would do. D. Aldis. *AlA*
Wind song. C. Sandburg. *NaM—SaW*
Sleep, baby boy. Unknown, tr. fr. the Italian. *FeF*
"Sleep, baby, sleep (thy father guards)." Mother Goose. *LiL*
Holy lullaby. *UnG*
"Sleep, baby, sleep (thy father watches the sheep)." Unknown, tr. fr. the German. *BrL-k—BrR-3—FeF—JoAc*
"Sleep, comrades, sleep and rest." See Decoration day
Sleep impression. Carl Sandburg. *SaW*
"Sleep is the gift of many spiders." See Drowsy
"Sleep, mouseling, sleep." See Lullaby
"Sleep, my babe, lie still and slumber." See Welsh lullaby
"Sleep, my little one, sleep." See Lullaby
"Sleep, sleep, beauty bright." See Cradle song
Sleep song. Carl Sandburg. *SaW*
"A sleeper from the Amazon." Unknown. *LoL*
"Sleepy Betsy from her pillow." See The bedpost
The sleepy man. John Ciardi. *CiI*
The sleepy song ("As soon as the fire burns red and low") Josephine Dodge Daskam Bacon. *HuSv*
Sleepy song ("Ere the moon begins to rise") Thomas Bailey Aldrich. *UnG*
Sleepy song ("Mother sings a sleepy-song") Marian Kennedy. *McAw*
Sleepyhead. Walter De La Mare. *ArTp*

Sleet storm. James S. Tippett. *BrS—PeF*
Sleigh bells at night. Elizabeth Jane Coatsworth. *BrS*
Sleighs. See Sleds and sleighs
"A slender young blackbird built in a thorn-tree." See The blackbird
Sliding ("Down the slide") Marchette Chute. *ChA—McAw*
Sliding ("We can slide") Myra Cohn Livingston. *BrS—LiW*
Slippery. Carl Sandburg. *ArTp—BrBc—FeF*
The **sloth.** Theodore Roethke. *McW*
Sloths
The sloth. T. Roethke. *McW*
Slow pokes. Laura Arlon. *McAw*
Slowly. James Reeves. *ReW*
"Slowly England's sun was setting o'er the hilltops far away." See Curfew must not ring tonight
"Slowly, silently, now the moon." See Silver
"Slowly the flakes come down through the ash-gray skies and the shouting." See First snowfall
"Slowly the tide creeps up the sand." See Slowly
"Slowly ticks the big clock." See The big clock
The **sluggard.** Isaac Watts. *NaM*
"A slumber did my spirit seal." William Wordsworth. *SmLg*
"Slung between the homely poplars at the end." See Ursa Major
"A small bird singing." See February bird
"The small child-angels." See By the crib
"Small gnats that fly." See One hard look
"Small shining drop, no lady's ring." See For a dewdrop
"Small skill is gained by those who cling to ease." Unknown
Signs, seasons, and sense. *UnG*
Small talk. Don Marquis. *CoSp*
"The smallest bird in the wide world." See The hummingbird
Smart, Christopher
"Glorious the sun in mid-career." *SmLg*
A hymn for Saturday. *ReG*
A lark's nest. *SmLg*
The instruments. *HoW*
Jubilate agno. *PlU* (sel.)
A lark's nest. See A hymn for Saturday
My cat Jeoffry. *HaP—HoW—UnG*
A song to David. *PlU* (sel.)
"Smart Mr Doppler." David McCord. *McFf*
Smells. Christopher Morley. *BrR-5*
Smells, Junior. Christopher Morley. *ArTp—BrL-k*
"Smiling girls, rosy boys." Mother Goose. *DeMg*
The gingerbread man. *OpO*
Smith, Bradford
"Winter is icumen in." *CoPs*
Smith, Charlotte T.
Lady-bird. at. *HuL-2—UnG*
Smith, Cicely Fox. See Fox-Smith, Cicely
Smith, Dulcie L.
Thy garden. tr. *PaS*

Smith, Goldwin
I'll twine white violets. *PaS*

Smith, James Steel
Change of seasons. *McAw*

Smith, Mary Louise Riley. See Smith, May Riley

Smith, May Riley (Mary Louise Riley Smith)
"O bells in the steeple." *DoP*

Smith, Samuel Francis
America. *FeF*

Smith, William Hawley
Prayer for a child. *DoP*

Smith, William Jay
Alice. *SmL*
Anteater. *SmB*
Antelope. *SmB*
Apples. *SmL*
Around my room. *SmL*
Betsy Robin. *SmL*
Big and little. *SmL*
Butterfly. *ArTp—CoI—SmB*
Camel. *SmB*
Cat. *SmB*
Coati-mundi. *SmB*
Cow. *SmB*
Crocodile. *SmB*
Dictionary. *SmL*
Dog. *SmB*
Dragon. *SmB*
Elephant. *SmB*
Fish. *SmB*
The floor and the ceiling. *CoH*
Fox and crow. *SmB*
Giraffe. *SmB*
Goony bird. *SmB*
Grandmother ostrich. *SmL*
Gull. *ArTp—SmB*
Hats. *SmL*
Having. *SmL*
Hen. *SmB*
Hippopotamus. *SmB*
Jack-in-the-box. *SmL*
Jittery Jim. *SmL*
Kangaroo. *SmB*
The King of Hearts. *SmL*
The king of Spain. *SmL*
The land of Ho-Ho-Hum. *SmL*
Laughing time. *FeF—SmL*
Lion. *SmB*
Love. *SmL*
The mirror. *SmL*
Mrs Caribou. *CoPm—SmL*
Mistress Mary. *SmL*
Mole. *SmB*
Molly Mock-Turtle. *SmL*
Monkey. *SmB*
Moon. *SmL*
My body. *SmL*
Opossum. *SmB—UnG*
Over and under. *SmL*
The owl. *CoI—SmL*
The panda. *SmL*
Parrot ("I bought me a parrot in Trinidad") *SmB*
Parrot ("A parrot I bought in Zambezi") *SmB*
A pavane for the nursery. *CoPs*
Penguin. *SmB*
People. *SmL*

Pick me up. *SmL*
Pig. *SmB*
Polar bear. *SmB*
The queen of the Nile. *SmL*
Raccoon. *ArTp—SmB*
Rhinoceros. *SmB*
Seal. *SmB—UnG*
Spilt milk: Whodunit. *SmL*
Swan. *SmB*
Tapir. *SmB*
Things. *SmL*
Tiger. *SmB*
Toaster. *ArTp—CoH—SmL*
Unicorn. *SmB*
Up the hill. *SmL*
Water buffalo. *SmB*
Whale. *SmB*
When candy was chocolate. *SmL*
Why. *SmL*
Woodpecker. *SmB*
Yak. *SmB—UnG*
Zebra. *SmB*

Smoke
Blue smoke. F. M. Frost. *BrS*
Smoke animals. R. B. Bennett. *HuL-2*
Smoke stack. A. M. Sullivan. *McW*
Smoke animals. Rowena Bastin Bennett. *HuL-2*
Smoke stack. A. M. Sullivan. *McW*
"Smooth and flat, grey, brown and white." See Stones by the sea
The **snail** ("At sunset, when the night-dews fall") James Reeves. *ReW*
The **snail** ("The frugal snail, with forecast of repose") Charles Lamb. *NaM—UnG*
Snail ("Little snail") Langston Hughes. *ArTp—FeF*
The **snail** ("The snail, who wears a spiral dome") Frances M. Frost. *FrLn*
Snail ("This sticky trail") David McCord. *McFf*
The **snail** ("To grass, or leaf, or fruit, or wall") Vincent Bourne, tr. fr. the Latin by William Cowper. *McW—UnG*
Snail hunters. See "Four and twenty tailors"
"Snail, snail." Mother Goose. *DeMg—JoAc*
To the snail. *OpO*
"Snail, snail, put out your horns." See "Snail, snail"
"The snail, who wears a spiral dome." See The snail

Snails
"Four and twenty tailors." Mother Goose. *DeMg—JoAc*
"Four and twenty tailors went to kill a snail." *LiL*
Snail hunters. *OpO*
"Johnnie Crack and Flossie Snail." From Under milk wood. D. Thomas. *FeF*
From Under milk wood. *CoH*
Little snail. H. Conkling. *ArTp—FeF—JoAc*
The lobster quadrille. From Alice's adventures in wonderland. L. Carroll. *FeF—HuL-2—HuSv—NaM—PeF*
The snail ("At sunset, when the night-dews fall") J. Reeves. *ReW*
The snail ("The frugal snail, with forecast of repose") C. Lamb. *NaM—UnG*

Snow everywhere. I. O. Eastwick. *EaI*

Snow fairies. I. P. Richardson. *BrL-k*

Snow-flakes. H. W. Longfellow. *HoW*

Snow in spring. I. O. Eastwick. *EaI*

Snow in the city. R. Field. *ArTp*

Snow in the suburbs. T. Hardy. *ReT*

Snow palace. J. Reeves. *ReW*

Snow picture. I. O. Eastwick. *EaI*

Snow toward evening. M. Cane. *ArTp*

The snowflake. W. De La Mare. *JoAc*

Snowflake world. I. O. Eastwick. *EaI*

Snowflakes ("I once thought that snowflakes were feathers") M. Chute. *ChA*

Snowflakes ("Little white feathers") M. M. Dodge. *BrL-k—HuL-1*

Snowflakes ("Snowflakes falling through the air") E. L. Cleveland. *BrL-k*

Snowflakes ("Whirling, swirling, rushing, twirling") M. Kennedy. *McAw*

Snowman ("My little snowman has a mouth") D. McCord. *McT*

The snowman ("We made a snowman in our yard") F. M. Frost. *BrL-k*

The snowman's resolution. A. Fisher. *PeF*

Snowstorm ("Oh did you see the snow come") R. W. Bacmeister. *BrL-k*

Snowstorm ("What a night. The wind howls, hisses, and but stops") J. Clare. *HoW*

A snowy day. Dafydd Ap Gwilym. *PaS*

Snowy morning. B. Young. *McAw*

Stopping by woods on a snowy evening. R. Frost. *ArTp—BrL-8—BrS—CoPs—FeF—FrR—FrY—HaP—HuL-2—HuSv—JoAc—McW—NaM—PeF—ReT—SmLg*

A story in the snow. P. R. Crouch. *ArTp—BrR-3*

Thaw. E. Tietjens. *McAw*

"Thin ice." From Five chants. D. McCord. *McFf*

To a snow-flake. F. Thompson. *PlI—ReT*

To a snowflake. *UnG*

To the snow. Mother Goose. *OpO*

Tracks in the snow. M. Chute. *BrS—ChA*

Velvet shoes. E. Wylie. *ArTp—BrS—FeF—HuSv—JoAc—PeF*

"White bird featherless." Mother Goose. *OpO*

    Snow and sun. *ReG*

White fields. J. Stephens. *BrR-4—BrS—CoPs—FeF—HuL-2—McAw—NaM*

Why does it snow. L. E. Richards. *BrS*

Winter. Jōsō. *PaS*

Winter in the wood. I. O. Eastwick. *HaY*

Snow ("Fence posts wear marshmallow hats") See On a snowy day

The snow ("It sifts from leaden sieves") Emily Dickinson. *UnG*

Snow ("A snow can come as quietly") Elizabeth Jane Coatsworth. *BrR-6—BrS* January. *CoPs*

Snow ("The snow fell softly all the night") Alice Wilkins. *ArTp—BrL-k—McAw*

The snow ("The sun that brief December day") See Snow-bound

Snow ("The three stood listening to a fresh access") Robert Frost. *FrR*

Snow and sun. See "White bird featherless"

The snow-bird. Frank Dempster Sherman. *ArTp—BrS*

Snow-birds. See Snowbirds

Snow-bound, sels. John Greenleaf Whittier

    The schoolmaster. *UnG*

    The snow. *HuSv*

        Snow-bound. *HoW*

    The uncle. *UnG*

    "Unwarmed by any sunset light" Lines from Snow-bound. *JoAc*

"A snow can come as quietly." See Snow

"Snow-dust driven over the snow." See Winter noon

Snow everywhere. Ivy O. Eastwick. *EaI*

Snow fairies. Isla Paschal Richardson. *BrL-k*

"Snow falls." See Winter in the wood

"The snow fell on the mountain." See Snow everywhere

"The snow fell softly all the night." See Snow

Snow-flakes. Henry Wadsworth Longfellow. *HoW*

"The snow had begun in the gloaming." See The first snowfall

Snow in spring. Ivy O. Eastwick. *EaI*

Snow in the city. Rachel Field. *ArTp*

Snow in the suburbs. Thomas Hardy. *ReT*

"Snow is out of fashion." See Snow in the city

"The snow is soft, and how it squashes." See Thaw

"Snow makes whiteness where it falls." See First snow

"The snow of February had buried Christmas." See The Christmas robin

Snow palace. James Reeves. *ReW*

Snow picture. Ivy O. Eastwick. *EaI*

"Snow, snow faster." See To the snow

The snow storm. See "Announced by all the trumpets of the sky"

"Snow time, sad time." See Christmastide

Snow toward evening. Melville Cane. *ArTp*

"Snow wind-whipt to ice." See Winter

Snowbirds

    The snow-bird. F. D. Sherman. *ArTp—BrS*

The snowdrop, sel. Mary Webb

    The first bee. *DeT*

Snowdrops (Flowers)

    Fair maid of February. E. Farjeon. *FaCb—FaN*

    Snowdrops. M. Vivian. *HuL-1*

Snowdrops. Mary Vivian. *HuL-1*

The snowflake. Walter De La Mare. *JoAc*

Snowflake world. Ivy O. Eastwick. *EaI*

"Snowflakes." See Snowflake world

Snowflakes ("I once thought that snowflakes were feathers") Marchette Chute. *ChA*

Snowflakes ("Little white feathers") Mary Mapes Dodge. *BrL-k—HuL-1*

Snowflakes ("Snowflakes falling through the air") Elizabeth L. Cleveland. *BrL-k*

Snowflakes ("Whirling, swirling, rushing, twirling") Marian Kennedy. *McAw*

"Snowflakes falling through the air." See Snowflakes

Snowman ("My little snowman has a mouth") David McCord. *McT*

The **snowman** ("We made a snowman in our yard") Frances M. Frost. *BrL-k*

"The **snowman's** hat was crooked." See The snowman's resolution

The **snowman's** resolution. Aileen Fisher. *PeF*

The **snows** of yester-year. François Villon, tr. fr. the French by Dante Gabriel Rossetti. *HoW*

Snowstorm ("Oh did you see the snow come") Rhoda W. Bacmeister. *BrL-k*

Snowstorm ("What a night. The wind howls, hisses, and but stops") John Clare. *HoW*

A **snowy** day. Dafydd Ap Gwilym, tr. fr. the Welsh by H. Idris Bell. *PaS*

"A **snowy** field. A stable piled." See Christmas at Freelands

Snowy morning. Barbara Young. *McAw*

"**Snub** nose, the guts of twenty mules are in your cylinders and transmission." See New farm tractor

Snuff
  "I had a little dog and they called him Buff." Mother Goose. *DeMg*
  Buff. *OpO*

The **snuff-boxes**. Unknown. *CoSp*

The **snyke**. James Reeves. *ReP*

"**So**, April, here thou art again." See Lady April

"**So** cold the first Thanksgiving came." See The first Thanksgiving

"**So** far as I can see." See Meditations of a tortoise dozing under a rosetree near a beehive at noon while a dog scampers about and a cuckoo calls from a distant wood

"**So** few sandpipers." See Beach

"**So** ghostly then the girl came in." Robert Hillyer. *GrCc*

"**So** here hath been dawning." See Today

"**So** here we are in April, in showy, blowy April." See April

So late into the night. See "So, we'll go no more a-roving"

"**So** lovely is the Lorelei." See L is for Lorelei

"**So** lucky I was in being born." See Yankee cradle

"**So** many little flowers." See Cycle

So many monkeys. Marion Edey. *ArTp*

"**So** many strange and magical sights there were to see." See The house beyond the meadow

"**So** much depends." See Spring and all

"**So** much that I would give you hovers out." See For a birthday

"**So**, now is come our joyful feast." See Our joyful feast

"**So** questioning, I was bold to dare." See The shape God wears

So run along and play. David McCord. *McT*

"**So** she went into the garden." See The great panjandrum himself

"**So** soft came the breath." See May day

"**So** still the pond in morning's gray." See The pond

"**So** sweet, so sweet the roses in their blowing." See In June

"**So** sweet the plum trees smell." See Plum trees

"**So** the foemen have fired the gate, men of mine." See The knight's leap

"**So** they camped upon the common in the gloaming of the day." See Mumfludgeons

So to speak. Carl Sandburg. *SaW*

"**So**, we'll go no more a-roving." George Gordon Byron. *HaP*

So late into the night. *HoW*

We'll go no more a-roving. *GrCc*

Soap
  Naughty soap song. D. Aldis. *AlA—BrL-k*

Soap bubbles
  Soap bubbles ("Dip the pipe in the suds just so") M. L. Allen. *AlP*
  Soap bubbles ("Fill the pipe") Unknown. *BrL-k*

Soap bubbles ("Dip the pipe in the suds just so") Marie Louise Allen. *AlP*

Soap bubbles ("Fill the pipe") Unknown. *BrL-k*

Soap, the oppressor. Burges Johnson. *BrR-4*

The **society** upon the Stanislow. Bret Harte. *UnMc*

"A **soft** answer turneth away wrath." See Proverbs, Bible, Old Testament

Soft steps. Georgette Agnew. *HuL-1*

"**Soft**, what light through yonder window breaks." See Romeo and Juliet

"**Softly** along the road of evening." See Nod

"**Softly**, drowsily." See A child's day

"**Softly** glows the sun." See April

"**Softly**, let the measure break." See Harp music

"**Softly** sighs the April air." See Bel m'es quan lo vens m'alena

"**Softly** the day dies out behind the pines." See Evening landscape

The **soldier**. Rupert Brooke. *UnMc*

"**Soldier** brave, sailor true." Mother Goose. *OpO*

Soldier, rest. See The lady of the lake

"**Soldier**, rest, thy warfare o'er." See The lady of the lake—Soldier, rest

Soldiers. See also Memorial day; Veterans day; War; also names of wars, as European war, 1914-1918; also names of battles, as Bannockburn, Battle of, 1314
  Abdullah Bulbul Amir. Unknown. *CoSp*
  At home. A. A. Milne. *MiWc*
  Ballad. W. H. Auden. *UnMc*
  Belisarius. H. W. Longfellow. *HoW*
  Buckingham palace. A. A. Milne. *HuL-2—MiWc*
  Bugs. W. Stokes. *NaM*
  Danny Deever. R. Kipling. *UnMc*
  The drum. E. Field. *BrR-6*
  The duke. Unknown. *DeT*
  The duke of Plaza-Toro. From The gondoliers. W. S. Gilbert. *CoH—FeF*
  The dumb soldier. R. L. Stevenson. *UnG*
  Epitaph for Chaeroneia. Aristotle. *PaS*
  Faithless Nelly Gray. T. Hood. *CoH*
  Fife tune. J. Manifold. *SmLg*

Fighting south of the ramparts. Unknown. *PaS*

General John. W. S. Gilbert. *CoH—UnG*

A grenadier. Mother Goose. *OpO*

"His golden locks time hath to silver turned." From Polyhymnia. G. Peele. *HaP*

How happy the soldier. Unknown. *SmLg*

More than flowers we have brought. N. B. Turner. *BrS*

"O tan-faced prairie boy." W. Whitman. *FeF*

"Oh, the grand old duke of York." Mother Goose. *DeMg—LiL*
   The brave old duke of York. *OpO*
   Duke o' York. *HuL-1*
   "The grand old duke of York." *ArTp*
   "Oh, the brave old duke of York." *JoAc*

An old song. Yehoash. *PaS*

Parliament soldiers. Mother Goose. *OpO*

The rebel soldier. Unknown. *SmLg*

The returned volunteer to his rifle. H. Melville. *GrCc*

Seven poems. M. Bashō. *PaS* (sel.)

"A sight in camp in the daybreak gray and dim." W. Whitman. *HaP*

The soldier. R. Brooke. *UnMc*

Soldier, rest. From The lady of the lake. W. Scott. *McW—NaM*
   "Soldier, rest, thy warfare o'er." *DeT*

Soldier's song. T. Hume. *HoW*

The spires of Oxford. W. M. Letts. *BrL-7*

"There was an old soldier and he had a wooden leg." Unknown. *WoF*

These fought. E. Pound. *HaP*

The triumph. E. Farjeon. *FaN*

"We be soldiers three." Unknown. *GrCc*

We be the king's men. From The dynasts. T. Hardy. *HuL-2*
   Men who march away. *DeT*

When Johnny comes marching home. P. S. Gilmore. *CoPs*

"Soldiers, as we come to lay." See More than flowers we have brought

Soldier's song. Tobias Hume. *HoW*

Soliloquy of a tortoise on revisiting the lettuce beds after an interval of one hour while supposed to be sleeping in a clump of blue hollyhocks. E. V. Rieu. *RiF*

"A solitary egret, left behind." See The white egret

Solitary pine. Prince Ichihara, tr. fr. the Japanese by Ishii and Obata. *PaS*

The solitary reaper. William Wordsworth. *HaP—PlU—ReT*

Solitude. See also Loneliness; Silence

"Alone." M. C. Livingston. *LiW*

Alone ("All through the woods it's as dark as dark") M. Chute. *ChA*

Alone ("From childhood's hour I have not been") E. A. Poe. *HaP*

Alone ("I never had walked quite so far") J. Paget-Fredericks. *BrR-3—HuSv*

Alone ("I was alone the other day") D. Aldis. *AlA*

Alone ("White daisies are down in the meadow") J. Farrar. *HaY*

Bereft. R. Frost. *FrR*

Immense hour. J. R. Jiménez. *PaS*

In neglect. R. Frost. *F, R*

In the dark. A. A. Milne. *MiWc*

The lake isle of Innisfree. W. B. Yeats. *FeF—JoAc*

The listeners. W. De La Mare. *FeF—ReT —UnMc*

Lucy Gray; or, Solitude. W. Wordsworth. *DeT*

Mr Flood's party. E. A. Robinson. *HaP— NaE*

The old familiar faces. C. Lamb. *HaP*

Skipping along alone. W. Welles. *ArTp— HuL-2*

The solitary reaper. W. Wordsworth. *HaP —PlU—ReT*

Solitude. A. A. Milne. *MiWc*

Solitude. A. A. Milne. *MiWc*

Solomon, King of Israel (about)
   "King David and King Solomon." Unknown Rhymed chuckles. *UnG*
   Solomon and the bees. J. G. Saxe. *UnG*

Sorrow. See Grief

Solomon and the bees. John Godfrey Saxe. *UnG*

"Solomon Grundy." Mother Goose. *DeMg —HuL-1—JoAc—LiL—OpO*
   Birthday rhyme. *BrBc*

Solovyov, Vladimir
   With wavering feet I walked. *PaS*

"Some bears are fierce, and most grow fiercer." See A warning about bears

"Some bears are fierce, and some are fiercer." See More about bears

"Some blank verse from a blank mind." Unknown. *MoY*

Some cook. John Ciardi. *CiM*

"Some day I'm going to have a store." See General store

"Some days are fairy days. The minute that you wake." See Sometimes

"Some days I go with Daddy for a walk." See Six and thirty

"Some days my thoughts are just cocoons— all dull and blind." See Days

Some fishy nonsense. Laura E. Richards. *ArTp*

"Some hae meat and canna eat." See A child's grace

"Some hae meat that canna eat." See A child's grace

"Some like movies." See Matters of taste

Some little mice. See "Some little mice sat in a barn to spin"

"Some little mice sat in a barn to spin." Mother Goose. *DeMg*
   Some little mice. *BrL-k*

"Some love ten." Unknown. *MoY*

"Some of the cats I know about." See My cat, Mrs Lick-a-chin

Some one. Walter De La Mare. *ArTp— BrL-k—HuL-2—HuSv—JoAc—NaM*
   Someone. *FeF*

"Some one is always sitting there." See The little green orchard

Some people. Rachel Field. *FeF*

"Some people say that apples are red." See Apples

Some questions to be asked of a rajah, perhaps by the Associated Press. Preston Newman. *CoH*

"Some say, compar'd to Bononcini." See Epigram on Handel and Bononcini

"Some say, that ever 'gainst that season comes." See Hamlet

"Some say the deil's deid." Unknown. *SmLg*

"Some say the world will end in fire." See Fire and ice

"Some shoes are black." Unknown. *MoY*

"Some things I can reach without standing on tiptoe." See Taller and older

"Some things persist by suffering change, others." See Homage to the philosopher

Some vegetables and flowers. Dorothy Aldis. *AlHd*

"Some years ago you heard me sing." See Sarah Byng

"Some years of late, in eighty-eight." Unknown. *SmLg*

Somebody and naebody. Eleanor Farjeon. *FaN*

"Somebody said that it couldn't be done." See It couldn't be done

"Somebody up in the rocky pasture." See The ant village

Somebody's birthday. Abbie Farwell Brown. *BrBc*

"Somebody's birthday every day." See Somebody's birthday

"Someday." See Skipping ropes

Someone ("Someone came knocking") See Some one

Someone ("There was a boy just one year old") John Ciardi. *BrBc—CiR*

"Someone came knocking." See Some one

"Someone painted pictures on my." See Jack Frost

Someone's face. John Ciardi. *CiM*

"Someone's face was all frowned shut." See Someone's face

Somersault. Dorothy Aldis. *AlA*

"Something around which it may twine." See God careth

Something better. David McCord. *McFf*

"Something inspires the only cow of late." See The cow in apple time

"Something lives on yonder hill." Unknown. *WiRm*

"Something there is that doesn't love a wall." See Mending wall

"Something told the wild geese." Rachel Field. *ArTp—BrS—CoPs—HaY—HuL-2 —HuSv—JoAc—McW*

Something very elegant. Aileen Fisher. *BrBc*

"Sometimes." See Automobile mechanics

Sometimes. Rose Fyleman. *BrS*

Sometimes I feel this way. John Ciardi. *CiY*

"Sometimes I have to cross the road." See Bobby Blue

"Sometimes I sit and think and think." See Thinking

"Sometimes I'm naughty." Unknown. *MoY*

"Sometimes in the summer." See Sprinkling

"Sometimes when I am at tea with you." See Things

Somewhere. Walter De La Mare. *FeF*

"Somewhere inside of me." See Altar smoke

"Son." See Father and I in the woods

The son. Ridgely Torrence. *McW*

"A son just born." Mary Britton Miller. *ArTp*

"Son, said my mother." See The ballad of the harp-weaver

Song ("And can the physician make sick men well") Unknown. *ReT*

Song ("April, April") William Watson. *CoPs—JoAc*

April. *UnG*

Song ("Christ keep the hollow land") William Morris. *ReT*

Song ("Do not fear to put thy feet") See The river god's song

Song ("The feathers of the willow") Richard Watson Dixon. *HaY—ReT—SmLg*

Song ("The glories of our blood and state") See Contention of Ajax and Ulysses

Song ("Go and catch a falling star") John Donne. *HaP*

Song ("Good morrow, 'tis St Valentine's day") See Hamlet

Song ("Grace and beauty has the maid") Gil Vicente, tr. fr. the Portuguese by Alice Jane McVan. *PaS*

Song ("I had a dove and the sweet dove died") John Keats. *FeF—ReT*

I had a dove. *CoI—DeT*

Song ("I have twelve oxen that be fair and brown") Unknown. *ReT*

Song ("I wandered by the brook-side") Richard Monckton Milnes, Lord Houghton. *DeT*

Song ("If thou art sleeping, maiden") Gil Vicente, tr. fr. the Spanish by Henry Wadsworth Longfellow. *PaS*

A song ("I'll sing you a song—nine verses long") Mother Goose. *OpO*

A song ("I'll sing you a song—the days are long") Mother Goose. *OpO*

Song ("The maidens came") Unknown. *ReT*

Song ("Neither in halls, nor yet in bowers") Unknown. *EaW*

Song ("O mistress mine, where are you roaming") See Twelfth night

Song ("O'er the smooth enamel'd green") John Milton. *ReT*

Song ("On the Eastern Way at the city of Lo-yang") Sung Tzŭ-hou, tr. fr. the Chinese by Arthur Waley. *PaS*

Song ("Once my heart was a summer rose") Edith Sitwell. *GrCc*

Song ("Stay, stay at home, my heart, and rest") Henry Wadsworth Longfellow. *DeT*

Song ("A sunny shaft did I behold") Samuel Taylor Coleridge. *CoPs—DeT*

Song ("Weep, weep, ye woodmen, wail") See Robin Hood's funeral

Song ("Who can say") Alfred Tennyson. *SmLg*

Song ("Who is the baby, that doth lie") See The brides' tragedy

Song ("Why do bells of [or for] Christmas ring") Eugene Field. *ArTp—DoP—HuL-1*
Christmas song. *HaY*
"Why do the bells of Christmas ring." *BrL-k*
Song ("Wind and wave and star and sea") David McCord. *McFf*
Song before supper. David McCord. *McFf*
Song for a blue roadster. Rachel Field. *ArTp—FeF*
Song for a camper. John Farrar. *HaY*
Song for a dance. See Superlative dance and song
Song for a hot day. Elizabeth Jane Coatsworth. *HuSv*
Song for a little cuckoo clock. Elizabeth Jane Coatsworth. *BrS*
Song for a little house. Christopher Morley. *BrR-6—FeF—HuSv—JoAc*
Song for December thirty-first. Frances M. Frost. *HaY*
A song for Hal. Laura E. Richards. *HuL-2*
Song for midsummer night. Elizabeth Jane Coatsworth. *HaY*
Song for my mother. See Song for my mother: Her words
Song for my mother: Her words. Anna Hempstead Branch. *BrS—HaY*
Her words. *FeF*
Song for my mother. *ArTp*
A song for St Cecilia's day, 1687. John Dryden. *PlU* (sel.)
A song for September. Eleanor Farjeon. *FaCb*
Song for two voices. Edith Sitwell. *GrCc*
A song from Cyprus. H. D. *GrCc*
A song in praise of the Lord. Unknown. *DoP*
Song in spring. Louis Ginsberg. *HaY*
Song in the wood. John Fletcher. *ReT*
Song: Lift-boy. See Lift-boy
The song my paddle sings. E. Pauline Johnson. *FeF*
A song of always. Efraim Rosenzweig. *ArTp*
Song of autumn. Paul Verlaine, tr. fr. the French by Arthur Symons. *PaS*
The song of D. James Reeves. *ReR*
A song of dagger-dancing. Tu Fu, tr. fr. the Chinese by Witter Bynner. *PlU* (sel.)
A song of greatness. Mary Austin. *ArTp—BrBc—FeF—JoAc*
The song of Hiawatha, sel. Henry Wadsworth Longfellow
Hiawatha's childhood. *ArTp—FeF—HuSv—JoAc*
The song of Mr Toad. See The wind in the willows
Song of myself, sels. Walt Whitman
"I believe a leaf of grass is no less than the journey-work of the stars." *ArTp*
Miracles. *HuSv—JoAc—McW—UnG*
An old-time sea-fight. *UnMc*
A song of Sherwood. Alfred Noyes. *ArTp—FeF—JoAc*
The song of Solomon, sels. Bible, Old Testament
Awake. *FeF*
The song of songs. *PaS*

The winter is past. *HaY—McAw*
"For, lo, the winter is past." *ArTp*
Lo, the winter is past. *FeF*
The song of songs. See The song of Solomon
Song of summer. Paul Laurence Dunbar. *BrL-8*
Song of the all-wool shirt. Eugene Field. *CoSp*
Song of the brook. See The brook
Song of the camels. See Twelfth night
The song of the creatures. See The mirror of perfection—Praise of created things
The song of the dumb waiter. James Reeves. *ReW*
Song of the engine bells. Elizabeth Jane Coatsworth. *BrR-5*
The song of the four winds. Thomas Love Peacock. *HoW*
The song of the Jellicles. T. S. Eliot. *LoL—SmLg*
The song of the mad prince. Walter De La Mare. *GrCc—SmLg*
The song of the Muses. Matthew Arnold. *HoW*
Song of the open road, sel. Walt Whitman
"Afoot and light-hearted, I take to the open road." *ArTp*
Song of the open road. Ogden Nash. *ThP*
Song of the parrot. Elizabeth Jane Coatsworth. *HuSv*
Song of the pop-bottlers. Morris Bishop. *CoH—FeF*
The song of the robin. Beatrice Bergquist. *BrL-k*
"The song of the saw." See Busy carpenters
Song of the sea wind. Austin Dobson. *HuL-2*
Song of the seasons. Blanche De Good Lofton. *HaY*
Song of the settlers. Jessamyn West. *FeF*
Song of the ship's cat. Elizabeth Jane Coatsworth. *BrR-4*
The song of the shirt. Thomas Hood. *UnMc*
The song of the toad. John Burroughs. *FeF*
Song of the train. David McCord. *FeF—JoAc—McFf*
Song of the very poor. Unknown, tr. fr. the Old French by Eleanor Farjeon. *FaCb—FaN*
Song of the wave. Robert Frost. *FrR*
Song of the wooden-legged fiddler. Alfred Noyes. *HuL-2*
The song of wandering Aengus. William Butler Yeats. *ArTp—CoPm—HaP—JoAc—McW—ReT—SmLg—UnG*
A song-offering. Rabindranath Tagore. *PaS*
Song on the water. Thomas Lovell Beddoes. *SmLg*
"The song that I'm going to sing." See The crafty farmer
Song: The owl. See The owl ("When cats run home and light is come")
Song to a tree. Edwin Markham. *FeF*
Song, to Celia. Ben Jonson. *HaP*
A song to David. Christopher Smart. *PlU* (sel.)
Song to night. Elizabeth Jane Coatsworth. *McW*

"**Space-time,** our scientists tell us, is impervious." See Reply to Mr Wordsworth

"**Spaced** in a helmet." See Man for Mars

"The **spacious** firmament on high." Joseph Addison. *BrL-7*

"**Spades** take up leaves." See Gathering leaves

"The **spangled** pandemonium." Palmer Brown. *ArTp*

Spain
Conquistador. E. J. Coatsworth. *UnG*
A feller I know. M. Austin. *FeF*
"Rain, rain, go to Spain." Mother Goose. *LiL—OpO*
Spanish Johnny. W. S. Cather. *FeF—McW*
Spanish waters. J. Masefield. *FeF—McW*
Tarantella. H. Belloc. *NaM—SmLg*

Spain—History. See also United States—History—War with Spain
The Armada. T. B. Macaulay. *SmLg*
La noche triste. R. Frost. *FrR*
"Some years of late, in eighty-eight." Unknown. *SmLg*
"The Spanish Armada met its fate." Mother Goose. *OpO*
Spanish ladies. Unknown. *SmLg*
The vindictives. R. Frost. *FrR*

"A **spaniel,** a woman, and a walnut tree." Unknown. *MoY*

Spanish Armada. See Spain—History

"The **Spanish** Armada met its fate." Mother Goose. *OpO*

Spanish dancer. Unknown. *WoJ*

"**Spanish** dancer do the splits." See Spanish dancer

Spanish Johnny. Willa Sibert Cather. *FeF—McW*

Spanish ladies. Unknown. *SmLg*

Spanish lullaby. Unknown, tr. fr. the Spanish by Louis Untermeyer. *DoP*

Spanish waters. John Masefield. *FeF—McW*

"**Spanish** waters, Spanish waters, you are ringing in my ears." See Spanish waters

"**Spanking** is something that must go." See Character building

"The **sparrow** hath found an house." See Psalms—Psalm LXXXIV

The **sparrow,** 1 ("The sparrow hath found an house") See Psalms—Psalm LXXXIV

The **sparrow,** 2 ("Are not two sparrows sold for a farthing") See Gospel according to Matthew

"**Sparrow,** you little brown gutter-mouse." See London sparrow

Sparrows
The blossom. W. Blake. *ReT*
"Jaybird pulls the turnin' plow." Unknown. *WoF*
"A little cock sparrow sat on a green tree." Mother Goose. *DeMg—LiL—OpO*
"A little sparrow built his nest, up in a waterspout." Unknown. *WoF*
London sparrow. E. Farjeon. *ReG*
The sparrow, 2. From Gospel according to Matthew, Bible, New Testament. *FeF*
The sparrow's dirge. J. Skelton. *SmLg*

The **sparrow's** dirge. John Skelton. *SmLg*

"**Speak** gently, spring, and make no sudden sound." See Four little foxes

Speak no evil. Unknown. *UnG*

"**Speak** roughly to your little boy." Lewis Carroll. *SmLg*

"**Speak,** sir, and be wise." See Basket

"**Speak,** speak, thou fearful guest." See The skeleton in armor

Speak to me. Unknown. *TaD*

"**Speak** to me, darlin', oh, speaky, spikey, spokey." See Speak to me

"**Speak** with contempt of none, from slave to king." See Speak no evil

"**Speaking** of Joe, I should have said." See Fred

"The **spearmen** heard the bugle sound." See Beth Gêlert

"A **speck** that would have been beneath my sight." See A considerable speck

"A **speck** went blowing up against the sky." See A visit from abroad

Speed
The master speed. R. Frost. *FrR*
Slowly. J. Reeves. *ReW*
Speed. M. Chute. *ChA*
"Swift things are beautiful." E. J. Coatsworth. *ArTp—HuL-2—HuSv*
The tortoise and the magistrate. E. V. Rieu. *RiF*

Speed. Marchette Chute. *ChA*

A **spell.** John Dryden. *HoW*

A **spell** for sleeping. Alastair Reid. *ReG*

Spell of creation. Kathleen Raine. *McW—SmLg*

Spelling
"Chicken in a car." Unknown. *WiRm*
"Chicken in the car and the car won't go." *WoF*
In school-days. J. G. Whittier. *FeF* (sel.)
"Knife and a fork." Unknown. *WiRm*
"Knife and a fork and a bottle and a cork." *WoF*
"M I crooked letter, crooked letter I." Unknown. *WiRm*
"P U umpkin." Unknown. *WiRm*
"Round and round the rugged rock." Mother Goose. *OpO*
Spelling bee. D. McCord. *McT*
The spelling bee at Angels. B. Harte. *CoSp*
"Timothy Titus took two ties." Mother Goose. *OpO*

Spelling bee. David McCord. *McT*

The **spelling** bee at Angels. Bret Harte. *CoSp*

Spells. James Reeves. *CoPm—ReG—ReW*

Spencer, Theodore
Entropy. *PlI*
A narrative. *McW*

Spencer, William Robert
Beth Gêlert. *UnG*

Spender, Stephen
Beethoven's death mask. *PlU*
I think continually of those. *HaP*
The swan. *PlU*

The **spendthrift.** Eleanor Farjeon. *FaCb—FaN*

Spenser, Edmund
The bower of bliss. See The faerie queene
The faerie queene, sels.
  The bower of bliss. *PlU*
  Old January. *HaY*
Like as a huntsman. *HaP*
A nosegay. See The shepherd's calendar
Old January. See The faerie queene
The shepherd's calendar, sel.
  A nosegay. *DeT*
Speyer, Leonora
"Measure me, sky." *BrBc—FeF—JoAc*
X-ray. *PlI*
"A **sphere**, which is as many thousand spheres." See Prometheus unbound
Spicer, Anne Higginson. See Higginson, Anne
The **spider.** See "A noiseless patient spider"
The **spider** ("With six small diamonds for his eyes") Robert P. Tristram Coffin. *PlI*
The **spider** and the fly. Mary Howitt. *DeT —FeF—PeF*
"**Spider.** Spider." See The spider's web
"The **spider** weaves his silver wire." See Of a spider
Spiders. See also Cobwebs
  Design. R. Frost. *FrR*
  Drowsy. C. Sandburg. *SaW*
  "Eency weency spider climbed the water spout." Mother Goose. *DeMg*
  The embarrassing episode of little Miss Muffet. G. W. Carryl. *CoSp—FeF*
  Ipsey wipsey. Mother Goose. *OpO*
  "Little Miss Muffet." Mother Goose. *ArTp —BrL-k—DeMg—HuSv—JoAc—LiL*
    Miss Muffet. *OpO*
  "Mrs Spider." M. C. Livingston. *LiWa*
  "A noiseless patient spider." W. Whitman. *HaP—NaE*
    The spider. *HoW*
  Of a spider. W. Thorley. *FeF*
  The spider. R. P. T. Coffin. *PlI*
  The spider and the fly. M. Howitt. *DeT— FeF—PeF*
  The spider's web. C. D. Cole. *HuL-1*
  Spiders in the sun. E. Farjeon. *FaCb— FaN*
  The true story of the web-spinner M. Howitt. *DeT*
  "Will you walk into my parlor." Unknown. *WiRm*
"**Spiders** are spinning their webs." See Mid-August
The **spider's** web. Charlotte Druitt Cole. *HuL-1*
Spilt milk: Whodunit. William Jay Smith. *SmL*
Spin dame. Mother Goose. *OpO*
"**Spin,** dame, spin." See Spin dame
Spinden, H. J.
  A lover's lament. tr. *PaS*
Spinners in the sun. Eleanor Farjeon. *FaCb —FaN*
Spinning
  "Cross-patch." Mother Goose. *DeMg— JoAc—LiL—NaE—OpO*
  "Six little mice sat down to spin." Mother Goose. *JoAc*
    Six little mice. *OpO*

"Some little mice sat in a barn to spin." Mother Goose. *DeMg*
  Some little mice. *BrL-k*
Spin dame. Mother Goose. *OpO*
The spinning wheel. J. F. Waller. *CoSp*
A tale. Mother Goose. *OpO*
"There was an old woman sat spinning." Unknown
  American Father Gander. *UnG*
"**Spinning** Jenny and Hoppin' John." Unknown. *WoF*
Spinning top. Frank Dempster Sherman. *BrL-k*
The **spinning** wheel. John Francis Waller. *CoSp*
Spinsterhood
  Molly Grime. E. Farjeon. *FaCb—FaN*
The **spires** of Oxford. Winifred M. Letts. *BrL-7*
Spirits. See Ghosts
Spirituals. See Negro spirituals
The **spit-bug.** William H. Matchett. *McW*
"**Splashing** water." See The herd-boy's song
The **splendour** falls. See The princess— Bugle song
"The **splendour** falls on castle walls." See The Princess—Bugle song
Splinter. Carl Sandburg. *ArTp—FeF*
The **Spoon** River anthology, sels. Edgar Lee Masters
  Achilles Deatheridge. *UnMc*
  Anne Rutledge. *CoPs—HaP*
  Fiddler Jones. *PlU—SmLg*
  Petit, the poet. *HaP—SmLg*
  William Jones. *PlI*
A **sporting** monk. See The Canterbury tales
Sports. See Athletes; Games; also names of games, as Baseball; also names of sports, as Fishermen and fishing
Sportsmanship
  "Winning, never boast; and, losing." A. Guiterman
    Proverbs. *ThP*
Spring. See also April; March; May; Seasons
  Alons au bois le may cueillir. Charles d'Orleans. *PaS*
  Apple blossoms. W. W. Martin. *BrR-6*
  April. S. Teasdale. *ArTp—CoPs—FeF— HaY—HuL-2—HuSv—JoAc*
  At Mrs Appleby's. E. U. McWebb. *ArTp —BrS—HuSv*
  Autumnal spring song. V. Miller. *HaP*
  Carmina burana. Unknown. *PaS* (sel.)
  Casual gold. M. E. Uschold. *HaY*
  A charm for spring flowers. R. Field. *ArTp*
  The coming of the spring. N. Perry. *HaY*
  Crisscross. C. Sandburg. *SaW*
  Daffodils. Kikuriō. *ArTp*
  Daffodowndilly. A. A. Milne. *MiWc*
  The dress of spring. M. Justus. *HaY*
  An Easter carol. C. G. Rossetti. *DoP*
  The echoing (ecchoing) green. W. Blake. *CoPs—HoW—JoAc*
  Everybody stared. I. O. Eastwick. *EaI*
  The fields of Ballyclare. D. A. McCarthy. *BrL-7*

First signs. E. Farjeon. *FaCb*
The first spring day. C. G. Rossetti. *HoW*
First spring morning. R. Bridges. *HaY*
Flower chorus. R. W. Emerson. *HuL-2*
Glad earth. E. C. Forbes. *HaY*
"The green leaf dances now." E. Farjeon. *FaCb*
The gusts of winter are gone. Meleager. *PaS*
Harbingers. E. Tatum. *BrR-6*
Hello. L. A. Garnett. *BrS*
"Here we come a-piping." Unknown. *BrS —JoAc*
"Here's spring." E. Farjeon. *FaCb*
I bended unto me. T. E. Brown. *CoPs*
In just spring. From Chanson innocente. E. E. Cummings. *CoH—JoAc—ReT*
　Chanson innocente. *FeF—NaM*
　"In just." *UnG*
In spring. E. Mörike. *PaS*
In spring in warm weather. D. Aldis. *AlA —BrBc*
In the spring ("In the season of spring is the season of growing") Ibycus. *PaS*
In the spring ("Now the bright crocus flames, and now") Meleager. *PaS*
"In time of silver rain." L. Hughes. *ArTp*
The invaders. A. A. Milne. *MiWc*
Jonathan Bing dances for spring. B. C. Brown. *BrS*
Joys. J. R. Lowell. *HuL-2*
Kerchoo. M. Fishback. *CoPs*
Kite days. M. Sawyer. *BrS—McAw*
The little valley in spring. Onitsura. *PaS*
The magic piper. E. L. Marsh. *BrS— HuL-2*
Miracle. L. H. Bailey. *HaY*
The miracle of spring. Bahar. *PaS*
The missing cuckoo. E. V. Rieu. *RiF*
A morning song. E. Farjeon. *FaCb—FaN*
Nakatsukasa. From Shui Shū. Unknown. *PaS*
Old Dan'l. L. A. G. Strong. *CoPs*
On the road to Nara. M. Bashō. *PaS*
Only the wind says spring. H. J. Miller. *UnG*
An open secret. Unknown. *BrR-4*
Over, under, over. I. O. Eastwick. *EaI*
A page's road song. W. A. Percy. *HaY*
Pippa's song. From Pippa passes. R. Browning. *FeF*
　Spring song. *UnG*
　"The year's at the spring." *DoP— HaY—HuSv—ThP*
A prayer in spring. R. Frost. *FrR—HaY*
Prisoned. M. C. Davies *HuL-2*
Pussy willow. K. L. Brown. *BrL-k*
The question. P. B. Shelley. *DeT*
"The rains of spring." Lady Ise. *ArTp*
Rainy day song. V. A. Storey. *HaY*
The return of spring. Charles d'Orleans. *GrCc*
Robin's song. E. L. M. King. *ArTp*
Rondeau. Charles d'Orleans. *PaS*
Scarcely spring. L. Untermeyer. *UnG*
Snow in spring. I. O. Eastwick *EaI*
Song in spring. L. Ginsberg. *HaY*

The song of Solomon, sels. Bible, Old Testament
　Awake. *FeF*
　The song of songs. *PaS*
　The winter is past. *HaY—McAw*
　　"For lo, the winter is past." *ArTp*
　　Lo, the winter is past. *FeF*
Spring ("All happy and glad in the sunshine I stood") D. A. Lord. *DoP*
Spring ("Everyone's bursting outdoors, outdoors") D. Aldis. *AlA*
Spring ("The last snow is going") H. Behn. *ArTp*
Spring ("The leaves are uncurling") M. Chute. *ChA—McAw*
Spring ("Now fades the last long streak of snow") A. Tennyson. *DeT*
The spring ("Now that the winter's gone, the earth hath lost") T. Carew. *GrCc— HaP—HoW*
　Now that the winter's gone. *CoPs*
Spring ("Sound the flute") W. Blake. *ArTp — FeF — HaY — JoAc — NaM — SmLg—UnG*
Spring ("The spring comes linking and jinking through the woods") W. Miller. *CoPs* (sel.)
Spring ("Spring, the sweet spring, is the year's pleasant king") T. Nashe. *DeT— HoW*
Spring and all ("By the road to the contagious hospital") W. C. Williams. *HaP*
Spring and all ("So much depends") W. C. Williams. *NaE—ReT*
Spring and fall. G. M. Hopkins. *HaP— ReT*
Spring and winter. From Love's labor's lost. W. Shakespeare. *ReT*
Spring cricket. F. Rodman. *BrS—FeF*
Spring, etc. R. Whittemore. *McW*
Spring grass. C. Sandburg. *FeF*
Spring in hiding. F. M. Frost. *HaY*
Spring is in the making. N. K. Duffy. *HaY*
Spring lullaby. F. M. Frost. *FrLn*
Spring morning A. A. Milne. *MiWc*
Spring night in a village. E. Farjeon. *FaCb*
Spring pools. R. Frost. *FrR*
Spring prayer. R. W. Emerson. *HuL-2*
Spring quiet. C. G. Rossetti. *ReT*
Spring rain ("Leaves make a slow") H. Behn. *ArTp—PeF*
Spring rain ("The storm came up so very quick") M. Chute. *ArTp—ChA—HuL-1 —McAw*
Spring-signs ("Everywhere the wind blows") M. Bowers. *McAw*
Spring signs ("When will it turn into spring") M. C. Livingston. *LiWa*
Spring song ("I know, I know, I know it") M. Justus. *McAw*
Spring song ("I love daffodils") H. Conkling. *CoPs*
Spring song ("If I could be where I wish to be") E. A. Chaffee. *BrL-7*
Spring song ("Spring is coming, spring is coming") W. Blake. *HuL-1*

Spring—*Continued*

Spring song for two voices. E. V. Rieu. *RiF*

The spring walk. T. Miller. *DeT*

Spring wind. N. B. Turner. *BrS*

Spring's arrival. Unknown. *FeF*

Springtime in Donegal. M. R. Stevenson. *HuSv*

Surprise. B. E. Martin. *McAw*

Three signs of spring. D. McCord. *McT*

To spring. W. Blake. *HoW*

Twist-rime on spring. A. Guiterman. *CoPs*

The vow to Cupid. Unknown. *PaS*

What bird so sings. J. Lyly. *ReT*

When blue sky smiles. O. B. Miller. *BrL-k*

"When daffodils begin to peer." From The winter's tale. W. Shakespeare. *SmLg*

Who calls. F. C. Sayers. *BrL-7—BrS*

Wise Johnny. E. Fallis. *ArTp—BrL-k—BrS*

Written in March. W. Wordsworth. *ArTp — BrR-6 — FeF — HaY — HuL-2 — McW—ReG—ReT—UnG*

In March. *DeT*

March. *JoAc*

The merry month of March. *NaE—NaM*

Young lambs. J. Clare. *UnG*

Spring ("All happy and glad in the sunshine I stood") Daniel A. Lord. *DoP*

Spring ("Everyone's bursting outdoors, outdoors") Dorothy Aldis. *AlA*

Spring ("The last snow is going") Harry Behn. *ArTp*

Spring ("The leaves are uncurling") Marchette Chute. *ChA—McAw*

The spring ("A little mountain spring I found") Rose Fyleman. *FeF*

Spring ("Now fades the last long streak of snow") Alfred Tennyson. *DeT*

The spring ("Now that the winter's gone, the earth hath lost") Thomas Carew. *GrCc—HaP—HoW*

Now that the winter's gone. *CoPs*

Spring ("Sound the flute") William Blake. *ArTp — FeF — HaY — JoAc — NaM —SmLg—UnG*

Spring ("The spring comes linking and jinking through the woods") William Miller. *CoPs* (sel.)

Spring ("Spring, the sweet spring, is the year's pleasant king") Thomas Nashe. *DeT—HoW*

Spring and all ("By the road to the contagious hospital") William Carlos Williams. *HaP*

Spring and all ("So much depends") William Carlos Williams. *NaE—ReT*

Spring and fall. Gerard Manley Hopkins. *HaP—ReT*

Spring and winter. See Love's labor's lost

"Spring bursts today." See An Easter carol

"Spring came late." See Spring song for two voices

"Spring comes hurrying." See Hello

"The spring comes linking and jinking through the woods." See Spring

Spring cricket. Frances Rodman. *BrS—FeF*

"Spring crosses over into summer." See Crisscross

Spring, etc. Reed Whittemore. *McW*

Spring grass. Carl Sandburg. *FeF*

"Spring grass, there is a dance to be danced for you." See Spring grass

Spring in hiding. Frances M. Frost. *HaY*

"The spring is coming by a many signs." See Young lambs

"Spring is coming, spring is coming." See Spring song

Spring is in the making. Nona Keen Duffy. *HaY*

The spring is past. See Elegy ("My prime of youth is but a frost of cares")

"The spring is past, and yet it hath not sprung." See Elegy ("My prime of youth is but a frost of cares")

"Spring is showery, flowery, bowery." Mother Goose. *ArTp*

"Spring is the morning of the year." See The goldenrod

"Spring is when the grass turns green and glad." See Lines written for Gene Kelly to dance to

Spring lullaby. Frances M. Frost. *FrLn*

Spring morning. A. A. Milne. *MiWc*

Spring night in a village. Eleanor Farjeon. *FaCb*

Spring pools. Robert Frost. *FrR*

Spring prayer. Ralph Waldo Emerson. *HuL-2*

Spring quiet. Christina Georgina Rossetti. *ReT*

Spring rain ("Leaves make a slow") Harry Behn. *ArTp—PeF*

Spring rain ("The storm came up so very quick") Marchette Chute. *ArTp—ChA—HuL-1—McAw*

"The spring rain is soft rain." See Rainy day song

Spring-signs ("Everywhere the wind blows") Mildred Bowers. *McAw*

Spring signs ("When will it turn into spring") Myra Cohn Livingston. *LiWa*

Spring song ("I know, I know, I know it") May Justus. *McAw*

Spring song ("I love daffodils") Hilda Conkling. *CoPs*

Spring song ("If I could be where I wish to be") Eleanor Alletta Chaffee. *BrL-7*

Spring song ("Spring is coming, spring is coming") William Blake. *HuL-1*

Spring song ("The year's at the spring") See Pippa passes—Pippa's song

Spring song for two voices. E. V. Rieu. *RiF*

"Spring, the sweet spring, is the year's pleasant king." See Spring

The spring walk. Thomas Miller. *DeT*

Spring wind. Nancy Byrd Turner. *BrS*

Springfield mountain. Unknown. *WoF*

"A springful of larks in a rolling." See October

Springs (Water)

The pasture ("I'm going out to clean the pasture spring") R. Frost. *ArTp—BrR-4 — FeF — FrR — FrY — HuL-2 — HuSv —JoAc—NaM—PeF*

The spring. R. Fyleman. *FeF*

Spring's arrival. Unknown, tr. fr. the German. *FeF*

Springtime in Donegal. Mabel Rose Stevenson. *HuSv*

"Springtime is a green time." See Four seasons

"Springtime, springtime." See Everybody stared

The sprinkler. Dorothy Aldis. *AlA*

"The sprinkler whirls its shiny drops." See The sprinkler

Sprinklers (Water)
The sprinkler. D. Aldis. *AlA*
Sprinkling. D. M. Pierce. *ArTp—BrLk*

Sprinkling. Dorothy Mason Pierce. *ArTp—BrL-k*

"Sprinkling, wrinkling, softly tinkling." See Waters

Sprod, G. N.
Request number. *CoH*

Squaw talk. David McCord. *McT*

Squire, Sir J. (John) C. (Collings or Collins)
The discovery. *CoPs—McW*
Sonnet. *FeF*
The march. *CoPs*
The ship. *DeT*
Sonnet. See The discovery

A squire. See The Canterbury tales

The squirrel. See "The winds they did blow"

The squirrel ("The squirrel, flippant, pert, and full of play") William Cowper. *UnG*

The squirrel ("Whisky, frisky") Unknown. *ArTp — BrL-k — FeF — HuL-1 — HuSv —JoAc*

"The squirrel, flippant, pert, and full of play." See The squirrel

Squirrels
Don't tell me. D. Aldis. *AlA*
"Five little squirrels." Unknown. *HuL-1—WiRm*
   "Five little squirrels sat up in a tree." *JoAc*
The flying squirrel. R. B. Bennett. *BrR-4*
Fred. D. McCord. *ArTp—McFf*
Joe. D. McCord. *ArTp—McFf*
A little squirrel. Unknown. *ArTp*
"The mountain and the squirrel." R. W. Emerson. *FeF—UnG*
   Fable. *BrR-4*
Our squirrel. D. Aldis. *AlHd*
Our tame baby squirrel. D. Aldis. *AlA*
"Peep, squirrel, peep." Unknown. *TaD*
Run, squirrel, run. Unknown. *TaD*
The squirrel ("The squirrel, flippant, pert, and full of play") W. Cowper. *UnG*
The squirrel ("Whisky, frisky") Unknown. *ArTp — BrL-k — FeF — HuL-1 — HuSv —JoAc*
The story of the baby squirrel. D. Aldis. *ArTp*
To a squirrel at Kyle-na-no. W. B. Yeats. *FeF—ReT*
"The winds they did blow." Mother Goose. *DeT*
   The squirrel. *OpO*

"The stable door was closed that night." See The first night

The staff of Aesculapius. Marianne Moore. *PlI*

Stage-coaches
The coachman. Mother Goose. *OpO*
The phantom mail coach. L. O. Welcome. *CoPm*

"The stair-carpet is Turkey red." See On the staircase

Stairs
Dr Klimwell's fall. *McT*
Halfway down. A. A. Milne. *FeF—MiWc*
Here I come. D. Aldis. *AlA*
The little man who wasn't there. H. Mearns. *CoH—FeF*
On the staircase. E. Farjeon. *BrS*
Stairs. O. Herford. *CoH*

Stairs. Oliver Herford. *CoH*

Stamp battalion. Edward Verrall Lucas. *HuSv*

"A stamp's a tiny, flimsy thing." See Stamp battalion

Standards. Nathalia Crane. *UnG*

Stanley-Wrench, Margaret
Shepherds' carol. *EaW*

A stanza on freedom. James Russell Lowell. *McW—ThP*

Stanzas for music, sel. George Gordon Byron
Thy sweet voice. *DeT*

"A star." See Thought on a star

The star. Jane Taylor. *ArTp—FeF—OpO*
Little star. *HuSv*
"Twinkle, twinkle, little star." *BrL-k*

"Star bright, starlight." See "Star-light, starbright"

The star in the pail. David McCord. *McFf*

"Star-light, star-bright." Mother Goose. *ArTp—OpO*
"Star bright, starlight." *HuSv*

"A star looks down at me." See Waiting both

The star-spangled banner. Francis Scott Key. *FeF*

The star-splitter. Robert Frost. *FrR—PlI*

"The star that bids the shepherd fold." See Comus

Starfish
Starfish ("Last night I saw you in the sky") W. Welles. *BrS—FeF*
The starfish ("Triangles are commands of God") Robert P. Tristram Coffin. *PlI*

Starfish ("Last night I saw you in the sky") Winifred Welles. *BrS—FeF*

The starfish ("When I see a starfish") David McCord. *McFf*

Starkey, James. See O'Sullivan, Seumas

The starlight night. Gerard Manley Hopkins. *ReT*

The starlighter. Arthur Guiterman. *BrS*

Starling. David McCord. *McT*

Starlings
Old blue saucepan. E. Farjeon. *FaN*
Starling. D. McCord. *McT*

Stars
All about fireflies all about. D. McCord. *McFf*
August night. E. M. Roberts. *HaY*
Baby toes. C. Sandburg. *FeF*
Bedtime. H. C. Crew. *BrR-3*
Candle and star. E. J. Coatsworth. *BrBc*
Canis Major. R. Frost. *FrR*
Capricorn. E. Farjeon. *FaCb—FaN*

"Stephen is just five years old." See Blanket street

Stephens, James
  Breakfast time. *BrR-3*
  Check. *ArTp—BrS—PeF*
    Night was creeping. *HuSv*
  Christmas at Freelands. *EaW*
  Deirdre. *GrCc*
  Little things. *ArTp—BrS—FeF—JoAc*
  Night was creeping. See Check
  The rivals. *BrR-6—FeF*
  Seumas Beg. *FeF—NaE*
  The shell. *NaM*
  The snare. *ArTp—CoI*
  A visit from abroad. *CoPm*
  The voice of God. *DoP*
  When you walk. *McW*
  The whisperer. *DoP*
  White fields. *BrR-4—BrS—CoPs—FeF—HuL-2—McAw—NaM*
  The white window. *ArTp—BrL-k—HuL-2—HuSv—JoAc*

Stetson, Charlotte Perkins
  A man must live. *ThP*

Stevens, Wallace
  Banjo boomer. *McW*
  Disillusionment of ten o'clock. *HaP*
  Earthy anecdote. *ReT*
  The emperor of ice-cream. *HaP*
  The man with the blue guitar. *PlU* (sel.)
  Mozart, 1935. *PlU*
  Peter Quince at the clavier. *GrCc*
  Ploughing on Sunday. *FeF—ReT*
  A rabbit as king of the ghosts. *ReT*
  Thirteen ways of looking at a blackbird. *HaP*

Stevenson, D. E.
  Six and thirty. *BrBc*

Stevenson, Lionel
  In a desert town. *HuSv*

Stevenson, Mabel Rose
  Springtime in Donegal. *HuSv*

Stevenson, Robert Louis
  At the sea-side. *ArTp—FeF—JoAc*
  Autumn fires. *ArTp—HaY—JoAc*
  Bed in summer. *DeT—HuL-1—HuSv—JoAc*
  Block city. *FeF*
  The Celestial Surgeon. *UnG*
  Christmas at sea. *CoSp*
  The cow. *ArTp—FeF—HuSv*
  De cœnatione micæ. tr. *SmLg*
  The dumb soldier. *UnG*
  Escape at bedtime. *ArTp—BrR-5—PeF—UnG*
  Farewell to the farm. *ArTp—FeF*
  The flowers. *FeF*
  Foreign lands. *HuL-1*
  From a railway carriage. *ArTp—FeF—HuL-2—PeF—ReG*
  Good and bad children. *SmLg*
  A good play. *ArTp—FeF—NaM*
  Happy thought. *ArTp*
  "I should like to rise and go." See Travel
  I will make you brooches. See My valentine
  The land of counterpane. *FeF—HuSv—JoAc—NaE*
  The land of Nod. *UnG*
  The land of story-books. *ArTp—FeF—UnG*

The little land. *HuSv—JoAc*
Marching song. *ArTp—FeF*
My bed is a boat. *HuSv*
My shadow. *ArTp—BrL-k—FeF—HuL-1—HuSv—JoAc—PeF*
My task. *ThP*
My valentine. *BrS—FeF*
  I will make you brooches. *HuL-2*
  Romance. *CoPs*
Pirate story. *ArTp—FeF—JoAc—UnG*
Rain. *ArTp—BrL-k—HuSv—JoAc*
Requiem. *HaP—McW—ThP—UnG*
Romance. See My valentine
The sick child. *CoPs—DeT*
The sun's travels. *FeF*
The swing. *ArTp—HuL-1—HuSv—JoAc—PeF*
Time to rise. *BrS—BrL-k—HuSv*
Travel. *ArTp—FeF—McW—NaM—SmLg—UnG*
  "I should like to rise and go." *HuSv*
The vagabond. *BrL-8*
Vailima. *DeT*
Where go the boats. *ArTp—BrR-3—HuL-2—SmLg*
Whole duty of children. *NaE*
The wind. *ArTp—HuL-1—HuSv—JoAc*
Windy nights. *ArTp—BrR-4—BrS—DeT—GrCc—HuL-1*
Winter-time. See Wintertime
Wintertime. *HuSv*
  Winter-time. *UnG*
Words. *UnG*

Stevenson, Robert Louis (about)
  Requiem. R. L. Stevenson. *HaP—McW—ThP—UnG*
  Vailima. R. L. Stevenson. *DeT*
A stick for a horse. Sybil Fountain. *HuL-1*

Still, John
  Drinking song. *HoW*
Still more about bears. John Ciardi. *CiY*
"Still sits the schoolhouse by the road." See In school-days
Still to be neat. Ben Jonson. *HaP*
"Still to be neat, still to be drest." See Still to be neat
Stirring the pudding. Eleanor Farjeon. *FaN*
"Stocking and shirt." James Reeves. *ReW*
Stocking fairy. Winifred Welles. *ArTp—FeF—HuL-2*

Stockings
  Christmas stocking. E. Farjeon. *FaCb—FaN*
  Shoes and stockings. A. A. Milne. *HuL-1—MiWc*
  "Stocking and shirt." J. Reeves. *ReW*
  Stocking fairy. W. Welles. *ArTp—FeF—HuL-2*
  Troubles. D. Aldis. *BrL-k—HuSv—JoAc*
"Stockings are a trouble; so many times my toes." See Troubles

Stokes, Will
  Bugs. *NaM*
The stolen child. William Butler Yeats. *CoPm*
"The stone goes straight." See Washington monument by night
Stones by the sea. James Reeves. *ReW*
Stop and go. Marie Louise Allen. *AlP*

Stop—go. Dorothy Baruch. *ArTp—BrL-k—FeF—HuL-1*

"Stop, look, and listen." Unknown. *HuL-1*

"Stop, stop, pretty water." See The runaway brook

Stopping by woods on a snowy evening. Robert Frost. *ArTp—BrL-8—BrS—CoPs — FeF — FrR — FrY — HaP — HuL-2 — HuSv — JoAc — McW — NaM — PeF—ReT—SmLg*

Stopping the swing. Mother Goose. *OpO*

"The store we like best is Emma's store." See Emma's store

Storey, Violet Alleyn
Dawn song—St Patrick's day. *HaY*
Neighborly. *ArTp*
Rainy day song. *HaY*

Stork, Charles Wharton
The eternal. tr. *PaS*
The heather. tr. *PaS*
Like an April day. tr. *PaS*
The pearl. tr. *PaS*

The storm ("From my bed so safe and warm") Dorothy Aldis. *AlA*

The storm ("We wake to hear the storm come down") Edward Shanks. *DeT*

Storm ("You crash over the trees") H. D. *ArTp*

"The storm came up so very quick." See Spring rain

Storm cellar. Herbert Merrill. *BrR-5*

Storm fear. Robert Frost. *FrR*

Storms. See also Rain; Snow; Weather; Winds
Blossoms and storm. Sadaiye. *PaS*
Broadcasting. M. D. Shacklett. *BrR-3*
The hurricane. P. Matos. *FeF*
A line-storm song. R. Frost. *FrR—GrCc*
A nautical extravaganza. W. Irwin. *CoSp*
A nautical extravagance. *HuSv*
The sailor's consolation. Attributed to C. Dibdin; also attributed to W. Pitt. *CoH—DeT—HuSv*
Sleet storm. J. S. Tippett. *BrS—PeF*
The steeple. E. Fleming. *HuL-2*
The storm ("From my bed so safe and warm") D. Aldis. *AlA*
The storm ("We wake to hear the storm come down") E. Shanks. *DeT*
Storm ("You crash over the trees") H. D. *ArTp*
Storm cellar. H. Merrill. *BrR-5*
Storm fear. R. Frost. *FrR*
The tempest. E. J. Coatsworth. *HuL-2*
Willful homing. R. Frost. *FrR*
"The wind begun to rock the grass." E. Dickinson. *GrCc*

Story. Dorothy Parker. *UnMc*

A story in the snow. Pearl Riggs Crouch. *ArTp—BrR-3*

The story of Augustus who would not have any soup. Heinrich Hoffmann. *DeT—NaM*
The story of Augustus. *ArTp*

The story of Johnny Head-in-air. Heinrich Hoffmann. *ArTp*

The story of little Suck-a-thumb. Heinrich Hoffmann. *NaE*

The story of Rimini. Leigh Hunt. *NaE* (sel.)

The story of Samuel Jackson. Charles Godfrey Leland. *CoSp*

The story of the baby squirrel. Dorothy Aldis. *ArTp*

Story-telling
American yarns. From The people, yes. C. Sandburg. *HuSv*
Yarns. *UnG*
The bedpost. R. Graves. *GrP*
Bible stories. L. W. Reese. *DoP*
Fairy days. W. M. Thackeray. *UnG*
Father's story. E. M. Roberts. *CoPs—FeF*
The first story. N. Crane. *BrR-5*
H is for happily ever after. E. Farjeon. *FaCb*
"I'll tell you a story." Mother Goose. *DeMg—JoAc—LiL*
Jack a nory. *OpO*
Jock o' Binnorie. R. Graves. *GrP*
King Stephen. R. Graves. *McW*
Little Orphant Annie. J. W. Riley. *FeF—HuSv—NaM*
The mother's tale. E. Farjeon. *BrBc—DoP*
O is for once upon a time. E. Farjeon. *FaCb*
Request number. G. N. Sprod. *CoH*
A stout miller. See The Canterbury tales—A miller

Stow, John (about)
A quill for John Stow. E. Farjeon. *FaN*

Strachan, Pearl
Morning overture: Chorus of dogs. *UnG*

Strange footprints. Vivian G. Gouled. *McAw*

"A strange foreboding is o'er me." See The Lorelei

The strange man. Unknown. *FeF*

"A strange night it was." See The shepherd's tale

"A strange, strange thing it is to know." See The sampler

Strange talk. L. E. Yates. *HuL-1*

"Strange, that such horror and such grace." See To a fair lady, playing with a snake

Strange tree. Elizabeth Madox Roberts. *FeF*

A strange wild song. See Sylvie and Bruno —The gardener's song

"Stranger, approach this spot with gravity." See On a dentist

"A stranger came to the door at eve." See Love and a question

The stranger cat. N. P. Babcock. *CoH*

The stranger in the pumpkin. John Ciardi. *CiM*

"The stranger in the pumpkin said." See The stranger in the pumpkin

Stranger still. Dorothy Aldis. *AlHd*

"The strangest of adventures." See Lord Arnaldos

The strangest wish. See The house beyond the meadow

Strawberries
Millions of strawberries. G. Taggard. *ArTp—FeF—NaM—UnG*
Strawberry jam. M. Justus. *FeF*
"Strawberry shortcake, blueberry pie." Unknown. *SmLg*
Wild strawberries. R. Graves. *SmLg*

"Strawberries that in gardens grow." See Wild strawberries

Strawberry jam. May Justus. *FeF*

"Strawberry shortcake, blueberry pie." Unknown. *SmLg*

"A stream far off beneath the moon." See The moonlit stream

"Stream, go hide yourself." See On a railroad right of way

The street musician. James Reeves. *ReBl*

Streets
    City streets and country roads. E. Farjeon. *ArTp—PeF*
    Corner-of-the-street. A. A. Milne. *MiWz*
    Eighth street west. R. Field. *BrS*
    Friday street. E. Farjeon. *HuL-1*
    The lonely street. W. C. Williams. *GrCc*
    A man with a little pleated piano. W. Welles. *FeF*
    Rum lane. J. Reeves. *ReBl*
    The street musician. J. Reeves. *ReBl*
    Yesterday in Oxford street. R. Fyleman. *ArTp—PeF*

"Strength and honour are her clothing." See Proverbs, Bible, Old Testament

"Strew on her roses, roses." See Requiescat

Strictly germ-proof. Arthur Guiterman. *BrL-8*

String quartet. Babette Deutsch. *PlU*

"Strolling along." See Docks

"A strolling fox, famished and underfed." See The greedy fox and the elusive grapes

Strong, George A.
    The modern Hiawatha. *CoH—FeF—NaM*

Strong, L. (Leonard) A. (Alfred) G. (George)
    Old Dan'l. *CoPs*

"A strong imagination from my youth has been combined." See The caulker

"The strong man awhile in his kingdom is lord." See The eternal

"Strut, Miss Susie." Unknown. *TaD*

Struther, Jan
    Carol. *EaW*
    Cat. *UnG*

Stuart, Jesse
    "My land is fair for any eyes to see." *ArTp—FeF*
    To call our own. *ThP*

Stuart, Muriel
    The seed shop. UnG

"Study and work." Unknown. *MoY*

"Stuff of the moon." See Nocturne in a deserted brickyard

Stupidity street. Ralph Hodgson. *BrS—DeT*

Stylites, Saint Simeon (about)
    Saint Simeon Stylites. E. Farjeon. *FaCb*

Su Tung-p'o
    Pear-trees by the fence. *PaS*

Suárez, Emma Gutiérrez
    Thoughts of a little girl. tr. *FeF*

Suasnavar, Constantino
    "I have lost my shoes." *FeF*

A subaltern's love-song. John Betjeman. *NaE*

Success. See also Ambition; Fame; Opportunity; Service; Thrift
    The blackbird in the lilac. J. Reeves. *ReBl*
    A blue ribbon at Amesbury. R. Frost. *FrR*

"He that would thrive." Mother Goose. *DeMg—OpO*

If. R. Kipling. *UnG*

"If I can stop one heart from breaking." E. Dickinson. *BrR-4*

It couldn't be done. E. A. Guest. *BrL-8*

"Seventh son of seventh son." E. Farjeon. *FaCb*
    Seventh son. *FaN*

"True success is that which makes." A. Guiterman
    Proverbs. *ThP*

"Success and happiness run in pairs." Unknown. *MoY*

The succession of the four sweet months. Robert Herrick. *HaY*
    The four sweet months. *HoW*
    July: The succession of the four sweet months. *FeF*

"Such a fine pullet ought to go." See A blue ribbon at Amesbury

Suckling, Sir John
    The constant lover. *ThP*
        "Out upon it, I have loved." *HaP*
    "Out upon it, I have loved." See The constant lover
    Why so pale and wan. *NaE*

Sudden gale in spring. Martha Banning Thomas. *BrR-5*

"Sudden refreshment came upon the school." See Physical geography

Sudden shower. John Clare. *CoPs*

"Suddenly the sky turned gray." See Snow toward evening

"Sugar and cream." Unknown
    Four questions. *WoJ*

"Sugar is sweet." Unknown. *MoY*

The sugar man. Charlotte Druitt Cole. *HuL-1*

"Sukey, you shall be my wife." Mother Goose. *OpO*

Sulky Sue. See "Here's Sulky Sue"

"A sulky witch and a surly cat." See Hallowe'en indignation meeting

Sullivan, A. M.
    The chronometer. *McW*
    Measurement. *McW*
    Smoke stack. *McW*

Sully-Prudhomme (René François Armand)
    The naked world. *PlI*
    The wheel. *PlI*

Summer. See also August; July; June; Seasons
    Barefoot days. R. Field. *FeF—HaY—HuL-2*
    "The big swing-tree is green again." M. J. Carr. *BrS*
    A boy's summer song. P. L. Dunbar. *BrS*
    Crisscross. C. Sandburg. *SaW*
    A dragon-fly. E. Farjeon. *FeF*
    Enchanted summer. H. Behn. *BeW*
    End-of-summer poem. R. B. Bennett. *BrS—FeF*
    Farewell to summer. E. Farjeon. *FaCb—FaN*
    Farm boy after summer. R. Francis. *HaP*
    Grasshopper Green. Unknown. *BrR-4—FeF—HuL-1*
    The grasshopper's song. H. N. Bialik. *FeF—HaY*

Novel experience. C. Wells. *BrR-3*

Prayer to the sun god. From Indian songs. L. Mertins. *HuSv*

"The puppy chased the sunbeam." I. O. Eastwick. *EaI*

Rise, sun. F. M. Frost. *FrLn*

Silver sheep. A. B. Payne. *BrS*

"Sing a song of sunshine." I. O. Eastwick. *BrS*

The sun. J. Drinkwater. *ArTp—FeF—PeF*

The sun is first to rise. E. J. Coatsworth. *HuSv*

The sun path. M. Bashō. *PaS*

Sunbeams. A. E. Poulsson. *BrR-3*

The sunlight ran on little feet. I. O. Eastwick. *EaI*

Sunning. J. S. Tippett. *ArTp—BrR-4—BrS —HuL-2*

Sunrise. C. E. S. Wood. *UnG*

The sun's travels. R. L. Stevenson. *FeF*

What the rattlesnake said. V. Lindsay. *JoAc*

"White bird featherless." Mother Goose. *OpO*

    Snow and sun. *ReG*

The sun. See "I'll tell you how the sun rose"

The sun ("I told the sun that I was glad") John Drinkwater. *ArTp—FeF—PeF*

The sun ("There's sun on the clover") Louise Fabrice Handcock. *McAw*

Sun and moon. See "I see the moon"

"Sun and rain at work together." See The red-gold rain

"The sun at noon to higher air." See March

"The sun descending in the west." See Night

"The sun does rise." See The echoing (ecchoing) green

"The sun draws." See On the beach

"The sun has long been set." William Wordsworth. *HaY*

"The sun is a huntress young." See An Indian summer day on the prairie

"The sun is always in the sky." See Breakfast time

The sun is first to rise. Elizabeth Jane Coatsworth. *HuSv*

"The sun is not abed, when I." See The sun's travels

The sun path. Matsuo Bashō, tr. fr. the Japanese by Harold G. Henderson. *PaS*

"The sun that brief December day." See Snow-bound—The snow

The sun that warms you. Eleanor Farjeon. *FaCb—FaN*

"The sun was bright when we went in." See At the theater

"The sun was shining on the sea." See Through the looking glass—The walrus and the carpenter

"The sun was warm but the wind was chill." See Early April

"Sun, you may send your haze gold." See Haze gold

Sunbeams. Anne Emilie Poulsson. *BrR-3*

Sunday. See Days of the week—Sunday

Sunday. Elizabeth Jane Coatsworth. *McW*

Sundials

    Lesson from a sun-dial. Unknown. *ArTp*

Sung Tzŭ-hou

    Song. *PaS*

"The sunlight ran." See The sunlight ran on little feet

The sunlight ran on little feet. Ivy O. Eastwick. *EaI*

"The sunlight speaks, and its voice is a bird." See The humming bird

Sunning. James S. Tippett. *ArTp—BrR-4— BrS—HuL-2*

Sunny bank; or, I saw three ships. See Carol ("As I sat on a sunny bank")

"Sunny Martinmas, you come." See Saint Martin

"A sunny shaft did I behold." See Song

Sunrise. Charles Erskine Scott Wood. *UnG*

Sunrise and sunset. See "I'll tell you how the sun rose"

"The sunrise tints the dew." See Crocuses

"The sun's a bright-haired shepherd boy." See Silver sheep

"The sun's in the window, and who do you guess." See It's time to get up

The sun's travels. Robert Louis Stevenson. *FeF*

"The sun's warm tongue is licking at." See In May

"The sun's way." See The sun path

"Sunset and evening star." See Crossing the bar

"Sunshine and weiners and pickles and ham." See Picnics

"Sunshine, forever." See Indian songs— Prayer to the sun god

"A sunshiny shower." Mother Goose. *DeMg —LiL—OpO*

Signs, seasons, and sense. *UnG*

"Superintindint was Flannigan." See Finnigin to Flannigan

Superlative dance and song. Francis Beaumont. *PlU*

    Song for a dance. *SmLg*

Supernatural. See Ghosts; Miracles; Witchcraft

Superstitions

    Company. Unknown. *WiRm*

    "The fair maid who, the first of May." Mother Goose. *DeMg*

    Finger nails. Mother Goose. *OpO*

    "Friday night's dream." Mother Goose. *DeMg—WiRm*

    "Go to bed first." Mother Goose. *OpO*

    Lonesome water. R. Helton. *CoPm—McW*

    "Monday's child is fair of face." Mother Goose. *BrBc—DeMg—HuSv—JoAc—LiL —SmLg*

        Birthdays. *OpO—ReG*

        Days of birth. *NaM*

        Signs, seasons, and sense. *UnG*

    "The robin of the red breast." Unknown. *CoPm*

        Bad luck. *DeT*

    Saint Swithin's wish. E. Farjeon. *FaCb— FaN*

    The sea wolf. V. McDougal. *FeF*

    "See a pin and pick it up." Mother Goose. *DeMg—JoAc—LiL*

        Signs, seasons, and sense. *UnG*

    "Seventh son of seventh son." E. Farjeon. *FaCb*

        Seventh son. *FaN*

"Sweet reader, whom I've never seen." See Apostrophic notes from the new-world physics

The sweet, red rose. Mary Mapes Dodge. *BrBc*

Sweet Robin Herrick. Eleanor Farjeon. *FaCb—FaN*

"Sweet sounds, oh, beautiful music, do not cease." See On hearing a symphony of Beethoven

Sweet story of old. Jemima Thompson Luke. *DoP*

Sweet was the song. Unknown. *CoPs*

"Sweet was the song the Virgin sung." See Sweet was the song

"Sweet william, silverweed, sally-my-handsome." See A spell for sleeping

Sweet William's ghost. Unknown. *MaB*

"Sweeten these bitter wild crabapples." See Crabapples

"Sweetest of sweets, I thank you: when displeasure." See Church-musick

"Sweetly sweetly singing." See Morning magic

The sweetness of nature. Unknown, tr. fr. the Irish by Frank O'Connor. *GrCc*

Swenson, May
The cloud-mobile. *UnG*
"Was worm." *UnG*

Swett, Susan Hartley
It is July. *HaY*

Swift, Jonathan
Baucis and Philemon. *CoSp*
The vowels. *DeT*

"Swift and busy, brash and bold." See Jack Frost

"Swift things are beautiful." Elizabeth Jane Coatsworth. *ArTp—HuL-2—HuSv*

"Swiftly the years, beyond recall." See New corn

"Swiftly walk o'er the western wave." See To night

Swimmers. Louis Untermeyer. *JoAc* (sel.)

Swimming. See also Bathing
"Come down to the water." E. Farjeon. *FaCb*
"A daring young lady of Guam." Unknown Limericks since Lear. *UnG*
"Little Jimmy Jimsonweed." Unknown. *WoF*
"Mother, may I go out to swim." Mother Goose. *FeF*
Caution. *OpO*
"Oh, Aunt Jenny." Unknown. *WiRm*
Our silly little sister. D. Aldis. *AlA—CoH—FeF—NaE*
Swimmers. L. Untermeyer. *JoAc* (sel.)
Swimming. C. Scollard. *FeF*

Swimming. Clinton Scollard. *FeF*

Swinburne, Algernon Charles
Atalanta in Calydon, sel.
Chorus from Atalanta in Calydon. *HaP—NaE*
August. *HoW*
A baby's feet. See Étude réaliste
A child's laughter. *BrBc*
Chorus from Atalanta in Calydon. See Atalanta in Calydon

Étude réaliste, sel.
A baby's feet. *FeF*
"Watchman, what of the night." *HoW*
White butterflies. *FeF*

The swing ("How do you like to go up in a swing") Robert Louis Stevenson. *ArTp—HuL-1—HuSv—JoAc—PeF*

The swing ("Now so high") Mary I. Osborn. *HuL-1*

Swing low, sweet chariot. Unknown. *FeF—SmLg*

"Swing out, oh bells." See The bells of peace

Swing song ("Here I go up in my swing") A. A. Milne. *MiWc*

A swing song ("Swing, swing") William Allingham. *FeF—HuL-1—NaM—PeF*

"Swing, swing." See A swing song

"Swing yo' lady roun' an' roun', do de bes' you know." See A frolic

Swinging
Back-yard swing. M. C. Livingston. *LiW*
"The big swing-tree is green again." M. J. Carr. *BrS*
The fairy swing. I. O. Eastwick. *EaI*
The other child. E. Farjeon. *FaCb*
Stopping the swing. Mother Goose. *OpO*
The swing ("How do you like to go up in a swing") R. L. Stevenson. *ArTp—HuL-1—HuSv—JoAc—PeF*
The swing ("Now so high") M. I. Osborn. *HuL-1*
Swing song ("Here I go up in my swing") A. A. Milne. *MiWc*
A swing song ("Swing, swing") W. Allingham. *FeF—HuL-1—NaM—PeF*
Swinging. Mother Goose. *OpO*

Swinging. Mother Goose. *OpO*

"The swinging mill bell changed its rate." See A lone striker

Swithin, Saint (about)
"St Swithin's day, if thou dost rain." Mother Goose. *DeMg—LiL*
Signs, seasons, and sense. *UnG*
Saint Swithin's wish. E. Farjeon. *FaCb—FaN*

Swords
An old song. Yehoash. *PaS*
Opportunity. E. R. Sill. *BrR-6—ThP—UnG*

Sycamore, William (about)
The ballad of William Sycamore. S. V. Benét. *JoAc*

The sycophantic fox and the gullible raven. Guy Wetmore Carryl. *CoH*

Sylvester. John Ciardi. *CiM*

"Sylvester wrote to Mary Lou." See Sylvester

Sylvie and Bruno, sels. Lewis Carroll
The gardener's song. *GrCc—JoAc—NaE*
He thought he saw. *CoH—HuL-2*
The mad gardener's song. *HoW*
A strange wild song. *HuSv*
The melancholy pig. *FeF*
A pig-tale. *HoW*

"A symbol from the first, of mastery." See The staff of Aesculapius

Symonds, John Addington
In February. *HaY*
The vow to Cupid. tr. *PaS*

Symons, Arthur
Song of autumn. tr. *PaS*

Sympathy. See also Consolation; Friendship; Kindness; Love
An angel singing. W. Blake. *DoP*
The dove and the ant. J. De La Fontaine. *JoAc*
The quality of mercy. From The merchant of Venice. W. Shakespeare. *BrL-8—ThP*
"There's snow on the fields." C. G. Rossetti. *DeT*

Symphony: First movement. John Hall Wheelock. *PlU*

Synge, John M. (Millington)
In Glencullen. *ReT*

Syrkin, Marie
An old song. tr. *PaS*

T

T., C. W.
Valentine. *HaY*

T is for talisman. Eleanor Farjeon. *FaCb*

Tabb, Father. See Tabb, John Banister

Tabb, John Banister (Father Tabb)
A child's prayer. *FeF*
Fern song. *DoP*
A lily of the field. *DoP*
My secret. *McW*

The **table** and the chair. Edward Lear. *HuSv—JoAc—UnG*

A **table** richly spread. John Milton. *SmLg*

"A **table** richly spread, in regal mode." See A table richly spread

Tables
The table and the chair. E. Lear. *HuSv—JoAc—UnG*
"Tables are round." Unknown. *MoY*

Tadema, Laurence Alma. See Alma-Tadema, Laurence

"**Tae** titly." Mother Goose. *OpO*

"**Taffy,** the topaz-coloured cat." See In honor of Taffy Topaz

"**Taffy** was a Welshman." Mother Goose. *DeMg—OpO*

"**Taffy** was born." See Baby Taffy

Taggard, Genevieve
Millions of strawberries. *ArTp—FeF—NaM —UnG*

Tagore, Rabindranath
The bird. *PaS*
Paper boats. *FeF*
A song-offering. *PaS*
Vocation. *FeF*

A **tail** to wag. Dorothy Aldis. *AlA*

The **tailor.** Thomas Lovell Beddoes. *HoW*

The **tailor** and the crow. See "A carrion crow sat on an oak"

"The **tailor** of Bicester." Mother Goose. *OpO*

Tailors
"A carrion crow sat on an oak." Mother Goose. *DeMg—JoAc—LiL*
The carrion crow. *OpO*
The tailor and the crow. *ReG*

"**Four** and twenty tailors." Mother Goose. *DeMg—JoAc*
"Four and twenty tailors went to kill a snail." *LiL*
Snail hunters. *OpO*
The old tailor. W. De La Mare. *BrR-5*
Sailor and tailor. Unknown. *DeT*
The tailor. T. L. Beddoes. *HoW*
"The tailor of Bicester." Mother Goose. *OpO*
Toad the tailor. N. E. Hussey. *HuL-1*

Tails
In the fashion. A. A. Milne. *MiWc*
Ode to the pig: His tail. W. R. Brooks. *LoL*
The pig's tail. N. Ault. *HuL-2*
"The raccoon's tail has rings all round." Unknown. *WoF*
A tail to wag. D. Aldis. *AlA*
Tails ("De coon's got a long ringed bushy tail") Unknown. *CoH*
Tails ("A dog's tail") M. C. Livingston. *LiW*
Tails ("The kangaroo has a heavy tail") R. B. Bennett. *BrR-4*
The tale of a dog. J. H. Lambert, Jr. *CoI*

Tails ("De coon's got a long ringed bushy tail") Unknown. *CoH*

Tails ("A dog's tail") Myra Cohn Livingston. *LiW*

Tails ("The kangaroo has a heavy tail") Rowena Bastin Bennett. *BrR-4*

"**Take** him, earth, for cherishing." See Cathemerinon

Take sky. David McCord. *McT*

"**Take** the local." Unknown. *MoY*

"**Take** the word pluck." Unknown. *MoY*

"**Take** this remark from Richard, poor and lame." See Poor Richard's wisdom

"**Take** this talisman of me." See T is for talisman

Taking off. Mary McB. Green. *ArTp—HuL-1*
The airplane. *McAw*

Talbot, Ethel
Crab-apple. *ArTp—BrBc*

A **tale.** Mother Goose. *OpO*

The **tale** of a dog. James H. Lambert, Jr. *CoI*

The **tale** of a tart. Frederic E. Weatherly. *HuL-1*

The **tale** of Custard the dragon. Ogden Nash. *FeF—UnG*

Talents
"The mountain and the squirrel." R. W. Emerson. *FeF—UnG*
Fable. *BrR-4*
Talents differ. L. E. Richards. *ArTp—HuL-1*

Talents differ. Laura E. Richards. *ArTp—HuL-1*

Tales of a wayside inn, sel. Henry Wadsworth Longfellow
Paul Revere's ride. *ArTp—BrL-7—CoSp—FeF—HuSv—JoAc—SmLg—UnG*

The **tales** the barbers tell. Morris Bishop. *CoH*

"The **talking** oak." See Be different to trees

"**Tall** ears." See What is it

"**Tall** people, short people." See People

"The tall pines pine." See The cow slips away

"Tall timber stood here once." See Improved farm land

Taller and older. Dorothy Aldis. *AlHd*

The taming of the shrew, sel. William Shakespeare
  "Why, then thou canst not break her to the lute"
    The taming of the shrew. *PlU*

Tamlane. Unknown. *MaB*

Tammy Tyrie. Mother Goose. *OpO*

T'ao Ch'ien
  I built my hut. *PaS*
  "A long time ago." *SmLg*
  New corn. *PaS*
  Reading the book of hills and seas. *PaS*

Tapestry trees. William Morris. *FeF*

Tapir. William Jay Smith. *SmB*

Tapirs
  Tapir. W. J. Smith. *SmB*

Tarantella. Hilaire Belloc. *NaM—SmLg*

The tardy playmate. Fannie R. Buchanan. *DoP*

Tarlingwell. James Reeves. *ReR*

Tartary. Walter De La Mare. *HuL-2—UnG*

Taste
  The alarmed skipper. J. T. Fields. *UnG*
  The worm. R. Bergengren. *BrS—FeF*

A tasty cook. See The Canterbury tales

Tate, Nahum
  "While shepherds watched their flocks by night." *JoAc*

"Tattoo was the mother of Pinkle Purr." See Pinkle Purr

Tatum, Edith
  Harbingers. *BrR-6*

Tatyanicheva, Lyudmila
  July. *PaS*

Taunts. See Teasing

Taurus. Eleanor Farjeon. *FaCb—FaN*

Taverns. See Inns and taverns

A tawnymoor. Mother Goose. *OpO*

Taxicabs
  Taxis. R. Field. *ArTp—FeF—HuL-2—JoAc*

Taxis. Rachel Field. *ArTp—FeF—HuL-2—JoAc*

The Tay bridge disaster. William McGonagall. *NaE*

Taylor, Ann (Ann Gilbert)
  Autumn, sel.
    The sound of a gun. *DeT*
  Pretty cow. *HuSv*
  The sound of a gun. See Autumn
  A true story. *DeT*
  —and Taylor, Jane
    An evening hymn for a little family. *DoP*

Taylor, Bayard
  A night with a wolf. *UnG*
  The three songs. *CoSp*

Taylor, Bert Leston (B. L. T., pseud)
  The dinosaur. *PlU*

Taylor, Jane
  God is so good. *DoP*
  "I like little pussy." See "I love little pussy"

"I love little pussy." *ArTp—BrL-k—DeMg—FeF--LiL*
  "I like little pussy." *JoAc*
  Kindness. *OpO*
  Little pussy. *UnG*
Kindness. See "I love little pussy"
Little pussy. See "I love little pussy"
Little star. See The star
The pigs. *DeT*
The star. *ArTp—FeF—OpO*
  Little star. *HuSv*
  "Twinkle, twinkle, little star." *BrL-k*
"Twinkle, twinkle, little star." See The star
—See also Taylor, Ann, jt. auth.

Taylor, Lillian F.
  Washing day. *HuL-1*

Taylor, Millicent
  On receiving a camp catalog. *BrR-6*

Tea
  Before tea. A. A. Milne. *MiWc*
  Jonathan Bing's tea. B. C. Brown. *McW*
  "Polly put the kettle on." Mother Goose. *DeMg—LiL*
    Tea-time. *OpO*
  The unfortunate giraffe. O. Herford. *CoH*

Tea parties
  The cats' tea-party. F. E. Weatherly. *ArTp—CoI*

  "In the pleasant green garden." K. Greenaway. *ArTp*

  Polite tea party. D. Aldis. *AlA*

  The tea party ("I had a new tea set") M. Chute. *ChA*

  Tea party ("Mister Beedle Baddlebug") H. Behn. *BeW*

The tea party ("I had a new tea set") Marchette Chute. *ChA*

Tea party ("Mister Beedle Baddlebug") Harry Behn. *BeW*

Tea-time. See "Polly put the kettle on"

"Teach me, Father, how to go." See A prayer

"Teach me, my God and King." See The elixir

Teachers and teaching. See also School
  America was schoolmasters. R. P. T. Coffin. *McW*
  "Come hither, little puppy dog." Mother Goose. *DeMg*
  Dr Brown. Unknown. *WoJ*
  "Doctor Faustus was a good man." Mother Goose. *DeMg—LiL*
    Doctor Foster. *OpO*
  "God made the bees (the bees made)." Unknown. *MoY*
  Here comes the teacher. Unknown. *WoJ*
  I wish. N. B. Turner. *BrS*
  The Irish schoolmaster. J. A. Sidney. *CoH*
  "Jay-bird, jay-bird, settin' on a rail." Unknown
    American Father Gander. *UnG*
  The purist. O. Nash. *CoH—NaM*
  The schoolmaster. From Snow-bound. J. G. Whittier. *UnG*
  The snuff-boxes. Unknown. *CoSp*
  "Teachers are religious souls." Unknown. *MoY*

"**Tell** me, Pyrrha, what fine youth." See Another to the same

"**Tell** me quick." Unknown. *MoY*

"**Tell** me, shepherd, tell me, pray." See Country gods

"**Tell** me, tell me everything." See Curiosity

"**Tell** me the reason I must wear." See Tell me

"**Tell** me where is fancy bred." See The merchant of Venice—Fancy

"**Tell**-tale-tit." Mother Goose. *DeMg*

The **tempest**, sels. William Shakespeare
"Be not afeard. The isle is full of noises" The tempest. *PlU*
"Come unto these yellow sands." *DeT*
Ariel's song. *ReT—SmLg*
"Full fathom five thy father lies." *SmLg*
Ariel's dirge. *NaE—ReT*
"Where should this music be? I' the air, or the earth" The tempest. *PlU*
"Where the bee sucks, there suck I." *ArTp*
Where the bee sucks. *JoAc—ReT*

The **tempest** ("In fury and terror") Elizabeth Jane Coatsworth. *HuL-2*

"The **temple** is clean." See A song of always

Ten brothers. Unknown, tr. fr. the Yiddish by Louis Untermeyer. *UnMc*

Ten little Indian boys. M. M. Hutchinson. *HuL-1*

Ten little nigger boys. Mother Goose. *OpO*

"**Ten** little nigger boys went out to dine." See Ten little nigger boys

"**Ten** little toes, ten little toes." See The ideal age for a man

Ten o'clock scholar. See "A diller, a dollar, a ten o'clock scholar"

"**Ten** snowy white pigeons are standing in line." See The pigeons

"**Ten** South Sea Island boys." See Fun with fishing

"**Ten** tired tortoises." See Ten to one

Ten to one. Ivy O. Eastwick. *EaI*

Tennant, E. Wyndham
"I saw green banks of daffodil." *ArTp*

Tennyson, Alfred, Lord
"And, star and system rolling past." See In memoriam
Blow, bugle, blow. See The princess—Bugle song
"Break, break, break." *HaP*
The brook. *DeT—FeF*
Song of the brook. *JoAc*
Bugle song. See The princess
The charge of the Light Brigade. *FeF—JoAc—UnMc*
A cradle song. See Sweet and low
Crossing the bar. *BrL-8—ThP*
Dainty little maiden. *HuL-2*
"Dark house, by which once more I stand." See In memoriam
The death of the old year. *CoPs* (sel.)
The dying swan. *HoW*
The eagle. *ArTp—FeF—HoW—ReT—SmLg—ThP—UnG*
Echo song. See The princess—Bugle song
"Flower in the crannied wall." *DoP—FeF—ThP*

"I trust I have not wasted breath." See In memoriam
In memoriam, sels.
"And, star and system rolling past" In memoriam. *PlI*
"Dark house, by which once more I stand" From In memoriam. *HaP*
"I trust I have not wasted breath" In memoriam. *PlI*
Ring out, wild bells. *ArTp—BrL-8—FeF—HoW*
The kraken. *HoW*
Lady Clare. *CoSp—FeF—HuSv—UnG*
The lady of Shalott. *HoW—UnMc*
Mariana. *HoW*
The mermaid. *CoPm—FeF—UnG*
The merman. *CoPm—FeF—UnG*
The oak. *FcF*
The owl. *NaM—SmLg—UnG*
Song: The owl. *FeF—ReT*
The white owl. *DeT*
The princess, sels.
Bugle song. *FeF—HuSv*
Blow, bugle, blow. *HoW—PlU*
Echo song. *DeT*
Song. *ReT*
"The splendor falls on castle walls." *ArTp*
The splendour falls. *SmLg*
Tears, idle tears. *HaP*
"This world was once a fluid haze of light" The princess. *PlI*
The Revenge. *UnMc*
Ring out, wild bells. See In memoriam
Song. *SmLg*
Song of the brook. See The brook
Song: The owl. See The owl
"The splendor falls on castle walls." See The princess—Bugle song
The splendour falls. See The princess—Bugle song
Spring. *DeT*
Sweet and low. *FeF—HuL-2—HuSv—JoAc—UnG*
A cradle song. *DeT*
Song. *ReT*
Tears, idle tears. See The princess
"This world was once a fluid haze of light." See The princess
The throstle. *CoPs—FeF—HuL-2—McW*
To Christopher North. *NaE*
Ulysses. *HaP*
"What does little birdie say." *BrL-k—HuL-1*
The white owl. See The owl

"**Terence** McDiddler." Mother Goose. *OpO*

Teresa of Avila, Saint
St Teresa's book-mark. *PaS*

The **term**. William Carlos Williams. *ReT*

Termites
Metropolitan nightmare. S. V. Benét. *PlI*

A **ternarie** of littles, upon a pipkin of jelly sent to a lady. Robert Herrick. *SmLg*

Terrapins. See Turtles

A **terrible** infant. Frederick Locker-Lampson. *CoH*

Texas
Little boys of Texas. R. P. T. Coffin. *McW*
Texas trains and trails. M. Austin. *ArTp*

Texas trains and trails. Mary Austin. *ArTp*

Thackeray, William Makepeace
Fairy days. *UnG*
Little Billee. *DeT—SmLg*
Pocahontas. *FeF—UnG*
A tragic story. tr. *BrL-7—CoH—DeT—FeF—NaM—UnG*
Twenty-one. *DeT*

"**Thank** you for the earth so sweet." Unknown. *AnI*
A child's grace. *BrL-k—HuL-1*

"**Thank** you for the world so sweet." See "Thank you for the earth so sweet"

"**Thank** you, pretty cow, that made." See Pretty cow

"**Thank** you very much indeed." See Thanks

Thankfulness. See also Thanksgiving day
Belisarius. H. W. Longfellow. *HoW*
"Blow, blow, thou winter wind." From As you like it. W. Shakespeare. *HoW—McW*
Blow, blow. *DeT*
For joy. F. E. Coates. *BrL-7*
God giveth all things. Unknown. *DoP*
God's gift. Unknown. *DoP*
"I thank you, God." I. Orleans. *DoP—HuL-1*
Lovely things. H. M. Sarson. *HuL-2*
Psalm C. From Psalms, Bible, Old Testament
Be thankful unto Him. *FeF*
"Make a joyful noise unto the Lord, all ye lands." *ArTp*
A psalm of praise. *BrS*
Psalm 100. *PlU*
Thanksgiving. *HuSv*
Psalm CXLVII. From Psalms, Bible, Old Testament
"Praise ye the Lord (for it is)." *ArTp*
Who maketh the grass to grow. *FeF*
"Thank you for the earth so sweet." Unknown. *AnI*
A child's grace. *BrL-k—HuL-1*
Thanks. N. Gale. *DoP—UnG*
Thanksgiving. L. Driscoll. *HaY*
Thanksgiving for the earth. E. Goudge. *DoP—HaY*
A thanksgiving to God for his house. R. Herrick. *DeT*
Thanksgivings for the beauty of His providence. T. Traherne. *SmLg*
This happy day. H. Behn. *ArTp—HuL-1*
We thank Thee. Unknown. *BrR-6—FeF*

Thanks. Norman Gale. *DoP—UnG*

Thanksgiving ("I thank you, God") Louise Driscoll. *HaY*

Thanksgiving ("I'm glad that I was good today") Marchette Chute. *ChA*

Thanksgiving ("Make a joyful noise unto the Lord, all ye lands") See Psalms—Psalm C

Thanksgiving day. See also Thankfulness
The first Thanksgiving. N. B. Turner. *HaY*
First Thanksgiving of all. N. B. Turner. *BrR-6—BrS—FeF*
The happy thank-you day. Unknown. *BrR-3*
"If I were a pilgrim child." R. B. Bennett. *HaY*
The pilgrims came. A. Wynne. *McAw*
The pumpkin. J. G. Whittier. *CoPs*
Thanksgiving. M. Chute. *ChA*

Thanksgiving day. L. M. Child. *BrS—FeF—HuSv—UnG*
Thanksgiving magic. R. B. Bennett. *ArTp—BrS*
Thanksgiving wishes. A. Guiterman. *CoPs*
The turkey's opinion. A. M. Pratt. *BrR-4*
Thanksgiving day. Lydia Maria Child. *BrS—FeF—HuSv—UnG*
"Thanksgiving day I like to see." See Thanksgiving magic
Thanksgiving for the body. Thomas Traherne. *PlI*
Thanksgiving for the earth. Elizabeth Goudge. *DoP—HaY*
Thanksgiving magic. Rowena Bastin Bennett. *ArTp—BrS*
A thanksgiving to God for his house. Robert Herrick. *DeT*
Thanksgiving wishes. Arthur Guiterman. *CoPs*
Thanksgivings for the beauty of His providence. Thomas Traherne. *SmLg*
That cat. Ben King. *CoH*
That duck. Brittan MacI. *McAw*
"That first Christmas night of all." See First Christmas night of all
"That October morning." See A memory
"That time of year thou mayst in me behold." See Sonnets
"That vengence I ask and cry." See Vengence on cats
That was the one. Dorothy Aldis. *AlA*
"That was the top of the walk, when he said." See The gypsy
That wind. Emily Brontë. *DeT*
"That wind, I used to hear it swelling." See That wind
"A thatcher of Thatchwood went to Thatchet a-thatching." Mother Goose. *DeMg—OpO*
That'll be all right you'll find. L. De Giberne Sieveking. *CoH*
That's July. Mary Frances Butts. *HaY*
That's June. Mary Frances Butts. *HaY*
"That's my last duchess painted on the wall." See My last duchess
Thaw. Eunice Tietjens. *McAw*

Thaxter, Celia (Leighton)
August. *FeF—HaY*
Little Gustava. *FeF*
March. *UnG*
On Easter day. *FeF—HaY*
The sandpiper. *FeF—JoAc*

Thayer, Ernest Lawrence
Casey at the bat. *CoSp—FeF—UnMc*

Thayer, Mary Dixon
How nice. *DoP*

Theaters. See also Actors and acting
At the theater. R. Field. *FeF*

"**Their** majesties and I sat where two streams." See The house beyond the meadow—First enchantment

Theme in yellow. Carl Sandburg. *ArTp—HaY—HuSv*

Then ("Twenty, forty, sixty, eighty") Walter De La Mare. *HuL-2—ReG*

Then ("When you can catch") Dorothy Aldis. *BrBc—HuL-1*

Then as now. Walter De La Mare. *McW*

"Then as now; and now as then." See Then as now

"Then came old January, wrapped well." See The faerie queene—Old January

"Then comes the winter, like a hale old man." See Winter

Then I met another man I could not see. John Ciardi. *CiI*

"Then sing, ye birds, sing, sing a joyous song." See The gladness of the May

"Then, when I'd seen them leave the bay." See And back

"Theophilus Thistle, the successful thistle sifter." Mother Goose. *DeMg*

Theophilus Thistledown. *LoL*

"Theophilus Thistledown, the successful thistle sifter." *OpO*

Theophilus Thistledown. See "Theophilus Thistle, the successful thistle sifter"

"Theophilus Thistledown, the successful thistle sifter." See "Theophilus Thistle, the successful thistle sifter"

"Ther' ain't no use in all this strife." See An easy-goin' feller

There. Rodney Bennett. *HuL-1*

"There also was a nun, a prioress." See The Canterbury tales—A prioress

"There are big waves and little waves." See Big waves and little waves

"There are fairies at the bottom of our garden." See Fairies

"There are forked branches of trees." See Little sketch

"There are four vibrators, the world's ex-actest clocks." See Four quartz crystal clocks

"There are golden ships." Unknown. *MoY*

"There are lions and roaring tigers, and enormous camels and things." See At the zoo

"There are lots and lots of people who are always asking things." See The friend

"There are lots of queer things that dis-coverers do." See Christopher Columbus

"There are loyal hearts, there are spirits brave." See Life's mirror

"There are mushrooms in the paddock." See The wagon in the barn

"There are no bells in all the world." See Sleigh bells at night

"There are not many blossoms yet." See First signs

"There are pumpkins in the field." See Fall days

"There are seven ages of woman." Unknown. *MoY*

"There are seven men in Moy castle." See Moy castle

There are so many ways of going places. Leslie Thompson. *BrR-3—FeF*

"There are strange things done in the mid-night sun." See The cremation of Sam McGee

"There are things." See Feet

"There are three words, the sweetest words." See Three words

"There are trails that a lad may follow." See Silver ships

"There are tulips in the garden." Unknown. *MoY*

"There are twelve months in all the year." See Robin Hood rescuing the widow's three sons

"There are twelve months throughout the year." See September

"There are white moon daisies in the mist of the meadow." See Summer song

"There are words like freedom." See Refu-gee in America

"There be four things which are little upon the earth." See Proverbs, Bible, Old Testament—Four things

"There be none of beauty's daughters." See Stanzas for music—Thy sweet voice

"There be two men of all mankind." See Two men

"There breaks on me, burning upon me." See Song to Steingerd

"There calleth me ever a marvelous horn." See Home-sickness

"There came a ghost to Margret's door." See Sweet William's ghost

"There came a giant to my door." See The giant

"There came a knight from out the west." See Clootie

"There came one who spoke of the shame of Jerusalem." See The rock—Choruses from The rock

"There fared a mother driven forth." See The house of Christmas

"There goes the Wapiti." See The Wapiti

"There is a blue star, Janet." See Baby toes

"There is a charming land." Adam Oehlen-schlager, tr. fr. the Danish by Robert Hillyer. *FeF*

"There is a garden in her face." Thomas Campion. *ReT*

"There is a lady who plays a piano." See The piano

"There is a little man all dressed in gray." See The merry man of Paris

"There is a memory stays upon old ships." See Old ships

"There is a moment country children know." See Village before sunset

"There is a moment in midsummer when the earth." See Midsummer pause

"There is a myth, a tale men tell." See The pearl

"There is a pale blue flower." Unknown. *MoY*

"There is a singer everyone has heard." See The oven bird

"There is a stream that flowed before the first beginning." See Water

"There is a warm and cozy whiff." See Ironing day

"There is a way the moon looks into the timber at night." See Timber moon

"There is a young lady, whose nose." Ed-ward Lear

Limericks. *JoAc*

"There is an eagle screaming from a roof." See The Painted desert—In Walpi

"There is an inn, a merry old inn." See The hobbit

"There is but one May in the year." Christina Georgina Rossetti. *ArTp—HuL-2*

"There is in my old picture-book." See Knights and ladies

"There is music in the jungle on the hills of Malabar." See Jungle night club

"There is no frigate like a book." Emily Dickinson. *BrS—HaY*
   A book. *FeF*

"There is one story and one story only." See To Juan at the winter solstice

"There is only one horse on the earth." See Prologue to The family of man—Names

"There is so much good in the worst of us." See Charity

"There is something in the autumn that is native to my blood." See A vagabond song

"There is stone in me that knows stone." See Rock

"There is wind where the rose was." See Autumn

"There isn't a prettier sight, I think." See Bare-back rider

There isn't time. Eleanor Farjeon. *FeF—HuL-2*

"There isn't time, there isn't time." See There isn't time

There lived a king. See The gondoliers

"There lived a king, as I've been told." See The gondoliers—There lived a king

"There lived a king into the east." See King Orpheo

"There lived a sage in days of yore." See A tragic story

"There lived a wife at Usher's well." See The wife of Usher's well

"There lived an old man in the kingdom of Tess." See The new vestments

"There lived years ago the beautiful Kung-sun." See A song of dagger-dancing

"There lives an old man at the top of the street." See The alchemist

"There met two mice at Scarborough." See The two mice

"There must be fairy miners." See Buttercups

"There must be magic." See Otherwise

"There once was a barber of Kew." See The barber of Kew

"There once was a dormouse who lived in a bed." See The dormouse and the doctor

"There once was a fat little pig named Alice." See Alice

"There once was a frog." See A legend of Lake Okeefinokee

"There once was a giant who needed new shoes." See The giant's shoes

"There once was a girl of New York." See The girl of New York

"There once was a green." See The frog on the log

"There once was a hunter from Littletown." See There was a hunter from Littletown

"There once was a man of Calcutta." Unknown. *LoL*

"There once was a monarch, a pompous old Persian." See The king and the clown

"There once was a mouse who lived on a hill." See The mouse who lived on a hill

There once was a puffin. Florence Page Jaques. *ArTp—HuL-2*

"There once was a witch of Willowby wood." See The witch of Willowby wood

There once was an owl. John Ciardi. *CiR*

"There once was an owl perched on a shed." See There once was an owl

"There once were two cats of Kilkenny." Mother Goose. *DeMg*
   The cats of Kilkenny. *UnG*
   The Kilkenny cats. *CoH—LoL*

"There overtook me and drew me in." See The gum-gatherer

"There piped a piper in the wood." See The magic piper

"There wanst was two cats at Kilkenny." See "There once were two cats of Kilkenny"

"There was a bee." Mother Goose. *DeMg*

"There was a bonny blade." See The dumb wife cured

There was a boy. See The prelude

"There was a Boy bedden in bracken." See Carol

"There was a boy just one year old." See Someone

"There was a boy of other days." See Lincoln

"There was a boy whose name was Jim." See Jim, who ran away from his nurse

"There was a boy; ye knew him well, ye cliffs." See The prelude—There was a boy

"There was a child, as I have been told." See The comical girl

There was a child went forth. Walt Whitman. *BrBc—UnG*

"There was a child went forth every day." See There was a child went forth

"There was a crooked man." Mother Goose. *BrL-k—ReG*
   The crooked man. *OpO*
   "There was a crooked man, and he went a crooked mile." *DeMg—HuSv—JoAc—LiL*

"There was a crooked man, and he went a crooked mile." See "There was a crooked man"

"There was a faith-healer of Deal." Unknown
   Limericks since Lear. *UnG*

"There was a fat man of Bombay." Mother Goose. *DeMg*

"There was a gentle hostler." See Gates and doors

"There was a giant in times of old." See The Dorchester giant

"There was a girl from Havana." Unknown. *MoY*

"There was a girl in our town." Mother Goose. *DeMg—OpO*

There was a hunter from Littletown. John Ciardi. *CiM*

"There was a jolly miller." See Love in a village

"There was a jolly miller once." See Love in a village—"There was a jolly miller"

"There was a jolly miller once lived on the river Dee." See Love in a village—"There was a jolly miller"

"There was a king, and he had three daughters." Mother Goose. *OpO*

"There was a king met a king." Mother Goose. *OpO*

"There was a knight, a most distinguished man." See The Canterbury tales—A knight

There was a lady. See "There was a lady loved a swine"

"There was a lady fair and gay." See The dream

"There was a lady loved a swine." Mother Goose. *DeMg*
The lady in love. *OpO*
There was a lady. *DeT*

"There was a little boy and a little girl." Mother Goose. *DeMg—OpO*

"There was a little boy went into a barn." See The scaredy

"There was a little, elvish man." See The man who hid his own front door

There was a little girl. See "There was a little girl, and she had a little curl"

"There was a little girl, and she had a little curl." Mother Goose. *AnI—DeMg*
Jemima. *SmLg—UnG*
The little girl. *OpO*
There was a little girl. *NaE*

"There was a little girl, and she wore a little curl." See "There was a little girl, and she had a little curl"

"There was a little girl, who had a little curl." See "There was a little girl, and she had a little curl"

"There was a little green house." Unknown Five very old riddles. *DeT*

"There was a little guinea-pig." Mother Goose. *DeMg*
The guinea-pig. *LoL—OpO—UnG*

"There was a little island." See The emperors of Rome

"There was a little maid, and she was afraid." See A little maid

"There was a little man." See "There was a little man, and he had a little gun"

"There was a little man, and he had a little gun." Mother Goose. *DeMg—JoAc*
Sam, the sportsman. *OpO*
"There was a little man." *HuL-1—LiL*

"There was a little man (and he wooed)." See The little man and the little maid

"There was a little one-eyed gunner." See One-eyed gunner

"There was a little pickle and he hadn't any name." See The highlander's song

"There was a little woman." See "There was an old woman, as I've heard tell"

"There was a little turtle." See The little turtle

"There was a maid, and a well-favoured maid." See Katherine Johnstone

"There was a man." See The sad goat

"There was a man and he had nought." Mother Goose. *DeMg*
The man with nought. *OpO*
There was a man. *DeT*

"There was a man, and he lived in England." See The Turkish lady

"There was a man and his name was Dob." Mother Goose. *DeMg*
Dob and Mob. *OpO*

"There was a man, he went mad." See The man who jumped

"There was a man in a lobster-boat." See Lobster music

"There was a man in another town." See Willy Wood

"There was a man in our town." Mother Goose. *DeMg*

"There was a man in Westmoreland." See Johnny Armstrong

"There was a man lived in the moon." See Aiken Drum

"There was a man named Mingram Mo." See Mingram Mo

"There was a man of double deed." Mother Goose. *OpO*

"There was a man of our town." Unknown. *TaD*

"There was a man of Thessaly." Mother Goose. *LiL*
Alexander's song. *JoAc*
Man of Thessaly. *OpO*

"There was a man of Uriconium." See Uriconium

"There was a man out your way." See A sea song

"There was a man rode through our town." Mother Goose. *OpO*

"There was a man who had a clock." See The sad tale of Mr Mears

"There was a man who had no eyes." Mother Goose. *OpO*

"There was a monk, a leader of the fashions." See The Canterbury tales—A sporting monk

There was a monkey. See "There was a monkey climbed up a tree"

"There was a monkey climbed up a tree." Mother Goose. *DeMg*
There was a monkey. *DeT—OpO*

"There was a naughty boy." John Keats. *CoH—DeMg—NaM—SmLg*
The naughty boy. *HuL-2—ReG*

"There was a pig that sat alone." See Sylvie and Bruno—The melancholy pig

"There was a piper had a cow." Mother Goose. *DeMg*
The piper. *OpO*

"There was a Presbyterian cat." Unknown. *SmLg*

"There was a pretty dandelion." See The dandelion

"There was a pussy in the stable." See In the stable

"There was a rat, for want of stairs." Mother Goose. *DeMg*
A rat. *OpO*

"There was a road ran past our house." See The unexplorer

"There was a ship of Rio." See The ship of Rio

"There was a ship sailed from the North Countree." See The Golden Vanity

"There was a snake that dwelt in Skye." See The fastidious serpent

"There was a thick-headed marine." Unknown
Limericks since Lear. *UnG*

"There was a thing a full month old." Mother Goose. *OpO*

"There was a time before our time." See Clipper ships and captains

"There was a tree stood in the ground." See The green grass growing all around

"There was a wee bit mousikie." Unknown. *NaM*

There was an old man ("There was an old man, an old, old, old") John Ciardi. *CiM*

"There was an old man, an old, old, old." See There was an old man

"There was an old man (and he had a calf)." Mother Goose. *DeMg—JoAc*
And that's all. *DeT—OpO*

"There was an old man and he lived in a wood." See Father Grumble

"There was a wee bit wifie." See A Scottish shoe

"There was a young girl of Asturias." Unknown
Limericks since Lear. *UnG*

"There was a young lady from Woosester." Unknown
Limericks since Lear. *UnG*

"There was a young lady named Bright." See Relativity

"There was a young lady of Bute." Edward Lear
Nonsense verses. *HuSv*

"There was a young lady of Hull." Edward Lear
Limericks. *NaM*

"There was a young lady of Niger." Cosmo Monkhouse. *LoL*
The young lady of Niger. *FeF*

"There was a young lady of Norway." Edward Lear. *ArTp*
Limericks. *JoAc*
Nonsense verses. *HuSv*
A young lady of Norway. *FeF*

"There was a young lady of station." Lewis Carroll
Limericks since Lear. *UnG*

"There was a young lady of Russia." Edward Lear
Limericks. *NaM*

"There was a young lady whose chin." Edward Lear. *ArTp*

"There was a young lady whose eyes." Edward Lear. *CoH*

"There was a young lady whose nose." Edward Lear. *FeF*
Limericks. *JoAc*

"There was a young man from Trinity." Unknown. *PlI*

"There was a young man of Bengal." Unknown
Limericks since Lear. *UnG*

"There was a young man of Herne bay." Unknown. *CoH*

"There was a young man of St Bees." William Schwenck Gilbert. *CoH*

"There was a young man so benighted." Unknown. *CoH*

"There was a young person named Tate." Carolyn Wells
Limericks since Lear. *UnG*

"There was a young prince in Bombay." Walter Parke. *CoH*

"There was a youth, and a well-loved youth." See The bailiff's daughter of Islington

"There was an ancient carver that carved of a saint." See The figure-head

"There was an ancient Grecian boy." See A tiger's tale

"There was an Indian, who had known no change." See The discovery

"There was an old bachelor who lived all alone." Unknown. *WoF*

"There was an old crow." See Short song

There was an old dog. Unknown. *DeT*

"There was an old dog, and he lived at the mill." See There was an old dog

"There was an old fellow called Lear." See Edward Lear went away to-day

"There was an old hen and she had a black foot." Unknown. *WoF*

"There was an old lady of Steen." Unknown
Limericks. *BrL-7*

"There was an old man from Antigua." Unknown. *CoH*

"There was an old man from the Rhine." Unknown
Limericks since Lear. *UnG*

"There was an old man in a boat." See The floating old man

"There was an old man in a pew." Edward Lear
Limericks. *NaM*

"There was an old man in a tree (who was horribly)." Edward Lear. *ArTp*
Lear's limericks. *UnG*
Limericks. *JoAc*

"There was an old man in a tree (whose whiskers)." Edward Lear
Limericks. *JoAc*

"There was an old man in a velvet coat." See Deceiver

"There was an old man lived out in the wood." See Green broom

"There was an old man named Michael Finnegan." Unknown. *ArTp*
American Father Gander. *UnG*

"There was an old man of Blackheath." Unknown. *CoH—LoL*

"There was an old man of Calcutta." See Arthur

"There was an old man of Dumbree." Edward Lear
Lear's limericks. *UnG*

"There was an old man of Ibreem." Edward Lear. *CoH*

"There was an old man of Peru." Unknown. *WiRm*

"There was an old man of Tarentum." Unknown. *CoH—LoL*

"There was an old man of the coast." Edward Lear
Limericks. *NaM*

"There was an old man of the east." Edward Lear
Limericks. *JoAc*

"There was an old man of the Hague." Edward Lear
Limericks. *NaE*

"There was an old man of Thermopylae." Edward Lear
Limericks. *NaE*

"There was an old man of Tobago." Mother Goose. *DeMg*

"There was an old man on the border." Edward Lear
Limericks. *JoAc*

"There was an old man on whose nose." Edward Lear
Limericks. *JoAc*

"There was an old man who lived in a wood." Mother Goose. *DeMg—HuSv*
The old man who lived in a wood. *NaM*

"There was an old man who lived in Middle Row." See The hen keeper

"There was an old man who said, Do." Unknown. *FeF—PlU*

"There was an old man who said, How." Edward Lear
Limericks. *NaE*
Nonsense verses. *HuSv*

"There was an old man who said, Hush." Edward Lear
Lear's limericks. *UnG*
Limericks. *JoAc*
Nonsense verses. *HuSv*

"There was an old man, who when little." Edward Lear
Lear's limericks. *UnG*
Limericks. *JoAc*

"There was an old man with a beard." Edward Lear. *ArTp—CoH—WiRm*
Just as he feared. *BrR-4*
Nonsense verses. *HuSv*
Old man with a beard. *FeF*

"There was an old owl who lived in an oak." See "There was an owl lived in an oak"

"There was an old person of Bradley." Edward Lear. *PlU*

"There was an old person of Dundalk." Edward Lear. *CoH*

"There was an old person of Ickley." Edward Lear
Limericks. *NaE*

"There was an old person of Tring." Unknown. *CoH*

"There was an old person of Ware." Edward Lear
Lear's limericks. *UnG*
Limericks. *JoAc*

"There was an old person whose habits." Edward Lear. *FeF*

"There was an old soldier and he had a wooden leg." Unknown. *WoF*

"There was an old stupid who wrote." Walter Parke. *CoH*

"There was an old tailor of Hickery Mo." See The old tailor

"There was an old wife and she lived all alone." See The old wife and the ghost

"There was an old woman (and nothing she had)." Mother Goose. *OpO*

"There was an old woman, and she had a little pig." See The old woman and the pig

"There was an old woman, and what do you think." Mother Goose. *DeMg—LiL—SmLg*
An old woman. *OpO*
"There was an old woman." *JoAc*

"There was an old woman, as I've heard tell." Mother Goose. *ArTp—JoAc—LiL*
Lauk a mercy. *DeT*
The little woman and the pedlar. *OpO*
The old woman. *UnG*
"There was a little woman." *DeMg*
There was an old woman. *BrR-3—CoPs—CoSp—NaM*

"There was an old woman called Nothing-at-all." Mother Goose. *DeMg*
Nothing-at-all. *OpO*

"There was an old woman had three cows." See The old woman's three cows

"There was an old woman had three sons." Mother Goose. *JoAc*

"There was an old woman, her name it was Peg." Mother Goose. *DeMg*
Peg. *OpO*

"There was an old woman in Surrey." Mother Goose. *DeMg*

"There was an old woman (lived down)." See Was she a witch

"There was an old woman (lived under a hill, she put a mouse)." Mother Goose. *DeMg*
An old woman. *OpO*

"There was an old woman (lived under the hill and if she's not gone)." Mother Goose. *DeMg—JoAc—LiL*
Under a hill. *OpO*

"There was an old woman (lived under the stairs)." See Apples and pears

"There was an old woman sat spinning." See A tale

"There was an old woman sat spinning." Unknown
American Father Gander. *UnG*

"There was an old woman (sold puddings and pies)." Mother Goose. *DeMg*
Old pudding-pie woman. *OpO*

"There was an old woman tossed up in a basket." Mother Goose. *DeMg—HuSv—JoAc—LiL*
An old woman. *OpO*
The old woman in the basket. *ReG*
Sweeping the sky. *HuL-1*
There was an old woman. *NaE*

"There was an old woman who lived in a shoe." Mother Goose. *AnI—ArTp—DeMg—HuSv—JoAc—LiL*
The old woman in a shoe. *OpO*

"There was an old woman (who lived in Dundee)." See The dame of Dundee

"There was an old woman who rode on a broom." Mother Goose. *DeMg*

"There was an old woman who sowed a corn seed." See The magic seeds

"There was an owl lived in an oak." Mother Goose. *DeMg*
An owl in an oak. *OpO*
Signs, seasons, and sense. *UnG*
There was an owl. *HuL-1*

"There was an ox, there was a flea." See Partners

"There was never a sound beside the wood but one." See Mowing

"**There** was no song nor shout of joy." See The ship

"**There** was no west, there was no east." See The demon of the gibbet

"**There** was once a giraffe who said, What." See The unfortunate giraffe

"**There** was once a little man, and his rod and line he took." See The usual way

"**There** was once a young lady of Ryde." Unknown
Limericks. *NaE*

"**There** was once an old sailor my grandfather knew." See The old sailor

"**There** was one—little Jack." See Dirty Jack

"**There** was this road." See The legs

"**There** was three kings into the east." See John Barleycorn

"**There** wasn't a sign until today." See Who did it

"**There** went three children down to the shore." See The black pebble

"**There** were four of us about that bed." See Shameful death

"**There** were four red apples on the bough." See August

"**There** were lots on the farm." See After Christmas

"**There** were three cooks of Colebrook." See Three cooks

"**There** were three gypsies a-come to my door." See The raggle taggle gypsies

"**There** were three in the meadow by the brook." See The code

"**There** were three jovial huntsmen." See "There were three jovial Welshmen"

"**There** were three jovial Welshmen." Mother Goose. *DeMg—JoAc*
  "There were three jovial huntsmen." *HuSv*
  "Three jolly huntsmen." *UnG*
  The three jovial Welshmen. *OpO*
  The three huntsmen. *PaOm*
  The three Welshmen. *NaM*

"**There** were three little birds in a wood." Unknown
Limericks since Lear. *UnG*

"**There** were three sailors of Bristol city." See Little Billee

"**There** were three sisters fair and bright." See The riddling knight

"**There** were three sisters in a hall." Mother Goose. *OpO*

"**There** were three sisters lived in a bower." See The bonnie banks of Fordie

"**There** were two birds sat on a stone." Mother Goose. *DeMg*
  Two birds. *OpO*

"**There** were two blackbirds." Mother Goose. *DeMg*

"**There** were two little bears who lived in a wood." See Twice times

"**There** were two sisters sat in a bower." See Binnorie

"**There** were two wrens upon a tree." See Four wrens

"**There** you sit." Shelley Silverstein. *CoPs*

"**There's** a book." See Seven today

"**There's** a cavern in the mountain where the old men meet." See Shoes and stockings

"**There's** a certain slant of light." Emily Dickinson. *HaP—SmLg*

"**There's** a chirrupy cricket as guest in my room." See The chirrupy cricket

"**There's** a circus in the sky." See Winter circus

"**There's** a girl out in Ann Arbor, Mich." Unknown
Limericks since Lear. *UnG*

"**There's** a humming in the sky." See Aeroplane

"**There's** a merry brown thrush sitting up in the tree." See The brown thrush

"**There's** a meter in music." Unknown. *MoY*

"**There's** a mouse house." See I wouldn't

"**There's** a patch of old snow in a corner." See A patch of old snow

"**There's** a place called Far-away meadow." See The last mowing

"**There's** a plump little chap in a speckled coat." See Bob White

"**There's** a tune, said a sly Bengalese." See The snake charmer

"**There's** a whisper down the line at 11:39." See Skimbleshanks: The railway cat

"**There's** a wonderful family named Stein." See Stein song

"**There's** an apple of gold, an apple of gold." See D is for dragon

"**There's** been an accident, they said." See Four ruthless rhymes—Mr Jones

"**There's** folks that like the good dry land, an' folks that like the sea." See When the drive goes down

"**There's** hardly a wheel rut left to show." See The old coach road

"**There's** many a strong farmer." See The happy townland

"**There's** no dew left on the daisies and clover." See Seven times one

"**There's** no smoke in the chimney." See The deserted house

"**There's** not a tint that paints the rose." See God is everywhere

"**There's** room in the bus." See Jittery Jim

"**There's** snow on the fields." Christina Georgina Rossetti. *DeT*

"**There's** soap-suds on the waves." See Morning at the beach

"**There's** someone at the door, said gold candlestick." See Green candles

"**There's** something about the going down of the sun." See Any sunset

"**There's** something in a flying horse." See Peter Bell—The crescent boat

"**There's** something in the air." See The coming of the spring

"**There's** sun on the clover." See The sun

"**There's** sun on the river and sun on the hill." See Come out with me

"**There's** that old hag Moll Brown, look, see, just past." See A witch

"**There's** thik wold hag, Moll Brown, look zee, jus' past." See A witch

Thermopylae, Battle of, 480 B.C.
The Greek dead at Thermopylae. Simonides. *PaS*

"**These** are my two drops of rain." See Waiting at the window

"A **thing** of beauty is a joy forever." See Endymion—A thing of beauty

Things ("Sometimes when I am at tea with you") Aline Kilmer. *ThP*

Things ("Trains are for going") William Jay Smith. *SmL*

Things I like. Marjorie H. Greenfield. *HuL-1*

"The **things** in life I really want." See The cheerful cherub—Vanity

Things of summer. Kathryn Jackson. *McAw*

Things that get lost. Burges Johnson. *BrR-6*

"The **things** to draw with compasses." See Circles

Things to remember ("The buttercups in May") James Reeves. *ReBl*

Things to remember ("A robin redbreast in a cage") See Auguries of innocence—A robin redbreast

"**Think** of a fly." Unknown. *MoY*

Thinking. Marchette Chute. *ChA*

"The **third-grade** angels, two by two." See Christmas pageant

The **thirsty** earth. See Anacreontics

"The **thirsty** earth soaks up the rain." See Anacreontics—The thirsty earth

Thirteen ways of looking at a blackbird. Wallace Stevens. *HaP*

"**Thirty** days hath September." Mother Goose. *DeMg—HuSv—JoAc—LiL*
   Days in the month. *OpO*
   Signs, seasons, and sense. *UnG*

"**Thirty** white horses." See "Thirty white horses upon a red hill"

"**Thirty** white horses upon a red hill." Mother Goose. *ArTp—DeMg*
   "Thirty white horses." *JoAc—OpO*
   "Twenty white horses." *HuSv*

"**This** ae night, this ae night." See A lyke-wake dirge

This and that. Florence Boyce Davis. *FeF*

"**This** autumn rainfall." See November rain

"**This** bag of cherries for my love." See Eardrops

"**This** book becomes a treasure rare." Unknown. *MoY*

"**This** bread." Eleanor Farjeon. *FaCb—FaN*

"**This** dawn when the mountain-cherry lifts." See Easter in the woods

"**This** day a year ago, to me." See February birthday

"**This** day relenting God." See Lines written after the discovery by the author of the germ of yellow fever

"**This** day Robin Herrick." See Sweet Robin Herrick

This dim and ptolemaic man. John Peale Bishop. *PlI*

"**This** Easter, Arthur Winslow, less than dead." See Death from cancer

"**This** face you got." See Phizzog

This happy day. Harry Behn. *ArTp—HuL-1*

This holy night. Eleanor Farjeon. *DoP*

"**This** I beheld, or dreamed it in a dream." See Opportunity

"**This** is a carol for the dog." See Christmas carol for the dog

"**This** is a cat that sleeps at night." See Cat

"**This** is a song, as small as a clover." See At the beginning of winter

"**This** is Charles Ives." See Ives

"**This** is Flag day." See Hang out the flags

This is Halloween. Dorothy Brown Thompson. *ArTp—HaY*

"**This** is I at work at my desk." John Ciardi. *CiR*

"**This** is Independence day." See Listen to the people: Independence day, 1941

"**This** is Mab, the mistress-fairy." See The satyr—Mab

"**This** is Mister Beers." See Mister Beers

"**This** is my rock." David McCord. *BrS—FeF—HuSv—McFf*

"**This** is not a laundry tab." Unknown. *MoY*

"**This** is our school." See School creed

"**This** is the birthday of our land." See Prayer on fourth of July

"**This** is the common amperzand." See The amperzand

"**This** is the day." See The cuckoo comes

"**This** is the day when all through the town." See Sunday

"**This** is the horrible tale of Paul." See The revolving door

"**This** is the house that Jack built." Mother Goose. *DeMg—HuSv—JoAc—LiL*
   The house that Jack built. *OpO*

This is the key. See "This is the key of the kingdom"

"**This** is the key of the kingdom." Mother Goose. *DeMg—OpO*
   This is the key. *NaM—ReT—SmLg*

"**This** is the key to the playhouse." See The playhouse key

"**This** is the land where hate should die." See The land where hate should die

"**This** is the month of the Thunder Moon." See The month of the Thunder Moon

"**This** is the month when hills turn white." See The long night moon: December

"**This** is the mouth-filling song of the race that was run by a Boomer." See The sing-song of old man kangaroo

"**This** is the night mail crossing the border." See Night mail

"**This** is the rooster." See The pullet

"**This** is the song of the unicorn." See U is for unicorn

"**This** is the sorrowful story." See The legends of evil

"**This** is the story of." See Brady's bend

"**This** is the superfluminous osc." See The osc

"**This** is the time of wonder, it is written." See It rolls on

"**This** is the way the ladies ride." Mother Goose. *ArTp—DeMg—LiL—OpO*

"**This** is the way we wash our clothes." See Wash-day

"**This** is the weather the cuckoo likes." See Weathers

"**This** is the week when Christmas comes." See In the week when Christmas comes

"**This** is the Word whose breaking heart." See Mathematics or the gift of tongues

"This is Willy Walker, and that's Tam Sim." Mother Goose. *OpO*

"This little cow eats grass." See The five toes

"This little pig had a rub-a-dub." Mother Goose. *OpO*

"This little pig says, I'm goin' to steal some corn." Unknown. *WoF*

"This little pig went to market." Mother Goose. *DeMg—HuSv—JoAc—LiL—OpO*

"This lonely hill has always." See The infinite

This man came from nowhere. John Ciardi. *CiI*

This man had six eyes. John Ciardi. *CiI*

This man lives at my house now. John Ciardi. *CiI*

This man talked about you. John Ciardi. *CiI*

This man went away. John Ciardi. *CiI*

"This morning, as I walked to school." See A story in the snow

"This morning, early, when my mother let me go." See The house beyond the meadow—A friendly visit

"This morning, in my garden." See November garden

"This morning, there flew up the lane." See Lady lost

"This motion was of love begot." See Love restored

"This pardoner had hair as yellow as wax." See A girlish pardoner

"This saying good-by on the edge of the dark." See Good-by and keep cold

"This spiky fellow, black and white." See The porcupine

"This sticky trail." See Snail

"This sweetness built our beauty." See America is corn

"This troubled world is sighing now." Unknown
Rhymed chuckles. *UnG*

"This was a mouse who played around." See Tracks in the snow

"This was the noblest Roman of them all." See Julius Caesar

"This way, this way, come and hear." See Song in the wood

"This will be a chocolate cake." See Cooking

"This wind brings all dead things to life." See A windy day

"This winter's weather it waxeth cold." See The old cloak

"This world was once a fluid haze of light." See The princess

"This year, next year." See The wedding

"This year the cuckoo has not come to us." See The missing cuckoo

"Thistle and darnel and dock grew there." See Nicholas Nye

Thistle-seed. Unknown, tr. fr. the Chinese by Isaac Taylor Headland. *JoAc*

"Thistle-seed, thistle-seed." See Thistle-seed

Thistledown. Lizette Woodworth Reese. *HaY*

Thistles
"Cut thistles in May." Mother Goose. *OpO*
"Theophilus Thistle, the successful thistle sifter." Mother Goose. *DeMg*
Theophilus Thistledown. *LoL*
"Theophilus Thistledown, the successful thistle sifter." *OpO*
Thistle-seed. Unknown. *JoAc*
Thistledown. L. W. Reese. *HaY*

Thomas, Charles Swain
"What are the great bells ringing." *BrL-8*

Thomas, Dylan
"Do not go gentle into that good night." *HaP*
Fern hill. *JoAc—McW—NaE—ReT—SmLg*
"The force that through the green fuse drives the flower." *PlI*
"In my craft or sullen art." *HaP*
"Johnnie Crack and Flossie Snail." See Under milk wood
October. *HaY*
Poem in October. *GrCc*
Poem in October. See October
Under milk wood, sel.
"Johnnie Crack and Flossie Snail." *FeF*
From Under milk wood. *CoH*

Thomas, Edith Lovell
Birthday presents. tr. *McAw*

Thomas, Edith Matilda
Autumn fashions. *HaY*

Thomas, Edward
If I should ever by chance. *NaM—SmLg*
The owl. *HaP*
Two houses. *SmLg*
What shall I give. *SmLg*

Thomas, Martha Banning
The chirrupy cricket. *BrR-5*
Sudden gale in spring. *BrR-5*

"Thomas a Tattamus took two tees." Mother Goose. *DeMg*

"Thomas Jefferson." Rosemary Carr and Stephen Vincent Benét. *ArTp—BrL-8—FeF*

Thomas the Rhymer. See True Thomas

Thompson, Blanche Jennings
Magic. *BrR-3*

Thompson, D'A. (D'Arcy) W.
The funny old man and his wife. *BrR-4*
"Two magpies sat on a garden rail." *NaM*

Thompson, Dorothy Brown
Arbor day. *BrS—McAw*
The boy Washington. *BrS*
Getting back. *BrS*
I like housecleaning. *FeF*
Lemonade stand. *BrS*
Maps. *ArTp—HuL-2*
Plans. *BrBc—HuL-1*
Round and round. *BrBc—McAw*
This is Halloween. *ArTp—HaY*

Thompson, Edith Osborne
The monkeys. *ArTp*

Thompson, Francis
Ex ore infantium. *DoP*
To a snow-flake. *PlI—ReT*
To a snowflake. *UnG*
To a snowflake. See To a snow-flake

Thompson, Irene
Caravans. *HuL-2*
The country child. *HuL-1*
Feet. *HuL-1*
The town child. *HuL-1*

Thompson, J. J. See Scott, Louise Binder and Thompson, J. J.

Thompson, Leslie
There are so many ways of going places. *BrR-3—FeF*

Thompson, Lulu E.
In Hardin county, 1809. *CoPs—CoSp*

Thompson, James
The city of dreadful night. *HoW*
Gifts. *ThP*
To the memory of Sir Isaac Newton. *PlI*
Winter. *DeT*

Thoreau, Henry David
"Low-anchored cloud." *PlI*
"Men say they know many things." *PlI*

Thorley, Wilfrid
Buttercups. *FeF*
Of a spider. *FeF*

The **thorn.** William Wordsworth. *NaE* (sel.)

Thorns
"I went to the woods and got it." Unknown. *WoF*

Thornton, Lalia Mitchell
Corn. *BrL-7*

Thornton, Seth G.
Bailada. tr. *PaS*

Thorpe, Rosa Hartwick
Curfew must not ring tonight. *FeF*

"**Those** lumbering horses in the steady plough." See Horses

Those who go forth before daylight. See Psalm of those who go forth before daylight

Thou blind man's mark. Philip Sidney. *HaP*

"**Thou** blind man's mark, thou fool's self-chosen snare." See Thou blind man's mark

"**Thou** blossom bright with autumn dew." See To a fringed gentian

"**Thou** fair-haired angel of the evening." See To the evening star

"**Thou** happy, happy elf." See To my son, aged three years and five months

"**Thou** hearest the nightingale begin the song of spring." See The lark's song

"**Thou** perceivest the flowers put forth their precious odors." See The wild thyme

"**Thou** still unravished bride of quietness." See Ode on a Grecian urn

"**Thou**, too, sail on, O ship of state." See The building of the ship—Sail on, O ship of state

"**Thou** wert the morning star among the living." See Morning star

"**Though** I be now a gray, gray friar." See Friar's hunting song

"**Though** I speak with the tongues of men and of angels." See First epistle of Paul to the Corinthians—Charity

"**Though** no kin to those fine glistening." See Christening-day wishes for my Godchild, Grace Lane Berkley II

"**Though** the evening comes with slow steps and has signalled for all songs to cease." See The bird

"**Though** three men dwell on Flannan isle." See Flannan isle

"**Though** your tasks are many." Unknown. *MoY*

Thought. See also Mind
A child's thought of God. E. B. Browning. *DoP—FeF*
Day-dreamer. Unknown. *ArTp*
Days. K. W. Baker. *ArTp*
Sand dunes. R. Frost. *FrR*
Thinking. M. Chute. *ChA*
A thought. A. A. Milne. *MiWc*
Thoughts of a little girl. M. Enriqueta. *FeF*
A **thought** ("Birthdays and Christmas") Marchette Chute. *ChA*
A **thought** ("If I were John and John were me") A. A. Milne. *MiWc*
A **thought** ("It is very nice to know") Dorothy Aldis. *AlA*
A **thought** ("When I look into a glass") William Henry Davies. *NaM*
Thought on a star. Myra Cohn Livingston. *LiW*
Thoughts for a cold day. Unknown. *HuL-1*
Thoughts of a little girl. María Enriqueta, tr. fr. the Spanish by Emma Gutiérrez Suárez. *FeF*

The **thousand** nights and one, sels. Unknown, tr. fr. the Arabian by E. Powys Mathers
Haroun's favorite song. *PaS*
Love. *PaS*
The power of love. *PaS*

"**Thousands** of sheep, soft-footed, black-nosed sheep." See Sheep

"**Thouzandz** of thornz there be." See The bee's song

Thread
"Old Mother Twitchett had (or has) but one eye." Mother Goose. *ArTp—DeMg—LiL—OpO*
A needle and thread. *ReG*
The **thread** was thin. Unknown. *WoJ*

Three a-bed. Mother Goose. *OpO*

Three acres of land. See "My father left me three acres of land"

Three against one. Mother Goose. *OpO*

"**Three** blind mice." See "Three blind mice, see how they run"

"**Three** blind mice, see how they run." Mother Goose. *AnI—DeMg*
"Three blind mice." *LiL—OpO*

Three brethren from Spain. Mother Goose. *OpO*
We are three lords. *HuL-1*

The **three** cats. Unknown. *DeT*

Three children sliding. See "Three children sliding on the ice"

"**Three** children sliding on the ice." John Gay. *DeMg—JoAc—LiL*
Three children sliding. *OpO*
A warning. *DeT*

Three cooks. Mother Goose. *OpO*

"**Three** crooked cripples went through Cripplegate." Mother Goose. *OpO*

"**Three** fishermen." See Trebizond, Jonah, and the minnows

The **three** foxes. A. A. Milne. *HuSv—MiWc—NaM*

Three ghostesses. See "Three little ghostesses"

"Three gooses: geese." See Goose, moose and spruce
"Three grey geese in a green field grazing." Mother Goose. *OpO*
The three horses. Ivy O. Eastwick. *EaI*
"Three horses came." See The three horses
The three huntsmen. See "There were three jovial Welshmen"
"Three jolly farmers." See Off the ground
"Three jolly gentlemen." See The huntsmen
The three jolly hunters. James Whitcomb Riley. *McW*
Three jolly huntsmen. See "There were three jovial Welshmen"
The three jovial Welshmen. See "There were three jovial Welshmen"
The three kings. See Three kings came riding
Three kings came riding. Henry Wadsworth Longfellow. *HuSv*
The three kings. *UnG*
"Three kings came riding from far away." See Three kings came riding
"Three little bugs in a basket." Unknown. *WoF*
"Three little ghostesses." Mother Goose. *WiRm*
Three ghostesses. *OpO*
"Three little kittens." Unknown, wrongly attributed to Eliza Lee Follen. *BrL-k—FeF—HuSv—OpO*
The little kittens. *ArTp—HuL-1*
"Three little kittens, they lost their mittens." *AnI—DeMg—LiL*
"Three little kittens, they lost their mittens." See "Three little kittens"
Three little mice. See Pussy and the mice
"Three little mice sat down to spin." See Pussy and the mice
The three little pigs. Alfred Scott-Gatty. *HuL-1*
"Three little princes." Mother Goose. *FaN*
"Three little puffins." Eleanor Farjeon. *ArTp—LoL*
"Three little witches." See Hallowe'en song
Three lovely holes. Winifred Welles. *HuSv*
Three miles to Penn. Eleanor Farjeon. *FaCb*
"Three of us afloat in the meadow by the swing." See Pirate story
Three ships. See "I saw three ships come sailing by"
Three signs of spring. David McCord. *McT*
The three singing birds. James Reeves. *CoPm—ReBl*
The three songs. Bayard Taylor. *CoSp*
Three spring notations on bipeds, sel. Carl Sandburg
Laughing child. *SaW*
"The three stood listening to a fresh access." See Snow
"Three strange men came to the inn." See A lady comes to an inn
"Three tall frowns." See How the frightful child grew better
Three things. Unknown. *UnG*
"Three things there are that will never come back." See Three things

Three things to remember. See Auguries of innocence—A robin redbreast
"Three thousand miles to hear a nightingale." See The quest
Three turkeys. Marjorie Fleming. *ReT*
A melancholy lay. *SmLg*
"Three turkeys fair their last have breathed." See Three turkeys
The three unlucky men. James Reeves. *ReBl*
The three Welshmen. See "There were three jovial Welshmen"
"Three wise men of Gotham." Mother Goose. *DeMg—JoAc—LiL*
The wise men of Gotham. *OpO*
Three words. Douglas Malloch. *ThP*
The three woulds. Unknown. *ThP*
Three young rats. See "Three young rats with black felt hats"
"Three young rats with black felt hats." Mother Goose. *DeMg—JoAc*
Three young rats. *LoL—OpO*
"Thrice the brinded cat hath mew'd." See Macbeth—The witches' spell
"Thrice toss these oaken ashes in the air." Thomas Campion. *SmLg*

Thrift
The ant and the cricket. Aesop. *UnG*
A bachelor of Maine. E. D. Deland. *CoH*
Little Minnie Mystery. J. Reeves. *ReBl*
"Penny and penny." Mother Goose. *OpO*
Today. T. Carlyle. *DoP—ThP*
The throstle. Alfred Tennyson. *CoPs—FeF—HuL-2—McW*
"Through Dangly woods the aimless doze." See The doze
"Through storm and wind." Mother Goose. *OpO*
"Through the Appalachian valleys, with his kit a buckskin bag." See Ballad of Johnny Appleseed
"Through the black, rushing smoke-bursts." See The song of the Muses
"Through the hushed air the whitening shower descends." See Winter
Through the looking glass, sels. Lewis Carroll
Humpty Dumpty's recitation. *UnG*
Jabberwocky. *ArTp—FeF—JoAc—UnG*
The walrus and the carpenter. *CoH—DeT—FeF—HuSv—JoAc—PeF—UnMc*
"The time has come, the walrus said." *ArTp*
The white knight's song. *SmLg*
Ways and means. *CoH*
"Through the street as I trot when the weather is hot." See The Hottentot tot
Through the window. David McCord. *McFf*
"Through yonder park there runs a stream." See Yonder
A thrush in the moonlight. Witter Bynner. *ThP*
"Thrush, linnet, stare and wren." See In Glencullen

Thrushes
The brown thrush. L. Larcom. *BrR-4—FeF*
Come in. R. Frost. *FrR—FrY*
The darkling thrush. T. Hardy. *HaP—NaE*

Four quartz crystal clocks. M. Moore. *PlI*

Gallop, gallop to a rhyme. M. Shannon. *BrS*

"How many seconds in a minute." C. G. Rossetti. *BrS*

I could give all to time. R. Frost. *FrR*

The infinite. G. Leopardi. *PaS*

Jonathan Bing's tea. B. C. Brown. *McW*

Long. J. Reeves. *ReR*

Lost time. F. Wolfe. *HuL-2*

A musical critic anticipates eternity. S. Sassoon. *PlI*

"Now, says Time." E. Farjeon. *FaCb—FaN*

Our clock. F. Eakman. *BrS*

Reply to Mr Wordsworth. A. MacLeish. *PlI* (sel.)

The sands. E. Farjeon. *FaCb*

Song. A. Tennyson. *SmLg*

There isn't time. E. Farjeon. *FeF—HuL-2*

Time. J. Ciardi. *CiM*

Time and eternity. J. Bunyan. *HoW*

"Time, you old gipsy man." R. Hodgson. *BrS—FeF—McW—NaM—ReT*

To his coy mistress. A. Marvell. *HaP*

Tomorrows. D. McCord. *McFf*

A vision. H. Vaughan. *PlI*

Waking time. I. O. Eastwick. *ArTp—BrS*

What does it matter. E. V. Rieu. *RiF*

"What is time." E. Farjeon. *FaCb—FaN*

Who was it. H. Heine. *PaS*

Wild thyme. E. Farjeon. *BrS*

Time—Past

Jim Jay. W. De La Mare. *BrS—UnG*

Miniver Cheevy. E. A. Robinson. *HaP—SmLg—UnMc*

The past. R. W. Emerson. *SmLg*

Two houses. E. Thomas. *SmLg*

Verse. O. St J. Gogarty. *SmLg*

Yesterday. H. Chesterman. *BrS*

Time. John Ciardi. *CiM*

Time and eternity. John Bunyan. *HoW*

A **time** for building. Myra Cohn Livingston. *LiWa*

"The **time** has come, the walrus said." See Through the looking-glass—The walrus and the carpenter

"The **time** of the brown gold comes softly." See Brown gold

"**Time** runs wild on the hilltops." See Wild thyme

Time to go. Susan Coolidge. *DoP*

"**Time** to go home." James Reeves. *ReBl*

Time to rise. Robert Louis Stevenson. *BrS—BrL-k—HuSv*

A **time** to talk. Robert Frost. *FrR—FrY*

"**Time** was when his half million drew." See Bewick Finzer

The **time** we like best. Dorothy Aldis. *AlA*

"**Time,** you old gipsy man." Ralph Hodgson. *BrS—FeF—McW—NaM—ReT*

"The **time** you won your town the race." See A Shropshire lad—To an athlete dying young

"**Timothy** Boon." Ivy O. Eastwick. *ArTp*

"**Timothy** Tiggs and Tomothy Toggs." See Some fishy nonsense

"**Timothy** Tim was a very small cat." See Tiger-cat Tim

"**Timothy** Titus took two ties." Mother Goose. *OpO*

"**Timothy** took his time to school." See Lost time

Timothy II. See The second epistle of Paul to Timothy

The **tin-whistle** player. Padraic Colum. *PlI*

"**Ting-a-ling-a-ling.**" See The telephone

"A **tingling,** misty marvel." See November morning

"**Tinker,** tailor." See Cherry stones

"**Tinker,** tailor." Mother Goose. *OpO*

Tinkers

"If ifs and ands." Mother Goose. *DeMg—LiL*

"The **tiny** young hunter arose with the morn." See The hunter

Tippett, James S. (Sterling)

A-caroling on Christmas eve. *McAw*

Autumn woods. *ArTp—McAw*

Busy carpenters. *HuSv*

Ducks at dawn. *ArTp—BrS*

Engine. *BrL-k*

Familiar friends. *BrL-k—HuL-2*

Ferry-boats. *ArTp*

Freight boats. *FeF—HuL-2—HuSv*

George Washington. *HaY*

Hang out the flags. *BrS*

Let's pretend. *McAw*

Old log house. *FeF*

The park. *ArTp—BrL-k—HuL-1*

Park play. *McAw*

Sh. *ArTp*

Sleet storm. *BrS—PeF*

Sunning. *ArTp—BrR-4—BrS—HuL-2*

Trains. *ArTp—BrR-3—FeF—HuL-1*

Trucks. *FeF—JoAc*

Tugs. *FeF*

Up in the air. *ArTp*

"**Tippy,** tippy, tiptoe." See Soft steps

Tiptoe Night. John Drinkwater. *BrS*

"**Tiptoe** Night comes down the lane." See Tiptoe Night

"**Tiptoe,** squirrel." See Run, squirrel, run

Tired Tim. Walter De La Mare. *ArTp—FeF—HuL-2—JoAc—NaE—PeF*

"'**Tis** a lesson you should heed." See Try, try again

"'**Tis** by study that we learn." Unknown. *MoY*

"'**Tis** fine to play." See A boy's summer song

"'**Tis** fine to see the old world, and travel up and down." See America for me

"'**Tis** hard to find in life." See The panchatantra—True friendship

"'**Tis** like stirring living embers when, at eighty, one remembers." See Grandmother's story of Bunker hill battle

"'**Tis** long since, long since, since I heard." See The tin-whistle player

'**Tis** merry in greenwood. See Harold the Dauntless

" 'Tis merry in greenwood—thus runs the old lay." See Harold the Dauntless—'Tis merry in greenwood

" 'Tis not what I am fain to hide." See My secret

" 'Tis spring; come out to ramble." See A Shropshire lad—The Lent lily

" 'Tis the laughter of pines that swing and sway." See The phantom light of the Baie des Chaleurs

'Tis the voice of the lobster. See Alice's adventures in wonderland

" 'Tis the voice of the lobster; I heard him declare." See Alice's adventures in wonderland—'Tis the voice of the lobster

" 'Tis the voice of the sluggard: I heard him complain." See The sluggard

" 'Tis told by one whom stormy waters threw." See The prelude—The prelude, Book VI

"Tit, tat, toe." Mother Goose. *OpO*

"Titty cum tawtay." Mother Goose. *OpO*

Titus, Lucretius Carus. See Lucretius

To a butterfly. William Wordsworth. *UnG*

To a child. Christopher Morley. *BrBc*

To a Christmas tree. Frances M. Frost. *BrR-6*

To a fair lady, playing with a snake. Edmund Waller. *GrCc*

To a girl ("What slender youth bedewed with liquid odours") Horace, tr. fr. the Latin by John Milton. *HoW*

To a girl ("Why came I so untimely forth") Edmund Waller. *HoW*

To a guardian mouse. Elizabeth Jane Coatsworth. *CoM*

To a little sister, aged ten. Alison Elizabeth Cummings. *BrBc*

"To a lodge that stood." See Vaudracour and Julia

To a monkey. Marjory Fleming. *UnG*

To a mouse. Robert Burns. *McW*

To a skylark. Percy Bysshe Shelley. *FeF*

To a snow-flake. Francis Thompson. *PlI—ReT*
To a snowflake. *UnG*

To a snowflake. See To a snow-flake

To a squirrel at Kyle-na-no. William Butler Yeats. *FeF—ReT*

To a waterfowl. William Cullen Bryant. *DeT*

To a young wretch. Robert Frost. *FrR*

To Althea from prison. Richard Lovelace. *HaP*

To an athlete dying young. See A Shropshire lad

To an oak dropping acorns. Eleanor Farjeon. *FaCb—FaN*

To and fro. Elizabeth Jane Coatsworth. *CoM*

To Anthea who may command him any thing. Robert Herrick. *GrCc*

To autumn ("O autumn, laden with fruit, and stained") William Blake. *HoW*

To autumn ("Season of mists and mellow fruitfulness") John Keats. *DeT—HaP—JoAc—UnG*

To baby. Kate Greenaway. *BrL-k*

To be answered in our next issue. Unknown. *McW*

"To be honest, to be kind." See My task

To be or not to be. See I sometimes think

"To be or not to be: that is the question." See Hamlet

To Beachy, 1912. Carl Sandburg. *ArTp*

To bed. See "Come, let's to bed"

"To begin with she wouldn't have fallen in." See Our silly little sister

To call our own. Jesse Stuart. *ThP*

To Christopher North. Alfred Tennyson. *NaE*

To Chuck—concerning a rendezvous in Siam. Jack Charles. *McW*

"To Cotton Mather once there came." See Ben Franklin's head

To daffodils. Robert Herrick. *JoAc—NaE*

To Dick, on his sixth birthday. Sara Teasdale. *BrBc*

"To drive Paul out of any lumber camp." See Paul's wife

To earthward. Robert Frost. *FrR*

"To every man there openeth." See The ways

"To find the western path." See Morning

"To give—and forgive." See Short sermon

"To grass, or leaf, or fruit, or wall." See The snail

"To hear an oriole sing." Emily Dickinson. *PlU*

To his coy mistress. Andrew Marvell. *HaP*

To his friend Master R. L., in praise of music and poetry. Richard Barnfield. *PlU*

To his lute. William Drummond, of Hawthornden. *PlU*

To his son, Vincent Corbet. Richard Corbet. *SmLg*

To James. Frank Horne. *BrBc*

To Jane. Percy Bysshe Shelley. *ReT*

To Jane: The invitation. Percy Bysshe Shelley. *ReT*
Away, away. *UnG*

To Juan at the winter solstice. Robert Graves. *HaP*

"To keep my friends." Unknown. *MoY*

To let. D. Newey-Johnson. *HuL-1*

"To make your candles last for aye." Mother Goose. *DeMg—DeT—OpO*

"To market, to market, to buy a fat pig." Mother Goose. *ArTp—DeMg—HuSv—JoAc—LiL*
To market. *HuL-1*
"To market, to market." *OpO*

"To market, to market, to buy a plum bun." Mother Goose. *DeMg*
"To market, to market." *OpO*

To Mr Punchinello. Mother Goose. *OpO*

To Mistress Margaret Hussey. John Skelton. *HaP—ReT*
"Merry Margaret." *UnG*
Mistress Margaret Hussey. *SmLg*

To Morfydd. Lionel Johnson. *ReT*

"To music bent, is my retired mind." Thomas Campion. *PlU*

To music, to becalme his fever. Robert Herrick. *PlU* (sel.)

To musick. Robert Herrick. *PlU*

"To my friend." Unknown. *MoY*

To my mother. Louis Ginsberg. *CoPs*

To my son, aged three years and five months. Thomas Hood. *FeF*
  A parental ode to my son, aged three years and five months. *CoH* (sel.)

"To my true king I offered free from stain." See Epitaph on a Jacobite

To nature seekers. Robert William Chambers. *NaM*

To night. Percy Bysshe Shelley. *HoW*

To Patricia on her christening day. Edith Ballinger Price. *BrBc*

"To people who allege that we." See The uses of ocean

"To plant a seed and see it grow." See Lesson

"To plant a tree. How small the twig." See Arbor day

To Potapovitch. Hart Crane. *PlU*

To Rose. Sara Teasdale. *BrBc*

"To sea, to sea, the calm is o'er." See Death's jest book—Sea song

To see a world. See Auguries of innocence —"To see the world in a grain of sand"

"To see a world in a grain of sand." See Auguries of innocence

"To see the world in a grain of sand." See Auguries of innocence

"To serve my country day by day." See A patriotic creed

To sleep. Jan Kochanowski, tr. fr. the Polish by Watson Kirkconnell. *PaS*

"To sleep easy all night." Mother Goose. *OpO*

To spring. William Blake. *HoW*

"To stretch asleep on the deck in the sun." See Song of the ship's cat

To summer. William Blake. *HoW*

To Susanna, reading. Eleanor Farjeon. *FaCb*

To the bat. See "Bat, bat, come under my hat"

To the cuckoo. See "Cuckoo, cuckoo, what do you do"

To the cuckoo ("O blithe new-comer, I have heard") William Wordsworth. *UnG*

To the dandelion. James Russell Lowell. *FeF* (sel.)—*JoAc* (sel.)

To the evening star. William Blake. *HoW*

To the fringed gentian. William Cullen Bryant. *JoAc*

To the ladybird. See "Ladybird, ladybird (fly away home)"

"To the Lords of Convention 'twas Claver'se who spoke." See The doom of Devorgoil—Bonny Dundee

To the magpie. Mother Goose. *OpO*

To the memory of Sir Isaac Newton. James Thomson. *PlI*

To the puss moth. Mother Goose. *OpO*

To the shop. Unknown, tr. fr. the Welsh by Rose Fyleman. *JoAc*

To the snail. See "Snail, snail"

To the snow. Mother Goose. *OpO*

"To the sun." See Last song

To the sun. See To the sun from a flower

To the sun from a flower. Guido Gezelle, tr. fr. the Belgian by Jethro Bithell. *FeF*
To the sun. *PaS*

To the Supreme Being. Michelangelo Buonarroti, tr. fr. the Italian by William Wordsworth. *PaS*

To the thawing wind. Robert Frost. *FrR*

To the wayfarer. Unknown. *ArTp—BrS*

To think. See Counters

"To think that two and two are four." Alfred Edward Housman. *PlI*

"To think to know the country and not know." See A hillside thaw

"To time it never seems that he is brave." See I could give all to time

To winter. William Blake. *HoW*

"To you, little girl-child, the fairies do give." See To a little sister, aged ten

The **toad.** Louis Kent. *McW*

Toad-flax. Eleanor Farjeon. *FaCb*

"A **toad** that lived on Albury heath." See A roundabout turn

Toad the tailor. N. E. Hussey. *HuL-1*

"**Toad** the tailor lived in a well." See Toad the tailor

"**Toad,** toad, old toad." See Toad-flax

Toads. See also Frogs; Tree toads
  "As I went walking down the road." Unknown. *WoF*
  At the garden gate. D. McCord. *FeF—McFf*
  A charm; or, An allay for love. R. Herrick. *SmLg*
  A friend in the garden. J. H. Ewing. *BrR-3—FeF—HuSv*
  "Little horned toad." Unknown. *FeF*
  The one-legged stool. E. Blyton *HuL-1*
  "Our Mr Toad." D. McCord. *ArTp—JoAc—McFf*
  A roundabout turn. R. E. Charles. *NaM*
  The song of Mr Toad. From The wind in the willows. K. Grahame. *CoH—FeF*
    "The world has held great heroes." *LoL*
  The song of the toad. J. Burroughs. *FeF*
  The toad. L. Kent. *McW*
  Toad-flax. E. Farjeon. *FaCb*
  Toad the tailor. N. E. Hussey. *HuL-1*

The **toadstool** wood. James Reeves. *ReBl*

"The **toadstool** wood is dark and mouldy." See The toadstool wood

Toadstools. See Mushrooms

A **toast** for Doctor Sam. Eleanor Farjeon. *FaN*

The **toaster.** William Jay Smith. *ArTp—CoH—SmL*

Toasts
  "Here's a health to the barley mow." Mother Goose. *DeMg*
  John Barleycorn. R. Burns. *SmLg*

"**Tomorrow** I'll reform, the fool does say." See Poor Richard's wisdom

"**Tomorrow** is Saint Valentine's day." See Hamlet—Song

"**Tomorrow** morn I'm sweet sixteen, and Billy Grimes the drover." See The courtship of Billy Grimes

"**Tomorrow** when the wind is high." See Tomorrow

Tomorrows. David McCord. *McFf*

"**Tomorrows** never seem to stay." See Tomorrows

Tom's little dog. Walter De La Mare. *ArTp*

Tongs
"Long legs, crooked thighs." Mother Goose. *DeMg—JoAc—LiL—OpO*

Tongue-twisters
"Betty Botter bought some butter." Mother Goose. *JoAc—OpO*
    Betty Baker bought some butter. *WoF*
    Betty Barter. *WiRm*
"A big black bug bit a big black bear." Unknown. *WiRm*
"Double bubble gum bubbles double." Unknown. *WiRm*
"How much wood would a wood-chuck chuck." Mother Goose. *ArTp—HuSv—JoAc—WiRm*
    If a woodchuck would chuck. *FeF*
"I need not your needles." Mother Goose. *OpO*
"I would, if I could." Mother Goose. *DeMg—OpO*
"The Leith police dismisseth us." Mother Goose. *OpO*
"Moses supposes his toeses are roses." Mother Goose. *OpO*
"My dame hath a lame tame crane." Mother Goose. *OpO*
"My grandmother sent me." Mother Goose. *OpO*
"My pop keeps a lollipop shop." Unknown. *WiRm*
"One old Oxford ox opening oysters." Unknown. *DeMg*
"Peter Piper picked a peck of pickled pepper." Mother Goose. *DeMg—HuSv—LiL—OpO*
    Peter Piper. *FeF*
    "Peter Piper pick'd a peck of pepper." *JoAc*
"Robert Rowley rolled a round roll 'round." Mother Goose. *HuSv—OpO*
"Say in one breath." Unknown. *DeMg*
"Six long slim sycamore saplings." Unknown. *WiRm*
Song of the pop-bottlers. M. Bishop. *CoH—FeF*
"Swan swam over the sea." Mother Goose. *DeMg—OpO*
    The swan. *FeF*
    "Swan, swim over the sea." *WiRm*
"A thatcher of Thatchwood went to Thatchet a-thatching." Mother Goose. *DeMg—OpO*
"Theophilus Thistle, the successful thistle sifter." Mother Goose. *DeMg*
    Theophilus Thistledown. *LoL*
    "Theophilus Thistledown, the successful thistle sifter." *OpO*

"Thomas a Tattamus took two tees." Mother Goose. *DeMg*
"Three crooked cripples went through Cripplegate." Mother Goose. *OpO*
"Three grey geese in a green field grazing." Mother Goose. *OpO*
"When a twister a-twisting, will twist him a twist." Mother Goose. *DeMg—OpO*
Tongues
The woman's tongue-tree. A. Guiterman. *CoPm*
"**Tonight.**" See Proposition
"**Tonight** is the night." See Hallowe'en
"**Tonight** when the hoar frost falls on the wood." See Christmas in the woods
Tony the turtle. E. V. Rieu. *HuL-2—RiF*
"**Tony** was a turtle." See Tony the turtle
"**Too** much thought." See Day-dreamer
Tooth trouble. David McCord. *McT*
"The **top** of a hill." See How to tell the top of a hill
"The **top** of the ridge is a cornfield." See Cornfield ridge and stream
Topsy-turviness
"If buttercups buzz'd after the bee." Unknown. *SmLg*
Topsyturvey-world. W. B. Rands. *ReG*
Topsyturvey-world. William Brighty Rands. *ReG*
Torrence, (Frederic) Ridgely
The singers in a cloud. *PlU*
The son. *McW*
"A **tortoise** ambling down the strand." See The tortoise and the magistrate
The **tortoise** and the magistrate. E. V. Rieu. *RiF*
The **tortoise** in eternity. Elinor Wylie. *FeF—PlI*
Tortoises. See Turtles
"The **tortoiseshell** cat." Patrick R. Chalmers. *HuL-2*
Toss me your golden ball. Eleanor Farjeon. *FaCb*
"**Toss** me your golden ball, laughing maid, lovely maid." See Toss me your golden ball
"**T'other** side of Duck-pond." Eleanor Farjeon. *FaN*
Togo, Hashimura, pseud. See Irwin, Wallace
Touch, Sense of
The eel. O. Nash. *FeF—JoAc*
Mud. P. C. Boyden. *ArTp—BrL-k*
"A **tough** kangaroo named Hopalong Brown." See Kangaroo
The **town** child. Irene Thompson. *HuL-1*
"A **town** of ten towers." See Tarlingwell
Towns. See also Cities and city life; also names of towns, as Jerusalem
"Between two hills." C. Sandburg. *SaW*
In a desert town. L. Stevenson. *HuSv*
Kilcash. F. O'Connor. *ReT*
Lo-yang. Emperor Ch'ien Wenti. *GrCc*
O nay. J. Reeves. *ReR*
Potomac town in February. C. Sandburg. *McW—NaE*

From a railway carriage. R. L. Stevenson. *ArTp—FeF—HuL-2—PeF—ReG*

If only. R. Fyleman. *HuSv*

If pigs could fly. J. Reeves. *ReBl*

In foreign parts. L. E. Richards. *CoH—LoL*

"In go-cart so tiny." K. Greenaway. *FeF*

Johnny Fife and Johnny's wife. M. P. Meigs. *ArTp—BrL-7—HuL-1*

Journey's end. A. A. Milne. *MiWc*

The land of Ho-Ho-Hum. W. J. Smith. *SmL*

The listeners. W. De La Mare. *FeF—ReT—UnMc*

"A long time ago." T'ao Ch'ien. *SmLg*

The long voyage. M. Cowley. *McW*

Maps. D. B. Thompson. *ArTp—HuL-2*

Mind you, now. J. Ciardi. *CiY*

On a steamer. D. W. Baruch. *FeF*

The quest. E. Farjeon. *FaCb*

Relativity. Unknown. *ArTp—PlI*

    Limericks. *BrL-7*

    A young lady named Bright. *FeF*

Somewhere. W. De La Mare. *FeF*

Song for a blue roadster. R. Field. *ArTp—FeF*

The sun's travels. R. L. Stevenson. *FeF*

There. R. Bennett. *HuL-1*

There are so many ways of going places. L. Thompson. *BrR-3—FeF*

The ticket agent. E. Leamy. *HuSv*

Train windows. M. C. Livingston. *LiW*

Travel ("I should like to rise and go") R. L. Stevenson. *ArTp—FeF—McW—NaM—SmLg—UnG*

    "I should like to rise and go." *HuSv*

Travel ("The railroad track is miles away") E. St V. Millay. *ArTp—FeF—HuL-2—HuSv—NaM*

The unexplorer. E. St V. Millay. *NaM*

Vacation time. R. B. Bennett. *BrS*

Where lies the land. A. H. Clough. *SmLg*

"Wonder where this horseshoe went." From From a very little sphinx. E. St V. Millay. *ArTp*

    The horseshoe. *HuSv*

    Wonder where. *PeF*

Travel ("I should like to rise and go") Robert Louis Stevenson. *ArTp—FeF—McW—NaM—SmLg—UnG*

"I should like to rise and go." *HuSv*

Travel ("The railroad track is miles away") Edna St Vincent Millay. *ArTp—FeF—HuL-2—HuSv—NaM*

A **traveller.** See "Pussy-cat, pussy-cat, where have you been"

Traveller's joy. Eleanor Farjeon. *FaCb*

Treasure

Derelict. Y. E. Allison. *PaOm*

Momotara. Unknown. *ArTp—HuL-2*

Spanish waters. J. Masefield. *FeF—McW*

Treasure. E. E. Long. *BrBc*

Treasure. Elizabeth-Ellen Long. *BrBc*

Treasures in heaven. See Gospel according to Matthew

Trebetherick. John Betjeman. *NaE*

Trebizond, Jonah, and the minnows. Humbert Wolfe. *HuL-2*

The **tree** ("I love thee when thy swelling buds appear") Jones Very. *CoPs—UnG*

The **tree** ("The tree's early leaf buds were bursting their brown") Björnstjerne Björnson, tr. fr. the Norwegian. *CoPs—FeF*

The **tree** and the chaff. See Psalms—Psalm I

"A **tree** ascending there, O pure transcension." See Sonnets to Orpheus

Tree at my window. Robert Frost. *FrR—FrY*

"**Tree** at my window, window tree." See Tree at my window

Tree birthdays. Mary Carolyn Davies. *BrBc*

"The **tree** frogs sing." See The rain-frogs

Tree gowns. James Reeves. *ReW*

Tree house. Dorothy Aldis. *AlHd*

"A **tree** may be laughter in the spring." See Winter night

"The **tree** stands very straight and still." Annette Wynne. *BrR-3*

"The **tree** the tempest with a crash of wood." See On a tree fallen across the road

The **tree** toad. Monica Shannon. *ArTp—FeF*

"The **tree** toad is a creature neat." See The tree toad

Tree toads. See also Frogs; Toads

The tree toad. M. Shannon. *ArTp—FeF*

Trees. See also Forests and forestry; also names of trees, as Oak trees

Arbor day ("On Arbor day") A. Wynne. *DoP*

Arbor day ("To plant a tree. How small the twig") D. B. Thompson. *BrS—McAw*

Archibald's example. E. A. Robinson. *GrCc*

Autumn fancies. Unknown. *FeF—HuSv*

Be different to trees. M. C. Davies. *FeF*

Brooms. D. Aldis. *AlA—BrR-4*

City trees. E. St V. Millay. *FeF*

Counting-out rhyme. E. St V. Millay. *NaM*

"Every time I climb a tree." From Five chants. D. McCord. *ArTp—McFf—UnG*

Five trees. E. Farjeon. *FaCb—FaN*

Glimpse in autumn. J. S. Untermeyer. *JoAc*

Good company. K. W. Baker. *FeF*

The gum-gatherer. R. Frost. *FrR*

"I had a little nut tree." Mother Goose. *DeMg—DeT—HuL-1—JoAc—OpO—ReG*

    "I had a little nut tree; nothing would it bear." *AnI—ArTp—HuSv—LiL*

    The nut tree. *NaM*

"If all the trees were one tree." Unknown. *WiRm*

Improved farm land. C. Sandburg. *SaW*

In October. B. Carman. *HaY*

"In spring I look gay." Mother Goose. *OpO*

Into my own. R. Frost. *FrR*

Little sketch. C. Sandburg. *SaW*

A nature lesson. C. Wells. *BrR-3*

Trees—*Continued*

Never two songs the same. C. Sandburg. *SaW*

On a tree fallen across the road. R. Frost. *FrR*

Our tree. M. Chute. *ChA*

Planting a tree. N. B. Turner. *HaY*

Pruning trees. Po Chü-i. *PaS*

A rare tree. Unknown. *PaS*

A salute to trees. H. Van Dyke. *HuSv*

Shade. T. Garrison. *BrL-7*

"Something lives on yonder hill." Unknown. *WiRm*

Song to a tree. E. Markham. *FeF*

The sound of the trees. R. Frost. *FrR*

Strange tree. E. M. Roberts. *FeF*

Tapestry trees. W. Morris. *FeF*

Timber moon. C. Sandburg. *SaW*

To the wayfarer. Unknown. *ArTp—BrS*

The tree ("I love thee when thy swelling buds appear") J. Very. *CoPs—UnG*

The tree ("The tree's early leaf buds were bursting their brown") B. Björnson. *CoPs—FeF*

Tree at my window. R. Frost. *FrR—FrY*

Tree birthdays. M. C. Davies. *BrBc*

Tree gowns. J. Reeves. *ReW*

"The tree stands very straight and still." A. Wynne. *BrR-3*

Trees ("I think that I shall never see") J. Kilmer. *FeF*

Trees ("Trees are the kindest things I know") H. Behn. *ArTp—BrS—HaY—HuL-2—JoAc—PeF*

The trees and the wind. E. Farjeon. *FaCb*

Trees in the moonlight. J. Reeves. *ReBl*

The two old women of Mumbling hill. J. Reeves. *ReW*

"Under the greenwood tree." From As you like it. W. Shakespeare. *ArTp—DeT—FeF—HoW*

In Arden forest. *JoAc*

What do we plant. H. Abbey. *ArTp—FeF*

Winter night. C. Hutchison. *ArTp*

The woman's tongue tree. A. Guiterman. *CoPm*

"Woodman, spare that tree." G. P. Morris. *FeF*(sel.)

Y is for Yggdrasil. E. Farjeon. *FaCb*

Trees ("I think that I shall never see") Joyce Kilmer. *FeF*

Trees ("Trees are the kindest things I know") Harry Behn. *ArTp—BrS—HaY—HuL-2—JoAc—PeF*

"The **trees** along this city street." See City trees

The **trees** and the wind. Eleanor Farjeon. *FaCb*

The **trees** are bare. See The bluebell

"The **trees** are bare, the sun is cold." See The bluebell—The trees are bare

"**Trees** are the kindest things I know." See Trees

"The **tree's** early leaf buds were bursting their brown." See The tree

"**Trees** growing—right in front of my window." See Pruning trees

Trees in the moonlight. James Reeves. *ReBl*

"**Trees** in the moonlight stand." See Trees in the moonlight

"The **trees** of the Lord are full of sap." See Psalms—Psalm CIV

Tremendous trifles. See "For want of a nail, the shoe was lost"

Treves, Frederici (about)

In the evening. T. Hardy. *PlI*

"**Triangles** are commands of God." See The starfish

Trick or treat. David McCord. *McFf*

Tricky. Gelett Burgess. *CoH*

Trifles. See Little things, Importance of

Triolet on a dark day. Margaret Fishback. *CoPs*

"**Trip** upon trenchers, and dance upon dishes." Mother Goose. *DeMg*

A melancholy song. *OpO*

Triple bronze. Robert Frost. *FrR*

"**Trit** trot to market to buy a penny doll." Mother Goose. *OpO*

The **triumph.** Eleanor Farjeon. *FaN*

The **triumph** of the whale. Charles Lamb. *PlI*(sel.)

Troilus and Cressida. William Shakespeare. *PlI*(sel.)

"**Troll** sat alone on his seat of stone." See The hobbit

"**Trot** along, pony." Marion Edey. *ArTp*

"A **trot**, and a canter, a gallop, and over." Mother Goose. *OpO*

Troubadours. See Minstrels and troubadours

Troubetzkoy, Ulrich

Christmas lullaby. *HaY*

Trouble. David Keppel. *ThP*

Trouble at the farm. Ivy O. Eastwick. *HuL-1*

"The **trouble** with a kitten is." See The kitten

Troubles. Dorothy Aldis. *BrL-k—HuSv—JoAc*

Trowbridge, John Townsend

Darius Green and his flying-machine. *NaM*

Evening at the farm. *FeF*

Evening on the farm. *NaM*

Evening on the farm. See Evening at the farm

Troy. James Reeves. *ReBl*

Trucks

The army horse and the army jeep. J. Ciardi. *CiR*

Country trucks. M. Shannon. *ArTp—FeF*

"F is the fighting firetruck." From All around the town. P. McGinley. *FeF*

Josh's song. M. C. Livingston. *LiWa*

Trucks. J. S. Tippett. *FeF—JoAc*

Trucks. James S. Tippett. *FeF—JoAc*

"**True** friends are like diamonds." Unknown. *MoY*

True friendship. See The panchatantra

True love. See Sonnets—"Let me not to the marriage of true minds"

A **true** story. Ann Taylor. *DeT*

The **true** story of the web-spinner. Mary Howitt. *DeT*

"True success is that which makes." Arthur Guiterman
Proverbs. *ThP*

The true tale of Eliza Ottley. Eleanor Farjeon. *FaCb*

True Thomas. Unknown. *CoSp—UnG—UnMc*
Thomas the Rhymer. *MaB*

"True Thomas lay on Huntlie bank." See True Thomas

"Truly the light is sweet." See Ecclesiastes—The light is sweet

"Truly, the light is sweet." See A man's bread

"The trumpets were curled away, the drum beat no more." See The swan

Truthfulness and falsehood
The boy and the wolf. Aesop. *UnMc*
"Dare to be true." G. Herbert. *UnG*
A dead liar speaks. M. Lewis. *UnG*
The eternal. E. Tegnér. *PaS*
The false knight upon the road. Unknown. *MaB*
For once, then, something. R. Frost. *FrR*
How much is true. J. Ciardi. *CiM*
Matilda. H. Belloc. *CoSp—SmLg*
My true love. I. O. Eastwick. *BrS*
A narrative. T. Spencer. *McW*
A nautical extravaganza. W. Irwin. *CoSp*
A nautical extravagance. *HuSv*
Ode on a Grecian urn. J. Keats. *HaP*
Plain language from truthful James. B. Harte. *CoH*
This man talked about you. J. Ciardi. *CiI*
True Thomas. Unknown. *CoSp—UnG—UnMc*
Thomas the Rhymer. *MaB*
"The wayfarer." S. Crane. *McW*

Try, try again. T. H. Palmer. *FeF*

Tu Fu
The little rain. *FeF*
The rain at night. *PaS*
A song of dagger-dancing. *PlU*(sel.)

Tuck, Edward
Age. *BrBc*

Tudor church music. Sylvia Townsend Warner. *PlU*

The tuft of flowers. Robert Frost. *FrR—FrY*

Tugs. James S. Tippett. *FeF*

Tulips
Tulips. P. Colum. *PlI*

Tulips. Padraic Colum. *PlI*

"The tulips now are pushing up." See April

"The tumblers of the rapids go white, go green." See Niagara.

Turkeys
After Christmas. D. McCord. *McT*
"Grasshopper settin' on a sweet potato vine." Unknown. *WoF*
The little girl and the turkey. D. Aldis. *AlA*
Three turkeys. M. Fleming. *ReT*
A melancholy lay. *SmLg*
The turkey's opinion. A. M. Pratt. *BrR-4*

The turkey's opinion. Anna M. Pratt. *BrR-4*

The Turkish lady. Unknown. *UnMc*

"Turn again Whittington." Unknown. *ReG*

"Turn out for Plow-Monday." See Plow-Monday

"Turn, Willie Mackintosh." See Willie Mackintosh

Turner, Elizabeth
How to write a letter. *NaM*

Turner, Nancy Byrd
Adventure. *HuSv*
Autumn. *HaY*
The bagpipe man. *ArTp—HuL-1—HuL-2*
Black and gold. *ArTp—BrR-6—HaY—HuL-2*
A boy of other days. See Lincoln
The buccaneer. *ArTp*
Chairoplane chant. *BrR-5*
Dark-eyed lad Columbus. *BrS*
"Down a sunny Easter meadow." *BrS*
Easter joy. *HaY*
The extraordinary dog. *ArTp*
February birthday. *BrBc*
First Christmas night of all. *BrBc*
The first Thanksgiving. *HaY*
First Thanksgiving of all. *BrR-6—BrS—FeF*
God's providence. *DoP*
I wish. *BrS*
In praise of water. *HuL-2*
Lincoln. *ArTp—FeF*
A boy of other days. *BrR-5*
The mail goes through. *BrR-6*
More than flowers we have brought. *BrS*
"Old Quin Queeribus." *ArTp—BrR-4—CoH—HuL-1—NaE*
The orchestra. *BrR-5*
The ordinary dog. *ArTp*
Planting a tree. *HaY*
A pop corn song. *BrL-k—FeF—HuL-1*
Prayer on fourth of July. *HaY*
The resolute cat. *HuL-1*
The sampler. *BrBc*
Spring wind. *BrS*
A sure sign. *ArTp—BrR-4*
Washington. *ArTp—BrL-7—FeF—HaY—PeF*
The weather factory. *BrR-4*
When young Melissa sweeps. *FeF*
"Whenever I say America." *HaY*
Wings and wheels. *ArTp—HuSv*

Turner, W. (Walter) J. (James)
Romance. *BrBc—CoPm—ReT*

The turnip seller. See "If a man who turnips cries"

The turnip vendor. See "If a man who turnips cries"

Turnips
"If a man who turnips cries." S. Johnson. *DeMg*
The turnip seller. *NaE*
The turnip vendor. *OpO*
Mr Finney's turnip. Unknown. *CoH—LoL*

"The turtle, clam, and crab as well." See Covering the subject

Turtle soup. See Alice's adventures in wonderland

The **twins** ("The two-ones is the name for it") Elizabeth Madox Roberts. *ArTp—BrBc—McAw*

The **twins** ("When one starts crying") Dorothy Aldis. *AlA—BrBc*

"**Twirl** about, dance about." See Dreidel song

Twirling. Mother Goose. *OpO*

"**Twirling** your blue skirts, travelling the sward." See Blue girls

"**Twist** about, turn about." See Jim crow

Twist-rime on spring. Arthur Guiterman. *CoPs*

"**Twist** the tinsel." See Round and round

"**'Twixt** optimist and pessimist." See The difference

"**Two** apples, a book." See Autumn eve

Two birds. See "There were two birds sat on a stone"

"**Two** bodies have I." Mother Goose. *OpO*

"**Two-boots** in the forest walks." See The intruder

"**Two** boys went fishing one bright summer day." Unknown. *WiRm*

"**Two** brothers we are." Mother Goose. *OpO*

"**Two** bubbles found they had rainbows on their curves." See Bubbles

"**Two** cats." See Diamond cut diamond

Two comical folk. See "In a cottage in Fife"

The **two** corbies. See The twa corbies

"**Two** days ago the wild-rose buds." See Puzzles

The **two** frogs. Unknown. *HuL-1*

"**Two** frogs fell into a milk-pail deep." See The two frogs

Two houses. Edward Thomas. *SmLg*

"**Two** hundred wagons, rolling out to Oregon." See The Oregon trail: 1843

"**Two** in a car." Unknown. *MoY*

"**Two** in a hammock." Unknown. *MoY*

Two in bed. Abram Bunn Ross. *ArTp—FeF*

"**Two** legs sat on three legs." See "Two legs sat upon three legs"

"**Two** legs sat upon three legs." Mother Goose. *DeMg—LiL—OpO*
"Two legs sat on three legs." *JoAc*

Two lessons. John Ciardi. *CiM*

"**Two** little beaks went tap, tap, tap." See To let

"**Two** little boys late one night." Unknown. *MoY*

"**Two** little clouds one summer's day." See The rainbow fairies

"**Two** little dicky birds." Mother Goose. *LiL—OpO*

"**Two** little dogs." Mother Goose. *OpO*

"**Two** little kittens one stormy night." See The quarrelsome kittens

"**Two** little mice went tripping down the street." See Well, I never

Two look at two. Robert Frost. *FrR*

"**Two** magpies sat on a garden rail." D'A. W. Thompson. *NaM*

Two men. Edwin Arlington Robinson. *UnG*

The **two** mice. J. Reeves. *ReBl*

"**Two** microbes sat on a pantry shelf." See The microbes

"**Two** of us, two of us climb the stairs." See Being twins

The **two** old bachelors. Edward Lear. *CoH*

"**Two** old bachelors were living in one house." See The two old bachelors

"The **two** old trees on Mumbling hill." See The two old women of Mumbling hill

The **two** old women of Mumbling hill. James Reeves. *ReW*

"The **two-ones** is the name for it." See The twins

The **two** paths. See Proverbs, Bible, Old Testament

Two people. E. V. Rieu. *RiF*

"**Two** people live in Rosamund." See Two people

The **two** rats. Unknown. *HuL-1*

Two rivers ("Says Tweed to Till") Unknown. *MaB*

Two rivers ("Thy summer voice, Musketaquit") Ralph Waldo Emerson. *GrCc*

"**Two** roads diverged in a yellow wood." See The road not taken

The **two** spirits. Percy Bysshe Shelley. *HoW*

"**Two** thousand feet beneath our wheels." See Cockpit in the clouds

Two tramps in mud time. Robert Frost. *FrR—FrY*

"**Two** young lambs." Eleanor Farjeon. *FaCb—FaN*

Twos. John Drinkwater. *JoAc*

"**'Twould** ring the bells of heaven." See The bells of heaven

The **tyger.** See The tiger ("Tiger, tiger, burning bright")

"**Tyger,** tyger, burning bright." See The tiger

Tymnès
A Maltese dog. *ArTp—SmLg*

Tynan, Katharine (Katharine Tynan Hinkson)
By the crib. *EaW*
Chanticleer. *ArTp*
Christmas eve in Ireland. *EaW*
Lambs. *DeT*
Sheep and lambs. *DoP*
Wild geese. *UnG*

Typewriters
Archy a low brow. D. Marquis. *CoH*
Qwerty-ù-i-op. A. Guiterman. *CoH*

Tyrtaeus
How can man die better. *PaS*

Tyutchev, Fyodor
As ocean holds the globe. *PaS*
Silentium. *PaS*
Twilight. *PaS*

Tywater. Richard Wilbur. *HaP*

U

"**U** is for umbrellas." See All around the town

U is for unicorn. Eleanor Farjeon. *FaCb*

Udall, Nicholas
　"I mun be married a Sunday." *GrCc*
Ulysses (about)
　Argus and Ulysses. E. Farjeon. *FaCb*
　Ulysses. A. Tennyson. *HaP*
Ulysses. Alfred Tennyson. *HaP*
Umamina. B. W. Vilikazi, tr. fr. the Zulu
　by R. M. Mfeka. *PaS*
The umbrella brigade. Laura E. Richards.
　ArTp—HuL-2—JoAc
Umbrellas
　The elf and the dormouse. O. Herford.
　　ArTp—FeF—HuL-1—PeF—UnG
　My funny umbrella. A. Wilkins. *BrL-k*
　My new umbrella. M. M. Hutchinson.
　　HuL-1
　No drip of rain. I. O. Eastwick. *McAw*
　"Opens like a barn door." Unknown.
　　WiRm
　"U is for umbrellas." From All around
　　the town. P. McGinley. *ArTp*
　The umbrella brigade. L. E. Richards.
　　ArTp—HuL-2—JoAc
　Umbrellas. R. B. Bennett. *BrR-3*
Umbrellas. Rowena Bastin Bennett. *BrR-3*
Un. James Reeves. *ReR*
Un-birthday cake. Aileen Fisher. *BrBc*
The uncharted. Rachel Field. *BrR-6*
The uncle. See Snow-bound
Uncle James. Barbara E. Todd. *HuL-1*
Uncles
　Bobby's first poem. N. Gale. *CoH—NaM*
　G is for giant. E. Farjeon. *FaCb*
　Incidents in the life of my Uncle Arly.
　　E. Lear. *CoH—NaM*
　Kiph. W. De La Mare. *ArTp*
　Manners. M. G. Van Rensselaer. *FeF*
　My singing aunt. J. Reeves. *ReBl*
　Surprise. H. Behn. *BrBc*
　The uncle. From Snow-bound. J. G.
　　Whittier. *UnG*
　Uncle James. B. E. Todd. *HuL-1*
"Uncut is your corn, Farmer Hearn." See
　Un
Under a hat rim. Carl Sandburg. *SaW*
Under a hill. See "There was an old woman
　(lived under the hill and if she's not
　gone)"
"Under a spreading chestnut tree." See
　The village blacksmith
"Under a toadstool." See The elf and the
　dormouse
Under ground. James Reeves. *ReW*
Under milk wood, sel. Dylan Thomas
　"Johnnie Crack and Flossie Snail." *FeF*
　　From Under milk wood. *CoH*
Under my lean-to. Eleanor Farjeon. *FaCb—
　FaN*
"Under the greenwood tree." See As you
　like it
"Under the ground." See Rabbit and lark
Under the ground. Rhoda W. Bacmeister.
　BrL-k—McAw
"Under the linden the music is gay." See
　A meeting
Under the moon. Ivy O. Eastwick. *EaI*

"Under the pines and hemlocks." See
　The deer
"Under the roof of my lean-to." See Under
　my lean-to
"Under the tree in the shade sits a toad."
　See The toad
"Under the wide and starry sky." See
　Requiem
"Under this sod and beneath these trees."
　See An epitaph
"Underneath an old oak tree." See The
　raven
"Underneath my belt." See When I was lost
"Underneath the boardwalk, way, way,
　back." See The secret cavern
Underneath the clothes. Madeleine Night-
　ingale. *HuL-1*
"Underneath the leaves of Nimes." See
　Saint Giles
Undersea. Marchette Chute. *HuL-1*
The unexplorer. Edna St V. Millay. *NaM*
"Unfold unfold." See In grato jubilo
The unfortunate giraffe. Oliver Herford.
　CoH
Ungrateful Jenny. See "Jenny Wren fell
　sick"
The unicorn ("The unicorn stood, like a
　king in a dream") E. V. Rieu. *RiF*
Unicorn ("The unicorn with the long white
　horn") William Jay Smith. *SmB*
The unicorn ("While yet the morning star")
　Ella Young. *ArTp—FeF*
"The unicorn stood, like a king in a dream."
　See The unicorn
"The unicorn with the long white horn."
　See Unicorn
Unicorns
　Dance song. Unknown. *SmLg*
　Inhuman Henry; or, Cruelty to fabulous
　　animals. A. E. Housman. *CoH*
　"The lion and the unicorn." Mother
　　Goose. *AnI—DeMg—JoAc—LiL—NaE*
　　Battle royal. *OpO*
　U is for unicorn. E. Farjeon. *FaCb*
　The unicorn ("The unicorn stood, like a
　　king in a dream") E. V. Rieu. *RiF*
　Unicorn ("The unicorn with the long
　　white horn") W. J. Smith. *SmB*
　The unicorn ("While yet the morning
　　star") E. Young. *ArTp—FeF*
"The unicorn's hoofs." See Dance song
United Nations
　Bed-time story. M. Cane. *UnG*
United States. See also names of states, as
　New Hampshire
　America. S. F. Smith. *FeF*
　America for me. H. Van Dyke. *BrR-5*
　America is corn. R. P. T. Coffin. *McW*
　America the beautiful. K. L. Bates. *FeF*
　America was schoolmasters. R. P. T.
　　Coffin. *McW*
　American names. S. V. Benét. *McW—
　　SmLg*
　The centennial meditation of Columbia,
　　sel. S. Lanier
　　Dear land of all my love. *HuSv*
　The gift outright. R. Frost. *FrR—McW—
　　SmLg*

"I am an American." E. Lieberman. *FeF*

I hear America singing. W. Whitman. *ArTp—BrL-7—BrR-5—CoPs—FeF—HuSv—JoAc—SmLg—UnG*

The land where hate should die. D. A. McCarthy *BrL-8*

Landscapes, sels. T. S. Eliot
    Cape Ann. *JoAc—NaE—ReT—SmLg*
    New Hampshire. *HaP—ReT—SmLg*
    Rannoch, by Glencoe. *SmLg*
    Usk. *SmLg*
    Virginia. *HaP—SmLg*

The long voyage. M. Cowley. *McW*

My land. T. O. Davis. *BrR-5*

Ode in a night of overhanging weather. V. McHugh. *McW*

The people, yes, sels. C. Sandburg
    American yarns. *HuSv*
        Yarns. *UnG*
    Children of the desert. *SaW*
    Children of the wind. *HuSv*
    Circles. *SaW*
    Mother and child. *SaW*
    Niagara. *SaW*
    Night too has numbers. *SaW*
    Prairie barn. *SaW*
    Proverbs. *SaW*

A record stride. R. Frost. *FrY*

Sail on, O ship of state. From The building of the ship. H. W. Longfellow. *FeF*
    The ship of state. *BrL-7*

The star-spangled banner. F. S. Key. *FeF*

Stately verse. Unknown. *ArTp—CoH—FeF*

Watch, America. R. Nathan. *McW*

"Whenever I say America." N. B. Turner. *HaY*

United States—History—Colonial period

The first Thanksgiving. N. B. Turner. *HaY*

First Thanksgiving of all. N. B. Turner. *BrR-6—BrS—FeF*

The landing of the Pilgrim Fathers. F. D. Hemans. *ArTp—BrR-5—FeF—UnG*

The pilgrims came. A. Wynne. *McAw*

School days in New Amsterdam. A. Guiterman. *FeF*

United States—History—Revolution. See also names of battles, as Bunker hill, Battle of, 1775

Brady's bend M. Keller. *CoSp*

Concord hymn. R. W. Emerson. *FeF—HuSv*

Epitaph for a Concord boy. S. Young. *McW*

Grandmother's story of Bunker hill battle. O. W. Holmes. *UnG*

The little black-eyed rebel. W. Carleton. *FeF—UnG*

Molly Pitcher. K. B. Sherwood. *UnG*

An old-time sea-fight. From Song of myself. W. Whitman. *UnMc*

Paul Revere's ride. From Tales of a wayside inn. H. W. Longfellow. *ArTp—BrL-7—CoSp—FeF—HuSv—JoAc—SmLg—UnG*

The revolutionary rising. T. B. Read. *BrL-8*

"T'other side of Duck-pond." E. Farjeon. *FaN*

Voices of heroes. H. Gregory. *GrCc*

"Yankee Doodle came to town." Mother Goose. *HuSv—JoAc*
    Yankee Doodle. *FeF—OpO*

"Yankee Doodle went to town." *DeMg*

United States—History—Westward movement. See also Cowboys; Frontier and pioneer life; Indians of America

Crossing the plains. J. Miller. *GrCc*

John Sutter. Y. Winters. *HaP*

The Oregon trail: 1851 J. Marshall. *HuSv*

The Oregon trail: 1843. A. Guiterman. *FeF*

The passing of the buffalo. H. Garland. *HuSv*

The railroad cars are coming. Unknown. *FeF*

Western wagons. R. C. and S. V. Benét. *BrR-5—McW*

The wilderness is tamed. E. J. Coatsworth. *BrR-5—FeF—HuSv*

United States—History—Civil war. See also Naval battles

Achilles Deatheridge. From The Spoon River anthology. E. L. Masters. *UnMc*

The aged stranger. B. Harte. *UnMc*

Barbara Frietchie. J. G Whittier. *CoPs—FeF—JoAc—UnG—UnMc*

Battle-hymn of the republic. J. W. Howe. *FeF—UnG*

Dixie. D. D. Emmett. *FeF* (sel.)

Hasting's mill. C. F. Smith. *McW*

Kentucky Belle. C. F. Woolson. *CoSp—UnG—UnMc*

Little Giffen. F. O. Ticknor. *UnMc*

The old man and Jim. J. W. Riley. *CoSp*

The portent. H. Melville. *HoW*

The rebel soldier. Unknown. *SmLg*

The returned volunteer to his rifle. H. Melville. *GrCc*

Shiloh. H. Melville. *HoW*

"A sight in camp in the daybreak gray and dim." W. Whitman. *HaP*

United States—History—World war I. See European war, 1914-1918

United States—History—World war II. See World war II, 1939-1945

Universe. See World

"United States is a nation." Unknown. *MoY*

The **unknown** color. Countee Cullen. *FeF*

The **unseen** power. Rumi, tr. fr. the Persian by R. A. Nicholson. *PaS*

Untermeyer, Jean Starr
    Glimpse in autumn. *JoAc*

Untermeyer, Louis
    Any sunset. *UnG*
    The boy and the wolf. tr. *UnMc*
    Briar-rose. tr. *HuL-2*
    Coal fire. *UnG*
    Day-dreamer. tr. *ArTp*
    Disenchanted. *UnG*
    Dog at night. *UnG*
    German slumber song. tr. *UnG*
    Good advice. tr. *ArTp*
    The greedy fox and the elusive grapes. tr. *UnMc*
    The heart. tr. *UnMc*
    Last words before winter. *UnG*
    Lesson from a sun-dial. tr. *ArTp*
    Leviathan. *UnG*

Vacation. Katharine Lee Bates. *BrR-6*

Vacation song ("Shine on me, oh, you gold, gold sun") Edna St Vincent Millay. *HaY*

Vacation song ("When study and school are over") Frank Dempster Sherman. *BrR-6*

Vacation time. Rowena Bastin Bennett. *BrS*

The vagabond. Robert Louis Stevenson. *BrL-8*

A vagabond song. Bliss Carman. *BrR-5—CoPs—FeF—HuL-2—JoAc—UnG*

Vagabonds. See Gipsies; Tramps; Wayfaring life

Vailima. Robert Louis Stevenson. *DeT*

Vain. James Reeves. *ReR*

Vain and careless. Robert Graves. *GrP*

"Vain is the Princess Vara." See Vain

Valentine, Saint. See Saint Valentine's day

A valentine ("Frost flowers on the window glass") Eleanor Hammond. *ArTp—HaY*

Valentine ("I got a valentine from Timmy") Shelley Silverstein. *CoPs*

Valentine ("No early buds of laughing spring") C. W. T. *HaY*

A valentine ("Oh, little loveliest lady mine") Laura E. Richards. *BrR-5—HaY*

Valentine for earth. Frances M. Frost. *ArTp—FrLn*

Valentine promise. Unknown. *CoPs*

Valentines. See Saint Valentine's day

Valentine's day. Aileen Fisher. *HaY*

Valhalla
V is for Valhalla. E. Farjeon. *FaCb*

The valiant. See Julius Caesar

"The valley was swept with a blue broom to the west." See Santa Fe sketch

The valley's singing day. Robert Frost. *PlU*

Vanada, Lillian Schulz
"Fuzzy wuzzy, creepy crawly." *ArTp—BrR-3*

Van Doren, Mark
The distant runners. *SmLg*
The god of galaxies. *PlI*
If they spoke. *PlI*
Music God. *PlU*
Old hundred. *PlU*

Van Dyke, Henry
America for me. *BrR-5*
The angler's reveille. *HuSv*
Four things. *DoP—UnG*
Four things to do. *ThP*
Four things to do. See Four things
If all the skies. *DoP*
A salute to trees. *HuSv*
Work. *BrR-6*

The vanishing Red. Robert Frost. *FrR*

Vanity. See Pride and vanity

Vanity. See The cheerful cherub

Van Rensselaer, Mariana Griswold (Mrs Schuyler Van Rensselaer; Mariana Griswold)
I wonder. *BrL-k*
Manners. *FeF*

Van Rensselaer, Mrs Schuyler. See Van Rensselaer, Mariana Griswold

Variation on a Polish folk song. Marya Zaturenska. *GrCc*

Variation on a sentence. Louise Bogan. *PlI*

Variation on a theme by Francis Kilvert. Rolfe Humphries. *PlU*

Vases. See Pottery

Vaudeville dancer. John Hall Wheelock. *PlU*

Vaudracour and Julia. William Wordsworth. *NaE* (sel.)

Vaughan, Henry
Awake, glad heart. *UnG*
Peace. *GrCc—SmLg*
A vision. *PlI*
The waterfall. *HoW*

"Vault on the opal carpet of the sun." See To Potapovitch

Vegetables. See also Gardens and gardening; also names of vegetables, as Potatoes
Some vegetables and flowers. D. Aldis. *AlHd*
Vegetables. E. Farjeon. *FeF*

Vegetables. Eleanor Farjeon. *FeF*

Velvet shoes. Elinor Wylie. *ArTp—BrS—FeF—HuSv—JoAc—PeF*

Venders. See Peddlers and venders

Vengence on cats. John Skelton. *HaP*

Venice, Italy
The city of falling leaves. A. Lowell. *ArTp*

Venus
Hymn to Venus. Lucretius. *GrCc*

Verlaine, Paul
"The sky is up above the roof." *FeF*
Song of autumn. *PaS*
"Tears flow in my heart." *PaS*
"The white moon." *PaS*

Vern. Gwendolyn Brooks. *ArTp*

Verse. Oliver St John Gogarty. *SmLg*

Very, Jones
The tree. *CoPs—UnG*

"A very grandiloquent goat." See The grandiloquent goat

Very lovely. Rose Fyleman. *ArTp*

Very nearly. Queenie Scott-Hopper. *FeF*

"Very old are the woods." See All that's past

"Very thin." See Snake

"Very, very queer things have been happening to me." See Queer things

Vespers. A. A. Milne. *MiWc*

"Vessels large may venture more." See Poor Richard's wisdom

Veterans day
The bells of peace. A. Fisher. *BrS*
Everyone sang. S. Sassoon. *CoPs—McW*
In Flanders fields. J. McCrae. *BrS*
Memorial garden (Canterbury). E. Farjeon. *FaCb—FaN*
When Johnny comes marching home. P. S. Gilmore. *CoPs*

The vicar of Wakefield, sel. Oliver Goldsmith
Elegy on the death of a mad dog. *HaP—McW—SmLg—UnMc*

Vicary square. James Reeves. *ReW*

Vice. See An essay on man

"Vice is a monster of so frightful mien." See An essay on man—Vice

Voices
For a mocking voice. E. Farjeon. *ArTp—CoPm*
Voices. H. Behn. *BeW*
Voices. Harry Behn. *BeW*
Voices of heroes. Horace Gregory. *GrCc*
Von Herder, Johann Gottfried. See Herder, Johann Gottfried von
The **vow** to Cupid. Unknown, tr. fr. the Latin by J. A. Symonds. *PaS*
The **vowels.** Jonathan Swift. *DeT*
"Voy wawm, said the dustman." See Hymn to the sun
Voyages. See Adventure and adventurers; Seamen; Travel
The **vulture.** Hilaire Belloc. *LoL*
"The **vulture** eats between his meals." See The vulture
Vultures
The vulture. H. Belloc. *LoL*

W

W., A.
Youth. *HuL-2*
W., A. G.
Left out. *BrR-3*
W., D. D.
"The Indians come down from Mixco." tr. *FeF*
W. James Reeves. *ReBl—ReG*
W is for witch. Eleanor Farjeon. *FaCb*
Waddell, Helen
Carmina burana. tr. *PaS* (sel.)
Cathemerinon, sels. tr. *PaS*
    "The earth is sweet with roses"
    "Take him, earth, for cherishing"
"The **earth** is sweet with roses." See Cathemerinon
In the woods alone. tr. *PaS*
The morning glory. tr. *PaS*
"Take him, earth, for cherishing." See Cathemerinon
Wade-Gery
The power of music. tr. *PlU* (sel.)
Wadsworth, Olive A., pseud. (Katherine Floyd Dana)
"Over in the meadow." *NaM*
"Wae's me, wae's me." See The ghost's lament
"Wag a leg, wag a leg." See Foot play
The **wagon** in the barn. John Drinkwater. *BrR-4—PeF*
"A **wagonload** of radishes on a summer morning." See Prairie—Summer morning
Wagons
The wagon in the barn. J. Drinkwater. *BrR-4—PeF*
Western wagons. R. C. and S. V. Benét. *BrR-5—McW*
Wagtails
Little Trotty Wagtail. J. Clare. *FeF*
Waiting ("Dreaming of honeycombs to share") Harry Behn. *ArTp—BrS—JoAc*

Waiting ("Waiting, waiting, waiting") James Reeves. *ReW*
Waiting ("We've hung our Christmas stockings") Dorothy Aldis. *AlA*
Waiting ("What is the hardest thing of all? Waiting") Ruth Apprich Jacob. *BrBc*
Waiting at the window. A. A. Milne. *MiWc*
Waiting both. Thomas Hardy. *McW*
Waiting for the barbarians. C. P. Cavafy, tr. by John Mavrogordato. *GrCc*
"Waiting, waiting, waiting." See Waiting
Wake. See The rubáiyat of Omar Khayyám of Naishapúr
"Wake all the dead, what ho, what ho." William Davenant. *SmLg*
"Wake up, Jacob." Unknown. *WiRm*
"Wake up, O world; O world awake." See The wakeupworld
Wake-up poems. See also Morning
Asleep and awake. D. McCord. *McFf*
Chanticleer. J. Farrar. *ArTp—BrR-3*
"The cock doth crow." Mother Goose. *ArTp—DeMg—LiL—OpO*
"Cocks crow in the morn." Mother Goose. *ArTp*
    Signs, seasons, and sense. *UnG*
Dawn came running. I. O. Eastwick. *EaI*
Early. D. Aldis. *AlA*
Get up, get up. Unknown. *CoH*
Getting out of bed. E. Farjeon. *BrS*
I woke up. Unknown. *WoJ*
In the morning. D. Aldis. *AlHd*
It's time to get up. J. Ciardi. *CiM*
Morning. M. C. Livingston. *LiW*
Reveille. M. O'Connor. *BrR-6*
Rise, sun. F. M. Frost. *FrLn*
"Robin and Richard were two pretty men." Mother Goose. *DeMg*
    "Robin and Richard." *OpO*
"Softly, drowsily." From A child's day. W. De La Mare. *HuL-2—JoAc*
    A child's day begins. *HuSv*
    A child's day, Part II. *ArTp*
Song. G. Vicente. *PaS*
A summer morning. R. Field. *ArTp—BrR-4—HuSv—PeF*
The tardy playmate. F. R. Buchanan. *DoP*
Time to rise. R. L. Stevenson. *BrS—BrL-k—HuSv*
Up time. Mother Goose. *OpO*
"Wake up, Jacob." Unknown. *WiRm*
The wakeupworld. C. Cullen. *JoAc*
Waking time. I. O. Eastwick. *ArTp—BrS*
Wide awake. M. C. Livingston. *LiWa*
"A wind runs by at morning." R. B. Bennett. *BrR-4*
"Waken, lords and ladies gay." See Hunting song
The **wakeupworld.** Countee Cullen. *JoAc*
Waking time. Ivy O. Eastwick. *ArTp—BrS*
Waley, Arthur
The autumn wind. tr. *SmLg*
Clearing at dawn. tr. *PaS*
The cranes. tr. *PaS*
Crossing the river. tr. *PaS*
Dance song. tr. *SmLg*
Dreaming that I went with Li and Yü to visit Yüan Chên. tr. *PaS*

Battle of, 1314; also subdivisions under countries, as United States—History—Civil war

Anthem for doomed youth. W. Owen. *NaE*

The battle of Blenheim. R. Southey. *HaP—UnG*

Burial of Sir John Moore. C. Wolfe. *UnMc*
The burial of Sir John Moore at Corunna, 1809. *DeT*

The dark hills. E. A. Robinson. *HaP*

"Early in the morning." L. Simpson. *HaP*

The gay young squires. E. Farjeon. *FaCb*

In time of the breaking of nations. T. Hardy. *HaP*

"Once more unto the breach, dear friends, once more." From King Henry V. W. Shakespeare. *HaP*

The silent slain. A. MacLeish. *GrCc*

The silver tassie. R. Burns. *GrCc*

Soldier's song. T. Hume. *HoW*

The spires of Oxford. M. Letts. *BrL-7*

These fought. E. Pound. *HaP*

Voices of heroes. H. Gregory. *GrCc*

The war god's horse song. Unknown. *SmLg*

The war-song of Dinas Vawr. From The misfortunes of Elphin. T. L. Peacock. *CoSp—HoW—NaE*

The **war** god's horse song. Unknown, tr. fr. the Navajo by Dave and Mary Roberts Coolidge. *SmLg*

The **war-song** of Dinas Vawr. See The misfortunes of Elphin

Ward, Lydia Avery Coonley (Lydia Avery Coonley)
Flag song. *HaY*

"**Warm** and buoyant in his oily mail." See The whale

Warm hands. See "Warm hands, warm"

"**Warm** hands, warm." Mother Goose. *LiL*
Warm hands. *OpO*

"The **warm** of heart shall never lack a fire." Elizabeth Jane Coatsworth. *ArTp*

Warner, Sylvia Townsend
Tudor church music. *PlU*

A **warning.** See "Three children sliding on the ice"

Warning ("The inside of a whirlpool") John Ciardi. *CiM*

Warning ("The robin and the redbreast") Mother Goose. *OpO*

A **warning** about bears. John Ciardi. *CiY*

Warning to children. Robert Graves. *GrP—SmLg*

Warships. See also Naval battles
Old Ironsides. O. W. Holmes. *FeF—UnMc*
The Revenge. A. Tennyson. *UnMc*
The Shannon and the Chesapeake. Unknown. *DeT*

Was she a witch. Laura E. Richards. *BrL-k*

"**Was** worm." May Swenson. *UnG*

Wash-day. Lilian McCrea. *HuL-1*

"The **wash** is hanging on the line." See Windy wash day

Wash the dishes. Mother Goose. *OpO*

"**Wash** the dishes, wipe the dishes." See Wash the dishes

"**Wash** the sheep, and shear the sheep." See July's song

"The **washcloth** is a savage whale." See Bath time

Washday. Elizabeth F. Upson. *BrR-3*

Washday song. Myra Cohn Livingston. *LiWa*

Washing ("What is all this washing about") John Drinkwater. *BrR-4—FeF—HuSv—JoAc*

Washing ("With soap and water") Marie Louise Allen. *AlP*

Washing day ("The old woman must stand") Mother Goose. *OpO*

Washing day ("Water and soap") Lillian F. Taylor. *HuL-1*

Washing up. Mother Goose. *OpO*

Washington, George (about)
The boy Washington. D. B. Thompson. *BrS*
Ever since. E. J. Coatsworth. *BrS*
Footnote to history. E. J. Coatsworth. *BrS*
George Washington ("George Washington is tops with me") S. Silverstein. *CoPs*
George Washington ("George Washington, the farmer") J. S. Tippett. *HaY*
George Washington ("Sing hey, for bold George Washington") R. C. and S. V. Benét. *FeF—UnMc*
Leetla Giorgio Washeenton. T. A. Daly. *CoPs—FeF*
Picture people. R. B. Bennett. *HaY*
Washington. N. B. Turner. *ArTp—BrL-7—FeF—HaY—PeF*
Washington monument by night. C. Sandburg. *CoPs—FeF*
Young Washington. A. Guiterman. *CoPs—FeF*

Washington. Nancy Byrd Turner. *ArTp—BrL-7—FeF—HaY—PeF*

"**Washington** led armies." See Footnote to history

Washington monument by night. Carl Sandburg. *CoPs—FeF*

The **wasp.** William Sharp. *FeF—JoAc*

Waspish. Robert Frost. *FrR*

Wasps
"Big at both ends and small in the middle." Unknown. *WoF*
The wasp. W. Sharp. *FeF—JoAc*
Waspish. R. Frost. *FrR*

"The **wasps** in the orchard." See Thieves in the orchard

The **wassail** song. Unknown. *CoPs—DeT*

"**Watch.**" See Just watch

Watch, America. Robert Nathan. *McW*

Watch me. Dorothy Aldis. *AlHd*

"**Watch** the little otters." See Otter creek

"A **watch** will tell the time of day." See Mr Coggs, watchmaker

Watches. See Clocks and watches

Watching clouds. John Farrar. *HuSv*

Watching the moon. David McCord. *HaY—McFf*

"**Watchman,** what of the night." Algernon Charles Swinburne. *HoW*

Watchmen
Then. W. De La Mare. *HuL-2—ReG*
"Wee Willie Winkie runs through the town." Mother Goose. *ArTp—DeMg—HuSv—JoAc—LiL*
    "Wee Willie Winkie." *BrS*
    Willie Winkie. *OpO*
Water. See also Tides; Waterfalls; Waves; Weather; Wells; also types of streams, as Rivers
"Come down to the water." E. Farjeon. *FaCb*
Going for water. R. Frost. *FrR—FrY*
In praise of water. N. B. Turner. *HuL-2*
Irrigation. From In my mother's house. A. N. Clark. *HuSv*
"Jack and Jill went up the hill." Mother Goose. *ArTp—DeMg—HuSv—JoAc—LiL*
    Jack and Jill. *BrL-k*
    Jack and Jill and old Dame Dob. *OpO*
"Little drops of water." E. C. Brewer; also attributed to J. F. Carney. *AnI—DeMg*
    Little things. *FeF—UnG*
Lonesome water. R. Helton. *CoPm—McW*
The noise of waters. From Chamber music. J. Joyce. *ArTp—FeF*
    "All day I hear the noise of waters." *SmLg*
Prairie waters by night. C. Sandburg. *SaW*
Spring pools. R. Frost. *FrR*
Water ("There is a stream that flowed before the first beginning") K. Raine. *PlI* (sel.)
Water ("The world turns softly") H. Conkling. *ArTp*
Water noises. E. M. Roberts. *BrR-4—McAw*
Water ("There is a stream that flowed before the first beginning") Kathleen Raine. *PlI* (sel.)
Water ("The world turns softly") Hilda Conkling. *ArTp*
"Water and soap." See Washing day
The **water** babies, sels. Charles Kingsley
    The lost doll. *FeF—NaM*
    Young and old. *BrBc*
    The old song. *McW*
Water buffalo. William Jay Smith. *SmB*
"Water is a lovely thing." See In praise of water
Water-lilies
    Water-lilies. A. A. Milne. *MiWc*
Water-lilies. A. A. Milne. *MiWc*
Water mills. See Mills
Water noises. Elizabeth Madox Roberts. *BrR-4—McAw*
The **waterfall.** Henry Vaughan. *HoW*
Waterfalls
    Behind the waterfall. W. Welles. *ArTp—CoPm—HuSv*
    Evening waterfall. C. Sandburg. *GrCc*
    Niagara. From The people, yes. C. Sandburg. *SaW*
    The waterfall. H. Vaughan. *HoW*
Waterloo, Battle of, 1815
    The field of Waterloo. T. Hardy. *SmLg*
Waters. Edith H. Newlin. *BrR-4*

Waverley, sel. Walter Scott
    "Hie away, hie away." *ArTp*
    Hie away. *NaM*
Watkins, Vernon
    In spring. tr. *PaS*
Watson, Sara Ruth
    Bouncing ball. *BrR-3*
Watson, Sir William
    April. See Song
    Song. *CoPs—JoAc*
        April. *UnG*
Watts, Isaac
    The bee. See "How doth the little busy bee"
    "Christ hath a garden walled around." *SmLg*
    Cradle hymn. *DoP*
    "How doth the little busy bee." *FeF*
        The bee. *UnG*
        Little busy bee. *HuSv*
    Little busy bee. See "How doth the little busy bee"
    The sluggard. *NaM*
Watts, Mabel
    April weather. *McAw*
    Maytime magic. *McAw*
Watts, Marjorie Seymour
    New shoes. *BrR-3*
    The policeman. *ArTp*
Waves. See also Ocean
    Big waves and little waves. E. Farjeon. *HuL-1*
    "The horses of the sea." C. G. Rossetti. *FeF*
    A song for Hal. L. E. Richards. *HuL-2*
    Song of the wave. R. Frost. *FrR*
"The way a crow." See Dust of snow
"Way back here." Unknown. *MoY*
Way down South. Unknown. *NaE*
"Way down South where bananas grow." See Way down South
"Way down South where the coconuts grow." Unknown. *WiRm*
"Way down yonder in the maple swamp." Unknown
    American Father Gander. *UnG*
"Way down yonder on the Piankatank." Unknown. *WiRm*
" 'Way high up the Mogollons." See The glory trail
The **way** of life. Lao-tzu, tr. fr. the Chinese by Witter Bynner. *McW*
"The way they scrub." See An indignant male
The **way** through the woods. Rudyard Kipling. *FeF—HaP—ReT—SmLg*
"The wayfarer." Stephen Crane. *McW*
Wayfaring life. See also Adventure and adventurers; Gipsies; Roads and trails
    "Afoot and light-hearted, I take to the open road." From Song of the open road. W. Whitman. *ArTp*
    Being gypsy. B. Young. *ArTp*
    The hermit's song. Unknown. *PaS*
    "Hie away, hie away." From Waverley. W. Scott. *ArTp*
        Hie away. *NaM*
    "I meant to do my work today." R. Le Gallienne. *ArTp—BrR-5—HuL-2—JoAc—UnG*

The joys of the road. B. Carman. *BrL-8*
The Portsmouth road. C. Fox-Smith. *HuL-2*
The raggle taggle gypsies. Unknown. *ArTp
—FeF—HuSv—UnG*
    The wraggle taggle gipsies. *NaE—ReT*
    The wraggle taggle gipsies, O. *HoW*
Roadways. J. Masefield. *BrR-5*
Roofs. J Kilmer. *BrL-8*
Sea-fever. J. Masefield. *ArTp—BrL-8—
FeF—HuL-2—HuSv—JoAc—PeF*
The sea gypsy. R. Hovey. *BrL-7—FeF—
UnG*
The vagabond. R. L. Stevenson. *BrL-8*
A vagabond song. B. Carman. *BrR-5—
CoPs—FeF—HuL-2—JoAc—UnG*
Waltzing Matilda. A. B. Paterson. *CoSp—
McW*
Wander-thirst. G. Gould. *ArTp—BrL-7—
HuL-2*
A wanderer's song. J. Masefield. *JoAc*
Wild thyme. E. Farjeon. *BrS*
A windy day. W. Howard. *FeF*
The **ways**. John Oxenham. *ThP*
Ways and means. See Through the looking
glass—The white knight's song
The **ways** of trains. Elizabeth Jane Coats-
worth. *ArTp*
Ways of traveling. Alice Wilkins. *McAw*
"**We** all look on with anxious eyes." See
When father carves the duck
"**We** always drive along until." See The
Harpers' farm
"**We** are all in the dumps." Mother Goose.
DeMg
    In the dumps. *OpO*
"**We** are little." See To and fro
"**We** are poor and lowly born." See The
child's hymn
"**We** are such stuff as dreams are made of,
and these." See Poem
"**We** are the flute, our music is all Thine."
See The unseen power
"**We** are three brethren out of Spain." See
Three brethren from Spain
We are three lords. See Three brethren
from Spain
"**We** are three lords come out of Spain."
See Three brethren from Spain
"**We** are tired of Rome and Sparta." See
The children's lament
"**We** are very little creatures." See The
vowels
"**We** asked for rain. It didn't flash and
roar." See Our hold on the planet
"**We** be soldiers three." Unknown. *GrCc*
We be the king's men. See The dynasts
"**We** be the king's men, hale and hearty."
See The dynasts—We be the king's men
"**We** beat up spider webs to make." See
Our guest
"**We** brought a rug for sitting on." See The
picnic
"**We** brought him home, I was so pleased."
See My new rabbit
"**We** built a ship upon the stairs." See A
good play
"**We** can slide." See Sliding
"**We** dance round in a ring and suppose."
See The secret sits

"**We** do lie beneath the grass." See Dirge
"**We** do not know who made them." See
Negro spirituals
"**We** fed our tame baby squirrel his milk."
See Our tame baby squirrel
"**We** feed the birds in winter." See Joe
We fish. Herman Melville. *UnG*
"**We** fish, we fish, we merrily swim." See
We fish
"**We** found a beautiful green silk bug." See
The green silk bug
"**We** go to the golden palace." See The
golden palace
"**We** grow to the sound of the wind." See
Dates
"**We** had a circus in our shed." See Our
circus
"**We** had a pleasant walk to-day." See The
spring walk
"**We** had expected everything but revolt."
See Nightmare number three
"**We** had to wait for the heat to pass." See
August night
"**We** had waffles-with-syrup for breakfast."
See Birthdays
"**We** hang the holly up once more." See
Christmas singing
"**We** have a band at school." See Our band
"**We** have a mountain at the end of our
street." See In a desert town
"**We** have a nice clean new green lawn." See
Something better
"**We** have a secret, just we three." See The
secret
We have been here before. Morris Bishop.
NaE
We have been together. Eva Byron. *ThP*
"**We** have been together through the fat
days and the lean." See We have been
together
"**We** have tomorrow." See Youth
We know a house. Dorothy Aldis. *AlA*
"**We** know a house, we know a house." See
We know a house
"**We** listened to a scurry." See Our squirrel
"**We** made a snowman in our yard." See
The snowman
"**We** make ourselves a place apart." See
Revelation
"**We** may shut our eyes." See Joys
"**We** met the Flying Dutchman." See The
Flying Dutchman
We must be polite. Carl Sandburg. *SaW*
"**We** mustn't pick the garden flowers." See
Wildflowers
"**We** never had seen such a sight before."
See Saddest of all
We never know how high. Emily Dickinson.
McW
"**We** never know how high we are." See We
never know how high
"**We** planted a garden." See Flowers
"**We** put more coal on the big red fire." See
Father's story
"**We** sat together close and warm." See The
young mystic
"**We** saw him so naughty and scratching and
hitting." See A dreadful sight

"We saw thee come in, a wee naked babe."
See Farewell to the old year

"We shall not cease from exploration." See
Four quartets

"We shared in one delightful house." See
The lament of the white mouse

"We smile at astrological hopes." See For
the conjunction of two planets

"We stopped at the branch on the way to
the hill." See The branch

"We thank our loving Father God." See
God giveth all things

We thank Thee. Unknown. *BrR-6—FeF*

"We the fairies blithe and antic." See Fairies'
song

"We too, we too, descending once again."
See The silent slain

"We used to be ten brothers." See Ten
brothers

"We used to picnic where the thrift." See
Trebetherick

"We wake to hear the storm come down."
See The storm

"We went down to the river's brink." See
Explanation, on coming home late

"We were camped on the plains at the head
of the Cimarron." See The Zebra Dun

"We were schooner-rigged and rakish, with
a long and lissome hull." See A ballad
of John Silver

"We were taken from the ore bed and the
mine." See The secret of the machines

"We were very tired, we were very merry."
See Recuerdo

"We, who play under the pines." See The
rabbits' song outside the tavern

"We who were born." See Dew on the grass

"We will go to the wood, says Robin to
Bobbin." See The wren hunt

Wealth
Belongings. M. Chute. *ChA*
"The fairies have never a penny to spend."
R. Fyleman. *FeF*
"If life were a thing that money could
buy." Unknown. *MoY*
"My land is fair for any eyes to see."
J. Stuart. *ArTp—FeF*
Proverbs of King Alfred. King Alfred.
McW
The rich man. F. P. Adams. *CoH*
Richard Cory. E. A. Robinson. *CoSp—
SmLg—ThP*
Rune of riches. F. Converse. *HuL-2*
Wealth. R. W. Emerson. *PlI*
What's the difference. O. F. Pearre.
BrL-8

Wealth. Ralph Waldo Emerson. *PlI*

"A **wealthy** young squire of Tamworth we
hear." See The golden glove

Weapons. See Arms and armor; also names
of weapons, as Guns

"**Wearied** arm and broken sword." See
Pocahontas

The **wearin'** of the green. Unknown. *CoPs*

Wearing of the green. Aileen Fisher. *HaY*

The **weary** blues. Langston Hughes. *PlU*

Weather. See also Clouds; Dew; Fog; Mist;
Rain; Rainbows; Seasons; Snow; Storms;
Weather vanes; Winds
April weather. M. Watts. *McAw*
"As a rule men are fools." Unknown.
MoY
Clearing at dawn. Li T'ai-po. *PaS*
The cloud. P. B. Shelley. *FeF—JoAc—
PlI* (sel.)
"A dog and a cat went out together."
Mother Goose. *DeMg*
Dogs and weather. W. Welles. *ArTp—
FeF—HuL-2—HuSv*
The elements. W. H. Davies. *McW*
The equinox. H. W. Longfellow. *DeT*
"Evening red and morning grey." Mother
Goose. *OpO*
  Signs, seasons, and sense. *UnG*
The gnome. H. Behn. *ArTp—BeW—FeF*
Hot weather. D. Aldis. *AlA*
A hot-weather song. D. Marquis. *HuSv*
"If bees stay at home." Mother Goose.
OpO
  Signs, seasons, and sense. *UnG*
"If Candlemas day be dry and fair." Un-
known. *CoPs*
"If Candlemas day be fair and bright."
Unknown. *CoPs—DeMg*
"If the oak is out before the ash." Mother
Goose. *OpO*
"Mackerel sky." Mother Goose. *OpO*
"March winds and April showers." Mother
Goose. *DeMg—LiL—OpO*
  Signs, seasons, and sense. *UnG*
The mitten song. M. L. Allen. *AlP—ArTp
—BrL-k—HuL-1*
October's bright blue weather. H. H. Jack-
son. *CoPs*
Open eye, pimpernel. E. Farjeon. *FaCb—
FaN*
"Rainbow at night." Unknown. *WiRm*
  Signs, seasons, and sense. *UnG*
"Rainbow in the morning." Unknown.
WiRm
"A red sky at night." Mother Goose. *LiL
—OpO*
"St Swithin's day, if thou dost rain."
Mother Goose. *DeMg—LiL*
  Signs, seasons, and sense. *UnG*
Silk coats. E. Farjeon. *FaN*
"A sunshiny shower." Mother Goose.
DeMg—LiL—OpO
  Signs, seasons, and sense. *UnG*
This and that. F. B. Davis. *FeF*
Tree at my window. R. Frost. *FrR—FrY*
Weather ("It is a windy day") M. Chute.
ChA
Weather ("Weather is the answer") H.
Conkling. *ArTp*
The weather factory. N. B. Turner. *BrR-4*
Weather vanes. F. M. Frost. *BrS*
Weathers. T. Hardy. *DeT—HuL-2—NaE
—SmLg*
"When a cow begins to scratch her ear."
Unknown. *WiRm*
"When clouds appear." Mother Goose.
OpO
  Signs, seasons, and sense. *UnG*
"When the clouds are upon the hills."
Mother Goose. *OpO*

"When the dew is on the grass." Mother
Goose. *OpO*
"When the wind is in the east." Mother
Goose. *DeMg—LiL—OpO*
Signs, seasons, and sense. *UnG*
The winds. T. Tusser. *HoW*
"Winter's thunder." Mother Goose. *LiL*
Signs, seasons, and sense. *UnG*
The young mystic. L. Untermeyer. *BrR-5*
Weather ("It is a windy day") Marchette
Chute. *ChA*
Weather ("Weather is the answer") Hilda
Conkling. *ArTp*
The **weather** factory. Nancy Byrd Turner.
BrR-4
"**Weather** is the answer." See Weather
Weather vanes
Compass song. D. McCord. *McFf*
The four letters. J. Reeves. *ReBl*
The gnome. H. Behn. *ArTp—BeW—FeF*
Weather vanes. F. M. Frost. *BrS*
Weather vanes. Frances M. Frost. *BrS*
Weather words. David McCord. *PlI*
**Weatherly (or Weatherley), Frederic (or
Frederick) E.**
A carol. *HaY*
The cats' tea-party. *ArTp—CoI*
The tale of a tart. *HuL-1*
The usual way. *BrL-7*
Weathers. Thomas Hardy. *DeT—HuL-2—
NaE—SmLg*
Weavers and weaving
What the gray cat sings. A. Guiterman.
CoPm—NaM
"**Web-spinner** was a miser old." See The
true story of the web-spinner
Webb, Mary
The first bee. See The snowdrop
Green rain. *FeF*
The snowdrop, sel.
The first bee. *DeT*
Webb, Thomas Harry Basil
An ancient prayer. *DoP*
Webster, Daniel (about)
Daniel Webster's horses. E. J. Coats-
worth. *CoPm*
Webster, John
"Call for the robin-redbreast and the
wren." See The white devil
A dirge. See The white devil—"Call for
the robin-redbreast and the wren"
The white devil, sel.
"Call for the robin-redbreast and the
wren." *SmLg*
A dirge. *ReT*
Wedding ("Pussicat, wussicat, with a white
foot") Mother Goose. *OpO*
The **wedding** ("This year") Mother Goose.
OpO
Weddings. See Brides and bridegrooms;
Marriage
"A **wee** bird sat upon a tree." Unknown.
JoAc
"The **wee** folk will be tripping." See When
a ring's around the moon
"**Wee**, glossy, cowering, timorous beastie."
See To a mouse
"**Wee** Tammy Tyrie." See Tammy Tyrie

"**Wee**, wee tailor." See The tailor
"**Wee** Willie Winkie." See "Wee Willie
Winkie runs through the town"
"**Wee** Willie Winkie runs through the town."
Mother Goose. *ArTp—DeMg—HuSv—
JoAc—LiL*
"Wee Willie Winkie." *BrS*
Willie Winkie. *OpO*
Weelkes, Thomas
Ay me, alas. *SmLg*
"A **weeny** little bug." See Little bug
"**Weep**, weep, ye woodmen, wail." See Robin
Hood's funeral
"**Weep** with me, all you that read." See An
epitaph on Salathiel Pavy
Welchmen
"Taffy was a Welshman." Mother Goose.
DeMg—OpO
"There were three jovial Welshmen."
Mother Goose. *DeMg—JoAc*
"There were three jovial huntsmen."
HuSv
The three huntsmen. *PaOm*
"Three jolly huntsmen." *UnG*
The three jovial Welshmen. *OpO*
The three Welshmen. *NaM*
Welcome, L. O.
The phantom mail coach. *CoPm*
The **welcome.** Dorothy Aldis. *AlA*
A **welcome** to Dr Benjamin Apthorp Gould.
Oliver Wendell Holmes. *PlI*
Welcome to the new year. Eleanor Farjeon.
HaY
"**Well** boss did it." See The hen and the
oriole
"**Well**, boys and girls." See Ma's gonna buy
me
The **well-dressed** children. Robert Graves.
GrP
"**We'll** fill our cups and drink to you." See
A toast for Doctor Sam
We'll go no more a-roving. See "So, we'll
go no more a-roving"
Well, I never. Unknown, tr. fr. the Spanish
by Rose Fyleman. *JoAc*
"**Well** I never, did you ever." Unknown.
SmLg
"**Well** I remember how you smiled." See On
the death of Ianthe
"**Well**, old man Noah built the ark." See
Noah
"**We'll** see what we'll see." See The people,
yes—Proverbs
"**Well**, son, I'll tell you." See Mother to son
"**We'll** to the woods and gather may." See
Alons au bois le may cueillir
"The **well** was dry beside the door." See
Going for water
Welles, Winifred
The angel in the apple tree. *HuSv*
Behind the waterfall. *ArTp—CoPm—HuSv*
Climb. *BrBc*
Curious something. *ArTp*
Dogs and weather. *ArTp—FeF—HuL-2—
HuSv*
Fireflies. *JoAc*
God's first creature was light. *PlI*
Green grass and white milk. *ArTp*

"Whales have calves." See The guppy

"What a fearful battle." See The chickens

"What a lovely lazy sight." See A lazy sight

"What a night. The wind howls, hisses, and but stops." See Snowstorm

What a piece of work is a man. Sophocles, tr. fr. the Greek by F. L. Lucas. *PaS*

"What a wonderful bird the frog are." See The frog

What am I. Dorothy Aldis. *HuSv—JoAc*

What am I, Life. John Masefield. *PlI*

"What am I, Life? A thing of watery salt." See What am I, Life

What am I up to. David McCord. *McT*

"What are little boys made of, made of." Mother Goose. *DeMg—JoAc*
 Natural history. *OpO*

"What are the bugles blowin' for, said Files-on-Parade." See Danny Deever

"What are the cries of Bethlehem at Christmas on the night." See The cries of Bethlehem

"What are the great bells ringing." Charles Swain Thomas. *BrL-8*

"What are they ringing." See Canterbury bells

"What are we waiting for all crowded in the forum." See Waiting for the barbarians

"What are you able to build with your blocks." See Block city

"What are you carrying Pilgrims, Pilgrims." See The island—Atlantic Charter, A. D. 1620-1942

"What are you doing, my lady, my lady." See Mouse and mouser

"What are you doing there, Robin a Bobbin." See Talents differ

What bird so sings. John Lyly. *ReT*

"What bird so sings, yet so does wail." See What bird so sings

"What brings you, sailor, home from the sea." See Luck

"What can I give Him." See Carol ("In the bleak mid-winter")

"What can I give you." See Fifth birthday gift

What can the matter be. See "Oh dear, what can the matter be"

What care I. Mother Goose. *OpO*

"What care I how black I be." See What care I

"What care I, what cares he." See The cowboy

"What constitutes a state." William Jones. *BrL-7*

"What could be lovelier than to hear." Elizabeth Jane Coatsworth. *BrS*
 Summer rain. *BrR-5*

"What did I do on my blooming vacation." See The jokesmith's vacation

What did I dream. Robert Graves. *GrP*

"What did I dream? I do not know." See What did I dream

"What did I find." See A is for abracadabra

"What did I learn at the zoo." See What did you learn at the zoo

What did you learn at the zoo. John Ciardi. *CiY*

"What do hens say." See Near and far

"What do the stars do." See The stars

"What do they call you." Mother Goose. *DeMg*

What do they do. See "What does the bee do"

"What do they mean—the stripes of red." See The flag we fly

What do we plant. Henry Abbey. *ArTp—FeF*

"What do we plant when we plant the tree." See What do we plant

"What do you see in the sky, brown ox." See The ox and the ass

"What do you sell, O ye merchants." See In the bazaars of Hyderabad

What do you think his daddy did. John Ciardi. *CiY*

What does it matter. E. V. Rieu. *RiF*

"What does it matter to you and me." See What does it matter

"What does little birdie say." Alfred Tennyson. *BrL-k—HuL-1*

"What does the bee do." Christina Georgina Rossetti. *ArTp—HuL-1*
 What do they do. *FeF*

"What does the train say." See The baby goes to Boston

"What dost thou think of drumsticks." See The turkey's opinion

"What fairings will ye that I bring." See The singing leaves

"What God gives, and what we take." Robert Herrick. *JoAc*

"What God never sees." Mother Goose. *OpO*

"What goes into a birthday cake." See The birthday cake

"What great yoked brutes with briskets low." See Crossing the plains

What happened. Dorothy Aldis. *AlA*

"What have you done with your sheep." See Little Bo-peep and Little Boy Blue

"What heart could have thought you." See To a snow-flake

"What I have to say of Clarence Fud." See Say yes to the music, or else

"What I like about Clive." See Lord Clive

"What I saw was just one eye." See Bird at dawn

"What I shall leave thee none can tell." See To his son, Vincent Corbet

What I would do. Dorothy Aldis. *AlA*

"What if the air has a nipping tooth." See A skater's valentine

"What is a butterfly. At best." See Poor Richard's wisdom

"What is all this washing about." See Washing

"What is an epigram? A dwarfish whole." See An epigram

What is it. Marie Louise Allen. *AlP*

"What is life." Unknown. *MoY*

"What is lovelier than the gold." See Casual gold

"**What** is pink? a rose is pink." Christina Georgina Rossetti. *ArTp*
　Color. *HuL-1*

"**What** is poetry? Who knows." Eleanor Farjeon. *HaY*

"**What** is song's eternity." See Song's eternity

"**What** is the day after Sunday." See Every week song

"**What** is the hardest thing of all? Waiting." See Waiting

"**What** is the matter with Mary Jane." See Rice pudding

"**What** is the rhyme for porringer." Mother Goose. *OpO*
　Poringer. *ReG*

"**What** is the world, O soldiers." See Napoleon

"**What** is this life if, full of care." See Leisure

"**What** is time." Eleanor Farjeon. *FaCb—FaN*

"**What** is under the grass." See Under the ground

"**What** kind of a man made this poetry scan." See The author

What kind of music. James Reeves. *ReW*

"**What** kind of music does Tom like best." See What kind of music

"**What** kind of pants do cowboys wear." Unknown. *WiRm*
　"**What** kind of pants does a cowboy wear." *WoF*

"**What** kind of pants does a cowboy wear." See "What kind of pants do cowboys wear"

"**What** little throat." See The blackbird by Belfast lough

"**What** lovely names for girls there are." See Girls' names

"**What** lovely things." See The scribe

"**What** makes the crickets crick all night." See Crickets

"**What** makes the ducks in the pond, I wonder, go." See Regent's park

"**What** man is he that yearneth." See Old age

"**What** matter if my words will be." See To my mother

What Molly Blye said. David McCord. *McT*

What night would it be. John Ciardi. *CiY*

"**What**, not know our Clean Clara." See Clean Clara

"**What** passing-bells for these who die as cattle." See Anthem for doomed youth

What piggy-wig found. Enid Blyton. *HuL-1*

"**What** ran under the rosebush." See Could it have been a shadow

What robin told. George Cooper. *ArTp—BrL-k—BrR-3—FeF*

What saw I a-floating. Eleanor Farjeon. *FaCb*

"**What** shall I call." See The christening

What shall I give. Edward Thomas. *SmLg*

"**What** shall I give my daughter the younger." See What shall I give

"**What** shall we do for bacon now." Unknown. *WoF*

"**What** shall we do for timber." See Kilcash

"**What** shall we drink of when we sup." See King's-cup

"**What** should we know." See Verse

"**What** should we name our baby." See The baby's name

"**What** slender youth bedewed with liquid odours." See To a girl

"**What** splendid names for boys there are." See Boys' names

What the gray cat sings. Arthur Guiterman. *CoPm—NaM*

What the leaves said. Unknown. *HuL-1*

What the rattlesnake said. Vachel Lindsay. *JoAc*

What the toys are thinking. Ffrida Wolfe. *ArTp*

What the winds bring. Edmund Clarence Stedman. *BrR-4—HuL-1*

What they are for. Dorothy Aldis. *AlA*

What they do. Eleanor Farjeon. *FaCb—FaN*

What they like. Unknown. *HuL-1*

"**What** time is it? said the one." See The chronometer

What time of day. See "Bell horses, bell horses, what time of day"

"**What** time the rose of dawn is laid across the lips of night." See The angler's reveille

What to do. William Wise. *ArTp*

"**What** to do on a rainy day." See What to do

"**What** tree may not the fig be gathered from." See Wild grapes

"**What** was he doing, the great god Pan." See A musical instrument

"**What** was our trust, we trust not." See E = MC²

"**What** was the name you called me." See Evening waterfall

"**What** will go into the Christmas stocking." See Christmas stocking

"**What** will we do with the baby-oh." Unknown. *WoF*

"**What** will you have for your birthday." See Birthday gifts

"**What** will you ride on." See Hey, my pony

"**What** worlds of wonder are our books." See Books

"**What** would you say if I said I saw." See At the farm

"**What**, write in your album." Unknown. *MoY*

"**What**, write in your book." Unknown. *MoY*

"**What** you got there." See Club fist

What you will learn about the brobinyak. John Ciardi. *CiR—NaE*

"**Whatever** comes my way today." See Prayer

"**Whatever** is inside that sheet." See A-ha

"**Whatever** you are, be that." Unknown. *MoY*

"**What's** in the cupboard." Mother Goose. *JoAc—OpO*

"**What's** in there." Mother Goose. *OpO*

What's the difference. O. F. Pearre. *BrL-8*

"What's the good of breathing." See The frost pane

"What's the greeting for a rajah riding on an elephant." See Some questions to be asked of a rajah, perhaps by the Associated Press

What's the news. See "What's the news of the day"

"What's the news of the day." Mother Goose. *DeMg*
What's the news. *OpO*

"What's this dull town to me." See Robin Adair

"What's your age." See Mother's party

"What's your name." Unknown
American Father Gander. *UnG*

"Whatsoever things are true." See The epistle of Paul to the Philippians

Wheat
Color in the wheat. H. Garland. *JoAc*
The sheaves. E. A. Robinson. *HaP*

The **wheel**. Sully-Prudhomme, tr. fr. the French by William Dock. *PlU*

Wheel barrows
"Goes through the mud." Mother Goose. *OpO*

Wheeler, Ella. See Wilcox, Ella Wheeler

The **wheelgoround.** Robert Clairmont. *CoPm*

Wheelock, John Hall
Mozart perhaps. *PlU*
Symphony: First movement. *PlU*
Vaudeville dancer. *PlU*

Wheels. See also Bicycles and bicycling
The wheel. Sully-Prudhomme. *PlU*
Wings and wheels. N. B. Turner. *ArTp—HuSv*

"The **wheel's** inventor, nameless demigod." See The wheel

When. Dorothy Aldis. *AlA—BrS*

"When a cow begins to scratch her ear." Unknown. *WiRm*

When a fellow's four. Mary Jane Carr. *BrBc*

"When a felon's not engaged in his employment." See The pirates of Penzance—The policeman's lot

"When a friend calls to me from the road." See A time to talk

"When a goose meets a moose." Zhenya Gay. *ArTp*

"When a great tree falls." See To be answered in our next issue

"When a man hath no freedom to fight for at home." George Gordon Byron. *HaP*

"When a mounting skylark sings." See Skylark and nightingale

When a ring's around the moon. Mary Jane Carr. *ArTp—HuL-2*

When a ship sails by. Rowena Bastin Bennett. *BrR-6*

"When a ship sails down the river." See When a ship sails by

"When a sighing begins." See Song of autumn

"When a twister a-twisting, will twist him a twist." Mother Goose. *DeMg—OpO*

"When all is zed and done." See Z

"When all the days are hot and long." See Swimming

"When all the ground with snow is white." See The snow-bird

"When all the other leaves are gone." See Oak leaves

"When all the world is young, lad." See The water babies—Young and old

"When an elf is as old as a year and a minute." See The seven ages of elf-hood

When Anabelle's it. Dorothy Aldis. *AlA*

"When Ann and I go out a walk." See The morning walk

"When Anne has parties for her dolls." See Polite tea party

"When, as the garish day is done." See The new moon

"When as the rye reach to the chin." George Peele. *SmLg*

"When at home alone I sit." See The little land

"When autumn wounds the bough." See Autumnal spring song

"When awful darkness and silence reign." See The dong with a luminous nose

When blue sky smiles. Olive Beaupré Miller. *BrL-k*

"When blue sky smiles and birds come back." See When blue sky smiles

"When Bobby and I played we were pirates." See Pirates

"When brother takes me walking." See The ordinary dog

"When brownies filled the milking-pail." See H is for happily ever after

When candy was chocolate. William Jay Smith. *SmL*

"When candy was chocolate and bread was white." See When candy was chocolate

"When cats run home and light is come." See The owl

"When Charlemagne went to war." See The gay young squires

"When Christ was born in Bethlehem." See Ballad of the Epiphany

"When clouds appear." Mother Goose. *OpO*
Signs, seasons, and sense. *UnG*

"When clouds appear like rocks and towers." See "When clouds appear"

"When Daddy." See Walking

"When Daddy shaves and lets me stand and look." See Daddy

"When daffodils begin to peer." See The winter's tale

"When daisies pied and violets blue." See Love's labor's lost—Spring and winter

"When descends on the Atlantic." See The equinox

When did the world begin. See The answers

"When did the world begin and how." See The answers

"When does the rent fall due of the parson's glebe." See First catch your hare

When father carves the duck. Ernest V. Wright. *CoH—CoPs*

"When father takes his spade to dig." See The robin

"When foxes eat the last gold grape." See Escape

"When friendship or love our sympathies move." See Hours of idleness

"**When** frost is shining on the trees." See At Mrs Appleby's

"**When** gadding snow makes hillsides white." See Winter

"**When** George's grandmamma was told." See George who played with a dangerous toy and suffered a catastrophe of considerable dimensions

"**When** God at first made man." See The pulley

"**When** God makes a lovely thing." See Little

"**When** God reveals His plans to men." See An eclipse

"**When** good King Arthur ruled this land." Mother Goose. *DeMg—JoAc—LiL*
The bag pudding. *DeT*
King Arthur. *OpO*

"**When** Goody O'Grumpity baked a cake." See Goody O'Grumpity

"**When** great-grandmother was ten years old." See The sampler

When Hannibal crossed the Alps. Eleanor Farjeon. *FaCb—HuL-2*

"**When** he came to tuck me in." See It was

"**When** he takes a bath, the antelope." See Antelope

"**When** he was young his cousins used to say of Mr Knight." See Hall and Knight; or, $z + b + x = y + b + z$

"**When** human folk put out the light." See Kitten's night thoughts

"**When** I a verse shall make." See His prayer to Ben Jonson

"**When** I am a man and can do as I wish." See The conjuror

"**When** I am big, I mean to buy." Mary Mapes Dodge. *BrBc*

"**When** I am dead and in my grave." Unknown. *MoY*

"**When** I am dead, my dearest." Christina Georgina Rossetti. *HaP*

"**When** I am grown an hombre." See Ambition

"**When** I am old and grow a bit." See Growing up

"**When** I am playing by myself." See Water noises

"**When** I am the president." Unknown American Father Gander. *UnG*

"**When** I am walking down the street." See New shoes

"**When** I carefully consider the curious habits of dogs." See Meditatio

"**When** I climb up." See Drinking fountain

"**When** I consider how my light is spent." See Sonnet on his blindness

"**When** I consider thy heavens." See Psalms —Psalm VIII

"**When** I grow old I hope to be." See Growing old

"**When** I grow up." See Plans

"**When** I grow up." William Wise. *BrBc*

When I grow up ("When I grow up I mean to go") Rupert Sargent Holland. *BrBc—BrR-5*

"**When** I grow up I mean to go." See When I grow up

"**When** I have drunk my orange juice." See In winter

"**When** I have fears that I may cease to be." John Keats. *HaP—UnG*

"**When** I hear the old men." See A song of greatness

"**When** I heard the learn'd astronomer." Walt Whitman. *SmLg*

"**When** I invite the giraffe to dine." See Giraffe

"**When** I lived in Singapore." See In foreign parts

"**When** I look at our green hill." See Green hill neighbors

"**When** I look into a glass." See A thought

"**When** I must come to you, O my God, I pray." See Francis Jammès: A prayer to go to Paradise with the donkeys

"**When** I play on my fiddle in Dooney." See The fiddler of Dooney

"**When** I put her in the swing." See The other child

"**When** I put on my mother's clothes." See Pretending

"**When** I remember again." See The sparrow's dirge

"**When** I ride my bicycle." See Different bicycles

"**When** I see a starfish." See The starfish

"**When** I see birches bend to left and right." See Birches

"**When** I see the dentist." See Tooth trouble

"**When** I shet my eyes now." See Old blue saucepan

"**When** I spin round without a stop." See Spinning top

"**When** I spread out my hand here today." See Sitting by a bush in broad sunlight

"**When** I swam underwater I saw a blue whale." See Whale

"**When** I think on the happy days." See Absence

"**When** I try to skate." See Skating

"**When** I visited America." See Translations from the Chinese—He comforts himself

"**When** I was a bachelor, I lived by myself." Mother Goose. *LiL*

"**When** I was a beggarly boy." See Aladdin

When I was a lad. Mother Goose. *OpO*

"**When** I was a lad and so was my dad." See When I was a lad

"**When** I was a little boy." Mother Goose. *BrL-k*
The bachelor's lament. *OpO*
"When I was a little boy I lived by myself." *DcMg*

"**When** I was a little boy (I had but little wit)." See Lack wit

"**When** I was a little boy I had no sense." Unknown. *WoF*

"**When** I was a little boy I lived by myself." See "When I was a little boy"

"**When** I was a little boy, I thought I was a bold one." Unknown. *WoF*

"**When** I was a little boy (I washed)." See Washing up

"**When** I was a little boy (my mammy kept)." Mother Goose. *OpO*

"When I was a little child." See Ha ha thisaway

"When I was a little girl." See A little girl

"When I was a youngster just going to school." See Books et veritas

"When I was at the party." See Betty at the party

"When I was bound apprentice in famous Lincolnshire." See The Lincolnshire poacher

"When I was but thirteen or so." See Romance

"When I was christened." David McCord. BrBc

"When I was down beside the sea." See At the sea-side

"When I was just a little boy." See The ships of Yule

"When I was just as far as I could walk." See The telephone

When I was lost. Dorothy Aldis. AlA

"When I was making myself a game." See Little rain

"When I was once in Baltimore." See Sheep

"When I was one." See The end

"When I was one." See Sophisticate

"When I was one-and-twenty." See A Shropshire lad

"When I was only six years old." See When I was six

"When I was seven." See Growing up

"When I was sick and lay abed." See The land of counterpane

When I was six. Zora Cross. BrBc—FeF

"When I was small I'm sure I heard." See The fairy and the bird

"When I was young and full o' pride." See Blow me eyes

"When I was young—and very young." See Wisdom

"When I was young I heard a tune." See For the eightieth birthday of a great singer

"When I was young I planted thee." See An old man's epitaph

"When I was young, I said to sorrow." See Sorrow

"When I went down to Kingdom cove." See Kingdom cove

"When I went out to play today." See Dandelions

"When I went paddling in the sea." See Paddling

When I went to get a drink. John Ciardi. CiI

"When ice cream grows on spaghetti trees." Unknown. MoY

"When icicles hang by the wall." See Love's labor's lost

"When I'm a little older." See My plan

When I'm invited. Dorothy Aldis. AlHd

"When I'm invited anywhere." See When I'm invited

"When I'm playing." See All a duck needs

"When I'm riding on a train." See Train ride

"When in disgrace with fortune and men's eyes." See Sonnets

"When in our London gardens." See The London owl

"When in the chronicle of wasted time." See Sonnets

"When, in the morning, fresh from sleep." See In the morning

"When in the night I await her coming." See The muse

"When it gets dark the birds and flowers." See Prayer for a child

"When it is the winter time." See Ice

"When it's just past April." See The flower-cart man

"When its rays fall on its cheeks the cat licks them, thinking them milk." See The moon

"When it's stormy outside." See Winter content

"When Jack Frost comes—oh, what fun." See Jack Frost

"When Jack's a very good boy." Mother Goose. DeMg

"When Jacky's a good boy." OpO

"When Jacky's a very good boy." NaE

"When Jacky's a good boy." See "When Jack's a very good boy"

"When Jacky's a very good boy." See "When Jack's a very good boy"

"When Jesus was a little Child." See Mother and Child

"When Joan, aged ten, just after tea." See Hers

"When John was christened, up he reached." See It really happened

When Johnny comes marching home. Patrick Sarsfield Gilmore. CoPs

"When Johnny comes marching home again, hurrah, hurrah." See When Johnny comes marching home

"When Joy and Molly on the lawn." See Jessica dances

"When Lady Jane refused to be." See Save the tiger

"When land is gone and money spent." Mother Goose. OpO

"When leaves of April glisten." See The concert

"When life shall give you, some beggared hour." See Persian proverb

"When lion sends his roaring forth." See The lion

"When little Dickie Swope's a man." See An impetuous resolve

"When little heads weary have gone to their bed." See The plumpuppets

"When love has passed its limits." See Medea—Chorus from Medea

"When love with unconfinèd wings." See To Althea from prison

"When Lucy McLockett." See Lucy McLockett

"When Markham Toots blew out the light." Unknown. WoF

"When Mary came to Bethlehem." See A carol for sleepy children

"When Mary was one." See Mary and the marigold

"When May has come, and all around." See The archer

"When the hounds of spring are on winter's traces." See Atalanta in Calydon—Chorus from Atalanta in Calydon

"When the house is silent." See Song for a little cuckoo clock

"When the hurricane unfolds." See The hurricane

"When the leaves are young." See The leaves

"When the mole goes digging." See The mole

"When the moon shines o'er the corn." See The field mouse

"When the morning sun is on the trumpet-vine blossoms." See Prairie—Songs

"When the night is cloudy." See In the hours of darkness

"When the night wind howls in the chimney cowls, and the bat in the moonlight flies." See Ruddigore—Sir Roderic's song

"When the nights are long and the dust is deep." See Thistledown

"When the other children go." See The invisible playmate

"When the pale moon hides and the wild wind wails." See The wolf

"When the picnic was over." See Beach fire

"When the ploughman, as he goes." See Morning

"When the pods went pop on the broom, green broom." See A runnable stag

"When the Princess Priscilla goes out." See The Princess Priscilla

"When the rain is raining." See Umbrellas

"When the ripe pears droop heavily." See The wasp

"When the scarlet cardinal tells." See It is July

"When the snow has gone away." See The procession

"When the sun." See Twinkletoes

"When the sun has slipped away." See The skunk

"When the sun is strong." See In August

"When the sun rose I was still lying in bed." See Hearing the early oriole

"When the tea is brought at five o'clock." See Milk for the cat

"When the voices of children are heard on the green." See Nurse's song

"When the walls of earth have fallen." Unknown. MoY

"When the wind blows." Mother Goose. OpO

"When the wind is in the east." Mother Goose. DeMg—LiL—OpO
Signs, seasons, and sense. UnG

"When the wind works against us in the dark." See Storm fear

"When the winds blow and the seas flow." Unknown. ArTp

"When they heard the captain humming and beheld the dancing crew." See The post captain

"When they said the time to hide was mine." See The rabbit

When thou must home. See "When thou must home to shades of underground"

"When thou must home to shades of underground." Thomas Campion. GrCc
When thou must home. HaP

"When times are hard." Unknown. MoY

"When, to a cheap and tawdry tune, the orchestra cried out." See Vaudeville dancer

"When to her lute Corinna sings." Thomas Campion. GrCc
Corinna. PlU

"When to the sessions of sweet silent thought." See Sonnets

"When trees did show no leaves." See The ending of the year

"When twilight comes to Prairie street." See The winning of the TV West

"When twilight creeps upon the land." See S is for sandman

"When twilight drops her curtain." Unknown. MoY

"When walking in a tiny rain." See Vern

"When waves invade the yellowing wheat." See Composed while under arrest

When we are men. Stella Mead. HuL-1

"When we get out the car." See The picnic box

"When we lived in the city." See Until we built a cabin

"When we went to the zoo." See Our visit to the zoo

"When we were building Skua light." See The dancing seal

"When we're." See Dangerous

"When will it turn into spring." See Spring signs

"When winds that move not its calm surface sweep." See The landsman

"When, with my little daughter Blanche." See Presence of mind

"When you are drinking." Unknown. MoY

"When you are dying." Unknown. MoY

"When you are hungry." Unknown. MoY

"When you are in the country." Unknown. MoY

"When you are lonely." Unknown. MoY

"When you are married (and have a pair)." Unknown. MoY

"When you are married (and have one)." Unknown. MoY

"When you are married (and have twenty-five)." Unknown. MoY

When you are old ("When you are old and gray and full of sleep") William Butler Yeats. HaP

"When you are old (and cannot see)." Unknown. MoY

"When you are old and gray and full of sleep." See When you are old

"When you are sick." Unknown. MoY

"When you are walking by yourself." See Kick a little stone

"When you are washing at a tub." Unknown. MoY

"When you are wealthy." Unknown. MoY

"When you can catch." See Then

"When you get married (and live across)." Unknown. MoY

"When you get married (and live next door)." Unknown. *MoY*

"When you get married (and live on figs)." Unknown. *MoY*

"When you get married (and live upstairs)." Unknown. *MoY*

"When you get married (and your husband)." Unknown. *MoY*

"When you get married (don't marry a flirt)." Unknown. *MoY*

"When you get old and your dress gets purple." Unknown. *MoY*

"When you grow old." Unknown. *MoY*

"When you put me up on the elephant's back." See Elephant

"When you send a valentine." Mildred J. Hill. *BrR-3—McAw*

"When you sing." See The winter's tale

"When you talk to a monkey." Rowena Bastin Bennett. *BrR-3*

When you walk. James Stephens. *McW*

"When you walk in a field." See When you walk

"When you want to go wherever you please." See The land of Ho-Ho-Hum

"When you watch for." See Feather or fur

When young Melissa sweeps. Nancy Byrd Turner. *FeF*

"When young Melissa sweeps a room." See When young Melissa sweeps

"When you're an anvil, hold still." See Poor Richard's wisdom

"When you're lying awake with a dismal headache, and repose is tabooed by anxiety." See Iolanthe—The Lord Chancellor's song

"Whence comes this rush of wings afar." See Carol of the birds

Whence is this fragrance. Unknown. *ReG*

"Whence is this fragrance all perfuming." See Whence is this fragrance

"Whenever a little child is born." Agnes Carter Mason. *BrBc*

"Whenever I ride on the Texas plains." See Texas trains and trails

"Whenever I say America." Nancy Byrd Turner. *HaY*

"Whenever I walk in a London street." See Lines and squares

"Whenever I walk to Suffern along the Erie track." See The house with nobody in it

"Whenever I'm a shining knight." See Knight-in-armour

"Whenever Richard Cory went down town." See Richard Cory

"Whenever the days are cool and clear." See The sandhill crane

"Whenever the moon and stars are set." See Windy nights

Where. David McCord. *McT*

"Where am I going? I don't quite know." See Spring morning

"Where are you coming from, Lomey Carter." See Old Christmas

"Where are you going." See Holiday

"Where are you going." Ivy O. Eastwick. *EaI*

"Where are you going, Mrs Cat." See Country cat

"Where are you going, my little kittens." See The little kittens

"Where are you going, my little pig." See Little piggy

"Where are you going, my pretty maid." See "Where are you going to, my pretty maid"

"Where are you going to, my pretty maid." Mother Goose. *DeMg—LiL*

The milkmaid. *OpO*

"Where are you going, my pretty maid." *HuL-1—JoAc*

"Where are you going, winsome maid." See Arrows of love

"Where are you going, you little pig." See Precocious piggy

"Where are your oranges." See The children's bells

"Where bright waters flood the spring shore." See Wild geese

"Where did Momotara go." See Momotara

"Where did they come from, said Peter to Jane." See The secret

"Where did you come from, baby dear." See The baby

"Where dips the rocky highland." See The stolen child

"Where do all the daisies go." Unknown. *BrL-k*

"Where do the rainbows end." See A rainbow piece

"Where do the stars grow, Little Garaine." See Little Garaine

"Where do you go when you go to sleep." See The army horse and the army jeep

"Where does Pinafore palace stand." See Lilliput-land

Where dreams are made. Burges Johnson. *BrR-4*

Where go the boats. Robert Louis Stevenson. *ArTp—BrR-3—HuL-2—SmLg*

"Where God had walked." See The first autumn

"Where had I heard this wind before." See Bereft

"Where hae ye been a' the day." See The croodin doo

"Where have these hands been." See Musician

"Where have you been." See Banbury fair

"Where have you been all the day." See "Oh where have you been, Billy boy, Billy boy"

"Where have you been all the day, Billy boy, Billy boy." See "Oh where have you been, Billy boy, Billy boy"

"Where have you been all the day, Randall, my son." See Lord Randal

"Where have you gone to, Yesterday." See Yesterday

Where I took hold of life. Robert P. Tristram Coffin. *BrBc*

"Where is Anne." See Buttercup days

Where is he. See "Where, oh, where has my little dog gone"

Where is heaven. Bliss Carman. *UnG*

"**Where** is heaven? Is it not." See Where is heaven

Where is it. Dorothy Aldis. *AlA*

"**Where** is that little pond I wish for." See Where

"**Where** is the grave of Sir Arthur O'Kellyn." See The knight's tomb

"**Where** is the nightingale." See A song from Cyprus

Where lies the land. Arthur Hugh Clough. *SmLg*

"**Where** lies the land to which the ship would go." See Where lies the land

"**Where** long the shadows of the wind had rolled." See The sheaves

"**Where,** oh, where is my little dog gone." Mother Goose. *WoF*

Where is he. *OpO*

"**Where** oh where is pretty little Susie." See The pawpaw patch

Where shall we dance. Gabriela Mistral, tr. fr. the Spanish by Alice Stone Blackwell. *PaS*

"**Where** shall we dance in a circle." See Where shall we dance

"**Where** shall we go." See August afternoon

"**Where** shall we meet, oh where shall we meet." See Friday street

Where shall wisdom be found. See The Bacchae

"**Where** should this music be? I' the air, or the earth." See The tempest

Where the bee sucks. See The tempest— "Where the bee sucks, there suck I"

"**Where** the bee sucks, there suck I." See The tempest

"**Where** the northern ocean darkens." See Watch, America

"**Where** the pools are bright and deep." See A boy's song

"**Where** the remote Bermudas ride." See Bermudas

"**Where** the slanting forest eves." See To nature seekers

"**Where** the water-lilies go." See Water-lilies

"**Where** wast thou when I laid the foundations of the earth." See Job—Job, Chapter 38

"**Where** we walk to school each day." See Indian children

"**Where** will your training lead." See The boy Washington

Where's Mary. Ivy O. Eastwick. *ArTp*

"**Where's** the Queen of Sheba." See Gone

"**Wherever** I am, there's always Pooh." See Us two

"**Wherever** I go, it also goes." See My body

"**Which** I wish to remark." See Plain language from truthful James

"**Which** is the way to Baby-land." See Baby-land

"**Which** is the way to London town." Unknown. *HuL-1*

"**Which** is the way to the nearest town." See Conversation with an April fool

"**Which** is the wind that brings the cold." See What the winds bring

"**Which** will you have, a ball or a cake." See Choosing

"**While** midnight clung to every shore." See Natura in urbe

"**While** moonlight, silvering all the walls." See The barn owl

"**While** my hair was still cut straight across my forehead." See The river-merchant's wife: A letter

While shepherds watched. Margaret Deland. *DoP*

While shepherds watched their flocks by night. *EaW*

While shepherds watched their flocks by night. See While shepherds watched

"**While** shepherds watched their flocks by night." Nahum Tate. *JoAc*

"**While** the hum and the hurry." See Under a hat rim

"**While** yet the morning star." See The unicorn

Whippoorwills
The mountain whippoorwill. S. V. Benét. *CoSp*
A nature note. R. Frost. *FrY*

The **whirl-blast.** William Wordsworth. *DeT*

"A **whirl-blast** from behind the hill." See The whirl-blast

"**Whirling** gusts of starry flakes." See Frost fairies

"**Whirling,** swirling, rushing, twirling." See Snowflakes

Whirlpools
Warning. J. Ciardi. *CiM*

"**Whisky,** frisky." See The squirrel

"The **whisky** on your breath." See My papa's waltz

The **whisperer.** James Stephens. *DoP*

"**Whispers.**" Myra Cohn Livingston. *LiW*

Whistle. See Whistles ("I want to learn to whistle")

"**Whistle** and hoe." Unknown. *WoF*

"**Whistle,** daughter, whistle." Mother Goose. *DeMg*
Inducements. *OpO*

"**Whistle** under the water." See Flute-priest song for rain

Whistle, whistle. Unknown. *HuL-2*

"**Whistle,** whistle, old wife, and you'll get a hen." See Whistle, whistle

Whistles. See also Whistling
Trains at night. F. M. Frost. *ArTp*
Whistles. R. Field. *ArTp—HuSv*
Whistles ("I never even hear") Rachel Field. *ArTp—HuSv*
Whistles ("I want to learn to whistle") Dorothy Aldis. *JoAc*
Whistle. *BrL-k*

Whistling. See also Whistles
The little whistler. F. M. Frost. *ArTp— HuSv—JoAc—PeF*
Where is it. D. Aldis. *AlA*
"Whistle, daughter, whistle." Mother Goose. *DeMg*
Inducements. *OpO*
Whistle, whistle. Unknown. *HuL-2*
Whistles. D. Aldis. *JoAc*
Whistle. *BrL-k*
Whistling boy. J. R. Quinn. *BrBc*
Whistling boy. John Robert Quinn. *BrBc*

"The whistling postman swings along." See The postman

White, E. B.
Apostrophic notes from the new-world physics. *PlI*
Natura in urbe. *McW*

"White bird featherless." Mother Goose. *OpO*

Snow and sun. *ReG*

The white blackbirds. Eleanor Farjeon. *FaCb*

White butterflies. Algernon Charles Swinburne. *FeF*

"The white cock's tail." See Ploughing on Sunday

"White daisies are down in the meadow." See Alone

The white devil, sel. John Webster
"Call for the robin-redbreast and the wren." *SmLg*
A dirge. *ReT*

The white egret. Li T'ai-po, tr. fr. the Chinese by E. D. Edwards. *PaS*

White fields. James Stephens. *BrR-4—BrS —CoPs—FeF—HuL-2—McAw—NaM*

"White flowers and white butterflies." Dorothy Aldis. *AlHd*

"White frost comes." See October night

"White hair, red eyes and little black ears." See The new pet

The white island. Robert Herrick. *HoW*

The white knight's song. See Through the looking glass

"The white man drew a small circle in the sand and told the red man." See The people, yes—Circles

"The white moon." Paul Verlaine, tr. fr. the French by Kate Flores. *PaS*

The white owl ("When cats run home and light is come") See The owl

The white owl ("When night is o'er the wood") F. J. Patmore. *CoPm*

The white rabbit. E. V. Rieu. *RiF*

The white rabbit's verses. See Alice's adventures in wonderland

"White Rose is a quiet horse." See The four horses

White season. Frances M. Frost. *ArTp— FeF*

"White sheep, white sheep." Unknown. *ArTp*
Clouds. *BrL-k—HuSv*

The white ships. David McCord. *McFf*

The white-tailed hornet. Robert Frost. *FrR*

"The white-tailed hornet lives in a balloon." See The white-tailed hornet

The white window. James Stephens. *ArTp —BrL-k—HuL-2—HuSv—JoAc*

"Whitely, whitely." See Snow picture

"Whither, midst falling dew." See To a waterfowl

"Whither, O splendid ship, thy white sails crowding." See A passer-by

Whitman, Walt
"Afoot and light-hearted, I take to the open road." See Song of the open road
The commonplace. *JoAc*

Give me the splendid silent sun. *FeF— JoAc*

"I believe a leaf of grass is no less than the journey-work of the stars." See Song of myself

I hear America singing. *ArTp—BrL-7— BrR-5—CoPs—FeF—HuSv—JoAc—SmLg —UnG*

Miracles. See Song of myself

"A noiseless patient spider." *HaP—NaE* The spider. *HoW*

O captain, my captain. *FeF—HuSv—SmLg*

"O tan-faced prairie boy." *FeF*

An old-time sea-fight. See Song of myself

"A sight in camp in the daybreak gray and dim." *HaP*

Song of myself, sels.
"I believe a leaf of grass is no less than the journey-work of the stars." *ArTp*
Miracles. *HuSv—JoAc—McW—UnG*
An old-time sea-fight. *UnMc*

Song of the open road, sel.
"Afoot and light-hearted, I take to the open road." *ArTp*

The spider. See "A noiseless patient spider"

There was a child went forth. *BrBc—UnG*

"When I heard the learn'd astronomer." *SmLg*

"Whoever you are holding me now in hand." *HaP*

Whitman, Walt (about)
Song of myself, sels. W. Whitman
"I believe a leaf of grass is no less than the journey-work of the stars." *ArTp*
Miracles. *HuSv—JoAc—McW—UnG*
An old-time sea-fight. *UnMc*
"Whoever you are holding me now in hand." W. Whitman. *HaP*

Whitney, Adeline D. (Dutson) T. (Train)
February. *HaY*

Whittemore, Reed
A projection. *McW*
Spring, etc. *McW*

Whittier, John Greenleaf
Barbara Frietchie. *CoPs—FeF—JoAc—UnG —UnMc*
The barefoot boy. *FeF* (sel.)
The brown dwarf of Rügen. *CoPm*
In school-days. *FeF* (sel.)
My playmate. *DeT*
The pumpkin. *CoPs*
The schoolmaster. See Snow-bound
Skipper Ireson's ride. *CoSp*
The snow. See Snow-bound
Snow-bound, sels.
The schoolmaster. *UnG*
The snow. *HuSv*
Snow-bound. *HoW*
The uncle. *UnG*
"Unwarmed by any sunset light" Lines from Snow-bound. *JoAc*
The uncle. See Snow-bound
"Unwarmed by any sunset light." See Snow-bound

Whittling
"I met a man that was trying to whittle." J. Ciardi. *CiI*

A wonderful man. A. Fisher. *BrS*

"Who are you, asked the cat of the bear." Elizabeth Jane Coatsworth. *ArTp*

"Who are you, Sea Lady." See Santorin

Who calls. Frances Clarke Sayers. *BrL-7—BrS*

"Who calls? Who calls? Who." See For a mocking voice

"Who came in the quiet night." See The little fox

"Who can say." See Song

"Who comes dancing over the snow." See The new year

"Who comes here." See A grenadier

"Who did." Unknown. *TaD*

Who did it. Dorothy Aldis. *AlA*

"Who does not love the juniper tree." See Juniper

"Who doth presume my mistress's name to scan." See Melander supposed to love Susan, but did love Ann

"Who drives the horses of the sun." See The happiest heart

Who goes with Fergus. William Butler Yeats. *SmLg*

"Who has seen the wind." Christina Georgina Rossetti. *ArTp—DeT—FeF—HuL-1—HuSv—JoAc—McAw—PeF*

"Who hath a book." Wilbur D. Nesbit. *ArTp—BrS*

"Who have no heaven come." See String quartet

"Who in the world would ever have guessed." See Easter eggs

Who is so pretty. Elizabeth Jane Coatsworth. *CoM*

"Who is that a-walking in the corn." Fenton Johnson. *GrCc*

"Who is the baby, that doth lie." See The brides' tragedy—Song

"Who killed Cock Robin." Mother Goose. *DeMg—DeT—JoAc*
  Cock Robin. *UnG*
  Death and burial of Cock Robin. *OpO*

"Who knocks at the Geraldine's door to-night." See Ballad of the little black hound

"Who knows if the moon's." E. E. Cummings. *CoPm*

"Who knows, when raindrops are descending." See Rain

Who likes the rain. Clara Doty Bates. *ArTp—BrR-3—HuL-1*

Who maketh the grass to grow. See Psalms —Psalm CXLVII

"Who minds if the wind whistles and howls." See Windy morning

"Who, or why, or which, or what." See The Akond of Swat

"Who raps at my window." See Halloween

"Who ride by night through the woodland so wild." See The erl-king

"Who said, Peacock pie." See The song of the mad prince

"Who says that it's by my desire." See People hide their love

"Who sees the first marsh marigold." See A charm for spring flowers

"Who serves his country best." See The better way

"Who shall tell what did befall." See Wealth

"Who so late." See At the garden gate

"Who stuffed that white owl? No one spoke in the shop." See The owl-critic

"Who tames the lion now." See Lord Alcohol

"Who taught the bird to build her nest." See Who taught them

Who taught them. Unknown. *DoP*

"Who thought of the lilac." See The lilac

"Who wants a birthday." David McCord. *BrBc—McFf*

"Who wants my jellyfish." See The jellyfish

"Who wants Wednesday? Who wants that day." See Auction

Who was it. Heinrich Heine, tr. fr. the German by Richard Garnett. *PaS*

"Who was it, tell me, that first of men reckon'd." See Who was it

"Who was it who wrote." See Christmas eve in the wainscoting

"Who went to sleep in the flower-bed." See The song of the dumb waiter

"Who will be an April fool." See April fool

"Who will go drive with Fergus now." See Who goes with Fergus

"Who will sing me the song of D." See The song of D

"Who would be." See The mermaid

"Who would be." See The merman

"Who would be loved, let him possess." See Perfect love

"Who would true valour see." See The pilgrim's progress—Pilgrim's song

"Whodunit." See Spilt milk: Whodunit

"Whoever you are holding me now in hand." Walt Whitman. *HaP*

Whole duty of children. Robert Louis Stevenson. *NaE*

"Who'll that be." Kenneth Patchen. *McW*

"Whoo. Whoo. Who cooks for you-all." Unknown. *WoF*

Whoopee ti yi yo. See Whoopee ti yi yo, git along, little dogies

Whoopee ti yi yo, git along, little dogies. Unknown. *ArTp—FeF—McW*
  Git along, little dogies. *HuSv—NaM*
  Whoopee ti yi yo. *BrR-5*

Who's in. Elizabeth Fleming. *BrL-k—PeF*

"Who's that bleating." Eleanor Farjeon. *FaCb—FaN*

Who's that ringing. See "Who's that ringing at my doorbell"

"Who's that ringing at my doorbell." Mother Goose. *SmLg*
  Visitor. *OpO*
  Who's that ringing. *HuL-1*

"Who's that ringing at the front door bell." See "Who's that ringing at my doorbell"

"Whose absolute dumbness circumscribed by sound." See On first hearing Beethoven

Whose little pigs. Mother Goose. *OpO*

"Whose little pigs are these, these, these." See Whose little pigs

"Whose woods these are I think I know." See Stopping by woods on a snowy evening

Will you. See "Will you be my little wife."

"Will you be my little wife." Kate Greenaway. *NaM*

Will you. *BrS*

"Will you gang wi' me, Leezie Lindsay." See Leezie Lindsay

"Will you have some pie." See Little bits

"Will you have some tea, sir." See Playing store

"Will you lend me your mare to ride but a mile." See Money works wonders

"Will you take a sprig of hornbeam." See Forester's song

"Will you take a walk with me." See The clucking hen

"Will you walk a little faster? said a whiting to a snail." See The lobster quadrille

"Will you walk into my parlor." Unknown. *WiRm*

"Will you walk into my parlor? said the spider to the fly." See The spider and the fly

Willful homing. Robert Frost. *FrR*

William I, King of England (about)
Norman William. E. Farjeon. *FaCb*

"William and Mary." See Four children

William Jones. See The Spoon River anthology

"William McTrimbletoe." Mother Goose. *OpO*

"William the Conqueror, ten sixty-six." Mother Goose. *OpO*

Williams, Gwyn
"Oh send to me an apple that hasn't any kernel." tr. *SmLg*

Williams, William Carlos
The dance. *SmLg*
The desert music. *PlU* (sel.)
Hemmed-in males. *HaP*
Lighthearted William. *HaP*
The lonely street. *GrCc*
Poem. *FeF—ReT*
Spring and all ("By the road to the contagious hospital") *HaP*
Spring and all ("So much depends") *NaE —ReT*
The term. *ReT*

Willie boy, Willie boy. See "Willy boy, Willy boy, where are you going"

Willie Mackintosh. Unknown. *MaB*

"Willie poisoned Auntie's tea." See Willie the poisoner

"Willie saw some dynamite." See Little Willie

"Willie, take your little drum." See Burgundian carol

Willie the poisoner. Unknown. *CoH*

Willie Winkie. See "Wee Willie Winkie runs through the town"

"Willie, with a thirst for gore." See Careless Willie

Willow trees
Catkin. Unknown. *BrL-k*
Pussy willow ("Pussy willow wakened") K. L. Brown. *BrL-k*
Pussy willow ("With her brown bead eyes") M. C. Livingston. *LiWa*
Pussy willows. R. B. Bennett. *JoAc*
The willows. W. P. Eaton. *FeF*

The willows. Walter Prichard Eaton. *FeF*

Willson, Dixie
The mist and all. *BrL-7—FeF—HaY— HuL-2—PcF*

Wilmot, John, Earl of Rochester. See Rochester, John Wilmot, Earl of

Willy boy. Mother Goose. *OpO*

"Willy boy, Willy boy." See Willy boy

"Willy boy, Willy boy, where are you going." Mother Goose. *DeMg—HuSv*
Willie boy, Willie boy. *HuL-1*

"Willy, Willy Wilkin." Mother Goose. *OpO*

Willy Wood. Mother Goose. *OpO*

"Wilt thou go a quest." See Q is for quest

Wind. See Winds

The wind. See "Arthur O'Bower has broken his band"

The wind ("I can get through a doorway without any key") James Reeves. *ReW*

The wind ("I love the blustering noisy wind") Marion Doyle. *BrR-3*

The wind ("I saw you toss the kites on high") Robert Louis Stevenson. *ArTp— HuL-1—HuSv—JoAc*

The wind ("Wind in the garden") David McCord. *McFf*

Wind ("Wind is to show") Leonard Feeney. *UnG*

The wind ("The wind, O the wind, it is made out of air") Marie Louise Allen. *AlP*

The wind and the moon. George Macdonald *NaM—UnG*

The wind and the rain. See Twelfth night— "When that I was and a little tiny boy"

"Wind and wave and star and sea." See Song

Wind and window flower. Robert Frost. *FrR*

"The wind begun to rock the grass." Emily Dickinson. *GrCc*

"Wind bloweth." See Autumn sigheth

"The wind blows." See Ripe corn

"The wind came running." Ivy O. Eastwick. *EaI*

"A wind came up out of the sea." See Daybreak

"The wind comes, singing." See Glad earth

"The wind doth wander up and down." See Destiny

"Wind from the north: the young spring day." See The song of the four winds

"The wind had no more strength than this." See Calm

"The wind has such a rainy sound." Christina Georgina Rossetti. *ArTp—HuL-2*

The wind in a frolic. William Howitt. *NaM —ReG*

"Wind in the garden." See The wind

Wind in the pine. Lew Sarett. *BrL-7*

The wind in the willows, sels. Kenneth Grahame
Christmas carol. *FeF*
Carol. *EaW*
Ducks' ditty. *ArTp—BrR-3—FeF—JoAc— McW—NaM—PeF*
The song of Mr Toad. *CoH—FeF*
"The world has held great heroes." *LoL*

"**Wind** is to show." See Wind
"The **wind** is walking the tallest trees." See Sudden gale in spring
"The **wind**, O the wind, it is made out of air." See The wind
The **wind** of January. Christina Georgina Rossetti. *HaY*
Wind on the hill. A. A. Milne. *MiWc*
"The **wind** one morning sprang up from sleep." See The wind in a frolic
"A **wind** runs by at morning." Rowena Bastin Bennett. *BrR-4*
Wind song. Carl Sandburg. *NaM—SaW*
"A **wind** sways the pines." See Dirge in woods
"The **wind** was a torrent of darkness among the gusty trees." See The highwayman
Wind weather. Virginia Brasier. *HuSv*
Wind-wolves. William D. Sargent. *ArTp*
The **windmill** ("Behold, a giant am I") Henry Wadsworth Longfellow. *NaM*
The **windmill** ("If you should bid me make a choice") Edward Verrall Lucas. *DeT —HuL-2*

Windmills. See Mills

Window. Carl Sandburg. *SaW*
The **window** box. Ivy O. Eastwick. *EaI*
"A **window** box of pansies." See Window boxes
Window boxes. Eleanor Farjeon. *FeF*
A **window** in the breast. Unknown, tr. fr. the Greek by Walter Headlam. *PaS*

Windows
  The frost pane. D. McCord. *HuSv—JoAc —McFf*
  Tree at my window. R. Frost. *FrR—FrY*
  Waiting at the window. A. A. Milne. *MiWc*
  The white window. J. Stephens. *ArTp— BrL-k—HuL-2—HuSv—JoAc*
  Window. C. Sandburg. *SaW*
  The window box. I. O. Eastwick. *EaI*
  Window boxes. E. Farjeon. *FeF*
  "W's for windows." From All around the town. P. McGinley. *ArTp*

Winds
  "Arthur O'Bower has broken his band." Mother Goose. *OpO*
    The wind. *SmLg*
  "At Brill on the hill." Mother Goose. *OpO*
  Baby song of the four winds. C. Sandburg. *SaW*
  "Blow, blow, thou winter wind." From As you like it. W. Shakespeare. *HoW— McW*
    Blow, blow. *DeT*
  Brooms. D. Aldis. *AlA—BrR-4*
  "But hark to the wind how it blows." T. S. Moore. *ArTp*
  Calm. M. Drayton. *DeT*
  Come little leaves. G. Cooper. *FeF*
  The dance of the leaves. I. P. Richardson. *BrR-3*
  The day is dancing. R. B. Bennett. *BrR-6*
  Daybreak. H. W. Longfellow. *DeT—McW*
  Do you fear the wind. H. Garland. *ArTp —JoAc*
  During wind and rain. T. Hardy. *HaP*

The hills of May. R. Graves. *GrP*
Holiday. E. Young. *ArTp—HuL-2*
The hurricane. P. Matos. *FeF*
Landscape. C. Sandburg. *SaW*
"Little wind, blow on the hill-top." K. Greenaway. *ArTp*
  Little wind. *JoAc*
March wind. M. E. Uschold. *HaY*
The March winds. G. W. W. Houghton. *HaY*
The message of the March wind. W. Morris. *HoW*
"My Lady Wind, my Lady Wind." Mother Goose. *DeMg*
The night wind ("Have you ever heard the wind go Yooooo") E. Field. *BrR-4 —FeF*
The night-wind ("In summer's mellow midnight") E. Brontë. *HaP*
"Nobody knows." I. O. Eastwick. *EaI*
"O wind, why do you never rest." C. G. Rossetti. *ArTp*
October winds. V. D. Randall. *HaY*
Ode to the west wind. P. B. Shelley. *HaP*
Only the wind says spring. H. J. Miller. *UnG*
Pirate wind. M. J. Carr. *BrS*
The September gale. O. W. Holmes. *CoH* (sel.)
The song of the four winds. T. L. Peacock. *HoW*
Song of the sea wind. A. Dobson. *HuL-2*
The song my paddle sings. E. P. Johnson. *FeF*
Spring wind. N. B. Turner. *BrS*
Sudden gale in spring. M. B. Thomas. *BrR-5*
Sweet and low. A. Tennyson. *FeF—HuL-2 —HuSv—JoAc—UnG*
  A cradle song. *DeT*
  Song. *ReT*
That wind. E. Brontë. *DeT*
Then I met another man I could not see. J. Ciardi. *CiI*
To Morfydd. L. Johnson. *ReT*
To the thawing wind. R. Frost. *FrR*
Trade winds. J. Masefield. *HuL-2*
The trees and the wind. E. Farjeon. *FaCb*
The unknown color. C. Cullen. *FeF*
Weather. M. Chute. *ChA*
Weather words. D. McCord. *PlI*
What the winds bring. E. C. Stedman. *BrR-4—HuL-1*
"When the wind blows." Mother Goose. *OpO*
"When the wind is in the east." Mother Goose. *DeMg—LiL—OpO*
  Signs, seasons, and sense. *UnG*
"When the winds blow and the seas flow." Unknown. *ArTp*
The whisperer. J. Stephens. *DoP*
"White sheep, white sheep." Unknown. *ArTp*
  Clouds. *BrL-k—HuSv*
"Who has seen the wind." C. G. Rossetti. *ArTp — DeT — FeF — HuL-1 — HuSv —JoAc—McAw—PeF*
The wind ("I can get through a doorway without any key") J. Reeves. *ReW*

The wind ("I love the blustering noisy wind") M. Doyle. *BrR-3*

The wind ("I saw you toss the kites on high") R. L. Stevenson. *ArTp—HuL-1—HuSv—JoAc*

The wind ("Wind in the garden") D. McCord. *McFf*

Wind ("Wind is to show") L. Feeney. *UnG*

The wind ("The wind, O the wind, it is made out of air") M. L. Allen. *AlP*

The wind and the moon. G. Macdonald. *NaM—UnG*

Wind and window flower. R. Frost. *FrR*

"The wind begun to rock the grass." E. Dickinson. *GrCc*

"The wind came running." I. O. East- wick. *EaI*

"The wind has such a rainy sound." C. G. Rossetti. *ArTp—HuL-2*

The wind in a frolic. W. Howitt. *NaM—ReG*

Wind in the pine. L. Sarett. *BrL-7*

Wind on the hill. A. A. Milne. *MiWc*

"A wind runs by at morning." R. B. Ben- nett. *BrR-4*

Wind song. C. Sandburg. *NaM—SaW*

Wind weather. V. Brasier. *HuSv*

Wind-wolves. W. D. Sargent. *ArTp*

The winds. T. Tusser. *HoW*

Winds a-blowing. M. Justus. *BrR-5*

"Winds of the Windy City." From The Windy City. C. Sandburg. *SaW*

The wind's song. E. Mörike. *PaS*

A windy day. A. Young. *ReT—UnG*

Windy morning. H. Behn. *ArTp—BeW*

Windy nights. R. L. Stevenson. *ArTp—BrR-4—BrS—DeT—GrCc—HuL-1*

Windy weather. H. Merrill. *BrL-8*

Winter night. M. F. Butts. *ArTp*

Worms and the wind. C. Sandburg. *McW*

Wouldn't you. J. Ciardi. *CiY*

Yellow balloon. I. O. Eastwick. *EaI*

The youth and the northwind. J. G. Saxe. *CoSp*

The **winds** ("North winds send hail, south winds bring rain") Thomas Tusser. *HoW*

Winds a-blowing. May Justus. *BrR-5*

"The **wind's** an old woman in front of the rain." See Wind weather

"A **wind's** in the heart of me, a fire's in my heels." See A wanderer's song

The **winds** of fate. Ella Wheeler Wilcox. *BrL-8*

"**Winds** of the Windy City." See The Windy City

"The **wind's** on the wold." See Inscription for an old bed

The **wind's** song. Edward Mörike, tr. fr. the German by William R. Hughes. *PaS*

"The **winds** they did blow." Mother Goose. *DeT*

The squirrel. *OpO*

"**Winds** through the olive trees." See Long, long ago

The **Windy** City, sels. Carl Sandburg
Night. *SaW*
"Winds of the Windy City." *SaW*

A **windy** day ("Have you been at sea on a windy day") Winifred Howard. *FeF*

A **windy** day ("This wind brings all dead things to life") Andrew Young. *ReT—UnG*

Windy morning. Harry Behn. *ArTp—BeW*

Windy nights. Robert Louis Stevenson. *ArTp—BrR-4—BrS—DeT—GrCc—HuL-1*

Windy wash day. Dorothy Aldis. *AlA—ArTp—JoAc*

Windy weather. Herbert Merrill. *BrL-8*

"**Wine** and cakes for gentlemen." Mother Goose. *OpO*

Wing, Helen
Crickets. *BrL-k*
Rain. *BrL-k*

Wings
An angel. Unknown. *DoP*
Psalm LV. From Psalms, Bible, Old Testament
Wings. *FeF*

Wings and wheels. N. B. Turner. *ArTp—HuSv*

Wings ("Be like the bird, who") See Be like the bird

Wings ("Oh that I had wings like a dove") See Psalms—Psalm LV

Wings and wheels. Nancy Byrd Turner. *ArTp—HuSv*

"**Winning**, never boast; and, losing." Arthur Guiterman
Proverbs. *ThP*

The **winning** of the TV West. John T. Alexander. *McW*

Winslow, Helen Maria
August. *HaY*

Winter. See also December; January; March; Seasons; Snow
Advice to a bird, species unknown. G. S. Galbraith. *BrL-8*
At the beginning of winter. E. J. Coats- worth. *CoM*
Bed in winter. D. Aldis. *AlA*
"Blow, blow, thou winter wind." From As you like it. W. Shakespeare. *HoW—McW*
Blow, blow. *DeT*
"Cold winter now is in the wood." E. J. Coatsworth. *ArTp*
Cover. F. M. Frost. *BrL-k*
A Devonshire rhyme. Unknown. *BrS*
Field mouse conference. E. J. Coatsworth. *CoM*
First winter's day. D. Aldis. *AlA*
Good hours. R. Frost. *FrR—FrY*
I will sing you one-o. R. Frost. *FrR*
Ice. D. Aldis. *ArTp—BrL-k*
In the clear cold. S. Yesenin. *PaS*
In winter. M. Chute. *ChA*
The last flower. J. T Moore. *CoPs*
Last words before winter. L. Untermeyer. *UnG*
Late winter on our beach. B. Eaton. *McAw*
The lion of winter. From A midsummer- night's dream. W. Shakespeare. *HoW*
Puck speaks. *ReT*
Puck's song. *NaM*
Looking for a sunset bird in winter. R. Frost. *FrR—FrY*

Winter gold. Carl Sandburg. *SaW*

Winter in the wood. Ivy O. Eastwick. *HaY*

"Winter is icumen in." Bradford Smith. *CoPs*

The winter is past. See The song of Solomon

Winter night ("The air is frosty now and brittle thin") Herbert Merrill. *BrL-7*

Winter night ("Blow, wind, blow") Mary Frances Butts. *ArTp*

Winter night ("A tree may be laughter in the spring") Collister Hutchison. *ArTp*

"The winter night is cold and chill." See Winter

Winter noon. Sara Teasdale. *HaY*

"Winter, now thy spite is spent." See The vow to Cupid

Winter rain. Christina Georgina Rossetti. *HoW*

Winter streams. Bliss Carman. *DeT—HaY*

Winter-time. See Wintertime

Winter-wear. Marie Louise Allen. *AlP*

Winters, Yvor
  John Day, frontiersman. *HaP*
  John Sutter. *HaP*

The winter's tale, sels. William Shakespeare
  "Daffodils." *ArTp*
  Flowers of middle summer. *HaY*
  "Jog on, jog on, the foot-path way." *ArTp—SmLg*
  The pedlar. *HoW*
  "When daffodils begin to peer." *SmLg*
  "When you sing"
    The winter's tale. *PlU*

"Winter's thunder." Mother Goose. *LiL*
  Signs, seasons, and sense. *UnG*

Wintertime. Robert Louis Stevenson. *HuSv*
  Winter-time. *UnG*

Winton, Elizabeth
  A summer walk. *BrR-4*

Wisconsin
  Limited crossing Wisconsin. From Prairie. C. Sandburg. *SaW*

Wisdom. See also Mind
  Advice from an elderly mouse. E. J. Coatsworth. *CoM*
  Four things. From Proverbs. Bible, Old Testament. *FeF—UnG*
  Where shall wisdom be found. From The Bacchae. Euripides. *PaS—PlU*
  Wisdom ("I stand most humbly") L. Hughes. *ArTp*
  Wisdom ("When I was young—and very young") D. W. Hicky. *BrBc*
  The wise hen. J. Ciardi. *CiY*
  "A wise old owl lived in an oak." Mother Goose. *DeMg—LiL—OpO*
  Wise Sarah and the elf. E. J. Coatsworth. *CoPm*

Wisdom ("I stand most humbly") Langston Hughes. *ArTp*

Wisdom ("When I was young—and very young") Daniel Whitehead Hicky. *BrBc*

Wise, William
  After the party. *FeF*
  Telegram. *ArTp*
  What to do. *ArTp*
  "When I grow up." *BrBc*

The wise hen. John Ciardi. *CiY*

Wise Johnny. Edwina Fallis. *ArTp—BrL-k —BrS*

The wise men of Gotham. See "Three wise men of Gotham"

"A wise old owl lived in an oak." Mother Goose. *DeMg—LiL—OpO*

Wise Sarah and the elf. Elizabeth Jane Coatsworth. *CoPm*

Wishes. See Wishes and wishing

Wishes and wishing
  "As a rule men are fools." Unknown. *MoY*
  "As many fishes as are in the sea." Unknown. *MoY*
  Beach fire. F. M. Frost. *ArTp—PeF*
  "Best what." Unknown. *MoY*
  The big Rock Candy mountain. Unknown. *UnMc*
  The chameleon. A. P. Herbert. *CoI—FeF*
  "Chicken when you're hungry." Unknown. *MoY*
  The duck. E. King. *BrL-k—HuSv*
  "Everybody says." D. Aldis. *AlA—BrL-k —FeF—HuL-1*
  "Faith, I wish I were a leprechaun." M. Ritter. *ArTp—FeF—HuL-2*
  The fisherman. D. McCord. *McFf*
  Flying kite. F. D. Sherman. *BrR-4*
  Good wish. Unknown. *SmLg*
  "The heart asks pleasure first." E. Dickinson. *HaP*
  A hinted wish. Martial. *BrL-8*
  The house beyond the meadow, sels. H. Behn. *BeH* (complete)
    The bears who once were giants
    First enchantment
    A friendly visit
    Goodbye to fairyland
    The magic map
    The strangest wish
    The thunder-and-lightning bug
  I found. M. C. Livingston. *LiW*
  "I keep three wishes ready." A. Wynne. *ArTp—PeF*
  "I wish I were a bunny." Unknown. *MoY*
  "I wish I were an elephant." Unknown. *MoY*
  "I wish you health." Unknown. *MoY*
  "I wish you luck." Unknown. *MoY*
  I would like to be—a bee. D. W. Baruch. *BrBc*
  I'd love to be a fairy's child. R. Graves. *BrBc—FeF—HuL-2*
  "If I was a farmer, I'd have an easy time." Unknown. *WoF*
  If I were king. A. A. Milne. *MiWc*
  "If wishes were horses." Mother Goose. *DeMg—LiL—OpO*
  "If you were a fish." Unknown. *MoY*
  An impetuous resolve. J. W. Riley. *BrBc*
  "In the storms of life." Unknown. *MoY*
  Kiph. W. De La Mare. *ArTp*
  A kite. Unknown. *ArTp*
  "Long may you live." Unknown. *MoY*
  Margaret. C. Sandburg. *SaW*
  "May you always be happy." Unknown. *MoY*
  "May you always be the same." Unknown. *MoY*

Wishes and wishing—*Continued*
"May you always meet Dame Fortune."
Unknown. *MoY*
"May you gently float." Unknown. *MoY*
"May your future be as bright." Unknown.
MoY
"May your joys be as deep as the ocean."
Unknown. *MoY*
"May your life be like arithmetic." Unknown. *MoY*
"May your life be long and sunny." Unknown. *MoY*
"May your life be strewn with roses." Unknown. *MoY*
"May your luck ever spread." Unknown.
MoY
"May your record be as clean." Unknown.
MoY
My plan. M. Chute. *BrBc—ChA—FeF*
O for the wings of a dove. From Hippolytus. Euripides. *PaS*
An old woman of the roads. P. Colum.
FeF—HuL-2—HuSv
Plans. D. B. Thompson. *BrBc—HuL-1*
Raccoon. W. J. Smith. *ArTp—SmB*
Rathers. M. Austin. *FeF*
"Sailing down the stream of life." Unknown. *MoY*
The shiny little house. N. M. Hayes.
HuL-1
Somewhere. W. De La Mare. *FeF*
"Star-light, star-bright." Mother Goose.
ArTp—OpO
"Star bright, starlight." *HuSv*
Stirring the pudding. E. Farjeon. *FaN*
"Take the word pluck." Unknown. *MoY*
Tartary. W. De La Mare. *HuL-2—UnG*
Tell me now. Wang-Chi. *SmLg*
Thanksgiving wishes. A. Guiterman. *CoPs*
Thou blind man's mark. P. Sidney. *HaP*
The three woulds. Unknown. *ThP*
Timbuctoo. M. Chute. *ChA*
To his son, Vincent Corbet. R. Corbet.
SmLg
"To my friend." Unknown. *MoY*
Under the moon. I. O. Eastwick. *EaI*
Vocation. R. Tagore. *FeF*
What I would do. D. Aldis. *AlA*
"When I am president." Unknown
American Father Gander. *UnG*
When I grow up. R. S. Holland. *BrBc—BrR-5*
"When the walls of earth have fallen." Unknown. *MoY*
Whistle, whistle. Unknown. *HuL-2*
The wife of Usher's well. Unknown.
ArTp—DeT—MaB
The wishes of an elderly man. W. Raleigh.
CoH—SmLg
Wishful. D. McCord. *McT*
Wishing. W. Allingham. *FeF*
The youth dreams. R. M. Rilke. *PaS*
The **wishes** of an elderly man. Walter Raleigh. *CoH—SmLg*
Wishful. David McCord. *McT*
Wishing. William Allingham. *FeF*
The **witch** ("I saw her plucking cowslips")
Percy H. Ilott. *HuL-1*

The **witch** ("The raven croak'd as she sate
at her meal") Robert Southey. *HoW*
A **witch** ("There's thik wold hag, Moll
Brown, look zee, jus' past") William
Barnes. *CoPm*
A country witch. *UnG*
Witch cat. Rowena Bastin Bennett. *BrS*
The **witch** of Coös. Robert Frost. *FrR*
The **witch** of Willowby wood. Rowena
Bastin Bennett. *CoPm*
Witch, witch. Rose Fyleman. *HuL-1*
"**Witch**, witch, where do you fly." See
Witch, witch
Witchcraft
Alison Gross. Unknown. *MaB*
Bewitched. W. De La Mare. *CoPm*
The broomstick train. O. W. Holmes.
CoPm(sel.)—*FeF*(sel.)
The fairy king. W. Allingham. *CoPm*
Hallowe'en ("Broomsticks and witches") M.
Chute. *ChA*
Hallowe'en ("Granny, I saw a witch go by")
M. A. Lawson. *ArTp—BrS*
Halloween ("The sky was yellow") I. O.
Eastwick. *EaI*
A Halloween meeting. G. O. Butler. *BrL-k*
Hallowe'en song. M. Barrows. *HuL-1*
The hare W. De La Mare. *ArTp*
"Hinx, minx, the old witch winks." Mother
Goose. *DeMg*
Hinx, minx. *OpO*
The little creature. W. De La Mare. *NaE*
Little Orphant Annie. J. W. Riley. *FeF—HuSv—NaM*
Molly Means. M. Walker. *CoSp*
Old Moll. J. Reeves. *ReW*
The ride-by-nights. W. De La Mare. *ArTp—BrS—FeF—HuL-2*
The tailor. T. L. Beddoes. *HoW*
W is for witch. E. Farjeon. *FaCb*
Was she a witch. L. E. Richards. *BrL-k*
The witch ("I saw her plucking cowslips")
P. H. Ilott. *HuL-1*
The witch ("The raven croak'd as she sate
at her meal") R. Southey. *HoW*
A witch ("There's thik wold hag, Moll
Brown, look zee, jus' past") W. Barnes.
CoPm
A country witch. *UnG*
Witch cat. R. B. Bennett. *BrS*
The witch of Coös. R. Frost. *FrR*
The witch of Willowby wood. R. B. Bennett.
CoPm
Witch, witch. R. Fyleman. *HuL-1*
The witches' charms. B. Jonson. *CoPm*(sel.)
—*ReT*
Witches' charm. *SmLg* (sel.)
Witches' song. E. J. Coatsworth. *CoPm*
The witches' spell. From Macbeth. W.
Shakespeare. *CoPm*
The witch's ballad. W. B. Scott. *NaE*
Witchwood. M. Justus. *BrS*
Witches. See Witchcraft
Witches' charm. See The witches' charms
The **witches'** charms. Ben Jonson. *CoPm*
(sel)—*ReT*
Witches' charm. *SmLg* (sel.)
Witches' song. Elizabeth Jane Coatsworth.
CoPm

The **witches'** spell. See Macbeth

The **witch's** ballad. William Bell Scott. *NaE*

Witchwood. May Justus. *BrS*

With a daisy. Emily Dickinson. *PlI*

"**With** blackest moss the flower-pots." See Mariana

"**With** fingers weary and worn." See The song of the shirt

"**With** flintlocked guns and polished stocks." See In Hardin county, 1809

"**With** flowers on my shoulders." Unknown. *WiRm*

"**With** glass like a bull's-eye." See Mrs MacQueen

"**With** her brown bead eyes." See Pussy willow

"**With** hey, ho, the wind and the rain." See King Lear

"**With** him there was his son, a youthful squire." See The Canterbury tales—A squire

"**With** my two arms I cannot span thy girth." See To an oak dropping acorns

"**With** plaintive fluting, sad and slow." See The street musician

"**With** rakish eye and 'plenished crop." See The crow

"**With** six days' toiling." See Day of rest

"**With** six small diamonds for his eyes." See The spider

"**With** soap and water." See Washing

"**With** sweetest milk and sugar first." See The nymph and her fawn

"**With** the apples and the plums." See The dessert

With thee conversing. John Milton. *HoW*

"**With** thee conversing, I forget all time." See With thee conversing

"**With** their trunks the elephants." See The elephants

With wavering feet I walked. Vladimir Solovyov, tr. fr. the Russian by Babette Deutsch. *PaS*

"**With** wavering feet I walked where dawn-lit mists were lying." See With wavering feet I walked

"**With** what deep murmurs through time's silent stealth." See The waterfall

Wither, George
 Our joyful feast. *BrS*

Withers, Carl
 "Charlie Chaplin went to France." wr. at. *NaM*

"**Within** a thick and spreading hawthorn bush." See The thrush's nest

Within her eyes. Dante, tr. fr. the Italian by Dante Gabriel Rossetti. *PaS*

"**Within** my house of patterned horn." See The tortoise in eternity

"**Within** the bush, her covert nest." See The linnet

"**Within** the flower there lies a seed." See Spell of creation

"**Within** your heart." See "Hold fast your dreams"

Wives. See Married life

Wizard frost. Frank Dempster Sherman. *HaY—JoAc*

"**Woe's** me, woe's me." See The ghost's lament

The **wolf.** Georgia Roberts Durston. *ArTp*

"The **wolf** also shall dwell with the lamb." See Isaiah—The peaceable kingdom

The **wolf** cry. Lew Sarett. *FeF*

Wolfe, Charles
 Burial of Sir John Moore. *UnMc*
  The burial of Sir John Moore at Corunna, 1809. *DeT*
 The burial of Sir John Moore at Corunna, 1809. See Burial of Sir John Moore

Wolfe, Ffrida
 Choosing shoes. *ArTp—BrR-3—HuL-1*
 Four and eight. *BrBc—BrS—HuL-1*
 Lost time. *HuL-2*
 What the toys are thinking. *ArTp*

Wolfe, Humbert
 The blackbird. *ArTp—FeF—HuSv—JoAc*
 Green candles. *CoPm*
 The lilac. *FeF*
 The return of the fairy. *CoPm*
 Trebizond, Jonah, and the minnows. *HuL-2*
 The zoo. *CoH—McW—NaM*

Wolves
 The boy and the wolf. Aesop. *UnMc*
 The children of the wolf. E. Farjeon. *FaCb*
 A night with a wolf. B. Taylor. *UnG*
 Wind-wolves. W. D. Sargent. *ArTp*
 The wolf. G. R. Durston. *ArTp*
 The wolf cry. L. Sarett. *FeF*
 W-o-o-o-o-o-ww. N. M. Hayes. *HuL-1*

Woman
 "God made the men." Unknown. *MoY*
 "He is a fool who thinks by force or skill." Unknown. *MoY*
 Lady lost. J. C. Ransom. *HaP*
 "A spaniel, a woman, and a walnut tree." Unknown. *MoY*
 "There are seven ages of woman." Unknown. *MoY*

"A **woman**, a spaniel, and walnut tree." Mother Goose. *DeMg*

A **woman** driving. Thomas Hardy. *GrCc*

"A **woman** who lived in Holland, of old." See Going too far

The **woman's** tongue tree. Arthur Guiterman. *CoPm*

Women—Portraits. See People—Portraits —Women

Women's eyes. Bhartrihari, tr. fr. the Sanskrit by Arthur W. Ryder. *PaS*

The **wonder** of wonders. See "I saw a peacock with a fiery tail"

Wonder where. See From a very little sphinx—"Wonder where this horseshoe went"

"**Wonder** where this horseshoe went." See From a very little sphinx

The **wonderful** Derby ram. See "As I was going to Derby"

A **wonderful** man. Aileen Fisher. *BrS*

The **wonderful** world. William Brighty Rands. *ArTp—FeF*

"**Wonders** are many, but there is no wonder." See What a piece of work is a man

"**Wondrous** things have come to pass." See Wizard frost

Words ("Bright is the ring of words") Robert Louis Stevenson. *UnG*

Words ("In woods are words") James Reeves. *ReR*

"Words fall as lightly as snow." See The cheerful cherub—Light words

Words from an old Spanish carol. Unknown, tr. fr. the Spanish by Ruth Sawyer. *EaW*
On Christmas morn. *FeF*

Words from the bottom of a well. Ethel Jacobson. *ThP*

"Words move, music moves." See Burnt Norton

Wordsworth, William
Address to my infant daughter. *NaE*
Alice Fell. *DeT*
Among the stars. See Peter Bell—The crescent boat
Brother and sister. *DeT*
Composed upon Westminster bridge. *ArTp—SmLg*
  Upon Westminster bridge. *HaP*
The crescent boat. See Peter Bell
Daffodils. *BrL-8—FeF—HaP—HuSv—JoAc—UnG*
  "I wandered lonely as a cloud." *ReT*
The gladness of the May. *HaY*
The green linnet. *DeT*
"I wandered lonely as a cloud." See Daffodils
In March. See Written in March
The kitten at play. *FeF*
  The kitten playing with the falling leaves. *UnG*
The kitten playing with the falling leaves. See The kitten at play
Louisa. *GrCc*
Lucy. *UnMc*
Lucy Gray; or, Solitude. *DeT*
March. See Written in March
The merry month of March. See Written in March
My heart leaps up. *BrBc—HaP—JoAc*
  "My heart leaps up when I behold." *ArTp*
"My heart leaps up when I behold." See My heart leaps up
Newton. See The prelude
Ode on intimations of immortality. *BrBc* (sel.)
  Our birth is but a sleep. *HaP* (sel.)
An old man. *SmLg*
On the frozen lake. See The prelude—Skating
Our birth is but a sleep. See Ode on intimations of immortality
The pet lamb. *DeT* (sel.)
Peter Bell, sel.
  The crescent boat. *ReT*
    Among the stars. *UnG*
The prelude, sels.
  Newton. *PlI*
  The prelude, Book VI. *PlI*
  Skating. *UnG*
    On the frozen lake. *SmLg*
    There was a boy. *SmLg*
The prelude, Book VI. See The prelude
The reverie of poor Susan. *DeT—HoW*

Skating. See The prelude
"A slumber did my spirit seal." *SmLg*
The solitary reaper. *HaP—PlU—ReT*
"The sun has long been set." *HaY*
There was a boy. See The prelude
The thorn. *NaE* (sel.)
To a butterfly. *UnG*
To the cuckoo. *UnG*
To the Supreme Being. tr. *PaS*
Upon Westminster bridge. See Composed upon Westminster bridge
Vandracour and Julia. *NaE* (sel.)
The whirl-blast. *DeT*
The world is too much with us. *ThP*
Written in March. *ArTp—BrR-6—FeF—HaY—HuL-2—McW—ReG—ReT—UnG*
  In March. *DeT*
  March. *JoAc*
  The merry month of March. *NaE—NaM*

Work
"All work and no play makes Jack a dull boy." Mother Goose. *OpO*
Always finish. Unknown. *ThP*
The ant and the cricket. Unknown. *DeT*
Automobile mechanics. D. W. Baruch. *ArTp—FeF*
Day of rest. B. Braley. *ThP*
"Evan Kirk." J. Ciardi. *CiM*
Father Grumble. Unknown. *BrR-5*
Father Short. Mother Goose. *OpO*
The glow within. B. Braley. *BrL-8*
Good advice. Unknown. *ArTp*
The gum-gatherer. R. Frost. *FrR*
A hymn of nature. Robert Bridges. *HaY*
I hear America singing. W. Whitman. *ArTp — BrL-7 — BrR-5 — CoPs — FeF —HuSv—JoAc—SmLg—UnG*
"I meant to do my work to-day." R. Le Gallienne. *ArTp—BrR-5—HuL-2—JoAc—UnG*
Labor day. M. Pomeroy. *CoPs*
The line-gang. R. Frost. *FrR*
A lone striker. R. Frost. *FrR*
A man's bread. J. P. Peabody. *HaY*
Psalm of those who go forth before daylight. C. Sandburg. *NaM*
  Those who go forth before daylight. *HuSv*
The song of the shirt. T. Hood. *UnMc*
"There was an old man who lived in a wood." Mother Goose. *DeMg—HuSv*
  The old man who lived in a wood. *NaM*
"There you sit." S. Silverstein. *CoPs*
The tuft of flowers. R. Frost. *FrR—FrY*
Two tramps in mud time. R. Frost. *FrR—FrY*
Work ("Let me but do my work from day to day") H. Van Dyke. *BrR-6*
Work ("No man is born into the world whose work") J. R. Lowell. *CoPs*
Work ("Let me but do my work from day to day") Henry Van Dyke. *BrR-6*
Work ("No man is born into the world whose work") James Russell Lowell. *CoPs*

"Workers earn it." See Money

"The working people long ago." See Labor day

World

"And, star and system rolling past." From In memoriam. A. Tennyson
 In memoriam. *PlI*

The answers. R. Clairmont. *CoH—UnG*
 When did the world begin. *McW*

Apostrophic notes from the new-world physics. E. B. White. *PlI*

Ark of the covenant. L. T. Nicholl. *PlI*

Atom from atom. R. W. Emerson. *PlI*

The child in the train. E. Farjeon. *FaCb—FaN*

Continent's end. R. Jeffers. *PlI*

The creation. J. W. Johnson. *ArTp—JoAc*

The crescent boat. From Peter Bell. W. Wordsworth. *ReT*
 Among the stars. *UnG*

The difference. M. C. Livingston. *LiW*

"The earth abideth forever." From Ecclesiastes, Bible, Old Testament. *FeF*

Earth and sea. A. S. Pushkin. *PaS*

Earth and sky. E. Farjeon. *CoPs—EaW—HuL-2*

The end of the world. A. MacLeish. *HaP*

Entropy. T. Spencer. *PlI*

Epistle to be left in the earth. A. MacLeish. *PlI*

Fire and ice. R. Frost. *FrR—FrY*

Geography. E. Farjeon. *BrR-6—FeF*

Glad earth. E. C. Forbes. *HaY*

God's house. A. Wynne. *DoP*

God's world. From Renascence. E. St V. Millay. *CoPs—JoAc—UnG*

Happiness makes up in height for what it lacks in length. R. Frost. *FrR*

Happy thought. R. L. Stevenson. *ArTp*

Hudibras, Canto III. S. Butler. *PlI*(sel.)

"I'm glad the sky is painted blue." Unknown. *LoL*

Little Garaine. G. Parker. *FeF*

"A man said to the universe." S. Crane. *PlI*

Measurement. A. M. Sullivan. *McW*

The motion of the earth. N. Nicholson. *PlI*

My father's watch. J. Ciardi. *PlI*

The naked world. Sully-Prudhomme. *PlI*

Night thought of a tortoise suffering from insomnia on a lawn. E. V. Rieu. *RiF*

Once a child. E. Dickinson. *PlI*

Physical geography. L. T. Nicholl. *PlI*

Pippa's song. From Pippa passes. R. Browning. *FeF*
 Spring song. *UnG*
 "The year's at the spring." *DoP—HaY—HuSv—ThP*

The prelude, Book VI. From The prelude. W. Wordsworth. *PlI*

Prometheus unbound. P. B. Shelley. *PlI* (sel.)

Psalm VIII. From Psalms, Bible, Old Testament. *PlI*
 Psalm eight. *PaS*
 "When I consider thy heavens." *FeF*

Psalm XIX. From Psalms, Bible, Old Testament
 "The heavens declare the glory of God." *FeF*

Psalm CIV. From Psalms, Bible, Old Testament
 The rich earth. *UnG*

Psalm XXIV. From Psalms, Bible, Old Testament
 "The earth is the Lord's." *FeF—JoAc*
 "The earth is the Lord's, and the fulness thereof." *ArTp*
 Psalm twenty-four. *PaS*

Questions at night. L. Untermeyer. *FeF—UnG*

"Remember, though the telescope extend." G. Dillon. *PlI*

Revolution. A. E. Housman. *PlI*

Richard Tolman's universe. L. Bacon. *PlI*

"Ring around the world." A. Wynne. *ArTp—HuSv—JoAc*

Rock. K. Raine. *PlI* (sel.)

A roundabout turn. R. E. Charles. *NaM*

Shells. K. Raine. *PlI*

"The spacious firmament on high." J. Addison. *BrL-7*

Spell of creation. K. Raine. *McW—SmLg*

Thanksgiving for the earth. E. Goudge. *DoP—HaY*

Then as now. W. De La Mare. *McW*

The thirsty earth. From Anacreontics. A. Cowley. *HoW*
 Drinking. *HaP*

"This world was once a fluid haze of light." From The princess. A. Tennyson
 The princess. *PlI*

"To see the world in a grain of sand." From Auguries of innocence. W. Blake. *DoP*
 Auguries of innocence. *PlI*
 To see a world. *UnG*

Troilus and Cressida. W. Shakespeare. *PlI* (sel.)

Valentine for earth. F. M. Frost. *ArTp—FrLn*

The wakeupworld. C. Cullen. *JoAc*

Warning to children. R. Graves. *GrP—SmLg*

The wheel. Sully-Prudhomme. *PlI*

The wonderful world. W. B. Rands. *ArTp—FeF*

The world is too much with us. W. Wordsworth. *ThP*

The world's music. G. Setoun. *DoP*

"The world has held great heroes." See The wind in the willows—The song of Mr Toad

"The world is full of women's eyes." See Women's eyes

"The world is full of wonderful smells." Zhenya Gay. *ArTp*

"The world is so full of a number of things." See Happy thought

The world is too much with us. William Wordsworth. *ThP*

"The world is too much with us; late and soon." See The world is too much with us

"The world is very flat." See Night thought of a tortoise suffering from insomnia on a lawn

"The world turns and the world changes."
See The rock

"The world turns softly." See Water

World war I, 1914-1918. See European war, 1914-1918

World war II, 1939-1945
Atlantic Charter, A. D. 1620-1942. From The island. F. B. Young. *ArTp—JoAc*
Dunkirk. R. Nathan. *UnMc*
High flight. J. G. Magee, Jr. *FeF—McW —UnMc*
Tywater. R. Wilbur. *HaP*

"The world's a very happy place." See The world's music

The world's music. Gabriel Setoun. *DoP*

The worm. Ralph Bergengren. *BrS—FeF*

Worms. See also Caterpillars
Angleworms. M. L. Allen. *AlP*
The earthworm. Unknown. *McAw*
Inch-worm. D. Aldis. *AlHd*
The nightingale and the glowworm. W. Cowper. *UnG*
Our little kinsmen. E. Dickinson. *FeF— PlI*
The worm. R. Bergengren. *BrS—FeF*
Worms and the wind. C. Sandburg. *McW*

Worms and the wind. Carl Sandburg. *McW*

"Worms would rather be worms." See Worms and the wind

"Would I might rouse the Lincoln in you all." Vachel Lindsay. *CoPs*

"Would you hear of an old-time sea-fight." See Song of myself—An old-time sea-fight

"Wouldn't it be lovely if the rain came down." See Very lovely

Wouldn't you. John Ciardi. *CiY*

The wraggle taggle gipsies, O. See The raggle taggle gypsies

"Wrapped in a cloak." See Fog, the magician

The wreck of the Hesperus. Henry Wadsworth Longfellow. *FeF*

The wreck of the Julie Plante. William Henry Drummond. *FeF*

Wrecks. See Shipwrecks

Wren, Sir Christopher (about)
"Sir Christopher Wren." E. C. Bentley. *NaM*

Wrens
Cock Robin. Mother Goose. *DeT*
Cock Robin's courtship. *OpO*
The cutty wren. Unknown. *HoW*
"The dove says, Coo, coo, what shall I do." Mother Goose. *DeMg*
Coo. *DeT*
The dove says. *OpO*
Fidget. Mother Goose. *OpO*
Four wrens. Mother Goose. *OpO*
Greed. Mother Goose. *OpO*
"I'm called by the name of a man." Mother Goose. *OpO*
"It was on a merry time." Mother Goose. *DeMg*
"Jenny Wren fell sick." Mother Goose. *JoAc*
Jenny Wren. *NaE*
Little Jenny Wren. *HuL-1*
Ungrateful Jenny. *OpO*

Little friend. Mother Goose. *OpO*
"Little Lady Wren." T. Robinson. *ArTp —FeF*
Mailbox wren. F. M. Frost. *FrLn*
On this day the wren and the robin stop singing. E. Farjeon. *FaN*
"The robin of the red breast." Unknown. *CoPm*
Bad luck. *DeT*
A summer story. D. Aldis. *AlHd*
The wren hunt. Mother Goose. *OpO*
"Wrens and robins in the hedge." C. G. Rossetti. *ArTp*

The wren hunt. Mother Goose. *OpO*

"The wren inspects." See Mailbox wren

"Wrens and robins in the hedge." Christina Georgina Rossetti. *ArTp*

"Wrens are merry, cardinals gay." See Mourning doves

Wright, Ernest V. (Vincent)
When father carves the duck. *CoH—CoPs*

Wright, Orville and Wilbur (about)
Wilbur Wright and Orville Wright. R. C. and S. V. Benét. *BrL-8*
The Wrights' biplane. R. Frost. *FrR*

Wright, Wilbur (about). See Wright, Orville and Wilbur (about)

The Wrights' biplane. Robert Frost. *FrR*

"Wrinkling with laughter that made no sound." See At a country fair

Write me a verse. David McCord. *McT*

Writers and writing. See also Books and reading; Poets and poetry; also names of authors, as Lear, Edward (about)
Archy's autobiography. D. Marquis. *CoH* (sel.)
The height of the ridiculous. O. W. Holmes. *BrL-8—CoH—HuSv—NaM*
Pangur Bán. Unknown. *PaS—SmLg*
Paper I. C. Sandburg. *SaW*
Paper II. C. Sandburg. *SaW*
The scribe. W. De La Mare. *SmLg*
Survey of literature. J. C. Ransom. *SmLg*

Written in March. William Wordsworth. *ArTp—BrR-6—FeF—HaY—HuL-2— McW—ReG—ReT—UnG*
In March. *DeT*
March. *JoAc*
The merry month of March. *NaE—NaM*

Written on the road. Mary Mapes Dodge. *BrBc*

The wrong house. A. A. Milne. *MiWc*

"W's for windows." See All around the town

Wu Ch'ing-jen
On a mountain road. *PaS*

Wu-ti, Emperor of Liang
The autumn wind. *SmLg*
People hide their love. *PaS*

Wul 'e plaize. Unknown. *DeT*

"Wul 'e plaize tü remimber." See Wul 'e plaize

Wylie, Elinor
Cold-blooded creatures. *PlI*
Escape. *JoAc—ReT*
Peter and John. *UnMc*
The tortoise in eternity. *FeF—PlI*
Velvet shoes. *ArTp—BrS—FeF—HuSv— JoAc—PeF*

Wynken, Blynken, and Nod. Eugene Field. *FeF—HuL-1—HuSv—JoAc—UnG*

"Wynken, Blynken, and Nod one night." See Wynken, Blynken, and Nod

Wynne, Annette
Arbor day. *DoP*
Columbus. *ArTp*
"Excuse us, animals in the zoo." *ArTp*
Fairy shoes. *BrL-k*
God's house. *DoP*
The golden rule. *DoP*
"Hearts were made to give away." *ArTp*
The house cat. *BrL-k—HuSv*
"I keep three wishes ready." *ArTp—PeF*
Indian children. *ArTp—HuSv—McAw*
"It was Saint Francis who came." *DoP*
"A letter is a gypsy elf." *BrR-5*
The pilgrims came. *McAw*
"Ring around the world." *ArTp—HuSv—JoAc*
"The tree stands very straight and still." *BrR-3*

X

X & Y. David McCord. *McFf*
X is for xoanon. Eleanor Farjeon. *FaCb*
X-ray. Leonora Speyer. *PlI*
X-rays
X-ray. L. Speyer. *PlI*
X-roads. James Reeves. *ReR*
"X shall stand for playmates ten." See Roman figures

Xerxes, King of Persia (about)
King Xerxes and the sea. E. Farjeon. *FaCb*

Y

"Y is a chesty letter." See X & Y
Y is for Yggdrasil. Eleanor Farjeon. *FaCb*
Ya se van los pastores. Dudley Fitts. *GrCc*
The yak ("As a friend to the children, commend me the yak") Hilaire Belloc. *CoH—FeF—HuL-2—JoAc*
Yak ("The long-haired yak has long black hair") William Jay Smith. *SmB—UnG*
Yaks
The yak ("As a friend to the children, commend me the yak") H. Belloc. *CoH—FeF—HuL-2—JoAc*
Yak ("The long-haired yak has long black hair") W. J. Smith. *SmB—UnG*
Yang Kuei-Fei
Dancing. *FeF*
Yankee cradle. Robert P. Tristram Coffin. *NaE*
Yankee Doodle. See "Yankee Doodle went to town"
"Yankee Doodle came to town." See "Yankee Doodle went to town"

"Yankee Doodle went to town." Mother Goose. *HuSv—JoAc*
Yankee Doodle. *FeF—OpO*
"Yankee Doodle came to town." *DeMg*
Yarmolinsky, Avrahm
Grapes. tr. *PaS*
The yarn of the Loch Achray. John Masefield. *CoSp*
The yarn of the Nancy Bell. William Schwenck Gilbert. *CoH—HuSv—NaE—NaM—SmLg—UnG*
Yates, L. E.
Strange talk. *HuL-1*
Ybarra, Thomas R.
Prose and poesy: A rural misadventure. *CoH*
"Ye highlands and ye lowlands." See The bonny earl of Murray
"Ye say they all have passed away." See Indian names
"Ye who pass by and would raise your hand against me." See To the wayfarer
"Yea, let me praise my lady whom I love." See He will praise his lady
"Yea, the coneys are scared by the thud of hoofs." See The field of Waterloo
Year. See also New year
"A cherry year." Mother Goose. *OpO*
The death of the old year. A. Tennyson. *CoPs*(sel.)
The ending of the year. E. Farjeon *EaW*
Farewell to the old year. E. Farjeon. *BrS*
"January brings the snow." S. Coleridge. *ArTp—DeMg*
A calendar. *UnG*
The garden year. *DeT—HuSv*
The months of the year. *HuL-2*
The spendthrift. E. Farjeon. *FaCb—FaN*
The year. Coventry Patmore. *ReT*
The year's round. *DeT*
"A year ago today." See Birthday garden
"The year his winter cloak lets fall." See Rondeau
"The year's at the spring." See Pippa passes —Pippa's song
The year's round. See The year
Yeats, William Butler
The ballad of Father Gilligan. *McW*
Brown penny. *GrCc—SmLg*
The cat and the moon. *CoPm—ReT—SmLg*
The dancer at Cruachan and Cro-Patrick. *PlU*
The fiddler of Dooney. *ArTp—PlU—SmLg*
For Anne Gregory. *GrCc—HaP*
The happy townland. *ReT*
An Irish airman foresees his death. *GrCc—SmLg*
The lake isle of Innisfree. *FeF—JoAc*
No second Troy. *HaP*
The old men admiring themselves in the water. *SmLg*
The pilgrim. *HaP*
The players ask for a blessing on the psalteries and on themselves. *PlU*
Red Hanrahan's song about Ireland. *SmLg*
The song of wandering Aengus. *ArTp—CoPm—HaP—JoAc—McW—ReT—SmLg—UnG*

The stolen child. *CoPm*
To a squirrel at Kyle-na-no. *FeF—ReT*
When you are old. *HaP*
Who goes with Fergus. *SmLg*
Yehoash, pseud. (Solomon Bloomgarden)
An old song. *PaS*
Yellow (Color)
Theme in yellow. C. Sandburg. *ArTp—HaY—HuSv*
Yellow balloon. Ivy O. Eastwick. *EaI*
"**Yellow** butterflies." See Korosta katzina song
"A **yellow** gig has Farmer Patch." See Yellow wheels
"The **yellow** goldenrod is dressed." See August
"The **yellow** hands go round and round." See Nursery clock
"**Yellow** the bracken." See Autumn
Yellow wheels. James Reeves. *ReBl*
Yeomans, Edward S.
Navaho prayer. *HuSv*
Yer's tu thee. Unknown. *DeT*
"**Yer's** tu thee, old apple-tree." See Yer's tu thee
"**Yes,** Nancy Hanks." See A reply to Nancy Hanks
Yesenin, Sergey
In the clear cold. *PaS*
Yesterday. Hugh Chesterman. *BrS*
"**Yesterday** I bought a penny fiddle." See The penny fiddle
Yesterday in Oxford street. Rose Fyleman. *ArTp—PeF*
"**Yesterday** in Oxford street, oh, what d'you think, my dears." See Yesterday in Oxford street
"**Yesterday** our postman stuck." See The holiday
"**Yesterday** the twig was brown and bare." See Miracle
"**Yesterday** upon the stair." Unknown. *WiRm*
Yet gentle will the griffin be. Vachel Lindsay. *HuSv*
"**Yet** if His Majesty, our Sovereign Lord." See Guests
The **yew-tree.** Eleanor Farjeon. *FaCb*
"The **yew-tree** in the churchyard." See The yew-tree
Yew trees
The yew-tree. E. Farjeon. *FaCb*
Yonder. James Reeves. *ReR*
"**Yonder** see the morning blink." Alfred Edward Housman. *NaM*
York, York for my money. William Elderton. *ReG*
You and I. Unknown. *ThP*
"**You** are nice to see." Unknown. *MoY*
"**You** are old, Father William, the young man said." See Alice's adventures in wonderland—Father William
"**You** are that legendary figure, never seen." See Homage to Vaslav Nijinsky
"**You** are the cake of my endeavor, and my jelly-roll forever." See The merry pieman's song

"**You** are wise, Mr Dodgson, the young child said." See Lewis Carroll came here to-day
"**You** ask me how God felt on that first day." See Crayons
"**You** ask me what—since we must part." See Gifts
"**You** asked me to sign my autograph." Unknown. *MoY*
"**You** bee, stop flying over." See Our picnic
"**You** can fall from the mountains." Unknown. *MoY*
"**You** can take a tub with a rub and a scrub in a two-foot tank of tin." See Katawampus—Pater's bathe
"**You** cannot choose your battlefields." See Standards
"**You** can't catch me." See Catching song
"**You** can't see fairies unless you're good." See Fairies
"**You** can't see time." See The cuckoo-clock shop
"**You** come to fetch me from my work to-night." See Putting in the seed
"**You** crash over the trees." See Storm
"**You** did late review my lays." See To Christopher North
"**You** drink a lot of soda." Unknown. *MoY*
"**You** eyes, you large and all-inquiring eyes." See For Arvia
"**You** got a gal and I've got none." See Li'l Liza Jane
"**You** have no enemies, you say." See No enemies
"**You** have seen the world, you have seen the zoo." See Swan
"**You** have your water and your grain." See My little birds
"**You** know Orion always comes up sideways." See The star-splitter
"**You** know the four poles in the garden." See Loganberry spooks
"**You** know w'at for ees school keep out." See Leetla Giorgio Washeenton
"**You** know, we French stormed Ratisbon." See Incident of the French camp
"**You** like to hear about gold." See The vindictives
"**You** love yourself, you think you're grand." Unknown. *MoY*
"**You** may call, you may call." See The bad kittens
"**You** may hang your hat on the nose of the rhino." See Rhinoceros
"**You** may not believe it, for hardly could I." See The pumpkin
"**You** might think I was in the way." See So run along and play
"**You** milkmaids in the hedgerows." See Milkmaids
"**You** mustn't call it hopsichord." David McCord. *McT*
"**You** never know with a doorbell." See Doorbells
"**You** ought to have seen what I saw on my way." See Blueberries
"**You** say there are fairies in England, sir." See Geneviève

You shall be queen. See "Lilies are white"
"You shepherd-boys who spend long hours." See Shepherds
You spotted snakes. See A midsummer-night's dream—Fairy lullaby
"You spotted snakes with double tongue." See A midsummer-night's dream—Fairy lullaby
"You take a bath, and sit there bathing." See Poems in praise of practically nothing
"You told me, Maro, whilst you live." See A hinted wish
"You were forever finding some new play." See The exposed nest
"You who like a boulder stand." See The wildebeest
You'd say it was a funeral. James Reeves. ReW
"You'd say it was a funeral, a funeral." See You'd say it was a funeral
"You'd say it was a wedding." James Reeves. ReW

Young, Andrew
  Christmas day. EaW
  The shepherd's hut. ReT
  A windy day. ReT—UnG
Young, Barbara
  Being gypsy. ArTp
  Hunger and thirst. McAw
  Lying awake. McAw
  Snowy morning. McAw
  Sophisticate. BrBc—BrS
  "Summer morning." McAw
Young, E. R.
  Railroad reverie. BrR-6
Young, Ella
  Holiday. ArTp—HuL-2
  Rain. ArTp
  The unicorn. ArTp—FeF
Young, Francis Brett
  Atlantic Charter, A. D. 1620-1942. See The island
  The island, sel.
    Atlantic Charter, A. D. 1620-1942. ArTp—JoAc
Young, Roland
  The flea. McW
Young, Stanley
  Epitaph for a Concord boy. McW
Young and old. See The water babies
Young Bekie. Unknown. MaB
"Young Bekie was as brave a knight." See Young Bekie
A young birch. Robert Frost. FrY
A young bride. Sappho, tr. fr. the Greek by Dante Gabriel Rossetti. PaS
The young calves. Robert P. Tristram Coffin. ArTp—HuSv
The young dandelion. Dinah Maria Mulock. UnG
"Young Jem at noon returned from school." See James and the shoulder of mutton
Young John. Unknown. MaB
A young lady named Bright. See Relativity
The young lady of Niger. See "There was a young lady of Niger"

A young lady of Norway. See "There was a young lady of Norway"
Young lambs. John Clare. UnG
"Young lambs to sell. Young lambs to sell." Mother Goose. DeMg
  The toy lamb seller. OpO
"Young maids, will you try charms tonight." See M is for midsummer eve
The young mystic. Louis Untermeyer. BrR-5
"Young Roger came tapping at Dolly's window." See Roger and Dolly
Young Sammy Watkins. Unknown. CoH
"Young Sammy Watkins jumped out of bed." See Young Sammy Watkins
"Young Stephen has a young friend John." See Sailor John
The young thing. See "Oh where have you been, Billy boy, Billy boy"
Young Washington. Arthur Guiterman. CoPs—FeF
"Your eye may see." See The difference
"Your flute." See The flute-players
"Your friends shall be the tall wind." See For a child
"Your future lies before you." Unknown. MoY
"Your head is like a ball of straw." Unknown. MoY
"Your heart is not a plaything." Unknown. MoY
"Your name is Achilles Deatheridge." See The Spoon River anthology—Achilles Deatheridge
"Your teeth are like the stars, she said." Unknown. MoY
"Your time is come, you apple-trees." See Apple-time
Youth. See also Boys and boyhood; Childhood recollections; Girls and girlhood; Youth and age
  Anthem for doomed youth. W. Owen. NaE
  "Blessèd Lord, what is it to be young." D. McCord. McT
  Call to youth. Horace. PaS
  A human instinct. From Translations from the Chinese. C. Morley. NaE
  The limitations of youth. E. Field. BrR-6
  Sea memories. H. W. Longfellow. FeF
  "When I was one-and-twenty." From A Shropshire lad. A. E. Housman. BrBc
  Youth. L. Hughes. BrBc
  Youth's the season. J. Gay. HoW
Youth ("I must laugh and dance and sing") A. W. HuL-2
Youth ("We have tomorrow") Langston Hughes. BrBc
Youth and age. See also Birthdays; Childhood recollections; Old age; Youth
  Age. E. Tuck. BrBc
  At a window. E. Farjeon. FaCb
  The autumn wind. Wu-ti, Emperor of Liang. SmLg
  Blue girls. J. C. Ransom. GrCc—HaP
  The corner. W. De La Mare. BrBc
  The fairy king. W. Allingham. CoPm

Father William. From Alice's adventures in wonderland. L. Carroll. *BrBc—CoH—FeF—HuL-2—LoL—McW—UnG*
> "You are old, Father William, the young man said." *ArTp*

Gather ye rosebuds. R. Herrick. *HaP—ReG*

Growing old. R. Henderson. *BrBc*

"His golden locks time hath to silver turned." From Polyhymnia. G. Peele. *HaP*

"If you never talked with fairies." E. M. Fowler. *BrBc*

Jenny kissed me. L. Hunt. *BrBc*

John Anderson, my jo. R. Burns. *HaP—HuSv—ThP*

"Life is short." Unknown. *MoY*

No joy without love. Mimnermus. *PaS*

Old men and young men. J. Holmes. *McW*

Old woman in May. J. Drinkwater. *HuL-2*

One, two, three. H. C. Bunner. *FeF*

Rabbi Ben Ezra. R. Browning. *BrBc*(sel)

Song. Sung Tzŭ-hou. *PaS*

Wisdom. D. W. Hicky. *BrBc*

Young and old. From The water babies. C. Kingsley. *BrBc*
> The old song. *McW*

Youth. A. W. *HuL-2*

The **youth** and the northwind. John Godfrey Saxe. *CoSp*

The **youth** dreams. Rainer Maria Rilke, tr. fr. the German by Ludwig Lewisohn. *PaS*

"**Youth** is conservative." See Translations from the Chinese—A human instinct

Youth's the season. John Gay. *HoW*

"**Youth's** the season made for boys." See Youth's the season

"**You've** read of several kinds of cats." See The ad-dressing of cats

Yucca
"Yucca." From In my mother's house. A. N. Clark. *JoAc*

"**Yucca**." See In my mother's house

"**Yvonne's** a little Norman wench." See Ball with Yvonne

Z

Z. David McCord. *McFf*

Z is for Zoroaster. Eleanor Farjeon. *FaCb*

"**Z**, Y, X, and W, V." Mother Goose. *OpO*

Zachary Zed. James Reeves. *ReR*

"**Zachary** Zed was the last man." See Zachary Zed

Zangwill, Israel
I have sought Thee daily. tr. *PaS*

Zaturenska, Marya
Daphne. *GrCc*
Variation on a Polish folk song. *GrCc*

Zebra. William Jay Smith. *SmB*

The **Zebra** Dun. Unknown. *CoSp—HuSv*

Zebras
"When the donkey saw the zebra." Unknown. *WiRm*
Zebra. W. J. Smith. *SmB*

Zhukovsky, Vasily
Remembrance. *PaS*

Zippers
My zipper suit. M. L. Allen. *AlP—ArTp—BrL-k*

Zodiac
Aquarius. E. Farjeon. *FaCb—FaN*
Aries. E. Farjeon. *FaCb—FaN*
Cancer. E. Farjeon. *FaCb—FaN*
Capricorn. E. Farjeon. *FaCb—FaN*
Gemini. E. Farjeon. *FaCb—FaN*
Leo. E. Farjeon. *FaCb—FaN*
Libra. E. Farjeon. *FaCb—FaN*
Pisces. E. Farjeon. *FaCb—FaN*
Sagittarius. E. Farjeon. *FaCb—FaN*
Scorpio. E. Farjeon. *FaCb—FaN*
Taurus. E. Farjeon. *FaCb—FaN*
Virgo. E. Farjeon. *FaCb—FaN*

The **zoo**. Humbert Wolfe. *CoH—McW—NaM*

Zoo manners. Eileen Mathias. *HuL-1*

"**Zooming** across the sky." See Up in the air

Zoos
At the zoo ("Giraffes are tall") M. Chute. *ChA*
At the zoo ("I've been to the zoo") M. C. Livingston. *LiW*
At the zoo ("There are lions and roaring tigers, and enormous camels and things") A. A. Milne. *FeF—MiWc*
"Excuse us, animals in the zoo." A. Wynne. *ArTp*
The monkeys. E. O. Thompson. *ArTp*
Our visit to the zoo. J. Pope. *HuL-2*
The prodigy. A. P. Herbert. *NaE*
"The spangled pandemonium." P. Brown. *ArTp—LoL*
Supper for a lion. D. Aldis. *AlA*
What did you learn at the zoo. J. Ciardi. *CiY*
Why nobody pets the lion at the zoo. J. Ciardi *CiR*
The zoo. H. Wolfe. *CoH—McW—NaM*
Zoo manners. E. Mathias. *HuL-1*

Zoroaster (about)
Z is for Zoroaster. E. Farjeon. *FaCb*

Zuñi Indians. See Indians of America—Zuñi

Directory of Publishers and Distributors

ABELARD-SCHUMAN. Abelard-Schuman, Limited, 6 W 57th St, New York 10019.
ABINGDON. Abingdon Press, 201 8th Av S, Nashville, Tenn. 37202.

CROWELL. Thomas Y. Crowell Company, 201 Park Av S, New York 10003.

DOUBLEDAY. Doubleday & Company, Inc, Garden City, New York, 11530.
DUTTON. E. P. Dutton & Company, Inc, 201 Park Av S, New York 10003.

GOLDEN. Golden Press, 850 3d Av, New York 10022.

HARCOURT. Harcourt, Brace & World, Inc, 757 3d Av, New York 10017.
HARPER. Harper & Row, Publishers, 49 E 33d St, New York 10016.
HASTINGS. Hastings House, Publishers, Inc, 10 E 40th St, New York 10016.
HOLT. Holt, Rinehart & Winston, Inc, 383 Madison Av, New York 10017.
HOUGHTON. Houghton Mifflin Company, 2 Park St, Boston 02107.

KNOPF. Alfred A. Knopf, Inc, 501 Madison Av, New York 10022.

LIPPINCOTT. J. B. Lippincott Company, East Washington Square, Philadelphia 19105.
LITTLE. Little, Brown & Company, 34 Beacon St, Boston 02106.

McGRAW. McGraw-Hill Company, 330 W 42d St, New York 10036.
MACMILLAN. The Macmillan Company, 866 3d Av, New York 10011.

OXFORD. Oxford University Press, Inc, 200 Madison Av, New York 10016.
OXFORD BK. Oxford Book Company, Inc, 387 Park Av S, New York 10016.

PANTHEON. Pantheon Books, Inc, 437 Madison Av, New York 10022.
PUTNAM. G. P. Putnam's Sons, 200 Madison Av, New York 10016.

RANDOM. Random House, Inc, 457 Madison Av, New York 10022.

SCOTT. Scott, Foresman & Company, 1900 E Lake Av, Glenview, Ill. 60025.

VIKING. The Viking Press, Inc, 625 Madison Av, New York 10022.

WALCK. Henry Z. Walck, Inc, 19 Union Square West, New York 10003.
WATTS. Franklin Watts, Inc, 575 Lexington Av, New York 10022.
WORLD PUB. The World Publishing Company, 2231 W 110th St, Cleveland 44102.